PROPERTY LAW

PRINCIPLES, PROBLEMS, AND CASES

■ ■ ■

By

Calvin Massey

Professor of Law
University of California
Hastings College of the Law

AMERICAN CASEBOOK SERIES®

WEST®

A Thomson Reuters business

Mat #41064650

American Casebook Series is a trademark registered in the U.S. Patent and Trademark Office.

© 2012 Thomson Reuters
610 Opperman Drive
St. Paul, MN 55123
1–800–313–9378

Printed in the United States of America

ISBN: 978–0–314–26810–5

For Martha and the *Heretics*
and
in memory of Sophie,
a great dog who was never property

PREFACE

Property is a sprawling subject. It has roots in civil and common law, some of which are very old and gnarly; yet it is heavily influenced by statutory alterations and bounded by federal and state constitutional and statute law. Property may be fixed—real estate—or highly mobile and personal—marketable securities, jewels, and the like. Our notions of what constitutes property are not fixed–either over time or, sometimes, even at the present moment. Property can be sliced and diced in many different ways—temporally, owned by one person or more than one at the same time, held by married couples or single persons, or consist of a present right of possession or a future right to possession. Property can be and is regulated, and the nature of those regulations fluctuate over time. Property can be transferred in a number of ways. Our mechanisms for determining who owns property are varied and, sometimes, complex.

All of these things make the editorial job difficult. Choices must be made—what to include, what to exclude, what to emphasize, what to minimize. The result is that no two property casebooks are alike. This book focuses on fundamentals, because it is my belief that beginning law students need a solid grounding in the basics of property—particularly real property—before they can delve into the depths of this vast field. I have tried to indicate those depths but I have not tried to do everything. In a four unit or five unit single semester survey course, one's ambitions must be tailored to the tyranny of the allocation of credits. I hope that this book can be fully used in a single semester. If not, instructors must make some choices of their own. I have tried to include enough material to provide varied options.

For students, I have included many problems. Thinking through the problems is a great way to apply what you have grasped from the reading. I trust that the problems will also be a focus of classroom discussion. I have tried to expose the doctrinal issues as much as possible, in the belief that a good part of the art of lawyering is skillful argument about which rule of law is preferable and the analytical power to see the problems that can arise by application of any doctrinal rule. But this book is not all doctrine. Policy questions and issues of theory are embedded in these materials as well.

Property is exciting. It is one of the foundations of freedom, yet its use, disposition, and possession raise large social issues that go beyond the interests of the property owner. Enjoy the journey.

CALVIN MASSEY

September 2011

SUMMARY OF CONTENTS

TABLE OF CONTENTS

TABLE OF CASES

The principal cases are in bold type. Cases cited or discussed in the text are in roman type. References are to pages. Cases cited in principal cases and within other quoted materials are not included.

---

xix

KK?

PROPERTY LAW

PRINCIPLES, PROBLEMS, AND CASES

CHAPTER ONE

WHAT IS PROPERTY AND HOW DOES IT ORIGINATE?

■ ■ ■

We may think that property is obvious; it is what we own; it is *ours*, not yours. But that simply begs the question of what things we can own, and raises an additional question of what it means to own something. A typical dictionary definition of property is of not much more help. Property, we are told, is "the right to possess, use, or dispose, and dispose of something; ownership;" or "a thing or things owned." Webster's New World Dictionary of the American Language (1968). Consider the following cases.

A. WHAT IS PROPERTY?

THE ANTELOPE

Supreme Court of the United States
23 U.S. (10 Wheat.) 66 (1825)

[In December of 1819, the *Columbia* left Baltimore with a crew of thirty-odd English speaking sailors most of whom were American citizens, bound for Africa. Once clear of American waters the *Columbia* changed her name to the *Arraganta* and hoisted the colors of José Artigas, a Uruguayan revolutionary (later to be revered by Uruguayans as the "Father of His Country"), who was at war with Spain and Portugal. Under the protection of a letter of marque from the Artigas government, the *Arraganta* intended to attack and seize Spanish and Portuguese vessels. The participation of American citizens in these acts was prohibited by the Neutrality Act of 1818, but the American sailors ignored that law. The *Arraganta* captured an American ship, the *Exchange*, which was engaged in the illegal slave trade, and took from it twenty-five Africans; burned several Portuguese vessels, from which she also took Africans; and captured a Spanish vessel, the *Antelope*, together with a considerable number of Africans. When the *Arraganta* was wrecked on the Brazilian coast a portion of her crew and all of the Africans were transferred to the *Antelope*, which was then put under the command of John Smith, a United

1

Contravention- an action that violates a law, treaty

States citizen. The *Antelope* headed for North America but was intercepted by the United States revenue cutter *Dallas*, John Jackson commanding. Because Jackson found over 280 Africans in chains aboard the *Antelope* he arrested the crew and brought the slaver into Savannah, Georgia.

The Spanish and Portuguese governments claimed the Africans to be their property. The United States asserted that because the Africans had been transported from foreign parts by American citizens, in contravention to the laws of the United States, they were entitled to their freedom by those laws, and by the law of nations. Captain Jackson claimed that the Africans belonged to him, as prizes of war, and in the alternative, sought a portion of their value as a marine salvage award if they belonged to Spain and Portugal, or a reward if they were set free. John Smith, the captain of the *Antelope*, sought restitution of the entire cargo of slaves.

PH

District Crt

The district court dismissed John Smith's claim because it was patently obvious that the venture of the *Arraganta*, née *Columbia*, was undertaken in violation of the Neutrality Act. The court dismissed the claim of the United States, except as to seven Africans deemed to have been taken from the *Exchange*, an American vessel. The residue was divided between the Spanish and Portuguese claimants. Captain Jackson was awarded his salvage claim. The United States appealed and the circuit court modified the district court's judgment. Because no evidence was offered to show which of the Africans were taken from the *Exchange*, and which from the Spanish and Portuguese ships, the circuit court decreed that, because about one-third of them had died, the loss should be averaged among these three different classes; and that sixteen should be designated, by lot, from the whole number, and freed according to the law of the United States, as being the fair proportion of the twenty-five Africans proved to have been taken from the *Exchange*.]

CHIEF JUSTICE MARSHALL delivered the opinion of the Court:

In prosecuting this appeal, the United States assert no property in themselves. They appear in the character of guardians, or next friends, of these Africans, who are brought, without any act of their own, into the bosom of our country, insist on their right to freedom, and submit their claim to the laws of the land, and to the tribunals of the nation. The Consuls of Spain and Portugal, respectively, demand these Africans as slaves, who have, in the regular course of legitimate commerce, been acquired as property by the subjects of their respective sovereigns, and claim their restitution under the laws of the United States. In examining claims of this momentous importance; claims in which the sacred rights of liberty and of property come in conflict with each other; ... this Court must not yield to feelings which might seduce it from the path of duty, and must obey the mandate of the law.

That the course of opinion on the slave trade should be unsettled, ought to excite no surprise. The Christian and civilized nations of the world, with whom we have most intercourse, have all been engaged in it. However abhorrent this traffic may be to a mind whose original feelings are not blunted by familiarity with the practice, it has been sanctioned in modern times by the laws of all nations who possess distant colonies, each of whom has engaged in it as a common commercial business which no other could rightfully interrupt. It has claimed all the sanction which could be derived from long usage, and general acquiescence. That trade could not be considered as contrary to the law of nations which was authorized and protected by the laws of all commercial nations; the right to carry on which was claimed by each, and allowed by each.

The course of unexamined opinion, which was founded on this inveterate usage, received its first check in America; and, as soon as these States acquired the right of self-government, the traffic was forbidden by most of them. In the beginning of this century, several humane and enlightened individuals of Great Britain devoted themselves to the cause of the Africans; and, by frequent appeals to the nation, in which the enormity of this commerce was unveiled, and exposed to the public eye, the general sentiment was at length roused against it, and the feelings of justice and humanity, regaining their long lost ascendency, prevailed so far in the British parliament as to obtain an act for its abolition. The utmost efforts of the British government, as well as of that of the United States, have since been assiduously employed in its suppression. It has been denounced by both in terms of great severity, and those concerned in it are subjected to the heaviest penalties which law can inflict. In addition to these measures operating on their own people, they have used all their influence to bring other nations into the same system, and to interdict this trade by the consent of all.

Public sentiment has, in both countries, kept pace with the measures of government; and the opinion is extensively, if not universally entertained, that this unnatural traffic ought to be suppressed. While its illegality is asserted by some governments, but not admitted by all; while the detestation in which it is held is growing daily, and even those nations who tolerate it in fact, almost disavow their own conduct, and rather connive at, than legalize, the acts of their subjects; it is not wonderful that public feeling should march somewhat in advance of strict law. . . .

The principle common to [British] cases is, that the legality of the capture of a vessel engaged in the slave trade, depends on the law of the country to which the vessel belongs. If that law gives its sanction to the trade, restitution will be decreed; if that law prohibits it, the vessel and cargo will be condemned as good prize. . . .

In the United States, different opinions have been entertained in the different Circuits and Districts; and the subject is now, for the first time, before this Court. The question, whether the slave trade is prohibited by the law of nations has been seriously propounded, and both the affirmative and negative of the proposition have been maintained with equal earnestness. That it is contrary to the law of nature will scarcely be denied. That every man has a natural right to the fruits of his own labour, is generally admitted; and that no other person can rightfully deprive him of those fruits, and appropriate them against his will, seems to be the necessary result of this admission. But from the earliest times war has existed, and war confers rights in which all have acquiesced. Among the most enlightened nations of antiquity, one of these was, that the victor might enslave the vanquished. This, which was the usage of all, could not be pronounced repugnant to the law of nations, which is certainly to be tried by the test of general usage. That which has received the assent of all, must be the law of all.

Slavery, then, has its origin in force; but as the world has agreed that it is a legitimate result of force, the state of things which is thus produced by general consent, cannot be pronounced unlawful. Throughout Christendom, this harsh rule has been exploded, and war is no longer considered as giving a right to enslave captives. But this triumph of humanity has not been universal. The parties to the modern law of nations do not propagate their principles by force; and Africa has not yet adopted them. Throughout the whole extent of that immense continent, so far as we know its history, it is still the law of nations that prisoners are slaves. Can those who have themselves renounced this law, be permitted to participate in its effects by purchasing the beings who are its victims?

Whatever might be the answer of a moralist to this question, a jurist must search for its legal solution, in those principles of action which are sanctioned by the usages, the national acts, and the general assent, of that portion of the world of which he considers himself as a part, and to whose law the appeal is made. If we resort to this standard as the test of international law, the question, as has already been observed, is decided in favour of the legality of the trade. Both Europe and America embarked in it; and for nearly two centuries, it was carried on without opposition, and without censure. A jurist could not say that a practice thus supported was illegal, and that those engaged in it might be punished, either personally, or by deprivation of property. In this commerce, thus sanctioned by universal assent, every nation has an equal right to engage. How is this right to be lost? Each may renounce it for its own people; but can this renunciation affect others?

No principle of general law is more universally acknowledged, than the perfect equality of nations. Russia and Geneva have equal rights. It results from this equality, that no one can rightfully impose a rule on another. Each legislates for itself, but its legislation can operate on itself alone. A right, then, which is vested in all by the consent of all, can be divested only be consent; and this trade, in which all have participated, must remain lawful to those who cannot be induced to relinquish it. As no nation can prescribe a rule for others, none can make a law of nations; and this traffic remains lawful to those whose governments have not forbidden it. If it is consistent with the law of nations, it cannot in itself be piracy. It can be made so only by statute; and the obligation of the statute cannot transcend the legislative power of the state which may enact it.

If it be neither repugnant to the law of nations, nor piracy, it is almost superfluous to say in this Court, that the right of bringing in for adjudication in time of peace, even where the vessel belongs to a nation which has prohibited the trade, cannot exist. The Courts of no country execute the penal laws of another; and the course of the American government on the subject of visitation and search, would decide any case in which that right had been exercised by an American cruiser, on the vessel of a foreign nation, not violating our municipal laws, against the captors. It follows, that a foreign vessel engaged in the African slave trade, captured on the high seas in time of peace, by an American cruiser, and brought in for adjudication, would be restored.

The general question being disposed of, it remains to examine the circumstances of the particular case. The *Antelope*, a vessel unquestionably belonging to Spanish subjects, was captured while receiving a cargo of Africans on the coast of Africa, by the *Arraganta*, a privateer which was manned in Baltimore, and [which seized slaves from other Spanish and Portuguese vessels.] Both vessels proceeded to the coast of Brazil, where the *Arraganta* was wrecked, and her captain and crew either lost or made prisoners. The *Antelope*, whose name was changed to the *General Ramirez*, after an ineffectual attempt to sell the Africans on board at Surinam, arrived off the coast of Florida, and was hovering on that coast, near that of the United States, for several days. Supposing her to be a pirate, or a vessel wishing to smuggle slaves into the United States, Captain Jackson, of the revenue cutter *Dallas*, went in quest of her, and finding her laden with slaves, commanded by officers who were citizens of the United States, with a crew who spoke English, brought her in for adjudication. She was libelled[1] by the Vice Consuls of Spain and Portugal, each of whom claim that portion of the slaves which were conjectured to belong to the subjects of their respective sovereigns; which claims are opposed by the United States on behalf of the Africans. . . .

It is contended, that the *Antelope*, having been wrongfully dispossessed of her slaves by American citizens, and being now, together with her cargo, in the power of the United States, ought to be restored, without further inquiry, to those out of whose possession she was thus wrongfully taken. No proof of property, it is said, ought to be required. Possession is in such a case evidence of property.

Conceding this as a general proposition, the counsel for the United States deny its application to this case. A distinction is taken between men, who are generally free, and goods, which are always property. Although, with respect to the last, possession may constitute the only proof of property which is demandable, something more is necessary where men are claimed. Some proof should be exhibited that the possession was legally acquired. A distinction has been also drawn between Africans unlawfully taken from the subjects of a foreign power by persons acting under the authority of the United States, and Africans first cap-

---

1. [Ed.—A libel, in this context, is a claim in admiralty court against a vessel or person.]

tured by a belligerent privateer, or by a pirate, and then brought rightfully into the United States, under a reasonable apprehension that a violation of their laws was intended. Being rightfully in the possession of an American Court, that Court, it is contended, must be governed by the laws of its own country; and the condition of these Africans must depend on the laws of the United States, not on the laws of Spain and Portugal....

[Because the *Antelope* was] hovering on the coast with intent to introduce slaves in violation of the laws of the United States, our treaty requires that property rescued from [such a vessel] shall be restored to the Spanish owner on his making proof of his property. [It is thus essential] to make some inquiry into the title of the claimants. In support of the Spanish claim, testimony is produced, showing the documents under which the *Antelope* sailed from Havana on the voyage on which she was captured; that she was owned by a Spanish house of trade in that place; that she was employed in the business of purchasing slaves, and had purchased and taken on board a considerable number, when she was seized as prize by the *Arraganta*. Whether, on this proof, Africans brought into the United States, under the various circumstances belonging to this case, ought to be restored or not, is a question on which much difficulty has been felt. It is unnecessary to state the reasons in support of the affirmative or negative answer to it, because the Court is divided on it, and, consequently, no principle is settled.[2] So much of the decree of the Circuit Court as directs restitution to the Spanish claimant of the Africans found on board the Antelope when she was captured by the Arraganta, is affirmed.

There is some difficulty in ascertaining their number. [Testimony on this point varied wildly.] Whatever doubts may attend the question whether the Spanish claimants are entitled to restitution of all the Africans taken out of their possession with the *Antelope*, we cannot doubt the propriety of demanding ample proof of the extent of that possession. Every legal principle which requires the plaintiff to prove his claim in any case, applies with full force to this point; and no countervailing consideration exists. The *onus probandi* as to the number of Africans which were on board when the vessel was captured, unquestionably lies on the Spanish libellants. Their proof is not satisfactory beyond ninety-three. The individuals who compose this number must be designated to the satisfaction of the Circuit Court.

We proceed next to consider the libel of the Vice–Consul of Portugal. It claims one hundred and thirty slaves, or more, "all of whom, as the libellant is informed and believes," are the property of a subject or subjects of his Most Faithful Majesty; and although "the rightful owners of such slaves be not at this time individually and certainly known to the libellant, he hopes and expects soon to discover them." [The testimony offered to prove that these Africans were the property of unknown Portuguese subjects consisted of the fact that they were taken from ships

---

2. [Ed.—Because Justice Todd was ill the case was heard by six justices. Under long-standing Supreme Court practice, an evenly divided Court leaves the lower court judgment in place.]

flying the Portuguese flag. There was no other proof] that the proprietors of the Africans now claimed by the Vice–Consul of Portugal were the subjects of his king; nor is there any allusion to the individuals to whom they belong. These vessels were plundered in March, 1820, and the libel was filed in August of the same year. From that time to this, a period of more than five years, no subject of the crown of Portugal has appeared to assert his title to this property, no individual has been designated as its probable owner. This inattention to a subject of so much real interest, this total disregard of a valuable property, is so contrary to the common course of human action, as to justify serious suspicion that the real owner dares not avow himself. That Americans, and others, who cannot use the flag of their own nation, carry on this criminal and inhuman traffic under the flag of other countries, is a fact of such general notoriety, that Courts of admiralty may act upon it. It cannot be necessary . . . to prove a fact which is matter of general and public history. This long, and otherwise unaccountable absence, of any Portuguese claimant, furnishes irresistible testimony, that no such claimant exists, and that the real owner belongs to some other nation, and feels the necessity of concealment. . . .

[handwritten margin note: no Portuguese claimed the Africans]

These Africans still remain unclaimed by the owner, or by any person professing to know the owner. They are rightfully taken from American citizens, and placed in possession of the law. No property whatever in them is shown. It is said that possession, in a case of this description, is equivalent to property. Could this be conceded, who had the possession? From whom were they taken by the *Arraganta*? It is not alleged that they are the property of the crown, but of some individual. Who is that individual? No such person is shown to exist, and his existence, after such a lapse of time, cannot be presumed.

The libel, which claims them for persons entirely unknown, alleges a state of things which is prima facie evidence of an intent to violate the laws of the United States, by the commission of an act which, according to those laws, entitles these men to freedom. Nothing whatever can interpose to arrest the course of the law, but the title of the real proprietor. No such title appears, and every presumption is against its existence.

We think, then, that all the Africans . . . which were brought in with the *Antelope*, otherwise called the *General Ramirez*, except those which may be designated as the property of the Spanish claimants, ought to be delivered up to the United States, to be disposed of according to law.[3] So much of the sentence of the Circuit Court as is contrary to this opinion, is to be reversed, and the residue affirmed.

UNITED STATES v. THE AMISTAD

Supreme Court of the United States
40 U.S. (15 Pet.) 518 (1841)

JUSTICE STORY delivered the opinion of the Court.

This is . . . an appeal from the decree of the Circuit Court of the District of Connecticut, sitting in admiralty. The leading facts . . . are as

---

3. [Ed.—Federal law at the time provided that Africans illegally imported into the United States as intended slaves must be handed over to the United States government, which was obligated to return them to Africa.]

follows: On the 27th of June, 1839, the schooner *L'Amistad*, being the property of Spanish subjects, cleared out from the port of Havana, in the island of Cuba, for Puerto Principe, in the same island. On board of the schooner were the captain, Ransom Ferrer, and Jose Ruiz, and Pedro Montez, all Spanish subjects. The former had with him a negro boy, named Antonio, claimed to be his slave. Jose Ruiz had with him forty-nine negroes, claimed by him as his slaves, and stated to be his property, in a certain ... document signed by the Governor General of Cuba. Pedro Montez had with him four other negroes, also claimed by him as his slaves, and stated to be his property, in a similar ... document also signed by the Governor General of Cuba. On the voyage, and before the arrival of the vessel at her port of destination, the negroes rose, killed the captain, and took possession of her. On the 26th of August, the vessel was discovered by Lieutenant Gedney, of the United States brig *Washington*, at anchor on the high seas, at the distance of half a mile from the shore of Long Island. ... The vessel, with the negroes and other persons on board, was brought by Lieutenant Gedney into the district of Connecticut, and there libeled for salvage in the District Court of the United States. ... On the 18th of September, Ruiz and Montez filed claims ... in which they asserted their ownership of the negroes as their slaves, and of certain parts of the cargo, and prayed that the same might be "delivered to them, or to the representatives of her Catholic majesty, as might be most proper." On the 19th of September, the ... United States ... filed ... a claim for the restoration of the vessel, cargo, and slaves [to the Spanish owners], pursuant to the treaty between the United States and Spain.... But if it should appear, that the negroes were persons transported from Africa, in violation of the laws of the United States, and brought within the United States contrary to the same laws; [the United States sought an] order for their removal to the coast of Africa, pursuant to the laws of the United States....[4] On the 19th of November, ... Antonio G. Vega, the vice-consul of Spain for the state of Connecticut, filed his libel, alleging that Antonio was a slave, the property of the representatives of Ramon Ferrer, and praying the Court to cause him to be delivered to the said vice-consul, that he might be returned by him to his lawful owner in the island of Cuba. On the 7th of January, 1840, the negroes, ... with the exception of Antonio, ... filed an answer, denying that they were slaves, or the property of Ruiz and Montez.... They [assert] in this answer that they were native born Africans; born free, and still of right ought to be free and not slaves; that they were, on or about the 15th of April, 1839, unlawfully kidnapped, and forcibly and wrongfully carried on board a certain vessel on the coast of Africa, which was unlawfully engaged in the

---

4. [Ed.—An act of Congress of March 3, 1819, ch. 224, provided that Africans illegally imported into the Untied States as intended slaves must be repatriated to Africa.]

slave trade, and were unlawfully transported in the same vessel to the island of Cuba, for the purpose of being there unlawfully sold as slaves; that Ruiz and Montez, well knowing [these facts], made a pretended purchase of them: that afterwards, on or about the 28th of June, 1839, Ruiz and Montez, confederating with Ferrer, (captain of the *Amistad*),

caused them, without law or right, to be placed on board of the *Amistad*,

to be transported to some place unknown to them, and there to be enslaved for life; that, on the voyage, they rose on the master, and took possession of the vessel, intending to return therewith to their native country, or to seek an asylum in some free state....

[The District Court] allowed salvage to Lieutenant Gedney and others, on the vessel and cargo, of one-third of the value thereof, but not on the negroes ...; it dismissed the ... claims of Ruiz and Montez ...; it allowed the claim of the Spanish vice-consul for Antonio ...; it rejected the claim ... of the United States on behalf of [Spain] for the restoration of the negroes under the treaty; but it decreed that they should be ... transported to Africa.... [The] United States appealed to the Circuit Court, except so far as related to the restoration of the slave Antonio. ... No appeal was interposed by Ruiz or Montez, or on behalf of the representatives of the owners of the *Amistad*. The Circuit Court ... affirmed the decree of the District Court.... And from that decree the present appeal has been brought to this Court....

[The] only parties now before the Court on one side, are the United States, intervening for the sole purpose of procuring restitution of the property as Spanish property, pursuant to the treaty.... The United States do not assert any property in themselves, or any violation of their own rights, or sovereignty, or laws, by the acts complained of. They do not insist that these negroes have been imported into the United States, in contravention of our own slave trade acts. They do not seek to have these negroes delivered up for the purpose of being transported to Cuba as pirates or robbers, or as fugitive criminals against the laws of Spain. They do not assert that the seizure, and bringing the vessel, and cargo, and negroes into port, by Lieutenant Gedney, for the purpose of adjudication, is a tortious act. They simply confine themselves to the right of the Spanish claimants to the restitution of their property....

[The] parties before the Court on the other side as appellees, are Lieutenant Gedney, on his libel for salvage, and the negroes, ... asserting themselves ... not to be slaves, but free native Africans, kidnapped in their own country, and illegally transported by force from that country; and now entitled to maintain their freedom. ... The main controversy is whether these negroes are the property of Ruiz and Montez, and ought to be delivered up....

[The] United States [argues] that the Court are bound to deliver them up, according to the treaty of 1795, with Spain, which has in this particular been continued in full force, by the treaty of 1819, ratified in 1821. ... The ninth article [of the treaty] provides, "that all ships and merchandise, of what nature soever, which shall be rescued out of the hands of any pirates or robbers, on the high seas, shall be brought into some port of either state, and shall be delivered to the custody of the officers of that port, in order to be taken care of and restored entire to the true proprietor, as soon as due and sufficient proof shall be made concerning the property thereof." ... To bring the case within the article, it is essential to establish, First, That these negroes, under all the circumstances, fall within the description of merchandise, in the sense of the treaty. Secondly, That there has been a rescue of them on the high seas, out of the hands of the pirates and robbers; which, in the present case, can only be, by showing that they themselves are pirates and robbers; and, Thirdly, That Ruiz and Montez, the asserted proprietors, are the true proprietors, and have established their title by competent proof.

If these negroes were, at the time, lawfully held as slaves under the laws of Spain, and recognised by those laws as property capable of being lawfully bought and sold; we see no reason why they may not justly be deemed within the intent of the treaty, to be included under the denomination of merchandise, and, as such, ought to be restored to the claimants: for, upon that point, the laws of Spain would seem to furnish the proper rule of interpretation. But ... neither of the other essential facts and requisites has been established in proof. ... It is plain beyond controversy ... that these negroes never were the lawful slaves of Ruiz or Montez, or of any other Spanish subjects. They are natives of Africa, and were kidnapped there, and were unlawfully transported to Cuba, in violation of the laws and treaties of Spain, and the most solemn edicts and declarations of that government. By those laws, and treaties, and edicts, the African slave trade is utterly abolished; the dealing in that trade is deemed a heinous crime; and the negroes thereby introduced into the dominions of Spain, are declared to be free. Ruiz and Montez are proved to have made the pretended purchase of these negroes, with a full knowledge of all the circumstances. ...

If, then, these negroes are not slaves, but are kidnapped Africans, who, by the laws of Spain itself, are entitled to their freedom, and were kidnapped and illegally carried to Cuba, and illegally detained and restrained on board of the *Amistad*; there is no pretence to say, that they are pirates or robbers. We may lament the dreadful acts, by which they asserted their liberty, and took possession of the *Amistad*, and endeavoured to regain their native country; but they cannot be deemed pirates or robbers in the sense of the law of nations, or the treaty with Spain, or the laws of Spain itself. ...

But it is argued, on behalf of the United States, that the ship, and cargo, and negroes were duly documented as belonging to Spanish subjects, and this Court have no right to look behind these documents [even though there is] the most satisfactory proofs that they have been obtained by the grossest frauds and impositions upon the constituted authorities of Spain. To this argument we can, in no wise, assent. There is nothing in the treaty which justifies or sustains the argument. ... [Although] public documents of the government, accompanying property found on board of the private ships of a foreign nation, certainly are to be deemed prima facie evidence of the facts which they purport to state, yet they are always open to be impugned for fraud; and whether that fraud be in the original obtaining of these documents, or in the subsequent fraudulent and illegal use of them, when once it is satisfactorily established, it overthrows all their sanctity, and destroys them as proof. Fraud will vitiate any, even the *—spoil* most solemn transactions; and an asserted title to property, founded upon it, is utterly void. The very language of the ninth article of the treaty of 1795, requires the proprietor to make due and sufficient proof of his property. And how can that proof be deemed either due or sufficient, which is but a connected, and stained tissue of fraud? This is not a mere rule of municipal jurisprudence. Nothing is more clear in the law of nations, as an established rule to regulate their rights, and duties, and intercourse, than the doctrine, that the ship's papers are but prima facie evidence, and that, if they are shown to be fraudulent, they are not to be held proof of any valid title....

It is also a most important consideration in the present case, which ought not to be lost sight of, that, supposing these African negroes not to be slaves, but kidnapped, and free negroes, the treaty with Spain cannot be obligatory upon them; and the United States are bound to respect their rights as much as those of Spanish subjects. The conflict of rights between the parties under such circumstances, becomes positive and inevitable, and must be decided upon the eternal principles of justice and international law. If the contest were about any goods on board of this ship, to which American citizens asserted a title, which was denied by the Spanish claimants, there could be no doubt of the right of such American citizens to litigate their claims before any competent American tribunal, notwithstanding the treaty with Spain. A fortiori, the doctrine must apply where human life and human liberty are in issue; and constitute the very essence of the controversy. The treaty with Spain never could have intended to take away the equal rights of all foreigners, who should contest their claims before any of our Courts, to equal justice; or to deprive such foreigners of the protection given them by other treaties, or by the general law of nations. Upon the merits of the case, then, there does not seem to us to be any ground for doubt, that these negroes ought to be deemed free; and that the Spanish treaty interposes no obstacle to the just assertion of their rights.

There is another [matter for] consideration.... [The] United States, in their original claim, filed it in the alternative, to have the negroes, if slaves and Spanish property, restored to the proprietors; or, if not slaves, but negroes who had been transported from Africa, in violation of the laws of the United States, and brought into the United States contrary to the same laws, then the Court to ... order ... the United States to remove such persons to the coast of Africa, to be delivered there to such agent as may be authorized to receive and provide for them. [The] District Court [ordered] the delivery of the negroes to the United States, to be transported to the coast of Africa, under the act of the 3d of March, 1819, ch. 224. [But] there is no ground to assert that the case comes within the purview of the act of 1819, or of any other of our prohibitory slave trade acts. These negroes were never taken from Africa, or brought to the United States in contravention of those acts. When the *Amistad* arrived she was in possession of the negroes, asserting their freedom; and in no sense could they possibly intend to import themselves here, as slaves, or for sale as slaves. In this view of the matter, that part of the decree of the District Court . . . must be reversed.

[The] decree of the Circuit Court, affirming that of the District Court, ought to be affirmed, except so far as it directs the negroes to be delivered to the President, to be transported to Africa, in pursuance of the act of the 3d of March, 1819; and, as to this, it ought to be reversed: and that the said negroes be declared to be free, and be dismissed from the custody of the Court, and go without delay.

NOTES AND QUESTIONS

1. *What determines what is property?* The Africans on board the *Antelope*, or at least some of them, were treated as property and consigned by a lottery to a lifetime of slavery. The Africans on board the *Amistad* were not regarded as property, but as people free to go where they chose. What principle or principles produced these different outcomes? Today, of course, the idea of humans being treated as property is abhorrent. How is it that conceptions of property can change so dramatically? Is property simply whatever a society declares to be property? If so, how does society manifest its views? The Fifth Amendment to the United States Constitution provides: "[N]or shall private property be taken for public use, without just compensation." In the last chapter of this book you will explore the distinction between regulations of property that diminish its value but do not constitute takings of that property and regulations that do constitute takings of property. Can that constitutional command be avoided simply by characterizing something that was property as not property? It's best to leave the answer to that question for the last chapter but, at this point, try to identify the factors that led the Supreme Court in *The Antelope* and in *The Amistad* to reach the conclusions it did on the antecedent question of whether the Africans involved were people or property. If the notion of property is socially contingent, identify the factors (as best you can) upon which that contingency hinges. Finally, is property a relationship between a person and a thing called property, or is it the relationship between persons with respect to something we call property? Keep that question in mind as we explore the remainder of this chapter.

2. *Some background.* In *The Antelope* Chief Justice John Marshall, still widely regarded as the most important person to serve as Chief Justice, suggested that the claim of Portuguese ownership of a portion of the Africans on board the ship was fictional, and that the real "owner" might be an American who could not reveal his identity because it was a serious crime for an American to engage in the African slave trade. Some evidence exists that the *Exchange*, from which Africans were taken by the *Arraganta*, neé *Colum-*

bia, and later transferred to the *Antelope*, was owned by Charles and James De Wolfe, merchants of Bristol, Rhode Island. James De Wolfe became a United States Senator during the pendency of the *Antelope* proceedings. See John Noonan, *The* Antelope: *The ordeal of the re-captured Africans in the Administrations of James Monroe and John Quincy Adams* (1977), which is the thorough account of the entire episode.

The *Amistad* events achieved considerable recent notoriety through the movie *Amistad*, released in 1997. Among the historical accounts are Howard Jones, *Mutiny on the Amistad: The Saga of a Slave Revolt and Its Impact on American Abolition, Law, and Diplomacy* (1987); Mary Cable, *The Black Odyssey: The Case of the Slave Ship Amistad* (1971); Iyunolu Osagie, *The* Amistad *Revolt* (2000); William Owens, *Slave Mutiny: The Revolt on the Schooner* Amistad (1953). John Quincy Adams played an important role in each case. During the *Antelope* events he was Secretary of State and hungered to be President, a post he ultimately achieved by the margin of one Maryland congressman's vote. Perhaps because of his political ambition at a time when the political support of slave states was crucial to the realization of that ambition, Adams was no friend to the *Antelope* Africans. Yet, seventeen years later, as a lawyer and ex-President, he argued passionately on behalf of the *Amistad* Africans. Perhaps moral ambition had eclipsed political ambition.

MOORE v. THE REGENTS OF THE UNIVERSITY OF CALIFORNIA

Supreme Court of California
51 Cal.3d 120 (1990), cert. denied, 499 U.S. 936 (1991)

[John Moore contracted "hairy-cell" leukemia. In 1976 he consulted David Golde, a physician, and other medical professionals at the UCLA medical center, who told him that the disease was life threatening and recommended that his spleen be removed. Moore consented to the splenectomy, which was performed. Unknown to Moore, the defendant medical professionals preserved a portion of his spleen for research purposes. Over the next seven years Moore traveled from Seattle to Los Angeles numerous times for further examinations by Golde and other medical defendants and extractions by them of blood, bone marrow, and other bodily substances. The defendants told Moore that these visits were necessary to his health although their principal, if not only, purpose was to assist the defendants in their medical research using Moore's spleen. That research culminated in the creation of a patented cell line from T-lymphocytes obtained from Moore's spleen (the Mo cell line). The Mo cell line enabled the production of a certain lymphokine, a protein that regulates the immune system, that had considerable therapeutic value. Creation of a cell line, a culture that will reproduce indefinitely, is no easy task. The defendants entered into agreements with biotech companies for the commercial development of the patented Mo cell line.

When Moore learned of these events he brought suit alleging, among many causes of action, breach of fiduciary duty and conversion. Conversion is a tort that consists of wrongful exercise of ownership of the personal property of another. Moore's contention was that his spleen, even after its removal from his body, and other bodily substances extracted from him, were his property. The trial court sustained defendants' demurrer to Moore's conversion claim and dismissed the complaint because the conversion claim was incorporated into the other causes of action. The California Court of Appeal reversed, finding that Moore had stated a claim for conversion. 249 Cal. Rptr. 494 (Ct. App. 1988). Although the Court of Appeal acknowledged that societal evolution "from regarding people as chattels to recognition of the individual dignity of each person necessitates prudence in attributing the qualities of property to human tissue, ... [there is] a dramatic difference between having property rights in one's own body and being the property of another." The Court of Appeal concluded that the essence of property was dominion, the rights to use, control, and dispose of that which is property. Because such rights are recognized in other areas of law with respect to bodily interests, the Court of Appeal concluded "that it would be subterfuge" to call these interests something other than property. According to the Court of Appeal, Moore had not abandoned his spleen by consenting to its removal. The skill and ingenuity of the defendants in creating the patented cell line was relevant to the measure of damages for conversion, said the court, not to the question of whether the spleen from which the cell line was derived was Moore's property. The California Supreme Court granted review.]

PANELLI, J., delivered the opinion of the Court.

We granted review in this case to determine whether plaintiff has stated a cause of action against his physician and other defendants for using his cells in potentially lucrative medical research without his permission. ... We hold that the complaint states a cause of action for breach of the physician's disclosure obligations, but not for conversion....

Our only task in reviewing a ruling on a demurrer is to determine whether the complaint states a cause of action. Accordingly, we assume that the complaint's properly pleaded material allegations are true....

A. *Breach of Fiduciary Duty and Lack of Informed Consent*

Moore ... alleges that Golde failed to disclose the extent of his research and economic interests in Moore's cells before obtaining consent to the medical procedures by which the cells were extracted. These allegations ... state a cause of action against Golde for invading a legally protected interest of his patient. This cause of action can properly be characterized either as the breach of a fiduciary duty to disclose facts material to the patient's consent or, alternatively, as the performance of medical procedures without first having obtained the patient's informed consent....

B. *Conversion*

Moore also attempts to characterize the invasion of his rights as a conversion—a tort that protects against interference with possessory and ownership interests in personal property. He theorizes that he continued to own his cells following their removal from his body, at least for the purpose of directing their use, and that he never consented to their use in potentially lucrative medical research. Thus, to complete Moore's argument, defendants' unauthorized use of his cells constitutes a conversion. As a result of the alleged conversion, Moore claims a proprietary interest in each of the products that any of the defendants might ever create from his cells or the patented cell line....

In effect, what Moore is asking us to do is to impose a tort duty on scientists to investigate the consensual pedigree of each human cell sample used in research. To impose such a duty, which would affect medical research of importance to all of society, implicates policy concerns far removed from the traditional, two-party ownership disputes in which the law of conversion arose. Invoking a tort theory originally used to determine whether the loser or the finder of a horse had the better title, Moore claims ownership of the results of socially important medical research, including the genetic code for chemicals that regulate the functions of every human being's immune system....

[handwritten margin note: not just a dispute over 1 item but all that came from the cells.]

We have recognized that, when the proposed application of a very general theory of liability in a new context raises important policy concerns, it is especially important to face those concerns and address them openly.... Moreover, we should be hesitant to "impose [new tort duties] when to do so would involve complex policy decisions." especially when such decisions are more appropriately the subject of legislative deliberation and resolution. ... Accordingly, we first consider whether the tort of conversion clearly gives Moore a cause of action under existing law. We do not believe it does. [Application of] the theory of conversion in this context would frankly have to be recognized as an extension of the theory. Therefore, we consider next whether it is advisable to extend the tort to this context.

1. *Moore's Claim Under Existing Law*

"To establish a conversion, plaintiff must establish an actual interference with his *ownership* or *right of possession*. ... Where plaintiff neither has title to the property alleged to have been converted, nor possession thereof, he cannot maintain an action for conversion." [Because] Moore clearly did not expect to retain possession of his cells following their removal, to sue for their conversion he must have retained an ownership interest in them. But there are several reasons to doubt that he did retain any such interest. First, no reported judicial decision supports Moore's claim, either directly or by close analogy. Second, California statutory law drastically limits any continuing interest of a patient in excised cells. Third, the subject matters of the Regents' patent—the patented cell line and the products derived from it—cannot be Moore's property.

Neither the Court of Appeal's opinion, the parties' briefs, nor our research discloses a case holding that a person retains a sufficient interest in excised cells to support a cause of action for conversion. We do not find this surprising, since the laws governing such things as human tissues, transplantable organs,[5] blood, fetuses, pituitary glands, corneal tissue, and dead bodies deal with human biological materials as objects sui generis, regulating their disposition to achieve policy goals rather than abandoning them to the general law of personal property. It is these specialized statutes, not the law of conversion, to which courts ordinarily should and do look for guidance on the disposition of human biological materials.

[Thus,] Moore relies, as did the Court of Appeal, primarily on decisions [that] hold that every person has a proprietary interest in his own likeness and that unauthorized, business use of a likeness is redressible as a tort. But [those holdings were not expressly based] on property law. Each court stated, following Prosser, that it was "pointless" to debate the proper characterization of the proprietary interest in a likeness. For purposes of determining whether the tort of conversion lies, however, the characterization of the right in question is far from pointless. Only property can be converted.

... Moore ... argues that "[i]f the courts have found a sufficient proprietary interest in one's persona, how could one not have a right in one's own genetic material, something far more profoundly the essence of one's human uniqueness than a name or a face?" However, as the defendants' patent makes clear ... the goal and result of defendants' efforts has been to manufacture lymphokines. Lymphokines, unlike a name or a face, have the same molecular structure in every human being and the same, important functions in every human being's immune system. Moreover, the particular genetic material which is responsible for the natural production of lymphokines, and which defendants use to manufacture lymphokines in the laboratory, is also the same in every person; it is no more unique to Moore than the number of vertebrae in the spine or the chemical formula of hemoglobin.[6] ...

---

5. [By the Court, n.22] See the Uniform Anatomical Gift Act, Health and Safety Code section 7150 et seq. The act permits a competent adult to "give all or part of [his] body" for certain designated purposes, including "transplantation, therapy, medical or dental education, research, or advancement of medical or dental science." (Health & Saf. Code, §§ 7151, 7153.) The act does not, however, permit the donor to receive "valuable consideration" for the transfer. (Health & Saf. Code, § 7155.)

6. [Footnote 29 of the Court relocated; Ed.—] Inside the cell, a gene produces a lymphokine by attracting protein molecules, which bond to form a strand of "messenger RNA" (mRNA) in the mirror image of the gene. The mRNA strand then detaches from the gene and attracts other protein molecules, which bond to form the lymphokine that the original gene encoded. In the laboratory, scientists sometimes use genes to manufacture lymphokines by cutting a gene from the chromosome and grafting it onto the chromosome of a bacterium. The resulting chromosome is an example of "recombinant DNA," or DNA composed of genetic material from more than one individual or species. As the bacterium lives and reproduces, the engrafted gene continues to produce the lymphokine that the gene encodes. It can be extremely difficult to identify the gene that carries the code for a particular lymphokine. "Since the amount of DNA in a human cell is enormous compared to the amount present in an individual gene, the search for any single gene within a cell is like searching for needle in a haystack." As the Regents' patent application explains, the significance of a cell that overproduces mRNA is to make the difficult search for a particular gene unnecessary. If one has an adequate source of mRNA—the gene's mirror image—it can be used to make a copy, or clone, of the original gene. The cloned gene can then be used in recombinant DNA, as already described, for large-scale production of lymphokines. [Ed.—In an earlier footnote, the Court noted that "Moore's T-lymphocytes were interesting to the defendants because they overproduced certain lymphokines, thus making the corresponding genetic material easier to identify." Thus, while it may have been literally true that the genetic material used to

[One] may earnestly wish to protect privacy and dignity without accepting the extremely problematic conclusion that interference with those interests amounts to a conversion of personal property. Nor is it necessary to force the round pegs of "privacy" and "dignity" into the square hole of "property" in order to protect the patient, since the fiduciary-duty and informed-consent theories protect these interests directly by requiring full disclosure.

The next consideration that makes Moore's claim of ownership problematic is California statutory law, which drastically limits a patient's control over excised cells. Pursuant to Health and Safety Code section 7054.4, "[n]otwithstanding any other provision of law, recognizable anatomical parts, human tissues, anatomical human remains, or infectious waste following conclusion of scientific use shall be disposed of by interment, incineration, or any other method determined by the state department [of health services] to protect the public health and safety." Clearly the Legislature did not specifically intend this statute to resolve the question of whether a patient is entitled to compensation for the nonconsensual use of excised cells. A primary object of the statute is to ensure the safe handling of potentially hazardous biological waste materials. Yet one cannot escape the conclusion that the statute's practical effect is to limit, drastically, a patient's control over excised cells. By restricting how excised cells may be used and requiring their eventual destruction, the statute eliminates so many of the rights ordinarily attached to property that one cannot simply assume that what is left amounts to "property" or "ownership" for purposes of conversion law....

Finally, the subject matter of the Regents' patent—the patented cell line and the products derived from it—cannot be Moore's property ... because the patented cell line is both factually and legally distinct from the cells taken from Moore's body. Federal law permits the patenting of organisms that represent the product of "human ingenuity," but not naturally occurring organisms. Human cell lines are patentable because "... growth of human tissues and cells in culture is difficult—often considered an art ...," and the probability of success is low. It is this *inventive effort* that patent law rewards, not the discovery of naturally occurring raw materials. Thus, ... the patent ... constitutes an authoritative determination that the cell line is the product of invention....

2. *Should Conversion Liability Be Extended?*

... There are three reasons why it is inappropriate to impose liability for conversion based upon the allegations of Moore's complaint. First, a fair balancing of the relevant policy considerations counsels against extending the tort. Second, problems in this area are better suited to legislative resolution. Third, the tort of conversion is not necessary to protect patients' rights. [Thus,] the use of excised human cells in medical research does not amount to a conversion.

---

manufacture lymphokines is not unique to Moore, the cell line derived from Moore's cells may have been possible because of the unusual quality of Moore's cells.]

Of the relevant policy considerations, two are of overriding importance. The first is protection of a competent patient's right to make autonomous medical decisions. That right ... is grounded in well-recognized and long-standing principles of fiduciary duty and informed consent. This policy weighs in favor of providing a remedy to patients when physicians act with undisclosed motives that may affect their professional judgment. The second important policy consideration is that we not threaten with disabling civil liability innocent parties who are engaged in socially useful activities, such as researchers who have no reason to believe that their use of a particular cell sample is, or may be, against a donor's wishes....

[A congressional report noted that uncertainty] "about how courts will resolve disputes between specimen sources and specimen users could be detrimental to both academic researchers and the infant biotechnology industry, particularly when the rights are asserted long after the specimen was obtained. ... Biological materials are routinely distributed to other researchers for experimental purposes, and scientists who obtain cell lines or other specimen-derived products, such as gene clones, from the original researcher could also be sued under certain legal theories [such as conversion]. ... Since inventions containing human tissues and cells may be patented and licensed for commercial use, companies are unlikely to invest heavily in developing, manufacturing, or marketing a product when uncertainty about clear title exists." Indeed, so significant is the potential obstacle to research stemming from uncertainty about legal title to biological materials that the [report concluded that] "resolving the current uncertainty may be more important to the future of biotechnology than resolving it in any particular way." We need not, however, make an arbitrary choice between liability and nonliability. Instead, [we think that liability] based upon existing disclosure obligations, rather than an unprecedented extension of the conversion theory, protects patients' rights of privacy and autonomy without unnecessarily hindering research.

To be sure, the threat of liability for conversion might help to enforce patients' rights indirectly [because] physicians might be able to avoid liability by obtaining patients' consent, in the broadest possible terms, to any conceivable subsequent research use of excised cells. Unfortunately, to extend the conversion theory would utterly sacrifice the other goal of protecting innocent parties. Since conversion is a strict liability tort, it would impose liability on all those into whose hands the cells come, whether or not the particular defendant participated in, or knew of, the inadequate disclosures that violated the patient's right to make an informed decision. In contrast to the conversion theory, the fiduciary-duty and informed-consent theories protect the patient directly, without punishing innocent parties or creating disincentives to the conduct of socially beneficial research.

Research on human cells plays a critical role in medical research ... because researchers are increasingly able to isolate naturally occurring, medically useful biological substances and to produce useful quantities of such substances through genetic engineering. . . . Products developed through biotechnology that have already been approved for marketing in this country include treatments and tests for leukemia, cancer, diabetes, dwarfism, hepatitis-B, kidney transplant rejection, emphysema, osteoporosis, ulcers, anemia, infertility, and gynecological tumors, to name but a few.

Future Policy Concerns

The extension of conversion law into this area will hinder research by restricting access to the necessary raw materials. Thousands of human cell lines already exist in tissue repositories [and] are routinely copied and distributed to other researchers for experimental purposes, usually free of charge. This exchange of scientific materials, which still is relatively free and efficient, will surely be compromised if each cell sample becomes the potential subject matter of a lawsuit.

To expand liability by extending conversion law into this area would have a broad impact. [It is estimated that about half] "of the researchers at medical institutions surveyed used human tissues or cells in their research." . . . In addition, "there are nearly 350 commercial biotechnology firms in the United States actively engaged in biotechnology research and commercial product development and approximately 25 to 30 percent appear to be engaged in research to develop a human therapeutic or diagnostic reagent. . . . Most, but not all, of the human therapeutic products are derived from human tissues and cells, or human cell lines or cloned genes."

In deciding whether to create new tort duties we have in the past considered the impact that expanded liability would have on activities that are important to society, such as research. . . . [Here,] the theory of liability that Moore urges us to endorse threatens to destroy the economic incentive to conduct important medical research. If the use of cells in research is a conversion, then with every cell sample a researcher purchases a ticket in a litigation lottery. Because liability for conversion is predicated on a continuing ownership interest, "companies are unlikely to invest heavily in developing, manufacturing, or marketing a product when uncertainty about clear title exists." . . .

If the scientific users of human cells are to be held liable for failing to investigate the consensual pedigree of their raw materials, we believe the Legislature should make that decision. . . . Finally, there is no pressing need to impose a judicially created rule of strict liability, since enforcement of physicians' disclosure obligations will protect patients against the very type of harm with which Moore was threatened. . . .

Leave it to Legislature

For these reasons, we hold that the allegations of Moore's third amended complaint state a cause of action for breach of fiduciary duty or lack of informed consent, but not conversion.

H

ARABIAN, J., concurring.

. . . I write separately to . . . speak of the moral issue. Plaintiff has asked us to recognize and enforce a right to sell one's own body tissue *for profit.* He entreats us to regard the human vessel—the single most venerated and protected subject in any civilized society—as equal with the basest commercial commodity. He urges us to commingle the sacred with the profane. He asks much. . . .

[Here, there are] conflicting moral, philosophical and even religious values at stake. . . . The ramifications of recognizing and enforcing a property interest in body tissues are not known, but are greatly feared— the effect on human dignity of a marketplace in human body parts, the impact on research and development of competitive bidding for such materials, and the exposure of researchers to potentially limitless and uncharted tort liability. . . .

Whether, as plaintiff urges, his cells should be treated as property susceptible to conversion is not, in my view, ours to decide. The question implicates choices which not only reflect, but which ultimately define our essence. . . . Where then shall a complete resolution be found? Clearly the Legislature, as the majority opinion suggests, is the proper deliberative forum. Indeed, a legislative response creating a licensing scheme, which establishes a fixed rate of profit sharing between researcher and subject, has already been suggested. Such an arrangement would not only avoid the moral and philosophical objections to a free market operation in body tissue, but would also address stated concerns by eliminating the inherent- ly coercive effect of a waiver system and by compensating donors regard- less of temporal circumstances. . . .

MOSK, J., dissenting.

I dissent . . . for all the reasons stated by the Court of Appeal, and for additional reasons that I shall explain. . . .

The majority [finds] "reasons to doubt" that Moore retained a suffi- cient ownership interest in his cells, after their excision, to support a conversion cause of action. . . . The majority's first reason is that "no reported judicial decision supports Moore's claim," [but neither] is there any reported decision rejecting such a claim. The issue is as new as its source—the recent explosive growth in the commercialization of biotech- nology.

[The majority says that we should] "look for guidance" to the Legisla- ture rather than to the law of conversion. Surely this argument is out of place in an opinion of the highest court of this state. [T]he law of conversion is a creature of the common law. "The inherent capacity of the common law for growth and change is its most significant feature. Its development has been determined by the social needs of the community which it serves. . . ." [While the Legislature may act], "in the common law system the primary instruments of this evolution are the courts. . . ."

The majority's second reason for doubting that Moore retained an ownership interest in his cells [is Calif. Health & Safety Code § 7504.4, but] it does not follow that—as the majority conclude—the statute "elimi- nates so many of the rights ordinarily attached to property" that what remains does not amount to "property" or "ownership" for purposes of the law of conversion. The concepts of property and ownership in our law are extremely broad. ... Being broad, the concept of property is also abstract: rather than referring directly to a material object such as a parcel of land or the tractor that cultivates it, the concept of property is often said to refer to a "bundle of rights" that may be exercised with respect to that object—principally the rights to possess the property, to use the property, to exclude others from the property, and to dispose of the property by sale or by gift. ... But the same bundle of rights does not attach to all forms of property. For a variety of policy reasons, the law limits or even forbids the exercise of certain rights over certain forms of property. For example, both law and contract may limit the right of an owner of real property to use his parcel as he sees fit. Owners of various forms of personal property may likewise be subject to restrictions on the time, place, and manner of their use. Limitations on the disposition of real property, while less common, may also be imposed. Finally, some types of personal property may be sold but not given away,[7] while others may be given away but not sold,[8] and still others may neither be given away nor sold.[9]

In each of the foregoing instances, the limitation or prohibition diminishes the bundle of rights that would otherwise attach to the property, yet what remains is still deemed in law to be a ... property interest. ... The same rule applies to Moore's interest in his own body tissue: ... at the time of its excision he at least had *the right to do with his own tissue whatever the defendants did with it*: i.e., he could have contracted with researchers and pharmaceutical companies to develop and exploit the vast commercial potential of his tissue and its products....

The majority's third and last reason for their conclusion that Moore has no cause of action for conversion under existing law is that "the subject matter of the Regents' patent—the patented cell line and the products derived from it—cannot be Moore's property ... because the patented cell line is both *factually* and *legally* distinct from the cells taken from Moore's body." Neither branch of the explanation withstands analysis. First, ... no distinction can be drawn between Moore's cells and the Mo cell line. ... [The] principal reason for establishing a cell line is not to "improve" the quality of the parent cells but simply to extend their life indefinitely, in order to [exploit] the qualities already present in such cells. ... Moore's cells naturally produced certain valuable proteins in larger than normal quantities; indeed, that was why defendants were eager to culture them in the first place. [It is] their capacity to produce proteins [—and] the commercial exploitation of that capacity ... that Moore seeks to

---

7. [n.9] A person contemplating bankruptcy may sell his property at its "reasonably equivalent value," but he may not make a gift of the same property. (See 11 U.S.C. § 548(a).)

8. [n. 10] A sportsman may give away wild fish or game that he has caught or killed pursuant to his license, but he may not sell it. (Fish & G. Code, §§ 3039, 7121.) The transfer of human organs and blood is a special case that I discuss below.

9. [n. 11] E.g., a license to practice a profession, or a prescription drug in the hands of the person for whom it is prescribed.

assert an interest. Second, the majority [says] that Moore cannot have an ownership interest in the Mo cell line because defendants patented it. The majority's point wholly fails to meet Moore's claim that he is entitled to compensation for defendants' unauthorized use of his bodily tissues *before* defendants patented the Mo cell line: ... the patent ... did not issue until ... more than seven years after the unauthorized use began. ... [While] the patent granted defendants the exclusive right to make, use, or sell the invention for a period of 17 years ... Moore does not assert any such right for himself. Rather, he seeks to show that he is entitled ... to some share in the profits that defendants have made and will make from their commercial exploitation of the Mo cell line....

[T]he majority next consider whether to "extend" the conversion cause of action to this context [and conclude not to do so.] I respectfully disagree....

[O]ur society acknowledges a profound ethical imperative to respect the human body as the physical and temporal expression of the unique human persona. One manifestation of that respect is our prohibition against direct abuse of the body by torture or other forms of cruel or unusual punishment. Another is our prohibition against indirect abuse of the body by its economic exploitation for the sole benefit of another person. The most abhorrent form of such exploitation, of course, was the institution of slavery. Lesser forms, such as indentured servitude or even debtor's prison, have also disappeared. Yet their specter haunts ... today's biotechnological research-industrial complex. It arises wherever scientists or industrialists claim, as defendants claim here, the right to appropriate and exploit a patient's tissue for their sole economic benefit— the right ... to freely mine or harvest valuable physical properties of the patient's body....

A second policy consideration adds notions of equity to those of ethics. Our society values fundamental fairness in dealings between its members, and condemns the unjust enrichment of any member at the expense of another. This is particularly true when, as here, the parties are not in equal bargaining positions. ... [T]he complaint alleges that the market for the kinds of proteins produced by the Mo cell line was predicted to exceed $3 billion by 1990. These profits are currently shared exclusively between the biotechnology industry and the universities that support that industry. ... [B]ut for the cells of Moore's body taken by defendants there would have been no Mo cell line at all. Yet defendants deny that Moore is entitled to any share whatever in the proceeds of this cell line. This is both inequitable and immoral. [But] "property rights in one's own tissue would provide a morally acceptable result by giving effect to notions of fairness and preventing unjust enrichment." ...

I do not doubt that the Legislature is competent to act on this topic. The fact that the Legislature may intervene if and when it chooses, however, does not in the meanwhile relieve the courts of their duty of enforcing—or if need be, fashioning—an effective judicial remedy for the wrong here alleged....

The inference I draw from the current statutory regulation of human biological materials, moreover, is the opposite of that drawn by the majority. By selective quotation of the statutes the majority seem to suggest that human organs and blood cannot legally be sold on the open market—thereby implying that if the Legislature were to act here it would impose a similar ban on monetary compensation for the use of human tissue in biotechnological research and development. But if that is the argument, the premise is unsound: contrary to popular misconception, it is not true that human organs and blood cannot legally be sold.

As to organs, the majority rely on the Uniform Anatomical Gift Act (Health & Saf. Code, § 7150 et seq.; hereafter the UAGA) for the proposition that a competent adult may make a post mortem gift of any part of his body but may not receive "valuable consideration" for the transfer. But the prohibition of the UAGA against the sale of a body part ... applies only to sales for "transplantation" or "therapy." Yet a different section of the UAGA authorizes the transfer and receipt of body parts for such additional purposes as "medical or dental education, research, or advancement of medical or dental science." (Health & Saf. Code, § 7153, subd. (a)(1)). No section of the UAGA prohibits anyone from selling body parts for any of those additional purposes; by clear implication, therefore, such sales are legal. Indeed, the fact that the UAGA prohibits *no* sales of organs other than sales for "transplantation" or "therapy" raises a further implication that it is also legal for anyone to sell human tissue to a biotechnology company for research and development purposes.

With respect to the sale of human blood the matter is much simpler: there is in fact no prohibition against such sales. ... It follows that the statutes regulating the transfers of human organs and blood do not support the majority's refusal to recognize a conversion cause of action for commercial exploitation of human blood cells without consent. On the contrary, because such statutes treat both organs and blood as property that can legally be sold in a variety of circumstances, they impliedly support Moore's contention that his blood cells are likewise property for which he can and should receive compensation, and hence are protected by the law of conversion.

The majority's final reason for refusing to recognize a conversion cause of action on these facts is that "there is no pressing need" to do so because the complaint also states another cause of action that is assertedly adequate to the task.... I disagree ... with the majority's ... conclusion that in the present context a nondisclosure cause of action is an adequate—in fact, a superior—substitute for a conversion cause of action. [These] obligations will primarily be enforced by the traditional judicial remedy of an action for damages for their breach....

The remedy is largely illusory. "[A]n action based on the physician's failure to disclose material information sounds in negligence. As a practical matter ... it may be difficult to recover on this kind of negligence theory because the patient must prove a *causal connection* between his or her injury and the physician's failure to inform." ... There are two barriers to recovery. First, "the patient must show that if he or she had been informed of all pertinent information, he or she would have declined to consent to the procedure in question." ... The second barrier to recovery is still higher ...: it is not even enough for the plaintiff to prove that he personally would have refused consent to the proposed treatment if he had been fully informed; he must also prove that in the same circumstances *no reasonably prudent person* would have given such consent....

The second reason why the nondisclosure cause of action is inadequate ... is that it fails to solve half the problem before us: it gives the patient only the right to *refuse* consent, i.e., the right to prohibit the commercialization of his tissue; it does not give him the right to *grant* consent to that commercialization on the condition that he share in its proceeds. ... [T]he patient can say no, but he cannot say yes and expect to share in the proceeds of his contribution. Yet ..., there are sound reasons of ethics and equity to recognize the patient's right to participate in such benefits. The nondisclosure cause of action does not protect that right....

Third, the nondisclosure cause of action fails to reach a major class of potential defendants: all those who are outside the strict physician-patient relationship with the plaintiff. Thus the majority concede that here only defendant Golde, the treating physician, can be directly liable to Moore on a nondisclosure cause of action....

In sum, the nondisclosure cause of action (1) is unlikely to be successful in most cases, (2) fails to protect patients' rights to share in the proceeds of the commercial exploitation of their tissue, and (3) may allow the true exploiters to escape liability. It is thus not an adequate substitute ... for the conversion cause of action....

NOTES

1. The "Bundle of Rights." The majority and the dissent agree that property is composed of a number of separate rights which, when bundled together, constitute property. These sticks in the bundle are said to consist of the right to possess, use, dispose, and exclude others from the thing we call property. But, as Justice Mosk noted, it may not be necessary to enjoy every stick in order to have property. But how many sticks (and which ones) may be removed without destroying the concept of property? Justice Mosk noted several examples of property that lack all the sticks in the bundle. Here are some more to ponder.

Disposition. In the early 1970s Congress enacted legislation that forbade the taking of bald and golden eagles, or the possession or sale of their parts, including feathers. Exempted from the ban were the possession and transportation of eagle feathers acquired before the ban took effect. In Andrus v.

Allard, 444 U.S. 51 (1979), the Supreme Court ruled that the laws did not effect a taking of property without just compensation. In so holding, the Court assumed that a property right was involved, because "the denial of one traditional property right does not always amount to a taking. At least where an owner possesses a full 'bundle' of property rights, the destruction of one 'strand' of the bundle is not a taking, because the aggregate must be viewed in its entirety. In this case, it is crucial that appellees retain the rights to possess and transport their property, and to donate or devise the protected birds."

Exclusion. Kaiser Aetna leased from Hawaii's Bishop Estate about 6,000 acres, including Kuapa Pond, a non-navigable pond separated from the Pacific by a barrier beach. Kaiser Aetna dredged the pond and constructed a dredged channel connecting the pond to the Pacific, then built a marina and developed building sites around the pond. The United States claimed that as, a result, the pond was a navigable waterway entitling the public to its use. In Kaiser Aetna v. United States, 444 U.S. 164 (1979), the Supreme Court ruled that although the pond had become navigable and thus was subject to a navigation servitude[10] in favor of the public, the imposition of that servitude without compensation constituted a taking of "one of the most essential sticks in the bundle of rights that are commonly characterized as property—the right to exclude others." *Id.* at 176.

A number of states require owners of land on which is located a private burial ground to make the burial ground available to the public on reasonable terms. A typical statute is Texas Health & Safety Code § 711.041(a):

> Any person who wishes to visit a cemetery or private burial grounds for which no public ingress or egress is available shall have the right to reasonable ingress and egress for the purpose of visiting the cemetery or private burial grounds. This right of access extends only to visitation during the hours [and over the "routes of reasonable ingress and egress"] determined by the owner or owners of the lands ... or at a reasonable time [selected by the visitor if 14 days notice is given to the owner,] and only for purposes usually associated with cemetery visits.

Similar statutes exist in Missouri, South Carolina, West Virginia, Alabama, Florida, Virginia, and other states. Do these statutes take property, in the form of the right to exclude, without compensation? Put an owner's terms

Consider State v. Shack, 58 N.J. 297 (1971). Tedesco, a farmer, employed migrant workers for whom he provided modest housing on his farm. Terejas, an employee of an organization funded by the United States that was dedicated to providing health services for migrant farm workers, entered Tedesco's farm for the purpose of removing 28 sutures in one of the workers housed on Tedesco's farm. Shack, a legal aid attorney, entered Tedesco's farm to consult with another worker on the farm. Tedesco denied access to the farm housing area to Tejeras and Shack and, when they refused to leave, summoned police who arrested them for criminal trespass. Tejeras and Shack appealed their convictions. The New Jersey Supreme Court set aside the

---

10.   You will encounter servitudes in Chapter 10. They take a number of forms but all involve the right to use or control the use of somebody else's property. The navigation servitude in *Kaiser Aetna* was a claimed right of the public to use Kaiser Aetna's property for marine navigation.

convictions because it concluded that Tejeras and Shack had "invaded no possessory right" of Tedesco. Why not?

> The reason is that [in New Jersey] the ownership of real property does not include the right to bar access to governmental services available to migrant workers. . . . Property rights serve human values. . . . Title to real property cannot include dominion over the destiny of persons the owner permits to come onto the premises. [Migrant farm workers,] a highly disadvantaged segment of our society, . . . are a community within but apart from the local scene. They are rootless and isolated. . . . It is their plight that summoned government to their aid [and that aid] would not be gained if the intended beneficiaries could be insulated from efforts to reach them. . . . A man's right in his real property is of course not absolute. It was a maxim of the common law that one should so use his property as not to injure the rights of others. Although hardly a precise solvent of actual controversies, the maxim does express the . . . proposition that rights are relative and there must be an accommodation when they meet. [It is] unthinkable that the farmer-employer can assert a right to isolate the migrant worker in any respect significant for the worker's well-being. [The] migrant worker must be allowed to receive visitors . . . of his own choice [at his living quarters], so long as there is no behavior hurtful to others. . . .

Why was the right to exclude not part of Tedesco's bundle of sticks called property? Could Tedesco validly prevent Tejeras and Shack from entering his farm to consult with his employees while they were on a lunch break from work?

Destruction. Do you have the right to destroy your own property? Baseball fans may recall that a Chicago restaurant paid over $100,000 to purchase and then destroy the baseball that was snatched by a Cubs fan out of the clutches of a Cubs outfielder at a pivotal moment in the 2003 National League Championship Series. Had the ball been caught, Cubs fans thought, the Cubs would have progressed to the World Series. The Cubs were cursed, and destruction of the baseball might exorcize the curse. After all, the restaurant would have the right to burn up $100,000 in currency, so why not a baseball purchased for that amount? But suppose that the restaurant purchased a Picasso sketch for $100,000; would it have the right to burn the Picasso? Joseph Sax, a law professor at Berkeley, thinks not. In Joseph L. Sax, Playing Darts with a Rembrandt: Public and Private Rights in Cultural Treasures (1999), Sax argues that owners of cultural artifacts should not possess any right to destroy them. Such a rule would have frustrated the Rockefeller family's destruction of a Diego Rivera mural they owned because it contained an image of Lenin, or Lady Churchill's destruction of a portrait of Winston Churchill by Graham Sutherland that she considered demeaning of Churchill, or the Taliban's 2001 destruction of the sixth century Bamiyan Buddhas. Yet, as Lior Strahilevitz, a law professor at the University of Chicago, has argued, there is an expressive element in these acts of destruction. See Lior Strahilevitz, The Right to Destroy, 114 Yale L. J. 781 (2005).

B. HOW IS PROPERTY INITIALLY ACQUIRED?

We turn now to the question of how property may initially be acquired. Of course, most property we encounter already has an owner, but how did that initial owner acquire the legal rights we call ownership?

1. DISCOVERY

Not much (if any) real property (at least on Earth) is undiscovered. But it could happen, as with a new volcanic island emerging from the sea, belching lava. Acquisition of property by discovery was much more relevant in what historians call the "age of discovery," the period of roughly from the early 1400s to the early 1600s in which European explorers began to map the planet and made contact with people living in the other continents of Earth. The legal consequences of European discovery became an issue in a United States Supreme Court decision, Johnson and Graham's Lessee v. M'Intosh, 21 U.S. (8 Wheat.) 543 (1823).

In 1818 William M'Intosh purchased a tract of land in present-day Illinois from the United States. Thomas Johnson and Thomas Graham claimed title to the property by virtue of two prior deeds, a 1773 deed from the Illinois tribe of Indians and an 1775 deed from the Piankeshaw tribe, and sought to eject M'Intosh from occupancy of the land. The Supreme Court ruled for M'Intosh. In writing for the Court, Chief Justice Marshall stated:

> The inquiry [is] confined to the power of Indians to give ... a title which can be sustained in courts of this country. [T]itle to lands ... must be admitted to depend entirely on the law of the nation in which they lie....

> On the discovery of this immense continent, the great nations of Europe were eager to appropriate to themselves so much of it as they could respectively acquire. Its vast extent offered an ample field to the ambition and enterprise of all; and the character and religion of its inhabitants afforded an apology for considering them as a people over whom the superior genius of Europe might claim an ascendency. The potentates of the old world found no difficulty in convincing themselves that they made ample compensation to the inhabitants of the new, by bestowing on them civilization and Christianity, in exchange for [their] unlimited independence. But, as they were all in pursuit of nearly the same object, it was necessary, in order to avoid conflicting settlements, and consequent war with each other, to establish a principle, which all should acknowledge as the law by which the right of acquisition, which they all asserted, should be regulated as between themselves. This principle was, that discovery gave title to the government by whose subjects, or by whose authority, it was made, against

Right to acquire
Oil + deal w/
Natives.

all other European governments, which title might be consummated by possession. The exclusion of all other Europeans, necessarily gave to the nation making the discovery the sole right of acquiring the soil from the natives, and establishing settlements upon it. It was a right with which no Europeans could interfere. It was a right which all asserted for themselves, and to the assertion of which, by others, all assented....

[T]he rights of the original inhabitants were, in no instance, entirely disregarded; but were necessarily, to a considerable extent, impaired. They were admitted to be the rightful occupants of the soil, with a legal as well as just claim to retain possession of it, and to use it according to their own discretion; but their rights to complete sovereignty, as independent nations, were necessarily diminished, and their power to dispose of the soil at their own will, to whomsoever they pleased, was denied by the original fundamental principle, that discovery gave exclusive title to those who made it. While the different nations of Europe respected the right of the natives, as occupants, they asserted the ultimate dominion to be in themselves; and claimed and exercised, as a consequence of this ultimate dominion, a power to grant the soil, while yet in possession of the natives. These grants have been understood by all, to convey a title to the grantees, subject only to the Indian right of occupancy....

By the treaty which concluded the war of our revolution, ... the powers of government, and the right to soil, which had previously been in Great Britain, passed definitively to these States. ... The States, having within their chartered limits different portions of territory covered by Indians, ceded that territory, generally, to the United States.... The United States, then, have unequivocally acceded to that great and broad rule by which its civilized inhabitants now hold this country. They hold, and assert in themselves, the title by which it was acquired. They maintain, as all others have maintained, that discovery gave an exclusive right to extinguish the Indian title of occupancy, either by purchase or by conquest; and gave also a right to such a degree of sovereignty, as the circumstances of the people would allow them to exercise....

You might note that the Illinois and Piankeshaw Indians had discovered the lands in question long before the European discoverers. Why, then, did European discovery trump Indian discovery?

2. CONQUEST

In *M'Intosh* the Supreme Court noted that the "Indian title of occupancy" could be terminated by purchase or conquest. On the subject of conquest, the Court declared:

Conquest gives a title which the Courts of the conqueror cannot deny. ... The title by conquest is acquired and maintained by force.

The conqueror prescribes its limits. Humanity, however, ... has established ... that the conquered shall not be wantonly oppressed, and that their condition shall remain as eligible as is compatible with the objects of the conquest. Most usually, they are incorporated with the victorious nation, and become subjects or citizens of the government with which they are connected. The new and old members of the society mingle with each other; the distinction between them is gradually lost, and they make one people. Where this incorporation is practicable, humanity demands, and a wise policy requires, that the rights of the conquered to property should remain unimpaired; that the new subjects should be governed as equitably as the old, and that confidence in their security should gradually banish the painful sense of being separated from their ancient connexions, and united by force to strangers.

But the tribes of Indians inhabiting this country were fierce savages, whose occupation was war, and whose subsistence was drawn chiefly from the forest. To leave them in possession of their country, was to leave the country a wilderness; to govern them as a distinct people, was impossible, because they were as brave and as high spirited as they were fierce, and were ready to repel by arms every attempt on their independence. What was the inevitable consequence of this state of things? The Europeans were under the necessity either of abandoning the country, and relinquishing their pompous claims to it, or of enforcing those claims by the sword, and by the adoption of principles adapted to the condition of a people with whom it was impossible to mix, and who could not be governed as a distinct society, or of remaining in their neighbourhood, and exposing themselves and their families to the perpetual hazard of being massacred. Frequent and bloody wars, in which the whites were not always the aggressors, unavoidably ensued. European policy, numbers, and skill, prevailed. As the white population advanced, that of the Indians necessarily receded. The country in the immediate neighbourhood of agriculturists became unfit for them. The game fled into thicker and more unbroken forests, and the Indians followed. The soil, to which the crown originally claimed title, being no longer occupied by its ancient inhabitants, was parcelled out according to the will of the sovereign power, and taken possession of by persons who claimed immediately from the crown, or mediately, through its grantees or deputies. ... [Thus,] the Indian inhabitants are to be considered merely as occupants, to be protected, indeed, while in peace, in the possession of their lands, but to be deemed incapable of transferring the absolute title to others. . . .

For a more nuanced view of the transfer of title to land occupied by Indians to European settlers, see Stuart Banner, How the Indians Lost Their Land: Law and Power on the Frontier (2005).

FLEMING v. PAGE

United States Supreme Court
50 U.S. (9 How.) 603 (1850)

[Joseph Fleming and William Marshall, partners in the trading firm of Fleming & Marshall, brought merchandise from Tampico, Mexico to Philadelphia in the spring of 1847. By an 1846 act of Congress, the United States imposed a tariff applicable to goods imported from foreign countries. Fleming and Marshall contended that because the goods had been brought from Tampico after it had been occupied by American troops during the Mexican War, Tampico was no longer a foreign port but, by virtue of American conquest, under American sovereignty and thus the tariff was inapplicable. Fleming and Marshall's argument succeeded in the lower courts but was appealed to the United States Supreme Courts.]

CHIEF JUSTICE TANEY delivered the opinion of the Court.

The question ... turns upon the construction of the act of Congress of July 30, 1846. The duties levied upon the cargo of the schooner *Catharine* were the duties imposed by this law upon goods imported from a foreign country. And if at the time of this shipment Tampico was not a foreign port within the meaning of the act of Congress, then the duties were illegally charged, and, having been paid under protest, the plaintiffs would be entitled to recover in this action the amount exacted by the collector.

The port of Tampico, at which the goods were shipped, and the Mexican State of Tamaulipas, in which it is situated, were undoubtedly at the time of the shipment subject to the sovereignty and dominion of the United States. The Mexican authorities had been driven out, or had submitted to our army and navy; and the country was in the exclusive and firm possession of the United States, and governed by its military authorities, acting under the orders of the President. But it does not follow that it was a part of the United States, or that it ceased to be a foreign country, in the sense in which these words are used in the acts of Congress. The country in question had been conquered in war. But the genius and character of our institutions are peaceful, and the power to declare war was not conferred upon Congress for the purposes of aggression or aggrandizement, but to enable the general government to vindicate by arms, if it should become necessary, its own rights and the rights of its citizens. A war, therefore, declared by Congress, can never be presumed to be waged for the purpose of conquest or the acquisition of territory; nor does the law declaring the war imply an authority to the President to enlarge the limits of the United States by subjugating the enemy's country. The United States, it is true, may extend its boundaries by conquest or treaty, and may demand the cession of territory as the condition of peace, in order to indemnify its citizens for the injuries they have suffered, or to reimburse the government for the expenses of the war. But this can be done only by the treaty-making power or the legislative authority, and is not a part of the power conferred upon the President by the declaration of war. His duty and his power are purely military. As commander-in-chief, he is authorized to direct the movements of the naval and military forces placed by law at his command, and to employ them in the manner he may deem most effectual to harass and conquer and subdue the enemy. He may invade the hostile country, and subject it to the sovereignty and authority of the United States. But his conquests do not enlarge the boundaries of this Union, nor extend the operation of our institutions and laws beyond the limits before assigned to them by the legislative power.

It is true, that, when Tampico had been captured, and the State of Tamaulipas subjugated, other nations were bound to regard the country, while our possession continued, as the territory of the United States, and to respect it as such. For, by the laws and usages of nations, conquest is a valid title, while the victor maintains the exclusive possession of the conquered country. The citizens of no other nation, therefore, had a right to enter it without the permission of the American authorities, nor to hold intercourse with its inhabitants, nor to trade with them. As regarded all other nations, it was a part of the United States, and belonged to them as exclusively as the territory included in our established boundaries.

But yet it was not a part of this Union. For every nation which acquires territory by treaty or conquest holds it according to its own institutions and laws. And the relation in which the port of Tampico stood to the United States while it was occupied by their arms did not depend upon the laws of nations, but upon our own Constitution and acts of Congress. The power of the President under which Tampico and the State of Tamaulipas were conquered and held in subjection was simply that of a military commander prosecuting a war waged against a public enemy by the authority of his government. And the country from which these goods were imported was invaded and subdued, and occupied as the territory of a foreign hostile nation, as a portion of Mexico, and was held in possession in order to distress and harass the enemy. While it was occupied by our troops, they were in an enemy's country, and not in their own; the inhabitants were still foreigners and enemies, and owed to the United States nothing more than the submission and obedience, sometimes called temporary allegiance, which is due from a conquered enemy, when he surrenders to a force which he is unable to resist. But the boundaries of the United States, as they existed when war was declared against Mexico, were not extended by the conquest; nor could they be regulated by the varying incidents of war, and be enlarged or diminished as the armies on either side advanced or retreated. They remained unchanged. And every place which was out of the limits of the United States, as previously established by the political authorities of the government, was still foreign; nor did our laws extend over it. Tampico was, therefore, a foreign port when this shipment was made.

1. Acquisition by Conquest: Might makes Right? Chief Justice Taney[11] made a distinction between conquest as a source of political authority and as a source of ownership. Conquest by military force, he said, produces political power, but ownership depends upon a treaty between the victor and the vanquished. That may be true under American law, but is it universal? Does China have both political authority and ownership of Tibet? From a Chinese perspective it possesses both attributes. The Seventeen Point Agreement signed in 1951 by delegates of the Dalai Lama and the People's Republic of China satisfies the form of a treaty cession but is regarded by many as a coerced cession. Is the same true with respect to the Treaty of Guadeloupe Hidalgo, which ceded much of today's American southwest from Mexico to the United States? From a practical standpoint, does it matter?

2. Conquest Today. The international community generally condemns conquest and agrees that title acquired by conquest is void. See, e.g., United Nations Resolution 3314 (14 December 1974), Article V of which provides that "[n]o territorial acquisition ... resulting from aggression is or shall be recognized as lawful."[12] What, then, is the status of the territories occupied by Israel after the 1967 Six–Day War that formerly were part of Egypt, Syria, and Jordan?

3. FIRST POSSESSION

Discovery may not be of much importance today, but it embodies a principle—first in time—that is still very much at work in our notions of property. It is an ingrained cultural principle that the first to come is the first to be served. It is an equally venerable legal principle that the first person to possess an unowned object—a shell on a beach of an uninhabited island, perhaps—is entitled to ownership of the object. Depending on the specific circumstances, that conclusion is subject to a fair number of exceptions, as we shall see. But on to the main point: If first possession is the root of ownership, why should it be so?

The English philosopher John Locke argued, in Chapter V of Book II of his Two Treatises of Government that "every man has a property in his

11. Roger Taney (pronounced "TAW-nee") was appointed by Andrew Jackson to succeed John Marshall. He was the first Roman Catholic to serve on the Court. Before mounting the bench he served as Jackson's Attorney General and, under a recess appointment, as Secretary of the Treasury. The Whig-dominated Senate refused to confirm him as Treasury Secretary. Undaunted, President Jackson nominated him to succeed Gabriel Duval as an Associate Justice but the Whigs blocked his confirmation. After an intervening election and the death of John Marshall, Jackson tried again, nominating Taney for the post of Chief Justice. Though the Whigs tried to kill the nomination, Taney was confirmed. He presided over a Court that accommodated state authority to regulate commerce. Taney is best known for his authorship of the *Dred Scott* case, Scott v. Sandford, 60 U.S. (19 How.) 393 (1857), which held that persons of African descent could not become citizens and prohibited federal regulation of slavery in the territories. During the Civil War Taney ruled, in his capacity as a Circuit Judge, that only Congress, and not President Lincoln, had the power to suspend the writ of habeas corpus. Ex parte Merryman, 17 F. Cas. 144 (1861). Lincoln and the Army ignored the ruling.

12. The full text of the resolution may be accessed at http://www.un.org/documents/ga/res/29/ares29.htm.

own person. This nobody has any right to but himself. The labor of his body, and the work of his hands, . . . are properly his. Whatsoever then he removes out of the state that nature has provided, . . . he has mixed his labor with, and joined it to something that is his own, and thereby makes it his property." After reading *Moore*, you may well doubt the universality of the premise that "every man has a property in his own person," but the idea that one possesses a right to reap the rewards of one's lawful labor is fairly uncontroversial, though it too has its limits. Consider, for example, the problem of a person who sows, tends, and harvests wheat in a field that, unknown to him, is not his own. Should the farmer or the owner of the field own the wheat? Or, should we award the wheat to the farmer and require him to pay damages to the field owner?

First possession, says Richard Epstein, a law professor at the University of Chicago, "promotes a system of decentralized ownership: private actions by private parties shape . . . individual entitlements in ways that do not involve the active role of the state, whose job [is] restricted to protecting entitlements previously acquired by private means. The rule [permits] a system of rights that is not dependent on the whim of the sovereign. . . ." Richard A. Epstein, Past and Future: The Temporal Dimension in the Law of Property, 64 Wash. U. L. Q. 667, 669 (1986). Moreover, first possession is likely to resolve ownership in favor of a single owner. When you study concurrent ownership in Chapter Five you will begin to understand some of the problems inherent in multiple owners of the same property. Finally, first possession is an inexpensive way to resolve ownership claims; its stability obviates a great deal of expense and uncertainty that would attach to more subjective measures of determining initial ownership.

Nevertheless, there are critics of the first possession rule. Carol Rose, a law professor at the University of Arizona, argues that the first possession rule embodies an "attitude . . . with respect to the relationship between human beings and nature. . . . [F]irst possession . . . reflects the attitude that human beings are outsiders to nature. . . . Its texts are those of cultivation, manufacture, and development. We cannot have our fish both loose and fast, as Herman Melville might put it. . . . [F]irst possession . . . gives preference to those who convince the world that they can catch the fish and hold it fast. This may be a reward to useful labor, but it is more precisely [a manifestation of the mores] understood by a commercial people." Carol M. Rose, Property and Persuasion 19–20 (1994).

Rose's allusion to fast fish and loose fish is to Chapter 89 of Herman Melville's masterpiece, *Moby Dick*. To explain how whales become property, Melville describes two rules: "I. A Fast–Fish belongs to the party fast to it. II. A Loose–Fish is fair game for anybody who can soonest catch it." Herman Melville, *Moby–Dick; or, The Whale* 406 (University of California Press, Arion Press edition, 1979). Now consider the application of those rules.

PIERSON v. POST

Supreme Court of Judicature of New York
3 Caines 175 (1805)

[Lodowick Post sued Jesse Pierson in justice court for wrongful taking of his property. The property in question was a fox. Post alleged that he had taken out his dogs and hounds and, "upon a certain wild and uninhabitable, unpossessed and waste land, called the beach," found and chased "one of those noxious beasts called a fox." While in hot pursuit of the fox Pierson appeared, killed the fox, and carried off his carcass. Post alleged that Pierson did this with full knowledge of Post's pursuit and in Post's sight. The justice court rendered a verdict for Post and Pierson appealed.]

TOMPKINS, J. delivered the opinion of the court.

... The question ... is, whether Lodowick Post, by the pursuit with his hounds in the manner alleged in his declaration, acquired such a right to, or property in, the fox, as will sustain an action against Pierson for killing and taking him away? The cause was argued with much ability by the counsel on both sides, and presents for our decision a novel and nice question. It is admitted that a fox is an animal *feræ naturæ,* and that property in such animals is acquired by occupancy only. These admissions narrow the discussion to the simple question of what acts amount to occupancy, applied to acquiring right to wild animals?

If we have recourse to the ancient writers upon general principles of law, the judgment below is obviously erroneous. Justinian's Institutes,[13] lib. 2. tit. 1. s. 13. and Fleta,[14] lib. 3. c. 2. p. 175, adopt the principle, that pursuit alone vests no property or right in the huntsman; and that even pursuit, accompanied with wounding, is equally ineffectual for that purpose, unless the animal be actually taken. The same principle is recognised by Bracton,[15] lib. 2. c. 1. p. 8. Puffendorf,[16] lib. 4. c. 6. s. 2. and 10, defines occupancy of beasts *feræ naturæ,* to be the actual corporal possession of them, and Bynkershoek[17] is cited as coinciding in this definition. It is indeed with hesitation that Puffendorf affirms that a wild beast mortally wounded, or greatly maimed, cannot be fairly intercepted by another, whilst the pursuit of the person inflicting the wound continues. The foregoing authorities are decisive to show that mere pursuit gave Post no legal right to the fox, but that he became the property of Pierson, who intercepted and killed him.

---

13. [Ed.] Justinian's Institutes is a sixth century A.D. Roman law treatise.

14. [Ed.] Fleta is a treatise on English law, written in Latin around 1290. Its author is unknown, but was clearly very learned in the law. The treatise carries the name Fleta because the author was imprisoned in Fleet prison, giving new meaning to the term "jailhouse lawyer."

15. [Ed.] Henry de Bracton was an English jurist of the thirteenth century. His work, The Laws and Customs of England, which is referred to here by the court, was written around 1260.

16. [Ed.] Samuel von Pufendorf was a German jurist of the 17th century. His work, The Laws of Nature and Man (1672), is cited here.

17. [Ed.] Cornelius van Bynkershoek was a Dutch jurist of the late 17th and early 18th centuries.

It therefore only remains to inquire whether there are any contrary principles, or authorities, to be found in other books, which ought to induce a different decision. Most of the cases which have occurred in England, relating to property in wild animals, have either been discussed and decided upon the principles of their positive statute regulations, or have arisen between the huntsman and the owner of the land upon which beasts *feræ naturæ* have been apprehended; the former claiming them by title of occupancy, and the latter *ratione soli*.[18] Little satisfactory aid can, therefore, be derived from the English reporters.

Barbeyrac,[19] in his notes on Puffendorf, does not accede to the definition of occupancy by the latter, but, on the contrary, affirms, that actual bodily seizure is not, in all cases, necessary to constitute possession of wild animals. He does not, however, *describe* the acts which, according to his ideas, will amount to an appropriation of such animals to private use, so as to exclude the claims of all other persons, by title of occupancy, to the same animals; and he is far from averring that pursuit alone is sufficient for that purpose. To a certain extent, and as far as Barbeyrac appears to me to go, his objections to Puffendorf's definition of occupancy are reasonable and correct. That is to say, that actual bodily seizure is not indispensable to acquire right to, or possession of, wild beasts; but that, on the contrary, the mortal wounding of such beasts, by one not abandoning his pursuit, may, with the utmost propriety, be deemed possession of him; since, thereby, the pursuer manifests an unequivocal intention of appropriating the animal to his individual use, has deprived him of his natural liberty, and brought him within his certain control. So also, encompassing and securing such animals with nets and toils, or otherwise intercepting them in such a manner as to deprive them of their natural liberty, and render escape impossible, may justly be deemed to give possession of them to those persons who, by their industry and labour, have used such means of apprehending them. Barbeyrac seems to have adopted, and had in view in his notes, the more accurate opinion of Grotius,[20] with respect to occupancy. . . . The case now under consideration is one of mere pursuit, and presents no circumstances or acts which can bring it within the definition of occupancy by Puffendorf, or Grotius, or the ideas of Barbeyrac upon that subject.

[Keeble v. Hickeringill, Q.B., 103 Eng. Rep. 1127; 11 Mod. 74, 130; 3 Salk. 9 (1707) is] clearly distinguishable . . . ; inasmuch as there the action was for maliciously hindering and disturbing the plaintiff in the exercise and enjoyment of a private franchise. . . . [Samuel Keeble owned Minott's

---

18.   [Ed.] Latin for "according to the soil," which operates as a legal idiom to award ownership of the unowned object to the owner of the soil on which it is found, at least in some circumstances.

19.   [Ed.] Jean Barbeyrac was a French Huguenot jurist of the late 17th century and first half of the 18th century who achieved fame by his translation of and notes upon Pufendorf's The Laws of Nature and Man. After revocation of the Edict of Nantes he spent his life in exile in Switzerland and Germany.

20.   [Ed.] Hugo Grotius (or Huig de Groot, or Hugo de Groot) was a Dutch jurist of the early 17th century who laid the foundation for modern international law.

Meadow, on which was a cleverly constructed pond designed to trap unwary ducks for the ultimate end of slaughter and sale for food. Edmund Hickeringill discharged shotguns and other firearms on his own land, with the result that the ducks were frightened away from Keeble's pond before they could be captured. Keeble brought suit and obtained a verdict of £20, which was sustained on appeal. Chief Justice Holt, who played an important role in the establishment of a constitutional monarchy after the abdication of James II, opined that an action lies "where a violent or malicious act is done to a man's occupation, profession, or way of getting a living," and concluded that Hickeringill's act of discharging firearms was for the malicious purpose of damaging Keeble's duck-snaring enterprise. But Judge Tompkins misread *Keeble*, as he noted that Chief Justice Holt] states, that the ducks were in the plaintiff's decoy pond, and *so in his possession,* from which it is obvious the court laid much stress in their opinion upon the plaintiff's possession of the ducks, *ratione soli.*[21]

We are the more readily inclined to confine possession or occupancy of beasts *feræ naturæ,* within the limits prescribed by the learned authors above cited, for the sake of certainty, and preserving peace and order in society. If the first seeing, starting, or pursuing such animals, without having so wounded, circumvented or ensnared them, so as to deprive them of their natural liberty, and subject them to the control of their pursuer, should afford the basis of actions against others for intercepting and killing them, it would prove a fertile source of quarrels and litigation.

However uncourteous or unkind the conduct of Pierson towards Post, in this instance, may have been, yet his act was productive of no injury or damage for which a legal remedy can be applied. We are of opinion the judgment below was erroneous, and ought to be reversed.

LIVINGSTON, J. My opinion differs from that of the court. [The] single question [is whether] a person who, with his own hounds, starts and hunts a fox on waste and uninhabited ground, and is on the point of seizing his prey, acquires such an interest in the animal, as to have a right of action against another, who in view of the huntsman and his dogs in full pursuit, and with knowledge of the chase, shall kill and carry him away?

This is a knotty point, and should have been submitted to the arbitration of sportsmen, without poring over Justinian, Fleta, Bracton, Puffendorf, Locke, Barbeyrac, or Blackstone,[22] all of whom have been

---

21. [Ed.—] For an interesting account of Keeble v. Hickeringill, see A. W. Brian Simpson, Leading Cases in the Common Law 45–75 (1995).

22. [Ed.] Sir William Blackstone (1723–1780) was a titanic figure in Anglo–American law. He was the first Vinerian Professor of Law at Oxford University (and thus the first law professor in England), a member of Parliament, and a judge. His four volume Commentaries on the Laws of England, written between 1765 and 1769 became the Bible of colonial American lawyers and its influence was strongly felt throughout the 19th century. Such was the influence of Blackstone that the edition of Blackstone's *Commentaries* prepared by St George Tucker, a Virginia lawyer, judge, and law professor of the early 19th century, which contained notes and annotations pertinent to America, was a staple of the American lawyer's library in the 19th century. Many

cited; they would have had no difficulty in coming to a prompt and correct conclusion. In a court thus constituted, the skin and carcass of poor *reynard* would have been properly disposed of, and a precedent set, interfering with no usage or custom which the experience of ages has sanctioned, and which must be so well known to every votary of Diana. But the parties have referred the question to our judgment, and we must dispose of it as well as we can, from the partial lights we possess, leaving to a higher tribunal, the correction of any mistake which we may be so unfortunate as to make. By the pleadings it is admitted that a fox is a "wild and noxious beast." Both parties have regarded him, as the law of nations does a pirate, "*hostem humani generis,*"[23] and although "*de mortuis nil nisi bonum,*"[24] be a maxim of our profession, the memory of the deceased has not been spared. His depredations on farmers and on barn yards, have not been forgotten; and to put him to death wherever found, is allowed to be meritorious, and of public benefit. Hence it follows, that our decision should have in view the greatest possible encouragement to the destruction of an animal, so cunning and ruthless in his career. But who would keep a pack of hounds; or what gentleman, at the sound of the horn, and at peep of day, would mount his steed, and for hours together, "*sub jove frigido,*"[25] or a vertical sun, pursue the windings of this wily quadruped, if, just as night came on, and his stratagems and strength were nearly exhausted, a saucy intruder, who had not shared in the honours or labours of the chase, were permitted to come in at the death, and bear away in triumph the object of pursuit? Whatever Justinian may have thought of the matter, it must be recollected that his code was compiled many hundred years ago, and it would be very hard indeed, at the distance of so many centuries, not to have a right to establish a rule for ourselves. In his day, we read of no order of men who made it a business, in the language of the declaration in this cause, "with hounds and dogs to find, start, pursue, hunt, and chase," these animals, and that, too, without any other motive than the preservation of Roman poultry; if this diversion had been then in fashion, the lawyers who composed his institutes, would have taken care not to pass it by, without suitable encouragement. If any thing, therefore, in the digests or pandects shall appear to militate against the defendant in error, who, on this occasion, was the foxhunter, we have only to say *tempora mutantur;*[26] and if men themselves change with the times, why should not laws also undergo an alteration?

It may be expected, however, by the learned counsel, that more particular notice be taken of their authorities. I have examined them all, and feel great difficulty in determining, whether to acquire dominion over

---

American frontier lawyers practiced law with little more than a copy of Tucker's edition of Blackstone's *Commentaries*.

   23. [Ed.] "The enemy of humankind."

   24. [Ed.] "Speak no ill of the dead."

   25. [Ed.] Literally, "under cold Jupiter," but better rendered as "under the cold heavens."

   26. [Ed.] "Times change."

a thing, before in common, it be sufficient that we barely see it, or know where it is, or wish for it, or make a declaration of our will respecting it; or whether, in the case of wild beasts, setting a trap, or lying in wait, or starting, or pursuing, be enough; or if an actual wounding, or killing, or bodily tact and occupation be necessary. Writers on general law, who have favoured us with their speculations on these points, differ on them all; but, great as is the diversity of sentiment among them, some conclusion must be adopted on the question immediately before us. After mature deliberation, I embrace that of Barbeyrac, as the most rational, and least liable to objection. If at liberty, we might imitate the courtesy of a certain emperor, who, to avoid giving offence to the advocates of any of these different doctrines, adopted a middle course, and by ingenious distinctions, rendered it difficult to say (as often happens after a fierce and angry contest) to whom the palm of victory belonged. He ordained, that if a beast be followed with *large dogs and hounds,* he shall belong to the hunter, not to the chance occupant; and in like manner, if he be killed or wounded with a lance or sword; but if chased with *beagles only,* then he passed to the captor, not to the first pursuer. If slain with a dart, a sling, or a bow, he fell to the hunter, if still in chase, and not to him who might afterwards find and seize him.

Now, as we are without any municipal regulations of our own, and the pursuit here, for aught that appears on the case, being with dogs and hounds of *imperial stature,* we are at liberty to adopt one of the provisions just cited, which comports also with the learned conclusion of Barbeyrac, that property in animals *feræ naturæ* may be acquired without bodily touch or manucaption, provided the pursuer be within reach, or have a *reasonable* prospect (which certainly existed here) of taking, what he has *thus* discovered an intention of converting to his own use.

When we reflect also that the interest of our husbandmen, the most useful of men in any community, will be advanced by the destruction of a beast so pernicious and incorrigible, we cannot greatly err, in saying, that a pursuit like the present, through waste and unoccupied lands, and which must inevitably and speedily have terminated in corporal possession, or bodily *seisin,* confers such a right to the object of it, as to make any one a wrongdoer, who shall interfere and shoulder the spoil. The justice's judgment ought, therefore, in my opinion, to be affirmed.

NOTES AND QUESTIONS

1. Possession or Policy? Is the rationale for the decision based on the principle of first possession or some vision of good public policy? If it is the latter, what is that vision? Is it possible that the judges' notions of public policy informed their views on first possession?

2. What constitutes possession? The judges in *Pierson,* as well as the authorities cited, disagree on what constitutes first possession. How should this problem be resolved? In expounding upon the two simple rules of whalers regarding fast-fish and loose-fish, Herman Melville had this to say:

But what plays the mischief with this masterly code is the admirable brevity of it, which necessitates a vast volume of commentaries to expound it. First: What is a Fast–Fish? Alive or dead a fish is technically fast, when it is connected with an occupied ship or boat, by any medium at all controllable by the occupant or occupants,—a mast, an oar, a nine-inch cable, a telegraph wire, or a strand of cobweb, it is all the same. Likewise a fish is technically fast when it bears a waif, or any other recognised symbol of possession; so long as the party waifing it plainly evince their ability at any time to take it alongside, as well as their intention to do so.

These are scientific commentaries, but the commentaries of the whalemen themselves sometimes consist in hard words and harder knocks—the Coke-upon-Littleton[27] of the fist. True, among the more upright and honorable whalemen allowances are always made for peculiar cases, where it would be an outrageous moral injustice for one party to claim possession of a whale previously chased or killed by another party. But others are by no means so scrupulous.

Herman Melville, *Moby–Dick, or, The Whale*, Ch. 89.

So, should the acts that constitute possession be defined by reference to physical dominion, public policy, custom, or something else? Melville alludes to custom as the method of resolving first possession and, in the heyday of whaling, courts frequently deferred to the customs of whalers. An example is Swift v. Gifford, 23 F. Cas. 558 (D. Mass. 1872). Gifford's ship, *Rainbow*, harpooned a whale in the Arctic Ocean, but although the harpoon and the attached line remained in the giant cetacean, it was not fast to the *Rainbow*'s boat. A whaleboat crew from Swift's ship pursued the beast, captured the whale, and surrendered it to Gifford in conformity with a custom in the Arctic whaling grounds that the "iron holds the whale," regardless of whether the iron is fast to the whaler's boat. Later, Swift sued to recover the value of the whale, claiming that customs among whalers could not trump the common law rules of the sort laid down in Pierson v. Post. The district judge ruled for Gifford, finding the custom to be reasonable and valid:

> The rule of law invoked in this case is one of very limited application. The whale fishery is the only branch of industry of any importance in which it is likely to be much used; and if a usage is found to prevail generally in that business, it will not be open to the objection that it is likely to disturb the general understanding of mankind by the interposition of an arbitrary exception. ... Every judge who has dealt with this subject has felt the importance of upholding all reasonable usages of the fishermen, in order to prevent dangerous quarrels in the division of their spoils.

Custom is not always adopted, however. Justice Story, in *The Reeside*, 20 F. Cas. 458 (C.C.D. Mass. 1837) (No. 11,657), inveighed against the "habit ... of setting up particular usages or customs in almost all kinds of business and

---

27. [Ed.] Thomas de Littleton was a 15th century English jurist, whose great contribution was his Treatise on Tenures, a compendium of English land law written in "law French." Sir Edward Coke (pronounced "Cook") was a late 16th century and early 17th century English jurist and judge who foreshadowed Blackstone's *Commentaries* by writing his four volume Institutes of the Lawes of England, the first volume of which is Coke's commentary on Littleton's Treatise on Tenures, usually referred to as Coke-upon-Littleton.

trade, to control, vary, or annul the general liabilities of parties under the common law, as well as under the commercial law. . . . [T]here is no small danger in admitting such loose and inconclusive usages and customs, often unknown to particular parties, and always liable to great misunderstandings and misinterpretations and abuses, to outweigh the well-known and well-settled principles of law."

On first possession generally, see Richard A. Epstein, Possession as the Root of Title, 13 Ga. L. Rev. 1221 (1979).

4. CREATION

When Thomas Edison invented the phonograph he created a new tangible object—a machine that could accurately record and reproduce sounds—and something intangible—an idea reduced to a practical manifestation. Each of the tangible and intangible entities were Edison's property. You might say the tangible phonograph was created by Edison's use of materials that he had purchased and already owned, so the phonograph was just a different (and useful) assembly of his property, but the intangible entity—the idea and the process of manifesting the idea—was a wholly new piece of property, never before owned by anyone. Recall that John Locke argued that a person's "labor . . . , and the work of his hands" is exclusively owned by that person. That notion is recognized in Art. I, § 8 of the United States Constitution, which grants to Congress the power to "promote the Progress of Science and useful Arts, by securing for limited Times to Authors and Inventors the exclusive Right to their respective Writings and Discoveries." Congress has, of course, acted on this authority by enacting laws providing protection for patents, trademarks, and copyrights. But apart from this statutory law, there is an imbedded notion in the common law that a creator of property is entitled to its ownership. Usually an inventor, such as Edison, will not hoard his invention, but will make it available for consumers to purchase and, for a fee, license others to manufacture the invention. But suppose that A copies what B has created. How should the common law deal with copycats?

INTERNATIONAL NEWS SERVICE
v. ASSOCIATED PRESS
United States Supreme Court
248 U.S. 215 (1918)

[AP was a not-for-profit association of newspapers, each of which contributed funds to enable the gathering of the news of the day and distribution of the resulting news dispatches to its member newspapers. INS, a for-profit corporation, also engaged in news-gathering and distributing that news to subscribing newspapers for a fee. INS and AP were zealous competitors in news-gathering. AP brought suit to enjoin INS from, among other things, "copying news from bulletin boards and from early editions of [AP's] newspapers and selling this, either bodily or after rewriting it, to [INS's] customers." A federal district court refused to enjoin this activity even though it thought it was an unfair trade practice because the law was unsettled on the point. The Court of Appeals held that the injunction should have been granted because it thought that INS had unlawfully invaded AP's property rights. The Supreme Court affirmed.]

JUSTICE PITNEY delivered the opinion of the Court.

. . . [AP] asserts that [INS's] admitted course of conduct . . . both violates [AP's] property right in the news and constitutes unfair competition in business. . . . [The] questions are: 1. Whether there is any property in news; 2. Whether, if there be property in news collected for the purpose of being published, it survives the instant of its publication in the first newspaper to which it is communicated by the news-gatherer; and 3. Whether defendant's admitted course of conduct in appropriating for commercial use matter taken from bulletins or early editions of Associated Press publications constitutes unfair competition in trade. . . .

[AP's] news matter is not copyrighted. It is said that it could not, in practice, be copyrighted, because of the large number of dispatches that are sent daily; and . . . news is not within the operation of the copyright act. [INS] invokes the analogies of the law of literary property and copyright, insisting as its principal contention that, assuming [AP] has a right of property in its news, it can be maintained (unless the copyright act be complied with) only by being kept secret and confidential, and that upon the publication with [AP's] consent of uncopyrighted news by any of [AP's] members in a newspaper or upon a bulletin board, the right of property is lost, and the subsequent use of the news by the public or by defendant for any purpose whatever becomes lawful. . . .

In considering the general question of property in news matter, it is necessary to recognize its dual character, distinguishing between the substance of the information and the particular form or collocation of words in which the writer has communicated it. No doubt news articles often possess a literary quality, and are the subject of literary property at the common law; nor do we question that such an article, as a literary production, is the subject of copyright by the terms of the act as it now stands. . . . But the news element—the information respecting current events contained in the literary production—is not the creation of the writer, but is a report of matters that ordinarily are *publici juris*; it is the history of the day. It is not to be supposed that the framers of the Constitution, when they empowered Congress "to promote the progress of science and useful arts, by securing for limited times to authors and inventors the exclusive right to their respective writings and discoveries," intended to confer upon one who might happen to be the first to report a historic event the exclusive right for any period to spread the knowledge of it.

We need spend no time, however, upon the general question of property in news matter at common law, or the application of the copyright act, since it seems to us the case must turn upon the question of unfair competition in business. . . . The peculiar value of news is in the spreading of it while it is fresh; and it is evident that a valuable property interest in the news, as news, cannot be maintained by keeping it secret. Besides, except for matters improperly disclosed, or published in breach of trust or confidence, or in violation of law, none of which is involved in this branch of the case, the news of current events may be regarded as common property. What we are concerned with is the business of making it known to the world, in which both parties to the present suit are engaged. . . . The parties are competitors in this field; and . . . each party is under a duty so to conduct its own business as not unnecessarily or unfairly to injure that of the other. . . . [The] question of what is unfair competition in business must be determined with particular reference to the character and circumstances of the business. The question here is not so much the rights of either party as against the public but their rights as between themselves. And although we . . . assume that neither party has any remaining property interest as against the public in uncopyrighted news matter after the moment of its first publication, it by no means follows that there is no remaining property interest in it as between themselves. For, to both of them alike, news matter, however little susceptible of ownership or dominion in the absolute sense, is stock in trade, to be gathered at the cost of enterprise, organization, skill, labor, and money, and to be distributed and sold to those who will pay money for it, as for any other merchandise. Regarding the news, therefore, as but the material out of which both parties are seeking to make profits at the same time and in the same field, we hardly can fail to recognize that for this purpose, and as between them, it must be regarded as *quasi* property, irrespective of the rights of either as against the public. . . .

The peculiar features of the case arise from the fact that, while novelty and freshness form so important an element in the success of the business, the very processes of distribution and publication necessarily occupy a good deal of time. [AP's] service, as well as [INS's], is a daily service to daily newspapers; most of the foreign news reaches this country at the Atlantic seaboard, principally at the City of New York, and because of this, and of time differentials due to the earth's rotation, the distribution of news matter throughout the country is principally from east to west; and, since in speed the telegraph and telephone easily outstrip the rotation of the earth, it is a simple matter for [INS] to take [AP's] news from bulletins or early editions of [AP's] members in the eastern cities and at the mere cost of telegraphic transmission cause it to be published in western papers issued at least as early as those served by [AP]. Besides this, and irrespective of time differentials, irregularities in telegraphic transmission on different lines, and the normal consumption of time in printing and distributing the newspaper, result in permitting pirated news to be placed in the hands of [INS's] readers sometimes simultaneously with the service of competing Associated Press papers, occasionally even earlier.

[INS] insists that when, with the sanction and approval of [AP], and as the result of the use of its news for the very purpose for which it is distributed, a portion of [AP's] members communicate it to the general public by posting it upon bulletin boards so that all may read, or by issuing it to newspapers and distributing it indiscriminately, [AP] no longer has the right to control the use to be made of it; that when it thus reaches the light of day it becomes the common possession of all to whom it is accessible; and that any purchaser of a newspaper has the right to communicate the intelligence which it contains to anybody and for any purpose, even for the purpose of selling it for profit to newspapers published for profit in competition with [AP's] members.

INS's argument

The fault in the reasoning lies in applying as a test the right of [AP] as against the public, instead of considering the rights of [AP] and [INS], competitors in business, as between themselves. The right of the purchaser of a single newspaper to spread knowledge of its contents gratuitously, for any legitimate purpose not unreasonably interfering with [AP's] right to make merchandise of it, may be admitted; but to transmit that news for commercial use, in competition with [AP]—which is what [INS] has done and seeks to justify—is a very different matter. In doing this [INS], by its very act, admits that it is taking material that has been acquired by [AP] as the result of organization and the expenditure of labor, skill, and money, and which is salable by [AP] for money, and that [INS] in appropriating it and selling it as its own is endeavoring to reap where it has not sown, and by disposing of it to newspapers that are competitors of [AP's] members is appropriating to itself the harvest of those who have sown. Stripped of all disguises, the process amounts to an unauthorized interference with the normal operation of [AP's] legitimate business precisely at the point where the profit is to be reaped, in order to divert a material portion of the profit from those who have earned it to those who have not; with special advantage to [INS] in the competition because of the fact that it is not burdened with any part of the expense of gathering the news. The transaction speaks for itself, and a court of equity ought not to hesitate long in characterizing it as unfair competition in business.

not able to be defended against

The contention that the news is abandoned to the public for all purposes when published in the first newspaper is untenable. Abandonment is a question of intent, and the entire organization of the Associated Press negatives such a purpose. . . .

It is said that the elements of unfair competition are lacking because there is no attempt by [INS] to palm off its goods as those of the [Associated Press], characteristic of the most familiar, if not the most typical, cases of unfair competition. But we cannot concede that the right to equitable relief is confined to that class of cases. In the present case the fraud upon [AP's] rights is more direct and obvious. Regarding news matter as the mere material from which these two competing parties are endeavoring to make money, and treating it, therefore, as *quasi* property for the purposes of their business because they are both selling it as such, [INS's] conduct differs from the ordinary case of unfair competition in trade principally in this that, instead of selling its own goods as those of complainant, it substitutes misappropriation in the place of misrepresentation, and sells [AP's] goods as its own.

[Affirmed.]

JUSTICE BRANDEIS dissenting.

There are published in the United States about 2,500 daily papers. More than 800 of them are supplied with domestic and foreign news of general interest by the Associated Press—a corporation ... which does not sell news or earn or seek to earn profits, but serves merely as an instrumentality by means of which these papers supply themselves at joint expense with such news. Papers not members of the Associated Press depend for their news of general interest largely upon agencies organized for profit. Among these agencies is the International News Service which supplies news to about 400 subscribing papers. It has, like the Associated Press, bureaus and correspondents in this and foreign countries; and its annual expenditure in gathering and distributing news is about $2,000,000. Ever since its organization in 1909, it has included among the sources from which it gathers news, copies (purchased in the open market) of early editions of some papers published by members of the Associated Press and the bulletins publicly posted by them. These items, which constitute but a small part of the news transmitted to its subscribers, are generally verified by the International News Service before transmission; but frequently items are transmitted without verification; and occasionally even without being re-written. In no case is the fact disclosed that such item was suggested by or taken from a paper or bulletin published by an Associated Press member.

No question of statutory copyright is involved. The sole question for our consideration is this: Was the International News Service properly enjoined from using, or causing to be used gainfully, news of which it acquired knowledge by lawful means (namely, by reading publicly posted bulletins or papers purchased by it in the open market) merely because the news had been originally gathered by the Associated Press and continued to be of value to some of its members, or because it did not reveal the source from which it was acquired?

News is a report of recent occurrences. The business of the news agency is to gather systematically knowledge of such occurrences of interest and to distribute reports thereof. The Associated Press contended that knowledge so acquired is property, because it costs money and labor to produce and because it has value for which those who have it not are ready to pay; that it remains property and is entitled to protection as long as it has commercial value as news; and that to protect it effectively the defendant must be enjoined from making, or causing to be made, any gainful use of it while it retains such value. An essential element of individual property is the legal right to exclude others from enjoying it. . . .

The general rule of law is, that the noblest of human productions—knowledge, truths ascertained, conceptions, and ideas—become, after voluntary communication to others, free as the air to common use. Upon these incorporeal productions the attribute of property is continued after such communication only in certain classes of cases where public policy has seemed to demand it. These exceptions are confined to productions which, in some degree, involve creation, invention, or discovery. But by no means all such are endowed with this attribute of property. The creations which are recognized as property by the common law are literary, dramatic, musical, and other artistic creations; and these have also protection under the copyright statutes. The inventions and discoveries upon which this attribute of property is conferred only by statute, are the few comprised within the patent law.

There are also many other cases in which ... the right to relief is often called a property right, but is such only in a special sense. In those cases, the plaintiff has no absolute right to the protection of his production; he has merely the qualified right to be protected as against the defendant's acts, because of the special relation in which the latter stands or the wrongful method or means employed in acquiring the knowledge or the manner in which it is used. Protection of this character is afforded where the suit is based upon breach of contract or of trust or upon unfair competition.

The knowledge for which protection is sought in the case at bar is not of a kind upon which the law has heretofore conferred the attributes of property; nor is the manner of its acquisition or use nor the purpose to which it is applied, such as has heretofore been recognized as entitling a plaintiff to relief. ... [AP] does not contend that the posting [of news] was wrongful or that any papers were wrongfully issued by its subscribers. On the contrary it is conceded that both the bulletins and the papers were issued in accordance with [AP's] regulations.... Under such circumstances, for a reader of the papers purchased in the open market, or a reader of the bulletins publicly posted, to procure and use gainfully, information therein contained, does not involve inducing anyone to commit a breach either of contract or of trust, or committing or in any way abetting a breach of confidence....

[AP] also relied upon the cases which hold that the common-law right of the producer to prohibit copying is not lost by the private circulation of a literary composition, the delivery of lecture, the exhibition of a painting, or the performance of a dramatic or musical composition. These cases rest upon the ground that the common law recognizes such productions as property which, despite restricted communication, continues until there is a dedication to the public under the copyright statutes or otherwise. But they are inapplicable for two reasons. (1) At common law, as under the copyright acts, intellectual productions are entitled to such protection only if there is underneath something evincing the mind of a creator or originator, however modest the requirement. The mere record of isolated happenings, whether in words or by photographs not involving artistic skill, are denied such protection. (2) At common law, as under the copyright acts, the element in intellectual productions which secures such protection is not the knowledge, truths, ideas, or emotions which the composition expresses, but the form or sequence in which they are expressed; that is, "some new collocation of visible or audible points,—of lines, colors, sounds, or words."

That news is not property in the strict sense is illustrated by the case of Sports and General Press Agency, Ltd. v. "Our Dogs" Publishing Co., Ltd., [1916] 2 K.B. 880, where the plaintiff, the assignee of the right to photograph the exhibits at a dog show, was refused an injunction against defendant who had also taken pictures of the show and was publishing them. The court said that, except in so far as the possession of the land occupied by the show enabled the proprietors to exclude people or permit them on condition that they agree not to take photographs (which condition was not imposed in that case), the proprietors had no exclusive right to photograph the show and could therefore grant no such right. And, it was further stated that, at any rate, no matter what conditions might be imposed upon those entering the grounds, if the defendant had been on top of a house or in some position where he could photograph the show without interfering with the physical property of the plaintiff, the plaintiff would have no right to stop him. If, when the plaintiff creates the event recorded, he is not entitled to the exclusive first publication of the news (in that case a photograph) of the event, no reason can be shown why he should be accorded such protection as to events which he simply records and transmits to other parts of the world, though with great expenditure of time and money.

If news be treated as possessing the characteristics not of a trade secret, but of literary property, then the earliest issue of a paper of general circulation or the earliest public posting of a bulletin which embodies such news would, under the established rules governing literary property, operate as a publication, and all property in the news would then cease. [AP contended that] a restriction is to be implied that the news shall not be used gainfully in competition with the Associated Press or any of its members. There is no basis for such an implication, [for it is] well settled that ... a general publication is effective to dedicate literary property to the public, regardless of the actual intent of its owner....

[AP] further contended that [INS's] practice constitutes unfair competition, ... and it is upon this ground that the decision of this court appears to be based. To appropriate and use for profit, knowledge and ideas produced by other men, without making compensation or even acknowledgment, may be inconsistent with a finer sense of propriety; but, with the exceptions indicated above, the law has heretofore sanctioned the practice. Thus it was held that one may ordinarily make and sell anything in any form, may copy with exactness that which another has produced, or may otherwise use his ideas without his consent and without the payment of compensation, and yet not inflict a legal injury; and that ordinarily one is at perfect liberty to find out, if he can by lawful means, trade secrets of another, however valuable, and then use the knowledge so acquired gainfully, although it cost the original owner much in effort and in money to collect or produce. . . .

Such taking and gainful use of a product of another which, for reasons of public policy, the law has refused to endow with the attributes of property, does not become unlawful because the product happens to have been taken from a rival and is used in competition with him. The unfairness in competition which hitherto has been recognized by the law as a basis for relief, lay in the manner or means of conducting the business; and the manner or means held legally unfair, involves either fraud or force or the doing of acts otherwise prohibited by law. In the "passing off" cases (the typical and most common case of unfair competition), the wrong consists in fraudulently representing by word or act that defendant's goods are those of plaintiff. In the other cases, the diversion of trade was effected through physical or moral coercion, or by inducing breaches of contract or of trust or by enticing away employees, [or] because defendant's purpose was . . . not competition but deliberate and wanton destruction of plaintiff's business. . . .

He who follows the pioneer into a new market, or who engages in the manufacture of an article newly introduced by another, seeks profits due largely to the labor and expense of the first adventurer; but the law sanctions, indeed encourages, the pursuit. . . . He who has made his name a guaranty of quality, protests in vain when another with the same name engages, perhaps for that reason, in the same lines of business; provided, precaution is taken to prevent the public from being deceived into the belief that what he is selling was made by his competitor. One bearing a name made famous by another is permitted to enjoy the unearned benefit which necessarily flows from such use, even though the use proves harmful to him who gave the name value. . . .

The means by which the International News Service obtains news gathered by the Associated Press is also clearly unobjectionable. It is taken from papers bought in the open market or from bulletins publicly posted. No breach of contract . . . or of trust [is present] and neither fraud nor force is involved. The manner of use is likewise unobjectionable. No reference is made by word or by act to the Associated Press, either in transmitting the news to subscribers or by them in publishing it in their papers. Neither the International News Service nor its subscribers is gaining or seeking to gain in its business a benefit from the reputation of the Associated Press. They are merely using its product without making compensation. That, they have a legal right to do; because the product is not property, and they do not stand in any relation to the Associated Press, either of contract or of trust, which otherwise precludes such use. . . .

[The] fact that [INS] does not refer to the Associated Press as the source of the news [does not] furnish a basis for the relief. [INS] and its subscribers, unlike members of the Associated Press, were under no contractual obligation to disclose the source of the news; and there is no rule of law requiring acknowledgment to be made where uncopyrighted matter is reproduced. The International News Service is said to mislead its subscribers into believing that the news transmitted was originally gathered by it and that they in turn mislead their readers. There is, in fact, no representation by either of any kind. . . .

Nor is the use made by the International News Service of the information taken from papers or bulletins of Associated Press members legally objectionable by reason of the purpose for which it was employed. The acts here complained of were not done for the purpose of injuring the business of the Associated Press. Their purpose was not even to divert its trade, or to put it at a disadvantage by lessening [INS's] necessary expenses. The purpose was merely to supply subscribers of the International News Service promptly with all available news. . . . [The protection AP seeks by injunction] consists merely in denying to other papers the right to use, as news, information which . . . had . . . been given to the public . . .; and to which the law denies the attributes of property. . . .

The great development of agencies now furnishing country-wide distribution of news, the vastness of our territory, and improvements in the means of transmitting intelligence, have made it possible for a news agency or newspapers to obtain, without paying compensation, the fruit of another's efforts and to use news so obtained gainfully in competition with the original collector. The injustice of such action is obvious. But to give relief against it would . . . require the making of a new rule in analogy to existing ones. The unwritten law possesses capacity for growth; and has often satisfied new demands for justice by invoking analogies or by expanding a rule or principle. This process has been in the main wisely applied and should not be discontinued. Where the problem is relatively simple, as it is apt to be when private interests only are involved, it generally proves adequate. But with the increasing complexity of society, the public interest tends to become omnipresent; and the problems presented by new demands for justice cease to be simple. Then the creation or recognition by courts of a new private right may work serious injury to the general public, unless the boundaries of the right are definitely established and wisely guarded. In order to reconcile the new private right with the public interest, it may be necessary to prescribe limitations and rules for its enjoyment; and also to provide administrative machinery for enforcing the rules. It is largely for this reason that, in the effort to meet the many new demands for justice incident to a rapidly changing civilization, resort to legislation has latterly been had with increasing frequency.

The rule for which [AP] contends would effect an important extension of property rights and a corresponding curtailment of the free use of knowledge and of ideas. . . . A large majority of the newspapers and perhaps half the newspaper readers of the United States are dependent for their news of general interest upon agencies other than the Associated Press. The channel through which about 400 of these papers received, as [AP] alleges, "a large amount of news relating to the European war of the greatest importance and of intense interest to the newspaper reading public" was suddenly closed. The closing to the International News Service of these channels for foreign news ... was due not to unwillingness on its part to pay the cost of collecting the news, but to the prohibitions imposed by foreign governments upon its securing news from their respective countries and from using cable or telegraph lines running therefrom. For aught that appears, this prohibition may have been wholly undeserved; and at all events the 400 papers and their readers may be assumed to have been innocent. For aught that appears, the International News Service may have sought then to secure temporarily by arrangement with the Associated Press the latter's foreign news service. For aught that appears, all of the 400 subscribers of the International News Service would gladly have then become members of the Associated Press, if they could have secured election thereto. It is possible, also, that a large part of the readers of these papers were so situated that they could not secure prompt access to papers served by the Associated Press. The prohibition of the foreign governments might as well have been extended to the channels through which news was supplied to the more than a thousand other daily papers in the United States not served by the Associated Press; and a large part of their readers may also be so located that they can not procure prompt access to papers served by the Associated Press.

A legislature, urged to enact a law by which one news agency or newspaper may prevent appropriation of the fruits of its labors by another, would consider such facts and possibilities and others which appropriate enquiry might disclose. Legislators might conclude that it was impossible to put an end to the obvious injustice involved in such appropriation of news, without opening the door to other evils, greater than that sought to be remedied....

Or legislators dealing with the subject might conclude, that the right to news values should be protected to the extent of permitting recovery of damages for any unauthorized use, but that protection by injunction should be denied.... If a legislature concluded to recognize property in published news to the extent of permitting recovery at law, it might, with a view to making the remedy more certain and adequate, provide a fixed measure of damages, as in the case of copyright infringement.

Or again, a legislature might conclude that it was unwise to recognize even so limited a property right in published news as that above indicated; but that a news agency should, on some conditions, be given full protection of its business; and to that end a remedy by injunction as well as one for damages should be granted, where news collected by it is gainfully used without permission. If a legislature concluded ... that under certain circumstances news-gathering is a business affected with a public interest, it might declare that, in such cases, news should be protected against appropriation, only if the gatherer assumed the obligation of supplying it, at reasonable rates and without discrimination, to all papers which applied therefor. If legislators reached that conclusion, they would probably go further, and prescribe the conditions under which and the extent to which the protection should be afforded; and they might also provide the administrative machinery necessary for ensuring to the public, the press, and the news agencies, full enjoyment of the rights so conferred.

Courts are ill-equipped to make the investigations which should precede a determination of the limitations which should be set upon any property right in news or of the circumstances under which news gathered by a private agency should be deemed affected with a public interest. Courts would be powerless to prescribe the detailed regulations essential to full enjoyment of the rights conferred or to introduce the machinery required for enforcement of such regulations. Considerations such as these should lead us to decline to establish a new rule of law in the effort to redress a newly-disclosed wrong, although the propriety of some remedy appears to be clear.

NOTE AND QUESTIONS

Competition or Theft? The majority opinion in *INS* has not endured. The general common law rule is better stated in a later case brought by a fabric manufacturer who designed and sold distinctive patterned silk, introducing new designs each season. The designs were not susceptible of copyright protection and it was impractical, if not impossible, to obtain a design patent. A competitor copied a popular pattern onto its own silk fabric and sold the fabric at a discount from the plaintiff's price. In Cheney Brothers v. Doris Silk Corp., 35 F.2d 279 (1930), the court stated: "In the absence of some recognized right at common law, or under the [copyright and patent] statutes . . . a man's property is limited to the chattels which embody his invention. Others may imitate these at their pleasure." Why is this so? Another court has offered this justification: "[While] at first glance it might seem intolerable that one manufacturer should be allowed to sponge on another by pirating the product of years of invention and development without license or recompense and reap the fruits sown by another, . . . this initial response to the problem has been curbed in deference to the greater public good. . . . For imitation is the life blood of competition. It is the unimpeded availability of substantially equivalent units that permits the normal operation of supply and demand to yield the fair price society must pay for a given commodity." American Safety Table Co. v. Schreiber, 269 F.2d 255, 271–272 (2d Cir. 1959).

This apparent paradox lies at the intersection of the market economy and the need to promote innovation. Exclusive ownership of property functions to allocate resources and enable the owner to make productive use of them. If one person possesses a barrel of oil it is axiomatic that nobody else can possess it at the same time. Exclusive ownership of a barrel of oil is efficient and sensible. But what about intangibles, such as information? More than one person can possess the news of the day, or the same silk fabric design, simultaneously, and it is indeed efficient to permit copycats to drive the price of the news (or fabric) down to a market-clearing equilibrium where supply equals demand. But will that outcome deter innovation? Therein lies the dilemma. How much protection do innovators need to continue to innovate? Congress has control over this question through its ability to enact statutory protection for copyrights, patents, and trademarks, but the same problem is present in considering the extent of those protections. Those knotty problems are at the heart of courses in Intellectual Property.

C. WHY RECOGNIZE PRIVATE PROPERTY?

Let us begin with a state of nature, when all things are unowned and people are free to claim possession of such things as they desire. If the resources are abundant and the people who appropriate this resource are few in comparison this arrangement may work fairly well. But even then it is riddled with waste and inefficiency.

Consider the decline of the American bison. Before the arrival of whites in large numbers on the plains of middle America, the indigenous tribes of the area took as many buffalo as they desired, but they did so in a wasteful manner. It is estimated that as many as 450,000 bison per year were slaughtered in the first half of the nineteenth century, often by stampeding a herd over cliffs and also by more individualized killing. The hides, some parts of the animal, and the best portions of the meat were used, but the rest of the carcass was left to rot. See Shepard Krech III, The Ecological Indian: Myth and History (1999). One study of the period concludes that the Indian slaughter was probably not enough to destroy the bison, but that natural predation, fire, and drought coupled with the aboriginal harvest might have exceeded the replacement rate of the bison. Andrew C. Isenberg, The Destruction of the Bison (2000). But the fate of the bison was surely sealed when white traders arrived offering items that were otherwise unavailable (and appealing) in exchange for buffalo hides. The final coup was the wholesale slaughter of bison to earn the value of the hide (for the burgeoning leather industry), the bones (for fertilizer and pigments), and the meat (for human consumption). Between 1872 and 1874 it is estimated that over 1.3 million buffalo hides were shipped on the Union Pacific railway alone. Buffalo bones are thought to have filled 5,000 railway boxcars annually. By the turn of the twentieth century the bison was reduced to remnant herds, mostly in Yellowstone National Park and various zoos. The American Bison Society, founded in 1905, was devoted to preservation of bison by acquiring ownership of herds and breeding them for pure preservation and also as a genetic pool to mingle with cattle to produce so-called "beefalo." Today there are estimated to be about 500,000 bison in North America, mostly on commercial ranches. Only about 15,000 bison are unowned wild animals.

What can we derive from this tale? One moral might be that told by Garret Hardin, in his famous essay The Tragedy of the Commons, 162 Science 1243 (1968). Suppose that a large and bountiful meadow of 1000 acres is owned in common by a community of herdsmen, who use it to graze their livestock. Each herder owns his own animals and consumes them for food. The community swells in size to 1000 people and each person grazes more animals to provide food for himself and his family. Each person has an incentive to add an additional animal to his herd grazing on the meadow, because the value of that animal is entirely captured by the animal's owner. Call that value 100 utils. On the other hand, the addition of another grazing animal means that the ability of the meadow to sustain its grass is diminished. Call that at loss of 200 utils. Each herder has an incentive to capture the entire 100 utils that results from grazing an additional animal, but loses only 1/5 of a util by doing so, because the negative value is shared among the entire community of herders. With enough mouths to feed, grazing pressure will increase until the meadow is reduced to bare dirt, the animals die, and the herders go hungry. Every person acted to maximize their individual advantage, but the end result is a catastrophic loss for all. Hence the "tragedy of the commons."

How might this tragedy be avoided? One solution is to apportion individual property rights in the meadow. Suppose that each person is given ownership of one acre of the meadow. Now that person gains 100 utils for each additional animal he places on his acre but he also incurs the loss of 200 utils by doing so. He will not overgraze. He will only graze as many animals as the acre will support. Perhaps he will shift to chickens instead of cattle or sheep. Perhaps he will eschew meat and raise vegetables instead. Whatever he does, he will incur the full benefit and full cost of his activity. This is one good reason why property operates to allocate scarce resources efficiently.

In the initial example an economist might say that the cost of overgrazing is a "negative externality," which means that the negative cost of the activity is not borne by the actor creating it. That cost is external to the actor; it is borne by the community as a whole. Making that external cost internal forces the actor to take it into account. Property helps to do this.

Of course, there are other ways to address negative externalities. One might rely entirely upon the command of the sovereign, backed by force of arms, to compel people to refrain from imposing negative externalities. The problem with this arrangement is that governments are never omniscient. How much grazing can the meadow endure? What if the community desires to allocate individual acres and let each person decide how to use that acre, but the distant sovereign decrees that carrots alone may be grown on the meadow? The extreme version of this approach is to abolish private property and administer all resources by governmental control. Strongly centralized economies, especially those that seek to eradicate private property, tend to be woefully inefficient, as the bleak history of communism in the twentieth century illustrates. This is not to say that all governmental regulation of private behavior is obnoxious, but it is to say that private property may tend toward more efficient utilization of resources. Selective governmental intervention may indeed be useful to control negative externalities.

The tragedy of the commons can also be addressed by cooperation. The problem with cooperation is that there is a tendency for people not to cooperate. If our community of herders were to try to persuade everyone to limit their grazing, a natural (albeit selfish) reaction would be to let other people limit their grazing and continue to graze as many animals as you desire. You would be a "free-rider," because you would be receiving benefits without contributing to their creation. Now suppose that the herders' meadow turns out to contain a mineral deposit under its surface, worth $1 billion after the full cost of its extraction is factored in. Mega Mining Corporation desires to purchase the meadow from the herders. Mega Mining reasons that it can pay anything up to $1 billion for the meadow and reap a profit, but of course the smaller the profit the less incentive it has to devote its funds to this venture (because there are other investment opportunities available to it). Mega Mining offers each herder $500,000, but conditions the offer on acceptance by every herder. One herder, a very sharp cookie indeed, realizes that the mineral deposit is worth $1 billion to Mega Mining and thus insists on payment of $400 million. Mega Mining refuses, reasoning that a $100 million profit is inadequate, given its other investment opportunities. The sharp herder is a holdout—his refusal to deal at a price attractive to Mega Mining dooms the entire transaction. Perhaps the holdout realizes his error and reduces his demand to $100 million. Mega Mining is willing to meet this price, but word leaks out and the remaining herders who have not accepted the $500,000 offer clamor for $100 million each. It does not take many such holdouts to raise the total price above $1 billion, at which point Mega Mining walks away from the deal, leaving all the herders worse off financially. These problems of collective action will surface repeatedly in your study of law, and the law of property addresses them by some of its rules.

Collective action does sometime work, however. In so-called limited access commons—resources that are open only to a relatively small number of people, often defined by kinship, confined location, common values or a common occupation which is not easy to enter—informal customs or rules may develop that limit exploitation of the common resource. A modern example is the division of Maine's lobster fishery into geographic zones, with considerable authority devolved upon the fishermen in each zone to set many (but not all) of their own rules governing exploitation of the resource. Because it is difficult to enter the Maine lobster fishery these tightly knit bands police themselves to a considerable degree, albeit under the general restriction of statutory limits on the take. The role of such arrangements and their practicality is the subject of Elinor Ostrom, Governing the Commons: The Evolution of Institutions for Collective Action (1990). Ostrom won the 2009 Nobel Prize in economics for her work in this field. See also Robert Ellickson, Order Without Law: How Neighbors Settle Disputes (1991). A related historical example is the practice of migrants traveling west by wagon train in the first half of the nineteenth century to create their own law to govern themselves during the journey. See John Phillip Reid, Law for the Elephant: Property and Social Behavior on the Overland Trail (1980).

Economic explanations for private property are not the only arguments for its existence. Private property delivers to its holder a certain degree of freedom and autonomy, and thus may serve the goal of human liberty. On the other hand, those who own no property lack the freedom and autonomy that property ownership produces, although the existence of private property offers the prospect of obtaining the greater freedom that comes with its acquisition. Disparities in the ownership of property raise political issues concerning the wisdom and propriety of redistributing wealth via taxation and spending, on which people strongly disagree, but such disparities do not negate the importance of recognizing private property. Social concerns may operate to limit how property may be used, transferred, or even possessed, but those concerns do not override the reasons why we recognize the institution of private property.

CHAPTER TWO

SUBSEQUENT POSSESSION AND GIFTS

■ ■ ■

While first possession occupied some of your attention in Chapter One as a device to acquire property initially, we now turn to the question of the role of possession with respect to property already owned by somebody. At first blush, it might seem obvious that a person who owns property but loses possession of it remains its owner. But that loss of possession might be a deliberate renunciation of ownership, or might be an inadvertent loss, or might constitute a loan, or might result from theft, or might be an intended transfer of ownership. In any case, when the owner of property cannot be located who should be entitled to possession of the property? If the possessor in fact has a right to continued possession, is that ownership? What is the legal status of a person who occupies somebody else's property for a long period of time? This chapter deals with these issues.

A. FOUND PROPERTY

ARMORY v. DELAMIRIE

Court of King's Bench
93 Eng. Rep.664, 1 Strange 505 (1722)

The plaintiff, being a chimney sweeper's boy, found a jewel and took it to the defendant's shop (who was a goldsmith) to know what it was. He delivered it into the hands of the defendant's apprentice who, under pretence of weighing it, took out the stones and called to the master to let him know it came to three halfpence. The master offered the plaintiff that money, which he refused to take and insisted on having the jewel again, whereupon the apprentice gave him back the socket without the stones. In an action of trover[1] against the master,

SIR JOHN PRATT, CHIEF JUSTICE,

Ruled the following points:

(i) That the finder of a jewel, though he does not by such finding acquire an absolute property or ownership, yet he has such a property as

---

1. Trover was the common law form of action to recover the value of personal property owned or possessed by the plaintiff and which was wrongfully taken by the defendant.

55

will enable him to keep it against all but the rightful owner, and consequently may maintain trover.

(ii) That the action well lay against the master who gives a credit to his apprentice and is answerable for his neglect.

(iii) As to the value of the jewel, several of the trade were examined to prove what a jewel of the finest water that would fit the socket would be worth; and Sir John Pratt, Chief Justice, directed the jury that, unless the defendant did produce the jewel and show it not to be of the finest water, they should presume the strongest against him and make the value of the best jewels the measure of their damages, which they accordingly did.

how much $ goldsmith has to pay

NOTES AND QUESTIONS

1. Relative Title. Armory v. Delamirie is frequently cited for the following proposition: "The general rule undoubtedly is, that the finder of lost property is entitled to it as against all the world except the real owner, and that ordinarily the place where it is found does not make any difference." Durfee v. Jones, 11 R.I. 588, 591 (1877). "Ever since . . . Armory v. Delamirie . . . the law has been steady and uniform that the finder of lost property has a right to retain it against all persons except the true owner." Bowen v. Sullivan, 62 Ind. 281, 288 (1878). Thus, as a general matter, prior possessors prevail over subsequent possessors.

For example, Clark found some logs adrift in Delaware Bay and secured them to a post in a creek bank, but a storm sent them adrift again. Maloney found them. Clark sued Maloney for the value of the logs and won. "It is a well settled rule of law that the loss of a chattel does not change the right of property; and for the same reason that the original loss of these logs by the rightful owner, did not change his absolute property in them, . . . so the subsequent loss did not divest the *special* property of the plaintiff. It follows, therefore, that as the plaintiff has shown a special property in these logs, which he never abandoned, and which enabled him to keep them against all the world but the rightful owner, he is entitled to a verdict." Clark v. Maloney, 3 Del. 68 (1840).

The same principle applies even when the prior possessor obtained possession wrongfully (e.g., by trespassing) and seeks return of the property. See Anderson v. Gouldberg, 51 Minn. 294 (1892). Anderson trespassed onto property and cut 93 pine logs. Gouldberg took the logs from the lumber mill where Anderson had deposited them. The Minnesota court concluded that Gouldberg could not prevail simply by proving that Anderson did not have clear title, but must prove that Gouldberg had a better title than Anderson. The "bare possession of property, though wrongfully obtained, is sufficient title to enable the party enjoying it to [recover it from] a mere stranger, who takes it from him. Any other rule," said the court, "would lead to an endless series of unlawful seizures and reprisals in every case where property had once passed out of the possession of the rightful owner."

To the contrary is Russell v. Hill, 125 N.C. 470 (1899), also involving logs. McCoy sold to Russell the right to cut timber on property that McCoy thought she owned, but in fact was not owned by her. Russell cut the timber and hauled the logs to a river bank for transport to a furniture company, but Hill took them before Russell could do so. The North Carolina Supreme Court upheld a verdict for Hill, reasoning that because Russell could neither prove he owned the logs nor had a present right to possession of them he was not entitled to a verdict for damages for the loss. See John V. Orth, *Russell v. Hill*: Misunderstood Lessons, 73 N.C. L. Rev. 2031, 2034 (1995): "What is troubling about *Russell* is the concern that an innocent person may be without remedy against a wrongful taker merely because the wrongdoer can assert *jus tertii* [—the fact that a third party, the true owner, has a better title than the innocent—], while what is troubling about *Anderson* is the concern that a party can defend possession even if wrongfully acquired. Both problems may be avoided by a rule that conditions the assertion of *jus tertii* on a showing that the prior possessor did not hold in good faith." Professor Richard Helmholz claims that the rule advocated by Professor Orth is in fact the rule most commonly applied today. Richard H. Helmholz, Wrongful Possession of Chattels: Hornbook Law and Case Law, 80 Nw. U. L. Rev. 1221 (1986). Aside from the concerns identified by Orth, what other problems might be encountered by application of the *Anderson* rule? By the *Russell* rule?

owner-bailor / not the owner-bailee [handwritten marginalia]

   2. *On Bailments.* Bailment is the term used to describe rightful possession of personal property by someone who is not their owner (the "bailee"). A voluntary bailment occurs when the owner (the "bailor") voluntarily entrusts his property to another, as you do when you leave your clothing at the cleaners. That sort of bailment is also a commercial transaction, but voluntary bailments can also be gratuitous, as when you loan your car to a friend. From the perspective of the owner, a bailment is involuntary when someone takes possession of his property without the owner's consent, as happens when property is lost or mislaid. Of course, from the perspective of the bailee the bailment is voluntary. The duty of care of a bailee traditionally depended on the nature of the relationship between the bailee and the bailor. Unfortunately, bailments have been classified in many different ways. In Coggs v. Bernard, 92 Eng. Rep. 107 (K.B. 1704), Chief Justice Holt classified bailments into six different categories, with differing degrees of care imposed on the bailee. Another approach has been to classify bailments by the benefits produced. Thus, where a bailment is primarily for the benefit of the bailee (e.g., a gratuitous loan) the bailee was held to very high degree of care; where a bailment is primarily for the benefit of the bailor (e.g., a finder of a lost wallet) the bailee was held to a standard of minimal care; and a bailment for the benefit of both parties (e.g., a commercial laundry) required the bailee to exercise ordinary and reasonable care under the circumstances. In some jurisdictions a gratuitous bailee need only exercise "slight care for the preservation of the thing deposited." Cal. Civ. Code § 1846 (2009). The evolution of these traditional standards is considered in Kurt Philip Antor, Note, Bailment Liability: Toward a Standard of Reasonable Care, 61 S. Cal. L. Rev. 2117 (1988); Shelden D. Elliott, 6 S. Cal. L. Rev. 91 (1933). Although the contemporary trend is toward a uniform standard of ordinary and reasonable

Eng common law [handwritten marginalia]

care, that standard is not yet uniform. See Richard H. Helmholz, Bailment Theories and the Liability of Bailees: The Elusive Standard of Reasonable Care, 41 U. Kan. L. Rev. 97 (1992).

A finder is, of course, a bailee. In *Armory* the chimney sweep was a bailee, albeit an involuntary bailee from the standpoint of the true owner. After Delamirie paid the sweep the full value of the jewels, suppose the true owner appeared in Delamirie's shop and demanded the return of the gems or their monetary value. Should Delamirie pay twice or should the true owner be the loser? In cases of voluntary bailments, the rule is that the "wrongdoer, having once paid full damages to the bailee, has an answer to any action by the bailor." The Winkfield, [1902] P. 42 (Court of Appeal 1901). But in the problem posed above, the bailee was not voluntarily chosen by the bailor. Should that make a difference?

GODDARD v. WINCHELL

Supreme Court of Iowa
86 Iowa 71 (1892)

an estate in land

GRANGER, J., delivered the opinion of the court:

The district court found the following facts ...: "[1] [T]he plaintiff, John Goddard, is ... the owner in fee simple of the north half of [a certain section of real estate] in Winnebago county, Iowa, and was such owner at the time of the fall of the meteorite hereinafter referred to. [2] [S]aid land was prairie land, and that the grass privilege for the year 1890 was leased to one James Elickson. [3] [On May 2, 1890] an aerolite passed over northern ... Iowa, and the aerolite ... fell onto the plaintiff's land ... and buried itself in the ground to a depth of three feet, and became imbedded.... [4] [T]he day after the aerolite in question fell it was dug out of the ground with a spade by one Peter Hoagland, in the presence of the tenant, Elickson; ... Hoagland took it to his house, and claimed to own same, for the reason that he had found same and dug it up. [5] [O]n May 5, 1890, Hoagland sold the aerolite ... to the defendant, H. V. Winchell, for one hundred and five dollars, and the same was at once taken possession of by [Winchell, who] knew at the time of his purchase that it was an aerolite, and that it fell on the prairie south of Hoagland's land. ... [6] [The] value of said aerolite [is stipulated to be] one hundred and one dollars ($101) [and it] weighs about sixty-six pounds, is of a black, smoky color on the outside, showing the effects of heat, and of a lighter and darkish gray color on the inside; [it] fell from the heavens on the second of May, 1890; [and] a member of Hoagland's family saw the aerolite fall, and directed him to it."

[The] district court found that the aerolite became a part of the soil on which it fell; that the plaintiff was the owner thereof; and that the act of Hoagland in removing it was wrongful. [Winchell insists] that the enlightened demands of the time in which we live call for, if not a modification, a liberal construction, of the ancient rule, "that whatever is affixed to the soil belongs to the soil," or, the more modern statement of the rule, that "a permanent annexation to the soil, of a thing in itself personal, makes it a part of the realty." [Winchell also invokes] a rule alike ancient and of undoubted merit—that of "title by occupancy"—and we are cited to the language of Blackstone, as follows: "Occupancy is the taking possession of those things which before belonged to nobody;" and "whatever movables are found upon the surface of the earth, or in the sea, and are unclaimed by any owner, are supposed to be abandoned by the last proprietor, and as such are returned into the common stock and mass of things, and therefore they belong, as in a state of nature, to the first occupant or finder." ...

The rule sought to be avoided [by Winchell] has alone reference to what becomes a part of the soil, and hence belongs to the owner thereof, because attached or added thereto. It has no reference whatever to an ... acquisition of property existing independent of other property. The rule invoked [by Winchell] has reference only to property of this independent character, for it speaks of movables "found upon the surface of the earth or in the sea." The term "movables" must not be construed to mean that which can be moved, for, if so, it would include much known to be realty; but it means such things as are not naturally parts of earth or sea, but are on the one or in the other. Animals exist on the earth and in the sea, but they are not, in a proper sense, parts of either. If we look to the natural formation of the earth and sea, it is not difficult to understand what is meant by "movables," within the spirit of the rule cited. To take from the earth what nature has placed there in its formation, whether at the creation or through the natural processes of the acquisition and depletion of its particular parts, as we witness it in our daily observations, whether it be the soil proper or some natural deposit, as of mineral or vegetable matter, is to take a part of the earth, and not movables....

[The] aerolite ... that "fell from the heavens" on the land of the plaintiff, and was found three feet below the surface, ... came to its position in the earth through natural causes. It was one of nature's deposits, with nothing in its material composition to make it foreign or unnatural to the soil. It was not a movable thing "on the earth." It was in the earth, and in a very significant sense immovable; that is, it was only movable as parts of earth are made movable by the hand of man. Except for the peculiar manner in which it came, its relation to the soil would be beyond dispute. It was in its substance, as we understand, a stone. It was not of a character to be thought of as "unclaimed by any owner," and, because unclaimed, "supposed to be abandoned by the last proprietor," as should be the case under the rule invoked by the appellant. In fact, it has none of the characteristics of the property contemplated by such a rule....

Through the action of the elements, wind and water, the soil of one man is taken and deposited in the field of another; and thus all over the country, we may say, changes are constantly going on. By these natural causes the owners of the soil are giving and taking as the wisdom of the controlling forces shall determine. By these operations one may be affected with a substantial gain, and another by a similar loss. These gains are of accretion, and the deposit becomes the property of the owner of the soil on which it is made.

A scientist of note has said that from six to seven hundred of these stones fall to our earth annually. If they are . . . departures from other planets, and if among the planets of the solar system there is this interchange, bearing evidence of their material composition, upon what principle of reason or authority can we say that a deposit thus made shall not be of that class of property that it would be if originally of this planet and in the same situation? . . . It is not easy to understand why stones or balls of metallic iron, deposited as this was, should be governed by a different rule than obtains from the deposit of boulders, stones, and drift upon our prairies by glacier action; and who would contend that these deposits from floating bodies of ice belong, not to the owner of the soil, but to the finder? Their origin or source may be less mysterious, but they, too, are "telltale messengers" from far-off lands, and have value for historic and scientific investigation.

It is said that the aerolite is without adaptation to the soil, and only valuable for scientific purposes. Nothing in the facts of the case will warrant us in saying that it was not as well adapted for use by the owner of the soil as any stone, or, as [Winchell] is pleased to denominate it, "ball of metallic iron." That it may be of greater value for scientific or other purposes may be admitted, but that fact has little weight in determining who should be its owner. We cannot say that the owner of the soil is not as interested in, and would not as readily contribute to, the great cause of scientific advancement, as the finder, by chance or otherwise, of these silent messengers. . . .

The rule is cited, with cases for its support, that the finder of lost articles, even where they are found on the property, in the building, or with the personal effects of third persons, is the owner thereof against all the world, except the true owner. The correctness of the rule may be conceded, but its application to the case at bar is very doubtful. The subject of this controversy was never lost or abandoned. Whence it came is not known, but, under the natural law of its government, it became a part of this earth, and, we think, should be treated as such. . . .

The judgment of the district court is affirmed.

Customer **McAVOY v. MEDINA** *Barber Shop Owner*
Supreme Judicial Court of Massachusetts
93 Mass. 548 (1866)

[McAvoy, a customer in Medina's barber shop, "saw and took up a pocket-book which was lying upon a table there, and said, 'See what I have found.' [Medina] came to the table and asked where he found it. [McAvoy] laid it back in the same place and said, 'I found it right there.' [Medina] then took it and counted the money, and [McAvoy] told him to keep it, and if the owner should come to give it to him; and otherwise to advertise it; which [Medina] promised to do. Subsequently [McAvoy] made three demands for the money, and [Medina] never claimed to [be entitled to keep it] till the last demand. It was agreed that the pocket-book was placed upon the table by a transient customer of the defendant and accidentally left there, and was first seen and taken up by the plaintiff, and that the owner had not been found.

The judge ruled that the plaintiff could not maintain his action, and a verdict was accordingly returned for the defendant; and the plaintiff appealed.]

DEWEY, J., delivered the opinion of the court:

It seems to be the settled law that the finder of lost property has a valid claim to the same against all the world except the true owner, and generally that the place in which it is found creates no exception to this rule. . . . But this property is not, under the circumstances, to be treated as lost property in that sense in which a finder has a valid claim to hold the same until called for by the true owner. This property was voluntarily placed upon a table in the defendant's shop by a customer of his who accidentally left the same there and has never called for it. The plaintiff also came there as a customer, and first saw the same and took it up from the table. The plaintiff did not by this acquire the right to take the property from the shop, but it was rather the duty of the defendant, when the fact became thus known to him, to use reasonable care for the safe keeping of the same until the owner should call for it. In the case of Bridges v. Hawkesworth the property, although found in a shop, was found on the floor of the same, and had not been placed there voluntarily by the owner, and the court held that the finder was entitled to the possession of the same, except as to the owner. But the present case more resembles that of Lawrence v. The State, [20 Tenn.] 1 Humph. (Tenn.) 228 [1839], and is indeed very similar in its facts. The court there take a distinction between the case of property thus placed by the owner and neglected to be removed, and property lost. It was there held that "to place a pocket-book upon a table and to forget to take it away is not to lose it, in the sense in which [we] speak of lost property." We accept this as the better rule, and especially as one better adapted to secure the rights of the true owner. . . . [McAvoy] acquired no original right to the property, and the defendant's subsequent acts in receiving and holding the property in the manner he did does not create any.

[Affirmed.] Customer

NOTES, QUESTIONS AND PROBLEMS

1. The Owner of the "Locus in Quo." The phrase *locus in quo* is Latin for "the place in which. . . ." In this context it means the place in which the property is found. Recall the judicial statement following *Armory* that "the finder of lost property is entitled to it as against all the world except the real

[handwritten: so if he ever did come back Mdlna would have it (his shop)]

owner, and ... ordinarily the place where it is found does not make any difference." Why did it make a difference in *Goddard* and *McAvoy*? The court in *McAvoy* claimed that its ruling was designed "to secure the rights of the true owner." How will this happen? Even if the Massachusetts court was correct in its judgment about the pocket-book, the aerolite (or meteorite) that landed on Goddard's field had no true owner, so what policy was furthered by awarding ownership to Goddard? Did Goddard prevail because he was the prior possessor?

Note that Goddard was an absentee owner and likely would never have known of the aerolite had not Peter Hoagland's family seen it land and Hoagland dug it out of the soil. Did Goddard reap where he did not sow, or did Hoagland (who sold the aerolite to Winchell) take what he did not own? Who should be entitled to possession of the aerolite? Why? What policy or policies should be advanced?

   2. *Problems.*

    a. Suppose that you are a guest at a dinner party where the food is supplied by commercial caterers who have been employed by the hostess. In your serving of salad you find a valuable diamond ring. Who has the better claim to possession: You, your hostess, or the caterer? Why?

[handwritten: according to McAvoy, to the hotel]

    b. Hotel Corp. employs Jane as a chambermaid. When cleaning a room, she finds an expensive watch under the bed. Jane reports the find to her employer, who tries in vain to locate the true owner. When Jane requests that the watch be returned to her, Hotel Corp. refuses to do so. Who should prevail? Why? Compare Erickson v. Sinykin, 223 Minn. 232 (1947) with Hamaker v. Blanchard, 90 Pa. 377 (1879).

    c. Landowner engages John to clean out a henhouse. In doing so, John finds several sacks of gold coins inside a well-rusted tin can. John tells Landowner of the find and Landowner keeps the gold, refusing John's demand for its return. Who should prevail? Why? Compare Danielson v. Roberts, 44 Ore. 108 (1904) with South Staffordshire Water Co. v. Sharman, [1896] 2 Q.B. 44.

[handwritten: Peel]

    d. Major Peel purchased a country estate in Shropshire just prior to the outbreak of Word War II, but never moved in. The UK government requisitioned the house to quarter soldiers. Corporal Hannah found a valuable brooch while adjusting a blackout curtain, and reported the find to his superiors. After several years, when no true owner had been located, the brooch was delivered to Peel, who sold it. Hannah demanded the sale proceeds from Peel. Who should prevail? Why? See Hannah v. Peel, [1945] 1 K.B. 509.

FAVORITE v. MILLER

Supreme Court of Connecticut
176 Conn. 310 (1978)

BOGDANSKI, J., delivered the opinion of the court:

On July 9, 1776, a band of patriots, hearing news of the Declaration of Independence, toppled the equestrian statue of King George III, which was located in Bowling Green Park in lower Manhattan, New York. The statue, of gilded lead, was then hacked apart and the pieces ferried over Long Island Sound and loaded onto wagons at Norwalk, Connecticut, to be hauled some fifty miles northward to Oliver Wolcott's bullet-molding foundry in Litchfield, there to be cast into bullets. On the journey to Litchfield, the wagoners halted at Wilton, Connecticut, and while the patriots were imbibing, the loyalists managed to steal back pieces of the statue. The wagonload of the pieces lifted by the Tories was scattered about in the area of the Davis swamp in Wilton and fragments of the statue have continued to turn up in that area since that time. . . .

In 1972, the defendant, Louis Miller, determined that a part of the statue might be located within property owned by the plaintiffs. On October 16 he entered the area of the Davis Swamp owned by the plaintiffs although he knew it to be private property. With the aid of a metal detector, he discovered a statuary fragment fifteen inches square and weighing twenty pounds which was embedded ten inches below the soil. He dug up this fragment and removed it from the plaintiffs' property. The plaintiffs did not learn that a piece of the statue of King George III had been found on their property until they read about it in the newspaper, long after it had been removed.

In due course, the . . . defendant agreed to sell it to the Museum of the City of New York for $5500. The museum continues to hold it pending resolution of this controversy.

In March of 1973, the plaintiffs instituted this action to have the fragment returned to them and the case was submitted to the court on a stipulation of facts. The trial court found . . . for the plaintiffs, from which judgment the defendant appealed to this court. The sole issue presented on appeal is whether the claim of the defendant, as finder, is superior to that of the plaintiffs, as owners of the land upon which the historic fragment was discovered. Traditionally, when questions have arisen concerning the rights of the finder as against the person upon whose land the property was found, the resolution has turned upon the characterization given the property. Typically, if the property was found to be "lost" or "abandoned," the finder would prevail, whereas if the property was characterized as "mislaid," the owner or occupier of the land would prevail.

Lost property has traditionally been defined as involving an involuntary parting, i.e., where there is no intent on the part of the loser to part with the ownership of the property. Abandonment, in turn, has been defined as the voluntary relinquishment of ownership of property without reference to any particular person or purpose; i.e., a "throwing away" of the property concerned; while mislaid property is defined as that which is intentionally placed by the owner where he can obtain custody of it, but afterwards forgotten. It should be noted that the classification of property as "lost," "abandoned," or "mislaid" requires that a court determine the intent or mental state of the unknown party who at some time in the past parted with the ownership or control of the property.

The trial court in this case applied the traditional approach and ruled in favor of the landowners on the ground that the piece of the statue found by Miller was "mislaid." The factual basis for that conclusion is . . . that "the loyalists did not wish to have the pieces [in their possession] during the turmoil surrounding the Revolutionary War and hid them in a place where they could resort to them [after the war], but forgot where they put them." . . . [We think] that any conclusion as to the mental state of persons engaged in events which occurred over two hundred years ago would be of a conjectural nature and as such does not furnish an adequate basis for determining rights of twentieth century claimants.

The defendant argues further that his rights in the statue are superior to those of anyone except the true owner (i.e., the British government). He presses this claim on the ground that the law has traditionally favored the finder as against all but the true owner, and that because his efforts brought the statue to light, he should be allowed to reap the benefits of his discovery . . .: "As with archeologists forever probing and unearthing the past, to guide man for the betterment of those to follow, explorers like Miller deserve encouragement, and reward, in their selfless pursuit of the hidden, the unknown."

There are, however, some difficulties with the defendant's position. The first concerns the defendant's characterization of himself as a selfless seeker after knowledge. The facts in the record do not support such a conclusion. The defendant admitted that he was in the business of selling metal detectors and that he has used his success in finding the statue as advertising to boost his sales of such metal detectors, and that the advertising has been financially rewarding. Further, there is the fact that he signed a contract with the City Museum of New York for the sale of the statuary piece and that he stands to profit thereby.

Moreover, even if we assume his motive to be that of historical research alone, that fact will not justify his entering upon the property of another without permission. It is unquestioned that in today's world even archeologists must obtain permission from owners of property and the government of the country involved before they can conduct their explorations. Similarly, mountaineers must apply for permits, sometimes years in advance of their proposed expeditions. On a more familiar level, backpackers and hikers must often obtain permits before being allowed access to certain of our national parks and forests, even though that land is public and not private. Similarly, hunters and fishermen wishing to enter upon private property must first obtain the permission of the owner before they embark upon their respective pursuits. . . .

[The] fact that the finder is trespassing is sufficient to deprive him of his normal preference over the owner of the place where the property was found. The basis for the rule is that a wrongdoer should not be allowed to profit by his wrongdoing. Another line of cases holds that property, other

The place in which

than treasure trove, which is found embedded in the earth is the property of the owner of the locus in quo. The presumption in such cases is that possession of the article found is in the owner of the land and that the finder acquires no rights to the article found.

The defendant, by his own admission, knew that he was trespassing when he entered upon the property of the plaintiffs. He admitted that he was told by Gertrude Merwyn, the librarian of the Wilton Historical Society, *before* he went into the Davis Swamp area, that the land was privately owned and that Mrs. Merwyn recommended that he call the owners, whom she named, and obtain permission before he began his explorations. He also admitted that ... the piece of the statue which he found was embedded in the ground ten inches below the surface and that it was necessary for him to excavate in order to take possession of his find.

In light of those undisputed facts the defendant's trespass was neither technical nor trivial. We conclude that the fact that the property found was embedded in the earth and the fact that the defendant was a trespasser are sufficient to defeat any claim to the property which the defendant might otherwise have had as a finder. [Affirmed.]

NOTES AND QUESTIONS

1. The Trespassing Finder. Miller was a deliberate trespasser, but he expended considerable effort and skill to locate the pieces of the statue. The landowners would likely have never discovered the statuary pieces but for Miller's efforts. Should Miller have been deprived of all the benefits of his efforts because he was a wrongdoer? Recall Anderson v. Gouldberg, which held that even wrongful prior possessor should prevail against a subsequent possessor. Did Favorite win because he was a *prior* possessor rather than a subsequent possessor? Or did Favorite win simply because Miller was a deliberate wrongdoer? What kind of behavior will be encouraged (or discouraged) by the rule in *Favorite*?

2. Treasure Trove. English common law provided that treasure trove (found treasure), which consisted of money, gold or other refined precious metal, or bullion hidden in the earth, belonged to the Crown. After revolt against the Crown, Americans discarded that notion but its residue is to be found in various old pronouncements of American courts that treasure trove belongs to the finder and not to the owner or occupant of the premises where it is found. See, e.g, Groover v. Tippins, 51 Ga.App. 47 (1935). But that rule is largely rejected today. An example is Morgan v. Wiser, 711 S.W.2d 220 (Tenn. App. 1985), in which appellees allegedly trespassed upon appellants' farm and, with the aid of a metal detector, located a buried cache of gold coins. The trial court applied the rule that treasure trove belongs to exclusively to the finder. The appeals court reversed:

The common-law rule of treasure-trove invites trespassers to roam at large over the property of others with their metal detecting devices and to dig wherever such devices tell them property might be found. If the discovery happens to fit the definition of treasure-trove, the trespasser may claim it as his own. . . . The invitation to trespassers inherent in the rule with respect to treasure-trove is repugnant to the common law rules dealing with trespassers in general.

Rather, treasure trove was to be treated like any other imbedded object. The Roman emperor Hadrian ruled that treasure trove was to be shared equally between the finder and the property owner. Is that a better rule?

COLUMBUS–AMERICA DISCOVERY GROUP v. ATLANTIC MUTUAL INSURANCE CO.

United States Court of Appeals
974 F.2d 450 (4th Cir. 1992)

RUSSELL, CIRCUIT JUDGE:

"When Erasmus mused that '[a] common shipwreck is a source of consolation to all', *Adagia,* IV.iii.9 (1508), he quite likely did not foresee inconcinnate free-for-alls among self-styled salvors." Without doubt the Dutch scholar also could not imagine legal brawls involving self-styled "finders" from Ohio, British and American insurance underwriters, an heir to the Miller Brewing fortune, a Texas oil millionaire, an Ivy League university, and an Order of Catholic monks. Yet that is what this case involves, with the prize being up to one billion dollars in gold.

This gold was deposited on the ocean floor, 8,000 feet below the surface and 160 miles off the South Carolina coast, when the S.S. *Central America* sank in a hurricane on September 12, 1857. The precise whereabouts of the wreck remained unknown until 1988, when it was located by the Columbus–America Discovery Group ("Columbus–America"). This enterprise has since been recovering the gold, and last year it moved in federal district court to have itself declared the owner of the treasure. Into court to oppose this manoeuvre came British and American insurers who had originally underwritten the gold for its ocean voyage and then had to pay off over a million dollars in claims upon the disaster. . . .

The district court . . . awarded Columbus–America the golden treasure in its entirety. It found that the underwriters had previously abandoned their ownership interests in the gold by deliberately destroying certain documentation. [We] find that the evidence was not sufficient to show that the underwriters affirmatively abandoned their interests in the gold. . . .

I. A. The year 1857 is justly famous in American history for its many notable events. Among these was the beginning of a fairly serious financial decline, the aptly named Panic of 1857. Associated with the Panic, and another reason why the year is so famous, is one of the worst disasters in American maritime history, the sinking of the S.S. *Central America.*

The *Central America* was a black-hulled, coal-fired, three-decked, three-masted sidewheeler with a cruising speed of eleven knots. Built in 1852, and launched the following year, she carried passengers, mail, and cargo between Aspinwall, Colombia (on the Caribbean side of the isthmus of Panama), and New York City, with a stopover in Havana. Most, if not all, of her passengers were headed to or from California, the route being one leg of the then quickest way between the west coast and the eastern seaboard—from California to the Pacific side of the isthmus of Panama aboard a steamship, across the isthmus on the Panama Railroad, and then from Aspinwall to New York aboard another steamship. Owned by the U.S. Mail and Steamship Company and originally named the S.S. *George Law* (until June 1857), the *Central America* completed forty-three voyages between Panama and New York in her four years of operation. During this period, the California gold rush was in full swing, and it has been said that the ship carried one-third of all gold shipped at that time from California to New York.

In August of 1857, over four hundred passengers and approximately $1,600,000 (1857 value) in gold (exclusive of passenger gold) left San Francisco for Panama aboard the S.S. *Sonora*. Many of the passengers were prospectors who had become rich and were returning home, either for good or to visit. Also on board were California Judge Alonzo Castle Monson, who resigned from the bench after losing his house and all his money in a famous poker game, and Mrs. Virginia Birch, a.k.a. "the notorious Jenny French," a former dance hall girl well known in San Francisco. As for the gold, it was being shipped by California merchants, bankers, and express companies, including Levi Straus and Wells Fargo, to New York banks, the banks wanting specie to stave off the effects of the financial downturn.

The travellers and the cargo reached Panama without incident, and they crossed the isthmus by rail. On September 3, over six hundred people came aboard the *Central America*, as well as $1,219,189 of the gold shipped on the *Sonora*, the remainder being shipped to England aboard a different vessel. The *Central America* first headed for Havana, which was reached on September 7. There, the ship [layed] over for a night, and some of the passengers debarked to catch another vessel for New Orleans. On September 8, under clear skies, the *Central America* left Havana for New York, carrying approximately 580 persons and her golden treasure.

On the second day out of Havana, the weather changed and a mighty storm came up. What the passengers and crew could not know was that they were headed directly into the teeth of a ferocious hurricane. As the storm worsened around the *Central America*, a leak developed and soon water was rushing into the boat. The water extinguished the fires in the ship's boilers, and this in turn caused the ship's pumping system to fail. All able male passengers began a systematic bailing of water out of the ship, but it was to no avail; after thirty frantic hours, the boiler fires would still not light and the water level continued to rise.

Knowing the situation was hopeless, Captain William Lewis Herndon managed to hail a passing ship, the brig *Marine*, and one hundred persons, including all but one of the women and children aboard, were safely transferred to the other ship. Time and conditions would not allow for any more transfers, however, and shortly after 8 p.m. on September 12, the *Central America* began making its quick descent to the bottom of the ocean.

After being flung into the sea, many of the men managed to come to the top and float there, desperately holding onto any buoyant material available. Six to nine hours after the sinking, fifty of these men were rescued by the Norwegian bark *Ellen*. Earlier, a small bird had thrice circled the *Ellen* and flown directly into the face of the ship's captain. Taking this as a sign, the captain changed his course to follow from whence the bird had come, and in so doing discovered the fifty floating survivors. Three other men were also rescued when, nine days later and 450 miles away, a ship spotted their lifeboat, which had been riding the Gulf Stream. In all, 153 persons were rescued, while approximately 425 lost their lives. Also lost were hundreds of bags of mail and the $1,219,189 in gold. At the time, there were rumors that other commercial shipments of gold were aboard, but these were quickly discounted. It is true, though, that a significant amount, probably several hundred thousand dollars worth (1857 valuation), of passenger gold was lost. Many passengers had with them their earnings from several years' labor in the California gold fields. Some kept this gold on their person, while others carried it in carpetbags or trunks. Also, passenger gold could have been checked with the ship's purser, although these records were lost with the ship. Captain Thomas W. Badger is one example of a passenger carrying gold, he having lost $17,500 of it stored in a carpetbag. Also, the newspapers reporting the disaster contained vivid accounts of men flinging down their hard earned treasure in disgust upon realizing their impending doom.

Needless to say, for the next several weeks newspapers around the country devoted much space to the disaster which befell the *Central America*. While people mourned the over four hundred persons who had valiantly lost their lives, they also feared that the loss of such a large amount of specie would exacerbate the country's already serious financial situation. The commercial shipments of gold had been insured, though, and the insurance underwriters began advertising in the newspapers that they would pay off their commitments upon the proper proofs being presented. Approximately one-third of the treasure had been underwritten by New York insurers while the rest was underwritten in London. Without doubt, most, if not all, of the claims were promptly paid off by the underwriters.

Under applicable law, then and now, once the underwriters paid the claims made upon them by the owners of the gold, the treasure became theirs. Thus, less than two weeks after the disaster, the underwriters began negotiating with the Boston Submarine Armor Company about possibly raising the ship and her cargo. Also, on June 28, 1858, two of the underwriters (Atlantic Mutual Insurance Company and Sun Mutual Insurance Company) contracted with Brutus de Villeroi, a Frenchman then living in Pennsylvania, to salvage the gold. The contract states that de Villeroi, "by means of his Invention of a Submarine boat" and at his own expense, would raise the treasure and receive a salvage award of seventy-five percent. At this time, though, no one was quite sure where the boat had gone down, or in how deep of water. At first, some estimated the ship was in only twenty-eight fathoms of water (168 feet), when in fact it was over 8,000 feet below the surface. As would be expected, nothing came of the salvage attempts in the late 1850s, and the issue, and the gold, would lay dormant for over a hundred and twenty years.

B. Beginning in the 1970s, a number of individuals and groups began discussing and planning the salvage of the *Central America*, as the decade before had seen a great advance in the technology necessary for deep sea salvage. Still, though, no one was positive where the ship had gone down or in what depth of water. . . . A number of those interested in salvaging the *Central America* contacted some of the various insurers who had underwritten the gold. The would-be salvors hoped to receive a relinquishment of the insurers' rights to the property, or at least form a salvage contract with the underwriters. While the underwriters negotiated with several groups about the salvage, they did not enter into any salvage contracts nor did they relinquish any of their rights to the gold. One of the groups that contacted several of the underwriters was . . . Columbus–America Discovery Group, the eventual salvor. Columbus–America asked the underwriters to convey to it any claims they might have regarding the gold, but this was not done.

Another group that was interested in salvaging the gold was Santa Fe Communications, Inc. ("Santa Fe"), whose interests are now owned by . . . Harry G. John and Jack R. Grimm.[2] In 1984, Santa Fe paid . . . Columbia University $300,000 for Columbia's Dr. William B. F. Ryan to conduct a sonar search over a 400 square mile area of the Atlantic Ocean. . . . Dr. Ryan identified seven "targets" on the ocean floor. Of these targets, he found only one, target #4, to be a good candidate for being the *Central America*. . . . Santa Fe, though, did not further pursue the matter, and on December 31, 1984, it transferred to a Catholic monastic order, the Province of St. Joseph of the Capuchin Order—St. Benedict Friary of Milwaukee, Wisconsin ("the Capuchins"), any and all rights and interests arising out of its undersea salvage operations. It now appears that target #4 was indeed the *Central America*. . . .

Shortly after the survey, Columbus–America President Thomas Thompson began contacting Dr. Ryan and others at Columbia and Santa Fe in an attempt to learn the results. . . . Thompson wrote Dr. Ryan and requested certain sonar photographs taken during the survey. . . . Columbia . . . agreed to provide the information [on the condition that the material] "would be for your sole use and would not be reproduced for others." Thompson agreed to this condition, but went ahead and placed the information he received into Columbus–America's files.

---

2. John is an heir to the Miller Brewing Company, while Grimm is a multimillionaire Texas oilman who has in the past led searches for Noah's Ark, the Loch Ness Monster, and the *Titanic*.

C. In 1987, after much effort and expense, Columbus–America believed it had found the *Central America*. . . . Columbus–America spent two years attempting to salvage the wreck they thought was the *Central America* [and] recovered several artifacts, as well as a good many lumps of coal, but at some point they recognized that they were salvaging the wrong ship. They then began to look at other likely targets, and, eventually, they discovered the right ship. . . .

Since 1989, Columbus–America, through its invention of a submersible robot which can pick up objects ranging from small gold coins to a ship's anchor weighing thousands of pounds, has been salvaging objects left on the ocean floor by the *Central America*. Undoubtedly, its major interest is in recovering the gold, and so far several hundred million dollars worth (present value) of gold coins, ingots, and bars have been recovered—it is estimated that the total haul may be worth up to one billion dollars. . . .

[Many] of the original underwriters of the gold, plus the Superintendent of Insurance of the State of New York for several insurance companies now defunct, filed claims with the district court asserting that they were the proper owners of the gold. [The district court] bifurcated the trial, so that the first part would concern only whether Columbus–America was entitled to finder or salvor status. If the district court found that the insurance companies had somehow abandoned the gold, Columbus–America would be considered its "finder," and thus its owner. On the other hand, if the underwriters had not abandoned the gold, they would still remain its owners and Columbus–America would be its "salvor." If the latter scenario were found to be true, a second phase of the trial would be necessary, wherein the Court would have to determine what each underwriter had insured and the amount of Columbus–America's salvage award. [The] district court held that the underwriters had abandoned the gold, and thus Columbus–America was its finder and sole owner. The Court based this finding of abandonment primarily on the supposed fact that the underwriters had *intentionally* destroyed any documentation they had once had concerning the case. . . . The underwriters . . . now appeal.

II. A. Historically, courts have applied the maritime law of salvage when ships or their cargo have been recovered from the bottom of the sea by those other than their owners. Under this law, the original owners still retain their ownership interests in such property, although the salvors are entitled to a very liberal salvage award. . . . [If] no owner should come forward to claim the property, the salvor is normally awarded its total value. . . .

A related legal doctrine is the common law of finds, which expresses "the ancient and honorable principle of 'finders, keepers.' " Traditionally, the law of finds was applied only to maritime property which had never been owned by anybody, such as ambergris, whales, and fish. A relatively recent trend in the law, though, has seen the law of finds applied to long lost and abandoned shipwrecks. . . .

"The primary concern of the law of finds is title. The law of finds defines the circumstances under which a party may be said to have acquired title to ownerless property. Its application necessarily assumes that the property involved either was never owned or was abandoned.... To justify an award of title (albeit of one that is defeasible), the law of finds requires a finder to demonstrate not only the intent to acquire the property involved, but also possession of that property, that is, a high degree of control over it...."

In sharp contrast to "the harsh, primitive, and inflexible nature of the law of finds" is the law of salvage. Admiralty favors the law of salvage over the law of finds because salvage law's aims, assumptions, and rules are more consonant with the needs of marine activity and because salvage law encourages less competitive and secretive forms of conduct than finds law. The primary concern of salvage law is the preservation of property on oceans and waterways. Salvage law specifies the circumstances under which a party may be said to have acquired, not title, but the right to take possession of property (e.g., vessels, equipment, and cargo) for the purpose of saving it from destruction, damage, or loss, and to retain it until proper compensation has been paid. Salvage [l]aw assumes that the property being salved is owned by another, and thus that it has not been abandoned. Admiralty courts have adhered to the traditional and realistic premise that property previously owned but lost at sea has been taken involuntarily out of the owner's possession and control by the forces of nature at work in oceans and waterways; in fact, property may not be "salvaged" under admiralty law unless it is in some form of peril.... Salvage law requires that to be a salvor a party must have the intention and the capacity to save the property involved, but the party need not have the intention to acquire it. Furthermore, although the law of salvage, like the law of finds, requires a salvor to establish possession over property before obtaining the right to exclude others, "possession" means something less in salvage law than in finds law. In the salvage context, only the right to compensation for service, not the right to title, usually results.... Moreover, unlike the would-be finder, who is either a keeper or a loser, the salvor receives a payment, depending on the value of the service rendered, that may go beyond quantum meruit. Admiralty's equitable power to make an award for salvage—recognized since ancient times in maritime civilizations—is a corollary to the assumption of non-abandonment and has been applied irrespective of the owner's express refusal to accept such service.... These salvage rules markedly diminish the incentive for salvors to act secretly, to hide their recoveries, or to ward off competition from other would-be salvors.... In short, although salvage law cannot alter human nature, its application enables courts to encourage open, lawful, and cooperative conduct, all in the cause of preserving property (and life).

Today, finds law is applied to previously owned sunken property only when that property has been abandoned by its previous owners. Abandonment in this sense means much more than merely leaving the property, for it has long been the law that "when articles are lost at sea the title of the owner in them remains." Once an article has been lost at sea, "lapse of time and nonuser are not sufficient, in and of themselves, to constitute an abandonment." In addition, there is no abandonment when one discovers sunken property and then, even after extensive efforts, is unable to locate its owner.

While abandonment has been simply described as "the act of deserting property without hope of recovery or intention of returning to it," in the lost property at sea context, there is also a strong *actus* element required to prove the necessary intent. "Abandonment is said to be a voluntary act which must be proved by a clear and unmistakable affirmative act to indicate a purpose to repudiate ownership." . . . [W]hen sunken ships or their cargo are rescued from the bottom of the ocean by those other than the owners, courts favor applying the law of salvage over the law of finds. Finds law should be applied, however, in situations where the previous owners are found to have abandoned their property. Such abandonment must be proved by clear and convincing evidence, though, such as an owner's express declaration abandoning title. Should the property encompass an ancient and long-lost shipwreck, a court may infer an abandonment. Such an inference would be improper, though, should a previous owner appear and assert his ownership interest; in such a case the normal presumptions would apply and an abandonment would have to be proved by strong and convincing evidence.

B. . . . First, the *Central America* herself was self-insured, and successors in interest to the U.S. Mail and Steamship Company have made no attempt to claim an ownership interest in the wreck. Also, there appears to have been a fairly significant amount of passenger gold aboard, but this case, almost surprisingly, has failed to see descendants of any of the passengers attempt to gain a share of the treasure. Thus, an abandonment may be found, and Columbus–America may be declared the finder and sole owner, as to any recovered parts of the ship, all passenger possessions, and any cargo besides the insured shipments. . . .

[T]he district court applied the law of finds and awarded Columbus–America the entire treasure . . . because at some point the insurers had abandoned their interests in the gold. . . . [The district court] ruled as it did because of only two [factors]: the underwriters did nothing to recover the gold after 1858, and they supposedly destroyed all documentation they had regarding payment of claims for the gold. . . .

[At trial,] the underwriters did not produce any of the original insurance contracts with the insureds, statements from shippers that goods were aboard, bills of lading, or canceled checks or receipts from paying off the claims. While such documents would have existed in 1857, none could be located in 1990. Thus, because an insurance executive testified that the usual practice *today* is for insurance companies to destroy worthless documents after five years, the district court found that the above documentation concerning the *Central America* must have been intentionally destroyed in the ordinary course of business. Such destruction, coupled with 130 years of non-use, equalled, according to the Court, an abandonment. . . .

Contrary to the district court, we cannot find any evidence that the underwriters intentionally or deliberately destroyed any of their documents about the *Central America*. Instead, the only evidence we have is that after 134 years, such documents that may have once existed can no longer be located. With such a passing of time, it seems as, if not more, likely that the documents were lost or unintentionally destroyed, rather than being intentionally destroyed.

. . . Yet, the underwriters did present several other original documents from their files concerning this case, and in at least one instance all the documents in an insurer's file on the *Central America* were stolen by a would-be salvor. Also, almost all of the evidence in the record actually seems to indicate a specific predisposition on the underwriters' part not to abandon the treasure. Shortly after the disaster, the underwriters negotiated with a salvage company about rescuing the gold, and the next year a salvage contract was formed between two of the insurers and Brutus de Villeroi. Nothing came of these efforts, and the issue lay dormant for 120 years. Still, it appears that the gold was not totally forgotten, for when the Atlantic Mutual Insurance Company ("Atlantic Mutual") wrote its official history in 1967, it devoted a couple of pages to the *Central America* tragedy and the company's salvage contract with de Villeroi. . . .

Because of drastic advances in deep water salvage, the late 1970s witnessed a good many would-be salvors contacting various underwriters regarding the *Central America*. Atlantic Mutual and The Insurance Company of North America ("INA") opened their archives to these salvors, and several in turn sought to form salvage arrangements with the insurers. . . . Throughout the early and mid–1980s, would-be salvors continued to contact the underwriters for information on the wreck. Salvage contracts were sporadically discussed, but at no time did the insurers ever agree to abandon their ownership interests in the gold.[3] As late as 1987, INA was negotiating a salvage contract with Boston Salvage Consultants, Inc., whereby INA would receive two percent of any treasure recovered. . . . In addition, not only the American insurers, but also the British, entered into various salvage negotiations, the latter through their Salvage Association. . . .

It is ironic that one of the salvors who contacted the underwriters in the 1980s was Columbus–America itself. The eventual salvor used Atlantic Mutual's extensive library for research and then, in 1987, it, through an attorney, wrote the following enigmatic letter to many of the underwriters:

---

3. One typical example is from 1980, when an Edwin R. Fite of Pascagoula, Mississippi, contacted Atlantic Mutual for information on the *Central America*, and also inquired as to "how much it would cost to purchase the insurance claims to this wreck?" Atlantic Mutual responded by suggesting that Mr. Fite contact the law firm it had hired for such requests, and the letter also stated, "we are not interested in relinquishing any rights with respect to the cargo."

We are writing to a number of insurance companies on behalf of one of our clients. Our client is acquiring the rights to various 19th Century marine wrecks. If [your company] claims or asserts any interest in vessels or cargo which were wrecked in the Atlantic Ocean during the 19th Century and would consider conveying its claim or asserted interest, please get in touch with me. Our client would also be interested in obtaining or seeing any existing records upon which [your company] might assert a claim to any 19th Century wrecked vessel or its cargo.

Of course, none of the underwriters responded affirmatively to such a broad and mystifying request.[4] . . .

[A]bandonment . . . must be proved by clear and convincing evidence. Here, we are unable to find the requisite evidence that could lead a court to conclude that the underwriters affirmatively abandoned their interest in the gold. Thus, we hold that the lower court clearly erred when it found an abandonment and applied the law of finds. Accordingly, the case is remanded to the district court for further proceedings.

C. On remand, the district court is to apply the law of salvage, and in so doing it must determine what percentage of the gold each underwriter insured. Equally, if not more, important, the Court must also determine the proper salvage award for Columbus–America. Although this is a decision that must be left to the lower court, we are hazarding but little to say that Columbus–America should, and will, receive by far the largest share of the treasure. . . .

Notes, Questions and Problems

1. Discerning Abandonment. The *Columbus–America* court thought that abandonment must be proved by clear and convincing evidence of a deliberate intention to renounce ownership of property. Should the persistent and long-standing failure of the true owner to take action to recover the property be treated as evidence of an intention to renounce ownership? Can abandonment be inferred from actions of the owner?

2. Problems:

a. In a 1977 documentary film, the artist Georgia O'Keefe said that after a year of painting as a young woman (circa 1908) she had thrown away all her paintings because each of them had been painted to please someone else and she wanted to create art that pleased herself. One of her later paintings, created in 1928, sold at auction in 2001 for $6.166 million. Suppose your client's great-grandfather found one of O'Keefe's discarded paintings in 1908 and it has been bequeathed to your client, who offers it for sale at auction. The estate of Georgia O'Keefe demands possession, claiming that O'Keefe did not abandon the painting. Who should prevail? What evidence is needed to prove abandonment?

4. Atlantic Mutual did write back [as follows:] "It is our intention to retain any rights that may be due us under general maritime law (or otherwise) and accordingly we do not wish to convey any claims or interest to your client."

b.   Suppose that you host a party attended by sixty guests. After the party you discover a bracelet apparently left behind by one of your guests. You inquire of the guests, but nobody claims the bracelet. After a dozen years Stranger, who accompanied one of your guests to the party but was herself not an invitee, claims that the bracelet is hers, and has evidence to prove her ownership of the item at the time of the party. Has Stranger abandoned ownership? What facts would you wish to know in order to answer the query?   *no*   *Did she search for it?*

c.   The evening before the weekly garbage pick-up, Owner places a box of books at his curbside garbage collection station. Packrat stops at the box and takes a copy of Scott Fitzgerald's *The Great Gatsby* home with him. Before the garbage man's arrival, Owner realizes he has placed a valuable first edition of *The Great Gatsby* in the trash, and he rushes out to retrieve the volume. Too late, but Neighbor informs Owner that Packrat took a book out of the box. Owner investigates and seeks to recover the book. In the case of Owner v. Packrat, who should prevail? Why?   *"mislaid"*

3.   *Salvage law or finders' law?* In *Columbus–America* the court was required to determine which law should apply—the maritime law of salvage or the more general law pertaining to found property. This specific problem is unique to shipwrecks and other finds involving marine property, because salvage is a concept confined to maritime distress. However, the problem the *Columbus–America* court confronted presents a larger issue: Should finders law produce "winner-take-all" results or should it deliver shared rewards?

Consider the facts in Goddard v. Winchell. Hoagland, the finder of the aerolite, entered Goddard's property with the permission of Goddard's lessee and had a reasonable expectation that the object he found and labored to uncover would be his. Winchell, the purchaser of the aerolite from Hoagland, paid fair market value for the object. Goddard, as owner of the land, had a reasonable expectation that the land (including the rocks in the soil) was his and would be returned to him after the expiration of the lease to Elickson. Should the principles of salvage law be imported generally into the law of finds? But what if the contenders for possession do not want to sell the object and divide the proceeds, but wish to keep it? What if only one of the contenders wishes to have possession rather than a sale?

B.   ADVERSE POSSESSION

Adverse possession is a doctrine that enables a person who possesses property he does not own to acquire ownership of it after the elapse of a sufficient amount of time. How can this happen? Every state has a statute of limitations that bars the owner of land from recovering possession of it from another person who is possession of it. These statutes differ in the length of time before which an action to recover possession is barred, the conditions under which the statutory period may be suspended or lengthened, and other matters. By case law in every state, these statutes only apply if the adverse possessor has taken and maintained possession in a certain manner. Thus, the law of adverse possession is an amalgam of   *mixture* statutory and case law. The result of expiration of the limitations period against an adverse possessor who has maintained his possession in the requisite manner is that nobody has a better title than the adverse possessor, and the adverse possessor can institute a suit to "quiet title" in his name.

At first glance, the law of adverse possession appears to be a curiosity, and perhaps obnoxious as well. Why should a lawful owner lose his title in favor of a squatter? There are at least three justifications offered for this state of affairs. First, it ensures stability of ownership. After a long period in which a stranger has possessed the true owner's property there may be some doubt about the title. Stale claims pose a problem of proof, although that may be easily overcome by the ubiquity of recorded titles to land. Second, adverse possession rewards a possessor who "earns" land he does not own by improving it or making it productive. Third, adverse possession penalizes the slothful true owner, who does not care enough about his land that for many years he fails to take action to eject the interloper. As a variation upon the adage "use it or lose it," this justification seems to say "protect it or lose it." Note that these justifications are not mutually exclusive. As you read the following materials, consider the extent to which these justifications are at work, and whether they are sound.

1. THE ELEMENTS OF ADVERSE POSSESSION

MARENGO CAVE CO. v. ROSS

Supreme Court of Indiana
212 Ind. 624 (1937)

ROLL, J. delivered the opinion of the court:

Appellee and appellant were the owners of adjoining land in Crawford County, Indiana. On appellant's land was located the opening to a subterranean cavity known as "Marengo Cave." This cave extended under a considerable portion of appellant's land and the southeastern portion thereof extended under lands owned by appellee. This action arose out of a dispute as to the ownership of that part of the cave that extended under appellee's land. Appellant was claiming title to all the cave and cavities including that portion underlying appellee's land. Appellee instituted this action to quiet his title as against appellant's claim. Appellant ... filed a cross-complaint wherein he sought to quiet its title to all the cave including that portion underlying appellee's land. There was a trial by jury which returned a verdict for the appellee....

In 1883 one Stewart owned the real estate now owned by appellant, and in September of that year some young people who were upon that land discovered what afterwards proved to be the entrance to the cavern since known as Marengo Cave, this entrance being approximately 700 feet from the boundary line between the lands now owned by appellant and appellee, and the only entrance to said cave. Within a week after discovery of the cave it was explored, and the fact of its existence received wide

FACTS

publicity through newspaper articles and otherwise. Shortly thereafter the then owner of the real estate upon which the entrance was located, took complete possession of the entire cave as now occupied by appellant and used for exhibition purposes, and began to charge an admission fee to those who desired to enter and view the cave, and to exclude therefrom those who were unwilling to pay for admission. This practice continued from 1883, . . . and during the following years the successive owners of the land upon which the entrance to the cave was located advertised the existence of said cave through newspapers, magazines, posters, and otherwise, in order to attract visitors thereto; also made improvements within the cave, including the building of concrete walks, and concrete steps where there was a difference in elevation of said cavern, widened and heightened portions of passageways; had available and furnished guides, all in order to make the cave more easily accessible to visitors desiring to view the same; and continuously, during all this time, without asking or obtaining consent from anyone, but claiming a right so to do, held and possessed said subterranean passages constituting said cave, excluding therefrom the "whole world" except such persons as entered after paying admission for the privilege of so doing, or by permission.

Ross

Appellee . . . purchased the real estate which he now owns in 1908. He first visited the cave in 1895, paying an admission fee for the privilege, and has visited said cave several times since. He has never, at any time, occupied or been in possession of any of the subterranean passages or cavities of which the cave consists, and the possession and use of the cave by those who have done so has never interfered with his use and enjoyment of the lands owned by him. For a period of approximately twenty-five years prior to the time appellee purchased his land, and for a period of twenty-one years afterwards, exclusive possession of the cave has been held by appellant, its immediate and remote grantors. . . .

A part of said cave at the time of its discovery and exploration extended beneath real estate now owned by appellee, but this fact was not ascertained until the year 1932, when the boundary line between the respective tracts through the cave was established by means of a survey made by a civil engineer. . . . Previous to this survey neither of the parties to this appeal, nor any of their predecessors in title, knew that any part of the cave was in fact beneath the surface of a portion of the land now owned by appellee. Possession of the cave was taken and held by appellant's remote and immediate grantors, improvements made, and control exercised, with the belief on the part of such grantors that the entire cave as it was explored and held, was under the surface of lands owned by them. There is no evidence of the dispute as to ownership of the cave, or any portion thereof, prior to the time when in 1929 appellee requested a survey, which was approximately forty-six years after discovery of the cave and the exercise of complete dominion thereover by appellant and its predecessors in title.

[Appellant Marengo Cave Company contends that] it owns that part [of the cave] underlying appellee's land by adverse possession. [An Indiana statute] provides as follows: "The following actions shall be commenced within the periods herein prescribed after the cause of action has accrued, and not afterward: . . . Sixth. . . . for the recovery of the possession of real estate, within twenty (20) years." . . .

[Appellee Ross's title] extends from the surface to the center,[5] but [his] actual possession is confined to the surface. Appellee and his immediate and remote grantors have been in possession of the land and estate here in question at all times, unless it can be said that the possession of the cave by appellant . . . has met all the requirements of the law relating to the acquisition of land by adverse possession. A record title may be defeated by adverse possession. All the authorities agree that before the owner of the legal title can be deprived of his land by another's possession, through the operation of the statute of limitation, the possession must have been actual, visible, notorious, exclusive, under claim of ownership and hostile to the owner of the legal title and to the world at large (except only the government) and continuous for the full period prescribed by the statute. The rule is not always stated in exactly the same words in the many cases dealing with the subject of adverse possession, yet the rule is so thoroughly settled that there is no doubt as to what elements are essential to establish a title by adverse possession. Let us examine the various elements that are essential to establish title by adverse possession and apply them to . . . the undisputed facts in this case.

(1) The possession must be actual. It must be conceded that appellant, in the operation of the "Marengo Cave," used not only the cavern under its own land but also that part of the cavern that underlaid appellee's land, and assumed dominion over all of it. Yet it must also be conceded that during all of [that] time appellee was in constructive possession, as the only constructive possession known to the law is that which inheres in the legal title and with which the owner of that title is always endowed. Whether the possession was actual under the peculiar facts in this case we need not decide.

(2) The possession must be visible. The owner of land who, having notice of the fact that it is occupied by another who is claiming dominion over it, nevertheless stands by during the entire statutory period and makes no effort to eject the claimant or otherwise protect his title, ought not to be permitted, for reasons of public policy, thereafter to maintain an action for the recovery of his land. But . . . in order that the possession of the occupying claimant may constitute notice in law, it must be visible and open to the common observer so that the owner or his agent on visiting the premises might readily see that the owner's rights are being invaded. What constitutes open and visible possession has been stated in general

---

5. [Ed.] A venerable principle of property law is the *ad coelum* doctrine, derived from the Latin maxim *cujus est solum, ejus est usque ad coelum et ad infernos*, which (roughly translated) means "whoever owns the soil owns up to the heavens and down to Hell." This principle cannot be applied literally, as the competing underground claims of surface owners necessarily collide as one nears the center of the earth, and satellites and aircraft must, as a practical matter, be permitted freely to traverse the airspace above the surface. Yet, it does have application to the immediate, accessible underground, which is what is at issue in this case.

A

terms, thus: it is necessary and sufficient if its nature and character is such as is calculated to apprise the world that the land is occupied and who the occupant is. [It must be] such an appropriation of the land by claimant as to appraise, or convey visible notice to the community or neighborhood in which it is situated that it is in his exclusive use and enjoyment. It has been declared that the [adverse possessor] "must unfurl his flag" on the land, and "keep it flying," so that the owner may see, if he will, that an enemy has invaded his domains, and planted the standard of conquest.

(3) The possession must be open and notorious. The mere possession of the land is not enough. It is knowledge, either actual or imputed, of the possession of his lands by another, claiming to own them bona fide and openly, that affects the legal owner thereof. Where there has been no actual notice, it is necessary to show that the possession of the disseisor was so open, notorious and visible as to warrant the inference that the owner must, or should have known of it. [Thus,] "it must be visible and open to the common observer ...[;] it must be clear and unequivocal." And ... the possession must be notorious. It must be so conspicuous that it is generally known and talked of by the public. "It must be manifest to the community." Thus, [where] "persons who have passed frequently over and along the premises have been unable to see any evidence of occupancy, evidently the possession has not been of the character required by the rule. ... Insidious, desultory, and fugitive acts will not serve that purpose. To have that effect the possession should be clear and satisfactory, not doubtful and equivocal."

adverse
possessor

(4) The possession must be exclusive. It is evident that two or more persons cannot hold one tract of land adversely to each other at the same time. "It is essential that the possession of one who claims adversely must be of such an exclusive character that it will operate as an ouster of the owner of the legal title...."

Ross

The facts ... show that appellee and his predecessors in title have been in actual and continuous possession of his real estate since the cave was discovered in 1883. At no time were they aware that anyone was trespassing upon their land. No one was claiming to be in possession of appellee's land. It is true that appellant was asserting possession of the "Marengo Cave." There would seem to be quite a difference in making claim to the "Marengo Cave," and making claim to a portion of appellee's land, even though a portion of the cave extended under appellee's land, when this latter fact was unknown to anyone. The ... "Marengo Cave" was thought [by all parties] to be altogether under the land owned by appellant, and this erroneous supposition was not revealed until a survey was made at the request of appellee and ordered by the court in this case. It seems to us that the following excerpt from Lewey v. H.C. Fricke Coke Co. (1895), 166 Pa. 536, 31 A. 261, is peculiarly applicable to the situation here presented ... :

no one knew the cave was under Ross's land until Ross requested a survey

"The title of the plaintiff extends from the surface to the center, but actual possession is confined to the surface. Upon the surface he must be held to know all that the most careful observation by himself and his employees could reveal.... But in the coal veins deep down in the earth he cannot see. Neither in person nor by his servants nor employees can he explore their recesses in search for an intruder. If an adjoining owner goes beyond his own boundaries in the course of his mining operations the owner on whom he enters has no means of knowledge within his reach. Nothing short of an accurate survey of the interior of his neighbor's mines would enable him to ascertain the fact. This would require the services of a competent mining engineer and his assistants, inside the mines of another, which he would have no right to insist upon. To require an owner under such circumstances to take notice of a trespass upon his underlying coal at the time it takes place is to require an impossibility; and to hold that the statute begins to run at the date of the trespass is in most cases to take away the remedy of the injured party before he can know that an injury has been done him. A result so absurd and so unjust ought not to be possible. ... The owner of land may be present by himself or his servants on the surface of his possessions no matter how extensive they may be. He is for this reason held to be constructively present wherever his title extends. He cannot be present in the interior of the earth. No amount of vigilance will enable him to detect the approach of a trespasser who may be working his way through the coal seams underlying adjoining lands. His senses cannot inform him of the encroachment by such trespasser upon the coal that is hidden in the rocks under his feet. He cannot reasonably be held to be constructively present where his presence is in the nature of things impossible. He must learn of such a trespass by other means than such as are within his own control, and until these come within his reach he is necessarily ignorant of his loss. He cannot reasonably be required to act until knowledge that action is needed is possible to him."

... Here the possession of appellant was not visible. No one could see below the earth's surface and determine that appellant was trespassing upon appellee's lands. This fact could not be determined by going into the cave. Only by a survey could this fact be made known. The same undisputed facts clearly show that appellant's possession was not notorious. Not even appellant itself nor any of its remote grantors knew that any part of the "Marengo Cave" extended beyond its own boundaries....

Even though it could be said that appellant's possession has been actual, exclusive and continuous all these years, we would still be of the opinion that appellee has not lost his land. It has been the uniform rule in equity that the statute of limitation does not begin to run until the injured party discovers, or with reasonable diligence might have discovered, the facts constituting the injury and cause of action. Until then the owner cannot know that his possession has been invaded. Until he has knowledge, or ought to have such knowledge, he is not called upon to act, for he does not know that action in the premises is necessary and the law does not require absurd or impossible things of anyone. . . .

We cannot assent to the doctrine that would enable one to trespass upon another's property through a subterranean passage and under such circumstances that the owner does not know, or by the exercise of reasonable care could not know, of such secret occupancy, for twenty years or more and by so doing obtained a fee simple title as against the holder of the legal title. The fact that appellee had knowledge that appellant was claiming to be the owner of the "Marengo Cave," and advertised it to the general public, was no knowledge to him that it was in possession of appellee's land or any part of it. We are of the opinion that appellant's possession for twenty years or more of that part of "Marengo Cave," underlying appellee's land, was not open, notorious, or exclusive, as required by the law applicable to obtaining title to land by adverse possession.

Judgment affirmed. *(For Ross — no adverse possession by Marengo Cave Co.)*

NOTES, QUESTIONS, AND PROBLEMS

1. Statutes of Limitation. The details of the various state statutes of limitation differ, mostly (but not exclusively) concerning the period of time that must elapse before the owner's suit to recover possession of his property is barred. Some statutes, such as the Indiana provision in *Marengo Cave*, require twenty years of adverse possession before the owner's claim is time-barred. Others, such as California and some other western states, require adverse possession for only five years. The elements of the possession needed to trigger running of the limitations statute are as stated in *Marengo Cave*, although some jurisdictions (mostly in the western United States) add a requirement that the occupier must also pay the taxes on the claimed property. See, e.g., Utah Code Ann. § 78B–2–214; Cal. Code Civ Proc. § 325.

2. Actual Possession. The Indiana Supreme Court said that it did not need to decide whether the Marengo Cave Company's occupation of the portion of the cave lying under Ross's land was actual possession, yet it seemed to concede that was so. The need for an actual entry is implicit in the limitations statute; there must be an entry in order to give rise to cause of action for ejectment in order for the limitations statute to begin running. But what constitutes "actual possession"? *Legal Title*

A typical definition of actual possession is that supplied by the Colorado Court of Appeals in Palmer Ranch, Ltd. v. Suwansawasdi, 920 P.2d 870, 873 (Colo. App. 1996): "Adverse possession by actual occupancy means to exercise the ordinary use of which the land is capable and such as an owner would make use of it. Thus, the nature of the property is critical in determining what acts by the claimant are required for actual possession." Thus, in Lessee of Ewing v. Burnet, 36 U.S. (11 Pet.) 41 (1837), the Court concluded that an occupier's extraction of sand and gravel out of a steep pit unsuited to any other use was actual possession: "Neither actual occupation, cultivation, or residence, are necessary to constitute actual possession when the property is so situated as not to admit of any permanent useful improvement: and the continued claim of the party has been evidenced by public acts of ownership, such as he would exercise over property which he claimed in his own right, and would not exercise over property which he did not claim."

On the other hand, some states specify by statute that only certain types of occupation qualify as actual possession. An example is California Code Civ. Proc. § 325, which states:

For the purpose of constituting an adverse possession by a person claiming title, not founded upon a written instrument, judgment, or decree, land is deemed to have been possessed and occupied in the following cases only:

1. Where it has been protected by a substantial inclosure.

2. Where it has been usually cultivated or improved.

Such statutes simply shift the judicial inquiry to what constitutes a "substantial inclosure" or usual cultivation or improvement. An example is Van Valkenburgh v. Lutz, 304 N.Y. 95 (1952). New York law was identical to California Code Civ. Proc. § 325 for purposes of determining actual possession. For longer than the 15 year statutory period, Lutz had occupied property belonging to Van Valkenburgh and his predecessor in interest. The occupation consisted of growing vegetables on the property, piling logs and brush at the boundaries of the vegetable garden, and construction of a 52 square foot shed on the property. Lutz's adverse possession claim prevailed in the trial court but the Court of Appeals reversed, concluding that the logs and brush were not a sufficient inclosure, the vegetable garden did not constitute "usual" cultivation because there was no proof that the garden encompassed all of the property, and that the shed was too small and crude to be a "usual" improvement. Judge Fuld, dissenting, argued to no avail that the point of the statute was to insure that the adverse possessor's occupation was so unequivocal that an owner inspecting his property would be on notice of the adverse occupation. Thus, satisfaction of each of the substantial inclosure and the usual cultivation or improvement requirements depended on "the nature and situation of the property and the uses to which it can be applied." In *Lutz*, those elements were met, said Fuld, because there was proof that Lutz's occupation was as usual and ordinary as could be expected of a "thrifty owner."

3. *Open and Notorious.* The Indiana court added the element of visibility to the open and notorious possession requirement, but is that really independent of open and notorious possession? Can there be open and notorious possession without such possession being visible? The point of the requirement is to ensure that the true owner should realize that a stranger is encroaching upon his property. It is sometimes said that open and notorious possession gives rise to a presumption that the true owner knows of the encroachment, a presumption that cannot be overcome after the limitations statute has expired. In *Marengo Cave*, what more could the cave company have done? Its occupation was open for the world to see and the possession was as notorious as advertising could make it. The adverse occupation was even visible, but not readily detectable. Should the fact that the cave company had made the cave accessible to the public through its industry have factored more in the court's analysis? The result of the court's decision, at least for a

time, was that the public was denied access to a significant portion of the cave.[6] To similar effect is Mannillo v. Gorski, 54 N.J. 378 (1969), in which the New Jersey Supreme Court was called upon to decide if Gorski's possession of Mannillo's property, an encroachment of 15 inches consisting of a portion of some concrete steps and walkway, was open and notorious. It was certainly visible, but, said the court:

> when the encroachment of an adjoining owner is of a small area and the fact of the intrusion is not clearly and self-evidently apparent to the naked eye but requires an on-site survey for certain disclosure as in urban sections where the division line is only infrequently delineated by any monuments, natural or artificial, [the] presumption [that the owner has notice of the encroachment] is fallacious and unjustified. ... Accordingly, [when there is] a minor encroachment along a common boundary ... only where the true owner has actual knowledge thereof may it be said that the possession is open and notorious.

What's a minor encroachment? Is it anything that to the naked eye would not be an obvious encroachment? Consider the following problems:

    a. Ross pays the fee and tours the Marengo Cave. The tour guide describes the cave as a serpentine shape extending for almost half a mile from the northwest to the southeast. Ross knows that his land is a quarter mile to the southeast from the cave entrance. Under those circumstances, should the cave company's possession be treated as open and notorious?

    b. Suppose that during the time Gorski's steps were encroaching upon Mannillo's property, but before the statutory period had expired, another neighbor had mentioned to Mannillo that he thought the steps looked "weird" and opined that "something is not right there." Should Mannillo be charged with a duty to investigate further and, failing such investigation, should Gorski's possession be treated as open and notorious?

    4. Continuous Possession. An adverse possessor must maintain his possession continuously for the statutory period. What happens when the adverse possessor occupies only seasonally? Suppose the adverse possession occurs in a community of mountain cabins that are mostly used during the summer, and the adverse possessor occupies the disputed property only during the summer?

> In determining whether the common-law requirement of "continuity of possession" has been met in an adverse possession claim to an estate in land, a court should consider not only the adverse possessor's physical

---

    6. Economic theories advanced by Ronald Coase would suggest that in the absence of transaction costs the entitlement to the disputed portion of the cave, even after Ross's victory, would be transferred to the cave company (assuming that the value of the entitlement is worth far more to the cave company than to Ross). For illustration, assume that the value of the entitlement to the cave company was 1000 and the value to Ross was 100. In theory, the right should be transferred at a price greater than 100 but less than 1000. In theory. In practice, transaction costs do exist. Each party in this bilateral monopoly (only one seller and one buyer) would seek to reap all of the potential gains from trade. They might dissipate those gains on lawyers, consultants, or the like; they might just be pig-headed and ignore their purely economic interests; or they might attach a non-monetary subjective value to the right that is sufficiently high to thwart transfer. The assumptions undergirding economic theories and reality sometimes collide, as illustrated by the following joke: An economist and a business executive fall into a deep pit by the side of the road. The business executive says, "We're toast." The economist says, "Not to worry. We'll assume a ladder."

presence on the land but also the claimant's other acts of dominion and control over the premises that would appropriately be undertaken by owners of properties of similar character, condition and location. Thus, we conclude that plaintiffs' occupancy of the summer cottage in a now-defunct resort town for one month during the summer, coupled with their regular efforts taken to secure and improve the premises and to eject trespassers during their absences for the 10–year statutory period while all neighboring structures collapsed due to vandalism or abandonment, satisfied the element of continuous actual possession. Ray v. Beacon Hudson Mt. Corp., 88 N.Y.2d 154, 156 (1996).

See also Whalen v. Smith, 183 Iowa 949, 953 (1918); Howard v. Kunto, 3 Wn. App. 393, 397–398 (1970).

5. Exclusive Possession. An adverse possessor must maintain his possession to the exclusion of other claimants. What if the possessor grants permission to others to use the property? "When use of the property was done with the permission of the party claiming adverse possession, that does not negate exclusivity because the act of obtaining permission recognizes the superior authority of possession of the party from whom permission was sought." Rucker Properties, LLC v. Friday, 41 Kan.App.2d 664, 673–674 (2009). But if the possession is shared with others who have not obtained permission from the adverse possessor, or with the true owner, exclusivity is not satisfied. For example, Union Gas stored natural gas by injecting it into an abandoned gas well on its property that led to an underground formation that extended underneath the DeTars' land. Union Gas's claim that it had acquired the subsurface formation by adverse possession foundered for lack of exclusive possession: "The element of exclusiveness is not met because Union shared occupancy of the subsurface with the DeTars' native gas." Union Gas System, Inc. v. Carnahan, 245 Kan. 80, 87 (1989). As in *Marengo Cave*, Union Gas also failed to show that its occupation was open and notorious.

6. Possession under Claim of Right, or "Hostility." The adverse possessor's entry must be made under a claim of right. Sometimes this requirement is expressed as hostility to the true owner, though in that formulation it does not mean that the possessor must harbor malice toward the owner. However expressed, this requirement means that the possessor must have a claim that is adverse to that of the owner. But what form must it take? There are three answers: 1) The possessor must know that his entry is wrongful but nevertheless intends to take and hold the occupied property; 2) The possessor must have a reasonable good faith belief that the property occupied belongs to him, and 3) The state of the mind of the possessor is irrelevant. The first approach, sometimes called the "aggressive trespass" standard, might be likened to Hitler's invasion of Poland in 1939. The second approach effectively limits adverse possession to reasonable mistakes concerning the boundaries of property the possessor already owns, or to cases where the possessor enters property described in a defective deed to him. The third approach takes the position that the limitations statute should begin to run from the moment there is a wrongful entry, regardless of why the possessor has entered, because the owner's cause of action to recover his land has been triggered by the entry. Generally, a jurisdiction's approach to what constitutes a claim of right is a matter of judicial interpretation, but some states specify by statute what is meant by a claim of right. An example is Kansas, which permits a claim of right to be established either "under a belief in ownership" or by an occupation that is "knowingly adverse." K.S.A. § 60–503 (2009). The Kansas courts have defined "belief in ownership" to mean "a state of mind which must be based on good faith under circumstances which justify such belief." Wallace v. Magie, 214 Kan. 481 (1974). But a possessor who lacks that good faith belief may still prevail if he can prove he knew his claim was adverse. Are there any possessors who would lack a claim of right under the Kansas statute?

The view that the adverse possessor must take and hold possession with a good faith belief that he is the owner of the land has an old pedigree. Moore v. Worley, 24 Ind. 81, 83 (1865), is an example: "To constitute a *possession adverse,* so as to bar a recovery, ... the party setting up the possession must, in making his entry upon the land, ... believe the land to be his, and that he has title thereto, although his title may not be rightful or valid." This view is not an anachronism; a recent Georgia case repeats the theme:

> We hold that the correct rule is that one must enter upon the land claiming in good faith the right to do so. To enter upon the land without any honest claim of right to do so is but a trespass and can never ripen into prescriptive title. [S]uch a person is called a "squatter." Here there was evidence that the Halperns knew the parcel of land was owned by another yet they simply took possession when their offer to purchase was declined. ... One may maintain hostile possession of land in good faith. ... [M]ost who have hostile possession of land do so with a good faith claim of right and therefore a jury or other factfinder may, in the absence of a contrary showing, infer from hostile possession that it is done in good faith that a claim of right exists. Halpern v. Lacy Investment Corp. 259 Ga. 264, 265 (1989).

Of equally ancient pedigree is the view that the adverse possessor must intend to take title to the land, whether or not he is aware he does not own it. An example is Preble v. Maine Central Railroad Co., 85 Me. 260 (1893), in which the plaintiff possessor acknowledged that he always thought the property he occupied was his own:

> [O]ne who by mistake occupies for [the statutory period] land not covered by his deed with no intention to claim title beyond his actual boundary ..., does not thereby acquire title by adverse possession to land beyond the true line. ... [T]his intention of the occupant to claim the ownership of land not embraced in his title is a necessary element of adverse possession. And in case of occupancy by mistake [the] intention to claim title to the extent of the occupancy must appear to be absolute and not conditional; otherwise the possession will not be deemed adverse to the true owner. It must be an intention to claim title to all land within a certain boundary on the face of the earth, whether it shall eventually be found to be the correct one or not. If for instance one in ignorance of his actual boundaries takes and holds possession by mistake up to a certain fence beyond his limits, upon the claim and in the belief that it is the true line, with the intention to claim title, and thus if necessary, to acquire "title by possession" up to that fence, such possession having the requi-

site duration and continuity, will ripen into title. .... If on the other hand a party through ignorance, inadvertence or mistake, occupies up to a given fence beyond his actual boundary, because he believes it to be the true line, but has no intention to claim title to that extent if it should be ascertained that the fence was on his neighbor's land, an indispensable element of adverse possession is wanting. In such a case the intent to claim title exists only upon the *condition* that the fence is on the true line. The intention is not absolute, but provisional, and the possession is not adverse. Id. at 264–266.

This so-called Maine doctrine is a variant of aggressive trespass in that, unlike aggressive trespass, it does not require the adverse possessor to know that his occupation is wrongful.[7]

In contrast with *Preble* is another venerable case, French v. Pearce, 8 Conn. 439 (1831), also involving a boundary dispute. The court stated that to constitute occupation under a claim of right

it is only necessary for a person to enter and take possession of land *as his own*; to take the rents and profits to himself; and to manage with the property as an owner manages with his own property; that is, the person thus possessing must act as if he were the true owner and accountable to no person for the land or its avails. ... The possession alone, and the qualities immediately attached to it, are regarded. No intimation is there as to the *motive* of the possessor. If he intends a wrongful disseisin, his actual possession for [the statutory period] gives him a title; or if he occupies what he believes to be his own, a similar possession gives him a title. Into the recesses of his mind, his motives or purposes, his guilt or innocence, no enquiry is made. It is for this obvious reason; that it is the visible and adverse possession, with an intention to possess, that constitutes its adverse character, and not the remote views or belief of the possessor. ... The very nature of the act [entry and possession] is an assertion of his own title, and the denial of the title of all others. It matters not that the possessor was mistaken, and had he been better informed, would not have entered on the land. Id. at 443, 445–446.

A modern embrace of the view that the state of mind of the possessor is irrelevant is in Mannillo v. Gorski, 54 N.J. 378 (1969). Gorski built steps and a walkway that encroached upon Mannillo's property by fifteen inches, but held possession of the encroachment for longer than the statutory period. On the issue of whether Gorski held with an adequate claim of right, or hostility, the New Jersey court first criticized the Maine doctrine as one that rewards "the intentional wrongdoer and disfavors an honest, mistaken entrant." Embracing the view articulated in *French*, the court said:

[When] the problem is which of two mistaken parties is entitled to land ..., the true owner does not rely upon entry of the possessor by mistake as a reason for not seeking to recover possession. Whether or not the entry is caused by mistake or intent, the same result eventuates—the true owner is ousted from possession. In either event his neglect to seek

---

7. By statute, Maine has repudiated the rule in *Preble*. M.R.S. § 810–A (2009) provides: "If a person takes possession of land by mistake as to the location of the true boundary line, the possessor's mistaken belief does not defeat a claim of adverse possession."

recovery of possession, within the requisite time, is in all probability the result of a lack of knowledge that he is being deprived of possession of lands to which he has title. Accordingly, we discard the requirement that the entry and continued possession must be accompanied by a knowing intentional hostility and hold that any entry and possession for the required time which is exclusive, continuous, uninterrupted, visible and notorious, even though under mistaken claim of title, is sufficient to support a claim of title by adverse possession. Id. at 386–387.

The state-of-mind is irrelevant version of claim of title is probably the most widely observed version in the United States, although there are a fair number of jurisdictions that cling to the good faith version. Aggressive trespass is in disfavor.

7. *Entry Under Color of Title.* Entry under "claim of title," or hostility, must be carefully distinguished from entry under "color of title." Claim of title describes the nature of the possessor's occupation: Does he occupy in the manner that a true owner would? Color of title describes a claim that is based on a written transfer of title—a deed, will, or court judgment—that happens to be defective and thus not valid. The defect might be improper execution, a lack of capacity on the part of the grantor, the fact that the grantor does not have title to convey, a wrong description of the property, or something else. A few states limit adverse possession to claimants under color of title. See, e.g, Ala. Code § 6–5–200 (2010). Most states, however, do not do so. While color of title is not generally necessary to sustain adverse possession, entry under color of title may produce some advantages. Some states provide for a shorter limitations statute for possession under color of title. See, e.g. Alaska Stat. § 9.45.052 (2010). All states regard an adverse possessor who enters under color of title and occupies *only a portion of the property described in the instrument* as in constructive possession of the entire described property. This means that even though the adverse possessor has actual possession of only a part of the property described in the defective instrument he is entitled to acquire by adverse possession all of the property described in the instrument. But consider the following problems:

a. In 1990, adverse possessor A enters the front 20 acres of Blackacre, a tract of 60 acres, under a defective deed that accurately describes Blackacre, and occupies those 20 acres for the statutory period in the manner necessary to acquire title by adverse possession. During that time B, a lessee from O, the true owner of Blackacre, occupies the back 40 acres of Blackacre. A sues O and B to quiet title of all of Blackacre in in A. What should be the result? Would the result change if the back 40 acres had been continuously occupied since 1985 by C, a squatter whose occupation was of the required manner?

A - color of title possibly

b. Adverse possessor A is the grantee of a defective deed describing Lot 1 and Lot 2. A enters Lot 1 and occupies for the statutory period in the manner necessary to acquire title by adverse possession. During that time, Lot 2 remains vacant. The true owner of Lots 1 and 2 is O. A sues O to quiet title of Lots 1 and 2 in his name. What should be the result? Would it matter if O owned Lot 1 and Z owned Lot 2?

8. *Why Not Compensation?* You will note that adverse possession operates in a binary manner: Title is either in the true owner or the adverse

possessor. It need not be this way. One can imagine a system in which title is shifted to the adverse possessor only upon payment of compensation to the true owner. Less globally, compensation might be required only when the adverse possessor lacks a good faith belief of ownership. An explanation for the lack of compensation might be that property has traditionally been protected by absolute rules, or "property rules." The idea is that interests protected by property rules may only be taken away with the owner's consent. In general, this means that transfer of interests protected by property rules is voluntary. By contrast, many interests are protected by "liability rules." Such interests may be taken away without the owner's consent so long as the owner is compensated for the loss. Transfer is involuntary. Eminent domain is an example. The government may take private property for public use so long as just compensation is paid. U.S. Const., Amend. V. Sometimes liability rules are inevitable. For example, should the negligent driver strike you and break your leg, your good health has been forcibly taken and the only available remedy is to impose monetary liability on the negligent driver. The concepts of "property rules" and "liability rules," particularly as applied to property interests, achieved broad significance in the wake of a path-breaking article by Guido Calabresi and Douglas Melamed, Property Rules, Liability Rules and Inalienability: One View of the Cathedral, 85 Harv. L. Rev. 1089 (1972).[8] These concepts will continue to appear from time to time in your study of property law.

As applied to adverse possession the true owner's interest is protected by a property rule until the adverse possessor has maintained the requisite occupation for the statutory period; thereafter the adverse possessor's interest is protected by a property rule. In this mode, property rules function like an on-off switch. But the true owner's interest could be protected by a property rule until the limitations statute has expired, and thereafter could continue to be protected by a liability rule. This arrangement would require the adverse possessor to provide judicially determined compensation to the true owner to obtain the prospective benefits of a property rule. Which rule is preferable and why?

2. OPERATIONAL DETAILS OF ADVERSE POSSESSION: TACKING, DISABLED OWNERS, AND GOVERNMENTAL IMMUNITY

This section deals with some of the issues that occur in applying a statute of limitations to claims of adverse possession and with the special instance of adverse possession claims against a governmental owner of property. "Tacking" is a concept that allows certain possessors to add (or tack) their period of possession onto that of a prior possessor in order to satisfy the statutory period of adverse possession. Most limitations statutes provide that the limitations period will be suspended from running (called "tolled") when the true owner (who possesses the cause of action

---

8. Calabresi later became Dean of the Yale Law School and a judge of the U.S. Court of Appeals for the Second Circuit. Melamed has had a long and successful career as an antitrust attorney; he is now Senior Vice President and General Counsel of Intel Corp.

for recovery of property) is under a specified disability at the time the cause of action accrues. Finally, although adverse possession claims traditionally could not be made against government owners of property, this rule has partially eroded.

HOWARD v. KUNTO

Court of Appeals of Washington
3 Wn App. 393, 477 P.2d 210 (1970)

PEARSON, J., delivered the opinion of the court.

Land surveying is an ancient art but not one free of the errors that often creep into the affairs of men. In this case, we are presented with the question of what happens when the descriptions in deeds do not fit the land the deed holders are occupying. Defendants appeal from a decree quieting title in the plaintiffs of a tract of land on the shore of Hood Canal in Mason County.

At least as long ago as 1932 the record tells us that one McCall resided in the house now occupied by the appellant-defendants, Kunto. McCall had a deed that described a 50–foot-wide parcel on the shore of Hood Canal. The error that brings this case before us is that the 50 feet described in the deed is not the same 50 feet upon which McCall's house stood. Rather, the described land is an adjacent 50–foot lot directly west of that upon which the house stood. In other words, McCall's house stood on one lot and his deed described the adjacent lot. Several property owners to the west of defendants, not parties to this action, are similarly situated.

Over the years since 1946, several conveyances occurred, using the same legal description and accompanied by a transfer of possession to the succeeding occupants. The Kuntos' immediate predecessors in interest, Millers, desired to build a dock. To this end, they had a survey performed which indicated that the deed description and the physical occupation were in conformity. Several boundary stakes were placed as a result of this survey and the dock was constructed, as well as other improvements. . . .

The Kuntos then took possession of the disputed property under a deed from the Millers in 1959. In 1960 the respondent-plaintiffs, Howard, who held land east of that of the Kuntos, determined to convey an undivided one-half interest in their land to the Yearlys. To this end, they undertook to have a survey of the entire area made. After expending considerable effort, the surveyor retained by the Howards discovered that according to the government survey, the deed descriptions and the land occupancy of the parties did not coincide. Between the Howards and the Kuntos lay the Moyers' property. When the Howards' survey was completed, they discovered that they were the record owners of the land occupied by the Moyers and that the Moyers held record title to the land occupied by the Kuntos. Howard approached Moyer and in return for a conveyance of the land upon which the Moyers' house stood, Moyer conveyed to the Howards record title to the land upon which the Kunto house stood. Until plaintiffs Howard obtained the conveyance from Moyer in April, 1960, neither Moyer nor any of his predecessors ever asserted any right to ownership of the property actually being possessed by Kunto and his predecessors. This action was then instituted to quiet title in the Howards and Yearlys. The Kuntos appeal from a trial court decision granting this remedy.

At the time this action was commenced on August 19, 1960,[9] defendants had been in occupance of the disputed property less than a year. The trial court's reason for denying their claim of adverse possession is succinctly stated in its memorandum opinion: "In this instance, defendants have failed to prove, by a preponderance of the evidence, a continuity of possession or estate to permit tacking of the adverse possession of defendants to the possession of their predecessors." . . .

[The question on appeal is:] May a person who receives record title to tract A under the mistaken belief that he has title to tract B (immediately contiguous to tract A) and who subsequently occupies tract B, for the purpose of establishing title to tract B by adverse possession, use the periods of possession of tract B by his immediate predecessors who also had record title to tract A?

In approaching [this question], we point out that the evidence, largely undisputed in any material sense, established that defendant or his immediate predecessors did occupy the premises, which we have called tract B, as though it was their own for far more than the 10 years as prescribed in RCW 4.16.020.[10] We also point out that [the trial court's judgment] is not challenged for its factual determinations but for the conclusions . . . that a predecessor's possession may not be tacked because a legal "claim of right" did not exist under the circumstances. . . .

The precise issue before us is novel in that none of the property occupied by defendant or his predecessors coincided with the property described in their deeds, but was contiguous.

In the typical case, which has been subject to much litigation, the party seeking to establish title by adverse possession claims *more* land than that described in the deed. In such cases it is clear that tacking is permitted. In Buchanan v. Cassell, 53 Wn.2d 611, 614, 335 P.2d 600 (1959) the Supreme Court stated: "This state follows the rule that a purchaser may tack the adverse use of its predecessor in interest to that of his own where the land was intended to be included in the deed between them, but was mistaken-

---

9. The inordinate delay in bringing this matter to trial appears from the record to be largely inexcusable. However, neither counsel who tried the case was at fault in any way. We have intentionally declined to consider defendant's motion (probably well founded) to dismiss this case for want of prosecution for the reason that a new trial of the same issues would be inevitable and in light of our disposition of the case on the merits, defendants are not prejudiced by disregarding the technical grounds.

10. This statute provides: "4.16.020 Actions to be commenced within ten years. The period prescribed in RCW 4.16.010 for the commencement of actions shall be as follows: Within ten years: Actions for the recovery of real property, or for the recovery of the possession thereof; and no action shall be maintained for such recovery unless it appears that the plaintiff, his ancestor, predecessor or grantor was seized or possessed of the premises in question within ten years before the commencement of the action."

ly omitted from the description." El Cerrito, Inc. v. Ryndak, 60 Wn.2d 847, 376 P.2d 528 (1962).

The general statement which appears in many of the cases is that tacking of adverse possession is permitted if the successive occupants are in "privity." See Faubion v. Elder, 49 Wn.2d 300, 301 P.2d 153 (1956). The deed running between the parties purporting to transfer the land possessed traditionally furnishes the privity of estate which connects the possession of the successive occupants. Plaintiff contends, and the trial court ruled, that where the deed does not describe *any* of the land which was occupied, the actual transfer of possession is insufficient to establish privity.

To assess the cogency of this argument and ruling, we must turn to the historical reasons for requiring privity as a necessary prerequisite to tacking the possession of several occupants. Very few, if any, of the reasons appear in the cases, nor do the cases analyze the relationships that must exist between successive possessors for tacking to be allowed. See W[illiam] Stoebuck, The Law of Adverse Possession In Washington in 35 Wash. L. Rev. 53 (1960).

The requirement of privity had its roots in the notion that a succession of trespasses, even though there was no appreciable interval between them, should not, in equity, be allowed to defeat the record title. The "claim of right," "color of title" requirement of the statutes and cases was probably derived from the early American belief that the squatter should not be able to profit by his trespass.[11]

However, it appears to this court that there is a substantial difference between the squatter or trespasser and the property purchaser, who along with several of his neighbors, as a result of an inaccurate survey or subdivision, occupies and improves property exactly 50 feet to the east of that which a survey some 30 years later demonstrates that they in fact own. It seems to us that there is also a strong public policy favoring early certainty as to the location of land ownership which enters into a proper interpretation of privity.

On the irregular perimeters of Puget Sound exact determination of land locations and boundaries is difficult and expensive. This difficulty is convincingly demonstrated in this case by the problems plaintiff's engineer encountered in attempting to locate the corners. It cannot be expected that every purchaser will or should engage a surveyor to ascertain that the beach home he is purchasing lies within the boundaries described in his deed. Such a practice is neither reasonable nor customary. Of course, 50-foot errors in descriptions are devastating where a group of adjacent owners each hold 50 feet of waterfront property.

The technical requirement of "privity" should not, we think, be used to upset the long periods of occupancy of those who in good faith received an erroneous deed description. Their "claim of right" is no less persuasive

---

11. The English common law does not require privity as a prerequisite for tacking. See F. Clark, Law of Surveying and Boundaries, § 561 (3d ed. 1959) at 568.

than the purchaser who believes he is purchasing *more* land than his deed described.

In the final analysis, however, we believe the requirement of "privity" is no more than judicial recognition of the need for some reasonable connection between successive occupants of real property so as to raise their claim of right above the status of the wrongdoer or the trespasser. We think such reasonable connection exists in this case. Where, as here, several successive purchasers received record title to tract A under the mistaken belief that they were acquiring tract B, immediately contiguous thereto, and where possession of tract B is transferred and occupied in a continuous manner for more than 10 years by successive occupants, we hold there is sufficient privity of estate to permit tacking and thus establish adverse possession as a matter of law. We see no reason in law or in equity for differentiating this case from Faubion v. Elder, 49 Wn.2d 300, 301 P.2d 153 (1956) where the appellants were claiming *more* land than their deed described and where successive periods of occupation were allowed to be united to each other to make up the time of adverse holding. . . . This application of the privity requirement should particularly pertain where the holder of record title to tract B acquired the same with knowledge of the discrepancy.

Judgment is reversed with directions to dismiss plaintiffs' action and to enter a decree quieting defendants' title to the disputed tract of land in accordance with the prayer of their cross complaint.

NOTES, QUESTIONS, AND PROBLEMS

1. *Two Types of Tacking.* The problem in *Kunto* was whether a successor to a valid title to property never occupied by either the successor or his predecessor could use the deed that described the unoccupied property as evidence of a transfer of his predecessor's adverse possession. A related problem is a deed that accurately describes the property transferred but where the seller has unwittingly occupied land contiguous to but outside the property described in the deed, and has done so for the statutory period. *Kunto* extended prior Washington law that had held that a successor could indeed tack the land occupied by the predecessor onto that actually conveyed so long as there was adequate evidence of intent to transfer the occupied land. Note 2, which follows, explores this type of tacking.

The other type of tacking is when there are series of adverse possessors, none of whom have occupied for the statutory period, but when the series of occupations are added together, there is an occupation for the statutory period. The problems in Note 3 explore this form of tacking.

2. *Two Meanings of Privity.* The Washington court in *Kunto* thought that privity to establish tacking should mean the existence of "some reasonable connection between successive occupants of real property so as to raise their claim of right above the status of the wrongdoer or the trespasser," and so held that privity existed even when the deed that constituted the transfer described land that had never been occupied by Kunto or his predecessor in

title. By contrast, the Pennsylvania Supreme Court, in Baylor v. Soska, 540 Pa. 435 (1995), reached the opposite conclusion. Hanacek occupied a strip of land adjacent to land she owned for the 21 year statutory period and then sold her property to the Baylors under a deed that described Hanacek's property without including the strip. Fifteen years later the Baylors sought to quiet title to the strip by adverse possession but lost because they could not tack Hanacek's possession onto their own. Privity, said the court, " 'refers to a succession of relationship to the same thing, whether created by deed or other acts or by operation of law. But a deed does not of itself create privity between the grantor and the grantee as to land not described in the deed but occupied by the grantor.... Nor is privity created by the bare taking of possession of land previously occupied by the grantor.' " The court reversed a trial court's conclusion that privity for tacking exists whenever

> the circumstances of the case indicate an intent to convey more land than that which is described. ... [T]he entire concept of "circumstances' " in the context of tacking is misplaced....

> There is good reason for this requirement. Interested parties have a right to discern from the record the state of the title of any parcel of land. If tacking were to be permitted because of vague, undefined "circumstances," there could and most likely would be no way for one not a party to the conveyance to know this. But the law mandates that a person asserting a claim of adverse possession make this assertion openly and notoriously to all the world. There must be no secret that the adverse possessor is asserting a claim to the land in question. If the adverse possessor's claim is to be passed on to a successor in title, therefore, there must be some objective indicia of record by which it can be discerned with some degree of certainty that a claim of title by adverse possession is being made and that the duration of this claim has been passed on to a successor in title.

> It might be argued that if the original adverse possessor were simply to remain on the land and there were no action in ejectment, nothing of record would appear to indicate the adverse possessor's interest, and therefore, there should be no requirement that the record reveal the adverse interest of a successor in title. First, nothing of record need appear concerning the successor's adverse possession claim. It is only the predecessor's claim which the successor seeks to tack that is at issue. Second, public policy requires that when an interest in land is conveyed to another, the interest of the successor in title be described as nearly as possible, withholding nothing which could and should at that time be made visible. Otherwise, needless complexity and uncertainty is introduced into conveyancing. Accordingly, we hold that the only method by which an adverse possessor may convey the title asserted by adverse possession is to describe in the instrument of conveyance by means minimally acceptable for conveyancing of realty that which is intended to be conveyed.

Which of these views is better? Why?

3. *Problems.* Assume in each of the following problems that the jurisdiction has a fifteen year limitation period.

a. Suppose that *A* enters Blackacre, owned by *O*, in 1990 and occupies in the required fashion until 2000, when *B* appears, shows *A* a fake deed to Blackacre from *O* to *B*, and demands that *A* leave. *A* does so. *B* occupies Blackacre in the required manner until 2010. *O* then sues *B* to recover possession of Blackacre. Who should win? *B*

b. Suppose that *A* enters Blackacre, owned by *O*, in 1990 and occupies in the required fashion until 2000, when *A* tells *B* that he is leaving to enter a monastery in Nepal. *B* occupies Blackacre in the required manner until 2010. *O* then sues *B* to recover possession of Blackacre. Who should win? Would it matter if *A* told *B* "Blackacre is yours; take over for me"? Would it matter if *A* executed a deed of all his interest in Blackacre to *B*?

c. Suppose that *A* enters Blackacre, owned by *O*, in 1990 and occupies in the required fashion until 2000, when *A* abruptly departs for the monastery in Nepal. *B*, a homeless person notices that *A*'s cottage on Blackacre is vacant and promptly moves in. *B* occupies in the required manner until 2010. *O* then sues *B* to recover possession of Blackacre. Who should win?

d. Suppose that *A* enters Blackacre, owned by *O*, in 1990 and occupies in the required fashion until 2000, when *B* appears and by force of arms, ejects *A* from Blackacre, and takes occupancy in the required manner. One year later *B* abandons Blackacre and *A* immediately resumes his occupation. In 2010 *O* sues *A* to recover possession of Blackacre. Who should win?

e. Suppose that *A* enters Blackacre, owned by *O*, in 1990 and occupies in the required fashion thereafter. In 1993 *O* dies, leaving Blackacre by his will to *B*. In 1997 *B* conveys Blackacre to *C*. In 2000 *C* dies. By his will *C* devises Blackacre to *D* for life, then to *E*. In 2006 *D* dies. In 2007 *E* sues to eject *A* from Blackacre. Who should win? *7 yrs only*

 4. *Disabled Owners.* States extend the limitations period for institution of an action to recover real property if certain specific disabilities on the part of the person entitled to recover possession are present *at the time the cause of action accrues*. An example is Ohio R.C. § 2305.04:

> An action to recover the title to or possession of real property shall be brought within twenty-one years after the cause of action accrued, but if a person entitled to bring the action is, at the time the cause of action accrues, within the age of minority or of unsound mind, the person, after the expiration of twenty-one years from the time the cause of action accrues, may bring the action within ten years after the disability is removed.

In the following problems apply this statute and assume that the age of majority is 18 years of age.

a. Suppose that in 1985 *A* occupies Whiteacre, owned by *O*, a 55 year old law professor. In 1990 *O* becomes insane and is hospitalized. In 2000 *O* is fully recovered from his mental illness and resumes a normal life. In 2008 *O* sues to eject *A* from Whiteacre. *A* has continuously occupied Whiteacre in the required fashion. Who should win? Why?

b. Suppose that in 1984 *O*, the owner of Redacre, dies and devises Redacre by will to *O1*, his four year old daughter. In 1985 *A* occupies Redacre

and maintains that occupation in the required manner. In 2008 *O1* sues to eject *A* from Redacre. Who should win? Why? *O1 if w/in 10 yrs of 18?*

c. Suppose that in 1985 *A* occupies Greenacre, owned by *O*, a 70 year old retired farmer. In 1986 *O* dies and devises Greenacre by will to *Z*, his four year old granddaughter. *A* maintains his occupation of Greenacre in the required manner. In 2008 *Z* sues to eject *A* from Greenacre. Who should win? Why? *2* *2004*

d. Suppose that in 1985 *A* occupies Blackacre, owned by *O*, who is insane. *O* dies insane in 2000 with one statutory heir, *H*, who is 10 years old. When will the limitations period expire? 2001, 2010, 2018, or some other date?

e. Suppose that in 1985 *A* occupies Blackacre, owned by *O*, who is four years old. In 1996 *O* becomes insane and then dies, still insane, in 2001. *O* has one statutory heir, *X*, who is 55 years of age and of sound mind. When will the limitations expire? 2001, 2009, 2011, or some other date? *2022 ?* *w/in 21 yrs of 2001*

5. *Adverse Possession Against the Government.* The traditional common law rule, rooted in notions of sovereign immunity, was that a person could not adversely possess property owned by the government. That rule continues, either by statute or constitutional provision, in many states. See, e.g., Calif. Civ. Code § 1007; Neb. Rev. Stat. § 25–202. Other states have modified the rule. In Connecticut and New Jersey, for example, adverse possession against the government may be maintained if the property in question is not held for a public use. Goldman v. Quadrato, 142 Conn. 398, 403 (1955); Devins v. Borough of Bogota, 124 N.J. 570 (1991). A corollary is that, in some states, adverse possession may lie against government property that is held in a proprietary, as opposed to governmental, capacity. See, e.g., Monthie v. Boyle Road Associates, LLC, 724 N.Y.S.2d 178 (App. 2001).

Given that the government may adversely possess private land, why should adverse possession against the government be prohibited? What reasons support limitations on adverse possession against the government?

3. ADVERSE POSSESSION OF PERSONAL PROPERTY

O'KEEFFE v. SNYDER

Supreme Court of New Jersey
83 N.J. 478 (1980)

[In 1976 Georgia O'Keeffe, the famous American artist, sued Barry Snyder, an art dealer, seeking return of three of her paintings that she alleged were stolen in 1946. In 1975 Snyder had purchased the three paintings from Ulrich Frank for $35,000. Snyder contended that he had title because he was a bona fide purchaser for value of the paintings and that he had title by adverse possession because the six years limitations statute for recovery of personal property had expired.]

POLLOCK, J., delivered the opinion of the court.

... The trial court granted summary judgment for Snyder on the ground that O'Keeffe's action was barred because it was not commenced within six years of the alleged theft. The Appellate Division reversed and entered judgment for O'Keeffe. A majority of that court concluded that the paintings were stolen, the defenses of expiration of the statute of limitations and title by adverse possession were identical, and Snyder had not proved the elements of adverse possession. Consequently, . . . O'Keeffe could still enforce her right to possession of the paintings.

The dissenting judge stated that the appropriate measurement of the period of limitation was not by analogy to adverse possession, but by application of the "discovery rule" pertaining to some statutes of limitation. He concluded that the six-year period of limitations commenced when O'Keeffe knew or should have known who unlawfully possessed the paintings, and that the matter should be remanded to determine if and when that event had occurred. . . . We reverse and remand the matter for a plenary hearing in accordance with this opinion.

O'Keeffe contended the paintings were stolen in 1946 from a [Manhattan art] gallery, An American Place, . . . operated by her late husband, the famous photographer Alfred Stieglitz. An American Place was a cooperative undertaking of O'Keeffe and some other American artists identified by her as Marin, Hardin, Dove, Andema, and Stevens. In 1946, Stieglitz arranged an exhibit which included an O'Keeffe painting, identified as Cliffs. According to O'Keeffe, one day in March, 1946, she and Stieglitz discovered Cliffs was missing from the wall of the exhibit. O'Keeffe estimates the value of the painting at the time of the alleged theft to have been about $150. About two weeks later, O'Keeffe noticed that two other paintings, Seaweed and Fragments, were missing from a storage room at An American Place. She did not tell anyone, even Stieglitz, about the missing paintings, since she did not want to upset him. . . .

O'Keeffe testified on depositions that at about the same time as the disappearance of her paintings, 12 or 13 miniature paintings by Marin also were stolen from An American Place. According to O'Keeffe, a man named Estrick took the Marin paintings and "maybe a few other things." Estrick distributed the Marin paintings to members of the theater world who, when confronted by Stieglitz, returned them. However, neither Stieglitz nor O'Keeffe confronted Estrick with the loss of any of the O'Keeffe paintings.

There was no evidence of a break and entry at An American Place on the dates when O'Keeffe discovered the disappearance of her paintings. Neither Stieglitz nor O'Keeffe reported them missing to the New York Police Department or any other law enforcement agency. Apparently the paintings were uninsured, and O'Keeffe did not seek reimbursement from an insurance company. Similarly, neither O'Keeffe nor Stieglitz advertised the loss of the paintings in Art News or any other publication. Nonetheless, they discussed it with associates in the art world and later O'Keeffe mentioned the loss to the director of the Art Institute of Chicago, but she did not ask him to do anything because "it wouldn't have been my way."

O'Keeffe does not contend that Frank or Snyder had actual knowledge of the alleged theft.

Stieglitz died in the summer of 1946, and O'Keeffe explains she did not pursue her efforts to locate the paintings because she was settling his estate. In 1947, she retained the services of Doris Bry to help settle the estate. Bry urged O'Keeffe to report the loss of the paintings, but O'Keeffe declined because "they never got anything back by reporting it." Finally, in 1972, O'Keeffe authorized Bry to report the theft to the Art Dealers Association of America, Inc., which maintains for its members a registry of stolen paintings. The record does not indicate whether such a registry existed at the time the paintings disappeared.

In September, 1975, O'Keeffe learned that the paintings were in the Andrew Crispo Gallery in New York on consignment from Bernard Danenberg Galleries. On February 11, 1976, O'Keeffe discovered that Ulrich A. Frank had sold the paintings to Barry Snyder, d/b/a Princeton Gallery of Fine Art. She demanded their return and, following Snyder's refusal, instituted this action for replevin.

Frank traces his possession of the paintings to his father, Dr. Frank, who died in 1968. He claims there is a family relationship by marriage between his family and the Stieglitz family, a contention that O'Keeffe disputes. Frank does not know how his father acquired the paintings, but he recalls seeing them in his father's apartment in New Hampshire as early as 1941–1943, a period that precedes the alleged theft. Consequently, Frank's factual contentions are inconsistent with O'Keeffe's allegation of theft. Until 1965, Dr. Frank occasionally lent the paintings to Ulrich Frank. In 1965, Dr. and Mrs. Frank formally gave the paintings to Ulrich Frank, who kept them in his residences in Yardley, Pennsylvania and Princeton, New Jersey. In 1968, he exhibited anonymously Cliffs and Fragments in a one day art show in the Jewish Community Center in Trenton. All of these events precede O'Keeffe's listing of the paintings as stolen with the Art Dealers Association of America, Inc. in 1972.

Frank claims continuous possession of the paintings through his father for over thirty years and admits selling the paintings to Snyder. Snyder and Frank do not trace their provenance, or history of possession of the paintings, back to O'Keeffe. ... For purposes of his [summary judgment] motion, Snyder conceded that the paintings had been stolen. On her cross motion, O'Keeffe urged that ... the statute of limitations had not run, and title to the paintings remained in her. ... Where there are cross motions for summary judgment, a party may make concessions for the purposes of his motion that do not carry over and support the motion of his adversary. ... The Appellate Division accepted O'Keeffe's contention that the paintings had been stolen. However, in his deposition, Ulrich Frank traces possession of the paintings to his father in the early 1940's, a date that precedes the alleged theft by several years. The factual dispute about the loss of the paintings by O'Keeffe and their acquisition by Frank, as well as the other subsequently described factual issues, warrant a remand for a plenary hearing. . . .

Without purporting to limit the scope of the trial, other factual issues include whether ... the paintings were not stolen but sold, lent, consigned, or given by Stieglitz to Dr. Frank or someone else without O'Keeffe's knowledge before he died; and [whether] there was any business or family relationship between Stieglitz and Dr. Frank so that the original possession of the paintings by the Frank family may have been under claim of right.

On the limited record before us, we cannot determine now who has title to the paintings. That determination will depend on the evidence adduced at trial. Nonetheless, we believe it may aid the trial court and the parties to resolve questions of law that may become relevant at trial.

Our decision begins with the principle that, generally speaking, if the paintings were stolen, the thief acquired no title and could not transfer good title to others regardless of their good faith and ignorance of the theft. Proof of theft would advance O'Keeffe's right to possession of the paintings absent other considerations such as expiration of the statute of limitations.

Another issue that may become relevant at trial is whether Frank or his father acquired a "voidable title" to the paintings under N.J.S.A. 12A:2–403(1). That section, part of the Uniform Commercial Code (U.C.C.), does not change the basic principle that a mere possessor cannot transfer good title. Nonetheless, the U.C.C. permits a person with voidable title to transfer good title to a good faith purchaser for value in certain circumstances.[12] If the facts developed at trial merit application of that section, then Frank may have transferred good title to Snyder, thereby providing a defense to O'Keeffe's action. No party on this appeal has urged factual or legal contentions concerning the applicability of the U.C.C. Consequently, a more complete discussion of the U.C.C. would be premature, particularly in light of our decision to remand the matter for trial.

On this appeal, the critical legal question is when O'Keeffe's cause of action accrued. The fulcrum on which the outcome turns is the statute of limitations ... which provides that an action for replevin of goods or chattels must be commenced within six years after the accrual of the cause of action. The trial court found that O'Keeffe's cause of action accrued on the date of the alleged theft, March, 1946, and concluded that her action was barred. The Appellate Division found that an action might have accrued more than six years before the date of suit if possession by

12. Under the U.C.C. a person has voidable title if he acquired the goods by fraud, deceived the transferor as to identity, acquired the goods by a dishonored check, or is a merchant who deals in such goods. Thus, if Dr. Frank had acquired the paintings by defrauding Stieglitz, or by means of a bad check, he would have had voidable title, which would have passed to Ulrich Frank as a gratuitous transferee, and ripened into a good title in Snyder if Snyder was not on notice of the prior chicanery. Also, if O'Keeffe had entrusted the paintings to Stieglitz for exhibition but not for sale, Stieglitz could have conveyed good title to an innocent third party because he was a merchant who dealt in art works. See U.C.C. § 2–403.

the defendant or his predecessors satisfied the elements of adverse possession. As indicated, the Appellate Division concluded that Snyder had not established those elements and that the O'Keeffe action was not barred by the statute of limitations. . . .

The purpose of a statute of limitations is to "stimulate to activity and punish negligence" and "promote repose by giving security and stability to human affairs." A statute of limitations achieves those purposes by barring a cause of action after the statutory period. In certain instances, this Court has ruled that the literal language of a statute of limitations should yield to other considerations. To avoid harsh results from the mechanical application of the statute, the courts have developed a concept known as the discovery rule. The discovery rule provides that, in an appropriate case, a cause of action will not accrue until the injured party discovers, or by exercise of reasonable diligence and intelligence should have discovered, facts which form the basis of a cause of action. The rule is essentially a principle of equity, the purpose of which is to mitigate unjust results that otherwise might flow from strict adherence to a rule of law. . . .

[T]he discovery rule applies to an action for replevin of a painting. . . . O'Keeffe's cause of action accrued when she first knew, or reasonably should have known through the exercise of due diligence, of the cause of action, including the identity of the possessor of the paintings. . . . In determining whether O'Keeffe is entitled to the benefit of the discovery rule, the trial court should consider, among others, the following issues: (1) whether O'Keeffe used due diligence to recover the paintings at the time of the alleged theft and thereafter; (2) whether at the time of the alleged theft there was an effective method, other than talking to her colleagues, for O'Keeffe to alert the art world; and (3) whether registering paintings with the Art Dealers Association of America, Inc. or any other organization would put a reasonably prudent purchaser of art on constructive notice that someone other than the possessor was the true owner.

The acquisition of title to real and personal property by adverse possession is based on the expiration of a statute of limitations. Adverse possession does not create title by prescription apart from the statute of limitations. To establish title by adverse possession to chattels, the rule of law has been that the possession must be hostile, actual, visible, exclusive, and continuous. Redmond v. New Jersey Historical Society, 132 N.J.Eq. 464, 474 (E. & A.1942), . . . involved a portrait of Captain James Lawrence by Gilbert Stuart, which was bequeathed by its owner to her son with a provision that if he should die leaving no descendants, it should go to the New Jersey Historical Society. The owner died in 1887, when her son was 14, and her executors delivered the painting to the Historical Society. The painting remained in the possession of the Historical Society for over 50 years, until 1938, when the son died and his children, the legatees under his will, demanded its return. The Historical Society refused, and the legatees instituted a replevin action. The Historical Society argued that the applicable statute of limitations . . . had run and that plaintiffs' action was barred. The Court of Errors and Appeals held that the doctrine of adverse possession applied to chattels as well as to real property, and that the statute of limitations would not begin to run against the true owner until possession became adverse. The Court found that the Historical Society had done nothing inconsistent with the theory that the painting was a "voluntary bailment or gratuitous loan" and had "utterly failed to prove that its possession of the portrait was 'adversary', 'hostile.'" The Court found further that the Historical Society had not asserted ownership until 1938, when it refused to deliver the painting to plaintiff, and that the statute did not begin to run until that date. Consequently, the Court ordered the painting to be returned to plaintiffs. . . .

[But] there is an inherent problem with many kinds of personal property that will raise questions whether their possession has been open, visible, and notorious. . . . For example, if jewelry is stolen from a municipality in one county in New Jersey, it is unlikely that the owner would learn that someone is openly wearing that jewelry in another county or even in the same municipality. Open and visible possession of personal property, such as jewelry, may not be sufficient to put the original owner on actual or constructive notice of the identity of the possessor. The problem is even more acute with works of art. Like many kinds of personal property, works of art are readily moved and easily concealed. O'Keeffe argues that nothing short of public display should be sufficient to alert the true owner and start the statute running. Although there is merit in that contention from the perspective of the original owner, the effect is to impose a heavy burden on the purchasers of paintings who wish to enjoy the paintings in the privacy of their homes. . . .

The problem is serious. According to an affidavit submitted in this matter by the president of the International Foundation for Art Research, there has been an "explosion in art thefts" and there is a "worldwide phenomenon of art theft which has reached epidemic proportions." The limited record before us provides a brief glimpse into the arcane world of sales of art, where paintings worth vast sums of money sometimes are bought without inquiry about their provenance. There does not appear to be a reasonably available method for an owner of art to record the ownership or theft of paintings. Similarly, there are no reasonable means readily available to a purchaser to ascertain the provenance of a painting. It may be time for the art world to establish a means by which a good faith purchaser may reasonably obtain the provenance of a painting. An efficient registry of original works of art might better serve the interests of artists, owners of art, and bona fide purchasers than the law of adverse possession with all of its uncertainties. Although we cannot mandate the initiation of a registration system, we can develop a rule for the commencement and running of the statute of limitations that is more responsive to the needs of the art world than the doctrine of adverse possession.

We are persuaded that the introduction of equitable considerations through the discovery rule provides a more satisfactory response than the doctrine of adverse possession. The discovery rule shifts the emphasis from the conduct of the possessor to the conduct of the owner. The focus of the inquiry will no longer be whether the possessor has met the tests of adverse possession, but whether the owner has acted with due diligence in pursuing his or her personal property. For example, under the discovery rule, if an artist diligently seeks the recovery of a lost or stolen painting, but cannot find it or discover the identity of the possessor, the statute of limitations will not begin to run. The rule permits an artist who uses reasonable efforts to report, investigate, and recover a painting to preserve the rights of title and possession.

Properly interpreted, the discovery rule becomes a vehicle for transporting equitable considerations into the statute of limitations for replevin. . . . If a chattel is concealed from the true owner, fairness compels tolling the statute during the period of concealment. That conclusion is consistent with . . . the law of replevin as it has developed apart from the discovery rule. In an action for replevin, the period of limitations ordinarily will run against the owner of lost or stolen property from the time of the wrongful taking, absent fraud or concealment. Where the chattel is fraudulently concealed, the general rule is that the statute is tolled. . . .

A purchaser from a private party would be well-advised to inquire whether a work of art has been reported as lost or stolen. However, a bona fide purchaser who purchases in the ordinary course of business a painting entrusted to an art dealer should be able to acquire good title against the true owner. Under the U.C.C. entrusting possession of goods to a merchant who deals in that kind of goods gives the merchant the power to transfer all the rights of the entruster to a buyer in the ordinary course of business. In a transaction under that statute, a merchant may vest good title in the buyer as against the original owner. The interplay between the statute of limitations as modified by the discovery rule and the U.C.C. should encourage good faith purchases from legitimate art dealers and discourage trafficking in stolen art without frustrating an artist's ability to recover stolen art works.

The discovery rule will fulfill the purposes of a statute of limitations and accord greater protection to the innocent owner of personal property whose goods are lost or stolen. Accordingly, we overrule Redmond v. New Jersey Historical Society to the extent that they hold that the doctrine of adverse possession applies to chattels. By diligently pursuing their goods, owners may prevent the statute of limitations from running. The meaning of due diligence will vary with the facts of each case, including the nature and value of the personal property. For example, with respect to jewelry of moderate value, it may be sufficient if the owner reports the theft to the police. With respect to art work of greater value, it may be reasonable to expect an owner to do more. In practice, our ruling should contribute to more careful practices concerning the purchase of art.

The considerations are different with real estate, and there is no reason to disturb the application of the doctrine of adverse possession to real estate. Real estate is fixed and cannot be moved or concealed. The owner of real property knows or should know where his property is located and reasonably can be expected to be aware of open, notorious, visible, hostile, continuous acts of possession on it.

Our ruling not only changes the requirements for acquiring title to personal property after an alleged unlawful taking, but also shifts the burden of proof at trial. Under the doctrine of adverse possession, the burden is on the possessor to prove the elements of adverse possession. Under the discovery rule, the burden is on the owner as the one seeking the benefit of the rule to establish facts that would justify deferring the beginning of the period of limitations.

Read literally, the effect of the expiration of the statute of limitations ... is to bar an action such as replevin. The statute does not speak of divesting the original owner of title. By its terms the statute cuts off the remedy, but not the right of title. Nonetheless, the effect of the expiration of the statute of limitations, albeit on the theory of adverse possession, has been not only to bar an action for possession, but also to vest title in the possessor. There is no reason to change that result although the discovery rule has replaced adverse possession. History, reason, and common sense support the conclusion that the expiration of the statute of limitations bars the remedy to recover possession and also vests title in the possessor. . . .

To summarize, the operative fact that divests the original owner of title to either personal or real property is the expiration of the period of limitations. In the past, adverse possession has described the nature of the conduct that will vest title of a chattel at the end of the statutory period. Our adoption of the discovery rule does not change the conclusion that at the end of the statutory period title will vest in the possessor.

We next consider the effect of transfers of a chattel from one possessor to another during the period of limitation under the discovery rule. Under the discovery rule, the statute of limitations on an action for replevin begins to run when the owner knows or reasonably should know of his cause of action and the identity of the possessor of the chattel. Subsequent transfers of the chattel are part of the continuous dispossession of the chattel from the original owner. The important point is not that there has been a substitution of possessors, but that there has been a continuous dispossession of the former owner. ... Nonetheless, subsequent transfers of the chattel may affect the degree of difficulty encountered by a diligent owner seeking to recover his goods. To that extent, subsequent transfers and their potential for frustrating diligence are relevant in applying the discovery rule. An owner who diligently seeks his chattel should be entitled to the benefit of the discovery rule although it may have passed through many hands. Conversely an owner who sleeps on his rights may be denied the benefit of the discovery rule although the chattel may have been possessed by only one person.

We reject the alternative of treating subsequent transfers of a chattel as separate acts of conversion that would start the statute of limitations running anew. At common law, apart from the statute of limitations, a subsequent transfer of a converted chattel was considered to be a separate act of conversion. . . . Adoption of that alternative would tend to undermine the purpose of the statute in quieting titles and protecting against stale claims.

The majority and better view is to permit tacking, the accumulation of consecutive periods of possession by parties in privity with each other. . . . Treating subsequent transfers as separate acts of conversion could lead to absurd results. As explained by Dean Ames: "If a converter were to sell the chattel, five years after its conversion, to one ignorant of the seller's tort, the disposed owner's right to recover the chattel from the purchaser would continue five years longer than his right to recover from the converter would have lasted if there had been no sale. In other words, an innocent purchaser from a wrong-doer would be in a worse position than the wrong-doer himself,—a conclusion as shocking in point of justice as it would be anomalous in law." . . .

We reverse the judgment of the Appellate Division in favor of O'Keeffe and remand the matter for trial in accordance with this opinion.

SOLOMON R. GUGGENHEIM FOUNDATION v. LUBELL

Court of Appeals of New York
77 N.Y.2d 311 (1991)

WACHTLER, C.J., delivered the opinion of the court.

The backdrop for this replevin action is the New York City art market, where masterpieces command extraordinary prices at auction and illicit dealing in stolen merchandise is an industry all its own. The Solomon R. Guggenheim Foundation, which operates the Guggenheim Museum in New York City, is seeking to recover a Chagall gouache worth an estimated $200,000. The Guggenheim believes that the gouache was stolen from its premises by a mailroom employee sometime in the late 1960s. The appellant Rachel Lubell and her husband, now deceased, bought the painting from a well-known Madison Avenue gallery in 1967 and have displayed it in their home for more than 20 years. Mrs. Lubell claims that before the Guggenheim's demand for its return in 1986, she had no reason to believe that the painting had been stolen.

On this appeal, we must decide if the museum's failure to take certain steps to locate the gouache is relevant to the appellant's Statute of Limitations defense. In effect, the appellant argues that the museum had a duty to use reasonable diligence to recover the gouache, that it did not do so, and that its cause of action in replevin is consequently barred by the Statute of Limitations. The Appellate Division rejected the appellant's argument. We agree with the Appellate Division that the timing of the museum's demand for the gouache and the appellant's refusal to return it are the only relevant factors in assessing the merits of the Statute of

unreachable delay in pressing a claim

Limitations defense. .... Appellant's affirmative defense of laches remains viable, however, and her claims that the museum did not undertake a reasonably diligent search for the missing painting will enter into the trial court's evaluation of the merits of that defense. Accordingly, the order of the Appellate Division should be affirmed.

The gouache, known alternately as *Menageries* or *Le Marchand de Bestiaux (The Cattle Dealer)*, was painted by Marc Chagall in 1912, in preparation for an oil painting also entitled *Le Marchand de Bestiaux*. It was donated to the museum in 1937 by Solomon R. Guggenheim....

Precisely when the museum first learned that the gouache had been stolen is a matter of some dispute. The museum acknowledges that it discovered that the painting was not where it should be sometime in the late 1960s, but claims that it did not know that the painting had in fact been stolen until it undertook a complete inventory of the museum collection beginning in 1969 and ending in 1970. ... The appellant, on the other hand, argues that the museum knew as early as 1965 that the painting had been stolen. It is undisputed, however, that the Guggenheim did not inform other museums, galleries or artistic organizations of the theft, and additionally, did not notify the New York City Police, the FBI, Interpol or any other law enforcement authorities. The museum asserts that this was a tactical decision based upon its belief that to publicize the theft would succeed only in driving the gouache further underground and greatly diminishing the possibility that it would ever be recovered....

Mr. and Mrs. Lubell had purchased the painting from the Robert Elkon Gallery for $17,000 in May of 1967. The invoice and receipt indicated that the gouache had been in the collection of a named individual, who later turned out to be the museum mailroom employee suspected of the theft. They exhibited the painting twice, in 1967 and in 1981, both times at the Elkon Gallery. In 1985, a private art dealer brought a transparency of the painting to Sotheby's for an auction estimate. The person to whom the dealer showed the transparency had previously worked at the Guggenheim and recognized the gouache as a piece that was missing from the museum. She notified the museum, which traced the painting back to the defendant. On January 9, 1986, Thomas Messer, the museum's director, wrote a letter to the defendant demanding the return of the gouache. Mrs. Lubell refused to return the painting and the instant action for recovery of the painting, or, in the alternative, $200,000, was commenced on September 28, 1987....

New York case law has long protected the right of the owner whose property has been stolen to recover that property, even if it is in the possession of a good-faith purchaser for value. There is a three-year Statute of Limitations for recovery of a chattel. The rule in this State is that a cause of action for replevin against the good-faith purchaser of a stolen chattel accrues when the true owner makes demand for return of the chattel and the person in possession of the chattel refuses to return it.

Until demand is made and refused, possession of the stolen property by the good-faith purchaser for value is not considered wrongful. . . .

While the demand and refusal rule is not the only possible method of measuring the accrual of replevin claims, it does appear to be the rule that affords the most protection to the true owners of stolen property. . . . Other States that have considered this issue have applied a discovery rule to these cases, with the Statute of Limitations running from the time that the owner discovered or reasonably should have discovered the whereabouts of the work of art that had been stolen (see, e.g., O'Keeffe v Snyder, . . .; Cal Civ Proc Code § 338 [c]). New York has already considered—and rejected—adoption of a discovery rule. In 1986, both houses of the New York State Legislature passed [a bill] which would have modified the demand and refusal rule and instituted a discovery rule in actions for recovery of art objects brought against certain not-for-profit institutions. This bill provided that the three-year Statute of Limitations would run from the time these institutions gave notice, in a manner specified by the statute, that they were in possession of a particular object. Governor Cuomo vetoed the measure [because] the statute "[did] not provide a reasonable opportunity for individuals or foreign governments to receive notice of a museum's acquisition and take action to recover it before their rights are extinguished." The Governor also stated that . . . the bill . . . would have caused New York to become "a haven for cultural property stolen abroad since such objects [would] be immune from recovery under the limited time periods established by the bill." . . . .

Further, the facts of this case reveal how difficult it would be to specify the type of conduct that would be required for a showing of reasonable diligence. Here, the parties hotly contest whether publicizing the theft would have turned up the gouache. According to the museum, some members of the art community believe that publicizing a theft exposes gaps in security and can lead to more thefts; the museum also argues that publicity often pushes a missing painting further underground. In light of the fact that members of the art community have apparently not reached a consensus on the best way to retrieve stolen art, it would be particularly inappropriate for this Court to spell out arbitrary rules of conduct that all true owners of stolen art work would have to follow to the letter if they wanted to preserve their right to pursue a cause of action in replevin. . . .

Further, our decision today is in part influenced by our recognition that New York enjoys a worldwide reputation as a preeminent cultural center. To place the burden of locating stolen artwork on the true owner and to foreclose the rights of that owner to recover its property if the burden is not met would, we believe, encourage illicit trafficking in stolen art. Three years after the theft, any purchaser, good faith or not, would be able to hold onto stolen art work unless the true owner was able to establish that it had undertaken a reasonable search for the missing art. This shifting of the burden onto the wronged owner is inappropriate. In our opinion, the better rule gives the owner relatively greater protection and places the burden of investigating the provenance of a work of art on the potential purchaser.

Despite our conclusion that the imposition of a reasonable diligence requirement on the museum would be inappropriate for purposes of the Statute of Limitations, our holding today should not be seen as either sanctioning the museum's conduct or suggesting that the museum's conduct is no longer an issue in this case. [A]lthough appellant's Statute of Limitations argument fails, her contention that the museum did not exercise reasonable diligence in locating the painting will be considered . . . in the context of her laches defense. The conduct of both the appellant and the museum will be relevant to any consideration of this defense at the trial level, and . . . prejudice [to Lubell] will also need to be shown. On the limited record before us there is no indication that the equities favor either party. Mr. and Mrs. Lubell investigated the provenance of the gouache before the purchase by contacting the artist and his son-in-law directly. The Lubells displayed the painting in their home for more than 20 years with no reason to suspect that it was not legally theirs. These facts will doubtless have some impact on the final decision regarding appellant's laches defense. . . .

NOTES AND QUESTIONS

1. Which Approach? Of the three approaches to the problem of limiting the time to recover possession of personal property—traditional adverse possession, the discovery rule, or the demand-and-refusal rule—which is preferable? Is your answer affected by what you perceive to be the purpose or purposes of adverse possession?

2. May Title be Derived from a Thief? The general rule in the United States is that good title may not be obtained from a thief. This is not a universal rule, however. France, for example, treats possession of personal property as equivalent to title, with the proviso that a stolen object may be recovered from its possessor if the true owner acts to recover it within three years of the theft. Civil Code § 2279. But § 2280 of the French Civil Code qualifies that rule by stipulating that if the possessor of the stolen object has purchased it in a public market, or from a dealer in such objects, the true owner may obtain its return only upon payment to the possessor of the price paid for the object by the possessor. Some other countries protect absolutely the possessor's interest in the object if it has been purchased in a public sale. Crime may pay, after all, at least to the unwitting possessor who benefits from the crime.

Who should bear the loss—the innocent purchaser or the victim of the theft? Some legal economists think that the party who might avoid the loss at the least expense should bear the loss. But how is a court to determine which party fits that description? In *Lubell*, for example, should the Guggenheim Museum be that party, because it could have tightened its security procedures (but at what cost, and with what effect?), or should Mrs. Lubell be that party, because she could have hired an investigator to determine whether the putative owner of the Chagall gouache had a valid title (but at what cost, and with what results)?

3. An image of O'Keeffe's painting, *Seaweed*, may be obtained by a Google™ search for "O'Keeffe Seaweed 1927." An image of the oil version of Chagall's *Le Marchand de Bestiaux (The Cattle Dealer)*, but not of the gouache study at issue in *Lubell*, may be obtained by a Google™ search for "Chagall the Cattle Dealer."

C. GIFTS

Title to property may be transferred by gift. To do so, the donor must intend to transfer ownership to the donee ("donative intent") and, in the case of personal property, possession must pass from the donor to the donee ("delivery"). The donee must accept the gift but acceptance is presumed upon delivery. To rebut the presumption a donee must explicitly refuse to accept the gift. In general, the object itself must be physically delivered to the donee, but this requirement is not rigid. If physical delivery is impractical, either constructive or symbolic delivery may suffice. Constructive delivery is the act of delivering something that enables the donee to obtain physical possession of the donated object, such as a key or a code to unlock a safe. Symbolic delivery is delivery of something that is symbolic of the donated object, such as a letter stating that the described object is now the property of the donee. Constructive or symbolic delivery has traditionally been limited to instances when physical delivery is not possible or impractical, but some states permit symbolic delivery by a written instrument of gift in all circumstances. See, e.g., Calif. Civil Code § 1147 (2009); In re Estate of Hall, 154 Cal. 527 (1908); Driscoll v. Driscoll, 143 Cal. 528 (1904). Constructive delivery is permitted by some states even when physical delivery is possible, so long as donative intent is clear and the circumstances indicate that the donor thought her acts were sufficient to transfer title. See Scherer v. Hyland, 75 N.J. 127 (1977). As one treatise writer has put it, "[d]iscerning a coherent judicial approach to questions of constructive delivery has proved almost impossible [because courts] have exhibited an understandable desire to affirm a gift where the donative intent is obvious." Thompson on Real Property (David A. Thomas ed.) § 13.04.

Physical delivery is valued highly supposedly because it is clear evidence to third parties of an irrevocable gift, provides *prima facie* evidence of the donee's ownership, and makes plain to the donor that he is parting with dominion and control of the object. See Philip Mechem, Gifts of Chattels and Choses in Action Evidenced by Commercial Instruments, 21 Ill. L. Rev. 341 (1926).

A further distinction must be made between gifts *inter vivos* (completed during life), gifts *causa mortis* (in contemplation of death), and testamentary gifts (which occur only at the death of the donor). A gift *inter vivos* is the completed gift, combining donative intent, delivery, and acceptance. A gift *causa mortis* is made in the expectation of impending death and is revocable if death does not occur. A testamentary gift is valid only if it is made in compliance with the formal requirements for a will, which usually involve a witnessed written instrument.

PROBLEMS

1. Father leaves a gold coin on his minor daughter's desk in her room. Gift? Suppose he does this every anniversary of his daughter's birthday. Gift? See Patterson v. Greensboro Loan & Trust Co., 157 N.C. 13 (1911). Suppose Father visits his adult daughter in her own home and a gold coin slides out of his pocket onto the sofa on which he is sitting. Daughter calls him the following day and he tells her to keep the coin. Gift?

invalid testamentary gift

delivery nature intent

2. Son admires Father's gold watch. Father states: "It's yours when I die." Gift? What if Father instead hands the watch to Son as he says: "Here, it's yours; but I want to retain possession of it until I die." Gift? What if Father says to Son as he hands him the watch: "Here, it's yours; but I would like to borrow it for as long as I wish;" and Son says, "That's OK with me." Gift? If so, what is the nature of Father's possession?

3. Husband and Wife rented a safe-deposit box as co-owners, specifically as joint tenants. (See Chapter Five on the nature of joint tenancy.) Husband placed in the box certain valuable securities and gave one of the two keys to the box to Wife, saying: "Here is your key to the safe-deposit box." Husband died, leaving a will that gave Wife a life estate in his property. (See Chapter Three on the nature of a life estate.) Wife claimed that she owned outright the contents of the box, specifically the valuable securities. Did Husband make a gift *inter vivos* to Wife of the contents of the box? No, said the Maryland Court of Appeals in Bauernschmidt v. Bauernschmidt, 97 Md. 35, 59–60 (1903), because Husband retained "dominion over the [contents of the box], precisely as he had control of it before the alleged gift was made[; thus,] there is obviously no perfected gift because there [was] no change of possession and there [was] still an opportunity to recant."

GRUEN v. GRUEN

Court of Appeals of New York
68 N.Y.2d 48 (1986)

SIMONS, J., delivered the opinion of a unanimous court.

Plaintiff commenced this action seeking a declaration that he is the rightful owner of a painting which he alleges his father, now deceased, gave to him. He concedes that he has never had possession of the painting but asserts that his father made a valid gift of the title in 1963 reserving a life estate for himself. His father retained possession of the painting until he died in 1980. Defendant, plaintiff's stepmother, has the painting now and has refused plaintiff's requests that she turn it over to him. She contends that the purported gift was testamentary in nature and invalid insofar as the formalities of a will were not met or, alternatively, that a donor may not make a valid inter vivos gift of a chattel and retain a life estate with a complete right of possession. [The trial court] found that

ISSUES

plaintiff had failed to establish any of the elements of an inter vivos gift and that in any event an attempt by a donor to retain a present possessory life estate in a chattel invalidated a purported gift of it. The Appellate Division held that a valid gift may be made reserving a life estate and, finding the elements of a gift established in this case, it reversed and remitted the matter for a determination of value. That determination has now been made and defendant appeals directly to this court ... from the subsequent final judgment entered ... awarding plaintiff $2,500,000 in damages representing the value of the painting, plus interest. We now affirm.

The subject of the dispute is a work entitled "Schloss Kammer am Attersee II" painted by a noted Austrian modernist, Gustav Klimt. It was purchased by plaintiff's father, Victor Gruen, in 1959 for $8,000. On April 1, 1963 the elder Gruen, a successful architect with offices and residences in both New York City and Los Angeles during most of the time involved in this action, wrote a letter to plaintiff, then an undergraduate student at Harvard, stating that he was giving him the Klimt painting for his birthday but that he wished to retain the possession of it for his lifetime. This letter is not in evidence, apparently because plaintiff destroyed it on instructions from his father. Two other letters were received, however, one dated May 22, 1963 and the other April 1, 1963. Both had been dictated by Victor Gruen and sent together to plaintiff on or about May 22, 1963. The letter dated May 22, 1963 reads as follows:

> Dear Michael:
>
> I wrote you at the time of your birthday about the gift of the painting by Klimt. Now my lawyer tells me that because of the existing tax laws, it was wrong to mention in that letter that I want to use the painting as long as I live. Though I still want to use it, this should not appear in the letter. I am enclosing, therefore, a new letter and I ask you to send the old one back to me so that it can be destroyed. I know this is all very silly, but the lawyer and our accountant insist that they must have in their possession copies of a letter which will serve the purpose of making it possible for you, once I die, to get this picture without having to pay inheritance taxes on it.
>
> Love,
>
> s/Victor

Enclosed with this letter was a substitute gift letter, dated April 1, 1963, which stated:

> Dear Michael:
>
> The 21st birthday, being an important event in life, should be celebrated accordingly. I therefore wish to give you as a present the oil painting by Gustav Klimt of Schloss Kammer which now hangs in the New York living room. You know that Lazette and I bought it some 5 or 6 years ago, and you always told us how much you liked it.
>
> Happy birthday again.

Love,

s/Victor

Plaintiff never took possession of the painting nor did he seek to do so. Except for a brief period between 1964 and 1965 when it was on loan to art exhibits and when restoration work was performed on it, the painting remained in his father's possession, moving with him from New York City to Beverly Hills and finally to Vienna, Austria, where Victor Gruen died on February 14, 1980. Following Victor's death plaintiff requested possession of the Klimt painting and when defendant refused, he commenced this action.

The issues framed for appeal are whether a valid inter vivos gift of a chattel may be made where the donor has reserved a life estate in the chattel and the donee never has had physical possession of it before the donor's death and, if it may, which factual findings on the elements of a valid inter vivos gift more nearly comport with the weight of the evidence in this case, those of [the trial court] or those of the Appellate Division. Resolution of the latter issue requires application of two general rules. First, to make a valid inter vivos gift there must exist the intent on the part of the donor to make a present transfer; delivery of the gift, either actual or constructive to the donee; and acceptance by the donee. Second, the proponent of a gift has the burden of proving each of these elements by clear and convincing evidence.

Donative Intent

There is an important distinction between the intent with which an inter vivos gift is made and the intent to make a gift by will. An inter vivos gift requires that the donor intend to make an irrevocable present transfer of ownership; if the intention is to make a testamentary disposition effective only after death, the gift is invalid unless made by will.

Defendant contends that the trial court was correct in finding that Victor did not intend to transfer any present interest in the painting to plaintiff in 1963 but only expressed an intention that plaintiff was to get the painting upon his death. The evidence is all but conclusive, however, that Victor intended to transfer ownership of the painting to plaintiff in 1963 but to retain a life estate in it and that he did, therefore, effectively transfer a remainder interest in the painting to plaintiff at that time. Although the original letter was not in evidence, testimony of its contents was received along with the substitute gift letter and its covering letter dated May 22, 1963. The three letters should be considered together as a single instrument and when they are they unambiguously establish that Victor Gruen intended to make a present gift of title to the painting at that time. But there was other evidence for after 1963 Victor made several statements orally and in writing indicating that he had previously given plaintiff the painting and that plaintiff owned it. Victor Gruen retained possession of the property, insured it, allowed others to exhibit it and made necessary repairs to it but those acts are not inconsistent with his retention of a life estate. Furthermore, whatever probative value could be attached to his statement that he had bequeathed the painting to his heirs, made 16 years later when he prepared an export license application so that he could take the painting out of Austria, is negated by the overwhelming evidence that he intended a present transfer of title in 1963. Victor's failure to file a gift tax return on the transaction was partially explained by allegedly erroneous legal advice he received, and while that omission sometimes may indicate that the donor had no intention of making a present gift, it does not necessarily do so and it is not dispositive in this case.

Defendant contends that even if a present gift was intended, Victor's reservation of a lifetime interest in the painting defeated it. ... Defendant recognizes that a valid inter vivos gift of a remainder interest can be made not only of real property but also of such intangibles as stocks and bonds. Indeed, several of the cases she cites so hold. That being so, it is difficult to perceive any legal basis for the distinction she urges which would permit gifts of remainder interests in those properties but not of remainder interests in chattels such as the Klimt painting here. The only reason suggested is that the gift of a chattel must include a present right to possession. [But] to permit a gift of the remainder in this case ... is consistent with the distinction, well recognized in the law of gifts as well as in real property law, between ownership and possession or enjoyment. Insofar as some of our cases purport to require that the donor intend to transfer both title and possession immediately to have a valid inter vivos gift, they state the rule too broadly and confuse the effectiveness of a gift with the transfer of the possession of the subject of that gift. The correct test is " 'whether the maker intended the [gift] to have *no effect* until after the maker's death, or whether he intended it to transfer *some present interest*' " (McCarthy v Pieret, 281 NY 407, 409 [emphasis added].... As long as the evidence establishes an intent to make a present and irrevocable transfer of title or the right of ownership, there is a present transfer of some interest and the gift is effective immediately. Thus, in Speelman v. Pascal [10 N.Y. 2d 313 (1961)], we held valid a gift of a percentage of the future royalties to the play "My Fair Lady" before the play even existed. There, as in this case, the donee received title or the right of ownership to some property immediately upon the making of the gift but possession or enjoyment of the subject of the gift was postponed to some future time.

Defendant suggests that allowing a donor to make a present gift of a remainder with the reservation of a life estate will lead courts to effectuate otherwise invalid testamentary dispositions of property. The two have entirely different characteristics, however, which make them distinguishable. Once the gift is made it is irrevocable and the donor is limited to the rights of a life tenant[,] not an owner. Moreover, with the gift of a remainder title vests immediately in the donee and any possession is postponed until the donor's death whereas under a will neither title nor possession vests immediately. Finally, the postponement of enjoyment of the gift is produced by the express terms of the gift not by the nature of the instrument as it is with a will.

Delivery

In order to have a valid inter vivos gift, there must be a delivery of the gift, either by a physical delivery of the subject of the gift or a constructive or symbolic delivery such as by an instrument of gift, sufficient to divest the donor of dominion and control over the property. As the statement of the rule suggests, the requirement of delivery is not rigid or inflexible, but is to be applied in light of its purpose to avoid mistakes by donors and fraudulent claims by donees. Accordingly, what is sufficient to constitute delivery "must be tailored to suit the circumstances of the case." The rule requires that " '[the] delivery necessary to consummate a gift must be as perfect as the nature of the property and the circumstances and surroundings of the parties will reasonably permit.' "

Defendant contends that when a tangible piece of personal property such as a painting is the subject of a gift, physical delivery of the painting itself is the best form of delivery and should be required. Here, of course, we have only delivery of Victor Gruen's letters which serve as instruments of gift. Defendant's statement of the rule as applied may be generally true, but it ignores the fact that what Victor Gruen gave plaintiff was not all rights to the Klimt painting, but only title to it with no right of possession until his death. Under these circumstances, it would be illogical for the law to require the donor to part with possession of the painting when that is exactly what he intends to retain.

Nor is there any reason to require a donor making a gift of a remainder interest in a chattel to physically deliver the chattel into the donee's hands only to have the donee redeliver it to the donor. As the facts of this case demonstrate, such a requirement could impose practical burdens on the parties to the gift while serving the delivery requirement poorly. Thus, in order to accomplish this type of delivery the parties would have been required to travel to New York for the symbolic transfer and redelivery of the Klimt painting which was hanging on the wall of Victor Gruen's Manhattan apartment. Defendant suggests that such a requirement would be stronger evidence of a completed gift, but in the absence of witnesses to the event or any written confirmation of the gift it would provide less protection against fraudulent claims than have the written instruments of gift delivered in this case.

Acceptance

Acceptance by the donee is essential to the validity of an inter vivos gift, but when a gift is of value to the donee, as it is here, the law will presume an acceptance on his part. Plaintiff did not rely on this presumption alone but also presented clear and convincing proof of his acceptance of a remainder interest in the Klimt painting by evidence that he had made several contemporaneous statements acknowledging the gift to his friends and associates, even showing some of them his father's gift letter, and that he had retained both letters for over 17 years to verify the gift after his father died. Defendant relied exclusively on affidavits filed by plaintiff in a matrimonial action with his former wife, in which plaintiff failed to list his interest in the painting as an asset. These affidavits were made over 10 years after acceptance was complete and they do not even approach the evidence in Matter of Kelly (285 NY 139, 148–149 [(1941)], where the donee, immediately upon delivery of a diamond ring, rejected it as "too flashy." We agree with the Appellate Division that interpretation of the affidavit was too speculative to support a finding of rejection and overcome the substantial showing of acceptance by plaintiff.

Accordingly, the judgment appealed from and the order of the Appellate Division brought up for review should be affirmed, with costs.

NOTES

1. Life Estates and Remainders. As you will learn in Chapters Three and Four, what is usually thought of as ownership is the fee simple absolute, the chief characteristic of which is that the *estate* endures forever, even as *owners of the estate* come and go. The fee simple absolute can be subdivided; in *Gruen*, Victor Gruen created a presently possessory estate that endured only for his life, and gave what remained of the fee simple absolute after deduction of his life estate to his son, Michael. Each of Victor's life estate and Michael's remainder were presently existing titles to property; it is just that in Michael's case the right to possession was postponed until Victor's death and in Victor's case the only right he kept was the right of possession until his death. But those rights were irrevocably transferred during Victor's life by his gift to Michael of the remainder interest and his retention of a life estate.

Had Victor sent a letter to Michael that stated "I give you the Klimt painting of Schloss Kammer am Attersee II when I die," he would not have effected a valid *inter vivos* gift because there would be no intention of transferring any ownership right at that moment. Rather, he would have created a defective testamentary transfer, or will, because such a letter would evidence only an intention to make a transfer in the future—at Victor's death—and wills are valid only if they are executed in accord with the proper formalities. In the hypothetical posed, Victor's purported testamentary transfer would, among other things, lack the required competent witnesses.

2. What About the Stepmother's Rights? Because the New York court concluded that the gift of a remainder was complete during Victor's life, and Victor's interest in the Klimt expired at his death, he had no property interest in the painting at his death; thus his widow, Kemija, acquired no rights to the painting under either Victor's will or by intestate succession. In Chapter 5 you will learn that surviving spouses in most states have what is known as an elective share, or forced share, that enables them to elect to take some portion of the deceased spouse's estate regardless of the terms of the will. That would be of no advantage to Kemija unless the jurisdiction had adopted Uniform Probate Code § 2–205(2)(i), which subjects to the elective share those assets transferred by the deceased spouse during life but in which the deceased retained a life estate.

3. The Story Behind the Case. Considerably more information about the background and aftermath of this case may be found in Susan F. French, *Gruen v. Gruen*: A Tale of Two Stories, in Property Stories 71 (Gerald Korngold & Andrew P. Morriss, eds.). Among the tidbits to be found there is the fact that, after Kemija Gruen lost the suit, she mailed to Michael Gruen a receipt providing access to bank vault in Zurich. Michael went to Zurich, presented the receipt, obtained the Klimt painting which was in the vault, and sold it at auction for about $5.3 million. It was a record price for a Klimt, but the buyer sold the painting ten years later for about $23.5 million. The painting is now in Rome's Galleria Nazionale d'Arte Moderna e Contemporanea. An image of the painting may be seen by searching Google™ images for "Schloss Kammer am Attersee II."

CHAPTER THREE

FREEHOLD ESTATES

■ ■ ■

A. NOMENCLATURE AND BACKGROUND

1. A BRIEF TAXONOMY OF ESTATES

An owner of real property owns an *estate in land*, which is to be distinguished from the land itself. The estates in land which will occupy your attention in this Chapter are possessory estates, which means that the holder of the estate is entitled to present possession of the land that is the subject of the estate in land. By contrast, a *future interest* (considered in Chapter Four), is a right to possession of the property at some point in the future. While a future interest is a presently existing property interest, the right to possession of the property is deferred until some future event or events have occurred.

Possessory interests may be freehold or non-freehold interests. A freehold interest is what lay people think of when they think of ownership of property but, as you will see, there are a variety of freehold interests. A non-freehold interest is what lay people think of when they think of a lease of property. A leasehold, or a non-freehold interest, gives its holder a right to possession but no right of ownership. Leaseholds are considered in Chapter Six.

The six possessory freehold estates are (1) the fee simple absolute, (2) the fee simple determinable, (3) the fee simple subject to condition subsequent, (4) the fee simple subject to an executory limitation, (5) the fee tail, and (6) the life estate. The principal difference between these estates is their duration. The fee simple absolute is eternal, or as eternal as any construct of mankind may be.[1] The traditional common law expression of this eternal quality was a grant to a person "and his heirs." The words "and his heirs" were regarded as words describing the duration of the estate, or "words of limitation," and the reference to the

---

1. Astronomers project that in about 5 billion years the Sun will become a red giant star, and will balloon outward as it loses mass. It will swallow Earth, cooking our home into a molten ball of rock, or perhaps a lovely ceramic marble. In any case, while the fee simple absolute may survive this tribulation, there are unlikely to be any owners of the estate around to enjoy it. See http://www.universetoday.com/12648/will-earth-survive-when-the-sun-becomes-a-red-giant/

grantee's heirs was taken to mean unlimited duration because someone will always be your heir, however remote or unwelcome they may be. (Even if you die intestate—without a will—and with no statutorily designated heirs, your property will escheat to the state, so in that sense the government is your fallback "heir" by default.) Although the owner of a fee simple absolute will change over time due to death or transfer (whether voluntary or involuntary, as by eminent domain) the estate remains. A fee simple absolute contains nothing in its creation that would cause it to end. Even if an estate of a lesser duration is carved out of the fee simple absolute, as for example by the creation of a life estate, some interest remains, which when added to the life estate, equals the fee simple absolute.

Example 3.1: O, owner of Blackacre in fee simple absolute, conveys Blackacre to "A for life." O has created in A an estate of lesser duration than his fee simple absolute—an estate that endures for A's life and no longer—so what happens to O's fee simple absolute? The answer is that O has created a future interest in himself by retaining that portion of his fee simple absolute that was left over after creation of the life estate in A. That future interest is called a reversion, because when A's life estate expires possession will revert to O. More precisely, O's reversion is a reversion in fee simple absolute, because when A's life estate expires O (or his successor in interest) owns what he owned before creation of the life estate.

The three defeasible fees, the fee simple determinable, the fee simple subject to condition subsequent, and the fee simple subject to an executory limitation, are each fees simple that may or will terminate upon the happening of a specified future event.

Example 3.2 (Fee Simple Determinable): O, owner of Blackacre in fee simple absolute, conveys Blackacre "to A and her heirs so long as Blackacre remains used for agriculture." A has a fee simple determinable; her right to possession (or her successor in interest's right to possession) will automatically cease when and if Blackacre is no longer devoted to agriculture. Because the fee simple determinable has a duration of less than eternity, O retains something, which is known as a possibility of reverter. If O's possibility of reverter becomes possessory he will once again have a fee simple absolute.

Example 3.3 (Fee Simple subject to Condition Subsequent): O, owner of Blackacre in fee simple absolute, conveys Blackacre "to A and her heirs; provided, however, that if Blackacre is not used for agriculture, O may re-enter and take possession." A has a fee simple subject to a condition subsequent; her right to possession (or her successor in interest's right to possession) will cease when and if Blackacre is no longer devoted to agriculture *and* O, or his successor in interest, exercises the right of entry. O retains a right of entry, sometimes termed a power of termination. If O's power of termination is validly exercised O (or his successor in interest) will once again have a fee simple absolute. The subtle differences between these two fees simple will be discussed in the section on defeasible fees.

Example 3.4 (Fee Simple subject to an Executory Limitation): O, owner of Blackacre in fee simple absolute, conveys Blackacre "to *A* and her heirs so long as Blackacre is used for agriculture, and if it is not so used, to *B* and her heirs." *A* has a fee simple subject to an executory limitation. *B* has an executory interest in fee simple absolute. The right to possession held by *A* or her successors in interest will automatically terminate if Blackacre is no longer devoted to agriculture. At that moment *B* will own Blackacre in fee simple absolute. *O* has transferred his future interest (a possibility of reverter had he kept it) to *B*.

The fee tail is archaic and virtually non-existent today. The concept was that the estate would endure only so long as the original grantee had lineal descendants. This made some sense in the English world of landed wealth, because the family manor (which represented most, if not all, of the family wealth) needed to be kept intact and in the family to preserve both the source of the wealth and its retention within the family. The fee tail was coupled with primogeniture, the principle that the eldest son was entitled to the property held in fee tail. This did first-born sons prosper as squires, while their younger male siblings entered the law, military service, or the church. Daughters were expected to marry, hopefully to wealthy men.[2]

Example 3.5: O, owner of Blackacre in fee simple absolute, conveys Blackacre "to *A* and the heirs of her body." *A* has a fee tail; the estate will endure only so long as *A* continues to have lineal descendants. *O* has retained a reversion in fee simple absolute. When and if *A*'s bloodline becomes extinct, the fee tail expires. At that moment, the reversion in *O* (or, more likely, his successors in interest) becomes possessory. The separate principle of primogeniture ensured that the fee tail estate would go to the eldest son.

The life estate is very much in evidence today, but primarily as an equitable interest created as part of a trust. The trust is an arrangement by which a person who owns property (the "settlor" or "trustor") may convey it to a trustee, who owns legal title to the property, but for the economic benefit of beneficiaries named in the trust instrument. The trustee may convey the property, because he has legal title, but must do so always for the economic benefit of the beneficiaries, who have equitable title to the property. The nature of those equitable interests can be created by the settlor in the trust instrument. Trusts may be revocable or irrevocable, and may be created during life (an *inter vivos* trust) or at

---

2. Consider the opening line of Jane Austen's *Pride and Prejudice*: "It is a truth universally acknowledged, that a single man in possession of a good fortune, must be in want of a wife." Or consider Mrs. Bennet's thoughts about the prospect of her daughter Jane marrying the very wealthy Mr. Bingley: "It was, moreover, such a promising thing for her younger daughters, as Jane's marrying so greatly must throw them in the way of other rich men." Austen completed her first draft of *Pride and Prejudice* in 1797, although the novel was first published in 1813.

one's death (a *testamentary* trust). Trusts are a staple of estate planning to transfer wealth from one generation to the next.

> *Example 3.6 (Life Estate in Trust): O,* owner in fee simple absolute of Blackacre and a large portfolio of marketable securities (the "Fund"), conveys Blackacre and the Fund, in trust, to *T,* the trustee, for the benefit of *A* for life, then to *A*'s children, outright and free of trust. *T* has legal title and may deal with Blackacre and the Fund as would *O,* except that *T* must do so only advancing or protecting the economic interests of *A* and *A*'s children, who have equitable ownership of Blackacre and the Fund. *A* owns a life estate. *A*'s children have a remainder. The precise nature of their remainder is best left to Chapter Four, when you will become immersed in the details of future interests.

2. SOME HISTORICAL BACKGROUND

The preceding taxonomy of present possessory interests did not come about by accident. America inherited English common law, and the English law of land tenures had 700 years of development before English colonists in America decided to shed their colonial status and become Americans.

The tale begins with the victory of the Norman invader, William the Conqueror, at the Battle of Hastings, in October of 1066. William, an illegitimate son of the Duke of Normandy, had succeeded to the duchy in 1035. He spent the next fifteen years crushing rebellious barons in his duchy. By 1051, his power consolidated, he began to eye England. Edward the Confessor, King of England, embroiled in a power struggle with Earl Godwin, Edward's father-in-law, sought Norman support by promising the crown of England to William after Edward's death. Edward had no authority to make the promise, but that did not matter to William. When Edward died in January 1066, he had reconciled with Godwin; thus, Harold Godwinson (Earl Godwin's son) was named King. An enraged William plotted revenge. Strong winds delayed his invasion in August and September, which turned out well for William because the Norwegian King decided to invade the north of England during the delay. Harold, awaiting William in the south, marched north and defeated the Norwegians, then returned to face William, who had landed unopposed in late September. A few weeks later, at Hastings, a tired band of Englishmen eventually succumbed to William. Not surprisingly, Harold was killed. William, the Conqueror, became William I.

William I moved quickly to strip the defeated Anglo–Saxons of their land and power. He fused together Anglo–Saxon customs with his continental notions to create a distinctive brand of land law. The feudal tenure system he created began with the King. All tenures in land were held by grant from the King, and each tenure required some continuing payment or service to continue the tenure. Those who held immediately from the King were usually obliged to provide a specific number of knights to fight

William's wars. But those tenants in chief could, and did, grant tenure of part of their own tenures to lesser lights, in return for a specified service, such as a number of knights. This was called subinfeudation. The lesser vassals could carve tenures out of their tenures in return for an annual service, whether it be knights, a portion of the annual crop, so many days of manual labor, or money rent. But they could not substitute another person in their stead to perform feudal services without the consent of the lord from whom they held tenure. At the bottom of this feudal pyramid of tenure holders was the person who possessed the land—the tenant in demesne (pronounced "demean"). He had *seisin*—the right to possess land.[3] Those above him who had granted the tenure were mesne lords (truly "land lords"), but they did not possess the land held in tenure by the tenant in desmesne; rather, they owned the right to the specified services. Of course, if the services were not performed the tenure was forfeited and the land reverted to the next higher mesne lord. This system created the idea that, in order to transfer seisin—the right to possess land—some service must be provided. Even if a mesne lord wished to grant his son tenure without performance of service, it was thought necessary to stipulate that some nominal service, perhaps even as whimsical as a rose on St Swithin's Day,[4] be provided. Moreover, the tenure system was highly personal. *T*, a tenant in demesne who held Blackacre from *L*, his mesne lord upon provision of twenty knights, held the tenure only for his own life because the relationship of *L* to *T* was treated as personal. At *T*'s death *L* was under no obligation to permit *T*'s heirs or assigns to assume the tenure. Indeed, as discussed below, *L* could and did demand payment to permit *T*'s heirs to acquire the tenure. The personal relationship of *L* and *T* was dramatically enforced by the requirement that in order for *T* to receive tenure from *L*, *T* was required publicly to pay homage and swear fealty to *L*.

All of these foregoing tenures were regarded as free tenures because they were held by free men, but the peasants were not so fortunate. They were allowed to occupy and till the land surrounding the manorial castle, but their right to do so was at the will of the lord of the manor rather than by performance of a specified service. Over time the peasants gained more security; they were thought to hold according to the customs of the manor, which amounted to a contract of sorts, and they could not be

---

3. Seisin meant more than possession; it was also the expression of the tenure holder's personal obligation to his lord to provide the required feudal services. Because those services accompanied any grant of land tenure, it was necessary that someone have seisin—and be obligated for performance of those services—at all times. As feudalism declined seisin, or possession, was dependent upon performance of a ritual to transfer ownership of land. The ritual, called livery of seisin, consisted of the grantor, in the presence of witnesses and upon the land in question, delivering to the grantee a handful of the earth or something else symbolic of the transfer of possession. The term persists today as a rather quaint way of expressing ownership, as for example, in judicial opinions that speak of a person dying while seized of certain lands. But don't think property law is devoid of ancient rituals; recall our discussion of the requirement of delivery to accomplish an *inter vivos* gift.

4. St Swithin's Day, July 15, is the British rough equivalent of Groundhog Day. The weather on St Swithin's Day supposedly shall continue for the next forty days. The British rhyme associated with St Swithin's Day since Elizabeth I is "St Swithin's Day if thou dost rain/For forty days it will remain./St Swithin's Day if thou be fair/For forty days 'twill rain nae mair."

ejected except in accordance with those customs. As feudalism eroded, their tenures came to be regarded as freeholds, just like those of the tenants in demesne.

An important part of this feudal system were the various incidents, or feudal forms of taxation, that were assessed upon the death of a tenant in demesne. If the deceased tenant's heir was a minor, possession reverted to the lord from whom the deceased held tenure. That lord had to surrender possession when the minor heir came of age, but in the meantime he could enjoy the use of the land and demand relief from the heir when he came of age. Relief was a payment of money to release the land from the grip of the lord. Even if the heir was an adult at the time of the death of the tenant in demesne, the lord from whom the tenure was held could demand relief. And if the tenant died without heirs his tenure died with him; the land escheated to the lord from whom it was held. Of course, the King, from whom all tenures flowed, had these rights with respect to all the tenures that came immediately from him. It is partly for this reason that in 1085 William I carried out the minutely detailed inventory of the land and assets of his realm that is known as the Domesday Book. William I needed to know what his subjects held in order to be certain that he was collecting all the incidents due him. In short, Domesday Book was a national audit to ensure that all the King's taxes were collected.

All of this provided an incentive for feudal holders of tenure to devise imaginative ways to avoid the feudal incidents. A favorite gambit of a mesne lord was to grant tenure for a nominal service—e.g., the rose on St Swithin's Day—because the death of the grantor meant that the lord from whom he held could not reach the land but could only demand the service due the deceased tenant. As a mesne lord aged, it became a good idea for him to grant his tenure to his sons for a sprig of rosemary or that familiar rose. The landlord was entitled to that service, but what was a sprig of rosemary in comparison to the cost of paying relief? Today's analog might be estate planning to avoid estate and gift taxes, which are harder to escape than were the feudal incidents.

To curb this tax avoidance Edward I persuaded Parliament to pass Statute Quia Emptores in 1290. This law prohibited subinfeudation by requiring that grantees assume all of the feudal obligations of the grantor. In return the statute permitted tenure holders to transfer their tenures without the consent of their mesne lord. By requiring this substitution Statute Quia Emptores hastened the end of feudalism. More importantly, it explicitly blessed the transfer of land tenures. The ability to transfer title freely—alienation—is critical to the reallocation of resources that is at the heart of the market economy, perhaps the greatest engine of wealth creation and material comfort in human history. The elimination of subinfeudation eventually compressed the feudal pyramid by the gradual attrition of mesne lords, until almost all tenures in land were held directly from the King. This produced an enhanced potential for royal tax collections via the enforcement of the still-extant feudal incidents. That reality also produced new imaginative devices to avoid the clutches of the King's tax men, and in response Henry VIII, ever greedy for revenue and wives, pushed the Statute of Uses through Parliament. But that tale is best reserved for our study of future interests in Chapter Four.

B. THE FEE SIMPLE ABSOLUTE

The fee simple absolute began as a reaction to feudalism. As noted above, the pyramidal tenure system was based on a personal relationship between mesne lord and tenant in demesne. At the death of the tenant the tenure ceased, and both consent of the mesne lord and payment of relief was necessary to allow the tenant's heirs to continue to hold the tenure. Over time, though, the mesne lords began to consent in advance to continuation of the tenure. The mechanism for doing so was a grant from L, the mesne lord, to "T and his heirs." This consent did not, however, eliminate the necessity of paying relief.

Until Statute Quia Emptores tenures in land were not freely alienable. Even a grant to "T and his heirs" meant only that the tenure could pass without the consent of the mesne lord (or his successor) to T's heirs, and then to the heirs of T's heirs, and so on, but always with payment of relief at each generational transfer. Quia Emptores, however, provided for free alienation of tenures in land. Inevitably, this changed the meaning of the grant to "T and his heirs." Now that phrase came to describe an estate that could endure forever—a fee simple absolute. But lawyers and judges being creatures of habit, they insisted that the inclusion of the phrase "and his heirs" was absolutely necessary to create a fee simple absolute. In English common law, and well into the era of American independence, its omission created only a life estate in the grantee.

It is important to note that a grant "to A and his heirs" consists of two distinct parts. The words "to A" are *words of purchase*—they denote who is the immediate recipient of the estate being conveyed. The words "and his heirs" are *words of limitation*—they denote the nature of the estate that A is receiving. In this case, "and his heirs" signify the eternal estate of the fee simple absolute. The words "and his heirs" give the heirs of A absolutely no interest in the estate conveyed to A but, as we shall soon see, words of limitation that create a lesser estate than a fee simple absolute (e.g., an estate that is not eternal, but is capable of coming to an end) do have the effect of creating future interests in the property conveyed.

American states that continued to apply the English common law held that it was essential to use "and his heirs" to create a fee simple absolute. An example is McMichael v. McMichael, 51 S.C. 555 (1898), in which the court was required to determine the estates conveyed by a deed granting land to "R. V. McMichael during his natural lifetime, and after his death to his children and assigns forever." McMichael possessed a life estate and his children possessed a remainder, but was the remainder in fee simple absolute? No, said the court; their remainder was of a life estate. Why?

The technical rule of the common law makes it essential to the creation of an estate in fee simple in a natural person by deed, that there be in the deed an express limitation to such person and his "heirs." This rule is generally and inflexibly enforced in the United States, except where abrogated or modified by statute. While many States have altered this rule by statute, no such statute, as applicable to deeds, has been adopted in this State, and our Courts have repeatedly and uniformly recognized and enforced the strict rule of the common law.

But even under the common law regime, exceptions to this harsh and technical rule were carved out. Grants to artificial entities (e.g., corporations) or devises in wills could create a fee simple absolute even without the magic words of limitation, so long as the testator's intent to do so was clear.

"its successors"

Today, this residue of the past has been eliminated. Either by statute or judicial decision, every American state has rejected the requirement that "and his heirs" be included in the grant to create a fee simple absolute. A typical statute is Ariz. Rev. Stat. § 33–432 (2010): "Every estate in lands granted, conveyed or devised, although other words necessary at common law to transfer an estate in fee simple are not added, shall be deemed a fee simple if a lesser estate is not limited by express words or does not appear to have been granted, conveyed or devised by construction or operation of law."

PROBLEMS

1. Suppose that in 2010 *O* conveys Blackacre "to *A* forever." What is the state of title of Blackacre? *Fee simple absolute*

2. Suppose that in 2010 *O* conveys Whiteacre "to *A* for one day short of forever." Cf. Johnson v. Whiton, 159 Mass. 424 (1893). *life estate*

C. THE FEE TAIL

The fee tail began as a device of the English landed gentry to ensure that any current owner of the fee could not alienate it, but must keep it for the next generation. Because land was wealth and status in medieval England it was important to preserve it within the family. The chosen device was a grant to "*A* and the heirs of his body." Unlike the words of limitation in the fee simple absolute (which indicated perpetual inheritability), these words of limitation were intended to restrict inheritance to *A*'s lineal descendants, so long as they continue to exist. But this intention was thwarted by judicial decisions that construed such a grant to give to *A* the power to convey a fee simple absolute if children were born to *A*, thus eliminating the intended inheritance rights of *A*'s lineal descendants, or issue. This was known as a fee simple conditional because the condition to this being a fee simple absolute was having issue.

This changed in 1285, when Parliament enacted Statute De Donis Conditionalibus. This statute replaced the fee simple conditional with the fee tail.[5] After Statute De Donis, a grant to "*A* and the heirs of his body" meant that *A*'s estate must descend to his lineal descendants for generation after generation, until the bloodline of *A* finally comes to an end. The words of limitation in the fee tail—"and the heirs of his body"—might as well be read as "for so long as the grantee shall have lineal descendants." Because the fee tail does not (or may not) endure forever, it must have either a reversion or remainder that follows it.

Example 3.7 (Fee Tail with Reversion): Suppose *O* grants Blackacre "to *A* and the heirs of his body." *A* has a fee tail and *O* has retained a reversion in fee simple absolute. Whenever *A*'s bloodline should expire the fee tail will expire and *O* (or *O*'s successor in interest) will own Blackacre in fee simple absolute.

Example 3.8 (Fee Tail with Remainder): Suppose *O* grants Blackacre "to *A* and the heirs of his body, and then to *B* and his heirs." *A* has a fee tail and *B* has a remainder in fee simple absolute. Whenever *A*'s bloodline should expire the fee tail will expire and *B* (or *B*'s successor in interest) will own Blackacre in fee simple absolute. *O* did not retain a reversion because he has parted with his fee simple absolute, breaking into two pieces: the fee tail in *A* and the remainder in fee simple absolute in *B*.

In England the fee tail was combined with primogeniture, the rule that the eldest son was entitled to property in fee tail. Thus it was ensured that property that was entailed would not be subdivided among all the lineal descendants, but would remain intact in the hands of a single person, the eldest heir.[6]

There were variations on the fee tail. A fee tail male limited the entail to male descendants (though, with primogeniture, this was not usually necessary). A fee tail female could also be created, but was rarely done, given the dominant role of men. A fee tail special was more common, usually as part of a marriage settlement, in which the estate was limited to issue of the husband and a particular, named, wife.

This worked well for the landed gentry but not so well for the Crown. Rebellious gentry, once convicted of treason, forfeited their estates to the Crown, but estates in fee tail gave the King only possession of the forfeited fee tail for the duration of the traitor's life. To curb this incentive to rebel

---

5. Only Iowa and South Carolina recognize the fee simple conditional because each of those states regard Statute De Donis as not being part of the law received in America upon separation from Great Britain. See Prichard v. Department of Revenue, 164 N.W.2d 113 (Iowa 1969); Scarborough v. Scarborough, 246 S.C. 51 (1965); Powell on Real Property § 14.04.

6. The problems created by the fee tail are at the heart of Jane Austen's classic, *Pride and Prejudice*. Mr. Bennet held Longbourn in fee tail. Because he had five daughters and no sons, his estate would descend to his nearest male relative, the oleaginous Rev. Collins. Hence the imperative of the Bennet daughters marrying well, and Mrs. Bennet's distress over Elizabeth Bennet's refusal of Mr. Collins's hand in marriage. But as Shakespeare declared in another time and place, "All's Well that Ends Well." Except, perhaps, for the vapid Mrs. Wickham, *neé* Lydia Bennet.

the King's courts permitted tenants in tail to destroy the fee tail and create a fee simple absolute. But it was not easy. A complicated collusive lawsuit was necessary to accomplish what became known as a common recovery, with the result that the court would issue a decree converting the fee tail into a fee simple absolute. For the byzantine details, see Taltarum's Case, Y.B. 12 Edw. IV 19 (1472); Alfred William Brian Simpson, A History of the Land Law 125–138 (2d ed. 1986). Thus was the King empowered to seek and obtain a common recovery with respect to fees tail forfeited to him by his treasonous barons, thus giving the King fee simple absolute and depriving the traitor's heirs of their expectancy. The gentry were not so easily deterred, however. As we shall discuss in Chapter Four, the development of future interests came about in no small part because the gentry sought new ways to control the ownership of their lands after their death.

The fee tail has been abolished as to legal estates in England since 1925. It is virtually extinct in the United States. Only Delaware, Maine, Massachusetts, and Rhode Island recognize it. In these states the holder of the fee tail may destroy it by conveying the estate during life. This disentailing conveyance creates a fee simple absolute in the grantee. However, if a holder of a fee tail in these states fails to disentail during his life, the fee tail will exist at his death, and the issue of the deceased will acquire fractional interests in fee tail. In Rhode Island, an attempt to create a fee tail by will (rather than by deed) creates a life estate in the grantee and a remainder in fee simple absolute in the grantee's issue.

The only contemporary issue of consequence concerning the fee tail involves the method by which it has been abolished. In the forty-six states that have abolished the fee tail, what is one to do with a conveyance that would have created a fee tail? Suppose that in one of these states O conveys Blackacre "to A and the heirs of his body, and in default of such issue to B and her heirs." A cannot have a fee tail, but what does she have? And what interest, if any, does B have?

There are three approaches to this problem:

1) In some states a putative fee tail is converted into a life estate in the grantee, with a remainder in fee simple in the grantee's issue. See, e.g., Rosenbledt v. Wodehouse, 25 Haw. 561, 568 (1920); Fla. Stat. § 689.14 (2010); Kan. Stat. § 58–502 (2009). Thus, the grant described above would create a life estate in A and a remainder in fee simple absolute in A's issue. B's remainder would be destroyed.

2) About half of the states treat a purported fee tail as creating a fee simple absolute in the grantee and destroy any reversions or remainders that would become possessory upon expiration of the fee tail. See, e.g., Pa. Stat. Ann. Title 20, § 2516 (2010). Thus, A would receive fee simple absolute and B's remainder would be destroyed.

3) Eight states—California, Michigan, Montana, New York, North Dakota, Oklahoma, South Dakota, Wyoming—provide that the grantee receives a defeasible fee simple, and convert the remainder following the

purported fee tail into an executory interest in fee simple absolute. An example is Calif. Civil Code §§ 763, 764. Section 763 states: "Estates tail are abolished, and every estate which would be at common law adjudged to be a fee tail is a fee simple; and if no valid remainder is limited thereon, is a fee simple absolute." Section 764 states: "Where a remainder in fee is limited upon any estate, which would by the common law be adjudged a fee tail, such remainder is valid as a contingent limitation upon a fee, and vests in possession on the death of the first taker, without issue living at the time of his death." Under these provisions the grant above would create in *A* a fee simple subject to an executory limitation, and create in *B* an executory interest. *A* would be entitled to possession and ownership of Blackacre subject to the condition that his fee would be divested in favor of *B* if *A* dies without issue surviving him. If *A* should die without surviving issue *A*'s fee simple is destroyed and *B*'s executory interest becomes possessory as a fee simple absolute. But if *A* should die survived by issue, *A*'s defeasible fee simple becomes a fee simple absolute and the executory interest of *B* is destroyed, or lapses, because the condition that would have divested *A* of his fee and vested it in *B* did not occur, and now can never occur.

For a compilation of the states and their rules on abolition of the fee tail, see Powell on Real Property § 14.07.

PROBLEMS

1. Suppose that *O* conveys Blackacre "to *A* and the heirs of her body, and in default of such issue, to *B* and his heirs." *A*, who is married to *C* and the mother of *D*, conveys her interest in Blackacre to *E*. *C* dies, then *A* dies, leaving *D* as her sole heir. What is the state of title in Blackacre in the four states that recognize the fee tail and in each of the three types of states that have abolished the fee tail?

2. Suppose that in Maine *O* conveys Blackacre "to *A* and the heirs of her body, and in default of such issue, to *B* and his heirs." *A*, who is married to *C* and the mother of *D*, dies testate. Under her will, *A* devises Blackacre to Ivy College, her alma mater. What is the state of title of Blackacre? If you think your answer is inconsistent with *A*'s apparent intent, what should *A* have done?

3. Suppose that *O* devises Blackacre "to my grand-daughter *A* and her heirs on her father's side." What is the state of title of Blackacre? See Johnson v. Whiton, 159 Mass. 424 (1893). To aid your consideration of this problem, remember that the phrase "and her heirs on her father's side" are words of limitation.

D.   THE LIFE ESTATE

Other than the fee simple absolute, the life estate is the single most significant freehold estate today. Yet it has little impact as a legal estate; its significance and utility are almost entirely as an equitable estate.

Recall that the trust divorces legal and equitable ownership, The trustee legally owns the property placed in trust, but has fiduciary obligations to exercise his ownership for the benefit of the equitable owners of the property, the beneficiaries of the trust. This device enables a person, usually (but not always) to create a testamentary trust (a trust created by the decedent's will), in which he splits legal and equitable ownership between the trustee and the beneficiaries, and also creates an equitable life estate followed by a remainder in fee simple absolute. A typical arrangement is one in which O, the decedent, by his will devises all his property to T in trust, with the income from the trust corpus to be paid to A, his surviving spouse, for her life, and then the principal of the trust to be paid outright, free of trust, to O's children, in equal portions, and if any child should predecease A, that child's share to pass by right of representation to the predeceased child's heirs. See also Example 3.6, supra.

The life estate did not originate as an equitable estate, however. As the fee tail became subject to the common recovery, lawyers began to use life estates to control inheritance. They could do so because the creator of the life estate has the power to designate who will possess the property once the life estate expires. Thus, in theory, O, owner of Blackacre in fee simple absolute, could devise Blackacre to "my son A for life, then to his eldest surviving son for life, then to A's eldest surviving grandson for life, then to A's eldest surviving great-grandson for life, and then ..." In theory. The common law controlled this by creating a variety of doctrines to destroy future interests that produce uncertainty as to the identity of the future possessor. The most important of these doctrines is the rule against perpetuities, to be discussed in Chapter Four. For the moment, however, we can concentrate on the mechanics of the life estate.

A conveyance or devise to "A for life" creates a life estate in A. A's life estate endures until A's death. During A's life, A can convey his life estate to someone else. If he does so, the transferee owns a life estate that lasts only so long as A is alive. Thus, if A conveys his life estate to B, B is said to own a life estate *pur autre vie* (for the life of another). The duration of B's life estate is measured by A's life. Every life estate will be followed by either a reversion in the grantor or a remainder in a transferee from the grantor. A grant from O to A for life creates a reversion in fee simple absolute in O. A grant from O to A for life, and then to B and her heirs creates a remainder in fee simple absolute in B.

PROBLEM

Suppose that O conveys Blackacre to A for life. A then conveys her life estate to B, who dies intestate, survived by C, his sole heir, A, and O. What is the state of title in Blackacre? See Collins v. Held, 174 Ind.App. 584 (1977).

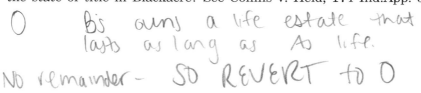

O   B's owns a life estate that lasts as long as A's life.

No remainder— SO REVERT to O (fee simple absolute)

WHITE v. BROWN

Supreme Court of Tennessee
559 S.W.2d 938 (1977)

BROCK, J., delivered the opinion of the court.

This is a suit for the construction of a will. The Chancellor held that the will passed a life estate, but not the [reversion], in certain realty, leaving the [reversion] to pass by inheritance to the testatrix's heirs at law. The Court of Appeals affirmed.

Mrs. Jessie Lide died on February 15, 1973, leaving a holographic will[7] which, in its entirety, reads as follows:

April 19, 1972

I, Jessie Lide, being in sound mind declare this to be my last will and testament. I appoint my niece Sandra White Perry to be the executrix of my estate. I wish Evelyn White to have my home to live in and <u>not</u> to be <u>sold</u>. I also leave my personal property to Sandra White Perry. My house is not to be sold.

Jessie Lide

(Underscoring by testatrix)

Mrs. Lide was a widow and had no children. Although she had nine brothers and sisters, only two sisters residing in Ohio survived her. These two sisters quitclaimed[8] any interest they might have in the residence to Mrs. White. The nieces and nephews of the testatrix, her heirs at law, are defendants in this action. Mrs. White, her husband, who was the testatrix's brother, and her daughter, Sandra White Perry, lived with Mrs. Lide as a family for some twenty-five years. After Sandra married in 1969 and Mrs. White's husband died in 1971, Evelyn White continued to live with Mrs. Lide until Mrs. Lide's death in 1973 at age 88.

Mrs. White, *Evelyn* joined by her daughter as executrix, filed this action to obtain construction of the will, alleging that she is vested with a fee simple title to the home. The defendants contend that the will conveyed only a life estate to Mrs. White, leaving the [reversion] to go to them under our laws of intestate succession. The Chancellor held that the will unambiguously conveyed only a life interest in the home to Mrs. White and refused to consider extrinsic evidence concerning Mrs. Lide's relationship with her surviving relatives. Due to the debilitated condition of the property and in accordance with the desire of all parties, the Chancellor ordered the property sold with the proceeds distributed in designated shares among the beneficiaries.

---

7. [Ed.] A holographic will is a will entirely in the testator's handwriting. Unlike typed or printed wills, such wills need not be witnessed in order to be valid.

8. [Ed.] A quit claim deed is a deed that passes to the grantee whatever interest the grantor may have in the property, but with no warranties that the grantor in fact has any interest in the property. See Chapter Seven.

I.   Our cases have repeatedly acknowledged that the intention of the testator is to be ascertained from the language of the entire instrument when read in the light of surrounding circumstances. . . . But, the practical difficulty in this case, as in so many other cases involving wills drafted by lay persons, is that the words chosen by the testatrix are not specific enough to clearly state her intent. Thus, in our opinion, it is not clear whether Mrs. Lide intended to convey a life estate in the home to Mrs. White, leaving the remainder interest to descend by operation of law, or a fee interest with a restraint on alienation. Moreover, the will might even be read as conveying a fee interest subject to a condition subsequent (Mrs. White's failure to live in the home).

In such ambiguous cases it is obvious that rules of construction, always yielding to the cardinal rule of the testator's intent, must be employed as auxiliary aids in the courts' endeavor to ascertain the testator's intent.

In 1851 our General Assembly enacted two such statutes of construction, thereby creating a statutory presumption against partial intestacy. Chapter 33 of the Public Acts of 1851 (now codified as T.C.A. §§ 64–101 and 64–501) reversed the common law presumption that a life estate was intended unless the intent to pass a fee simple was clearly expressed in the instrument. T.C.A. § 64–501 provides: "Every grant or devise of real estate, or any interest therein, shall pass all the estate or interest of the grantor or devisor, unless the intent to pass a less estate or interest shall appear by express terms, or be necessarily implied in the terms of the instrument." Chapter 180, Section 2 of the Public Acts of 1851 (now codified as T.C.A. § 32–301) was specifically directed to the operation of a devise. In relevant part, T.C.A. § 32–301 provides: "A will . . . shall convey all the real estate belonging to [the testator] or in which he had any interest at his decease, unless a contrary intention appear by its words and context."

Thus, under our law, unless the "words and context" of Mrs. Lide's will clearly evidence her intention to convey only a life estate to Mrs. White, the will should be construed as passing the home to Mrs. White in fee. "If the expression in the will is doubtful, the doubt is resolved against the limitation and in favor of the absolute estate." Meacham v. Graham, 98 Tenn. 190, 206, 39 S.W. 12, 15 (1897). . . . Several of our cases demonstrate the effect of these statutory presumptions against intestacy by construing language which might seem to convey an estate for life, without provision for a gift over after the termination of such life estate, as passing a fee simple instead. In Green v. Young, 163 Tenn. 16, 40 S.W.2d 793 (1931), the testatrix's disposition of all of her property to her husband "to be used by him for his support and comfort during his life" was held to pass a fee estate. Similarly, in Williams v. Williams, 167 Tenn. 26, 65 S.W.2d 561 (1933), the testator's devise of real property to his children "for and during their natural lives" without provision for a gift over was held to convey a fee. And, in Webb v. Webb, 53 Tenn.App. 609, 385 S.W.2d 295 (1964), a devise of personal property to the testator's wife "for her maintenance, support and comfort, for the full period of her natural life" with complete powers of alienation but without provision for the remainder passed absolute title to the widow.

II. Thus, if the sole question for our determination were whether the will's conveyance of the home to Mrs. White "to live in" gave her a life interest or a fee in the home, a conclusion favoring the absolute estate would be clearly required. The question, however, is complicated somewhat by the caveat contained in the will that the home is "not to be sold"—a restriction conflicting with the free alienation of property, one of the most significant incidents of fee ownership. We must determine, therefore, whether Mrs. Lide's will, when taken as a whole, clearly evidences her intent to convey only a life estate in her home to Mrs. White.

Under ordinary circumstances a person makes a will to dispose of his or her entire estate. If, therefore, a will is susceptible of two constructions, by one of which the testator disposes of the whole of his estate and by the other of which he disposes of only a part of his estate, dying intestate as to the remainder, this Court has always preferred that construction which disposes of the whole of the testator's estate if that construction is reasonable and consistent with the general scope and provisions of the will. A construction which results in partial intestacy will not be adopted unless such intention clearly appears. . . .

The intent to create a fee simple or other absolute interest and, at the same time to impose a restraint upon its alienation can be clearly expressed. If the testator specifically declares that he devises land to A "in fee simple" or to A "and his heirs" but that A shall not have the power to alienate the land, there is but one tenable construction, viz., the testator's intent is to impose a restraint upon a fee simple. To construe such language to create a life estate would conflict with the express specification of a fee simple as well as with the presumption of intent to make a complete testamentary disposition of all of a testator's property. By extension, as noted by Professor Casner in his treatise on the law of real property: "Since it is now generally presumed that a conveyor intends to transfer his whole interest in the property, it may be reasonable to adopt the same construction, [conveyance of a fee simple] even in the absence of words of inheritance, if there is no language that can be construed to create a remainder." 6 American Law of Property § 26.58 (A. J. Casner ed. 1952).

In our opinion, testatrix's apparent testamentary restraint on the alienation of the home devised to Mrs. White does not evidence such a clear intent to pass only a life estate as is sufficient to overcome the law's strong presumption that a fee simple interest was conveyed. Accordingly, we conclude that Mrs. Lide's will passed a fee simple absolute in the home to Mrs. White. Her attempted restraint on alienation must be declared void as inconsistent with the incidents and nature of the estate devised and contrary to public policy.

The decrees of the Court of Appeals and the trial court are reversed and the cause is remanded to the chancery court for such further proceedings as may be necessary, consistent with this opinion. . . .

HARBISON, J., joined by HENRY, C.J., dissenting.

. . . I am unable to agree that the language of the will of Mrs. Lide did or was intended to convey a fee simple interest in her residence to her sister-in-law, Mrs. Evelyn White. The testatrix expressed the wish that Mrs. White was "to have my home to live in and *not* to be sold." The emphasis is that of the testatrix, and her desire that Mrs. White was not to have an unlimited estate in the property was reiterated in the last sentence of the will, to wit: "My house is not to be sold." . . .

The will does not seem to me to be particularly ambiguous, and like the Chancellor and the Court of Appeals, I am of the opinion that the testatrix gave Mrs. White a life estate only, and that upon the death of Mrs. White the [reversion] will pass to the heirs at law of the testatrix.

The cases cited by petitioners in support of their contention that a fee simple was conveyed are not persuasive, in my opinion. Possibly the strongest case cited by the appellants is Green v. Young, 163 Tenn. 16, 40 S.W.2d 793 (1931), in which the testatrix bequeathed all of her real and personal property to her husband "to be used by him for his support and comfort during his life." . . . There was no limitation whatever upon the power of the husband to use, consume, or dispose of the property, and the Court concluded that a fee simple was intended. In the case of Williams v. Williams, 167 Tenn. 26, 65 S.W.2d 561 (1933), a father devised property to his children "for and during their natural lives" but the will contained other provisions not mentioned in the majority opinion which seem to me to distinguish the case. Unlike the provisions of the present will, other clauses in the *Williams* will contained provisions that these same children were to have "all the residue of my estate personal or mixed of which I shall die possessed or seized, or to which I shall be entitled at the time of my decease, to have and to hold the same to them and their executors and administrators and assigns forever." Further, following some specific gifts to grandchildren, there was another bequest of the remainder of the testator's money to these same three children. The language used by the testator in that case was held to convey the fee simple interest in real estate to the children, but its provisions hardly seem analogous to the language employed by the testatrix in the instant case.

In the case of Webb v. Webb, 53 Tenn.App. 609, 385 S.W.2d 295 (1964), the testator gave his wife all the residue of his property with a clear, unqualified and unrestricted power of use, sale or disposition. Thereafter he attempted to limit her interest to a life estate, with a gift over to his heirs of any unconsumed property. Again, under settled rules of construction and interpretation, the wife was found to have a fee simple estate, but, unlike the present case, there was no limitation whatever upon the power of use or disposition of the property by the beneficiary.

On the other hand, in the case of Magevney v. Karsch, 167 Tenn. 32, 65 S.W.2d 562 (1933), a gift of the residue of the large estate of the testator to his daughter, with power "at her demise [to] dispose of it as she pleases...." was held to create only a life estate with a power of appointment, and not an absolute gift of the residue. In other portions of the will the testator had given another beneficiary a power to use and dispose of property, and the Court concluded that he appreciated the distinction between a life estate and an absolute estate, recognizing that a life tenant could not dispose of property and use the proceeds as she pleased.

In the present case the testatrix knew how to make an outright gift, if desired. She left all of her personal property to her niece without restraint or limitation. As to her sister-in-law, however, she merely wished the latter have her house "to live in," and expressly withheld from her any power of sale. The majority opinion holds that the testatrix violated a rule of law by attempting to restrict the power of the donee to dispose of the real estate. Only by thus striking a portion of the will, and holding it inoperative, is the conclusion reached that an unlimited estate resulted.

In my opinion, this interpretation conflicts more greatly with the apparent intention of the testatrix than did the conclusion of the courts below, limiting the gift to Mrs. White to a life estate. I have serious doubt that the testatrix intended to create any illegal restraint on alienation or to violate any other rules of law. It seems to me that she rather emphatically intended to provide that her sister-in-law was not to be able to sell the house during the lifetime of the latter—a result which is both legal and consistent with the creation of a life estate.

In my opinion the judgment of the courts below was correct and I would affirm.

NOTES AND QUESTIONS

1. *Constructional Principles.* The Tennessee court emphasizes that the grantor's intention controls, and that the legal presumptions apply when the grantor's intention is ambiguous. But as the cases mentioned by the majority and dissent suggest, divination of the grantor's intent is somewhat subjective. Consider the differing outcomes of the following cases.

a. *Dickson v. Alexandria Hospital, Inc.*, 177 F.2d 876 (4th Cir. 1949). George L. Simpson died in 1907, survived by his widow, Virginia Simpson, and two sons, George Robbins Simpson and French Cameron Simpson. His holographic will read, in pertinent part:

> [F]irst I do not wish any appraisment [*sic*] of my estate; Secondly I do not wish my wife Virginia Simpson, whom I appoint my executrix, to give any security; Thirdly, I give to my wife Virginia Simpson, my property on Cameron and Columbus Streets, including furniture and contents of my home. Fourthly I give to each of my boys Geo. Robbins Simpson and French Cameron Simpson, the sum of ten thousand dollars, this money to be paid over to them when Geo. Robbins Simpson shall have reached the

age of twenty-five years and when French Cameron Simpson shall have reached the age of twenty-five years. The remainder of my property to go to my wife Virginia Simpson as long as she remains my widow. In the event of her marrying then said remainder of my property is to be equally divided between my sons Geo. Robbins and French Cameron Simpson.

George Robbins Simpson died intestate and unmarried on August 24, 1934. French Cameron Simpson died January 27, 1940, leaving a will whereby he devised and bequeathed his entire estate to his widow, Paulette Dickson, the plaintiff and appellant in this case. Virginia Simpson, widow of George L. Simpson, died March 19, 1944, without having remarried. Her will left her entire residuary estate to Alexandria Hospital, Inc.

Dickson argued that George L. Simpson created a defeasible life estate in Virginia Simpson, one-half of which, at the death of Virginia Simpson, passed to Paulette Dickson, as sole beneficiary under the will of her deceased husband, French Cameron Simpson. Alexandria Hospital contended that George L. Simpson's will created a defeasible fee simple in Virginia Simpson, and because Virginia Simpson having died without remarrying, a fee simple title to the residuum passed to it by her will. The trial court held that Virginia Simpson took a defeasible fee simple estate, which became absolute when she died without having remarried, and dismissed the complaint. The Court of Appeals affirmed that ruling.

Virginia's common law, as modified by statute, applied. A Virginia statute provided: "Where any real estate is conveyed, devised, or granted to any person without any words of limitation, such devise, conveyance, or grant shall be construed to pass the . . . whole estate or interest which the testator or grantor had power to dispose of in such real estate, unless a contrary intention shall appear by the will, conveyance, or grant." The court relied on four facts to conclude that George L. Simpson's intent was to give his widow

> a fee simple, defeasible only by her remarriage. . . . [In his will,] which testator himself wrote, . . . (1) he provided that there be no appraisement, (2) he appointed his wife his executrix, (3) he provided that she give no security, and (4) he devised to his wife, in fee simple, his residence, including its furniture and contents. He would hardly have provided that there be no appraisement if he had wished his wife to be accountable to his sons for the residuum of his estate. The fact that he appointed her his executrix, without security, and gave her outright his home with all its contents, strongly indicates not only his love for her, but his trust in her loyalty and good judgment. The testator then made specific devises of $10,000.00 to each of his sons, payable to them when they reached the age of twenty-five. This would seem to indicate that it was the testator's intention to give each son $10,000.00 with which to start his business career, and rely upon his wife to make such provision for them from the residuary estate as in her judgment might be wise and proper. In the event of a diversion of her affections by remarriage, the testator specifically provided that the residuum of his estate should go to his sons.

The court quoted with approval from a legal encyclopedia: "A devise to a testator's widow, which is absolute except for a provision terminating the estate, or providing for a gift over, in the event of her remarriage, creates a defeasible fee subject to be defeated by her remarriage. .... It is generally held that, where an estate has been devised in fee, subject to be defeated by the happening of some future event or contingency, if the happening of such event or contingency becomes impossible of occurrence, the defeasible fee becomes a fee simple absolute...."

Thus, the court concluded that George L. Simpson had created a defeasible fee simple title to the residuum in the widow, Virginia Simpson, which became a fee simple absolute when she died without having remarried.

    b. Tillerson v. Taylor, 282 Mo. 204 (1920). In 1888 Joseph Montgomery died testate, survived by his wife, Edna Montgomery, and nine siblings, but no children or other lineal descendants. Joseph Montgomery's will provided:

> ... I give and bequeath unto my esteemed wife, Edna Montgomery, all my property, both real and personal ..., to have and to hold the same and enjoy during her widowhood or so long as she remains my widow. If she remarries or in the event of her remarrying again, I desire that all the property should be divided equally between my brothers and sisters and my wife and her brothers and sisters all sharing alike and equal with my wife....

Edna Montgomery never remarried and died in 1917. In her will she left her property to her cousin Julia Taylor. Joseph Montgomery's siblings claimed that they owned certain real estate that had passed from Joseph to Edna on the theory that Joseph had created a life estate in Edna with a remainder in his siblings. Julia Taylor asserted that she owned the realty because Joseph Montgomery's will created a fee simple in Edna, defeasible in favor of his siblings if Edna remarried; but since Edna had not remarried Edna's interest became a fee simple absolute and thus passed via her will to Julia Taylor.

A Missouri statute provided:

> In all devises of lands or other estate in this State, in which the words "heirs and assigns," or "heirs and assigns forever," are omitted, and no expressions are contained in such will whereby it shall appear that such devise was intended to convey an estate for life only, and no further devise be made of the devised premises, to take effect after the death of the devisee to whom the same shall be given, it shall be understood to be the intention of the testator thereby to devise an absolute estate in the same, and shall convey an estate in fee simple to the devisee, for all such devised premises.

The court reasoned that the statute makes "a devise which otherwise would pass the fee, will [pass] only an estate for life if expressions are contained in the will which show the testator intended to give no greater estate than one for life, or if there is a devise over of the property after the death of the first taker." Because Joseph Montgomery's will used the expressions "to have and to hold the same and enjoy during her widowhood," and, "so long as she remains my widow," "in the clause wherein the gift to her is made, as a definition of the quantity of the estate given[, the will created in Edna] only an estate for life, and apter words for that purpose could not be chosen." Taylor's counsel argued that "an intestacy would result as to the remainder of the husband's estate, if she did not marry again, and as the law leans against intestacy, such an interpretation of the will is to be avoided." But, said the court, the "presumption that a testator intended to dispose of his whole estate and to die intestate as to none of it, must give way, when the words of a will are inconsistent with a purpose to give more than a life estate; and all the stronger is the rule when the words used have always been treated as passing a life estate."

In each of these cases property was left to a surviving spouse "so long as she remains my widow."[9] Yet, the two courts ascribe opposite legal results to this declaration of the testator's intent. Are the facts relied upon in *Dickson* sufficiently different from those in *Tillerson* to justify the result? Are the differences between the Virginia and Missouri statutes sufficient to produce different results? A good lesson to be derived from these cases is to be explicit about the estates which a grantor intends to create. Don't leave it up to the courts to do it for you or your client.

2. *More on Intent and Valuation of a Life Estate.* In *White*, the Tennessee Supreme Court, relying on the statutory presumptions, tentatively concluded that Jessie Lide had devised to Evelyn White a fee simple absolute, but then dismissed Jessie's directive that the house not be sold as an invalid restraint on the fee simple absolute she had created. Does this simply beg the question of whether Jessie actually intended to create a fee simple absolute? Is it implausible to construe the command that the house not be sold as an emphatic way for Jessie to ensure that Evelyn has a place in which to live for the remainder of her life? On that construction, is it so clear that Jessie created a fee simple absolute?

But dig a little deeper into Jessie's intent. It is reasonably clear that Jessie wanted to provide a home for Evelyn for the remainder of her life, yet we learn that Evelyn is the plaintiff and joined with the defendants in seeking to sell the home. The Chancellor found that Evelyn had a life estate and ordered the property sold, with the sale proceeds to be divided between Evelyn, as the life tenant, and the holders of the reversion. So Evelyn should receive a lump sum equal to the value of her life estate. Will this be enough to effectuate Jessie's intent to provide a home for Evelyn?

To answer this we need to know how this division is to be made. It can only be done by deciding what proportion of the proceeds are attributable to each estate, but how is this to be done? Because the life estate will expire at the end of Evelyn's life, one can make an actuarial computation of its duration, based on Evelyn's actuarial life expectancy. But that is not enough data. Here's why. Assume that Jessie's house is worth $10,000 (recall that it was dilapidated and this case arose in the late 1970s, before several decades of feverish speculation and inflation of house prices culminated in the bursting of the Great Housing Bubble in 2008). If the house is sold, the life tenant is

9. The question of whether the limitation terminating the defeasible estate upon remarriage is a void restraint upon marriage was not addressed by either of these cases because, although such limitations or conditions are generally void, they are valid if imposed to provide support to the surviving spouse until remarriage, rather than simply to hinder remarriage, See note 3 following *Mahrenholz*, in section E, Defeasible Estates. Knost v. Knost, 229 Mo. 170, 178 (1910), decided some years prior to *Tillerson*, provides a delicious reflection upon the sexism implicit in exempting estates defeasible upon remarriage granted to widows, but not to widowers, from the general rule of invalidity of restraints upon marriage.

entitled to the income from the proceeds for the duration of her life, but in order to calculate the expected income we need to assume a rate of return from investment of the proceeds. The investment must be prudent because the corpus must be passed on intact to the remaindermen, so let us assume that the proceeds are invested in a government obligation that has a maturity date coinciding with the actuarial demise of the life tenant. Let's assume that Evelyn is 75 years old. Her actuarial life expectancy is 12.43 years, which for ease of illustration we will round down to 12 years. (Maybe she is 75 years and six months of age; months matter in these calculations.) As of August 2010, the yield on a U.S. Treasury obligation maturing in 10 years is 2.65%. Let's round that up to 3% to account for the 12 year life expectancy. Now we can compute that Evelyn will receive $300 per year for each of the next 12 years. But we cannot simply multiply 300 by 12, because we are trying to ascertain what portion of $10,000 that is available now belongs to Evelyn. To do this we need to compute a sum that, when invested at 3% annually, will produce $300 per year but will be exhausted at the end of 12 years—the price of an annuity for that period. To calculate that price we must keep in mind that a dollar received a year from now is not worth as much as one received today, because if you had it today you could invest it and earn interest. (You could also spend it on café latte, but that would be improvident.) Thus, we ask the question: How much money today is needed, when invested at 3%, to produce a dollar a year from now? The answer is 97.1 cents. Then we ask the question: How much money today is needed, when invested at 3%, to produce a dollar two years from now? 94.3 cents. We add these amounts for each of the 12 years and we have a sum of $9.954. But this is for $1; we want to know how much is needed now to produce an annuity of $300 for 12 years, so we multiply $300 by $9.954 and the result is $2,986.20. The remaining $7,023.80 of the $10,000 sale proceeds goes to the holders of the reversion.

Does this exercise shed any light on Jessie's intentions? Should it do so? Would (or should) it make any difference if Jessie's house was in the path of prime commercial development, and was worth $100,000, when otherwise it would only be worth $10,000?

3. Restraints on Alienation. The Tennessee Supreme Court accepts as axiomatic that a restraint on alienation of a fee simple absolute is void. Why? The court says that a restraint is "inconsistent with the incidents and nature" of a fee simple absolute and also that it is "contrary to public policy." Some states express this rule in an unhelpful tautology. See, e.g., Calif. Civil Code § 711: "Conditions restraining alienation, when repugnant to the interest created, are void." But this simply raises the question of why any interest, fee simple absolute or otherwise, should be held to possess the attribute of alienability. The problem is exacerbated when one considers the types of restraints.

Restraints may disable the grantee from the exercising the power to alienate, which is what the court thinks Jessie Lide had in mind, but there are two other types of restraints. A grantor may stipulate that alienation causes forfeiture of the estate alienated. Thus, *O* conveys Blackacre "to *A* so long as Blackacre is never alienated by *A*." *A* has a fee simple determinable and *O* has retained a possibility of reverter. This form of restraint is surely consistent with the "incidents and nature" of a fee simple determinable. A grantor could also extract a promise from the grantee that she will not alienate the estate transferred to her. Breach of the promise enables the grantor to seek damages or an injunction. Promissory restraints are common in leases but not otherwise.

Curiously enough, the prevailing rule with respect to donative transfers—gifts of property, whether by will or trust or other written instrument—is that all three of these restraints are treated the same way when imposed on a fee simple. Restatement of Property 2d (Donative Transfers) § 4.1 (1) provides that a disabling restraint is void with respect to any interest if it "would make it impossible for any period of time from the date of the donative transfer to transfer such interest." Section 4.2 (1) permits forfeiture restraints upon life estates, but otherwise invalidates forfeiture restraints "if the restraint, if effective, would make it impossible for any period of time from the date such interest becomes a present interest to transfer such interest without causing a forfeiture thereof." Section 4.3 treats promissory restraints identically to forfeiture restraints. Section 4.2 (2) details the circumstances under which a forfeiture or promissory restraint that is not absolute may be valid. Essentially, they are valid if limited in duration, or permit a variety of transfers, or prohibit transfer only to a limited number of persons, or have the effect of increasing the property's value, or are imposed on an interest that is not itself readily marketable even without the restraint, or are imposed on property that is not readily marketable. Note that these rules, which are advisory and not binding on any court (though influential), apply only to donative transfers. But who in his right mind would pay to acquire an estate that is burdened with an absolute, or even very significant, restraint on alienation? So if it is illogical to think that an absolute restraint on alienation of a presently possessory interest (other than a life estate) is repugnant to the nature of the interest, why is logical to think that a partial restraint on alienation of such an interest is consistent with the nature of that interest?

Recall that the court in *White* also stated that restraints on alienation are against public policy. The policy in question is to favor free alienability of estates in land, because unfettered transferability is critical to reallocation of resources. If *O* owns a shuttered auto assembly plant and *A* desires that facility to make solar panels, it is in the society's interest for that transfer to occur. If *A* wants *O*'s assembly plant to make hula hoops or pet rocks, it is still in the public interest to permit the transfer. A market economy presupposes that resources can be allocated easily and efficiently. When that cannot occur, the market economy is frustrated and economic activity is hampered.

MELMS v. PABST BREWING CO.

Supreme Court of Wisconsin
104 Wis. 7 (1899)

[In 1864 Charles Melms constructed a large home at a cost of $20,000, quite expensive for the era. Melms owned and operated a brewery adjacent to his home. In 1869 Melms died, devising to his widow a life estate in his home and a fee simple absolute in the brewery. Later, Melms's widow sold the home and the brewery to Pabst Brewing. By 1890 the character of the neighborhood had changed dramatically, such that it was no longer desirable for residential purposes. Breweries, factories, and railway tracks predominated, leaving the old Melms homestead as an isolated relic of a former residential quarter. The Melms homestead was twenty to thirty feet above street level. Because the Melms homestead could not be rented for enough to pay the taxes and insurance, Pabst Brewing demolished the building and graded the lot down to street level. At the time, Pabst was under the mistaken impression that it owned the Melms homestead in fee simple absolute.

"For the life of another"

The plaintiffs (were owners of the reversion that followed the life estate *pur autre vie* held by Pabst Brewing. In this suit they contended that Pabst had committed waste, and sought damages. In a non-jury trial, the trial judge found that the demolition and grading had increased the value of the property and, thus, there was no waste.]

Winslow, J., delivered the opinion of the court. *affirmed*

Our statutes recognize waste, and provide [for] the recovery of double damages therefor; but they do not define it. It may be either voluntary or permissive, and may be of houses, gardens, orchards, lands, or woods; but, in order to ascertain whether a given act constitutes waste or not, recourse must be had to the common law. . . . In the present case a large dwelling house, expensive when constructed, has been destroyed, and the ground has been graded down, by the owner of the life estate, in order to make the property serve business purposes. That these acts would constitute waste under ordinary circumstances cannot be doubted. It is not necessary to delve deeply into the Year Books, or philosophize extensively as to the meaning of early judicial utterances, in order to arrive at this conclusion. The following definition of waste was approved by this court in Bandlow v. Thieme, 53 Wis. 57 [(1881)]: "It may be defined to be any act or omission of duty by a tenant of land which does a lasting injury to the freehold, tends to the permanent loss of the owner of the fee, or to destroy or lessen the value of the inheritance, or to destroy the identity of the property, or impair the evidence of title." In the same case it was also said: "The damage being to the inheritance, and the heir or the reversioner having the right of action to recover it, imply that the injury must be of a lasting and permanent character." And in Brock v. Dole, 66 Wis. 142 [(1886)], it was also said that "any material change in the nature and character of the buildings made by the tenant is waste, although the value of the property should be enhanced by the alteration."

These recent judicial utterances in this court settle the general rules which govern waste, without difficulty, and it may be said, also, that these rules are in accord with the general current of the authorities elsewhere. But, while they are correct as general expressions of the law upon the subject, and were properly applicable to the cases under consideration, it must be remembered that they are general rules only, and, like most general propositions, are not to be accepted without limitation or reserve under any and all circumstances. Thus the ancient English rule which prevented the tenant from converting a meadow into arable land was early softened down, and the doctrine of meliorating waste was adopted, which, without changing the legal definition of waste, still allowed the tenant to change the course of husbandry upon the estate if such change be for the betterment of the estate. Bewes, Waste, 134 *et seq.*, and cases cited. Again, and in accordance with this same principle, the rule that any change in a building upon the premises constitutes waste has been greatly modified, even in England; and it is now well settled that, while such change may constitute technical waste, still it will not be enjoined in equity when it clearly appears that the change will be, in effect, a meliorating change which rather improves the inheritance than injures it. Doherty v. Allman, 3 App. Cas. 709; In re McIntosh, 61 Law J. Q.B. 164. Following the same general line of reasoning, it was early held in the United States that, while the English doctrine as to waste was a part of our common law, still the cutting of timber in order to clear up wild land and fit it for cultivation, if consonant with the rules of good husbandry, was not waste, although such acts would clearly have been waste in England. Tiedeman, Real Prop. (2d ed.), § 74; Rice, Mod. Law Real Prop. §§ 160, 161; Wilkinson v. Wilkinson, 59 Wis. 557 [(1884)].

These familiar examples of departure from ancient rules will serve to show that, while definitions have remained much the same, the law upon the subject of waste is not an unchanging and unchangeable code, which was crystallized for all time in the days of feudal tenures, but that it is subject to such reasonable modifications as may be demanded by the growth of civilization and varying conditions. And so it is now laid down that the same act may be waste in one part of the country while in another it is a legitimate use of the land, and that the usages and customs of each community enter largely into the settlement of the question. Tiedeman, Real Prop. (2d ed.), § 73. This is entirely consistent with, and in fact springs from, the central idea upon which the disability of waste is now, and always has been, founded, namely, the preservation of the property for the benefit of the owner of the future estate without *permanent* injury to it. This element will be found in all the definitions of waste, namely, that it must be an act resulting in permanent injury to the inheritance or future estate. It has been frequently said that this injury may consist either in diminishing the value of the inheritance, or increasing its burdens, or in destroying the identity of the property, or impairing the evidence of title.

The last element of injury so enumerated, while a cogent and persuasive one in former times, has lost most, if not all, of its force at the present time. It was important when titles were not registered, and descriptions of land were frequently dependent upon natural monuments or the uses to which the land was put; but since the universal adoption of accurate surveys and the establishment of the system of recording conveyances, there can be few acts which will impair any evidence of title.

But the principle that the reversioner or remainderman is ordinarily entitled to receive the identical estate, or, in other words, that the identity of the property is not to be destroyed, still remains, and it has been said that changes in the nature of buildings, though enhancing the value of the property, will constitute waste if they change the identity of the estate. Brock v. Dole, 66 Wis. 142 [(1886)]. This principle was enforced in the last-named case, where it was held that a tenant from year to year of a room in a frame building would be enjoined from constructing a chimney in the building against the objection of his landlord. The importance of this rule to the landlord or owner of the future estate cannot be denied. Especially is it valuable and essential to the protection of a landlord who rents his premises for a short time. He has fitted his premises for certain uses. He leases them for such uses, and he is entitled to receive them back at the end of the term still fitted for those uses; and he may well say that he does not choose to have a different property returned to him from that which he leased, even if, upon the taking of testimony, it might be found of greater value by reason of the change. Many cases will be found sustaining this rule; and that it is a wholesome rule of law, operating to prevent lawless acts on the part of tenants, cannot be doubted, nor is it intended to depart therefrom in this decision. The case now before us, however, bears little likeness to such a case, and contains elements so radically different from those present in Brock v. Dole that we cannot regard that case as controlling this one. . . .

The defendants are the grantees of a life estate, and their rights may continue for a number of years. The evidence shows that the property became valueless for the purpose of residence property as the result of the growth and development of a great city. Business and manufacturing interests advanced and surrounded the once elegant mansion, until it stood isolated and alone, standing upon just enough ground to support it, and surrounded by factories and railway tracks, absolutely undesirable as a residence and incapable of any use as business property. Here was a complete change of conditions, not produced by the tenant, but resulting from causes which none could control. Can it be reasonably or logically said that this entire change of condition is to be completely ignored, and the ironclad rule applied that the tenant can make no change in the uses of the property because he will destroy its identity? Must the tenant stand by and preserve the useless dwelling-house, so that he may at some future time turn it over to the reversioner, equally useless? Certainly, all the analogies are to the contrary. As we have before seen, the cutting of timber, which in England was considered waste, has become in this country an act which may be waste or not, according to the surrounding conditions and the rules of good husbandry; and the same rule applies to the change of a meadow to arable land. The changes of conditions which justify these departures from early inflexible rules are no more marked nor complete than is the change of conditions which destroys the value of residence property as such and renders it only useful for business purposes. Suppose the house in question had been so situated that it could have been remodeled into business property; would any court of equity have enjoined such remodeling under the circumstances here shown, or ought any court to render a judgment for damages for such an act?

Clearly, we think not. Again, suppose an orchard to have become permanently unproductive through disease or death of the trees, and the land to have become far more valuable, by reason of new conditions, as a vegetable garden or wheat field, is the life tenant to be compelled to preserve or renew the useless orchard, and forego the advantages to be derived from a different use? Or suppose a farm to have become absolutely unprofitable by reason of change of market conditions as a grain farm, but very valuable as a tobacco plantation, would it be waste for the life tenant to change the use accordingly, and remodel a now useless barn or granary into a tobacco shed? All these questions naturally suggest their own answer, and it is certainly difficult to see why, if change of conditions is so potent in the case of timber, orchards, or kind of crops, it should be of no effect in the case of buildings similarly affected.

It is certainly true that a case involving so complete a change of situation as regards buildings has been rarely, if ever, presented to the courts, yet we are not without authorities approaching very nearly to the case before us. Thus, in the case of Doherty v. Allman, 3 App. Cas. 709, . . . a court of equity refused an injunction preventing a tenant for a long term from changing storehouses into dwelling-houses, on the ground that by change of conditions the demand for storehouses had ceased and the property had become worthless, whereas it would be productive when fitted for dwelling-houses. Again, in the case of Sherrill v. Connor, 107 N.C. 630 [(1890)], which was an action for permissive waste against a tenant in dower,[10] who had permitted large barns and outbuildings upon a plantation to fall into decay, it was held that, as these buildings had been built before the Civil War to accommodate the operation of the plantation by slaves, it was not necessarily waste to tear them down, or allow them to remain unrepaired, after the war, when the conditions had completely changed by reason of the emancipation and the changed methods of use resulting therefrom; and that it became a question for the jury whether a prudent owner of the fee, if in possession, would have suffered the unsuitable barns and buildings to fall into decay, rather than incur the cost of repair. This last case is very persuasive and well reasoned, and it well states the principle which we think is equally applicable to the case before us. In the absence of any contract, express or implied, to use the property for a specified purpose, or to return it in the same condition in which it was received, a radical and permanent change of surrounding conditions, such as is presented in the case before us, must always be an important, and sometimes a controlling, consideration upon the question whether a physical change in the use or the buildings constitutes waste.

In the present case this consideration was regarded by the trial court as controlling, and we are satisfied that this is the right view. This case is not to be construed as justifying a tenant in making substantial changes in the leasehold property, or the buildings thereon, to suit his own whim

---

10. [Ed.] Dower was the common law analog to the spousal elective share. At the death of her husband, a wife was entitled to a life estate in one-third of the real property of which the husband was seised during their marriage. See Chapter Four.

or convenience, because, perchance, he may be able to show that the change is in some degree beneficial. Under all ordinary circumstances the landlord or reversioner, even in the absence of any contract, is entitled to receive the property at the close of the tenancy substantially in the condition in which it was when the tenant received it; but when, as here, there has occurred a complete and permanent change of surrounding conditions, which has deprived the property of its value and usefulness as previously used, the question whether a life tenant, not bound by contract to restore the property in the same condition in which he received it, has been guilty of waste in making changes necessary to make the property useful, is a question of fact for the jury under proper instructions, or for the court where, as in the present case, the question is tried by the court. [Affirmed.]

NOTES, QUESTIONS AND PROBLEMS

1. The Concept of Waste. Whenever two or more people have ownership interests of the same property, the possibility of conflict exists. This is true if *A* and *B* are concurrent owners—entitled to possess the same property at the same time—or if *A* has the right to present possession and *B* has the right to future possession. The former problem is discussed more thoroughly in Chapter Five; the latter problem occurs whenever a present possessory interest is followed by a future interest. In either case, though, the owner in possession has an incentive to maximize the present value of the stream of income that is associated with his possession. Thus, a life tenant may rationally seek to reap value from his possession without regard to the long term effects of his action. For example, the life tenant may plant crops intensively to maximize present revenue, even though this may ultimately result in soil exhaustion after his tenure ends. Or he may harvest timber before it reaches its optimum maturity. The law of waste operates to prevent this disproportionate allocation of the value of the asset.

As *Melms* indicates, the law of waste is highly contextual. In addition to the factors discussed in *Melms*, the nature of the ownership interests involved is an additional factor. Some present possessory interests are of short duration, as a leasehold from month-to-month or for a single year; others are of long duration, as a life estate held by a healthy, sober, prudent 18 year old, or a leasehold for 99 years. Some future interests that follow present possession are certain to become possessory; others make possession contingent on uncertain future events. (The details will become clear in Chapter Four.) The identity of the owners of some future interests are known, but other future interests are held by people as yet unknown. Should the law of waste be more restrictive of the present possessor when the present possessor's interest is short and the future interest is certain to become possessory? Conversely, should the law of waste permit a wider range of action for present possessors when the future interest holder is unknown, or future possession is uncertain or very remote?

2. Types of Waste. There are two distinct forms of waste: Affirmative waste and permissive waste. Affirmative waste results from voluntary actions that inflict substantial injury on the estate, almost always taking the form of a substantial reduction in the value of the property. Permissive waste results from a failure to act, with the result that the property suffers significant damage.

Some voluntary acts that substantially reduce the value of the property are, nevertheless, not waste. For example, if an activity that drains value from the property exists at the time the life estate is created, the life tenant may continue to extract value to the detriment of the remainderman. The principal example is mineral extraction. If a mine exists when the life estate is created, the life tenant can continue to exploit it. See Westmoreland Coal Company's Appeal, 85 Pa. 344, 346 (1877). "The reasoning behind the doctrine is that if the life tenant did open new mines, he would be committing waste, whereas if he simply continues to use mines of the former owner, he is then merely enjoying the use of the land in the same manner in which it was enjoyed when his estate came into being." Doverspike v. Chambers, 357 Pa.Super. 539, 544 (1986).

As seen in *Melms* some voluntary acts that are destructive but which increase the value of the property are not waste, although sometimes this phenomenon is called meliorating waste. In accord with *Melms* is New York, Ontario and Western Railway Co. v. Livingston, 238 N.Y. 300, 307 (1924), where the New York Court of Appeals, speaking through Justice Cardozo, said: "We do not overlook the argument that a life tenant who turns a farm into a railroad yard commits an act of waste. The effect of the so-called waste in this instance was to add $49,000 to the value. The act, if waste at all, was at the utmost meliorating waste, improving instead of injuring the remainderman's inheritance." But see Brokaw v. Fairchild, 245 N.Y.S. 402 (App. Div. 1930).

3. *Problems.*

a. Suppose that *O*, owner of Greenacre in fee simple absolute, devises Greenacre for life to *A*, then to the Nature Conservancy. Greenacre is an ecological treasure, harboring rare but legally unprotected flora and fauna. *A* proposes to build an apartment complex on Greenacre, which is conceded will increase its market value from $100,000 to $1.0 million. Should the Nature Conservancy be entitled to enjoin the construction on the ground that it constitutes waste? Should the answer be different if *A* has already built the apartment complex and the Nature Conservancy is seeking damages for alleged waste?

b. Suppose that *O*, owner of Blackacre in fee simple absolute, devises Blackacre to *A* for life, then to *B* and her heirs. Blackacre is an exceptionally fine example of the architectural work of H.H. Richardson, the 19th century architect whose work often featured Romanesque elements. In his will *O* adds that he is giving *B* the remainder in Blackacre because *B* appreciates Richardson's work and is likely to preserve it. *A* proposes to convert Blackacre to law offices (with only minimal alterations to its interior) and to build a large addition in the steel-and-glass style of Philip Johnson's "Glass House." The evidence is undisputed that these changes will increase the market value of Blackacre to $3.5 million from its present value of $1.0 million. Should *B* be entitled to enjoin the changes on the ground that they constitute waste?

Should the answer be different if A has built the addition and B is seeking damages for alleged waste? $\sf N$

NOTE: LEGAL OR EQUITABLE LIFE ESTATES?

Life estates may be legal or equitable. For example, a legal life estate in Blackacre occurs when O, owner of Blackacre in fee simple absolute, transfers it to A for life. An equitable life estate in Blackacre occurs when O, owner of Blackacre, transfers it in trust to T, as trustee, for the benefit of A. Usually, however, an equitable life estate will be more precise, as for example if O transfers Blackacre in trust to T, to pay the income for life to A and so much of the principal as may be necessary to provide for the health, education, and maintenance of A. Almost all life estates created today are equitable.

There are multiple reasons why equitable life estates are preferable to legal life estates. Here is a problem to help you see why this so.

Recall the facts of White v. Brown. Suppose that Evelyn White were held to own a life estate. Evelyn wanted to sell the house and the reversion holders were willing to join in that sale to deliver a fee simple absolute to the buyer. (The combination of Evelyn's life estate and the reversion in fee simple absolute equal a present possessory fee simple absolute.) Suppose, however, that only Evelyn wished to sell the house. By herself, she could only sell her life estate, for which there are unlikely to be many buyers, or at least many buyers at a price that would be attractive to Evelyn. Further suppose that Evelyn's income is meager, so modest that she is reduced to severe penury, but the house is rapidly appreciating in value because it lies in the path of rapid commercial development. Evelyn asks a court to order the sale of the entire fee simple absolute (the combination of her life estate and the reversion), and to place the proceeds under the management of the court so that she can receive the income from the proceeds, while preserving the corpus for the reversion holders. (Assume that the proceeds are invested in blue-chip common stocks that pay a dividend; Evelyn would receive the dividend income—an amount sufficient to enable her to escape grinding poverty—and the capital appreciation, if any, would accrue to the benefit of the reversion.) The reversion holders object because they contend that a sale is premature; the property will continue to appreciate in value at a rate that exceeds whatever rate of capital appreciation can be expected with respect to the invested proceeds. In short, the reversion holders think the real estate is a better long term investment than blue-chip common stocks. What should the court do?

In Baker v. Weedon, 262 So.2d 641 (Miss. 1972), the Mississippi Supreme Court accepted the premise that such a sale could be forced when it "is necessary for the best interest of all the parties," but reversed a chancery court decision to order such a sale, remanding the case to the lower court to consider a partial sale in the event the life tenant and the remaindermen could not agree to join together to borrow sufficient funds, secured by a mortgage on the property, to provide an adequate income for the life tenant. But if the life tenant and the future interest holders cannot agree to sell or mortgage the property, how is a court to determine what is in the best interest of *all* parties? What is in the best interest of the life tenant may not be in the best interest of the reversion holder, and the reverse may be equally true.

These problems can be overcome with an equitable life estate. The trustee, who owns the property in fee simple absolute may sell or lease the property, and he may borrow funds, pledging the property as security via a mortgage. A legal life tenant may only sell her life estate and has no power to lease it for a term longer than her life. Nor is it very likely that a lender would accept a mortgage of a life estate as adequate security for a loan. Problems of waste can be minimized because the trustee has fiduciary obligations to each of the life tenant and the remainderman, and the trust document can specify how to manage assets, such as minerals or timber, that are subject to depletion.

Moreover, the trustee may be the life tenant. Of course, in that circumstance the life tenant, as trustee, is clothed with a fiduciary obligation to the remainderman, but the flexible management described above can be accomplished without violating that fiduciary duty. Legal life estates in personal property are even more problematic. Personal property, particularly marketable securities, are easily moved and sold. What security does the remainderman have to protect against the consumption of the asset by the life tenant? The law of waste, you may say, but what value is an action for damages against a life tenant who has squandered all his assets, including the marketable securities in which he owned only a life estate, at the roulette table? But the transferee of the securities only has a life estate, so the remainderman can trace the securities into the hands of the possessor once the life tenant has died, and claim them from the possessor. Perhaps, but how easy is this going to be with respect to a 100 share block of Intel that has changed hands many thousands of times after the life tenant has disposed of it? To address this problem some states impose by law a trust obligation on the life tenant, or require the life tenant to post security or account periodically to a court for the assets.

The short answer to these problems is: Never create a legal life estate; only create life estates as beneficial interests in a trust.

E.   DEFEASIBLE ESTATES

While any estate may be defeasible—cut short—upon the occurrence of a specified condition, the focus of this section is upon defeasible fees simple. There are three types of defeasible fees: fee simple determinable, fee simple subject to condition subsequent, and fee simple subject to an executory limitation. Refer to Examples 3.2, 3.3, and 3.4, supra.

The fee simple determinable automatically ends when the specified condition occurs. For example, *O*, who owns Blackacre in fee simple absolute, conveys Blackacre "to *A* and her heirs so long as Blackacre is used for agricultural purposes." *A* has a fee simple determinable and *O* has retained a possibility of reverter. *A* and her successors in interest are entitled to possess Blackacre, perhaps forever, if Blackacre is continually devoted to agriculture. But if Blackacre is converted into apartments the fee simple in *A* and her successors automatically ceases, and *O*'s possibility of reverter becomes a fee simple absolute. From the moment that Blackacre is no longer used for agriculture the continued occupation of Blackacre by *A* or her successors is wrongful.

The fee simple subject to a condition subsequent does not end automatically when the specified condition occurs. The grantor, who holds a power of termination (sometimes called a right of entry) must exercise that right to terminate the fee simple subject to a condition subsequent. For example, *O*, who owns Blackacre in fee simple absolute, conveys Blackacre "to *A* and her heirs; provided, however, that if Blackacre is not used for agricultural purposes *O* may re-enter and take possession." *A* has a fee simple subject to condition subsequent and *O* has retained a power of termination, or right of entry. As was true of the fee simple determinable, *A* and her successors in interest are entitled to possess Blackacre, perhaps forever, if Blackacre is continually devoted to agriculture. But if Blackacre is converted into apartments the fee simple in *A* and her successors does not automatically cease. Until *O* exercises his power of termination (right of entry) *A*'s occupation of Blackacre is not wrongful; her fee simple continues until *O* takes action to exercise his right to recover possession in fee simple absolute.

Given these consequences, it is important to understand why one expression of the same condition creates a fee simple determinable and a different expression creates a fee simple subject to condition subsequent. The theory is that the grantor in the fee simple determinable has never parted with all that he owns; he has only provisionally transferred his interest. This is thought to be expressed by such phrases as "so long as . . .," or "until . . .," or "during . . .," or "while . . .," that are part of the grant itself. The grantor has only parted with his property so long as a future event does not occur, or only until a future event occurs. By contrast, if a grantor linguistically parts with his entire interest and then adds, as an afterthought or addendum, that he has a right to get the property back if some future event occurs, the grantor is seen as having parted with all that he owned, and only after that transfer has he stipulated that he has a right to recover the estate upon the occurrence of the future event. This is thought to be expressed by such language following the grant to *A* as "provided, that if . . ." or "but if . . .," or "on the condition that . . .," or "however, if. . . ." Another way to distinguish the two is to think that the fee simple determinable employs a condition precedent to the transfer and the fee simple subject to condition subsequent uses a condition subsequent to the transfer. This might be seen more clearly if you imagine the grant in the fee simple determinable to be phrased: "so long as Blackacre is used for agricultural purposes, to *A*." A visual metaphor that may help is to imagine a person giving a tennis ball to another person. If a string from the tennis ball remains attached to the grantor and unwinds as he gives the ball to the grantee, and stays attached even as the grantee walks away with the ball, you have a fee simple determinable. But if the tennis ball has no string attached to it, but instead the grantor has kept an infinitely extendable hook to snatch the ball back after the gift is complete, you have a fee simple subject to a condition subsequent.

Note that in each of the fee simple determinable and the fee simple subject to condition subsequent the grantor retains the future interest that can or will become possessory upon occurrence of the stated condition. When the grantor does not retain that future interest, but instead transfers it to another transferee *at the time the fee simple is created*, the fee is called a fee simple subject to an executory limitation. However, if a grantor transfers his possibility of reverter or power of termination *after* its creation, it is still called by its original name and continues to have the attributes it had when owned by the grantor. An example of the fee simple subject to an executory limitation is a conveyance by *O*, owner of Blackacre in fee simple absolute, "to *A* and her heirs so long as Blackacre is used for agricultural purposes, and then to *B* and her heirs." A fee simple subject to an executory limitation would also be created by a conveyance of Blackacre "to *A* and her heirs; provided, however, that if Blackacre is not used for agricultural purposes, to *B* and her heirs." In each of these cases *A* would own a fee simple subject to an executory limitation and *B* would own an executory interest. (The reason these future interests are called executory interests will be explained in Chapter Four.) If the condition occurs, the fee will automatically cease and the executory interest will become a possessory fee simple absolute. This is true even if the language of the condition subsequent is used to create the interests.

But, to repeat, if a transferee acquires the grantor's future interest it still has the qualities it originally had. That means that a transferee of a power of termination must exercise the power to terminate the fee simple subject to a condition subsequent. For example, if *O* conveys Blackacre "to *A* so long as Blackacre is used for agricultural purposes," and later conveys to *B* his possibility of reverter, *B* owns a possibility of reverter that will automatically become possessory upon breach of the condition. If *O* conveys Blackacre "to *A* and her heirs; provided, however, that if Blackacre is not used for agricultural purposes *O* may re-enter and take possession," and then *O* later conveys to *B* his power of termination, *B* owns a power of termination which he must exercise to retake possession and terminate *A*'s fee simple subject to a condition subsequent. Note that under English common law neither the possibility of reverter or power of termination (right of entry) could be transferred during life nor by will, but could only pass by inheritance. That rule has largely been eliminated in American states, and most states now permit inter vivos transfer of these interests, but not all do so. Some, such as Illinois, adhere to the common law rule. See § 765 ILCS 330/1. Some only permit transfer to the defeasible fee owner (a release); some permit transfer of the possibility of reverter but not the power of termination (right of entry); and Colorado, Maine, and Massachusetts destroy powers of termination upon the attempt to convey the interest. The latter rule is illogical; as the Iowa Supreme Court observed in rejecting this doctrine: "It seems rather fantastic to us, that a conveyance which is ineffective to convey what it attempts to convey is nevertheless an effective means of destroying it." Reichard v. Chicago, B. & Q. Ry. Co., 231 Iowa 563, 576 (1942). See also Powell on Real Property § 21.02.

MAHRENHOLZ v. COUNTY BOARD OF SCHOOL TRUSTEES OF LAWRENCE COUNTY

Appellate Court of Illinois
93 Ill.App.3d 366 (1981)

JONES, J., delivered the opinion of the court.

This case involves an action to quiet title to real property located in Lawrence County, Illinois. Its resolution depends on the judicial construction of language in a conveyance of that property. The case is before us on the pleadings, plaintiffs' third amended complaint having been dismissed by a final order. The pertinent facts are taken from the pleadings.

On March 18, 1941, W. E. and Jennie Hutton executed a warranty deed in which they conveyed certain land, to be known here as the Hutton School grounds, to the trustees of School District No. 1, the predecessors of the defendants in this action. The deed provided that "this land to be used for school purpose only; otherwise to revert to Grantors herein." W. E. Hutton died intestate on July 18, 1951, and Jennie Hutton died intestate on February 18, 1969. The Huttons left as their only legal heir their son Harry E. Hutton. The property conveyed by the Huttons became the site of the Hutton School. Community Unit School District No. 20 succeeded to the grantee of the deed and held classes in the building constructed upon the land until May 30, 1973. After that date, children were transported to classes held at other facilities operated by the District. The District has used the property since then for storage purposes only.

Earl and Madeline Jacqmain executed a warranty deed on October 9, 1959, conveying to the plaintiffs over 390 acres of land in Lawrence County and which included the 40–acre tract from which the Hutton School grounds were taken. When and from whom the Jacqmains acquired the land is not shown and is of no consequence in this appeal. The deed from the Jacqmains to the plaintiffs excepted the Hutton School grounds, but purported to convey the disputed future interest. . . .

On May 7, 1977, Harry E. Hutton, son and sole heir of W. E. and Jennie Hutton, conveyed to the plaintiffs all of his interest in the Hutton School land. This document was filed in the recorder's office of Lawrence County on September 7, 1977. On September 6, 1977, Harry Hutton disclaimed his interest in the property in favor of the defendants. The disclaimer was in the form of a written document entitled "Disclaimer and Release." It contained the legal description of the Hutton School grounds and recited that Harry E. Hutton disclaimed and released any possibility of reverter or right of re-entry for condition broken, or other similar interest, in favor of the County Board of School Trustees for Lawrence County, Illinois, successor to the Trustees of School District No. 1 of

Lawrence County, Illinois. The document further recited that it was made for the purpose of releasing and extinguishing any right Harry E. Hutton may have had in the "interest retained by W. E. Hutton and Jennie Hutton ... in that deed to the Trustees of School District No. 1, Lawrence County, Illinois dated March 18, 1941, and filed on the same date...." The disclaimer was filed in the recorder's office of Lawrence County on October 4, 1977....

The plaintiffs filed a third amended complaint on September 13, 1978. This complaint recited the interests acquired from the Jacqmains and from Harry Hutton. On March 21, 1979, the trial court entered an order dismissing this complaint. In the order the court found that the "warranty deed dated March 18, 1941, from W.E. Hutton and Jennie Hutton to the Trustees of School District No. 1, conveying land here concerned, created a fee simple subject to a condition subsequent followed by the right of re-entry for condition broken, rather than a determinable fee followed by a possibility of reverter."

Plaintiffs have perfected an appeal to this court. The basic issue presented by this appeal is whether the trial court correctly concluded that the plaintiffs could not have acquired any interest in the school property from the Jacqmains or from Harry Hutton. Resolution of this issue must turn upon the legal interpretation of the language contained in the March 18, 1941, deed from W. E. and Jennie Hutton to the Trustees of School District No. 1: "this land to be used for school purpose only; otherwise to revert to Grantors herein." In addition to the legal effect of this language we must consider the alienability of the interest created and the effect of subsequent deeds.

The parties appear to be in agreement that the 1941 deed from the Huttons conveyed a defeasible fee simple estate to the grantee, and gave rise to a future interest in the grantors, and that it did not convey a fee simple absolute, subject to a covenant.[11] The fact that provision was made for forfeiture of the estate conveyed should the land cease to be used for school purposes suggests that this view is correct. The future interest remaining in this grantor or his estate can only be a possibility of reverter or a right of re-entry for condition broken. As neither interest may be transferred by will nor by *inter vivos* conveyance (Ill. Rev. Stat. 1979, ch. 30, par. 37b) [now § 765 ILCS 330/1], and as the land was being used for school purposes in 1959 when the Jacqmains transferred their interest in the school property to the plaintiffs, the trial court correctly ruled that the plaintiffs could not have acquired any interest in that property from the Jacqmains by the deed of October 9, 1959.

---

11. [Ed.] Chapter Ten discusses servitudes—contractual arrangements among landowners that limit land use but which are enforceable by or against subsequent possessors. One type of servitude is a covenant. Here, the court rejects the idea that the condition expressed in the Hutton deed was only a promise about land use attached to a fee simple absolute. As you will learn in Chapter Ten, the remedies for breach of such a promise are either an injunction or damages, but not forfeiture of the estate, which is the automatic or discretionary result of breach of the condition in a defeasible fee.

Consequently this court must determine whether the plaintiffs could *Issue* have acquired an interest in the Hutton School grounds from Harry Hutton. The resolution of this issue depends on the construction of the language of the 1941 deed of the Huttons to the school district. As urged by the defendants, and as the trial court found, that deed conveyed a fee simple subject to a condition subsequent, followed by a right of re-entry for condition broken. As argued by the plaintiffs, on the other hand, the deed conveyed a fee simple determinable followed by a possibility of reverter. In either case, the grantor and his heirs retain an interest in the property which may become possessory if the condition is broken. We emphasize here that although ... rights of re-entry for condition broken and possibilities of reverter are neither alienable nor devisable, they are inheritable. (Deverick v. Bline (1949), 404 Ill. 302, 89 N.E.2d 43.) ... If the grantor had a possibility of reverter, he or his heirs become the owner of the property by operation of law as soon as the condition is broken. If he has a right of re-entry for condition broken, he or his heirs become the owner of the property only after they act to retake the property.

It is alleged, and we must accept, that classes were last held in the Hutton School in 1973. Harry Hutton, sole heir of the grantors, did not act to legally retake the premises but instead conveyed his interest in that land to the plaintiffs in 1977. If Harry Hutton had only a naked right of re-entry for condition broken, then he could not be the owner of that property until he had legally re-entered the land. Since he took no steps for a legal entry, he had only a right of re-entry in 1977, and that right cannot be conveyed *inter vivos*. On the other hand, if Harry Hutton had a possibility of reverter in the property, then he owned the school property as soon as it ceased to be used for school purposes. Therefore, assuming (1) that cessation of classes constitutes "abandonment of school purposes" on the land, (2) that the conveyance from Harry Hutton to the plaintiffs was legally correct, and (3) that the conveyance was not pre-empted by Hutton's disclaimer in favor of the school district, the plaintiffs could have acquired an interest in the Hutton School grounds if Harry Hutton had inherited a possibility of reverter from his parents.

The difference between a fee simple determinable (or determinable fee) and a fee simple subject to a condition subsequent, is solely a matter of judicial interpretation of the words of a grant. As Blackstone explained, there is a fundamental theoretical difference between a conditional estate, such as a fee simple subject to a condition subsequent, and a limited estate, such as a fee simple determinable.

A distinction is however made between a *condition in deed* and a *limitation*, which Littleton denominates also a *condition in law*. For when an estate is so expressly confined and limited by the words of it's [*sic*] creation, that it cannot endure for any longer time than till the contingency happens upon which the estate is to fail, this is denominated a *limitation*: as when land is granted to a man, *so long as* he is parson of Dale, or *while* he continues unmarried, or *until* out of the rents and profits he shall have made £500, and the like. In such case the estate determines as soon as the contingency happens, (when he ceases to be parson, marries a wife, or has received the £500) and the next subsequent estate, which depends upon such determination, becomes immediately vested, without any act to be done by him who is next in expectancy. But when an estate is, strictly speaking, upon *condition in deed* (as if granted expressly *upon condition* to be void upon the payment of £40. by the grantor, or *so that* the grantee continues unmarried, or *provided* he goes to York, etc.) the law permits it to endure beyond the time when such contingency happens, unless the grantor or his heir or assigns take advantage of the breach of the condition, and make either an entry or a claim in order to avoid the estate. (Emphasis in original.) 2 W. Blackstone, Commentaries *155.

A fee simple determinable may be thought of as a limited grant, while a fee simple subject to a condition subsequent is an absolute grant to which a condition is appended. In other words, a grantor should give a fee simple determinable if he intends to give property for so long as it is needed for the purposes for which it is given and no longer, but he should employ a fee simple subject to a condition subsequent if he intends to compel compliance with a condition by penalty of a forfeiture. Following Blackstone's examples, the Huttons would have created a fee simple determinable if they had allowed the school district to retain the property *so long as* or *while* it was used for school purposes, or *until* it ceased to be so used. Similarly, a fee simple subject to a condition subsequent would have arisen had the Huttons given the land *upon condition that* or *provided that* it be used for school purposes. In the 1941 deed, though the Huttons gave the land "to be used for school purpose only, otherwise to revert to Grantors herein," no words of temporal limitation, or terms of express condition, were used in the grant. The plaintiffs argue that the word "only" should be construed as a limitation rather than a condition. The defendants respond that where ambiguous language is used in a deed, the courts of Illinois have expressed a constructional preference for a fee simple subject to a condition subsequent. (Storke v. Penn Mutual Life Insurance Co. (1945), 390 Ill. 619, 61 N.E.2d 552.) Both sides refer us to cases involving deeds which contain language analogous to the 1941 grant in this case.

We believe that a close analysis of the wording of the original grant shows that the grantors intended to create a fee simple determinable followed by a possibility of reverter. Here, the use of the word "only" immediately following the grant "for school purpose" demonstrates that the Huttons wanted to give the land to the school district only as long as it was needed and no longer. The language "this land to be used for school purpose only" is an example of a grant which contains a limitation within the granting clause. It suggests a limited grant, rather than a full grant subject to a condition, and thus, both theoretically and linguistically, gives rise to a fee simple determinable.

The second relevant clause furnishes plaintiffs' position with additional support. It cannot be argued that the phrase "otherwise to revert to grantors herein" is inconsistent with a fee simple subject to a condition subsequent. Nor does the word "revert" automatically create a possibility of reverter. But, in combination with the preceding phrase, the provisions by which possession is returned to the grantors seem to trigger a mandatory return rather than a permissive return because it is not stated that the grantor "may" re-enter the land.

The terms used in the 1941 deed, although imprecise, were designed to allow the property to be used for a single purpose, namely, for "school purpose." The Huttons intended to have the land back if it were ever used otherwise. Upon a grant of exclusive use followed by an express provision for reverter when that use ceases, courts and commentators have agreed that a fee simple determinable, rather than a fee simple subject to a condition subsequent, is created. (1 Simes & Smith, The Law of Future Interests § 286, at 344 n.58 (2d ed. 1956).) Our own research has uncovered cases from other jurisdictions and sources in which language very similar to that in the Hutton deed has been held to create a fee simple determinable:

> [A conveyance] "for the use, intent and purpose of a site for a School House . . . [and] whenever the said School District removes the School House from said tract of land or whenever said School House ceases to be used as the Public School House . . . then the said Trust shall cease and determine and the said land shall revert to [the grantor and his heirs.]" (Consolidated School District v. Walter (1954), 243 Minn. 159, 160, 66 N.W.2d 881, 882.)

> "[I]t being absolutely understood that when said land ceases to be used for school purposes it is to revert to the above grantor, his heirs." (United States v. 1119.15 Acres of Land (E.D. Ill. 1942), 44 F. Supp. 449.)

> "That I, S.S. Gray (Widower), for and in consideration of the sum of Donation to Wheeler School District to be used by said Wheeler Special School District for school and church purposes and to revert to me should school and church be discontinued or moved." (Williams v. Kirby School District No. 32 (1944), 207 Ark. 458, 461, 181 S.W.2d 488, 490.)

> "It is understood and agreed that if the above described land is abandoned by the said second parties and not used for school purposes then the above described land reverts to the party of the first part." (School District No. 6 v. Russell (1964), 156 Colo. 75, 76, 396 P.2d 929, 930.) . . .

Thus, authority from this State and others indicates that the grant in the Hutton deed did in fact create a fee simple determinable. We are not persuaded by the cases cited by the defendants for the terms of conveyance in those cases distinguish them from the facts presented here. . . .

The estate created in Latham v. Illinois Central R.R. Co. (1912), 253 Ill. 93, 97 N.E. 254, was held to be a fee simple subject to a condition subsequent. Land was conveyed to a railroad in return for the railroad's agreement to erect and maintain a passenger depot and a freight depot on the premises. The deed was made to the grantee, "their successors and assigns forever, for the uses and purposes hereinafter mentioned, and for none other." Those purposes were limited to "railroad purposes only." The deed provided "that in case of non-user of said premises so conveyed for the uses and purposes aforesaid, that then and in that case the title to said premises shall revert back to [the grantors], their heirs, executors, administrators and assigns." The property was granted to the railroad to have and hold forever, "subject, nevertheless, to all the conditions, covenants, agreements and limitations in this deed expressed." The estate in *Latham* may be distinguished from that created here in that the former was a grant "forever" which was subjected to certain use restrictions while the Hutton deed gave the property to the school district only as long as it could use it. . . .

The defendants also direct our attention to the case of McElvain v. Dorris (1921), 298 Ill. 377, 131 N.E. 608. There, land was sold subject to the following condition: "This tract of land is to be used for mill purposes, and if not used for mill purposes the title reverts back to the former owner." When the mill was abandoned, the heirs of the grantor brought suit in ejectment and were successful. The Supreme Court of Illinois did not mention the possibility that the quoted words could have created a fee simple determinable but instead stated[:] "Annexed to the grant there was a condition subsequent, by a breach of which there would be a right of re-entry by the grantor or her heirs at law. A breach of the condition in such a case does not, of itself, determine the estate, but an entry, or some act equivalent thereto, is necessary to revest the estate, and bringing a suit in ejectment is equivalent to such re-entry."

It is urged by the defendants that McElvain v. Dorris stands for the proposition that the quoted language in the deed creates a fee simple subject to a condition subsequent. We must agree with the defendants that the grant in *McElvain* is strikingly similar to that in this case. However, the opinion in *McElvain* is ambiguous in several respects. First, that portion of the opinion which states that "Annexed to the grant there was a condition subsequent . . ." may refer to the provision quoted above, or it may refer to another provision not reproduced in that opinion. Second, even if the court's reference is to the quoted language, the holding may reflect only the court's acceptance of the parties' construction of the grant. . . . After all, as an action in ejectment was brought in *McElvain*, the difference between a fee simple determinable and a fee simple subject to a condition subsequent would have no practical effect and the court did not discuss it.

To the extent that *McElvain* holds that the quoted language establishes a fee simple subject to a condition subsequent, it is contrary to the weight of Illinois and American authority. A more appropriate case with which to resolve the problem presented here is North v. Graham (1908), 235 Ill. 178, 85 N.E. 267. Land was conveyed to trustees of a church under a deed which stated that "said tract of land above described to revert to the party of the first part whenever it ceases to be used or occupied for a meeting house or church." Following an extended discussion of determinable fees, the court concluded that such an estate is legal in Illinois and that the language of the deed did in fact create that estate. North v. Graham, like this case, falls somewhere between those cases in which appears the classic language used to create a fee simple determinable and that used to create a fee simple subject to a condition subsequent....

Although the word "whenever" is used in the North v. Graham deed, it is not found in a granting clause, but in a reverter clause. The court found this slightly unorthodox construction sufficient to create a fee simple determinable, and we believe that the word "only" placed in the granting clause of the Hutton deed brings this case under the rule of North v. Graham.

We hold, therefore, that the 1941 deed from W. E. and Jennie Hutton to the Trustees of School District No. 1 created a fee simple determinable in the trustees followed by a possibility of reverter in the Huttons and their heirs. Accordingly, the trial court erred in dismissing plaintiffs' third amended complaint which followed [from] its holding that the plaintiffs could not have acquired any interest in the Hutton School property from Harry Hutton. We must therefore reverse and remand this cause to the trial court for further proceedings.

We refrain from deciding the following issues: (1) whether the 1977 conveyance from Harry Hutton was legally sufficient to pass his interest in the school property to the plaintiffs, (2) whether Harry Hutton effectively disclaimed his interest in the property in favor of the defendants by virtue of his 1977 disclaimer, and (3) whether the defendants have ceased to use the Hutton School grounds for "school purposes." Reversed and remanded.

NOTES, QUESTIONS, AND PROBLEMS

1. Consequences. Sometimes there is no consequence to the difference between a determinable fee and one subject to a condition subsequent. That appeared to have been so in McElvain v. Dorris, discussed by the court in *Mahrenholz.* But it was not the case in *Mahrenholz* itself. The difference between automatic termination of the determinable fee and the requirement that a right of entry must be exercised to terminate the fee simple subject to condition subsequent turned out to have considerable significance in *Mahrenholz.* It can also be important should adverse possession become an issue, as the following problems illustrate.

2. *Ambiguous Grants.* Suppose a grantor conveys Blackacre "to *A* so long as he uses it exclusively for organic farming, otherwise to revert to me; but if *A* should fail to use Blackacre for organic farming, or ever apply pesticides or chemical fertilizers to the soil, I retain the right to enter and

reclaim possession and ownership of Blackacre." How should this grant be interpreted? Although the general principle is to give effect to the grantor's intentions, here the grantor's intentions point in two entirely different directions. What factors or policies should govern judicial determination of the nature of the grant when the grantor's intentions are as muddled as this example?

At least two states, California and Kentucky, make this problem simple by statutory elimination of the fee simple determinable and its associated future interest, the possibility of reverter. In those states, a grant that would at common law create a fee simple determinable is held to create a fee simple subject to a condition subsequent. See Calif. Civil Code § 885.020; Ky. Rev. Stat. § 381.218.

3. Problems. In each of the problems below assume that at all times *A* has occupied Blackacre in the fashion of a true owner, sufficient to meet all the elements of adverse possession. The jurisdiction whose law governs has a 10 year limitations period for recovery of possession of real property and also recognizes the equitable doctrine of laches, defined as an unreasonable delay in asserting a right which causes sufficient prejudice to an adverse party to render granting of relief inequitable.

a. In 1990, *O*, owner of Blackare in fee simple absolute, conveyed Blackacre "to *A* so long as Blackacre is never used to raise or breed llamas." In 1991, after visiting Peru, *A* imported a herd of llama which he pastured on Blackacre. *A* bred the llamas and placed a large sign at the entrance of Blackacre, reading "Purebred Peruvian Llamas For Sale." In 2010 *O* sought to eject *A*, and *A*'s defense is that he owns Blackacre in fee absolute. Who should prevail? Why?

b. In 1990, *O*, owner of Blackare in fee simple absolute, conveyed Blackacre "to *A*, but if Blackacre is ever used to raise or breed llamas, *O* retains the right to re-enter and retake possession." In 1991, after visiting Peru, *A* imported a herd of llama which he pastured on Blackacre. *A* bred the llamas and placed a large sign at the entrance of Blackacre, reading "Purebred Peruvian Llamas For Sale." In 2010 *O* sought to eject *A*, and *A*'s defense is that he owns Blackacre in fee absolute. Who should prevail? Why? Would (should) it make any difference to the outcome if in 1995 *O* visited Blackacre and took photographs of *A* posing with the llamas? If, after taking the photos, *O* sent copies of them to *A* with a note inscribed, "Those llamas are so beautiful! You do a great job of breeding them. /s/ *O*"?

4. What constitutes breach? The condition that may terminate a defeasible fee is often phrased at a level of generality that is sufficient to breed disputes concerning alleged breach of the condition. For example, what are school purposes? In *Mahrenholz*, the undisputed facts were that classes were no longer held in the Hutton School, but that the building was used as a storage facility by the school district. Is that use a "school purpose"? See Mahrenholz v. County Board of School Trustees of Lawrence County (*Mahrenholz II*), 544 N.E.2d 128 (Ill. App. 1989).

Problem: Suppose that *A* owns Blackacre, a 320 acre plot, "so long as Blackacre is used for agricultural purposes." *A* opens a retail farm produce stand on Blackacre, which is otherwise devoted to crops, a farmhouse, a barn,

[Handwritten marginal notes:]

giving a stranger property right.

SoL

AP case
10yr SoL

estate was FSD
= goes to A
in FSA

FSS to CS

what photo—
likely O
But have to
look at
laches
So could be
A

then def. A

A - FSD
O - POR

often defined in

silos, and storage sheds for farm machinery. Later, *A* builds several large structures that house thousands of chickens laying eggs. *A* hires a substantial work force to attend to the egg laying operation. Later, *A* expands the farm produce stand to house a large restaurant that specializes in omelettes made from Blackacre eggs and Blackacre produce. Later, *A* leases the mineral rights to BP, which drills for and finds oil underneath Blackacre. The oil wells and associated machinery and access routes consume 10 acres of Blackacre. The remaining portion of Blackacre remains in crop production. At what point, if any, has *A* breached the condition? See Williams v. McKenzie, 203 Ky. 376 (1924).   *BUT — Does not say "ONLY" for agriculture*

Qs for jury

5. *Condemnation of Defeasible Fees.* When a government exercises its power of eminent domain and takes property that is held in defeasible fee, it takes the entire fee simple absolute. This means that the government takes not only the possessory defeasible fee but also the future interest that follows, whether it be a possibility of reverter, power of termination (right of entry), or an executory interest. Who should receive the proceeds? If the effect of the taking is to breach the condition, does the future interest holder receive the proceeds, or should the fee owner receive them on the theory that he did nothing to break the condition?

Problems:

a. Suppose that *O* conveys Parkacre, a 30 acre tract of land, as a gift, to City "so long as the property is used as a public park." City uses Parkacre as a public park for years, until State condemns 25 acres of it for use as a new limited access highway. The condemnation proceeds are $300,000. To whom should they be paid?

The Restatement (First) of Property, § 53, Comment b (1936), took the position that when "viewed from the time of the commencement of an eminent domain proceeding, and not taking into account any changes in the use of the land sought to be condemned which may result as a consequence of such proceeding, the event upon which a possessory estate in fee simple defeasible is to end is an event the occurrence of which, within a reasonably short period of time, is not probable, then the damages for a taking thereof by an eminent domain proceeding are ascertained as though the estate were a possessory estate in fee simple absolute and the entire amount thereof is awarded to the owner of the estate in fee simple defeasible." But when "the event upon which a possessory estate in fee simple defeasible is to end is an event the occurrence of which, within a reasonably short period of time, is probable, then the amount of damages is ascertained as though the estate were a possessory estate in fee simple absolute, and the damages, so ascertained, are divided between the owner of the estate in fee simple defeasible and the owner of the future interest in such shares as fairly represent the proportionate value of the present defeasible possessory estate and of the future interest." Rest. (1st) Property § 53, Comment c (1936).

In Ink v. City of Canton, 4 Ohio St.2d 51 (1965), the Ohio Supreme Court concluded, on facts similar to the problem, that breach of the condition was not imminent but awarded the City the value of the condemned property as a public park, and the remaining portion of the proceeds to the holder of the possibility of reverter. The proceeds awarded to the City were held to be subject to the condition that they be used to maintain the truncated park and, if not so used, to revert to the holder of the possibility of reverter. Does this make sense? How does one determine the value of a public park? Was the possibility of reverter holder paid for the interest and still permitted to keep it? In thinking through the question of division of the proceeds, should it matter if the defeasible fee owner received it as a gift, rather than in an arms-length commercial transaction in which the grantee purchased the defeasible fee?

b.) Suppose that *O* conveys Blackacre, a 30 acre tract of land, as a gift, to City "so long as the property is used as a public library." City uses Blackacre as a public library for years, until City decides without warning that it prefers to convert Blackacre into a public parking garage. City condemns the possibility of reverter and argues that because there was no probability that, at the moment of condemnation and without considering the new use, the condition would be breached in the reasonably foreseeable future, no compensation is due to the holder of the possibility of reverter. Is the City correct? See City of Palm Springs v. Living Desert Reserve, 70 Cal.App.4th 613 (1999).

ALBY v. BANC ONE FINANCIAL

Supreme Court of Washington
156 Wn. 2d 367 (2006)

C. W. JOHNSON, J., delivered the opinion of the court.

The issue in this case is whether a restriction in a deed, which provides that the deeded property automatically reverts to the grantor if the property is mortgaged or encumbered during the life of the grantor, is a valid restraint on alienation. We find the clause to be reasonable and justified by the interests of the parties and, therefore, valid. We affirm the Court of Appeals. . . .

In 1992, Eugene and Susan Alby sold part of their family farm to their niece, Lorri Brashler, and her husband, Larry Brashler. Although the property's market value was $100,000, the parties agreed to a purchase price of $15,000. The contract and the deed contained nearly identical clauses providing for automatic reverter to the Albys if the property were subdivided, mortgaged, or otherwise encumbered during either of the Albys' lifetimes. . . . The parties included these restrictions as a means of ensuring that the land remained within the family during the Albys' lifetimes.[12]

---

12. Susan Alby's uncontested affidavit states:

Because this piece of property had been in the Alby family for several generations, Gene and I wanted to make sure that the property always stayed in the family. After several discussions with Lorri about what she and her husband, Larry R. Brashler, could afford to pay for the home, my husband Gene and I decided that $15,000.00 was what Lorri and her husband could afford, even though we believed the property and home was of considerably greater valued [*sic*]. Since we were so concerned about the property staying in the family, we consulted with an attorney . . . to make a contract with the proper and appropriate language so that Lorri and her husband could not do three things:

1. Sell the property to someone who was not a member of the family;

2. Divide the property in any way; and

Notwithstanding the restrictions, the Brashlers obtained a loan for $92,000 from First Union Mortgage Corporation by executing a deed of trust for the property on February 26, 1999. This loan was recorded on March 3, 1999. The Brashlers executed a second deed of trust to obtain a second loan for $17,250 from CIT Group on March 31, 1999. This loan was recorded on April 2, 1999. CIT Group assigned the loan to petitioner, Banc One Financial (Banc One). The Brashlers defaulted on their payments on their first loan and the lender held a trustee's sale on October 27, 2000. Banc One purchased the property at the sale for $100,822.16 and recorded the trustee's deed on November 2, 2000.

On April 18, 2002, Susan Alby filed a quiet title action ... against Banc One, arguing the title to the property automatically reverted to her when the Brashlers encumbered the property. On competing motions for summary judgment, the trial court quieted title in Banc One and declared the clause void against public policy as an unreasonable restraint on alienation. The Court of Appeals reversed, concluding that the clause is valid because it is not a restraint on alienation and even if it were, the restraint is reasonable. Alby v. Banc One Fin., 119 Wn. App. 513, 82 P.3d 675 (2003). We granted review to determine whether the clause is a restraint on alienation, and if so, whether it is reasonable. . . .

Banc One and Susan Alby agree that the interest conveyed to the Brashlers is a fee simple determinable ... because the estate would revert to the Albys if the property were mortgaged or encumbered during their lifetimes. ... Fee simple determinable estates are subject to the rule against restraints on alienation, which prohibits undue or unreasonable restraints on alienation. Black's Law Dictionary defines a "restraint on alienation" as "[a] restriction ... on a grantee's ability to sell or transfer real property; a provision that conveys an interest and that, even after the interest has become vested, prevents or discourages the owner from disposing of it at all or from disposing of it in particular ways or to particular persons."

Here we have a restraint on alienation because the clause prevented the Brashlers from disposing of the property in a particular way: they could not mortgage or encumber the property without the property automatically reverting to the Albys. Additionally, though the clause did not directly prevent the Brashlers from selling the property, it limited the property's marketability because it prevented potential buyers from financing the purchase of the property.

---

3. Encumber the property with a mortgage or deed of trust.

We even told Lorri that we would buy the property back from her and her husband should they ever decide that they did not want it. My husband Gene Alby, now deceased, received this property from his mother. His father had received part of this property from his father who immigrated to the United States from Norway. This property has been in the Alby family for all these generations and *for this reason,* my husband and I had the [attorney] place the necessary language in the real estate contract and deed that should Lorri and her husband attempt to do any of the above mentioned acts, the property would automatically revert back to us.

(emphasis added) (Although neither the contract nor the deed contains restrictions on selling the property to someone who is not a member of the family, the Albys reserved a right of first refusal in the contract.).

Because we find the prohibition on mortgaging or encumbering to be a restraint on alienation, we must next determine the validity of the restraint. Washington follows the reasonableness approach to restraints on alienation. "Unreasonable restraints on alienation of real property are . . . invalid; reasonable restraints on alienation . . . are valid if justified by the *legitimate interests of the parties.*" McCausland v. Bankers Life Ins. Co., 110 Wn.2d 716, 722, 757 P.2d 941 (1988) (emphasis added). In determining whether a restraint is reasonable, we balance the utility of the purpose served by the restraint against the injurious consequences that are likely to flow from its enforcement.[13] *See* Restatement (Third) of Property § 3.4, at 440 (2000). Whether a restraint is limited in scope or time is often highly significant. In addition to the scope and duration of the restraint, we look at the purpose of the restraint and whether the restraint is supported by consideration.

The balance in this case is between the operation of a free market in land and the right to maintain property in family ownership for a limited time period. Family ownership is not always subordinated to immediate and free alienability. The fact that restraints may negatively affect marketability does not necessarily render them unreasonable. The Albys conveyed a restrained interest in long-held family property to their niece and her husband for a substantially reduced price with the purpose of maintaining family ownership of the property through the Albys' lifetimes. This restraint prevents the property from being mortgaged or encumbered but does not restrict the right to sell or transfer the property. The restraint has a limited scope of preventing only mortgaging or encumbering, a limited duration of the Albys' lifetimes, and a legitimate purpose of keeping the property in the family. The restraint is also supported by the consideration apparent in the significantly reduced purchase price. The recorded deed provides notice to potentially affected parties. Balancing the relevant factors, we conclude that the potentially injurious consequences of not mortgaging or encumbering the property and reducing its marketability are outweighed by the utility of enforcing the limited restraint to keep the property in the family for the Albys' lifetimes.

We next consider the legitimate interests of the parties. The Albys have a legitimate interest in keeping the property in the family and in preventing the property from being lost through foreclosure. The Brashlers have a legitimate interest in realizing the right to freely dispose of their property. However, the Brashlers' interest in free alienation is limited by the fact that they agreed to the restraint in consideration for the substantially reduced price. Enforcement of the restraint still provides

---

13. Restraints on alienation of land are used for a variety of legitimate purposes: retaining land in families; preserving affordable housing; furthering conservation, preservation, and charitable purposes to which land is devoted; and facilitating land investment and creating investment opportunities. Potentially harmful consequences that may flow from restraints on alienation include impediments to the operation of a free market in land, limits on the prospects for improvement, development, and redevelopment of land, and limits on the mobility of landowners and would-be purchasers. Restatement (Third) of Property § 3.4 [Comment] c at 442 (2000).

the Brashlers with a legitimate interest in owning the property with every aspect of absolute ownership except the right to mortgage or encumber the property. Both parties also have legitimate interests in enforcing the terms of their contract.

When evaluating the reasonableness of any agreement placing a restraint on alienation, courts should be reluctant to invoke common law principles disfavoring restraints to invalidate a bargained for contract freely agreed to by the parties. The parties here contracted to transfer property with the purpose of keeping the family farm in the family during the lifetimes of the grantors. We find nothing unreasonable about this purpose. We conclude that the restraint, which prevents the Brashlers from mortgaging or encumbering the property, is reasonable and justified by the legitimate interests of the parties. Accordingly, we affirm the Court of Appeals and remand to superior court with directions to enter summary judgment in favor of and quieting title in Susan Alby.

SANDERS, OWENS, FAIRHURST, and J.M. JOHNSON, JJ., concur.

ALEXANDER, C.J. (dissenting).

. . . While I agree that a reasonableness test applies to restraints on alienation, I would hold that the restraint in this case was not reasonable because the cherished value that our state places on free alienability outweighs the value to the Alby family of maintaining the property in family ownership.

We determine whether a restraint on alienation is reasonable or unreasonable based on "factual determinations and consideration of the equities," and on an assessment of the "legitimate interests of the parties." Determining reasonableness also requires "weighing the utility of the restraint against the injurious consequences of enforcing the restraint." Restatement (Third) of Property § 3.4, at 440 (2000). . . . Eugene and Susan Albys' interest was keeping the property in the Alby family. Lorri and Larry Brashlers' interest, on the other hand, was that of realizing the right of a property owner to freely dispose of his or her property interest, which, as this court has recognized, is among the "fundamental attribute[s] of property ownership." . . .

According to Susan Alby, the parties here "freely contracted for the exchange," with full knowledge and after an opportunity to freely negotiate the terms of their bargain. She argues that, although the Brashlers' right to exercise one of the incidents of property ownership was limited by the terms of the deed, this limitation was reflected in the selling price of the property as they paid significantly below market price. However, nothing in the record supports the claim that the Albys and the Brashlers bargained for a reduction in price in exchange for an estate that did not include the full right of alienation or that the reduction in price was consideration for conveyance of a reduced estate. The real estate contract that the parties signed indicated that the Albys considered the sale of the property to Lorri Brashler to be "in essence a gift to her." Indeed, Susan Alby's own affidavit reflects that the property was sold to the Brashlers at a reduced price, not in exchange for agreeing to a lesser estate, but as a favor to Lorri Brashler. . . . Susan Alby's affidavit also suggests that the Albys placed the restraint on alienation into the contract and deed *after* having agreed with the Brashlers on a selling price. For the foregoing reasons, I believe that the sale of the property at a reduced price was not a bargained-for exchange in consideration for the conveyance of a reduced estate.

Susan Alby notes that the restraint imposed on the alienability of the property in this case was limited both in scope and duration because it was a restriction on mortgaging or encumbering only and expired upon the death of both of the grantors. However, this limitation effectively rendered the property unalienable during the life of the grantors. The duration of the restriction is unknown; it could be a significant period of time, depending on Susan Alby's longevity.[14] During this period, the Brashlers would effectively be relegated to the status of leaseholders of the property, with the right of possession only. Furthermore, the restriction "runs with the land" and therefore limits the rights of not only the Brashlers, the immediate purchasers of the property, but all subsequent purchasers, for the lifetime of the grantor.

The utility of maintaining property in family ownership has been viewed in the law as subordinate to the value of free alienability of property. The doctrine of restraint on alienation . . . arose, in large part, to ensure that the desire of individuals to retain ownership of property within their family did not harm the economic interests of the nation by destroying the free market for property. . . . Maintaining the property within the Alby family no doubt has certain value to Susan Alby individually and to her family. Continued ownership of the property would allow them to maintain possession over land to which they no doubt have an emotional attachment. However, allowing Susan Alby to limit the alienability of the property for the sole purpose of maintaining it in the Alby family has injurious consequences both to the Brashlers and to the general public. The Brashlers are deprived of their right to freely dispose of their property, a right recognized as being one of the "fundamental attribute[s] of property ownership," [and] the property is effectively removed from the marketplace, causing economic consequences affecting society as a whole.

MADSEN and BRIDGE, JJ., concur with ALEXANDER, C.J.

CHAMBERS, J. (dissenting).

. . . I part company with my colleagues because the encumbrance clause at issue in this case was, in my view, an unreasonable restraint on alienation because it prevented Lorri and Larry Brashler, or their successors, from transferring their interest in the property in a particular and very common way: by way of mortgage or encumbrance. The encumbrance clause also had the effect of seriously discouraging disposition of the

---

14. Over 14 years have elapsed since the relevant language was placed in the real estate contract and deed. Because Susan Alby is now only 66 years of age, the restriction, if not void, could be in effect for many more years.

property by limiting the ability of a potential buyer to finance the purchase primarily through a mortgage. . . . Given the nature of the estate and the restraint, I would hold that the restraint was per se unreasonable. . . . [S]o holding would clarify the law.

Restraints on alienation fall into two categories: direct and indirect. Direct restraints are those provisions in an instrument which, by their terms or implications, "purport[] to prohibit or penalize the exercise of the power of alienation" of property. Direct restraints take one of three forms: promissory, disabling, or forfeiture. A promissory restraint is an agreement by the holder of an interest not to alienate, with contractual liability, if the agreement is breached. A disabling restraint is a provision in the document creating the interest that renders void any attempt to alienate the interest. A forfeiture restraint is a condition that terminates the fee upon an attempt to alienate. Such a restraint exists when "an instrument of conveyance provides that if the grantee attempts to alienate, the land shall go to the grantor by way of possibility of reverter or right of entry or to a third person by way of executory interest." . . . See also Restatement (Second) of Property § 3.2, at 147 (1983).

The automatic reverter clause here is a direct forfeiture restraint. Although there are no Washington decisions on point, the general rule is that even limited forfeiture restraints that interfere with the alienability of property [are,] if unreasonable, . . . void. It is desirable that the law be clear, understandable, and predictable. The reasonableness test embraced by the majority and dissent does not promote predictability. To send every contested restraint to a court hearing to balance the interests sought to be protected by the restraint against the benefits of alienability serves neither clarity nor predictability. I would hold that . . . a direct and automatic reverter upon the attempt to alienate is unreasonable as a matter of law. I therefore respectfully dissent.

NOTES, QUESTIONS, AND PROBLEMS

1. *Problems.*   *Fee simple absolute — against public policy to alienate*

a. Suppose that *O* conveys Blackacre to *A* "so long as it is never sold or otherwise transferred." What estate does *A* own? See Freeman v. Phillips, 113 Ga. 589 (1901).

b. Suppose that *O* devises to Historical Society, a non-profit corporation, a parcel of land adjacent to its building, "so long as said property is used by Historical Society for the purposes of its organization, and if not so used to revert to me and become a part of my residuary estate." Historical Society files suit to quiet title in the parcel, seeking a decree that it owns a fee simple absolute. What should be the result? Should it matter that Historical Society intends to lease the property to a developer for an office complex, but use the lease revenue to support its charitable purposes? Should it matter if Historical Society proposes to sell the property to a developer but lease it back to use as a parking garage for the Society as well as a revenue source, derived from charging the public for parking spaces? See Merchants Bank & Trust Co. v.

New Canaan Historical Society, 133 Conn. 706 (1947); Mt. Brow Lodge No. 82, Independent Order of Odd Fellows v. Toscano, 257 Cal.App.2d 22 (1967). But see Falls City v. Missouri Pacific Railway Co., 453 F.2d 771 (8th Cir. 1971) (applying Nebraska law).

    c. Suppose that *O* devises a single family residence to *A*, "so long as *A* and his heirs shall use the devised property as a residence." What estate does *A* own? Should it matter if the devise instead was "so long as *A* or his successors or assigns shall use the devised property as a residence"? See Wills v. Pierce, 208 Ga. 417 (1951); Cast v. National Bank of Commerce, Trust & Sav. Ass'n of Lincoln, 186 Neb. 385 (1971).

    What factors should be considered in order to decide these problems? Is the reasonableness analysis of the Washington Supreme Court in *Alby* sufficient?

    2. Restraints on Marriage. Conditions that operate as restraints on marriage are generally disfavored, but there are a number of exceptions to that principle. See Restatement (Second) Property (Donative Transfers) § 6.1, which declares invalid such restraints as to a *first* marriage, except where the "dominant motive" of the donor is to "provide support until marriage."

    Problems: Suppose *O* devises Blackacre to *A*, his daughter who has never married, "until such time as she marries." Valid? Would (should) the result be different if *O* devised Blackare "to *A* and her heirs; but if she ever marries, to Hole-in-One, my golf club." In Lewis v. Searles, 452 S.W.2d 153, 156 (Mo. 1970), the Missouri Supreme Court was confronted with a devise to the testator's widow "so long as she remains single and unmarried." The court thought that "the very wording of the will ... expresses an intent of the testator to provide *support* for [his widow] while she remained unmarried.... The provision did not constitute a penalty for marrying [..., because she] was not to be *cut off* if she did marry." (First italics in original; second italics supplied.)

    As *Lewis* suggests, the validity of conditions terminating fees or life estates upon remarriage are generally valid, though the trend is toward treating as valid conditions that are intended to provide support until remarriage, but to invalidate conditions that are intended only to frustrate or prevent remarriage. This rule is as often implemented by statute as by judicial decision. See, e.g. Calif. Civil Code § 710: "Conditions imposing restraints upon marriage ... are void; but this does not affect limitations where the intent was not to forbid marriage, but only to give the use until marriage."

    The Restatement (Second) Property (Donative Transfers) § 7.1, asserts that except for two circumstances, conditions or limitations encouraging divorce or marital separation are void. One exception is for conditions that do not call for future action, as when a devise is "to *A* if she shall be divorced from *B* at the time of my death," or when the grantee is already divorced or separated at the time the grant is effective. The other exception is for grants that clearly intend to provide support in the event of divorce or separation, but not to encourage the act.

    For more on the entire topic, see Powell on Real Property § 78.02.

CHAPTER FOUR

FUTURE INTERESTS

■ ■ ■

A. INTRODUCTION

A future interest is a presently existing property right that gives its holder (or his successors in interest) a right to possession of property at some point in the future. That right to possession may be certain or it may be contingent on future events. Because a fee simple absolute endures for eternity, no future interest follows upon it. But whenever an estate of lesser duration than the fee absolute is created a future interest will follow it. This is somewhat like the law of conservation of energy in physics—energy can be neither created nor destroyed, it can only be transformed from one state to another. The fee simple absolute cannot be destroyed, it can only be transformed into different states. In this chapter we are concerned about the consequences of temporal division of the fee simple absolute—splitting it into a presently possessory interest of a duration of less than eternity and a future possessory interest.

There are a finite number of future interests recognized by American law, but these are enough to handle almost any situation. There are three types of future interests that may be retained by the grantor: a reversion, a possibility of reverter, and a power of termination (right of entry). There are three types of future interests that may be created in a transferee from the grantor: a vested remainder, a contingent remainder, and an executory interest.

The following chart may help.

Present Interest	Future Interest in Grantor	Future Interest in Third Party
Fee simple absolute	None	None
Fee simple determinable	Possibility of reverter	Executory interest
Fee simple subject to condition subsequent	Power of termination (Right of entry)	Executory Interest
Fee tail	Reversion	Remainder or Executory Interest
Life Estate	Reversion	Remainder or Executory Interest

Leaseholds, which will be discussed in Chapter Six, are also present possessory estates that endure for less than eternity, so any type of leasehold will have a future interest that follows expiration of the leasehold. When that future interest is retained by the grantor it is a reversion; when it is created in a third party transferee of the grantor, it will be either a remainder or an executory interest.

Future interests are the building blocks of estate planning, the branch of law that focuses on wealth preservation and transmission to succeeding generations. If you intend to become an estate planner, a firm command of these tools is essential. But even if you are not planning on that career, these concepts can occur in other branches of law, often with surprising and unpleasant consequences, as we shall see when we consider the rule against perpetuities. Moreover, the study of future interests is an excellent exercise in analytic thinking, which is what the study and practice of law demands and highly prizes. Finally, unlike some areas of the law, there are right and wrong answers here. It's not all subtle shades of grey.

B. FUTURE INTERESTS RETAINED BY THE GRANTOR

Of the three types of future interests that may be retained by the grantor, the most common by far is the reversion.

1. REVERSION

A reversion occurs whenever an owner of a vested estate conveys or devises a vested estate of lesser duration than the one he owns, and either makes no provision for who owns the property when the lesser estate naturally expires, or makes such a provision that is contingent upon the occurrence of uncertain future events. Natural expiration means, in this context, that the estate comes to the end of its duration, rather than being cut short by the occurrence of some future event, as occurs with the defeasible fees. As indicated earlier, the fee simple absolute endures forever, but lesser estates do not. The fee tail may endure for a very long time, or it may come to an end in one lifetime. The life estate is certain to end with the death of the life tenant. A leasehold will end when its term expires, whether it be a term of years, a periodic tenancy (e.g., month-to-month), or a tenancy at will (terminable at any time by either party). Reversions might be thought of as simply the portion of the larger estate that was not conveyed or desired, and thus will come back to the grantor or his successors in interest when the lesser estate expires. Remainders are freely transferable during life, may be devised by will, or may be inherited.[1] See, e.g., N.C. Gen. Stat. § 39–6.3; Calif. Civil Code § 699.

Example 4–1: O conveys Blackacre "to *A* for life." *A* has a life estate, an estate the duration of which is measured by *A*'s life span. *O* has retained a reversion in fee simple absolute. When *A* dies, and her

---

1. A few states may adhere to the old common law rule that a contingent remainder may not be transferred *inter vivos*, although in those states a contingent remainder may pass at death to the heirs or devisees. See Powell on Real Property § 21.02 (4).

life estate comes to its natural end, the reversion in *O* automatically becomes possessory as a fee simple absolute.

In Example 4–1 *O*, or his successor in interest, has a certainty of acquiring possession. It does not matter if *A* outlives *O*, for at the end of the life estate *O*'s successor in interest will own Blackacre in fee simple absolute. Those successors could be *O*'s heirs (if *O* dies intestate), or *O*'s devisees under his will (if *O* dies testate), or *O*'s immediate or remote transferees (if, during his life, *O* conveyed his reversion to *B*, who in turn conveyed it to *C*). But not every reversion is certain of becoming possessory.

> *Example 4–2:* *O* conveys Blackacre "to *A* for life, but if *B* should become a judge before *A* dies, then to *B* and her heirs." *A* has a life estate, and *O* has a reversion, but it is not certain to become possessory. *O*'s reversion will become a possessory fee simple absolute only if *B* fails to become a judge during *A*'s life. If *B* does become a judge before *A* dies, *B*'s future interest will become a possessory fee simple absolute. *B*'s future interest is a contingent remainder. If it becomes possessory *O*'s reversion will be destroyed.

Reversions are considered vested at the moment of their creation, because the grantor never parted with a portion of what he owned. See Powell on Real Property § 20.02. Reversions are freely alienable, whether by transfer during life, by will, or by inheritance. Remainders, whether vested or contingent, will be discussed shortly, in section C, dealing with future interests in transferees.

PROBLEMS

1. Assume that *O* owns Blackacre in fee simple absolute and makes the following conveyances of Blackacre. In which instances does *O* retain a reversion? *[handwritten: POR (when bloodline dies out)]*

   a. *O* "to *A* and the heirs of her body." *[handwritten: A has Fee Tail | most jurisdictions O left w/ nothing]*

   b. *O* "to *A* for life, then to *B* for 20 years." *[handwritten: indicat. VR in TE | O has Reversion in FSA]*

   c. *O* "to *A* for life, then to *B* and her heirs." *[handwritten: no reversion — future interest in B]*

   d. *O* "to *A* for life, then to *B* and her heirs if during *A*'s life *B* should climb Mount Everest and return to tell the tale." *[handwritten: Cont. remainder B, possible reverpion to O, possible FSA in B]*

2. *O*, owner of Blackacre in fee simple absolute, conveys Blackacre "to *A* for life." After that conveyance *A* takes possession of Blackacre, but then conveys Blackacre "to *B* for life." At this point, when *O*, *A*, and *B* are all alive, what is the state of title in Blackacre? *[handwritten: A - LE   B - LE   O - reversion]*

   a. Suppose *B* dies, while *O* and *A* remain alive. What is the state of title in Blackacre? *[handwritten: A - LE]*

   b. Suppose *A* dies, while *B* and *O* remain alive. What is the state of title in Blackacre? *[handwritten: B - LE, then O reversion]*

   c. Suppose *O* dies intestate, leaving one heir, *H*, while *A* and *B* remain alive. What is the state of title in Blackacre? *[handwritten: B life, A life, H reversion]*

3. O, owner of Blackacre in fee simple absolute, conveys Blackacre "to *A* for life." After that conveyance *A* takes possession of Blackacre, but then conveys Blackacre "to *B* and her heirs." *A* dies, survived by *O* and *B*. What is the state of title in Blackacre?

[handwritten: O by reversion / A only conveyed LE]

2. POSSIBILITY OF REVERTER

A possibility of reverter is created when the grantor conveys an estate, whether of the same or lesser duration as that he owns, but only until a specified future event occurs. See Chapter Three, section E, concerning defeasible estates.

Example 4–3: O, owner of Blackacre in fee simple absolute, conveys Blackacre "to *A* and her heirs so long as *A* never becomes a lawyer." *O* has conveyed an estate of the same duration—forever—to *A*, but there is a catch. If *A* should become a lawyer, the estate will come to an unnatural, abrupt end. It will terminate (or "determine") and *O*'s possibility of reverter will become a possessory fee simple absolute. But if *A* dies intestate, leaving one heir, *H*, without ever having become a lawyer the divesting condition can never occur, so *H* has a fee simple absolute in Blackacre. *O*'s possibility of reverter is destroyed. When *A* is in possession of Blackacre, however, she does not own a fee simple *absolute*, but a fee simple *determinable*.

[handwritten: LE in A / O reversion + poss of rev.]

Problem: Suppose *O* had conveyed Blackacre "to *A* for life so long as she does not become a lawyer." What is the state of title in Blackacre?

As with reversions, a possibility of reverter is considered vested in the grantor at the moment of its creation. In Example 4–3, while *A* is alive *O*'s possibility of reverter is vested subject to complete divestment (or defeasance) if *A* dies without ever having become a lawyer. See Powell on Real Property § 20.02.

3. POWER OF TERMINATION (RIGHT OF ENTRY)

A power of termination (also called a right of entry) is created when the grantor conveys an estate of the same or lesser duration as that he owns, but then stipulates that the estate may be terminated by the grantor if a specified future event occurs. See Chapter Three, section E, concerning defeasible estates.

Example 4–4: O, owner of Blackacre in fee simple absolute, conveys Blackacre "to *A* and her heirs; but if *A* should ever become a lawyer *O* has the power to terminate *A*'s estate by exercising his right to re-enter and retake possession of the premises." *O* has conveyed an estate of the same duration—forever—to *A*, but *O* has retained the power to end *A*'s estate if *A* ever becomes a lawyer. If *A* should become a lawyer, and *O* exercises his power, the estate will come to an unnatural, abrupt end and *O*'s power of termination will become a possessory fee simple absolute. But if *A* dies intestate, leaving one heir, *H*, without ever having become a lawyer the divesting condition can never occur, so *H* has a fee simple absolute in Blackacre. *O*'s power of termination can never be exercised now, so it is destroyed. When *A* is in possession of Blackacre, however, she does not own a fee simple *absolute*, but a fee simple *subject to a condition subsequent*.

As with reversions and possibilities of reverter, a power of termination (right of entry) is considered vested in the grantor at the moment of its creation. See Powell on Real Property § 20.03; Palmer v. Union Bank, 17 R.I. 627, 632 (1892) (a right of entry is "a present vested and transmissible interest"). In Example 4–4, while *A* is alive *O*'s power of termination (right of entry) is vested subject to complete divestment (or defeasance) if *A* dies without ever having become a lawyer. See Powell on Real Property § 20.03.

C. FUTURE INTERESTS IN TRANSFEREES FROM THE GRANTOR

As mentioned earlier, the three types of future interests that a grantor may create in a third party transferee (someone other than the grantee) are a vested remainder, a contingent remainder, or an executory interest. These interests are freely transferable and retain their labels, even if transferred back to the original grantor. However, as we will see, future events can change their nature and, thus, their name. For example, a contingent remainder can become a vested remainder upon the occurrence of a specified future event. How this transformation occurs will become clear in this section.

A remainder is created when a grantor conveys an estate of lesser duration than that which he owns and, instead of retaining a reversion, conveys to a third party the future interest that remains after the lesser estate has been created. A remainder may be either vested or contingent. A vested remainder is one in which the owner is known and there is no condition precedent to the holder's right to future possession. The natural expiration of a prior estate is not a condition precedent to possession; it is merely the end of the lesser estate that, once ended, causes the remainder to become possessory.

> *Example 4–5:* *O*, owner of Blackacre in fee simple absolute, conveys Blackacre "to *A* for life, and then to *B* and her heirs." *A* has a presently possessory life estate and *B* has a vested remainder in fee simple absolute. There is no condition precedent to *B*'s right to take possession when the life estate in *A* expires.

A contingent remainder is one given to an unknown person or which has, as a condition of possession, some condition precedent which must be satisfied.

> *Example 4–6:* *O*, owner of Blackacre in fee simple absolute, conveys Blackacre "to *A* for life, and then to *B* and her heirs if *B* shall be admitted to the bar." At the time of the grant, *B* is an infant. *A*

has a presently possessory life estate, *B* has a contingent remainder in fee simple absolute, and *O* has retained a reversion. *B*'s right to possession of Blackacre upon the expiration of *A*'s life estate is contingent upon *B*'s admission to the bar. Because *B* might not be admitted to the bar before *A*'s life estate expires *O* has a reversion, which will become possessory in that event.

Example 4–6 contains some additional elements. Suppose that *B* has not been admitted to the bar when *A* dies. Is *B*'s contingent remainder destroyed, or does it survive? What happens if *B* is admitted to the bar after *A*'s death? The ancient doctrine of destructibility of contingent remainders (more on that topic in section E) held that a contingent interest that had not vested at the time the prior freehold estate expired was destroyed. Under that doctrine *B*'s remainder would be destroyed if she had not been admitted to the bar before *A*'s death. But the doctrine of destructibility of contingent remainders is virtually extinct in the United States today, so *B*'s remainder would not be destroyed. It would be given a new name, an executory interest. We shall explore executory interests in some detail in section C.2.

Remainders are passive. They quietly await the expiration of the prior estate. Executory interests are aggressive. They strike suddenly to take away a vested interest—whether a present possessory interest or a vested future interest—from its owner. A remainder waits its turn; an executory interest cuts into line and grabs the prize from its current owner.

> *Example 4–7:* *O*, owner of Blackacre in fee simple absolute, conveys Blackacre "to *A* for life, and then to *B* and her heirs if *B* shall be admitted to the bar." *A* dies, survived by *B*, who has not been admitted to the bar, and *O*. Because *B* has not satisfied the condition precedent to her right to possession of Blackacre, possession reverts to *O*. But because *B*'s remainder is not destroyed it is now called an executory interest. This means that *O* does not own Blackacre in fee simple absolute; instead, *O* has a fee simple subject to an executory interest. If *B* should later be admitted to the bar *B*'s interest will become possessory by cutting off *O*'s possession. *B* will then own Blackacre in fee simple absolute.

This loss of a vested interest to an executory interest is a bit like the loss of the Roman Empire, or bankruptcy. It happens gradually, then suddenly. *O* might have foreseen the loss by observing *B*'s matriculation in law school. Perhaps the day of reckoning was postponed as *B* failed the bar exam a few times. But one day, suddenly, *B* was sworn in as a lawyer. The sword of Damocles dropped and severed *O* from his possessory estate.

1. REMAINDERS

As indicated above, remainders are either vested or contingent. A vested remainder is one that is given to a known person and which has no condition precedent that must be satisfied before the remainder becomes possessory. Remember: The natural expiration of the preceding estate or estates is not considered a condition precedent. A contingent remainder, by contrast, is the result of any remainder that is created in an unknown person *or* makes possession subject to the occurrence of some specified event.

a. Vested Remainders

Vested remainders may be indefeasibly vested, vested subject to complete divestment, or vested subject to partial divestment. An indefeasibly vested remainder is one created in a known person, has no condition precedent attached to it, and cannot be divested (taken away) by the occurrence of some future event.

> *Example 4–8:* O, owner of Blackacre in fee simple absolute, conveys Blackacre "to my daughter A for life, and then to my son B and his heirs." B has an indefeasibly vested remainder. We know who he is, there is no condition precedent to his right to take possession upon the end of A's life estate, and there is no subsequent condition, the occurrence of which would take away, or divest, B of his interest.

Question: What is the state of title in Blackacre if B, facing bankruptcy, conveys all his property to T, to hold in trust for the benefit of his creditors, and then dies intestate, leaving H as his sole heir? B is survived by H, O, and A. When A dies → goes to H.

A vested remainder can be subject to complete divestment upon the occurrence of some event after the remainder has become vested.

> *Example 4–9:* O, owner of Blackacre in fee simple absolute, conveys Blackacre "to my daughter A for life, and then to my son B and his heirs, but if my son C should ever register as a Republican, to C and his heirs." At the time of the conveyance C is a partisan Democrat. B has a vested remainder because he is an ascertained person and there is no condition precedent to his right to obtain possession at the end of A's life estate. But there is a condition *subsequent*—the possibility that C may register as a Republican. If that occurs, C would divest B of his entire interest. C has an executory interest.

Question: What is the state of title in Blackacre if A dies, survived by B and C, who remains an ardent Democrat?

A vested remainder can also be subject to partial divestment, sometimes called a vested remainder subject to open. The reason it is often called "subject to open" is because this type of remainder involves a gift to a class of people. If one member of the class exists and there is no condition precedent to that person's entitlement to possession upon expiration of the prior estate, that known person has a vested remainder. But new members of the class might later exist, and as they come into being they acquire a vested remainder, with the result that the prior class member or members owning a vested interest must necessarily have their investments diluted, or partially divested. The simplest class gift is to a class of a known person's children.

> *Example 4–10:* O, owner of Blackacre in fee simple absolute, devises Blackacre "to my daughter A for life, then to A's children and their heirs." At the time of O's death A has one child, *A1*. Because we know who *A1* is and there is no condition precedent to her right to take possession of Blackacre upon A's death, *A1* has a vested remainder. But A then gives birth to *A2*. Now, *A2* also has a vested remainder. *A1*'s vested remainder has been partially divested to accommodate *A2*. Each of *A1* and *A2* hold a vested remainder subject to partial divestment, or subject to open, because the class of A's children remains open—new members could appear. As each new child of A is born the existing class members will suffer a partial divestment of their vested remainders. The class is open to new members, hence the vested remainders are called "subject to open," although subject to partial divestment is a more descriptive label.

Questions:

a. What is the state of title in Blackacre after A has given birth to *A1*, *A2*, and *A3* and then successfully undergoes irreversible surgery to prevent further pregnancies?

b. What is the state of title in Blackacre after A has given birth to *A1*, *A2*, and *A3* and then dies, leaving no other survivors?

b. Contingent Remainders

As indicated earlier a remainder is contingent if *either* (1) its owner is not known (not ascertainable), *or* (2) there is a condition *precedent* that must be satisfied before a known owner of the remainder is entitled to possession upon the expiration of the prior estate.

> *Example 4–11:* O, owner of Blackacre in fee simple absolute, conveys Blackacre "to A for life, then to A's children." At the time of the conveyance, A has no children. The class of A's children is not in existence; we cannot determine who they are. The class of A's children has a contingent remainder.[2]

> *Example 4–12:* O, a property professor and owner of Blackacre in fee simple absolute, conveys Blackacre "to A for life, then to the first person in my Property class of 2012 who becomes a judge." Although every member of the Property class is a known person we cannot yet ascertain which member, if any, will ever become a judge. The members of the Property class each own a contingent remainder.

Questions:

---

2. The common law glossed over the knotty problem of how a non-existent person or persons could own anything. Ownership was said to be *in nubibus* (in the clouds), *in pendenti* (in suspension), or *in gremio legis* (in the bosom of the law).

a. Suppose that *B*, a member of the Property class, is the first member of the class to become a judge. *A* is alive. What is the state of title in Blackacre? [handwritten: A - LE   B - future interest]

b. Suppose that *O* dies intestate, leaving one heir, *H*. Then *A* dies, at a time when no member of the Property class has become a judge. What is the state of title in Blackacre? [handwritten: H - FSA ?]

c. Suppose that *O* dies intestate, leaving one heir, *H*, a child 3 years of age. Then *A* dies, at a time when no member of the Property class has become a judge. Then *H* dies intestate, leaving no heirs. Eventually, all the members of the Property class die, none of them ever having become judges. What is the state of title in Blackacre? [handwritten: H's heirs - FSA]

A remainder may also be contingent because there is a condition precedent to obtaining possession upon the expiration of the prior estate.

Example 4–13: *O*, owner of Blackacre in fee simple absolute, conveys Blackacre "to *A* for life, then to *B* and his heirs if *B* becomes a priest before *A*'s death." *B* has a contingent remainder. His right to possession at the end of *A*'s life estate depends upon whether he has become a priest before that moment.

Question: What happens to *B*'s remainder if *B* never becomes a priest? [handwritten: Destroyed]

Example 4–14: *O*, owner of Blackacre in fee simple absolute, devises Blackacre "to *A* for life, then to *B* and his heirs if *B* becomes a priest before *A*'s death, and if *B* does not become a priest before *A*'s death, to *C* and her heirs." *B* has a contingent remainder because he must satisfy the condition precedent of becoming a priest before *A*'s death in order to be entitled to possession at the expiration of *A*'s life estate. *C* also has a contingent remainder because there is a condition precedent to *C*'s right to possession: *B* must not become a priest prior to *A*'s death. These remainders are alternative contingent remainders. A single condition is stated with different takers depending on the outcome of the condition.

Question: In Example 4–14, is there a reversion? If so, who owns it?

There are two situations that look very similar to alternative contingent remainders, but which are characterized differently. Consider the following examples.

Example 4–15: *O*, owner of Blackacre in fee simple absolute, devises Blackacre "to *A* for life, then to *B* and his heirs; but if *B* does not become a priest before *A*'s death, to *C* and her heirs." *B* has a vested remainder subject to complete divestment. We know who he is, and there is no condition precedent to his right to possession upon the expiration of the preceding estate. *C* has an executory interest, because if *B* does not become a priest before *A*'s death, *C*'s interest will become vested and divest *B*.

Question: In Example 4–15, is there a reversion? If so, who owns it?

Note that the apparent effect of the grants in Example 4–14 and Example 4–15 is identical. Only the wording is different; it is the same difference that exists between the language that creates a fee simple determinable and that which creates a fee simple subject to a condition subsequent. You may be wondering why, in Example 4–15, *B* has a vested remainder. Surely his right to possession of Blackacre depends upon his becoming a priest before *A* dies. The answer lies in the unlikely possibility that *A*'s life estate could expire before *A* dies. This could happen if *A* renounces her life estate. Renunciation of a devise or bequest under a will does happen. If *A* should renounce her life estate, the next succeeding estate is entitled to possession. In Example 4–15, that is *B*'s vested remainder. *B* may possess Blackacre in fee simple subject to *C*'s executory interest, but if *B* does not become a priest before *A* dies, *B* will be divested of his fee in favor of *C*.

Example 4–16: O, owner of Blackacre in fee simple absolute, conveys Blackacre "to *A* for life, then to *B* and her heirs if *B* survives *A*; and if *B* should not survive *A*, to *C* and his heirs if *C* should ever return from Tierra del Fuego." *B* has a contingent remainder because *B* must satisfy the condition precedent of surviving *A* in order to possess Blackacre. *C* also has a contingent remainder because *B* must not survive *A* for *C* to have any right to possession. If that were the entire grant, it would be alternative contingent remainders. But there is more: *C*'s right to possession is also subject to an additional condition precedent—his return from Tierra del Fuego. Resolution of the alternative in the alternative contingent remainder—whether *B* survives *A*—does not fully resolve *C*'s contingent right to possession.

When a grant of a remainder is ambiguous, there is a preference to construe it as a vested remainder. Such a construction eliminates uncertainty about ownership and promotes alienability of property. As you will see in section D, the common law achieved this end by the doctrine of destructibility of contingent remainders. That doctrine destroyed a contingent remainder if it had not vested by the time the preceding estate expired. Today, the destructibility doctrine is defunct, but the rule against perpetuities serves much the same function. Vested interests, such as indefeasibly vested remainders, are not subject to the rule against perpetuities, but contingent remainders, executory interests, and vested remainders subject to divestment are subject to the rule. The complexities of the rule against perpetuities will be explored in section D.

There are a few other consequential differences between vested and contingent remainders. First, as noted earlier, a few states may cling to the old rule that contingent remainders may not be transferred *inter vivos*, while vested remainders are freely transferable, Almost all states, however, permit free transferability of any type of remainder. Second, some states do not permit owners of a contingent remainder to sue for waste or partition (a subject to be discussed in Chapter Five), while owners of vested remainders (including vested remainders subject to complete or partial divestment) may do so. The rationale is that an owner of a contingent remainder has no certainty of acquiring possession, so lacks a sufficient interest in the property to warrant such claims. But this rationale is equally applicable to a vested remainder subject to *complete divestment*.

PROBLEMS

1. O, owner of Blackacre in fee simple absolute, conveys Blackacre "to A and B for so long as both of them are alive, and then to the survivor of A and B in fee simple absolute." What is the state of title in Blackacre?

2. O, owner of Blackacre in fee simple absolute, conveys Blackacre "to A for life, and if A should die, to B and her heirs." What is the state of title in Blackacre?

3. O, owner of Blackacre in fee simple absolute, conveys Blackacre "to A for life, and then to such of A's children who graduate from law school."

a. At the time of the grant A has two children, B, a high school senior, and C, a middle school student. What is the state of title in Blackacre?

b. Eight years later B graduates from law school. A is alive. What is the state of title in Blackacre?

c. Five years after B graduates from law school, B dies intestate, leaving H as his sole heir. At that time C is a second year law student and A is alive. What is the state of title in Blackacre?

d. Two years after B's death, C graduates from law school. A is alive. What is the state of title in Blackacre?

2. EXECUTORY INTERESTS

a. Introduction

There are two types of executory interests: shifting executory interests and springing executory interests. Each type divests a holder of a vested interest and transfers that interest to the holder of the executory interest. Put another way, an executory interest terminates someone's vested interest before its natural expiration, and places ownership of that person's vested interest in the holder of the executory interest.

A *shifting executory interest* divests a vested interest held in another transferee from the grantor. It shifts the vested interest from one transferee and places in a different transferee.

> *Example 4–17: O*, owner of Blackacre in fee simple absolute, conveys Blackacre "to A for life, then to B and her heirs, but if B should die without issue surviving her, to C and her heirs." B has a vested remainder in a fee simple subject to an executory limitation—C's executory interest. The only way that C can acquire possession is for the stated event—B's death without surviving issue—to occur, and that event will cut short B's fee simple, which would otherwise ripen into a fee simple absolute, which will endure forever.

Questions:

a. If *A* dies, survived by *B* and *C*, what is the state of title in Blackacre? *B*   *C exec interest*

b. If *B* dies, leaving no issue but survived by *A* and *C*, what is the state of title in Blackacre? *A - LE , C - exec. interest*

c. If *B* dies, survived by *D*, her only child, and by *A* and *C*, what is the state of title in Blackacre? *A - LE , D*

A *springing executory interest* divests a vested interest held by the transferor at some time in the future after the interest is created. The interest that vests in the executory interest holder springs from the grantor, but not at the moment the grantor makes the grant.

> *Example 4–18:* *O*, owner of Blackacre in fee simple absolute, conveys Blackacre "to my daughter *A* upon the occasion of her marriage." *A* is twelve years of age and unmarried at the time of the grant. *O* has a fee simple subject to an executory limitation and *A* has a springing executory interest. *A*'s interest cannot possibly divest *O* until some time has elapsed after the grant. When that happens, the interest that will then be vested in *A* will "spring" out of *O*.

PROBLEMS

1. *O*, owner of Blackacre in fee simple absolute, conveys Blackacre "to *A* for life, then to *B* if *B* shall deliver a eulogy at *A*'s funeral." What future interests are created by this conveyance?

2. *O*, owner of Blackacre in fee simple absolute, conveys Blackacre "to *A* for life, then to *B* and her heirs if *B* shall survive *A*, but if *B* shall not so survive, then to *C* and his heirs if *C* shall have married *D*." What future interests are created by this conveyance?

3. *O*, owner of Blackacre in fee simple absolute, conveys Blackacre "to *A* for life, then to *B* for 15 years, then to *C*'s heirs." At the time of the conveyance *C* is divorced but has one child, *Z*. What future interests are created by this conveyance? Suppose that *A* dies and, a year later, *C* dies, survived by *O*, *B*, and *Z*. What future interests exist after those events occur?

4. *O*, owner of Blackacre in fee simple absolute, conveys Blackacre "to *A* for life, then to *B*'s children and their heirs." At the time of the grant *B* is alive and has one child, *X*. What future interests are created by this conveyance? Suppose that *B* has a second child, *Y*, and then dies, survived by *X*, *Y*, *O*, and *A*. What future interests exist after those events occur?

5. *O*, owner of Blackacre in fee simple absolute, conveys Blackacre "to *A* for life, then to such of *B*'s children who reach age 21 and their heirs." At the time of the grant *B* is alive and has two children, *C* (age 19), and *D* (age 17). What future interests are created by this conveyance? Suppose that three years later *C* dies, survived by *O*, *A*, *B* and *D*. What future interests exist after *C*'s death?

6. *O*, owner of Blackacre in fee simple absolute, conveys Blackacre "to *A* and his heirs so long no pesticides are ever used on or applied to Blackacre, and then to *B* and her heirs." What is the state of title in Blackacre?

b. Historical Background

Knowledge of the historical evolution of executory interests aids understanding of these interests. The administration of justice in England after the Norman Conquest was divided into two types of courts: the courts of law and the courts of equity. The law courts adjudicated the legal rights and obligations of parties. The equity courts had no power to do this, but could punish people for what were thought to be unfair, or inequitable, assertion of those rights. The equity courts arose from the fact that the King had a council, which included among its members the King's Chancellor, a trusted and learned advisor. Losers in the law courts could appeal to the King in Council to prevent enforcement of legal rights on grounds of unfairness, or simply as an act of mercy. Because the Chancellor was an ecclesiastical official—often a canon lawyer—the council frequently deferred to his judgment. Over the course of four centuries after William I's conquest this practice was eventually institutionalized as the Court of Chancery. The importance of this to land law was that although the law courts could and did determine the legal rights to land, the equity courts—the Chancery courts—could restrain the holders of those legal rights from exercising them if it was deemed unfair (inequitable) to do so.

Medieval lawyers seized on this dichotomy to avoid the strictures of the common law and the payment of the feudal death taxes. Recall that after Statute Quia most land tenures were held directly from the Crown. Thus, upon the death of a landowner, its was necessary to pay relief to the Crown to permit the landowner's heirs or assigns to possess and enjoy the property. Enforcement of these death taxes was aided by two common law rules. First, the law courts invalidated any attempt to create a future interest that would cut short a freehold estate. In other words, the modern shifting executory interest was impermissible. Second, the law courts voided any attempt to create a freehold estate at some time in the future because the ritual act of livery of seisin could not be accomplished at the time of the grant. By this rule, the modern springing executory interest was impermissible. The Chancellor, however, was interested in fairness, not seisin, so his courts of equity could and did command people to do what was fair in the eyes of the chancery judges. That fact enabled these legal rules to be avoided by an inventive device that kept legal title in one person and simultaneously created equitable rights in other persons and imposed an equitable obligation upon the legal owner. In short, an early version of the modern trust was the scheme concocted by medieval lawyers to do what the law would not permit and, in some cases, to avoid death taxes.

> *Example 4–19:* To create a springing interest, *O*, father of his unmarried daughter *A* and holder of Blackacre from the Crown, enters Blackacre and delivers a clod of its earth (the ritual of livery of seisin) to "*T* and his heirs, to hold for the use of *A* and her heirs if *A* should marry." *T* was called the "feoffee to uses" because livery of seisin was also called enfeoffment and the recipient of seisin was the

feoffee. As a result, legal title was in *T* because *T* was seised of the feudal obligations, but an equitable right was created in *A*. The courts of chancery would force *T*, upon pain of imprisonment if necessary, to hold Blackacre for the benefit of *A* and to permit her the use of Blackacre after her marriage.

Example 4–20: To create a shifting interest, *O*, father of two sons, *A* and *B*, and holder of Blackacre from the Crown, enters Blackacre and delivers a clod of its earth "to *T* and his heirs, to hold for the use of *A* and his heirs, but if *A* should inherit Pemberly, the family manorial estate, then to hold for the use of *B* and his heirs." As with Example 4–19, *T*, the feoffee to uses, would hold legal title but the equity courts would force *T* to preserve Blackacre for the benefit and use of *A* and, if the subsequent condition occurred, for *B*.

Example 4–21: To avoid the cumbersome procedure of livery of seisin, *O*, holder of Blackacre from the Crown, executes a deed of Blackacre "to *A* and his heirs." Because of the absence of livery of seisin the law courts regarded *O* as the owner of Blackacre, but the equity courts would impose upon *O* an obligation to hold title for the benefit and use of *A*.

Example 4–22: Because prior to 1540 it was not possible to devise property by will, *O*, owner of Blackacre, might transfer seisin "to *T* and his heirs, to hold for the use of such persons as *O* may appoint by his last will and testament."

Example 4–23: To avoid death taxes, *O*, owner of Blackacre, might transfer seisin "to *X*, *Y*, and *Z* and their heirs, to hold for the use of *O*'s eldest surviving son, and then to the use of *O*'s eldest surviving son's eldest surviving son, and then to such person or persons as that person may appoint by his last will and testament." Because seisin stayed in the hands of *X*, *Y*, and *Z* no death taxes would be due at the death of each beneficiary of Blackacre. If any of *X*, *Y* or *Z* should become dangerously old, *X*, *Y*, and *Z* could transfer seisin to themselves and *U*, *V*, and *W*, thus keeping seisin frozen and avoiding the evil day when the land tenure would revert to the Crown and relief must be paid.

Naturally, the King was not pleased by these gambits, particularly avoidance of his death taxes. As sovereigns are wont to do, he demanded legislation to increase taxes, otherwise known as closing loopholes. With the Statute of Uses, reluctantly enacted in 1535 by a Parliament under great pressure from Henry VIII, the loophole was closed. The Statute of Uses simply "executed" the use, by converting the beneficial (or equitable) interest in a use into a legal interest. Now, once a legal executory interest became possessory as a fee simple, payment of relief would be due to the Crown.

The Statute of Uses did not apply, however, if the feoffee to uses had active duties, and was not merely a passive holder of seisin. That is precisely what a modern trustee is required to do—actively manage the trust corpus for the benefit of the equitable owners. Nor did the statute apply to personal property, such as money or marketable securities, the financial assets that are the staple of today's trusts. The statute was construed to be inapplicable to a "use upon a use," such as when *O* enfeoffs *T* for the use of *A* for the use of *B*. The first use was executed, giving *A* fee simple absolute, but *A* continued to have the obligation to hold the property for the benefit of *B*, an obligation enforced in the courts of equity. Thus, by these three exceptions to the scope of the Statute of Uses, space was preserved for the modern trust to develop and flourish. Finally, although for a time after its enactment, it was thought to be necessary to "raise a use" in order to have the Statute of Uses execute the use and convert the beneficial interest into a legal executory interest, in time that requirement was abandoned. Thus, any instrument, whether deed or will, may create an executory interest.

c. The Modern Form of the Use: The Trust

As discussed earlier, the trust is an exceedingly flexible device. It permits management of a pool of assets to be vested in a trustee who, because she has fee simple absolute, can freely alienate the trust corpus or otherwise deal with it as the legal owner. Yet, the fiduciary obligations imposed upon the trustee ensure that the trustee will prudently manage those assets solely for the advantage of the trust beneficiaries. The creator of the trust can create as many equitable future interests as he may desire, subject only to the legal limits imposed by the rule against perpetuities and the practical limits imposed by today's version of death taxes, the federal estate and gift tax laws. Finally, it is possible for a person to place assets in trust for the benefit of another person, but make the beneficial interest in the trust inalienable by the beneficiary, which keeps the interest immune from seizure by creditors of the beneficiary. See Broadway National Bank v. Adams, 133 Mass. 170 (1882), the leading case upholding the validity of such a so-called "spendthrift trust," on the theory that creditors would not be defrauded by such trusts because they can determine before extending credit what assets of the borrower might be available for repayment. This particular use of the trust was and is controversial. John Chipman Gray, the nineteenth century master of trusts and the rule against perpetuities, fulminated that

> it is against public policy that a man "should have an estate to live on, but not an estate to pay his debts with" [or] should have the benefits of wealth without the responsibilities. ... [It] is not the function of the law to join the futile effort to save the foolish and the vicious from the consequences of their own vice and folly. ... That grown men ... not paying their debts should live in luxury on inherited wealth [is thoroughly] undemocratic. ... The general intro-duction of spendthrift trusts would be to form a privileged class, who could indulge in every speculation, could [practice] every fraud, and, provided they kept on the safe side of the criminal law, could yet roll

in wealth. They would be an aristocracy, though certainly the most contemptible aristocracy with which a country was ever cursed.

John Chipman Gray, Restraints on the Alienation of Property 174 (1883). Today, some states even permit a person to place her own assets in trust for her own benefit, but with the proviso that the beneficial interest is inalienable. These "asset protection trusts" would surely move Professor Gray to new heights of condemnation, but contemporary critics also exist. See, e.g., Stewart Sterk, Asset Protection Trusts: Trust Law's Race to the Bottom?, 85 Cornell L. Rev. 1035 (2000).

Do not be misled, however, by this controversial dark side of trusts. The trust is an invaluable tool to manage pools of capital for the benefit of numerous beneficiaries, and thus has wide application in a variety of commercial and financial contexts, as well as its traditional use as a device to preserve and manage family wealth for purposes of inter-generational transfer.

PROBLEM

O devises a large sum of financial assets in trust for the benefit of "my daughter *A* for her life, then outright and free of trust in equal portions to the class of *A*'s children and my son *B*'s children and their heirs, but if any child of *B* should fail to survive *B*, such child's share shall pass to his or her issue that survive *B*." At the time of *O*'s death, *A* has one child, *K*, and *B* has one child, *X*. What are the equitable future interests in this trust? Then *A* has a second child, *L*, and *B* has a second child, *Y*. Now, what are the equitable future interests in the trust? After some period of time *K* dies, survived by her husband, *H*, to whom she has devised all her property, and her child, *P*. Then *Y* dies, survived by his wife, *W*, to whom he has devised all his property, and his child *Q*. Then *B* and *A* die in quick succession. Who are the owners of the property that will be distributed from the trust?

3. CONSEQUENCES OF THE FUTURE INTERESTS CLASSIFICATION SCHEME

There are significant consequences between indefeasibly vested interests and interests that are not certain to become possessory in the future—contingent remainders, executory interests, and vested remainders subject to complete divestment. Indefeasibly vested interests are not subject to destruction under the rule against perpetuities, while the interests that are uncertain of becoming possessory are subject to destruction by that rule. At common law important consequences flowed from the distinction between contingent remainders and executory interests. Contingent remainders were destroyed if they did not become possessory at the moment the preceding freehold estate expired, because somebody must always hold seisin (and thus be obligated to perform the feudal services), and the contingent remainderman could not hold seisin in the estate due to the fact that the condition precedent to a right to possession had not yet occurred. To avoid that gap in seisin, contingent remainders were destroyed if they had not vested prior to expiration of the preceding estate. But that rule, discussed below, did not apply to executory interests because they had the quality of cutting short a vested interest and immediately transferring possession (and thus seisin) to the executory interest holder. Contingent remainders were subject to the Rule in Shelley's Case (see below) but executory interests were not so subject. Today, however, with the virtual abolition of each of the Rule in Shelley's Case and the doctrine of destructibility of contingent remainders, those consequences are of most interest to legal historians.

Accordingly, the prestigious American Law Institute, creator of the various restatements of law, has urged American jurisdictions to simplify the classification system for future interests,. The Restatement (Third) of Property, Wills and other Donative Transfers, treats all future interests as just that: future interests. No distinction is drawn between possibilities of reverter, powers of termination (rights of entry), reversions, remainders, and executory interests. Under the Restatement (Third) any future interest that is not certain of becoming possessory is classified as a contingent future interest. Thus, possibilities of reverter, powers of termination, contingent remainders, vested remainders subject to complete divestment, and executory interests would all be called contingent future interests. Either a vested or contingent future interest may be subject to open. Except for future interests that are subject to a valid restraint on alienation, the Third Restatement stipulates that any future interest is alienable during life, and (except for future interests that terminate upon the holder's death) at death by either will or inheritance.

Example 4–24: O, owner of Blackacre in fee simple absolute, conveys Blackacre "to A and her heirs so long as it used exclusively as dude ranch, and if not so used to revert to O." O would ordinarily have a possibility of reverter and A would have a fee simple determinable. Under the Third Restatement system, A has a defeasible fee simple and O has a contingent future interest.

Example 4–25: O, owner of Blackacre in fee simple absolute, conveys Blackacre "to A for life, and then to B and her heirs if B becomes a judge." Ordinarily, O has a reversion and B has a contingent remainder. Under the Third Restatement system, each of B and O have contingent future interests.

Example 4–26: Suppose that in Example 4–25 B becomes a judge while A is alive. Ordinarily, B would have an indefeasibly vested remainder and O's reversion would be destroyed. Under the Third Restatement system, B has an indefeasibly vested future interest and O's contingent future interest is destroyed.

Example 4–27: O, owner of Blackacre in fee simple absolute, conveys Blackacre "to A for life, and then to B and her heirs, but if B ever becomes a judge, to revert to O." Ordinarily, B would have a vested remainder subject to complete divestment and O's reversion would also be vested subject to complete divestment. Under the Third Restatement system, each of *B* and *O* have a contingent future interest.

Example 4–28: *O*, owner of Blackacre in fee simple absolute, conveys Blackacre "to *A* for life, and then to *B*'s children and their heirs." Each of *A* and *B* are alive. *B* has one child, *C*. Ordinarily, *C* would have a vested remainder subject to partial divestment. The unborn children of *B* would have a contingent remainder, perhaps held "in the bosom of the law." Under the Third Restatement system, *C* has a vested future interest subject to open (or partial divestment). The unborn children of *B* have a contingent future interest subject to open (or partial divestment), perhaps still held "in the bosom of the law."

D. THE PROBLEM OF UNCERTAIN OWNERSHIP: RULES PROMOTING MARKETABILITY OF PROPERTY BY DESTROYING CONTINGENT FUTURE INTERESTS

Uncertainty about the ownership of property makes it unmarketable, and thus prevents its reallocation to others who might use it more wisely or productively. In order to transfer an estate that has been divided into a present possessory interest and a future interest, it is necessary to obtain the consent of all interest holders to effect the transfer. That is difficult enough even when the future interest is an indefeasibly vested remainder, but when it is contingent upon uncertain future events the task becomes even harder. In some cases it may well be insuperable, as when a contingent remainder is held by an open class of people.

Example 4–29: *O*, owner of Blackacre in fee simple absolute, devises Blackacre "to my daughter *A* for life, then to *A*'s children for life, then to such of my son *B*'s children who survive *A*." At the time of the grant neither *A* nor *B* have any children. Should *A* wish to sell a fee simple absolute in Blackacre it would be impossible to do so because she would need two open classes of unknown (indeed, as yet nonexistent) people to join in the conveyance. Not until the death of each of *A* and *B* would the entire identity of these open classes be known with certainty.

To address this and other problems of marketability posed by uncertainty of future possession, the common law created several rules, most of which are nearly, but not completely, extinct today. One of them, however, the rule against perpetuities, is a robust survivor that, in its common law form, can and does plague modern lawyers.

1. DESTRUCTIBILITY OF CONTINGENT REMAINDERS

The medieval legal mind could not tolerate any gap in seisin, because there must always be someone obligated (seised) to perform the feudal services. Even after feudalism disappeared the hobgoblin of seisin continued to roam through English land law, somewhat like Banquo's ghost in *Macbeth*. Thus, the destructibility doctrine held that a legal contingent remainder in land was destroyed if, at the expiration of the preceding freehold estate, it was still contingent. The remainderman was not entitled to possession because the contingency had not occurred, so he could not stand seised.

Example 4–30: O, owner of Blackacre in fee simple absolute, conveys it "to A for life, then to B and his heirs if B has become a Post–Captain in the Royal Navy." At A's death B is still a Lieutenant, hoping for promotion to Post–Captain. Too bad for B; not only is his military ambition stalled, his contingent remainder in Blackacre is destroyed. O's reversion becomes possessory in fee simple absolute.

The destructibility rule also created opportunities for the avaricious. The doctrine of merger held that if a possessory freehold and the next *vested* estate were held by the same person, the two interests would merge into one possessory freehold. That meant that if there was an intervening contingent remainder at the time the possessory freehold and the next vested estate came into the same hands, the contingent remainder was destroyed.

Example 4–31: O, owner of Blackacre in fee simple absolute, conveys it "to my second son, A, for life, then to my nephew, B and his heirs if B has become a Post–Captain in the Royal Navy." O dies, leaving his eldest son, H, as his sole heir. While B is still beseeching the Admiralty for a promotion from Lieutenant to Post–Captain, H purchases the life estate in Blackacre from his brother A. (Perhaps he offers a sum of money that is more than the value of a life estate alone, but less than the value of a fee simple absolute in Blackacre.) At that moment H owns the present possessory freehold (a life estate *pur autre vie*, measured by the life of A) and the next *vested* estate, the reversion that had been retained by O and acquired through inheritance. Merger causes the two vested interests to be collapsed into one fee simple absolute, squeezing out B by destroying his contingent remainder.

Despite the apparent implacable force of the destructibility rule, it was actually riddled with exceptions. It did not apply to equitable contingent remainders (a contingent remainder that was a beneficial interest in a trust corpus). Thus, property could be placed in trust and held there until the contingency was satisfied, then to be distributed free of the trust. This made sense to minds imprisoned by seisin, because the trustee always had seisin.

Example 4–32: O, owner of Blackacre in fee simple absolute, conveys it "to T, as trustee, to hold for A for life, then to hold for such of A's children who reach age 21." At the time of the conveyance into trust, A is alive and has two children, X and Y, ages 7 and 5, respectively. Two years later A dies. If the contingent remainder held by X and Y had not been made an equitable contingent remainder, it would have been destroyed at A's death. As it is, the remainder stays alive. When and if X and Y each attain the age of 21, they will receive the benefit of their portion of Blackacre.

The destructibility rule could be evaded by creating an executory interest instead of a contingent remainder. The two interests are each contingent, and function almost identically, but an executory interest posed no possibility of a gap in seisin, so it was exempt from destruction if the divesting condition had not occurred at the time a freehold estate expired.

Example 4–33: O, owner of Blackacre in fee simple absolute, conveys it "to A for life, then to revert to O, but if B should ever become a Post–Captain in the Royal Navy, to B and his heirs." This grant accomplishes the same purpose as the grant in Example 4–30, but unlike that one, if B has not been promoted to Post–Captain by A's death, seisin will revert to O, and B's executory interest stays alive.

Of course, O could also avoid the destructibility rule by granting B a vested remainder subject to complete divestment, but this would give B possession prior to his promotion to Post–Captain.

Example 4–34: O, owner of Blackacre in fee simple absolute, conveys it "to A for life, then to B and his heirs, but if B should never become a Post–Captain in the Royal Navy, to revert to O." O might not wish to use this tool because he might want the possibility of acquiring Blackacre to be an incentive for B to exert himself in his naval career. Under this grant, at A's death B can move into Blackacre, let his naval career stagnate or end, and enjoy the use and possession of Blackacre for the remainder of his life. The only incentive to B here is to acquire the more valuable and readily transferable fee simple absolute.

Finally, because leaseholds were not freehold estates, and thus a leaseholder did not hold seisin (which was held by the landlord), a contingent interest following a leasehold was not subject to the destructibility rule. Such an interest was regarded as an executory interest because it did not follow upon expiration of a freehold estate.

Example 4–35: O, owner of Blackacre in fee simple absolute, conveys it "to A for a term of ten years, then to B and his heirs if B shall have returned from Sir Francis Drake's expedition around the world." B holds an executory interest. If at the end of A's ten-year term B has not returned, possession reverts to O and B can divest O upon his return.

The destructibility rule has gradually shriveled into practical oblivion. At least 23 states have abolished the rule by statute. See, e.g., Calif. Civil Code §§ 741, 742. See also Powell on Real Property § 23.04. In other states the rule has been repudiated by judicial decision. See, e.g., Abo Petroleum Corp. v. Amstutz, 93 N.M. 332 (1979); Johnson v. Amstutz, 101 N.M. 94 (1984). In about a quarter of the states there has been no definitive elimination of the rule by either statute or judicial decision, but the consensus of opinion is that the doctrine is dead. Those states that are silent on the point may simply be tardy in writing the obituary. As long ago as 1936 the Restatement (First) of Property, § 240, stated that the destructibility rule does not exist in America. Given that it arose out of concern for avoiding gaps in seisin, there is no good reason to preserve the rule. Anything it can do, the rule against perpetuities can do better.[3]

PROBLEMS

1. In a jurisdiction that applies the rule of destructibility of contingent remainders, *O* devises Blackacre "to my daughter *A* for life, then in fee simple absolute to such of my grandchildren, *B* and *C*, who survive their father, *D*." What is the state of title in Blackacre after each of the following events, considered separately from each other?

a. *D* dies, survived by *B* and *C*, while *A* is alive; then *A* dies.

b. *A* dies while *B*, *C*, and *D* are alive.

c. While *A*, *B*, *C*, and *D* are alive, *A* conveys her life estate to *D*.

2. In a jurisdiction that has abolished the rule of destructibility of contingent remainders, *O* devises Blackacre "to my daughter *A* for life, then in fee simple absolute to such of her children who graduate from college with a bachelor's degree." What is the state of title in Blackacre after each of the following events, considered separately from each other?

a. *A* dies, survived by her children, *B*, age 10, and *C*, age 8, each of whom are enrolled in elementary school.

b. While *A* is alive *B* graduates from Harvard with a B.A. degree, then dies. *A* dies from shock upon hearing the news, survived by *C*, age 20 and a junior at Yale.

2. THE RULE IN SHELLEY'S CASE

Dating from 1581,[4] the rule derived from Wolfe v. Shelley (Shelley's Case), 1 Co. Rep. 93b, 76 Eng. Rep. 206 (1581), limited opportunities for tax avoidance and promoted alienability. It did this by prohibiting the

---

3. See Irving Berlin's song Anything You Can Do, composed for the 1946 musical "Annie Get Your Gun." This duet, which features the lyric "anything you can do I can do better; I can do anything better than you," was first sung by the inimitable Ethel Merman and Ray Middleton.

4. Arguably, the rule in Shelley's Case originated in Abel's Case, Y.B. 18 Ed. II, 577 (1324). The Provost of Beverley's Case, Y.B. 40 Ed. III, 9 (1366) is said by Richard Powell to be a "clear application" of the rule. 3 Powell on Real Property § 31.07, n.6. For the early history of the rule, see 3 Holdsworth, History of English Law 107–111 (4th ed. 1935).

creation of a remainder in the heirs of the owner of the preceding life estate. The effect of this was to ensure that those heirs, whoever, they turned out to be, could not acquire title by *inter vivos* transfer (which would enable them to avoid payment of the feudal incidents at the death of the life tenant) but must acquire title, if at all, by devise or inheritance (which made them subject to the feudal incidents). The rule also had the collateral effect of promoting alienability. Although feudal incidents were eliminated eighty years after the rule was created, the rule continued to thrive because it made land more easily transferable. As with the rule of destructibility of contingent remainders, it was riddled with exceptions, a fact that made it terribly complex. For a glimpse into those complexities see 3 Powell on Real Property § 31.07.

Here is the rule, as stated by Lord Coke in his report on Shelley's Case: "When the ancestor by any gift or conveyance takes an estate of freehold, and in the same gift or conveyance an estate is limited either mediately, or immediately, to his heirs in fee or in tail; that always in such cases the heirs are words of limitation of the estate and not words of purchase." Reduced to its essence and to its most common application, the rule stipulates that if (1) a single instrument (2) creates a life estate[5] in *A*, and (3) purports to create a remainder in *A*'s heirs or the heirs of *A*'s body, and (4) each of the life estate and the remainder are legal interests or each of the life estate and the remainder are equitable interests, the remainder is treated as a remainder in fee simple absolute in *A* (or, if the attempt was to create a remainder in the heirs of *A*'s body, a remainder in fee tail in *A*).

Independently of the rule in Shelley's Case, the merger doctrine could apply. If the remainder in *A* created by the rule is the next vested estate following the life estate in *A*, the life estate and the vested remainder would be merged into a possessory fee interest in *A*. Now, assuming that *A* wished to retain possession of the property during his life, *A*'s heirs could acquire the property only by devise or inheritance from *A*, not via the *inter vivos* transfer that created *A*'s interest.

Example 4–36: O, owner of Blackacre in fee simple absolute, conveys Blackacre "to *A* for life, then to the heirs of *A*." Before application of the rule in Shelley's Case, the heirs of *A*, a class of unknown persons (because we can never be certain of a person's heirs until his death), would own a contingent remainder. The rule operates to convert that remainder into a vested remainder in fee simple absolute owned by *A*. Because the possessory freehold and the next vested estate are owned by the same person, the merger doctrine fuses these interests into a possessory fee simple absolute in *A*, a result that also makes Blackacre alienable immediately. Of course, if there had been an intervening vested estate, merger would not occur.

---

5. The rule originated with respect to freehold interests in land, but there are precedents finding the rule applicable to personal property as well. See, e.g., Ham v. Ham, 21 N.C. 598 (1837), citing 4 James Kent, Commentaries on American Law 223.

Nor would merger occur if the remainder in *A* created by the rule were not vested, but contingent.

The rule applied to remainders, but not executory interests. See Restatement (Second) of Property, Donative Transfers § 30.1, comment e; Barnard v. Moore, 71 Colo. 401 (1922). The rule is a rule of law, not a rule of construction, and thus applies regardless of the grantor's intent. See Perrin v. Blake, 96 Eng. Rep. 392 (1769); cases collected in 3 Powell on Real Property § 31.07, n. 54.

NOTES AND PROBLEMS

1. In the United Kingdom and in some American states the rule applies only when the remainder in the heirs (or heirs of the body) of the life tenant refers to an *indefinite* line of succession, rather than to a specific and more limited class of the heirs of the life tenant. Even though the rule applies regardless of the grantor's intentions, when confronted with an ambiguous grant, courts in these jurisdictions strive to determine whether the grantor meant to create a remainder in the indefinite heirs of the life tenant or a specific set of heirs. If the former, the words used are words of limitation and the rule applies. If the latter, the words are words of purchase and the rule does not apply. For example, a devise of Blackacre "to *A* for life, and then to the persons who would have inherited Blackacre from *A* had he owned the same in fee simple at the time of his death" was held to be a grant to a specific set of takers, the heirs of *A* that exist only at the moment of his death. Earnhart v. Earnhart, 127 Ind. 397 (1891). A clearer expression of a specific set of heirs was a devise "to John, for ... life, and [then] to the children or other lawful heirs of his body, who may survive him...." Gordon v. Cadwalader, 164 Cal. 509, 515 (1912).

The majority rule in America, though, was that if the terms "heirs" or "heirs of the body" were used in the remainder, that was enough to invoke the rule in Shelley's Case. "Thus, a conveyance of land 'to A for life, then to the persons who will inherit real property from A on his death intestate' comes within the Rule in Shelley's Case under the approach of these American cases, but does not under the English approach." 3 Powell on Real Property § 31.07. See also the cases collected in 3 Powell on Real Property § 31.07, n.35.

2. What is the effect of the rule in Shelley's Case on each of the following transfers? In each case, prior to the transfer *O* owned a fee simple absolute in the land.

a. *O* conveys "to *A* for life, and then to the heirs of *A* if *A* resides in Surrey at his death."

b. *O* conveys "to *A* for 90 years if he should live so long, and then to the heirs of *A*."

c. *O* conveys "to *A* for life, and one day after *A*'s death, to the heirs of *A*."

d.   *O* conveys "to *T* and his heirs, in trust, to pay the rents and profits for life to *A*, and then to distribute the trust corpus, outright and free of trust, to the heirs of *A*."

e.   *O* conveys "to *A* for life." A week later, *O* conveys his reversion "to the heirs of *A*."

f.   *O* conveys "to *A* for life, then to *B* for life, and then to the heirs of *A*."

g.   *O* conveys "to *A* for the life of *C*, and then to the heirs of *A*."

3. The Good News: Abolition. The Rule in Shelley's Case has been abolished by statute or judicial decision in all but a tiny handful of American states. However, that abolition is prospective; the rule continues to apply to interests created before its abolition. As time elapses after abolition, the occasions for applying the rule diminish. But abolition is still fairly recent in some jurisdictions. See, e.g., North Carolina (1987), Illinois (1953); Ohio (1941). Thus, you may need to know and apply the rule.

3. THE DOCTRINE OF WORTHIER TITLE

The common law regarded the acquisition of title in land by inheritance or devise as "worthier" than the acquisition of title in any other manner. Why this was so is a matter of some speculation. It may have been the preference of the King's judges, seeking to preserve the Crown's ability to secure feudal incidents that accrued upon the passage of title at death. Some evidence that this was the reason may be inferred from the fact that the doctrine of worthier title did not apply to conveyances of personal property, because there were no feudal incidents due at passage of personal property by inheritance. But it may also have reflected a cultural preference for the landed gentry's habit of passing the manor along to the eldest son. The doctrine promotes alienability of land, so it may have arisen to accomplish that end. Whatever the reason, the common law prohibited a person from making an *inter vivos* conveyance of a future interest in land to his own heirs. Stated simply, the doctrine of worthier title holds that when a grantor makes an inter vivos conveyance of land to another person, with a limitation over in favor of the grantor's own heirs, either by remainder or executory interest, the purported future interest in the grantor's heirs is not recognized; instead, a reversion is created in the grantor. The doctrine was a rule of law, not of construction.

Example 4–37: O, owner of Blackacre in fee simple absolute, conveys it "to *A* for life, then to the heirs of *O*." The putative contingent remainder in the unknown class of *O*'s heirs is void; instead, there is a reversion in fee simple absolute in *O*. Blackacre is now more easily alienable because *O* can convey his reversion. If worthier title did not exist, Blackacre would remain inalienable until *A*'s death. (If *O* was alive at that moment, the contingent remainder in *O*'s heirs would be destroyed by the destructibility doctrine, leaving *O* with a reversion that would be immediately possessory. If *O* predeceased *A* then *O*'s heirs would be known and their vested remainder would become a possessory fee simple absolute.) Worthier title accelerates the moment of alienability.

No doubt because of its feudal origins, worthier title had largely disappeared in practice from American law when, in one of his less acute moments, New York Court of Appeals Judge Benjamin Cardozo (later Justice Cardozo) revived the doctrine as a rule of construction, rather than a rule of law. See Doctor v. Hughes, 225 N.Y. 305 (1919). A limitation in favor of the grantor's heirs raises a presumption that the grantor did not intend to convey anything to the grantor's heirs, thus producing a reversion in the grantor. But this presumption can be overcome by contrary evidence. Judge Cardozo also extended the application of his version of worthier title to personal property, thus making it widely applicable to trusts, most of which are funded by financial assets and other personal property. The Cardozo version bred litigation over the grantor's intent and provided no stability to the law governing wills and trusts, an area where grantors desire and need certainty. Thus, New York abolished worthier title altogether, as have most other states. Unhappily, the doctrine of worthier title as a rule of construction may still exist in some American states.

When the doctrine of worthier title as a rule of law stalked the land, there was a parallel rule that applied to devises of land. If a testator devised property to a person with a limitation over to the testator's heirs, the future interest in the heirs was treated as property that passes through intestate succession to the heirs. In feudal times, there might have been some reason to prefer inheritance to devise, but there are no reasons today for such a rule. Accordingly, the testamentary branch of worthier title is a dead letter. See, e.g., City National Bank v. Andrews, 355 So.2d 341, 343–344 (Ala. 1978): "[T]he wills branch of the worthier title doctrine has few, if any, defenders. It has been condemned by legal scholars [because it] 'invites litigation, ensnares the unwary draftsman[,] frustrates the wary draftsman[, and] applies to devises to people who are the most natural objects of the testator's bounty....' [It] is an anachronism in the law and should not be applied."

For more discussion of worthier title, see 3 Powell on Real Property § 381.

PROBLEMS

1. Assume that the *inter vivos* branch of worthier title, as a rule of law, is in effect. *O*, owner of Blackacre in fee simple absolute, conveys it "to *A* for life, then to my heirs." *O* later borrows money from *C* and defaults on the loan. *O* dies; *H* is his sole heir. *C* sues *O*'s estate on the unpaid debt and, while the case is pending, *A* dies. *H* intervenes in the litigation, asserting that Blackacre belongs to him and is exempt from *C*'s claim as a creditor of *O*. Does Blackacre belong to *H* or is it an asset of *O*'s estate that may be seized by *C*, as a creditor of *O*?

2. Assume that the *inter vivos branch* of worthier title, as a rule of law, is in effect. Assume that the Rule in Shelley's Case has been abolished. *O*, owner of Blackacre in fee simple absolute, conveys it "to *T* and his heirs, in trust, to pay the income from the trust corpus to *O* for life, then to distribute the trust corpus outright and free of trust to the heirs of *O*." Later, *O* dies, survived by *H*, his sole heir, and *A*. *O*'s will devises all of his property to *A*. Who owns the trust corpus? Would it make any difference to your answer if the Rule in Shelley's Case, as well as the doctrine of worthier title, were recognized by the jurisdiction in which this problem arises?

4. THE RULE AGAINST PERPETUITIES

a. The Common Law Version

The Rule Against Perpetuities is the modern device to prevent uncertain ownership of property from preventing its present alienability. A bit of legal history aids understanding of why the Rule developed as it did.

The Duke of Norfolk's Case, 3 Ch. Cas. 1; 22 Eng. Rep. 931 (Chancery 1682). In seventeenth century England, the Earl of Arundel and Duke of Norfolk, possessed of considerable property, had a problem: His eldest son, Thomas, was insane and he needed to do something to protect the family manor from the consequences of his son's illness. The Earl consulted Orlando Bridgman, the foremost conveyancer of the time, who drafted a trust lasting about 200 years to keep the property out of Thomas's control. The property in trust was for the benefit of his second son, Henry, but if Thomas should die without issue during Henry's life, to go to the third son, Charles, and the heirs of his body, and in tail, successively, to the Duke's other sons, Edward, Francis, and Bernard. It was a good bet that Thomas would die without issue as the Duke was keeping him locked up and away from female company. If Henry then became the Earl and Duke he would succeed via primogeniture to the family manor, and the portion left initially to Henry could be spared for Charles. The second son, Phillip, needed no provision from the Duke as he was a Cardinal in Rome, making it highly unlikely that Phillip would wish to trade his status and the comforts of Roman cuisine and climate for the life of a squire in damp, culinarily challenged, England. In the event, Thomas died childless during Henry's life.

When presented with this arrangement, Lord Nottingham decided that "perpetual clogs upon the estate" are void because they "fight against God [and] pretend to such a stability in human affairs, as the nature of them admits not of...." By this, Lord Nottingham meant that man, unlike God, lacked omniscience and thus could only provide for what he knows. The Duke could provide for his known sons, which he did in the grant to Henry and then over to Charles in tail, but the successive remainders in tail in Edward, Francis, and Bernard, contingent upon the expiration of Charles's bloodline and then further contingent upon the expiration of the bloodline of each son in order, were well outside the human knowledge of the Duke. Now he was pretending he was God, and that he could do, but since the only issue was the validity of the executory interest in Charles, Lord Nottingham said he did not have to decide the precise moment at which a grantor's desires pretend to be those of the Deity. A more earthly statement of the issue is to ask when the uncertainty of future possession is prolonged so long that the contingent future interests should be destroyed. Over the next century or so the courts concluded that creation of contingent future interests was acceptable so long as the uncertainty would be removed by the end of the lives of the persons living and known by the grantor at the time the grant is effective, plus an additional 21 years (being the time for the next generation to reach adulthood). The rationale was that a grantor could know and assess the capabilities of those living at the time he makes the grant, and ought to have the ability to keep possession in abeyance until the generation after those he knows have become adults. Or, you could say that after that period has expired the grantor, like Icarus, would fly too close to the Sun.

In the late nineteenth and early twentieth century, the incredibly learned Harvard professor of law, John Chipman Gray, who became the undisputed authority on the Rule Against Perpetuities, distilled it into one sentence: "No interest is good unless it must vest, if at all, not later than twenty-one years after some life in being at the creation of the interest." John Chipman Gray, The Rule Against Perpetuities 191, § 201 (4th ed. 1942). Beware the apparent simplicity of the Rule. Hidden in this sentence is enormous complexity that can and does create a variety of traps for the lawyer whose concentration wavers or whose powers of analytical thought are not well honed. Professor Gray's distillation of the Rule is the common law Rule Against Perpetuities. There are modern modifications to the Rule that will be discussed in later subsections, but in order to understand those modifications it is necessary to grasp the common law version. But before embarking on that task, consider these words of the master, Professor Gray:

> In many legal discussions there is, in the last resort, nothing to say but that one judge or writer thinks one way, and another writer or judge thinks another way. There is no exact standard to which appeal can be made. In questions of remoteness this is not so; there is ... a definite recognized rule: if a decision agrees with it, it is right; if does not agree with it, it is wrong. In no part of the law is the reasoning so mathematical in its character; none has so small a human element. ... If the answer to a problem does not square with the multiplication table one may call it wrong, although it be the work of Sir Isaac Newton; and so if a decision conflicts with the Rule against Perpetuities, one may call it wrong, however learned and able the court that has pronounced it." John Chipman Gray, The Rule Against Perpetuities xi (4th ed. 1942)

Those magisterial comments are tempered by this observation: "No one can read the perpetuities cases ... without some sense of nausea." W. Barton Leach & James K. Logan, Cases and Text on Future Interests and Estate Planning 672 (1961).

Analysis of the validity of future interests under the common law begins with deciding which future interests are subject to the Rule. The Rule is concerned about when a future interest will *vest in interest*, not when it will vest in possession. Vesting in interest occurs when the uncertainty about who will be entitled to possession in the future is removed. Vesting in possession occurs when the owner of a future interest is entitled to possession.

> *Example 4–38:* O, owner of Blackacre in fee simple absolute, conveys it "to A for life, then to B if B passes the bar examination." At the time of the grant, B is a law student and has not passed the bar examination. B has a contingent remainder. It is uncertain whether B will ever be entitled to possession. Three years after the conveyance, and while A is alive, B passes the bar examination. B has now *vested in interest*; her contingent remainder has become an indefeasibly vested remainder because she is a known person and the condition precedent to her ultimate right to possession has been satisfied. But B will not *vest in possession* until A's life estate ends. That could be many years later. Under the Rule Against Perpetuities we do not care when B will vest in possession; we only want to know when B will vest in interest.

Vesting in interest and vesting in possession can occur at the same moment, but that is not of concern to the Rule.

> *Example 4–39:* O, owner of Blackacre in fee simple absolute, conveys it "to A for life, and then to B if B survives A." While A and B are alive B has a contingent remainder. It will vest in interest, if it vests at all, at the moment that A dies, survived by B, and that happens also to be the moment B vests in possession. Of course, B's contingent remainder might not vest at all, if B predeceases A.

Because the Rule is concerned with vesting in interest, the only future interests that are subject to the Rule are those that are uncertain to become possessory. Those contingent future interests have not yet vested in interest. The future interests that fit that description are contingent remainders, executory interests, vested reminders subject to complete divestment, and vested remainders subject to open (or subject to partial divestment). The reason vested remainders subject to complete divestment are subject to the Rule is that, although vested for classification purposes, in fact there exists uncertainty whether such a remainder will ever become possessory. The divesting condition could occur before its holder is entitled to possession. Vested remainders subject to open are subject to the Rule because they occur when there is a class gift, and there are some special rules about class gifts which you will encounter shortly. Interests that are not subject to the Rule are indefeasibly vested remainders, reversions, possibilities of reverter, and rights of entry (powers of termination). Even though there exists uncertainty when a possibility of reverter or a right of entry will become possessory, if ever, the common law regarded those interests as vested at the moment of creation because they were what was retained by the grantor after he had conveyed an estate of lesser duration. Those interests never left the grantor, so they must be vested. That reasoning ignores the obvious uncertainty of possession but fits the idea that possession would ultimately come back to the grantor (or his successors), as soon as the limiting condition was broken (and, in the case of the right of entry, the right was asserted), so the interest retained by the grantor must be indefeasibly vested.

Before proceeding further, it is critical to understand that the Rule is a rule of logical proof. Your task is to prove that a future interest subject to the Rule will vest within the perpetuities period, or to prove that there is a *possibility* (no matter how unlikely) that it will not vest within the perpetuities period. If you can prove the former proposition, the contingent interest is valid. If you can prove the latter proposition, the contingent future interest is void and will be stricken from the grant. The Rule is concerned about *possibilities*, however outlandish, not probabilities. This exercise applies to the interest at the moment it is created, even if the inquiry occurs long after the interest has become effective. Thus, the Rule focuses on what might happen, not what has actually happened. Note that the Rule is a rule of law, not a rule of construction. It matters not a whit what the grantor may have intended if the grantor creates a contingent future interest that can be shown to have even a *possibility* of remote vesting: vesting after the perpetuities period has expired. That interest is void; dead on arrival.

In order to prove that an interest subject to the Rule is either valid or invalid, you must identify the period during which the interest must vest, or fail to vest, in order to be valid. An interest is valid under the Rule if it will certainly vest *or* fail to vest within either (1) 21 years after it becomes effective, (2) during the life of some person alive when it became effective, (3) upon the death of some person alive when it became effective, or (4) 21 years after the death of some person alive when it became effective. An interest created by an *inter vivos* conveyance is effective at the moment of the conveyance. An interest created by will is effective at the moment of the testator's death, not when the will is written.

The Rule thus requires you to identify some person *alive when the interest becomes effective* whose life can serve as the "validating" or "measuring" life for the interest in question. That could be a single person, or a class of persons, but it must be a person or persons whose life or lives is germane to the grant—a person or persons who can affect vesting of the interest. In essence, you must first determine the events that can affect vesting and then you identify the persons who can affect those events.

Example 4-40: At *O*'s death he devises Blackacre "to my wife, *W*, for life, then to my children for their lives, and then to my grandchildren then living." *O* is survived by *W*, and two children, *A* and *B*. *W* has a presently possessory interest that is not subject to the Rule. The class of *O*'s children is a closed class consisting of *A* and *B*, so each of them have an indefeasibly vested remainder in a life estate, that is not subject to the Rule. The open and unknown class of O's grandchildren has a contingent remainder, that is subject to the Rule. When will it vest, *or* fail to vest? We first determine the events that will remove the contingency. There are two events: (1) At the moment that the class of O's grandchildren is closed, we will know who all of them are, and (2) at the moment each of A and B die we will know which of O's grandchildren are then living. We will know who all of O's grandchildren are when both A and B are dead, and that is also the moment when we will know which of them will be alive. Thus, we can use the closed class of O's children—A and B—as the measuring or validating lives. At the end of their lives the contingent remainder in O's grandchildren will either vest in living grandchildren or fail to vest because there no living grandchildren. The contingent remainder is valid.

Example 4–40 illustrates how one can prove the validity of a future interest subject to the Rule. By identifying a measuring life (or lives), the expiration of which will allow us to determine whether the future interest will vest *or* fail to vest at that moment, we can prove that the uncertainty will be removed within the period of the Rule. Here is another example.

Example 4–41: O conveys Blackacre "to A for life, and then to the first of A's children to attain the age of 21." A is alive at the time of the grant and has no children. The unknown class of A's children has a contingent remainder. When A dies we will know the identity of all of A's children. If A has no children the contingent remainder will be certain to fail to vest at the end of A's life. If A has children the contingent remainder will be certain to vest *or* fail to vest no later than 21 years after A's death. Even if A has one child, B, and dies at the moment of childbirth we will know whether B will reach age 21 no later than 21 years after A's death. A is the validating or measuring life.

Proof of the invalidity of an interest can be more difficult. In essence you must concoct a possible scenario in which the interest could vest or fail to vest after the perpetuities period has expired.

Example 4–42: O conveys Blackacre "to A for life, and then to the first of A's children to attain the age of 25." At the time of the grant A is alive and has no children. At A's death we will know the identity of all of A's children but the remainder may still be contingent for 25 more years. Suppose that A has a child, B, at her death. B cannot reach the age of 25 within 21 years after A's death. A cannot serve as a validating life. It does not matter if A had a child at the time of the grant, so long as that child is less than 25 years of age at the time. Suppose at the time of the grant A had a child, C, who was 20 years of age. C could die the next day, A could give birth to B, and them immediately die. The remainder could vest in B 25 years later. Too late. The remainder is destroyed. That leaves a life estate in *A* and a reversion in *O*.

In the foregoing examples the validating (or measuring) life is a person or class of persons mentioned in the grant. This need not be the case. The validating or measuring life may be someone unmentioned but whose life is relevant to the question of when the future interest will vest.

> *Example 4–43:* *O* conveys Blackacre "to my nephews who reach age 21." At the time of the grant *O* has two siblings, *R* and *S*, and each of *O*'s parents has predeceased him. The springing executory interest in *O*'s nephews is valid because we will know the identity of all of *O*'s nephews when both *R* and *S* have died, and the nephews will either reach age 21 or not within 21 years after the death of the last to die of *R* and *S*. We can use the class of *O*'s siblings as validating lives because that class is closed. *O*'s parents are dead so there can be no more siblings of *O* created.

Example 4–43 also illustrates a key fact about classes of people. In order to use a class of people as validating lives, *every member of the class* must be alive at the moment the future interest becomes effective. If in Example 4–43 *O*'s parents had been alive at the time of the grant, we could not use the class of *O*'s siblings as validating lives. *R*, *S*, and all living nephews of *O* could die the next day after the grant is made; *O*'s parents then conceive and give birth to *P*, an event which causes *O* and *O*'s parents to die of heart failure. Thirty years later *P* gives birth to *Q*, a nephew of *O*. Twenty-one years later *Q* reaches age 21. This is long after 21 years have elapsed from the death of all persons relevant to the grant who were alive at the time of the grant.

When a future interest is created in a class of people some special rules apply. For classification purposes a remainder in *A*'s children created while *A* is alive and has one child, *B*, creates a vested remainder subject to open in *B*. But that remainder is not vested for perpetuities purposes. The reason is that, for perpetuities purposes, a future interest in a class of people is not considered vested with respect to any member of the class until it is vested in *every member of the class*. The earliest moment that will happen is when (1) the class is closed, so that no new members may enter, and (2) any conditions precedent to vesting have been satisfied by *every member* of the closed class.

> *Example 4–44:* *O* devises Blackacre "to my daughter *A* for life, then to *A*'s children for their lives, and then to *A*'s grandchildren." *O* is survived by *A*, *A*'s two children, *B* and *C*, and *A*'s one grandchild, *D*. For classification purposes *B* and *C* have a vested remainder in a life estate subject to open, and *D* has a vested remainder in fee simple subject to open. However, none of these remainders are vested for perpetuities purposes. The class of *A*'s children will close when *A* dies. Because there is no condition precedent to *A*'s children's possession of their life estate, the remainders held by *B* and *C* (and any new entrants to the class, should *A* have more children) will vest at the

Crt fand the interest to TI's was too remote, violating RoPerp.

end of *A*'s life. (If all of *A*'s children predecease *A*, their interests will have expired naturally, because their interests were in a life estate.) *A* is the validating life for the remainder in her children. However, the class of *A*'s grandchildren will not close until all of *A*'s children have died. *A* could have another child, *E*, after *O*'s death (the effective date of the grant). Then *A*, *B*, *C*, and *D* could all die. Thirty years later *E* gives birth to *F*, a grandchild of *A*. *E* then dies. Now the class of *A*'s grandchildren is closed and every member of that class will have vested, but it is too late. The possibility of remote vesting, however unlikely, is enough to invalidate the entire remainder in *A*'s grand-children.

Although a class ordinarily closes when every possible member of the class has been identified, there is an exception to this principle. Under the rule of convenience, a presumption arises that the grantor intended the class to close around all living members of the class when any member of the class is entitled to *possession*. The rule of convenience is not a rule of law, but is a principle of construction; if a grantor does not wish it to apply the grantor may state that it is not his intention for it to apply, or to provide other evidence of that contrary intention.

> *Example 4–45:* *O* devises Blackacre "to such of *A*'s children who reach age 25." *O* is survived by *A* and *A*'s two children, *B* (age 26), and *C* (age 21). Under the rule of convenience *B* is entitled to possession. That closes the class around *B* and *C*. *C* will either reach age 25 or not within her own life, so *C* can serve as the validating life for the entire class. If the rule of convenience did not apply the entire class interest would be void. *A* could have another child, *Z*, and then *A*, *B*, and *C* could all immediately die. *Z* could reach age 25 more than 21 years after the expiration of all relevant lives in being at the time the grant became effective. That scenario of remote vesting would invalidate the grant as to every member of the class, including the unfortunate *B*. On the other hand, while application of the rule of convenience saves the interest from destruction by the Rule Against Perpetuities, it also cuts out from the gift any later born children of *A*. *Z* would not share in the enjoyment of Blackacre, a result that is likely to engender sibling resentment.

You understand the common law Rule Against Perpetuities if you grasp the reasons for the result of the following case and can identify and explain how the bequest could have been altered to make the bequest valid in its entirety.

JEE v. AUDLEY

Court of Chancery, 1787
1 Cox 324, 29 Eng. Rep. 1186 (1787)

Edward Audley, by his will, bequeathed as follows,

Also my will is that £1000 shall be placed out at interest during the life of my wife, which interest I give her during her life, and at her death I give the said £1000 unto my niece Mary Hall[6] and the issue of her body lawfully begotten, and to be begotten, and in default of such issue I give the said £1000 to be equally divided between the daughters then living of my kinsman John Jee and his wife Elizabeth Jee.

It appeared that John Jee and Elizabeth Jee were living at the time of the death of the testator, had four daughters[7] and no sons,[8] and were of a very advanced age. Mary Hall was unmarried and of the age of about 40;[9] the wife was dead.[10] The present bill was filed by the four daughters of John and Elizabeth Jee to have the £1000 secured for their benefit upon the event of the said Mary Hall dying without leaving children. And the question was, whether the limitation to the daughters of John and Elizabeth Jee was not void as being too remote; and to prove it so, it was said that this was to take effect on a general failure of issue of Mary Hall; and though it was to the daughters of John and Elizabeth Jee, yet it was not confined to the daughters living at the death of the testator, and consequently it might extend to after-born daughters, in which case it would not be within the limit of a life or lives in being and 21 years afterwards, beyond which time an executory devise is void.

On the other side it was said, that though the late cases had decided that on a gift to children generally, such children as should be living at the time of the distribution of the fund should be let in, yet it would be very hard to adhere to such a rule of construction so rigidly, as to defeat the evident intention of the testator in this case, especially as there was no real possibility of John and Elizabeth Jee having children after the testator's death, they being then 70 years old;[11] that if there were two ways of construing words, that should be adopted which would give effect to the disposition made by the testator; that the cases, which had decided that after born children should take, proceeded on the implied intention of the testator, and never meant to give an effect to words which would totally defeat such intention.

MASTER OF THE ROLLS [SIR LLOYD KENYON]. Several cases ... have settled that children born after the death of the testator shall take a share

---

6. [Ed.—] Her name was actually Mary Hale. This and the factual corrections that are in the subsequent notes are the product of the meticulous historical research of A. W. Brian Simpson. See. A. W. Brian Simpson, Leading Cases in the Common Law 76–99 (1995). None of these factual errors, if known by Sir Lloyd Kenyon, the judge, would have had any relevance to his decision of the issues in the case. The moral, if there is one, is that court reporters and journalists can not always be relied upon to be accurate.

7. [Ed.—] The Jees had three daughters, Elizabeth, Mary, and Sarah. At the time of the case Mary, age 40, and Sarah, about 34 or 35 years of age, were married. Elizabeth was about 38 years old and unmarried.

8. [Ed.—] The Jees had two sons, John and Edward. Their existence was not material to the issues in the case.

9. [Ed.—] Mary Hale was actually about 53 years of age. She was, indeed, unmarried.

10. [Ed.—] She was very much alive. The widow of Edward Audley, Elizabeth Audley, died in late 1791 or early 1792. It is a mystery how the report of the case could have gotten this wrong, because the named defendant was Elizabeth Audley and she had entered an answer in the litigation.

11. [Ed.—] John and Elizabeth Jee were actually in their early 60s.

in these cases; the difference is, where there is an immediate devise, and where there is an interest in remainder; in the former case the children living at the testator's death only shall take; in the latter those who are living at the time the interest vests in possession; and this being now a settled principle, I shall not strain to serve an intention at the expense of removing the landmarks of the law; it is of infinite importance to abide by decided cases, and perhaps more so on this subject than any other. The general principles which apply to this case are not disputed: the limitations of personal estate are void, unless they necessarily vest, if at all, within a life or lives in being and 21 years or 9 or 10 months afterwards.[12] This has been sanctioned by the opinion of judges of all times, from the time of the Duke of Norfolk's Case to the present: it is grown reverend by age, and is not now to be broken in upon; I am desired to do in this case something which I do not feel myself at liberty to do, namely to suppose it impossible for persons in so advanced an age as John and Elizabeth Jee to have children; but if this can be done in one case it may in another, and it is a very dangerous experiment, and introductive of the greatest inconvenience to give a latitude to such sort of conjecture. Another thing pressed upon me, is to decide on the events which have happened; but I cannot do this without overturning very many cases. The single question before me is, not whether the limitation is good in the events which have happened, but whether it was good in its creation; and if it were not, I cannot make it so. Then must this limitation, if at all, necessarily take place within the limits prescribed by law? The words are "in default of such issue I give the said £1000 to be equally divided between the daughters then living of John Jee and Elizabeth his wife." If it had been to "daughters now living," or "who should be living at the time of my death," it would have been very good; but as it stands, this limitation may take in after-born daughters; . . . and the effect of law on such limitation cannot make any difference in construing such intention. If then this will extended to after-born daughters, is it within the rules of law? Most certainly not, because John and Elizabeth Jee might have children born ten years after the testator's death, and then Mary Hall might die without issue 50 years afterwards; in which case it would evidently transgress the rules prescribed. I am of opinion therefore, though the testator might possibly mean to restrain the limitation to the children who should be living at the time of his death, I cannot, consistently with decided cases, construe it in such restrained sense, but must intend it to take in after-born children. This therefore not being within the rules of law, and as I cannot judge upon subsequent events, I think the limitation void. Therefore dismiss the bill, but without costs.

NOTES, QUESTIONS, AND PROBLEMS

1. Analysis of the Bequest. The first requirement is to understand what interests Edward Audley created when his will became effective at his death.

---

12. [Ed.—] The addition of "9 or 10 months afterwards" reflects the universally accepted doctrine in property law that a child is considered to be in existence at the moment of conception if that child is later born alive.

<u>His wife is given a present possessory life estate in</u> the income from £1,000 but the judge treats her as having predeceased Audley, so on that understanding the bequest has lapsed and <u>Mary Hall has possession</u>. (If the judge had the facts straight Mary would appear to have an indefeasibly vested remainder in fee tail.) But what does she possess? By the language "unto my niece Mary Hall and the issue of her body lawfully begotten," Mary Hall appears to have been given a fee tail. But a fee tail could not be created in personal property because the Statute De Donis, which authorized the fee tail, applied only to land. An attempt to create a fee tail in personal property would instead create a fee simple, so Mary Hall has a fee simple subject to the executory limitation in favor of the Jee daughters. (Given the widow Audley's existence Mary actually had a vested remainder in a fee simple subject to complete divestment by the Jee daughters' executory interest.) The event that would divest Mary Hall's fee simple in favor of the Jee daughters is "default of such issue" of Mary Hall. This could mean either (1) if Mary Hall has no issue at the time of her death (often called *definite failure of issue*), or (2) when Mary Hall's bloodline finally expires (often called *indefinite failure of issue*). Sir Lloyd Kenyon, later Baron Kenyon, construed this to mean "general failure of issue," or indefinite failure of issue. While Mary Hall's bloodline could expire at her death, if she should die childless, it could also expire many generations hence. When Baron Kenyon postulated that Mary Hall could "die without issue 50 years afterwards" he meant the latter possibility, not that Mary Hall might die childless "50 years afterwards." In this locution George Washington is dead without issue, but Theodore Roosevelt is not dead without issue. It is the possibility that Mary Hall's bloodline will expire at some unknown time in the future, perhaps centuries later, that leads to the conclusion that Audley's executory interest in the Jee daughters might vest too remotely.

Construct the scenario of remote vesting. Hint: Your scenario must include a child being born to John and Elizabeth Jee after Edward Audley's death as well as a child being born to Mary Hall after Audley's death. It does not matter how unlikely it is that a septuagenarian can conceive and deliver a child; the Rule presumes that a person of any age may do so.[13]

Explain why none of the following can serve as validating lives: Mary Hall, John and Elizabeth Jee, the four Jee daughters alive at Edward Audley's death.

2. The Judge's Supposition. Sir Lloyd Kenyon opined in dicta that if Edward Audley's bequest to the Jee daughters "had been to 'daughters now living,' or 'who should be living at the time of my death,' it would have been very good." Consider each part of the statement in isolation, inasmuch as

---

13. Is this presumption unreasonable in an age in which adoption is freely permitted and eggs and sperm may be frozen for later fertilization? It has always been a staple of perpetuities law that a person may not beget a child after one's death, but in the age of *in vitro* fertilization of frozen, preserved gametic material, should this presumption be abandoned? For example, a testamentary grant to the testator's grandchildren has always been held to be valid because the class of the testator's children in closed at testator's death and thus they may serve as the validating lives for the executory interest in testator's grandchildren. But such a grant would be void if perpetuities law were to indulge in the presumption that people can have children after their death. Perhaps because of the destabilizing effect of such a presumption, courts have not yet done so.

Kenyon phrased them in the disjunctive. Is either statement, standing alone, wrong? Are both wrong? Is only one wrong? Why?

In what way does Kenyon's statement need to be altered to make it entirely correct? Explain why that alteration serves to save the executory interest in the Jee daughters from destruction under the Rule Against Perpetuities.

3. Background.

a. Edward Audley's Intentions. What do you suppose Edward Audley intended? At the time Edward made his will, 1769, Mary Hall was unmarried and 35 years of age, the midway point of life, according to Dante Alighieri.[14] This is Jane Austen's England, a time in which economic security for a woman was provided mostly by marriage, hence the imperative that drives the ambitions of Mrs Bennet in *Pride and Prejudice,* and which explains her anger at Elizabeth Bennet's refusal of the hand of the odious Rev. Collins. Edward Audley undoubtedly wished to provide some measure of economic security for Mary Hall and, to a lesser extent, for the Jee daughters in the event that Mary never married and bore a child. But the Rule Against Perpetuities is impervious to intentions. Without changing or adding to Audley's will how would the bequest have to be interpreted to accomplish Audley's intentions?

b. The Remedy Sought by the Jee Daughters. In their suit, the Jee daughters alleged that Mary Hall had possession of the £1000, that they had asked Mary Hall and Elizabeth Audley to appoint trustees to hold the money, or to deposit the fund with the court, and they had refused to do so. Thus they wanted some security that the fund would be preserved for them, or as the report styles it, "secured for their benefit." Because the executory interest in the Jee daughters was void, there was no need to address the remedy. But what if it had been valid? What remedy can (should) a court deliver? Suppose the court ordered the money turned over in trust to a court-appointed trustee; would the court be required to monitor the trustee? Is this practical or reasonable? Maybe the case would never have arisen if Edward Audley had bequeathed the £1000 to an independent trustee for the income benefit of his widow for life, then for the income benefit of Mary Hall and the heirs of her body lawfully begotten, and in default of such issue to the Jee daughters then living. The perpetuities problem would remain in this grant; it just might not have fallen into the clutches of Sir Lloyd Kenyon.

As mentioned in the footnotes, more background on the case may be obtained in A.W. Brian Simpson, Leading Cases in the Common Law 76–99 (1995).

4. Problems.

a. O conveys Blackacre "to *A* for life, then to *A*'s widow for life, then to *C* if she is then alive, but if not to *C*'s heirs." Which, if any, of the future interests created in this grant are valid? Why?

---

14. "Midway this way of life we're bound upon,/ I woke to find myself in a dark wood,/ Where the right road was wholly lost and gone." Dante Alighieri, Inferno, Canto I (Dorothy L. Sayers, trans.)

b. *O* conveys Blackacre "to *A* for life, then to *A*'s children who reach 25." *A* has a child, *B*, age 26, living at the time of the conveyance. Is the remainder valid? Why? *Yes*

c. *O* devises Blackacre "to *A* for life, then to *A*'s widow for life, then to *A*'s lineal descendants then living." Which, if any, of the future interests in this devise are valid? Why? *A's widow,*

d. *O*, survived by *A* and *B*, devises property "to *A* for life, then to *A*'s children for their lives, and then to *B* if *A* dies childless." Which, if any, of the future interests in this devise are valid? *A's children + B* *O-POR; b/c A's children have UO*

e. *O*, survived by *A* and *B*, devises property "to *A* for life, then to *A*'s children for their lives, and then to *B*'s children." Which, if any, of the future interests in this devise are valid? *A's children.*

f. *O*, survived by *A* and *B*, devises property "to *A* for life, then to *A*'s children for their lives, and then to *B*'s children then living." Which, if any, of the future interests in this devise are valid? *A's children, B's*

g. *O*, survived by *A* and *B*, devises property "to *A* for life, then to *A*'s children for their lives, and then to *O*'s grandchildren." Which, if any, of the future interests in this devise are valid? *A's children* *O's children closed due*

h. *O*, survived by *A* and *B*, devises property "to *A* for life, then to *A*'s children for their lives, and then to *A*'s grandchildren." Which, if any, of the future interests in this devise are valid? *A's children* *A's children not a closed class!*

i. *O* conveys Blackacre "to *A* for life, then to *B* if *B* attains the age of 25." *B* is 3 years old at the time of the conveyance. Is the remainder valid?

j. *O* conveys Blackacre "to the first member of the Yale undergraduate class of 2008 who shall become President of the United States, and if none, to *B* and her heirs." *B* is 3 years old at the time of the grant.

5. *Modern Application of the Rule Against Perpetuities.* The most common place in which a perpetuities problem will be encountered is in a trust that is designed to preserve family wealth for several generations.[15] A possible arrangement might involve a testamentary trust that requires the trustee to pay the income for life to the testator's surviving spouse ("*Spouse*"), then to pay the income for life to the testator's children ("*Children*"), then to pay the income for life to the testator's grandchildren ("*Grandchildren*"), and then to distribute the trust corpus, free of trust, to the testator's great-grandchildren ("*Greats*"). You will note that the remainders to the *Children* and the *Grandchildren* are valid but the remainder in the *Greats* is void. To avoid destruction of the last remainder and still preserve the trust to accomplish as much of its intended purpose as possible, the trust drafter might insert a clause terminating the trust at the expiration of the perpetuities period, if it has not already terminated.

> Notwithstanding any other provision in this instrument this trust shall terminate if it has not previously terminated 21 years after the death of the survivor of all of my issue, of whatever degree of descent, living at my death. In the event this trust terminates under this provision, the

---

15. But note the occurrence of a perpetuities problem in the next case, which is a commercial real estate transaction.

principal and undistributed income of the trust shall then be distributed to my *Children*'s issue then living by right of representation, or, if no issue of my *Children* is then living, to Doctors Without Borders (Medecins Sans Frontieres).

Another approach is to create an artificial class of lives that will serve as the validating lives. In the clause recited above, instead of making the trust terminate 2i years after "the death of the survivor of all my issue, of whatever degree of descent, living at my death," the trust might be made to terminate 21 years after "the death of the survivor of all the descendants of Joseph P. Kennedy, Sr., living at my death," or 21 years after "the death of the survivor of of all the descendants of Queen Elizabeth II living at my death." The danger in this gambit is that if "the number of individuals specified as the measuring lives . . . is so large that it would be an impossible administrative burden to locate them initially, let alone determine the death of the survivor," the clause is not effective. See Restatement (Second) of Property, Donative Transfers § 1.3, comment a (1983); Uniform Statutory Rule Against Perpetuities Act § 1, comment, part B. The class of Joseph P. Kennedy, Sr.'s living descendants is a borderline example. According to http://en.wikipedia.org/wiki/List_of_descendants_of_Joseph_P._and_Rose_Fitzgerald_Kennedy there are 96 currently (as of September 2010) living descendants of Joseph P. Kennedy, Sr.[16] Keeping track of this clan and determining when the last one dies might be just the sort of administrative burden that the Restatement envisions. Although the currently living descendants of Queen Elizabeth II are fewer in number (as of September 2010, there are eleven in the class, according to http://europeandynasties.com/Descendants_of_ElizabethIIi_Windsor.htm), and it would probably be easier to identify when the last survivor of Elizabeth II dies than it would be to identify the last of the Kennedy clan, one must ask whether it is really worth the effort to use this artificial class as the measuring life. It is better to use the descendants of the testator.

NOTE: EXECUTORY INTERESTS FOLLOWING DEFEASIBLE FEES

When a grantor creates a defeasible fee in *A* and at the same time places the future interest following that defeasible fee in *B*, instead of retaining it as a possibility of reverter or right of entry, *B* holds an executory interest that is subject to the Rule Against Perpetuities. However, if the grantor had retained a possibility of reverter or right of entry his future interest would be treated as indefeasibly vested and immune from the Rule. Thus, the identical contingency can endure forever if it is preserved in the grantor but may be destroyed if it is created in a grantee. Odd as that may be, it pales in comparison to the different results that obtain after destruction of an executory interest that follows a defeasible fee using the language of fee simple determinable and destruction of an executory interest that follows a defeasible fee phrased as a fee simple subject to a condition subsequent.

Example 4–46: O, owner of Blackacre in fee simple absolute, conveys it "to *A* and his heirs so long as Blackacre is never used for industrial purposes, and then to *B* and his heirs." The executory interest in *B* is

---

16. This assumes that Wikipedia is accurate, which may not be the case.

void under the Rule Against Perpetuities because the uncertainty of divestment may be prolonged for centuries. More than 21 years after *O*, *A*, and *B* have died a successor to *A* may build a factory on Blackacre, thus triggering the divesting condition. This scenario of remote vesting kills the executory interest at its inception. The interest is stricken from the grant, so it ends after "industrial purposes." That means that *O* has, by operation of law, retained a possibility of reverter that is exempt from the Rule Against Perpetuities. This result could have been avoided had *O* conveyed a fee simple determinable to *A*, retaining a possibility of reverter, and subsequently conveying his possibility of reverter to *B*, if local law permits such an *inter vivos* transfer.

Contrast that result with the following example.

> *Example 4–47: O*, owner of Blackacre in fee simple absolute, conveys it "to *A* and his heirs; but if Blackacre is ever used for industrial purposes, then to *B* and his heirs." As in Example 4–46, the executory interest in *B* is void under the Rule Against Perpetuities because the uncertainty of divestment may be prolonged for centuries. Because of the possibility of remote vesting, the executory interest is void at its creation. The interest is stricken from the grant, so it ends after "*A* and his heirs." That produces a fee simple absolute in *A* in Blackacre. As in Example 4–46, *O* could have avoided this result by first granting a fee simple subject to a condition subsequent to *A*, retaining an explicit right of entry which is exempt from the Rule Against Perpetuities, then transferring that right of entry to *B* if local law permits such an *inter vivos* transfer.

It is hard to justify these disparate results, which stem entirely from the linguistic construction of the grants of the preceding defeasible fees. Apart from historical tradition, it is equally difficult to justify the fact that possibilities of reverter and rights of entry are immune from destruction by the Rule while the analogous executory interests are subject to destruction. As Justice Holmes once opined: "It is revolting to have no better reason for a rule of law than that it was laid down in the time of Henry IV. It is still more revolting if the grounds upon which it was laid down have vanished long since, and the rule simply persists from blind imitation of the past." Oliver Wendell Holmes, The Path of the Law, 10 Harv. L. Rev. 457, 469 (1897).

Contemporary jurisdictions have reacted to this state of affairs in three different ways.

First, the Rule Against Perpetuities could be applied to possibilities of reverter and rights of entry. This approach has been adopted in the United Kingdom. See Perpetuities and Accumulations Act 1964, Ch. 55, § 12. The effect is not only to eliminate the preferential treatment accorded these interests under the Rule, but also produces a fee simple absolute in the holder of the putatively defeasible fee. This happens because the possibility of reverter that would be created by destruction of the executory interest following a determinable fee is also destroyed by the Rule.

Second, some states have enacted statutes that automatically destroy possibilities of reverter, rights of entry, and executory interests following a defeasible fee, unless the divesting condition occurs within a specific number of years after the creation of these interests. See Fla. Stat. § 689.18, which destroys all "reverter or forfeiture provision of unlimited duration" in conveyances of land 21 years after their creation; N.C. Gen. Stat. § 41–32, which subjects possibilities of reverter, rights of entry, and executory interests following a defeasible fee to destruction if they do not vest in possession within 60 years after their creation; Ky. Rev. Stat § 381.219, which subjects rights of entry (the only form of interest that in Kentucky a grantor can retain following a defeasible fee) to destruction thirty years after their creation if the divesting event has not occurred by then; and Conn. Gen. Stat. § 45a–505 (2010), which destroys executory interests following a defeasible fee, possibilities of reverter, and rights of entry thirty years after their creation if the divesting condition has not occurred. These statutes typically preserve possibilities of reverter and rights of entry from destruction by the Rule Against Perpetuities but, of course, substitute a statutory destruction rule in its place. Typically these statutes extend exemption from the Rule Against Perpetuities to executory interests following defeasible fees but, of course, the price of exemption is subjection to the statutory destruction rule.

A variation on the second method is contained in California law. California subjects all of these future interests following a defeasible fee to destruction thirty years after their creation, but allows them to continue in perpetuity so long as the holder of the interest records his intention to preserve the interest not later than thirty years after its creation or previous such recording. See Calif. Civil Code §§ 885.010 and 885.030. As with the second method, these interests are immune from the Rule but subject to the statutory destruction rule.

The third approach is that of the Uniform Statutory Rule Against Perpetuities, adopted by about half the states and discussed in section 4.b, infra. Under USRAP, executory interests following a defeasible fee are valid for ninety years, but USRAP leaves possibilities of reverter and rights of entry exempt from the Rule.

Finally, an executory interest following a defeasible fee is exempt from both the Rule Against Perpetuities and any statutory destruction rule if the defeasible fee and the subsequent executory interest are each owned by charities. (immune)

> *Example 4–48: O*, owner of Blackacre in fee simple absolute, conveys it "to Alma Mater College so long as it used for educational purposes, and if not, to the National Trust for Historical Preservation." The executory interest in the National Trust is immune from the Rule and, in jurisdictions that have adopted a statutory destruction rule, is also exempt from destruction under that rule.

THE SYMPHONY SPACE, INC. v. PERGOLA PROPERTIES, INC.

Court of Appeals of New York
88 N.Y.2d 466 (1996)

CHIEF JUDGE KAYE delivered the opinion of the court.

This case presents the novel question whether options to purchase commercial property are exempt from the prohibition against remote vesting embodied in New York's Rule against Perpetuities (EPTL 9–1.1 [b]). Because an exception for commercial options finds no support in our law, we decline to exempt all commercial option agreements from the statutory Rule against Perpetuities. ... [The] option defendants seek to enforce violates the statutory prohibition against remote vesting and is therefore unenforceable.

I. Facts.

The subject of this proceeding is a two-story building situated on the Broadway block between 94th and 95th Streets on Manhattan's Upper West Side. In 1978, Broadwest Realty Corporation owned this building, which housed a theater and commercial space. Broadwest had been unable to secure a permanent tenant for the theater—approximately 58% of the total square footage of the building's floor space. Broadwest also owned two adjacent properties, Pomander Walk (a residential complex) and the Healy Building (a commercial building). Broadwest had been operating its properties at a net loss. Plaintiff Symphony Space, Inc., a not-for-profit entity devoted to the arts, had previously rented the theater for several one-night engagements. In 1978, Symphony and Broadwest engaged in a transaction whereby Broadwest sold the entire building to Symphony for the below-market price of $10,010 and leased back the income-producing commercial property, excluding the theater, for $1 per year. Broadwest maintained liability for the existing $243,000 mortgage on the property as well as certain maintenance obligations. As a condition of the sale, Symphony, for consideration of $10, also granted Broadwest an option to repurchase the entire building. [The] transaction did not involve Pomander Walk or the Healy Building.

The purpose of this arrangement was to enable Symphony, as a not-for-profit corporation, to seek a property tax exemption for the entire building—which constituted a single tax parcel—predicated on its use of the theater. The sale-and-leaseback would thereby reduce Broadwest's real estate taxes by $30,000 per year, while permitting Broadwest to retain the rental income from the leased commercial space in the building, which the trial court found produced $140,000 annually. The arrangement also furthered Broadwest's goal of selling all the properties, by allowing Broadwest to postpone any sale until property values in the area increased and until the commercial leases expired. Symphony, in turn, would have use of the theater at minimal cost, once it received a tax exemption.

Thus, on December 1, 1978, Symphony and Broadwest—both sides represented by counsel—executed a contract for sale of the property from Broadwest to Symphony for the purchase price of $10,010. The contract specified that $10 was to be paid at the closing and $10,000 was to be paid by means of a purchase-money mortgage. The parties also signed several separate documents, each dated December 31, 1978: (1) a deed for the property from Broadwest to Symphony; (2) a lease from Symphony to Broadwest of the entire building except the theater for rent of $1 per year and for the term January 1, 1979 to May 31, 2003, unless terminated earlier; (3) a 25–year, $10,000 mortgage and mortgage note from Symphony as mortgagor to Broadwest as mortgagee, with full payment due on December 31, 2003; and (4) an option agreement by which Broadwest obtained from Symphony the exclusive right to repurchase all of the property, including the theater.

It is the option agreement that is at the heart of the present dispute. Section 3 of that agreement provides that Broadwest may exercise its option to purchase the property ... "(a) at any time after July 1, 1979, so long as the Notice of Election specifies that the Closing is to occur during any of the calendar years 1987, 1993, 1998 and 2003...." [If the option were to be exercised the purchase price was $15,000 if the closing occurred by the end of 1987, $20,000 if it occurred by year-end 1993; $24,000 if by year-end 1998; and $28,000 if by year-end 2003.] Finally, section 6 established that the option constituted "a covenant running with the land, inuring to the benefit of heirs, successors and assigns of Broadwest."

Symphony ultimately obtained a tax exemption for the theater. In the summer of 1981, Broadwest sold and assigned its interest under the lease, option agreement, mortgage and mortgage note, as well as its ownership interest in the contiguous Pomander Walk and Healy Building, to ... Pergola Properties, Inc., [and others for $4.8 million.] Subsequently, defendants initiated a cooperative conversion of Pomander Walk, which was designated a landmark in 1982, and the value of the properties increased substantially. An August 1988 appraisal of the entire blockfront, including the Healy Building and the unused air and other development rights available from Pomander Walk, valued the property at $27 million assuming the enforceability of the option. By contrast, the value of the leasehold interest plus the Healy Building without the option were appraised at $5.5 million....

[In 1985, on behalf of itself and the other owners of the option, Pergola notified Symphony Space that it was exercising the option under section 3 (a) of the option agreement, and set a closing date of January 5, 1987. Symphony sought a declaratory judgment that the option agreement violated the New York statutory prohibition against remote vesting. The trial court granted Symphony's motion for summary judgment and denied Pergola's motion for summary judgment. The trial] court concluded that the Rule against Perpetuities applied to the commercial option.... that the option violated the Rule and that Symphony was entitled to exercise its equitable right to redeem the mortgage. ... [The Appellate Division affirmed these rulings. We] now affirm.

II. Statutory Background.

The Rule against Perpetuities evolved from judicial efforts during the 17th century to limit control of title to real property by the dead hand of landowners reaching into future generations. Underlying both early and modern rules restricting future dispositions of property is the principle that it is socially undesirable for property to be inalienable for an unreasonable period of time. These rules thus seek "to ensure the productive use and development of property by its current beneficial owners by simplifying ownership, facilitating exchange and freeing property from unknown or embarrassing impediments to alienability." . . .

In New York, the rules regarding suspension of the power of alienation and remoteness in vesting—the Rule against Perpetuities—have been statutory since 1830. . . . New York's current statutory Rule against Perpetuities is found in EPTL 9–1.1. Subdivision (a) sets forth the suspension of alienation rule and deems void any estate in which the conveying instrument suspends the absolute power of alienation for longer than lives in being at the creation of the estate plus 21 years (*see,* EPTL 9–1.1 [a] [2]). [This rule is unique to New York and was not at issue in this case. New York prohibits suspension of alienation, which exists when there are insufficient existing persons to convey a fee simple absolute. When a trust is involved, New York considers alienation to be suspended whenever either the trustee cannot convey a fee simple absolute in the trust corpus *or* the beneficiaries cannot convey an equitable fee simple absolute in the trust corpus. In this case, the combination of Symphony Space and Pergola and its fellow option holders (all known and existing persons) could convey a fee simple absolute.] The prohibition against remote vesting is contained in subdivision (b), which states that "[n]o estate in property shall be valid unless it must vest, if at all, not later than twenty-one years after one or more lives in being at the creation of the estate and any period of gestation involved" (EPTL 9–1.1 [b]). This Court has described subdivision (b) as "a rigid formula that invalidates any interest that may not vest within the prescribed time period" and has "capricious consequences." . . . [These] rules . . . constitute non-waivable legal prohibitions.

In addition to these statutory formulas, New York also retains the more flexible common-law rule against unreasonable restraints on alienation. Unlike the statutory Rule against Perpetuities, which is measured exclusively by the passage of time, the common-law rule evaluates the reasonableness of the restraint based on its duration, purpose and designated method for fixing the purchase price.

Against this background, we consider the option agreement at issue.

III.   *Validity of the Option Agreement*   As arguments

Defendants proffer three grounds for upholding the option: that the statutory prohibition against remote vesting does not apply to commercial options; that the option here cannot be exercised beyond the statutory period; and that this Court should adopt the "wait and see" approach to the Rule against Perpetuities. We consider each in turn.

A.   *Applicability of the Rule to Commercial Options*

Under the common law, options to purchase land are subject to the rule against remote vesting [because they] are specifically enforceable and give the option holder a contingent, equitable interest in the land. This creates a disincentive for the landowner to develop the property and hinders its alienability, thereby defeating the policy objectives underlying the Rule against Perpetuities.

Typically, however, options to purchase are part of a commercial transaction. For this reason, subjecting them to the Rule against Perpetuities has been deemed "a step of doubtful wisdom." As one vocal critic, Professor W. Barton Leach, has explained,

> [t]he Rule grew up as a limitation on family dispositions; and the period of lives in being plus twenty-one years is adapted to these gift transactions. The pressures which created the Rule do not exist with reference to arms-length contractual transactions, and neither lives in being nor twenty-one years are periods which are relevant to business men and their affairs. (Leach, Perpetuities: New Absurdity, Judicial and Statutory Correctives, 73 Harv L Rev 1318, 1321–1322)....

It is now settled in New York that, generally, EPTL 9–1.1 (b) applies to options. In Buffalo Seminary v McCarthy [86 App. Div. 2d 435 (1982)], the court held that an unlimited option in gross to purchase real property was void under the statutory rule against remote vesting, and we affirmed [in Buffalo Seminary v. McCarthy, 58 N.Y.2d 867 (1983)]. ... Although the particular option at issue in *Buffalo Seminary* was part of a private transaction between neighboring landowners, the reasoning employed in that case establishes that EPTL 9–1.1 (b) applies equally to commercial purchase options. In reaching its conclusion in *Buffalo Seminary,* the court explained that ... the Legislature specifically intended to incorporate the American common-law rules governing perpetuities into the New York statute. ... Inasmuch as the common-law prohibition against remote vesting applies to both commercial and noncommercial options, it likewise follows that the Legislature intended EPTL 9–1.1 (b) to apply to commercial purchase options as well.

 Consequently, creation of a general exception to EPTL 9–1.1 (b) for all purchase options that are commercial in nature, as advocated by defendants, would remove an entire class of contingent future interests that the Legislature intended the statute to cover. While defendants offer compelling policy reasons—echoing those voiced by Professor Leach—for refusing to apply the traditional rule against remote vesting to these commercial option contracts, such statutory reformation would require legislative action....

Our decision in Metropolitan Transp. Auth. v Bruken Realty Corp. [67 N.Y.2d 156 (1986)] is not to the contrary. In *Bruken,* we held that EPTL 9–1.1 (b) did not apply to a preemptive right in a "commercial and governmental transaction" that lasted beyond the statutory perpetuities period. In doing so, we explained that, *unlike options,* preemptive rights (or rights of first refusal) only marginally affect transferability:

> An option grants to the holder the power to compel the owner of property to sell it whether the owner is willing to part with ownership or not. A preemptive right, or right of first refusal, ... merely

requires the owner, when and if he decides to sell, to offer the property first to the party holding the preemptive right so that he may meet a third-party offer or buy the property at some other price set by a previously stipulated method." . . .

Bruken merely recognized that the Legislature did not intend EPTL 9–1.1 (b) to apply to those contingent future interests in real property that encourage the holder to develop the property by insuring an opportunity to benefit from the improvements and to recapture any investment. In these limited circumstances, enforcement [of the right of first refusal] would promote the purposes underlying the rule. . . . [Since *Bruken*,] we have . . . emphasized that options to purchase are to be treated differently than preemptive rights, underscoring that preemptive rights impede alienability only minimally whereas purchase options vest substantial control over the transferability of property in the option holder. We have also clarified that even preemptive rights are ordinarily subject to the statutory rule against remote vesting. Only where the right arises in a governmental or commercial agreement is the minor restraint on transferability created by the preemptive right offset by the holder's incentive to improve the property.

Here, the option agreement creates precisely the sort of control over future disposition of the property that we have previously associated with purchase options and that the common-law rule against remote vesting—and thus EPTL 9–1.1 (b)—seeks to prevent. As the Appellate Division explained, the option grants its holder absolute power to purchase the property at the holder's whim and at a token price set far below market value. This Sword of Damocles necessarily discourages the property owner from investing in improvements to the property. Furthermore, the option's existence significantly impedes the owner's ability to sell the property to a third party, as a practical matter rendering it inalienable. . . .

That defendants, the holder of this option, are also the lessees of a portion of the premises does not lead to a different conclusion here. Generally, an option to purchase land that originates in one of the lease provisions, is not exercisable after lease expiration, and is incapable of separation from the lease is valid even though the holder's interest may vest beyond the perpetuities period. Such options—known as options "appendant" or "appurtenant" to leases—encourage the possessory holder to invest in maintaining and developing the property by guaranteeing the option holder the ultimate benefit of any such investment. Options appurtenant thus further the policy objectives underlying the rule against remote vesting and are not contemplated by EPTL 9–1.1 (b).

To be sure, the option here arose within a larger transaction that included a lease. Nevertheless, not all of the property subject to the purchase option here is even occupied by defendants. The option encompasses the entire building—both the commercial space and the theater—yet defendants are leasing only the commercial space. With regard to the theater space, a disincentive exists for Symphony to improve the property, since it will eventually be claimed by the option holder at the predetermined purchase price. Furthermore, the option is not contained in the lease itself, but in a separate agreement. Indeed, section 5 of the option agreement specifies that the right to exercise the option is wholly independent from the lease. . . . The duration of the option, moreover, exceeds the term of the lease. Consequently, defendants could compel Symphony to sell them the property even after they have ceased possession as lessee.

Put simply, the option here cannot qualify as an option appurtenant and significantly deters development of the property. If the option is exercisable beyond the statutory perpetuities period, refusing to enforce it would thus further the purpose and rationale underlying the statutory prohibition against remote vesting.

B.   Duration of the Option Agreement
1.   Duration Under Section 3 (a) of the Agreement

Defendants alternatively claim that section 3 (a) of the agreement does not permit exercise of the option after expiration of the statutory perpetuities period. According to defendants, only the possible closing dates fall outside the permissible time frame.

Where, as here, the parties to a transaction are corporations and no measuring lives are stated in the instruments, the perpetuities period is simply 21 years. [The] parties' agreement . . . expressly provides that the option may be exercised "*at any time* after July 1, 1979," so long as the closing date is scheduled during 1987, 1993, 1998 or 2003. Even factoring in the requisite [180 day] notice, then, the option could potentially be exercised as late as July 2003—more than 24 years after its creation in December 1978. Defendants' contention that section 3 (a) does not permit exercise of the option beyond the 21–year period is thus contradicted by the plain language of the instrument.

Nor can EPTL 9–1.3—the "saving statute"—be invoked to shorten the duration of the exercise period under section 3 (a) of the agreement. That statute mandates that, "[u]nless a contrary intention appears," certain rules of construction govern with respect to any matter affecting the Rule against Perpetuities. The specified canons of construction include that "[i]t shall be presumed that the creator intended the estate to be valid" and "where the duration or vesting of an estate is contingent upon . . . the occurrence of any specified contingency, it shall be presumed that the creator of such estate intended such contingency to occur, if at all, within twenty-one years from the effective date of the instrument creating such estate." By presuming that the creator intended the estate to be valid, the statute seeks to avoid annulling dispositions due to inadvertent violations of the Rule against Perpetuities.

The provisions of EPTL 9–1.3, however, are merely rules of construction. While the statute obligates reviewing courts, where possible, to avoid constructions that frustrate the parties' intended purposes, it does not authorize courts to rewrite instruments that unequivocally allow interests to vest outside the perpetuities period. Indeed, by their terms, the rules of construction in EPTL 9–1.3 apply only if "a contrary intention" does not appear in the instrument.

. . . For example, where a deed contains contradictory phrases, one of which is valid under the Rule, or where one of two possible interpretations of a term in an agreement would comply with the Rule, the court will adopt the construction validating the disposition. By contrast, an option containing no limitation in duration demonstrates the parties' intent that it last indefinitely, and EPTL 9–1.3 does not permit "an extensive rewriting of the option agreement . . . so as to make it conform to the permissible period."

The unambiguous language of the agreement here expresses the parties' intent that the option be exercisable "at any time" during a 24–year period pursuant to section 3 (a). The section thus does not permit a construction that the parties intended the option to last only 21 years. Given the contrary intention manifested in the instrument itself, the saving statute is simply inapplicable. . . .

C. "Wait and See" Approach

Defendants next urge that we adopt the "wait and see" approach to the Rule against Perpetuities: an interest is valid if it actually vests during the perpetuities period, irrespective of what might have happened. The option here would survive under the "wait and see" approach since it was exercised by 1987, well within the 21–year limitation. This Court, however, has long refused to "wait and see" whether a perpetuities violation in fact occurs. As explained in Matter of Fischer [307 N.Y. 149, 157(1954)], "[i]t is settled beyond dispute that in determining whether a will has illegally suspended the power of alienation, the courts will look to what might have happened under the terms of the will rather than to what has actually happened since the death of the testator."

The very language of EPTL 9–1.1, moreover, precludes us from determining the validity of an interest based upon what actually occurs during the perpetuities period. Under the statutory rule against remote vesting, an interest is invalid "unless it *must* vest, if at all, not later than twenty-one years after one or more lives in being" (EPTL 9–1.1 [b] [emphasis added]). That is, an interest is void from the outset if it *may* vest too remotely. Because the option here could have vested after expiration of the 21–year perpetuities period, it offends the Rule. We note that the desirability of the "wait and see" doctrine has been widely debated. Its incorporation into EPTL 9–1.1, in any event, must be accomplished by the Legislature, not the courts.

We therefore conclude that the option agreement is invalid under EPTL 9–1.1 (b). . . .

IV. Remedy

As a final matter, defendants argue that, if the option fails, the contract of sale conveying the property from Broadwest to Symphony should be rescinded due to the mutual mistake of the parties. . . . A contract entered into under mutual mistake of fact is generally subject to rescission. CPLR 3005 provides that when relief against mistake is sought, it shall not be denied merely because the mistake is one of law rather than fact. Relying on this provision, defendants maintain that neither Symphony nor Broadwest realized that the option violated the Rule against Perpetuities at the time they entered into the agreement and that both parties intended the option to be enforceable.

CPLR 3005, however, does not equate all mistakes of law with mistakes of fact. . . . CPLR 3005 "does not permit a mere misreading of the law by any party to cancel an agreement." Here, the parties' mistake amounts to nothing more than a misunderstanding as to the applicable law, and CPLR 3005 does not direct undoing of the transaction.

The remedy of rescission, moreover, lies in equity and is a matter of discretion. Defendants' plea that the unenforceability of the option is contrary to the intent of the original parties ignores that the effect of the Rule against Perpetuities—which is a statutory prohibition, not a rule of construction—is always to defeat the intent of parties who create a remotely vesting interest. As explained by the Appellate Division, there is "an irreconcilable conflict in applying a remedy which is designed to void a transaction because it fails to carry out the parties' true intent to a transaction in which the mistake made by the parties was the application of the Rule against Perpetuities, the purpose of which is to defeat the intent of the parties."

The Rule against Perpetuities reflects the public policy of the State. Granting the relief requested by defendants would thus be contrary to public policy, since it would lead to the same result as enforcing the option and tend to compel performance of contracts violative of the Rule. Similarly, damages are not recoverable where options to acquire real property violate the Rule against Perpetuities, since that would amount to giving effect to the option.

[Affirmed.]

NOTES AND QUESTIONS

1. Options and Preemptive Rights. The New York court found an option, a device that compels a sale, to be more objectionable than a preemptive right (or a right of first refusal), which gives the right holder the first opportunity to purchase when the owner wishes to sell. While under the common law Rule both types of rights were generally subject to the Rule, the prevailing common law opinion today is that options are subject to the Rule and jurisdictions are divided on whether the Rule should apply to preemptive rights. The movement is away from treating preemptive rights as subject to the Rule. In addition to *Bruken Realty*, cited by the court in *Symphony Space*, see Old Port Cove Holdings, Inc. v. Old Port Cove Condominium Ass'n One, Inc., 986 So.2d 1279, 1285 n.2, 1286 n.3 (Fla. 2008), for a listing of the states and decisions in either camp.

The Uniform Statutory Rule Against Perpetuities, § 4.1, abolishes application of the Rule to options and other commercial transactions, a move that leaves such arrangements subject to the judicial and legislative tests formulated to identify unreasonable restraints on alienation. By statute, Illinois limits the duration of preemptive rights and options that do not run with the land to 40 years. 765 ILCS § 305/4(a)(7). Massachusetts limits the duration of such rights that do not run with the land to 30 years. Mass. Gen. Laws Ch. 184A, § 5(a).

2. *More Perpetuities Puzzles.* The New York court did not discuss two aspects of perpetuities law that might have produced a different outcome.

a. *Option or Power of Termination?* Was the option in substance the retention by Broadwest of a power of termination? It is hornbook law that a power of termination (right of entry) retained by the grantor is immune from destruction under the Rule. The entire point of this transaction was to transfer title to Symphony Space temporarily, with Broadwest retaining the power to terminate Symphony's fee. But the form appeared to matter more than the substance. Suppose that Broadwest had conveyed the building "to Symphony Space only so long as Symphony Space permits Broadwest to retain possession of the premises described in the lease and agreement attached hereto and made a part hereof according to its terms, and until Broadwest exercises its purchase option that is contained in that lease and agreement and tenders the consideration prescribed for exercise of the option." Would (should) that have produced a different result? Consider the following conveyance: "In receipt of $100,000, O conveys Blackacre to A and his heirs, but if Blackacre is ever used to cultivate sugar beets, O or his heirs, successors, or assigns may, upon payment of $100,000 to A or his heirs, successors, or assigns, re-enter and retake possession of Blackacre." Does this create a power of termination in O, an interest immune from the Rule, an option, or a right of first refusal?

b. *Separable, or Split, Contingencies.* The common law Rule has long recognized that if a grantor creates a future interest in another person that is dependent upon either of two expressed contingencies, one of which is void for remoteness and the other is valid, the contingent future interest is valid. See Longhead v. Phelps, 2 Wm. Black. 704; 96 Eng. Rep. 414 (K.B. 1770); Holmes v. Connecticut Trust & Safe Deposit Co., 92 Conn. 507 (1918); Whitman's Estate, 248 Pa. 285 (1915); John Chipman Gray, The Rule Against Perpetuities §§ 341–348 (1886); Gray, The Rule Against Perpetuities §§ 341–353.3 (4th ed. 1942); Edward C. Halbach, Jr. & Eugene Scoles, Problems and Materials on Future Interests 257 (1977). But this principle does not apply unless the grantor has expressly separated the contingencies. See Proctor v. Bishop of Bath and Wells, 2 Hy. Bl. 358, 126 Eng. Rep. 594 (1794); John Chipman Gray, The Rule Against Perpetuities 369, §§ 331–333 (4th ed. 1942).

Thus, if O, survived by A and B, devises property "to B if no child of A attains the age of 25," the devise is void, even though it silently expresses two contingencies: (1) to B if A dies childless, or (2) to B if A has children and they all die before reaching age 25. But if O were to have made these two contingencies explicit, the devise would be valid. All O need do is devise the property "to B if either (1) A dies childless, or (2) A has children and they all die before reaching age 25." The second contingency is void for remoteness but the first is not, so the springing executory interest in *B* is valid.

This is the law in New York, as it has been for some time. See Schettler v. Smith, 41 N.Y. 328, 336–337 (1869). *Symphony Space* poses a riddle: Why didn't the Court of Appeals discuss this rule? One answer might be that the option dates were not expressly separated, because each date was contained in section 3(a) of the agreement. But the agreement also stipulated separate option prices for each of those dates, so the option could be read as consisting of four separate options: 1987 at $15,000; 1993 at $20,000; 1998 at $24,000; and 2003 at $28,000. Yet, the Appellate Division treated this as an appeal to the court to modify the agreement "to excise that portion which permits exercise of the option outside the perpetuities period," 214 App. Div 2d 66, 79 (1995), and the Court of Appeals thought this was an attempt to invoke New York's savings statute. Perhaps this was a failure of the lawyers for Pergola to frame the issue with clarity, or perhaps it was a wilful desire of the judges to elide the issue. Consider the Appellate Division's view of the equities of the claims: "[D]uring the period of its ownership Symphony has utilized the property for constructive purposes inuring to the public good and made a positive contribution to the neighborhood while defendants have done nothing to enhance the property or its value to the neighborhood, other than allowing it to deteriorate, and that any increase in the property's value has been in spite of, rather than because of, their efforts or interest in the property." Id. at 82. On the other hand, the dissent in the Appellate Division had quite a different take on the matter: "What we have here is a tax gimmick transaction beneficial to both sides. The plaintiff got a theater with tax exemption and the defendants found a way to keep a tie on the property at little overhead expense [while] waiting for the pot of gold at the end of the rainbow to materialize. Now that the pot is about to boil over, the plaintiff tries to void the bargain it made. It is not for us to manufacture a reason to keep a worthwhile community project from ending. The show had a solid run and it was contemplated that the curtain would come down." Id. at 82–83.

3. Attorney Malpractice? Did the attorney for Broadwest commit malpractice? Did the attorney for the Pergola group, in reviewing the Broadwest/Symphony Space agreement prior to the transaction by which the Pergola group acquired the option right, commit malpractice? See Lucas v. Hamm, 56 Cal.2d 583 (1961) (finding that California perpetuities law at the time was so complex and esoteric that it did not fall beneath the standard of care to violate the Rule.) But see Wright v. Williams, 47 Cal.App.3d 802, 809 n.2 (1975) (questioning whether that is still the case). Most commentators think that Lucas v. Hamm was wrongly decided. See, e.g., Robert H. Sitkoff & Maz Schanzenbach, Jurisdictional Competition for Trust Funds: An Empirical Analysis of Perpetuities and Taxes, 115 Yale L. J. 356, 369 n.37 (2005). See also Millwright v. Romer, 322 N.W.2d 30, 33 (Iowa 1982), involving a will that contained invalid future interests. In the malpractice action against the attorney who drafted the will, the issue was whether the limitations statute, which commenced to run upon plaintiffs' discovery of the cause of action, had expired. The majority said the statute began to run at the testator's death because "[e]very citizen is assumed to know the law and is charged with knowledge of [its] provisions." The plaintiffs contended to no avail that the statute began to run when they first learned that the will's provisions might violate the Rule. The dissent castigated the majority reasoning in this catechism: "Question: How do we bar a claim that a lawyer was negligent for misunderstanding the rule against perpetuities? Answer: By pretending lay persons understand it."

4. Background and Aftermath. Symphony Space today is a thriving non-profit art center devoted to an eclectic mix of the arts. Its web site is www.symphonyspace.org. For more on the case see Jeffrey Evans Stake, Property Stories 265–297 (2d ed. 2009).

5. Some Levity. After you have wrestled with the common law Rule Against Perpetuities you may enjoy a delightful spoof of the Rule that is contained in Peter F. Sloss, Alice's Adventures in Jurisprudencia 60–75 (1982). In that satire Lady Annabelle bequeaths her entire estate in trust for the income benefit of all of the pets and domestic animals that she kept on her property and that survived her, and upon the death of the last of these creatures the income to be accumulated for 21 additional years and then the principal and accumulated income to be distributed free of trust to Lady Annabelle's heirs. Among the animal beneficiaries is a Galapagos turtle, a creature with a maximum life expectancy of almost 200 years. For perpetuities purposes only, is the bequest valid? If you are troubled by the fact that the tortoise may be the sole income beneficiary for some time, consider a different will by which Lady Annabelle bequeaths her estate in trust for the income benefit of her issue now living or to be born, by right of representation, for their respective lives, and 21 years after Gerhard, her pet Galapagos tortoise dies, the principal and accumulated income to be distributed free of trust to her then living issue. Peter Sloss's version of Alice quotes the tortoise: "I'm a creature, like all others, to be treated just the same." Id. at 73.

b. Statutory and Judicial Modification of the Rule Against Perpetuities

The emphasis the common law Rule Against Perpetuities places upon possibilities, however outlandish, that might occur when viewed at the inception of the future interest subject to the Rule, may aid the logic of the Rule, but produces bizarre results never intended by the grantor. Understandably, legislatures reacted to that in a number of ways.

Some states have enacted specific conclusive presumptions that eliminated the most improbable possibilities. For example, Illinois stipulates that for perpetuities purposes a reference in a grant to one's widow, widower, or spouse refers to a person living at the time the perpetuities period commences, that a person under age 13 or over age 65 is incapable of producing a child, that the production of a child or more remote descendant by adoption is disregarded, and that any administrative contingency that is a condition precedent to vesting of a future interest (e.g., closure of an estate, appointment of an executor, etc.) is deemed to occur, if at all, within some life in being at the moment the interest became effective, plus 21 years if necessary. 765 ILCS § 305/4(c)(1) (2010). On this type of reform, see generally Powell on Real Property § 75A.04.

Another device has been to instruct courts to reform the grant to make the interests created under it valid under the Rule, hewing as closely as possible to the grantor's intentions. These statutes may be limited to specific instances or may grant considerable general authority to courts to do so. An example of the specifically limited approach is an Illinois law that requires that age contingencies be reduced to age 21 if any greater age would result in invalidity of the contingent future interest. 765 ILCS § 305/4(c)(2) (2010). An example of the general approach is Tex. Prop. Code § 5.043(a) (2010), which directs courts to "reform or construe" any interest that violates the Rule in order "to effect the ascertainable general intent of the creator of the interest." Texas courts are obliged to "liberally construe and apply this provision to validate an interest to the fullest extent consistent with the creator's intent." For more discussion of this *cy pres* ("as close as possible") approach, see Powell on Real Property § 75A.03.

Yet another reform, called "wait-and-see," seeks to defer determination of whether the Rule has been violated until actual subsequent events have occurred. The earliest, and most limited version of this approach was to wait until the end of the life of the first possessor, almost always a life tenant, to determine validity. See, e.g, Quigley's Estate, 329 Pa. 281 (1938); In re McCreary's Estate, 328 Pa. 513 (1938). In 1947 Pennsylvania was the first state to extend the wait to the end of the entire perpetuities period, but it did so in an incoherent fashion. The Pennsylvania method is to invalidate any future interests that are not vested at "the expiration of the period allowed by the common law rule against perpetuities as measured by actual rather than possible events." Pa. Cons. Stats. § 6104(b) (2010). The fallacy in this is that there is no such period. "[T]here is 'a perpetuity period' only with respect to *valid* interests. Invalid interests are . . . invalid because there is no life that can be identified that makes them valid." Lawrence W. Waggoner, Perpetuity Reform, 81 Mich. L. Rev. 1718, 1763 (1983). The problem is that, for wait-and-see to be coherent, a principle must be formulated to determine whose lives we wait to expire, for that determines how long we wait to see if the contingent interests expire. Implicit in the common law Rule is such a principle—the measuring or validating lives we use to validate a grant are those whose lives are relevant to the events that will cause contingent interests to vest. Professors Jesse Dukeminier and Lawrence Waggoner argued that these are the lives that have a "causal relationship" to vesting, and so we should wait for those lives, and no others, to expire. See Jesse Dukeminier, Perpetuities: The Measuring Lives, 85 Colum. L. Rev. 1648 (1985); Lawrence W. Waggoner, Perpetuity Reform, 81 Mich. L. Rev. 1718 (1983). The only state that has explicitly incorporated the causal relationship principle into a wait-and-see statute is Kentucky. See Ky Rev. Stats. § 381.216 (2010): "In determining whether an interest would violate the rule against perpetuities the period of perpetuities shall be measured by actual rather than possible events; provided, however, the period shall not be measured by any lives whose continuance does not have a causal relationship to the vesting or failure of the interest." Yet in those states that have adopted wait-and-see for the common law period it seems implicit that the lives for whom we wait are those relevant to vesting.

Some wait-and-see states require courts to reform the instrument to make valid any interest not yet vested at the end of the wait-and-see period. See, e.g., Ky. Rev. Stats. § 381.216 (2010), which stipulates: "Any interest which would violate [the rule against perpetuities] as thus modified shall be reformed, within the limits of that rule, to approximate most closely the intention of the creator of the interest." See also Ohio Rev. Code § 2131.08(c) (2010); Iowa Code § 558.68(3) (2010). Other wait-and-see states invalidate interests that have not yet vested at the expiration of the wait-and-see period. See, e.g., Pa. Cons. Stats. § 6104(b) (2010). For more on wait-and-see, consult Powell on Real Property § 75A.02.

The most recent, and probably the most dramatic development, is the arrival of the Uniform Statutory Rule Against Perpetuities. USRAP, as it is known by its acronym, replaces the common law Rule by the following two-part test:

A nonvested property interest is invalid unless:

(1) when the interest is created, it is certain to vest or terminate no later than 21 years after the death of an individual then alive; or

(2) the interest either vests or terminates within 90 years after its creation.

USRAP § 1

The first part of the test is simply the common law Rule Against Perpetuities, but if an interest should be void under the common law Rule it is still valid it vests, or fails to vest, 90 years after its creation. And that is not all. Section 3 of USRAP commands courts to "reform a disposition in the manner that most closely approximates the transferor's manifested plan of distribution" if, at the end of the 90 year period, the interest has not vested. USRAP has been adopted in about half the states.

c. Estate Taxation and the Possible Death of the Rule Against Perpetuities

The common law Rule has two main purposes: increase alienability of property and decrease the ability of dead people to dictate who will possess what was their property when they were alive (usually termed "dead hand control"). Alienability is enhanced by chopping off remote contingent interests, which tends to produce a fee simple absolute in a single owner or set of owners sooner than the grantor intended, Curbing dead hand control is thought to prevent property from being frozen into place while ambient circumstances, unanticipated by the grantor, have made that static arrangement inefficient or otherwise unsuitable. But the common law Rule is both underinclusive and overinclusive with respect to each of those objectives. Some interests that are vested for perpetuities purposes involve uncertainty concerning future rights to possession. Contingent beneficial interests in trusts are subject to the Rule even though the trustee has full power to alienate the property held in trust.

The difference between contingent legal interests and contingent equitable interests might have been enough, by itself, to encourage states to abandon the common law Rule with respect to beneficial interests in trusts, so long as the trustee had the full power to alienate, but the impetus to do so was spurred on by the enactment in 1986 of significant changes to federal taxation of estates and gifts. For our immediate purposes, the congressional policy that it implemented was to prevent people from passing property from one generation to another without paying an estate or gift tax. To that end, Congress created the "generation skipping transfer tax," or GST. The estate tax applies to property owned by a testator at his death, but if the decedent owns a life estate he owns nothing at his death. His life estate is not a transmissible interest, and so it is not subjected to estate taxation. The federal estate tax provides a credit against the tax, which means in practice that, as of 2011 (barring some change in the law, always a possibility) an amount of $1 million per person may be transferred without incurring a federal estate tax liability. Prior to 1986, the general principle described above enabled testators to devise property in successive life estates to several generations and avoid estate taxes on the trust corpus.

> *Example 4–49:* O bequeaths his property "to T in trust, to pay the income for life to my son A, and then to pay the income for life to A's children, and then to distribute the principal and accumulated income to A's grandchildren, provided, however, that the trust shall terminate not later than 21 years after the death of A and all of A's issue living at my death." While T's estate will be subject to the federal estate tax, there will be no estate tax imposed on the transfer of the income interest for life to A's children on the occasion of A's death, because A has no transmissible interest at his death. Nor would there be any estate tax levied on the distribution to A's grandchildren because this is a distribution from O's estate, which has already paid an estate tax on that amount. An estate tax would be levied at the death of each of A's grandchildren because they would possess a fee simple absolute at their death.

The GST tax changed this. If a testator creates a life estate that avoids the estate tax by allowing the property to be passed to the next generation without estate taxation, as in Example 4–49, a generation skipping transfer tax is levied on the transfer. Thus, while the transfer from A to his children in Example 4–49 is still exempt from the federal *estate tax* it is now subject to the *GST tax*, which mimics the estate tax. As part of that mimicry, there is an exemption from the GST tax of $1 million (as of 2011, barring changes in the law) per transferor. Thus, O in Example 4–49 could allocate his exemption entirely to the transfer from A to A's children. What is important for the development of perpetuities law, however, is that *O* could also choose to allocate his GST exemption to a trust that contains one *or more* generation skipping transfers.

That latter possibility stimulated states to encourage creators of these GST-exempt trusts to locate them in their jurisdiction. To do so, they simply repealed the Rule Against Perpetuities outright, or did so for interests in trust, so long as the trustee had the power of alienation. At least 17 states permit perpetual trusts, and another five permit trusts to endure for a minimum of 150 years (Washington) to a maximum of 1000 years (Utah and Wyoming). Some of these states require trust settlors to opt out of the Rule, but that is easy to do, and the opt-out requirement has the effect of making the Rule a default rule for those who are either ill-informed or wish to enter the labyrinth and endure the limits of the Rule. According to one empirical study, the abandonment of the Rule in these states has produced billions of dollars flowing into perpetual trusts sited in these jurisdictions. See Robert H. Sitkoff & Maz Schanzenbach, Jurisdictional Competition for Trust Funds: An Empirical Analysis of Perpetuities and Taxes, 115 Yale L. J. 356 (2005). Thus, it is federal tax law and the lure of economic activity that is associated with trust management that has triggered the partial collapse of the Rule.

There are problems with a perpetual trust. Beneficial interests can become ever more subdivided as the pool of descendants from the settlor grows larger over time. If the trust assets do not increase commensurately the point of the trust—income maintenance for a dynasty of descendants—is lost. On the other hand, a $1 million contribution to a GST trust (or $2 million if we assume a married couple funding the trust), made now by settlors with a 50 year life expectancy should generate considerable capital appreciation before any income is paid out at the death of the survivor. Lest you scoff at the idea of a 28 year old couple having sufficient means to do so, consider the proliferation of young hedge fund managers or cyber-entrepreneurs such as Mark Zuckerberg, founder of Facebook and one of the richest men in America at age 26. So, $2 million invested at a compounded return of 7% (the historical average return for U.S. stocks from 1802 to 1997) would produce a fund of $65.5 million in 50 years. At that point, assume that the income begins to be distributed to the beneficiaries. Assuming that the income on that fund is the long term dividend yield on U.S. stocks of about 3.5% the annual income distributed will be about $2.3 million. But the principal may continue to appreciate at a compounded rate of 7% and, if so, in another hundred years that fund will be about $56 billion. Of course, these rosy predictions may not pan out, as the human judgment of securities fund managers sometimes picks losers (think Enron) as well as winners. Even so, a perpetual GST trust, especially when funded by the young and rich, can grow to very large amounts over time.

This phenomenon raises some interesting policy questions. As a society, do we wish to encourage the creation of dynastic pools of wealth? Some argue that this erodes democracy by fostering an aristocracy of wealth that enables that aristocracy to magnify political power. See, e.g.,

James L. Repetti, Democracy, Taxes, and Wealth, 76 N.Y.U. L. Rev. 825 (2001); Ray D. Madoff, Immortality and the Law 68–70 (2010). On the other hand, persons armed with foresight, wealth, and financial acumen that choose to provide for their remote descendants create some societal benefits. Economists assert that national saving is the key to investment and economic prosperity. Perpetual trusts are a form of savings and investment. In a nation with a phenomenally low savings rate (it hit zero in 2005 and has averaged about 2.5% of disposable personal income in the first decade of the 21st century) this might be a boon. (To be sure, historical savings rates in the United States have been much higher, averaging about 8% of disposable personal income from 1947 to about 1982.)

To compound matters, many people claim that the estate tax should be abolished, because it taxes the accumulation of wealth that has already been taxed in the form of the income tax. This is not entirely true, as some of that accumulation is produced by unrealized (and thus untaxed) capital gains. But suppose the estate tax were to be repealed; would the incentive to create perpetual GST-exempt trusts disappear? Certainly the tax incentive would disappear, and we would then see whether Americans are as dynasty minded as the tax code appears to make them out to be. Were that to occur there might be a revival of enthusiasm for the Rule Against Perpetuities, whether in its common law form, modified by statute, or replaced by USRAP. As Mark Twain wrote in 1897 upon the occasion of the publication of his obituary, "the reports of my death are greatly exaggerated."

Chapter Five

Concurrent Owners and Marital Property

■ ■ ■

A. INTRODUCTION

Just as property ownership can be divided in time—between present possessors and future possessors—it can be divided among multiple owners of the same interest. Thus, there can be multiple owners of a possessory estate, and there can be multiple owners of a future interest. The focus of this chapter is on the forms of multiple ownership and the principles governing the relations of multiple owners of the same interest in property,

There are five forms of multiple ownership known to the common law—tenancy in common, joint tenancy, tenancy by the entirety, tenancy in partnership, and co-parceny. In the United States today marital property has become a form of concurrent ownership for many purposes, so that topic is included in this chapter. There are three forms of marital property—the tenancy by the entirety, the common law marital property system as modified by statute, and community property, a creature of the civil law that has found a home in a small number of states, mostly in the west. Co-parceny is extinct, as it existed only as an aspect of the English law of primogeniture, the rule that land must be inherited by the eldest male son. In the absence of any sons, land was permitted to be inherited by all the decedent's daughters in equal shares, or co-parceny. Tenancy in partnership is commonplace, and is best studied in a course on Business Associations. Two or more persons who conduct a business for profit as co-owners are business partners. In every jurisdiction their relations are governed by statutes and interpretive case law. Thus, the focus of this chapter is on the remaining forms of concurrent ownership.

1. TENANCY IN COMMON

Tenancy in common is the default form of co-ownership in America. It is characterized by an equal right of each tenant in common to possess the property, although each tenant in common owns an individually alienable, devisable, or inheritable fraction of the whole. Thus, it is often said that tenants in common own separate but undivided interests.

Example 5–1: O conveys Blackacre to B, C, and D, as tenants in common. Each of B, C, and D own equal 1/3 interests in Blackacre, and each may convey their interest separately during life, or pass it by will or interstate succession. If B conveys his interest to E, C dies and devises his interest to F, and D dies intestate, leaving a sole heir, H, Blackacre is owned in equal 1/3 interests by E, F, and H.

In every state there is a presumption that a grant to two or more persons is a grant in tenancy in common. That presumption may be rebutted by evidence in the grant that a joint tenancy is intended. See, e.g., Mass. Ann. Laws Ch. 184, § 7 (2010). Some states presume that a grant to a husband and wife creates a tenancy by the entirety (a unique form of joint tenancy that is limited to married couples). See, e.g., Alaska Stat. § 34.15.110(b) (2010).

2. JOINT TENANCY

The key fact about joint tenancy is that each joint tenant has a right of survivorship, which means that upon the death of a joint tenant the remaining joint tenant or tenants own the entire interest. The decedent joint tenant may not pass his interest by will or intestacy. At his death his interest dies with him, leaving the surviving joint tenant or tenants as the sole owner or owners. If a joint tenant conveys his interest during life, he breaks the joint tenancy and conveys to the transferee an interest as a tenant in common. Thus, it is said that joint tenants own undivided interests in the whole. Because each joint tenant enjoys an equal interest, the common law insisted that this equality be manifested in the creation of a joint tenancy. To that end, the so-called "four unities" were essential to the creation of a joint tenancy. There must be unity of time, title, interest, and possession. See 2 William Blackstone *180–182.

The unity of time meant that each joint tenant must acquire their interest at the same moment in time. The unity of title meant that each joint tenant must acquire their interest by the same grant or by a commonality of adverse possession. The unity of interest meant two things: each joint tenant must have the same estate (as measured by its duration) and have an equal interest in that estate. The unity of possession meant that each joint tenant must have an equal right to possession of the whole. Close readers will note that this latter unity is a part of the tenancy in common, though none of the other unities has any application to a tenancy in common. Not only must the four unities be present at creation of the joint tenancy, under the common law if any one of the unities was later destroyed the joint tenancy was destroyed and converted into a tenancy in common. Thus, if a joint tenant transferred his interest in a joint tenancy to a third party the unities of time and title were severed and the transferee owned as a tenant in common.

Example 5–2: In a single deed, *O* conveys Blackacre "to *A* and *B*, as joint tenants and not as tenants in common." *A* and *B* own Blackacre as joint tenants. Later, *A* conveys his interest to *C*. *B* and *C* now own Blackacre as tenants in common.

However, as you will observe in section B of this chapter, the importance of the unities has broken down. The unity of time may, under some circumstances, be disregarded, particularly when a sole owner wishes to create a joint tenancy in himself and another. The unity of interest has also begun to be discarded in the circumstance where joint tenants provide unequal contributions to effect purchase and maintenance of the property, and intend for their ownership interests to be unequal. These matters and others will be discussed in section B.

The common law presumed that a grant to two or more persons was in joint tenancy, so long as the four unities were present. This may have arisen to prevent subdivision of the feudal services. Tracts of land held in joint tenancy were thus kept intact, keeping the feudal services from being parceled out. By contrast, tenancy in common facilitated this subdivision. But as feudalism became as extinct as the dinosaurs, there were no longer any reasons to presume the creation of a joint tenancy. As noted above, the presumption has been reversed today, in favor of presuming creation of a tenancy in common. To create a joint tenancy it is generally a good idea to say so explicitly, as "joint tenants, and not as tenants in common" or in "joint tenancy, not tenancy in common" rather than simply stating "jointly." The latter locution is ambiguous, as it could mean "concurrently," or as "co-owners," leaving it unclear what form of concurrent ownership was intended. Unfortunately, this can get tricky. Virginia, for example, abolished the joint tenancy by Va. Code Ann. § 55–20 (2010), but then provided an exception in Va. Code Ann. § 55–21 "when it manifestly appears from the tenor of the instrument transferring such property . . . that it was intended the part of the one dying should then belong to the others." But a conveyance to grantees "as joint tenants, and not as tenants in common," was held in Hoover v. Smith, 248 Va. 6 (1994), to be an insufficient manifestation of intent to create a right of survivorship. Explicit mention of the right of survivorship was necessary. Thoughtless addition of the right of survivorship, however, may also be a trap. In Michigan, for example, a grant as "joint tenants, with right of survivorship" creates a joint life estate in the possessory tenants with a contingent remainder in the survivor. See Albro v. Allen, 434 Mich. 271 (1990). The same principle applies in Kentucky, where a grant "with survivorship" to the grantees, "jointly and to the survivor," was also held to create a joint life estate followed by a contingent remainder in the survivor. Sanderson v. Saxon, 834 S.W.2d 676 (Ky. 1992). The effect of the Michigan and Kentucky rule is that such a grant prevents severance of the joint tenancy by an *inter vivos* transfer of one joint tenant's interest to a third party. The survivorship right is indestructible unless both parties consent. Make sure you consult the relevant jurisdiction's law before you blithely convey property in joint tenancy.

Joint tenancy may have originated as a device to avoid the feudal incidents due upon death of the tenure holder. By enfeoffing a third party, who in turn enfeoffed the original owner and his presumptive heir in joint tenancy, there would be no incidents due at the death of the father (the original owner) because the son would continue in uninterrupted ownership. See 2 Frederick Pollock & Frederic William Maitland, The History of English Law 20. Although the Statute of Wills (1540) permitted bequests of personal property, real property was not devisable but only inheritable, and the strict rule of primogeniture ensured that land would descend to the eldest son. To avoid this, landowners began to convey property to a trusted and cooperative "strawman," who would in turn reconvey it to the original owner and his desired co-owners as joint tenants. Upon the original owner's death the land would not be in his estate (and thus escape the rule of primogeniture) because the surviving joint tenant or tenants would own the land. Eventually, as land became devisable by will, this use of the joint tenancy was unnecessary.

There are many modern uses for the joint tenancy, however. The principal advantage of the joint tenancy is that it enables avoidance of probate. Property that passes by will or intestate succession is subject to a court-supervised process called probate, which is both expensive and time consuming. There are a number of probate avoidance devices, which will be encountered in a course on Wills, Trusts, and Estates, but the joint tenancy is one of the simplest such devices and a favorite of married couples. Because the surviving joint tenant owns the property in its entirety at the death of the decedent joint tenant, the property is not in the estate of the decedent. Most married couples wish to leave their property to their surviving spouse, and joint tenancy is a simple solution that avoids a court-supervised transfer of ownership to the surviving spouse. This is not an estate tax avoidance device, however. Federal tax law specifically includes the portion of a joint tenancy owned by a decedent in the decedent's estate that is subject to the federal estate tax. Because there is an unlimited deduction from the estate tax for property that passes to one's spouse this is not a tax problem when spouses own property in joint tenancy, but a joint tenancy between a parent and child (or anyone other than a husband and wife) garners no such deduction and either an estate or gift tax may be the result. If a sole owner of property creates a joint tenancy for no consideration with himself and someone not his spouse (such as a child), one-half of the value at the time of the transfer is a gift subject to the gift tax. If a sole owner transfers property to himself and a non-spouse in joint tenancy in receipt of market value for the interest conveyed to the non-spouse, there is no gift (and hence no gift tax) but at the death of one joint tenant the decedent's estate for federal estate tax purposes includes the portion of the property's value attributable to the decedent joint tenant's interest in the property. See 26 U.S.C. § 2040.

3.   TENANCY BY THE ENTIRETY

This form of co-ownership was limited by the common law to married couples. To create a tenancy by the entirety five unities were required— the four needed to create a joint tenancy plus the fifth unity of marriage. The common law strongly presumed that a conveyance to a husband and wife created a tenancy by the entirety, so long as the other four unities were present. As with the joint tenancy, each tenant by the entirety has a right of survivorship. Unlike the joint tenancy, neither tenant by the entirety may defeat that right by an *inter vivos* transfer. The rationale for this was the husband and wife were one person. Under the common law that person was the husband, a state of affairs that has been universally rejected in American law.

Nevertheless, the tenancy by the entirety lives on. It terminates, of course, upon the death of one of the marital partners. Likewise, because divorce terminates the marriage it also terminates the tenancy by the entirety. With the advent of same-sex marriage and its legal kin, civil unions or domestic partnerships, tenancy by the entirety has become available to same-sex partners in those jurisdictions that recognize same-sex marriage or extend to civil unions or domestic partnerships the same legal status as marriages *and* recognize the tenancy by the entirety. A majority of the states recognize tenancy by the entirety, but its status varies considerably even among those states. Sixteen states have either abolished the tenancy by the entirety or never recognized it, and its existence in another four states is not clear. See Powell on Real Property § 52.01[3]. The United Kingdom abolished the tenancy by the entirety in 1925. Law of Property Act, 15 & 16 Geo. V, ch. 2, § 37.

Some aspects of the tenancy by the entirety, such as the rights of creditors of one marital partner with respect to property owned in tenancy by the entirety, generate considerable disagreement among the jurisdictions that recognize the interest. Because the resolution of that issue, and others concerning the tenancy by the entirety, involve policies germane to marital property, the topic is reserved for that section of this chapter.

B.   FORMATION AND SEVERANCE OF THE JOINT TENANCY

Medieval common law required two persons to transfer property, because a transfer meant a transfer of seisin—the obligation to perform the feudal duties—from one person to another. But even after feudalism evaporated into the mist of time the concept of "two to transfer" lived on. Accordingly, at common law, a transfer of Blackacre from *A*, its sole owner, to *A* and *B*, as joint tenants, was ineffective to create a joint tenancy. One objection was that the unity of time was absent, because *A* already had the interest he purported to create by his transfer. But the real objection was rooted in the anachronistic notion of seisin—because *A* already held seisin he could not possibly transfer seisin to himself. Under the common law the only way *A*, an owner of property, could create a joint tenancy in himself and *B* was to convey his interest to *C*, a trusted confederate, who would then reconvey the property to *A* and *B*, as joint tenants. Thus were the four unities observed. Given the obsolescence of seisin and the ease with which these "straw man" conveyances could be used to create a joint tenancy of this sort, some states began to bow to reality and provided by statute that a joint tenancy could be created between *A*, a sole owner, and *B* simply by a conveyance from *A* to *A* and *B*, as joint tenants. See, e,g., Calif. Civil Code § 683; Ga. Code Ann. § 44–6–190(a); Mich. Stat. Ann. § 26–565; Minn. Stat. § 500.19(3); Utah Code. Ann. § 57–1–5(3); Wash. Rev. Code Ann. § 64.28.010; Wis. Stat. Ann. § 700.19(5). A few others have done the same thing by judicial decision. See, e.g., Nunn v. Keith, 289 Ala. 518 (1972); Capitol Savings Bank v. Snelson, 998 S.W.2d 862 (Mo. Ct. App. 1999). But a number of states still adhere to the four unities. See generally Powell on Real Property § 51.01[2].

Even though each joint tenant owns an undivided interest in the whole it is universally acknowledged that each joint tenant has the right unilaterally to sever the joint tenancy. This can be done by an act that destroys one of the four unities or by any other act that is manifestly inconsistent with joint tenancy. Once severed, the relationship among owners is that of tenants in common. But, as you will see in the cases that follow, the principle is easier to state than to apply.

RIDDLE v. HARMON

Court of Appeal of California, First District
102 Cal.App.3d 524 (1980)

POCHE, J., delivered the opinion of the court.

We must decide whether Frances Riddle, now deceased, unilaterally terminated a joint tenancy by conveying her interest from herself as joint tenant to herself as tenant in common. The trial court determined, via summary judgment quieting title to her widower, that she did not....

Facts

Mr. and Mrs. Riddle purchased a parcel of real estate, taking title as joint tenants. Several months before her death, Mrs. Riddle retained an attorney to plan her estate. After reviewing pertinent documents, he advised her that the property was held in joint tenancy and that, upon her death, the property would pass to her husband. Distressed upon learning this, she requested that the joint tenancy be terminated so that she could dispose of her interest by will. As a result, the attorney prepared a grant deed whereby Mrs. Riddle granted to herself an undivided one-half interest in the subject property. The document also provided that[:] "The purpose of this Grant Deed is to terminate those joint tenancies formerly existing between the Grantor, Frances P. Riddle, and Jack C. Riddle, her husband...." He also prepared a will disposing of Mrs. Riddle's interest in the property. Both the grant deed and will were executed on December 8, 1975. Mrs. Riddle died 20 days later.

The court below refused to sanction her plan to sever the joint tenancy and quieted title to the property in her husband. The executrix of the will of Frances Riddle appeals from that judgment....

An indisputable right of each joint tenant is the power to convey his or her separate estate by way of gift or otherwise without the knowledge or consent of the other joint tenant and to thereby terminate the joint tenancy. If a joint tenant conveys to a stranger and that person reconveys to the same tenant, then no revival of the joint tenancy occurs because the unities are destroyed. The former joint tenants become tenants in common.

At common law, one could not create a joint tenancy in himself and another by a direct conveyance. It was necessary for joint tenants to acquire their interests at the same time (unity of time) and by the same conveyancing instrument (unity of title). So, in order to create a valid joint tenancy where one of the proposed joint tenants already owned an interest in the property, it was first necessary to convey the property to a disinterested third person, a "strawman," who then conveyed the title to the ultimate grantees as joint tenants. This remains the prevailing practice in some jurisdictions. Other states, including California, have disregarded this application of the unities requirement "as one of the obsolete 'subtle and arbitrary distinctions and niceties of the feudal common law,' [and allow the creation of a valid joint tenancy without the use of a strawman]." By amendment to its Civil Code, California became a pioneer in allowing the *creation* of a joint tenancy by direct transfer. Under authority of Civil Code section 683, a joint tenancy conveyance may be made from a "sole owner to himself and others," or from joint owners to themselves and others.... Accordingly, in California, it is no longer necessary to use a strawman to *create* a joint tenancy. This court is now asked to reexamine whether a strawman is required to *terminate* a joint tenancy.

Twelve years ago, in Clark v. Carter, [265 Cal.App.2d 291, 295 (1968)], the Court of Appeal considered the same question and found the strawman to be indispensable. As in the instant case, the joint tenants in *Clark* were husband and wife. The day before Mrs. Clark died, she executed two documents without her husband's knowledge or consent: (1) a quitclaim deed conveying her undivided half interest in certain real property from herself as joint tenant to herself as tenant in common, and (2) an assignment of her undivided half interest in a deed of trust from herself as joint tenant to herself as tenant in common. These documents were held insufficient to sever the joint tenancy. After summarizing joint tenancy principles, the court reasoned that "[Under] California law, a transfer of property presupposes participation by at least two parties, namely, a grantor and a grantee. Both are essential to the efficacy of a deed, and they cannot be the same person. A transfer of property requires that title be conveyed by one living person to another. ... Foreign authority also exists to the effect that a person cannot convey to himself alone, and if he does so, he still holds under the original title. Similarly, it was the common law rule that ... the grantor could not make himself the grantee by conveying an estate to himself."

That "two-to-transfer" notion stems from the English common law feoffment ceremony with livery of seisin. If the ceremony took place upon the land being conveyed, the grantor (feoffor) would hand a symbol of the land, such as a lump of earth or a twig, to the grantee (feoffee). In order to complete the investiture of seisin it was necessary that the feoffor completely relinquish possession of the land to the feoffee. It is apparent from the requirement of livery of seisin that one could not enfeoff oneself—that is, one could not be both grantor and grantee in a single transaction. Handing oneself a dirt clod is ungainly. Just as livery of seisin has become obsolete, so should ancient vestiges of that ceremony give way to modern conveyancing realities....

[Yet,] resourceful attorneys have worked out an inventory of methods to evade the rule that one cannot be both grantor and grantee simultaneously. The most familiar technique for unilateral termination is use of an intermediary "strawman" blessed in the case of Burke v. Stevens [264 Cal.App.2d 30 (1968)]. There, Mrs. Burke carried out a secret plan to terminate a joint tenancy that existed between her husband and herself in certain real property. The steps to accomplish this objective involved: (1) a letter written from Mrs. Burke to her attorney directing him to prepare a power of attorney naming him as her attorney in fact for the purpose of terminating the joint tenancy; (2) her execution and delivery of the power of attorney; (3) her attorney's execution and delivery of a quitclaim deed conveying Mrs. Burke's interest in the property to a third party, who was an office associate of the attorney in fact; (4) the third party's execution and delivery of a quitclaim deed reconveying that interest to Mrs. Burke on the following day. The *Burke* court sanctioned this method of terminating the joint tenancy ...: "While the actions of the wife, from the standpoint of a theoretically perfect marriage, are subject to ethical criticism, and her stealthy approach to the solution of the problems facing her is not to be acclaimed, the question before the court is not what should have been done ideally in a perfect marriage, but whether the decedent and her attorneys acted in a legally permissible manner."

Another creative method of terminating a joint tenancy appears in Reiss v. Reiss [45 Cal. App. 2d 740 (1941)]. There a trust was used. For the purpose of destroying the incident of survivorship, Mrs. Reiss transferred bare legal title to her son, as trustee of a trust for her use and benefit. The son promised to reconvey the property to his mother or to whomever she selected at any time upon her demand. The court upheld this arrangement[:] "[T]he clearly expressed desire of Rosa Reiss to terminate the joint tenancy arrangement was effectively accomplished by the transfer of the legal title to her son for her expressed specific purpose of having the control and the right of disposition of her half of the property."

In view of the rituals that are available to unilaterally terminate a joint tenancy, there is little virtue in steadfastly adhering to cumbersome feudal law requirements. "It is revolting to have no better reason for a rule of law than that so it was laid down in the time of Henry IV. It is still more revolting if the grounds upon which it was laid down have vanished long since, and the rule simply persists from blind imitation of the past." [Oliver Wendell Holmes, The Path of the Law, 10 Harv. L. Rev. 457, 469 (1897).] Common sense as well as legal efficiency dictate that a joint tenant should be able to accomplish directly what he or she could otherwise achieve indirectly by use of elaborate legal fictions....

Rejects the old ways

Our decision does not create new powers for a joint tenant. A universal right of each joint tenant is the power to effect a severance and destroy the right of survivorship by conveyance of his or her joint tenancy interest to another "person." ... We discard the archaic rule that one cannot enfeoff oneself which, if applied, would defeat the clear intention of the grantor. There is no question but that the decedent here could have accomplished her objective—termination of the joint tenancy—by one of a variety of circuitous processes. We reject the rationale of the *Clark* case because it rests on a common law notion whose reason for existence vanished about the time that grant deeds and title companies replaced colorful dirt clod ceremonies as the way to transfer title to real property. One joint tenant may unilaterally sever the joint tenancy without the use of an intermediary device.

The judgment is reversed.

NOTES, QUESTIONS, AND PROBLEMS

1. *Secret Severance.* In *Riddle*, as well as in the other cases discussed by the court, the acts constituting severance of the joint tenancy were concealed from the other joint tenant. That means that the joint tenancy was severed without the knowledge of the other joint tenant. Presumably the other joint tenant continued to think he had a right of survivorship *and* had no ability to dispose of joint tenancy property by his will. Thus, if secret severance occurs, the putative joint tenant (now a tenant in common, though he does not know it) will not make any specific provision for passage of his interest at his death. If he has a will, his interest will pass to the residuary takers; if he dies intestate, his interest will pass to his statutory heirs. Perhaps the decedent's interest in the severed joint tenancy is his single largest asset. If so, because he thinks he cannot dispose of it by will, he may either not make a will or regard the residuary clause of his will as taking care of the inconsequential odds and ends of his estate.

But there might be room for more sinister mischief in the secret severance. Consider Calif. Civil Code § 683.2(c), enacted partially in response to *Riddle*:

(c) Severance of a joint tenancy of record by deed, written declaration, or other written instrument ... is not effective to terminate the right of survivorship of the other joint tenants as to the severing joint tenant's interest unless one of the following requirements is satisfied:

(1) Before the death of the severing joint tenant, the deed, written declaration, or other written instrument effecting the severance is recorded in the county where the real property is located.

(2) The deed, written declaration, or other written instrument effecting the severance is executed and acknowledged before a notary public by the severing joint tenant not earlier than three days before the death of that joint tenant and is recorded in the county where the real property is located not later than seven days after the death of the severing joint tenant.

What might be the problem that this section is intended to address? Is it effective to deal with that problem? Is it effective to deal with the problem of the joint tenant who doesn't know he is no longer a joint tenant?

2. *Murder and Other Fatal Tragedies.* A joint tenant who murders his fellow joint tenant will not benefit from the right of survivorship. Uniform Probate Code § 2–803(c)(2) provides that the "felonious and intentional killing" of one joint tenant by another severs the joint tenancy and turns it into a tenancy in common. The killer, who has larger problems, keeps his share but loses the right of survivorship.

People die in common accidents, and sometimes they are joint tenants. Under the Uniform Simultaneous Death Act § 3 (1953), if there is "no sufficient evidence" of whether A or B, joint tenants, died first, one-half is distributed as if A died first, and one-half is distributed as if B died first. This rule results in some grisly inquiries. For example, A and B were in a car that collided head-on with another car. Within minutes A was found without pulse or respiration, unresponsive to a bright light directed into his open eyes. B was found without pulse or respiration but bleeding profusely from the ears. Who died first? See Estate of Schmidt, 261 Cal.App.2d 262 (1968). A and B, riding in a car that suddenly veered off the road into an icy pool of water, were found dead. A, who suffered from a greatly enlarged heart, was found floating and gasped several times as artificial respiration was applied, while B was found under water entombed in the car, apparently a drowning victim. Daniels v. Bush, 211 Miss. 1 (1951). Uniform Probate Code § 2–702(c), which incorporates a more recent version of the Simultaneous Death Act, provides that unless there is clear and convincing evidence that one person survived the other by 120 hours (5 days), one-half is distributed as if A died first, and one-half is distributed as if B died first. This eliminates most of the grisly inquiries. About 20 states have adopted this version of the simultaneous death act.

3. *Problems.* O conveys Blackacre to A, B, and C, as joint tenants. What is the state of title in Blackacre after each of the following events, considered independently of each other?

a.   A conveys his interest in Blackacre to B.

b.   A conveys his interest in Blackacre to D, then B dies intestate, survived by his sole heir, H, and A, C, and D.

    c. A conveys a "full life estate" in Blackacre to *B*, then *C* dies intestate, survived by *H*, his sole heir, and *A* and *B*. Then *B* dies, leaving a will by which he devises all his property to *D*.

TENHET v. BOSWELL

Supreme Court of California
18 Cal.3d 150 (1976)

MOSK, J., delivered the opinion of the court.

A joint tenant leases his interest in the joint tenancy property to a third person for a term of years, and dies during that term. We conclude that the lease does not sever the joint tenancy, but expires upon the death of the lessor joint tenant.

Raymond Johnson and plaintiff Hazel Tenhet owned a parcel of property as joint tenants. Assertedly without plaintiff's knowledge or consent, Johnson leased the property to defendant Boswell for a period of 10 years at a rental of $150 per year with a provision granting the lessee an "option to purchase."[1] Johnson died some three months after execution of the lease, and plaintiff sought to establish her sole right to possession of the property as the surviving joint tenant. After an unsuccessful demand upon defendant to vacate the premises, plaintiff brought this action to have the lease declared invalid. The trial court sustained demurrers to the complaint, and plaintiff appealed from the ensuing judgment of dismissal. . . .

    II. An understanding of the nature of a joint interest in this state is fundamental to a determination of the question whether the present lease severed the joint tenancy. Civil Code section 683 [requires] an express declaration for the creation of joint interests, [but] does not abrogate the common law rule that four unities are essential to an estate in joint tenancy: unity of interest, unity of time, unity of title, and unity of possession. The requirement of four unities reflects the basic concept that there is but one estate which is taken jointly; if an essential unity is destroyed the joint tenancy is severed and a tenancy in common results. Accordingly, one of two joint tenants may unilaterally terminate the joint tenancy by conveying his interest to a third person. Severance of the joint tenancy, of course, extinguishes the principal feature of that estate—the *jus accrescendi* or right of survivorship. Thus, a joint tenant's right of survivorship is an expectancy that is not irrevocably fixed upon the creation of the estate; it arises only upon success in the ultimate gamble—survival—and then only if the unity of the estate has not theretofore been destroyed by voluntary conveyance, by partition proceedings, by involuntary alienation under an execution, or by any other action which operates to sever the joint tenancy.

---

1. The lease did not disclose that the lessor possessed only a joint interest in the property. To the contrary, the "option to purchase" granted to the lessee, which might more accurately be described as a right of first refusal, implied that the lessor possessed a fee simple. . . .

issue

opposing views

Our initial inquiry is whether the partial alienation of Johnson's interest in the property effected a severance of the joint tenancy under these principles. It could be argued that a lease destroys the unities of interest and possession because the leasing joint tenant transfers to the lessee his present possessory interest and retains a mere reversion. Moreover, the possibility that the term of the lease may continue beyond the lifetime of the lessor is inconsistent with a complete right of survivorship. On the other hand, if the lease entered into here by Johnson and defendant is valid only during Johnson's life, then the conveyance is more a variety of life estate *pur autre vie* than a term of years. Such a result is inconsistent with Johnson's freedom to alienate his interest during his lifetime.

We are mindful that the issue here presented is "an ancient controversy, going back to Coke and Littleton." (2 Am. Law of Prop. (1952) § 6.2, p. 10.) Yet the problem is like a comet in our law: though its existence in theory has been frequently recognized, its observed passages are few. Some authorities support the view that a lease by a joint tenant to a third person effects a complete and final severance of the joint tenancy. [Alexander v. Boyer, 253 Md. 511, 521–522 (1969); 2 Am. Law of Prop. (1952) § 6.2, p. 10.] Such a view is generally based upon what is thought to be the English common law rule. Others adopt a position that there is a temporary severance during the term of the lease. If the lessor dies while the lease is in force, under this view the existence of the lease at the moment when the right of survivorship would otherwise take effect operates as a severance, extinguishing the joint tenancy. If, however, the term of the lease expires before the lessor, it is reasoned that the joint tenancy is undisturbed because the joint tenants resume their original relation. (See, e.g., 2 Reeves on Real Property (1909) § 680, p. 965....) The single conclusion that can be drawn from centuries of academic speculation on the question is that its resolution is unclear.

As we shall explain, it is our opinion that a lease is not so inherently inconsistent with joint tenancy as to create a severance, either temporary or permanent. Under Civil Code sections 683 and 686 a joint tenancy must be expressly declared in the creating instrument, or a tenancy in common results. ... Inasmuch as the estate arises only upon express intent, and in many cases such intent will be the intent of the joint tenants themselves, we decline to find a severance in circumstances which do not clearly and unambiguously establish that either of the joint tenants desired to terminate the estate.

If plaintiff and Johnson did not choose to continue the joint tenancy, they might have converted it into a tenancy in common by written mutual agreement. They might also have jointly conveyed the property to a third person and divided the proceeds. Even if they could not agree to act in concert, either plaintiff or Johnson might have severed the joint tenancy, with or without the consent of the other, by an act which was clearly indicative of an intent to terminate, such as a conveyance of her or his entire interest. Either might also have brought an action to partition the property, which, upon judgment, would have effected a severance. Because a joint tenancy may be created only by express intent, and because there are alternative and unambiguous means of altering the nature of that estate, we hold that the lease here in issue did not operate to sever the joint tenancy.

III.   Having concluded that the joint tenancy was not severed by the lease and that sole ownership of the property therefore vested in plaintiff upon her joint tenant's death by operation of her right of survivorship, we turn next to the issue whether she takes the property unencumbered by the lease. ... By the very nature of joint tenancy ... the interest of the non-surviving joint tenant extinguishes upon his death. And as the lease is valid only "in so far as the interest of the lessor in the joint property is concerned," it follows that the lease of the joint tenancy property also expires when the lessor dies.

This conclusion is borne out by decisions in this state involving liens on and mortgages of joint tenancy property. In Zeigler v. Bonnell, [52 Cal. App. 2d 217 (1942)], the Court of Appeal ruled that a surviving joint tenant takes an estate free from a judgment lien on the interest of a deceased cotenant judgment debtor. The court reasoned that[:] "... The judgment lien of [the creditor] could attach only to the interest of his debtor.... That interest terminated upon [the debtor's] death." After his death "the deceased joint tenant had no interest in the property, and his judgment creditor has no greater rights." A similar analysis was followed in People v. Nogarr, [164 Cal.App.2d 591 (1958)], which held that upon the death of a joint tenant who had executed a mortgage on the tenancy property, the surviving joint tenant took the property free of the mortgage. The court reasoned that "as the mortgage lien attached only to such interest as [the deceased joint tenant] had in the real property[,] when his interest ceased to exist the lien of the mortgage expired with it." As these decisions demonstrate, a joint tenant may, during his lifetime, grant certain rights in the joint property without severing the tenancy. But when such a joint tenant dies his interest dies with him, and any encumbrances placed by him on the property become unenforceable against the surviving joint tenant. For the reasons stated a lease falls within this rule.

Any other result would defeat the justifiable expectations of the surviving joint tenant. Thus if A agrees to create a joint tenancy with B, A can reasonably anticipate that when B dies A will take an unencumbered interest in fee simple. During his lifetime, of course, B may sever the tenancy or lease his interest to a third party. But to allow B to lease for a term continuing *after* his death would indirectly defeat the very purposes of the joint tenancy. For example, for personal reasons B might execute a 99–year lease on valuable property for a consideration of one dollar a year. A would then take a fee simple on B's death, but would find his right to use the property—and its market value—substantially impaired. This circumstance would effectively nullify the benefits of the right of survivorship, the basic attribute of the joint tenancy. On the other hand, we are not insensitive to the potential injury that may be sustained by a person in good faith who leases from one joint tenant. In some circumstances a lessee might be unaware that his lessor is not a fee simple owner but merely a joint tenant, and could find himself unexpectedly evicted when the lessor dies prior to expiration of the lease. This result would be avoided by a prudent lessee who conducts a title search prior to leasing, but we appreciate that such a course would often be economically burdensome to the lessee of a residential dwelling or a modest parcel of property. Nevertheless, it must also be recognized that every lessee may one day face the unhappy revelation that his lessor's estate in the leased property is less than a fee simple. For example, a lessee who innocently rents from the holder of a life estate is subject to risks comparable to those imposed upon a lessee of joint tenancy property.

More significantly, we cannot allow extraneous factors to erode the functioning of joint tenancy. The estate of joint tenancy is firmly embedded in centuries of real property law and in the California statute books. Its crucial element is the right of survivorship, a right that would be more illusory than real if a joint tenant were permitted to lease for a term continuing after his death. Accordingly, we hold that under the facts alleged in the complaint the lease herein is no longer valid. . . .

Notes, Questions, and Problems

1. *Unbroken Unities or Intent to Sever?* At common law a grant of a leasehold was a conveyance, and a conveyance was thought to break the unity of title, so severance would result. Today, as will be seen in Chapter Six, leaseholds have a dual quality—both contracts and conveyances—and that chameleon-like nature is one reason some courts do not adhere slavishly to the unities. But some courts do so. See, e.g., Alexander v. Boyer, 253 Md. 511 (1969). The alternative to worship at the altar of the unities is to examine whether the event in question manifests an intention to sever, and in doing so to assess the policy implications of a finding of severance or not.

2. *Mortgages and Judgment Liens.* In addition to grants of a lesser estate to a third party, such as a lease or a life estate (as in *Tenhet*), the question of whether severance has occurred also erupts in grants of a mortgage or deed to trust to property held in joint tenancy to secure a debt incurred by only one joint tenant and when there is an attachment or levy upon a debtor joint tenant's interest in joint tenancy.

Mortgage or Deed of Trust. A mortgage is a lien on property that secures repayment of a debt incurred by a borrower. If the debt is not paid the mortgagee is entitled to proceed to perfect the lien by foreclosing upon the property—acquiring title to it at a foreclosure sale or taking that portion of the proceeds of the sale that is sufficient to extinguish the debt. A deed of trust is a similar such security device. The borrower secures payment of the debt by executing a deed to the property to a trustee, who is charged with the obligation of either reconveying the property to the borrower upon full payment of the debt or, in the event of default, selling the property to raise funds with which to pay the debt.

Problem: Suppose that *A* and *B* own Blackacre as joint tenants. *A* borrows money from *C* and grants *C* a mortgage or deed of trust on Blackacre. *A* dies and his estate defaults on the debt to *C*. *C* seeks to foreclose on Blackacre. *B* asserts that he is sole owner of Blackacre and that it is not encumbered by the mortgage in favor of *C*. What should be the result and why? Should it matter whether a mortgage or deed of trust transfers title to the mortgagee or trustee or, instead, creates a lien that does not transfer title until and unless a foreclosure sale or trustee's sale occurs? Should it matter whether the lender and mortgagee is in the business of making loans secured by mortgages on real property or is a non-commercial lender, such as a family member or a seller of property who finances the sale by accepting a note from the buyer secured by a mortgage of the property?

In People ex rel. Dep't of Public Works v. Nogarr, 164 Cal.App.2d 591 (1958), a husband and wife owned property as joint tenants. Without the knowledge or consent of *W*, *H* borrowed a sum of money from his parents ("*P*") and gave them a mortgage on the property to secure the debt. *H* died and a year later the state condemned the property. *W* contended that she was entitled to the entire condemnation proceeds because the joint tenancy had not been severed. *P* contended that the joint tenancy had been severed by the mortgage and thus they were entitled to satisfy *H*'s unpaid debt out of the one-half of the proceeds attributable to *H*'s separate interest. The California appellate court concluded that the joint tenancy had not been severed. It regarded a mortgage as a mere lien that did not transfer title, and thus did not break the four unities. The court noted that *P* could have enforced the lien by foreclosure and sale prior to *H*'s death and thus severed the joint tenancy. The mortgage died along with *H*.

A similar case is Harms v. Sprague, 119 Ill.App.3d 503 (1983). *A* purchased a house from *S* by paying part cash and executing a promissory note to *S* for the balance of the purchase price. To secure payment of the note *A*'s friend, *B*, co-signed the note and executed a mortgage encumbering property ("Blackacre") owned in joint tenancy with his brother, *C*. Then *B* died, leaving a will that devised all his property to *A*, who was in default on the debt to *S*. *C* sought to quiet title in Blackacre in himself. *S* and *A* contended that *B*'s mortgage of Blackacre severed the joint tenancy. The Illinois appellate court ruled that no severance had occurred. The mortgage was a mere lien, although the court noted in dicta that it would not matter if title had been transferred by the mortgage because such a transfer of title was merely a temporary security device, rather than a permanent transfer. Thus, unities aside, the hypothecation of Blackacre did not adequately manifest an intent to sever the joint tenancy. As in *Nogarr*, the mortgage died with *B*, because *B* could only encumber his own interest, and that interest ended at *B*'s death.

The converse situation was presented in Brant v. Hargrove, 129 Ariz. 475 (Ct. App. 1981). *H* granted a mortgage on property held in joint tenancy with *W*. Then *W* died and *W*'s estate contended that *H*'s act had severed the joint tenancy. As in *Nogarr* and *Harms* the court ruled that no severance had occurred.

In *Nogarr* and *Harms*, there is an unspoken question: Who should bear the risk of loss? If the joint tenancy is not severed the mortgage holder's security is wiped out if the executing joint tenant dies before the debt is paid or a foreclosure sale is completed. If the joint tenancy is severed in this scenario, the joint tenant who did not consent to the mortgage loses half of the property.

There is another problem with severance in these cases: What happens if the debt is paid and the mortgage extinguished while all joint tenants are alive? Does the severance continue or is the joint tenancy put back together?

Attachment or Levy Upon a Debtor's Interest in Joint Tenancy. Jurisdictions differ concerning the point at which a creditor's seizure of a debtor's interest in a joint tenancy severs the joint tenancy. Some states hold that the mere filing of a lien, without levy or execution upon the lien, does not sever the joint tenancy. See, e.g., Ladd v. State ex rel. Oklahoma Tax Comm., 1984 Okla. 60, 688 P.2d 59 (1984). Others hold that the joint tenancy is severed only at the moment of an execution sale. See, e.g., First National Bank v. Energy Fuels Corp., 200 Colo. 540 (1980).

3. *Divorce.* The traditional rule was that divorce did not terminate a joint tenancy between husband and wife, because the four unities were unaffected by the collateral termination of the marriage that probably induced the joint tenancy. This approach, which is oblivious to the reality of joint tenancies between married couples, has been addressed by some statutes that treat divorce as severing the joint tenancy and creating a tenancy in common. See, e.g, Ohio Rev. Code Ann. § 5302.20(c)(5) (2010); Mich. Cons. Laws § 552.102 (2010) (severance upon divorce unless divorce decree is to the contrary). Without statutory rules to govern, courts today seem to focus on the intent of the parties as the criterion for decision. See Richard H. Helmholz, Realism and Formalism in the Severance of Joint Tenancies, 77 Neb. L. Rev. 1, 21 (1998). Such courts either frankly reject the unities as controlling (see, e.g., Mamalis v. Bornovas, 112 N.H. 423 (1972)), or simply ignore the unities to examine the parties' intent. See, e.g., Estate of Gebert, 95 Cal.App.3d 370 (1979).

> *Problem: A* and *B*, a married couple, own Blackacre as joint tenants. They separate and seek judicial dissolution of their marriage. At the time of separation, and before the divorce is accomplished, they enter into an agreement by which they stipulate that neither party may unilaterally transfer their interest before the divorce is final and that, if the two should agree to sell Blackacre, they will share the net proceeds equally. Then *A* dies before the divorce is final. *A*'s estate contends that the agreement severed the joint tenancy; *B* contends that there was no severance and that she is the sole owner of Blackacre. What should be the result?

In thinking about this problem, recall that severance can be effected by an agreement of the parties. Compare Sondin v. Bernstein, 126 Ill.App.3d 703 (1984); In re Marriage of Dowty, 146 Ill.App.3d 675 (1986); In re Estate of Violi, 65 N,Y, 2d 392 (1985); and Mann v. Bradley, 188 Colo. 392 (1975). If this agreement is insufficient to sever, and that is what the parties truly intended, how could it be changed to accomplish that end?

For an erudite treatment of the origins and implication of severance, see Robert W. Swenson & Ronan E. Degnan, Severance of Joint Tenancies, 38 Minn. L. Rev. 466 (1954).

Note: Bank Accounts

A common problem is the status of bank accounts held in joint tenancy. The problem arises for two reasons. First, people open joint tenancy bank accounts for at least three different reasons: (1) to create a true joint tenancy, in which either joint tenant has a right to the deposited funds during life and the survivor owns the account at the death of the other joint tenant; (2) a convenience account, which is an informal attorney-in-fact relationship, in which the depositor joint tenant intends for the other joint tenant to have access to the account to pay the bills and provide for the comfort of the depositor joint tenant, but not to own the account at the death of the depositor joint tenant; and (3) a "pay-on-death," or P.O.D., account, in which the depositor does not intend that the other joint tenant have any present access to the funds but does wish the other joint tenant to own the account at the depositor's death. The second reason for problems with these accounts is that is easier for banks to insist on joint tenancy as the only form of co-ownership than to permit these tailored forms of ownership. There is no need for the bank to inquire whether a withdrawal is authorized and no need to inquire who is entitled to the account upon the death of one joint tenant.

Although states have been hesitant to recognize pay-on-death accounts, because they are in effect a will substitute without the usual formalities associated with a will that are thought to provide certainty concerning the decedent's desires for disposition of his property, they have become permitted by statute in some jurisdictions. See, e.g., Calif. Fin. Code § 852; Calif. Probate Code §§ 5100 et seq. But even in those jurisdictions that recognize P.O.D. accounts the problem remains to distinguish between the convenience account and the true joint tenancy. The burden is on those who contend a joint tenancy account is a convenience account to prove it, usually by clear and convincing evidence.

C.   RIGHTS AND OBLIGATIONS OF CONCURRENT OWNERS TOWARD EACH OTHER

When two or more people own the same property at the same time they each have an equal right to the whole, but that avoids answering the question of how they may or must conduct themselves to avoid injury to each other. Each of two siblings may have an equal right to the whole pie, but they cannot each eat the entire pie. The law that has developed on this topic seeks to dampen or resolve conflict between co-owners. If there are two broad principles that undergird that process it is the desire to achieve efficient outcomes without sacrificing fairness or, put the other way, to achieve fairness without sacrificing efficiency. These principles, even at the high level of generality at which they are pitched, serve only to introduce another potential conflict. From this may be glimpsed the fact that the law here seeks to do the best it can without tilting too much in either direction. That is not easy, and courts and legislators may regard the trade-off between fairness and efficiency differently, both on the wholesale level of articulating general rules and the retail level of their application to individual cases.

1. PARTITION

In general, every co-owner has the unconditional right to seek partition of the property owned concurrently. This right is almost always asserted when the co-owners cannot agree voluntarily to terminate their co-ownership or to sell the property and divide the proceeds. Partition is often efficient because it eliminates the problems of concurrent ownership but it can be unfair because partition can be used to compel results that one co-owner might desire and the others do not desire, or to place one co-owner at a disadvantage with respect to the other co-owner or owners.

Partition began as a legal remedy available only to co-parceners, because they had involuntarily become co-owners, and was limited to a physical division and allocation of the property held in co-parceny. By statutes enacted in the mid-sixteenth century partition became available to joint tenants and tenants in common as well. The English equity courts then extended and refined the remedy. Today, partition is provided by statute in every American jurisdiction but courts supplement the statutes by exercise of their equitable powers.

JOHNSON v. HENDRICKSON

Supreme Court of South Dakota
71 S.D. 392 (1946)

SICKEL, J., delivered the opinion of the court.

This is an action for the partition of real property. Henry W. Bauman and Katie B. Bauman were husband and wife. Their children [were] Grace, Arthur, and Vernon. The husband died intestate in 1904, leaving an estate consisting of an improved quarter section[2] of land in Clark County. The [land was inherited] as follows: One-third to the widow, two-ninths to each of the three children, all subject to the homestead right of the widow. The widow then married the defendant Karl Hendrickson. The children of this marriage consisted of twin boys named Kenneth and

---

2. [Ed.—] A section is a one square mile consisting of 640 acres, more or less. At the very beginning of American independence it was decided to survey the entire United States. Eventually this was done for the territory west of the original thirteen colonies (excepting Kentucky, Tennessee, Vermont, Maine, Texas, and West Virginia) on a grid. The vertical axis consists of range lines, six miles apart, and the horizontal axis consists of township lines, also six miles apart. Each square within this grid is subdivided into 36 smaller squares, called sections. Some corrections to these lines are made to account for the fact that the Earth's curvature causes all north-south lines to converge at the poles. Thus, not every section is exactly 640 acres. In the broad expanse of the agricultural west, it is not uncommon for a farm to be composed of several sections, or at least a good chunk of a single section.

Karrol. Katie B. Hendrickson, widow of Henry W. Bauman, wife of Karl Hendrikson and mother of all the children, never moved from this land during her lifetime. Karl Hendrickson, her husband, lived there with her until she died, and still lives upon the land. All the children lived on this land during their minority and at various periods of time after attaining their majority. The mother died in May 1944 and left her property by will as follows: To her husband, Karl Hendrikson, one-half; to each of the children of the second marriage one-fourth; to the children of her first marriage, five dollars each. Thus, the ownership of the quarter section of land involved in this action is as follows: Grace Bauman Johnson, Arthur Bauman and Vernon Bauman, two-ninths each; Karl Hendrickson, one-sixth; Kenneth and Karrol Hendrickson, one-twelfth each. These interests are subject to the homestead rights of Karl Hendrickson in the one-third interest owned by Katie B. Hendrickson at the time of her death. Plaintiffs in this action are the three children of the first marriage of Katie B. Hendrickson. They allege in their complaint that the land is so situated that it cannot be partitioned among the various owners either individually or in groups, without prejudice to such owners, and ask that it be sold in one tract. Defendants deny that the partition in kind would be prejudicial to the owners. The circuit court . . . adjudged that the land be sold. From this decree the defendants have appealed.

(A) Appellants [urge that] partition in kind be made by allotting to them, as owners collectively of a one-third interest in the land, the southeast forty-acre tract with all the buildings and improvements situated thereon, and the hog house now on the southwest forty-acre tract, and by allotting to the three respondents, as owners of a two-thirds interest in the land, the other three forty-acre tracts with no buildings, but upon which is situated a forty-acre slough. The first question presented then is whether the court was justified in deciding that the land be sold.

SDC 37.1412 provides in part: "If it appear to the satisfaction of the Court that the property, or any part of it, is so situated that partition cannot be made without great prejudice to the owners, the Court may order a sale thereof. . . ." The language of this statute means that a sale may be ordered if it appear to the satisfaction of the court that the value of the share of each cotenant, in case of partition, would be materially less than his share of the money equivalent that could probably be obtained for the whole. Idema v. Comstock, 131 Wis. 16 [(1907)]; . . . Williamson Inv. Co. v. Williamson, 96 Wash. 529 [(1917)]. The above rule was approved by this court in the case of Kluthe v. Hammerquist, 45 S.D. 476 [(1922)]. . . . [A] sale is justified if it appears to the satisfaction of the court that the value of the land when divided into parcels is substantially less than its value when owned by one person. This land is now owned by six persons. The largest individual interest is two-ninths and the smallest is one-twelfth. Partition in kind would require the division of the land into not less than four parcels: Two-ninths to each of the three respondents, and one-third to appellants, collectively. It is a matter of common knowledge in this state that the division of this quarter section of land, located as it is, into four or more separate tracts would materially depreciate its value, both as to its salability and as to its use for agricultural purposes. The fact that it would be an advantage to appellants to have the farm partitioned according to their demands because of their ownership of adjoining land, is immaterial.

[Appellants propose that] the court allot to appellants, who own a one-third interest in the farm, approximately one-third of the acreage contained therein, leaving to respondents who own the other two-thirds interest in the land, the remaining acreage, forty acres of which is worthless slough, to be divided amongst the three of them. They then ask the court to determine the value of the respective tracts of land so partitioned, also the value of the improvements on the land allotted to appellants, and that the court direct appellants to pay respondents their two-thirds share of the excess. SDC 37.1427 makes the following provision for an award of owelty: "When it appears that the partition cannot be made equal between the parties according to their respective rights, without prejudice to the rights and interests of some of them, and a partition be ordered, the Court may adjudge compensation to be made by one party to another, on account of the inequality. . . ." This statute applies only to those cases in which a partition in kind be ordered. The circuit court did not decree a partition in kind, but rightfully decided that the farm be sold, on the ground that partition in kind would materially lessen the value of the interests of the several owners. Since the land is to be sold there will be no allotment of shares in the land to anybody. The proceeds of the sale will be apportioned according to the interests of the several owners, and hence there is no occasion for owelty in this case. . . .

The widow inherited from her first husband an undivided one-third interest in the farm. After she married appellant Karl Hendrickson in 1909 she continued to occupy the farm as a homestead with her children, her second husband, and the children of the second marriage. During such occupancy they remodeled the house, built the barn, hog house, granary, wash house, milk house, chicken house, fences, and two wells, at a cost of over $9,000. Appellants Karl Hendrickson and the two sons of the second marriage claim in this action that as the devisees of Katie B. Hendrickson, and present owners of an undivided one-third interest in the farm they are entitled to credit for such improvements. The rule at common law is that a tenant in common cannot compel his cotenants to contribute to his expenditures for improvements placed by him on the common property without the consent or agreement of the cotenants. . . .

[A court in equity may] generally make suitable allowance, on partition, for improvements made in good faith by a cotenant in possession, to the extent that the value of the property has been enhanced thereby. . . . Here the evidence shows that improvements consisting of a house, barn, granary, chicken house, and shed, all old, were situated upon this farm in 1909. In 1910 a granary was built, in 1911 a chicken house and in subsequent years the barn was torn down and a new one constructed in its place. The house was repaired and remodeled, a hog house, wash house, garage, milk house, fences, and wells were also constructed in the following years. In the year 1909 the mortgage on the homestead was $2500. It was increased to as much as $7,000 to pay for improvements, debts, and to buy another quarter section of land across the road. Arthur Bauman was born in 1893 and remained at home until he was twenty-seven years of age. Grace Bauman was born in 1895 and remained at home until her mother died in 1944. Vernon Bauman was born in 1898 and remained at home until he was thirty-six years of age. These three children of the first marriage worked but received no wages while at home, and none of them had separate incomes, except the daughter from some chickens and Vernon from some farming which he did on his own account. During all the time that these three children of the first marriage remained at home they and their mother occupied the homestead as such, and owned it as tenants in common. The second husband and the children of the second marriage were members of the same family. The mother was the head of this family. She owned all the personal property and managed all the family affairs. The improvements, [e]ncumbrances, and additional land were made and paid for out of the land by the combined efforts of all. The respondents made substantial contributions to the family income out of which these things were accomplished, during their minority, and also during their majority. The family had the use of the greater part of the improvements over a period of more than thirty years. These improvements and the payment of the mortgage have greatly enhanced the value of the estate. Karl Hendrickson and his two sons now own a one-third interest in the homestead, improved and free from debt, and the additional quarter section of land. The circuit court determined that under these circumstances an allowance to Karl Hendrickson and his sons for the improvements made and the indebtedness paid would be inequitable, and this conclusion is amply supported by the evidence. . . .

[Affirmed.]

ARK LAND COMPANY v. HARPER

Supreme Court of Appeal of West Virginia
215 W.Va. 331 (2004)

DAVIS, J., delivered the opinion of the court.

. . . This is a dispute involving approximately 75 acres of land situate in Lincoln County, West Virginia. The record indicates that "the Caudill family has owned the land for nearly 100 years." The property "consists of a farmhouse, constructed around 1920, several small barns, and a garden[.]" Prior to 2001, the property was owned exclusively by the Caudill family. However, in 2001 Ark Land acquired a 67.5% undivided interest in the land by purchasing the property interests of several Caudill family members. Ark Land attempted to purchase the remaining property interests held by the Caudill heirs, [consisting of Harper and her fellow appellants,] but they refused to sell. Ark Land sought to purchase all of the property for the express purpose of extracting coal by surface mining.

After the Caudill heirs refused to sell their interest in the land, Ark Land filed a complaint in the Circuit Court of Lincoln County in October of 2001 ... seeking to have the land partitioned and sold. ... On October 30, 2002, the circuit court entered an order directing the partition and sale of the property. ... From this ruling the Caudill heirs appealed....

The dispositive issue is whether the evidence supported the circuit court's conclusion that the property could not be conveniently partitioned in kind, thus warranting a partition by sale. During the proceeding before the circuit court, the Caudill heirs presented expert testimony by Gary F. Acord, a mining engineer. Mr. Acord testified that the property could be partitioned in kind. Specifically, Mr. Acord testified that lands surrounding the family home did not have coal deposits and could therefore be partitioned from the remaining lands. On the other hand, Ark Land presented expert testimony which indicated that such a partition would entail several million dollars in additional costs in order to mine for coal.

We note at the outset that "partition means the division of the land held in cotenancy into the cotenants' respective fractional shares. If the land cannot be fairly divided, then the entire estate may be sold and the proceeds appropriately divided." 7 Powell on Real Property, § 50.07[1] (2004). It has been observed that, "in the United States, partition was established by statute in each of the individual states. Unlike the partition in kind which existed under early common law, the forced judicial sale was an American innovation." Phyliss Craig-Taylor, Through a Colored Looking Glass: A View of Judicial Partition, Family Land Loss, and Rule Setting, 78 Wash. U.L.Q. 737, 752 (2000). [By] virtue of W. Va. Code § 37–4–1 et seq., "the common law right to compel partition has been expanded by [statute] to include partition by sale."[3]

Partition by sale, when it is not voluntary by all parties, can be a harsh result for the cotenant(s) who opposes the sale. This is because

3. All jurisdictions provide for partition in kind or by sale. *See* Ala. Code § 35–6–57 (Law. Co-op. 1991); Alaska Stat. tit. 9, § 09.45.290 (Lexis 2000); Ariz. Rev. Stat. Ann. § 12–1218 (West 2003); Ark. Stat. Ann. § 18–60–420 (Lexis 2003); Cal. Civ. Proc. Code § 872.820 (West 1980); Colo. Rev. Stat. § 38–28–107 (Bradford 2002); Conn. Gen. Stat. Ann. § 52–500 (West 1991); Del. Code Ann. tit. 25, § 729 (Michie 1989); D.C. Code Ann. § 16–2901 (Lexis 2001); Fla. Stat. Ann. § 64.071 (West 1997); Ga. Code Ann. § 44–6–166.1 (Michie 1991); Haw. Rev. Stat. § 668–7 (1993); Idaho Code § 6–512 (Lexis 1998); 735 Ill. Comp. Stat. § 5/17–101 (West 2003); Ind. Code Ann § 32–17–4–12 (Lexis 2002); Iowa Code Ann. Rule 1.1201 (West 2002); Kan. Stat. Ann. § 60–1003 (1994); Ky. Rev. Stat. Ann. § 389A.030 (Lexis 1999); La. Stat. Ann. Civ. Code art. 1336 (West 2000); Me. Rev. Stat. Ann. tit. 18–A, § 3–911 (West 1998); Md. Real Prop. Code Ann. § 14–107 (Lexis 2003): Mass. Gen. Laws Ann. ch. 241, § 31 (West 1988); Mich. Comp. Laws § 600.3332 (West 2000): Minn. Stat. Ann. § 558.14 (West 2000); Miss. Code Ann. § 11–21–27 (West 1999); Mo. Ann. Stat. § 528.340 (Vernon 1953); Mont. Code Ann. § 70–29–202 (West 2003); Neb. Rev. Stat. § 25–2181 (1995); Nev. Rev. Stat. Ann. § 39.120 (2003); N.H. Rev. Stat. Ann. § 547–C:25 (Michie 1997); N.J. Stat. Ann. § 2A:56–2 (West 2000); N.M. Stat. Ann. § 42–5–7 (Michie 1978); N.Y. Real Prop. Acts. Proc. Law § 922 (West 1979); N.C. Gen. Stat. § 46–22 (Lexis 2003); N.D. Cent. Code § 32–16–12 (Michie 1996); Ohio Rev. Code Ann. § 5307.09 (Anderson 1989); Okla. Stat. Ann. tit. 12, § 1509 (West 1993); Or. Rev. Stat. § 105.245 (2003); Pa. Cons. Stat. Ann., R. Civ. Pro. Rule 1558 (West 2002); R.I. Gen. laws § 34–15–16 (Michie 1995); S.C. Code Ann. § 15–61–50 (Law. Co-op. 1977); S.D. Codified Laws Ann. § 21–45–28 (Michie 1987); Tenn. Code Ann. § 29–27–201 (Lexis 2000); Tex. Code Ann. Property § 23.001 (West 2000); Utah Code Ann. § 78–39–12 (Lexis 2002); Vt. Stat. Ann. tit. 12, § 5174 (Lexis 2002); Va. Code Ann. § 8.01–83 (Lexis 2000); Wash. Rev. Code Ann. § 7.52.080 (West 1992); Wis. Stat. Ann. § 842.11 (West 1994); Wyo. Stat. § 1–32–109 (Lexis 2003).

" '[a] particular piece of real estate cannot be replaced by any sum of money, however large; and one who wants a particular estate for a specific use, if deprived of his rights, cannot be said to receive an exact equivalent or complete indemnity by the payment of a sum of money.' " Wight v. Ingram–Day Lumber Co., 195 Miss. 823 (Miss. 1944) (quoting Lynch v. Union Inst. for Savings, 159 Mass. 306 (1893)). Consequently, "partition in kind . . . is the preferred method of partition because it leaves cotenants holding the same estates as before and does not force a sale on unwilling cotenants." Powell, § 50.07[4][a]. The laws in all jurisdictions "appear to reflect this long-standing principle by providing a presumption of severance of common ownership in real property by partition in-kind[.]" Craig–Taylor, 78 Wash. U.L.Q. at 753. "Thus, partitioning sale statutes should be construed narrowly and used sparingly because they interfere with property rights." John G. Casagrande, Jr., Acquiring Property Through Forced Partitioning Sales: Abuses and Remedies, 27 Boston C.L. Rev. 721, 775 (1986). . . .

[This Court has] set out the following standard of proof that must be established to overcome the presumption of partition in kind: "[A] party desiring to compel partition through sale is required to demonstrate [(1)] that the property cannot be conveniently partitioned in kind, [(2)] that the interests of one or more of the parties will be promoted by the sale, and [(3)] that the interests of the other parties will not be prejudiced by the sale." In its lengthy order requiring partition and sale, the circuit court [concluded that an allotment of] "the manor house and the surrounding 'bottom land' unto the [Caudill heirs], cannot be [e]ffected without undeniably prejudicing [Ark Land's] interests;" [and that] "while its uniform topography superficially suggests a division-in-kind . . ., the access road, the bottom lands and the relatively flat home site is, in fact, integral to establishing the fair market value of the subject property in its entirety, as its highest and best use as mining property. . . ." [The circuit court also concluded the Caudill heirs] "do not wish to sell, or have the Court sell, their interests in the subject property, solely due to their sincere sentiment for it as the family's 'home place' [but other] family members . . . did not feel the same way. . . . [It] is just and reasonable for the Court to conclude that the interests of all the subject property's owners will not be financially prejudiced, but will be financially promoted, by sale of the subject property and distribution among them of the proceeds, according to their respective interests. The subject property's value as coal mining property, its uncontroverted highest and best use, would be substantially impaired by severing the family's 'home place' and allotting it to them separately."

We are troubled by the circuit court's conclusion that partition by sale was necessary because the economic value of the property would be less if partitioned in kind. We have long held that the economic value of property *may* be a factor to consider in determining whether to partition in kind or to force a sale. . . . However, our cases *do not* support the conclusion that economic value of property is the exclusive test for determining whether

$ not only factor to consider!

to partition in kind or to partition by sale. In fact, we explicitly stated in Hale v. Thacker, 122 W. Va. 648, 650, 12 S.E.2d 524, 526 (1940), "that many considerations, other than monetary, attach to the ownership of land, and courts should be, and always have been, slow to take away from owners of real estate their common-law right to have the same set aside to them in kind."

Other courts have also found that monetary consideration is not the only factor to contemplate when determining whether to partition property in kind or by sale. In the case of Eli v. Eli, 1997 SD 1, 557 N.W.2d 405 (S.D. 1997), the South Dakota Supreme Court addressed the issue of the impact of monetary considerations in deciding whether to partition property in kind or by sale. In that case over 100 acres of land were jointly owned by three members of the Eli family. The land had been owned by the Eli family for almost 100 years, and was used solely as farm land. Two of the co-owners sought to have the land partitioned and sold. A trial judge found that the land would be worth less if partitioned in kind, therefore the court ordered the land be sold at public auction. The co-owner who sought a partition in kind appealed the trial court's decision. The South Dakota Supreme Court found that the trial court erroneously relied upon the fact that the property would be worth less if partitioned in kind. In reversing the trial court's decision, the *Eli* court reasoned as follows:

> Monetary considerations, while admittedly significant, do not rise to the level of excluding all other appropriate considerations. . . . The sale of property "without [the owner's] consent is an extreme exercise of power warranted only in clear cases." We believe this to be especially so when the land in question has descended from generation to generation. While it is true that the Eli brothers' expert testified that if partitioned, the separate parcels would sell for $50 to $100 less per acre, this fact alone is not dispositive. One's land possesses more than mere economic utility; it "means the full range of the benefit the parties may be expected to derive from their ownership of their respective shares." Such value must be weighed for its effect upon all parties involved, not just those advocating a sale. 557 N.W.2d at 409–410 (internal citations omitted).

See also . . . Fike v. Sharer, 280 Ore. 577, 571 P.2d 1252, 1254 (Or. 1977) ("Sentimental reasons, especially an owner's desire to preserve a home, may also be considered [in a partition suit]").

Similarly, in Delfino v. Vealencis, 181 Conn. 533, 436 A.2d 27 (Conn. 1980), two plaintiffs owned a 20.5 acre tract of land with the defendant. The defendant used part of the property for her home and a garbage removal business. The plaintiffs filed an action to force a sale of the property so that they could use it to develop residential properties. The trial court concluded that a partition in kind could not be had without great prejudice to the parties, and that the highest and best use of the property was through development as residential property. The trial court therefore ordered that the property be sold at auction. The defendant appealed. The Connecticut Supreme Court reversed for the following reasons:

> The [trial] court's ... observations relating to the effect of the defendant's business on the probable fair market value of the proposed residential lots ... are not dispositive of the issue. *It is the interests of all of the tenants in common that the court must consider; and not merely the economic gain of one tenant, or a group of tenants.* The trial court failed to give due consideration to the fact ... that the [defendant] has made her home on the property; and that she derives her livelihood from the operation of a business on this portion of the property, as her family before her has for many years. A partition by sale would force the defendant to surrender her home and, perhaps, would jeopardize her livelihood. It is under just such circumstances, which include the demonstrated practicability of a physical division of the property, that the wisdom of the law's preference for partition in kind is evident. [436 A.2d at 32–33 (emphasis added).]

[We] now make clear and hold that, in a partition proceeding in which a party opposes the sale of property, the economic value of the property is not the exclusive test for deciding whether to partition in kind or by sale. Evidence of long-standing ownership, coupled with sentimental or emotional interests in the property, may also be considered in deciding whether the interests of the party opposing the sale will be prejudiced by the property's sale. [This latter factor should ordinarily control when it is shown that the property can be partitioned in kind, though it may entail some economic inconvenience to the party seeking a sale.] In the instant case, the Caudill heirs were not concerned with the monetary value of the property. Their exclusive interest was grounded in the long-standing family ownership of the property and their emotional desire to keep their ancestral family home within the family.[4] It is quite clear that this emotional interest would be prejudiced through a sale of the property.

The expert for the Caudill heirs testified that the ancestral family home could be partitioned from the property in such away as to not deprive Ark Land of any coal. The circuit court summarily and erroneously dismissed this uncontradicted fact because of the increased costs that Ark Land would incur as a result of a partition in kind. [But] the additional economic burden that would be imposed on Ark Land, as a result of partitioning in kind, is not determinative under the facts of this case. . . .

[P]rior to 2001, Ark Land had no ownership interest in the property. Conversely, for nearly 100 years the Caudill heirs and their ancestors

---

4. The circuit court's order suggests that, because some family members sold their interest in the property, no real interest in maintaining the family home existed. While it may be true that the family members who sold their interest in the property did not have any emotional attachment to the family home, this fact cannot be dispositively attributed to the Caudill heirs. The interest of the Caudill heirs cannot be nullified or tossed aside, simply because other family members do not share the same sentiments for the family home.

owned the property and used it for residential purposes.[5] In 2001 Ark Land purchased ownership rights in the property from some Caudill family members. When the Caudill heirs refused to sell their ownership rights, Ark Land immediately sought to force a judicial sale of the property. In doing this, Ark Land established that its proposed use of the property, surface coal mining, gave greater value to the property. This showing is self-serving. In most instances, when a commercial entity purchases property because it believes it can make money from a specific use of the property, that property will increase in value based upon the expectations of the commercial entity. This self-created enhancement in the value of property cannot be the determinative factor in forcing a pre-existing co-owner to give up his/her rights in property. To have such a rule would permit commercial entities to always "evict" pre-existing co-owners, because a commercial entity's interest in property will invariably increase its value.

We are very sensitive to the fact that Ark Land will incur greater costs in conducting its business on the property as a result of partitioning in kind. However, Ark Land voluntarily took an economical gamble that it would be able to get all of the Caudill family members to sell their interests in the property. Ark Land's gamble failed. ... The fact that Ark Land miscalculated on its ability to acquire outright all interests in the property cannot form the basis for depriving the Caudill heirs of their emotional interests in maintaining their ancestral family home. The additional cost to Ark Land that will result from a partitioning in kind simply does not impose the type of injurious inconvenience that would justify stripping the Caudill heirs of the emotional interest they have in preserving their ancestral family home. ...

[The] circuit court erred in determining that the property could not be partitioned in kind. We ... reverse the circuit court's order requiring sale of the property. This case is remanded with directions to the circuit court to enter an order requiring the property to be partitioned in kind, consistent with the report and testimony of the Caudill heirs' mining engineer expert, Gary F. Acord.

Reversed and Remanded.

MAYNARD, C.J., concurring, in part, and dissenting, in part:

I ... agree that evidence of longstanding ownership along with sentimental or emotional attachment to property are factors that should be considered and, in some instances, control the decision of whether to partition in kind or sale jointly-owned property Which is the subject of a partition proceeding.

I dissent in this case, however, because I do not believe that evidence to support the application of those factors was presented here. [None] of the appellants have resided at the subject property for years. At most, the property has been used for weekend retreats. While this may have been

---

5. No one lives permanently at the family home. However, the family home is used on weekends and for special family events by the Caudill heirs.

the family "homeplace," a majority of the family has already sold their interests in the property to the appellee. Only a minority of the family members, the appellants, have refused to do so. I believe that the sporadic use of the property by the appellants in this case does not outweigh the economic inconvenience that the appellee will suffer as a result of this property being partitioned in kind.

I am also troubled by the majority's decision that this property should be partitioned in kind instead of being sold because I don't believe that such would have been the case were this property going to be put to some use other than coal mining. For instance, I think the majority's decision would have been different if this property was going to be used in the construction of a four-lane highway. Under those circumstances, I believe the majority would have concluded that such economic activity takes precedence over any long-term use or sentimental attachment to the property on the part of the appellants. In my opinion, coal mining is an equally important economic activity. This decision destroys the value of this land as coal mining property because the appellee would incur several million dollars in additional costs to continue its mining operations. As a result of the majority's decision in this case, many innocent coal miners will be out of work....

NOTES, QUESTIONS, AND PROBLEMS

1. Partition Remedies. The courts say that partition in kind is the norm and partition by sale is exceptional. Yet, most residential real estate is not capable of partition in kind, and other legal restrictions upon subdivision of tracts may render partition in kind impossible or impractical. Thus, partition by sale may result more frequently than the doctrine would seem to acknowledge. However, the property at issue in *Johnson* and *Ark Land* was each capable of division in kind, yet the outcomes were different. Why did *Ark Land* take into account the value to the Caudill heirs of retaining the family home while the *Johnson* court did not give any weight to the desire of the Hendricksons' to stay in the family farmstead?

The *Johnson* court also noted that the Hendricksons' desire to be allocated the portion nearest to their wholly owned adjacent 40 acre farm was "immaterial." In accord with that sentiment is Gray v. Crotts, 58 N.C.App. 365 (1982). To effect a partition in kind property was divided into four equally valuable tracts and then allotted by lottery to each of the four co-tenants. One of the co-tenants objected, claiming that he had either a right to be allotted the parcel that adjoined his home or that it was equitable to do so. The court rejected both contentions. Although it acknowledged that it was permissible to take that fact into account, there is neither an obligation for a court to do so nor is it inequitable to ignore a co-tenant's ownership of adjacent land. Why is this so? Should it be so?

The economic loss to the Ark Land Company resulting from partition in kind was estimated to be the millions of dollars. Assuming that a partition by sale would have captured that value, why should the subjective value that the Caudill heirs attached to their erstwhile but largely unused family home outweigh this palpable economic value? If the answer is that fairness trumps efficiency, was it fair to Ark Land to strip them of their portion of this value in order to subsidize the Caudill heirs? Should the Caudill heirs have been required to compensate Ark Land for the loss?

Note the West Virginia court's contention that "when a commercial entity purchases property because it believes it can make money from a specific use of the property, that property will increase in value based upon the expectations of the commercial entity," and that this is a "self-created enhancement" in value that should be discounted or ignored. Is this true? To have a partition by sale there must be willing buyers, and those buyers will assess the value of the property independently of the interests of the co-tenants. On the other hand, suppose that the only bidder is Ark Land. Will the sale price truly reflect its fair market value? If *A* can afford to buy out *B*'s interest, but *B* cannot afford to buy out *A*'s interest, will partition by sale inevitably be inequitable? Does the answer turn on whether there is an adequate number of rival bidders to ensure that the property sells for its fair market value?

2.   *Owelty and its kin.* The court in *Johnson* noted that owelty—compensation from one co-tenant to another—will be awarded when there is a partition in kind and the value of the parcels are unequal. Owelty can also be ordered when there is a partition by sale and the sale price reflects value added by improvements made by one of the co-tenants, who should be compensated for the added value shared among all co-tenants. Suppose that partition in kind is impractical or impossible and that partition by sale does not adequately protect the interest of all parties. Should a court award the entire parcel to one of the co-tenants and require that co-tenant to pay to the other co-tenants their share of the fair market value of the property? What problems, if any, do you see in this solution? See, e.g., Zimmerman v. Marsh, 365 S.C. 383 (2005). Marsh owned a one-half interest in a beach house in which she lived. The other half was owned by Berg. Zimmerman, a real estate agent, purchased Berg's interest and within minutes of recording the deed filed a partition action, seeking sale of the property, which was ordered by the trial court. The South Carolina Supreme Court reversed, ordering that the property be allotted to Marsh upon her payment to Zimmerman of one-half of the fair market value of the whole. See also Wilk v. Wilk, 173 Vt. 343 (2002). Eight siblings inherited equal interests in a developed one acre parcel. John Wilk, who operated a business on the property, purchased six of those interests from his siblings. His brother Joseph, who operated a junkyard on an adjacent parcel refused to sell to John. In a partition action the court ordered Joseph to sell his one-eighth interest to John for one-eighth of the fair market value of the whole. The court stressed the need to permit such forced sales in order to keep family farms and other family-owned properties intact.

3.   *Metes and bounds division.* *A* and *B* owned a tract of land that they leased to *C* for a 10 year term. Then *C* offered to purchase the leased premises. Without *B*'s consent, *A* conveyed his interest in the leased premises, described by its metes and bounds, and his interest in the lease, to *C*. *B* sued *A* and *C* to cancel the deed; the trial court refused to do and also granted *C*'s request that partition of the tract be made in kind, in accordance with the

metes and bounds conveyance from *A* to *C*. In affirming those rulings the Third Circuit stated:

> While some of the earlier authorities hold that such a conveyance is void, we think that the better rule, which is followed by a majority of the states and which was applied by the district court in this case, is that such a conveyance is voidable only[,] and as between the parties is valid and is to be given full effect if it can be done without prejudice or injury to the non-conveying cotenant. [Partition by the metes and bounds conveyances] may only be had if it can be accomplished without prejudice or injury to the non-consenting cotenant. ... In the absence of any evidence that [*B*] will be prejudiced or injured by the deeds ... or by the partition ... we cannot hold that the district court erred in giving effect to the deeds ... and in awarding to [*C*] the partition [he] sought. Kean v. Dench, 413 F.2d 1, 3–5 (3rd Cir. 1969).

4. *Agreements not to partition.* If *A* and *B*, co-owners of Blackacre, agree never to seek to partition Blackacre, is the agreement valid? What principles are applicable to resolution of this question? See Raisch v. Schuster, 47 Ohio App.2d 98, 100–102 (1975). Would the answer be different if the agreement stipulated that it was for the purpose of preserving the property as a family home and would terminate when each of the minor children of the co-owners have reached age 21? See *Id.* See also Ex parte Watts, 130 N.C. 237 (1902). What if the agreement stated that it would expire at the death of all of the co-owners? See Condrey v. Condrey, 92 So.2d 423, 426 (Fla. 1957).

[handwritten margin note: reasonable or unreasonable Restraint on alienability — usually dependent on length of time]

5. *Who can partition? Of future interests.* The partition issues which we have examined thus far have involved concurrent ownership of present possessory interests. Suppose that *O* conveys Blackacre to *A* for life, and then to *B* and *C* in fee simple absolute. May *B* or *C* obtain partition of their concurrently owned remainder? Should it make any difference to your answer if *O* had instead conveyed Blackacre to *A* for life, and then to *B* and *C*, should they each survive *A*, in fee simple absolute? For analysis of this and other partition problems involving future interests, see Powell on Real Property § 50.07 and § 21.05[2]. *[handwritten: Depends on State you are in]*

6. *Problem: O* dies, leaving a will by which she bequeathed "all of my tangible personal property to my children, *A* and *B*." Included in that property is a needlepoint cushion that *O* had made with a market value of $50 but which is much loved for its sentimental value by each of *A* and *B*. They quarrel over which should possess the cushion and one of them seeks partition of the cushion. What should the court do? See Estate of McDowell, 74 Misc.2d 663, 664–665 (N.Y. Sur. Ct. 1973).

7. *Efficiency.* Co-ownership exacerbates inefficiency because of the inherent conflict that lurks in the differing desires of co-owners, and because it increases the incentive on the part of any individual co-owner to exploit the common asset for individual benefit. To the extent the costs of such exploitation can be shifted onto the other co-owners they incur a negative externality which, from the perspective of the exploiting co-owner, is a windfall gain. Because each co-owner has the same incentive, the possibility of friction among co-owners is amplified. Partition may be a reaction to that possibility, but the law governing the rights and obligations of co-owners who choose to

remain in concurrent ownership also addresses these problems. It is to that topic that we now turn.

2. CONFLICT CONCERNING POSSESSION, REVENUES, COSTS, AND IMPROVEMENTS

Property ownership brings financial rewards in the form of rents and profits, and imposes costs in the form of taxes, insurance, maintenance, and payments upon debt that may be incurred to acquire the property. Because developed property is a wasting asset, sometimes maintenance can be turned into improvements. How should these costs and benefits be shared? At first it may seem simple to say that they should be shared in proportion to the co-tenants' ownership shares, but complications arise. What if one co-tenant occupies the entire property and the other co-tenants make no complaint about that? What if one co-tenant improves the property at his own expense without asking the others for their consent? What constitutes an improvement? What if one co-tenant pays the bills and keeps the rents? What remedies do co-tenants have against each other? These issues and others are the subject of this subsection.

a. Exclusive Possession

SPILLER v. MACKERETH

Supreme Court of Alabama
334 So.2d 859 (1976)

JONES, J., delivered the opinion of the court.

[Spiller and Mackereth owned a commercial building as tenants in common. The building was rented to a third party, Auto–Rite, who vacated. Spiller then used the entire building as a warehouse to store his goods. Mackereth's lawyer sent a letter to Spiller demanding that he either vacate one-half of the building or pay to Mackereth rent for that half. Spiller did not respond to the letter, did not vacate, and did not pay rent. Instead, Spiller sought to partition the property and Mackereth counterclaimed for rent. The trial court ordered partition by sale and awarded Mackereth $2,100 in rent. Spiller appealed.]

... We reverse ... the rental award. Since there is no real dispute concerning the ... facts, ... we will limit our review to the trial Judge's application of the law to the facts. [W]e start with the general rule that in absence of an agreement to pay rent or an ouster of a cotenant, a cotenant in possession is not liable to his cotenants for the value of his use and occupation of the property. Since there was no agreement to pay rent, there must be evidence which establishes an ouster before Spiller is required to pay rent to Mackereth. The difficulty ... lies in the definition of the word "ouster." Ouster is a conclusory word which is used loosely in cotenancy cases to describe two distinct fact situations. The two fact

ouster

situations are (1) the beginning of the running of the statute of limitations for adverse possession and (2) the liability of an occupying cotenant for rent to other cotenants. Although the cases do not acknowledge a distinction between the two uses of "ouster," it is clear that the two fact situations require different elements of proof to support a conclusion of ouster.

Ouster + AP

The Alabama cases involving adverse possession require a finding that the possessing cotenant asserted complete ownership to the land to support a conclusion of ouster. The finding of assertion of ownership may be established in several ways. Some cases find an assertion of complete ownership from a composite of activities such as renting part of the land without accounting [to the other cotenant], hunting the land, cutting timber, assessing and paying taxes and generally treating the land as if it were owned in fee for the statutory period. See Howard v. Harrell, 275 Ala. 454, 156 So.2d 140 (1963). Other cases find the assertion of complete ownership from more overt activities such as a sale of the property under a deed purporting to convey the entire fee. Elsheimer v. Parker Bank & Trust Co., 237 Ala. 24, 185 So. 385 (1938). But whatever factual elements are present, the essence of the finding of an ouster in the adverse possession cases is a claim of absolute ownership and a denial of the cotenancy relationship by the occupying cotenant.

Ouster + Liability for rent

In the Alabama cases which adjudicate the occupying cotenant's liability for rent, a claim of absolute ownership has not been an essential element. [An] occupying cotenant [is] liable to out of possession cotenants [when] the occupying cotenant refuses a demand of the other cotenants to be allowed into use and enjoyment of the land, regardless of a claim of absolute ownership.

The ... adverse possession rule is precluded in this case by Spiller's acknowledgement of the cotenancy relationship as evidenced by filing the bill for partition. We can affirm the trial Court if the record reveals some evidence that Mackereth actually sought to occupy the building but was prevented from moving in by Spiller. To prove ouster, Mackereth's attorney relies upon the [demand] letter ... as a sufficient demand and refusal to establish Spiller's liability for rent. This letter, however, did not demand equal use and enjoyment of the premises; rather, it demanded only that Spiller either vacate half of the building or pay rent. the question of whether a demand to vacate or pay rent is sufficient to establish an occupying cotenant's liability for rent has not been addressed in Alabama; however, it has been addressed by courts in other jurisdictions. In jurisdictions which adhere to the majority and Alabama rule of nonliability for mere occupancy, several cases have held that the occupying cotenant is not liable for rent notwithstanding a demand to vacate or pay rent. Grieder v. Marsh, 247 S.W.2d 590 (Tex.Civ.App. 1952); Brown v. Havens, 17 N.J.Super. 235, 85 A.2d 812 (1952).

There is a minority view which establishes liability for rents on a continued occupancy after a demand to vacate or pay rent. Re Holt's

Estate, 14 Misc.2d 971, 177 N.Y.S.2d 192 (1958). We believe that the majority view on this question is consistent with Alabama's approach to the law of occupancy by cotenants[:] . . . "Tenants in common [have] an equal right to occupy; and unless the one in actual possession denies to the other the right to enter, or agrees to pay rent, nothing can be claimed for such occupation."

Thus, before an occupying cotenant can be liable for rent in Alabama, he must have denied his cotenants the right to enter. It is axiomatic that there can be no denial of the right to enter unless there is a demand or an attempt to enter. Simply requesting the occupying cotenant to vacate is not sufficient because the occupying cotenant holds title to the whole and may rightfully occupy the whole unless the other cotenants assert their possessory rights. Besides the [demand] letter, Mackereth's only attempt to prove ouster is a showing that Spiller put locks on the building. However, there is no evidence that Spiller was attempting to do anything other than protect the merchandise he had stored in the building. Spiller testified that when Auto–Rite moved out they removed the locks from the building. Since Spiller began to store his merchandise in the building thereafter, he had to acquire new locks to secure it. There is no evidence that either Mackereth or any of the other cotenants ever requested keys to the locks or were ever prevented from entering the building because of the locks. There is no evidence that Spiller intended to exclude his cotenants by use of the locks. Again, we emphasize that as long as Spiller did not deny access to his cotenants, any activity of possession and occupancy of the building was consistent with his rights of ownership. Thus, the fact that Spiller placed locks on the building, without evidence that he intended to exclude the other cotenants, is insufficient to establish his liability to pay rent. . . .

[We] are unable to find any evidence which supports a legal conclusion of ouster. We are, therefore, compelled to reverse the trial Court's judgment awarding Mackereth $2,100 rental. . . .

NEWMAN v. CHASE

Supreme Court of New Jersey
70 N.J. 254 (1976)

MOUNTAIN, J., delivered the opinion of the court.

[Arthur and Dorothy Chase owned a single-family residence as tenants by the entirety. Arthur went bankrupt and Newman acquired Arthur Chase's one-half interest in the Chase family home by purchasing it from Arthur Chase's bankruptcy trustee. Newman thus became a tenant in common with Dorothy Chase. Under New Jersey law, Newman acquired Arthur's present right to possession during the joint lives of Arthur and Dorothy and Arthur's future interest in fee simple absolute of the whole in the event he survived Dorothy. (This results from the peculiarities of the tenancy by the entirety, discussed in section C, Marital Interests.)

Procedure

Newman sought partition of the present interest. Although this is general-ly an unconditional right, the court denied partition, stating that "where, as in the present case, a bankrupt husband lives with his young family in a modest home, we hold that it is within the equitable discretion of the court to deny partition to a purchaser of the husband's interest, leaving the creditor to resort to some other remedy." Newman sought another remedy: imposition of liability for rent.]

With respect to the residential property involved in this case . . . [the] only benefit inuring to the tenant in possession is the value of her use and occupation of the property—in effect, the imputed rental value of the house. As a general rule, since each cotenant has an undivided interest in the whole estate, each is entitled to occupy the entire property. Thus, absent ouster of the other cotenants, a cotenant in possession is not required to account to them for the value of use and occupation. We think, however, that where one cotenant, with her family, remains in possession of a one-family house which is not susceptible of joint occupancy, and refuses to accede to plaintiff's demands for access to the property, such conduct clearly constitutes an ouster. Mrs. Chase is thus accountable to Mr. Newman for one-half the imputed rental value of the house.

[A later New Jersey case, Bauer v. Migliaccio, 235 N.J. Super. 127 (1989), ruled that in these circumstances the co-tenant out of possession must at least make a demand for possession, "thereby giving the co-tenant the option of choosing to vacate before an obligation to [pay rent] accrues."]

CUMMINGS v. ANDERSON

Supreme Court of Washington
94 Wn. 2d 135 (1980)

ROSELLINI, J., delivered the opinion of the court.

[In anticipation of marriage Patty Cummings and Wally Anderson acquired, as tenants in common, the purchaser's rights under an install-ment sale contract for a house.[6] Approximately 80% of the purchase price remained to be paid. They then married and lived together in the house. Six months later Cummings moved out of the house. She testified] that she had left the premises to protect her children from involvement in and observation of the sexual activities of [Anderson's] son, then in his early teens. She said that she had told [Anderson] that one of them would have to leave, and he had said it would have to be her. His testimony was that she had left the home without notice and without explanation. She did not contend that her departure had been occasioned by any conduct or omission of [Anderson. Cummings brought suit for partition and for one-

---

6. [Ed.—] An installment sale contract leaves title to the property in the vendor until the full purchase price has been paid, at which point title is transferred to the buyer. The same economic result could be achieved by transferring title to the buyer upon the buyer's execution of a promissory note for the purchase price, payable to the seller in installments, and secured by a mortgage or deed of trust encumbering the property.

half the rental value of the house during the time it was occupied exclusively by Anderson.] The trial court found that [Cummings] had not been ousted by [Anderson].

The respondent urges reversal of the Court of Appeals upon the question of her entitlement to rent. She relies upon the conduct of [Anderson's] son as constituting ouster, but cites no authority which supports that contention. It is the rule in Washington that, in the absence of an agreement to pay rent, or limiting or assigning rights of occupancy, a cotenant in possession who has not ousted or actively excluded the cotenant is not liable for rent based upon his occupancy of the premises. In order for ouster to exist, there must be an assertion of a right to exclusive possession.

An appealing argument is made that, in a situation such as this, where the property is not adaptable to double occupancy, the mere occupation of the property by one cotenant may operate to exclude the other. Had the respondent not abandoned her obligations under the contract of purchase at a time when over four-fifths of the purchase price remained to be paid, we would be much inclined to agree that she is entitled to receive rent. Under the circumstances as they exist, she has not demonstrated a sufficient equitable interest to warrant this extension of the rule. . . .

NOTES, QUESTIONS, AND PROBLEMS

1. *What constitutes ouster?* The Alabama Supreme Court says that ouster (at least when adverse possession between co-tenants is not the issue) occurs when the co-tenant in possession excludes other co-tenants from possession after they have demand possession, and that a demand letter is not enough proof of such ouster. The New Jersey Supreme Court says that even a demand letter is unnecessary to prove ouster when the property is a single family home that is exclusively possessed by one co-tenant as the family home. The Washington Supreme Court rules that offensive conduct by the minor son of a co-tenant is insufficient to constitute ouster when the other co-tenant moves out to avoid that offensive conduct. What should be the criteria to prove ouster? Should different rules apply to residential and commercial property? If so, why? Why is a demand for possession communicated by letter, followed by the refusal of the co-tenant in possession to acquiesce, not enough proof of ouster?

Which, if any, of the following scenarios constitute ouster? In each case, *A* and *B*, tenants in common, occupy Blackacre jointly.

a. *A* is an habitual drunkard and threatens *B* with physical violence when he is intoxicated, but never actually lands a blow. *B* moves out and files suit, seeking rent from *A*.

b. *A* is engaged in criminal activity in Blackacre, which brings people into Blackacre whom *B* fears might erupt into violence. *B* moves out and files suit, seeking rent from *A*.

c. Blackacre is a commercial building that *A* and *B* each use to store goods. *B* moves out voluntarily because she has found a better warehouse. *A* occupies all of Blackacre. *B* sends a letter to *A* demanding rent. *A* replies: "Because you moved out, you have lost all interest you had in Blackacre. I refuse your demand because you have no claim on Blackacre." *B* files suit, seeking rent from *A*.

2. *Ouster and adverse possession.* In order for the co-tenant in possession to claim that his possession is adverse to the co-tenant(s) out of possession (and thus start the limitations statute to begin to run) it must be clear that the co-tenant in possession has not only refused the demand for possession of the co-tenant(s) out of possession but has also unequivocally denied that the co-tenant(s) out of possession have any ownership rights or, what is the same thing, unequivocally claimed that he is the sole owner. Does this require an explicit statement by the co-tenant in possession that he is the sole owner, or can this be inferred from the actions of the co-tenant in possession?

In Horne v. Ward, 585 So.2d 877 (Ala. 1991), the Wards acquired a three-fourths interest as tenants in common in a house and yard known as the "Pearce lot." McChesney owned the remaining one-fourth interest. After the relevant limitations statute had expired McChesney conveyed his one-fourth interest in the Pearce lot to Horne. The Wards contended that the McChesney–Horne deed was a nullity because they had acquired McChesney's interest in the Pearce lot by adverse possession. The court said

> "possession of one tenant in common is presumed to be the possession of all; and such possession does not become adverse to the cotenant until he is actually ousted or short of ouster, the adverse character of the possession of one is actually known to the other, or the possession of one is so open and notorious in its hostility and exclusiveness as to put the cotenant on notice of its adverse character." "Before the possession of a cotenant may be regarded as adverse to his cotenant, he must repudiate the cotenant's interest in the property by act or declaration." This means that there must be some express denial of title and right to possession of the fellow cotenant brought home to him openly and unequivocally.

Because there was no ouster (in the adverse possession sense of demand for possession, refusal, and denial of the demanding co-tenant's ownership interest), the question was whether the Wards had either provided actual notice to McChesney of their claim or that their occupation of the Pearce lot was "so open and notorious in its hostility and exclusiveness as to have put McChesney on notice of its adverse character." Mrs. Ward testified that she had mailed three letters to McChesney informing him that they claimed the whole title, but admitted that one had been returned by the Postal Service, and could not recall even the city to which the other two had been addressed. Mrs. Ward also testified that she had mailed a similar letter to McChesney's mother and had told his aunt that they were claiming the whole title. That was not good enough to establish actual notice. Nor was the Wards' occupation sufficient to have constituted constructive notice. While the Wards occupied as a true owner would—openly using the home and garden and paying the taxes—that was not enough to put McChesney on notice of an adverse claim as to *title*. No doubt the Wards' occupation was sufficient to meet the requirements of adverse possession against a stranger, but as between co-tenants something stronger, more dramatic, was needed. Would it have been sufficient if the Wards had erected a large sign on the property reading: "Attention McChesney: The current occupants, the Wards, claim ownership of the entire property as the sole owners."?

In Wright v. Wright, 270 Ga. 530 (1999), the Georgia Supreme Court upheld a finding of adverse possession by one co-tenant against other co-tenants. Aitchley owned a one-half interest in a farm; his siblings owned the other half interest. Aitchley was in exclusive possession of the farm from 1950 until his death in the 1990s. During that time he had conveyed a fee simple absolute title to a tiny portion of the farm to a stranger, warranting in the deed that he owned the whole title, had paid the taxes, made major improvements, and granted easements to strangers. His siblings admitted that they were aware that Aitchley regarded the farm as his own but were afraid to confront him because of his "tyrannical" nature and violent temper.

Some states impose even stricter requirements to establish adverse possession against a co-tenant. Hawaii, for example, requires actual notice to the co-tenant of the adverse claim, except (1) where the tenant in possession has no reason to suspect the existence of a co-tenancy, (2) where a tenant in possession makes a good faith effort to locate co-tenants but is unable to find them, and (3) where the co-tenants out of possession have actual knowledge of the adverse claim. See City and County of Honolulu v. Bennett, 57 Haw. 195, 209 (1976).

3. *Co-owners as fiduciaries.* Generally, co-tenants do not owe fiduciary duties to each other, except in special circumstances such as those discussed below. However, some states do treat co-tenants as fiduciaries of each other, regardless of any special circumstances. See, e.g, City and County of Honolulu v. Bennett, 57 Haw. 195, 209 (1976); Hendrix v. Hendrix, 256 Ark. 289, 293 (1974); Webster v. Knop, 6 Utah 2d 273, 277–278 (1957). In those states that do not impose a general fiduciary obligation between co-tenants, there are two common exceptions that result in such a fiduciary duty.

First, when co-tenants are related to one another, a fiduciary obligation may be implied from the familial relationship. This is especially so when one co-tenant seeks to extinguish the interest of his relatives and fellow co-tenants by adverse possession. See, e.g, Ex parte Walker, 739 So.2d 3 (Ala. 1999).

Second, when one co-tenant acquires title to concurrently owned property at a foreclosure sale or at a sheriff's sale for unpaid taxes it is generally held that the acquiring co-tenant has acted for all the co-tenants. Thus, should the acquiring co-tenant claim that he has a superior title to the prior concurrent title, his claim will be ignored on the ground that, as a fiduciary, he is obliged to hold title for all his co-tenants, so long as they reimburse the acquirer for their pro rata share of the acquisition. See, e.g., Massey v. Prothero, 664 P.2d 1176 (Utah 1983).

4. *Why require ouster?* Not every state requires ouster as a precondition to establishing liability for rent on the part of the tenant in exclusive possession. See, e.g., West v. Weyer, 46 Ohio St. 66, 72 (1888); Cohen v.

Cohen, 157 Ohio St. 503, 510 (1952). Which rule is better? Why? The Ohio statute at issue in *Cohen* provided that a co-tenant "may recover from another his share of rents and profits received by such [co-tenant] from the estate, according to the justice and equity of the case." If ouster is not required and liability for rent on the part of the co-tenant in possession hinges on the "justice and equity of the case," what factors should be helpful (or determinative) to the outcome?

b.   Accounting for Revenue, Expenses, Repairs, and Improvements

Because each co-owner has equal rights to the whole, and human nature being what it is, co-owners can act independently of one another to receive revenue or other benefits from the property, to construct improvements, undertake maintenance or repairs, or pay expenses (such as taxes, mortgage loan payments, or insurance) that are attributable to the entire property. If informal mechanisms of accounting fail, co-owners may bring an action for an accounting or for contribution from the other co-tenants. Such claims can be combined with a partition action, but need not be so combined. This subsection provides a synopsis of the rights and obligations of co-tenants with respect to these matters and concludes with a classic case that illustrates the practical difficulties of the remedies available to co-owners when strong disagreement erupts.

Revenue. A co-owner who receives rental income from a third party with respect to the property must account to his co-owners for that income. The recipient co-owner must deliver to his other co-owners the portion of his net rental income that exceeds his share. Thus, if *A*, owner of a one-half interest in Blackacre with *B*, receives gross rental income of $10,000 for a lease of Blackacre and another $5,000 in mineral royalties for oil extracted from Blackacre, but incurs $3,000 in expenses to obtain those rents and royalties, *A* is obligated to remit to *B* $6,000, which is one-half of the net receipts. The liability of a co-tenant in exclusive possession for rent to the co-tenants not in possession was treated in the preceding subsection.

Expenses. Necessary expenses—those essential to preservation of the ownership interests of the co-tenants—are the responsibility of all owners. Thus, if one co-tenant pays more than his share of taxes, debt service, insurance, or other reasonably necessary expenses, he is entitled to recover the excess from his fellow co-tenants via a suit for contribution. What if the co-tenant who has paid more than his share is in exclusive possession of the property? Should that co-tenant be entitled to contribution from his fellow owners? Should the resolution of this issue have anything to do with whether a co-tenant in exclusive possession should be liable for rent regardless of ouster?

Repairs and Improvements. In general, a co-owner who undertakes to repair or improve the property does so at his own expense. Absent an agreement among co-owners, contribution from co-owners is not generally an available remedy, on the ground that the wisdom or even necessity of these expenditures is inherently subjective and thus too uncertain to admit of principled resolution in the courts. On the other hand, in an accounting action courts will usually grant a credit to a co-owner for his expenditures upon necessary repairs. One wonders why courts are capable of determining which repairs are necessary in an accounting action if they are not able to do so in a contribution action. Perhaps the difference is that if such claims were permitted in contribution actions, claims brought by the co-tenant who has incurred the expense would be legion; but permitting an offset in an accounting is far less likely to produce an avalanche of claims because accounting actions are usually brought by a co-tenant who believes that he has been short-changed in receipt of revenues (and it is probable that the co-tenant making the expenditure on repairs is the one who is receiving the revenue).

But co-tenants who expend funds on improvements are not entirely without a remedy. Though contribution is barred to them they are usually entitled to receive the value of their improvements in a partition action. The mechanism for doing so depends on whether the partition is in kind or by sale. If partition is in kind the improving co-tenant may be awarded that portion of the property that has been improved, so long as that division does not prejudice the other co-tenants. If prejudice would result by such a division, then the property may be divided in such a manner as to avoid prejudice, but the improving co-tenant may be awarded owelty from the non-improving co-tenants. The amount of owelty should equal the value added to the physical share awarded to the non-improving co-tenants that is attributable to the improvements. If partition is by sale, distribution of the sale proceeds is made in such a manner to compensate the improving co-tenant for the valued added to the sale price by the improvement.

Note that the courts are concerned with actual fair market value in reckoning improvements. If an improvement costs more than its actual market value the "improver" gets nothing for his pains. If an improvement costs less than its market value the improver gets rewarded. That is how the market works for sole owners, and it should operate the same for concurrent owners. Some states, however, provide that an improving co-tenant may only receive the *lesser* of the improvement's cost or its market value. What is the likely effect of that latter rule? Is it a better or worse rule than the general rule?

Waste. A co-owner is generally liable to his fellow owners for waste. Most states have enacted statutes that subject a co-owner committing waste to treble damages. See, e.g. Alaska Stat. § 09.45.740 (2010); Calif. Code Civ. Proc. § 732 (2009). For a list of such statutes, see Powell on Real Property § 56.08 n.2. Waste is treated the same way as it is with respect to claims for waste made by the holder of an indefeasibly vested future interest against a present possessor. Some states provide that some activities that might not be waste, such as mining, may be enjoined if engaged in without the consent of all co-owners. See, e.g, Chosar Corp. v.

Owens, 235 Va. 660 (1988). Contra, McCord v. Oakland Quicksilver Mining Co., 64 Cal. 134 (1883).

SWARTZBAUGH v. SAMPSON

Court of Appeal of California, Fourth District
11 Cal.App.2d 451 (1936)

MARKS, J., delivered the opinion of the court.

This is an action to cancel two leases executed by John Josiah Swartzbaugh, as lessor, to Sam A. Sampson, as lessee, of two adjoining parcels of land in Orange County. A motion for nonsuit was granted at the close of plaintiff's case and this appeal followed.

Defendant [John] Swartzbaugh and plaintiff [Lola Swartzbaugh] are husband and wife. They owned, as joint tenants with the right of survivorship, sixty acres of land in Orange County planted to bearing walnuts. In December, 1933, defendant Sampson started negotiations with plaintiff and her husband for the leasing of a small fraction of this land fronting on Highway 101 for a site for a boxing pavilion. Plaintiff at all times objected to making the lease and it is thoroughly established that Sampson knew she would not join in any lease to him. The negotiations resulted in the execution of [a] lease, dated February 2, 1934, [by John Swartzbaugh and Sam Sampson]. A second lease of property adjoining the site of the boxing pavilion was signed by [John] Swartzbaugh and Sampson. This was also dated February 2, 1934, but probably was signed after that date. Plaintiff's name does not appear in any of the three documents and Sampson was advised that she would not sign any of them. [The lease rental was $15 per month.]

The walnut trees were removed from the leased premises. Sampson went into possession, erected his boxing pavilion and placed other improvements on the property[, at an estimated cost of $10,000]. Plaintiff was injured in February, 1934, and was confined to her bed for some time. This action was started on June 20, 1934. Up to the time of the trial plaintiff had received no part of the rental of the leased property. Sampson was in possession of all of it under the leases to the exclusion of plaintiff.

There is but one question to be decided in this case which may be stated as follows: Can one joint tenant who has not joined in the leases executed by her cotenant and another maintain an action to cancel the leases where the lessee is in exclusive possession of the leased property?

This question does not seem to have been decided in California and there is not an entire uniformity of decision in other jurisdictions. In decisions on analogous questions where courts reached like conclusions they did not always use the same course of reasoning in reaching them. It seems necessary, therefore, that we consider briefly the nature of the estate in joint tenancy and the rights of the joint tenants in it. An estate in joint tenancy can be severed by destroying one or more of the necessary unities, either by operation of law, by death, by voluntary or certain involuntary acts of the joint tenants, or by certain acts or omissions of one joint tenant without the consent of the other. It seems to be the rule in England that a lease by one joint tenant for a term of years will effect a severance, at least during the term of the lease. We have found no case in the United States where this rule has been applied. From the reasoning used and conclusions reached in many of the American cases its adoption in this country seems doubtful.

One of the essential unities of a joint tenancy is that of possession. Each [joint] tenant owns an equal interest in all of the fee and each has an equal right to possession of the whole. . . . Ordinarily one joint tenant out of possession cannot recover exclusive possession of the joint property from his cotenant. He can only recover the right to be let into joint possession of the property with his cotenant. He cannot eject his cotenant in possession. Ordinarily one joint tenant cannot maintain an action against his cotenant for rent for occupancy of the property or for profits derived from his own labor. [He may, however, compel the tenant in possession to account for rents collected from third parties.] . .

It is a general rule that the act of one joint tenant without express or implied authority from or the consent of his cotenant cannot bind or prejudicially affect the rights of the latter. In the application of the foregoing rule the courts have imposed a limitation upon it . . . in cases where one joint tenant in possession leases all of the joint property without the consent of his cotenant and places the lessee in possession. . . . [The] joint tenant in possession is entitled to the possession of the entire property and by his lease merely gives to his lessee a right he, the lessor, had been enjoying, [which] puts the lessee in the enjoyment of a right of possession which he, the lessor, already had and by so doing does not prejudicially affect the rights of the cotenant out of possession, it being conceded that the joint tenant not joining in the lease is not bound by its terms and that he can recover from the tenant of his cotenant the reasonable value of the use and enjoyment of his share of the estate, if the tenant under the lease refuses him the right to enjoy his moiety of the estate. . . .

In 2 Thompson on Real Property, page 929, section 1715, it is said: "One joint tenant may make a lease of the joint property, but this will bind only his share of it." The same rule is thus stated in 1 Landlord and Tenant, Tiffany, 405: "One of two or more joint tenants cannot, by making a lease of the whole, vest in the lessee more than his own share, since that is all to which he has an exclusive right. Such a lease is, however, valid as to his share." The foregoing authorities support the conclusion that a lease to all of the joint property by one joint tenant is not a nullity but is a valid and supportable contract in so far as the interest of the lessor in the joint property is concerned.

While the qualities of estates of joint tenancy and a tenancy in common differ, the rights of possession are quite similar. . . . In the case of Lee Chuck v. Quan Wo Chong & Co., 91 Cal. 593 [(1891)], the plaintiff, a tenant in common, brought an action to oust defendant who was holding under a lease from another tenant in common, the Supreme Court reversed the judgment in favor of plaintiff and said: "... All that the plaintiff was entitled to ... was to be let into possession with the defendant—to enjoy his moiety. ... One tenant in common may, 'by either lease or license, ... confer upon another person the right to occupy and use the property of the co-tenancy as fully as such lessor or licensor himself might have used or occupied it if such lease or license had not been granted. ... If the lessee has the exclusive possession of the premises, he is not liable to any one but his lessor for the rent, unless the other cotenants attempt to enter and he resists or forbids their entry, or unless, being in possession with them, he ousts or excludes some or all of them.' ...'"

[W]here one tenant leases the common property to a stranger to the title the other tenants in common cannot cancel the lease or recover exclusive possession of the entire property.... Tiffany, in 1 Real Property, 684, says that the effect of a lease by one cotenant is to give the lessee the right to share in the possession of the leased property for the term of the lease. This coincides with statements made in Lee Chuck v. Quan Wo Chong & Co. ... that all a cotenant out of possession is entitled to is to be let into possession with the lessee of his cotenant to enjoy his moiety. This rule has not been uniformly adopted and its application in this state has not been directly decided.

As far as the evidence before us in this case is concerned, the foregoing authorities force the conclusion that the leases from [John] Swartzbaugh to Sampson are not null and void but valid and existing contracts giving to Sampson the same right to the possession of the leased property that [John] Swartzbaugh had. It follows they cannot be cancelled by plaintiff in this action.... *H*

Plaintiff expresses the fear that as one of the leases runs for five years, with an option for an additional five years, she may lose her interest in the leased premises by prescription. It is a general rule that a lessee in possession of real property under a lease cannot dispute his landlord's title nor can he hold adversely to him while holding under the lease. [Because] the lessee of one cotenant holds the possession of his lessor and ... a cotenant in possession holds for the other cotenant and not adversely, Sampson would have great difficulty in establishing any holding adverse to plaintiff without a complete and definite ouster. As a general rule an adverse possessor must claim the property in fee and a lessee holding under a lease cannot avail himself of the claim of adverse possession. ... There is no showing that plaintiff ever demanded that Sampson let her into possession of her moiety of the estate nor is there anything to indicate that he is holding adversely to her.

Judgment affirmed.

no ouster!

NOTES AND QUESTIONS

1. No severance. The court expressed doubt that a lease by one joint tenant could constitute a severance of the joint tenancy, and that conclusion was squarely held to be the case in Tenhet v. Boswell, supra. Without severance, then, the joint tenancy continued intact but the lease validly transferred to Sampson the right to possession held by John Swartzbaugh with respect to the leased premises. Lola Swartzbaugh had two objections to the lease—the lease rental of $15 per month was too low and the boxing pavilion would introduce objectionable and licentious behavior. Neither of those objections was redressed by the court's ruling.

2. What can Lola Swartzbaugh do now? What remedies are available to Lola Swartzbaugh after the court's decision? Consider the advantages and limitations of partition, seeking rent from Sampson, demanding an accounting from John Swartzbaugh. Which, if any, of them is most likely to deliver to Lola Swartzbaugh that which she desires?

D. MARITAL PROPERTY

There are two different systems of marital property in the United States. One is the common law system that was inherited from the United Kingdom; the other is the community property regime that has its origins in continental Europe and which arrived in America through Spanish and French colonization. The common law system's central organizing principle is that each spouse owns their own property. Ownership is determined by title; the spouse who acquires property and in whose name title is vested is the owner, and the other spouse has no claim upon it. The common law system dominates American law; all but ten states apply the common law approach. The community property system holds that husband and wife constitute a marital community—an economic partnership—and that, in general, all the property acquired by either spouse belongs to the community. Each spouse has an equal claim to the assets of the marital community. Community property is recognized by Louisiana (due to its French antecedents), Arizona, California, Idaho, Nevada, New Mexico, Texas, and Washington (reflective for the most part of Spanish colonization or influence), Wisconsin (which has made a relatively recent and conscious choice to adopt community property principles), and Alaska (which has also recently offered community property as an elective to married couples).

The two systems tend to converge when it comes to division of property at divorce because most common law states have enacted equitable division statutes that can deliver approximately the same results as community property. Division of property at death, however, is a different matter. The two systems have widely different views on the ability of each spouse to control the distribution of their property at death. This section will first examine the common law system, then turn to community property, and conclude with a subsection on cohabiting unmarried partners and same-sex marriage and its legal equivalents.

1. COMMON LAW MARITAL PROPERTY

Today's version of the common law marital property system is much altered from its original structure. In its heyday the common law considered a husband and wife to be one person, but that person was definitely the husband. A woman lost her separate legal identity upon marriage and her personal property (with the exception of her clothing and related personal property) became that of her husband. Although a wife could continue to own real property as her separate property, her husband was entitled to possession of her real property, including that which she might acquire after marriage. Because this possessory right of the husband was reachable by his creditors, the wife of an unfortunate or reckless husband could do nothing to prevent his creditors from occupying her land during her marriage to the debtor husband. It is perhaps no wonder that, under such a legal regime, marriage was regarded in a somewhat cold-blooded manner.

This state of affairs in America began to break down in the nineteenth century. An 1809 Connecticut law allowed women to make wills, but the first Married Women's Property Act was an Arkansas statute of 1835. It provided that the property of a married woman could not be reached by her husband's creditors. A cascade of similar laws occurred in the 1840s. By 1848 the Seneca Falls Declaration of Sentiments offered the following as but a few of the "injuries and usurpations" of men toward women: "He has made her, if married, in the eye of the law, civilly dead. He has taken from her all right in property, even to the wages she earns." In the same year New York enacted the first of the next generation of Married Women's Property Acts. The New York Act declared that the property of a married woman (whether acquired before or during marriage) was her sole and separate property, that her husband had no right to its possession or income therefrom, and that it was not subject to the claims of her husband's creditors. These statutes became generally adopted in the 1850s and were universal by the end of the nineteenth century. See generally Richard H. Chused, Married Women's Property Law: 1800–1850, 71 Geo. L. J. 1359 (1983).

a. Tenancy by the Entirety

One feature of the common law system of marital property is the tenancy by the entirety, an estate that is limited to married couples and which is in essence a joint tenancy with an indestructible right of survivorship in each spouse. The theory of the tenancy by the entirety was grounded in the legal fiction that a married couple were one person. Thus, each spouse owned the entirety of the property (not simply an undivided interest in the whole), and neither spouse, acting alone, could alienate the property or any part of it, thus preserving inviolate the survivorship right held by each spouse. With the advent of the Married Women's Property Acts, however, a logical quandary arose. The tenancy by the entirety was seen by some states as inconsistent with the idea that a husband and wife were equals, possessed of separate and independent capacity to own and deal with property. Because "the one legal person of the common law" had been turned into "two distinct persons" and each spouse was now "capable of taking [title] separately, it is impossible that they should take [title] by entireties, as if they constituted a single person." Walthall v. Goree, 36 Ala. 728, 735 (1860). Today 25 states recognize the tenancy by the entirety and 25 states do not recognize it.[7] Problems arise, however, when creditors of one spouse seek to seize the interest of the debtor spouse in property held in tenancy by the entirety.

KING v. GREENE

Supreme Court of New Jersey
30 N.J. 395 (1959)

BURLING, J., delivered the opinion of the court.

This is an action seeking possession of lands.... The Superior Court, Law Division, hearing the matter on stipulated facts, granted plaintiff's motion for summary judgment. Defendants appealed....

[Marie and Philip King owned three lots on Patterson Avenue in Shrewsbury, New Jersey as tenants by the entirety. In 1931 Philip sued Marie and obtained a judgment against her for $1,225.00. Philip executed his judgment by a sheriff's sale in 1932 of Marie's interest in the lots. Crowell purchased Marie's interest at the sale. Later, Philip conveyed his own interest in the Patterson Avenue lots to Smock. At the same time, Crowell conveyed his own interest in the lots to Smock. At a later date Smock conveyed his interest in the lots to Greene. In 1957, some nineteen years after Philip King's death, Marie King,] as surviving spouse of Philip King, instituted the present action for possession, contending that she is the sole owner of the property and that the 1932 sheriff's deed conveyed only one-half the rents, issues and profits of the property during the joint lives of the spouses and did not convey her right of survivorship. She alleges that when her husband died in 1938 the life estate for the joint lives of the spouses terminated and she became entitled to the fee. Defendants' contention is that the sheriff's deed conveyed plaintiff's right of survivorship as well as a life interest.

The trial court concluded that the sheriff's deed did not include the right of survivorship and entered a summary judgment for plaintiff which declared that she is the present holder of a fee simple in the premises....

The question at issue is whether the purchaser at an execution sale under a judgment entered against the wife in a tenancy by the entirety acquires the wife's right of survivorship. ... Involved are two fundamental problems: (A) the nature of an estate by the entirety at common law,

---

7. The states that recognize the tenancy by the entirety are Alaska, Arkansas, Delaware, Florida, Hawaii, Illinois, Indiana, Kentucky, Maryland, Massachusetts, Michigan, Mississippi, Missouri, New Jersey, New York, North Carolina, Oklahoma, Ohio, Oregon, Pennsylvania, Rhode Island, Tennessee, Vermont, Virginia, and Wyoming.

and (B) the effect upon the estate by the entirety of the Married Women's 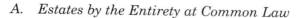 Act. . . .

A. *Estates by the Entirety at Common Law*

At the outset we note that the industry of counsel and our own independent research have failed to reveal any English case decided prior to 1776, touching upon the question of whether a voluntary or involuntary conveyance of a husband's interest in a tenancy by the entirety carries with it his right of survivorship.

The unique form of concurrent ownership at common law, labeled estates by the entirety, may be traced into antiquity at least as far back as the 14th and 15th Centuries. . . . The estate was unique because of the common law concept of unity of husband and wife and the positing of that unity in the person of the husband during coverture. A husband and wife cannot hold by moieties or in severalty, said Littleton, "and the cause is, for that the husband and wife are but one person in law. . . ." Coke on Littleton, sec. 291. Blackstone, in his judicial capacity, noted [that] "husband and wife, being considered in law as one person, they cannot, during the coverture take separate estates; and therefore upon a purchase made by them both, they cannot be seised by moieties, but both and each has the entirety. . . ." Green v. King, 2 Wm. Blackstone 1211, 1214, 96 Eng. Rep. 713, 714 (C.P. 1777). . . .

The unity of the spouses theory was early recognized in New Jersey as the foundation upon which estates by the entirety rested. . . . Thus, in an estate by the entirety the husband had absolute dominion and control over the property during the joint lives. The husband was entitled to the rents, issues and profits during the joint lives of himself and his wife, with the right to use and alienate the property as he desired, and the property was subject to execution for his debts.

The remaining question is, could the husband unilaterally alienate his right of survivorship at common law? Our study of the authorities convinces us that he could. The entire thrust of the authorities on the common law, with one notable exception, is to the effect that the only distinction between a joint tenancy and a tenancy by the entirety at common law was that survivorship could not be affected by unilateral action in the latter estate.

It was settled in England as early as the 14th Century that the husband could not defeat the wife's right of survivorship. In that case, reported in 2 Coke on Littleton, sec. 291, William Ocle was found guilty of treason (he murdered Edward II) and his estate was forfeited. Edward III granted the forfeited lands (owned jointly with the wife) to someone else. It was held that the husband's act of treason could not deprive the wife of her right of survivorship. . . . But to say that the husband cannot by his voluntary or involuntary act defeat the wife's right of survivorship is not to say that his own right of survivorship, subject to wife's right of survivorship, should he predecease her, cannot be alienated. The notion that the husband could not alienate his interests stems from Blackstone's comment, writing in 1765 to the following effect:

> And therefore, if an estate in fee be given to a man and his wife, they are neither properly joint tenants, nor tenants in common, for husband and wife being considered as one person in law, they cannot take the estate by moieties, but both are seised of the entirety ...; the consequence of which is that *neither the husband nor the wife can dispose of any part without the assent of the other, but the whole must remain in the survivor*." 2 Blackstone's Commentaries (Tucker, ed. (1802), 181) (Emphasis supplied)....

Blackstone's enigmatic statement that "neither the husband nor the wife can dispose of any part without the assent of the other, but the whole must remain in the survivor" was early limited in New Jersey. In Den ex dem. Wyckoff v. Gardner, 20 N.J.L. 556 (Sup. Ct. 1846), decided prior to the Married Women's Act, and hence under common-law principles, the issue was whether the husband could mortgage the premises in an estate by the entirety without the consent of his wife. In that case, Carpenter, J., held: "... The husband has the right of possession and control during coverture. Though he cannot convey the estate ... so as to prejudice her rights in case she survive; yet he may demise, alien or mortgage his interest during his own life." ...

Thus, the view that neither spouse could alienate his interest in the estate without the consent of the other, was interpreted to mean that the husband could not alienate so as to prejudice the wife's rights in the estate, and it is clear that the wife's only right at common law was her right of survivorship. No prejudice would result to the wife's interests at common law by the husband's alienation of his right of survivorship. If he predeceased her, she would take a fee. If she predeceased him, her interests were cut off anyway. During his lifetime she had no interest in the estate. That the husband could alienate his right of survivorship at common law is buttressed by the fact that at common law, in instances where property was held in the wife's name alone, the husband had the right to possession and had the absolute control over the rents, issues and profits during coverture. He could freely alienate that interest and it was subject to execution by his creditors. It would be incongruous to suggest that the husband could convey at the common law no greater interest in property held jointly by his wife and himself than in property held solely by his wife. Most courts and commentators have taken the position that at common law the husband's right of survivorship was alienable, so that the purchaser or grantee would take the entire fee in the event the wife predeceased the husband and the interest was subject to execution for his debts. [Case citations omitted.] ...

It is our view that the husband could, at common law, alienate his right of survivorship, or, more properly, his fee simple subject to defeasance.

Statute

B.   Effect of the Married Women's Act of 1852 Upon Estates by the Enitirety

[The Married Women's Act of 1852, codified at N.J. Stat. § 37:2–12] provides: "The real and personal property of a woman which she owns at the time of her marriage, and the real and personal property, and the rents, issues and profits thereof, of a married woman, which she receives or obtains in any manner whatever after her marriage, shall be her separate property as if she were a *feme sole*." . . .

The Court of Errors and Appeals in Buttlar v. Rosenblath, 42 N.J. Eq. 651 (E. & A. 1887), settled the question of the effect of the Married Women's Act upon estates by the entirety. After holding that the act does not destroy the estate, it was held that the effect and purpose of the act was to put the wife on a par with the husband. It was held [that] "the just construction of this legislation, and the one in harmony with its spirit and general purpose, is that the wife is endowed with the capacity, during the joint lives, to hold in her possession, as a single female, one-half of the estate in common with her husband, and that the right of survivorship still exists as at common law." . . .

Subsequent decisions have confirmed that presently husband and wife, by virtue of the Married Women's Act, hold as tenants in common for their joint lives; that survivorship exists as at common law and is indestructible by unilateral action; and that the rights of each spouse in the estate are alienable, voluntarily or involuntarily, the purchaser becoming a tenant in common with the remaining spouse for the joint lives of the husband and wife. It is clear that the Married Women's Act created an equality between the spouses in New Jersey, insofar as tenancies by the entirety are concerned. If, as we have previously concluded, the husband could alienate his right of survivorship at common law, the wife, by virtue of the act, can alienate her right of survivorship. And it follows, that if the wife takes equal rights with the husband in the estate, she must take equal disabilities. Such are the dictates of complete equality. Thus, the judgment creditors of either spouse may levy and execute upon their separate rights of survivorship. . . .

The judgment appealed from is reversed and the cause is remanded for the entry of a judgment in accordance with the views expressed in this opinion.

SAWADA v. ENDO

Supreme Court of Hawaii
57 Haw. 608 (1977)

MENOR, J., delivered the opinion of the court.

This is a civil action brought by the plaintiffs-appellants, Masako Sawada and Helen Sawada, in aid of execution of money judgments in their favor, seeking to set aside a conveyance of real property from judgment debtor Kokichi Endo to Samuel H. Endo and Toru Endo,

P

defendants-appellees herein, on the ground that the conveyance as to the Sawadas was fraudulent.

On November 30, 1968, the Sawadas were injured when struck by a motor vehicle operated by Kokichi Endo. On June 17, 1969, Helen Sawada filed her complaint for damages against Kokichi Endo. Masako Sawada filed her suit against him on August 13, 1969. The complaint and summons in each case was served on Kokichi Endo on October 29, 1969. On the date of the accident, Kokichi Endo was the owner, as a tenant by the entirety with his wife, Ume Endo, of a parcel of real property situate at Wahiawa, Oahu, Hawaii. By deed, dated July 26, 1969, Kokichi Endo and his wife conveyed the property to their sons, Samuel H. Endo and Toru Endo. . . . No consideration was paid by the grantees for the conveyance. Both were aware at the time of the conveyance that their father had been involved in an accident, and that he carried no liability insurance. Kokichi Endo and Ume Endo, while reserving no life interests therein, continued to reside on the premises.

On January 19, 1971, after a consolidated trial on the merits, judgment was entered in favor of Helen Sawada and against Kokichi Endo in the sum of $8,846.46. At the same time, Masako Sawada was awarded judgment on her complaint in the amount of $16,199.28. Ume Endo, wife of Kokichi Endo, died on January 29, 1971. She was survived by her husband, Kokichi. Subsequently, after being frustrated in their attempts to obtain satisfaction of judgment from the personal property of Kokichi Endo, the Sawadas brought suit to set aside the conveyance which is the subject matter of this controversy. The trial court refused to set aside the conveyance, and the Sawadas appeal.

I.   The determinative question in this case is, whether the interest of one spouse in real property, held in tenancy by the entireties, is subject to levy and execution by his or her individual creditors. This issue is one of first impression in this jurisdiction.

A brief review of the present state of the tenancy by the entirety might be helpful. Dean Phipps, writing in 1951,[8] pointed out that only nineteen states and the District of Columbia continued to recognize it as a valid and subsisting institution in the field of property law. Phipps divided these jurisdictions into four groups. He made no mention of Alaska and Hawaii, both of which were then territories of the United States.

In the Group I states (Massachusetts, Michigan, and North Carolina) the estate is essentially the common law tenancy by the entireties, unaffected by the Married Women's Property Acts. As at common law, the possession and profits of the estate are subject to the husband's exclusive dominion and control. In all three states, as at common law, the *husband* may convey the entire estate subject only to the possibility that the wife may become entitled to the whole estate upon surviving him. As at common law, the obverse as to the wife does not hold true. Only in Massachusetts, however, is the estate in its entirety subject to levy by the

---

8.   [Oval A.] Phipps, "Tenancy by Entireties," 25 Temple L.Q. 24 (1951).

husband's creditors. In both Michigan and North Carolina, the use and income from the estate is not subject to levy during the marriage for the separate debts of either spouse.[9]

In the Group II states (Alaska, Arkansas, New Jersey, New York, and Oregon)[10] the interest of the debtor spouse in the estate may be sold or levied upon for his or her separate debts, subject to the other spouse's contingent right of survivorship. Alaska, which has been added to this group, has provided by statute that the interest of a debtor spouse in any type of estate, except a homestead as defined and held in tenancy by the entirety, shall be subject to his or her separate debts.

In the Group III jurisdictions (Delaware, District of Columbia, Florida, Indiana, Maryland, Missouri, Pennsylvania, Rhode Island, Vermont, Virginia, and Wyoming) an attempted conveyance by either spouse is wholly void, and the estate may not be subjected to the separate debts of one spouse only.[11]

Grp III

In Group IV, the two states of Kentucky and Tennessee hold that the contingent right of survivorship appertaining to either spouse is separately alienable by him and attachable by his creditors during the marriage. The use and profits, however, may neither be alienated nor attached during coverture.

It appears, therefore, that Hawaii is the only jurisdiction still to be heard from on the question. Today we join that group of states and the District of Columbia which hold that under the Married Women's Property Acts the interest of a husband or a wife in an estate by the entireties is not subject to the claims of his or her individual creditors during the joint lives of the spouses. . . .

Hawaii has long recognized and continues to recognize the tenancy in common, the joint tenancy, and the tenancy by the entirety, as separate and distinct estates. That the Married Women's Property Act of 1888 was not intended to abolish the tenancy by the entirety was made clear by the language of Act 19 of the Session Laws of Hawaii, 1903 (now HRS § 509–1). . . . The effect of the Married Women's Property Acts was to abrogate the husband's common law dominance over the marital estate and to place the wife on a level of equality with him as regards the exercise of

---

9. [Ed.—] Massachusetts has since altered its rule to permit creditors of either spouse to levy upon the spouse's interest in property held in tenancy by the entirety. Massachusetts is now a Group II state, according to the taxonomy of the court in *Sawada*, except that a principal residence held in tenancy by the entirety is not susceptible to levy by a creditor of one spouse. See Coraccio v. Lowell Five Cents Savings Bank, 415 Mass. 145 (1993). North Carolina has granted each spouse equal rights with respect to the entirety and has continued to insulate tenancies by the entirety from creditors' claims against one spouse, thus placing it in Group III. See N.C. Gen. Stat. § 39–13.6 (2010). Michigan has also granted each spouse equal rights in tenancies by the entirety and appears to continue to adhere to its view, developed when the Michigan tenancy by the entirety was the pure common law version, that property held in tenancy by the entirety is immune from creditor's claims against one spouse. Thus, Michigan may also be counted among Group III. See Mich. Comp. Laws § 557.71.

10. [Ed.—] As noted, Massachusetts has also joined this group.

11. [Ed.—] This group also includes Illinois, Michigan, North Carolina, and, by virtue of the *Sawada* decision, Hawaii.

ownership over the whole estate. The tenancy was and still is predicated upon the legal unity of husband and wife, but the Acts converted it into a unity of equals and not of unequals as at common law. No longer could the husband convey, lease, mortgage or otherwise encumber the property without her consent. The Acts confirmed her right to the use and enjoyment of the whole estate, and all the privileges that ownership of property confers, including the right to convey the property in its entirety, jointly with her husband, during the marriage relation. Jordan v. Reynolds, 105 Md. 288, 66 A. 37 (1907); Hurd v. Hughes, 12 Del. Ch. 188, 109 A. 418 (1920).... They also had the effect of insulating the wife's interest in the estate from the separate debts of her husband. Jordan v. Reynolds.

Neither husband nor wife has a separate divisible interest in the property held by the entirety that can be conveyed or reached by execution. A joint tenancy may be destroyed by voluntary alienation, or by levy and execution, or by compulsory partition, but a tenancy by the entirety may not. The indivisibility of the estate, except by joint action of the spouses, is an indispensable feature of the tenancy by the entirety.

In Jordan v. Reynolds, ... the Maryland court held that no lien could attach against entirety property for the separate debts of the husband, for that would be in derogation of the entirety of title in the spouses and would be tantamount to a conversion of the tenancy into a joint tenancy or tenancy in common. In holding that the spouses could jointly convey the property, free of any judgment liens against the husband, the court said:

> To hold the judgment to be a lien at all against this property, and the right of execution suspended during the life of the wife, and to be enforced on the death of the wife, would, we think, likewise encumber her estate, and be in contravention of the constitutional provision heretofore mentioned, protecting the wife's property from the husband's debts. It is clear, we think, if the judgment here is declared a lien, but suspended during the life of the wife, and not enforceable until her death, if the husband should survive the wife, it will defeat the sale here made by the husband and wife to the purchaser, and thereby make the wife's property liable for the debts of her husband. 105 Md. at 295, 296, 66 A. at 39.

In Hurd v. Hughes, ... the Delaware court, recognizing the peculiar nature of an estate by the entirety, in that the husband and wife are the owners, not merely of equal interests but of the whole estate, stated:

> The estate [by the entireties] can be acquired or held only by a man and woman while married. Each spouse owns the whole while both live; neither can sell any interest except with the other's consent, and by their joint act and at the death of either the other continues to own the whole, and does not acquire any new interest from the other. There can be no partition between them. From this is deduced the indivisibility and unseverability of the estate into two interests, and hence that the creditors of either spouse cannot during their joint

lives reach by execution any interest which the debtor had in land so held. . . . One may have doubts as to whether the holding of land by entireties is advisable or in harmony with the spirit of the legislation in favor of married women; but when such an estate is created due effect must be given to its peculiar characteristics. 12 Del. Ch. at 190, 109 A. at 419.

. . . We are not persuaded by the argument that it would be unfair to the creditors of either spouse to hold that the estate by the entirety may not, without the consent of both spouses, be levied upon for the separate debts of either spouse. No unfairness to the creditor is involved here. We agree with the court in Hurd v. Hughes . . .: "But creditors are not entitled to special consideration. If the debt arose prior to the creation of the estate, the property was not the basis of credit, and if the debt arose subsequently the creditor presumably had notice of the characteristics of the estate which limited his right to reach the property." 12 Del. Ch. at 193, 109 A. at 420. We might also add that there is obviously nothing to prevent the creditor from insisting upon the subjection of property held in tenancy by the entirety as a condition precedent to the extension of credit. . . .

Were we to view the matter strictly from the standpoint of public policy, we would still be constrained to hold as we have done here today. In Fairclaw v. Forrest, [76 U.S. App. D.C. 197, 130 F. 2d 829 (1942)], the court makes this observation: "The interest in family solidarity retains some influence upon the institution [of tenancy by the entirety]. It is available only to husband and wife. It is a convenient mode of protecting a surviving spouse from inconvenient administration of the decedent's estate and from the other's improvident debts. It is in that protection the estate finds its peculiar and justifiable function." 130 F.2d at 833.

It is a matter of common knowledge that the demand for single-family residential lots has increased rapidly in recent years, and the magnitude of the problem is emphasized by the concentration of the bulk of fee simple land in the hands of a few. The shortage of single-family residential fee simple property is critical and government has seen fit to attempt to alleviate the problem through legislation. When a family can afford to own real property, it becomes their single most important asset. Encumbered as it usually is by a first mortgage, the fact remains that so long as it remains whole during the joint lives of the spouses, it is always available in its entirety for the benefit and use of the entire family. Loans for education and other emergency expenses, for example, may be obtained on the security of the marital estate. This would not be possible where a third party has become a tenant in common or a joint tenant with one of the spouses, or where the ownership of the contingent right of survivorship of one of the spouses in a third party has cast a cloud upon the title of the marital estate, making it virtually impossible to utilize the estate for these purposes.

If we were to select between a public policy favoring the creditors of one of the spouses and one favoring the interests of the family unit, we would not hesitate to choose the latter. But we need not make this choice for, as we pointed out earlier, by the very nature of the estate by the entirety as we view it, and as other courts of our sister jurisdictions have viewed it, "... a broad immunity from claims of separate creditors remain among its vital incidents." In re Estate of Wall, [142 U.S. App. D.C. 187, 440 F.2d 215, 218 (1971)].

Having determined that an estate by the entirety is not subject to the claims of the creditors of one of the spouses during their joint lives, we now hold that the conveyance of the marital property by Kokichi Endo and Ume Endo, husband and wife, to their sons, Samuel H. Endo and Toru Endo, was not in fraud of Kokichi Endo's judgment creditors.

Affirmed.

KIDWELL, J., dissenting.

... The majority reaches its conclusion by holding that the effect of the Married Women's Act was to equalize the positions of the spouses by taking from the husband his common law right to transfer his interest, rather than by elevating the wife's right of alienation of her interest to place it on a position of equality with the husband's. I disagree. I believe that a better interpretation of the Married Women's Acts is that offered by the Supreme Court of New Jersey in King v. Greene, 30 N.J. 395, 412, 153 A.2d 49, 60 (1959)....

One may speculate whether the courts which first chose the path to equality now followed by the majority might have felt an unexpressed aversion to entrusting a wife with as much control over her interest as had previously been granted to the husband with respect to his interest. Whatever may be the historical explanation for these decisions, I feel that the resultant restriction upon the freedom of the spouses to deal independently with their respective interests is both illogical and unnecessarily at odds with present policy trends. Accordingly, I would hold that the separate interest of the husband in entireties property, at least to the extent of his right of survivorship, is alienable by him and subject to attachment by his separate creditors, so that a voluntary conveyance of the husband's interest should be set aside where it is fraudulent as to such creditors, under applicable principles of the law of fraudulent conveyances.

NOTES, QUESTIONS, AND PROBLEMS

1. *Federal Tax Liens and Forfeitures.* If the split among the states on a creditor's ability to seize a spouse's interest in property held by the entirety was not enough to sort out, consider the special status afforded the federal government as a creditor. The United States Supreme Court held, in United States v. Craft, 535 U.S. 274 (2002), that a spouse's interest in a tenancy by the entirety was subject to attachment to satisfy a federal tax lien against one spouse. The Court ignored state law that barred this result by asserting that

federal law determines what "property" is subject to seizure to satisfy a tax lien.

Uncertainty has thus been generated about the ability of the federal government to seize entireties property under other federal statutes. Federal law provides for a civil *in rem* action to obtain forfeiture of property used to commit certain drug crimes and of property owned by the convicted felon even though it was not used to commit the drug crime. The law exempts from forfeiture any interest in the property held by an innocent person. This poses no analytical problem with respect to property held in tenancy in common or joint tenancy. Only the interest of the criminal is forfeited and the innocent owners retain their interests. If a joint tenancy is involved the forfeiture effects severance and the government is now a tenant in common with the innocent owner(s). But a tenancy by the entirety raises much more difficult issues. If the government can seize the whole, the innocent owner exemption is eviscerated; but if the government can seize nothing the forfeiture statute is nullified. In United States v. 1500 Lincoln Avenue, 949 F.2d 73 (3d Cir. 1991), the court concluded that the only way to slice this Gordian knot was to permit the government to seize the felonious husband's survivorship interest and permit the innocent wife to keep possession of the whole. In that case the property was a pharmacy which was used to accomplish the drug crimes for which the husband was convicted. Suppose the wife wants to sell out; will anybody purchase her interest? If not, what must the wife do to obtain a marketable title?

In contrast is United States v. Lee, 232 F.3d 556 (7th Cir. 2000). *H* was convicted of crimes that triggered the forfeiture statute, but the family home, held in tenancy by the entirety, was not used to commit the crimes. The court thought that the government ought not be permitted to seize any part of *H*'s interest, because that would deprive *W* of the ability to control and manage the property without government approval.

Which of these rules better accomplishes the twin aims of the forfeiture statute—to deprive the criminal of his ill-gotten gains and to preserve inviolate the interest of the innocent owner?

2. *Tort and Contract Creditors.* The Hawaii court observes that creditors can protect themselves by refusing to extend credit on the basis of property owned in tenancy by the entirety. The Sawada sisters had no chance to do this because they were hit in a crosswalk by the car piloted by 82 year old Kokichi Endo. Tort creditors do not get to choose their debtors. Should the Hawaii court have carved out an exception to its rule for tort creditors? On the other hand, the residence owned by Kokichi and Ume Endo as tenants by their entirety was their only asset of any consequence. Should this matter? For more on this case, See Patricia Cain, The Story of *Sowado* [sic] *v. Endo*, Property Stories 100–122 (2d ed. 2009).

By contrast, the rule articulated by the New Jersey court protected the assignees of a creditor who knew (or should have known) that the interest they acquired was in a tenancy by the entirety. The assignees must have known this fact as well. However logical the New Jersey court's analysis of the alteration of the tenancy by the entirety by the Married Women's Act may have been, did the New Jersey court give undue consideration to the fact that contract creditors and their assignees can protect themselves in advance of their action?

3. *Problem.* *H* and *W* own Blackacre as tenants by the entirety. *H* incurs a contractual debt to *C*, defaults on that debt, and disappears. *C* obtains a judgment against *H* and executes that judgment by purchasing *H*'s interest in Blackacre at a sheriff's sale. Under the various approaches taken to this problem, what has *C* acquired?

b. Divorce

Upon divorce, the common law system allotted to each spouse the property to which they held title. That was simple, but inequitable in a time of traditional sex roles that enabled the husband (typically the income earner) to amass assets in his name while the wife (typically the homemaker) had little opportunity to do so. But the common law tempered that inequity by imposing on the husband an obligation of continuing support of his former wife, usually called alimony but now more frequently referred to as maintenance.

That system has been drastically altered as cultural perceptions of the nature of marriage and the role of women within marriage and society have changed. Every American jurisdiction has replaced the common law system of property division upon divorce with some version of equitable distribution or equitable division. Whatever the term used the concept is similar. Title to property may be ignored by a court in order to divide the property of the spouses in an equitable manner. There are many factors that courts may take into account to deliver these equitable results, but the overriding concern is to deliver to each spouse a fair share of the combined assets of the couple. Jurisdictions vary as to the property that is subject to equitable division. Some states include all the property of each spouse, regardless of when or how it was obtained. Other states limit equitable division to a lesser set of that property, denominated marital property. But even under these statutes there are wide variations. Some marital property definitions are so expansive that it includes every conceivable tangible or intangible asset of the soon-to-be-former spouses. Others define marital property in much the same way that community property is defined—typically the assets derived from the earnings of either spouse during the marriage.

With the advent of equitable division, however, came the decline of alimony or maintenance. Although maintenance remains an option within marital dissolution, the occasions for its invocation and the duration of the award have each diminished. The quid pro quo for the common law system's division of property by title was a guarantee of lifelong support. The quid pro quo for equitable division of marital property is the renunciation of the guarantee of lifelong support. In its place is a discretionary power to award continuing support for some period after divorce when it is necessary to do so to achieve fairness.

ARCHER v. ARCHER

Court of Appeals of Maryland
303 Md. 347 (1985)

MURPHY, J., delivered the opinion of the court.

The question presented is whether a medical degree and license to practice medicine obtained by a spouse during marriage constitutes "marital property" within the contemplation of the Property Disposition in Divorce and Annulment Law (the Act), Maryland Code (1984), § 8–201(e) of the Family Law Article[:]

(1) "Marital property" means the property, however titled, acquired by [one] or both parties during the marriage.

(2) "Marital property" does not include property:

(i) acquired before the marriage;

(ii) acquired by inheritance or gift of a third party;

(iii) excluded by valid agreement; or

(iv) directly traceable to any of these sources.

I. Jeanne (Appellant) and Thomas (Appellee) Archer were married on August 6, 1977. At that time, Thomas had just completed his first year of medical school. Jeanne, having completed two years towards an undergraduate degree, discontinued her studies to work full time. She continued to work after the birth of the Archers' two children in 1981 and 1982. During the marriage, Thomas attended medical school for three years, obtained his medical degree and license and completed two years of his residency. The United States Navy paid Thomas'[s] medical school expenses, together with a tax-free stipend of approximately $500 per month, in exchange for Thomas'[s] four-year commitment to serve the Navy upon graduation. In addition to the stipend, Thomas'[s] earnings during the marriage consisted of approximately $1,500 each summer from work done while in medical school and $15,000 to $18,000 per annum while completing two years of his residency requirement.

The Archers were temporarily separated for most of 1979 and were permanently separated in October of 1982. They were divorced by decree of the Circuit Court for Prince George's County on July 12, 1984; the decree awarded Jeanne custody of the two children, child support of $250 per child per month and alimony of $100 per month for a period not to exceed one year. The decree also required Thomas to maintain medical and life insurance for the benefit of the two children.

The question of whether Thomas'[s] medical degree and license constituted marital property for purposes of making a monetary award to Jeanne under § 8–205(a) of the Family Law Article was separately considered. That section provides that after the court determines "which property is marital property, and the value of the marital property, [it] may grant a monetary award as an adjustment of the equities and rights of the

parties concerning marital property, whether or not alimony is awarded."
In determining the amount and method of payment of a monetary award,
the court is enjoined by § 8–205(a) to consider each of ten specified
factors, including "the contributions, monetary and non[-]monetary, of
each party to the well-being of the family"; "the economic circumstances
of each party at the time the award is to be made"; "how and when
specific marital property was acquired, including the effort expended by
each party in accumulating the marital property"; and "any other factor
that the court considers necessary or appropriate to consider in order to
arrive at a fair and equitable monetary award." Section 8–205(b) permits
the court to reduce to judgment "any monetary award made under this
section, to the extent that any part of the award is due and owing."

The trial court ... held that a medical degree or license was not
marital property under the Act and thus denied Jeanne's prayer for a
monetary award. In so holding, the court adopted the reasoning of the
Colorado Supreme Court in its determination of a similar issue in In re
Marriage of Graham, 194 Colo. 429, 574 P.2d 75, 77 (1978):

> An educational degree, such as an M.B.A., is simply not encompassed
> even by the broad views of the concept of 'property.' It does not have
> an exchange value or any objective transferable value on an open
> market. It is personal to the holder. It terminates on death of the
> holder and is not inheritable. It cannot be assigned, sold, transferred,
> conveyed, or pledged. An advanced degree is a cumulative product of
> many years of previous education, combined with diligence and hard
> work. It may not be acquired by the mere expenditure of money. It is
> simply an intellectual achievement that may potentially assist in the
> future acquisition of property. In our view, it has none of the
> attributes of property in the usual sense of that term.

Jeanne appealed, contending that a medical degree/license is marital
property under the Act and, as such, subject to equitable distribution upon
divorce by a monetary award. We granted certiorari ... to consider this
issue of first impression in Maryland.

II.   The ... Act indicates that non-monetary contributions within a
marriage should be recognized in the event that a marriage is dissolved;
that a spouse whose activities do not include the production of income
may nevertheless have contributed toward the acquisition of property by
either or both spouses during the marriage; that when a marriage is
dissolved, the property interests of the spouses should be adjusted fairly
and equitably, with careful consideration given to both monetary and non-
monetary contributions made by the respective spouses; and that the
accomplishment of these objectives necessitates that there be a departure
from the inequity inherent in Maryland's old "title" system of dealing
with the marital property of divorcing spouses.

III.   Jeanne maintains that the definition of "marital property"—"all
property, however titled, acquired ... during the marriage"—must be
liberally construed to effect its broad remedial purposes and that the term

therefore encompasses nontraditional forms of "property" such as a medical degree or license. She recognizes, however, that of the twenty-four jurisdictions which have considered the matter, courts in all but two jurisdictions have uniformly held that a professional degree or license is not marital property subject to equitable division. Virtually all of these courts, consistent with the rationale advanced by the Colorado Supreme Court in In re Marriage of Graham, supra, have held that an advanced degree or professional license lacks the traditional attributes of "property," being neither transferable, assignable, devisable, nor subject to conveyance, sale, pledge or inheritance. Some courts, by way of an additional reason for concluding that a degree/license is not marital property, have held that such items are too speculative to value. Other courts have said that efforts to characterize spousal contributions as an investment or commercial enterprise deserving of recompense demean the concept of marriage. Still other courts have found that the future earning capacity of a degree or license-holding spouse is personal, a mere expectancy and a post-marital effort—not divisible as "marital property." And some other courts, in declining to find that a graduate degree or professional license is marital property, express the view that such items are best considered when awarding alimony.

Notwithstanding the overwhelming number of jurisdictions which hold that a degree or license is not marital property, Jeanne urges adoption of a minority view advanced by an intermediate appellate court in Michigan and a trial court in Massachusetts, both holding that a professional degree or license is marital property. Woodworth v. Woodworth, 126 Mich.App. 258, 337 N.W.2d 332 (1983); Reen v. Reen, 8 Fam.L.Rep. (BNA) 2193 (Mass.Prob. and Fam.Ct. Dec. 23, 1981). In *Reen*, the court held, without elaboration, that a husband's license to practice orthodontia constituted marital property. *Woodworth* held that a husband's law degree, earned during marriage, was marital property. In rejecting the majority view, the court held that the fact that an educational degree or license does not conform with traditional property concepts—not being transferable, assignable nor subject to sale, conveyance or pledge—was outweighed by the need to achieve the "most equitable solution" when one spouse sacrifices and works for the benefit of the other who pursues a professional degree and enhances his earning capacity. 337 N.W.2d at 335. That marriage is not a commercial enterprise or investment from which dashed expectations or efforts ought to be recompensed was, in the Michigan court's opinion, merely a characterization of "marriage while it endures"; it failed, the court said, to focus upon dissolution of the marriage and how best to compensate, not for a failed expectation, but for one spouse's share of the fruits of a degree which she helped the other earn. Id. at 336. The view that valuation of a degree is too speculative to constitute marital property was also rejected, it being concluded that courts have been adept at calculating future earnings in a number of contexts, such as personal injury, wrongful death and workers' compensation cases. Lastly, the view that the non-degree spouse's contributions are best considered when awarding alimony was also rejected; the court reasoned that the purpose of alimony was for spousal support, involving a variety of factors in the determination of whether alimony should be awarded, including financial condition and the ability to be self-supporting. In the case of a spouse who has worked and supported the other spouse through graduate school, the court said that the former will usually be capable of self-support. Moreover, as Michigan courts have discretion to terminate an alimony award upon remarriage of the spouse who is awarded alimony, the court concluded that the award of alimony was not an adequate means for recognizing the contributions of a spouse who has helped the other through graduate school. . . .

Our cases have generally construed the word "property" broadly, defining it as a term of wide and comprehensive signification embracing " 'everything which has exchangeable value or goes to make up a man's wealth—every interest or estate which the law regards of sufficient value for judicial recognition.' " Deering v. Deering, 292 Md. 115, 125, 437 A.2d 883 (1981); Diffendall v. Diffendall, 239 Md. 32, 36, 209 A.2d 914 (1965). In Bouse v. Hutzler, 180 Md. 682, 686, 26 A.2d 767 (1942), we said that the word "property," when used without express or implied qualifications, "may reasonably be construed to involve obligations, rights and other intangibles as well as physical things." "Goodwill," for example, has been characterized as a legally protected valuable property right. Schill v. Remington Putnam Co., 179 Md. 83, 88–89, 17 A.2d 175 (1941).

In *Deering*, we recognized a spouse's pension rights to be a form of marital property subject to equitable distribution. . . . [We] concluded that a spouse's pension rights, "to the extent accumulated during the marriage," constitute a form of "marital property" subject to distribution. In so holding, we noted that regardless of the type of retirement plan, vested or unvested, non-contributory or contributory, the critical issue was "whether a property right has been acquired during the marriage and whether equity warrants its inclusion in the marital estate in light of its limitations." We said that as " 'pension benefits represent a form of deferred compensation for services rendered, the employee's right to such benefits is a contractual right, derived from the terms of the employment contract. Since a contractual right is not an expectancy but a . . . form of property, . . . an employee acquires a [judicially recognized] property right to pension benefits when he enters upon the performance of his employment contract.' "

While . . . we have in some contexts construed the term "property" in a broad sense, there is nothing in the Maryland Act to suggest that the General Assembly intended that a medical degree or license, earned during marriage, would constitute "marital property" subject to equitable distribution upon divorce by a monetary award. We therefore hold, in accordance with the majority view, that a professional degree or license does not possess any of the basic characteristics of property within the ambit of marital property under § 8–201(e) of the Act. While pension rights, as in *Deering*, constitute a current asset which the individual has a

med. degree

contractual right to receive, such rights are plainly distinguishable from a mere expectancy of future enhanced income resulting from a professional degree. The latter is but an intellectual attainment; it is not a present property interest. It is personal to the holder; it cannot be sold, transferred, pledged or inherited. It does not have an assignable value nor does it represent a guarantee of receipt of a set monetary amount in the future, such as pension benefits. Quite simply, a degree/license does not have an exchange value on an open market. In re Marriage of Graham, supra, 574 P.2d at 77. At best, it represents a potential for increase in a person's earning capacity made possible by the degree and license in combination with innumerable other factors and conditions too uncertain and speculative to constitute "marital property" within the contemplation of the legislature. Moreover, . . . income earned after the marriage is dissolved as a result of the degree/license would in no event constitute "marital property" within the definition of that term in § 8–201(e), since it would not have been acquired during the marriage.

The cases thus lead inexorably to the conclusion that the trial judge in this case correctly found that Thomas'[s] medical degree and license were not encompassed within the legislatively intended definition of marital property in the Maryland statute.

IV.   Jeanne does not challenge the amount of her alimony award and we do not, therefore, consider its adequacy in the circumstances of this case. We note that under § 11–106 of the Family Law Article, the chancellor was empowered to take into account such matters as the husband's earning capacity in making an alimony award. Specifically, § 11–106 enjoins the chancellor to consider a number of enumerated factors "necessary for a fair and equitable award" including, among others, "the contributions, monetary and non-monetary, of each party to the well-being of the family"; "the ability of the party from whom alimony is sought to meet that party's needs while meeting the needs of the party seeking alimony"; and "the financial needs and financial resources of each party."

[If] public policy dictates that some economic compensation be made to a spouse who makes monetary and non-monetary contributions to the other spouse's acquisition of a professional degree/license, equitable results can be achieved under § 11–106. Indeed, this section permits the chancellor to consider the circumstances surrounding the acquisition by one spouse of a professional degree/license, as well as that spouse's potential income. [Any income actually earned as a result of one spouse's acquisition of a professional degree/license, together with the sacrifices of the other spouse toward its attainment, are factors which may, and presumably were in this case, considered by the court in making its alimony award to Jeanne.]

[Affirmed.]

affects alimony award only

reimbursement alimony?

NOTES AND QUESTIONS

1. *A Different Perspective.* **June and Melvin Mahoney** married in 1971. They each contributed to household expenses until 1975, when Melvin entered the M.B.A. program at the Wharton School of the University of Pennsylvania. During the two years of Melvin's M.B.A. program, June contributed $24,000 to the household finances and Melvin paid his $6,500 tuition by a combination of veteran's benefits and a grant from the Air Force. The parties separated in late 1978 and divorced in 1980. June sought recovery of $15,250, being one-half of the household and tuition expenses incurred in the M.B.A. student period. In **Mahoney v. Mahoney,** 91 N.J. 488 (1982), the New Jersey Supreme Court concluded that valuation of an M.B.A. or the enhanced future earnings power attributable to the degree was too uncertain to qualify as marital property. Nor was the reimbursement that June sought proper: "Marriage is not a business arrangement in which the parties keep track of debits and credits, their accounts to be settled upon divorce." Id. at 500. On the other hand equity required what the court called reimbursement alimony:

> To provide a fair and effective means of compensating a supporting spouse who has suffered a loss or reduction of support, or has incurred a lower standard of living, or has been deprived of a better standard of living in the future, the Court now introduces the concept of reimbursement alimony into divorce proceedings. . . . [R]egardless of the appropriateness of permanent alimony or the presence or absence of marital property to be equitably distributed, there will be circumstances where a supporting spouse should be reimbursed for the financial contributions he or she made to the spouse's successful professional training. Such reimbursement alimony should cover *all* financial contributions towards the former spouse's education, including household expenses, educational costs, school travel expenses and any other contributions used by the supported spouse in obtaining his or her degree or license. . . .

> Marriage should not be a free ticket to professional education and training without subsequent obligations. This Court should not ignore the scenario of the young professional who after being supported through graduate school leaves his mate for supposedly greener pastures. One spouse ought not to receive a divorce complaint when the other receives a diploma. Those spouses supported through professional school should recognize that they may be called upon to reimburse the supporting spouses for the financial contributions they received in pursuit of their professional training. And they cannot deny the basic fairness of this result. Id. at 501, 503.

Mahoney also suggested that " 'rehabilitative alimony' may be more appropriate in cases where a spouse who gave up or postponed her own education to support the household requires a lump sum or a short-term award to achieve economic self-sufficiency." Id. at 504.

By the time of the divorce June had obtained a master's degree in microbiology. Suppose that she then wanted to attend medical school. How far should the concepts of rehabilitative and reimbursement alimony then be applied? Should Melvin be required to finance June's medical school? Two years of medical school? No rehabilitative alimony, on the theory that with a master's degree in microbiology she could fend for herself? How much reimbursement alimony should June receive?

2. *The New York Perspective.* Almost all states subscribe either to the Maryland view described in *Archer* or the New Jersey view of *Mahoney*. New York, however, is the most aggressive in extending marital property to include professional or career attainments and the enhanced earnings potential of one spouse developed during marriage.

O'Brien v. O'Brien. Michael and Loretta O'Brien married in 1971 when she was a teacher and he had a semester remaining to complete college. He completed college and sufficient additional courses to enter medical school in Mexico. Loretta worked as a tutor and teacher in Guadalajara to finance Michael's studies. Upon their return to New York in 1976 Loretta resumed her former job as a teacher, while Michael completed medical school, an internship, and a residency. Two months after he obtained his medical license he sued to dissolve the marriage. In the landmark case of *O'Brien v. O'Brien*, 66 N.Y.2d 576 (1985), the New York Court of Appeals construed the New York equitable division statute to include as marital property the professional license of a marital partner. The statute defines marital property as "all property acquired by either or both spouses during marriage" and commands courts, when making an equitable division of marital property, to consider "any equitable claim to . . . or direct or indirect contribution made to the marital property by the party not having title, including . . . contributions and services as a spouse . . . and homemaker, and to the career or career potential of the other party, [and] the . . . difficulty of evaluating any . . . interest in a . . . profession." N.Y. Dom. Rel. Law § 236 (2010). The New York court interpreted this to mean that the "explicit reference in the statute to the contributions of one spouse to the other's profession or career [means] that these contributions represent investments in the economic partnership of the marriage and that the product of the parties' joint efforts, the professional license, should be considered marital property."

Elkus v. Elkus. The sweep of the New York statute has been extended to include the enhanced value of a person's career and celebrity status obtained during marriage. The opera star Frederica von Stade Elkus married her voice coach at the beginning of her career, when she had minor roles that garnered $2,250 in her first year of marriage. Seventeen years later, on the eve of divorce, Frederica von Stade was an international opera star, earning over $600,000 in the final year of the marriage. Her increased earning power was marital property subject to equitable division, said the New York intermediate appellate court:

> While it is true that the plaintiff was born with talent, and, while she had already been hired by the Metropolitan Opera at the time of her marriage to the defendant, her career, at this time, was only in the initial stages of development. During the course of the marriage, the defendant's active involvement in the plaintiff's career, in teaching, coaching, and critiquing her, as well as in caring for their children, clearly contributed to the increase in its value. Accordingly, to the extent the appreciation in the

[handwritten marginalia: Can take advantage of higher future earnings]

plaintiff's career was due to the defendant's efforts and contributions, this appreciation constitutes marital property. Elkus v. Elkus, 169 App. Div. 2d 134, 140 (N.Y. App. 1991).

What happens if Frederica von Stade remarries and that marriage ends in dissolution? If you were her lawyer, what would you advise her to do prior to the second marriage in order to protect her financial interests? *Prenup!*

3.   *Professional Goodwill.* Not only have courts rejected the notion that the increased earnings power attributable to a professional degree and license obtained by one spouse during marriage is marital property, courts have also rejected the contention that goodwill—the value that inheres in continued patronage of a business or professional practice—of a professional practice is marital property. See, e.g., Prahinksi v. Prahinski, 321 Md. 227 (1990), which involved *H*'s solo law practice was limited almost entirely to issuing title opinions. *W* worked as *H*'s secretary and participated in the title search work. Upon divorce, the court concluded that goodwill of a professional practice is personal and not marital property.

However, most states reject this view and treat professional goodwill as an intangible asset that can be equitably divided, even though the professional license and qualification cannot be divided. See, e.g., Dugan v. Dugan, 92 N.J. 423 (1983), involving goodwill attributable to *H*'s solo law practice. The New Jersey court distinguished goodwill and future earnings capacity: "Future earning capacity *per se* is not goodwill. However, when that future earning capacity has been enhanced because reputation leads to probable future patronage from existing and potential clients, goodwill may exist and have value. When that occurs the resulting goodwill is property subject to equitable distribution." Id. at 433.

c.   Death

The common law recognized several doctrines that gave a surviving spouse certain rights in the property of the decedent spouse. A wife was entitled to half of her husband's personal property if there were no surviving issue of the marriage, and one-third if there were surviving issue. In an era when wealth mostly inhered in land ownership, dower and curtesy were far more important.

Dower was the right of a surviving wife to a life estate in one-third of all freehold real property of which the husband was seised at any time during marriage and which could be inherited by the issue of the marriage. Thus, it excluded property held in joint tenancy. Of course, if the joint tenants were husband and wife, a surviving wife would have sole ownership, but if the joint tenants were the husband and a stranger to the marriage a surviving wife had no dower right in that property. Dower existed throughout the marriage but did not become possessory until death of the husband. Dower was inalienable by the husband. Thus, unless a wife released her dower right, any conveyance of property by a husband (or seizure of that property by a creditor of the husband) was subject to the inchoate dower right of the wife. Dower may have been an adequate portion for the widows of the landed gentry but was hardly adequate for widows of the landless or those who owned a home but no lands producing income.

Curtesy was the analogue to dower. A surviving husband was entitled to a life estate in the whole of each freehold estate in land of which the wife was seised during marriage, *if* issue of the marriage capable of inheriting the estate was born alive.

Dower and curtesy are almost extinct in America. Arkansas, Kentucky, and Ohio recognize dower but have extended it to widowers and abolished curtesy.[12] Michigan recognizes dower but not curtesy,[13] a form of sex discrimination that is presumptively invalid under the equal protection clause of the Constitution's Fourteenth Amendment. If challenged, Michigan would bear the exceedingly difficult burden of proving that its actual purpose in preserving dower, but not curtesy, was an important interest, untainted by archaic sex stereotypes, and that this asymmetry is substantially related to accomplishment of that actual purpose. See Orr v. Orr, 440 U.S. 268 (1979) (holding that an Alabama statute subjecting husbands, but not wives, to potential liability for alimony violated the equal protection clause); Stokes v. Stokes, 271 Ark. 300 (1981); Boan v. Watson, 281 S.C. 516 (1984) (applying the federal and state equal protection clauses to invalidate a statute granting dower to wives but not curtesy to husbands). Iowa retains dower for husbands and wives but has converted it to a share of the decedent's property in fee simple absolute, unless relinquished by the survivor.[14] Because every common law state but one provides to the surviving spouse a share of the decedent spouse's property via intestate succession or the elective share (discussed below) the practical consequence of dower is the necessity of obtaining the release of each spouse of their dower rights upon any transfer of real estate owned by either spouse alone. As we shall see, dower and curtesy are not a part of the community property regime but community property secures the interest of each spouse in community property at the death of a spouse.

Dower and curtesy have largely been replaced by the spousal elective share. Every common law state but Georgia has an elective share statute. The concept is that a surviving spouse may elect to take the portion of the decedent spouse's property that is provided in the statute rather than to take the portion allotted to the survivor by the decedent's will. In these states, it is impossible to disinherit completely one's spouse. States vary as to the fraction of the decedent's property that is awarded under the elective share statute, but the usual portion is one-third or one-half. Some states require a surviving spouse to take *either* the property devised and bequeathed under the will *or* the elective share, but some permit the surviving spouse who opts for the elective share to take under the will and set off that amount against the elective share portion. In those states

---

12. See Ark. Code Ann. § 28–11–301 (2010); Ky. Rev. Stat. § 392.020 (2010); Ohio Rev. Code Ann. § 2103.2 (2010).

13. See Mich. Comp. Laws § 558.1 (2010).

14. See Iowa Code Ann. § 633.212 (2010).

recognizing dower, a surviving spouse has a choice of one of three options: assert dower, take the elective share portion, or take under the decedent spouses's will.

In recent years, as some states have adopted the most current version of the Uniform Probate Code, but often with important substantive changes, there has emerged considerable variation concerning the property that is subject to the elective share. The traditional rule has been that the elective share only applies to the property owned by the decedent spouse at his or her death, but that rule has been abrogated by statute or judicial decision in many states. Under the Uniform Probate Code a variety of transfers occurring before death may be included in the pool of property used to compute the elective share. The entire subject is complicated; the details are best left for a course in Wills, Trusts, and Estates.

The rationale for the elective share varies. Most states profess that because the surviving spouse contributed to the accumulation of wealth by the decedent spouse, it is unfair to permit the decedent to deprive the survivor of some share of that wealth. Other states regard the elective share as a form of spousal support. Judge Posner, the leading luminary of economic explanations for legal rules, argues that the elective share reduces transaction costs. Because one spouse's unpaid domestic labor permits the other spouse to save income that would otherwise be devoted to purchasing that domestic labor the accumulated savings (i.e., wealth) of the decedent spouse is larger than it would otherwise be. Without an elective share, spouses would be forced to negotiate for contracts to make a bequest. The elective share eliminates the transaction costs of such negotiations. See Richard Posner, Economic Analysis of the Law 561 (5th ed. 1998).

PROBLEMS

1. Assume that the following people are all domiciled in Arkansas—a state that recognizes dower in each of the husband and wife—and that Blackacre is located in Arkansas. *H* and *W*, husband and wife, own Blackacre as joint tenants. *W* conveys her interest in Blackacre to *A*, who is married to *B*. *A* later conveys his interest in Blackacre to *C*, who is married to *D*. Then *W* dies. Does *H* have any dower rights in Blackacre? Then *A* dies. Does *B* have any dower rights in Blackacre? Then *C* dies. What is the state of title in Blackacre?

2. *H* and *W* are husband and wife. *O* conveys Blackacre "to *H* for life, and then to *Z* and her heirs." At *H*'s death, does *W* have any dower rights in Blackacre?

3. *H* and *W* are husband and wife. During marriage, *H* acquires title to Blackacre in fee simple absolute, then conveys Blackacre to *A*. *W* dies, leaving a will by which she bequeaths all her property, "including my dower rights," to *B*. Then *H* dies. Does *B* have dower rights to Blackacre?

4. *H* and *W* are husband and wife. It is the second marriage for each. *H* has an adult child, *X*, by his first marriage. *W* has an adult child, *Z*, by her first marriage. During the marriage *H* purchases a life insurance policy in the amount of $250,000 on his life, naming *W* as beneficiary. *H* and *W* own a home, valued at $100,000, as joint tenants, and a beachfront condominium, valued at $100,000, as tenants in common. *H* also owns marketable securities worth $150,000, a collection of antique autos which are worth $100,000 all together, and a savings account worth $100,000. At *H*'s death his will leaves the savings account to *Z* and remainder of his property to *X*. The jurisdiction does not recognize dower and has an elective share statute that provides that a surviving spouse may renounce the will and take one-half of the property owned by the decedent spouse at his or her death. If *W* makes that election, how will these assets be distributed? What could *H* have done prior to death to ensure that his apparent intent is accomplished?

5.   In a state that recognizes dower, is it possible for one spouse to acquire and dispose of real property without dower attaching to those properties? If so, how can this be accomplished?

2. COMMUNITY PROPERTY

a. Introduction and Comparison With the Common Law

The eight states that have true community property as the default system of marital property are Arizona, California, Idaho, Louisiana, Nevada, New Mexico, Texas, and Washington. Alaska offers community property as an option to married couples. See Alaska Stat. §§ 34.77.030, 34.77.090, 34.77.100 (2010). Wisconsin has adopted the Uniform Marital Property Act, which mimics community property in all but the name. See Wis. Stat. § 766.001 et seq. (2010).

In general, community property consists of the earnings of either spouse during marriage (and the assets derived therefrom), but does not include the separate property of either spouse. That separate property is generally the property owned by each spouse at the commencement of the marriage, and property acquired by each spouse by gift or inheritance during marriage. A married couple may vary these rules by agreement or by conduct. If they commingle separate and community property it is presumed to be community property and, unless the separate property can be traced and proven to be separate it is community property. They may agree that property that would otherwise be community property is separate property. Thus, spouses in a community property state (including Wisconsin) have the option of creating a common law system by agreement, accepting the default community property rules, or turning all property acquired during marriage, from whatever source, into community property. Yet, spouses in common law states other than Alaska do not have this option. Why not? Is this just sclerosis of legal thought, or is there a good reason to deny a married couple these options?

The details of community property may vary from state to state. For example, in Alaska, Arizona, California, Nevada, New Mexico, and Washington the income from separate property retains its character as separate property, but in Idaho, Louisiana, Texas, and Wisconsin that income is treated as community property. Upon divorce some states require an equal division of community property; other states require only that there be an equitable division of community property. In all community property states, divorcing spouses are entitled to keep their separate property. Generally, community property does not cease until the divorce is accomplished, but Arizona, California, and Washington hold that community property ceases to be created at the moment the marital partners separate. But what constitutes separation? See, e.g., Calif. Fam. Code § 771(a) (separation occurs when the spouses are "living separate and apart"); Marriage of Norviel, 102 Cal.App.4th 1152, 1158 (2002), holding that "two factors [are] prerequisites to separation. First, at least one spouse must entertain the subjective intent to end the marriage; second, there must be objective evidence of conduct furthering that intent." Accord, Marriage of Hardin, 38 Cal.App.4th 448, 451 (1995).

Because community property can exist only for married couples, community property states do not recognize the tenancy by the entirety, dower, or curtesy. Each of those common law interests address the marital relationship, but do so in a way that is fundamentally at odds with the rationale for community property. The common law approach to marriage was to make the husband the master of the wife's property, but give her in return a measure of support for the remainder of her life. The community property approach treats both spouses as equal partners in the economic life of the marriage. Just as a marriage relationship acquires a life that transcends the individual identities of the partners, the marital community acquires a legal life that transcends the separate legal interests of the marital partners.

While a community property state does not permit a husband and wife to own property as tenants by the entirety, it is possible for a husband and wife to take title as joint tenants or tenants in common. When they do so, the property is *not* community property; each spouse has a separate interest in the joint tenancy or tenancy in common. Though ill-informed people sometimes attempt to take title as "joint tenants in community property" that result is not possible. Given the presumption that property acquired during marriage is community property, such a botched attempt is likely to result in community property, absent strong evidence to the contrary. Of course, unmarried people in a community property state can also take title as tenants in common or joint tenants; those estates are not limited to married couples, as is true of community property.

During the marriage neither spouse may unilaterally convey their share of the community property to a stranger to the marriage, though they may convey it to their spouse. Thus, it is not possible to turn community property into separate property *without the consent of the other spouse*. Recall that a joint tenancy may be severed unilaterally by a joint tenant, and that this can be done to transmute a joint tenancy into a tenancy in common without changing the identity of the co-owners. *A*, a joint tenant with *B*, can convey her interest to *A* as a tenant in common, and thus sever the joint tenancy without altering the identities of the co-owners, *A* and *B*.[15] Nor may either spouse seek partition, as would be possible with a joint tenancy or tenancy in common.

At death, each spouse may devise their one-half interest in the community property as they please. Because the surviving spouse has a one-half interest, there is no need to create an elective share. The surviving spouse's protection against disinheritance is built in to the community property system. Moreover, federal tax law confers a significant financial advantage upon the surviving spouse in a community property state. When an asset is sold at a profit the difference between the taxpayer's "basis" (usually its acquisition cost, unless it was received as a gift, in which case it is the donor's cost) and the net sale price is taxable income. However, the federal estate tax provides that the tax basis of a decedent's property is "stepped-up" at death from acquisition cost to current market value as of the date of death. With community property that stepped-up basis applies to the entire community property, including the half owned by the surviving spouse. If the same property were held in joint tenancy, the surviving spouse would only receive a stepped-up basis as to the one-half owned by the decedent spouse. This can produce a big difference in tax liability when those assets are later sold.

> *Example 5–3 (Joint Tenancy): H* and *W* purchased Blackacre, a commercial building, for $100,000, taking title as joint tenants. At *H*'s death the market value of Blackacre was $500,000. The acquisition cost of each of *H* and *W*'s undivided interests is $50,000. The basis in *H*'s share is stepped-up at death to market value, or $250,000. Thus, *W*'s basis in the entirety of Blackacre is $300,000 (*H*'s stepped-up basis of $250,000 plus *W*'s original basis of $50,000). If years later *W* should sell Blackacre for $800,000, her taxable gain would be $500,000.

> *Example 5–4 (Community Property): H* and *W* purchased Blackacre, a commercial building, for $100,000, taking title as community property. At *H*'s death the market value of Blackacre was $500,000. *H*'s will devised his share of the community property to *W*. *W*'s basis in Blackacre is stepped up to $500,000 because federal tax law permits the stepped up basis to apply to the entirety of the community property. If years later *W* should sell Blackacre for $800,000, her taxable gain would be $300,000.

While it may seem that this tax advantage is available only to residents of community property states, that is not strictly correct. A couple who reside in a common law state who are determined to reap this advantage have two cumbersome options. First, they could move to a community property state, establish bona fide residency, then execute a written agreement to make all their property community property (or, better yet, create a revocable trust of which they are trustees and

---

15. As noted earlier in the discussion of the joint tenancy, in some states this requires a straw man intermediary, but in other states the conveyance may be accomplished directly.

beneficiaries, declare in that trust instrument that all property held in trust is community property, and transfer title of all their property into the trust). After all this is done, they could move back to Indiana or wherever they came from, and the property would continue to be treated as community property because property acquires its character at acquisition unless the parties later agree to change its character in conformity with local law. Once its character is fixed by agreement or the trust arrangement it keeps that character unless they later agree otherwise. Second, they could create an Alaska community property trust of the type roughly described above, although they would be required to make an Alaska resident the trustee, and transfer title of their property to the trust. Neither option is free of considerable transaction costs, so the tax avoidance imperative must be significant to make these legal contortions worthwhile.

PROBLEM

H and *W* are married and reside in a community property state. *W* inherits $100,000 and invests it a portfolio of securities held by Monolithic Financial in a brokerage account that is in the name of *H* and *W* and that is otherwise funded by earnings of *H* and *W*. Later, *W* sells some of the stock in that portfolio and uses the proceeds to purchase a condominium in Hawaii, taking title in joint tenancy with *H*. *W* then dies, leaving a will by which she devises all her separate and community property to *X*. Who owns the Hawaii condominium?

b.   Administration of Community Property

In every community property state each of husband and wife have equal power to manage the community property. That means in practice that either spouse, acting alone, may manage the property. Spouses are fiduciaries toward each other in connection with their management of community property. That means that they must exercise good faith but not necessarily impeccable judgment.

Important consequences flow from these rules. For example, creditors of either spouse may generally satisfy their claims from the entire community property. In general, transfers of real property held as community property require each spouse to join in the transfer, but the rule is different for personal property. Although most community property states hold that a gift of community property by one spouse may be set aside, they also protect bona fide purchasers of such property. Thus, if one spouse gives away a valuable Persian rug the gift may be cancelled at the behest of the other spouse, but if one spouse sells that same rug to a dealer in Oriental rugs the sale may not be avoided by the other spouse. A gift of community property by one spouse is voidable in its entirety at the behest of the other spouse. See Droeger v. Friedman, Sloan & Ross, 54 Cal.3d 26 (1991); Britton v. Hammell, 4 Cal.2d 690, 692 (1935). However, after the death of the donor spouse such gifts are voidable to the extent of one-half of the gift, on the theory that the decedent donor spouse was entitled freely to dispose of his or her share of the community property. See Trimble v. Trimble, 219 Cal. 340 (1933). If a spouse breaches this fiduciary duty by making gifts during life his estate may also be liable for the breach. See Fields v. Michael, 91 Cal.App.2d 443 (1949).

c. Common Problems

There are a number of common problems that can produce unexpected consequences. One problem occurs when a mixture of separate and community property is used to acquire an asset. A related problem is posed when one spouse owns a business as her separate property, then marries, and continues to operate her business after marriage. A third problem occurs when one spouse receives an award of damages for his or her personal injuries. Yet another common problem occurs when a married couple moves from a common law to a community property state, or from a community property to a common law state.

Asset Acquisition. There are two common patterns that occur. First, an asset, such as a house, can be acquired, and title passes to the purchaser at that time, but subject to a mortgage securing a loan that financed the purchase. Second, a contract may be entered into to purchase an asset but title will not pass until all the installment payments under the contract have been made. There are three different rules that community property states employ to characterize the nature of the asset acquired. Some states use the "inception of right" rule, under which the character of the property is fixed at the moment the contract or credit transaction is initiated.

> *Example 5–5:* While single, *H* enters into an installment sale contract to purchase a house. He makes several payments using his separate property, and then marries *W*. The remainder of the installment payments are made using funds earned by each spouse after their marriage. Under inception of right the house is the separate property of *H* because at the moment the installment sale contract was signed by *H* he was single and his rights under the contract were his separate property. Even though community funds were used to complete the installment payments under the contract the house remains the separate property of *H*. However, the community will be entitled to reimbursement from *H* of the community funds used to acquire the house. That means that the house remains *H*'s separate property and any appreciation in value will inure to *H*'s sole benefit. The community simply gets its money back.

Some states use the "time of vesting" rule, under which the character of the property is determined when title passes.

> *Example 5–6:* Assume the facts of Example 5–5. Under the time of vesting rule, title to the house did not pass until all the installment payments under the contract were completed. At that moment *H* and *W* were married and the property is treated as community property. However, *H* may be entitled to reimbursement from the community

for his payments made with his separate property. Under this rule *H* and *W* will share equally any appreciation in value of the house, but *H* will get his money back.

Finally, some states employ a "pro rata" rule, under which the property acquired is partly community and partly separate, in proportion to the funds of each kind that were used to acquire the property.

Example 5–7: Assume the facts of Example 5–5, but also assume that *H*'s payments using his separate property totaled $10,000 and that the total of payments made using community funds was $90,000. After acquisition of title the house a 10% interest in the house is owned by *H* as his separate property and a 90% interest in the house is owned by the marital community. Under this rule 10% of any appreciation in value of the house will be *H*'s alone, and 90% of that appreciation will inure to the community.

Spousal Business. If one spouse owns and operates a business prior to marriage (making that business his or her separate property), continues to do so after marriage, and the value of that business increases during the marriage, how should the increased value be treated? The problem usually surfaces in the context of divorce but can also arise when the business is sold and its former owner wishes to preserve the proceeds of sale as separate property. There is no universal answer. One approach is akin to the inception of right view of assets acquired with a mix of community and separate property: The business is separate property but its owner is required to pay to the marital community the value of the business manager's efforts expended in managing the business, after deducting from that sum the actual earnings the owner received (which inured to the benefit of the community).

Problem: Suppose that *H* owned and managed a swimming pool service company, worth $200,000 at his marriage to *W*. During the five year length of the marriage *H* drew a salary of $50,000 per year for his management. Managers of comparable companies in the area received an average annual salary of $65,000. Upon divorce the company is worth $500,000. How much will *H* be required to pay to the marital community?

A second approach is to determine whether the increased value of the business is greater than the average increase in value of similar businesses. Though that determination is not always easy to make, the point of the exercise is to determine whether the increased value is attributable to exceptional skill on the part of the owner/manager spouse or is attributable to factors that are not the product of the owner/manager spouse's particular efforts. If the former is the case, this approach holds that the excess of actual increased value over average increased value belongs to the community because it is attributable to the "earnings" skill of the spouse, but if there is no excess value the incremental value of the business is separate property.

Problem: Suppose that *H* owned and managed an auto repair shop, worth $500,000 at his marriage to *W*. Upon divorce five years later, the business is worth $1 million. The average percentage increase in value of other comparable auto repair shops in the area is 50% over the same five year period. How much of the increased value of *H*'s business belongs to the marital community? Suppose that the average percentage increase in value of other auto repair shops in the area over the same five year period had been 110%. How much of the increased value of *H*'s business belongs to the marital community?

Damages for Personal Injuries. The question presented in such cases is whether the damages are community property because they were acquired during marriage but not by gift or inheritance, or whether they are the recipient spouse's separate property because the injuries suffered were visited on that spouse alone. At one time all the community property states declared that such damages were community property. That is no longer the case. The current prevailing rule with respect to damages received by a spouse for his or her personal injury is that the portion representing lost earnings and reimbursement for community expenses is community property while the portion that is compensation for individual pain and suffering is separate property.

Migration. The United States is a highly mobile society, so married couples frequently move from a common law state to a community property state, or from a community property to a common law state. The problems, however, are quite different.

In general, when a couple moves from a common law state to a community property state the property retains the character it had in their former state. Thus, to the extent either spouse owns property in their name it retains its character as separate property. Moreover, the elective share, which would protect each spouse from compete disinheritance, is lost because community property states do not have elective share statutes. (The rationale for this is that community property rules make the elective share unnecessary.) The intersection of these two principles can produce considerable inequity, particularly in the case of retired couples.

Example 5–8: *H* and *W* have been married for many years in New Jersey. During that time *H* has invested his saved earnings in stocks and bonds, and has acquired a securities portfolio, held in his name at Titanic Financial, worth $1 million. *W* has devoted herself to raising the couple's children, making a pleasant and comfortable home, and performing volunteer work in her community. She has no assets of consequence. *H* and *W* retire and move to Austin, Texas to be near their grown children. They sell their New Jersey home and purchase one in Austin, taking title as community property. *H* has a secret relationship with *Z*, a woman he met in Austin. At *H*'s death his will leaves all his property to *Z*. As a result, *Z* takes *H*'s securities portfolio at Titanic Financial and H's half of the community property (the home H and W acquired in Austin).

What could W have done to protect herself against this outcome?

California and a few other community property states recognize the doctrine of "quasi-community property," which holds that property brought into the state by new residents is treated as if it were community property if it was acquired during marriage and would be community property if the acquisition had occurred in California. (Texas does not have quasi-community property.) Under the quasi-community property rule, all that H could leave to Z, in Example 5–8, would be his half interest in the quasi-community property and the community property. At death, the law of the decedent's domicile controls his personal property and real property located within the jurisdiction, but real property elsewhere is governed by the law of its state of location. Thus, quasi-community property controls only personal property and real property located within the state. If a decedent spouse owns real property in his own name in a common law state, the other spouse will have an elective share option with respect to that property (except, of course, in Georgia, the lone common law state that refuses to provide an elective share).

When a married couple move from a community property state to a common law state they frequently assume that they must leave community property principles behind. This is not completely true. Absent later voluntary change, the character of property is fixed at the time of its acquisition. Thus, community property that is taken to a common law state retains its character as community property. Migrating couples often assume (or are told) that they may not take title to the new house in the common law state as community property, even when the funds used to purchase that house are community property. One way to avoid these nettlesome objections from bankers, realtors, and others unacquainted with legal realities is to create a revocable trust in which the settlors, trustees, and beneficiaries are the married couple, and which states in the trust agreement that all the property in trust is community property. Once title to the couple's community property is transferred to the trust, it is a fairly simple matter to use trust assets to acquire property in the name of the trust in the common law state. The advantage to retaining community property is the step up in tax basis on all of the community property at the death of the first spouse to die. Couples may also simply prefer community property as a more sensible way to deal with marital property.

3. SAME–SEX COUPLES AND UNMARRIED COHABITANTS

Special problems are posed when people cohabit in an enduring relationship without benefit of marriage. There are a wide variety of patterns within this general relationship. Opposite-sex or same-sex couples may simply live together without any express or implied agreement to govern their relationship; they may have an express agreement; or an agreement may be implied from statements or actions of the parties. The varied legal responses to these phenomena are discussed in this subsection.

a. Common Law Marriage

At one time the doctrine of common law marriage was widespread, but today only about a dozen jurisdictions in the United States continue to recognize it. A man and a woman who agree to be husband and wife and cohabit as such are married under this doctrine, but because it is exceedingly rare for such a couple to have a written agreement to this effect, proof of a common law marriage depends either on testimony of the putative spouses or circumstantial evidence, such as tax returns or statements on credit applications or other documents. A presumption of common law marriage arises when the parties held themselves out to the world as a married couple. Most states that do not recognize common law marriage do recognize the validity of common law marriage when it occurs in another jurisdiction that permits common law marriage. Once common law marriage is established the marital partners are entitled to all the benefits and obligations of marriage. For a discussion of common law marriage, see Ellen Kandoian, Cohabitation, Common Law Marriage, and the Possibility of a Shared Moral Life, 75 Geo. L. J. 1829 (1987).

Some states recognize the doctrine of the putative spouse, a concept borrowed from civil law. See, e.g., Calif. Family Code § 2251. An unmarried person who participates in a marriage ceremony that turns out to be invalid (perhaps because the other partner is already married) but acts in the good faith belief that he or she is married is entitled to be treated as if he or she was a legal spouse. See Estate of Leslie, 37 Cal.3d 186 (1984). That good faith belief must be objectively reasonable and present at the time the invalid marriage ceremony occurs. See Batey v. Batey, 933 P.2d 551 (1997); Marriage of Guo & Sun, 186 Cal.App.4th 1491 (2010). But see Marriage of Tejeda, 179 Cal.App.4th 973 (2009), interpreting the California statute to mean that if one partner is a putative spouse the marriage is a "putative marriage" and both partners are entitled to be treated as legal spouses. What happens if a partner has a good faith belief in the validity of the marriage ceremony but later learns that the marriage is bogus? Does one's status as a putative spouse abruptly end, or should that status, once acquired, continue thereafter? See Burks v. Apfel, 233 F.3d 1220 (10th Cir. 2000); Tatum v. Tatum, 241 F.2d 401, 411 (9th Cir. 1957); Gallaher v. State Teachers' Retirement System, 237 Cal.App.2d 510 (1965); In re Roberts, 2007 Cal. App. Unpub. Lexis 6613.

b. Cohabitation

In general, cohabiting partners have no property rights in each other's property. They may, of course, hold property in joint tenancy and thus confer those rights upon each other, but the rights of marital partners are non-existent. When unmarried partners attempt to replicate marital property rights by agreement among themselves, the question arises whether such agreements will be recognized.

Marvin v. Marvin, 18 Cal.3d 660 (1976), was the California Supreme Court's answer to this question. Michelle Triola and the actor Lee Marvin lived together for seven years pursuant to an alleged oral agreement that while "the parties lived together they would combine their efforts and earnings and would share equally any and all property accumulated as a result of their efforts whether individual or combined." Triola claimed she gave up her career as a singer to devote herself full time as Marvin's "companion, homemaker, housekeeper and cook." Id. at 666. The California court stated that

> courts should enforce express contracts between non-marital partners except to the extent that the contract is explicitly founded on the consideration of meretricious sexual services. . . . In the absence of an express contract, the courts should inquire into the conduct of the parties to determine whether that conduct demonstrates an implied contract, agreement of partnership or joint venture, or some other tacit understanding between the parties. The courts may also employ the doctrine of quantum meruit, or equitable remedies such as constructive or resulting trusts, when warranted by the facts of the case.

This conclusion was warranted, said the court, because "the prevalence of non-marital relationships in modern society and the social acceptance of them, marks this as a time when our courts should by no means apply the doctrine of the unlawfulness of the so-called meretricious relationship to the instant case. . . . The mores of the society have indeed changed so radically in regard to cohabitation that we cannot impose a standard based on alleged moral considerations that have apparently been so widely abandoned by so many." *Marvin* has been followed in some states (see, e.g., Connell v. Francisco, 127 Wn. 2d 339 (1995); Carroll v. Lee, 148 Ariz. 10 (1986)) and has been applied to same-sex cohabitants. See Gormley v. Robertson, 120 Wn. App. 31 (2004); Whorton v. Dillingham, 202 Cal. App.3d 447 (1988).

Not every court is convinced by *Marvin*. In Hewitt v. Hewitt, 77 Ill.2d 49 (1979), Victoria Hewitt sought "an equal share of the profits and properties accumulated" by Robert Hewitt on the basis of equitable estoppel, implied contract, fraud that warranted imposition of a constructive trust, and unjust enrichment. In 1960, when Victoria and Robert were students at Grinnell College, Victoria became pregnant. Robert then told her that they were husband and wife and would live as such, no formal ceremony being necessary, and that he would " 'share his life, his future, his earnings and his property' " with her. Victoria and Robert immediately announced to their respective parents that they were married and thereafter held themselves out as husband and wife. Victoria devoted her efforts to Robert's professional education and his establishment in dental practice, obtaining financial assistance from her parents for this purpose.

Victoria asserted that she assisted Robert "in his career with her own special skills," that Robert "was without funds at the time of the marriage," but "as a result of her efforts" he "has accumulated large amounts of property, owned either jointly with her or separately," and that "she has given him every assistance a wife and mother could give, including social activities designed to enhance his social and professional reputation." The Illinois Supreme Court rejected these theories in their entirety, reasoning that to adopt them would revive common law marriage, which Illinois had eliminated by statute.

Some courts have taken an intermediate position, ruling that only express agreements between unmarried cohabitants are enforceable. See Kinkenon v. Hue, 207 Neb. 698, 702 (1981); Koslowski v. Koslowski, 80 N.J. 378, 384 (1979); Morone v. Morone, 50 N.Y.2d 481 (1980).

What should be the approach taken by courts to the problem of the division of property of unmarried cohabitants when the relationship ends? Should courts refuse any redress? Should the answer depend on the existence of an express or implied contract? Should common law marriage be revived everywhere? Should cohabitants be treated as married if they share a residence and otherwise act as a married couple would for a significant (or specified) period of time?

c. Same–Sex Marriage

The question of whether marriage may be limited to opposite-sex couples has become controversial and emotional. As of November 2011 only six states and the District of Columbia permit same-sex marriage: Connecticut, Iowa, Massachusetts, New Hampshire, New York, and Vermont. Of those six, only New Hampshire and New York effected the change through legislative action. The other four states did so by judicial decision of the state's highest court, relying on the state constitution. See Kerrigan v. Commissioner of Public Health, 289 Conn. 135, 262–263 (2008); Varnum v. Brien, 763 N.W.2d 862, 906 (Iowa 2009); Goodridge v. Department of Public Health, 440 Mass. 309, 341–344 (2003); Baker v. State, 170 Vt. 194, 224–225 (1999). In *Baker*, the Vermont Supreme Court ruled that same-sex civil unions must receive the same legal status as marriages. In 2009, the Vermont and New Hampshire legislatures each acted to define marriage "as the legally recognized union of two people." Vt. Stat. Ann. § 8 (2010); N.H. Rev. Stat. Ann. § 457:1–a (2010). The District of Columbia followed suit in 2010. D.C. Code § 46–401 (2010). New York did so in 2011. Maine's legislature enacted similar legislation in May of 2009, but it was repealed by a voter referendum that November. California's Supreme Court ruled in In re Marriage Cases, 43 Cal.4th 757 (2008), that limiting marriage to opposite sex partners violated the state constitution, but California voters amended the state constitution in November 2008 to overturn that ruling and restore the limitation. Other state courts have considered and rejected constitutional attacks upon the validity of limiting marriage to opposite-sex partners. See, e.g., Conaway v. Deane, 401 Md. 219 (2007); Hernandez v. Robles, 7 N.Y.3d 338 (2006);

Andersen v. King County, 158 Wn. 2d 1 (2006). Federal constitutional challenges to the validity of confining marriage to opposite-sex partners are at various stages of the judicial process as of November 2011. The United States Supreme Court has yet to rule on whether same-sex marriage is a right protected by the United States Constitution.

In those states recognizing same-sex marriage all of the status benefits and obligations of marriage *under state law* are available to the marital partners. Federal law, in the form of the Defense of Marriage Act ("DOMA"), 110 Stat. 2419 (1996), denies the benefits of marriage under federal law to married couples of the same-sex. 1 U.S.C. § 7 stipulates: "In determining the meaning of any Act of Congress, or of any ruling, regulation, or interpretation of the various administrative bureaus and agencies of the United States, the word 'marriage' means only a legal union between one man and one woman as husband and wife, and the word 'spouse' refers only to a person of the opposite sex who is a husband or a wife." Among the federal status benefits of marriage are the ability to file a joint income tax return, the marital deduction under the federal estate tax, spousal benefits under Social Security, and many others. This asymmetry between federal and state law creates some difficult problems. Many states impose an inheritance or estate tax that is linked in some fashion to the federal estate tax liability. If a decedent spouse leaves his or entire estate to the surviving spouse, federal law provides an unlimited deduction for that transfer, resulting in no tax liability. But if the decedent spouse is of the same sex as the survivor, federal law provides no deduction, and a federal estate tax liability will result. Because of the federal tax liability a state estate tax may be assessed while such a tax would not be imposed upon the estate of a decedent whose spouse is of the opposite sex. Does this result violate the equal protection provisions of the relevant state constitution? Challenges to the validity of DOMA under the federal equal protection guarantee are presently pending in the federal courts.

A number of states have enacted laws that enable same-sex partners to register as domestic partnerships and obtain all or many of the legal status benefits available under state law to married couples. These states include California, Colorado, Hawaii, Illinois, Maine, Maryland, Nevada, New Jersey, Oregon, Rhode Island, Washington, and Wisconsin. The scope of the benefits provided under these laws varies widely. Some, such as N.J. Stat. § 37:1–28 et seq. (2010), provide status benefits equivalent to marriage. Others, such as Maryland and Colorado, provide much more limited benefits. See Md. Health–General Code Ann. §§ 6–101, 6–201 through 6–203 (2010) (providing for visitation, accompaniment, and health care agency for domestic partners); Colo. Rev. Stat. §§ 15–22–101 through 112 (2010) (The Designated Beneficiary Act, which enables unmarried persons to designate another person as their beneficiary for purposes of health care, medical emergencies, incapacity, death, and administration of decedent's estates). Of course, even those laws that provide identical status benefits to marriage do not enable the partners to obtain the status benefits of marriage under federal law.

About 19 states have constitutional prohibitions of same-sex marriage and their equivalent civil unions or domestic partnerships. Another ten states have constitutional bans on same-sex marriage alone. An additional ten states have statutory prohibitions of same-sex marriage. This pattern produces the question of whether states that ban same-sex marriage must recognize same-sex marriages that are valid in the state where the marriage occurred. The DOMA enacted 28 U.S.C. § 1738C, which provides: "No State, territory, or possession of the United States, or Indian tribe, shall be required to give effect to any public act, record, or judicial proceeding of any other State, territory, possession, or tribe respecting a relationship between persons of the same sex that is treated as a marriage under the laws of such other State, territory, possession, or tribe, or a right or claim arising from such relationship." States are not forbidden by DOMA to recognize same-sex marriages that were legal where they were contracted. Thus, New York, Vermont, and the District of Columbia recognize out-of-state same-sex marriages and their equivalents (civil unions or domestic partnerships); Connecticut, Iowa, Maryland, Massachusetts, and New Hampshire recognize out-of-state same-sex marriages only; California, New Jersey, and Oregon recognize out-of-state same-sex marriages and their equivalents, but only as domestic partnerships or civil unions; and Washington recognizes only out-of-state civil unions or domestic partnerships. The other states do not recognize any of these forms of same-sex union. This patchwork raises some problems. What if a same-sex couple, legally married in Vermont, move to Texas and seek a divorce? See In re J.B. and H.B., 326 S.W.3d 654 (Tex. App. 2010) (divorce denied); Kern v. Taney, 11 Pa. D. & C. 5th 558 (2010) (divorce denied). On the choice of law rules that govern whether states will recognize same-sex unions, see William Baude, Beyond DOMA: Choice of State Law in Federal Statutes, 64 Stan L. Rev. ___ (2012).

PROBLEMS

1.   *A* and *B*, each of the same-sex, become registered domestic partners under Washington law (Wash. Rev. Code Ann.§ 26.60.010 et seq.), which gives them the same legal rights as married couples, and acquire a securities portfolio as community property. They then move to Texas. Is their securities portfolio still community property? Suppose they move to New York; what result? Or Nebraska?

2.   *A* and *B*, each of the same-sex, marry in Massachusetts. They purchase a vacation house in Maryland and take title as tenants by the entirety. Are they tenants by the entirety? What if they purchased the vacation home in Michigan?

CHAPTER SIX

LANDLORD AND TENANT

■ ■ ■

Somewhat more than one-third of American households rent rather than own their homes. The pure common law treated leaseholds as non-freehold estates because the transfer of possession under a lease was regarded as personal, and did not involve any transfer of seisin. That distinction is of no consequence today. But the common law also regarded the creation of a leasehold as a conveyance, because it creates a present possessory estate and a reversion in the owner of the fee. While that is still true, contemporary approaches to leaseholds also borrow from contract principles. Moreover, courts today are apt to treat commercial leases differently from residential leases in key respects. They do so because they assume that the parties to commercial leases are able to bargain for terms that reflect their mutual desires, but residential lease transactions often involve a "take it or leave it" lease offered by the landlord. See, e.g., Wesson v. Leone Enterprises, Inc., 437 Mass. 708 (2002). In general, the doctrines discussed in this chapter are the same for commercial and residential leases; where doctrines differ, the differences will be made explicit. In this chapter we will explore the types of leaseholds, questions surrounding delivery of possession, subleases and assignments, tenant obligations and landlord remedies, landlord obligations and tenant remedies, and governmental regulation of leaseholds.

A. TYPES OF LEASEHOLD ESTATES

There are three true types of leaseholds—the specific term (more usually called a term of years), the periodic tenancy, and the tenancy at will—and one "tenancy" that is not really a tenancy at all—the holdover "tenancy," also called the tenancy at sufferance. Because the holdover tenancy involves a wrongful extension of possession after the tenancy has expired, it poses the problem of how to treat that possessor, and thus will be considered in this section.

1. SPECIFIC TERM

A lease for a fixed or computable period creates a leasehold for a term of years, or a specific term. Thus, the term can be one week, one day, one year, a thousand years, or a billion years. Usually, such leases are for a term of years, such as five years. To renew such a lease, a new agreement is necessary to create a new leasehold. The lease will terminate automatically at the end of the period, and the landlord's reversion will become possessory. Continued possession by the tenant is wrongful. Most states apply the Statute of Frauds to such leases, and require that leases for more than one year must be in writing. Some states impose limits on the length of a specific term. In California, for example, commercial leases of agricultural land may not endure for more than 51 years, and commercial leases of urban land may not be for more than 99 years. Cal. Civ. Code §§ 717, 718. La. Civ. Code Art. 2679 limits the durations of leases to 99 years. Other states permit much longer leases. See, e.g, Atlantic & St. Lawrence R.R. v. State, 60 N.H. 133 (1880); Keliipuleole v. Wilson, 85 Haw. 217 (1997). A term of years may be defeasible, as when O leases Blackacre to A "for 5 years or until O sooner terminates the lease," or "for 5 years or until A ceases to use Blackacre as a law office." See, e.g., Philpot v. Field, 633 S.W.2d 546 (Tex. App. 1982); Myers v. The East Ohio Gas Co., 51 Ohio St.2d 121 (1977).

PROBLEMS

1. O leases Blackacre to A for a five year term beginning when O has completed construction of the building that A will occupy under the lease. O has an application pending for governmental approval of his construction plans. Is the lease valid?

2. O leases Blackacre to A for a five year term beginning when B, who has a life estate in Blackacre, shall die. Valid?

3. O leases Blackacre to A for so long as oil is extracted from Blackacre. Does the lease create a term of years?

2. PERIODIC TENANCY

A periodic tenancy results when possession is transferred for a specific period that will automatically be renewed for that period until and unless a party has given adequate notice to the other party of termination of the lease. The usual example is a lease from "month to month" or from "year to year." To terminate a periodic tenancy the common law required that notice be given in advance for at least the period of the tenancy, but not longer than six moths in advance. For example, notice to terminate a month to month periodic tenancy must be given at least one month in advance of the next renewal period, but notice to terminate a year to year tenancy must be given at least six months in advance of the renewal period. The common law notice periods are often changed by statutes.

PROBLEMS

1. O leases Blackacre to A "in exchange for rent of $12,000, to be paid in monthly installments of $1,000." Is this a periodic tenancy or a term of years? What if the lease said, "in exchange for rent of $12,000, to be paid in monthly installments of $1,000, each installment representing one month of occupancy"? What if the lease said, "for the calendar year 2010, in exchange for rent of $12,000, to be paid in monthly installments of $1,000"?

2. In a jurisdiction that observes the common law rules on notice, O leases Blackacre to A "for year to year, beginning on January 1, 2012." On August 1, 2012 A provides O with written notice of his election to terminate the tenancy as of the end of December 31, 2012. On December 31 A moves out. O advertises Blackacre for rent and rents it to a new tenant for occupancy beginning on March 1, 2013. O demands that A pay rent for January and February of 2013. Is O entitled to that rent?

3. In a jurisdiction that observes the common law rules on notice, O leases Blackacre to A "for month to month, beginning on January 1, 2012." On May 10, 2012, A provides O with written notice of his election to terminate the tenancy as of the end of May, 2012. On June 1, A moves out. O advertises Blackacre for rent and rents it to a new tenant for occupancy beginning on October 1, 2012. O demands that A pay rent for June, July, August, and September of 2012. Is O entitled to all, or any portion, of that rent?

3. TENANCY AT WILL

Under a tenancy at will the tenant has possession for no defined period of time. Either party may terminate the tenancy at any time. Problems can arise when a lease of no definite term grants to one party the right to terminate at any time, but is silent with respect to the other party. Ordinarily, this creates a tenancy at will, and each party has the right to terminate the tenancy at any time. But not always; sometimes courts find that such asymmetry produces something other a tenancy at will.

For example, in Garner v. Gerrish, 63 N.Y.2d 575 (1984), the New York Court of Appeals confronted a lease by which the landlord, in return for $100 monthly rent, granted Gerrish possession for a term that ended whenever Gerrish chose to terminate the lease. The court concluded that the lease created a "life tenancy terminable at the will of the tenant." The court did not specify whether this was a determinable leasehold for life or whether it was a determinable freehold life estate. If it is a determinable life estate, how is the $100 monthly "rent" to be characterized? Is there any significance to the distinction between a determinable life estate and a determinable lease for life? If so, what is it?

4. HOLDOVERS, OR TENANCY AT SUFFERANCE

When a tenant lawfully in possession stays on after his tenancy has expired he is, strictly speaking, no longer a tenant at all. However, his status differs from that of a trespasser, who never had any right to possess the property at any time. The general rule is that where a tenant holds over after the expiration of the term provided for in his lease, the landlord may either evict the holdover and also obtain damages or may consent to a new tenancy to which the provisions of the expired lease are applicable. The choice is entirely that of the landlord. See Donnelly Advertising Corp. of Maryland v. Flaccomio, 216 Md. 113 (1958). But once a landlord has made his election and communicated it to the tenant he cannot change his mind without the tenant's consent. See Crechale & Polles, Inc. v. Smith, 295 So.2d 275 (Miss. 1974). Most states treat a new tenancy resulting from the landlord's exercise of his option to do so as a periodic tenancy, though the period may differ. If the original lease term was longer than one year, it is common to treat the new tenancy as one from year-to-year. An original month-to-month is usually treated as a new month-to-month. An original lease for one year may be treated as new periodic tenancy from year-to-year or as a periodic tenancy defined by the period that rent was payable under the old lease, usually month-to-month.

Statutes may alter the landlord's traditional options. Rent control laws may prevent the landlord from evicting a holdover by forcing a new lease on the landlord. Some states impose statutory damages upon holdovers, often double or treble rent, although a few convert a holdover into a tenancy at will with the rental obligation fixed at the reasonable value of possession of the premises, which might be more or less than the stipulated lease rentals under old lease. In many of the states that impose liability for double or treble rent, the common law right of the landlord to choose to impose a new term on the tenant is abrogated, leaving the landlord with the choice of either eviction and statutory damages, or negotiating a new lease with the consent.

There are often three parties that are affected by holdovers: the landlord, the holdover, and the new tenant who has made plans to move in upon the expiration of the old lease. How should these interests be accommodated? Consider the following possibilities: (1) The common law rule; (2) Only eviction and multiple rent as damages; or (3) Eviction and imposition of liability upon the holdover for actual damages to each of the landlord and the new tenant.

On holdovers generally, see Powell on Real Property § 17.06.

PROBLEMS

1.   *T* occupies Blackacre under a lease from *L* that expires June 30, 2012. *T* uses Blackacre for commercial purposes. *T* makes arrangements with a moving company to move all of *T*'s possessions out on June 30. On the appointed day, both *T*'s employees and the moving company's employees strike. *T*'s employees erect a picket line around Blackacre. No other moving company will cross the picket line. The strike lasts two weeks. *L* sues *T* for double damages, as stipulated under state law. Is *T* liable? See Feiges v. Racine Dry Good Co., 231 Wis. 270 (1939); Herter v. Mullen, 159 N.Y. 28 (1899).

2. *T* occupies Blackacre under a lease from *L* that expires May 15, 2012. *L* vacates Blackacre on May 15, but leaves behind a desk and a chair. What are *L*'s remedies, if any? See Comedy v. Vito, 492 A.2d 276 (D.C. Ct. App. 1985). What if *L* vacated at 2:00 a.m. on May 16, 2012, but left nothing behind? See Commonwealth Building Corp. v. Hirschfield, 307 Ill.App. 533 (1940).

3. *T* occupies Blackacre under a five year lease from *L* that expires August 31, 2012. *L* sends *T* a letter that if he has not vacated by midnight on August 31, 2012, he will treat *L* as a trespasser. *T* does not vacate, but stays on for three months. During that time, *T* sends monthly rent checks to *L*, which *L* deposits after sending *L* another letter stating that *L*'s acceptance of the rent checks constitutes his election to create a new lease for year to year, as permitted under state law. *L* vacates after three months of holding over. May *T* recover from *L* rent for the next nine months?

5. LEASEHOLD, LICENSE, OR EASEMENT?

Disputes may arise whether a possessory right creates a leasehold, license, or an easement. In Chapter 10 you will encounter easements, which generally give someone a right to use another's land. Examples include an easement for access, or an easement to permit utility lines to pass over or under property. Once created, easements may not be revoked at the will of the grantor. A lawful occupant of land creates a license when he permits another to enter or use that land in a way that would otherwise be a trespass. A shopkeeper grants a license to a prospective customer when the customer enters the shop. A theater grants the moviegoer a license when the admission ticket is sold. Generally, a license may be revoked at any time or for any reason. The moviegoer who starts chatting on his cell phone in the middle of the feature film is likely to have his license revoked.

DE BRUYN PRODUCE CO. v. ROMERO

Court of Appeals of Michigan
202 Mich.App. 92 (1993)

REILLY, J., delivered the opinion of the court.

De Bruyn Produce Company is involved in the growing, harvesting, packing, and shipping of vegetables. ... Defendants are migrant workers from Texas who worked for plaintiff in Ionia, Michigan, during the 1987 season. Defendants were recruited in Texas. Before defendants came to Michigan, the parties executed a number of documents that described the conditions of employment, including housing. Defendants were paid $3.35

an hour and lived in mobile homes provided by plaintiff. Plaintiff required a deposit of $150 for each housing unit to cover the cost of any damage to the unit. Five dollars was to be deducted from each paycheck to cover the deposit.

Defendants Pablo Romero and Gustavo Romero, together with Gustavo's wife and child, lived in a mobile home that was set aside for a family. Single men, including defendant Jorge Resendez, were housed in separate mobile homes. After Gustavo's wife and child moved out, Pablo and Gustavo were asked by a representative of plaintiff to move to another mobile home occupied by single men. Another family was expected to arrive and was to be housed in the mobile home formerly occupied by the Romero family. Rather than move to another mobile home, Pablo and Gustavo left the farm and ceased working for plaintiff. Resendez also apparently left because of housing conditions. Gerardo Montes' employment was terminated by plaintiff.

Defendants sought legal counsel, and when the parties could not agree regarding the nature of defendants' rights with respect to the housing provided on the farm, plaintiff ... sought a declaration of the nature of the legal relationship between plaintiff and defendants with respect to defendants' occupancy of the housing provided by plaintiff and the applicability of the summary proceedings act, MCL 600.5701 *et seq.*; MSA 27A.5701 *et seq.* Additionally, plaintiff asked the court to determine whether the deposit on the mobile home was a security deposit within the meaning of the landlord-tenant relationship act, MCL 554.601 *et seq.*; MSA 26.1138(1) *et seq.* Lastly, plaintiff sought a declaration regarding the applicability of the Michigan Consumer Protection Act, MCL 445.901 *et seq.*; MSA 19.418(1) *et seq.*, and the Truth in Renting Act, MCL 554.631 *et seq.*; MSA 26.1138(31) *et seq.*

The trial court ... held that the relationship between plaintiff and defendants was regulated by the Migrant and Seasonal Agricultural Worker Protection Act (AWPA), 29 USC 1801 *et seq.* On the basis of the language of the documents executed by the parties, the testimony of the parties, "the controlling federal statute provisions and purposes," and Michigan law, the trial court determined that a landlord-tenant relationship had not existed and that the only legal relationship between the parties was one of employer-employee. The court ruled that because defendants were not tenants, they had no estate at will requiring termination by statutory notice and, therefore, the notice provisions of the summary proceedings act did not apply. ... Finally, the trial court held that the landlord-tenant relationship act, the Michigan Consumer Protection Act, and the Truth in Renting Act were all inapplicable to the employer-employee relationship between plaintiff and defendants....

The AWPA regulates the relationship between migrant workers and agricultural employers and imposes specific duties upon employers. See, e.g., 29 USC 1821–1823. It is clear that the overriding concern of the legislation is to protect migrant workers from exploitation. Although the

AWPA serves to regulate the relationship between migrant workers and their employers, it does not occupy the entire field of regulation so as to preempt state regulation. Rather, it "is intended to supplement State law, and compliance with [the statute] Shall not excuse any person from compliance with appropriate State law and regulation." 29 USC 1871. . . .

The underlying issue to be resolved is the nature of the relationship between plaintiff and defendants with regard to the housing provided by plaintiff. Defendants argue that the trial court erred in finding that the relationship was solely one of employer and employee. They assert that the documents in the employment packet, when read together, constitute a lease. We disagree. . . . *not a lease*.

A lease is a conveyance by the owner of an estate of a portion of the interest therein to another for a term less than his own for a valuable consideration. A lease gives the tenant the possession of the property leased and the exclusive use or occupation of it for all purposes not prohibited by the terms of the lease. In order for an agreement to be a valid lease, it must contain the names of the parties, an adequate description of the leased premises, the length of the lease term, and the amount of the rent. Consideration for a lease may be in services as well as in money. We conclude that the documents relied on by defendants do not constitute a lease or create a landlord-tenant relationship between the parties.

The document entitled "Worker Information Sheet" was provided to defendants in an effort to comply with the disclosure provisions of the AWPA, 29 USC 1821(a), [which requires disclosure of "the transportation, housing, and any other employee benefit to be provided, if any, and any cost to be charged for each of them."] It included a section that stated:

> housing: (For migrant workers who will be housed, the kind of housing available and cost, if any) Type: *Mobile Home* Charges: *Deposit* Other: *Available only to those offered housing agreements and are currently employed by De Bruyn Produce Co. Tenantcy [sic] is week to week.*

The document evidenced that defendants were informed, in compliance with the AWPA, of the housing situation.

Another document entitled "Housing Units" described conditions for use of the housing units and stated in pertinent part:

> 1. To be occupied by De Bruyn Produce Company employees, and their immediate family only.
>
> 2. "Housing Units" tenantcy [sic] is strictly on a week-to-week basis.
>
> 3. Upon termination of employment, the housing unit is expected to be vacated within 2 days.

This document was also supplied to defendants in conformance with 29 USC 1821(c). We agree with the trial court's interpretation of the language that housing is "[t]o be occupied by De Bruyn Produce Company employees, and their immediate family only" as meaning that employment is required as a condition of housing and occupancy is limited to an employee's immediate family, not that the workers are given exclusive possession and control of the premises, as asserted by defendants. Moreover, we agree with the trial court that the language "tenantcy [sic] is on a week-to-week basis," when read in context, refers to occupancy of the housing unit and does not serve to create a lease.

Also included in the package was a document explaining the company's policy regarding the $150 deposit for housing and authorizing the company to deduct $5 each pay period to cover the deposit. There was also a list entitled "Occupant's Responsibilities."

In spite of the use of the word "tenantcy," it is clear from the language of these documents, when read in context, that there was no landlord-tenant relationship created and that housing was contingent upon the employer-employee relationship. None of these documents contain language evidencing an intent to form a landlord-tenant relationship. There is no provision regarding conveyance for consideration or monetary rent, nor is there any provision indicating an agreement that defendants' services were to be considered as rent. There is no language conveying a possessory interest in specific, designated property, or providing for defendants' exclusive use and possession of any property. Additionally, it is undisputed that workers who were not provided housing made the same wage as those who were provided with housing. We believe these facts defeat defendants' argument that their services were intended as rent.

The situation presented in this case is distinguishable from that in *Grant v Detroit Ass'n of Women's Clubs*, 443 Mich 596; 505 NW2d 254 (1993). In *Grant*, the use and occupancy of an apartment by the plaintiff was provided pursuant to an employment contract in exchange for the plaintiff's services as a full-time caretaker. The plaintiff's occupancy in that case was not a marginal consequence of employment. Rather, according to the terms of the employment contract, the plaintiff's occupancy was the "sole and full compensation" for the plaintiff's services. In the present case, however, there was no agreement between the parties that defendants' occupancy of the mobile homes would be compensation for their services. Defendants were paid a wage that was the same as that paid to other workers who were not provided with housing.

We are convinced that the documents in the employment package do not constitute a lease agreement separate and distinct from the parties' employment contract. Thus, defendants' right to occupy the premises owned by plaintiff was dependent on the continuation of the employment relationship with plaintiff and not on any separate rights of tenancy. See also *Vasquez v Glassboro Service Ass'n, Inc*, 83 NJ 86; 415 A2d 1156 (1980), where the court, in addressing the right of a farm worker to remain on an employer's property after the employment had ended, found that the special characteristics of migrant workers' housing, the absence of a contractual provision for the payment of rent, the lack of privacy, the intermittent occupancy, and the interdependence of employment and housing supported the determination that the migrant worker in that case was not a tenant.

The determination that defendants' occupancy was not based upon a landlord-tenant relationship does not mean that defendants could have been summarily removed from the premises at any time. Plaintiff correctly acknowledges that it is prevented from exercising "self-help" in order to regain possession of the property and that it must resort to judicial process. However, ... plaintiff contends that it is not required to comply with the notice requirements [applicable to termination of a tenancy at will or tenancy at sufferance, which require one month's notice].

To facilitate resort to judicial process, the summary proceedings act provides ... for the recovery of possession of realty in an expeditious manner. Pursuant to MCL 600.5714(1); MSA 27A.5714(1), a person entitled to certain premises may seek to recover possession through summary proceedings "(e) When a person takes possession of premises by means of a forcible entry, holds possession of premises by force after a peaceable entry, or comes into possession of premises by trespass without color of title or other possessory interest."

[Only] subsection 1(e) ... address[es] the unique situation presented in this case where an employee occupies property with the consent of his employer. As we have already determined, defendants did not have possession of the housing units pursuant to a lease agreement. ... [T]here is nothing to indicate that defendants were tenants at will or at sufferance. ... An employee who continues to occupy housing provided by an employer after the termination of the employment relationship may be considered to be a tenant by sufferance if the employer allows him to remain in possession for a sufficient period to imply acquiescence in the occupancy. Further, if the employee remains on the property pursuant to the express consent of the employer, he may become a tenant at will. However, there were no facts before the trial court indicating either consent or laches on the part of plaintiff. In fact, plaintiff, in requesting a declaratory judgment, is seeking to determine which judicial remedies are applicable so that it may properly act and avoid creating a tenancy at will or at sufferance. Accordingly, we conclude that the provisions of MCL 600.5714(1)(c)(iii); MSA 27A.5714(1)(c)(iii), [which require notice to quit to a tenant before instituting summary proceedings,] are ... not applicable in this case.

Although plaintiff has not specifically addressed the distinction between a refusal by its migrant workers to move to different living quarters during the period of employment when ordered by the employer and a refusal to leave living quarters after employment has terminated, we believe either situation may be resolved under subsection 1(e). Under either situation, the refusal to leave peaceably, thus requiring removal by force, constitutes a holding by force, and the plaintiff is entitled to recover possession by summary proceedings under subsection 1(e).

The next question is whether the summary proceedings act is the only judicial process available to plaintiff in seeking to dispossess defendants. We conclude that it is not. Pursuant to § 5750 of the act, the remedy provided by summary proceedings "is in addition to, and not exclusive of, other remedies, either legal, equitable or statutory." ... Thus, we conclude that pursuant to § 5750 the plaintiff is not precluded from seeking other forms of relief, such as statutory and common-law equitable relief, including an injunction.

The next issue presented is whether the trial court erred in determining that the provisions of the landlord tenant relationship act (LTRA), did not apply under the circumstances of this case. The LTRA serves to regulate relationships between landlords and tenants relative to rental agreements and the payment, repayment, and use of security deposits. The act is intended to protect tenants, especially from the situation where a landlord "surreptitiously usurp[s] substantial sums held to secure the performance of conditions under the lease." Oak Park Village v Gorton, 128 Mich App 671, 680; 341 NW2d 788 (1983). For the purposes of the LTRA, a tenant is defined as "any person who occupies a rental unit for residential purposes with the landlord's consent for an agreed upon consideration." We agree with the trial court that defendants are not tenants within the meaning of the LTRA. Although defendants occupied the housing units with plaintiff's consent, the occupancy was not based on "an agreed upon consideration." Defendants did not pay rent. Furthermore, the documents executed by the parties and the situation surrounding defendants' occupancy do not support a finding that defendants' travel from Texas or availability for work operated as "agreed upon consideration." The fact that defendants were paid the same wage as workers who were not provided housing indicates that defendants' services were not intended as consideration for the housing. Lastly, the language of the statute itself implies that "agreed upon consideration" means a monetary payment of rent. See MCL 554.602; MSA 26.1138(2) (a security deposit shall not exceed 1 1/2 months' rent).

Defendants also assert that the trial court erred in determining that the Truth in Renting Act was not applicable in this case. The Truth in Renting Act regulates rental agreements for residential premises. The term "rental agreement" as used in the act is defined as "a written agreement embodying the terms and conditions concerning the use and occupancy of residential premises, but does not include an agreement the terms of which are limited to 1 or more of the following: the identity of the parties, a description of the premises, the rental period, the total rental amount due, the amount of rental payments, and the times at which payments are due." We agree with ... the trial court that the act has no application to the present case. The documents in the employment packet do not establish a "written *agreement* embodying the terms and conditions concerning the use and occupancy" of the housing units.

Rather, the documents were informational, providing defendants with information regarding the terms and conditions of their occupancy as required by § 1821 of the AWPA. We do not believe that these documents come within the scope of the Truth in Renting Act.

Lastly, defendants argue that the trial court erroneously found that the Michigan Consumer Protection Act was not relevant to the relationship between the parties. We disagree. The MCPA prohibits certain unconscionable, deceptive or unfair acts, practices, or methods in the conduct of trade or commerce. The act defines "trade or commerce" to include the rental of real property. We do not believe that the conduct of plaintiff involved in this case, i.e., the providing of housing to defendant farm workers, falls within the definition of "trade and commerce" as utilized in the MCPA. As we have already determined, defendants did not occupy the housing units pursuant to a lease agreement with plaintiff. Nor did they pay rent. Rather the use of the housing units was provided as a benefit of employment. We find that the situation in this case is distinguishable from that in Rodriguez v Berrybrook Farms, Inc, 672 F Supp 1009 (WD Mich, 1987). In *Rodriguez*, the court found that where "labor camp owners charge a monetary fee for housing, *a fortiori*, they fall within the clear language of [the MCPA]." In the present case, defendants were not charged for the occupancy of the housing units.

Affirmed.

NOTES, QUESTIONS, AND PROBLEM

1. *Vasquez and the role of Contracts*. Vasquez v. Glassboro Service Ass'n, Inc, 83 N.J. 86 (1980), involved a contract between Vasquez, a Puerto Rican migrant farm worker, and the employment association. Under the contract the worker agreed to pick crops for stipulated wages. The employer agreed to provide temporary housing at the farm site, which turned out to be a mattress, bedding, and a locker in a barracks, for the time of employment. All benefits ceased upon termination of employment, including a return air ticket to Puerto Rico, but the contract called for a hearing on the discharge no later than five days later. Vasquez was fired for unsatisfactory work, and his hearing, which occurred a few hours later, confirmed the firing. He was told to leave the barracks immediately and moved in with a friend because he had no funds to return to Puerto Rico. He sued to regain his housing and enjoin the defendant from evicting him except in accord with New Jersey law governing tenant evictions.

The New Jersey Supreme Court concluded that farm workers provided housing on the farm were not tenants, but then went on to rule that the contract was unconscionable and thus unenforceable. The contract was an adhesion contract—"take it or leave it"—that was the product of significant inequality of bargaining power between the parties. The "crux" of its unconscionability was "its failure to provide the worker with a reasonable opportunity to find alternative housing [and] in its disregard for his welfare after termination of his employment." The New Jersey court then stated that courts should fashion equitable remedies to prevent these effects.

There was also a contract in *De Bruyn*, but the Michigan court's approach stopped at the determination that no tenancy was created. The Michigan court implicitly accepted the notion that people are free to negotiate contracts and they should be left with their bargain. It is sometimes argued that judicial intervention to strike down "unconscionable" bargains compromises autonomy and is inefficient; people are the best judges of their own utility maximization preferences. Moreover, it is said that judicial intervention leaves the poor even worse off because the condition that constrained them—lack of money—is not caused by the other party and judicial intervention will cause landlords to withdraw from the market or refuse to do business with people who lack equal bargaining power. The farm employer, for example, may hire people with no provision for housing them. Finally, it may be that judicial intervention is unwarranted in many cases of adhesion lease contracts because the landlord's use of an adhesion contract is due to his desire to minimize the transaction costs of negotiating and drafting a new agreement with each tenant. This might be especially true of large landlords with many rental units in the same building. Adhesion leases, on this view, are a potential problem only when the landlord has a monopoly on housing in the relevant market. See Richard Posner, Economic Analysis of the Law 115–116 (6th ed. 2003).

The opposite argument, embraced by the New Jersey court, is that gross disparities in bargaining power lead one party to take advantage of the other, and judicial intervention evens the playing field. See Robert Hale, Bargaining, Duress, and Economic Liberty, 43 Colum. L. Rev. 603 (1943). As noted, this may be the case when the landlord has a monopoly, but when the tenant has other alternatives this may not be so. A related argument, lying somewhere between the two poles, is that all contracts should be susceptible to regulation to ensure some basic minimum standards are enforced. The problem with this view is that there is enormous disagreement over what those standards should be. Your basic minimum may be my gross overreaching into the realm of individual liberty, and you may regard my sense of prudent limitation as oblivious ignorance of social reality. That is what elections are sometimes about. But in the absence of legislative action, why should judges be empowered to substitute their views on these vexed questions for those of the parties?

2. More Licenses and, Perhaps, Easements. The courts usually say that the intent of the parties determines when an arrangement is a lease, license, or easement. Yet, in doing so, they often look to what the substance of the deal may be. In Golden West Baseball Co. v. City of Anaheim, 25 Cal.App.4th 11 (1994), the California Court of Appeal was called upon to decide whether an agreement, denominated a lease, that gave the then-Anaheim Angels baseball team the exclusive use and control of Anaheim Stadium and its parking facilities on 81 game dates per year was a lease or something else. The Court concluded that "possession and control of the stadium premises on approximately 81 dates which vary from year to year" could not "be considered 'exclusive against all the world including the owner,' where the owner operates all concession and parking facilities and provides security." What, then, was the interest held by the Angels, if it was not a lease? The court suggested "two possibilities," but concluded that neither mattered "to the outcome of this case." Golden West might own an easement or it might have an irrevocable license. See also Charlton v. Champaign Park District, 110 Ill.App.3d 554 (1982) (agreement granting a company the right to construct and operate a waterslide in a public park created a license when the government retained control over pricing and conduct of the company's employees); Hayden v. City of Houston, 305 S.W.2d 798 (Tex. Civ. App.1957) (license created by agreement giving company the right to operate parking facilities at municipal airport where the city retained control over allocation of areas to free or paid parking); Keller v. Southwood North Medical Pavilion, Inc., 959 P.2d 102 (Utah 1998) (clause in lease of office space granting lessee the right to affix a sign on a street monument owned by landlord created a license to use the monument space because no specific space was set aside for occupation by tenant's sign). Assuming that they desired to do so, how could the parties in any of these cases have secured the rights and obligations of a tenant for what turned out to be a license?

3. *Problems.*

a.   State University requires its incoming freshmen to live in university dormitories. Each incoming student is required to sign a housing contract, which guarantees a dorm room for the student, obliges the student to pay a specified sum of money for occupancy of the room, and stipulates that the university can terminate the contract and summarily remove the student without notice for any violations of law that the student may commit in the dorm room. S, a freshman at State University is apprehended smoking marijuana in his dorm room, in violation of federal and state law. State University officials immediately tell him to pack his bags and leave the dorm because they have cancelled the housing contract. State law requires that landlords may evict tenants only by a judicial proceeding requiring notice to the tenant, an evidentiary hearing, and a court order of eviction. Is S's summary removal pursuant to the contract valid? Would it make any difference if dormitory living was optional? See Houle v. Adams State College, 190 Colo. 406 (1976).

b.   Z, a student at State University, occupies a dormitory room under the terms of the housing contract described in the previous problem. Z is the victim of a criminal assault in a common area of her dormitory, perpetrated by an unknown assailant who entered through doors to the dormitory that the university keeps unlocked as a matter of policy. State law imposes an obligation upon landlords to take reasonable precautions against criminal assault of its tenants, and prior cases have held that failure to lock outside entrances is a breach of this duty. No such obligation is imposed on grantors of licenses. Z sues State University for its negligence and seeks recovery of damages for her personal injuries. State University moves for summary judgment in its favor. How should the court rule? Why? If your answer to this problem is not consistent with your answer to the prior problem, explain and justify the difference.

See Miller v. State, 62 N.Y.2d 506 (1984); Burch v. University of Kansas, 243 Kan. 238 (1988); Green v. Dormitory Authority of the State of New York, 173 App. Div. 2d 1 (1991).

B. INITIAL POSSESSION

There are several issues concerning initial possession. The first issue—governmental prohibition of various forms of discriminatory tenant selection—occurs even before a lease is executed. Once a lease is entered into, however, a second problem can arise if the existing tenant fails to vacate in a timely fashion. If the new tenant arrives on the date he is entitled to possession and the old tenant is still in possession, has the landlord fulfilled his obligation to deliver possession?

1. UNLAWFUL DISCRIMINATION

The federal Fair Housing Act, 42 U.S.C. §§ 3601 et seq., was enacted in 1968 primarily to address the problem of private racial discrimination in the sale or rental of housing. The Act has been amended several times since then, and covers such discrimination on the basis of "race, color, religion, sex, familial status, or national origin." 42 U.S.C. § 3604. States have enacted similar statutes, the coverage of which is sometimes broader. For example, some states also forbid housing discrimination on the basis of sexual orientation.

§ 3604. Discrimination in the sale or rental of housing and other prohibited practices.

As made applicable by [42 U.S.C. § 3603] and except as exempted by [42 U.S.C. §§ 3603(b) and 3607], it shall be unlawful—

(a) To refuse to sell or rent after the making of a bona fide offer, or to refuse to negotiate for the sale or rental of, or otherwise make unavailable or deny, a dwelling to any person because of race, color, religion, sex, familial status, or national origin.

(b) To discriminate against any person in the terms, conditions, or privileges of sale or rental of a dwelling, or in the provision of services or facilities in connection therewith, because of race, color, religion, sex, familial status, or national origin.

(c) To make, print, or publish, or cause to be made, printed, or published any notice, statement, or advertisement, with respect to the sale or rental of a dwelling that indicates any preference, limitation, or discrimination based on race, color, religion, sex, handicap, familial status, or national origin, or an intention to make any such preference, limitation, or discrimination.

(d) To represent to any person because of race, color, religion, sex, handicap, familial status, or national origin that any dwelling is not available for inspection, sale, or rental when such dwelling is in fact so available.

(e) For profit, to induce or attempt to induce any person to sell or rent any dwelling by representations regarding the entry or prospective entry into the neighborhood of a person or persons of a particular race, color, religion, sex, handicap, familial status, or national origin.

(f)(1) To discriminate in the sale or rental, or to otherwise make unavailable or deny, a dwelling to any buyer or renter because of a handicap of—

(A) that buyer or renter;

(B) a person residing in or intending to reside in that dwelling after it is so sold, rented, or made available; or

(C) any person associated with that buyer or renter.

(2) To discriminate against any person in the terms, conditions, or privileges of sale or rental of a dwelling, or in the provision of services or facilities in connection with such dwelling, because of a handicap of—

(A) that person; or

(B) a person residing in or intending to reside in that dwelling after it is so sold, rented, or made available; or

(C) any person associated with that person.

(3) For purposes of this subsection, discrimination includes—

(A) a refusal to permit, at the expense of the handicapped person, reasonable modifications of existing premises occupied or to be occupied by such person if such modifications may be necessary to afford such person full enjoyment of the premises except that, in the case of a rental, the landlord may where it is reasonable to do so condition permission for a modification on the renter agreeing to restore the interior of the premises to the condition that existed before the modification, reasonable wear and tear excepted.[;]

(B) a refusal to make reasonable accommodations in rules, policies, practices, or services, when such accommodations may be necessary to afford such person equal opportunity to use and enjoy a dwelling; or

(C) in connection with the design and construction of covered multifamily dwellings for first occupancy after the date that is 30 months after [September 13, 1988], a failure to design and construct those dwellings in such a manner that—

(i) the public use and common use portions of such dwellings are readily accessible to and usable by handicapped persons;

(ii) all the doors designed to allow passage into and within all premises within such dwellings are sufficiently wide to allow passage by handicapped persons in wheelchairs; and

    (iii) all premises within such dwellings contain the following features of adaptive design:

        (I) an accessible route into and through the dwelling;

        (II) light switches, electrical outlets, thermostats, and other environmental controls in accessible locations;

        (III) reinforcements in bathroom walls to allow later installation of grab bars; and

        (IV) usable kitchens and bathrooms such that an individual in a wheelchair can maneuver about the space. . . .

(4) Compliance with the appropriate requirements of the American National Standard for buildings and facilities providing accessibility and usability for physically handicapped people (commonly cited as "ANSI A117.1") suffices to satisfy the requirements of paragraph (3)(C)(iii).

(5)(A) If a State or unit of general local government has incorporated into its laws the requirements set forth in paragraph (3)(C), compliance with such laws shall be deemed to satisfy the requirements of that paragraph. . . .

(7) As used in this subsection, the term "covered multifamily dwellings" means—

    (A) buildings consisting of 4 or more units if such buildings have one or more elevators; and

    (B) ground floor units in other buildings consisting of 4 or more units.

(8) Nothing in this title shall be construed to invalidate or limit any law of a State or political subdivision of a State, or other jurisdiction in which this title shall be effective, that requires dwellings to be designed and constructed in a manner that affords handicapped persons greater access than is required by this title.

(9) Nothing in this subsection requires that a dwelling be made available to an individual whose tenancy would constitute a direct threat to the health or safety of other individuals or whose tenancy would result in substantial physical damage to the property of others.

Section 3603 exempts from these provisions (other than the prohibition in § 3604(c)) the sale or rental of a single family home if the sale or rental is effected without the use of a broker or sales agent or the employment of any advertisement that would violate § 3604(c). Section 3603 also exempts (except for § 3604(c)) rentals of "rooms or units in dwellings containing living quarters occupied or intended to be occupied by no more than four families living independently of each other, if the owner actually maintains and occupies one of such living quarters as his residence." Section 3607 exempts religious entities and private clubs in some circumstances and provides that the prohibition of familial status discrimination does not apply to housing limited to so-called "retirement communities" or assisted living facilities catering to older people.

NOTES, PROBLEMS, AND QUESTIONS

1. *Scope of the Fair Housing Act and other Laws.* The portion of the Fair Housing Act quoted above is only one part of a larger pattern of legal prohibitions on discriminatory practices. Other parts of the Fair Housing Act prohibit discriminatory practices pertaining to loans that are secured by mortgages on housing and with respect to real estate brokerage. Remedies available to injured parties include damages and injunctive relief.

With the adoption of the Thirteenth, Fourteenth, and Fifteenth Amendments Congress acquired power to enforce their provisions by enacting "appropriate legislation." The Thirteenth Amendment bans slavery, whether sanctioned by law or practiced privately. Key provisions of the Fourteenth Amendment forbid states from denying their residents equal protection of the laws or depriving them of life, liberty, or property without due process of law, and from denying to citizens the privileges and immunities of their federal citizenship. The Fifteenth Amendment forbids states from denying the franchise on account of "race, color, or previous condition of servitude." The 1866 Civil Rights Act, codified at 42 U.S.C. § 1982, was intended to eliminate private racial discrimination in housing: "All citizens of the United States shall have the same right, in every State and Territory, as is enjoyed by white citizens thereof to inherit, purchase, lease, sell, hold, and convey real and personal property." The promise of this law was delayed by the Supreme Court's conclusion in the Civil Rights Cases, 109 U.S. 3 (1883), that congressional power to enforce the substance of the Fourteenth and Fifteenth Amendments was limited to laws directed at state action, not private behavior. The Court also held that, although the Thirteenth Amendment gave Congress power to act upon private behavior, prohibitions of private racial discrimination were sufficiently unrelated to the Amendment's ban of slavery to be outside the enforcement power granted under the Thirteenth Amendment. So matters stood until the Supreme Court, in Jones v. Alfred H. Mayer Co., 392 U.S. 409 (1968), ruled that 42 U.S.C. § 1982 was a valid exercise of congressional power to enforce the Thirteenth Amendment. The Court said that Congress could "rationally ... determine what are the badges and incidents of slavery," and that it was rational for Congress to conclude that private racial discrimination in housing was such a badge or incident.

Even so, 42 U.S.C. § 1982 is both broader and more limited than the Fair Housing Act. It is broader in that there are no exemptions from its coverage. It is more limited in that it applies only to racial discrimination, does not prohibit discriminatory advertising, does not extend to collateral services or facilities, and requires proof of intentional racial discrimination.

A plaintiff makes out a prima facie case of a Fair Housing Act violation by proof of *either* discriminatory *intent* or discriminatory *impact*. See, e.g,. Betsey v. Turtle Creek Associates, 736 F.2d 983 (4th Cir. 1984); Resident Advisory Board v. Rizzo, 564 F.2d 126 (3d Cir. 1977). To use race as the example, proof that a housing pattern or practice produces racially disparate results is ordinarily sufficient to prove discriminatory impact. An individual plaintiff might have to show that after he was denied the housing it was made available to someone of another race or continued to be left on the market. The burden then shifts to the defendant to prove that his action was a bona fide business necessity (e.g., the individual denial was due to the plaintiff's unemployed status coupled with an extremely bad credit rating). Even then, the plaintiff has one last chance to prove that the business necessity was actually a pretext for forbidden discrimination (e.g., the unit was rented to a person of another race who was unemployed and had an equally poor credit rating).

2. Problems.

a. *L* owns a building in which 90% of the tenants are African–American. *L* leases the building to University for housing of its students. The lease stipulates that University will pay rental in an amount that is equal to the present total rentals of the building (regardless of how fully it is occupied by University students), assume the expense of insurance, maintenance and management of the building, repair all damage and wear and tear at its expense, and pay the rent in two lump sums (half in September and half in January) each year. Although University maintains a non-discriminatory housing policy, about 90% of the University students that will occupy the building are white. *L* refuses to renew any lease with its existing tenants in order to deliver occupancy to University but offers comparable housing in another building it owns. Does this violate either 42 U.S.C. § 1983 or 42 U.S.C. § 3604? See Dreher v. Rana Management, Inc., 493 F.Supp. 930 (E.D. N.Y. 1980).

b. Suppose Norman places the following advertisement in a newspaper that circulates mostly among college students:

> Roommate needed: White computer geek wants fellow geek to share rent/utilities equally in a 2BR apt. 1 block from computing center. No smokers; no neurotics; fluent English essential. Send e-mail to ngeek@ uunniversity.edu.

Bill, an African–American computer geek who is not a smoker, is rejected by Norman as a roommate. Is either or both of 42 U.S.C. § 1982 and 42 U.S.C. § 3604 violated?

c. *L*, a public housing authority in Detroit, a city that has experienced pronounced ''white flight,'' decides to prefer white applicants when the proportion of white to non-white tenants falls below 25%. All parties agree that *L*'s motivation is solely its desire to maintain racially integrated housing. Is § 3604 violated?

d. *L*, a public housing authority, has a number of criteria it uses to consider whether it will make subsidized public housing available to applicants. Among them is the "ability to live independently with only minimal aid." Does this violate the Fair Housing Act?

e. *T*, a tenant of *L*, suffers from schizophrenia and manifests this condition by loud screaming and slamming of doors in his apartment at all hours of the day and night. This has produced numerous complaints from other tenants. After *L* has soundproofed the front door of *T*'s apartment, but to no effect, *L* refuses *T*'s request that he or the complaining tenants be relocated to another apartment or, alternatively, that *L* soundproof the entirety of *T*'s apartment. *L* refuses to renew the month-to-month tenancy of *T*. Has the Fair Housing Act been violated?

f. *L* refuses to rent to *T* because *T* is law student and *L* believes that law students are troublesome and litigious. Has the Fair Housing Act been violated?

3. *State Laws and Constitutional Protection of Religious Beliefs.* Many states prohibit housing discrimination on the basis of marital status or sexual orientation, in addition to the forms of discrimination prohibited by the Fair Housing Act. Suppose that in such a state *L* refuses to rent an apartment to an unmarried opposite-sex couple and to an unmarried same-sex couple. In each case *L* honestly states that his refusal is based on his religious beliefs. Under Employment Division v. Smith, 494 U.S. 872 (1990), laws of general applicability that incidentally frustrate religious beliefs are valid, and do not violate the First Amendment's guarantee of free exercise of religion. State constitutions may provide more extensive protection to religious belief, and some do so, usually by requiring the state to prove it has a compelling reason to infringe substantially religious belief or conduct, and that the particular infringement is necessary to achieve that compelling interest. In Swanner v. Anchorage Equal Rights Commission, 874 P.2d 274 (Alaska 1994), the Alaska Supreme Court concluded that Alaska's ban of marital status discrimination violated neither the federal nor Alaska Constitution. The law was of general applicability and even though the Alaska Constitution requires the government to prove the necessity of the ban to achieve its compelling interest of combating discrimination, that burden was sustained, in part because of the landlord's voluntary participation in the commercial housing market.

The Massachusetts Constitution imposes a similarly strict burden of justification on governments, but in Attorney General v. Desilets, 418 Mass. 316 (1994), the Massachusetts Supreme Judicial Court concluded that a trial was necessary to determine whether, in each individual case, the state had a sufficiently compelling interest to justify the infringement of religious belief. Three justices thought that the state could never justify the infringement, and one justice thought that only proof of a disturbance of the public peace would suffice.

In substantial accord with *Swanner* is Smith v. Fair Employment & Housing Commission, 12 Cal.4th 1143 (1996), although the California Supreme Court did not think that the burden on the objecting landlord was substantial. See also Levin v. Yeshiva University, 96 N.Y.2d 484 (2001), involving only the question of whether a university's limitation of certain housing to married students violated the state's prohibition of discrimination on the basis of sexual orientation. Constitutional claims based on religious belief were not raised.

2. DELIVERY OF POSSESSION

A landlord has a duty to deliver possession of the leased premises to the tenant. There is no dispute about this when the premises are vacant on the date that the term begins. But if the premises are occupied on that date, problems erupt. There are three types of occupants that might be in possession when the tenant expects to move in: the landlord, a wrongful occupant (such as a holdover tenant or a trespasser), or a third party with a valid claim to possession. Wrongful occupants are either holdover tenants or trespassers. There are a variety of possible third parties with a valid claim to possession. For example, the landlord might have rented the same premises to two different tenants for the same time period, or the landlord might have a defective title to the fee, and the rival owner of the fee is in possession. The usual problem, though, is the presence of a holdover tenant.

When that happens, does the tenant have the right to terminate the lease, or seek damages from the landlord? The answer depends upon whether the landlord has discharged his duty to deliver possession. This duty is an implied term of every lease. The so-called American rule is that the landlord has fulfilled his duty so long as he has given the tenant the legal right to possession. The English rule, by contrast, is that the landlord has a duty to deliver actual possession to the tenant. The American rule may have predominated at an earlier time, but today most American states apply the English rule. See Restatement (Second) of Property, Landlord and Tenant § 6.2 (1977); Uniform Residential Landlord and Tenant Act § 2.103. Note that in some states the parties may alter this duty by explicit provisions in the lease. See Rest. (2d) Property, Landlord & Tenant § 6.2. The URLTA is ambiguous on this point. See URLTA §§ 1.403, 2.103. Thus, in general the parties may contract for the American rule in an English rule state, or for the English rule in an American rule state.

Under the American rule, the landlord's duty is breached if he has rented the space to two tenants for the same time, if a third party has a better title to the property than does the landlord, or if the landlord himself is in possession and frustrating the tenant's ability to move in. Each of those examples is a breach of the duty to deliver a legal right to possession. But if the premises are occupied by a wrongful occupant, such as a holdover tenant, the landlord has delivered the legal right to possession. Under the American rule, the wrongful occupant is the tenant's problem. The new tenant must evict the holdover and, if possible, obtain damages from the holdover for the denial of occupancy.

The English rule imposes on the landlord the duty to deal with the holdover. The landlord must evict the holdover, and the landlord is liable for damages to the incoming tenant for his failure to deliver actual possession. Of course, the landlord can recover damages from the hold-over, but if that damage recovery is capped at, say, double rent for the holdover period, and the incoming tenant's damages exceed that amount, the landlord may be left out-of-pocket.

Who should bear the risk that an outgoing tenant may become a holdover? A common justification for the American rule is that the landlord should not be held liable for a third party's wrong. Another justification is that the new tenant has adequate remedies against the holdover. Of course, in every jurisdiction the landlord is also able to proceed against the wrongful occupant, so the presence of an adequate remedy possessed by the incoming tenant says nothing about which party—landlord or new tenant—should be required to bear the burden of ousting the wrongdoer. The English rule is usually justified by the argument that, especially with respect to holdovers (the usual problem), the landlord is in a better position to prevent the problem from occurring in the first place. Another argument for the English rule is that actual possession is what a tenant reasonably expects to have, and placing the burden on the landlord to deliver actual possession is better calculated to make that happen.

Arguments for each rule. [handwritten marginal note]

PROBLEMS

1. In an English rule state, *L* leases Suite 101 in Blackacre Towers to *T* for a one year term beginning on March 1, 2013. On that date, Suite 101 is vacant but *T* is delayed moving in. On March 5, *X*, a tenant who occupies Suite 102, adjacent to Suite 101, finds the door to Suite 101 unlocked, stores 250 boxes of documents in Suite 101, and changes the lock. On March 10, *T* attempts to move in but finds that his key will not work. After engaging a locksmith to open the door, *T* discovers the boxes within. What are *T*'s remedies? See Fabrique, Inc. v. Corman, 796 S.W.2d 790 (Tex. App. 1990).

2. In an English rule state, *L* leases "the entirety of Whiteacre" to *T* for a one year term commencing on July 1, 2013. Whiteacre consists of one large ground level space, a storage attic, and full basement. When *T* moves in, he notes that the basement contains a large quantity of boxes and equipment that belong to *L*. Does *T* have a remedy against *L*? Would the answer be different in an American rule state? See, e.g., Warren v. Greenfield, 407 Pa.Super. 600, 595 A.2d 1308 (1991).

3. *L* leases Redacre to *T* for a five year term, beginning August 1, 2013. At the time *T* executes the lease he knows that *L* had leased Redacre to *Y* for a five year term ending on September 30, 2015, but that *Y* had never taken possession of Redacre, had no intention of doing so, and that *L* had taken no action of any kind against *Y*. After going into possession, *T* receives a letter from *Y*, informing him that *Y* has a valid lease and that he may take possession of Redacre "at any moment." *T* stays put in Redacre but stops paying rent. *L* sues *T* for rent and *T* counterclaims to recover rent that he has already paid. What result? Compare Campbell v. Hensley, 450 S.W.2d 501 (Ky. App. 1970), and Sloan v. Hart, 150 N.C. 269 (1909), with Moore v.

Cameron Parish School Board, 563 So.2d 347 (La. App. 1990), and Morrison v. Weinstein, 151 Ark. 255 (1921).

C. SUBLEASES AND ASSIGNMENTS OF LEASEHOLDS

In general, a tenant may freely transfer the leasehold unless the lease contains limitations upon this right, the tenancy is one at will, or the lease involves personal services and transfer would substantially impair the prospect of performance of those services. See Restatement (Second) of Property, Landlord and Tenant § 15.1. Some states have enacted statutes that deny to tenants the ability to transfer without the landlord's consent. See, e.g, Alaska Stat. § 34.03.060 (2010).

A transfer may be either an *assignment* or a *sublease.* Important consequences flow from which type of transfer has occurred.

JABER v. MILLER

Supreme Court of Arkansas
219 Ark. 59 (1951)

SMITH, J., delivered the opinion of the court.

This is a suit brought by Miller to obtain cancellation of fourteen promissory notes, each in the sum of $175, held by the appellant, Jaber. [Miller's] theory is that these notes represent monthly rent upon a certain business building in Fort Smith for the period beginning January 1, 1950, and ending March 1, 1951. The building was destroyed by fire on December 3, 1949, and [Miller] contends that his obligation to pay rent then terminated. [Jaber] contends that the notes were given not for rent but as deferred payments for the assignment of a lease formerly held by Jaber. The chancellor, in an opinion reflecting a careful study of the matter, concluded that the notes were intended to be rental payments and therefore should be canceled.

In 1945 Jaber rented the building from its owner for a five-year term beginning March 1, 1946, and ending March 1, 1951. The lease reserved a monthly rent of $200 and provided that the lease would terminate if the premises were destroyed by fire. Jaber conducted a rug shop in the building until 1949, when he sold his stock of merchandise at public auction and transferred the lease to Norber & Son. Whether this instrument of transfer is an assignment or a sublease is the pivotal issue in this case.

In form the document is an assignment rather than a sublease. It is entitled "Contract and Assignment." After reciting the existence of the five-year lease the instrument provides that Jaber "hereby transfers and assigns" to Norber & Son "the aforesaid lease contract ... for the remainder of the term of said lease." It also provides that "in consideration of the sale and assignment of said lease contract" Norber & Son have paid Jaber $700 in cash and have executed five promissory notes for $700 each, due serially at specified four-month intervals. Norber & Son agree to pay to the owner of the property the stipulated rental of $200 a month, and Jaber reserves the right to retake possession if Norber & Son fail to pay the rent or the notes. The instrument contains no provision governing the rights of the parties in case the building is destroyed by fire.

Later on the plaintiff, Miller, obtained a transfer of the lease from Norber & Son. Miller, being unable to pay the $700 notes as they came due, arranged with Jaber to divide the payments into monthly installments of $175 each. He and the Norbers accordingly executed the notes now in controversy, which Jaber accepted in substitution for those of the original notes that were still unpaid. When the premises burned Miller contended that Jaber's transfer to Norber & Son had been a sublease rather than an assignment and that the notes therefore represented rent. Miller now argues that, under the rule that a sublease terminates when the primary lease terminates, his sublease ended when the fire had the effect of terminating the original lease.

In most jurisdictions the question of whether an instrument is an assignment or a sublease is determined by principles applicable to feudal tenures. In a line of cases beginning in the year 1371 the English courts worked out the rules for distinguishing between an assignment and a sublease. . . . The doctrine established in England is quite simple: If the instrument purports to transfer the lessee's estate for the entire remainder of the term it is an assignment, regardless of its form or of the parties' intention. Conversely, if the instrument purports to transfer the lessee's estate for less than the entire term—even for a day less—it is a sublease, regardless of its form or of the parties' intention.

The arbitrary distinction drawn at common law is manifestly at variance with the usual conception of assignments and subleases. We think of an assignment as the outright transfer of all or part of an existing lease, the assignee stepping into the shoes of the assignor. A sublease, on the other hand, involves the creation of a new tenancy between the sublessor and the sublessee, so that the sublessor is both a tenant and a landlord. The common law distinction is logical only in the light of feudal property law.

In feudal times every one except the king held land by tenure from some one higher in the hierarchy of feudal ownership. "The king himself holds land which is in every sense his own; no one else has any proprietary right in it; but [the] person whom we may call its owner . . . holds the land of the king either immediately or mediately. In the simplest case he holds it immediately of the king; only the king and he have rights in it. But it well may happen that between him and the king there stand other persons; Z holds immediately of Y, who holds of X, who holds of V, who holds . . . of A, who holds of the king." Pollock and Maitland, History of English Law (2d Ed.), vol. I, p. 232. In feudal law each person owed duties, such as that of military service or the payment of rent, to his overlord. . . .

It is evident that in feudal theory a person must himself have an estate in the land in order to maintain his place in the structure of ownership. Hence if a tenant transferred his entire term he parted with his interest in the property. The English courts therefore held that the transferee of the entire term held of the original lessor, that such a transferee was bound by the covenants in the original lease, and that he was entitled to enforce whatever duties that lease imposed upon the landlord. The intention of the parties had nothing to do with the matter; the sole question was whether the first lessee retained a reversion that enabled him to hold his place in the chain of ownership.

The injustice of these inflexible rules has often been pointed out. Suppose that *A* makes a lease to *B* for a certain rental. *B* then executes to *C* what both parties intend to be a sublease as that term is generally understood, but the sublease is for the entire term. If *C* in good faith pays his rent to *B,* as the contract requires, he does so at his peril. For the courts say that the contract is really an assignment, and therefore *C*'s primary obligation is to *A* if the latter elects to accept *C* as his tenant. Consequently *A* can collect the rent from the subtenant even though the sublessor has already been paid. . . .

Not only may the common law rule operate with injustice to the subtenant; it can be equally harsh upon the sublessor. Again suppose that *A* makes a lease to *B* for a certain rental. *B* then makes to *C* what *B* considers a profitable sublease for twice the original rent. But *B* makes the mistake of attempting to sublet for the entire term instead of retaining a reversion of a day. The instrument is therefore an assignment, and if the original landlord acquires the subtenant's rights there is a merger which prevents *B* from being able to collect the increased rent. That was the situation in Webb v. Russell, 3 T. R. 393, 100 Eng. Reprint 639 [(1789)]. The court felt compelled to recognize the merger, but in doing so Lord Kenyon said [the result was] "of a most unrighteous ... nature." Kent, in his Commentaries (14th Ed.), p. 105, refers to this case as "reaching an inequitable result;" Williams and Eastwood, in their work on Real Property, p. 206, call it an "unpleasant result." Yet when the identical question arose in California the court felt bound to hold that the same distasteful merger had taken place. Smiley v. Van Winkle, 6 Calif. 605 [(1856)].

A decided majority of the American courts have adopted the English doctrine in its entirety. Tiffany, Landlord & Tenant, § 151. A minority of our courts have made timid but praiseworthy attempts to soften the harshness of the common law rule. ... [Some] courts have gone as far as possible to find something that might be said to constitute a reversion in what the parties intended to be a sublease. In some States, notably Massachusetts, it has been held that if the sublessor reserves a right of reentry for nonpayment of rent this is a sufficient reversionary estate to make the instrument a sublease. Dunlap v. Bullard, 131 Mass. 161 [(1881)]; Davis v. Vidal, 105 Tex. 444 [(1912)]. ... [Miller] urges us to follow the Massachusetts rule and to hold that since Jaber reserved rights of reentry his transfer to Norber & Son was a sublease. We are not in sympathy with this view. It may be true that a right of re-entry for condition broken has now attained the status of an estate in Arkansas. See Moore v. Sharpe, 91 Ark. 407 [(1909)]. Even so, the Massachusetts rule was adopted to carry out the intention of parties who thought they were making a sublease rather than an assignment. Here the instrument is in form an assignment, and it would be an obvious perversion of the rule to apply it as a means of defeating intention. . . .

[We] do not feel compelled to adhere to an unjust rule which was logical only in the days of feudalism. The execution of leases is a very practical matter that occurs a hundred times a day without legal assistance. The layman appreciates the common sense distinction between a sublease and an assignment, but he would not even suspect the existence of the common law distinction. "Every one knows that a tenant may in turn let to others, and the latter thereby assumes no obligations to the owner of the property; but who would guess that this could only be done for a time falling short by something—a day or an hour is sufficient—of the whole term? And who, not familiar with the subject of feudal tenures, could give a reason why it is held to be so?" It was of such a situation that Holmes was thinking when he said: "It is revolting to have no better reason for a rule than that so it was laid down in the time of Henry IV. It is still more revolting if the grounds upon which it was laid down have vanished long since, and the rule simply persists from blind imitation of the past." The Path of the Law, 10 Harv. L. Rev. 457, 469. The rule now in question was laid down some years before the reign of Henry IV.

The English distinction between an assignment and a sublease is not a rule of property in the sense that titles or property rights depend upon its continued existence. A lawyer trained in common law technicalities can prepare either instrument without fear that it will be construed to be the other. But for the less skilled lawyer or for the layman the common law rule is simply a trap that leads to hardship and injustice by refusing to permit the parties to accomplish the result they seek.

For these reasons we adopt as the rule in this State the principle that the intention of the parties is to govern in determining whether an instrument is an assignment or a sublease. If, for example, a tenant has leased an apartment for a year and is compelled to move to another city, we know of no reason why he should not be able to sublease it for a higher rent without needlessly retaining a reversion for the last day of the term. The duration of the primary term, as compared to the length of the sublease, may in some instances be a factor in arriving at the parties' intention, but we do not think it should be the sole consideration. . . .

In the case at bar it cannot be doubted that the parties intended an assignment and not a sublease. The document is so entitled. All its language is that of an assignment rather than that of a sublease. The consideration is stated to be in payment for the lease and not in satisfaction of a tenant's debt to his landlord. The deferred payments are evidenced by promissory notes, which are not ordinarily given by one making a lease. From the appellee's point of view it is unfortunate that the assignment makes no provision for the contingency of a fire, but the appellant's position is certainly not without equity. Jaber sold his merchandise at public auction, and doubtless at reduced prices, in order to vacate the premises for his assignees. Whether he would have taken the same course had the contract provided for a cancellation of the deferred payments in case of a fire we have no way of knowing. A decision either way works a hardship on the losing party. In this situation we do not feel called upon to supply a provision in the assignment which might have been, but was not, demanded by the assignees.

Reversed.

NOTES AND PROBLEMS

1. Distinguishing subleases and assignments. As the *Jaber* court indicates, there are two dominant approaches to the problem. The approach taken by the *Jaber* court is to look to the intentions of the parties, regardless of how they may style the arrangement or whether the entire remaining interest of the original lessee is transferred. The traditional approach is to determine whether the original lessee has retained a reversion—of any duration, however short. If he has, a sublease is the result; if he has not done so, an assignment is the result. A variation on this approach is to treat the original lessee's retention of a right of entry (power of termination) as a sufficient "reversion" to constitute creation of a sublease.

> *Example 6–1: L* leases Blackacre to *T1,* who later transfers his entire interest in the lease to *T2,* under an instrument that gives *T1* the right to retake possession if *T2* should default on the rent payments. This variation accepts the common law rule but broadens the concept of a "reversion" beyond what the common law would recognize as sufficient to create a sublease. Under the intentions approach, it might well be argued that the parties intended to create a sublease because the retention of a power of termination is evidence of a mutual desire to allow the original lessee to regain possession (and his tenancy) in the event the transferee should default.

2. Privity of Estate and Privity of Contract. In order to fully understand the consequences of the distinction between a sublease and an assignment it is essential to grasp the differences between these two terms. *Privity,* by itself, is simply a shorthand way to describe the relationship between two parties with respect to a third thing. The term acquires different meanings, depending on the nature of that "third thing." Thus, *privity of estate* describes the voluntary relationship two parties have with respect to an estate in land, while *privity of contract* describes the voluntary relationship of two parties with respect to an agreement between themselves or others.

> *Example 6–2: L* leases Blackacre to *T1* for a five year term, beginning January 1, 2012. *T1* takes possession of Blackacre. *L* and *T1* are in privity of estate because they have voluntarily carved a leasehold out of *L*'s

freehold estate. *L* and *T1* are also in privity of contract by virtue of their voluntary entry into the contract that is the lease.

A sublease creates a new contract between the original lessee and the sub-lessee, so privity of contract exists between them but not between the landlord and the sub-lessee, as there is no contract between them. Nor is there privity of estate between the landlord and the sub-lessee, because (according to the traditional common law rule) the sub-lessee has an estate that is of lesser duration than the estate held by the original tenant under the head lease.

By contrast, an assignment transfers the entirety of the estate held by the original tenant to the transferee, thus placing the transferee in privity of estate with the landlord and ending the original tenant's privity of estate. But that transfer does not relieve the original tenant of liability on the lease contract he made with the landlord. The original tenant remains in privity of contract with the landlord. Of course, the landlord can agree to release the original tenant of that contractual liability—called a novation—but unless the landlord does so the original tenant remains liable for the performance of the lease terms, including rent.

It is also possible that the transferee may enter into privity of contract with the landlord, by agreeing to assume the obligations of the original tenant under the head lease. This is true even if the agreement to assume the head lease obligations is only between the original tenant and the transferee. The agreement to assume is for the benefit of the landlord; thus the landlord is in privity of contract with the transferee as a third-party beneficiary of the assumption agreement.

3. Problems.

a. *L* leases office space to *T1* for a five year term ending on July 31, 2017, for a monthly rental of $1000, pursuant to a lease that permits transfer of the leasehold upon the consent of *L*. In June 2013, *T1* obtains *L*'s consent to a transfer of the leasehold to *T2*. *T1* and *T2* then enter into a "Transfer Agreement" by which *T1* "assigns, transfers, and leases" the office space to *T2* for the period "beginning immediately and ending on July 31, 2017," for a monthly rental of $1050, payable to *T1*. The Transfer Agreement gives *T1* the right to retake possession should *T2* default in the payment of rent. *T2* pays the rent to *T1*, but *T1* makes no rent payments to *L*. *L* then terminates the lease to *T1*, as he is permitted to do under that lease, and seeks to evict *T2* and collect back rent from *T2*. *T2* asserts that he is not liable for back rent because he paid it to *T1* and is entitled to retain possession because he has not defaulted on the rent and *L* consented to the Transfer Agreement. What result? Would the result be different if *T1* surrendered the lease to *L* and *L* accepted the surrender?

b. *L* leases a commercial store to *T1* for a term ending on June 30, 2015. On April 1, 2014, *L* consents to the assignment of the lease from *T1* to *T2*, "so long as *T2* expressly agrees to assume and perform all of *T1*'s obligations under the lease." *T1* and *T2* then enter into an agreement entitled "Assignment and Assumption," under which *T1* assigns "all of his right, title, and interest" in the lease to *T2* and *T2* "assumes and agrees to perform all of the tenant's obligations under the lease from *L* to *T1*." On December 31, 2014 *T2* stops paying rent. *L* diligently attempts to rent the store but cannot do so. *L* seeks to recover the last six months of rent. Is *T1* liable? Is *T2* liable?

    c. *L* leases a warehouse to *T1* for a ten year term ending on August 31, 2021. In July 2015 *T1* subleases the warehouse, with *L*'s consent, to *T2* for a two year term ending on July 31, 2017. As of January 1, 2017, *T2*, who is current on the rent, assigns his sublease, with *T1*'s consent, to *T3*, who agrees to assume the obligations of the master lease for the period of his sub-tenancy. *T3* never makes any rent payments. On August 1, 2017 *T1* retakes possession and resumes making rent payments to *L*. However, *L* seeks to recover rent for the period from Jan. 1, 2017 through July 31, 2017. Is *T1* liable for that rent? Is *T2* liable? Is *T3* liable? What are the rights and obligations of *T1, T2,* and *T3* to each other?

KENDALL v. ERNEST PESTANA, INC.

Supreme Court of California
40 Cal.3d 488 (1985)

BROUSSARD, J., delivered the opinion of the court.

This case concerns the effect of a provision in a commercial lease[1] that the lessee may not assign the lease or sublet the premises without the lessor's prior written consent. The question we address is whether, in the absence of a provision that such consent will not be unreasonably withheld, a lessor may unreasonably and arbitrarily withhold his or her consent to an assignment.[2] This is a question of first impression in this court.

    I. ... The allegations of the complaint may be summarized as follows. The lease at issue is for 14,400 square feet of hangar space at the San Jose Municipal Airport. The City of San Jose, as owner of the property, leased it to Irving and Janice Perlitch, who in turn assigned their interest to respondent Ernest Pestana, Inc. Prior to assigning their interest to respondent, the Perlitches entered into a 25–year sublease with one Robert Bixler commencing on January 1, 1970. The sublease covered an original five-year term plus four 5–year options to renew. The rental rate was to be increased every 10 years in the same proportion as rents increased on the master lease from the City of San Jose. The premises were to be used by Bixler for the purpose of conducting an airplane maintenance business. Bixler conducted such a business under the name "Flight Services" until, in 1981, he agreed to sell the business to appellants Jack Kendall, Grady O'Hara and Vicki O'Hara. The proposed sale included the business and the equipment, inventory and improvements on the property, together with the existing lease. The proposed assignees had a stronger financial statement and greater net worth than the current lessee, Bixler, and they were willing to be bound by the terms of the lease.

---

    1. We are presented only with a commercial lease and therefore do not address the question whether residential leases are controlled by the principles articulated in this opinion.

    2. Since the present case involves an assignment rather than a sublease, we will speak primarily in terms of assignments. However, our holding applies equally to subleases....

The lease provided that written consent of the lessor was required before the lessee could assign his interest, and that failure to obtain such consent rendered the lease voidable at the option of the lessor.[3] Accordingly, Bixler requested consent from the Perlitches' successor-in-interest, respondent Ernest Pestana, Inc. Respondent refused to consent to the assignment and maintained that it had an absolute right arbitrarily to refuse any such request. The complaint recites that respondent demanded "increased rent and other more onerous terms" as a condition of consenting to Bixler's transfer of interest.

The proposed assignees brought suit for declaratory and injunctive relief and damages seeking ... a declaration "that the refusal of Ernest Pestana, Inc. to consent to the assignment of the lease is unreasonable and is an unlawful restraint on the freedom of alienation...." The trial court sustained a demurrer to the complaint without leave to amend and this appeal followed.

II. The law generally favors free alienability of property, and California follows the common law rule that a leasehold interest is freely alienable. [Kassan v. Stout, 9 Cal.3d 39, 43 (1973).] Contractual restrictions on the alienability of leasehold interests are, however, permitted. [Id.] "Such restrictions are justified as reasonable protection of the interests of the lessor as to who shall possess and manage property in which he has a reversionary interest and from which he is deriving income." (Schoshinski, American Law of Landlord and Tenant (1980) § 8:15, at pp. 578–579. See also 2 Powell on Real Property, para. 246[1], at p. 372.97.) The common law's hostility toward restraints on alienation has caused such restraints on leasehold interests to be strictly construed against the lessor.[4] [Chapman v. Great Western Gypsum Co., 216 Cal. 420 (1932).] This is particularly true where the restraint in question is a "forfeiture restraint," under which the lessor has the option to terminate

---

3. Paragraph 13 of the sublease between the Perlitches and Bixler provides: "Lessee shall not assign this lease, or any interest therein, and shall not sublet the said premises or any part thereof, or any right or privilege appurtenant thereto, or suffer any other person (the agents and servants of Lessee excepted) to occupy or use said premises, or any portion thereof, without written consent of Lessor first had and obtained, and a consent to one assignment, subletting, occupation or use by any other person, shall not be deemed to be a consent to any subsequent assignment, subletting, occupation or use by another person. Any such assignment or subletting without this consent shall be void, and shall, at the option of Lessor, terminate this lease. This lease shall not, nor shall any interest therein, be assignable, as to the interest of lessee, by operation of a law [sic], without the written consent of Lessor."

4. There are many examples of the narrow effect given to lease terms purporting to restrict assignment. Covenants against assignment without the prior consent of the lessor have been held not to affect the lessee's right to sublease [Stevinson v. Joy, 164 Cal. 279, 286 (1912)], to mortgage the leasehold [Chapman v. Great Western Gypsum Co.], or to assign his or her interest to a cotenant [Hoops v. Tate, 104 Cal. App. 2d 486 (1951)]. Such covenants also do not prevent transfer of a leasehold interest by will [Burns v. McGraw, 75 Cal. App. 2d 481 (1946)], by bankruptcy [Farnum v. Hefner, 79 Cal. 575, 580 (1889)], by the personal representative of a deceased tenant [Joost v. Castel, 33 Cal. App. 2d 138, 141 (1939)] or by transfer among partners [Safeway Stores, Inc. v. Buhlinger, 85 Cal. App. 717, 718–719 (1927)] or spouses [Buck v. Cardwell, 161 Cal. App. 2d 830, 835 (1958)]. Covenants against assignment furthermore do not prohibit transfer of the stock of a corporate tenant [Ser–Bye Corp. v. C.P. & G. Market, Inc., 78 Cal. App. 2d 915, 920–921 (1947)] or assignment of a lease to a corporation wholly owned by the tenant [Sexton v. Nelson, 228 Cal. App. 2d 248, 258–259 (1964)].

the lease if an assignment is made without his or her consent. [Karbelnig v. Brothwell, 244 Cal. App. 2d 333, 341 (1966); Civ. Code, § 1442 ("A condition involving a forfeiture must be strictly interpreted against the party for whose benefit it is created.")].

Nevertheless, a majority of jurisdictions have long adhered to the rule that where a lease contains ... a clause stating that the lease cannot be assigned without the prior consent of the lessor, the lessor may arbitrarily refuse to approve a proposed assignee no matter how suitable the assignee appears to be and no matter how unreasonable the lessor's objection. The harsh consequences of this rule have often been avoided through application of the doctrines of waiver and estoppel, under which the lessor may be found to have waived (or be estopped from asserting) the right to refuse consent to assignment.

The traditional majority rule has come under steady attack in recent years. A growing minority of jurisdictions now hold that where a lease provides for assignment only with the prior consent of the lessor, such consent may be withheld *only where the lessor has a commercially reasonable objection to the assignment*, even in the absence of a provision in the lease stating that consent to assignment will not be unreasonably withheld. [Boss Barbara, Inc. v. Newbill, 97 N.M. 239 (1982); Jack Frost Sales v. Harris Trust & Sav. Bank, 104 Ill. App.3d 933 (1982); Fernandez v. Vasquez, 397 So.2d 1171 (Fla. App. 1981); Warmack v. Merchants Nat. Bank of Fort Smith, 272 Ark. 166 (1981); Funk v. Funk, 102 Idaho 521 (1981); Hendrickson v. Freericks, 620 P.2d 205 (Alaska 1980); Homa–Goff Interiors, Inc. v. Cowden, 350 So.2d 1035 (Ala. 1977); Shaker Building Co. v. Federal Lime & Stone Co., 28 Ohio Misc. 246 (1971); Rest.2d Property, § 15.2(2) (1977); Annot., 21 A.L.R.4th 188 (1983).]

For the reasons discussed below, we conclude that the minority rule is the preferable position....

III. The impetus for change in the majority rule has come from two directions, reflecting the dual nature of a lease as a conveyance of a leasehold interest and a contract. [Medico–Dental etc. Co. v. Horton & Converse, 21 Cal.2d 411, 418 (1942).] The policy against restraints on alienation pertains to leases in their nature as *conveyances*. Numerous courts and commentators have recognized that "[in] recent times the necessity of permitting reasonable alienation of commercial space has become paramount in our increasingly urban society." [Schweiso v. Williams, 150 Cal. App. 3d 883, 887 (1984).] Civil Code section 711 provides: "Conditions restraining alienation, when repugnant to the interest created, are void." It is well settled that this rule is not absolute in its application, but forbids only *unreasonable* restraints on alienation. [Wellenkamp v. Bank of America, 21 Cal.3d 943, 948 (1978).] Reasonableness is determined by comparing the justification for a particular restraint on alienation with the quantum of restraint actually imposed by it. "[The] greater the quantum of restraint that results from enforcement of a given clause, the greater must be the justification for that enforcement." [*Wellenkamp.*]

In Cohen v. Ratinoff, 147 Cal. App. 3d 321 (1983), the court examined the reasonableness of the restraint created by an approval clause in a lease: "Because the lessor has an interest in the character of the proposed commercial assignee, we cannot say that an assignment provision requiring the lessor's consent to an assignment is inherently repugnant to the leasehold interest created. We do conclude, however, that *if such an assignment provision is implemented in such a manner that its underlying purpose is perverted by the arbitrary or unreasonable withholding of consent, an unreasonable restraint on alienation is established.*" (Id., italics added.)[5]

The Restatement Second of Property adopts the minority rule on the validity of approval clauses in leases: "A restraint on alienation without the consent of the landlord of a tenant's interest in leased property is valid, *but the landlord's consent to an alienation by the tenant cannot be withheld unreasonably,* unless a freely negotiated provision in the lease gives the landlord an absolute right to withhold consent." (Rest.2d Property, § 15.2(2) (1977), italics added.)[6] A comment to the section explains: "The landlord may have an understandable concern about certain personal qualities of a tenant, particularly his reputation for meeting his financial obligations. The preservation of the values that go into the personal selection of the tenant justifies upholding a provision in the lease that curtails the right of the tenant to put anyone else in his place by transferring his interest, but this justification does not go to the point of allowing the landlord arbitrarily and without reason to refuse to allow the tenant to transfer an interest in leased property." [Id., comment a.) Under the Restatement rule, the lessor's interest in the character of his or her tenant is protected by the lessor's right to object to a proposed assignee on reasonable commercial grounds. (See id., reporter's note 7 at pp. 112–113.) The lessor's interests are also protected by the fact that the original lessee remains liable to the lessor as a surety even if the lessor consents to the assignment and the assignee expressly assumes the obligations of the lease. [Peiser v. Mettler, 50 Cal.2d 594, 602 (1958).]

The second impetus for change in the majority rule comes from the nature of a lease as a *contract*. As ... observed in *Cohen* ... "there has been an increased recognition of and emphasis on the duty of good faith and fair dealing inherent in every contract." Thus, "[in] every contract there is an implied covenant that neither party shall do anything which will have the effect of destroying or injuring the right of the other party to

5. [Footnote relocated, Ed.—] Statutes have been enacted in at least four states prohibiting lessors from arbitrarily refusing consent to the assignment of leases. (Alaska Stat., § 34.03.060 (1975) [residential leases only]; Del. Code Ann., tit. 25, § 5512, subd. (b) (1974) [residential, commercial and farm leases]; Hawaii Rev. Stat., § 516–63 [residential leases only]; N.Y. Real Prop. Law, § 226–b (McKinney 1982) [residential leases only])....

6. This case does not present the question of the validity of a clause absolutely prohibiting assignment, or granting absolute discretion over assignment to the lessor. We note that under the Restatement rule such a provision would be valid if freely negotiated.

receive the fruits of the contract. . . ." [Universal Sales Corp. v. California Press Mfg. Co., 20 Cal.2d 751, 771 (1942).] "[Where] a contract confers on one party a discretionary power affecting the rights of the other, a duty is imposed to exercise that discretion in good faith and in accordance with fair dealing." [California Lettuce Growers v. Union Sugar Co., 45 Cal.2d 474, 484 (1955).] Here the lessor retains the discretionary power to approve or disapprove an assignee proposed by the other party to the contract; this discretionary power should therefore be exercised in accordance with commercially reasonable standards. . . .

Under the minority rule, the determination whether a lessor's refusal to consent was reasonable is a question of fact. Some of the factors that the trier of fact may properly consider in applying the standards of good faith and commercial reasonableness are: financial responsibility of the proposed assignee; suitability of the use for the particular property; legality of the proposed use; need for alteration of the premises; and nature of the occupancy, i.e., office, factory, clinic, etc. Denying consent solely on the basis of personal taste, convenience or sensibility is not commercially reasonable. Nor is it reasonable to deny consent "in order that the landlord may charge a higher rent than originally contracted for." [*Schweiso*.] This is because the lessor's desire for a better bargain than contracted for has nothing to do with the permissible purposes of the restraint on alienation—to protect the lessor's interest in the preservation of the property and the performance of the lease covenants. "[The] clause is for the protection of the landlord *in its ownership and operation of the particular property*—not for its general economic protection." [Krieger v. Helmsley–Spear, Inc., 62 N.J. 423 (1973), italics added.]

In contrast to the policy reasons advanced in favor of the minority rule, the majority rule has traditionally been justified on three grounds. Respondent raises a fourth argument in its favor as well. None of these do we find compelling.

First, it is said that a lease is a conveyance of an interest in real property, and that the lessor, having exercised a personal choice in the selection of a tenant and provided that no substitute shall be acceptable without prior consent, is under no obligation to look to anyone but the lessee for the rent. This argument is based on traditional rules of conveyancing and on concepts of freedom of ownership and control over one's property. A lessor's freedom at common law to look to no one but the lessee for the rent has, however, been undermined by the adoption in California of a rule that lessors—like all other contracting parties—have a duty to mitigate damages upon the lessee's abandonment of the property by seeking a substitute lessee. (See Civ. Code, § 1951.2.) Furthermore, the values that go into the personal selection of a lessee are preserved under the minority rule in the lessor's right to refuse consent to assignment on any commercially reasonable grounds. Such grounds include not only the obvious objections to an assignee's financial stability or proposed use of the premises, but a variety of other commercially reasonable objections as well. [See, e.g., Arrington v. Walter E. Heller International Corp., 30 Ill.

App.3d 631 (1975) (desire to have only one "lead tenant" in order to preserve "image of the building" as tenant's international headquarters); Warmack v. Merchants Nat. Bank of Fort Smith, 272 Ark. 166 (1981) (desire for good "tenant mix" in shopping center); List v. Dahnke, 638 P. 2d 824 (Colo. App. 1981) (lessor's refusal to consent to assignment of lease by one restaurateur to another was reasonable where lessor believed proposed specialty restaurant would not succeed at that location).] The lessor's interests are further protected by the fact that the original lessee remains a guarantor of the performance of the assignee.

The second justification advanced in support of the majority rule is that an approval clause is an unambiguous reservation of absolute discretion in the lessor over assignments of the lease. The lessee could have bargained for the addition of a reasonableness clause to the lease (i.e., "consent to assignment will not be unreasonably withheld"). The lessee having failed to do so, the law should not rewrite the parties' contract for them. [But] the clause is not [as] "clear and unambiguous" as respondent suggests. [For example,] the court in Gamble v. New Orleans Housing Mart, Inc., 154 So.2d 625 (La. App. 1963), stated: "... This does not *prohibit* or *interdict* subleasing. To the contrary, it permits subleasing provided only that the lessee first obtain the written consent of the lessor. *It suggests or connotes that, when the lessee obtains a subtenant acceptable or satisfactory to the lessor, he may sublet.* ... Otherwise the provision simply would prohibit subleasing." (Id., at p. 627, final italics added.) ... [The] assertion that an approval clause "clearly and unambiguously" grants the lessor absolute discretion over assignments is untenable. It is not a rewriting of a contract, as respondent suggests, to recognize the obligations imposed by the duty of good faith and fair dealing, which duty is implied by law in every contract.

The third justification advanced in support of the majority rule is ... the doctrine of stare decisis. It is argued that the courts should not depart from the common law majority rule because "many leases now in effect covering a substantial amount of real property and creating valuable property rights were carefully prepared by competent counsel in reliance upon the majority viewpoint." [But] the majority viewpoint has been far from universally held and has never been adopted by this court. Moreover, the trend in favor of the minority rule should come as no surprise to observers of the changing state of real property law in the 20th century. The minority rule is part of an increasing recognition of the contractual nature of leases and the implications in terms of contractual duties that flow therefrom. . . .

A final argument in favor of the majority rule is [that] "the lessor has a right, under circumstances such as these, to realize the increased value of his property." Respondent essentially argues that any increase in the market value of real property during the term of a lease properly belongs to the lessor, not the lessee. We reject this assertion. One California commentator has written: "[When] the lessee executed the lease he acquired the contractual right for the exclusive use of the premises, and all of the benefits and detriment attendant to possession, for the term of the contract. He took the downside risk that he would be paying too much rent if there should be a depression in the rental market. . . . Why should he be deprived of the contractual benefits of the lease because of the fortuitous inflation in the marketplace[?] By reaping the benefits he does not deprive the landlord of anything to which the landlord was otherwise entitled. The landlord agreed to dispose of possession for the limited term and he could not reasonably anticipate any more than what was given to him by the terms of the lease. His reversionary estate will benefit from the increased value from the inflation in any event, at least upon the expiration of the lease." (4 Miller & Starr, Current Law of Cal. Real Estate (1977) 1984 supp., § 27:92 at p. 321.) Respondent . . . is trying to get *more* than it bargained for in the lease. A lessor is free to build periodic rent increases into a lease, as the lessor did here. Any increased value of the property beyond this "belongs" to the lessor only in the sense . . . that the lessor's reversionary estate will benefit from it upon the expiration of the lease. We must therefore reject respondent's argument in this regard.[7] . . .

IV. In conclusion, both the policy against restraints on alienation and the implied contractual duty of good faith and fair dealing militate in favor of adoption of the rule that where a commercial lease provides for assignment only with the prior consent of the lessor, such consent may be withheld only where the lessor has a commercially reasonable objection to the assignee or the proposed use. Under this rule, appellants have stated a cause of action against respondent Ernest Pestana, Inc. The order sustaining the demurrer to the complaint, which we have deemed to incorporate a judgment of dismissal, is reversed.

LUCAS, J., dissenting.

I respectfully dissent. In my view we should follow the weight of authority which, as acknowledged by the majority herein, allows the commercial lessor to withhold his consent to an assignment or sublease arbitrarily or without reasonable cause. The majority's contrary ruling, requiring a "commercially reasonable objection" to the assignment, can only result in a proliferation of unnecessary litigation.

The correct analysis is contained in the opinion of Justice Carl Anderson for the Court of Appeal in this case. I adopt the following portion of his opinion as my dissent: . . .

The plain language of the lease provides that the lessee *shall not* assign the lease "without written consent of Lessor first had and obtained. . . . Any such assignment or subletting without this consent shall be void, and shall, at the option of Lessor, terminate this lease." The lease does not require that "consent may not unreasonably be withheld"; the lease does not provide that "the lessor may refuse

---

7. Amicus Pillsbury, Madison & Sutro request that we make clear that, "whatever principle governs in the absence of express lease provisions, nothing bars the parties to commercial lease transactions from making their own arrangements respecting the allocation of appreciated rentals if there is a transfer of the leasehold." This principle we affirm; we merely hold that the clause in the instant lease established no such arrangement.

consent only where he has a good faith reasonable objection to the assignment." Neither have the parties so contracted, nor has the Legislature so required. Absent such legislative direction, the parties should be free to contract as they see fit.

Appellant urges this court to rewrite the contract by adding a limitation on the lessor's withholding of consent—"that such consent may not be unreasonably withheld." He urges that such must be implied in the term "without written consent of lessor first had and obtained"; and he places the burden on the lessor to add language to negate that, if such be his intent—language such as "such consent may be arbitrarily, capriciously and/or unreasonably withheld."

However, it is obvious that the attorney for the lessor agreeing to such a term was entitled to rely upon the state of the law then existing in California. And at such time (Dec. 12, 1969), it is clear that California followed the "weight of authority" in these United States and allowed such consent to be arbitrarily or unreasonably withheld absent a provision to the contrary. . . .

Some jurisdictions have overruled the common law, at least as to residential leases, by legislative action. This would appear to be the wisest procedure, if only to effect the repeal prospectively and thereby give force to those contracts entered into when the common law prevailed. . . . [T]hose jurisdictions which reject the temptation to follow what the minority call "the trend" do so because they simply refuse to rewrite unambiguous language within a lease. They so refuse in order to uphold the integrity of the contract and the inalienable rights of citizens to seek and obtain enforcement thereof by the courts. . . .

To rewrite this contract (as appellant would have us do) for the benefit of one who was not an original party thereto, and to the detriment of one who stands in privity with one who was, and to hold that there is a triable issue of fact concerning whether respondents unreasonably withheld their consent when they had already contracted for that right, creates only mischief by breeding further uncertainty in the interpretation of otherwise unambiguously written contracts. To so hold only encourages needless future litigation.

We respectfully suggest that if California is to adopt the minority rule and reject the majority rule which recognizes the current proviso as valid, unambiguous and enforceable, that it do so by clear affirmative legislative action. To so defer to the legislative branch, protects not only this contract but "those tens of thousands of landlords, tenants and lawyers who have relied on our unbroken line of judicial precedent." . . .

NOTES AND QUESTIONS

1. Statutory Postscript. The California Supreme Court noted that the *Kendall* case did not present the question of whether a landlord and tenant could agree to include in the lease an absolute prohibition of transfer of the tenant's interest. The California legislature answered that question in 1989 by enacting a new chapter of the Calif. Civil Code, §§ 1995.010 through 1995.340. That chapter applies only to "transfer of a tenant's interest in a lease of real property for other than residential purposes" Cal. Civ. Code § 1995.010. It provides that a "restriction on transfer of a tenant's interest in a lease may absolutely prohibit transfer." § 1995.230. The Law Revision Commission Comment (1989) to that section noted that it "settles the question raised in Kendall v. Ernest Pestana, Inc., of the validity of a clause absolutely prohibiting assignment or sublease. A lease term actually prohibiting transfer of the tenant's interest is not invalid as a restraint on alienation. Such a term is valid subject to general principles governing freedom of contract, including the adhesion contract doctrine, where applicable." See also Harara v. Conoco Phillips Co., 377 F. Supp. 2d 779 (N.D. Cal. 2005). Section 1995.240 provides that a "restriction on transfer of a tenant's interest in a lease may provide that the transfer is subject to any express standard or condition, including, but not limited to, a provision that the landlord is entitled to some or all of any consideration the tenant receives from a transferee in excess of the rent under the lease." See Carma Developers (California), Inc. v. Marathon Development California, Inc., 2 Cal.4th 342 (1992), upholding the validity of a provision in a commercial lease that gave the landlord the right to terminate the lease and enter into a new lease with an intended transferee in order to reap a higher rent from the transferee. Section 1995.250 permits transfer to be conditioned upon the landlord's consent, so long as that consent is either not withheld unreasonably or "withheld subject to express standards or conditions." Thus, in California the *Kendall* rule only applies to non-residential leases, and then only to those leases that contain a consent restriction that fails to state the express standards or conditions upon which consent may be withheld. With respect to residential leases that contain a consent restriction, the landlord may withhold consent for any reason. Of course, if any lease fails to contain any consent restriction, the tenant is free to transfer his interest.

California Civil Code section 1995.340 states that "a restriction on transfer of a tenant's interest in a lease applies to a subsequent transfer by a tenant, an assignee, or a subtenant notwithstanding the landlord's consent to a prior transfer or the landlord's waiver of a standard or condition for a prior transfer," unless there is an express provision to the contrary in the lease or given in writing by the landlord.

2. Residential Leases. Residential leases typically contain a requirement that the landlord's consent is necessary for any transfer of the lessee's interest. Should the landlord be able to refuse his consent to transfer for any reason? In Slavin v. Rent Control Board of Brookline, 406 Mass. 458 (1990), the Massachusetts Supreme Judicial Court held that a landlord in a residential lease that prohibited transfer of the leasehold without the landlord's consent could withhold consent for any reason. The tenant of a rent-controlled apartment had brought in an unauthorized co-occupant, thus partially transferring possession, without obtaining consent. The landlord then sought to evict on the ground that the tenant had violated a lease obligation, but the Rent Control Board refused eviction because the landlord had categorically refused to permit the tenant to bring in a replacement co-occupant. The Massachusetts court reasoned that, at least with respect to rent-controlled apartments, there was no danger of the landlord withholding consent to reap an "unfair financial gain," nor was there any proof that free transferability of residential leaseholds was necessary to provide access to residential housing.

3. *Which Rule?* The implied requirement of reasonableness is still the minority view, but it is increasingly being adopted in the commercial context. See Julian v. Christopher, 320 Md. 1 (1990); Newman v. Hinky Dinky Omaha–Lincoln, Inc., 229 Neb. 382 (1988). But that trend is not universal. In Massachusetts, for example, the Supreme Judicial Court extended the *Slavin* rule to include commercial leases. See Merchants Row Corp. v. Merchants Row, Inc., 412 Mass. 204 (1992). See also First Federal Savings Bank v. Key Markets, Inc., 559 N.E.2d 600 (Ind. 1990).

The argument for the majority rule—no implied requirement of reasonableness—is that the parties are free to negotiate whatever provisions they desire to govern transferability of the leasehold, and if they fail to include a reasonableness requirement the courts should not supply one. The arguments for the minority rule—reasonableness requirement implied—are twofold. Tenants often have unequal bargaining power and parties to a contract are required to act in good faith and deal fairly with each other.

Assess these arguments in the context of each of commercial leases and residential leases. If tenants are generally at a bargaining disadvantage in the residential context, why are courts more reluctant to impose an implied obligation of reasonableness in that context than in the commercial setting?

4. *Problems.*

a. *L* leases a commercial building to *T1*, pursuant to a lease that requires the landlord's consent to any transfer of the leasehold. *T1* obtains *L*'s consent to an assignment to *T2*, who does not assume the lease obligations. Then *T2* assigns the leasehold to *T3* without even asking for, much less obtaining, *L*'s consent to the assignment. *T3* defaults on the rent and skips town. May *L* recover rent from *T2*? If California law applies, what result?

b. What if, in the previous problem, *L* had accepted rent from *T3* for several months before *T3*'s default?

c. In a jurisdiction applying the reasonableness rule, *L* leases office space to *T* under a lease requiring landlord consent to any transfer of the leasehold. *T* seeks consent for a assignment of the lease to the State Parole Board. *L* had considered leasing space to the State Parole Board before entering into the lease to *T*. Other tenants of the building learn of the proposed transfer and register their objections to *L*, even threatening to sue *L* if the State Parole Board moves in. *L* then refuses to consent. Unreasonable?

d. In a jurisdiction applying the reasonableness rule, *L* leases a strip-mall unit to *T* under a lease requiring landlord consent to any transfer of the leasehold. *T* seeks consent for a assignment of the lease to a restaurant that would offer only Arabic dishes prepared in accordance with *halal*, the Islamic dietary law. To accommodate the restaurant, the premises would need substantial alteration that would render it unlikely to be rented for any purpose other than a restaurant. There are many restaurants in the area, and they frequently fail for lack of sufficient patronage. While there is a large Islamic segment to the community, there is also considerable prejudice against Muslims. *L* refuses consent. Make and assess the best arguments in support of and in opposition to the validity of *L*'s refusal.

D. TENANT DEFAULT: OBLIGATIONS AND REMEDIES

Tenant default can take several forms. Most common is failure to pay rent, but a tenant can be in default by his breach of any number of possible lease covenants, such as an obligation not to alter the premises without permission of the landlord, or a promise to permit the landlord to have reasonable access, or an agreement not to transfer the leasehold. When the tenant defaults on one or more of his lease obligations, landlords have a variety of remedies. If the tenant is still in possession, the landlord will want to recover possession. That is the topic of subsection 1 on self-help and its alternatives. In addition, the landlord may wish to recover back rent and damages. If the tenant has stopped paying rent and departed from the leased premises, recovery of possession is not an issue but recovery of rent and damages remains as a remedy. Section 2, dealing with the duty to mitigate damages, considers the issues presented when the landlord seeks rent and damages after the tenant has abandoned the premises.

1. RECOVERY OF POSSESSION: SELF–HELP AND SUMMARY PROCEEDINGS

SPINKS v. TAYLOR

Supreme Court of North Carolina
303 N.C. 256 (1981)

[Taylor leased an apartment to Spinks in Greensboro, North Carolina, *F / P* pursuant to a lease that provided that Taylor could terminate the lease in the event of tenant default by providing five days notice of intent to terminate, and thereafter Taylor could "re-enter and take possession of the leased premises, without process or by legal process from the Court having jurisdiction over the premises." Nine months later, after Spinks had failed to pay the rent, Taylor had notified her of the delinquency and given her ten days to cure the default, but Spinks had failed to do so. Taylor padlocked the apartment, depriving her of access. Taylor left a notice on the door stating that she could regain access by paying the back rent and could recover her personal property by contacting the property manager. Spinks brought suit for damages caused by the alleged wrongful padlocking of the premises. Each party moved for summary judgment after stipulating to the facts described here. The trial court granted Taylor's motion for summary judgment and denied Spinks's motion. The court of appeals affirmed.]

BRANCH, C.J., delivered the opinion of the court.

Plaintiffs first contend that the trial court erred in granting summary judgment for defendant since North Carolina law does not recognize a landlord's right to use peaceful self-help to evict tenants who are subject to forfeiture for non-payment of rent. Defendant maintains on the other hand that at common law a landlord had the right to reenter peacefully and take possession of leased premises subject to forfeiture, and that nothing in the statutory or case law of this state abrogates that common law right.

At early common law, a lessor was permitted to reenter leased premises and use necessary force, not amounting to death or bodily harm, to take possession. In 1381, however, Parliament enacted the statute of Forcible Entry, 5 Richard II stat. 1, c. 8, making forcible entry without legal process a crime. That statute provided:

> That none from henceforth make any entry into any lands and tenements but in case where entry is given by the law; and in such case, not with strong hand nor with multitude of people, but only in peaceable and easy manner. And if any man from henceforth do to the contrary, and thereof be duly convict, he shall be punished by imprisonment of his body, and thereof ransomed at the King's will.

In England it was held that, while the use of necessary force may be a crime under the forcible entry statute, a dispossessed tenant still had no civil remedy in the absence of excess force. In numerous jurisdictions in this country, including North Carolina, statutes similar to that of 5 Richard II were enacted, and the various constructions placed upon the statutes in the states have produced at least three distinct approaches to the question of self-help evictions.

First, a number of states adhere to the English rule that a landlord may use necessary and reasonable force to expel a tenant and may do so without resort to legal process. E.g., Virginia Iron, Coal & Coke Co. v. Dickenson, 143 Va. 250, 129 S.E. 228 (1925). A second line of authority holds that a landlord must in any case resort to the remedy provided by law, usually summary ejectment proceedings, in order to evict an overstaying tenant. E.g., Reader v. Purdy, 41 Ill. 279 (1866). Finally, a third line of cases, and one which tends to overlap the second line, holds that a landlord entitled to immediate possession may "gain possession of the leased premises by peaceable means, and necessity for recourse to legal process exists only where peaceable means fail and force would otherwise be necessary." Within this third category are cases which hold that, while peaceful means technically may be used, *any* retaking which is against the will of the tenant constitutes a forceful retaking and thus is not permitted. E.g., Reader v. Purdy, supra.

Turning now to the law of North Carolina, we find that our forcible entry statute reads substantially as did the old English statute and that Mosseller v. Deaver, 106 N.C. 494, 11 S.E. 529 (1890), is the pivotal case dealing with the issue before us. In *Mosseller* the landlord entered the tenant's house while the tenant was present.... The trial judge instructed the jury that the landlord " 'had the right to go there and put him out by force, if no more force was used than was necessary for that purpose.' " Id. at 495, 11 S.E. at 530. This Court disapproved such an instruction, relying on Reader v. Purdy, supra, and noted that public policy required "the owner *to use peaceful means or resort to the courts* in order to regain his possession...." Id. [Emphasis added.] It seems clear to us, then, that this state recognizes the right of a lessor to enter peacefully and repossess leased premises which are subject to forfeiture due to nonpayment of rent.

Even so, plaintiffs urge that the existence of statutory summary ejectment procedures precludes the use of self-help measures in evicting a tenant in default of rental payments. We are not inadvertent to the fact that some jurisdictions view the statutory remedies as exclusive and as precluding self-help. E.g., Malcolm v. Little, 295 A. 2d 711 (Del. 1972). However, nothing in our summary ejectment statutes indicates a legislative intent to make those remedies exclusive. Furthermore, despite the widespread existence of summary statutory remedies, the majority view still recognizes some degree of self-help.

Having determined that the law of this state permits a landlord to employ peaceable self-help measures in repossessing leased premises, we turn now to an inquiry into what acts constitute acts of force which would subject a landlord to civil liability for the reentry. In Reader v. Purdy, supra, relied upon by this Court in *Mosseller*, the court examined the prohibition against the use of force:

> It is urged that the owner of real estate has a right to enter upon and enjoy his own property. Undoubtedly, if he can do so without a forcible disturbance of the possession of another; but the peace and good order of society require that he shall not be permitted to enter against the will of the occupant.... He may be wrongfully kept out of possession, but he cannot be permitted to take the law into his own hands and redress his own wrongs. The remedy must be sought through those peaceful agencies which a civilized community provides for all its members. ... If the right to use force be once admitted, it must necessarily follow as a logical sequence, that so much may be used as shall be necessary to overcome resistance, even to the taking of human life. ... In this State, it has been constantly held that *any entry is forcible*, within the meaning of this law, that is made against the will of the occupant. Id. at 285–286. [Emphasis added.]

We find the reasoning of *Reader* persuasive and perceive no reason for departing from its rule. We therefore hold that while a landlord is permitted to use peaceful means to reenter and take possession of leased premises subject to forfeiture, he may not do so against the will of the tenant; an objection by the tenant elevates the reentry to a forceful one, and the landlord's sole lawful recourse at that time is to the courts.

In the instant case, ... [Spinks] alleges that she requested access to the apartment to get certain items of clothing but was denied admission. This allegation contradicts the assertion by defendant that if an ousted tenant requested entrance to the apartment to obtain personal property, he would be allowed to enter. A refusal by the landlord to permit a tenant to enter the premises, for whatever purposes, would elevate the taking to a forceful taking and subject the landlord to damages. Whether in this case there was such a refusal is a material issue of fact to be decided by a jury. That being so, entry of summary judgment for defendant as to plaintiff Spinks was improper....

[Reversed and remanded.]

NOTES AND QUESTIONS

1. *The Decline of Self–Help.* As the North Carolina court noted, peaceable self-help has long been an available remedy to landlords to recover possession. The scope of that remedy has shrunk. One way that has occurred is the method chosen by the court in *Spinks*—defining peaceable down, to paraphrase Daniel Patrick Moynihan.[8] To similar effect is Gulf Oil Corp. v. Smithey, 426 S.W.2d 262 (Tex. Civ. App. 1968). While purportedly not altering the common law rule, the Texas court held that the landlord's entry in the tenant's absence by picking the locks and locking the tenant out, although accomplished without actual violence, was forcible as a matter of law. This gambit leaves open the possibility that self-help is still available in some undefined circumstances. But what might those circumstances be? After *Spinks* self-help is available only if the tenant consents. Under what circumstances would a tenant be likely to consent? If entry in the tenant's absence was critical to the Texas court's ruling, does Texas subscribe to the same principle as North Carolina? See also Karp v. Margolis, 159 Cal. App. 2d 69 (1958).

Berg v. Wiley, 264 N.W.2d 145 (Minn. 1978), represents a more forthright, or at least more direct, approach to self-help. Berg leased from Wiley a building to use as a restaurant. Berg breached various provisions of the lease and Wiley notified Berg that he would retake possession, as he was entitled to do under the lease, unless the violations were cured within two weeks. Once that period had elapsed without cure, Wiley picked the locks in Berg's absence and locked out Berg. Berg sought and was awarded damages for wrongful eviction. The Minnesota Supreme Court affirmed, finding that Wiley's self-help was wrongful as a matter of law:

> Minnesota has historically followed the common-law rule that a landlord may rightfully use self-help to retake leased premises from a

---

8. Daniel Patrick Moynihan, Defining Deviancy Down: How We've Become Accustomed to Alarming Levels of Crime and Destructive Behavior, 62:1 The American Spectator 17–30 (Winter 1993).

tenant in possession without incurring liability for wrongful eviction provided two conditions are met: (1) The landlord is legally entitled to possession, such as where a tenant holds over after the lease term or where a tenant breaches a lease containing a reentry clause; and (2) the landlord's means of reentry are peaceable. . . .

It has long been the policy of our law to discourage landlords from taking the law into their own hands, and our decisions and statutory law have looked with disfavor upon any use of self-help to dispossess a tenant in circumstances which are likely to result in breaches of the peace. . . . To facilitate a resort to judicial process, the legislature has provided a summary procedure . . . whereby a landlord may recover possession of leased premises upon proper notice and showing in court in as little as 3 to 10 days. . . . To further discourage self-help, our legislature has provided treble damages for forcible evictions . . . and has provided additional criminal penalties for intentional and unlawful exclusion of a tenant. . . .

[Because the] record shows a history of vigorous dispute and keen animosity between the parties[, . . .] the singular reason why actual violence did not erupt at the moment of Wiley's changing of the locks was Berg's absence and her subsequent self-restraint and resort to judicial process. [We] cannot find Wiley's means of reentry peaceable under the common-law rule. Our long-standing policy to discourage self-help which tends to cause a breach of the peace compels us to disapprove the means used to dispossess Berg. . . .

We recognize that the growing modern trend departs completely from the common-law rule to hold that self-help is never available to dispossess a tenant who is in possession and has not abandoned or voluntarily surrendered the premises. This growing rule is founded on the recognition that the potential for violent breach of peace inheres in any situation where a landlord attempts by his own means to remove a tenant who is claiming possession adversely to the landlord. Courts adopting the rule reason that there is no cause to sanction such potentially disruptive self-help where adequate and speedy means are provided for removing a tenant peacefully through judicial process. At least 16 states have adopted this . . . rule, holding that judicial proceedings, including the summary procedures provided in those states' unlawful detainer statutes, are the exclusive remedy by which a landlord may remove a tenant claiming possession. . . .

While we . . . disapprove the lockout of Berg in her absence under the common-law rule . . . , we . . . adopt as preferable the modern view. . . . To make clear our departure from the common-law rule for the benefit of future landlords and tenants, we hold that, subsequent to our decision in this case, the only lawful means to dispossess a tenant who has not abandoned nor voluntarily surrendered but who claims possession adversely to a landlord's claim of breach of a written lease is by resort to judicial process. . . .

As the Minnesota court noted, its ruling applied prospectively to all landlords and tenants, even though the actual dispute in *Berg* arose from a commercial lease. See also Jordan v. Talbot, 55 Cal.2d 597 (1961) (residential lease); Kassan v. Stout, 9 Cal.3d 39 (1973) (commercial lease). However, some jurisdictions hold that self-help is available in the commercial setting but possibly not in the residential setting. See, e.g., Watson v. Brown, 67 Haw. 252 (1984), in which the landlord locked out the tenant following tenant default. The Hawaii Supreme Court held that the presence of a statutory unlawful detainer remedy did not foreclose self-help, as a matter of law, in the commercial context. The court reasoned that the parties to commercial leases are generally possessed of fairly equal bargaining power. The court expressed no opinion on self-help in residential settings. Are there sound reasons to permit self-help in the commercial context but not in the residential context?

The Restatement (Second) of Property, Landlord and Tenant, § 14.03 states that in the absence of any law forbidding self-help, that remedy should be available only when accomplished

(1) within a reasonable time after the lease terminates;

(2) without causing physical harm, or the reasonable expectation of physical harm, to the tenant, or anyone else on the leased property with the permission of the tenant; and

(3) by using reasonable care to avoid damage to the property of the tenant, or of others on the leased property with the tenant's permission.

Moreover, the same Restatement section provides that any "agreement that undertakes to eliminate any of those requirements is against public policy and void." Suppose that a commercial lease expressly gives the landlord the right to use self-help in accordance with the Restatement limitations. Should self-help be permitted or should the *Berg* rule apply?

2. *Summary Proceedings to Recover Possession.* Every American jurisdiction today has adopted some form of a summary procedure to enable landlords to recover possession of property that is being unlawfully detained by others. These statutes were enacted in reaction to the stark alternatives available to a landlord to recover possession: self-help or resort to an ordinary lengthy lawsuit to eject the wrongful possessor. These summary proceedings, sometimes referred to as unlawful detainer, were designed to provide a quick resolution of the single issue of right to possession. That meant that other issues that might be raised as a counterclaim or defense, such as a setoff against alleged unpaid rent of a debt owed to the tenant by the landlord, could not be heard in the unlawful detainer proceeding. By focusing on the right to possession alone, and providing a calendar preference for hearing and decision, it was thought that these proceedings would be short and simple, and thus an effective alternative to either an ejectment suit or self-help. But that has not happened. Because the issue is the right to possession, many states permit tenants to raise defenses that are relevant to the landlord's claimed right to recover possession, such as the asserted failure of the landlord to comply with his implied warranty that the leased premises are inhabitable. As the range of possible disputed material issues of fact increase, the likelihood of a speedy conclusion to the "summary" proceeding diminishes. Yet, if the landlord has breached his obligations and thus may not be entitled to recover possession, these proceedings do what they are supposed to do—provide a forum for decision of the right of possession. To fuse cliches, while justice

delayed may be justice denied, a rush to judgment may not be justice. There is, however, no constitutional requirement that states permit tenants to assert the defense of landlord breach of the implied warranty of habitability in unlawful detainer actions. In Lindsey v. Normet, 405 U.S. 56 (1972), the United States Supreme Court held that due process was not violated by Oregon's requirement that unlawful detainer actions be tried within a week after their commencement or by its preclusion of the defense of breach of the warranty of habitability. On the latter point, the Court reasoned that tenants could vindicate that interest in a separate action.

2. DUTY TO MITIGATE DAMAGES

When a tenant has abandoned the premises before expiration of the lease term, the traditional common law rule permits the landlord to do nothing but wait until the end of the term and sue for unpaid rent. Unless the lease contains an acceleration clause—a provision that stipulates that, upon tenant default, the entire rent for the remainder of the lease term is immediately due and payable—the rent only becomes due as the payment period arrives. Thus, rent under a ten year lease that is due monthly is not owing until each month passes. Of course, should a tenant default and abandon the premises after one month of a ten year lease with rent due monthly, a landlord is not likely to wait until the next 119 months have elapsed before seeking the rent. If the landlord wants to recover rent immediately, he must seek damages for the tenant breach, and the measure of those damages will be the present value of the difference between the actual rent and the fair rental value for the remainder of the term. See, e.g., Calif. Civil Code § 1951.2. Of course, if fair rental value and actual rent are the same, the landlord's damages are nil. That rule creates an incentive for the landlord to accept the tenant's surrender of the lease and re-let the premises to someone new. Or, the landlord could simply wait for the term to expire and sue the tenant for the rent.

When a tenant abandons he is regarded as offering to surrender the lease. If a landlord accepts that surrender he has agreed to forego any right to recover the *rent* that would have become due after the surrender, but he retains the right to recover unpaid rent for periods prior to the surrender. However, his right to recover *damages* attributable to the tenant's breach may depend on whether there is a lease provision that so stipulates or, in the absence of such a provision, whether the governing law permits such recovery. See, e.g., Calif. Civil Code § 1951.2; Lennon v. U.S. Theatre Corp., 920 F.2d 996 (D.C. Cir. 1990) (applying D.C. law). The measure of damages is the present value of the shortfall, if any, between the lease rent and the fair rental value for the remainder of the lease, plus the out-of-pocket costs incurred by the landlord in reletting the premises (which the landlord would not have to do, but for the tenant's breach and abandonment).

The landlord does not have to accept the tenant's offer of surrender. Under the traditional rule, he could sit back, wait for the term to expire, and sue the tenant for the rent. Of course, that result is woefully inefficient, because an apartment or commercial space stays empty even though there may be other prospective occupants who would be happy to pay rent to have possession of the premises. Whether the landlord should be permitted to have that option is the subject of the following case, a landmark in landlord-tenant law.

SOMMER v. KRIDEL

Supreme Court of New Jersey
74 N.J. 446 (1977)

PASHMAN, J., delivered the opinion of the court.

... I. A. *Sommer v. Kridel*

This case was tried on stipulated facts. On March 10, 1972 the defendant, James Kridel, entered into a lease with the plaintiff, Abraham Sommer, owner of the "Pierre Apartments" in Hackensack, to rent apartment 6–L in that building.[9] The term of the lease was from May 1, 1972 until April 30, 1974, with a rent concession for the first six weeks, so that the first month's rent was not due until June 15, 1972. One week after signing the agreement, Kridel paid Sommer $690. Half of that sum was used to satisfy the first month's rent. The remainder was paid under the lease provision requiring a security deposit of $345. Although defendant had expected to begin occupancy around May 1, his plans were changed. He wrote to Sommer on May 19, 1972, explaining

> I was to be married on June 3, 1972. Unhappily the engagement was broken and the wedding plans cancelled. Both parents were to assume responsibility for the rent after our marriage. I was discharged from the U.S. Army in October 1971 and am now a student. I have no funds of my own, and am supported by my stepfather. In view of the above, I cannot take possession of the apartment and am surrendering all rights to it. Never having received a key, I cannot return same to you. I beg your understanding and compassion in releasing me from the lease, and will of course, in consideration thereof, forfeit the 2 month's rent already paid. Please notify me at your earliest convenience.

Plaintiff did not answer the letter.

Subsequently, a third party went to the apartment house and inquired about renting apartment 6–L. Although the parties agreed that she was ready, willing and able to rent the apartment, the person in charge told her that the apartment was not being shown since it was already rented to Kridel. In fact, the landlord did not re-enter the apartment or exhibit it to anyone until August 1, 1973. At that time it was rented to a new tenant for a term beginning on September 1, 1973. The new rental

---

9. Among other provisions, the lease prohibited the tenant from assigning or transferring the lease without the consent of the landlord. If the tenant defaulted, the lease gave the landlord the option of re-entering or re-letting, but stipulated that failure to re-let or to recover the full rental would not discharge the tenant's liability for rent.

was for $345 per month with a six week concession similar to that granted Kridel.

Prior to re-letting the new premises, plaintiff sued Kridel in August 1972, demanding $7,590, the total amount due for the full two-year term of the lease. Following a mistrial, plaintiff filed an amended complaint asking for $5,865, the amount due between May 1, 1972 and September 1, 1973. The amended complaint included no reduction in the claim to reflect the six week concession provided for in the lease or the $690 payment made to plaintiff after signing the agreement. Defendant filed an amended answer to the complaint, alleging that plaintiff breached the contract, failed to mitigate damages and accepted defendant's surrender of the premises. He also counterclaimed to demand repayment of the $345 paid as a security deposit. The trial judge ruled in favor of defendant[, concluding] that "justice and fair dealing" imposed upon the landlord the duty to attempt to re-let the premises and thereby mitigate damages. He also held that plaintiff's failure to make any response to defendant's unequivocal offer of surrender was tantamount to an acceptance, thereby terminating the tenancy and any obligation to pay rent. [He] dismissed both the complaint and the counterclaim. The Appellate Division reversed ... and we granted certification.

B. *Riverview Realty Co. v. Perosio*

This controversy arose in a similar manner. On December 27, 1972, Carlos Perosio entered into a written lease with plaintiff Riverview Realty Co. The agreement covered the rental of apartment 5–G in a building owned by the realty company at 2175 Hudson Terrace in Fort Lee. As in the companion case, the lease prohibited the tenant from subletting or assigning the apartment without the consent of the landlord. It was to run for a two-year term, from February 1, 1973 until January 31, 1975, and provided for a monthly rental of $450. The defendant took possession of the apartment and occupied it until February 1974. At that time he vacated the premises, after having paid the rent through January 31, 1974.

The landlord filed a complaint on October 31, 1974, demanding $4,500 in payment for the monthly rental from February 1, 1974 through October 31, 1974. Defendant answered the complaint by alleging that there had been a valid surrender of the premises and that plaintiff failed to mitigate damages. The trial court granted the landlord's motion for summary judgment against the defendant, fixing the damages at $4,050 plus $182.25 interest. The Appellate Division affirmed the trial court, holding that it was bound by prior precedents, including Joyce v. Bauman, [174 A. 693 (N.J. 1934)]. Nevertheless, it freely criticized the rule which it found itself obliged to follow:

> There appears to be no reason in equity or justice to perpetuate such an unrealistic and uneconomic rule of law which encourages an owner to let valuable rented space lie fallow because he is assured of full recovery from a defaulting tenant. Since courts in New Jersey and

elsewhere have abandoned ancient real property concepts and applied ordinary contract principles in other conflicts between landlord and tenant there is no sound reason for a continuation of a special real property rule to the issue of mitigation. . . .

We granted certification.

II.   As the lower courts in both appeals found, the weight of authority in this State supports the rule that a landlord is under no duty to mitigate damages caused by a defaulting tenant. This rule has been followed in a majority of states. . . .

Nevertheless, while there is still a split of authority over this question, the trend among recent cases appears to be in favor of a mitigation requirement. The majority rule is based on principles of property law which equate a lease with a transfer of a property interest in the owner's estate. Under this rationale the lease conveys to a tenant an interest in the property which forecloses any control by the landlord; thus, it would be anomalous to require the landlord to concern himself with the tenant's abandonment of his own property. [In] Muller v. Beck, [110 A. 831 (N.J. 1920)], where essentially the same issue was posed, the court clearly treated the lease as governed by property, as opposed to contract, precepts,[10] [observing] that "the tenant has an estate with which the landlord may not interfere." . . .

Yet the distinction between a lease for ordinary residential purposes and an ordinary contract can no longer be considered viable. As Professor Powell observed, evolving "social factors have exerted increasing influence on the law of estates for years." 2 Powell on Real Property (1977 ed.), § 221[1] at 180–81. The result has been that

> [t]he complexities of city life, and the proliferated problems of modern society in general, have created new problems for lessors and lessees and these have been commonly handled by specific clauses in leases. This growth in the number and detail of specific lease covenants has reintroduced into the law of estates for years a predominantly contractual ingredient.

Thus, in 6 Williston on Contracts (3d ed. 1962), § 890A at 592, it is stated:

> There is a clearly discernible tendency on the part of courts to cast aside technicalities in the interpretation of leases and to concentrate their attention, as in the case of other contracts, on the intention of the parties . . .

This Court has taken the lead in requiring that landlords provide housing services to tenants in accordance with implied duties which are hardly consistent with the property notions expressed in Muller. . . . See Braitman v. Overlook Terrace Corp., 68 N.J. 368 (1975) (liability for failure to repair defective apartment door lock); Berzito v. Gambino, 63 N.J. 460 (1973) (construing implied warranty of habitability and covenant

---

10. It is well settled that a party claiming damages for a breach of contract has a duty to mitigate his loss. . . .

to pay rent as mutually dependent); Marini v. Ireland, 56 N.J. 130 (1970) (implied covenant to repair); Reste Realty Corp. v. Cooper, 53 N.J. 444 (1969) (implied warranty of fitness of premises for leased purpose)....

Application of the contract rule requiring mitigation of damages to a residential lease may be justified as a matter of basic fairness.[11] Professor McCormick first commented upon the inequity under the majority rule when he predicted in 1925 that eventually

> the [formalistic] logic ... which permits the landlord to stand idly by the vacant, abandoned premises and treat them as the property of the tenant and recover full rent, will yield to the more realistic notions of social advantage which in other fields of the law have forbidden a recovery for damages which the plaintiff by reasonable efforts could have avoided. [McCormick, "The Rights of the Landlord Upon Abandonment of the Premises by the Tenant," 23 Mich. L. Rev. 211, 221–22 (1925).]

Various courts have adopted this position.

The pre-existing rule cannot be predicated upon the possibility that a landlord may lose the opportunity to rent another empty apartment because he must first rent the apartment vacated by the defaulting tenant. Even where the breach occurs in a multi-dwelling building, each apartment may have unique qualities which make it attractive to certain individuals. Significantly, in *Sommer* there was a specific request to rent the apartment vacated by the defendant; there is no reason to believe that absent this vacancy the landlord could have succeeded in renting a different apartment to this individual.

We therefore hold that antiquated real property concepts which served as the basis for the pre-existing rule, shall no longer be controlling where there is a claim for damages under a residential lease. Such claims must be governed by more modern notions of fairness and equity. A landlord has a duty to mitigate damages where he seeks to recover rents due from a defaulting tenant. If the landlord has other vacant apartments besides the one which the tenant has abandoned, the landlord's duty to mitigate consists of making reasonable efforts to re-let the apartment. In such cases he must treat the apartment in question as if it was one of his vacant stock.

As part of his cause of action, the landlord shall be required to carry the burden of proving that he used reasonable diligence in attempting to re-let the premises. We note that there has been a divergence of opinion concerning the allocation of the burden of proof on this issue. While generally in contract actions the breaching party has the burden of proving that damages are capable of mitigation, here the landlord will be in a better position to demonstrate whether he exercised reasonable diligence in attempting to re-let the premises.

---

11. However, we reserve for another day the question of whether a landlord must mitigate damages in a commercial setting.

III. The *Sommer v. Kridel* case presents a classic example of the unfairness which occurs when a landlord has no responsibility to minimize damages. Sommer waited 15 months and allowed $4658.50 in damages to accrue before attempting to re-let the apartment. Despite the availability of a tenant who was ready, willing and able to rent the apartment, the landlord needlessly increased the damages by turning her away. While a tenant will not necessarily be excused from his obligations under a lease simply by finding another person who is willing to rent the vacated premises, here there has been no showing that the new tenant would not have been suitable. We therefore find that plaintiff could have avoided the damages which eventually accrued, and that the defendant was relieved of his duty to continue paying rent. Ordinarily we would require the tenant to bear the cost of any reasonable expenses incurred by a landlord in attempting to re-let the premises, but no such expenses were incurred in this case.[12]

In *Riverview Realty Co.*, no factual determination was made regarding the landlord's efforts to mitigate damages, and defendant contends that plaintiff never answered his interrogatories. Consequently, the judgment is reversed and the case remanded for a new trial. Upon remand and after discovery has been completed, the trial court shall determine whether plaintiff attempted to mitigate damages with reasonable diligence, and if so, the extent of damages remaining and assessable to the tenant. As we have held above, the burden of proving that reasonable diligence was used to relet the premises shall be upon the plaintiff.

In assessing whether the landlord has satisfactorily carried his burden, the trial court shall consider, among other factors, whether the landlord, either personally or through an agency, offered or showed the apartment to any prospective tenants, or advertised it in local newspapers. Additionally, the tenant may attempt to rebut such evidence by showing that he proffered suitable tenants who were rejected. However, there is no standard formula for measuring whether the landlord has utilized satisfactory efforts in attempting to mitigate damages, and each case must be judged upon its own facts....

NOTES, QUESTIONS, AND PROBLEM

1. More on Surrender. The New Jersey court did not have to answer the question of whether Sommer accepted Kridel's offer to surrender by his failure to respond to the offer. Why might the answer to that question matter? Suppose that Sommer had accepted Kridel's offer of surrender, then rented the apartment to Newtenant, who paid the rent until there were two months left on Kridel's original term, and then departed for parts unknown. Sommer would not be able to recover those two months' rent from Kridel, but if Sommer had explicitly refused to accept the offer of surrender and had relet the apartment as an accommodation to Kridel, Sommer would be able to

---

12. ... Because we hold that plaintiff breached his duty to attempt to mitigate damages, we do not address defendant's argument that the landlord accepted a surrender of the premises.

collect the last two months' rent from Kridel, because that lease would still be in effect. When a landlord relets on the tenant's account he is, in essence, acting as the tenant's rental agent in finding what amounts to a sublessee.

What constitutes an acceptance of the tenant's offer to surrender? Surrender is easy when it is explicit; had Sommer replied to Kridel, "I accept your offer of surrender," there would be no dispute on that point. Problems arise when offer and acceptance must be implied by conduct. For example, some states hold that the act of reletting the premises is an implied acceptance of surrender. But there is no implied acceptance of surrender if the landlord notifies the tenant that he is not accepting surrender but, instead, is reletting the premises on the tenant's account, and any unpaid rent by the replacement tenant is the continuing responsibility of the original tenant. See, e.g., Atkinson v. Rosenthal, 33 Mass.App. 219, 222 (1992). But if the landlord fails to so notify the tenant, and takes action that is clearly inconsistent with the original tenant's right to occupy (such as changing the locks or drastic alterations of the premises) an implied acceptance of surrender is the likely result. Id. at 221.

2. *More on the Duty to Mitigate.* The overwhelming majority of states impose on landlord and tenant a duty to mitigate damages. Some have done so by statute, others have done so by judicial decision. See, e.g., Alaska Stat. § 34.03.230(c). In those states that have adopted the duty to mitigate, the duty applies to all leases, whether commercial or residential. See, e.g, Austin Hill Country Realty v. Palisades Plaza, 948 S.W.2d 293 (Tex. 1997). Some states continue to apply the common law rule to all leases. See, e.g., Bowdoin Square, LLC v. Winn–Dixie Montgomery, Inc., 873 So.2d 1091 (Ala. 2003); Ex parte Kaschak, 681 So.2d 197 (Ala. 1996). Others draw a distinction between commercial and residential leases, finding no duty to mitigate in the commercial context.

In Holy Properties, Ltd. v. Kenneth Cole Productions, Inc., 87 N.Y.2d 130 (1995), involving a commercial lease, the New York Court of Appeals found no duty to mitigate. The tenant vacated the premises three years shy of the end of a ten year lease. Landlord obtained a judgment of almost $719,000 for the remainder of the rent under the lease. The Court of Appeals affirmed:

> The issue is whether ... the landlord had a duty to mitigate its damages after the tenant's abandonment of the premises and subsequent eviction. The law imposes upon a party subjected to injury from breach of contract, the duty of making reasonable exertions to minimize the injury. Leases are not subject to this general rule, however, for, unlike executory contracts, leases have been historically recognized as a present transfer of an estate in real property. Once the lease is executed, the lessee's obligation to pay rent is fixed according to its terms and a landlord is under no obligation or duty to the tenant to relet, or attempt to relet abandoned premises in order to minimize damages. When defendant abandoned these premises prior to expiration of the lease, the landlord had three options: (1) it could do nothing and collect the full rent due under the lease; (2) it could accept the tenant's surrender, reenter the premises and relet them for its own account thereby releasing the tenant from further liability for rent, or (3) it could notify the tenant that it was

entering and reletting the premises for the tenant's benefit. If the landlord relets the premises for the benefit of the tenant, the rent collected would be apportioned first to repay the landlord's expenses in reentering and reletting and then to pay the tenant's rent obligation. Once the tenant abandoned the premises prior to the expiration of the lease, however, the landlord was within its rights under New York law to do nothing and collect the full rent due under the lease.

Defendant urges us to reject this settled law and adopt the contract rationale recognized by some courts in this State and elsewhere. We decline to do so. Parties who engage in transactions based on prevailing law must be able to rely on the stability of such precedents. In business transactions, particularly, the certainty of settled rules is often more important than whether the established rule is better than another or even whether it is the "correct" rule. This is perhaps true in real property more than any other area of the law, where established precedents are not lightly to be set aside.

Defendant contends that even if it is liable for rent after abandoning the premises, plaintiff terminated the landlord-tenant relationship shortly thereafter by instituting summary proceedings. After the eviction, it maintains, its only liability was for contract damages, not rent, and under contract law the landlord had a duty to mitigate. Although an eviction terminates the landlord-tenant relationship, the parties to a lease are not foreclosed from contracting as they please. If the lease provides that the tenant shall be liable for rent after eviction, the provision is enforceable. In this case, the lease expressly provided that plaintiff was under no duty to mitigate damages and that upon defendant's abandonment of the premises or eviction, it would remain liable for all monetary obligations arising under the lease.

New York law on residential leases is in disarray. Compare Whitehouse Estates, Inc. v. Post, 662 N.Y.S.2d 982 (App. Div. 1997) (no duty), with 29 Holding Corp. v. Diaz, 775 N.Y.S.2d 807 (2004) (duty imposed). In Rios v. Carrillo, 861 N.Y.S.2d 129, 131 (App. 2008), the Appellate Division relied on *Holy Properties* to conclude that there was no duty to mitigate where the lease contained an explicit tenant obligation to pay rent even after abandonment. In *Holy Properties* the presence of a lease provision holding the tenant liable for rent even after eviction and termination of the lease was given effect. Careful drafting and reading of leases is important.

Finally, note that the duty to mitigate does not mean that landlord is liable to the tenant or anyone else if he refuses to attempt to relet the premises. If the landlord makes no effort to relet, and leaves the unit vacant, his breach of the duty to mitigate limits his claims against the tenant to the sum of (1) rent unpaid before abandonment, and (2) the present value of the difference between the lease rentals and the fair market value of the vacant unit. In those states that have adopted the Uniform Residential Landlord and Tenant Act, however, the lease terminates by operation of law if the landlord fails to use "reasonable efforts" to rent the vacant unit "at a fair rental." URLTA § 4.203. As a result, the landlord can collect nothing from the tenant after the lease is terminated.

3. *Problem.* Recall that the duty to mitigate, as articulated in *Sommer*, imposes on the landlord the obligation to treat the abandoned apartment as one of his stock of available apartments, which presumably means that his effort to rent apartments must be equal with respect to the abandoned unit and all others. But what if an existing tenant wishes to move into the vacated unit and the landlord agrees?

L leases office suite 101 to *T* for three years at a rent of $1,000 per month. With a year remaining on the term, *T* abandons. *T1*, an existing tenant of *L* who occupies office suite 202 at a rent of $800 per month, proposes to *L* that the lease to suite 202 be terminated and a new lease between *T1* and *L* for suite 101 be executed. *L* agrees, and the new lease to suite 101 is for three years at a monthly rent of $1,100. Then *L* sues *T* for $9,600 in damages, consisting of twelve months of lost rental on suite 202. What result? Would it make any difference if the lease between *T* and *L* provided that *T* would be liable for all consequential damages (defined as those reasonably foreseeable by the parties) resulting from *T*'s abandonment or breach?

4. *Policy and Practicality.* The argument for the duty to mitigate is that it promotes efficiency. The duty creates an incentive to utilize the fallow resource. The landlord is no worse off (but consider the problem immediately above), and the tenant is relieved of a dead weight cost. The arguments against are the need to adhere to settled expectations that landlords and tenants took into account in making their bargain (but change can occur prospectively), and that there are no efficiency gains. The landlord is required to expend effort he need not have expended had the tenant not breached, and that even though he may be compensated for this effort by the tenant in breach, he should receive compensation for the breach itself. If all the landlord gets is the rent he would have otherwise received from the tenant in breach, he has not been compensated for the breach. Part of the landlord's benefit of the bargain was to avoid having to look for a new tenant until the lease expired. If the tenant wants to quit early, he should pay the landlord fair compensation for the loss of this benefit, and payment for the out-of-pocket costs of finding a new tenant is not adequate because there are hidden transactional costs that are not out-of-pocket. (Perhaps because of the duty to mitigate, in general, a large landlord has to hire two additional rental agents he would not have hired but for the duty; however, their costs are not out-of-pocket expenses attributable to any particular tenant in breach.) Which argument is sounder?

Question: As a practical matter, what advice should you give to a tenant who wants to abandon before the lease term expires? How can the tenant mitigate damages?

5. *Security Deposits.* One device commonly employed by landlords to protect themselves from damage to the premises inflicted by the tenant or the tenant's failure to pay rent is to require a security deposit, often in an amount equal to one or more monthly rental payments. Most states regulate security deposits in varying ways. Some states limit the amount of the deposit that may be required. Some states require that deposits be placed in separate interest-bearing accounts and that the deposit, plus interest but less reason-

able expenses incurred to pay for damages caused by the tenant, be returned to the tenant at the end of the lease term. Some states impose on the landlord a fiduciary duty to the tenant with respect to the security deposit. Some states require the landlord to provide an itemized list of the deductions from the deposit. Some states impose a penalty for violation of these requirements, often some multiple of the deposit.

E.   DUTIES CONCERNING THE PREMISES

Many of the duties imposed on landlord and tenant with respect to the premises are duties that arise from specific provisions in the lease, but some duties are implied by law. This section focuses primarily on these implied duties.

1.   TENANT DUTIES

a.   No Waste, Nuisance, or Illegal Activity

Leases commonly contain provisions that prohibit the tenant from committing waste of the premises, harboring or committing a nuisance, or engaging in any illegal activity on the premises. In the absence of such provisions, though, tenants are still liable for waste that they may commit. The Restatement (Second) of Property, Landlord and Tenant, § 12.2, delineates the scope of the tenant's implied obligation not to commit waste. Unless the lease is to the contrary, a "tenant is entitled to make changes in the physical condition of the leased property which are reasonably necessary in order for the tenant to use the leased property in a manner that is reasonable under all the circumstances." But if the tenant goes beyond this and commits waste that cannot be restored or, if capable of restoration, is not accomplished within a reasonable time after the landlord demands restoration, the landlord may "terminate the lease and recover damages; continue the lease and recover damages; and in an appropriate case, obtain equitable relief."

But what constitutes waste? Suppose the ceiling in T's apartment is defective and, without authorization, T replaces it with gypsum sheetrock that is too thin to comply with the applicable building and housing code. At the same time T wires and installs a ceiling light and wall switch. Is this waste? See Rumiche Corp. v. Eisenreich, 40 N.Y.2d 174 (1976).

The common law of every state imposes a duty upon a possessor of real property to use that property in a fashion that does not injure the ability of another possessor to have reasonable use and enjoyment of his property. A breach of this duty constitutes an actionable nuisance, the usual remedy for which is an injunction to stop the activity that constitutes a nuisance. Nuisance will be considered in detail in Chapter Nine. As you may realize, nuisance is a bit circular. If A uses his land in some manner that is not compatible with his neighbor B's use of his land, and B's use is not compatible with A's use, which use is a nuisance? We will grapple with that knotty problem in Chapter Nine but, for the moment, a relatively simple case illustrates the scope of the tenant's obligation not to commit nuisance.

> *Example 6–3: L* leases an apartment to *T1*, who habitually plays hard rock music at full amplification at all hours of the day and night. Under a lease from *L*, *T2* occupies an apartment immediately adjacent to *T1* and is unable to sleep or engage in normal conversation as a result of *T1*'s activities. *T1*'s activity will no doubt be treated as a nuisance and *T2* may enjoin *T1* from committing the nuisance. But unless *T1*'s activity constitutes a breach of a lease provision prohibiting nuisance, *L* may have no remedy. In subsection 2(a), we will consider whether *T2* has any remedies against *L* with respect to the nuisance committed by *T1*.

Only the most poorly drafted lease would fail to include a covenant that the tenant will not engage in illegal activity on the premises, and providing that breach of the covenant entitles the landlord to terminate the lease. In the absence of such a provision, however, the landlord may still be able to evict and terminate the lease if the jurisdiction's statutory law so provides. See, e.g., N.Y. Real Property Law § 231: "Whenever the lessee or occupant ... of any building or premises, shall use or occupy the same, or any part thereof, for any illegal trade, manufacture or other business, the lease or agreement for the letting or occupancy of such building or premises, or any part thereof shall thereupon become void, and the landlord of such lessee or occupant may enter upon the premises so let or occupied." See also RRW Realty v. Flores, 686 N.Y.S.2d 278 (Civ. Ct. 1999).

b. Commercial Duty to Operate

Leases of commercial property intended for some form of retail use often split the rent into two parts—a base rent in a fixed amount and a rent that is a percentage of the tenant's gross sales. Conflict can arise in several dimensions under these leases. Suppose the tenant ceases to operate the retail business but continues to pay the base rent for the remainder of the term. Or, suppose the tenant changes the nature of the retail business, causing patronage, gross sales, and the percentage rent to fall sharply. A well drafted lease might contain provisions explicitly requiring the tenant to continue to operate the business in a fashion carefully and precisely described, but in the absence of such provisions, is there a duty to operate? If so, what is the scope of the duty?

When a tenant is in default of an express lease covenant to operate, a suit for damages is likely to be the landlord's sole remedy. Courts are unwilling to force a tenant to continue to operate an unprofitable business, and damages are likely to be an adequate remedy. See, e.g., Summit Towne Centre, Inc. v. Shoe Show of Rocky Mount, Inc., 573 Pa. 637 (2003). Economic efficiency is surely not advanced by making a tenant continue to operate a business at a loss.

When there is no express lease covenant to operate continuously, the question is whether such an obligation can be implied from other provisions of the lease.

COLLEGE BLOCK v. ATLANTIC RICHFIELD COMPANY

Court of Appeal of California, Second District
206 Cal.App.3d 1376 (1988)

ASHBY, ACTING P.J., delivered the opinion of the court.

In 1965 . . . College Block owned a parcel of undeveloped real property [and] College Block signed a 20–year lease with . . . Atlantic Richfield Company (ARCO) in which ARCO agreed to build and operate a gasoline service station on the property. . . . Pursuant to the lease, ARCO constructed and then operated for approximately 17 years a gasoline service station on the property. The rent . . . was determined by a percentage of the gasoline delivered, and irrespective of the gallons delivered, College Block was to receive a minimum of $1,000 per month.

On January 1, 1983, 39 months prior to the expiration of the lease, ARCO closed the station. When ARCO ceased operations, it paid College Block $1,000 per month for the months remaining on the lease. ARCO contended that it was responsible only for the minimum monthly rental because the lease did not contain an express covenant requiring it to operate the station. College Block brought suit alleging that ARCO was also responsible for additional sums College Block would have received had the station remained in business. College Block contended that it was entitled to damages because as a matter of law a covenant of continued operation was implied into the lease.

[The trial court] ruled as a matter of law that there was an implied covenant in the lease which required ARCO to operate a gasoline station for the entire 20–year lease period. Based upon this ruling, the parties subsequently stipulated that had the station been in operation, College Block would have received approximately $3,250 per month. A judgment based on this amount was . . . entered. . . .

[We] disagree with ARCO's contention that the language of the lease is ambiguous, but agree that further evidence must be considered before implying the covenant of continued operation into the lease. . . .

The issue of whether there is an implied covenant of continued operation arises because the lease did not fix the rent, but guaranteed a minimum payment plus a percentage based upon the gasoline delivered. In having a percentage lease, the parties contemplated a lengthy association (20 years) during which rents would periodically be established by the market place. A percentage lease provides a lessor with a hedge against inflation and automatically adjusts the rents if the location becomes more valuable. It is advantageous to the lessee if the "location proves undesirable or his enterprise proves unsuccessful." Thus, both parties share in the inherent business risk. Inherent within all percentage leases is the fundamental idea that the business must continually operate if it is to be successful. To make a commercial lease mutually profitable when the rent is a minimum plus a percentage, or is based totally on a percentage, a covenant to operate in good faith will be implied into the contract if the minimum rent is not substantial. Lippman v. Sears, Roebuck & Co., 44 Cal.2d 136 (1955)....

To effectuate the intent of the parties, implied covenants will be found if after examining the contract as a whole it is so obvious that the parties had no reason to state the covenant, the implication arises from the language of the agreement, and there is a legal necessity. *Lippman.* A covenant of continued operation can be implied into commercial leases containing percentage rental provisions in order for the lessor to receive that for which the lessor bargained.

We first examine the lease to determine that to which the parties bargained. The lease between ARCO and College Block required ARCO to build and operate a gasoline service station on the undeveloped property owned by College Block. Other provisions in the lease allowed ARCO to build and maintain any edifices ARCO desired in operating a service station, obligated ARCO to pay all applicable property taxes and insurance, prohibited College Block from conducting a gasoline station on other properties College Block owned or controlled, gave ARCO the right of first refusal if College Block received an offer to sell the property, and limited ARCO's use of the property to that of the gasoline service station.

In addition, the rent was tied to the operation of the station. The rent provision, an essential part of the lease, did not set a minimum payment irrespective of whether the property was utilized as a service station, but rather "irrespective of the number of gallons ... delivered." "Without an on-going service station operation, no basis would exist to calculate the rent." Continental Oil Co. v. Bradley, 198 Colo. 331 (1979). The wording of this provision suggests that continued operation of the business was contemplated.

Further, it is incongruent to limit College Block's abilities to lease properties it owned or controlled for use as another gasoline station under the non-competition clause, thus foreclosing College Block from securing another station if ARCO abandoned the premises, and to limit ARCO's ability to operate any other type of business on the property, yet to conclude that ARCO could cease operations when it desired. ... Both parties were entitled to the expectations as bargained for in the lease....

ARCO's contention that there is no implied covenant of continued operation is based on Article 7 of the lease[, which] allows ARCO "[at] any time during the term of this lease ... [to] remove from said premises any and all buildings, structures, improvements...." ARCO argues that [because] "it is impossible for ARCO to operate a service station while simultaneously exercising its right to remove all buildings and equipment from the leased property" it therefore could cease operating the station at any time as long as College Block was paid the specified minimum rent.

Crt does not agree

need Trial

ARCO's interpretation of this provision is inconsistent with the spirit of the entire contract. ... [When] this provision is viewed in conjunction with all other provisions of the contract, the party's intent becomes evident—ARCO was expected to continually operate a station for the entire length of the lease. Article 7 was an obvious recognition that ARCO would need the right to refurbish, replace, and upgrade its station over the 20–year lease period. However, leaving this property idle was not in the contemplation of the parties. ARCO could tear down the gasoline station, replace it, and refurbish it. However, ARCO was still obligated to operate a station for the entire leasehold period. ...

We now turn to whether the $1,000 rent minimum was "substantial." Contracts which determine rents by a percentage of sales inherently contain uncertainties. As discussed above, this type of contract is designed to adjust to the commercial realities of the day by reconciling the rent to the amount of sales. If a business is not profitable, courts are reluctant to force the lessee to continue to operate the business. However, as in all contracts, both parties are entitled to their reasonable expectations at the time the contract was entered into. [Calif. Civ. Code, § 1636.] If both parties contemplated continued operations of the business, a covenant of continued operation will be implied into a commercial lease containing a specified minimum plus a percentage when the guaranteed minimum is not substantial or adequate. ...

"A substantial minimum" cannot be precisely defined and factual information on this issue must be examined before a covenant will be implied. By evaluating the facts surrounding the formulation of the contract, the courts determine if the specified sum provides the lessor with what was reasonably expected. ... [The trial] court erred by ruling that there was an implied covenant of continued operation in the lease prior to receiving evidence on this factual issue.

The lease between ARCO and College Block was executed approximately 17 years prior to the cessation of operations. In the interim, great changes in property values, gasoline prices, and the amount of sales could have occurred. Before finding, as a matter of law, that a covenant of continued operation will be implied, the trier of fact must find that the $1,000, the guaranteed minimum, was not substantial and did not provide College Block with a fair return on its investment. The parties should be given an opportunity to submit evidence as to the facts and circumstances surrounding the contract to determine if, at the time the contract was entered into, the guaranteed rent was "substantial." We remand to the trial court so evidence may be heard on this issue....

NOTES, QUESTIONS, AND PROBLEM

1. *Covenants Limiting Use.* Commercial leases often contain a covenant that limits the tenant's use of the premises to a defined activity; e.g., a restaurant, or a retail clothing store, or a bookstore. Should such a covenant carry with it the implication that the tenant will continuously operate, e.g., a

restaurant, or should it be interpreted to mean only that the tenant cannot use the property for anything other than a restaurant? See, e.g., Dickey v. Philadelphia Minit–Man Corp., 377 Pa. 549, 552 (1954).

2. *Major Tenants.* Shopping center operators often desire to have a major tenant, usually called an anchor tenant, to attract large numbers of shoppers who might linger and patronize the peripheral tenants. If an anchor tenant ceases to operate, however, the oxygen is sucked out of the shopping atmosphere. Does that fact imply that by agreeing to be an anchor tenant, the tenant is obligated to operate continuously?

Yes, said the court in Columbia East Associates v. Bi–Lo, Inc., 299 S.C. 515 (App. 1989). The tenant, a supermarket chain, entered into a 20 year lease as the major tenant in a shopping center and agreed that the premises would be used solely as a grocery supermarket. Later, a competitor in a nearby shopping center ceased operations and Bi–Lo acquired the space, apparently to prevent any other competitor to move in. Bi–Lo then moved its store into the new space and made no real effort to sublease the old premises, though it had the right to do so. Instead, Bi–Lo paid the landlord the base rent, depriving it of any percentage rents. The court found Bi–Lo to be in breach of an implied covenant of continued operation, but that conclusion may have been influenced by the tenant's evident desire to stifle competition by keeping its old premises unavailable to any competitor.

No, said the Utah Supreme Court in Oakwood Village LLC v. Albertsons, Inc., 2004 Utah 101. For a fixed rent, the landlord had leased ground for 65 years to the tenant, who constructed a grocery supermarket at its own expense. The landlord had constructed a shopping center around the anchor tenant. Twenty-one years into the lease the tenant moved its store to another nearby location, continued to pay the rent, and even though it had the right to sublet or assign, it left the old space unoccupied in order to prevent a competitor from moving in. The court characterized the tenant's behavior as "perhaps not nice," but found no implied covenant to operate. Several factors contributed to this conclusion: (1) the absence of a percentage rent clause, (2) the "absence of any, let alone a restrictive, 'use of premises' clause," and (3) the tenant's "right to sublet or assign the lease, without the landlord's consent and with no restriction on the type of sublettees or assignees." Taken together, these facts undermined the contention that part of the bargain was an implicit promise on the tenant's part to operate continuously. The landlord made a bad bargain and entered into a poorly drafted lease. "Long term commercial leases," said the court, are risky by nature. "Each party took the risk that unpredictable market forces would at some later day render the ... terms unfavorable to themselves. Despite this risk, both parties willingly agreed to the terms in the lease. It is not our role to intervene now, construing the ... unambiguous terms to mean something different from what the parties intended them to mean at the outset."

3. *Problem.* For a fixed base rent and a percentage of T's gross sales, L leases commercial space to T "for the operation of a restaurant facility and for no other purpose," and T promises to "keep the leased premises open for business during normal business hours for a restaurant." T operates a full service restaurant open for lunch and supper, then opens a similar restaurant

under the same name nearby, and converts the first facility to a lunch only take-out menu, causing a significant drop in the percentage rent. Should a covenant of continued operation be implied? If so, has *T* violated the covenant? What additional facts would you need to know in order to answer these queries?

2. LANDLORD DUTIES

a. Quiet Enjoyment and Constructive Eviction

BLACKETT v. OLANOFF

Supreme Judicial Court of Massachusetts
371 Mass. 714 (1977)

WILKINS, J., delivered the opinion of the court.

The defendant in each of these consolidated actions for rent successfully raised constructive eviction as a defense against the landlords' claim. The judge found that the tenants were "very substantially deprived" of quiet enjoyment of their leased premises "*for a substantial* time" (emphasis original). He ruled that the tenants' implied warranty of quiet enjoyment was violated by late evening and early morning music and disturbances coming from nearby premises which the landlords leased to others for use as a bar or cocktail lounge (lounge). The judge further found that, although the landlords did not intend to create the conditions, the landlords "had it within their control to correct the conditions which ... amounted to a constructive eviction of each [tenant]." He also found that the landlords promised each tenant to correct the situation, that the landlords made some attempt to remedy the problem, but they were unsuccessful, and that each tenant vacated his apartment within a reasonable time. Judgment was entered for each tenant; the landlords appealed; and we transferred the appeals here. We affirm the judgments.

The landlords argue that they did not violate the tenants' implied covenant of quiet enjoyment because they are not chargeable with the noise from the lounge. The landlords do not challenge the judge's conclusion that the noise emanating from the lounge was sufficient to constitute a constructive eviction, if that noise could be attributed to the landlords.[13] Nor do the landlords seriously argue that a constructive eviction could not be found as matter of law because the lounge was not on the same premises as the tenants' apartments. The landlords' principal contention, based on the denial of certain requests for rulings, is that they are not responsible for the conduct of the proprietors, employees, and patrons of the lounge.

---

13. There was evidence that the lounge had amplified music (electric musical instruments and singing, at various times) which started at 9:30 P.M. and continued until 1:30 A.M. or 2 A.M., generally on Tuesdays through Sundays. The music could be heard through the granite walls of the residential tenants' building, and was described variously as unbelievably loud, incessant, raucous, and penetrating. The noise interfered with conversation and prevented sleep. There was also evidence of noise from patrons' yelling and fighting.

Our opinions concerning a constructive eviction by an alleged breach of an implied covenant of quiet enjoyment sometimes have stated that the landlord must perform some act with the intent of depriving the tenant of the enjoyment and occupation of the whole or part of the leased premises. See Katz v. Duffy, 261 Mass. 149, 151–152 (1927), and cases cited. There are occasions, however, where a landlord has not intended to violate a tenant's rights, but there was nevertheless a breach of the landlord's covenant of quiet enjoyment which flowed as the natural and probable consequence of what the landlord did, what he failed to do, or what he permitted to be done. Charles E. Burt, Inc. v. Seven Grand Corp., 340 Mass. 124, 127 (1959) (failure to supply light, heat, power, and elevator services). Westland Housing Corp. v. Scott, 312 Mass. 375, 381 (1942) (intrusions of smoke and soot over a substantial period of time due to a defective boiler). Shindler v. Milden, 282 Mass. 32, 33–34 (1933) (failure to install necessary heating system, as agreed). Case v. Minot, 158 Mass. 577, 587 (1893) (landlord authorizing another lessee to obstruct the tenant's light and air, necessary for the beneficial enjoyment of the demised premises). Skally v. Shute, 132 Mass. 367, 370–371 (1882) (undermining of a leased building rendering it unfit for occupancy). Although some of our opinions have spoken of particular action or inaction by a landlord as showing a presumed intention to evict, the landlord's conduct, and not his intentions, is controlling.

The judge was warranted in ruling that the landlords had it within their control to correct the condition which caused the tenants to vacate their apartments. The landlords introduced a commercial activity into an area where they leased premises for residential purposes. The lease for the lounge expressly provided that entertainment in the lounge had to be conducted so that it could not be heard outside the building and would not disturb the residents of the leased apartments. The potential threat to the occupants of the nearby apartments was apparent in the circumstances. The landlords complained to the tenants of the lounge after receiving numerous objections from residential tenants. From time to time, the pervading noise would abate in response to the landlord's complaints. We conclude that, as matter of law, the landlords had a right to control the objectionable noise coming from the lounge and that the judge was warranted in finding as a fact that the landlords could control the objectionable conditions.

This situation is different from the usual annoyance of one residential tenant by another, where traditionally the landlord has not been chargeable with the annoyance. See Katz v. Duffy, 261 Mass. 149 (1927) (illegal sale of alcoholic beverages); DeWitt v. Pierson, 112 Mass. 8 (1873) (prostitution).[14] Here we have a case more like Case v. Minot, 158 Mass. 577

---

14. The general, but not universal, rule in this country is that a landlord is not chargeable because one tenant is causing annoyance to another (A.H. Woods Theatre v. North American Union, 246 Ill. App. 521, 526–527 [1927] [music from one commercial tenant annoying another commercial tenant's employees]), even where the annoying conduct would be a breach of the landlord's covenant of quiet enjoyment if the landlord were the miscreant. See Paterson v. Bridges, 16 Ala. App. 54, 55 (1917); Thompson v. Harris, 9 Ariz. App. 341, 345 (1969), and cases

(1893), where the landlord entered into a lease with one tenant which the landlord knew permitted that tenant to engage in activity which would interfere with the rights of another tenant. There, to be sure, the clash of tenants' rights was inevitable, if each pressed those rights. Here, although the clash of tenants' interests was only a known potentiality initially, experience demonstrated that a decibel level for the entertainment at the lounge, acoustically acceptable to its patrons and hence commercially desirable to its proprietors, was intolerable for the residential tenants.

Because the disturbing condition was the natural and probable consequence of the landlords' permitting the lounge to operate where it did and because the landlords could control the actions at the lounge, they should not be entitled to collect rent for residential premises which were not reasonably habitable. Tenants such as these should not be left only with a claim against the proprietors of the noisome lounge. To the extent that our opinions suggest a distinction between nonfeasance by the landlord, which has been said to create no liability, and malfeasance by the landlord, we decline to perpetuate that distinction where the landlord creates a situation and has the right to control the objectionable conditions.

Judgments affirmed.

NOTES, QUESTIONS, AND PROBLEMS

1. Actual Eviction. If a landlord prevents the tenant from access to the leased premises an actual eviction has occurred, which extinguishes the tenant's liability to pay rent. A physical lockout of the tenant is an actual eviction. See, e.g. Aldrich v. Olson, 12 Wn. App. 665, 667 (1975). The landlord's failure to perform a lease obligation that is necessary for the tenant to have possession is an actual eviction. See, e.g., Esmieu v. Hsieh, 92 Wn. 2d 530 (1979).

Sometimes a landlord may physically dispossess the tenant of a portion of the leased premises. Such an actual partial eviction gives the tenant the right to move out and stop paying rent without liability for its non-payment. But if a tenant stays on after an actual partial eviction, jurisdictions split on the result. The traditional rule has been that the tenant may lawfully cease paying all rent until the actual partial eviction ceases. See, e.g, Smith v.

cited; 1 American Law of Property § 3.53 (A.J. Casner ed. 1952); Annot., 38 A.L.R. 250 (1925). Contra, Kesner v. Consumers Co., 255 Ill. App. 216, 228–229 (1929) (storage of flammables constituting a nuisance); Bruckner v. Helfaer, 197 Wis. 582, 585 (1929) residential tenant not liable for rent where landlord, with ample notice, does not control another tenant's conduct).

The rule in New York appears to be that the landlord may not recover rent if he has had ample notice of the existence of conduct of one tenant which deprives another tenant of the beneficial enjoyment of his premises and the landlord does little or nothing to abate the nuisance. See Cohen v. Werner, 85 Misc. 2d 341, 342 (N.Y. App. T. 1975); Rockrose Assocs. v. Peters, 81 Misc. 2d 971, 972 (N.Y. Civ. Ct. 1975) (office lease); Home Life Ins. Co. v. Breslerman, 168 Misc. 117, 118 (N.Y. App. T. 1938). But see comments in Trustees of the Sailors' Snug Harbor in the City of New York v. Sugarman, 264 App. Div. 240, 241 (N.Y. 1942) (no nuisance).

A tenant with sufficient bargaining power may be able to obtain an agreement from the landlord to insert and to enforce regulatory restrictions in the leases of other, potentially offending, tenants....

McEnany, 170 Mass. 26 (1897), in which the Massachusetts court held that the landlord's modest physical encroachment upon the leased premises entitled the tenant who remained in possession to suspend all rent payments. A 34 foot long shed under the landlord's possession encroached on tenant's lot by about a foot. Future Supreme Court Justice Oliver Wendell Holmes wrote the opinion.

A variation on the *Smith* rule is that adopted by the California intermediate appeals court in Dussin Investment Company v. Bloxham, 96 Cal.App.3d 308 (1979). To trigger a complete suspension of the obligation to pay rent, there must be proof that the tenant has been deprived of a "substantial portion of the premises." To be sure, the Massachusetts court in *Smith* noted that a *de minimis* dispossession would not suspend the rent obligation. The difference between *Smith* and *Bloxham* is that a physical dispossession that is more than *de minimis* but less than of a "substantial portion of the premises" ends the rental obligation under the *Smith* rule, but not under *Bloxham*. Instead, under *Bloxham* the tenant is entitled only to a partial abatement of rent in an amount that reflects the proportion of the premises denied to the tenant. The Restatement (Second) of Property, Landlord and Tenant, §§ 6.1, 11.1 (1977), applies the partial abatement rule to all cases of actual partial eviction.

2. Constructive Eviction. Constructive eviction results from the landlord's breach of the covenant of quiet enjoyment. Older common law held that this covenant existed only if it was in the lease. Today, the covenant is almost universally implied into every lease. Upon breach of the covenant the tenant may vacate and terminate the lease, or stay and sue for injunctive relief or damages. The rationale for the tenant's ability to vacate and terminate is that the covenant of quiet enjoyment and the covenant to pay rent are mutually dependent. Breach of the covenant of quiet enjoyment also denies the tenant the benefit of his entire bargain—useful possession—and thus entitles the tenant to terminate. This doctrine of dependent covenants is a departure from the usual rule that lease covenants are independent, meaning that a breach by the landlord of a lease covenant does not permit the tenant to breach an independent covenant.

A tenant who stays in possession after a breach of the covenant of quiet enjoyment usually loses the ability to withhold rent. Note that the court in *Blackett* observed that the tenants had vacated within a "reasonable time." The rationale for requiring the tenant to vacate is that the tenant's decision to remain suggests that the tenant did not consider the breach to be so significant as to amount to an eviction. See, e.g., Barash v. Pennsylvania Terminal Real Estate Corp., 26 N.Y.2d 77 (1970). The Restatement (Second) of Property, Landlord and Tenant §§ 6.1, 11.3, would permit the tenant to stay in possession and withhold rent. Generally, however, a tenant who claims total constructive eviction must vacate. This puts the tenant to a hard choice: If he vacates and abandons and it turns out that he was wrong about constructive eviction he has lost his leasehold and is liable for damages. Is there a way out of this dilemma?

The rule as to total constructive eviction has been softened by the development of the theory of partial constructive eviction. Under this approach, if the landlord's conduct is sufficiently egregious that it denies to the tenant the quiet enjoyment of a significant portion of the premises the tenant may stay and abate the rent. See Restatement (Second) of Property, Landlord and Tenant, § 6.1. Under the Restatement, "the rent is abated to the amount of that proportion of the rent which the fair rental value after the event giving the right to abate bears to the fair rental value before the event." Id., § 11.1. This approach is identical to the Restatement's approach to partial actual eviction. Some, but by no means all, courts have adopted the defense of partial constructive eviction. See, e.g, East Haven Associates, Inc. v. Gurian, 313 N.Y.S.2d 927 (Civ. Ct. 1970), adopting the theory and applying rent abatement as the remedy. See also Minjak Co. v. Randolph, 528 N.Y.S.2d 554 (App. Div. 1988). Contra, Brine v. Bergstrom, 4 Wn. App. 288 (1971).

Minjak is especially instructive. *L* leased a 1700 square foot loft in the Chelsea district of Manhattan to *T* for use as residence and music studio. A year later the tenant on the floor above permitted water to pour repeatedly into *T*'s loft, ruining clothing, and onto *T*'s grand piano and other musical instruments. Then the upstairs tenant began sandblasting, which caused sand to seep into *T*'s clothes, bed, food, and eyes. Then *L* commenced construction work, causing great clouds of dust to invade *T*'s loft, settling everywhere. *L*'s workmen removed plastic sheeting that *T* employed in a futile effort to stem the tide of dust and debris. Then *L* demolished portions of the stairs, leaving unmarked holes in them for the unwary. Then *L* jackhammered into *T*'s loft, showering the loft with yet more debris, some of which fell on *T*. Then *L*'s workmen decided to mix their concrete on the floor of *T*'s loft. The trial court awarded an 80% rent abatement for this partial constructive eviction, reasoning that *T* stayed on and could use a small portion as a residence though its value as a studio was almost wholly lost. The trial court also awarded punitive damages. The judgment was affirmed.

What constitutes a breach of the covenant of quiet enjoyment? First, the conduct that allegedly constitutes breach must be that of the landlord or persons who are either the landlord's agents or interest holders through the landlord (such as a lessee). Of course, if the landlord never had good title and the actions that interfere with the tenant's quiet enjoyment come from the true and paramount owner, the landlord will be held to have breached the quiet enjoyment covenant. In one sense, that is just a subcategory of landlord action—delivering possession without authority to do so. See Reste Realty Corp. v. Cooper, 53 N.J. 444, 457 (1969).

As *Minjak* illustrates, when the conduct is truly astounding—amounting to the creation of conditions that are intolerable—there is little doubt that the tenant has been deprived of quiet enjoyment. One might wonder why the tenant in *Minjak* stayed on through this evident nightmare, but as anyone who has lived in Manhattan can testify, it is not easy to find an affordable replacement for 1700 square feet of space. Even there, though, because the tenant chose to endure the suffering, he obtained only a rent abatement (though the punitive damages must have been some balm).

But what if the landlord's behavior is not so egregious? Or if the acts are not those of the landlord, but might be controllable by the landlord? The problems below raise these issues and others.

3. Problems.

a. Recall the facts from Example 6–2. *L* leases an apartment to *T1*, who habitually plays hard rock music at full amplification at all hours of the day and night. Under a lease from *L*, *T2* occupies an apartment immediately adjacent to *T1* and is unable to sleep or engage in normal conversation as a result of *T1*'s activities. *T2* requests *L* to take steps to stop the aural interference. *L* declines to do so. Has *L* breached the covenant of quiet enjoyment? Would the answer be different if the lease to *T1* contained a covenant that *T1* would not commit a "nuisance or other action that would deprive other tenants in the building of their quiet enjoyment of their premises"?

b. *L* leases commercial space to *T* for the purpose of operating a school offering language instruction mostly to young Latino members of a church known, among other things, for its members' abstention from alcoholic beverages. *L*'s property manager constantly disparages Latinos to *T*'s manager, yells, swears, and employs ethnic slurs when conversing with *T*, and, after granting permission to *T* to host a fiesta on the premises, accuses *T* of intending to serve alcoholic beverages to minors at the fiesta. *T*'s manager explains that the church members abstain from alcohol and that the state Governor and Mexican consul will attend, thus indicating that underage consumption of alcohol will be extremely unlikely. Without any evidence of underage drinking *L*'s property manager summons police to the fiesta to deal with alleged underage drinking, thus completely disrupting the fiesta. *T* vacates and pleads constructive eviction as a defense to *L*'s suit for rent. What result? Suppose that the property manager confined his ethnic slurs to comments made only to *T*'s manager, and otherwise cooperated with *T* to deliver what *T* was promised under the lease?

c. *L* leases an apartment in a building to *T*. Unknown third parties commit crimes in and around the building, consisting of assaults, robberies, and burglaries. *L* installs better lighting, new and improved locks, and requests that the local police patrol the area more heavily. The crimes continue. *T* vacates and *L* sues for rent. *T* claims constructive eviction as a defense. What result?

b. Implied Warranty of Habitability

Landlord
WADE v. JOBE
Tenant

Supreme Court of Utah
818 P.2d 1006 (Utah 1991)

DURHAM, J.

In June 1988, defendant Lynda Jobe (the tenant) rented a house in Ogden, Utah, from plaintiff Clyde Wade (the landlord). Jobe had three young children. Shortly after she took occupancy, the tenant discovered numerous defects in the dwelling, and within a few days, she had no hot water. Investigation revealed that the flame of the water heater had been extinguished by accumulated sewage and water in the basement which also produced a foul odor throughout the house. The tenant notified the landlord, who came to the premises a number of times, each time pumping the sewage and water from the basement onto the sidewalk and relighting the water heater. These and other problems persisted from July through October 1988. In November 1988, the tenant notified the landlord that she would withhold rent until the sewage problem was solved permanently. The situation did not improve, and an inspection by the Ogden City Inspection Division (the division) in December 1988 revealed that the premises were unsafe for human occupancy due to the lack of a sewer connection and other problems. Within a few weeks, the division made another inspection, finding numerous code violations which were a substantial hazard to the health and safety of the occupants. The division issued a notice that the property would be condemned if the violations were not remedied.

After the tenant moved out of the house, the landlord brought suit . . . to recover the unpaid rent. The tenant filed a counterclaim, seeking an offset against rent owed because of the uninhabitable condition of the premises and seeking damages, attorney fees, and declaratory relief under the Utah Consumer Sales Practices Act, Utah Code Ann. §§ 13–11–1 to–23. . . . At trial, the landlord was awarded judgment of unpaid rent of $770, the full rent due under the parties' original agreement. The tenant was denied any offsets, and her counterclaim was dismissed, the court holding that the Utah Consumer Sales Practices Act did not apply to landlord/tenant transactions and, if it did, the landlord had not engaged in any deceptive act. This appeal followed, raising two issues: First, may a tenant recover at common law for breach of a warranty of habitability? Second, does the Utah Consumer Sales Practices Act apply to residential rental transactions, and if the Act is applicable, did the landlord in this case commit an unconscionable or deceptive act in violation of it?

The discussion concerning the warranty of habitability contained in the first section of this opinion reflects the unanimous view of the members of this court. The second section, discussing whether the renting of residential housing is a consumer transaction within the meaning of the Utah Consumer Sales Practices Act (UCSPA), reflects only the view of the author and Justice Zimmerman. The remaining members of the court do not consider it necessary in this case to reach this question because of the likelihood that defendant will receive adequate relief on her counterclaims under the warranty of habitability doctrine . . . They may or may not prove to be right, but I include my views on the UCSPA for the benefit of the trial court and the bar nonetheless. . . .

I. *Warranty of Habitability*

At common law, the leasing of real property was viewed primarily as a conveyance of land for a term, and the law of property was applied to landlord/tenant transactions. At a time when the typical lease was for agricultural purposes, it was assumed that the land, rather than any improvements, was the most important part of the leasehold. [Javins v. First Nat'l Realty Corp., 428 F.2d 1071, 1077 (D.C. Cir.), *cert. denied,* 400

U.S. 925 (1970).] Under the rule of caveat emptor, a tenant had a duty to inspect the premises to determine their safety and suitability for the purposes for which they were leased before entering a lease. Moreover, absent deceit or fraud on the part of the landlord or an express warranty to the contrary, the landlord had no duty to make repairs during the course of the tenancy. Under the law of waste, it was the tenant's implied duty to make most repairs.

Unlike tenants in feudal England, most modern tenants bargain for the use of structures on the land rather than the land itself. Modern tenants generally lack the necessary skills or means to inspect the property effectively or to make repairs. *Javins,* 428 F.2d at 1078–79. Moreover, the rule of caveat emptor assumes an equal bargaining position between landlord and tenant. Modern tenants, like consumers of goods, however, frequently have no choice but to rely on the landlord to provide a habitable dwelling. See *Javins,* 428 F.2d at 1079. Where they exist, housing shortages, standardized leases, and racial and class discrimination place today's tenants, as consumers of housing, in a poor position to bargain effectively for express warranties and covenants requiring landlords to lease and maintain safe and sanitary housing. *Javins,* 428 F.2d at 1079; Green v. Superior Court, 10 Cal. 3d 616, [624–625] (1974).

In consumer law, implied warranties are designed to protect ordinary consumers who do not have the knowledge, capacity, or opportunity to ensure that goods which they are buying are in safe condition. The implied warranty of habitability has been adopted in other jurisdictions to protect the tenant as the party in the less advantageous bargaining position.

The concept of a warranty of habitability is in harmony with the widespread enactment of housing and building codes which reflect a legislative desire to ensure decent housing. It is based on the theory that the residential landlord warrants that the leased premises are habitable at the outset of the lease term and will remain so during the course of the tenancy. *See Javins,* 428 F.2d at 1081. The warranty applies to written and oral leases, *see Javins,* 428 F.2d at 1077 n.29, and to single-family as well as to multiple-unit dwellings. The warranty of habitability has been adopted, either legislatively or judicially, in over forty states and the District of Columbia. See 2 R. Powell, The Law of Real Property ¶ 233 [2], at §§ 16B–50 to–51 n.42 (cases), ¶ 233[3], at § 16B–64 (statutes) (1991).

In recent years, this court has conformed the common law in this state to contemporary conditions by rejecting the strict application of traditional property law to residential leases, recognizing that it is often more appropriate to apply contract law. Similarly, we have expanded landlord liability in tort. [Stephenson v. Warner, 581 P.2d 567 (Utah 1978) (landlord must use ordinary care to ensure leased premises are reasonably safe)]. Consistent with prevailing trends in consumer law, products liability law, and the law of torts, we reject the rule of caveat emptor and recognize the common law implied warranty of habitability in residential[15] leases.

---

15. We do not decide whether the warranty is implied in commercial leases.

The determination of whether a dwelling is habitable depends on the individual facts of each case. To guide the trial court in determining whether there is a breach of the warranty of habitability, we describe some general standards that the landlord is required to satisfy. We note initially that the warranty of habitability does not require the landlord to maintain the premises in perfect condition at all times, nor does it preclude minor housing code violations or other defects. Moreover, the landlord will not be liable for defects caused by the tenant. *See Javins*, 428 F.2d at 1082 n.62. Further, the landlord must have a reasonable time to repair material defects before a breach can be established. As a general rule, the warranty of habitability requires that the landlord maintain "bare living requirements," and that the premises are fit for human occupation. *See* Mease v. Fox, 200 N.W.2d 791 (Iowa 1972); Hilder v. St. Peter, 144 Vt. 150, [159] (1984). Failure to supply heat or hot water, for example, breaches the warranty. A breach is not shown, however, by evidence of minor deficiencies such as the malfunction of venetian blinds, minor water leaks or wall cracks, or a need for paint.

Substantial compliance with building and housing code standards will generally serve as evidence of the fulfillment of a landlord's duty to provide habitable premises. Evidence of violations involving health or safety, by contrast, will often sustain a tenant's claim for relief. *See* Green v. Superior Court, 517 P.2d at 1182–83. At the same time, just because the housing code provides a basis for implication of the warranty, a code violation is not necessary to establish a breach so long as the claimed defect has an impact on the health or safety of the tenant. Hilder v. St. Peter, [144 Vt. at 159].

In the instant case, in support of her claim that the premises were not in habitable condition, the tenant presented two city housing inspection reports detailing numerous code violations which were, in the words of the trial judge, "a substantial hazard to the health and safety of the occupants." Those violations included the presence of raw sewage on the sidewalks and stagnant water in the basement, creating a foul odor. At trial, the tenant testified that she had repeatedly informed the landlord of the problem with the sewer connection and the resulting lack of hot water, but the landlord never did any more than temporarily alleviate the problem. The landlord did not controvert the evidence of substantial problems. .... [Because] we have now recognized the warranty [we] remand this case to the trial court to determine whether the landlord has breached the implied warranty of habitability as defined in this opinion. If the trial court finds a breach of the warranty of habitability, it must then determine damages.

A. Remedies. Under traditional property law, a lessee's covenant to pay rent was viewed as independent of any covenants on the part of the landlord. Even when a lessor expressly covenanted to make repairs, the lessor's breach did not justify the lessee's withholding rent. Under the prevailing contemporary view of the residential lease as a contractual transaction, however, the tenant's obligation to pay rent is conditioned upon the landlord's fulfilling his part of the bargain. The payment of rent by the tenant and the landlord's duty to provide habitable premises are, as a result, dependent covenants.

Once the landlord has breached his duty to provide habitable conditions, there are at least two ways the tenant can treat the duty to pay rent. The tenant may continue to pay rent to the landlord or withhold the rent.[16] If the tenant continues to pay full rent to the landlord during the period of uninhabitability, the tenant can bring an affirmative action to establish the breach and receive a reimbursement for excess rents paid. Rent withholding, on the other hand, deprives the landlord of the rent due during the default, thereby motivating the landlord to repair the premises.[17]

Some jurisdictions have taken the position that ... damages for the uninhabitable conditions existing prior to the tenant's withholding must be recovered in a separate action. We reject this reasoning; it is more in keeping with the policy behind our adoption of the warranty of habitability to provide for retroactive abatement of the rent during the period of the landlord's default whether or not the tenant withholds rent.[18]

B. Damages. In general, courts have applied contract remedies when a breach of the warranty of habitability has been shown. One available remedy, therefore, is damages. Special damages may be recovered when, as a foreseeable result of the landlord's breach, the tenant suffers personal injury, property damage, relocation expenses, or other similar injuries. *See* Restatement (Second) of Property, Landlord & Tenant § 10.2 (1977). General damages recoverable in the form of rent abatement or reimbursement to the tenant are more difficult to calculate.

Several different measures for determining the amount of rent abatement to which a tenant is entitled have been used by the courts. The first of these is the fair rental value of the premises as warranted less their fair rental value in the unrepaired condition. Under this approach, the contract rent may be considered as evidence of the value of the premises as warranted. Another measure is the contract rent less the fair rental value of the premises in the unrepaired condition. Methodological difficulties inherent in both of these measures, combined with the practical difficulties of producing evidence on fair market value,[19] however, limit the

---

16. In addition, some jurisdictions recognize rent application, also known as "repair and deduct," allowing the tenant to use the rent money to repair the premises. Because this remedy has not been relied on or sought in the instant case, we do not at this time make a ruling on its availability in Utah.

17. The majority of jurisdictions that permit rent withholding allow the tenant to retain the funds subject to the discretionary power of the court to order the deposit of the rent into escrow. ... [We] think this type of escrow account would provide a useful protective procedure in the right circumstances.

18. Before the tenant may receive a rent abatement, she must put the landlord in breach by giving her actual or constructive notice of the defects and a reasonable time in which to make repairs.

19. Under either approach, at least one market value is almost certain to require expert testimony. The production of such testimony will increase the cost, in time and money, of the typical case.

efficacy of those measures for dealing with residential leases. For this reason, a number of courts have adopted what is called the "percentage diminution" (or percentage reduction in use) approach which places more discretion with the trier of fact.

Under the percentage diminution approach, the tenant's recovery reflects the percentage by which the tenant's use and enjoyment of the premises has been reduced by the uninhabitable conditions. In applying this approach, the trial court must carefully review the materiality of the particular defects and the length of time such defects have existed. It is true that the percentage diminution approach requires the trier of fact to exercise broad discretion and some subjective judgment to determine the degree to which the defective conditions have diminished the habitability of the premises. It should be noted, however, that despite their theoretical appeal the other approaches are not objectively precise either. Furthermore, they involve the use of an expert witness's subjective opinion of the "worth" of habitable and uninhabitable premises.

As the foregoing discussion demonstrates, the determination of appropriate damages in cases of a breach of the warranty of habitability will often be a difficult task. None of the approaches described above is inherently illegitimate, but we think that the percentage diminution approach has a practical advantage in that it will generally obviate the need for expert testimony and reduce the cost and complexity of enforcing the warranty of habitability. We acknowledge the limitation of the method but conclude that it is as sound in its result as any other and more workable in practice. We will have to depend on development of the rule in specific cases to determine whether it will be universally applicable.

II. *Consumer Sales Practices Act*

A. Applicability. The Utah Consumer Sales Practices Act (UCSPA), Utah Code Ann. §§ 13–11–1 to–23, prohibits deceptive or unconscionable acts or practices by a supplier in connection with a consumer transaction. A consumer transaction is broadly defined as

> a sale, lease, assignment, award by chance, or other written or oral transfer or disposition of goods, services, or other property, both tangible and intangible (except securities and insurance), to a person for primarily personal, family, or household purposes. ... It includes any offer or solicitation, any agreement, any performance of an agreement with respect to any of these transfers or dispositions.

... The Act does not expressly include or exclude residential leases, nor was there any indication in the floor debate prior to the statute's enactment whether the legislature intended to include landlord/tenant transactions within its application.

The UCSPA was modeled after the Uniform Consumer Sales Practices Act[, which] has been adopted in only three states: Utah, Kansas, and Ohio. There is great diversity in the language, scope, degree of enforcement, and judicial interpretation of the various state consumer protection laws. Most relevant here are the differences in the statutory language used to define what is considered to be a "commercial transaction" or "trade or commerce" subject to any given law. The Uniform Consumer Sales Practices Act states that it applies to the "sale, lease, assignment, award by chance, or other disposition of *an item of goods, a service, or an intangible.*" Unif. Consumer Sales Practices Act § 2(1) (emphasis added). [The] comment to section 2(1) states, that "land transactions ... are excluded altogether" from the scope of the model act. The Utah version of the model act contains no such comment. Moreover, the language of the Utah statute is different, stating that it applies to "goods, services, or other property *both tangible and intangible.*" Utah Code Ann. § 13–11–3(2) (emphasis added). As a general rule, "tangible" property can be either real or personal. The Utah Legislature's addition of the word "tangible" to the language of the definition of consumer transaction is consistent with the conclusion that the Utah act was meant to apply to residential leases and other land transactions. The UCSPA states that it should be "construed liberally" to promote ... uniformity in the law between Utah and the other states enacting similar consumer protection laws. ... [T]herefore, it is instructive to look at the law as it has developed in other jurisdictions.

Defendant cites a number of cases from other states and the federal courts which apply consumer protection laws to residential leases. Most of the consumer protection statutes interpreted in those cases are modeled after the Uniform Trade Practices and Consumer Protection Law, which ... differ[s] from the Uniform Consumer Sales Practices Act and the UCSPA. The statutory definition of "trade and commerce" subject to the former is much broader, expressly including the sale of real property....

Notwithstanding this difference, this author and Justice Zimmerman think the Utah consumer protection statute applies to residential leases. The UCSPA specifically includes the "lease" of tangible and intangible property.... Moreover, that the UCSPA does not expressly mention the leasing of *real property* argues in favor of, rather than against, its application; the legislature has mandated a liberal construction of the Act, and it was explicit in excepting other transactions from its jurisdiction.

The contemporary view of landlord/tenant relations and the public policy behind the consumer protection laws also support the applicability of the UCSPA to residential leasing. ... Functionally, the tenant, much like a buyer of a used car, is a consumer of housing....

One of the stated purposes of the UCSPA is "to protect consumers from suppliers who commit deceptive and unconscionable sales practices." Utah Code Ann. § 13–11–2(2). The legislative intent ... was to balance the unequal bargaining positions between supplier and consumer. The tenant is entitled to protection under these remedial laws as much as any other consumer. In view of (1) the legislature's mandate to construe the UCSPA liberally, (2) the stated purpose of keeping Utah law consistent with ... the consumer protection laws of other states, and (3) the absence of any language or other expression of legislative intent to the contrary, this author and Justice Zimmerman would hold that the renting of residential housing is a consumer transaction within the meaning of the UCSPA.

B. *Violations of the Act.* Section 13–11–4(2) of the UCSPA enumerates several acts which are considered deceptive *per se.* Under that section, the tenant asserts that the landlord engaged in a deceptive act by indicating that the premises were "of a particular standard, quality, grade, style, or model" when they were not. . . . The UCSPA requires that the supplier act "with intent to deceive." Utah Code Ann. § 13–11–4(2). . . . The determination of whether a person had the intent is one of fact for the lower court. . . . In this case, . . . there does not appear to be any evidence that the landlord knew of the problem with the sewer connection when he rented the premises. There is therefore no reason for us to disturb the trial court's findings . . . that the landlord did not engage in a deceptive act under the UCSPA.

The tenant also asserts that the landlord's actions were unconscionable under section 13–11–5 of the UCSPA. Under the statute, unconscionability does not require proof of specific intent but can be found by considering circumstances which the supplier "knew *or had reason to know.*" Utah Code Ann. § 13–11–5(3) (emphasis added). The determination of unconscionability is a question of law. Utah Code Ann. § 13–11–5(2). This court is therefore free to review the record and make its own conclusions as to this determination. . . .

[T]here is no evidence that the landlord knew when he rented the premises that there was a problem with the sewer connection, nor is there any indication that he had reason to know of the problem at that time. Further, . . . the tenant had the opportunity to inspect the premises before she rented the house [but] she did not go down into the basement when she first looked at the house. Thus, at the time the lease was signed, the tenant had a meaningful choice in whether or not to rent the house, and the bargaining power of the parties was relatively equal since both had the same opportunity to inspect the premises. As a matter of law, the landlord did not act unconscionably in renting the premises to the tenant initially.

The relative positions of the parties changed dramatically, however, once the tenant moved into the house, discovered the problems, and informed the landlord. According to the housing inspector's testimony, by December 1988 the premises exhibited " 'dozens' of violations of the Utah Housing Code which posed substantial dangers to the health and safety of the occupants, including the presence of raw sewage on the sidewalks, and stagnant water in the basement with a foul odor." The landlord's repeated failure to repair the sewage problem after he had knowledge of its existence was unconscionable. At that point, the tenant's only choice was either living without hot water, with foul odors permeating her residence and standing water and raw sewage in the basement, or moving out of the house and incurring the substantial expenditure of time, energy, and money that relocation requires. This amounted to no meaningful choice at all. . . . [F]rom that point until the premises were ordered vacated, the bargain became one with terms "so one-sided as to oppress" the tenant. . . .

The division investigated the premises twice during December 1988. The tenant . . . called the housing inspectors once, [but] it was the landlord who called the inspectors the second time. The purpose of that second call, by the landlord's own admission, was to have the house condemned "so [the tenant] would move out." The landlord's efforts were successful; the second inspection resulted in a notice ordering vacation of the premises until the "life-safety" threats were corrected. The landlord's direct admission that he had the house effectively condemned for the purpose of evicting the tenant rather than repairing the sewer system is shocking. Tenants in Utah have a right to be evicted only by judicial process. The landlord's actions violated state policy disfavoring self-help evictions. He also abused the building inspection process. His acts were unconscionable under the UCSPA. . . .

A consumer has an express statutory right to bring an action under the UCSPA even if he seeks or is entitled to damages or otherwise has an adequate remedy at law. Utah Code Ann. § 13–11–19(1). The tenant in this case should not be precluded from bringing an action under the statute *and* under the common law warranty of habitability.

Conclusion

The decision of the trial court dismissing the tenant's counterclaim for declaratory relief under the UCSPA is affirmed. Its determination regarding the implied warranty of habitability, however, is reversed. We remand this case to the trial court to determine whether the landlord breached the implied warranty of habitability as defined in this opinion. If the trial court determines that he was not in breach, the landlord will be entitled to payment for all the past due rent. If the trial court determines that his breach of the warranty of habitability totally excused the tenant's rent obligation (i.e., rendered the premises virtually uninhabitable), the landlord's action to recover rent due will fail. If the trial court determines that the landlord's breach partially excused the tenant's rent obligation, the tenant will be entitled to a percentage rent abatement for the period during which the house was uninhabitable.

NOTES, QUESTIONS, AND PROBLEMS

1. Source of the Warranty of Habitability. The implied warranty of habitability was initially created by judicial decision. The first court to do so was the Hawaii Supreme Court, in Lemle v. Breeden, 51 Haw. 426 (1969). A year later, the decision in Javins v. First National Realty Corp., 428 F.2d 1071 (D.C. Cir. 1970), to create an implied warranty of habitability under D.C. law spurred acceptance of the idea. Today, almost all states have adopted the implied warranty of habitability, either by statute or judicial decision. A few have rejected it. See, e.g., Cohran v. Boothby Realty Co., 379 So.2d 561 (Ala. 1980); Miles v. Shauntee, 664 S.W.2d 512 (Ky. 1983); Bedell v. Los Zapatistas, Inc., 805 P.2d 1198 (Colo. App. 1991). A warranty of habitability is imposed under the URLTA § 2.104(a). In every jurisdiction that imposes a warranty of habitability, the warranty may not be waived by agreement. See, e.g., Knight v. Hallsthammar, 29 Cal.3d 46 (1981); Leardi v. Brown, 394 Mass. 151 (1985); Park West Management Corp. v. Mitchell, 47 N.Y.2d 316 (1979); Hilder v. St. Peter, 144 Vt. 150 (1984); N.Y. Real Prop. Law § 235–b(2); URLTA §§ 1.403, 1.404.

The measure of what constitutes habitability varies from state to state. Some states tie the concept to compliance with applicable building or housing codes. See, e.g., Worden v. Ordway, 105 Idaho 719 (1983); Teller v. McCoy, 162 W.Va. 367 (1978); Winchester Management Corp. v. Staten, 361 A.2d 187 (D.C. App. 1976). Others, such as the Utah court in *Wade*, start with housing codes but are willing to find a breach if there is any condition that would have a material adverse impact on the health and safety of the tenant such that bare minimal living conditions are not present. See also Lemle v. Breeden, 51 Haw. 426 (1969). This standard leaves much to the determination of the fact finder.

2. Remedies. The court in *Wade* sets out some of the remedies available to a tenant when the warranty of habitability is breached, but it is useful to summarize the full range of possibilities here.

a. Rescission: Termination of the Lease. The tenant may move out and stop paying rent. This is implicit in the conclusion that the habitability warranty and the rental obligation are dependent covenants. Note that this permits the tenant to terminate the lease even under circumstances that might not support a claim of constructive eviction due to breach of the covenant of quiet enjoyment.

b. Stay in Possession and Withhold Rent. Unlike constructive eviction, which requires the tenant to move out, after landlord breach of the warranty of habitability a tenant may stay and withhold rent. The landlord may bring suit for the unpaid rent, but breach of the habitability warranty is a defense. The tenant may be required to pay a portion of the rent, as discussed in connection with "rent abatement" (see below), but not until there has been a judicial determination of breach. The corollary to this principle is that the tenant is entitled to assert breach of the warranty of habitability as a defense in an eviction proceeding, even in a summary proceeding. The landlord's right to possession is dependent on compliance with the warranty.

There are a number of states that have statutes regulating rent withholding. It is common for these statutes to require that the tenant notify the landlord of the defects and give the landlord a chance to rectify the problem before rent may be withheld. Note that the court in *Wade* created a requirement of notification before the warranty of habitability can be invoked. See also Hilder v. St. Peter, 144 Vt. 150, 162–163 (1984). Some states require that the local housing authorities confirm the presence of the violations that constitute breach of the warranty of habitability before the tenant may withhold rent. As the Utah court in *Wade* noted, in some states deposit of the withheld rent into an escrow account is within judicial decision, but in other states deposit into an escrow account is required. In any case, it is a good idea for the tenant to deposit rent into an escrow account. If the tenant is held to be liable for back rent and cannot pay it, he may be evicted. Deposit into an escrow account avoids the temptation to spend the rent money on the rosy expectation that the tenant will never have to pay any back rent.

c. *Rent Abatement.* This remedy is a variation upon rent withholding. A tenant may stay in possession and pay only a portion of the stipulated rental, or a tenant may seek a return from the landlord of a portion of rent previously paid when the premises were uninhabitable. This remedy applies when the landlord's breach of the warranty of habitability only partially destroys the utility of the premises to the tenant. If the landlord's breach deprives the tenant of any use of the premises, the rent obligation will be completely suspended.

When rent abatement applies some formula must be employed to determine how much of the rent obligation remains. The court in *Wade* lays out the options.

> *Proportion of Uninhabitable Fair Rental Value to Habitable Fair Rental Value.* Under this test, the fair rental value of the premises in a habitable condition is first determined, then the fair rental value of the property in its actual condition is determined, and the proportion that the "as is" value bears to the value in habitable conditions determines the proportion of the rent abatement.

> *Example 6–4*: The lease rental is $200 per month, the fair rental value in habitable condition is $250, and the fair rental value of the premises in its "as is" condition is $50, or 1/5 of the fair rental value. The lease rental is abated to 1/5 of the stated rent: $40 per month.

Note that this method does not presume that the lease rental is equal to the fair rental value in a habitable condition.

> *Proportion of Uninhabitable Fair Value to Lease Rental.* Under this test, the fair rental value of the premises in its uninhabitable condition is compared to the lease rental, and the rent is abated to its actual fair rental value. See, e.g., Park West Management Corp. v. Mitchell, 47 N.Y.2d 316, 329 (1979).

> *Example 6–5*: The lease rental is $200 per month and the fair rental value of the premises in its "as is" condition is $50. The lease rental is abated to $50.

Note that under this test the tenant receives no additional benefit for having leased property at less than its fair value in a habitable condition.

> *Percentage Diminution of Use.* Under this test, which the Utah court in *Wade* preferred, the fact-finder determines what percentage of the premises' utility to the tenant has been lost due to the landlord's breach of the warranty of habitability.

> *Example 6–6*: The lease rental is $200 per month. The jury determines that the landlord's breach of the warranty of habitability has reduced the tenant's use of the premises by 90%. The rent is abated to $20 per month.

d. Repair and Deduct. Under statutes in some states, a tenant may make repairs to the premises and deduct the cost of those repairs from the rent. See, e.g., Jangla Realty Co. v. Gravagna, 447 N.Y.S.2d 338 (Civ. Ct. 1981). Those statutes sometimes limit the amount of the deduction that may be made. The repair and deduct remedy is not exclusively the product of statutes, however; some states have permitted it by judicial decision. See, e.g., Pugh v. Holmes, 486 Pa. 272, 293–294 (1979); Marini v. Ireland, 56 N.J. 130 (1970). To invoke repair-and-deduct, the tenant must notify the landlord of the specific defects and the action the tenant will take if the repairs are not accomplished by the landlord within a reasonable time. In *Jangla* the landlord's failure to repair a broken door lock within 18 hours after a burglary of the premises was a failure to repair within a reasonable time. Repairs must be reasonably priced and cannot exceed the amount of the rent available to apply against the cost, which, at most, is the rent owed for the remainder of the lease term.

e. Damages. In addition to the above rent reduction remedies, a tenant might assert an independent claim against the landlord for compensatory damages. For such a claim to succeed, the tenant must prove that the landlord's breach damaged personal property of the tenant, or caused the tenant to incur expenses in addition to and distinct from the rent. For example, if the landlord's breach causes water to come through a roof, ruining valuable personal property of the tenant, the landlord may be liable for that loss. See, e.g, Minjak Co. v. Randolph, 528 N.Y.S.2d 554 (App. Div. 1988); Hilder v. St. Peter, 144 Vt. 150 (1984).

f. Injunctive Relief. When damage remedies are inadequate, a tenant may be able to obtain an injunction to force the landlord to fix the defects that render the premises uninhabitable.

g. Criminal Sanctions. In some jurisdictions, a landlord's wilful violation of housing codes may be a crime. Of course, enforcement of these sanctions is within the discretion of public prosecutors.

h. Administrative Enforcement. Housing inspectors, charged with the responsibility of enforcing local housing and building codes, possess an array of sanctions that can be applied to landlords, including civil penalties or injunctive relief. Aggrieved tenants can institute enforcement proceedings by requesting inspection of the premises which, if it reveals code violations, is likely to lead to further enforcement action by the inspectors.

i. Consumer Protection Statutes. Finally, as Justices Durham and Zimmerman contended in *Wade*, state consumer protection statutes may apply to the rental of housing that is or becomes uninhabitable. This possibility opens the door to a separate and distinct basis of landlord liability and remedies for violation of those statutes. As noted in *Wade*, these statutes might be violated by landlord conduct that is unconscionable. While it is likely that unconscionable conduct will also be the conduct that constitutes breach of the warranty of habitability, there may be circumstances where there is no breach but the landlord's conduct is unconscionable. For example, in a jurisdiction that finds no breach if the condition of the premises complies with the housing code, the landlord's attempt to make life sufficiently miserable for the complaining tenant to induce them to vacate could constitute unconscionable behavior under the applicable consumer protections statute. Or, the remedies available under the consumer protection statute might be more extensive than the usual rent reduction remedies available to a tenant after landlord breach of the warranty of habitability.

3. Commercial Leases. In most states in which the question has arisen, courts have held that the warranty of habitability does not apply to commercial leases. See, e.g., Hong v. Estate of Graham, 101 Haw. 421 (2003); Golub v. Colby, 120 N.H. 535 (1980); B.W.S. Investments v. Mid–Am Restaurants, Inc., 459 N.W.2d 759 (N.D. 1990). The warranty has also been found inapplicable to agricultural leases. Knapp v. Simmons, 345 N.W.2d 118 (Iowa 1984).

An exception is Davidow v. Inwood North Professional Group, 747 S.W.2d 373 (Tex. 1988), in which the Texas Supreme Court found the warranty applicable to a commercial lease. Davidow, a physician, leased space for his medical practice. The roof leaked, producing rot and mildew and water dripping on patients. "Pests and rodents often infested the office. The hallways remained dark because hallway lights were [not] replaced for months. Cleaning and maintenance were not provided. The parking lot was constantly filled with trash. Hot water was not provided, and on one occasion Dr. Davidow went without electricity for several days because Inwood failed to pay the electric bill." The court concluded that

> there is an implied warranty of suitability by the landlord in a commercial lease that the premises are suitable for their intended commercial purpose. This warranty means that at the inception of the lease there are no latent defects in the facilities that are vital to the use of the premises for their intended commercial purpose and that these essential facilities will remain in a suitable condition. If, however, the parties to a lease expressly agree that the tenant will repair certain defects, then the provisions of the lease will control.

See also Reste Realty Corp. v. Cooper, 53 N.J. 444, 460–461 (1969).

The remedies available to the commercial tenant, even when a warranty of suitability is implied, depends upon whether that warranty and the obligation to pay rent are dependent covenants. In *Davidow* the Texas court ruled that they were: "The tenant's obligation to pay rent and the landlord's implied warranty of suitability are ... mutually dependent." That means, in theory, that the full range of remedies following landlord's breach of the warranty of suitability should be available to the commercial tenant.

An intermediate approach is that taken by Wesson v. Leone Enterprises, Inc., 437 Mass. 708, 719–720 (2002). The Massachusetts Supreme Judicial Court declined to rule that there was a warranty of suitability implied in commercial leases but did hold that the express covenants contained in a commercial lease, including the rent covenant, are mutually dependent. See also Teodori v. Werner, 490 Pa. 58, 65 (1980); Richard Barton Enterprises, Inc. v. Tsern, 928 P.2d 368, 378 (Utah 1996); Terry v. Gaslight Square Associates, 182 Ariz. 365, 370 (App. 1994).

4. Illegal Leases. Leases that are prohibited by law are illegal and unenforceable. An example might be a lease that contains a racially restrictive occupancy covenant. The District of Columbia courts have extended that doctrine to apply to a lease of premises that the landlord knows or should know, *at the inception of the lease*, does not comply with applicable housing codes (except for minor or technical violations). See Brown v.Southall Realty Co., 237 A.2d 834 (D.C. App 1968); Diamond Housing Corp. v. Robinson, 257 A.2d 492 (D.C. App. 1969). Violations that occur after the inception of the lease may be a violation of the warranty of habitability but do not render the lease illegal. See Saunders v. First National Realty Corp., 245 A.2d 836 (D.C. App. 1968). A tenant who stays in possession under an illegal lease may still be liable for the reasonable value of the occupation. In most cases, there is not much practical difference between an illegal lease and a landlord violation of the warranty of habitability. But if a lease is illegal and the tenant's only other remedy is to claim constructive eviction, the tenant may stay on and suspend rent, a remedy not available with respect to constructive eviction.

c. Retaliatory Eviction

Many leaseholds are periodic month-to-month tenancies or tenancies at will. Under a tenancy at will, a landlord may terminate the tenancy at any time; under a month-to-month tenancy the leasehold can be terminated with the proper notice, usually a single month in advance. One can readily see how these rules may be employed by landlords to oust tenants who complain about the conditions of the premises. In response to this reality, most states today prohibit such retaliatory evictions, and that is endorsed by the Restatement (Second) of Property, Landlord and Tenant §§ 14.8, 14.9. Prohibitions upon retaliatory evictions have been adopted by statute and judicial decision. A fairly typical statute is 9 Vt. Stat. § 4465:

a) A landlord of a residential dwelling unit may not retaliate by establishing or changing terms of a rental agreement or by bringing or threatening to bring an action against a tenant who:

(1) has complained to a governmental agency charged with responsibility for enforcement of a building, housing or health regulation of a violation applicable to the premises materially affecting health and safety; . . . or

(3) has organized or become a member of a tenant's union or similar organization.

(b) If the landlord acts in violation of this section, the tenant is entitled to recover damages and reasonable attorney's fees and has a defense in any retaliatory action for possession.

(c) If a landlord serves notice of termination of tenancy on any grounds other than for nonpayment of rent within 90 days after notice by any municipal or state governmental entity that the premises are not in compliance with applicable health or safety regulations, there is a rebuttable presumption that any termination by the landlord is in retaliation for the tenant having reported the noncompliance.

Under a Vermont-type statute, if a landlord seeks to evict after more than 90 days have elapsed since the landlord was notified of the violation that was detected by tenant complaint, the tenant can still assert retaliatory eviction as a defense, but now the tenant loses the benefit of the rebuttable presumption and must prove that the eviction proceeding is retaliatory.

This approach is not the only one taken by states to the problem of retaliatory eviction. By judicial decision, some jurisdictions have permitted tenants to assert a defense of retaliatory eviction, finding such a defense to be necessary in order to further the public policy of enforcement of housing codes. See Edwards v. Habib, 397 F.2d 687 (D.C. Cir. 1968), *cert. denied* 393 U.S. 1016 (1969); Schweiger v. Superior Court, 3 Cal.3d 507 (1970); Building Monitoring Systems, Inc. v. Paxton, 905 P.2d 1215 (Utah 1995).

What happens after the landlord has made the repairs needed to cure a code violation? Is the landlord forever barred from seeking eviction or refusing to renew the lease? Courts have taken two approaches to this problem. One method is to require the landlord to prove that his subsequent actions are not retaliatory. See, e.g., Robinson v. Diamond Housing Corp., 463 F.2d 853 (D.C. Cir. 1972); Schweiger v. Superior Court, 3 Cal.3d 507, 517 (1970). This is, of course, a question for the trier of fact. But once a landlord has been shown to have acted in retaliation, how is he to prove that his intentions are now blameless?

PROBLEM

L rents apartment units in a building that is deteriorating because the rents (at fair market value) are too low, and the property taxes too high, to permit *L* economically to repair the building. *L* seeks to evict *T*, a month-to-month tenant, for non-payment of the rent. *T* defends successfully on the ground that *L* is in breach of the warranty of habitability. Then *L* notifies *T* that he elects to terminate the periodic tenancy. When *T* fails to vacate *L* sues to evict her. *T* defends on the ground that *L*'s motive for refusing to renew the periodic tenancy is in retaliation for her assertion of the warranty of habitability as a defense in the prior suit. *L* responds that he wishes to cease operations as a landlord of the building because it is not economic to do so, but he wishes to withdraw units slowly to minimize the cost of ceasing business, and his plan is to withdraw units from the market as soon as they appear to be uninhabitable. What result? See Robinson v. Diamond Housing Corp., 463 F.2d 853 (D.C. 1972).

Perhaps in response to the quandary presented by the problem, other courts have ruled that, after the tenant has completed the repairs needed to cure violations, the landlord may evict the tenant without any proof of his motive so long as the landlord can sustain the burden of proving "that he has given the tenant a reasonable opportunity to procure other housing." Building Monitoring Systems v. Paxton, 905 P.2d 1215, 1219 (Utah 1995). In agreement is Markese v. Cooper, 333 N.Y.S.2d 63, 75 (Co. Ct. 1972).

Other laws may restrict a landlord's ability to terminate or refuse to renew a lease. For example, rent control statutes usually prohibit eviction or refusal to renew without good cause, often defined in limited terms. Anti-discrimination laws, of course, also apply to limit landlord discretion.

Note that the Vermont statute prohibits eviction for participation in a "tenant's union." But what if eviction is in retaliation for something unrelated to the tenancy, or only marginally connected to it?

IMPERIAL COLLIERY COMPANY v. FOUT

Supreme Court of Appeals of West Virginia
179 W.Va. 776 (1988)

MILLER, J., delivered the opinion of the court.

Danny H. Fout ... appeals a summary judgment dismissing his claim of retaliatory eviction based on the provisions of W. Va. Code, 55–3A–3(g), which is our summary eviction statute. Imperial Colliery had instituted an eviction proceeding and Fout sought to defend against it, claiming that his eviction was in retaliation for his participation in a labor strike.

This case presents two issues: (1) whether a residential tenant who is sued for possession of rental property under W. Va. Code, 55–3A–1, *et seq.*, may assert retaliation by the landlord as a defense, and (2) whether the retaliation motive must relate to the tenant's exercise of a right incidental to the tenancy.

Fout is presently employed by Milburn Colliery Company as a coal miner. For six years, he has leased a small house trailer lot in Burnwell, West Virginia, from Imperial Colliery Company. It is alleged that Milburn and Imperial are interrelated companies. A written lease was signed by Fout and an agent of Imperial in June, 1983. This lease was for a primary period of one month, and was terminable by either party upon one month's notice. An annual rental of $1.00 was payable in advance on January 1 of each year. No subsequent written leases were signed by the parties.

On February 14, 1986, Imperial advised Fout by certified letter that his lease would be terminated as of March 31, 1986. Fout's attorney corresponded with Imperial before the scheduled termination date. He advised that due to various family and monetary problems, Fout would be unable to timely vacate the property. Imperial voluntarily agreed to a two-month extension of the lease. A second letter from Fout's attorney, dated May 27, 1986, recited Fout's personal problems and requested that Imperial's attempts to oust Fout be held "in abeyance" until they were resolved. A check for $1.00 was enclosed to cover the proposed extension. Imperial did not reply.

On June 11, 1986, Imperial sued for possession of the property.... Fout answered and ... asserted as a defense that Imperial's suit was brought in retaliation for his involvement in the United Mine Workers of America and ... in a selective strike against Milburn. ... Imperial moved for summary judgment. The circuit court granted Imperial's motion[, reasoning] that the retaliation defense "must derive from, or in some respect be related to, exercise by the tenant of rights incident to his capacity as a 'tenant.'" Since Fout's participation in the labor strike was admittedly unrelated to his tenancy, the defense was dismissed and possession of the property was awarded to Imperial. It is from this order that Fout appeals.

Our initial inquiry is whether retaliation by the landlord may be asserted by the tenant as a defense in a suit [for eviction]. ... It appears that the first case that recognized retaliatory eviction as a defense to a landlord's eviction proceeding was Edwards v. Habib, 397 F.2d 687 (D.C. Cir. 1968), *cert. denied,* 393 U.S. 1016 (1969). There, a month-to-month tenant who resided in a District of Columbia apartment complex reported to a local health agency a number of sanitary code violations existing in her apartment. The agency investigated and ordered that remedial steps be taken by the landlord, who then advised Edwards that her lease was terminated. When the landlord sued for possession of the premises, Edwards alleged the suit was brought in retaliation for her reporting of the violations. A verdict was directed for the landlord and Edwards appealed. On appeal, the court reviewed at length the goals sought to be advanced by local sanitary and safety codes. It concluded that to allow retaliatory evictions by landlords would seriously jeopardize the efficacy of the codes. A prohibition against such retaliatory conduct was therefore to be implied, even though the regulations were silent on the matter.

Many states have protected tenant rights either on the *Edwards* theory or have implied such rights from the tenant's right of habitability. Others have utilized statutes analogous to section 5.101 of the Uniform Residential Landlord and Tenant Act, which is now adopted in fifteen jurisdictions. Similar landlord and tenant reform statutes in seventeen other states also provide protection for tenancy-related activities.

Only New Jersey and Minnesota appear to go beyond the tenancy-related rights enumerated above. The New Jersey statute allows the defense of retaliation to be raised, and provides for recovery of damages, where a landlord's acts are "a reprisal for the tenant's efforts to secure or enforce any rights under the laws of ... the State of New Jersey ... or of the United States[.]" N. J. Stat. Ann. § 2A:42–10.10.

Under W. Va. Code, § 37–6–30, a tenant is, with respect to residential property, entitled to certain rights to a fit and habitable dwelling. In Teller v. McCoy, 162 W. Va. 367 (1978), we spoke at some length of the common law right of habitability which a number of courts had developed to afford protection to the residential tenant. We concluded that these rights paralleled and were spelled out in more detail in W. Va. Code, § 37–6–30. In *Teller,* we also fashioned remedies for the tenant where there had been a breach of the warranty of habitability. However, we had no occasion to discuss the retaliatory eviction issue in Teller.

The central theme underlying the retaliatory eviction defense is that a tenant should not be punished for claiming the benefits afforded by health and safety statutes passed for his protection. These statutory benefits become a part of his right of habitability. If the right to habitability is to have any meaning, it must enable the tenant to exercise that right by complaining about unfit conditions without fear of reprisal by his landlord.

After the seminal decision in *Edwards,* other categories of tenant activity were deemed to be protected. Such activity was protected against retaliation where it bore a relationship to some legitimate aspect of the tenancy. For example, some cases provided protection for attempts by tenants to organize to protect their rights as tenants. Others recognized the right to press complaints directly against the landlord via oral communications, petitions, and "repair and deduct" remedies. E.g., Robinson v. Diamond Housing Corp., 463 F.2d 853 (D.C. Cir. 1972). A few courts recognize that even where a tenant's activity is only indirectly related to the tenancy relationship, it may be protected against retaliatory conduct if such conduct would undermine the tenancy relationship.

Typical of these cases is Windward Partners v. Delos Santos, 59 Haw. 104 (1978). There a group of month-to-month tenants gave testimony before a state land use commission in opposition to a proposal to redesignate their farm property from "agricultural" to "urban" uses. The proposal was sponsored by the landlord, a land developer. As a result of coordinated activity by the tenants, the proposal was defeated. Within six months, the landlord ordered the tenants to vacate the property and brought suit for possession. The Hawaii Supreme Court noted that statutory law provided for public hearings on proposals to redesignate property, and specifically invited the views of the affected tenants. The court determined that the legislative policy encouraging such input would be jeopardized "if ... [landlords] were permitted to retaliate against ... tenants for opposing land use changes in a public forum." 59 Haw. at 116....

The Legislature, in giving approval to the retaliation defense, must have intended to bring our State into line with the clear weight of case law and statutory authority outlined above. We accordingly hold that retaliation may be asserted as a defense to a summary eviction proceeding ... if the landlord's conduct is in retaliation for the tenant's exercise of a right incidental to the tenancy.

Fout seeks to bring this case within the *Windward* line of authority. He argues principally that Imperial's conduct violated a public policy which promotes the rights of association and free speech by tenants. We do not agree, simply because the activity that Fout points to as triggering his eviction was unrelated to the habitability of his premises. ... [We conclude] that the retaliatory eviction defense must relate to activities of the tenant incidental to the tenancy. First Amendment rights of speech and association unrelated to the tenant's property interest are not protected under a retaliatory eviction defense in that they do not arise from the tenancy relationship. Such rights may, of course, be vindicated on other independent grounds. [Affirmed.]

d. Landlord Liability in Tort to Tenants for Personal Injuries

Landlords have traditionally been held not to be liable for the injuries sustained by their tenants arising from the condition of the premises that are under the possession and control of the tenant. The rationale for this rule is rooted in the conception of a lease as a conveyance of property. An old Virginia case, Caudill v. Gibson Fuel Co., Inc., 185 Va. 233 (1946), described it thusly:

> Where the right of possession and enjoyment of the leased premises passes to the lessee, . . . in the absence of concealment or fraud by the landlord as to some defect in the premises, known to him and unknown to the tenant, the tenant takes the premises in whatever condition they may be in, thus assuming all risk of personal injury from defects therein. An agreement by the landlord to repair does not affect the rule, so far as concerns the landlord's liability for personal injuries due to defects in the premises . . ., although the existence of the defect is attributable to the failure to repair. . . . Generally[,] no recovery can be had for personal injuries on account of the landlord's failure to repair, and . . . his covenant to repair renders him liable only to an action for the breach of covenant, in which recovery is limited to the costs of repairs and any loss of use suffered by the tenant after the lapse of a reasonable time from giving the notice in which to make repairs. Id. at 239–41.

The traditional rule continues to apply in many states. See, e.g., Isbell v. Commercial Investment Associates, 273 Va. 605 (2007); Hatfield v. Palles, 537 F. 2d 1245 (4th Cir. 1976) (applying S.C. law). The rule is softened by a variety of exceptions, which courts tend to interpret broadly. Those exceptions, as identified by the Restatement (Second) of Property, Landlord and Tenant §§ 17.1–17.7, are: 1) Concealment of an existing dangerous defect; 2) Negligent maintenance of areas remaining under landlord control; 3) Breach of an agreement to repair the premises; 4) Negligent repairs; 5) Violation of a statutory duty to repair or breach of an implied warranty of habitability; and 6) Negligent lease of defective property to which the public will be admitted. In general, under the traditional rule a "landlord owes no greater duty to the invitees or guests of his tenant than he owes to the tenant himself." Regan v. Seattle, 76 Wn.2d 501, 504 (1969).

Increasingly, states have abandoned the traditional rule in favor of applying general negligence standards to landlords. As early as 1898 at least one court observed that landlords ought not be exempt from general negligence principles. Wilcox v. Hines, 100 Tenn. 538, 549 (1898), stated that a lease of defective property causing injury to the lessee "is the ordinary case of liability for personal misfeasance." But the modern trend originated with Sargent v. Ross, 113 N.H. 388 (1973). The New Hampshire court thought that the relative tort immunity of landlords was a relic of the agrarian past and rooted in unrealistic notions of leases as purely conveyances of land. The general negligence standard has been adopted by a significant minority of states.

Strict liability is another alternative. California adopted this approach in Becker v. IRM Corporation, 38 Cal.3d 454 (1985), only to repudiate it ten years later in favor of the general negligence standard. Peterson v. Superior Court (Banque Paribas), 10 Cal.4th 1185 (1995). In *Becker*, the California Supreme Court held landlords strictly liable for personal injuries suffered by their tenants from latent defects in the premises, reasoning that landlords were better able to identify and correct such defects than tenants, and that landlords could defray the costs resulting from strict liability through modestly higher rents for all tenants, offset to some degree by landlord recovery on claims of equitable indemnity against builders or makers of defective components. To similar effect is Johnson v. Scandia Associates, Inc., 641 N.E.2d 51 (Ind. App. 1994), in which the court indicated that "professional landlords" might be be held strictly liable for injuries to their tenants caused by latent defects in the premises. The strict liability approach may survive only in Louisiana, where it is imbedded in La. Civ.Code Art. 2317. See Matherne v. Somme, 638 So.2d 437 (La. Ct. App. 1994).

In repudiating California's experiment with strict liability, the court in *Peterson* observed that strict liability made the landlord the insurer of tenant safety even when the defect that causes tenant injury is neither known to the landlord nor should have been known. While strict liability may be justified with respect to defective products because the cost of insuring this risk will be diffused along the entire chain of commercial manufacturing and distribution, this is not so in the case of landlords and tenants. Rather, the likely result is simply to increase costs to tenants, thus forcing tenants as a class to insure themselves. See Alice Perlman, Becker v. IRM Corporation: Strict Liability in Tort for Residential Landlords, 16 Golden Gate L. Rev. 349, 360 (1986).

PROBLEMS

Analyze the following problems under the traditional rule and the general negligence standard.

1. L leases land to T for operation as a wildlife refuge. T brings a Bengal tiger onto the premises and films a video for a commercial advertisement using the tiger. F, an invitee of T who is participating in the filming, is mauled by the tiger and seriously injured. F sues L in tort to recover damages for her personal injuries. What result? Compare Frobig v. Gordon, 124 Wn.2d 732 (1994), and Thomas v. Shelton, 740 F.2d 478 (7th Cir. 1984) (applying Indiana law), with Strunk v. Zoltanski, 62 N.Y.2d 572, 576 (1984).

2. L, who is aware that his apartment building is in a high crime area, leases an apartment in the building to T. Later, T is seriously injured by a criminal assault committed in the building's common entryway by local thugs who do not live in the building. *T* sues *L* for damages attributable to the assault. What result? Would the result be the same if the lease contained a provision that "*L* will provide reasonable security in common areas"? Compare Feld v. Merriam, 506 Pa. 383(1984), with Kline v. 1500 Massachusetts Avenue Apartment Corporation, 439 F.2d 477 (D.C. Cir. 1970).

3. *L* leases an apartment to *T* in a building that is in a very low crime area. After *T* moves in, he complains to *T1*, another tenant of *L*, that *T1*'s habit of smoking cigars in *T1*'s apartment is annoying. *T1* is sufficiently angered that he assaults *T*, inflicting severe injuries. The use of tobacco products in the building is legal and there is no provision in the lease with *T1* that forbids their use. *T* sues *L* to recover damages for his personal injuries inflicted by *T1*. What result?

F. RENT CONTROL

Rent control is the shorthand term for statutes enacted, mostly by municipalities such as New York City, San Francisco, and Berkeley, California, that limit rent increases to approved amounts, deny to landlords the ability to terminate leases or refuse to renew them except for defined "good cause," and often impose fees, registration requirements and other duties upon landlords. The Berkeley, California law, Berkeley Municipal Code Chap. 13.76.010 *et seq.*, available at http://www.ci.berkeley.ca.us/ContentDisplay.aspx?id=9296, has been described as "the strictest rent control in the nation."[20]

The functional reality of rent control is that it amounts to a governmental seizure of the landlord's reversion and compelled transfer of an indefinite leasehold carved out of that reversion to the in-place tenant, contingent upon the tenant's compensation to the landlord of an amount that may or may not represent a reasonable rate of return on the landlord's investment. In Chapter 12 you will encounter the constitutional problem of regulatory takings—the phenomenon of governmental regulations that amount to a taking of private property for a public use without payment of just compensation, in violation of the takings clause of the Fifth Amendment to the United States Constitution. Although rent control might look like a regulatory taking, and some have argued that it is, the United States Supreme Court has rejected such claims and upheld the validity of rent control laws. See, e.g., Yee v. City of Escondido, 503 U.S. 519 (1992); Pennell v. City of San Jose, 485 U.S. 1 (1988). Richard Epstein, Takings: Private Property and the Power of Eminent Domain (1985), argues that rent control should be treated as taking for two reasons. First, it amounts to a naked transfer of property from private owner *A* to private owner *B* without any public use. Id. at 176–177. Second, there is no just compensation provided to the landlord even if the forced transfer is of public use. Id. at 186–188. For an extended discussion of regulatory takings issues, including rent control, from an economic

20. ASUC Renter's Legal Assistance, accessible on the Internet at http://www.ocf.berkeley.edu/?asucrla/index.php?page=rentcontrol.

policy perspective, see William Fischel, Regulatory Takings: Law, Economics, and Politics (1995).

The stated goal of rent control is almost always to preserve housing for low to middle income households, usually coupled with the contention that there is a shortage of housing in the market to be regulated. Some argue that rent control does not achieve this objective; others argue that rent control does accomplish the job. Those policy arguments, for and against rent control, boiled down to their essentials, follow.

Against Rent Control. Almost all economists agree that rent control is inefficient, ineffective, and counter-productive to its stated objective. Rents serve two basic functions: 1) recovery of the cost of building and providing shelter, and 2) creation of an incentive to construct new housing and maintain existing housing. In an unregulated, competitive market, a housing shortage drives rents up, which becomes an incentive to construct new housing. As new housing comes on the market, rents may stabilize or drop, but existing landlords will have an incentive to use the increased rents to improve the quality of their rental housing in order to retain tenants who might otherwise opt for fresher surroundings. (Of course, the transaction costs of moving deter tenant mobility, so this incentive may not be as strong as the incentive to build new housing.) If rent control is applied to this market, the incentive to build new housing dissipates or ends, and landlords have no incentive to maintain their buildings at any level beyond what may be minimally required. Moreover, some existing landlords may decide that they can earn a higher return on their investment by converting their property to condominium units and selling those units, or converting the property to a non-residential use. Thus, the supply of housing may actually be decreased by imposition of rent control.

In addition to inhibiting construction of new housing and providing incentives for deterioration of existing housing, rent control is said to produce at least four other harmful economic effects: reduction in property tax revenues, increased administrative costs that are not productive, reduced mobility as in-place tenants become reluctant to give up their below-market housing (and attendant inefficiencies as people may forego more productive labor opportunities to keep their artificially cheap housing), and higher entry costs for would-be tenants as they search for housing that has been made artificially scarce (e.g., "key money"— payments to in-place tenants to induce a sublease, or payments to brokers to find available space).

Moreover, it is said that rent control disadvantages the poor. If there are more tenants than spaces landlords will prefer tenants with the best credit ratings and highest incomes, as they reason those tenants pose a lesser risk. And landlords will skimp on maintenance, with the result that the cheapest units in the market (which may already be cheap due to their unattractive qualities) become even more unattractive. Several studies have demonstrated that most of the economic benefit of rent control is reaped by higher income households, and young, well-educated professionals. See Pollakowski, An Examination of Subsidies Generated by Rent Stabilization in New York City (Cambridge: Joint Center for Housing Studies of Harvard University, 1989); Devine, Who Benefits from Rent Controls? (Oakland: Center for Community Change, 1986).

Finally, rent control might have the perverse effect of removing residential units from the market. In the East Harlem section of Manhattan, landlords are content to rent the ground floor commercial spaces and leave the apartments vacant because the maintenance costs and aggravation of dealing with residential tenants under New York's rent control law is deemed to be greater than the foregone rent rolls. See "In East Harlem, 'Keep Out' Signs Apply Even to Renters," New York Times, October 31, 2011, available at the following site: http://www.nytimes.com/2011/10/31/nyregion/east-harlem-landlords-keep-apartments-sealed-up.html?r=1&hp

For Rent Control. There are two main branches of the arguments for rent control One is to contend that the economic arguments against rent control are wrong; the other is to contend that economic arguments do not matter.

The economic case for rent control has multiple facets. It is claimed that the market for housing is not competitive—because landlords and tenants have unequal bargaining power landlords are able to extract oligopoly gains from tenants. Rent control merely counters this power. Rent control usually allows for regulated increases in rents, even for existing tenants, so landlords receive a "fair return" on their investment. (Query: Is a "fair return" large enough to stimulate new construction?) To the extent rent control exempts new construction the presence of rent control will not impede creation of new housing. (Query: But will the uncertainty about whether newly constructed housing will continue to be exempted impede that investment?)

The other main argument is that rent control benefits existing in-place tenants, and that is a reason, independent of the economic effects of rent control, to impose rent control. Tenants, especially elderly tenants on relatively fixed incomes, can have the security of knowing that the proportion of their income that must be expended on shelter will remain stable. See, e.g., Margaret J. Radin, Residential Rent Control, 15 Phil. & Pub. Affairs 350 (1986). Critics, of course, argue that rental subsidies to these targeted beneficiaries are more efficient than rent control, which applies to the entire rental housing stock. For more arguments in this vein, see Mark Kelman, On Democracy Bashing: A Skeptical Look at the Theoretical and "Empirical" Practice of the Public choice Movement, 74 Va. L. Rev. 199 (1988); William Simon, Social–Republican Property, 38 UCLA L. Rev. 1335 (1991).

Whatever its merits, rent control is not widely established in America. Outside of a few colonies in California and New York, there are not many rent control laws. Indeed, by voter referendum adopted in 1994, Massachusetts abolished rent control, thus nullifying local rent control ordinances. See Mass Gen Laws Ch. 40P, particularly § 4.

CHAPTER SEVEN

VOLUNTARY REAL PROPERTY TRANSFERS

■ ■ ■

Most transfers of real property are voluntary. Involuntary transfers are the exception; they occur primarily through adverse possession or the government's exercise of its power of eminent domain. The United States Constitution requires that property owners dispossessed by eminent domain receive "just compensation," but in general no compensation is due when the property owner is stripped of ownership by adverse possession. Eminent domain is the topic of Chapter 12; adverse possession was covered in Chapter 2.

Voluntary transfers may take the form of a sale or gift. Gifts of real property during the life of the donor were addressed in Chapter 2; gifts of real property that occur at the donor's death are the subject of courses in Wills, Trusts, and Decedent's Estates. A sale of real property, which is the subject of this chapter, involves an amalgam of contract and property law. Although this chapter focuses on sales of residential real estate, the process is fundamentally similar with respect to more complex transfers of commercial real estate.

A. THE PROCESS OF SALE

The first decision a seller must make is whether to engage a broker to represent him in offering the property for sale. If a broker is hired, and the property listed for sale through the broker, a contract between the seller and the broker (called a listing agreement) specifies the terms of that representation. Brokers charge a commission, which may vary from place to place and within localities. The usual commission is 5% or 6% of the sale price, although all brokerage commissions are negotiable. The listing agent (the broker who has entered into the listing agreement with the seller) usually keeps half of the commission and the other half is paid to the buyer's agent. To save money, some sellers seek to sell their property without the aid of a broker. Because brokers control access to the Multiple Listing Service in their community (a comprehensive listing of properties offered for sale) it may be more difficult for a seller who chooses to forego a broker to make the availability of the property known to prospective buyers. Discount brokers may charge a seller a reduced or flat fee to list and market the property but usually these arrangements require the seller to pay the buyer's agent the customary fee (often 3% of the sales price).

Once a willing and able buyer is found, seller and buyer enter into a contract for the sale of the property, which will specify the terms of the sale and the conditions that must be satisfied before the buyer and seller are obliged to close the transaction. The buyer pays a deposit against the purchase price, usually called earnest money, that is entirely negotiable but is often a modest percentage of the purchase price. The contract of sale is typically a form contract prepared by the realtors' association in the community where the property is located. In most residential transactions the contract is entered into without the benefit of legal assistance. Of course, buyers or sellers may engage legal counsel to review the contract before signing it, but this rarely happens. In sellers' markets there is often a scramble to make an offer acceptable to the seller, and buyers thus dispense with legal advice. While this is not true of buyers' markets, even then it is unusual for attorneys to be employed at the point at which the contract is created. Even though the standard form agreements used by realtors have been drafted by counsel for the realtors' association, their terms may not fully reflect the expectations of either buyer or seller. Once the contract of sale is entered into the contract is executory until performance has occurred and title transferred by delivery of a deed. At that point the contract is fully executed. The contract often includes conditions that must be satisfied before performance is due, and those conditions— inspections of the property by experts, and especially obtaining financing—usually cannot be met immediately. Thus, there is frequently a delay of a month or two before the contract is fully executed. Because of the protracted period that the contract is executory, legal rules have developed to address a variety of events that can occur.

At the closing, or settlement, the purchase price is delivered to the seller and the buyer receives a deed to the property, thus transferring legal title to the new owner. In most transactions, the buyer also executes a mortgage in favor of a third party lender, who has loaned a substantial portion of the purchase price to the buyer. The closing will also involve an apportionment of certain prepaid expenses of ownership, such as taxes, and payment of various expenses incurred as part of the transaction, such as real estate transfer taxes, title insurance or title searches, and recording fees. Expenses chargeable to the seller are deducted from the purchase price, while expenses chargeable to the buyer require the buyer to contribute additional funds at closing to settle the transaction. If the seller has a mortgage lien outstanding the closing will also involve paying the seller's mortgage lender and release of the mortgage. All of these funds transfers will be specified in a closing statement that will specify where the funds are coming from, where they are going, and what they are for.

Closings take place in one of two ways. In many localities, particularly in the west, the closing is handled through an escrow agent, often a title insurance company. In an escrow, the parties deposit into escrow the funds needed to complete the purchase, the documentation relevant to release or creation of mortgages, and the documentation needed to transfer title (including, of course, the deed). Each party will deliver to the escrow agent a set of escrow instructions that tells the escrow agent when and to whom to deliver the funds or documents placed in escrow. The escrow agent holds the items deposited into escrow until all the instructions are satisfied and then deals with them in accordance with the instructions. In other localities, particularly in the east, the closing is a face-to-face transaction presided over by an attorney or title company officer. Documents are inspected and signed by the buyer and seller, funds change hands, a deed and (if applicable) a mortgage encumbering the buyer's title and a release of the mortgage encumbering the seller's title are delivered. As a part of the closing in an escrow transaction, the deed, mortgage, and mortgage release will be recorded by the escrow agent. In a face-to-face closing, those documents are often delivered to the respective parties and they are responsible for recording them in the appropriate government office for recording of deeds and other instruments affecting title to real property. Recording is a topic discussed in Chapter 8.

The deed usually contains various promises, or warranties, on the part of the seller concerning title. Unless the deed stipulates that the contract of sale survives the closing and delivery of the deed to the buyer, the contract (now fully executed) is replaced by the deed as the embodiment of the contractual obligations of the parties. Thus, after the closing, the seller remains liable for breach of those deed warranties. However, regardless of the displacement of the contract of sale by the deed, a seller remains liable for fraud practiced upon the buyer and may have other liabilities stemming from statutory obligations.

B. BROKERS AND LISTING AGREEMENTS

The listing agreement is a contract between a seller and a broker who agrees to list the property for sale and expend best efforts to locate prospective buyers and show the property to them. In return, the seller agrees to pay a commission to the broker, usually 5% or 6% of the sales price. The listing agreement will specify the terms of sale that the seller desires and will accept, the asking price for the property being the key term. Listing agreements expire after a specified period of time, often six months, has elapsed. An important difference among listing agreements is the degree of exclusivity that the broker is given with respect to the sale of the property. The most exclusive arrangement is an *exclusive right to sell*, under which the broker is entitled to the commission if the property sells during the period the listing agreement is effective, no matter whether the sale is due to the broker's efforts. A somewhat less exclusive arrangement is an *exclusive agency*, under which the broker earns his commission if the property is sold due to the effort of any broker, but not if the property is sold only by the seller's efforts. An *open listing* is non-exclusive and the broker is entitled to a commission only if he is the first to produce a ready, willing, and able buyer on terms acceptable to the owner as set forth in the listing agreement.

MAPES v. CITY COUNCIL OF THE
CITY OF WALSENBURG

Court of Appeals of Colorado
151 P.3d 574 (Colo. App. 2006)

LOEB, J., delivered the opinion of the court.

In this case for recovery of a real estate brokerage commission, plaintiff, Larry Mapes, ... appeals the district court's order granting the motion to dismiss of defendant, the City Council of the City of Walsenburg. We reverse and remand....

Mapes, a real estate broker, and the City entered into an open listing contract for the sale of a ranch owned by the City. The contract provided for a listing price of $506,000, with a minimum earnest money deposit of $10,000, and a six percent sales commission. Shortly after entering into the contract, Mapes located a buyer who made an offer of $510,000, with an earnest money deposit of $10,000, and no contingencies. However, some six weeks later, the City entered into a contract to sell the property to another party.

Mapes filed this action for breach of contract to recover his sales commission. The City filed a motion to dismiss for failure to state a claim upon which relief could be granted.... The district court entered an order granting the City's motion. ... This appeal followed....

This case turns on the interpretation of the parties' open listing contract. Mapes contends that the district court erred in concluding as a matter of law that the unambiguous terms of the open listing contract preclude any award to him even if he procured a ready, willing, and able buyer. The court found that, under the contract, a broker is not entitled to a commission if the seller decides to sell to a third-party buyer not procured by the broker. We agree that this ruling was error....

We evaluate the contract as a whole and construe the language in harmony with the plain and generally accepted meaning of the words employed. We will enforce the contract as written unless there is an ambiguity in the language. In determining whether an ambiguity exists, we must ask whether the disputed provision is reasonably susceptible on its face of more than one interpretation. Written contracts that are complete and free from ambiguity will be found to express the intention of the parties and will be enforced according to their plain language....

The open listing contract here is on a standardized form, the printed portions of which have been approved by the Colorado Real Estate Commission. With an open listing, a broker is not the exclusive agent for the sale of the property and is only entitled to compensation upon the sale of the property to a buyer whom the agent has introduced to the selling principal. The open listing is an offer for a unilateral contract creating in the broker the power of acceptance by procuring a purchaser ready, willing, and able to buy on the terms proposed by the owner. *See* Garrett v. Richardson, 149 Colo. 449 (1962); 1 Corbin on Contracts § 2.30, at 260–64 (J. M. Perillo, ed., rev. ed. 1993).... The broker earns a commission by finding a ready, willing, and able purchaser before other agents or the owner finds such a purchaser, and before the owner revokes the offer.

Paragraph 1 of the contract here provides [that] "this Contract shall apply only to a Sale of the Property by Broker during the Listing Period ... or upon Broker procuring a buyer who is ready, willing and able to complete the Sale as proposed by Seller (collectively, Broker Sale). In the case of any other Sale, this Listing Contract is null and void and of no effect." Paragraph 3(e) defines a Sale as "the voluntary transfer or exchange of any interest in the Property or the voluntary creation of the obligation to convey any interest in the Property, including a contract or lease." Paragraph 13, titled "Compensation to Brokerage Firm," provides, in pertinent part [that in] "the case of a Broker Sale, Seller agrees that [the broker's commission is earned upon] Broker finding a buyer who is ready, willing and able to complete the transaction as specified herein by Seller...." The contract further provides ... that the six percent commission is "payable ... upon fulfillment of subsection 13(b)(2), [providing that Broker has procured a buyer ready, willing, and able to purchase on seller's terms,] and where either the offer made by such buyer is defeated by Seller or by the refusal or neglect of Seller to consummate the Sale as agreed upon."

... The City contends that Mapes cannot recover a commission under the open listing contract because he was not the procuring cause of the sale of the property and, pursuant to Paragraph 1, the contract was rendered null and void and of no effect when the City contracted to sell the property to a third party rather than to Mapes's potential buyer. Mapes contends that ... he is entitled to a commission because he was the first broker to procure a buyer ready, willing, and able to purchase the property on the City's terms, even if the City refused to enter into a purchase contract with his client and subsequently sold the property to a third party. We agree with Mapes.

Under the plain language of Paragraph 1 of the contract, a Broker Sale occurs when ... Mapes procures a buyer during [the listing] period who is ready, willing, and able to "complete the sale" as proposed by the City.

This provision follows the general rule that a real estate broker is entitled to receive a commission when he or she has procured for his or her client a party who is ready, willing, and able to enter into a contract with the seller on the terms that the latter has stipulated. *See* McCullough v. Thompson, 133 Colo. 352 (1956); Bossow v. Bowlway Lanes, Inc., 161 Ill. App. 3d 983 (1987); Staubus v. Reid, 652 S.W.2d 293, 293–94 (Mo. Ct. App. 1983) (open listing agreement awards sole commission to the first broker to produce a ready, willing, and able buyer, and who first notifies the seller that he or she has such a buyer). If a seller does not perform once a qualified buyer is produced by the broker, the seller cannot thereby escape the payment of the agreed-upon commission. *See* City of Pueblo v. Leach Realty Co., 149 Colo. 92, 94 (1962). The rule applies even if the seller refuses to consummate the transaction and the deal fails because of such refusal. [*Id.*;] Trimmer v. Ludtke, 105 Ariz. 260 (1969)(in open listing, where broker produces ready, willing, and able purchaser according to terms of listing agreement but seller refuses to enter contract of sale, broker is nevertheless entitled to a commission because the broker has fully performed that for which he or she was employed and cannot be frustrated by breach of agreement by seller); Restatement (Second) of Agency § 445 (1957); Richard Lord, Williston on Contracts § 62:19, at 371 (2002).

Although the owner is "not required to convey the property to the prospective buyer, he is liable for a commission to the broker," and the owner is "precluded from rejecting any valid offer in accordance with the original terms so as to avoid liability for a commission." E.R. Archambeau, Jr., Real Estate Brokerage Commissions in Colorado, 35 Dicta 297, 302 (1958). The fact that a contract is an open listing rather than an exclusive listing is immaterial. . . . Mapes procured a buyer ready, willing, and able to "complete the sale" on the City's terms.

The City contends that, because a sale took place to another party, the contract was null and void and of no effect, pursuant to Paragraph 1. We reject this contention. According to Paragraph 13 . . . of the contract, once Mapes finds a buyer who is ready, willing, and able to complete the sale . . . , he achieves a Broker Sale and earns his commission. Moreover, under Paragraph 13(c) of the contract, when Mapes finds such a buyer, and the buyer's offer is defeated by the seller, the commission is due and payable. A sale is defeated when the seller refuses to consummate the sale at the agreed upon price. *See also* C.R.S. § 12–61–201 (No real estate agent or broker is entitled to a commission for finding a purchaser who is ready, willing, and able to complete the purchase of real estate as proposed by the owner until the same is consummated or is defeated by the refusal or neglect of the owner to consummate the same as agreed upon.).

Here, Mapes alleged that he procured a qualified buyer and that the City then defeated the buyer's offer by selling the property to another party. In our view, the City's interpretation of Paragraph 1 of the contract would render the terms of Paragraph 13 meaningless if the contract became null and void whenever another sale took place, regardless of whether Mapes had first achieved a Broker Sale by procuring a buyer who was ready, willing, and able to complete the sale on the City's terms. We conclude the contract can be null and void pursuant to Paragraph 1 only if another sale takes place before a Broker Sale occurs.

This result is consistent with the law concerning the circumstances under which a seller may revoke a broker's authority pursuant to an open listing contract. In general, a broker's authority under an open listing is effectively terminated by express revocation or otherwise, most commonly by the sale of the property. *See* W.W. Chambers, Inc. v. Audette, 385 A.2d 10, 14 (D.C. 1978). However, once a broker has produced a buyer who is ready, willing, and able to purchase the property upon the terms set forth in the listing, the seller may no longer revoke the broker's authority under the open listing and be relieved of the obligation to pay the commission. Therefore, under Paragraph 1 of the contract, . . . "any other sale" of the property could only serve to revoke Mapes's authority under the open listing and render the contract null and void where such sale occurs prior to Mapes's having performed under the contract by procuring a ready, willing, and able buyer.

The City argues that the interpretation of the contract we adopt here will have a chilling effect on the use of open listing contracts in Colorado because the City may have to pay two commissions, one to Mapes and one to the broker for the other party who purchased the property after Mapes had procured a qualifying offer from a ready, willing, and able buyer. However, under the terms of the contract, that is an economic risk that the City voluntarily assumed. Although it was not obligated to sell the property to Mapes's proposed buyer, the City may not avoid paying Mapes a commission, once he had performed under the open listing, merely because it chose to sell the property to someone else. Moreover, we perceive no practical concern that a seller under an open listing may ultimately have to pay more than two commissions, because once a broker submits an unconditional offer from a ready, willing, and able buyer, the seller may revoke the authority of other brokers under the open listing. . . .

Because Mapes alleged facts in his complaint that, if true, would entitle him to a commission under the unambiguous terms of the contract, we conclude the district court erred as a matter of law by granting the City's motion to dismiss. The order is reversed, and the case is remanded for further proceedings consistent with this opinion.

NOTES

1. Buyer's failure to perform. In *Mapes*, the issue was the seller's refusal to deal with a "ready, willing, and able" buyer that the broker had procured before the owner entered into a contract of sale with a third party. An even clearer case for the broker's right to a commission is presented when the seller has entered into a contract of sale and then refuses or fails to close. But what if it is the buyer who refuses or fails to close?

The traditional rule was that a broker had earned his commission by finding a buyer ready, willing, and able "to conclude a bargain on the terms on which the broker was authorized to sell." Hinds v. Henry, 36 N.J.L. 328, 332 (1873). The term "able" meant the financial capacity to consummate the sale; thus in cases in which the seller had refused to enter into a contract the burden was generally placed on the broker to prove the buyer's financial ability to perform in order to earn the commission. See, e.g., Gartner v. Higgins, 100 R.I. 285 (1965); De Harport v. Green, 215 Ore. 281, 283 (1959). But by entering into a contract with the buyer, the seller was deemed to have accepted the buyer as able to perform. See, e.g., Courter v. Lydecker, 71 N.J.L. 511, 513 (1904); Matz v. Bessman, 1 N.J.Misc. 5 (1923): Although the buyer was financially unable to close, the broker was entitled to his commission because "after the broker procured the customer and the defendant accepted him, the broker was not an insurer of either the solvency or the willingness of the customer."

The contrary rule is that the broker is not entitled to a commission in cases where the seller remains willing to perform but the buyer backs out. See, e.g., Riggs v. Turnbull, 105 Md. 135 (1907); Butler v. Baker, 17 R.I. 582 (1892); Ellsworth Dobbs, Inc. v. Johnson, 50 N.J. 528 (1967); Dennis Reed, Ltd. v. Goody, [1950] 2.K.B. 277, 1 All Eng. Rep. 919 (1950). The rationale of these decisions is that "ordinarily when an owner of property lists it with a broker for sale, his expectation is that the money for the payment of commission will come out of the proceeds of the sale." *Ellsworth Dobbs*, 50 N.J. at 547. The traditional rule

> permits a broker to satisfy his obligation to the owner simply by tendering a human being who is physically and mentally capable of agreeing to buy the property on mutually satisfactory terms, so long as the owner enters into a sale contract with such person. . . . Once he enters into a contract of sale with the broker's customer, he is considered to have accepted the purchaser as fully capable of the ultimate performance agreed upon. If it later appears that the purchaser is not financially able to close . . ., or even that he never did have the means to do so, the owner must pay the broker his commission, so long as he acted in good faith. Such a rule, considered in the context of the real relationship between broker and owner, empties the word "able" of substantially all of its significant content and imposes an unjust burden on vendors of property. [F]airness requires that the arrangement between broker and owner be interpreted to mean that the owner hires the broker with the expectation of becoming liable for a commission only in the event a sale of the property is consummated, unless the title does not pass because of the owner's improper or frustrating conduct. . . . [W]e hold that even if both broker and seller, on execution of the contract of sale, in good faith believe the buyer to be financially able to perform, and it turns out otherwise at the crucial time, the seller cannot be held for the commission.

Id. at 547–548, 552.

    2. *Buyer's liability for a brokerage commission.* Normally, buyers are not liable for the broker's commission, which is part of the contract between broker and seller, unless they have contractually agreed to pay that commission. But this is not always the case. A buyer who induces a seller to sell the property to him outside of the terms of the listing agreement (e.g., immediately after the listing agreement expires or a month or so later) may be liable for tortious interference with contract. Of course, the broker's more direct remedy is to sue the seller but if the seller is insolvent or has disappeared the

broker's only recourse may be against the buyer. Another theory of buyer liability is that of implied contract. Where a buyer has retained a broker to locate suitable property, the broker does so, and the buyer knows that a commission will be due to the broker from the seller, "the law will imply a promise on the part of the buyer to complete the transaction with the owner." Ellsworth Dobbs, Inc. v. Johnson, 50 N.J. 528, 559 (1967). To similar effect are Livermore v. Crane, 26 Wn. 529 (1901); Probst v. Di Giovanni, 232 La. 811, 95 So.2d 321 (1957). Contra: Rich v. Emerson–Dumont Distributing Co., 55 Mich.App. 142 (1974); Professional Realty Corp. v. Bender, 216 Va. 737 (1976) (also rejecting the theory that the broker was an intended third-party beneficiary of the buyer's contract of sale with the seller).

3. *Who does the broker represent?* The broker who has entered into a listing agreement with the seller is clearly the seller's agent, but what about another broker who has been asked by a prospective buyer to find and show properties? The prospective buyer may reasonably think that her broker is her agent, but the broker's incentive is to earn a commission that is paid by the seller. That places the "buyer's broker" in a conflict: It is in the "buyer's broker's" interest to encourage a higher price than might be necessary to secure a deal in order to reap a larger commission, but that is certainly not in the buyer's interest. Buyers may, of course, hire a broker to work exclusively for them, but compensation from the buyer will be required. In some instances the listing broker may also be assisting the buyer (a "dual agency"), presenting an even starker conflict of interest. Most states require that these conflicts be fully disclosed to both buyer and seller. See, e.g., Calif. Civ. Code §§ 2079.12 through 2079.24; Ga. Code §§ 10–6A–10, 10–6A–12.

4. *Listing broker's obligations to the buyer.* Ordinarily, a listing broker owes fiduciary duties only to the seller, not to the buyer. Of course, a listing broker is liable for his intentional misrepresentation of facts known to him, but should a listing broker be liable for innocent misrepresentations? One view is that because a listing broker is hired by the seller as his sales agent, the broker has "no duty to verify independently representations made by a seller unless [he is] aware of facts that 'tend to indicate that such representation[s are] false.' " Provost v. Miller, 144 Vt. 67, 70 (1984), *quoting* Lyons v. Christ Episcopal Church, 71 Ill.App.3d 257, 259–60 (1979). This view imposes on the listing broker a duty of reasonable care to investigate claims made by the seller that are "pivotal to the transaction from the buyer's perspective." Hoffman v. Connall, 108 Wn.2d 69, 75 (1987), *quoting* Tennant v. Lawton, 26 Wn. App. 701, 706 (1980).

Another view is that buyers should be entitled to rely on brokers' statements, and thus a listing broker is liable to a buyer for innocent misrepresentations. See, e.g., Bevins v. Ballard, 655 P.2d 757 (Alaska 1982); Spargnapani v. Wright, 110 A.2d 82 (D.C. App. 1954). This rule is sometimes criticized as creating an incentive for brokers to stay mum about the property because, without a corresponding duty to investigate, the chances of liability may be minimized by saying next to nothing. See Note, Realtor Liability for Innocent Misrepresentation and Undiscovered Defects: Balancing the Equities Between Broker and Buyer, 20 Val. U. L. Rev. 255, 269 (1986). Calif. Civ. Code § 2079 imposes on listing brokers a duty to make "a reasonably competent and diligent visual inspection" of a residential structure of less than 4 units and to disclose to prospective buyers "all facts materially affecting the value or desirability of the property that an investigation would reveal." Other states reject the notion that a listing broker should be under an obligation to inspect and disclose. See, e.g., Kubinsky v. Van Zandt Realtors, 811 S.W.2d 711 (Tex. App. 1991).

Another pitfall for brokers that can result in liability to a buyer is to engage in the unauthorized practice of law. The mere filling in the blanks of a standard form real estate contract is not regarded as the practice of law, but what happens when a broker or other third party crosses the line into legal practice and, by doing so, damages the buyer? A revealing answer is provided by Bowers v. Transamerica Title Insurance Co., 100 Wn. 2d 581 (1983). Transamerica acted as the escrow agent in the sale of realty from Bowers to Quantum Construction. Evans, a Transamerica employee who was not an attorney, prepared each of seller's and buyer's escrow instructions, a promissory note for $35,000 from Quantum to Bowers, representing a significant portion of the purchase price, and a deed. Evans asked Quantum whether the note was to be secured by a mortgage on the property. Quantum's representative replied that the agreement spoke of a "note," not one secured by a mortgage or deed or trust encumbering the property. Evans did not put this query to Bowers, but prepared an unsecured note which was delivered to Bowers at the closing. Quantum immediately borrowed over $30,000 from a third party lender, secured by a mortgage on the property, and then declared bankruptcy. Quantum's principals skipped town and Bowers sued Transamerica under a Washington consumer protection statute. The Washington Supreme Court held that Evans, as Transamerica's agent, had engaged in the unauthorized practice of law, and then declared that an unauthorized legal practitioner is held to the same standard of care as a licensed attorney. Evans's failure to advise each of Bowers and Quantum that it was advisable to obtain independent legal counsel fell beneath this standard. Note that Evans's negligence consisted of the *failure* to give legal advice. Thus, Evans acquired a duty to give legal advice by engaging in the unauthorized practice of law.

Queries: Would Transamerica have avoided liability if Evans had advised Bowers to obtain independent legal counsel but Bowers had declined to do so? Suppose that the listing agent for Bowers had done what Evans did, but had also advised Bowers to obtain legal counsel and Bowers had declined to do so? Suppose that Transamerica had not engaged in any unauthorized practice of law and a broker that is independent of the listing broker and who had assisted Quantum in the purchase prepared the note and gave it to Transamerica, along with instructions that this note is to be unsecured.

C. THE CONTRACT OF SALE

Contracts for sale of real property are, in some respects, like all other contracts—a legally adequate expression of a meeting of the minds as to the transaction—but must also deal with the distinctive nature of transfers of real estate. The statute of frauds requires that agreements to convey realty must be in writing. The subject property must be described with sufficient specificity to identify it. This is particularly so when the contract applies to real property and also to personal property contained within the realty. A contract of sale should specify the title to be conveyed, how that title is to be ascertained or insured, and the nature of the deed that transfers title. The contract should express clearly all conditions precedent to the buyer's or seller's obligation to close the deal, and indicate what constitutes satisfaction of each of those conditions. A key condition is the buyer's ability to obtain financing; thus, a contract should specify the amount and terms of such financing. The time period during which each of these conditions must be satisfied is essential, and a closing date must be set. The contract should also detail what happens if the property is destroyed or damaged before the closing, who pays the various closing costs, and include remedies for either party's breach. Of course, not all contracts for sale are well-drafted, and the law necessarily must supply default rules to fill in the gaps left by the contracting parties.

1. THE STATUTE OF FRAUDS AND ITS EXCEPTIONS

The original Statute of Frauds, enacted in 1677 during the reign of Charles II, barred any action to enforce a contract for the sale of land or any interest in land "unless the agreement upon which such action shall be brought, or some memorandum or note thereof, shall be in writing and signed by the party to be charged therewith" or his authorized agent. Every American state has enacted some version of the Statute of Frauds. See, e.g., Cal. Civ. Code § 1624; Tex. Bus. & Com. Code § 26.01. In addition to contracts of sale the Statute of Frauds applies to leases in excess of a year. In most states the Statute of Frauds applies to real estate brokerage agreements as well as to contracts of sale. See, e.g., Cal. Civ. Code § 1624(a)(4). While there are many issues germane to the Statute of Frauds, the focus in this subsection is upon two key issues: 1) What constitutes a sufficient writing? 2) What are the exceptions to the Statute of Frauds that permit an oral contract to be enforced in equity, by an action for specific performance?

a. Sufficient Writing

The writing need not be a formal contract, but it must name the parties, contain all the essential elements of a contract though they may be expressed in general terms, describe the property with sufficient particularity to be identified, state the price, and be signed by the party against whom it is sought to be enforced. See generally Powell on Real Property § 81.02.

In Irvmor Corp. v. Rodewald, 253 N.Y. 472 (1930), the seller signed a memorandum indicating his receipt of earnest money toward the purchase and sale of an identified property for $25,000 on terms specified in the memo, but the memo did not identify the buyer. The purported buyer's suit to enforce the agreement was dismissed. Said Justice Cardozo, "This is nothing more than an offer lanced into the void." Id. at 476. The rationale is "that unless the names of both parties appear the contract may be foisted upon any one by perjury, which is the very thing the Statute of Frauds was enacted to prevent." Tobias v. Lynch, 192 App. Div. 54, 56 (N.Y. 1920).

Incomplete property descriptions cause problems, but are not necessarily fatal. At the least, the writing must identify the property, however informally, in a fashion that will enable it to be identified with certainty and specificity. The writing must also indicate the interest to be conveyed, but unless there are words to the contrary the presumption that the seller intends to convey his entire interest will apply.

JONES v. HUDSON

Supreme Court of Appeals of West Virginia
160 W.Va. 518 (1977)

NEELY, J., delivered the opinion of the Court.

This case concerns a contract for the sale of land voided by the Circuit Court of Jackson County on the ground that the description of the property attempted to be conveyed was vague, indefinite, and insufficient as a matter of law. Plaintiffs below, as buyers, brought an action seeking specific performance of the contract, and . . . the circuit court entered an order granting defendant-sellers' motion to dismiss the action. . . . [W]e reverse.

In its entirety the contract reads as follows:

August 14, 1973 Everett and Eva Hudson do hereby sell to William K. and Mary R. Jones One-hundred (100) acres, more or less, located on the waters of Big Run. Buyer is to receive the two and one-half (2–1/2) shares of the mineral rights that are presently owned by the Hudsons. Buyer is also to receive the three (3) cows and one (1) heifer calf in with the price listed below. Buyer is also to get all the hay. Total price for farm and things listed above is Twenty Thousand and Eight-hundred dollars ($20,800.00)

Sellers Everett Hudson Eva Hudson

Buyers William K. Jones Mary R. Jones

Received from William K. and Mary R. Jones Three-hundred Dollars ($300.00) as down payment on farm. Leaving balance of Twenty-thousand and five hundred dollars ($20,500.00)

Everett Hudson Eva Hudson

[Under] West Virginia's Statute of Frauds, . . . no contract for the sale of land is enforceable unless in writing, signed by the party against whom enforcement is sought. The contract in question appears generally to satisfy those requirements, and in particular, defendants below admitted they signed the contract.

The case, however, is not that simple. Longstanding judicial construction of the Statute of Frauds has engrafted onto it a requirement that contracts for the sale of land include a certain description of the land to be conveyed. The harshness of this rule has been significantly mitigated by the Court's frequent application of the maxim, "In description, that is certain which can be made certain." Holley's Executor v. Curry, 58 W. Va. 70, 73 (1905). . . .

The land's approximate size is recorded: ". . . One-hundred (100) acres, more or less. . . ." The land's location is mentioned: ". . . on the waters of Big Run." While this reference to Big Run helps locate the land, there is little else in the contract to help locate Big Run. Since . . . both buyers and sellers were residents of Jackson County, it is likely that Big Run may be found in Jackson County. Since the buyers were to get "all the hay" together with "three (3) cows and one (1) heifer calf" we may logically infer the land was farm property. Our inference is supported by the contract's notation that the buyers received from the sellers a $300.00 down payment "on farm." Finally, we may infer that the Hudsons, as sellers, undertook to sell land which they owned, rather than land which they did not own. This common sense inference finds support in other jurisdictions' case law. See, Danforth v. Chandler, 237 Mass. 518 (1921); Scott v. Marquette Nat. Bank, 173 Minn. 225 (1927); Price v. McKay, 53 N.J.Eq. 588 (1895); and Edwards v. Phillips, 70 Okla. 9 (1918).

Thus it fairly appears that the subject matter of the disputed contract is a 100 acre farm on Big Run, most likely owned by the Hudsons and located in Jackson County. This description lays a satisfactory foundation for the admission of extrinsic evidence to make more certain that which in our view stands a good chance of being made more certain. Naturally, we may be mistaken in our view, and when evidence is taken, the sellers will have every opportunity to bring out ambiguities not now apparent and to rebut such evidence as the buyers present in their behalf. Nonetheless, on the record before us, we cannot say that the description is insufficient as a matter of law and incapable of being made certain by extrinsic evidence.

Accordingly, . . . the order of the Circuit Court of Jackson County is reversed and the case is remanded for further proceedings not inconsistent with this opinion.

NOTES AND PROBLEM

1. Contrary views. Although the West Virginia court's approach is frequently applied, some states adhere to a much stricter view of the requisite description. Washington, for example holds that "a contract for the conveyance of land is void under the statute of frauds, when such a contract does not contain a description of the land sufficient to locate it without recourse to oral testimony." See Martin v. Seigel, 35 Wn. 2d 223 (1949); Fosburgh v. Sando, 24 Wn. 2d 586 (1946). In *Martin*, the property was described as 309 E. Mercer in the "City of Seattle, County of King, State of Washington." The seller, against whom the contract was sought to be enforced, had also signed a listing agreement that provided the lot and block number of the recorded addition in the county's real estate records, although that description omitted a ten foot portion of an adjacent lot that was also part of "309 E. Mercer." The Washington court required that the description include a full and accurate reference to the lot and block number in a described addition or subdivision as recorded in the realty records of the jurisdiction, along with the city, county, and state in which the property is located. In Pitek v. McGuire, 51 N.M. 364 (1947), a written earnest money receipt for the purchase of "property on E. Central Avenue, Albuquerque, N.M." was insufficient because the seller owned six lots fronting 150 feet on E. Central Avenue. The court noted that if the writing had referred to all of seller's property on E. Central Avenue, or lots fronting 150 feet on E. Central Avenue the description would have been sufficient.

2. *Problem.* O owns two parcels of land in Dunn County and he owns no other real estate. One parcel is a 130 acre farm, including barns and a dwelling. The other parcel is a one acre parcel enclosed by a fence and including a renovated schoolhouse used as O's residence. O signs a contract of sale with P by which he agrees to convey to P "my farm in Dunn County for a price of $18,000." O refuses to close and P sues to enforce the contract by compelling O's specific performance. What result? See Wadsworth v. Moe, 53 Wis.2d 620 (1972).

3. *Of Signatures, E-mails, Typewriters, and Telegrams.* The Statute of Frauds requires that the party to be charged must have signed the writing, but contract law requires that there be mutuality of obligations before a contract may be enforceable. Nevertheless, courts often hold that it does not matter if the plaintiff had failed to sign the writing so long as the defendant had done so. See, e.g., Cottom v. Kennedy, 140 Ill.App.3d 290 (1986); Sewell v. Dolby, 171 Kan. 640 (1951). The rationale for dispensing with formal mutuality is that the plaintiff has bound himself to the contract by seeking to enforce it.

Does a typewritten signature suffice as a signature? Is an e-mail a writing? These related issues, especially that concerning e-mail correspondence, are likely to generate a spate of litigation as computer communication becomes ever more ubiquitous. In Hillstrom v. Gosnay, 188 Mont. 388 (1980), a telegram containing all of the requisite elements concluded with the phrase "Please consider this my written acceptance," followed by the typed name of the sender and seller. The Montana Supreme Court found that to be sufficient to satisfy the Statute of Frauds. In Zier v. Lewis, 352 Mont. 76 (2009), the same Montana court ruled that a package of writings, including exchanges of e-mail, was insufficient, but not because of a perceived difference between e-mail and telegrams. Id. at 81 n1. A Massachusetts trial court has found an exchange of e-mail to be sufficient, where the communications contained all the requisite elements and the name of the sender was typed at the bottom of each e-mail. Shattuck v. Klotzbach, 14 Mass. L. Rep. 360, 2001 WL 1839720 (Mass. Super. 2001). Other courts are more skeptical. See Vista Developers Corp. v. VFP Realty LLC, 847 N.Y.S.2d 416 (2007). Yet, Rosenfeld v. Zerneck, 776 N.Y.S.2d 458 (2004), opined that the typed name in an e-mail constituted a signature, but the substance of the e-mail was insufficient to constitute a written agreement. While some concern may exist that e-mail communications are so easy to make and transmit that they lack the deliberation inherent in a traditional writing, it is likely that the developing law on this topic will focus on the substance of the communications rather than their medium. Congress has weighed in by enacting the "E–Sign" act, 15 U.S.C. § 7001(a)(1) of which provides that a "signature, contract, or other record . . . may not be denied legal effect, validity, or enforceability solely because it is in electronic form." This provision only applies to "any transaction in or affecting interstate or foreign commerce," so it may be that it does not apply to many local real estate transactions. Moreover, to the extent that § 7001 purports to apply to a class of transactions that do not *substantially* affect interstate or foreign commerce it likely exceeds congressional power to enact it under the commerce clause. See United States v. Lopez, 514 U.S. 549 (1995).

b. Exception: Part Performance

The equitable doctrine of part performance permits a party who has partly performed an oral agreement to compel the other party to perform the contract. Two key questions arise: 1) Are the acts of partial performance sufficient to conclude that, in the interest of fairness, the oral contract should be enforced? 2) Has the party seeking specific performance sustained his burden of proving, by clear and convincing evidence, the existence of the oral contract that the plaintiff claims to have partly performed?

BURNS v. McCORMICK

Court of Appeals of New York
233 N.Y. 230 (1922)

CARDOZO, J., delivered the opinion of the court.

In June, 1918, one James A. Halsey, an old man and a widower, was living, without family or housekeeper, in his house in Hornell, New York. He told the plaintiffs, so it is said, that if they gave up their home and business in Andover, New York, and boarded and cared for him during his life, the house and lot with its furniture and equipment would be theirs upon his death. They did as he asked, selling out an interest in a little draying business in Andover, and boarding and tending him till he died, about five months after their coming. Neither deed nor will, nor memorandum subscribed by the promisor, exists to authenticate the promise. The plaintiffs ask specific performance. The defense is the Statute of Frauds. . . .

We think the defense must be upheld. Not every act of part performance will move a court of equity, though legal remedies are inadequate, to enforce an oral agreement affecting rights in land. There must be performance "unequivocally referable" to the agreement, performance which alone and without the aid of words of promise is unintelligible or at least extraordinary unless as an incident of ownership, assured, if not existing. "An act which admits of explanation without reference to the alleged oral contract or a contract of the same general nature and purpose is not, in general, admitted to constitute a part performance." Woolley v. Stewart, 222 N. Y. 347, 351 [(1918)]. What is done must itself supply the key to what is promised. It is not enough that what is promised may give significance to what is done. The housekeeper who abandons other prospects of establishment in life and renders service without pay upon the oral promise of her employer to give her a life estate in land, must find her remedy in an action to recover the value of the service. Her conduct, separated from the promise, is not significant of ownership either present or prospective. On the other hand, the buyer who not only pays the price, but possesses and improves his acre, may have relief in equity without producing a conveyance. Canda v. Totten, 157 N. Y. 281 [(1898)]; McKinley v. Hessen, 202 N. Y. 24 [(1911)]. His conduct is itself the symptom of a promise that a conveyance will be made. Laxer tests may prevail in other jurisdictions. We have been consistent here. *Woolley*; Wheeler v. Reynolds, 66 N. Y. 227, 231, 232 [(1876)]; *McKinley*; *cf.* Van Epps v. Redfield, 69 Conn. 104 [(1897)]; Ellis v. Cary, 74 Wis. 176 [(1889)].

Promise and performance fail when these standards are applied. The plaintiffs make no pretense that during the lifetime of Mr. Halsey they occupied the land as owners or under claim of present right. They did not even have possession. The possession was his; and those whom he invited to live with him were merely his servants or his guests. He might have shown them the door, and the law would not have helped them to return. Whatever rights they had, were executory and future. The tokens of their title are not, then, to be discovered in acts of possession or dominion. The tokens must be found elsewhere if discoverable at all. The plaintiffs did, indeed, while occupants of the dwelling, pay the food bills for the owner as well as for themselves, and do the work of housekeepers. One who heard of such service might infer that it would be rewarded in some way. There could be no reasonable inference that it would be rewarded at some indefinite time thereafter by a conveyance of the land. The board might be given in return for lodging. The outlay might be merely an advance to be repaid in whole or part. "Time and care" might have been bestowed "from a vague anticipation that the affection and gratitude so created would, in the long run, ensure some indefinite reward." Maddison v. Alderson, [(1881–1885) All E.R. 742; L.R. 8 App. Cas. 467, 486 (1883)]. This was the more likely since there were ties of kinship between one of the plaintiffs and the owner. Even if there was to be a reward, not merely as of favor, but as of right, no one could infer, from knowledge of the service without more, what its nature or extent would be. Mr. Halsey paid the taxes. He paid also for the upkeep of the land and building. At least, there is no suggestion that the plaintiffs had undertaken to relieve him of those burdens. He was the owner while he lived. Nothing that he had accepted from the plaintiffs evinces an agreement that they were to be the owners when he died.

We hold, then, that the acts of part performance are not solely and unequivocally referable to a contract for the sale of land. Since that is so, they do not become sufficient because part of the plaintiffs' loss is without a remedy at law. At law, the value of board and services will not be difficult of proof. The loss of the draying business in Andover does not permit us to disregard the statute, though it may go without requital. We do not ignore decisions to the contrary in other jurisdictions. Sears v. Redick, 211 F. 856 (8th Cir. 1914); Aldrich v. Aldrich, 287 Ill. 213 (1919); Best v. Gralapp, 69 Neb. 811 (1903); Schutt v. Missionary Society, 41 N. J. Eq. 115 (1886). They are not law for us. Inadequacy of legal remedies, without more, does not dispense with the requirement that acts, and not words, shall supply the framework of the promise. That requirement has its origin in something more than an arbitrary preference of one form over others. It is "intended to prevent a recurrence of the mischief" which the statute would suppress. [*Maddison*] The peril of perjury and error is latent in the spoken promise. Such, at least, is the warning of the statute, the estimate of policy that finds expression in its mandate. Equity, in assuming what is in substance a dispensing power, does not treat the statute as irrelevant, nor ignore the warning altogether. It declines to act on words, though the legal remedy is imperfect, unless the words are confirmed and illuminated by deeds. A power of dispensation, departing from the letter in supposed adherence to the spirit, involves an assumption of jurisdiction easily abused, and justified only within the limits imposed by history and precedent. The power is not exercised unless the policy of the law is saved.

In conclusion, we observe that this is not a case of fraud. No confidential relation has been abused. No inducement has been offered with the preconceived intention that it would later be ignored. The most that can be said against Mr. Halsey is that he made a promise which the law did not compel him to keep, and that afterwards he failed to keep it. We cannot even say of his failure that it was willful. He had made a will before the promise. Negligence or mere inertia may have postponed the making of another. The plaintiffs left the preservation of their agreement, if they had one, to the fallible memory of witnesses. The law exacts a writing....

NOTES AND QUESTIONS

1. The Nature of the Performance. Judge Cardozo, in *Burns*, articulated the so-called evidentiary theory of part performance—that the performance must be "unequivocally referable" to the oral agreement. Under this theory, apparently the *only* explanation of the promisee's actions must be that it was performance of the oral agreement. Cardozo suggested that acts of possession under a claim of rightful possession might be sufficient. But consider Dixieland Food Stores, Inc. v. Geddert, 505 So.2d 371 (Ala. 1987). As a commercial lease was nearing expiration, the parties allegedly agreed orally to extend the lease for five years at an increased rental. Dixieland, the lessee, remained in possession after expiration of the original lease and paid the original, lower, rental. The Alabama Supreme Court held that Dixieland's actions were insufficient to constitute part performance. Possession, said the court, "must be *exclusively* referable to the contract in issue." This possession was inadequate because it was consistent with the old lease, not the new lease. It is frequently said that an oral contract for the sale of land may be specifically enforced where the "purchaser with the assent of the vendor (a) makes valuable improvements on the land, or (b) takes possession thereof or retains a possession thereof existing at the time of the bargain, and also pays a portion or all of the purchase price." Restatement of Contracts (First) § 197. Under this section, what did Dixieland fail to do to establish part performance?

Consider Gardner v. Gardner, 454 N.W.2d 361 (Iowa 1990). Harry Gardner owned a life estate in some Iowa farmland. The remainder in fee simple absolute was owned by Harry's siblings. Harry was in financial trouble and wanted to use the farmland as security for a loan. Harry's siblings orally agreed that they would convey their remainder to Harry, and Harry agreed that he would reconvey it if he could not obtain a loan. The siblings conveyed their interest to Harry, he could not obtain a loan, and he refused to reconvey. His brothers, James and Mark Gardner, sought to compel performance of the oral agreement on the basis that they had performed the agreement. The Iowa Supreme Court agreed. Why was the deed from Mark and James to Harry, conveying their remainder interest, sufficient performance to enforce the alleged oral agreement? Couldn't their action be explained by the brothers' desire to make a gift to Harry? In what way was it an *unequivocal reference* to the oral agreement? If the answer to these questions seems difficult to reconcile with the principle adopted by *Burns*, consider whether the next section, on equitable estoppel, sheds any light on the matter.

2. *The Necessity of an Agreement.* The Statute of Frauds prevents *enforcement* of oral agreements for the sale of land, but the exceptions to the Statute do not dispense with the necessity of proving the existence of an agreement. The evidentiary theory of Judge Cardozo in *Burns* is bottomed on the notion that only performance that is unequivocally referable to the agreement is likely to be probative evidence of the existence of the agreement. But what if the defendant admits the existence of the agreement? Should Cardozo's rule apply in that context? In *Gardner* the court noted that there was some evidence that Harry Gardner had admitted the existence of the oral agreement. Was that enough, by itself, to conclude that Harry's siblings' conveyance was sufficient performance? Professor Corbin, in his treatise on contracts, declared: "Where the oral testimony of the contract is not disputed, or where it is ample, disinterested and convincing, the court need not depend so strongly upon the part performance. ... The question how strongly ... part performance [is evidence of an oral agreement] is a question of degree, directly depending upon the degree of certainty in the accompanying testimony and the degree of injustice and wrong to be avoided." 2 Corbin on Contracts, § 430 (1950).

c. Exception: Equitable Estoppel

HICKEY v. GREEN

Appeals Court of Massachusetts
14 Mass.App. 671, 442 N.E.2d 37 (1982)

CUTTER, J., delivered the opinion of the court.

This case is before us on a stipulation of facts. . . . Mrs. Gladys Green owns a lot (Lot S) in the Manomet section of Plymouth. In July, 1980, she advertised it for sale. On July 11 and 12, Hickey and his wife discussed with Mrs. Green purchasing Lot S and "orally agreed to a sale" for $15,000. Mrs. Green on July 12 accepted a deposit check of $500, marked by Hickey on the back, "Deposit on Lot . . . Massasoit Ave. Manomet . . . Subject to Variance from Town of Plymouth." Mrs. Green's brother and agent "was under the impression that a zoning variance was needed and [had] advised . . . Hickey to write" the quoted language on the deposit check. It turned out, however, by July 16 that no variance would be required. Hickey had left the payee line of the deposit check blank, because of uncertainty whether Mrs. Green or her brother was to receive the check and asked "Mrs. Green to fill in the appropriate name." Mrs. Green held the check, did not fill in the payee's name, and neither cashed nor endorsed it. Hickey "stated to Mrs. Green that his intention was to sell his home and build on Mrs. Green's lot."

"Relying upon the arrangements . . . with Mrs. Green," the Hickeys advertised their house on Sachem Road in newspapers on three days in July, 1980, and agreed with a purchaser for its sale and took from him a deposit check for $500 which they deposited in their own account. On July 24, Mrs. Green told Hickey that she "no longer intended to sell her property to him" but had decided to sell to another for $16,000. Hickey told Mrs. Green that he had already sold his house and offered her $16,000 for Lot S. Mrs. Green refused this offer.

The Hickeys filed this complaint seeking specific performance. Mrs. Green asserts that relief is barred by the Statute of Frauds. . . . The trial judge granted specific performance. Mrs. Green has appealed.

The present rule applicable in most jurisdictions in the United States is succinctly set forth in Restatement (Second) of Contracts § 129 (1981). The section reads: "A contract for the transfer of an interest in land may be specifically enforced notwithstanding failure to comply with the Statute of Frauds if it is established that the party seeking enforcement, *in reasonable reliance on the contract* and on the continuing assent of the party against whom enforcement is sought, *has so changed his position that injustice can be avoided only by specific enforcement*" (emphasis supplied).[1] . . .

---

1. Comments a and b to § 129, read (in part): "a. . . . This section restates what is widely known as the 'part performance doctrine.' Part performance is not an accurate designation of such acts as taking possession and making improvements when the contract does not provide for such acts, but such acts regularly bring the doctrine into play. The doctrine is contrary to the words of the Statute of Frauds, but it was established by English courts of equity soon after the enactment of the Statute. . . . Enforcement has . . . been justified on the ground that repudiation after 'part performance' amounts to a 'virtual fraud.' A more accurate statement is that courts with equitable powers are vested by tradition with what in substance is a dispensing power based on the promisee's reliance, *a discretion to be exercised with caution* in the light of all the circumstances . . . [emphasis supplied].

"b. . . . Two distinct elements enter into the application of the rule of this Section: first, the extent to which the evidentiary function of the statutory formalities is fulfilled by the conduct of the parties; second, the reliance of the promisee, providing a compelling substantive basis for relief in addition to the expectations created by the promise."

The present facts reveal a simple case of a proposed purchase of a residential vacant lot, where the vendor, Mrs. Green, knew that the Hickeys were planning to sell their former home (possibly to obtain funds to pay her) and build on Lot S. The Hickeys, relying on Mrs. Green's oral promise, moved rapidly to make their sale without obtaining any adequate memorandum of the terms of what appears to have been intended to be a quick cash sale of Lot S. So rapid was action by the Hickeys that, by July 21, less than ten days after giving their deposit to Mrs. Green, they had accepted a deposit check for the sale of their house, endorsed the check, and placed it in their bank account. Above their signatures endorsing the check was a memorandum probably sufficient to satisfy the Statute of Frauds.... At the very least, the Hickeys had bound themselves in a manner in which, to avoid a transfer of their own house, they might have had to engage in expensive litigation. No attorney has been shown to have been used either in the transaction between Mrs. Green and the Hickeys or in that between the Hickeys and their purchaser.

There is no denial by Mrs. Green of the oral contract between her and the Hickeys. This, under § 129 of the Restatement, is of some significance.[2] There can be no doubt (a) that Mrs. Green made the promise on which the Hickeys so promptly relied, and also (b) she, nearly as promptly, but not promptly enough, repudiated it because she had a better opportunity. The stipulated facts require the conclusion that in equity Mrs. Green's conduct cannot be condoned. This is not a case where either party is shown to have contemplated the negotiation of a purchase and sale agreement. If a written agreement had been expected, even by only one party, or would have been natural (because of the participation by lawyers or otherwise), a different situation might have existed. It is a permissible inference from the agreed facts that the rapid sale of the Hickeys' house was both appropriate and expected. These are not circumstances where negotiations fairly can be seen as inchoate....

No public interest behind [the Statute of Frauds] will be violated if Mrs. Green fairly is held to her precise bargain by principles of equitable estoppel....

NOTES

1. *Distinction without a difference?* In *Hickey*, the Massachusetts court quoted Restatement (Second) of Contracts, § 129, and emphasized the elements of equitable estoppel: a promise made and (with the assent of the promisor) reasonable detrimental reliance on the promise. Yet, the comments to that section of the Restatement claim that the section merely restates the

---

2. Comment d of Restatement (Second) of Contracts § 129, reads [in part:] "d. ... [It] is commonly said that the action taken by the purchaser must be unequivocally referable to the oral agreement. But this requirement is not insisted on *if the making of the promise is admitted or is clearly proved*. The promisee *must act in reasonable reliance on the promise, before the promisor has repudiated* it, and the action must be such that the remedy of restitution is inadequate. If these requirements are met, *neither taking of possession nor payment of money nor the making of improvements is essential* ..." (emphasis supplied).

doctrine of part performance. Which is it? Perhaps the estoppel theory of *Hickey* is a liberalization of part performance. If so, how should *Burns* be decided under the *Hickey* rationale? In thinking about that query, recall Comments b and d to Rest. (2d) Contracts.

In Montoya v. New Mexico Human Services Department, 108 N.M. 263 (App. 1989), the New Mexico Court of Appeals held that "there is no essential difference between the circumstances that make it inequitable to deny enforcement to an oral contract to sell real property and those that make it inequitable to refuse to enforce a promise to give real property. Thus, we hold that if there is proof of the elements of promissory estoppel, an oral gift of real property is enforceable...."

Consider Walker v. Ireton, 221 Kan. 314 (1977). Ireton and Walker agreed orally to sell Ireton's farm to Walker, who tendered checks for a portion of the purchase price to Ireton, although Ireton never cashed the checks. Walker also moved a piece of farm equipment onto the Ireton farm and sold another farm he owned in reliance upon the oral contract with Ireton. Ireton backed out of the deal; Walker sued and the trial court granted Ireton's motion for summary judgment. The Kansas Supreme Court affirmed.

> Here there is no claim that there was any relationship of trust or confidence between the parties. There are no allegations or evidence of false misrepresentation of existing facts. The worst which can be said is that Ireton repeatedly promised that he would perform the oral contract and that he would enter into a written contract to evidence the same. ... [T]he parties understood a written contract was to be prepared. Ireton simply refused to sign a written contract on four or five different occasions. Although Walker made a ... down payment he never took possession of the land ... and made no improvements thereon. Walker placed a hay rake on ... the farm but this could not be considered a delivery of possession of the land.

> The acts of reliance which Walker has asserted are limited ... to delivery of [an uncashed] check as an installment on the purchase price, payment of [an] abstract expense and [an] attorney fee for an abstract examination, the placing of a hay rake on a pasture ..., and the fact that Walker sold a farm near Hedville ... in reliance on Ireton's promise to sell his farm. ... The fact that Walker sold another farm in expectation that the Iretons would sell their farm to him does not justify specific performance under the circumstances of the case. As a general rule an act which is purely collateral to an oral contract, although done in reliance on such contract is not such a part performance as to authorize the enforcement of the contract by a court of equity. An exception is recognized, however, where the agreement was made to induce the collateral act or where the collateral act was contemplated by the parties as a part of the entire transaction....

> Walker does not contend that he advised the Iretons of his intention to sell the Hedville farm in advance of the sale or that the Iretons had any knowledge concerning the sale of the Hedville farm until after it had already been sold. [The] resale of the Hedville farm by Walker to others [was] a matter wholly collateral to the Ireton contract and not within the

contemplation of the parties nor within the scope of any understanding between Ireton and Walker.

2. *Inchoate agreements.* Suppose that when the Hickeys and Mrs. Green had reached an oral agreement they had also said, "Of course, we will get our lawyers to write it up; but this is the deal." If there had never been a written agreement drawn up, but the Hickeys had then sold their house in reliance on the oral agreement, should the result be the same?

In thinking about this problem, consider King v. Wenger, 219 Kan. 668 (1976). Ethel Wenger owned a life estate in 160 acres of Kansas farmland. Loraine Wenger and Lorene Ralston, sisters, owned the remainder in fee simple absolute. Following a telephone conversation between King, Loraine Wenger, and Ralston (who was in Colorado), King and Loraine Wenger each signed a written memorandum containing all the requisite elements of a contract. Loraine Wenger signed for herself and for Lorene Ralston. At the time of the signing, the parties agreed to meet with King's lawyer later in the day to draw up and sign a formal contract. No such formal contract was ever signed, partly because Loraine Wenger did not approve of additional terms inserted by King's lawyer. Instead, the Wenger–Ralston group entered into a contract with other buyers. King's suit for specific performance was rejected because the Kansas courts concluded that the actions of the parties after the memorandum was signed indicated that their intent was not to be bound until the formal contract was executed. Until then, there was no meeting of the minds.

2. CONDITIONS TO PERFORMANCE

The contract of sale may contain any number of conditions to the performance of either buyer or seller. This section examines some common disputes that are likely to lead to litigation.

a. Time for Performance

Contracts for sale will contain a closing date, but the significance of the specified date may vary with the transaction. In some deals, the parties may be flexible as to the timing of the closing, but in other transactions, one or both parties may regard the closing date to be of critical importance, perhaps because other, unrelated, transactions hinge on closing as of the set date. When timing is critical, the parties may include a provision that "time is of the essence." When such a provision is included, courts interpret it strictly. In Nadeau v. Beers, 73 Wn. 2d 608, 610 (1968), time was stipulated to be of the essence. The buyer tendered a certified check for the purchase price three days after the close of a 120 day period in which the closing was to occur. (The buyer mistakenly thought that the 120 day period meant four calendar months.) The Washington Supreme Court declared:

> The ... agreement in question is ... free from ambiguity as to those points essential for decision. Time is made the essence of the agreement, and a termination date is fixed. Payment was not tendered

until after the agreement by its terms had expired. Absent conduct giving rise to estoppel or waiver, no further action on the part of [the sellers] was required to effectuate the termination. There is no forfeiture involved, for the agreement, by operation of its time provisions, became legally defunct.

But what happens if the contract does not specify that time is of the essence? In Kasten Construction Co. v. Maple Ridge Construction Co., 245 Md. 373 (1967), the contract of sale called for a closing within 60 days but did not say that time was of the essence. The closing date was extended once, but the seller refused to extend it further. The delay was due to difficulties encountered by the buyer in arranging financing. Five days after the extended closing date, the buyer notified the seller that it would be able to close in three weeks. The seller contended that the contract had expired. The buyer sought and obtained a decree of specific performance, which was upheld on appeal by the Maryland Court of Appeals:

> In a case involving specific performance, where the intention of the parties is always the controlling factor, the general rule is that time is not of the essence of the contract of sale and purchase of land unless a contrary purpose is disclosed by its terms or is indicated by the circumstances and object of its execution and the conduct of the parties. Of course, one may lose his right to specific performance by gross laches and unreasonable delay in paying the purchase money. Ordinarily, however, time is held to be of the essence only when it is clear that the parties have expressly so stipulated or their intention is inferable from the circumstances of the transaction, the conduct of the parties or the purpose for which the sale was made. . . . [E]ven though the buyer was somewhat neglectful in not paying the balance of the purchase money on the day it was due, [it cannot] be said that the delay, particularly in view of the fact that the seller was in no hurry to perform its part of the contract, was unreasonable. *Id.* at 377–378.

See also Duprey v. Donahoe, 52 Wn. 2d 129, 135 (1958), an action in equity for specific performance: "When, as here, no time is specified in the . . . agreement for the final payment and delivery of the instruments of conveyance, the time of payment and delivery is a reasonable time after acceptance of the offer."

But the general rule is different in actions at law, in which the remedy sought is damages. See Lusker v. Tannen, 456 N.Y.S.2d 354, 357 (App. Div. 1982): "[T]he rule of equity is that time of performance will not be considered of the essence of the contract unless it affirmatively appears that the parties regarded it as a material consideration. . . . The fact that the party may not have an action at law is a reason for a decree for specific performance. On the other hand, the general rule of law is that the stipulated time of performance in executory contracts is of the essence unless a contrary intent appears." Accord, GDJS Corp. v. 917 Properties, Inc., 473 N.Y.S.2d 453, 455 (App. Div. 1984): "[I]n an action at law to recover the down payment or for damages upon breach of an agreement, it is generally held that the time for performance stipulated in the contract is of the essence unless a contrary intent appears, either from the agreement or the conduct of the parties. Thus, in such an action, the specification in the contract of a date for closing, without more, made time of the essence. Nevertheless, the parties, by their conduct, may evince an intent that time not be of the essence and, in such instances, even where the action is at law, the refusal to grant a reasonable adjournment may amount to a repudiation of the agreement.''

Note that this rule is not universally observed. In one Arizona case, the sale contract called for a closing on December 15, 1982 and a lease of the premises by the buyer from May until the closing. The buyer took possession under the lease, then informed the seller that he would not perform either the lease or the sale. The seller told buyer that he would not enforce the lease but would insist on performance of the sale. Without any further contact or notice the buyer appeared on December 15 at the escrow agent and tendered performance. The seller did not perform because he was out of town on that day, although the court later concluded that the seller would have performed had he known of buyer's intention to perform. Seller tendered full performance a day later but the buyer contended that the contract was now void and instituted a suit at law to recover his earnest money deposit. The Arizona Court of Appeals declared: "In a land sale contract, time is usually not regarded as being of the essence. When a contract for the sale and purchase of land does not make time of the essence as it relates to closing, a party can breach the contract only by refusing to perform after demand that closing take place at a reasonable time and place." Miller v. Long Family Partnership, 151 Ariz. 306, 308 (1986). The court drew no distinction between actions at law or in equity.

b. Marketable Title

Every contract of sale of real property contains an implied promise on the part of the seller to deliver marketable title, unless the parties have explicitly agreed on some other standard. The parties could agree, for example, that the seller would deliver title "satisfactory to the buyer," or that the seller would deliver title "free from any doubts or imperfections whatever." Such an obligation would leave a buyer with an easy exit, as most titles come with some liens or imperfections (such as a utility easement, or even for taxes accrued but not yet due). On the other hand, the parties could stipulate that title is satisfactory unless the buyer can prove that the title is actually defective. Marketable title occupies a somewhat shadowy middle ground. What constitutes marketable title? It does *not* mean that the property is not easily saleable, or that there are defects in the structure or the land that make it highly unlikely that it could be resold. Rather, it focuses upon the state of the title itself—the quality of ownership that is to be conveyed:

A marketable title ... is one which can be readily sold or mortgaged to a person of reasonable prudence, the test of the marketability of a title being whether there is an objection thereto such as would interfere with a sale or with the market value of the property. The law assures to a buyer a title free from reasonable doubt, but not from every doubt, and the mere possibility or suspicion of a defect, which according to ordinary experience has no probable basis, does not demonstrate an unmarketable title. "If 'the only defect in the title' is 'a very remote and improbable contingency,' ... a conveyance will be decreed." Norwegian Evangelical Free Church v Milhauser, 252 N.Y. 186, 190 (1929).

Regan v. Lanze, 40 N.Y.2d 475, 481–482 (1976).

DUKAS v. TOLMACH

Supreme Court of New York, Appellate Division
153 N.Y.S. 2d 392 (App. 1956)

RABIN, J., delivered the opinion of the court.

Plaintiff, claiming that defendants' title is unmarketable, sues to recover the amount of the deposit paid by him on a contract for the purchase of a residential property from defendants [and for reimbursement of his] expenses. ... The claim of unmarketability is based upon [allegations that two stone retaining walls, lawn, and plantings encroach on a city street from about three inches to over 17 feet, and a driveway and the stone and masonry entranceway to the house encroach about 17 feet on the street.]

The property was sold by a metes and bounds description. All of the alleged encroachments are outside of the metes and bounds and no part of the building itself encroaches upon city property. The proof shows quite clearly however that all of these claimed encroachments including the retaining walls, the driveway and the stairway all emanate from the parcel sold and appear as an integral part thereof. Defendants take the position that since they did not sell plaintiff any of the land on which these encroachments lie they are in a position to convey good title in accordance with the contract—that is by the metes and bounds description.

The question posed ... is whether under these facts (the so-called encroachments being clearly established by the evidence) defendants' title is marketable. We think it is not. A purchaser may not be compelled to accept a title which will subject him to a lawsuit or which will require him to expend substantial sums of money in order to comply with the law.

There would seem to be little doubt that the city authorities can compel removal of any or all of these encroachments. Section 82d6–6.0 of the Administrative Code of the City of New York provides: "The president of the borough having jurisdiction may serve written notice upon the owner of any premises requiring such owner to remove or alter any unauthorized projection, encroachment or incumbrance, on or *in front* of his premises, within a period to be specified in such notice." (Emphasis added.) Thus if the purchaser were to accept the property as tendered he would then have a parcel which carries with it a burden—the burden of removing the abutting encroachments at the city's request. Nor can it be said that the title is marketable because the city has not, and may not in the immediate future demand the removal of the encroachments. The purchaser did not contract for a title thus burdened. If a vendor wishes to convey subject to an incumbrance affecting title—even though the incumbrance be contained in a deed of record—the contract must provide that the property is sold subject thereto. So too, any encroachment, whether within or without the record lines, should be excepted in the contract if such encroachment would constitute a burden on the property. Particularly is that so, where as here, the owner can be compelled at considerable expense to remove the encroachments.

[It is] obvious from a view of the encroachments ... that a very substantial sum as compared to the purchase price would be required [to remove them]. The removal of the retaining walls with some adequate substitute for support of the adjoining land, the removal of the paved driveway and consequent lowering of the garage, the removal of the stairway and replacement, would unquestionably involve a considerable expenditure. We conclude that defendants' title is unmarketable.

An additional reason given by the purchaser for the rejection of title was that the title company refused to insure without listing these encroachments as exceptions. The contract provides that: "The seller shall give and the purchaser shall accept a title such as ____ will approve and insure." While the name of the title company to which this title was to be submitted was left blank it was clearly contemplated by the parties that title to be given would be a title that would be insurable as per the contract with only such exceptions as were referred to in the contract. Defendants conceded that Lawyers Mortgage and Title Company was selected by the plaintiff with their *approval* and recommendation. In the light of this admission plaintiff had the right to a title that the Lawyers Mortgage and Title Company would insure and defendants should not be permitted to make capital of the fact that the name of the title company was omitted. When the parties have agreed that the title must be one that a title company will insure, refusal by the title company to insure is a good ground for rejection. We believe that on the facts of this case the purchaser had the clear right to reject title as unmarketable....

NOTES AND QUESTIONS

1. Encroachments and Violations of Codes or Covenants. A number of marketable title cases involve encroachments, violations of municipal ordinances, or covenants limiting use of the property (that latter being a topic addressed in Chapter 10).

In Lohmeyer v. Bower, 170 Kan. 442 (1951), the court made a distinction between the bare existence of ordinances and covenants and actual conditions that violate those ordinances and covenants. Bower agreed to sell a single story residence to Lohmeyer, under a contract that called for Bower to deliver marketable title subject "to all restrictions and easements of record applying to this property." The property was subject to a covenant requiring that it be two stories in height, and was situated on the lot so that it violated a city ordinance requiring structures to be set back from the lot line a minimum distance. The court noted that the existence of the ordinance did not render title unmarketable but "it is the violation of the restrictions imposed by both the ordinance and the [covenant], not the existence of those restrictions, that render the title unmarketable" because those violations exposed Lohmeyer to the "hazard of litigation."

In Bethurem v. Hammett, 736 P.2d 1128 (Wyo. 1987), Bethurem agreed to purchase from Hammett a residence via an installment sale contract. Under an installment sale title does not pass until all installments of the purchase price have been made. Two years into the deal Bethurem learned that the property substantially encroached on a city street and sought to rescind the contract. The contract stipulated that the seller would deliver marketable title, subject to "defects . . . readily visible upon inspection." The Wyoming court held that, as a matter of law, title was not marketable. A dissenting judge thought that the question of whether the encroachments were "readily visible" was a matter that should have been submitted to the trier of fact. Note that the seller under an installment sale contract has no obligation to deliver title until all the installment payments have been made. That allows a seller to cure some title defects before the day of reckoning arrives, so the buyer cannot back out on the basis of unmarketable title until title is actually delivered. However, when the seller can never cure the defect, as was the case in *Bethurem*, the buyer need not wait until the day title is to pass to raise the objection of unmarketable title.

Brown v. Herman, 75 Wn.2d 816 (1969), stands in contrast. Herman sold a business to Brown under an installment sale contract. Brown stopped paying because the premises were constructed within 8 feet of a city street in violation of a city ordinance, and the business violated an applicable covenant. Herman sued to enforce the contract, Brown sought rescission based on claimed unmarketable title, and the court found title to be marketable. The court determined that Brown was fully aware that the business violated the restrictive covenant and that "the most casual observation of the property would disclose that the building was closer to the [street] than 8 feet."

2. The Nature of the Deed. In section D.2 of this chapter you will encounter various types of deeds, some of which contain warranties concerning the state of title. The *quit claim deed*, however, contains no warranties of title. By delivering a quit claim deed the seller makes no promise of any kind about the title; he says, in effect, "I convey any right, title, or interest I may have in the property, but there are no promises that I have any right, title, or interest to convey." As you will see, quit claim deeds serve useful functions, but a prudent buyer might not wish to receive title via a quit claim deed. Suppose a contract of sale calls for conveyance of described realty via quit claim deed; may the buyer raise a defense of unmarketable title if there is a defect in the title?

Wallach v. Riverside Bank, 206 N.Y. 434 (1912), addressed that issue. Seller and Buyer entered into a contract for the sale of 165 and 167 E. 108th Street in New York City, title to be delivered via a quit claim deed. At the closing Buyer refused to accept the deed because a title search disclosed that Seller did not have clear title. It turned out that Seller owned the property "subject to an inchoate right of dower vested by statute in the wife of a prior grantor." Acceptance of the quit claim deed would mean that Buyer would receive a title blemished by the possibility that the dower holder would demand her rights to partial ownership and possession. Seller contended that Buyer was getting what he bargained for; after all, the contract did not specify that Seller must deliver marketable title. The Court of Appeals found for the Buyer:

> [Buyer] did not agree to accept a defective title. He agreed to buy "all the premises" described by clear and unmistakable boundaries, and by implication of law this means in an executory contract a good title to the whole thereof, free and clear from incumbrances. Although the writing does not say so, the law says so, and the law is part of the writing. When a vendor agrees to sell a piece of land the law imputes to him a covenant that he will convey a marketable title unless the vendee stipulates to accept something less. . . . The agreement of the plaintiff to accept a quitclaim deed as the means of transfer was not a waiver of the defect. A quitclaim deed is as effective as any to convey all the title the grantor has, and a deed with all the covenants known cannot strengthen a defective title, but can simply protect from loss on account thereof. The sale was subject to existing liens and to existing restrictions of record, and it could be subject to no other defect unless it was also specified. *Id.* at 437–438.

Suppose that the Seller in *Wallach* was aware of the inchoate dower right that was a blot on title but also knew that the holder of that right was ninety-eight years old, in failing health, had taken vows of poverty, and was living in a cloister in Tierra del Fuego. Believing the title defect to be almost certain of never materializing, but without any means to cure the defect, what could Seller do to avoid the requirement of delivering marketable title? In answering this question, recall that Buyer in *Wallach* was willing to accept a quit claim deed, at least at the moment the executory contract of sale was created.

3. Without Market Value but with Marketable Title. If the title that the seller can deliver carries no reasonable risk of litigation as to its validity, it does not matter that the property may not have any market value. For example, property that has no access from a public thoroughfare is not likely to be very easy to sell, if at all, but if the title is good the seller has delivered marketable title. See Sinks v. Karleskint, 130 Ill.App.3d 527 (1985). Similarly, property that is tainted by toxic waste (and thus carries strict liability on the part of the owner for the cost of remediation) is surely almost impossible to sell, but title to such property is marketable if it is without defects. See HM Holdings, Inc. v. Rankin, 70 F.3d 933, 936 (7th Cir. 1995), applying Indiana law and noting "that every court that has addressed the issue has refused to expand the marketable title doctrine to make the presence of hazardous waste an encumbrance on title." The seeming harshness of these rules is substantially mitigated by the fact that buyers can either inspect the property with great care, bargain for explicit seller warranties that no such problems exist, or both.

3.   DISCLOSURE OBLIGATIONS

The traditional rule has been *caveat emptor*—buyer beware. Under this approach, a seller has no obligation to disclose anything unless there is a fiduciary relationship between buyer and seller or the seller has taken steps to conceal a known defect from discovery by the buyer. See, e.g., London v. Courduff, 529 N.Y.S.2d 874 (App. Div. 1988); Moser v. Spizzirro, 295 N.Y.S.2d 188 (App. Div. 1968), *aff'd*, 25 N.Y.2d 941 (1969); 17 E. 80th Realty Corp. v. 68th Associates, 569 N.Y.S.2d 647 (App. Div. 1991). Under *caveat emptor* only fraud or intentional misrepresentation results in seller liability. But *caveat emptor* has eroded. This has occurred in several ways. By statute, some states impose on sellers the obligation to disclose a variety of known specified issues, such as encroachments, soil or structural problems, the existence of underground storage tanks, and alterations made without permits or in violation of local ordinances. See, e.g., Cal. Civ. Code § 1102.6. Other states have changed the common law to require sellers to disclose all defects known to them. Failure to do so results in the same consequences as if the seller had intentionally misrepresented the premises.

JOHNSON v. DAVIS

Supreme Court of Florida
480 So.2d 625 (1985)

ADKINS, J., delivered the opinion of the court.

. . . In May of 1982, the Davises entered into a contract to buy for $310,000 the Johnsons' home, which at the time was three years old. The contract required a $5,000 deposit payment, an additional $26,000 deposit payment within five days and a closing by June 21, 1982. The crucial provision of the contract . . . is Paragraph F which provided:

F.   *Roof Inspection*: Prior to closing at Buyer's expense, Buyer shall have the right to obtain a written report from a licensed roofer stating that the roof is in a watertight condition. In the event repairs are required either to correct leaks or to replace damage to facia or soffit, seller shall pay for said repairs which shall be performed by a licensed roofing contractor.

The contract further provided for payment to the "prevailing party" of all costs and reasonable fees in any contract litigation.

Before the Davises made the additional $26,000 deposit payment, Mrs. Davis noticed some buckling and peeling plaster around the corner of a window frame in the family room and stains on the ceilings in the family room and kitchen of the home. Upon inquiring, Mrs. Davis was told by Mr. Johnson that the window had had a minor problem that had long since been corrected and that the stains were wallpaper glue and the result of ceiling beams being moved. There is disagreement among the parties as to whether Mr. Johnson also told Mrs. Davis at this time that there had never been any problems with the roof or ceilings. The Davises thereafter paid the remainder of their deposit and the Johnsons vacated the home. Several days later, following a heavy rain, Mrs. Davis entered the home and discovered water "gushing" in from around the window frame, the ceiling of the family room, the light fixtures, the glass doors, and the stove in the kitchen.

Two roofers hired by the Johnsons' broker concluded that for under $1,000 they could "fix" certain leaks in the roof and by doing so make the roof "watertight." Three roofers hired by the Davises found that the roof was inherently defective, that any repairs would be temporary because the roof was "slipping," and that only a new $15,000 roof could be "watertight." The Davises filed a complaint alleging breach of contract, fraud and misrepresentation, and sought recission of the contract and return of their deposit. The Johnsons counterclaimed seeking the deposit as liquidated damages.

The trial court ... awarded the Davises $26,000 plus interest and awarded the Johnsons $5,000 plus interest. Each party was to bear their own attorneys' fees. The Johnsons appealed and the Davises cross-appealed.... The Third District [intermediate appellate court] found for the Davises affirming the trial court's return of the majority of the deposit to the Davises ($26,000), and reversing the award of $5,000 to the Johnsons as well as the court's failure to award the Davises costs and fees. Accordingly, the court remanded with directions to return to the Davises the balance of their deposit and to award them costs and fees.

The [intermediate appellate court concluded that there was no breach] of the roof inspection provision of the contract. ... We agree.... The contract contemplated the possibility that the roof may not be watertight at the time of inspection and provided a remedy if it was not in such a condition. The roof inspection provision of the contract did not impose any obligation beyond the seller correcting the leaks and replacing damage to the facia or soffit. The record is devoid of any evidence that the seller refused to make needed repairs to the roof. In fact, the record reflects that the Davises' never even demanded that the areas of leakage be repaired either by way of repair or replacement. Yet the Davises insist that the Johnsons breached the contract justifying recission. We find this contention to be without merit.

We also agree with the [intermediate appellate court's] conclusions under a theory of fraud and find that the Johnsons' statements to the Davises regarding the condition of the roof constituted a fraudulent misrepresentation entitling respondents to the return of their $26,000 deposit payment. In the state of Florida, relief for a fraudulent misrepresentation may be granted only when the following elements are present: (1) a false statement concerning a material fact; (2) the representor's knowledge that the representation is false; (3) an intention that the representation induce another to act on it; and, (4) consequent injury by the party acting in reliance on the representation. The evidence adduced at trial shows that after the buyer and the seller signed the purchase and sales agreement ... the Johnsons affirmatively repeated to the Davises that there were no problems with the roof. ... The ... statement made by the Johnsons was a false representation of material fact, made with knowledge of its falsity, upon which the Davises relied to their detriment as evidenced by the $26,000 paid to the Johnsons.

The doctrine of *caveat emptor* does not exempt a seller from responsibility for the statements and representations which he makes to induce the buyer to act, when under the circumstances these amount to fraud in the legal sense. [The] false representations need not have been made at the time of the signing of the purchase and sales agreement in order for the element of reliance to be present. The fact that the false statements as to the quality of the roof were made after the signing of the purchase and sales agreement does not excuse the seller from liability when the misrepresentations were made prior to the execution of the contract by conveyance of the property. It would be contrary to all notions of fairness and justice for this Court to place its stamp of approval on an affirmative misrepresentation by a wrongdoer just because it was made after the signing of the executory contract when all of the necessary elements for actionable fraud are present. Furthermore, the Davises' reliance on the truth of the Johnsons' representation was justified and is supported by this Court's decision in Besett v. Basnett, 389 So.2d 995 (1980), where we held "that a recipient may rely on the truth of a representation, even though its falsity could have been ascertained had he made an investigation, unless he knows the representation to be false or its falsity is obvious to him." *Id.* at 998.

In determining whether a seller of a home has a duty to disclose latent material defects to a buyer, the established tort law distinction between misfeasance and nonfeasance, action and inaction, must carefully be analyzed. The highly individualistic philosophy of the earlier common law consistently imposed liability upon the commission of affirmative acts of harm, but shrank from converting the courts into an institution for forcing men to help one another. This distinction is deeply rooted in our case law. Liability for nonfeasance has therefore been slow to receive recognition in the evolution of tort law. In theory, the difference between misfeasance and nonfeasance, action and inaction is quite simple and obvious; however, in practice it is not always easy to draw the line and determine whether conduct is active or passive. That is, where failure to disclose a material fact is calculated to induce a false belief, the distinction between concealment and affirmative representations is tenuous. Both proceed from the same motives and are attended with the same consequences; both are violative of the principles of fair dealing and good faith; both are calculated to produce the same result; and, in fact, both essentially have the same effect.

Still there exists in much of our case law the old tort notion that there can be no liability for nonfeasance. The courts in some jurisdictions, including Florida, hold that where the parties are dealing at arm's length and the facts lie equally open to both parties, with equal opportunity of examination, mere nondisclosure does not constitute a fraudulent concealment. . . . These unappetizing cases are not in tune with the times and do not conform with current notions of justice, equity and fair dealing. One should not be able to stand behind the impervious shield of *caveat emptor* and take advantage of another's ignorance. Our courts have taken great strides since the days when the judicial emphasis was on rigid rules and ancient precedents. Modern concepts of justice and fair dealing have given our courts the opportunity and latitude to change legal precepts in order to conform to society's needs. Thus, the tendency of the more recent cases has been to restrict rather than extend the doctrine of *caveat emptor*. The law appears to be working toward the ultimate conclusion that full disclosure of all material facts must be made whenever elementary fair conduct demands it.

The harness placed on the doctrine of *caveat emptor* in a number of other jurisdictions has resulted in the seller of a home being liable for failing to disclose material defects of which he is aware. This philosophy was succinctly expressed in Lingsch v. Savage, 213 Cal. App. 2d 729, 29 Cal. Rptr. 201 (1963):

> It is now settled in California that where the seller knows of facts materially affecting the value or desirability of the property which are known or accessible only to him and also knows that such facts are not known to or within the reach of the diligent attention and observation of the buyer, the seller is under a duty to disclose them to the buyer.

In Posner v. Davis, 76 Ill. App. 3d 638, 395 N.E. 2d 133, . . . (1979), [the court relied on *Lingsch* to conclude] that the sellers knew of and failed to disclose latent material defects and thus were liable for fraudulent concealment. *Id.* at 137. Numerous other jurisdictions have followed this view in formulating law involving the sale of homes. *See* Flakus v. Schug, 213 Neb. 491, 329 N.W.2d 859 (1983) (basement flooding); Thacker v. Tyree, 297 S.E.2d 885 (W.Va. 1982) (cracked walls and foundation problems); Maguire v. Masino, 325 So.2d 844 (La.Ct.App. 1975) (termite infestation); Weintraub v. Krobatsch, 64 N.J. 445, 317 A.2d 68 (1974) (roach infestation); Cohen v. Vivian, 141 Colo. 443, 349 P.2d 366 (1960) (soil defect).

We are of the opinion, in view of the reasoning and results in *Lingsch, Posner* and the aforementioned cases decided in other jurisdictions, that the same philosophy regarding the sale of homes should also be the law in the state of Florida. Accordingly, we hold that where the seller of a home knows of facts materially affecting the value of the property which are not readily observable and are not known to the buyer, the seller is under a duty to disclose them to the buyer. This duty is equally applicable to all forms of real property, new and used.

In the case at bar, the evidence shows that the Johnsons knew of and failed to disclose that there had been problems with the roof of the house. Mr. Johnson admitted during his testimony that the Johnsons were aware of roof problems prior to entering into the contract of sale and receiving the $5,000 deposit payment. Thus, we agree with the [intermediate appellate court] and find that the Johnsons' fraudulent concealment also entitles the Davises to the return of the $5,000 deposit payment plus interest. We further find that the Davises should be awarded costs and fees. . . .

BOYD, C.J., dissenting.

I respectfully but strongly dissent to the Court's expansion of the duties of sellers of real property. This ruling will give rise to a flood of litigation and will facilitate unjust outcomes in many cases. If, as a matter of public policy, the well settled law of this state on this question should be changed, the change should come from the legislature. Moreover, I do not find sufficient evidence in the record to justify rescission or a finding of fraud even under present law. I would quash the decision of the district court of appeal. . . .

Homeowners who attempt to sell their houses are typically in no better position to measure the quality, value, or desirability of their houses than are the prospective purchasers with whom such owners come into contact. Based on this and related considerations, the law of Florida has long been that a seller of real property with improvements is under no duty to disclose all material facts, in the absence of a fiduciary relationship, to a buyer who has an equal opportunity to learn all material information and is not prevented by the seller from doing so. This rule provides sufficient protection against overreaching by sellers [and] is not the least bit "unappetizing." . . .

[The] elements of actionable fraud . . . were not established by sufficient evidence in this case. There was no competent, substantial evidence to show that Mr. Johnson made a false statement knowing it to be false. There was absolutely no evidence that the statement was made with the intention of causing Mrs. Davis to do anything; she had already contracted to purchase the house. There was no competent evidence that Mrs. Davis in fact relied on Mr. Johnson's statement or was influenced by it to do anything. And the only detriment or injury that can be found is that, when the Davises subsequently decided not to complete the transaction, they stood to forfeit the additional $26,000 deposit paid in addition to the original $5,000. The Davises had already agreed to pay the additional deposit at the time of the conversation. They had to pay the additional deposit if they wanted to preserve their rights under the contract. They chose to do so. Mr. Johnson's statements, even if we believe Mrs. Davis'[s] version of them rather than Mr. Johnson's, did not constitute the kind of representation upon which a buyer's reliance is justified.

I do not agree with the Court's belief that the distinction between nondisclosure and affirmative statement is weak or nonexistent. It is a distinction that we should take special care to emphasize and preserve. Imposition of liability for seller's nondisclosure of the condition of improvements to real property is the first step toward making the seller a guarantor of the good condition of the property. Ultimately this trend will significantly burden the alienability of property because sellers will have to worry about the possibility of catastrophic post-sale judgments for damages sought to pay for repairs. The trend will proceed somewhat as follows. At first, the cause of action will require proof of actual knowledge of the undisclosed defect on the part of the seller. But in many cases the courts will allow it to be shown by circumstantial evidence. Then a rule of constructive knowledge will develop based on the reasoning that if the seller did not know of the defect, he should have known about it before attempting to sell the property. Thus the burden of inspection will shift from the buyer to the seller. Ultimately the courts will be in the position of imposing implied warranties and guaranties on all sellers of real property.

Although as described in the majority opinion this change in the law sounds progressive, high-minded, and idealistic, it is in reality completely unnecessary. Prudent purchasers inspect property, with expert advice if necessary, before they agree to buy. Prudent lenders require inspections before agreeing to provide purchase money. Initial deposits of earnest money can be made with the agreement to purchase being conditional upon the favorable results of expert inspections. It is significant that in the present case the major portion of the purchase price was to be financed by the Johnsons who were to hold a mortgage on the property. If they had been knowingly trying to get rid of what they knew to be a defectively constructed house, it is unlikely that they would have been willing to lend $200,000 with the house in question as their only security. . . .

This case should be remanded for findings by the trial court based on the evidence already heard. The action for rescission based on fraud should be dismissed. The only issue is whether the Johnsons were in compliance with the contract at the time of the breach by the Davises. Resolving this issue requires a finding of whether the roof could have been put in watertight condition by spot repairs or by re-roofing and in either case whether the sellers were willing to fulfill their obligation by paying for the necessary work. If so, the Johnsons should keep the entire $31,000 deposit.

NOTES, QUESTIONS, AND PROBLEMS

1. Scope of the Duty to Disclose. Under the Florida court's rule, a seller must disclose anything known to him "materially affecting the value of the property." But what is material? One test is that "a misrepresentation of fact is material when it would be likely, under the circumstances, to affect the conduct of a reasonable person with reference to the transaction in question." Van Camp v. Bradford, 63 Ohio Misc.2d 245, 255 (Com. Pl. 1993). See also

Restatement of Contracts § 470(2) (1932). Yet, the same court opined that when "the individual making the misrepresentation is aware that the recipient is peculiarly disposed to attach importance to a particular subject, subjective considerations have a bearing on the subject matter; in such an instance, the misrepresentation should be deemed material, regardless of its significance to a reasonable person under similar circumstances." Id.

What is the likely effect of extending seller liability in the fashion that the Florida court did in Johnson v. Davis? Will it hamper alienability, as the dissenting justice charged? Is it a problem if houses with disclosed latent defects become harder to sell than those that do not have such defects? Or will the enhanced disclosure obligation mean that sellers will disclose everything that might possibly be a problem, no matter how trivial, and that excessive disclosure will hinder alienability generally?

    2. Stigmatic or Psychological Defects. Dorris Reed purchased a house from Robert King, who did not tell her that ten years earlier a woman and her four children had been brutally murdered in the residence. After Reed learned the truth she sued to rescind the purchase on the ground of fraudulent concealment of a material defect. In Reed v. King, 145 Cal.App.3d 261 (1983), the California Court of Appeal held that Reed had stated a cause of action:

> Reed alleges the fact of the murders has a quantifiable effect on the market value of the premises. We cannot say this allegation is inherently wrong and, in the pleading posture of the case, we assume it to be true. If information known or accessible only to the seller has a significant and measurable effect on market value and, as is alleged here, the seller is aware of this effect, we see no principled basis for making the duty to disclose turn upon the character of the information. Id. at 267.

To similar effect is Van Camp v. Bradford, 63 Ohio Misc.2d 245, 255 (Com. Pl. 1993), in which the seller failed to disclose to the buyer, a single woman, that an occupant of the house had been recently raped at knifepoint in the house, another rape had occurred in a neighboring residence, and two others had been committed in the same general vicinity.

Lest stigmatic defects be thought to consist of tangible horrors, consider Stambovsky v. Ackley, 572 N.Y.S.2d 672 (App. Div. 1991). After buying a house in Nyack, N.Y., plaintiff learned that local lore held that the house was haunted by poltergeists. Seller and her family had reportedly seen ghosts there over a nine year period and had made known to the community their sightings. The Appellate Division of the New York Supreme Court ruled that "as a matter of law, the house is haunted." Seller's public revelation of the house's alleged inhabitation by ghosts created a reputation of the house that went "to the very essence of the bargain between the parties, greatly impairing both the value of the property and its potential for resale." Accordingly, seller's failure to disclose the house's haunted reputation provided a basis for rescission. As the court said of ghosts, invoking the title song to the 1984 movie *Ghost Busters*: "Who you gonna call? Ghost Busters!" Apparently, the real answer is the courts.

About half the states have reacted to these and other cases finding sellers liable for failure to disclose stigmatic or psychological defects by enacting "stigma shield" statutes, that excuse sellers from any obligation to disclose such defects. See, e.g., Ariz. Rev. Stat. § 32–2156, which exempts sellers from liability for non-disclosure of the facts that the property has been (1) the site of a "natural death, suicide, homicide," or other felony; (2) occupied by a person exposed to the HIV virus or carrying AIDS, or (3) located in the vicinity of a sex offender.

3. *Implied Warranty of Habitability.* The home at issue in Johnson v. Davis was not newly constructed. While jurisdictions split on the question of the scope of the duty to disclose defects in used homes, there is virtual unanimity that builders of *new* homes should be held to an implied warranty that the home is habitable. The Utah Supreme Court explained this development in Davencourt at Pilgrims Landing Homeowners Ass'n v. Davencourt at Pilgrims Landing LC, 2009 Utah 65, 221 P.3d 234 (2009):

> Today, by common law or statutory law, an overwhelming majority of jurisdictions recognize an implied warranty in the purchase of new residential property. Forty-five states have adopted an implied warranty in some form and Hawaii appears to have done so in dicta. Forty-three states provide for an implied warranty of habitability. ... Delaware, Nebraska, and Ohio expressly reject the implied warranty of habitability; yet those three states each provide for an implied warranty of workman-like manner. Out of the four states that have not adopted any implied warranty, two states, New Mexico and North Dakota, have not directly addressed or answered the issue. The two remaining states, Georgia and Utah, have expressly rejected implied warranties. But Georgia does so because it allows recovery under negligence theory. This leaves Utah in a minority of one....

> Courts recognize that "[b]uilding construction by modern methods is complex and intertwined with governmental codes and regulations." For a builder-vendor or developer-vendor engaged in the business of selling houses, the construction and/or sale of a new home is a daily event, whereas for a buyer the purchase of a new home is a significant and unique transaction. Given these modern realities ..., "[a] home buyer should be able to place reliance on the builder or developer who sells him a new house." Some courts reason that the implied warranty will "inhibit the unscrupulous, fly-by-night, or unskilled builder" [while others reason that an] implied warranty ... takes into account the equitable consideration that between two innocent parties, the one in the better position to prevent the harm ought to bear the loss. ... Hence, in protecting the innocent home purchaser by holding the responsible party accountable, the law has come to recognize that no longer does the purchaser of a new residence stand on an equal bargaining position with the builder-vendor or developer-vendor.

> Moreover, the concept of an implied warranty is "consistent with the expectations of the parties." The essence of the transaction is an implicit engagement upon the part of the seller to transfer a house suitable for habitation. If the purchaser expected anything less, there would be no sale. ... [We] now join the overwhelming majority of states. Under Utah law, in every contract for the sale of a new residence, a vendor in the business of building or selling such residences makes an implied warranty

to the vendee that the residence is constructed in a workmanlike manner and fit for habitation.

A number of states hold that a subsequent owner of the newly constructed home may also sue the builder/seller for breach of this implied warranty, regardless of the lack of contractual privity, so long as the claim is brought within a reasonable time period after the construction is finished, based on a latent defect that become manifest after the subsequent purchase and which could not have been reasonably discovered prior to the purchase, and the defect is proven to have been caused by the builder's failure to construct in a workmanlike manner in accord with accepted building standards. See, e.g., Lempke v. Dagenais, 130 N.H. 782 (1988); Tusch Enterprises v. Coffin, 113 Ida. 37 (1987); Richards v. Powercraft Homes, Inc., 139 Ariz. 242 (1984); Aronsohn v. Mandara, 98 N.J. 92 (1984). See Powell on Real Property § 84A.06 n.26. But this rule is not universal; some states continue to hold that privity of contract is necessary to sue on an implied warranty theory. See, e.g., Real Estate Marketing, Inc. v. Franz, 885 S.W.2d 921 (Ky. 1994); Barnes v. MacBrown & Co., 264 Ind. 227 (1976). But privity is not generally a barrier to a suit founded on negligence of the builder, rather than implied warranty. See, e.g., Coburn v. Lenox Homes, Inc., 173 Conn. 567, 574–575 (1977).

  4. Disclaimers and "As Is" Clauses. To avoid the possibility that a disgruntled buyer may falsely claim that the seller lied about the condition of the property, a seller may include a clause in the written contract of sale, by which the buyer agrees that there are no representations other than those in the contract and that the buyer is not relying on any oral statements of the seller or his agents. States disagree on the effectiveness of these provisions. One view is that if the written agreement contains explicit statements that the seller has made no representations concerning the property other than in the agreement, the buyer has not relied on any representations other than those in the written contract, the written contract is the entire agreement, and the buyer has had ample opportunity to inspect the property and takes it "as is," the buyer has waived any claim based on oral representations made outside of the contract. A vivid example is Moore v. Prudential Residential Services Ltd. Partnership, 849 So.2d 914 (Ala. 2002). Buyer, experienced in real estate transactions, allegedly asked Sellers if they had ever had water seepage in the house and Sellers had responded that they had not had any water problems. The sale contract stipulated that Buyer had the responsibility to inspect the property and determine its condition, including leaks, Buyer had not relied on any representation of Sellers or their agents, Buyer took the property "as is," and the written contract was the entire agreement. Even though there was corroboration of the alleged oral falsehoods the Alabama Supreme Court affirmed a grant of summary judgment in Sellers' favor. To similar effect is Danann Realty Corp. v. Harris, 5 N.Y.2d 317 (1959); Alires v. McGehee, 277 Kan. 398 (2004); Prudential Insurance Company of America v. Italian Cowboy Partners, Ltd., 270 S.W.3d 192 (Tex. App. 2008). The arguments in favor of this position are that it provides certainty in contracts and protects the ability of buyers and sellers to make voluntary choices about the nature of their bargain. If a buyer is actually induced to enter the contract on the basis of oral representations he should not sign a contract that states otherwise.

The argument against this position is that it permits the seller to insulate himself from the consequences of his own fraud: "If a party has actually induced another to enter into a contract by means of fraud ... language may not be devised to shield him from the consequences of such fraud. The law does not temporize with trickery or duplicity. ... [F]raud vitiates every agreement it touches." *Danann Realty*, 5 N.Y.2d at 323, 326 (Fuld, J., dissenting). Most states hold that such contractual provisions do not insulate the seller from liability for affirmative falsehoods. See, e.g., Cal. Civ. Code § 1668: "All contracts which have for their object, directly or indirectly, to exempt anyone from responsibility for his own fraud, or willful injury to the person or property of another, or violation of law, whether willful or negligent, are against the policy of the law." In McClain v. Octagon Plaza, LLC, 159 Cal.App.4th 784 (2008), a lessee of commercial space alleged that the landlord had intentionally or negligently misrepresented the square footage of the premises, thus inflating the base rent. The lease contained a disclaimer of oral representations and a recital that the lessee had ample opportunity to measure the area of the leased premises. The lessee contended that the landlord had purported to be offended by the lessee's desire to do just that, and had assured the prospective tenant that they were honest and that the stated area was accurate. The California Court of Appeal held that Civ. Code § 1668 operated to permit the lessee's claim to proceed.

Both sellers and buyers can be dishonest. How does an honest seller protect himself against the possibility that his buyer is dishonest, and will falsely claim that the seller made representations that, if made, would be fraud?

5. *Problems.*

a. Possible Defect. Blackacre, owned by Seller, has a pond, fed by an underground spring, with an outlet stream that flows across Blackacre, then Whiteacre, to empty into a river. The pond has never overflowed. Seller, who reads scientific journals and is keenly aware of predicted global climate change, says nothing to Buyer about the possibility of the pond overflowing. After Buyer purchases Blackacre, the pond overflows during a season of especially heavy rains, causing substantial damage to the residence situated on Blackacre. A prominent scientist opines that the heavy rains are attributable to global climate change. Buyer sues Seller, seeking rescission due to Seller's alleged breach of his duty to disclose this latent defect. What result?

b. Mountain Lion. Pinetop, owned by Seller, consists of ten acres of woods and meadow in the mountain west. Although Seller knows that a person was mauled severely by a mountain lion in national forest land immediately adjacent to Pinetop, he fails to tell Buyer, who is from another state, of this incident. Buyer tells Seller that she is a dog breeder and that she plans to use Pinteop as a site to breed Brittany Spaniels. After the purchase, Buyer learns of the mountain lion attack and seeks rescission due to Seller's alleged breach of the duty to disclose. What result?

c. Cholera Epidemic. Row House, owned by Seller, is located in a densely populated city that has had a recent cholera outbreak, caused by flooding and contamination of the water supply. Although Row House was undamaged by the flooding, it was used during the cholera epidemic to house cholera patients, some of whom died in Row House. Seller fails to tell Buyer these facts because the water supply to Row House is untainted. After Buyer closes on the deal, he learns of these facts and sues to rescind. Cholera is caused by ingestion of the bacterium *vibrio cholerae*, found in contaminated food and water, and causes severe dehydration due to a watery diarrhea that contains the bacteria. What result in a *caveat emptor* jurisdiction? In a state that has adopted the Florida rule but has not enacted a stigma shield law? In a state that has adopted the Florida rule but that has also enacted a clone of the Arizona stigma shield law?

4. REMEDIES FOR BREACH

If a contract of sale is breached the party not in default has a choice of one of three remedies: specific performance, rescission, or damages. The details, however, depend upon whether it is the buyer or seller who is the non-defaulting party.

a. Buyer's Remedies

Specific Performance. This equitable remedy is available if damages are inadequate, but because of the presumption that each parcel of real estate is unique it is relatively easy for a buyer ready and able to perform to require the seller in breach to convey title in return for receipt of the contract price. In an age of mass-produced housing, is it still true that every parcel of realty is unique, thus affording a buyer the ability to obtain specific performance?

> *Example 7–1*: Seller and Buyer enter into a contract for the sale of a condominium unit in a high-rise building. The building contains 200 units consisting of four different floor plans, so that there are four sets of 50 units each that have identical floor plans. After Seller's breach Buyer seeks specific performance. Seller contends that there is nothing unique about a condominium unit that is identical in its floor plan to 49 other units. Should Buyer be entitled to specific performance?

In Giannini v. First National Bank of Des Plaines, 136 Ill.App.3d 971 (1985), a defaulting seller of a condominium unit in a complex developed by the seller argued that the buyer should not be able to compel specific performance "because a condominium is not so unique as to require such relief." The court rejected the contention as without merit: "Illinois courts have long held that where the parties have fairly and understandingly entered into a valid contract for the sale of real property, specific performance of the contract is a matter of right and equity will enforce it, absent circumstances of oppression and fraud. ... Thus '[w]here land, or any estate therein, is the subject matter of the agreement, the inadequacy of the legal remedy is well settled, and the equitable jurisdiction is firmly established.' "

Rescission. If the buyer does not wish to force the seller to perform he may rescind the contract and recover his deposit. To enforce this remedy the buyer is given a lien upon the property to secure return of the deposit. See, e.g., N.D. Cent. Code § 35–20–03: "One who pays to the owner any part of the price of real property under an agreement for the sale thereof has a special lien upon the property, independent of possession, for such part of the amount paid as the person may be entitled to recover in case of a failure of consideration."

Damages. If a buyer does not want specific performance and rescission will not adequately compensate him for seller's breach he may seek to recover damages, measured by the sum of (1) the difference between the contract price and the fair market value of the parcel at the time of breach, (2) return of the buyer's deposit, and (3) actual out-of-pocket expenses caused by seller's breach. In many jurisdictions, however, there is an exception to this measure of damages. When a seller defaults because he cannot deliver good title and the seller has at all times acted in good faith to obtain and deliver good title the buyer is not entitled to recover his expectation damages—the difference between the contract price and the market value at the time of breach. In Horton v. O'Rourke, 321 So.2d 612 (Fla. App. 1975), the seller could not deliver good title although "he dealt above board, made every effort and went to considerable expense to clear the title defect and to consummate ultimately the contract to convey." The trial court awarded the buyer his expectation damages, measured "by the difference between the value of the land when it should have been conveyed less the contract price as yet unpaid." The Florida Court of Appeal reversed:

> [This] measure of damages[,] giving purchasers *in a land sale contract* the benefit of their bargain is error in the absence of a showing of bad faith. . . . In Florida and many other jurisdictions, the courts follow the English rule announced in Flureau v. Thornhill, [96 Eng. Rep. 638 (1776),] whereby in the absence of bad faith the damages recoverable for breach by the vendor of an executory contract to convey title to real estate are the purchase money paid by the purchaser together with interest and expenses of investigating title. Id. at 613.

b. Seller's Remedies

Damages. A seller who seeks damages has elected to keep the property but wants compensation for the loss resulting from buyer's breach. The measure of damages is the sum of (1) the contract price minus the fair market value of the property *at the time of breach* and (2) other out-of-pocket expenses incurred by the seller related to the breach. But whe should the measure of damages be in a falling market?

> *Example 7–2*: On May 1, Seller and Buyer One agree on the of Blackacre for $500,000. On June 1, Buyer One breaches contract. Blackacre is worth $475,000 on that date. After dili seeking a new buyer, on September 1, Seller enters into a c with Buyer Two to sell Blackacre for $450,000. Buyer Two p Seller sues Buyer One for damages. Should the measure of be $25,000 plus out-of-pocket expenses or $50,000 plus

Awarding Seller $25,000 in damages allows Buyer One to shift the further decline of market value onto Seller. Awarding Seller $50,000 in damages allows Seller to recoup the full decline in market value from Buyer One even though some of that decline occurred after Buyer One's breach. But Seller will argue that his expectations were that he would conclude a sale at $500,000 and that it was Buyer One's breach that made it necessary for Seller to find Buyer Two. Thus, the further decline in value was incurred because of Buyer One's breach. In Kuhn v. Spatial Design, Inc., 585 A.2d 967 (N.J. Super. App. Div. 1991), involving facts similar to those of Example 7–2, the New Jersey Appellate Division of the Superior Court declared:

> [When assessing] damages resulting from a breach in a falling market . . . two basic rules must be consulted. One is that contract damages are designed to put the injured party in as good a position as if performance had been rendered as promised. The other, from Hadley v. Baxendale, is that damages should be such as may fairly be considered either arising naturally, *i.e.*, according to the usual course of things, from the breach, or such as may reasonably be supposed to have been in the contemplation of both parties, at the time they contracted, as the probable result of the breach. In the usual course of things, a $515,000 house cannot be resold the instant a contract buyer breaches, and a reasonable time for resale must therefore be allowed. . . . In a falling market, buyers take longer to find, and they buy at reduced prices. A rule that restricts damages for breach of a contract to buy real estate to the difference between contract price and value at the time of breach (plus expenses) works fairly only in a static market. A damage rule works fairly in a declining market only if it takes account of slowing sales and falling values. In such cases, where the seller puts the property back on the market and resells, the measure is not contract price less value at the time of breach, but rather the resale price, if it is reasonable as to time, method, manner, place and terms.

Kuhn notwithstanding, the general rule is that measure of damages is the difference between the contract price and the market value at time of breach, not subsequent resale.

Retention of the Buyer's Deposit. When a buyer breaches the contract a seller may elect to keep the deposit made by the buyer toward the purchase price, so long as the deposit is a reasonably modest portion of the price. Ten percent of the purchase price is a commonly accepted upper limit, but in Uzan v. 845 UN Ltd. Partnership, 778 N.Y.S.2d 171 (App. Div. 2004), the seller was permitted to retain a deposit of over $8 million that was 25% of the purchase price of two luxury penthouse apartments on the 90th floor of Trump World, the tallest residential building in the world. The buyers, two billionaire brothers, possessed equal bargaining power with the seller, a partnership controlled by Donald Trump. The buyers refused to perform because the terrorist attacks of September 11, 2001 caused them to consider the building to be at risk for a future such attack, but they implausibly contended that Trump "had prior special knowledge that certain tall buildings, such as Trump World, were potential targets for terrorists." Id. at 174.

Suppose, however, that the deposit, even if it is a reasonably small portion of the purchase price, exceeds the actual damages to the seller. Should the seller be entitled to keep the entire deposit? If the contract explicitly states that the seller will retain the deposit as liquidated damages upon breach by the buyer, and the amount of the deposit is a reasonable amount (generally 10% or less of the purchase price), it is virtually universally agreed that the seller is entitled to keep the deposit. In the absence of a liquidated damages provision, the venerable common law rule, still followed in most jurisdictions, is that where the buyer "makes a part payment on the purchase price, but fails to fulfill the contract without lawful excuse, he cannot recover the payment . . . even though the vendor may have made a profit by reason of his default." Quillen v. Kelley, 216 Md. 396, 401–402 (1958). The usual rationale for this rule is that it approximates the result of a liquidated damages clause—it is difficult to estimate actual damages and retention of a deposit of 10% or less of the purchase price is a fair estimate of damages. See, e.g., Maxton Builders, Inc. v. Lo Galbo, 68 N.Y.2d 373, 382 (1986).

The minority rule is represented by Restatement (Second) of Contracts, § 374(1): "[T]he party in breach is entitled to restitution for any benefit that he has conferred by way of part performance . . . in excess of the loss he has caused by his own breach." Thus, in Kutzin v. Pirnie, 124 N.J. 500 (1991), the buyer breached after he had deposited $36,000 toward a purchase price of $365,000. After breach the seller sold the house to another party for $352,500. After including $3,825 in expenses related to the breach, the sellers' damages were $17,325. The New Jersey Supreme Court ordered the return to the buyer of the balance of their deposit, or $18,675. When the buyer can prove that the damages are less than the deposit, it is unjust enrichment of the seller to permit the seller to retain the entire deposit. Accord, Seekins v. King, 66 R.I. 105, 110 (1941); Schwartz v. Syver, 264 Wis. 526, 531 (1953); Wilkins v. Birnbaum, 278 A.2d 829, 831 (Del. 1971).

But even the minority rule does not apply if the contract specifically calls for forfeiture of the deposit as liquidated damages. See Restatement (Second) of Contracts, § 374(2): "To the extent that under the manifested intent of the parties, a party's performance is to be retained in the case of breach, that party is not entitled to restitution if the value of th performance as liquidated damages is reasonable in light of the anticip' ed loss caused by the breach and the difficulties of proof of loss." W 10% of the purchase price is the benchmark of reasonableness, the v limit on liquidated damages may be much greater if the stated sum fact a reasonable estimate of damages at the time the contract is Thus, in Chamberlain v. Bagley, 11 N.H. 234 (1840), liquidated ⟨ of 42% of the contract price was reasonable, and in Brewster v

13 N.H. 275 (1842), liquidated damages of five times the contract price were held to be reasonable.

Rescission. If a seller elects to rescind, in theory the deal should be unwound and the buyer's deposit returned. In fact, the seller is usually entitled to keep the deposit, either because the contract so stipulates, or because the seller has elected to keep the deposit in lieu of other damages. This leaves the seller with title and the deposit. Because the buyer acquires equitable title at the moment the contract becomes effective, however, most states provide that the seller immediately acquires a lien against the buyer's equitable title to secure the buyer's performance. See, e.g., N.D. Cent. Code § 35–20–01: "One who sells real property has a special or vendor's lien thereon, independent of possession, for so much of the price as remains unpaid and unsecured otherwise than by the personal obligation of the buyer." This lien is not of much significance because the seller retains legal title until the closing, but can be used to clear title in the unlikely event that a buyer in breach continues to assert equitable title as a blot upon the title the seller could otherwise deliver to a third party.

Specific Performance. The established rule is that specific perform-ance is equally available to sellers and buyers. See, e.g., O'Halloran v. Oechslie, 402 A.2d 67 (Me. 1979), in which a defaulting buyer was ordered to specifically perform. Even in the absence of "direct evidence of the uniqueness of the property to be conveyed" or proof of the inadequacy of "monetary damages," a court "may assume the inadequacy of money damages in a contract for the purchase of real estate and order the specific performance of the contract without an actual showing of the singular character of the realty." Id. at 70.

But if damages are truly an adequate remedy specific performance may not be obtainable. For example, in Suchan v. Rutherford, 90 Ida. 288 (1966), buyer refused to complete the purchase of Idaho farmland, and the trial court ordered specific performance. The Idaho Supreme Court re-versed:

> The land here involved is not unique. It is irrigated farm land common to the general area in which it is located. Sales of similar land are frequent and it is not difficult to establish its market value. It cannot be seriously contended that the remedy at law via damages was not adequate, plain, speedy, and complete in this case, [which was] commenced ... thirty-seven days after execution of the contract. [Buyer] had not taken possession of the property. There was no rental value, nor any depreciation or enhancement in the value of the property, to be considered. Vendors' damages were readily ascertain-able. They could have been made whole with a minimum of delay and inconvenience. A judgment for the amount determined would have ended the controversy promptly. Id. at 296, 303.

The Idaho court was at pains to note that the denial of specific performance was not simply because it was the vendor seeking the remedy. However, that distinction was made in Centex Homes Corp. v. Boag, 320 A.2d 194 (N.J. Super. Ch. 1974). Centex was the developer of six 31 story buildings containing 3,600 condominium residential units. Boag agreed to purchase a unit, then backed out of the deal when he was transferred to Chicago. Centex sought to compel specific performance, arguing "that since the subject matter of the contract is the transfer of a fee interest in real estate, the remedy of specific performance is available to enforce the agreement." The court disagreed:

> The principle underlying the specific performance remedy is equity's jurisdiction to grant relief where the damage remedy at law is inadequate. The text writers generally agree that at the time this branch of equity jurisdiction was evolving in England, the presumed uniqueness of land as well as its importance to the social order of that era led to the conclusion that damages at law could never be adequate to compensate for the breach of a contract to transfer an interest in land. Hence specific performance became a fixed remedy in this class of transactions. ... While the inadequacy of the damage remedy suffices to explain the origin of the vendee's right to obtain specific performance in equity, it does not provide a *rationale* for the availability of the remedy at the instance of the vendor of real estate. Except upon a showing of unusual circumstances or a change in the vendor's position, such as where the vendee has entered into possession, the vendor's damages are usually measurable, his remedy at law is adequate and there is no jurisdictional basis for equitable relief. ... [S]pecific performance relief should no longer be automatically available to a vendor of real estate, but should be confined to those special instances where a vendor will otherwise suffer an economic injury for which his damage remedy at law will not be adequate, or where other equitable considerations require that the relief be granted. Id. at 389, 392–393.

5. EQUITABLE CONVERSION: RISK OF LOSS

One reason for the general availability of specific performance to either seller or buyer is the notion that, from the moment the contract is entered into, equitable title has passed to the buyer. Although legal title remains in the seller until the closing, under the theory of equitable title the seller holds legal title in trust. Because in equity "[t]hat which ought to have been done is to be regarded as done," Cal. Civ. Code § 3529, specific performance flows inexorably. This doctrine is known as equitable conversion. The concept is that, at the moment a valid contract for the sale of realty is created, the seller's interest is converted into personal property and the buyer's interest is converted into real property. A number of consequences flow from this idea, but this subsection is concerned with its effect on the risk of loss of the property during the time the contract is executory.

From the theory of equitable conversion it also follows that the bᵁ has assumed the risk of loss from the moment the contract is made.

though the seller may remain in possession. This principle was embedded in English law by Paine v. Meller, 6 Ves. 349, 31 Eng. Rep. 1088 (Ch. 1801). Thus, if the property is destroyed by fire the buyer continues to be obligated to complete the purchase. The United Kingdom repudiated this harsh rule in the Law of Property Act of 1925, § 47, but it continues to exist in American law. For an application of the Paine v. Meller rule, see Bleckley v. Langston, 112 Ga.App. 63 (1965). The so-called Massachusetts rule, which is said to be the minority position but which is gaining adherents, holds that if the property is substantially or entirely destroyed before legal title has passed, the loss falls on the vendor:

> [T]he contract is to be construed as subject to the implied condition that it no longer shall be binding if, before the time for the conveyance to be made, the buildings are destroyed by fire. The loss by the fire falls upon the vendor, the owner; and if he has not protected himself by insurance, he can have no reimbursement of this loss; but the contract is no longer binding upon either party. If the purchaser has advanced any part of the price, he can recover it back.

Libman v. Levenson, 236 Mass. 221, 224 (1920). Accord, Wells v. Calnan, 107 Mass. 514 (1871). Under the Uniform Vendor and Purchaser Risk Act, if "all or a material part" of the property is destroyed the risk of loss is placed on the seller unless either legal title has passed to the buyer or the buyer has taken possession, in which cases the buyer assumes the risk of loss. Section 1(a) of the Act states that, in those circumstances, "the vendor cannot enforce the contract, and the purchaser is entitled to recover any portion of the price that he has paid." Section 1(b) states that if either legal title or possession has passed to the buyer before the contract is fully executed "the purchaser is not ... relieved from a duty to pay the price, nor is he entitled to recover any portion thereof that he has paid." The Act has been adopted in twelve states: California, Hawaii, Illinois, Michigan, Nevada, New York, North Carolina, Oklahoma, Oregon, South Dakota, Texas, and Wisconsin. See, e.g., Mich. Comp. Laws § 565.701. The Massachusetts rule, or that of the Uniform Vendor and Purchaser Risk Act, responds to the reality that the seller has better control over the property until title or possession changes hands, and is far more likely to have insured the property against casualty loss. All of these issues may be avoided by a provision in the sale contract allocating the risk of loss prior to closing and providing for insurance on the property.

PROBLEM

In a state observing the common law of equitable conversion, Seller and Buyer enter into a contract of sale for Blackacre, a residence, for $200,000. Buyer makes a deposit of $20,000. The contract is silent about insurance or risk of loss. Seller has insured Blackacre against casualty loss for $175,000. Before the closing, Blackacre burns to the ground. Seller receives $175,000 in insurance proceeds and insists upon Buyer's performance. Must Buyer perform? If so, what amount is due from Buyer to Seller at the closing? What result under the Massachusetts rule? Under the Uniform Vendor and Purchaser Act, could Buyer demand specific performance if Seller should refuse to close?

D. DEEDS

When the contract for sale of land is executed, title is conveyed to the purchaser by deed. The deed has independent significance from the contract of sale. Not only does it convey title, most deeds contain warranties as to the nature of the title that passes from seller to buyer.

1. FORMALITIES

To be effective to convey title, a deed must be in writing, identify accurately the grantor(s) and grantee(s), contain an adequate description of the property and the interest being conveyed, declare the grantor's intent to convey that interest to the grantee, and be signed by the grantor. The deed need not contain any signature of the grantee. Generally, the grantor's signature does not have to be acknowledged by a notary public, although a few states do impose that requirement. However, for a deed to be recorded in the governmental records of real estate titles it must bear a notarial acknowledgment. In Chapter 8 the importance of recording will be discussed; recording is necessary to protect the grantee against other claimants to title but the failure to record does not destroy the validity of the deed itself.

It is the usual practice to recite in the deed the receipt by the seller of nominal consideration (e.g., "for $1 and other good and valuable consideration") in order to raise the presumption that the buyer is a bona fide purchaser for value and thus entitled to certain protections afforded by the recording acts, as will be discussed in Chapter 8. Nominal consideration is usually recited because the parties may not wish to disclose publicly the actual sale price. However, many states and local jurisdictions impose transfer taxes that are computed on the actual sale price, and the amount of the transfer tax may become a matter of public record.

Problems can and do arise with the description of the property to be conveyed by deed. The description must be sufficiently definite to identify a specific parcel of land that can be distinguished from all other parcels. The description serves to identify the boundaries of the land and place the buyer on notice of what he receives and also what encroachments, if any, may exist with respect to the conveyed parcel. Generally, parol evidence of the description is not admissible, but that rule is not inexorable. If the written description contains a latent ambiguity parol evidence is usually admissible to clarify the description. Thus, a description of property as "1101–1/2 East Plant Street" when the legal address was 1101 East Plant Street and there were two buildings served by that address, contained a latent ambiguity which parol evidence could clarify. Bajrangi v. Madnethel Enterprises, Inc., 589 So.2d 416 (Fla. App. 1991).

The description may be complete by itself or it may incorporate by reference other facts of documents. A complete self-contained description is one by metes and bounds—that describes the property with sufficient precision that a surveyor could locate its boundaries. A metes and bounds description begins with a easily located monument, such as street intersection or edge, a survey marker, a creek boundary, or a boundary fence. From there the description requires a series of "calls," each containing a course and distance, until the boundaries have been enclosed. It is the custom for the calls to begin northwards for a specified distance at some specified angle (stated in degrees and minutes), then east or west, then south, and then to the beginning. Thus, such a description could be as follows: "Beginning at a steel survey marker on the north side of Elm Street located 102 feet east of the intersection of Elm and Pine Streets, north 10 degrees west for 110 feet, thence east 5 degrees south for 125 feet, thence south 10 degrees west for 104 feet, thence west along the boundary of Elm Street to the point of beginning." The calls of a metes and bounds description need not use angles, as the final call in the hypothetical description above illustrates. However, if the call lies along a road or way that is customary and not a public thoroughfare or platted in the government real estate records, litigation can develop over the true location of the boundary. Also, a tiny error in the angle can produce a major error over a long distance. Metes and bounds descriptions can be inaccurate due to the use of transitory monuments. Thus, a description that begins with "the old oak tree" or "the sugar maple marked with a double blaze" will become ambiguous over time as the oak tree or sugar maple die.

When a metes and bounds description is internally inconsistent, incomplete, or otherwise mistaken on its face, courts try to determine the intent of the parties. To do so, courts employ a series of constructional rules: Original survey markers prevail over natural monuments (e.g. trees), which prevail over artificial monuments (e.g., a rock cairn), which prevail over references to known boundary lines (e.g., to the U.S. Forest Service boundary), which prevail over courses of direction (e.g, "north six degrees west"), which prevail over distances (e.g, "110 feet"), which prevail over area descriptions (e.g. "2.2 acres"), which prevail over place names (e.g., "the Simmons homestead"). But this hierarchy is simply an aid to discovery of the parties' intentions and is not a Procrustean bed.

Frequently, deed descriptions incorporate some survey by reference. In most of the United States the land has been subdivided by official United States government surveys into "townships" of thirty six square miles, which are further subdivided into 36 sections, each of one square mile. To do this, the survey has established "principal meridians," running north and south, and "base lines," running east and west. Every six miles to the east or west of a principal meridian are "range lines." Every six miles to the north or south of a base line is a "township line."

Running north from a base line each succeeding township is denominated T1N, T2N, and so on. A similar denomination applies to townships running south of the base line. Running west of the principal meridian each succeeding range is denominated R1W, R2W, and so on, and a similar label is applied to ranges running east of the principal meridian. Thus, the thirty-six square mile "township that lies two townships south of the base line and three ranges east of the principal meridian" is called T2S, R3E. Within that township are thirty six sections, each of one square mile, numbered as follows:

6	5	4	3	2	1
7	8	9	10	11	12
18	17	16	15	14	13
19	20	21	22	23	24
30	29	28	27	26	25
31	32	33	34	35	36

Within that township, each section is likely to be further subdivided. Thus, a description of land as the SW 1/4 of Section 20, of Township 2 South, Range 3 E of an identified principal meridian and base adequately describes the 160 acres that occupies that corner of the identified section.

Here is an illustration of the system, taken from the National Atlas of the United States:

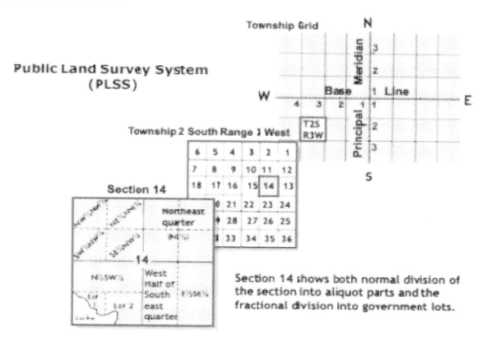

Section 14 shows both normal division of the section into aliquot parts and the fractional division into government lots.

A description may incorporate a reference to a recorded plat map or subdivision map. These are usually surveyed plots of land showing individual lots, usually prepared by the developer or subdivider of the property, and recorded in the public real estate records of the jurisdiction in which the property is located. Thus, a reference in the deed description to "Lot 13 of the Jones Addition, as recorded in the Burgess County Recorder's Office at Book 42, page 221" is sufficient to describe the conveyed property.

To convey title, a deed must be delivered to the grantee with the grantor's intention to so convey title. Normally, this will occur at the closing. As with the requirement of delivery in the law of gifts, delivery ensures that the grantor really means to divest himself of title. A physical delivery of a deed without any intention of conveying title is not effective.

Example 7–3: William Shealy owned a 1/4 interest in a 65 acre tract known as Roland Place. The other 3/4 were owned in equal portions by his brothers, Frank, Charles, and Wilson. Twelve years before his death William executed a deed conveying his 1/4 interest in Roland Place to his brother Wilson. He placed the deed in a sealed envelope and gave it to his brother Charles, without revealing its contents. William told Charles: "Keep this for me. . . . You'll be told when to open it, and you'll know what to do with it." After William's death, Charles opened the envelope and gave the deed to Wilson, who then recorded it. First Union Bank, trustee of a testamentary trust created by William's will, sued to void the deed, claiming that it had not been delivered and thus William's interest had passed by his will into the trust of which First Union was trustee. The South Carolina Court of Appeals found no delivery. William had not indicated any present intention to part with title; he retained effective control over the deed and continued to receive his share of income from Roland Place. Also, the delivery to Wilson after William's death was ineffective because the transfer of an interest at death must be done by will, not by deed. First Union National Bank of South Carolina v. Shealy, 325 S.C. 351 (1996).

Questions of delivery almost never arise in the sale of land, because almost nobody is so witless as to pay for property without receiving a deed in return. Delivery issues arise most often when property is given without consideration, as in *Shealy*.

2. WARRANTIES OF TITLE

There are three different types of deeds: a *general warranty* deed, a *special warranty* deed, and a *quit claim* deed. The general warranty deed contains the following six warranties of title and is the seller's promise that there are no defects, whether they arose before or after the seller took title. A special warranty deed contains the same six warranties but only as to the seller's own actions; it makes no warranties with respect to the actions of prior owners or others. Many states have codified the six deed warranties and provided for a *statutory warranty* deed that automatically incorporates the deed warranties. A quit claim deed contains no warranties of title. It operates to convey whatever interest the grantor may have in the described property. If the grantor has no interest at all, he has not breached any deed warranty by delivery of a quit claim deed. Quit claim deeds are useful to clear disputed titles; a person with a disputed or uncertain interest in property may deliver a quit claim deed to expunge whatever interest he may have from the title, and can do so without making any promises about the title that he may or may not have.

The six deed warranties may be divided into present and future covenants. The present covenants are breached, if at all, at the moment of delivery of the deed, and the limitations period for suit based on breach of one or more of those covenants begins at that moment. The future covenants are breached, if at all, after title has passed and the covenant is broken by some future development, such as the assertion of a superior title or the disruption of the grantee's possession. The limitations period begins to run from that moment.

Present Covenants

1. Seisin. The covenant of *seisin* is the grantor's promise that he owns what he conveys to the grantee. For example, a grantor who owns a life estate breaches the covenant if he purports to convey a fee simple; a grantor who owns a one-third interest in the property in fee simple breaches the covenant if he purports to convey a 100% interest in fee simple.

2. Right to Convey. The covenant of the *right to convey* is the grantor's promise that he has the right to convey the granted interest. There is considerable overlap with the covenant of seisin, as a grantor who breaches the covenant of seisin will also breach this covenant, but it is possible that a grantor has not breached the covenant of seisin but does breach this covenant. For example, an owner of property burdened with a valid restraint upon alienation would not breach the covenant of seisin but would breach the covenant of the right to convey. This could occur if the grantor was a trustee holding legal title under a trust instrument that denies to the trustee the power of alienation, or if the grantor owns a life estate that may not be alienated.

3. No Encumbrances. The covenant *against encumbrances* is the grantor's promise that there are no encumbrances—mortgages, liens, unpaid taxes, leases, easements, irrevocable licenses, covenants or other use restrictions—upon the property except those that have been recited in the deed itself. In most jurisdictions, an open, visible, notorious physical encumbrance on the land is deemed to have been known and accepted by the buyer, and thus does not constitute an encumbrance to which the warranty applies. See, e.g., Barnum v. Lockhart, 75 Ore. 528 (1915) (existing railroad); Leach v. Gunnarson, 290 Ore. 31 (1980) (affirming the principle but finding that a adjacent owner's right to use a spring was not open and visible).

What about violations of governmental land use regulations that are neither known by the seller or reasonably discoverable by the buyer? A Connecticut appellate court held that latent violations—those not of record, unknown to the seller, and which have not triggered enforcement action at the time of the conveyance—do not constitute an encumbrance. Frimberger v. Anzellotti, 25 Conn.App. 401 (1991). Vermont courts disagree. In Bianchi v. Lorenz, 166 Vt. 555, 558 (1997), the Vermont Supreme Court ruled that "an encumbrance is present at least when the seller can determine from municipal records that the property violates local zoning regulations at the time of conveyance, and the violation substantially impairs the purchaser's use and enjoyment of the property." Accord, Hunter Broadcasting, Inc. v. City of Burlington, 164 Vt. 391 (1995). Which rule is better? Why? Under the Vermont rule, what can a seller do to protect against breach of the covenant against encumbrances? What should be the measure of damages for breach of this covenant? Recall that most states hold that a violation of a zoning ordinance makes title unmarketable but under the Connecticut rule a latent zoning violation does not constitute an encumbrance. Does this make sense?

The traditional rule is that the present covenants are enforceable only by the immediate grantee. The rationale is that such covenants are personal to the immediate grantee, breach of the covenants occurs, if at all, at the moment of conveyance (thus creating a chose in action owned by the immediate grantee), and the common law did not permit assignment of a chose in action. But this rationale has broken down with general acceptance of the assignability of a chose in action. Thus, a grantee who becomes a grantor impliedly assigns the benefit of these covenants to the remote grantee. But note that the statute of limitations begins to run at the moment of the conveyance by the remote grantor.

PROBLEMS

1. Able owns a life estate in Blackacre, and Foster has an indefeasibly vested remainder in fee simple absolute in Blackacre. In 2000 Able conveys to Baker, by general warranty deed reciting $1 consideration (but for actual consideration of $100,000), a fee simple absolute in Blackacre. Baker takes possession. In 2006 Baker conveys to Conrad, by general warranty deed reciting $10,000 consideration (but for actual consideration of $120,000), a fee simple absolute in Blackacre. In 2011 Conrad conveys to Dunston, by special warranty deed reciting $1 consideration (but for actual consideration of $125,000), a fee simple absolute in Blackacre Able dies in 2012. Foster sues Dunston to recover possession of Blackacre and wins. The jurisdiction permits choses in action to be assigned and has a seven year statute of limitations for claims founded on deed warranties. See, e.g., Rockafellor v. Gray, 194 Iowa 1280 (1922); Schofield v. The Iowa Homestead Co., 32 Iowa 317 (1871).

a. In 2012, can Dunston successfully sue Conrad? On what covenant?

b. In 2012, can Dunston successfully sue Baker? On what covenant?

c. If Dunston can successfully sue either Baker or Conrad what is the measure of damages?

d.   How, if at all, would your answers change if the limitations statute was four years?

2.   Arnold owns Blackacre. For actual consideration of $100,000 Barney, an occupant of Blackacre who has not acquired title by adverse possession, delivers to Charles a general warranty deed to Blackacre. Charles does not take possession. A year later, for $95,000 cash Charles conveys Blackacre by general warranty deed to Draco. After the closing, Draco discovers that Arnold is the true owner and that Arnold has taken vows of poverty and entered a severely cloistered monastery. As a result Arnold has made no attempt to recover possession or assert his paramount title. The jurisdiction treats interruptions in possession by adverse possessors as triggering a new limitations period.

a.   Who, if anyone, may Draco successfully sue on any of the present deed covenants?

b.   What are the damages, if any, that Draco may recover?

3.   A conveys Redacre to B by general warranty deed, receiving $100,000 as the purchase price. B conveys Redacre by general warranty deed to C in receipt of $90,000. Then TO, the true owner who has paramount title, ousts C from possession. The limitations statute has not expired with respect to any potential claim. C sues B on the covenant of seisin and collects $90,000. B then sues A on the covenant of seisin. What is the proper measure of B's damages? What might you wish to know to answer this question?

Future Covenants

4.   *General Warranty.* The covenant of *general warranty* is the grantor's promise that he will defend against any *lawful* claims of others to a title superior to that of the grantee, and will pay the grantee the value of any loss that he may sustain by someone's successful assertion of a superior title to the property. Note that the scope of this covenant depends on the type of deed. A general warranty deed warrants against all defects of title, whenever they might have occurred. A special warranty deed warrants only against title defects that are the result of the grantor's actions. A quit claim deed, of course, contains no warranties. This covenant is not breached by the assertion of a spurious claim to superior title; only the successful assertion of a superior title in another person constitutes breach of the covenant. Thus, legal fees expended by a grantee to defend successfully against an unmeritorious claim are the burden of the grantee because the claim of superior title was not lawful. See, e.g., McDonald v. Delhi Savings Bank, 440 N.W.2d 839 (Iowa 1989).

5.   *Quiet Enjoyment.* The covenant of *quiet enjoyment* is the grantor's promise that the grantee's possession will not be disturbed by someone holding superior title to the property. Breach of this covenant occurs when and if a holder of superior title actually interferes with the grantee's possession.

6.   *Further Assurances.* The covenant of *further assurances* is the grantor's promise that he will take all necessary steps to perfect the grantee's title. For example, this could involve executing additional documents, removing an

adverse possessor, extinguishing a lien, easement, or some other encumbrance.

The traditional common law rule is that the contract of sale is merged into the deed, which means that any promises or covenants of the seller in the contract become replaced by the deed warranties. Thus, the buyer's post-closing contract rights inhere in the deed alone. This rule is justified by the notion that the buyer's acceptance of the deed is conclusive proof that the buyer was satisfied that the contract had been fully performed. The merger doctrine has fallen into disfavor, however. A major exception is that any promises in the sale contract that are independent of or collateral to the transfer of title remain alive and can be enforced by the buyer. See, e.g. Knight v. Heddon, 112 Ga. 853 (1965) (contractual guarantee of a dry basement and a working fireplace survived the closing). The Uniform Land Transactions Act, § 1–309, squarely rejects the merger doctrine and leaves the contract provisions alive and susceptible of enforcement.

BROWN v. LOBER

Supreme Court of Illinois
75 Ill.2d 547 (1979)

UNDERWOOD, J., delivered the opinion of the court.

[By a general warranty deed of December 21, 1957 containing no exceptions to the title, William and Faith Bost conveyed 80 acres to the Browns. Ten years earlier, in 1947, a prior owner of the 80 acres had conveyed title but had reserved ownership of 2/3 of the mineral rights. In 1958 and 1968 the Browns had their title examined for loan purposes, but it was not until 1976, when they had contracted with Consolidated Coal to convey the mineral rights to the 80 acres for $6,000, that they learned that they actually owned only 1/3 of those rights. As a result, the contract was renegotiated and the Browns sold their 1/3 interest in the mineral rights to Consolidated Coal for $2,000. The holder of the other 2/3 of the mineral rights had never sought to exert his rights. Because the Bosts had died, the Browns sued the executor of the Bosts' estate, seeking damages of $4,000 for breach of the covenants of seisin and quiet enjoyment. The trial court ruled for the Bosts' executor. The intermediate appellate court reversed as to the claim for breach of the covenant of quiet enjoyment. The Illinois Supreme Court agreed to hear the Browns' appeal.]

The trial court held that although there had been a breach of the covenant of seisin, the suit was barred by the 10–year statute of limitations.... This court has stated repeatedly that the covenant of seisin is a covenant *in praesenti* and, therefore, if broken at all, is broken at the time of delivery of the deed. Since the deed was delivered to the plaintiffs on December 21, 1957, any cause of action for breach of the covenant of seisin would have accrued on that date. The ... cause of action for breach of the covenant of seisin was properly determined by the trial court to be barred by the statute of limitations since plaintiffs did not file their complaint until May 25, 1976, nearly 20 years after their alleged cause of action accrued....

The appellate court [held] that the cause of action on the covenant of quiet enjoyment was not barred by the statute of limitations ... [because] plaintiffs' cause of action did not accrue until 1976, when plaintiffs discovered that they only had a one-third interest in the subsurface coal rights and renegotiated their contract with the coal company for one-third of the previous contract price. The primary issue ... is when, if at all, the plaintiffs' cause of action for breach of the covenant of quiet enjoyment is deemed to have accrued.

This court has stated on numerous occasions that, in contrast to the covenant of seisin, the covenant of warranty or quiet enjoyment is prospective in nature and is breached only when there is an actual or constructive eviction of the covenantee by the paramount titleholder. Biwer v. Martin (1920), 294 Ill. 488; Barry v. Guild (1888), 126 Ill. 439; Scott v. Kirkendall (1878), 88 Ill. 465; Bostwick v. Williams (1864), 36 Ill. 65; Moore v. Vail (1855), 17 Ill. 185. The cases are also replete with statements to the effect that the mere existence of paramount title in one other than the covenantee is not sufficient to constitute a breach of the covenant of warranty or quiet enjoyment: "[T]here must be a union of acts of disturbance and lawful title, to constitute a breach of the covenant for quiet enjoyment, or warranty...." (Barry v. Guild (1888), 126 Ill. 439, 446.) "[T]here is a general concurrence that something more than the mere existence of a paramount title is necessary to constitute a breach of the covenant of warranty." (Scott v. Kirkendall (1878), 88 Ill. 465, 467.) "A mere want of title is no breach of this covenant. There must not only be a want of title, but there must be an ouster under a paramount title." Moore v. Vail (1855), 17 Ill. 185, 189.

The question is whether plaintiffs have alleged facts sufficient to constitute a constructive eviction. They argue that if a covenantee fails in his effort to sell an interest in land because he discovers that he does not own what his warranty deed purported to convey, he has suffered a constructive eviction and is thereby entitled to bring an action against his grantor for breach of the covenant of quiet enjoyment. We think that the decision of this court in Scott v. Kirkendall (1878), 88 Ill. 465, is controlling on this issue and compels us to reject plaintiffs' argument.

In *Scott*, an action was brought for breach of the covenant of warranty by a grantee who discovered that other parties had paramount title to the land in question. The land was vacant and unoccupied at all relevant times. This court, in rejecting the grantee's claim that there was a breach of the covenant of quiet enjoyment, quoted the earlier decision in Moore v. Vail (1855), 17 Ill. 185, 191:

> "Until that time, (the taking possession by the owner of the paramount title), he might peaceably have entered upon and enjoyed the premises, without resistance or molestation, which was all his grantors covenanted he should do. They did not guarantee to him a perfect title, but the possession and enjoyment of the premises."

Relying on this language in *Moore*, the *Scott* court concluded:

> We do not see but what this fully decides the present case against the appellant. It holds that the mere existence of a paramount title does not constitute a breach of the covenant. That is all there is here. There has been no assertion of the adverse title. The land has always been vacant. Appellant could at any time have taken peaceable possession of it. He has in no way been prevented or hindered from the enjoyment of the possession by any one having a better right. It was but the possession and enjoyment of the premises which was assured to him, and there has been no disturbance or interference in that respect. True, there is a superior title in another, but appellant has never felt "its pressure upon him."

Admittedly, *Scott* dealt with surface rights while the case before us concerns subsurface mineral rights. We are, nevertheless, convinced that the reasoning employed in *Scott* is applicable to the present case. While plaintiffs went into possession of the surface area, they cannot be said to have possessed the subsurface minerals. "Possession of the surface does not carry possession of the minerals.... To possess the mineral estate, one must undertake the actual removal thereof from the ground or do such other act as will apprise the community that such interest is in the exclusive use and enjoyment of the claiming party." Failoni v. Chicago & North Western Ry. Co. (1964), 30 Ill. 2d 258, 262. Since no one has, as yet, undertaken to remove the coal or otherwise manifested a clear intent to exclusively "possess" the mineral estate, it must be concluded that the subsurface estate is "vacant." As in *Scott*, plaintiffs "could at any time have taken peaceable possession of it. [They have] in no way been prevented or hindered from the enjoyment of the possession by any one having a better right." (88 Ill. 465, 468.) Accordingly, until such time as one holding paramount title interferes with plaintiffs' right of possession (*e.g.*, by beginning to mine the coal), there can be no constructive eviction and, therefore, no breach of the covenant of quiet enjoyment.

What plaintiffs are apparently attempting to do on this appeal is to extend the protection afforded by the covenant of quiet enjoyment. However, we decline to expand the historical scope of this covenant to provide a remedy where another of the covenants of title is so clearly applicable. As this court stated in Scott v. Kirkendall (1878), 88 Ill. 465, 469:

> To sustain the present action would be to confound all distinction between the covenant of warranty and that of seizin, or of right to convey. They are not equivalent covenants. An action will lie upon the latter, though there be no disturbance of possession. A defect of title will suffice. Not so with the covenant of warranty, or for quiet enjoyment, as has always been held by the prevailing authority.

The covenant of seisin, unquestionably, was breached when the Bosts delivered the deed to plaintiffs, and plaintiffs then had a cause of action. However, despite the fact that it was a matter of public record that there was a reservation of a two-thirds interest in the mineral rights in the earlier deed, plaintiffs failed to bring an action for breach of the covenant of seisin within the 10–year period following delivery of the deed. The likely explanation is that plaintiffs had not secured a title opinion at the time they purchased the property, and the subsequent examiners for the lenders were not concerned with the mineral rights. Plaintiffs' oversight, however, does not justify us in overruling earlier decisions in order to recognize an otherwise premature cause of action. The mere fact that plaintiffs' original contract with Consolidated had to be modified due to their discovery that paramount title to two-thirds of the subsurface minerals belonged to another is not sufficient to constitute the constructive eviction necessary to a breach of the covenant of quiet enjoyment. . . .

QUESTIONS AND PROBLEMS

1.   What now? After this decision, what can the Browns do? Which of the following possibilities (there may be others) is efficacious?

a.   Locate the owner of the remaining 2/3 of the mineral rights, purchase those rights from the owner, and then sue the Bosts' executor.

b.   Hire contractors to excavate the coal, and then sell the mined coal.

c.   Locate the owner of the remaining 2/3 of the mineral rights, and then sue that owner to quiet title in the Browns, on the theory that the Browns have acquired the mineral rights by adverse possession.

2.   Adverse possession by the grantor. Suppose that in 1990 *O*, owner of fee simple absolute in Blackacre, conveys Blackacre to *A*, who never takes possession. In 2000, *A* conveys title to Blackacre to *B*, who also never takes possession. From 1990 to the present *O* remains in possession of Blackacre. In 2010 *B* files suit against *O* to recover possession of Blackacre. The jurisdiction has a 15 year limitations statute for suits to recover possession of real property. *O* contends that he has title to Blackacre by virtue of his adverse possession. What result?

3.   AFTER–ACQUIRED TITLE, OR ESTOPPEL BY DEED

What happens when a grantor conveys title to property that he does not own, and then later acquires title to that property? Should the answer depend on what warranties of title are contained in the deed?

SCHWENN v. KAYE

Court of Appeal of California
155 Cal.App.3d 949 (1984)

COMPTON, J., delivered the opinion of the court.

Plaintiff in this action to quiet title to oil royalties appeals from the judgment entered in favor of defendants. We affirm.

Plaintiff Lillian Schwenn acquired real property in Long Beach in 1965. The property was generating oil and gas royalties pursuant to a lease with Atlantic Richfield Company (not a party to this appeal). In 1969, plaintiff conveyed the oil and gas royalties as a gift to her daughter and son-in-law by grant deed which was duly recorded. In 1974, plaintiff sold the real property to defendants Richard and Johanna Kaye. Neither the written offer to purchase nor the original escrow instructions made any mention of oil and gas rights, royalties or leases. During the escrow, the preliminary title report revealed that the property was subject to the oil and gas lease, but for unexplained reasons did not reveal the 1969 conveyance of the rights in the oil and gas lease. As a result of the indication regarding the lease, an amendment to escrow was signed by plaintiff's agent to the effect that such lease would be "assigned, if assignable," (presumptively to the Kayes) after the close of escrow.[3]

After escrow closed, Atlantic Richfield was notified of the sale and thereafter sent royalty payments to the defendants. When plaintiff complained to Atlantic Richfield that the payments belonged to her daughter and son-in-law, she was told that no further royalties would be paid without a court order determining who was entitled to the royalty payments. In anticipation of litigation, plaintiff asked her daughter and son-in-law to reconvey the oil and gas rights to her. Plaintiff's explanation for this request was that she did not want them to be involved in litigation over a gift she had made to them.

After a court trial, title was quieted in favor of defendants Kaye on the basis of the doctrine of after-acquired title. This common law doctrine was codified in Civil Code section 1106 which provides: "Where a person purports by proper instrument to grant real property in fee simple, and subsequently acquires any title, or claim of title thereto, the same passes by operation of law to the grantee, or his successors."

The thrust of plaintiff's argument on appeal is that she mistakenly allowed the doctrine of after-acquired title to govern this case when she asked her daughter to reconvey the oil and gas rights to her. Plaintiff contends that she never intended such a result and therefore, her true intent ought to have been considered by the court and equitable principles applied in order to preserve her family's interest in the royalties. We disagree. Such a result would be contrary to the law and to the policy underlying the doctrine of after-acquired title. Civil Code section 1106 has as its genesis the common law doctrine of estoppel by deed. That doctrine generally precludes a grantor of real property from asserting, as against the grantee, any right or title in derogation of the deed. The policy behind the doctrine is to protect an unwitting grantee who relies upon the good title of the grantor when the latter does not possess legal or perfect title to the property. Cecil v. Gray (1915) 170 Cal. 137, 140. . . . The net effect is the same as if the grantor specifically provided in the deed that he

---

3. [T]he evidence is susceptible of the inference that plaintiff was actively concealing from defendants the fact that she had already conveyed the oil and gas rights. She knew the lease was not assignable by her and she obviously didn't intend to reacquire it in order to "assign" it to defendants.

conveyed all of the title and estate which he then possessed or which he might at any time thereafter acquire.

In the case at bench, plaintiff delivered a grant deed into escrow. . . . No reservation of rights or other limiting language appeared in the deed. A fee simple title is presumed to pass by a grant of real property, unless it appears *from the grant* that a lesser estate was intended. . . . Application of these general principles to the facts of the instant case make it clear that plaintiff granted [to] defendants fee simple title to the property[,] including any oil and gas rights and the royalties attendant thereto. The fact that she had previously deeded away the oil and gas rights did not invalidate the subsequent grant deed, but probably would have subjected her to liability for breach of [the covenant of seisin] had she not later reacquired the rights. When plaintiff subsequently acquired title to the oil and gas rights, the title passed to the defendants by operation of law, thereby obviating the need for bringing an action for breach of covenant.

Plaintiff's argument that the trial court erred in excluding parol evidence of her intent is none too clear. It is patently clear, however, that any reason she had for reacquiring the oil and gas rights is simply irrelevant. The applicability of the common law doctrine or Civil Code section 1106 does not depend on the grantor's motive in reacquiring the property. . . . If plaintiff's argument is that she never intended to grant the oil and gas rights to defendants in the original grant deed, this argument also is of no avail. . . . In essence plaintiff's argument is simply that because defendants were aware of the lease from the title report and the above mentioned amendment to the escrow instructions and because defendants had constructive notice of the assignment of the lease by plaintiff to her children, defendants had no reasonable expectation of receiving the oil and gas rights. The argument further is that because of defendants' efforts in obtaining the royalty payments from Arco, plaintiff was led to believe, mistakenly, that she needed to reacquire the title in order to have standing to litigate the issue. From this rather convoluted argument, plaintiff extrapolates that equity should shield her from her mistaken belief by raising an estoppel against defendants invoking the effect of Civil Code section 1106. . . . The trial court's finding that defendants, because of the recordation, had constructive notice of plaintiff's prior transfer is of no consequence since the doctrine of after-acquired title applies even if the grantee had knowledge of the deficiency. . . .

The judgment is affirmed.

PROBLEMS

1. In 2000, *O*, owner of Blackacre in fee simple absolute, conveys the mineral rights to Blackacre to *A*. In 2005, *O* conveys Blackacre to *B* by a quit claim deed that recites that "*O* hereby releases and quit claims to *B*, his heirs and assigns, any right, title or interest that *O* may have in Blackacre." In 2010, *A* conveys the mineral rights to Blackacre to *O*. Who owns the mineral rights in Blackacre?

2. Assume the same facts as Problem 1, except that the deed from *O* to *B* recites that "*O* hereby releases and quit claims to *B*, his heirs and assigns, *O*'s fee simple absolute in Blackacre." Who owns the mineral rights in Blackacre?

3. In 1946 Ernest, owner of 120 acres of Iowa farmland, died intestate, survived by his wife Inez and six children. In April 1947, before settlement of Ernest's estate, one of the children, Albert, conveyed a 1/3 interest in the 120 acres to Inez. In August 1947 the heirs of Ernest agreed to settle the estate by granting Albert, Ernest Jr. and Harold each a 1/3 interest in the 120 acres. In September of 1947, by special warranty deed, the remaining heirs of Ernest Sr., including Inez, conveyed their interests in the 120 acres in equal portions to Albert, Harold, and Ernest Jr. In 1965 Inez conveyed her interest in the 120 acres, by quit claim deed, to Ernest Jr. In 1973, by quit claim deed Harold conveyed his interest in the 120 acres to Ernest Jr. In 1974, Ernest Jr. conveyed by quit claim deed his entire interest in the 120 acres to Wright. What is the state of title in the 120 acres?

E. FINANCING DEVICES

Most people do not have enough cash to purchase real estate without someone lending them a portion of the purchase price. Typically, a buyer will make a cash down payment of somewhere between 10% and 25% of the purchase price and the balance of the purchase price will be obtained by borrowing the funds from someone else. The buyer will execute a promissory note in favor of the lender, containing the terms of payment of the borrowed money, including the interest rate, monthly payment, and maturity date. There are two principal sources of loans to enable a purchaser to complete the transaction: third party lenders (such as a bank or other institutional lender) and the seller. Most sellers are not anxious to become lenders by taking a portion of the purchase price in the form of the buyer's promissory note, so the great majority of real estate transactions involve a third party lender. The lender, of course, will demand some security for repayment of his loan, and that security will almost always consist of the property itself. There are two common devices by which the property is pledged as collateral security for the payment of the loan.

One is a mortgage, by which the lender becomes the mortgagee. In most states, the mortgagee has a lien against the title to the property which will be released when the loan is fully paid. If the borrower should default the mortgagee may proceed to foreclose on the mortgage, obtaining a judicial decree ordering the property to be sold at a foreclosure sale to the highest bidder. The proceeds of the sale are remitted to the mortgagee to extinguish the debt; any excess goes to the borrower. Frequently there is no excess and sometimes the foreclosure sale will not realize enough cash to extinguish the debt. In that event the borrower is personally liable for the unpaid portion of the debt and the lender may obtain a "deficiency judgment" for that amount, unless either by statute or agreement the lender's recourse is limited to the property alone (so-called non-recourse financing, or a non-recourse loan). Sometimes there are no bidders at the foreclosure sale and the lender acquires title by being the only bidder.

The other security device is the deed of trust, by which the buyer deeds title to the property to a trustee, who holds title in trust for the benefit of the buyer and lender. If the borrower-buyer defaults on the loan, the trustee is authorized and directed to sell the property at a trustee's sale (which operates in much the same way as a mortgage foreclosure sale). If the borrower pays the loan in full the trustee is directed to reconvey title to the buyer. Note that the deed of trust does not involve any judicial oversight, as is the case with foreclosure upon a mortgage. Another formal difference between a mortgage and a deed of trust is that title remains with the buyer in the case of a mortgage but has moved to the trustee in the case of a deed of trust. That difference is largely without significance today, as most courts treat the two devices as but different ways to give the lender an inchoate right to seize and sell the property in the event of borrower default.

Under either device states permit a defaulted mortgagor some period of time after the foreclosure sale or trustee's sale to redeem the property by paying the entire outstanding balance of the loan, plus accrued interest and whatever additional costs incurred by the buyer at the foreclosure or trustee's sale that the jurisdiction allows to be charged as a cost of redemption. States may permit the buyer to cut off the redemption right by bringing an action to quiet title in which the defaulted mortgagor must pay up or assert some defect in the process that invalidates the sale.

Mortgages are readily transferable by the mortgagee and, subject to contractual limits described below, by the mortgagor. A purchaser of encumbered property, of course, takes the property subject to the encumbrance. But a buyer of such property might agree to take the property "subject to the mortgage" or to "assume the mortgage." If a transferee takes "subject to the mortgage" he makes no promise to be personally responsible for payment of the loan secured by the mortgage. Thus, in the event of default the mortgagee's remedy with respect to the transferee is only the property. The mortgagee could, of course, seek and obtain a deficiency judgment against the original mortgagor, if such judgments are permitted in the jurisdiction. By contrast, if the transferee assumes the mortgage he promises that he will be personally responsible for payment of the mortgage loan. That does not relieve the original mortgagor of personal liability, however, unless the mortgagee has granted a release of that liability to the original mortgagor. In periods of rising interest rates a buyer of encumbered real property may desire to assume a mortgage, or acquire title subject to the mortgage, if the interest rate on the existing loan is lower than could be obtained with new financing. Lenders appreciate this fact, too. A common device used by lenders is to make the entire loan balance due on sale or transfer of the encumbered property. That forces the new owner to refinance at a higher interest rate. Of course, in a period in which rates are declining a due on sale clause backfires, but even if a due on sale clause was absent, a new buyer would no doubt refinance to obtain the benefit of lower interest rates. Thus, there is no risk to the lender to include a due on sale clause.

A seller who chooses to lend to the buyer a portion of the purchase price has several options. He can take a mortgage or deed of trust on the property, just as would a third party lender. Or he can enter into an installment sale contract, by which the buyer agrees to purchase the property for a specified price and to pay that price in periodic installments over a specified time period. Under an installment sale contract, title stays with the seller until all payments have been made. Problems arise when a buyer defaults before all the payments have been made. May the seller keep the property and the payments? May the seller keep the property but return the payments to the buyer? Or is the entire transaction the functional equivalent of a mortgage loan? If so, must the seller comply with all the requirements pertaining to foreclosure? These questions will be explored in this section, but first we shall examine some of the obligations involved in a mortgage foreclosure.

MURPHY v. FINANCIAL DEVELOPMENT CORPORATION

Supreme Court of New Hampshire
126 N.H. 536 (1985)

Douglas, J., delivered the opinion of the court.

The plaintiffs brought this action seeking to set aside the foreclosure sale of their home, or, in the alternative, money damages. The Superior Court, adopting the recommendation of a Master, entered a judgment for the plaintiffs in the amount of $27,000 against two of the defendants, Financial Development Corporation and Colonial Deposit Company (the lenders). The plaintiffs purchased a house in Nashua in 1966, financing it by means of a mortgage loan. They refinanced the loan in March of 1980, executing a new promissory note and a power of sale mortgage, with Financial Development Corporation as mortgagee. The note and mortgage were later assigned to Colonial Deposit Company.

In February of 1981, the plaintiff Richard Murphy became unemployed. By September of 1981, the plaintiffs were seven months in arrears on their mortgage payments, and had also failed to pay substantial amounts in utility assessments and real estate taxes. After discussing unsuccessfully with the plaintiffs proposals for revising the payment schedule, rewriting the note, and arranging alternative financing, the lenders gave notice on October 6, 1981, of their intent to foreclose. During the following weeks, the plaintiffs made a concerted effort to avoid foreclosure. They paid the seven months' mortgage arrearage, but failed to pay some $643.18 in costs and legal fees associated with the foreclosure proceedings. The lenders scheduled the foreclosure sale for November 10, 1981, at the site of the subject property. They complied with all of the statutory requirements for notice. At the plaintiffs' request, the lenders agreed to postpone the sale until December 15, 1981. They advised the plaintiffs that this would entail an additional cost of $100, and that the sale would proceed unless the lenders received payment of $743.18, as well as all mortgage payments then due, by December 15. Notice of the postponement was posted on the subject property on November 10 at the originally scheduled time of the sale, and was also posted at the Nashua City Hall and Post Office. No prospective bidders were present for the scheduled sale.

In late November, the plaintiffs paid the mortgage payment which had been due in October, but made no further payments to the lenders. An attempt by the lenders to arrange new financing for the plaintiffs through a third party failed when the plaintiffs refused to agree to pay for a new appraisal of the property. Early on the morning of December 15, 1981, the plaintiffs tried to obtain a further postponement, but were advised by the lenders' attorney that it was impossible unless the costs and legal fees were paid. At the plaintiffs' request, the attorney called the president of Financial Development Corporation, who also refused to postpone the sale. Further calls by the plaintiffs to the lenders' offices were equally unavailing. The sale proceeded as scheduled at 10:00 a.m. on December 15, at the site of the property. Although it had snowed the previous night, the weather was clear and warm at the time of the sale, and the roads were clear. The only parties present were the plaintiffs, a representative of the lenders, and an attorney, Morgan Hollis, who had been engaged to conduct the sale because the lenders' attorney, who lived in Dover, had been apprehensive about the weather the night before. The lenders' representative made the only bid at the sale. That bid of $27,000, roughly the amount owed on the mortgage, plus costs and fees, was accepted and the sale concluded.

Later that same day, Attorney Hollis encountered one of his clients, William Dube, a representative of the defendant Southern New Hampshire Home Traders, Inc. (Southern). On being informed of the sale, Mr. Dube contacted the lenders and offered to buy the property for $27,000. The lenders rejected the offer and made a counter offer of $40,000. Within two days a purchase price of $38,000 was agreed upon by Mr. Dube and the lenders, and the sale was subsequently completed.

The plaintiffs commenced this action on February 5, 1982. The lenders moved to dismiss, arguing that any action was barred because the plaintiffs had failed to petition for an injunction prior to the sale. The master denied the motion. After hearing the evidence, he ruled for the plaintiffs, finding that the lenders had "failed to exercise good faith and due diligence in obtaining a fair price for the subject property at the foreclosure sale. . . ." The master also ruled that Southern was a bona fide purchaser for value, and thus had acquired legal title to the house. That ruling is not at issue here. He assessed monetary damages against the lenders equal to "the difference between the fair market value of the subject property on the date of the foreclosure and the price obtained at said sale." Having found the fair market value to be $54,000, he assessed damages accordingly at $27,000. He further ruled that "[t]he bad faith of the 'Lenders' warrants an award of legal fees." The lenders appealed.

The first issue before us is whether the master erred in denying the motion to dismiss. The lenders, in support of their argument, rely upon RSA 479:25, II, which gives a mortgagor the right to petition the superior court to enjoin a proposed foreclosure sale, and then provides: "Failure to institute such petition and complete service upon the foreclosing party, or his agent, conducting the sale prior to sale shall thereafter bar any action or right of action of the mortgagor based on the validity of the foreclosure." If we were to construe this provision as the lenders urge us to do, it would prevent a mortgagor from challenging the validity of a sale in a case where the only claimed unfairness or illegality occurred during the sale itself—unless the mortgagor had petitioned for an injunction before any grounds existed on which the injunction could be granted. We will not construe a statute so as to produce such an illogical and unjust result. The only reasonable construction of the language in RSA 479:25, II relied upon by the lenders is that it bars any action based on facts which the mortgagor knew or should have known soon enough to reasonably permit the filing of a petition prior to the sale. The master could not have found that this was such an action, because the only unfairness referred to in his report involves the amount of the sale price. Thus, his denial of the lenders' motion to dismiss was proper.

The second issue before us is whether the master erred in concluding that the lenders had failed to comply with the often-repeated rule that a mortgagee executing a power of sale is bound both by the statutory procedural requirements *and* by a duty to protect the interests of the mortgagor through the exercise of good faith and due diligence. ... The master found that the lenders, throughout the time prior to the sale, "did not mislead or deal unfairly with the plaintiffs." They engaged in serious efforts to avoid foreclosure through new financing, and agreed to one postponement of the sale. The basis for the master's decision was his conclusion that the lenders had failed to exercise good faith and due diligence in obtaining a fair price for the property.

This court's past decisions have not dealt consistently with the question whether the mortgagee's duty amounts to that of a fiduciary or trustee. This may be an inevitable result of the mortgagee's dual role as seller and potential buyer at the foreclosure sale, and of the conflicting interests involved. We need not label a duty, however, in order to define it. In his role as a seller, the mortgagee's duty of good faith and due diligence is essentially that of a fiduciary. Such a view is in keeping with "[t]he 'trend ... towards liberalizing the term [fiduciary] in order to prevent unjust enrichment.'" Lash v. Cheshire County Savings Bank, Inc., 124 N.H. 435, 438, 474 A.2d 980, 981 (1984) (quoting Cornwell v. Cornwell, 116 N.H. 205, 209, 356 A.2d 683, 686 (1976)). A mortgagee, therefore, must exert every reasonable effort to obtain "a fair and reasonable price under the circumstances," Reconstruction Corp. v. Faulkner, 101 N.H. 352, 361, 143 A.2d 403, 410 (1958), even to the extent, if necessary, of adjourning the sale or of establishing "an upset price below which he will not accept any offer." Lakes Region Fin. Corp. v. Goodhue Boat Yard, Inc., 118 N.H. [103,] 107, 382 A.2d [1108,] 1111 [(1978)].

What constitutes a fair price, or whether the mortgagee must establish an upset price, adjourn the sale, or make other reasonable efforts to assure a fair price, depends on the circumstances of each case. Inadequacy of price alone is not sufficient to demonstrate bad faith unless the price is so low as to shock the judicial conscience. Mueller v. Simmons, 634 S.W.2d 533, 536 (Mo. App. 1982); Rife v. Woolfolk, 289 S.E.2d 220, 223 (W. Va. 1982); Travelers Indem. Co. v. Heim, 352 N.W.2d 921, 923–24 (Neb. 1984).

We must decide, in the present case, whether the evidence supports the finding of the master that the lenders failed to exercise good faith and due diligence in obtaining a fair price for the plaintiffs' property. We first note that "[t]he duties of good faith and due diligence are distinct.... One may be observed and not the other, and any inquiry as to their breach calls for a separate consideration of each." Wheeler v. Slocinski, 82 N.H. [211,] 213, 131 A. [598,] 600 [(1926)]. In order "to constitute bad faith there must be an intentional disregard of duty or a purpose to injure." *Id.* at 214, 131 A. at 600–01. There is insufficient evidence in the record to support the master's finding that the lenders acted in bad faith in failing to obtain a fair price for the plaintiffs' property. The lenders complied with the statutory requirements of notice and otherwise conducted the sale in compliance with statutory provisions. The lenders postponed the sale one time and did not bid with knowledge of any immediately available subsequent purchaser. Further, there is no evidence indicating an intent on the part of the lenders to injure the mortgagor by, for example, discouraging other buyers.

There is ample evidence in the record, however, to support the master's finding that the lenders failed to exercise due diligence in obtaining a fair price. "The issue of the lack of due diligence is whether a reasonable man in the [lenders'] place would have adjourned the sale," *id.* at 215, 131 A. at 601, or taken other measures to receive a fair price. In early 1980, the plaintiffs' home was appraised at $46,000. At the time of the foreclosure sale on December 15, 1981, the lenders had not had the house reappraised to take into account improvements and appreciation. The master found that a reasonable person in the place of the lenders would have realized that the plaintiffs' equity in the property was at least $19,000, the difference between the 1980 appraised value of $46,000 and the amount owed on the mortgage totaling approximately $27,000. At the foreclosure sale, the lenders were the only bidders. The master found that their bid of $27,000 "was sufficient to cover all monies due and did not create a deficiency balance" but "did not provide for a return of any of the plaintiffs' equity."

Further, the master found that the lenders "had reason to know" that "they stood to make a substantial profit on a quick turnaround sale." On the day of the sale, the lenders offered to sell the foreclosed property to

William Dube for $40,000. Within two days after the foreclosure sale, they did in fact agree to sell it to Dube for $38,000. It was not necessary for the master to find that the lenders knew of a specific potential buyer before the sale in order to show lack of good faith or due diligence as the lenders contend. The fact that the lenders offered the property for sale at a price sizably above that for which they had purchased it, only a few hours before, supports the master's finding that the lenders had reason to know, at the time of the foreclosure sale, that they could make a substantial profit on a quick turnaround sale. For this reason, they should have taken more measures to ensure receiving a higher price at the sale.

While a mortgagee may not always be required to secure a portion of the mortgagor's equity, such an obligation did exist in this case. The substantial amount of equity which the plaintiffs had in their property, the knowledge of the lenders as to the appraised value of the property, and the plaintiffs' efforts to forestall foreclosure by paying the mortgage arrearage within weeks of the sale, all support the master's conclusion that the lenders had a fiduciary duty to take more reasonable steps than they did to protect the plaintiffs' equity by attempting to obtain a fair price for the property. They could have established an appropriate upset price to assure a minimum bid. They also could have postponed the auction and advertised commercially by display advertising in order to assure that bidders other than themselves would be present. Instead, as Theodore DiStefano, an officer of both lending institutions, testified, the lenders made no attempt to obtain fair market value for the property but were concerned *only* with making themselves "whole." On the facts of this case, such disregard for the interests of the mortgagors was a breach of duty by the mortgagees.

Although the lenders *did* comply with the statutory requirements of notice of the foreclosure sale, these efforts were not sufficient in this case to demonstrate due diligence. At the time of the initially scheduled sale, the extent of the lenders' efforts to publicize the sale of the property was publication of a legal notice of the mortgagees' sale at public auction on November 10, published once a week for three weeks in the Nashua Telegraph, plus postings in public places. The lenders did not advertise, publish, or otherwise give notice to the general public of postponement of the sale to December 15, 1981, other than by posting notices at the plaintiffs' house, at the post office, and at city hall. That these efforts to advertise were ineffective is evidenced by the fact that no one, other than the lenders, appeared at the sale to bid on the property. This fact allowed the lenders to purchase the property at a minimal price and then to profit substantially in a quick turnaround sale.

We recognize a need to give guidance to a trial court which must determine whether a mortgagee who has complied with the strict letter of the statutory law has nevertheless violated his additional duties of good faith and due diligence. A finding that the mortgagee had, or should have had, knowledge of his ability to get a higher price at an adjourned sale is the most conclusive evidence of such a violation. More generally, we are in agreement with the official Commissioners' Comment to section 3–508 of the Uniform Land Transactions Act:

> The requirement that the sale be conducted in a reasonable manner, including the advertising aspects, requires that the person conducting the sale use the ordinary methods of making buyers aware that are used when an owner is voluntarily selling his land. Thus an advertisement in the portion of a daily newspaper where these ads are placed or, in appropriate cases such as the sale of an industrial plant, a display advertisement in the financial sections of the daily newspaper may be the most reasonable method. In other cases employment of a professional real estate agent may be the more reasonable method. It is unlikely that an advertisement in a legal publication among other legal notices would qualify as a commercially reasonable method of sale advertising.

13 Uniform Laws Annotated 704 (West 1980). As discussed above, the lenders met neither of these guidelines.

While agreeing with the master that the lenders failed to exercise due diligence in this case, we find that he erred as a matter of law in awarding damages equal to "the difference between the fair market value of the subject property ... and the price obtained at [the] sale." Such a formula may well be the appropriate measure where *bad faith* is found. See Danvers Savings Bank v. Hammer, 122 N.H. 1, 5, 440 A.2d 435, 438 (1982). In such a case, a mortgagee's conduct amounts to more than mere negligence. Damages based upon the *fair market value*, a figure in excess of a *fair* price, will more readily induce mortgagees to perform their duties properly. A *fair* price may or may not yield a figure close to *fair market value*; however, it will be that price arrived at as a result of due diligence by the mortgagee. Where, as here, however, a mortgagee fails to exercise due diligence, the proper assessment of damages is the difference between a fair price for the property and the price obtained at the foreclosure sale. We have held, where lack of due diligence has been found, that " 'the test is not "fair market value" as in eminent domain cases nor is the mortgagee bound to give credit for the highest possible amount which might be obtained under different circumstances, as at an owner's sale.' " Silver v. First National Bank, 108 N.H. 390, 392, 236 A.2d 493, 495 (1967) (quoting Reconstruction Corp. v. Faulkner, 101 N.H. 352, 361, 143 A.2d 403, 410 (1958)).

Accordingly, we remand to the trial court for a reassessment of damages consistent with this opinion.

Because we concluded above that there was no "bad faith or obstinate, unjust, vexatious, wanton, or oppressive conduct," on the part of the lenders, we see no reason to stray from our general rule that the prevailing litigant is not entitled to collect attorney's fees from the loser. Therefore, we reverse this part of the master's decision.

BROCK, J., dissenting:

I agree with the majority that a mortgagee, in its role as seller at a foreclosure sale, has a fiduciary duty to the mortgagor. ... On the record presently before us, however, I cannot see any support for the master's finding that the lenders here failed to exercise due diligence.... I would remand the case to the superior court for further findings of fact.

... The master's report stated that the lenders "did not establish an upset price or minimum bid," ... but there is nothing in the record ... to indicate what an appropriate upset price would have been under the conditions present here. The master correctly noted that "[a] foreclosure sale ... usually produces a price less than the property's fair market value," so it is virtually certain that any upset price would have been less than that amount.

I also cannot accept the majority's statement that the lenders' offer to sell the house for $40,000 constitutes support for a finding that they "should have taken more measures to ensure receiving a fair price at the sale." The offer was certainly relevant to the question of what the lenders knew about the house's value. Standing alone, however, it says nothing about what a reasonable person in the lenders' position would have done to ensure a fair price under the circumstances of this particular sale.

... Although the [master's] report nowhere states specifically *what* the lenders should have done, its clear implication is that they should have made a higher bid at the foreclosure sale.

There is no authority for such a conclusion. The mortgagee's fiduciary duty extends only to its role as a *seller*. Once the mortgagee has exerted every reasonable effort to obtain a fair price (which may sometimes include setting an upset price and adjourning the sale if no bidder meets that price), it has no further obligation in its role as a potential buyer.

As the majority notes, a low price is not of itself sufficient to invalidate a foreclosure sale, unless the price is "so low as to shock the judicial conscience." The price here was clearly not that low. Cf. Shipp Corp., Inc. v. Charpilloz, 414 So. 2d 1122, 1124 (Fla. Dist. Ct. App. 1982) (bid of $1.1 million was not grossly inadequate compared to a market value of between $2.8 and $3.2 million).

Because it is unclear whether the master applied the correct standard regarding the mortgagees' duty, and because the record as presently constituted cannot support a determination that the lenders violated that standard, I respectfully dissent.

NOTES, QUESTIONS, AND PROBLEMS

1. Fair Price. The court reflects the consensus of legal opinion when it states that a low price, by itself, is insufficient to void a foreclosure sale. Something else must be present, such as fraud. See, e.g., note 4. But the court asserts that a low price that "shocks the judicial conscience" is enough to invalidate such a sale. How is this factor to be assessed? How can a mortgagee be sure that the sale price is not so low as to be shocking? What constitutes a "fair price," as distinguished from fair market value? In thinking through this issue, consider the following problems:

a. The mortgagor, A, owes $20,000 on the note to the lender and mortgagee, L. The fair market value of the property subject to the mortgage was $40,000 prior to an economic recession that caused A to lose his job and to default on the loan. The recession has meant that houses such as the one subject to L's mortgage lien are not easily saleable, and then at a significant decline from pre-recession values. Only two similar properties have sold in the prior year, one for $32,000 and the other for $18,000. A number of similar homes are offered for sale at prices ranging from $28,000 to $38,000. Each of them has been on the market for over a year. At the foreclosure sale L, the only bidder, buys the property for $10,000. Is the sale valid? Should it matter whether the jurisdiction permits or prohibits deficiency judgments?

b. The mortgagor, X, a real estate developer, owes $1.1 million on the note to the lender and mortgagee, Y. The property subject to the mortgage is a commercial office building that is under construction. Seventy-five percent of the space has been leased for an annual rental of $600,000 but because X is in default the lease agreements permit the lessees to rescind without penalty. The vacancy rate for commercial office space in the community where the building is located is very low, about 1%. Y calculates that the value of the building, when completed and fully leased, is ten times the annual rents, or $8.0 million. However, it will require expenditure of another $900,000 to complete the building. Y lacks the expertise to complete the building without the assistance of a skilled contractor. X has been acting as the contractor for construction of the building. At the foreclosure sale Y is the only bidder and acquires the building for the loan balance of $1.1 million. Is the sale valid?

2. *Mortgagee's Duty.* What should the mortgagee in *Murphy* have done to ensure that the foreclosure sale produced a "fair" price, albeit less than fair market value? In short, what does the obligation of due diligence entail?

3. *Alternatives to Foreclosure.* A mortgagor in default has alternatives to waiting for the mortgagee to foreclose. If the mortgagor has substantial equity in the property, as did the Murphys, there is an obvious incentive for the mortgagor to sell the property himself. Even though the sale must be completed quickly (and thus may not derive top dollar) it will likely produce a sale price that will recoup a substantial amount of the mortgagor's equity. Note that if the mortgagor sells the property he can deliver good title to the purchaser, but the purchaser at a foreclosure sale takes a title that is subject to the mortgagor's right to redeem the property. That latter fact means that a prudent purchaser at a foreclosure sale is unlikely to pay more than the amount of the unpaid debt. That fact also explains why William Dube did not bid at the foreclosure sale, but negotiated a purchase from Financial Development after the sale: Because Dube acquired title from Financial Development he was a bona fide purchaser for value and thus insulated from the possibility that the Murphys could strip him of title by paying the outstanding mortgage loan balance. The New Hampshire court held that the mortgagee breached its duty to use due diligence to obtain a "fair price," but should the mortgagor be held to a duty to mitigate its own loss? Why should a mortgagor be permitted

to sit back passively, allow the mortgagee to sell the property at foreclosure sale, and then complain that the price is too low to be fair?

If the mortgagor has no equity in the property (because the outstanding debt on the mortgage loan exceeds the fair market value of the property) there is no incentive for the mortgagor to sell the property on his own. However, if the jurisdiction permits deficiency judgments the mortgagor faces the possibility of a personal judgment for the difference between the foreclosure sale price and the unpaid loan balance. To avoid this, a mortgagor might offer to convey a deed in lieu of foreclosure to the mortgagee, in return for the mortgagee's waiver of any right to seek a deficiency judgment. The mortgagee avoids the time and expense of judicial foreclosure and obtains a clean title; the mortgagor avoids any further liability. Of course, this requires agreement between the parties.

4. *Proving Title or Lien.* In order to foreclose the mortgagee must prove that he holds title or has a valid lien that may be vindicated by a foreclosure sale. This was not usually a problem when mortgages were held by the lender, and that lender would have recorded the mortgage in the real estate records of the jurisdiction in which the property is located, but in the late twentieth century mortgages were increasingly turned into marketable securities. The method for doing so is complicated, but boils down to an assignment by the original mortgagee (often a so-called mortgage originator) of the mortgage loan to a financial institution which then assigns it (along with thousands of other mortgage loans) to a trust that then offers fractional ownership interests in the trust to investors in the global capital markets. When the real estate market crashed in 2007 and 2008, and many mortgagors defaulted on their loans, foreclosures by trustees of these mortgage-backed securities trusts began to occur. One problem that has surfaced is that the chain of assignments is often not recorded and poorly documented. Foreclosures occurred and, in some cases, the mortgagee-purchaser then obtained an assignment from the original mortgagee, but after the foreclosure sale had occurred. When faced with the question of whether a foreclosure sale by an entity that could not prove its ownership of the mortgage at the time of the sale is valid, the Massachusetts Supreme Judicial Court said that the sale was void. Securities prospectuses that asserted the fact of the assignment was insufficient; actual documentary proof of assignment was necessary. See U.S. Bank National Association v. Ibanez, 458 Mass. 637 (2011). While this conclusion appears to be obvious, the fact that holders of securitized mortgages would proceed to foreclosure without clear evidence of ownership of the mortgage is an indication of the cavalier treatment of property interests as they were transformed into securities marketable in the global capital markets.

5. *Unfair or deceptive lending practices.* During the housing bubble of the first six years or so of the twenty-first century a variety of mortgage lending practices became common. Instead of a borrower dealing directly with a lender, who shouldered the risk of the loan after it was made, mortgages began to originate with mortgage brokers, who then forwarded the loan application to a lender who, after review, would decide whether to lend. The broker received from the lender a fee for his services. Once the loan was made, the lender would sell it to a financial institution, who would then assign the mortgage with hundreds of others to a trustee, who would hold

them as the collateral backing a marketable security, sold as fractional interests in the pooled mortgage loan assets, in the global capital markets. Thus, the originators of the mortgage had little incentive to worry about the risk of payment so long as the loan could be sold for securitization. The packagers of securitized mortgage loans had little incentive to worry about this risk so long as they could persuade global investors that the overall risk of the pool of mortgages was negligible.

Added to this was the policy of the United States government to increase home ownership by lower income households. To that end, Congress enacted a variety of laws that were designed to pressure lenders to make such loans and to facilitate the ability of lenders to shed the risk associated with these loans. See, e.g. the Community Reinvestment Act, 12 U.S.C. §§ 2901–2901 (requiring federally regulated lenders to meet the "credit needs" of the communities they serve), and the awkwardly named Federal Housing Enterprises Financial Safety and Soundness Act, 12 U.S.C. §§ 4561–4567 (requiring Fannie Mae and Freddie Mac to purchase such mortgage loans). Fannie Mae—the Federal National Mortgage Association—is a governmentally regulated entity owned by private stockholders that is obliged to purchase mortgage loans for securitization. Freddie Mac—the Federal Home Loan Mortgage Corporation—is a public government entity that also is charged to buy mortgages and securitize them. Thus, due to government policy Fannie Mae and Freddie Mac were ready and willing to purchase many so-called sub-prime loans—loans made to less credit-worthy borrowers who might not ordinarily qualify for a loan, usually at rates higher than those otherwise available (because of the higher risk of default).

In Commonwealth v. Fremont Investment and Loan, 452 Mass. 733 (2008), the Massachusetts Attorney General obtained an injunction preventing foreclosure sales of certain mortgages originating with Fremont. The Attorney General relied on a Massachusetts statute prohibiting "[u]nfair methods of competition and unfair or deceptive acts or practices in the conduct of any trade or commerce...." The Massachusetts Supreme Judicial Court affirmed. Fremont offered adjustable rate loans, in which the initial rate (the so-called "teaser rate") was low but would adjust upward dramatically in two to three years. Fremont made these loans to people whose monthly debt obligations was as high as 50% of their income, and computed that ratio without taking into account the increase in monthly debt payments that would be produced by the adjustable interest rate. Fremont also loaned an amount equal to 100% of the purchase cost of the property (meaning that no down payment was necessary). The Massachusetts court relied on these factors to approve the trial judge's reasoning that Fremont

> should have recognized that [such] loans ... were "doomed to foreclosure" unless the borrower could refinance the loan at or near the end of the introductory rate period, and obtain in the process a new and low introductory rate. The [practice of lending 100% of the purchase price], however, would make it essentially impossible for subprime borrowers to refinance unless housing prices increased, because if housing prices remained steady or declined, a borrower with a mortgage loan having a loan-to-value ratio of one hundred per cent or a substantial prepayment penalty was not likely to have the necessary equity or financial capacity

to obtain a new loan. The [trial] judge stated that, "[g]iven the fluctuations in the housing market and the inherent uncertainties as to how that market will fluctuate over time ... it is unfair for a lender to issue a home mortgage loan secured by the borrower's principal dwelling that the lender reasonably expects will fall into default once the introductory period ends unless the fair market value of the home has increased at the close of the introductory period. To issue a home mortgage loan whose success relies on the hope that the fair market value of the home will increase during the introductory period is as unfair as issuing a home mortgage loan whose success depends on the hope that the borrower's income will increase during that same period." Id. at 739–740.

The Massachusetts court conceded that there was "no evidence ... that Fremont encouraged or condoned misrepresentation of borrowers' incomes ..., or that Fremont deceived borrowers by concealing or misrepresenting the terms of its loans."

In the absence of misrepresentation or deception, why should a lender be required to refrain from making a loan that a borrower desires?

SKENDZEL v. MARSHALL

Supreme Court of Indiana
261 Ind. 226 (1973)

HUNTER, J., delivered the opinion of the court.

... Plaintiff-respondents originally brought suit to obtain possession of certain real estate through the enforcement of a forfeiture clause in a land sale contract. Plaintiff-respondents suffered a negative judgment, from which they appealed. The Court of Appeals reversed, holding that the defendant-petitioners had breached the contract and that the plaintiff-respondents had not waived their right to enforce the forfeiture provisions of the contract.

In December of 1958, Mary Burkowski, as vendor, entered into a land sale contract with Charles P. Marshall and Agnes P. Marshall, as vendees. The contract provided for the sale of certain real estate for the sum of $36,000.00, payable as follows: "$500.00, at the signing, execution and delivery of this contract, the receipt whereof is hereby acknowledged; $500.00 or more on or before the 25th day of December, 1958, and $2500.00 or more on or before the 15th day of January, 1960, and $2500.00 or more on or before the 15th day of January of each and every year thereafter until the balance of the contract has been fully paid, all without interest and all without relief from valuation and appraisement laws and with attorney fees." The contract also contained a fairly standard section which provided for the treatment of prepayments—but which the Court of Appeals found to be of particular importance. It provided as follows:

Should Vendees have made prepayments or paid in advance of the payments herein required, said prepayments, if any, shall at any time thereafter be applied in lieu of further principal payments required as herein stated, to the extent of such prepayments only.

The following is the forfeiture/liquidated damages provision of the land sale contract.

It is further agreed that if any default shall be made in the payment of said purchase price or any of the covenants and/or conditions herein provided, and if any such default shall continue for 30 days, then, after the lapse of said 30 days' period, *all moneys and payments previously paid shall, at the option of the Vendor without notice or demand, be and become forfeited and be taken and retained by the Vendor as liquidated damages* and thereupon this contract shall terminate and be of no further force or effect; provided, however, that nothing herein contained shall be deemed or construed to prevent the Vendor from enforcing specific performance of this agreement in the event of any default on the part of the Vendees in complying, observing and performing any of the conditions, covenants and terms herein contained.... (Emphasis added.)

The vendor, Mary Burkowski, died in 1963. The plaintiffs in this action are the assignees (under the vendor's will) of the decedent's interests in the contract. They received their assignment from the executrix of the estate of the vendor on June 27, 1968. One year after this assignment, several of the assignees filed their complaint in this action alleging that the defendants had defaulted through non-payment.

The schedule of payments made under this contract was shown ... to be as follows:

Date	Amount Paid	Total of Paid Principal
12/1/1958	$500	$500
12/25/1958	500	1,000
3/26/1959	5,000	6,000
4/5/1960	2,500	8,500
5/23/1961	2,500	11,000
4/6/1962	2,500	13,500
1/15/1963	2,500	16,000
6/30/1964	2,500	18,500
2/15/1965	2,500	21,000

No payments have been made since the last one indicated above—$15,000.00 remains to be paid on the original contract price. In response to the plaintiff's attempt to enforce the forfeiture provision, the defendants raised the affirmative defense of waiver. The applicable rule is well established and was stated by the Court of Appeals as follows: "Where a contract for the sale and purchase of land contains provisions similar to those in the contract in the case at bar, *the vendor may waive strict compliance with the provisions of the contract by accepting overdue or irregular payments,* and having so done, equity requires the vendor give specific notice of his intent that he will no longer be indulgent and that he will insist on his right of forfeiture unless the default is paid within a reasonable and specified time." It follows that where the vendor has not waived strict compliance by acceptance of late payments, no notice is required to enforce its provisions. In essence, the Court of Appeals found that there was no waiver because the vendors were obligated to accept prepayment, and, the payments made, although irregular in time and amount, were prepayments on the unpaid balance through and including the payment due on January 15, 1965." The Court concluded that . . . "the vendors waived no rights under the contract, because they were obliged to accept prepayment." [Thus,] the vendors could not have insisted on forfeiture until January 16, 1968.

If forfeiture is enforced against the defendants, they will forfeit outright the sum of $21,000, or well over one-half the original contract price, as liquidated damages, *plus possession.* Forfeitures are generally disfavored by the law. In fact, ". . . [e]quity abhors forfeitures and beyond any question has jurisdiction, which it will exercise in a proper case to grant relief against their enforcement." . . . Pomeroy defines this doctrine of equitable interference to relieve against penalties and forfeitures as follows:

> Wherever a penalty or a forfeiture *is used merely to secure the payment of a debt,* or the performance of some act . . ., equity . . . will relieve against such penalty or forfeiture by awarding compensation instead thereof, proportionate to the damages actually resulting from the non-payment, or non-performance. . . . The test which determines whether equity will or will not interfere in such cases *is the fact whether compensation can or cannot be adequately made for a breach of the obligation which is thus secured. If the penalty is to secure the mere payment of money, compensation can always be made, and a court of equity will relieve the debtor party upon his paying the principal and interest* . . . The granting of relief in such circumstances is based on the ground that it is wholly against conscience to say that because a man has stipulated for a penalty in case of his omission to do a particular act—*the real object of the parties being the performance of the act*—if he omits to do the act, he shall suffer a loss which is *wholly disproportionate to the injury sustained by the other party.*"
> Pomeroy, *Equity Jurisprudence,* § 433, 5th Edition (1941). (Emphasis added.)

[While reasonable] liquidated damage provisions are permitted by the law[,] the issue before this Court is whether a $21,000 forfeiture is a "reasonable" measure of damages. If the damages are unreasonable, i.e., if they are disproportionate to the loss actually suffered, they must be characterized as penal rather than compensatory. Under the facts of this case, a $21,000 forfeiture is clearly excessive.

The authors of American Law Reports have provided an excellent analysis of forfeiture provisions in land contracts:

[T]here is no single rule for the determination of whether a contractual stipulation is one for liquidated damages or a penalty, each case depending largely upon its own facts and equities, and this apothegm is fully applicable to the decisions involving provisions in land contracts for the forfeiture of payments. ... Granting this, however, certain tendencies of decision are clearly discernible in the cases. If, for example, the contract involved calls for deferred payments of the purchase price which are relatively small in amount and extend over a number of years, and if it appears that at the time of the purchaser's breach and the consequent invocation of the forfeiture clause by the vendor a comparatively small proportion of the total price remains unpaid, the courts are prone to find that the forfeiture clause was one for a penalty, at least if, as is usually the case, such a holding will tend to give the purchaser another chance to complete the purchase. On the other hand, if the amount of the payments received by the vendor at the time the purchase was abandoned represents but a small percentage of the total purchase price, and if the purchaser's breach occurred soon after the execution of the agreement (and particularly if the circumstances indicate that the purchase was made for speculative purposes or that the breach represented an effort on the part of the purchaser to escape an unfortunate turn in the market), the courts tend to hold that the forfeiture clause was one for liquidated damages with the result that the purchaser cannot recover back the payments made. 6 A. L. R. 2d 1401 (1949.)

If we apply the specific equitable principle announced above—namely, that the amount paid be considered in relation to the total contract price—we are compelled to conclude that the $21,000 forfeiture as liquidated damages is inconsistent with generally accepted principles of fairness and equity. The vendee has acquired a substantial interest in the property, which, if forfeited, would result in substantial injustice.

Under a typical conditional land contract, the vendor retains legal title until the total contract price is paid by the vendee. Payments are generally made in periodic installments. *Legal* title does not vest in the vendee until the contract terms are satisfied, but equitable title vests in the vendee at the time the contract is consummated. When the parties enter into the contract, all incidents of ownership accrue to the vendee. The vendee assumes the risk of loss and is the recipient of all appreciation in value. The vendee, as equitable owner, is responsible for taxes. The vendee has a sufficient interest in land so that upon sale of that interest, he holds a vendor's lien. This Court has held, consistent with the above notions of equitable ownership, that a land contract, once consummated constitutes a present sale and purchase. The vendor " 'has, in effect, exchanged his property for the unconditional obligation of the vendee, the performance of which is secured by the retention of the legal title.' " Stark v. Kreyling, 207 Ind. 128, 135 (1934). The Court, in effect, views a conditional land contract as a sale with a security interest in the form of legal title reserved by the vendor. Conceptually, therefore, the retention of the title by the vendor is the same as reserving a lien or mortgage. Realistically, vendor-vendee should be viewed as mortgagee-mortgagor. To conceive of the relationship in different terms is to pay homage to form over substance.

The piercing of the transparent distinction between a land contract and a mortgage is not a phenomenon without precedent. In addition to the *Stark* case, there is an abundance of case law from other jurisdictions which lends credence to the position that a land sales contract is in essence a mortgage. . . .

It is also interesting to note that the drafters of the Uniform Commercial Code abandoned the distinction between a conditional sale and a security interest. Section 1–201 of the UCC defines "security interest" as "an interest in personal property or fixtures which secures payment or performance of an obligation . . . retention or reservation of title by a seller of goods notwithstanding shipment or delivery to the buyer is limited in effect to a reservation of 'security interest.' " We can conceive of no rational reason why conditional sales of real estate should be treated any differently.[4]

We believe this position is entirely consistent with the evolving case law in the area. A conditional land contract in effect creates a vendor's lien in the property to secure the unpaid balance owed under the contract. This lien is closely analogous to a mortgage—in fact, the vendor is commonly referred to as an "equitable mortgagee." In view of this characterization of the vendor as a lienholder, it is only logical that such a lien be enforced through foreclosure proceedings. Such a lien "has all the incidents of a mortgage," one of which is the right to foreclose.

There is a multitude of cases upholding the vendor's right to foreclose. The remedy is most often referred to as a foreclosure of an executory contract. . . . A 1924 New York case best describes this remedy:

> Out of the nature of the relationship created by a land contract, where the vendee is in possession, there have developed certain equitable remedies, among which is the right of the vendor in a proper case to sell out the interest of the vendee for the purpose of satisfying his lien under the contract, in case of default, and while it seems a misnomer, for convenience this remedy is spoken of as foreclosure, and the action as one to foreclose the contract. Conners v. Winans (1924), 122 Misc. 824, 204 N. Y. Supp. 142, 145.

See also, Keller v. Lewis (1878), 53 Cal. 113, for another excellent characterization. . . .

The foreclosure of a land sale contract is undeniably comprehended by [Indiana law pertaining to judicial actions to foreclose liens on real estate.]

---

4. In fact, the Commissioners on Uniform State Laws have recognized the transparency of any such distinctions. Section 3–102 of the Uniform Land Transactions Code (working draft of first tentative draft) reads as follows: "This Article applies to security interests created by contract, including mortgage . . . land sales contract . . . and any other lien or title retention contract intended as security."

The vendor's interest clearly constitutes a "lien upon real estate" and should, therefore, be treated as one. The basic foreclosure statute ... provides for a six-month period of redemption, commencing with the filing of the complaint [and] establishes the procedures attendant to the foreclosure sale. ... We believe there to be great wisdom in requiring judicial foreclosure of land contracts pursuant to the mortgage statute. Perhaps the most attractive aspect of judicial foreclosure is the period of redemption, during which time the vendee may redeem his interest, possibly through refinancing.

Forfeiture is closely akin to strict foreclosure—a remedy developed by the English courts which did not contemplate the equity of redemption. American jurisdictions, including Indiana, have, for the most part, rejected strict foreclosure in favor of foreclosure by judicial sale:

> The doctrine of strict foreclosure developed in England at a time when real property had, to a great extent, a fixed value; the vastly different conditions in this country, in this respect, led our courts to introduce modifications to the English rules of foreclosure. Generally, in consonance with equity's treatment of a mortgage as essentially a security for the payment of the debt, foreclosure by judicial sale supplanted strict foreclosure as the more equitable mode of effectuating the mutual rights of the mortgagor and mortgagee; and there is at the present time, in the majority of the American states, no strict foreclosure as developed by the English courts—either at law or in equity—by which a mortgagee can be adjudged absolute owner of the mortgaged property. The remedy of the mortgagee is by an action for the sale of the mortgaged premises and an application of the proceeds of such sale to the mortgage debt, and although usually called an action to foreclose, it is totally different in its character and results from a strict foreclosure. The phrase "foreclosure of a mortgage" has acquired, in general, a different meaning from that which it originally bore under the English practice and the common law imported here from England. In this country, the modern meaning of the term "foreclosure" denotes an equitable proceeding for the enforcement of a lien against property in satisfaction of a debt. 55 Am. Jur. 2d, *Mortgages,* § 549 (1971).

Guided by the above principles, we are compelled to conclude that judicial foreclosure of a land sale contract is in consonance with the notions of equity developed in American jurisprudence. A forfeiture—like a strict foreclosure at common law—is often offensive to our concepts of justice and inimical to the principles of equity. This is not to suggest that a forfeiture is an inappropriate remedy for the breach of *all* land contracts. In the case of an abandoning, absconding vendee, forfeiture is a logical and equitable remedy. Forfeiture would also be appropriate where the vendee has paid a minimal amount on the contract at the time of default and seeks to retain possession while the vendor is paying taxes, insurance, and other upkeep in order to preserve the premises. Of course, in this latter situation, the vendee will have acquired very little, if any, equity in the property. However, a court of equity must always approach forfeitures with great caution, being forever aware of the possibility of inequitable dispossession of property and exorbitant monetary loss. We are persuaded that forfeiture may only be appropriate under circumstances in which it is found to be consonant with notions of fairness and justice under the law....

Turning our attention to the case at hand, ... the vendor-assignees were ... asking for strict application of the contract terms at law which we believe would have led to unconscionable results requiring the intervention of equity. ... [T]he trial court correctly refused the remedy sought by the vendor-assignees, but in so refusing it denied all remedial relief to the plaintiffs. ... [T]his Court has the undeniable authority to remand with guidelines which will give substantial relief to plaintiffs under their secured interests and will prevent the sacrifice of the vendees' equitable lien in the property.

[The] cause is reversed and remanded with instructions to enter a judgment of foreclosure on the vendors' lien.... Said judgment shall include an order for the payment of the unpaid principal balance due on said contract, together with interest at 8% per annum from the date of judgment. The order may also embrace any and all other proper and equitable relief that the court deems to be just, including the discretion to issue a stay of the judicial sale of the property, [and] shall be consistent with the principles and holdings developed within this opinion....

PRENTICE, J., concurring.

I have some concern that our opinion herein might be viewed by some as indicating an attitude of indifference towards the rights of contract vendors. Such a view would not be a true reflection. Because the installment sales contract, with forfeiture provisions, is a widely employed and generally accepted method of commerce in real estate in this state, it is appropriate that a vendee seeking to avoid the forfeiture, to which he agreed, be required to make a clear showing of the inequity of enforcement. In any given transaction anything short of enforcing the forfeiture provision may be a denial of equity to the vendor. It has been set forth in the majority opinion that if the vendee has little or no real equity in the premises, the court should have no hesitancy in declaring a forfeiture. It follows that if the vendee has indicated his willingness to forego his equity, if any, whether by mere abandonment of the premises, by release or deed or by a failure to make a timely assertion of his claim, he should be barred from thereafter claiming an equity.

If the court finds that forfeiture, although provided for by the terms of the contract, would be unjust, it should nevertheless grant the vendor the maximum relief consistent with equity against a defaulting vendee. In so doing, it should consider that, had the parties known that the forfeiture provision would not be enforceable, other provisions for the protection of the vendor doubtlessly would have been incorporated into the agreement. Generally, this would require that the transaction be treated as a note and mortgage with such provisions as are generally included in such documents customarily employed in the community by prudent investors. Terms customarily included in such notes and mortgages but frequently omitted from contracts include provisions for increased interest during periods of default, provision for the acceleration of the due date of the entire unpaid principal and interest upon a default continuing beyond a reasonable grace period, provisions for attorneys' fees and other expenses incidental to foreclosure, for the waiver of relief from valuation and appraisement laws and for receivers.

NOTES AND QUESTIONS

1. The theory of forfeiture. Forfeiture of the defaulting installment buyer's payments might be founded on one of two alternative theories: rescission of the contract, or termination of the contract by the buyer's breach.

Rescission. If rescission is the theory, the buyer and seller should each be restored to their position *ex ante.* The seller should recover possession of the property and should receive a reasonable amount to compensate him for his loss of possession during the time the contract was in force. That amount is, in essence, the fair rental value of the property. The buyer should get his money back (except for the portion of his payments that represent fair rental) and the value of any improvements he may have made to the property. In theory, because the object of rescission is to put the parties in their positions before entering into the contract, the seller should also receive an amount equal to any decline in market value of the property between the contract and rescission dates. The buyer should receive credit against his rental obligation for the value of any increase in value between those dates.

If the rescission theory were to be applied to the facts of *Skendzel,* what should be the result?

Termination. The termination approach holds that the buyer's breach of the contract excuses any further performance by the seller. The contract has terminated by the buyer's breach. Thus, the seller is entitled to damages caused by the buyer's breach. The seller's expectation is receipt of the full contract price, but after breach he is left with the property and the cumulative total of the buyer's payments. If the sum of those values equals the purchase price, forfeiture is called for. If the sum is less than the purchase price, the buyer should be obliged to pay the difference. If the sum is greater than the purchase price, the buyer should receive from the seller the difference.

If the termination theory were to be applied to the facts of *Skendzel,* what should be the result? Assume that the fair market value of the property at the time of breach was equal to the original contract price.

Given these two theories of determining the amount that might be subject to forfeiture, why did the Indiana court treat this contract as a mortgage?

2. When is an installment contract a mortgage, and when it is a contract? The Indiana court noted that forfeiture is appropriate when the buyer has little or no equity. Thus, the Indiana approach has sometimes been characterized as "convertibility"—the installment contract is enforceable according to its terms (including forfeiture of payments) until the moment is reached when the buyer's equity is large enough to convert the contract into the functional equivalent of a mortgage. When is that moment reached? Would it be better to treat such contracts as mortgages from the moment of inception, or to take the logic of rescission or termination seriously and deal with each contract by applying those principles rigorously?

The Kentucky Supreme Court, in Sebastian v. Floyd, 585 S.W.2d 381 (Ky. 1979), held that installment sale contracts are to be treated as mortgages from the moment of inception. Though the Indiana approach is convertibility, in practice installment sale contracts become mortgages in almost every circumstance. Foreclosure is required even when the buyer's payments are almost entirely interest, or when the buyer's equity results entirely from an increase in the property value. See Looney v. Farmers Home Administration, 794 F.2d 310 (7th Cir. 1986). Forfeiture is limited to the situation where the buyer either seeks to continue in possession or the seller's security is impaired, even though the buyer's equity is minimal. See Morris v. Weigle, 270 Ind. 121 (1978). Indiana courts do not permit the contracting parties to waive these requirements. Parker v. Camp, 656 N.E.2d 882 (Ind. App. 1995). The court held unenforceable a contractual provision defining "substantial equity" to be payment of at least 75% of the purchase price, where the buyer in default had paid 43% of the total purchase price.

Some states, such as Illinois, permit forfeiture in a great many circumstances. An Illinois statute, 735 ILCS 5/9–101 through 5/9–321, applies to installment sales contracts entered into after 1987 and requires foreclosure only where the contract calls for payments to be made for longer than five years and the buyer has paid 80% or more of the purchase price. Contract principles otherwise apply.

CHAPTER EIGHT

ASSURANCE OF GOOD TITLE

■ ■ ■

This chapter addresses the system for assuring that the interests that people acquire in land—whether title or mortgage liens—are good against the rest of the world. The problem arises because people are not always noble or honest. A person might, for example, convey the same property to two different people, each of whom is ignorant of the other claimant to title. Or an owner might borrow money from two different people, giving a mortgage on his home to each of them.

Example and Problem 8–1: O, owner of Blackacre, conveys title to Blackacre to A for $100,000. Then O conveys Blackacre to B for $100,000. B has no knowledge of the prior transfer to A. O takes the $200,000, loses it all in a poker game, and disappears. As between the two innocent purchasers, A and B, who should bear the loss?

Example and Problem 8–2: X, owner of Whiteacre, borrows $100,000 from Y, giving Y a mortgage of Whiteacre. Then X borrows $50,000 from Z, giving a mortgage of Whiteacre to Z. Later, X defaults on each loan and Y and Z each seek to foreclose. Whiteacre's fair market value is $100,000, and the jurisdiction forbids deficiency judgments. How should the $100,000 value of Whiteacre be apportioned between Y and Z?

The common law resolved these problems by application of the "first in time" rule. Thus, A prevails in Example 8–1 and Y receives the entire $100,000 proceeds in Example 8–2. The justification for the first-in-time rule was that once an owner had conveyed his interest he had nothing that he could convey to the second transferee. But the common law has been supplanted by various other methods of resolving these conflicts. The principal method is the recording system, in which interests in real estate are recorded in a government registry for the county in which the real estate is located. By itself, recording is ineffective; it is the addition of recording acts that specify the consequences of recording, or failing to record, and that seek to establish a priority between conflicting interests, that makes the recording system effective. Under the recording system the answers to Examples 8–1 and 8–2 will depend on whether the interests were recorded; if so, the order in which recording took place, and whether the subsequent acquirer (*B*, in Example 8–1 and *Z*, in Example 8–2) had notice of the prior interest. As it turns out, there is no singular answer. Because there are three distinct types of recording acts, there could be different answers.

The recording system and recording acts do not eliminate all problems, however, as you will learn in this chapter. One way for a buyer or lender to obtain additional protection is to purchase title insurance, in which an insurer examines the record state of title and, for a premium, insures the lender or buyer that they have good title, subject to whatever exceptions are contained in the insurance policy. Of course, title insurance is only as good as the fiscal solvency of the insurer and, even then, useless if a title defect turns out to be one of the excepted possibilities. Nevertheless, title insurance is widely used in the United States. An alternative to title insurance is to obtain a lawyer's opinion letter stating that title is vested in the buyer or lender, again subject to such exceptions or limitations that the lawyer may include. As with title insurance, this form of title assurance is only as deep as the lawyer's assets (or those of his malpractice insurer) and as wide as the opinion's exceptions permit.

An alternative to recording is the system of registered title, or Torrens registration, named after its inventor. Under this system titles are registered in a government office and that registration is the conclusive title. While title registration would seem to offer the promise of eliminating disputes entirely, it does have some defects, such as ministerial errors in the registration process. This system is not widely used in the United States.

Section A of this chapter discusses the recording system and recording acts. Section B deals with title insurance. Section C is a brief discussion of title registration.

A. ESTABLISHING PRIORITY OF TITLE: RECORDING ACTS AND THE CHAIN OF TITLE

1. INTRODUCTION

The recording system is a public record of real estate transactions maintained by a public official, usually called the Recorder, in each county. While nobody is obligated to record a transaction, the recording act of the jurisdiction will establish grave consequences to a failure to record should there be rival claimants to title. The point of the recording acts is to protect bona fide purchasers for value and lien creditors who record their interests from the claims of the holder of a prior unrecorded interest. A person who acquires an interest in real property is presumed to know the contents of the recorded instruments in the chain of title—the sequence of conveyances of interests in a particular parcel.

Recording acts do not affect the validity of deeds; they are designed to sort out rival claims. Thus, if each of two rival claimants have failed to record their deeds from O, the record owner of real estate, the deeds are valid but the recording acts are of no help. In such an instance the common law principle of first-in-time applies, and the claimant who first received a deed from O prevails. In addition to facilitating resolution of the priority of rival claims, the recording system provides to the public a common place for determining who owns land in the jurisdiction. Anyone may consult these records. The recording system also provides secure evidence of the transaction. A Recorder copies and thus records the original deed or mortgage, and then returns the original to the person who submitted it for recording. In most jurisdictions the recorded copy is admissible in evidence even in the absence of the original document. To be eligible for recording, the instrument must affect an interest in land and must bear a notarial acknowledgment of the signature of the maker. The former requirement is common sense; the latter is designed to ensure that the public records are reliable.

The recording system is searchable only because the recording officer maintains an index of the instruments recorded. There are two types of indexes. The most common type is the grantor-grantee index. Less common is the tract index.

The tract index lists all instruments recorded that pertain to an identifiable tract of land. The reason this type of index is not universally available is that for many years parcels were described by metes and bounds, rather than by some identifying tract or parcel identification number. Only in relatively recent years have parcels been identified by a recorded subdivision map or by a parcel identification number that the taxing authorities use for property tax purposes. Because not every piece of realty has a parcel identification number or can be identified in some other way, tract indexes are not widespread. Where such an index is available, though, it becomes an easy matter to locate all the instruments that bear upon the state of title of the parcel in question. Nebraska, North Dakota, Oklahoma, South Dakota, Utah, and Wyoming have tract indexes in all counties. Other states either do not have them or they exist on a county-by-county basis. The Uniform Simplification of Land Transfers Act, § 6–207, requires creation of a tract index, and also obliges anyone who presents an instrument for recording to provide "information fixing the location sufficiently to enable the recording officer to determine where in the geographic index the document is to be recorded." Id. at § 2–302(a)(4).

The most common index is the grantor-grantee index. This actually consists of two indexes—a grantor index and a grantee index. The grantor index is an alphabetical and chronological listing by the surname of the grantor of any instrument. The recorder will usually consolidate those listings into volumes that encompass a particular time period. For example, there may be one volume for grants made prior to 1900, separate volumes for grants for each decade thereafter, yearly volumes for the current decade, monthly volumes for the current year, and a daily volume for the current month. The method of consolidation—whether by decade, quarter-century, year, or some other period—is in the discretion of the recorder. The grantee index is indexed alphabetically by surname.

Example 8–3: On October 1, 1941 Jones executes a deed to Smith, which is recorded that day. In the grantor index for the decade of the 1940s this deed will be listed, perhaps under column headings of "Date," "Grantor," "Grantee," "Book and Page," and "Description." Thus the Jones–Smith entry would read "10–1–41; Jones; Smith; Bk 221, Pg 114; Deed." The date is the date of recording, the grantor and grantee are obvious, the Book and Page numbers refer to the exact spot in the public records where a copy of the instrument may be located, and the description is usually a capsule summary of the type of instrument. In this example a searcher would not know from the index itself what piece of property Jones has deeded to Smith. To learn whether the deed is to 123 Elm Street or 1211 Tenth Avenue, it is necessary to read the deed itself. The grantee index is similar—just the order of grantee and grantor are reversed. In the grantee index the entry would read "10–1–41; Smith; Jones; Bk 221, Pg 114; Deed."

A search of these public records is indispensable to determine the state of title of any parcel. Thus, if you were asked in 2012 by William Client to determine the state of title of 123 Elm Street, a property that Client wishes to purchase from Bernard Evans, you must search the chain of title. Here is a description of that search process. Starting from today, you would consult the grantee index under Evans, going backward in time until you locate a deed to Evans from Marjorie Black, recorded in 1991. You would turn to the relevant Book and Page and find that deed. Assuming it was to 123 Elm Street, you would then consult the grantee index back in time from 1991 until you find a deed to Black from Steven Harper recorded in 1967. After determining that the referenced deed is to 123 Elm Street you return to the grantee index and search backward from 1967 until you find a deed to Harper from Harold Smith recorded in 1955. Again, after determining that the deed is to 123 Elm Street, you go back to the grantee index and search from 1955 backward until you find a deed to Smith from Sally Jones recorded October 1, 1941. If this deed is also to 123 Elm Street you repeat the search until you find an adequate *root of title*. As you will learn, many states have laws that bar claims made by people founding their claim on some transaction older than a specified period. These acts permit the title searcher to stop at the point he has located a source, or root, of the title chain that is older than the statutory period. Let's assume that the period in this jurisdiction is 80 years. In 2012, your root of title must be a source prior to 1932. Thus, you search the grantee index back from 1941 until you find a deed to 123 Elm Street from Jack Spratt to Sally Jones, recorded and dated in 1930. Now you must turn to the grantor index, starting with the date of the 1930 Spratt/Jones deed, and search forward in time under Jones to determine if Jones made any other conveyances (e.g., mortgages, easements, deeds of an interest less than fee simple absolute) to 123 Elm Street. Once you find the 1941 deed to Smith you then search forward under Smith for the same purpose until you find the 1955 Smith/Harper deed. Suppose in doing so you discover that the Smith to Harper deed was executed on July 1, 1951 but was not recorded until 1955. Now you have to go back to July 1, 1951 and search forward under Harper to see if Harper made any conveyances between 1951 and 1955 as well as from 1955 to 1967, when Harper conveyed to Black. The reason is simple: Harper acquired title in 1951 and he might have transferred all or a portion of his title before he got around to recording his deed from Smith.

Once you have established a chain of title you can determine what the current owner actually owns. Let's assume that in 1953 Harper conveyed an easement for parking to Edwards, the owner of the neighboring property, "and his heirs and assigns." Now you know that Evans, the current owner, owns fee simple absolute subject to the easement. Let's also assume that Black granted a mortgage to MegaBank in 1991 and that your search of the grantor index forward from 1991 under MegaBank has not revealed any release of that mortgage. Now you know that Evans must have taken title subject to the mortgage or assumed the obligation. Either way, the mortgage to MegaBank is an outstanding lien against Evans's title.

This is a simplified version of the task that a title searcher would conduct. In addition to the search of the records in the recorder's office, you would also consult other sources of liens or transfers, which might include judgments in the probate court (accomplishing a transfer by will or intestacy), mechanic's liens or tax liens that might be documented outside of the real estate records, or building and zoning code records that might reveal violations of those provisions.

With the advent of powerful computer technology, recorders have increasingly turned to computers to create the indexes. This does not mean that old written records have been scanned into the computer systems, but does mean that records from the late twentieth century forward are likely to be readily available in a computer retrieval system. In jurisdictions that have scanned the recorded instruments themselves into the computer system, or stored them in some computer readable format, the searcher's task is made even simpler by virtue of the ability to obtain an image of the recorded instrument with a few keystrokes and clicks.

2. THE TYPES OF RECORDING ACTS

There are three common types of recording acts: race, notice, and race-notice.

Race Statute. A race statute gives priority to a subsequent acquirer of an interest in real property if he records that interest before a prior acquirer records his interest. Put another way, a prior interest is not enforceable against a subsequent purchaser for value unless it is recorded before the subsequent purchaser records his interest. N.C. Gen. Stat. § 47–18 is an example:

No conveyance of land, or contract to convey, or option to convey, or lease of land for more than three years shall be valid to pass any property interest as against lien creditors or purchasers for a valuable consideration from the donor, bargainor or lessor but from the time of registration thereof in the county where the land lies, or if the land is located in more than one county, then in each county where any portion of the land lies to be effective as to the land in that county.

Reduced to its essentials it may be restated as follows: No conveyance of an interest in real property shall be valid against a purchaser for valuable consideration until it is recorded in the public records of the county in which the property is located. Louisiana Civil Code, Art. 3338, is a different version of a race statute. It may be paraphrased as follows: No conveyance of an interest in real property shall be valid against "a third person unless the instrument is registered by recording it in the appropriate mortgage or conveyance records. . . ." Delaware's statute, 25 Del. Code § 153, provides: "A deed concerning lands or tenements shall have priority from the time that it is recorded in the proper office without respect to the time that it was signed, sealed and delivered." Note that the Louisiana version is not limited to bona fide purchasers for value, but prefers any third person (whether or not they have paid value) to the holder of the unrecorded prior interest. The Delaware version probably has the same effect, because it contains no limitation to subsequent acquirers for value.

Example and Problem 8–4: On January 1, 2012, *O*, owner of Blackacre in fee simple absolute, conveys Blackacre to *A* for valuable consideration. On February 1, 2012, *O* conveys Blackacre to *B* for valuable consideration. On February 2, 2012 *B* records his deed to Blackacre. On February 15, 2012 *A* records his deed to Blackacre. Who prevails if *A* sues *B* to quiet title in *A*? Would (should) it make any difference to the outcome if on February 1, 2012 *B* had actual knowledge of the *O* to *A* deed?

Only three states, Delaware, Louisiana and North Carolina, have pure race statutes. A handful of states have race statutes that apply only to mortgages or other liens.

Notice Statutes. Under a notice statute, a subsequent purchaser for value has priority over an unrecorded prior interest if the subsequent purchaser lacks notice of the prior interest. Phrased differently, an unrecorded prior interest is not enforceable against a subsequent purchaser for value who has no notice of the prior interest. A typical notice statute might read as follows: No conveyance of an interest in real property is valid against a subsequent purchaser for valuable consideration who lacks notice of the prior interest, unless the prior interest is recorded. See Ala. Code § 35–4–90; Ariz. Rev. Stat. § 33–412.

Example and Problem 8–5: On June 1, 2012, *O*, owner of Blackacre in fee simple absolute, conveys Blackacre to *A* for valuable consideration. *A* does not record the deed. On July 1, 2012, *O* conveys Blackacre to *B* for valuable consideration. *B* lacks actual notice of the prior *O* to *A* deed to Blackacre. On August 1, 2012 *A* records his deed to Blackacre. On August 15, 2012 *B* records his deed to Blackacre. Who prevails if *A* sues *B* to quiet title in *A*? What result if neither deed was recorded? What result if *A* recorded his deed on June 30, 2012?

About half the states have adopted notice statutes.

Race–Notice Statutes. Under a race-notice statute priority goes to a subsequent purchaser for value who acquires his interest without notice of the prior interest, but only if the subsequent purchaser records his interest before the holder of the prior interest records his interest. In other words, a prior interest is not enforceable against a subsequent purchaser for value who (i) lacks notice of the prior interest and (ii) records his interest first. A typical race-notice statute might read as follows: No conveyance of an interest in real property is valid against any subsequent purchaser or mortgagee who acquires the interest in good faith, for a valuable consideration, and first records the interest. See, e.g., N.Y. Real Prop. Law § 291; Wash. Rev. Code § 65.08.070.

Example and Problem 8–6: On October 1, 2012, *O*, owner of Blackacre in fee simple absolute, conveys Blackacre to *A* for valuable consideration. *A* does not record the deed. On November 1, 2012, *O* conveys Blackacre to *B* for valuable consideration. *B* lacks notice of the prior *O* to *A* deed to Blackacre. On November 15, 2012 *A* records his deed to Blackacre. On December 1, 2012 *B* records his deed to Blackacre. Who prevails if *A* sues *B* to quiet title in *A*? What result if neither deed was recorded? What result if *A* recorded his deed on October 15, 2012?

About half the states have adopted race-notice statutes.

The Shelter Rule. An important corollary to the recording acts is the shelter rule, which holds that once a bona fide purchaser has perfected title under the recording act, that status is passed on to his immediate and remote transferees, even though they may not be independently entitled to the protection of the recording act. See, e.g., Hendricks v. Lake, 12 Wn. App. 15 (1974). The rationale for the shelter rule is that it is necessary to deliver to the bona fide purchaser the value of his purchase. Without the rule, the subsequent market for the purchaser's interest could evaporate entirely.

Example and Problem 8–7: O, record owner of Blackacre, conveys title to *A*, who pays good value. *A* fails to record. Then *O* conveys to *B*, who pays value and lacks notice of the prior transfer. *A* then records his deed, followed by *B*'s recording of his deed. *B* then conveys to *C*, who pays value and has constructive notice from the record of *A*'s interest. In a notice jurisdiction, *C* prevails over *A*, despite his knowledge of the *O* to *A* deed, because *B* prevails over *A* (due to his lack of notice at the time he acquired the interest for value) and *C* is deemed by the shelter rule to stand in *B*'s shoes and succeed to *B*'s title. But what should be the result in a race jurisdiction? In a race-notice jurisdiction?

The shelter rule does not apply if the grantor later acquires title from a subsequent bona fide purchaser for value. The rationale is that the shelter rule would otherwise be converted into an instrument of fraud or inequity. See, e.g, Chergosky v. Crosstown Bell, Inc., 463 N.W.2d 522 (Minn. 1990); Clark v. McNeal, 114 N.Y. 287 (1889).

> *Example 8–8:* In a notice jurisdiction *O* conveys Blackacre to *A*, who fails to record. *O* conveys to *B*, who knows of the unrecorded *O* to *A* deed. *B* records. Brooding over his defective title, *B* conveys to *C*, who pays value and is ignorant of the *O* to *A* deed, under a deed that gives *B* the option to repurchase Blackacre. *C* records. Then *B* exercises the option and *C* conveys Blackacre to *B*. Then *B* sues *A* to quiet title in *B*. *A* prevails. *A*'s title was better than *B*'s title because *B* had notice of the *O* to *A* deed. Although *C* was a bona fide purchaser for value without notice *B* cannot cleanse his defective title by laundering title through *C*. *A* still has better title than *B*.

NOTE AND PROBLEMS

1. Problem. O, owner of Blackacre in fee simple absolute, conveys title to *A*, who fails to record. Then *O* conveys title to Blackacre to *B*, who pays value for Blackacre, lacks notice of the prior deed, and fails to record the deed. *A* then records and, after recording, conveys title to *C*, who pays value but knows of the *O* to *B* transfer. Then *B* records his deed. Then *C* records.

Who prevails in a race jurisdiction? In a notice jurisdiction? In a race-notice jurisdiction? What if *C* was ignorant of the *O* to *B* transfer?

2. Problem. O owns Blackacre, a commercial office building worth $450,000, in fee simple absolute. *O* borrows $75,000 from *A* and gives *A* a mortgage to Blackacre to secure payment of the loan. *A* fails to record the mortgage. *O* then borrows $150,000 from *B*, who is aware of the prior mortgage to *A*, and executes a mortgage of Blackacre in favor of *B*, who records the mortgage. *O* then borrows $50,000 from *C* and gives *C* a mortgage to Blackacre. *C* has no notice of *A*'s mortgage. *C* records its mortgage. A severe economic recession ensues. Tenants in Blackacre default or leave at the end of their lease terms. As a result, *O* cannot make his mortgage payments and he defaults. At the foreclosure sale, Blackacre fetches $225,000. How much of this $225,000 should each of *A*, *B*, and *C* receive? The jurisdiction has enacted a notice statute. Would it make any difference if it was a race-notice statute?

In analyzing this problem, start with the proposition that we ought to give each party his reasonable expectations, insofar as we can. What other methods might be used to deal with allocation of these funds?

3. Problem. Assume the same facts as in Problem 2, except that Blackacre is initially worth $200,000, each of *A*, *B*, and *C* have loaned *O* $25,000, and that the funds available for distribution after foreclosure are only $25,000. How should they be distributed?

4. Problem. Assume the same facts as in Problem 3, except that the funds available for distribution after foreclosure are $40,000. How should they be distributed?

5. Liability for failure to record. Buyers frequently rely upon other people—lawyers or escrow agents—to record their deed. Mortgagees, which are usually institutions, may rely on others or do the job themselves. But if third parties are relying on a lawyer or other agent to record for them, they are likely to have a claim for the negligence of the agent in failing to record. Privity of contract is not usually a limit on the exposure of the agent. Courts increasingly are apt to find that the agent has a duty of care to any person who might be reasonably foreseen to be injured by the actor's negligence. See, e.g., Petrillo v. Bachenberg, 139 N.J. 472 (1995); Prudential Insurance Co. of America v. Dewey, Ballantine, Bushby, Palmer & Wood, 80 N.Y.2d 377 (1992); Biakanja v. Irving, 49 Cal.2d 647 (1958).

3. WHAT CONSTITUTES NOTICE?

Notice may come in several forms. The most obvious is actual knowledge, but notice may be imputed and, under some circumstances, an obligation is imposed to ask questions or take other actions that might lead to the discovery of facts.

a. Actual Notice

Actual knowledge sounds simple, but when it is key to priority under a notice or race-notice statute, it can prove to be inefficient because it may necessitate investigation into matters that are not of record and which may be difficult to uncover.

Example 8–9: O, owner of Blackacre, conveys to A, who fails to record. Then O conveys to B, who has no knowledge of the unrecorded O to A deed. After this transaction A records; then B records. Later, B desires to sell Blackacre to C, but C examines the record and finds the O to A deed on record. In order to be certain that B can deliver a perfected title to Blackacre C or his agents must investigate matters off the record, such as B's files, e-mail records, newspaper notices (if any) concerning the O to A transfer, signs (if any) on Blackacre itself, and any other matter that might bear on what B knew or reasonably should have known at the time he acquired his deed from O. Recall that if B actually lacked notice C will inherit B's perfected title through the shelter rule.

b. Record Notice

Because the point of a public record is to give notice to the world of the interests recorded therein, any subsequent purchaser is deemed to have notice of that which is in the record. This is, of course, the concept of constructive notice—whether or not the subsequent purchaser actually knows of the prior interest, he is deemed to have notice of it if it is in the record. But this general statement needs qualification. What if the instrument of record was never entitled to be recorded in the first place? What if the name of the grantor or grantee is misspelled? What if the description of the property in the deed is so encompassing that it covers a large number of separate parcels?

MESSERSMITH v. SMITH

Supreme Court of North Dakota
60 N.W.2d 276 (N.D. 1953)

MORRIS, C. J., delivered the opinion of the Court.

This is [an] action to quiet title to three sections of land in Golden Valley County. The records in the office of the register of deeds of that county disclose the following pertinent facts concerning the title: For some time prior to May 7, 1946, the record title owners of this property were Caroline Messersmith and Frederick Messersmith. On that date, Caroline Messersmith executed and delivered to Frederick Messersmith a quit claim deed to the property which was not recorded until July 9, 1951. Between the date of that deed and the time of its recording the following occurred: On April 23, 1951, Caroline Messersmith, as lessor, executed a lease to Herbert B. Smith, Jr., lessee, which was recorded May 14, 1951. On May 7, 1951, Caroline Messersmith, a single woman, conveyed to Herbert B. Smith, Jr., by mineral deed containing a warranty of title, an undivided one-half interest in and to all oil, gas and other minerals in and under or that may be produced upon the land involved in this case. This deed was recorded May 26, 1951. On May 9, 1951, Herbert B. Smith, Jr., executed a mineral deed conveying to E. B. Seale an undivided one-half interest in all of the oil, gas and other minerals in and under or that may be produced upon the land. This deed was also recorded in the office of the Register of Deeds of Golden Valley County, on May 26, 1951. Seale answered plaintiff's complaint by setting up his deed and claiming a one-half interest in the minerals as a purchaser without notice, actual or constructive, of plaintiff's claim. To this answer the plaintiff [Frederick Messersmith] replied by way of a general denial and further alleged that the mineral deed by which Seale claims title is void; that it was never acknowledged, not entitled to record and was obtained by fraud, deceit and misrepresentation. The defendant Herbert B. Smith, Jr., defaulted.

For some time prior to the transactions herein noted, Caroline Messersmith and her nephew, Frederick S. Messersmith, were each the owner of an undivided one-half interest in this land, having acquired it by inheritance. The land was unimproved except for being fenced. It was never occupied as a homestead. Section 1 was leased to one tenant and Sections 3 and 11 to another. They used the land for grazing. One party had been a tenant for a number of years, paying $150.00 a year. The amount paid by the other tenant is not disclosed. The plaintiff lived in Chicago. Caroline Messersmith lived alone in the City of Dickinson where she had resided for many years. She looked after the renting of the land, both before and after she conveyed her interest therein to her nephew. She never told her tenants about the conveyance.

On April 23, 1951, the defendant Smith, accompanied by one King and his prospective wife, went to the Messersmith home and negotiated an oil and gas lease with Miss Messersmith covering the three sections of land involved herein. According to Miss Messersmith, all that was discussed that day concerned royalties. According to the testimony of Mr. Smith and Mr. King, the matter of the mineral deed was discussed. Two or three days later, Smith and King returned. Again the testimony varies as to the subject of conversation. Miss Messersmith said it was about royalties. Smith and King say it was about a mineral deed for the purchase of her mineral rights. No agreement was reached during this conversation. On May 7, 1951, Smith returned alone and again talked with Miss Messersmith. As a result of this visit, Miss Messersmith executed a mineral deed for an undivided one-half interest in the oil, gas and minerals under the three sections of land. Smith says this deed was acknowledged before a notary public at her house. She says no notary public ever appeared there. She also says that Smith never told her she was signing a mineral deed and that she understood she was signing a "royalty transfer." The consideration paid for this deed was $1400.00, which is still retained by Miss Messersmith. After leaving the house Smith discovered a slight error in the deed. The term "his heirs" was used for the term "her heirs." He returned to the home of Miss Messersmith the same day, explained the error to her, tore up the first deed, and prepared another in the same form, except that the error was corrected. According to Smith's testimony, he took the second deed to the same notary public to whom Miss Messersmith had acknowledged the execution of the first deed and the notary called Miss Messersmith for her acknowledgment over the telephone and then placed on the deed the usual notarial acknowledgment, including the notary's signature and seal. The notary, who took many acknowledgments about that time, has no independent recollection of either of these acknowledgments. It is the second deed that was recorded on May 26, 1951, and upon which the defendant, E. B. Seale, relied when he purchased from the defendant, Herbert B. Smith, Jr., the undivided one-half interest in the minerals under the land in question.

The trial court reached the conclusion that the transaction resulting in the mineral deeds to Smith was not fraudulent and he so found. While Miss Messersmith was an elderly woman, 77 years of age, she appears to have been in full possession of her faculties and a person of considerable business experience. She owned a number of other farms upon which she had executed oil and gas leases previous to the time she made the lease of this land to Smith. Although Miss Messersmith is very positive that she did not know she signed a mineral deed, she is very vague as to what she thought she was signing. She knew she had already signed an oil and gas lease to all of the land in favor of Smith, so she does not contend that she thought she was signing another lease. On cross examination she was asked: "Q[:] Well, will you tell the Court what you thought you were signing? A[:] Thought that I was selling a certain percentage of it on royalty. That's what I thought."

A day or two after signing the deed she wrote to the plaintiff, her nephew, and he wrote a letter back by air mall. She did not send him a copy of the mineral deed. In fact, there is nothing in the record that indicates a copy was ever made. She testifies that Smith tore up the first deed in her presence and put the pieces in his pocket. He took the second deed with him. Without consultation with anyone, except the correspondence with her nephew, she wrote the defendant Smith on May 26, 1951, as follows:

My dear Mr. Smith.

Am sorry to say that, I didn't have the right to sell that mineral right to you. I should have consulted my nephew in any deals like this. He is 1/2 owner in this land and should have been consulted. He is very much put out about it and when I stop to give it a serious thought I realize that he should have had a voice in this deal and of course signed the deed with me. I would like to buy it back. The money $1400.00 is here and what ever expense connected with it, shall be sent you.

Don't think that there are any other deals on. There are not. I am anxious to get this fixed right, so there will be peace in my home. My nephew, 40 years old, feels that he ought to have some voice in this business, and now realizing this I take all blame. As far as the leasing is concerned that is O.K. with him. But when it comes to giving an oil gas & mineral deed without his consent that is different. You will understand.

Let me hear from you immediately. I realize that he should have been consulted and that he should have signed with me, if he had favored it.

This letter indicates that she fully understood that she signed a mineral deed. She complains of no fraud in its procurement. . . .

The determination that the mineral deed from Caroline Messersmith to Herbert B. Smith, Jr., was not fraudulently obtained by the grantee does not mean that the defendant, who in turn received a deed from Smith, is entitled to prevail as against the plaintiff in this action. At the time Miss Messersmith executed the mineral deed she owned no interest in the land, having previously conveyed her interest therein to the plaintiff. Smith in turn had no actual interest to convey to the defendant Seale. If Seale can assert title to any interest in the property in question, he must do so because the plaintiff's deed was not recorded until July 9, 1951, while the deed from Caroline Messersmith to Smith and the deed from Smith to the defendant Seale were recorded May 26, 1951, thus giving him a record title prior in time to that of the plaintiff.

Section 47–1907 NDRC 1943 contains this provision: "An instrument entitled to be recorded must be recorded by the register of deeds of the county in which the real property affected thereby is situated."

Section 47–1908 NDRC 1943 provides: "An instrument is deemed to be recorded when, being duly acknowledged or proved and certified, it is deposited in the register's office with the proper officer for record."

The defendant Seale asserts that priority of record gives him a title superior to that of the plaintiff by virtue of the following statutory provision, Section 47–1941 NDRC 1943:

Every conveyance of real estate not recorded as provided in section 47–1907 shall be void as against any subsequent purchaser in good faith, and for a valuable consideration, of the same real estate, or any part or portion thereof, whose conveyance, whether in the form of a warranty deed, or deed of bargain and sale, or deed of quitclaim and release, of the form in common use or otherwise, first is recorded, or as against an attachment levied thereon or any judgment lawfully obtained, at the suit of any party, against the person in whose name the title to such land appears of record, prior to the recording of such conveyance. The fact that such first recorded conveyance of such subsequent purchaser for a valuable consideration is in the form, or contains the terms, of a deed of quitclaim and release aforesaid, shall not affect the question of good faith of the subsequent purchaser, or be of itself notice to him of any unrecorded conveyance of the same real estate or any part thereof.

Section 47–1945 NDRC 1943, in part, provides: "The deposit and recording of an instrument proved and certified according to the provisions of this chapter are constructive notice of the execution of such instrument to all purchasers and encumbrancers subsequent to the recording."

As against the seeming priority of record on the part of Seale's title, the plaintiff contends that the deed from Caroline Messersmith to Smith was never acknowledged and, not having been acknowledged, was not entitled to be recorded, and hence, can confer no priority of record upon the grantee or subsequent purchasers from him. It may be stated as a general rule that the recording of an instrument affecting the title to real estate which does not meet the statutory requirements of the recording laws affords no constructive notice. J. I. Case Co. v. Sax Motor Co., 64 N.D. 757 [(1934)]. The applicability of the rule is easily determined where the defect appears on the face of the instrument, but difficulty frequently arises where the defect is latent. Perhaps the most common instance of this nature arises when an instrument is placed of record bearing a certificate of acknowledgment sufficient on its face despite the fact that the statutory procedure for acknowledgment has not been followed.

The certificate of acknowledgment on the mineral deed to Smith, while it is presumed to state the truth, is not conclusive as to the fact of actual acknowledgment by the grantor. In Severtson v. Peoples, 28 N.D.

372 [(1914)], this court [concluded that a notarial acknowledgment is void if the party whose signature is acknowledged by a notary has not actually appeared in person before the notary, but that the party attacking the validity of an acknowledgment that is "regular on its face" has the burden of proving its falsity by "very strong and convincing" evidence.] It avails the [subsequent] purchaser nothing to point out that a deed is valid between the parties though not acknowledged by the grantor ... for Caroline Messersmith, having previously conveyed to the plaintiff, had no title. The condition of the title is such that Seale must rely wholly upon his position as an innocent purchaser under the recording act.

[Although the notarial acknowledgment on the deed from Messersmith to Smith is in proper form and declares that Caroline Messersmith "personally appeared" before the notary, in fact] Caroline Messersmith did not appear before the notary and acknowledge that she executed the deed that was recorded. In the absence of the fact of acknowledgment the deed was not entitled to be recorded, regardless of the recital in the certificate. The deed not being entitled to be recorded, the record thereof did not constitute notice of its execution ... or contents.... The record appearing in the office of the register of deeds not being notice of the execution or contents of the mineral deed, the purchaser from the grantee therein did not become a "subsequent purchaser in good faith, and for a valuable consideration" within the meaning of Section 47–1941 NDRC 1943.

In this case we have the unusual situation of having two deeds covering the same property from the same grantor, who had no title, to the same grantee. The only difference between the two was a minor defect in the first deed, for which it was destroyed. The evidence is conflicting as to whether or not the first deed was acknowledged. The second deed clearly was not. It is argued that the transaction should be considered as a whole, with the implication that if the first deed was actually acknowledged, the failure to secure an acknowledgment of the second deed would not be fatal to the right to have it recorded and its efficacy as constructive notice. We must again point out that the right which the defendant Seale attempts to assert is dependent exclusively upon compliance with the recording statutes. His claim of title is dependent upon the instrument that was recorded and not the instrument that was destroyed. Assuming that Smith is right in his assertion that the first deed was acknowledged before a notary public, we cannot borrow that unrecorded acknowledgment from the destroyed deed and, in effect, attach it to the unacknowledged deed for purposes of recording and the constructive notice that would ensue.

In Dixon v. Kaufman, 79 N.D. 633 [(1953)], we sustained the title ... of purchasers for value and without notice whose title rested upon a deed bearing a certificate of acknowledgment regular on its face but which in fact had not been acknowledged by the grantors. In that case the grantors were the actual owners of the property at the time they signed the deed and ... the delivery of the deed without acknowledgment was sufficient to pass title which the grantees then had. . . . In that case plaintiffs sought relief from the consequences of their own acts which would result in loss to innocent parties. The situation here is entirely different. The plaintiff seeks relief from the consequences of the acts of a third party, Caroline Messersmith, who, after deeding to the plaintiff her entire interest in the property, executed the mineral deed to Smith. This deed . . . conveyed no title . . ., for the grantor had nothing to convey. For the loss which resulted from her acts, the plaintiff in this case is not to blame. His failure to record his deed will not defeat the title which he holds unless there appears against it a record title consisting of instruments executed and recorded in the manner prescribed by our recording statutes. The title asserted by the defendant Seale does not meet these requirements and the trial court erred in rendering judgment in his favor. [Reversed.]

[Seale petitioned the Supreme Court of North Dakota for a rehearing, which petition was denied in the following opinion.]

MORRIS, C.J., delivered the opinion of the Court.

[It] appears that there may be a misapprehension concerning the scope of our opinion. We would emphasize the fact that at the time Caroline Messersmith signed and delivered the deed to Herbert B. Smith, Jr., she had no title to convey. Smith therefore obtained no title to convey to E. B. Seale who, as grantee of Smith, claims to be an innocent purchaser. The title had already been conveyed to Frederick Messersmith. The deed to Smith had never been acknowledged and was therefore not entitled to be recorded, although it bore a certificate of acknowledgment in regular form. Seale, whose grantor had no title, seeks through the operation of our recording statutes to divest Frederick Messersmith of the true title and establish a statutory title in himself.

We are here dealing with a prior unrecorded valid and effective conveyance that is challenged by a subsequent purchaser to whom no title was conveyed and who claims that the recording laws vest title in him by virtue of a deed that was not acknowledged in fact and therefore not entitled to be placed of record. This situation differs materially from a case where an attack is made by a subsequent purchaser on a prior recorded deed which actually conveyed title to the grantee but was not entitled to be recorded because of a latent defect. The questions presented by the latter situation we leave to be determined when they arise.

The petition for rehearing is denied.

NOTES AND QUESTIONS

1. *What could Seale have done?* Assume that E.B. Seale, who purchased Smith's interest in good faith and for valuable consideration, examined the records before closing the deal. He would have found a chain of title that showed Caroline Messersmith as the record owner of an undivided one-half interest in the three sections or real property at issue. Then he would have found a recorded deed from Caroline Messersmith to Smith of an undivided

one-half interest in the mineral rights to those three sections. From the record it would appear that Caroline had conveyed her mineral rights to Smith. Because North Dakota is a race-notice jurisdiction, Seale might have made off-record inquiries to determine if Smith knew about any unrecorded prior conveyances, but Smith did not know of the unrecorded deed to Frederick Messersmith, and Caroline's letter to him did not make him aware of aware of it, even after the fact. So what could Seale have done to protect himself?

Suppose that the Caroline to Frederick deed had no notarial acknowledgment, but Frederick had persuaded an unscrupulous notary to affix an acknowledgment of Caroline's signature on the deed, and had then recorded it before Smith recorded his deed. Would Seale be better able to protect himself in that situation? It is this pattern that the North Dakota court says is materially different from the actual case. If so, in which pattern is the subsequent innocent purchaser better able to protect himself?

The North Dakota rule is a minority position. The prevailing opinion may be seen in an old Wyoming case, Boswell v. First National Bank of Laramie, 16 Wyo. 161 (1907), in which the court said that the invalidity of a defective acknowledgment

> may be conceded in respect to instruments which ... disclose the defect upon their face or the face of the certificate of acknowledgment. Where, however, the infirmity is not apparent upon the face of the deed or instrument or certificate of acknowledgment, but the acknowledgment appears to be fair and regular and to have been properly taken, and the instrument is one which would not be invalidated as between the parties to it by a defective acknowledgment, the recording of the instrument in the proper office will operate as constructive notice thereof, notwithstanding the latent defect. This rule is sustained by abundant authority and is founded upon public policy to carry out the purpose of the recording acts and preserve the reliability of the public records of transfers and conveyances. It is readily to be seen that a contrary rule would render unsafe any reliance upon the record of deeds or instruments requiring acknowledgment to entitle them to be recorded. Id. at 181–182.

See also Mills v. Damson Oil Corp., 686 F.2d 1096 (5th Cir. 1982); Mills v. Damson Oil Corp., 437 So.2d 1005 (Miss. 1983). Six years after *Messersmith*, North Dakota amended its race-notice statute to reverse the ruling in *Messersmith*. See N.D. Cent. Code § 47–19–41, which added the phrase "whether entitled to recording or not" after the essence of the race-notice priority statement, and for good measure included the following two sentences: "No action affecting any right, title, interest or lien, to, in or upon real property shall be commenced or maintained or defense or counterclaim asserted or recognized in court on the ground that a recorded instrument was not entitled to be recorded. The record of all instruments whether or not the same were entitled to be recorded shall be deemed valid and sufficient as the legal record thereof."

    2. Notice Statute. Suppose North Dakota had a pure notice statute. Would the result in *Messersmith* have been the same?

3. Added Context: Oil Boom. Although it was surely aware of it, the court in *Messersmith* made no mention of the fact that at the time of the Messersmith–Smith–Beale transactions there was a mad scramble to obtain mineral rights in western North Dakota, because the Williston Basin pool of oil had just been discovered.

> On April 4, 1951, Amerada Corp. . . . struck oil on [Clarence] Iverson's farm, [eight miles south of Tioga, N.D.,] spurring an oil frenzy that has lasted six decades throughout the Williston Basin [of western North Dakota, eastern Montana, and parts of South Dakota, Saskatchewan, and Manitoba.] The Clarence Iverson No. 1 [well] produced 585,000 barrels for 28 years. Clarence Iverson died in 1986, a wealthy man "who never got used to all that money," his [77 year old] son, [Cliff,] said. Cliff Iverson still raises durum [wheat] on the farm and lives in the pink home where he grew up—though he can afford not to. He said he'll retire when his 51–year–old cab-less combine wears out. "Guys that are used to living simply are hard to change," Iverson said. Today, nodding oil pumps are scattered throughout the region, and roads are heavy with oil traffic. James MacPherson, The Bismarck Tribune, Aug. 30, 2008.[1]

In what way might this context have affected the court, even unconsciously?

4. The Zimmer *Rule.* A proposition related to the *Messersmith* rule is that taken in Zimmer v. Sundell, 237 Wis. 270 (1941). The court held that a subsequent purchaser who records nevertheless is not treated as having recorded if there is an earlier link in his chain of title that is unrecorded. To be of record, one must not only record one's own deed but be certain that the deeds of each predecessor in title are also recorded. Does this make sense? Consider the following problems.

Problems:

a.   *O*, owner of Blackacre, conveys title to *A*, who fails to record. Then *O* conveys Blackacre to *B* who also fails to record. Then *B* conveys his interest to *C*, who pays value and is ignorant of the *O* to *A* deed. *C* records. As between *C* and *A* who prevails?

b.   *O*, owner of Blackacre, conveys title to *A*, who fails to record. Then *O* conveys Blackacre to *B* who also fails to record. Then *B* conveys his interest to *C*, who pays value and is ignorant of the *O* to *A* deed. *C* records. Then *O* conveys Blackacre to *D*, who pays value and is ignorant of the *O* to *A* and *O* to *B* deeds. As between *C* and *D* who prevails?

BRADY v. MULLEN

Supreme Court of New Hampshire
139 N.H. 67 (1994)

THAYER, J., delivered the opinion of the court.

The plaintiff, Thomas Brady, . . . appeals the Superior Court's . . . order denying his petition in equity for declaratory relief. . . . We affirm.

---

1.   The article, providing an account of the discovery and the size of the oil deposit, is at http://www.bismarcktribune.com/news/state-and-regional/article_3aa93790–be1f–526e–81ae–4f39c876b3 b2.html

... On September 14, 1984, David T. Brady recorded a $40,000 attachment against "Eric B. Welsh" in the Hillsborough County Registry of Deeds (1984 attachment). On September 25, 1984, Eric R. Welch sold certain real estate in Manchester for value to the defendants, William and Peggy Mullen. After recovering judgment against "Eric B. Welsh" in July 1986, Brady notified the defendants of his claim against their property pursuant to the 1984 attachment. The defendants, maintaining that they lacked actual notice of the 1984 attachment when they purchased their property, refused to acknowledge Brady's claim.

In July 1989, Brady filed a petition in equity for declaratory judgment, seeking ... a ruling that he had a valid claim against the defendants' property pursuant to the 1984 attachment. Brady argued, under the legal doctrine of *idem sonans*, that the misspelling of Eric R. Welch's name in the writ of attachment did not render the 1984 attachment fatally defective because the misspelled name, when spoken, sounds similar to the actual name, and the law does not regard the spelling of names as much as it does their sound. ... In October 1990, Brady assigned his interest in this action to the plaintiff. ... In August 1993, [after a hearing, the Superior Court] ruled that the confessed facts, together with the applicable law, failed to support a claim for relief.

On appeal, the plaintiff argues ... that New Hampshire still adheres to the doctrine of *idem sonans* and that this doctrine applies to legal instruments recorded in the registry of deeds. ... The phrase *idem sonans*, literally "of the same sound," refers, at common law, to two differently spelled names that have nearly indistinguishable pronunciations. Generally, under the legal doctrine of *idem sonans*, a mistake or variance in the spelling of a party's name is immaterial to the disposition of a legal proceeding if both modes of spelling have the same sound. Early New Hampshire case law recognized the doctrine of *idem sonans* in both the criminal and civil contexts, primarily to avoid invalidating relevant documents merely because they misspelled or varied the complete spelling of certain names. See, e.g., State v. Perkins, 70 N.H. 330, 47 A. 268 (1900) (birth record); Hart v. Lindsey, 17 N.H. 235 (1845) (military records); Tibbets v. Kiah, 2 N.H. 557 (1823) (deed). We have never addressed whether the doctrine of *idem sonans* applies to attachment liens recorded in the registry of deeds. We hold that it does not.

The ability of *idem sonans* to rescue an otherwise deficient document boils down to a question of notice. Put another way, does a document containing a discrepancy or variation in the spelling of a name still put the party against whom the document is to be applied on adequate notice of the obligations or consequences flowing from it? At common law, a party typically invoked the doctrine of *idem sonans* to avoid the invalidation of a document, despite a variance in the spelling of a particular name in the document, when the document had already been exchanged between, or acknowledged by, people who knew each other. See, e.g., *Tibbets*, 2 N.H. at 557–58. Thus, in the typical case, the misspelling of a name that sounded like the actual name would not invalidate the document being contested because relevant parties would have been on notice of the document's existence or of pertinent conditions contained within it.

By contrast, application of the *idem sonans* doctrine to an attachment index search involves different considerations. The attachment index is alphabetically based, integrated into the general land records and absent any identifying context, other than the name of the person attached and the character of the filing. It is designed, primarily, to alert third parties to the existence of attachment or judgment liens on real estate that third parties propose to acquire. The key to proper notice, in this index context, is the proper spelling of the attachment defendant's name and the resulting proper alphabetical placement. The plaintiff would rely on the doctrine of *idem sonans* to support the constructive notice (or, more appropriately, to impute actual notice) to the defendants in this case. Such notice would negate the defendants' claim of status as bona fide purchasers and would have subjected them to plaintiff's judgment lien. ... We do not hold this to be a proper application of the doctrine of *idem sonans*.

The defendants cite authority from other jurisdictions that, in our view, perfectly illustrates the problem of applying the doctrine of *idem sonans* to names that are misspelled in attachment-lien indices:

> We have experienced a tremendous growth in the population and the economy, and those developments have spawned countless real estate sales and a volume of litigation resulting in an abundance of indexed judgment liens. ... To impose rigidly the doctrine of *idem sonans* to name indexes now maintained for judgment liens would tax all land abstractors beyond reasonable limits and require them to be poets, phonetic linguists, or multilingual specialists. The additional time necessary to examine name indexes under such a stringent doctrine would make the examinations financially prohibitive.

National Packaging Corp. v. Belmont, 47 Ohio App. 3d 86, 547 N.E.2d 373, 376 (1988); see also Orr v. Byers, 198 Cal. App. 3d 666, 244 Cal. Rptr. 13, 16–17 (Ct. App. 1988). We will not attenuate the judgment creditor's burden to take appropriate measures to ensure satisfaction of the attachment lien merely to accommodate the judgment creditor's spelling error. See *Orr*, 244 Cal. Rptr. at 17. We concur with the court in *Orr* that "the simple alternative is to require [attachment creditors] simply to spell the names of their ... debtors properly." Id. Thus, title examiners, or the people for whom they conduct searches, are not charged with constructive notice of a lien when the only reference to that lien is a misspelled name in the attachment-lien index at the registry of deeds.

Because we hold that the doctrine of *idem sonans* does not apply to attachment-lien indices, we do not reach the issue of whether, in fact, the contested names are of the same sound.

Affirmed.

NOTES AND QUESTIONS

1. What if idem sonans *applied?* The New Hampshire court did not reach the question of whether Welch and Welsh are *idem sonans.* In Orr v. Byers, 198 Cal.App.3d 666 (1988), the California Court of Appeal noted that Elliott and Eliot were *idem sonans,* but proceeded to reject the *idem sonans* doctrine in the context of a recorded judgment lien. In Green v. Meyers, 98 Mo.App. 438 (1903), the Missouri Court of Appeals held that Seibert and Sibert were "not only *idem sonans* ... but they are, practically, the same name." Thus, a purchaser of property from Eleanor Sibert was charged with notice of a recorded judgment lien against E.G. Seibert. The court refused to decide whether constructive notice would apply if the names were *idem sonans* but the spellings began with different capital letters, "as, for instance, 'Kane' and 'Cain'...."

2. Should idem sonans *apply to a tract index?* In a tract index, all transactions are indexed by tract. Does that make the *idem sonans* problem irrelevant for judgment liens or tax liens?

"Mother Hubbard" Clauses

Sometimes a grantor will include in the grant of specific property a clause conveying all his interests in all other real property he owns in the vicinity. Such clauses are commonly referred to as "Mother Hubbard" clauses, after the first verse of the venerable English nursery rhyme: "Old Mother Hubbard/ Went to the cupboard,/ To give the poor dog a bone:/ When she came there,/ The cupboard was bare,/ And so the poor dog had none." Such clauses empty the grantor's cupboard of ownership.

Example and Problem 8–10: O, record owner of Blackacre and Whiteacre, each consisting of a separate quarter section tract of land located in Sitting Bull County, conveys Blackacre to *A* by a deed that describes it as "NE 1/4 of Section 12 in T2S, R4W of the Able and Baker base and meridian," but which also states that "by this deed *O* intends to convey, and does convey, to *A* all the right, title, and interest that *O* possesses in all other real property located in Sitting Bull County." *A* records the deed. Later, *O* conveys Whiteacre, described as the "SW 1/4 of Section 11 in T2S, R4W of the Able and Baker base and meridian," to *B,* who pays valuable consideration and has examined the records of Sitting Bull County. Who owns Whiteacre: *O, A,* or *B?* Sitting Bull County is in a state that has enacted a notice statute.

We can start by eliminating *O* as the owner. As between *O* and *A,* the deed is sufficient to transfer title to *A.* See, e.g., Whitehead v. Johnston, 467 So.2d 240 (Ala. 1985). The problem is whether *B* had constructive notice of the prior transfer of Whiteacre to *A.* On what should this turn? States that require maintenance of a grantor/grantee index specify in the statute establishing the recording system that the index must include a brief description of the property. States that permit or require the use of a tract index obviously require that the property be identified in order for the conveyance to be indexed. Suppose that in Example 8–10 Sitting Bull County maintains both a grantor/grantee index and a tract index. When in searching the grantor/grantee index B finds the indexed grant from O to A, it contains only a reference to the "NE 1/4 of Section 12 in T2S, R4W of the Able and Baker base and meridian" as the described property. Should B be charged with a duty to examine the actual deed to be sure it did not include a Mother Hubbard clause? If B does examine the actual deed and discovers a Mother Hubbard clause, B must examine the grantee index to ascertain what other property O has acquired, and then go forward through the grantor index for each of them to see if O still had title at the time of the O to A deed. Suppose that B examined only the tract index for Whiteacre. He would find nothing of record. Should B be required to search both indexes?

Luthi v. Evans, 223 Kan. 622 (1978), is a leading case holding that no constructive notice is imparted by a recorded instrument containing a Mother Hubbard clause. In Kansas, B wins. Is the argument for holding that Mother Hubbard clauses do not impart constructive notice stronger or weaker with respect to a tract index as opposed to a grantor/grantee index?

Note that states are divided on the question of whether an instrument that is indexed incorrectly imparts constructive notice. The majority rule continues to be that the index is not the record, and it is the record itself that later purchasers are deemed to know. Thus, a wrongly indexed instrument, though virtually impossible to locate using normal search methods, imparts constructive notice. See, e.g., Haner v. Bruce, 146 Vt. 262 (1985). But increasingly courts recognize that an recorded instrument that is next to impossible to find does not impart constructive notice. See, e.g., Hochstein v. Romero, 219 Cal.App.3d 447 (1990). How much, if any, should the policy questions surrounding wrongly indexed instruments influence the question of whether a Mother Hubbard clause gives notice?

c. Inquiry Notice

A person who acquires an interest in real property is charged with a duty to inquire about the possibility that another person may have an interest in that property if there are facts that would cause a reasonable person to make further inquiry.

GORZEMAN v. THOMPSON

Court of Appeals of Oregon
162 Ore. App. 84 (1999)

[The facts in this tale of familial discord have been edited to focus on the issue of inquiry notice. The other issues in the case reveal a mother (Faye Thompson) at odds with defendant Thomas Jerry Thompson and in sympathy with the plaintiffs.]

BREWER, J., delivered the opinion of the court.

Defendant Thomas Jerry Thompson appeals from a judgment in favor of plaintiffs Chloe and Peter Gorzeman in this action for judicial foreclosure of a trust deed under which plaintiffs are the beneficiaries and defendant Faye Thompson was the grantor. [We] affirm.

Chloe Gorzeman and defendant are the children of Faye Thompson. Peter Gorzeman is married to Chloe. Faye was engaged in various business ventures with defendant in Jackson County between 1970 and the early 1990s. They jointly owned the Royal Coachman Motel and sometimes resided together in living quarters at the motel. In 1988, Faye purchased and moved into a residence in Shady Cove referred to as the Heather Lane property. Defendant also moved into the Heather Lane residence in order to help Faye renovate the property. After she acquired title to the Heather Lane property, Faye deeded the property to herself and defendant with mutual rights of survivorship. Although the deed was executed in 1988, it was not recorded at that time.

. . . Because Faye needed money for living expenses, home improvements and debts, including mortgage payments on the Heather Lane property, plaintiffs loaned money to Faye at various times during 1991 and 1992. In early 1992, Faye and Chloe jointly determined the total amount of money that plaintiffs had loaned to Faye, plus the outstanding mortgage loan balance and unpaid real estate taxes against the Heather Lane property. Plaintiffs then paid off the mortgage debt and property taxes in order to consolidate Faye's debts into a single loan. In March 1992, Faye executed a promissory note in favor of plaintiffs, secured by a trust deed executed the same date against the Heather Lane property. The note was in the principal sum of $46,000, the amount of the consolidated loan. The note provided for nine percent interest and monthly payments, including interest, in the amount of $400.26. The note provided that it was secured by a trust deed against the Heather Lane property. However, the trust deed provided that it was given

> [to] secur[e payment] of . . . **$400.26** . . . with interest thereon according to the terms of a promissory note of even date . . . , [with] the final payment of principal and interest . . . to be due and payable [no later than] June 1st, 2014. (Emphasis added.)

The . . . trust deed . . . , with a copy of the note attached, was recorded in the official records of Jackson County in April 1992. Plaintiffs testified that they had no knowledge of defendant's interest in the property at the time the trust deed was recorded in April 1992.

From April 1992 until July 1994, Faye made regular monthly payments to plaintiffs on the note. She made no payments on the note thereafter. By mid–1994, Faye's health had deteriorated and she moved to California in order to live near plaintiffs. In the summer of 1994, Faye listed the Heather Lane property for sale. After learning that Faye planned to sell the property, defendant recorded the survivorship deed in June 1994. . . .

Faye learned that the trust deed erroneously stated that the debt she owed plaintiffs was in the amount of $400.26 rather than the true amount, $46,000. Faye's attorney advised her that she could re-record the trust deed after correcting the amount recited for the indebtedness. [A properly executed and notarized] corrected trust deed was ... recorded in the Jackson County official records in July 1995....

In November 1996, plaintiffs filed this action on the promissory note and to foreclose the corrected trust deed. Plaintiffs alleged that the promissory note was in default by reason of nonpayment since 1994. Plaintiffs also alleged that the corrected trust deed was entitled to priority over defendant's survivorship deed because the survivorship deed was recorded after the trust deed was originally recorded in 1992. ... The case was tried to the court without a jury. The trial court [found that plaintiffs were bona fide creditors for value who had no notice of Thomas Thompson's interest in the Heather Lane property at the time they extended credit to Faye.] Because defendant and Faye lived together and defendant provided care for Faye between 1992 and 1994, the court found it reasonable to expect that defendant knew that Faye was making monthly payments on the loan from plaintiffs. As a consequence, the court found that defendant knew or should have known of the existence of an encumbrance on the Heather Lane property that required monthly payments of $400.26. The court found that, because plaintiffs' trust deed was previously recorded, defendant was on notice of its existence before he recorded the survivorship deed in 1994. The court also found "that [defendant] could have discovered the trust deed at the time he recorded his deed by having a title search performed. By inquiring further at the time he recorded the 1988 deed, or at an earlier time, [defendant] would have discovered the note and trust deed and learned from a review of said note and trust deed that the original encumbrance was, in fact, $46,000 requiring a monthly payment of $400.26." ... [The] trial court concluded that plaintiffs' corrected trust deed was entitled to priority over defendant's deed. The court entered judgment in favor of plaintiffs against Faye on the promissory note in the amount of $47,681.75, plus interest, costs, and attorney fees. The judgment foreclosed the corrected trust deed and declared defendant's interest in the property to be subordinate to the full amount of the corrected lien. This appeal followed. [Faye Thompson died during the pendency of the appeal.]

Defendant [argues] that plaintiffs had notice of his interest in the property because of the fact that he lived in the residence with Faye from time to time over a period of several years and had owned other property jointly with her. However, the trial court expressly found that plaintiffs had no knowledge of the existence of defendant's interest in the property before the trust deed was recorded in 1992. Moreover, defendant's mere residence in his mother's home and the fact that they had owned the motel jointly afforded no constructive notice that he had an unrecorded ownership interest in the Heather Lane property....

Defendant next contends that the trial court erred in concluding that plaintiffs' trust deed was entitled to priority over his own interest in the property. ... Under [Oregon's race-notice] statute, an unrecorded conveyance such as defendant's deed is valid as between grantor and grantee. The priority contest is determined by three factors: (1) the good faith of the subsequent purchaser; (2) whether the subsequent purchaser paid a valuable consideration; and (3) whether the subsequent purchaser's conveyance is filed first for record. [Because] plaintiffs acquired their interest in the property in good faith and for value [and] their interest was recorded first, plaintiffs have satisfied each of the requirements under the statute. Therefore, the trust deed, as first recorded in 1992, is entitled to priority over defendant's deed. Defendant nevertheless contends that the trust deed is entitled to record priority only to the extent of $400.26, the face amount shown in the originally recorded instrument. He reasons that, because the survivorship deed was recorded before the trust deed was corrected and re-recorded in 1995, the trust deed is not entitled to priority for the much larger full amount owed on the promissory note. [We] disagree.

The notice that will deprive the grantee under a subsequently recorded deed of priority can be either actual or constructive. Constructive notice encompasses both notice chargeable under the recording statute and inquiry notice. A properly recorded trust deed constitutes record notice to third persons of the rights of the parties under the instrument. Inquiry notice, on the other hand, arises when the existence of a claimed interest in real property may be determined through investigation based on facts available to the claimant that would cause a reasonable person to make such inquiry. Recorded instruments may themselves provide inquiry notice. See Lewis v. Investors Leased Group II, 118 Ore. App. 361, 366, 848 P.2d 113 (1993)....

We need not decide whether record notice alone was sufficient because, for the following reasons, we conclude that the trust deed did provide inquiry notice of the correct amount of the debt. In this case, a reasonable person examining the record title to the property at the time defendant's deed was recorded would have questioned the accuracy of the minimal obligation shown on the first page of the trust deed for several reasons. First, the trust deed recited that the obligation was payable in monthly installments with the final payment not falling due until June 1, 2014, or 22 years after the date of the instrument. It is implausible that such a lengthy amortization period would apply to a secured debt in the amount of $400.26. More importantly, a copy of the promissory note was recorded with the trust deed. An obligation and the instrument securing it must be construed together. The note correctly stated that the principal indebtedness was $46,000 and that monthly payments were payable in the amount of $400.26, the amount mistakenly shown as the principal balance on the first page of the trust deed. Moreover, the note recited a 22–year amortization schedule, coinciding with the schedule stated in the trust deed. The note also provided that it was secured by property located at: 110 Heather Lane, Shady Cove, Oregon." Finally, the trust deed recited the identical street address for the property it encumbered.

In High v. Davis, 283 Ore. 315, 333, 584 P.2d 725 (1978), a mortgagee's interest in ranch property was held subordinate to the recreational rights of members of a hunting and fishing club. Although the recreational interests were recorded before the mortgage was recorded, they were not properly acknowledged and did not clearly describe the encumbered property. Therefore, the recorded documents did not provide adequate record notice of the interests. However, the recreational interests were shown as exceptions on the title report the mortgagee received before advancing loan funds. The Oregon Supreme Court held that the lender had a duty to inquire of the interest holders in order to determine the extent of the interest claimed. Because the lender failed to inquire, it was charged with notice of the facts that would have been discovered by such an inquiry, and the recreational interests were accorded priority over the mortgage lien. 283 Ore. at 332–34.

If anything, defendant's claim to priority in this case is weaker than the mortgagee's position in *High*. In that case, the lender changed its position by loaning funds to the owner when it recorded its interest in the property. In this case, defendant did not change his position in reliance on the typographical error in the originally recorded trust deed. He simply recorded his deed six years after the date of the conveyance without investigating the title to the property for intervening interests.

We hold that, under these circumstances, a reasonable person in defendant's position recording an interest in the property would have discovered the recorded trust deed and would have inquired further in order to verify the correct amount of the debt secured by the trust deed. Such an inquiry would have disclosed the true amount of the obligation. Therefore, the originally recorded note and trust deed furnished constructive notice of the amount of the debt secured so as to achieve priority to the full extent of that debt over defendant's subsequently recorded deed. . . . Defendant's remaining arguments do not merit discussion. Affirmed.

COHEN v. THOMAS & SON TRANSFER LINE, INC.

Supreme Court of Colorado
196 Colo. 386 (1978)

GROVES, J., delivered the opinion of the court.

Parties to this appeal are Thomas & Son Transfer Line, Inc., the lessee ["Thomas & Son"], and the Cohens who purchased the leased premises from the lessors. The district court denied [Thomas & Son's] claim for specific performance of a right of first refusal against the Cohens. The Colorado Court of Appeals reversed. We granted certiorari, and now affirm.

The question is whether the Cohens, who had constructive notice of [Thomas & Son's] tenancy, had a duty to inquire of [Thomas & Son] concerning [their] rights in the leased property. In 1968, the lessors, who are not parties to this appeal, leased 10 contiguous lots to [Thomas & Son] for five years at a monthly rental of $400. The lease contained provisions regarding holding over, a right of first refusal and an option to renew. The latter two provisions were typewritten below other printed provisions of the lease. It was never recorded.

After the lease expired on May 1, 1973, [Thomas & Son] retained possession and continued to pay rent. No discussion occurred concerning any extension or renewal of the lease, but [Thomas & Son] agreed to pay $550 per month beginning November 1, 1973. Throughout, the entire property was used by the occupant as a truck terminal. On July 26, 1974, the lessors sold the leased property, together with four additional lots, to the Cohens. [Thomas & Son] first learned of the sale on August 5, 1974, and protested both to the lessors and the Cohens. Prior to their purchase of the property, the Cohens were aware of [Thomas & Son's] tenancy and questioned the lessors about the existence of a lease. The lessors responded that the written lease had expired and that [Thomas & Son] had a month-to-month tenancy. The Cohens did not ask to see the expired lease, nor did they question [Thomas & Son] directly.

The trial court concluded that, since the lease did not require notice to the lessor, the lessee had exercised its option to renew by remaining in possession and continuing to pay rent after May 1, 1973. The court of appeals agreed. The parties disputed whether the right of first refusal provision was part of the renewed leasing agreement. The district court held that, since the first refusal option was embodied in a typewritten provision set off by parentheses which was separate from the rest of the lease terms, it consequently was not renewed along with the other terms of the tenancy. The court of appeals reversed, stating that where a lease provides that its extension or renewal is to be on the same terms and conditions as were in the original lease, the renewal extends a right of first refusal option.

Since the parties have not appealed the decision that the lease was renewed in its entirety, the only remaining question is whether the Cohens took title subject to [Thomas & Son's] right of first refusal. The notice provisions of the Colorado recording statute provide: "All . . . instruments . . . affecting the title to real property . . . may be recorded in the office of the county clerk and recorder . . . and no such instrument or document shall be valid as against any class of persons with any kind of rights, except between the parties thereto and such as have notice thereof. . . ." Section 38–35–109, C.R.S. 1973. Both courts below correctly determined that [Thomas & Son's] possession put the Cohens on constructive notice of the terms of the lessee's tenancy. Having such notice, the Cohens took title subject to any rights of the lessee which reasonable inquiry would have revealed. Section 38–35–109, C.R.S. 1973; Shamrock Land & Cattle Co. v. Hagen, 30 Colo. App. 127, 489 P.2d 607 (1971). . . .

Under these circumstances, we conclude that reasonable inquiry would have included inquiry of the lessee who was the sole tenant in possession. Keck v. Brookfield, 2 Ariz.App. 424, 409 P.2d 583 (1965). We do not agree with the Cohens' contention that the prospective purchaser with constructive notice has a duty to inquire concerning only possessory rights. The rule that prospective purchasers must inquire of lessees in possession as to their rights does not have universal application. Exceptions typically have been applied in cases where possession was consistent with record title; where the tenant occupied only part of the leased property or the tenant's possession was not sufficiently visible to put a prospective purchaser on inquiry notice; and where various equitable defenses were pertinent. Schlegel v. Kinzie, 158 Okla. 93, 12 P.2d 223 (1932); Scott v. Woolard, 12 Wash. App. 109, 529 P.2d 30 (1974); Feld v. Kantrowitz, 98 N.J. Eq. 167, 130 A. 6 (1925), *aff'd* 99 N.J. Eq. 706, 134 A. 920 (1926). The exceptions pertain to issues not presented by this case. We note them to show that the proper parties and the scope of inquiry may vary according to circumstances.

Neither do we have a situation involving multiple tenants. Here, the lessee as the sole tenant was the proper party of whom to inquire. The Cohens had actual knowledge of [Thomas & Son's] possession for 13 years and did not avail themselves of an opportunity for inquiry when they inspected the leased premises shortly before they purchased the property.

We conclude that, having notice of the tenancy by virtue of the lessee's possession, the Cohens had a duty to inquire of the lessee concerning its rights in the leased property. They take subject to all rights which would have been revealed by reasonable inquiry, including [Thomas & Son's] right of first refusal. Judgment affirmed.

PHELAN v. BRADY

Court of Appeals of New York
119 N.Y. 587 (1890)

O'BRIEN, J., delivered the opinion of the court.

On the 23d day of July, 1886, the plaintiff loaned to the defendant John E. Murphy the sum of $2,000, and took from him his bond, whereby he promised to pay the same with interest semi-annually in two years thereafter. On the same day, and as collateral security for the payment of the bond, Murphy and his wife executed, acknowledged and delivered to the plaintiff a mortgage upon certain real estate in the city of New York. The premises thus mortgaged consisted of a tenement building, or block, containing forty-three rooms or apartments, then occupied by twenty different occupants or families, as tenants from month to month, except that three of these apartments were occupied by the defendant Margaret Brady and her husband, who kept a liquor store in part of the building, and they occupied two living rooms in the rear of the store, the wife claiming to be the owner of the premises and collecting rents from the other tenants.

The plaintiff, at the time he made the loan, had no actual notice or knowledge of any title to the premises in Mrs. Brady, or any claim on her part to be the owner. When the first installment of interest became due upon the mortgage, default was made, and the plaintiff brought this action to foreclose under a provision in the mortgage making the whole sum due upon default in the payment of the interest when due. Margaret Brady being in possession was made a party to the action, and she answered, setting up the defense that prior to the execution and delivery of the plaintiff's mortgage, and on or about the 5th of May, 1886, she became the absolute owner in fee-simple of the premises described in the complaint and in the mortgage and of the whole thereof, and that upon becoming such owner, she took possession of the same, and that she has ever since continued in actual, open and notorious occupation and possession of the premises as such owner, and has ever since and still owns the same in fee-simple.

The trial court found that in March, 1886, Margaret Brady employed one Michael J. Murphy, an attorney, to examine the title to the premises in question and purchase the same for her, and before May 7, 1886, she gave said Murphy, as her attorney, the sum of $6,700 to be used as part of the purchase-money; that Murphy procured a contract for the sale of the premises to be made between Mary S. Trimble, who then owned the same, and his son John E. Murphy the defendant, in which contract the said John E. Murphy appeared to be the purchaser of the premises; that upon the execution of this contract, about March 19, 1886, Michael J. Murphy paid to Mrs. Trimble part of the sum of $6,700, which he had received for that purpose from Mrs. Brady, and the rest of that sum was paid to her on the 7th of May, 1886; that the balance of the purchase-price, namely $16,000, was secured to be paid to Mrs. Trimble by a purchase-money mortgage; that on the same day the purchase-price was thus paid, Mrs. Brady's lawyer took from Mrs. Trimble a deed of the premises to his son John E. Murphy, and the deed was duly recorded on that day; that on the 1st of May, 1886, Mrs. Brady took possession of the premises under the contract claiming to own the same, and has ever since remained in possession and occupied the same herself and by her tenants; that she rented certain rooms in the building to tenants immediately thereafter; that she discharged the housekeeper who had before that date rented the premises and collected the rents for Mrs. Trimble, and moved herself into the rooms formerly occupied by the housekeeper, and that she has received the rents ever since the 1st of May, 1886; that on the fifth of May of that year a deed conveying the premises to Mrs. Brady was executed and duly acknowledged by the defendant John E. Murphy and his wife, and by him delivered to his son Michael J. Murphy as agent and attorney for Mrs. Brady; that [John E.] Murphy never had any interest in the premises, never paid any part of the consideration money and never had possession of the same or any part thereof; that the said Michael J. Murphy retained the deed to Mrs. Brady in his possession until not later than the 25th of August, 1886, when he delivered the same to her and the same was recorded by her on the 26th of August, 1886, subsequent to the execution, delivery and record of the plaintiff's mortgage.

The trial court held that Mrs. Brady's title and possession was sufficient to defeat any claim under the plaintiff's mortgage, and dismissed the complaint, and this judgment has been affirmed by the General Term.

At the time of the execution and delivery of the mortgage to the plaintiff, the defendant Mrs. Brady was in the actual possession of the premises under a perfectly valid but unrecorded deed. Her title must, therefore, prevail as against the plaintiff. It matters not, so far as Mrs. Brady is concerned, that the plaintiff in good faith advanced his money upon an apparently perfect record title of the defendant John E. Murphy. Nor is it of any consequence, so far as this question is concerned, whether the plaintiff was in fact ignorant of any right or claim of Mrs. Brady to the premises. It is enough that she was in possession under her deed and the contract of purchase, as that fact operated in law as notice to the plaintiff of all her rights.

It may be true, as has been argued by the plaintiff's counsel, that when a party takes a conveyance of property situated as this was, occupied by numerous tenants, it would be inconvenient and difficult for him to ascertain the rights or interests that are claimed by all or any of them. But this circumstance cannot change the rule. Actual possession of real estate is sufficient notice to a person proposing to take a mortgage on the property, and to all the world of the existence of any right which the person in possession is able to establish.

The circumstance that Mrs. Brady and her husband occupied the store and a living apartment in the building prior to the time that she went into possession under her contract of purchase as tenants under Mrs. Trimble, the then owner, cannot aid the plaintiff. It does not appear that he ever heard of that fact till after the commencement of this suit, and we cannot perceive how it would affect the result if he had. The trial court found that prior to making the loan the plaintiff was upon the premises for other purposes, and that then, by making inquiry, he could have ascertained the rights of Mrs. Brady in the property, and while the absence of such a finding would not change the result, it shows that the plaintiff's loss is to be attributed to his confidence in Murphy, who probably deceived him, and to his failure to take notice of Mrs. Brady's possession.

The judgment should be affirmed, with costs.

NOTE, QUESTIONS, AND PROBLEMS

1. The Scope of the Duty to Inquire. Before lending to Murphy and taking a mortgage on the apartment building to secure the debt, was Phelan required to inquire of each tenant the status of their occupation? Apparently so, for actual possession triggers inquiry notice, according to the New York court. How far can this go?

Consider Miller v. Green, 264 Wis. 159 (1953). Green owned a 63 acre farm, which she leased to Miller for the year 1950. In early November Green entered into a contract of sale of the farm to Miller for $3,500 and Miller made a $400 down payment. In late November Green deeded the farm to Hines in return for $3,300, Hines recorded his deed in December 1950 but Miller did not record his contract of sale until March of 1951. Wisconsin is a race-notice state. At the time Hines bought the farm the crops that Miller had raised had been harvested, his livestock had been removed, and the structures on the farm were dilapidated and uninhabited.

However, starting November 4, 1950 (the date that the Millers contracted to purchase this farm tract), Miller's father, in behalf of the Millers, hauled between 50 and 60 loads of manure to the farm. First the manure was spread over the land, but then after a snowstorm came it was piled on a pile about 100 feet from the road, such pile being about 60 feet long and several feet high. Such hauling of manure was taking place on November 29, 1950 (the date that ... Hines made the $500 down payment on the purchase price), and continued until about December 8 or 9, 1950. Also in November, prior to the snowstorm, approximately two acres of land had been plowed by Miller, which plowed land was plainly visible from the abutting highway before the snowstorm. The Hines farm was located about one-half mile from this 63–acre tract, although the distance by highway was about one and one-half miles. Part of the tract was visible from the Hines home [but] Hines ... denied that he drove past the tract on the abutting highway during November, 1950, and denied having seen the plowing of the land, the hauling of the manure, or the manure pile on the land.... Id. at 161–162.

The Wisconsin Supreme Court ruled that this was sufficient possession to place Hines on inquiry notice of Miller's prior interest.

In general, the scope of the inquiry duty ought to be limited to the inquiry that can be reasonably expected from an ordinary person acquiring real estate who is in the purchaser's position at the time of the transaction. See Francis S. Philbrick, Limits of Record Search and Therefore of Notice, 93 U. Pa. L. Rev. 259, 271 (1944).

2. Problem: Hotel Occupants. Suppose your client wishes to acquire a motel or hotel consisting of several hundred rooms. Must you inquire of each occupant of a hotel room or suite concerning the nature of their occupancy rights? Consider that many motels offer extended stay suites. Indeed, for many years in the 1930s and 1940s United States Supreme Court Justice Stanley Reed lived in the Mayflower Hotel for most of any given year. What if a hotel occupant has an agreement that guarantees the occupant long term possession? If inquiry is too onerous, what can your client do to protect himself against the unrecorded interest of an occupant?

3. Problem: Shopping Center. Suppose your client wishes to acquire a shopping center that has sixty separate commercial tenants. After examining the record you discover that almost none of the leases are recorded. What sort of inquiry must you conduct? What is the safest course of conduct you can take to protect your client against tenant interests that are not of record?

4. Problem: Single Family Residence. Suppose your client wishes to purchase a single family residence from *O*, the record owner. You investigate and find that the occupants of the residence are *O*, his wife, and their adult son and daughter-in-law. Must you inquire of *O*'s wife, son, and daughter-in-law as to their interests, or may you safely assume that they are licensees from *O* whose right to occupancy ends upon transfer of title to your client?

5. Inquiry Notice: A Good or Bad Idea? What benefits are delivered by inquiry notice? What are its costs? Is it desirable?

4. WHO IS ENTITLED TO THE PROTECTION OF THE RECORDING ACTS?

Ordinarily, only bona fide purchasers are protected by the recording acts. With respect to race statutes, North Carolina's law expressly limits its protection to bona fide purchasers for value, a conclusion confirmed by its courts. See Hill v. Pinelawn Memorial Park, Inc., 304 N.C. 159, 165 (1981): "Our registration statute does not protect all purchasers, but only innocent purchasers for value." The Louisiana and Delaware statutes contain no such limit. To be a bona fide purchaser one must pay valuable consideration. This principle excludes recipients of gratuitous transfers—donees and devisees—but it also excludes some transferees who have paid minimal value, but not enough to qualify as "valuable consideration."

However, it is critical to pay attention to the specific statutory language of the relevant jurisdiction. For example, Colorado's race-notice statute, Colo. Rev. Stat. 38–35–109(1), provides: "No ... unrecorded instrument or document shall be valid against any person with any kind of rights in or to such real property who first records and those holding rights under such person...." In Eastwood v. Shedd, 166 Colo. 136 (1968), the Colorado Supreme Court construed an earlier version of this statute to protect a donee who recorded first against the claims of a prior donee. The Colorado legislature had amended its race-notice statute to substitute "shall be valid as against any class of persons with any kind of rights" for the deleted text: "shall take effect as to subsequent bona fide purchasers and encumbrancers by mortgage judgment or otherwise not having notice thereof." The court rejected the prior donee's contention that the legislature must have intended the words "any class of persons with any kind of rights" to include only transferees for value. *Eastwood* involved rival donees; should the result be the same if the holder of the prior unrecorded interest had paid substantial value and the subsequent recorded interest was that of a donee?

Colorado's statute is unique. Most states only protect bona fide purchasers or creditors who pay valuable consideration for their interest. For example, Florida's statute declares: "No conveyance, transfer, or mortgage of real property, or of any interest therein, nor any lease for a term of 1 year or longer, shall be good ... against creditors or subsequent purchasers for a valuable consideration and without notice, unless the same be recorded according to law...." Fla. Stat. § 695.01(1). Several questions emerge from such statutes. What constitutes valuable consideration? When does a creditor or subsequent purchaser give valuable consideration?

An old Missouri case, Strong v. Whybark, 204 Mo. 341 (1907), held that an 1863 transfer for "natural love and affection and five dollars" was valuable consideration. A later Missouri court, in Allaben v. Shelbourne,

357 Mo. 1205 (1948), concluded that a single dollar was not valuable consideration. Putting aside the increased purchasing power of five dollars in 1863 (equal to ten dollars in 1948 and about 90 dollars today), *Strong* is a distinctly minority view. The overwhelming consensus is that such a modest payment is not valuable consideration. For example, in Anderson v. Anderson, 435 N.W.2d 687, 689 (N.D. 1989), the North Dakota Supreme Court cited eminent commentators and cases for the proposition that

> for protection under a recording act as a good faith purchaser for value, the purchase must be for a valuable and not a nominal consideration. The consideration does not have to be an equivalent value in order to be valuable, but it must be substantial and not merely nominal. . . . The recital of a nominal consideration in a deed is insufficient to establish a valuable consideration or to raise a presumption of value for a good faith purchase. [The] party claiming to be a good faith purchaser has the burden of proof to establish valuable consideration from evidence other than the deed.

The court concluded that a deed recital of consideration of ten dollars, without proof of additional real value paid, was insufficient.

But as the North Dakota court observed, fair market value need not be paid. Between these extremes lies a vast gray area. A bargain purchase may suffice. For example, in Horton v. Kyburz, 53 Cal.2d 59 (1959), the California Supreme Court noted that the purpose of the recording act "is to protect those who honestly believe they are acquiring a good title, and who invest some substantial sum in reliance on that belief," quoting Beach v. Faust, 2 Cal.2d 290, 292 (1935). Then it concluded that the following efforts, performed in reliance upon the grantor's promise to convey title to a ranch worth about $150,000 at the time of the conveyance, was valuable consideration: 1) Fixing or building over a half-mile of fencing, 2) Paying half the cost of drilling three new water wells, 3) Reroofing a barn and placing a foundation under it, 4) Constructing a water distribution system from the new wells, 5) Renovating an outbuilding, 6) Building a three-car garage, and 7) Clearing brush and seeding the cleared area.

DANIELS v. ANDERSON

Supreme Court of Illinois
162 Ill.2d 47 (1994)

FREEMAN, J., delivered the opinion of the court.

Plaintiff, William L. Daniels, brought an action in the circuit court of Cook County against several defendants, including James Anderson, the estate of Stephen Jacula, and Nicholas Zografos. Daniels sought . . . the specific performance of a real estate sales contract. Following a bench trial, the trial court entered judgment in favor of Daniels. The appellate court affirmed. We allowed Zografos' petition for leave to appeal and now affirm the appellate court. . . .

In March 1977, Anderson and Jacula owned a 10–acre tract of real estate [that] is divided into four lots. Two of the four lots (the Daniels Property) are situated side-by-side, east and west, and face the south side of 79th Street at 11445 79th Street. Each lot is an acre. ... The third lot (the Contiguous Parcel) lies directly south of the Daniels Property. In other words, the south boundary of the Daniels Property is also the north boundary of the Contiguous Parcel....

In March 1977, Daniels contracted with Anderson and Jacula to buy the Daniels Property. The written contract [contained a provision by which Anderson and Jacula granted Daniels] "the first right to purchase (on the same terms and conditions, and for the same price, as any bona-fide offer in writing made to Seller)" [the Contiguous Parcel.] Daniels and his wife moved into the single-family home on the Daniels Property when they entered into the 1977 sales contract. In March 1979, the ... Danielses received a deed [to the Daniels Property but which] did not mention Daniels' ... right of first refusal of the Contiguous Parcel. Daniels did not record the 1977 sales contract at this time.

In June 1979, Jacula and his wife acquired sole ownership of the Contiguous Parcel.... In September 1985, Zografos contracted with the Jaculas to buy the Contiguous Parcel for $60,000. Daniels never received an offer to buy the Contiguous Parcel. Since Daniels had not recorded the 1977 contract by this time, a title search for this sale to Zografos reflected that Daniels did not have any interest in the Contiguous Parcel. Pursuant to the 1985 contract, Zografos paid the Jaculas $10,000 initially.... On February 18, 1986, Zografos paid $15,000 and, on March 22, he paid another $15,000. At the closing on August 22, Zografos paid the remaining $20,000. Shortly after that date, Zografos recorded a warranty deed to the Contiguous Parcel....

Daniels brought this action in December 1989. Daniels sought specific performance of his right of first refusal of the Contiguous Parcel. ... At the close of a hearing, the trial court found as follows. Daniels' right of first refusal of the Contiguous Parcel, as provided by the 1977 sales contract, was legally enforceable. Zografos had actual notice of Daniels' right prior to Zografos' purchase of that parcel. Therefore, Zografos was not a *bona fide* purchaser of the Contiguous Parcel and he took title thereto subject to Daniels' right. Also, Jacula breached the 1977 sales contract by selling the Contiguous Parcel to Zografos without first offering it to Daniels. Based on these findings, the trial court entered a judgment that provided as follows. Zografos was ordered to convey the Contiguous Parcel to Daniels on the same terms and conditions as Zografos received the property.... Daniels was ordered to pay Zografos the full purchase price and reimburse him for approximately $11,000 in property taxes that Zografos had paid on the Contiguous Parcel during his ownership....

The appellate court affirmed the trial court's judgment in all material respects....

Zografos ... contends [that] he was a *bona fide* purchaser of the Contiguous Parcel.... A *bona fide* purchaser is a person who takes title to real property in good faith for value without notice of outstanding rights or interests of others. A *bona fide* purchaser takes such title free of any interests of third persons, except such interests of which he has notice. Zografos testified that he did not know of Daniels' right of first refusal until Daniels' wife told him in June 1986. By that time, Zografos had already contracted to buy the Contiguous Parcel and had paid $40,000 of the $60,000 purchase price. The trial court found that Zografos was not a *bona fide* purchaser based solely on this June 1986 notice.

In the appellate court, Zografos contended that he was a *bona fide* purchaser of the Contiguous Parcel despite his June 1986 notice of Daniels' interest. Zografos invoked the doctrine of equitable conversion in support of his *bona fide* purchaser defense. He argued that although he did not take legal title to the Contiguous Parcel until August 1986, he became the equitable owner of the Contiguous Parcel in September 1985, when he entered into the contract. Thus, Zografos reasoned, he became a *bona fide* purchaser because he took equitable title prior to receiving the June 1986 notice of Daniels' interest. The appellate court concluded that Zografos waived this theory.

Zografos repeats this theory before this court. We agree with the appellate court that Zografos did not assert this theory in any pleading, memorandum, argument, or post-trial motion in the trial court. Rather, Zografos raised this theory for the first time on appeal. "It has frequently been held that the theory upon which a case is tried in the lower court cannot be changed on review, and that an issue not presented to or considered by the trial court cannot be raised for the first time on review." Kravis v. Smith Marine, Inc. (1975), 60 Ill. 2d 141, 147, 324 N.E.2d 417.... Zografos ... argues that ... his presentation in the trial court encompassed the doctrine. ... Zografos' attempt to avoid the waiver rule fails. Although the parties addressed the issue of when Zografos received notice of Daniels' right of first refusal, the ... record shows that Zografos did *not* contend in the trial court that he *had already owned* the Contiguous Parcel prior to the June 1986 notice. ... We uphold the appellate court's finding that Zografos has waived application of the doctrine of equitable conversion.

We must next address, absent consideration of the equitable conversion doctrine, the issue of when during the executory stages of a real estate installment contract does the buyer become a *bona fide* purchaser. Zografos contends that, during this executory period, the buyer can rely solely on the public records and ignore even actual notice of an outstanding, unrecorded interest. This contention is erroneous. The legal principles are quite established. As we earlier noted, a *bona fide* purchaser, by definition, takes title to real property *without notice* of the interests of others. A buyer who, prior to the payment of *any* consideration receives notice of an outstanding interest, pays the consideration at his or her peril with respect to the holder of the outstanding interest. Such a buyer is not protected as a *bona fide* purchaser and takes the property bound by the outstanding interest. The law reasons that consummation of the purchase, after notice of the outstanding interest, is a fraud upon the holder of that interest.

Where a buyer receives notice of an outstanding interest subsequent to paying *some,* but prior to paying the full purchase price, authorities differ on whether the buyer is a *bona fide* purchaser. As the appellate court noted, some of the authorities state that partial payment of the consideration is insufficient to render the buyer a *bona fide* purchaser. However, a majority of jurisdictions have relaxed this harsh rule. Instead, they apply a *pro tanto* rule, which protects the buyer to the extent of the payments made prior to notice, but no further. (R. Cunningham, W. Stoebuck, D. Whitman, Property 795 (1984); 8 J. Grimes, Thompson on Real Property § 4322, at 418–19 (1963); 5 B. Jones, Tiffany on Real Property § 1305 (3d ed. 1939).) This court recognized this *pro tanto* rule in *dicta* in Redden v. Miller, 95 Ill. 336, 346 (1880).

Courts have identified at least three methods to apply this *pro tanto* protection. First, the most common method is to award the land to the holder of the outstanding interest and award the buyer the payments that he or she made. The second method is to award the buyer a fractional interest in the land proportional to the amount paid prior to notice. The third method is to allow the buyer to complete the purchase, but to pay the remaining installments to the holder of the outstanding interest. (R. Cunningham, W. Stoebuck, D. Whitman, Property 795–96 (1984); 8 J. Grimes, Thompson on Real Property § 4322, at 418 (1984).) Courts exercise considerable latitude in these cases, taking into account the relative equities of the parties. . . .

In the present case, the trial court ordered Zografos to convey the Contiguous Parcel to Daniels and ordered Daniels to pay Zografos the full purchase price. The trial court also ordered Daniels to reimburse Zografos for the property taxes that Zografos had paid on the property. We agree with the appellate court that the trial court's disposition of this issue, between Daniels and Zografos, satisfied these well-settled principles of equity. We cannot say that the trial court abused its discretion. . . . [Affirmed.]

NOTES, QUESTIONS, AND PROBLEMS

1. *Equitable Conversion.* Suppose that Zografos had raised the equitable conversion claim in the trial court. Should that change the result?

2. *Which Solution?* The court says that there are three possible remedies: (1) Benefit of the bargain to the subsequent buyer; (2) Fractional ownership; or (3) Restitution to the subsequent buyer. The Illinois court opts for the third possibility, a result often justified by one or both of two arguments: 1) Unless the buyer has actually paid for the property he is not injured by preferring the prior interest holder, and 2) A buyer who continues

to pay the seller after he has notice of a prior claim does so gratuitously, because there has been a failure of consideration, thus relieving the buyer of his obligations. Are these justifications sound? If a subsequent buyer makes partial payment and then loses his interest in the property, is it true that he has suffered no injury? Is the latter argument a sufficient reason to distinguish between the buyer who owes the balance of the purchase price to the seller and a buyer who borrows funds from third party to pay the seller all cash at the closing? What factors ought to be taken into account in deciding which remedy is best?

In thinking about these issues, consider the following problems:

a. *O* owns Blackacre and Whiteacre in fee simple. *O* borrows money from *A* and gives *A* a mortgage on each of Blackacre and Whiteacre to secure payment. The mortgage is not recorded. Then *O* sells Blackacre to *B* for $5,000 cash, received by *O* at the closing. *B* records his deed to Blackacre. On the same day, *O* sells Whiteacre to *C* for $5,000. At the closing *O* receives $500 from *C* and *C*'s note for $4,500, representing the balance of the purchase price. *C* records his deed to Whiteacre. Neither *B* nor *C* knew about the prior mortgage to *A* when they received and recorded their deeds. *O* stops paying *A* and *A* seeks to foreclose on his mortgage. Should *B* prevail over *A* because he had paid the full price before he had actual notice? Should *A* prevail over *C* because at the time *C* received actual notice (by the foreclosure action) he still owed *O* $4,500? See Davis v. Ward, 109 Cal. 186 (1895).

b. *X* owns Blackacre in fee simple. *X* borrows money from *Y* and gives *Y* a mortgage on Blackacre. Before the mortgage is recorded *X* agrees to sell Blackacre to *Z* for $5,000. At the closing *Z* pays $500 cash and delivers his note in favor of *X* for $4,500. *Z* receives a deed to Blackacre and records the deed. A day later *Y* records his mortgage. A month later *Z* pays the remaining $4,500 plus interest to *Z*. Three years later *Y* seeks to foreclose on the mortgage. Who should prevail? Suppose that instead of giving *X* his note for $4,500, *Z* borrowed $4,500 from *ABC Financial Corp.* and gave *ABC Financial* a note for $4,500. Should that make a difference to the outcome? See Lewis v. Superior Court, 30 Cal.App.4th 1850 (1994)

3. Creditors. Not all creditors that acquire an interest in real property have given valuable consideration. For example, a creditor that has extended unsecured credit and later takes a mortgage on real property to secure payment of the debt has not given value for the interest unless the creditor alters the terms of the debt in some way that is detrimental to the lender and advantageous to the debtor.

Example 8–11: *O* borrows $100,000 from *A* and gives *A* his promissory note in return. The note requires *O* to pay interest of 6% annually, in equal monthly payments of $500, and to pay the outstanding principal balance on the third anniversary of the date of the note. *O* encounters financial difficulty and asks *A* to extend the due date. *A* agrees to extend the due date to the tenth anniversary of the date of the note, but in return demands and receives a mortgage on Blackacre, which is owned by *O* subject to a prior unrecorded mortgage in favor of *B* and of which *A* is unaware. *A* records. *A* has given valuable consideration and has priority over *B*. See Van Cleve v. Meyers, 108 N.J.Eq. 421 (1931); O'Brien v.

Fleckenstein, 180 N.Y. 350 (1905); Sweeney v. Bixler, 69 Ala. 539, 542 (1881) (dicta).

Example 8–12: O borrows $20,000 from A and gives A his promissory note in return. The note bears interest at 6% annually, calls for monthly interest payments of $100, and is due upon A's demand. After O misses several interest payments, A demands and receives a mortgage on Blackacre, owned by O subject to a prior unrecorded mortgage in favor of B and of which A is unaware. In return, A promises to forebear from instituting suit on the note "for the time being." A records. Then B records. A has not given valuable consideration. See Gabel v. Drewrys, Ltd., U.S.A., 68 So.2d 372 (1953). But if O had given A a deed to Blackacre in extinguishment of the debt, and A had recorded the deed before B recorded his prior mortgage, A would have given valuable consideration and would prevail. After all, A surrendered his personal claim against all of O's assets by taking the deed. See Fox v. Templeton, 229 Va. 380 (1985).

A related problem exists when a judgment creditor records his judgment as a lien against real property owned by the judgment debtor. In general, unless the jurisdiction's recording act contains provisions protecting the judgment creditor's recorded lien from prior unrecorded claims, the judgment creditor is treated like the creditor who has taken a mortgage to secure a pre-existing debt without altering his position detrimentally. See, e.g., Geller v. Meek, 496 N.E.2d 103 (Ind. App. 1986). An example of a statute explicitly protecting judgment creditors is Calif. Civ. Code § 1214:

> Every conveyance of real property or an estate for years therein, other than a lease for a term not exceeding one year, is void as against any subsequent purchaser or mortgagee of the same property, or any part thereof, in good faith and for a valuable consideration, whose conveyance is first duly recorded, and as against any judgment affecting the title, unless the conveyance shall have been duly recorded prior to the record of notice of action.

Mechanics' liens, which are a lien for value previously provided (in the form of goods and services) are generally treated the same way as judgment creditors' liens.

4. Quit Claim Deeds. Some jurisdictions treat the grantee of a quit claim deed as lacking bona fide purchaser status, on the theory that the refusal or failure of the grantor to warrant title places the grantee on constructive notice of all defects in the title. See Equitable Trust Co. v. Roland, 721 S.W.2d 530, 534 (Tex. App. 1986). Other states regard a quit claim as sufficiently suspicious that the grantee is under a duty to inquire about title defects. See Winkler v. Miller, 54 Iowa 476 (1880). But most states reject these reasons. Either by statute or judicial decision these doctrines have been widely rejected. See 14 Powell on Real Property § 82.02[1][d][iii][B]. The reason for their rejection is that a purchaser who pays value must be thought to have been satisfied as to the state of title, and a purchaser who does not pay value will be unprotected in any case. Thus, there is no good reason to disfavor quit claim deeds, which serve many useful functions and are not always an indicator of defective title.

5. WHAT COMPOSES THE CHAIN OF TITLE?

The chain of title is the expression used to denote the collection of recorded instruments that trace the passage of title back from the present record owner to an adequate root of title. Recall that when searching a grantor-grantee index the title searcher goes backward in time from the present record owner, searching through the grantee index to locate the instrument that conveyed title to the present owner, and then backward through time to locate when the grantor of that instrument received title as a grantee, and so on until an adequate root of title is found. That describes, as it were, one side of a series of links that compose a chain, but the other side of those links is not yet established. The searcher goes forward in time from the root of title through the grantor index to locate when the root of title owner granted title to the next in line, and then searches forward to determine when that grantee granted title to the next person in the chain, until the links are finally welded together into a chain when the grant to the present record owner is located. A tract index is much simpler. In a tract index the searcher examines the records that pertain to the tract of land in question back to the root of title. The chain of title is already laid out. Of course, in both types of search the title examiner must read the instruments themselves, for the index merely tells the searcher that the instrument exists and where to locate it in the records.

These indexing methods lead to some common problems, which will be discussed in this subsection. For a comprehensive discussion of these problems, see Harry M. Cross, The Record Chain of Title Hypocrisy, 57 Colum. L. Rev. 787 (1957).

a. Improper Indexing

What happens when an instrument is improperly indexed, or the recorder simply fails to index the instrument? In a grantor-grantee index, suppose the grant from Burnim Woods to Malcolm Canmohr is indexed as from Burnim to Malcolm, instead of from Woods to Canmohr. A title searcher, looking for a grant to Canmohr will not find it in the index; nor will the searcher looking for a grant from Woods find such a grant in the index. Although most states treat anything of record as part of the record, no matter how impossible it may be to find it by normal search methods, the emerging trend is to regard a wrongly indexed instrument (or one not indexed at all) as not recorded. Compare Haner v. Bruce, 146 Vt. 262 (1985), with Hochstein v. Romero, 219 Cal.App.3d 447 (1990). See also Section A.3.b of this chapter, in the discussion of "Mother Hubbard" clauses. Improper indexing can occur in tract indexes if the instrument is noted in the wrong tract, as when a deed to 123 Maple Street is indexed in the tract record for 1223 Maple Street.

b. "Wild" Deeds

What happens if an owner, readily identifiable in the chain of title by the usual search methods, makes a transfer that is unrecorded, but the transferee later deeds the property to his grantee and that subsequent deed is recorded?

>   *Example 8–13:* O, the record owner of Blackacre, deeds Blackacre to W, who does not record the deed. Later, O deeds Blackacre to A, who is unaware of the O to W deed, and records the O to A deed. Then W deeds Blackacre to X, who records. A then conveys Blackacre to B, who records. As between X and B, who should prevail?

What happens if a person who does not have title purports to transfer his interest to a grantee who records, and then transfers his interest after he actually acquires title to a different grantee, who records?

>   *Example 8–14:* S purports to convey Whiteacre to F by quit claim deed, but S actually has no interest in Whiteacre. F records the deed. Then O, who is the true record owner of Whiteacre, deeds Whiteacre to S, who records the deed. Then S deeds Whiteacre to P, who pays valuable consideration and knows nothing of the S to F deed. P records his deed. As between F and P, who should prevail? Would it make any difference if the S to F deed was a general warranty deed instead of a quit claim deed?

The following cases explore the issues raised by Examples 8–13 and 8–14. Note that these problems will not arise in a properly indexed tract index because all of the recorded instruments will appear in the tract index, thus eliminating the need for a special rule to deal with wild deeds—those not in the chain of title that is revealed by a search of a grantor-grantee index.

BOARD OF EDUCATION OF MINNEAPOLIS v. HUGHES

Supreme Court of Minnesota
118 Minn. 404 (1912)

BUNN, J., delivered the opinion of the court.

[This is a suit] to determine adverse claims to a lot in Minneapolis. ... The trial resulted in a decision in favor of plaintiff, and defendant [Hughes] appealed....

On May 16, 1906, Carrie B. Hoerger ... owned the lot in question, which was vacant and subject to unpaid delinquent taxes. ... Hughes offered to pay $25 for this lot. His offer was accepted, and he sent his check for the purchase price of this and two other lots bought at the same time to Ed. Hoerger, husband of the owner, together with a deed to be executed and returned. The name of the grantee in the deed was not inserted; the space for the same being left blank. It was executed and acknowledged by Carrie B. Hoerger and her husband on May 17, 1906, and delivered to defendant Hughes by mail. The check was retained and cashed. Hughes filled in the name of the grantee, but not until shortly prior to the date when the deed was recorded, which was December 16, 1910. On April 27, 1909, Duryea & Wilson, real estate dealers, paid Mrs. Hoerger $25 for a quitclaim deed to the lot, which was executed and delivered to them, but which was not recorded until December 21, 1910.

On November 19, 1909, Duryea & Wilson executed and delivered to plaintiff a warranty deed to the lot, which deed was filed for record January 27, 1910. It thus appears that the deed to Hughes was recorded before the deed to Duryea & Wilson, though the deed from them to plaintiff was recorded before the deed to [Hughes].

The questions for our consideration may be thus stated: (1) Did the deed from Hoerger to Hughes ever become operative? (2) If so, is he a subsequent purchaser whose deed was first duly recorded, within the language of the recording act?

The decision of the first question involves a consideration of the effect of the delivery of a deed by the grantor to the grantee with the name of the latter omitted from the space provided for it, without express authority to the grantee to insert his own or another name in the blank space. It is settled that a deed that does not name a grantee is a nullity, and wholly inoperative as a conveyance, until the name of the grantee is legally inserted. [Therefore,] the deed to defendant Hughes was not operative as a conveyance until his name was inserted as grantee. [In any case,] Hughes had implied authority from the grantor to fill the blank with his own name as grantee, and that when he did so the deed became operative. . . . [A] deed which is a nullity when delivered because the name of the grantee is omitted becomes operative without a new execution or acknowledgment if the grantee, with either express or implied authority from the grantor, inserts his name in the blank space left for the name of the grantee. . . .

When the Hughes deed was recorded, there was of record a deed to the lot from Duryea & Wilson to plaintiff, but no record showing that Duryea & Wilson had any title to convey. The deed to them from the common grantor had not been recorded. We hold that this record of a deed from an apparent stranger to the title was not notice to Hughes of the prior unrecorded conveyance by his grantor. He was a subsequent purchaser in good faith for a valuable consideration, whose conveyance was first duly recorded; that is, Hughes' conveyance dates from the time when he filled the blank space, which was after the deed from his grantor to Duryea & Wilson. He was, therefore, a "subsequent purchaser," and is protected by the recording of his deed before the prior deed was recorded. The statute cannot be construed so as to give priority to a deed recorded before, which shows no conveyance from a record owner. It was necessary, not only that the deed to plaintiff should be recorded before the deed to Hughes, but also that the deed to plaintiff's grantor should be first recorded. Our conclusion is that the learned trial court should have held on the evidence that defendant L. A. Hughes was the owner of the lot.

Order reversed. . . .

FAR WEST SAVINGS AND LOAN ASSOCIATION v. McLAUGHLIN

Court of Appeal of California, Second District
201 Cal.App.3d 67 (1988)

CROSKEY, J., delivered the opinion of the court.

... McLaughlin ... appeal[s] from a summary judgment granted in favor of plaintiff and respondent Far West Savings and Loan Association (Far West). Far West claims priority for its deed of trust over an earlier recorded encumbrance given to McLaughlin by an unrecorded grantee whose deed placing him in the chain of title was not recorded until the same date as Far West's deed of trust. [We] hold ... that Far West did not have actual knowledge or notice of the earlier encumbrance, [and so] we affirm the judgment. . . .

On June 1, 1982, Frederick Geiger (Geiger) acquired record title to real property in Sylmar located at 13553 Polk Street. A purchase money deed of trust from Geiger to Hancock Savings and Loan Association for $92,000 was also recorded that same day. On July 8, 1982, Geiger executed a grant deed transferring the property to GTB Properties (GTB). However, *that document was not recorded until July 1, 1983*, almost a year later. Meanwhile, on August 3, 1982, GTB executed a deed of trust for $51,888.49 in favor of McLaughlin ("GTB deed of trust") and *on August 10, 1982, this document was recorded*. On July 1, 1983, as part of Escrow No. 2134 at Burbank Escrow, the following three documents were recorded in the following sequential order: (1) a purported "reconveyance" of the GTB deed of trust executed by the Vice President of Burbank Escrow as trustee;[2] (2) the Geiger grant deed to GTB (dated July 8, 1982); and (3) a grant deed conveying the property from GTB to Thomas and Jean Stapleton (Stapleton). On the same date, as part of Escrow No. 2231 at Burbank Escrow a purchase money deed of trust executed by Stapleton in favor of Far West for $105,300, was also recorded. From the $105,300 loan made by Far West, the outstanding first trust deed obligation to Hancock Savings and Loan Association was satisfied.

On February 3, 1984, after Stapleton had failed to make timely payments, Far West recorded a Notice of Default and Election to Sell under Deed of Trust in order to foreclose Stapleton's interest in the Sylmar property. On May 15, 1984, Far West recorded a Notice of Trustee's Sale and, on July 5, 1984, acquired title to the property at a nonjudicial foreclosure sale. Subsequently, McLaughlin informed Far West of their intention to foreclose under the GTB deed of trust and denied that Far West (1) was a bona fide encumbrancer for value or (2) had subsequently taken title as a bona fide purchaser for value.

---

2. For reasons that are not explained in the record, this "reconveyance" was executed by an officer of Burbank Escrow, a "nonparty" to the original deed of trust. Chicago Title Insurance Company was the named trustee and as such was the proper party to execute the reconveyance. As a result, such "reconveyance" was a nullity.

On April 9, 1985, Far West filed a complaint for declaratory relief seeking a declaration that its interest in the property was unencumbered by any claim or right of McLaughlin. Far West denies the priority of the GTB deed of trust on several grounds: (1) it "is a 'wild' Deed of Trust which does not appear within the chain of title, . . ." and that accordingly, Far West cannot be charged with constructive notice thereof; [and] (2) Far West "did not have actual knowledge of [McLaughlin's] claim to the subject property. . . ." [The trial court granted Far West's motion for summary judgment and entered judgment accordingly.] This appeal followed. . . .

The GTB Deed of Trust Was a "Wild" Document Which Was Never in the Chain of Title

Proper recordation of a real property instrument is necessary to impart constructive notice of its contents. (Civ. Code, §§ 1213, 1214.)[3] If an instrument cannot be located by searching the "grantor" and "grantee" indices of the public records, the instrument does not constitute constructive notice and later bona fide purchasers or encumbrances are not charged with knowledge of its existence.

The GTB deed of trust was recorded *before GTB obtained record title*. Therefore, it must be termed a "wild" document, i.e., one recorded outside the chain of title. As such, a search of the grantor/grantee indices could not have disclosed its existence. "One who is not connected by any conveyance whatever with the record title to a piece of property and makes a conveyance thereof, does not thereby create any defect in the record title of another when such title is deducible by intermediate effective conveyances from the original owners to that other. . . . Such a deed would not even be constructive notice." Bothin v. The California Title Ins. Co., 153 Cal. 718, 723 (1908). . . .

This same rule applies to a conveyance by a person who is in the chain of title, but who makes a conveyance *prior to his acquisition of record title*. His conveyance, at the time it is made, is that of a stranger to the title; and, although he afterwards gains record title and makes another conveyance, the second grantee is not bound, in his search of the record, to determine whether his grantor, or any grantor in the chain, made a conveyance *before such grantor became a part of the chain*. The second grantee who purchases for value and records first will prevail by virtue of the terms of the recording statute. He has no constructive notice of the deed to the first grantee, for the record of such deed, made before

3. Civil Code section 1213 provides in pertinent part: "Every conveyance of real property acknowledged or proved and certified and recorded as prescribed by law from the time it is filed with the recorder for record is constructive notice of the contents thereof to subsequent purchasers and mortgagees; . . ."

Civil Code section 1214 provides: "Every conveyance of real property, other than a lease for a term not exceeding one year, is void as against any subsequent purchaser or mortgagee of the same property, or any part thereof, in good faith and for a valuable consideration, whose conveyance is first duly recorded, and as against any judgment affecting the title, unless such conveyance shall have been duly recorded prior to the record of notice of action."

the grantor had title, *is not in the chain of title.* For the first grantee to prevail he would have to have recorded his deed *again* (1) *after* record title had come to his grantor and (2) *before* the second grantee had given value.

McLaughlin did not later record again after GTB acquired record title; therefore, the GTB deed of trust remained outside the chain of title. Contrary to McLaughlin's argument, the later recordation, on July 1, 1983, of the July 8, 1982, Geiger grant deed to GTB did not bring the GTB deed of trust into the chain of title. To accomplish that, McLaughlin would have had to record the GTB deed of trust again, *after the grant deed to GTB had been recorded, and before Far West gave value.* This, of course, did not happen. . . .

Finally, from the record before us, no evidence was presented showing that Far West had any actual knowledge of McLaughlin's deed of trust. . . .

The judgment of dismissal is affirmed. . . .

SABO v. HORVATH

Supreme Court of Alaska
559 P.2d 1038 (Alaska 1976)

BOOCHEVER, C.J., delivered the opinion of the court.

This appeal arises because Grover C. Lowery conveyed the same five-acre piece of land twice—first to William A. Horvath and Barbara J. Horvath and later to William Sabo and Barbara Sabo. Both conveyances were by separate [quit claim deeds.] Lowery's interest in the land originates in a patent from the United States Government under 43 U.S.C. § 687a (1970) ("Alaska Homesite Law").[4] Lowery's conveyance to the Horvaths was prior to the issuance of patent, and his subsequent conveyance to the Sabos was after the issuance of patent. The Horvaths recorded their deed . . . on January 5, 1970; the Sabos recorded their deed on December 13, 1973. The transfer to the Horvaths, however, predated patent and title, and thus the Horvaths' interest in the land was recorded "outside the chain of title." Mr. Horvath brought suit to quiet title, and the Sabos counterclaimed to quiet their title.

[The] superior court ruled that Lowery had an equitable interest capable of transfer at the time of his conveyance to the Horvaths and further said the transfer contemplated more than a "mere quitclaim"—it warranted patent would be transferred. The superior court also held that Horvath had the superior claim to the land because his prior recording had given the Sabos constructive notice. . . . The Sabos' appeal raises the following issues:

1. . . . [When] did Lowery obtain a present equitable interest in land which he could convey?

---

4. [Ed.—Under this statute, a person may claim a five acre parcel of federally owned public land in Alaska as a homestead, and after proving to the satisfaction of the Interior Secretary that the parcel is in fact a homestead, may purchase title to the land for $10. The deed from the United States to the homesteader is termed a patent.]

2. Are the Sabos, as grantees under a quitclaim deed, "subsequent innocent purchaser[s] in good faith"?

3. Is the Horvaths' first recorded interest, which is outside the chain of title, constructive notice to Sabo?

We affirm the trial court's ruling that Lowery had an interest to convey at the time of his conveyance to the Horvaths. We further hold that Sabo may be a "good faith purchaser" even though he takes by quitclaim deed. We reverse the trial court's ruling that Sabo had constructive notice and hold that a deed recorded outside the chain of title is a "wild deed" and does not give constructive notice under the recording laws of Alaska.[5]

The facts may be stated as follows. Grover C. Lowery occupied land . . . on October 10, 1964 for purposes of obtaining Federal patent. Lowery . . . made his application to purchase on June 6, 1967 with the Bureau of Land Management (BLM). On March 7, 1968, the BLM . . . recommended that patent issue to Lowery. On October 7, 1969, a request for survey was made by the United States Government. On January 3, 1970, Lowery issued a "Quitclaim Deed" to the Horvaths; Horvath recorded the deed on January 5, 1970. . . . Horvath testified that when he bought the land from Lowery, he knew patent and title were still in the United States Government, but he did not re-record his interest after patent had passed to Lowery. Following the sale to the Horvaths, [Lowery was issued] the patent on August 10, 1973.

Almost immediately after the patent was issued, Lowery advertised the land for sale in a newspaper. He then executed a second . . . "quitclaim" [deed] to the Sabos on October 15, 1973. The Sabos duly recorded this document on December 13, 1973. . . .

The first question this court must consider is whether Lowery had an interest to convey at the time of his transfer to the Horvaths. [After a lengthy examination of the federal "Alaska Homesite Law," the court concluded] that at the time Lowery executed the deed to the Horvaths he had complied with the statute to a sufficient extent so as to have an interest in the land which was capable of conveyance.

Since the Horvaths received a valid interest from Lowery, we must now resolve the conflict between the Horvaths' first recorded interest and the Sabos' later recorded interest. The Sabos, like the Horvaths, received their interest in the property by a quitclaim deed. They are asserting that their interest supersedes the Horvaths under Alaska's statutory recording system. AS 34.15.290 provides that:

A conveyance of real property . . . is void as against a subsequent innocent purchaser . . . for a valuable consideration of the property

---

5. Because we hold Lowery had a conveyable interest under the Federal statute, we need not decide issues raised by the parties regarding after-acquired property and the related issue of estoppel by deed.

... whose conveyance is first duly recorded. An unrecorded instrument is valid ... as against one who has actual notice of it.

Initially, we must decide whether the Sabos, who received their interest by means of a quitclaim deed, can ever be "innocent purchaser[s]" within the meaning of AS 34.15.290. Since a "quitclaim" only transfers the interest of the grantor, the question is whether a "quitclaim" deed itself puts a purchaser on constructive notice. Although the authorities are in conflict over this issue, the clear weight of authority is that a quitclaim grantee can be protected by the recording system, assuming, of course, the grantee purchased for valuable consideration and did not otherwise have actual or constructive knowledge as defined by the recording laws.[6] We choose to follow the majority rule and hold that a quitclaim grantee is not precluded from attaining the status of an "innocent purchaser."

In this case, the Horvaths recorded their interest from Lowery prior to the time the Sabos recorded their interest. Thus, the issue is whether the Sabos are charged with constructive knowledge because of the Horvaths' prior recordation. Horvath is correct in his assertion that in the usual case a prior recorded deed serves as constructive notice pursuant to AS 34.15.290, and thus precludes a subsequent recordation from taking precedence. Here, however, the Sabos argue that because Horvath recorded his deed prior to Lowery having obtained patent, they were not given constructive notice by the recording system. They contend that since Horvaths' recordation was outside the chain of title, the recording should be regarded as a "wild deed." It is an axiom of hornbook law that a purchaser has notice only of recorded instruments that are within his "chain of title."[7] If a grantor (Lowery) transfers prior to obtaining title, and the grantee (Horvath) records prior to title passing, a second grantee who diligently examines all conveyances under the grantor's name from the date that the grantor had secured title would not discover the prior conveyance. The rule in most jurisdictions which have adopted a grantor-grantee index system of recording is that a "wild deed" does not serve as constructive notice to a subsequent purchaser who duly records.[8]

---

6. *See Note, Deeds–Quitclaim Grantee as a Bona Fide Purchaser,* 28 Ore.L.Rev. 258 n. 1 (1949) and the many cases cited therein. *See generally,* Annot., 59 A.L.R. 632 (1929); Annot., 162 A.L.R. 556, 560–62 (1946); 77 Am.Jur.2d, Vendor and Purchaser, §§ 711–13....

7. 1 R. Patton & C. Patton, Patton on Land Titles § 69, at 230–33 (2d ed. 1957). *Cities Service Oil Co. v. Adair,* 273 F.2d 673, 676 (10th Cir. 1959); *Stafford v. Ballinger,* 199 Cal.App.2d 289, 18 Cal.Rptr. 568, 572 (1962); *Pierson v. Bill,* 138 Fla. 104, 189 So. 679, 684 (1939); *Jenkins v. Bates,* 230 Miss. 406, 92 So.2d 655, 657 (1957); *Baker v. Koch,* 114 Ohio App. 519, 183 N.E.2d 434, 437 (1960); *Portman v. Earnhart,* 343 S.W.2d 294, 297 (Tex.Civ.App. 1960); *Lone Star Gas Co. v. Sheaner,* 297 S.W.2d 855, 857 (Tex.Civ.App. 1957); *Hyson v. Dodge,* 198 Va. 792, 96 S.E.2d 792, 796 (1957).

8. 1 R. Patton & C. Patton, Patton on Land Title § 69, at 230–33 (2d ed. 1957); *Lacey v. Humphres,* 196 Ark. 72, 116 S.W.2d 345, 347 (1938); *Etchison v. Dail,* 182 Ark. 350, 31 S.W.2d 426, 427 (Ark. 1930); *Brown v. Copp,* 105 Cal.App.2d 1, 232 P.2d 868, 871 (1951); *Hawley v. McCabe,* 117 Conn. 558, 169 A. 192, 194 (1933); *Ward v. Parks,* 166 Ga. 149, 142 S.E. 690, 692 (1928); *Manson v. Berkman,* 356 Ill. 20, 190 N.E. 77, 79 (1934); *Blumenthal v. Serota,* 129 Me. 187, 151 A. 138, 141 (1930); *Smith v. Williams,* 132 Okl. 141, 269 P. 1067, 1073 (1928); *Brown v. Ackerman,* 17 S.W.2d 771 (Tex.Com.App. 1929).

Alaska's recording system utilizes a "grantor-grantee" index. Had Sabo searched title under both grantor's and grantee's names but limited his search to the chain of title subsequent to patent, he would not be chargeable with discovery of the pre-patent transfer to Horvath.

On one hand, we could require Sabo to check beyond the chain of title to look for pre-title conveyances. While in this particular case the burden may not have been great, as a general rule, requiring title checks beyond the chain of title could add a significant burden as well as uncertainty to real estate purchases. To a certain extent, requiring title searches of records prior to the date of a grantor acquired title would thus defeat the purposes of the recording system. The records as to each grantor in the chain of title would theoretically have to be checked back to the later of the grantor's date of birth or the date when records were first retained.

On the other hand, we could require Horvath to re-record his interest in the land once title passes, that is, after patent had issued to Lowery. As a general rule, re-recording an interest once title passes is less of a burden than requiring property purchasers to check indefinitely beyond the chain of title.

It is unfortunate that in this case due to Lowery's double conveyances, one or the other party to this suit must suffer an undeserved loss. We are cognizant that in this case, the equities are closely balanced between the parties to this appeal. Our decision, however, in addition to resolving the litigants' dispute, must delineate the requirements of Alaska's recording laws. Because we want to promote simplicity and certainty in title transactions, we choose to follow the majority rule and hold that the Horvaths' deed, recorded outside the chain of title, does not give constructive notice to the Sabos and is not "duly recorded" under the Alaskan Recording Act, AS 34.15.290. Since the Sabos' interest is the first duly recorded interest and was recorded without actual or constructive knowledge of the prior deed, we hold that the Sabos' interest must prevail. The trial court's decision is accordingly [reversed].

NOTES AND QUESTIONS

1. The Truly Wild Deed. Example 8–13 involves a deed that is impossible to discover by normal search methods of a grantor-grantee index. That is the pattern presented by *Hughes.* Reduced to schematics, the Minnesota court saw the facts as follows: Hoerger conveyed to D & W, who did not record. Then D & W conveyed to Board, who records. Then Hoerger conveyed to Hughes, who records. Then D & W records the Hoerger to D & W deed. Hughes prevailed against Board. Hughes lacked actual notice of the Hoerger to D & W deed, and a diligent search of the index could not possibly reveal the D & W to Board deed, because there was nothing in the record to connect Hoerger, the record owner, to D & W. Searching for the D & W to Board deed is a search for the proverbial needle in a haystack.

But note that the court says that the first deed from Hoerger—in blank but delivered to Hughes in 1906—was ineffective until Hughes filled in his name, at the time he recorded it on December 16, 1910. Yet the court says that Hughes was empowered by Hoerger to fill in his name, which he could have done at any time after May 17, 1906. So why wasn't the deed effective upon delivery? If it was effective at that moment, would that have changed the result? Remember that Minnesota is a race-notice state. Suppose Minnesota was a pure notice state; would the result depend on when Hughes's deed became effective?

2. *Recording too early:* Far West *and* Sabo. When Far West loaned a portion of the purchase price of the Sylmar property to Stapleton, and recorded its deed of trust to secure that loan, Far West had constructive notice only of the Geiger to GTB deed but could not have known from the record about the GTB to McLaughlin deed unless it went back in time to search for possible transfers made by GTB before it appeared as a record owner. If it had done so it would have found the GTB to McLaughlin deed of trust, recorded on August 10, 1982, almost a year before GTB appeared as the record owner. The question is whether a searcher should be obliged to do so. Such a duty means that the search must be pushed back in time to the date of birth of each grantor, or at least to the point in past time that establishes a root of title. While not impossible, this is a substantial burden. The same problem appears in *Sabo.* If the Lowery to Horvath deed was treated as recorded and thus in the chain of title Sabo would be required to search back in time from the moment that Lowery acquired record title.

Suppose that the Alaska Supreme Court had ruled that Lowery had no interest to convey to Horvath when he gave Horvath a deed. Would that alter the result? What if Lowery had no interest to convey to Horvath but he had delivered to Horvath a general warranty deed?

3. *The Grantor Who Changes Names.* What happens if a grantor changes his or her name between the time they acquired title and their later transfer of title? The most oft-married woman is supposed to be Linda Wolfe, married 23 times.[10] Born Linda Lou Taylor in 1941, she presumably assumed 21 different surnames since her first marriage in 1957 to George Scott (because she married Jack Gourley three times). Suppose that Linda Wolfe had been a real-estate wheeler-dealer, frequently buying and selling properties and that during the interim between marriages she used her maiden name. Thus, imagine that in January she acquired title to Blackacre as Linda Gourley, but in July sold Blackacre as Linda Taylor. Is this a wild deed? Should the answer depend on whether the jurisdiction uses a grantor-grantee index or a tract index?

4. *Recording Too Late.* What rule should apply when the recipient of a prior deed records after a later donee has recorded his subsequent deed?

Problems:

a. *O* conveys Blackacre to *A* for valuable consideration. *A* does not record his deed. Then *O* conveys Blackacre as a gift to *B*, and *B* records the deed. Then *A* records his deed. Then *B* conveys Blackacre to *C*, who pays

---

10. See http://www.telegraph.co.uk/news/newstopics/howaboutthat/4796811/Grandmother-is-most-married-woman-after-tying-the-knot-23-times.html.

valuable consideration and is ignorant of the *O* to *A* deed. As between *A* and *C*, who should prevail?

b. *O* conveys Blackacre to *A* for valuable consideration. *A* does not record his deed. Then *O* conveys Blackacre to *B*, who pays valuable consideration and is ignorant of the *O* to *A* deed. *B* records the deed. Then *A* records his deed. Then *B* conveys Blackacre to *C* as a gift and, for good measure, tells *C* that *A* has recorded a deed to Blackare from *O*. As between *A* and *C*, who should prevail?

Compare Morse v. Curtis, 140 Mass. 112 (1885), with Woods v. Garnett, 72 Miss. 78 (1894). A more recent comparison is Jefferson County v. Mosley, 284 Ala. 593 (1969), and Spaulding v. H.E. Fletcher Co., 124 Vt. 318 (1964).

As with the other chain of title problems encountered so far, note that this problem will not occur in a tract index. At the time *C* acquires title the tract index will display the recorded *O* to *A* deed, so there is no additional burden placed on a title searcher.

Consider the following problem.

Example and Problem 8–15: *O* owns Lots 1 and 2, adjacent to one another. Each of Lots 1 and 2 are separate tracts. *O* conveys Lot 1 to *A* by a deed that recites that *O*, on behalf of himself and his successors in interest in Lot 2, grants *A* and his successors in interest an easement for parking on Lot 2. *A* records the deed. Later, *O* conveys Lot 2 to *B* under a general warranty deed that makes no mention of the parking easement. *B* refuses to allow *A* to park on Lot 2. *A* sues to enforce the easement. Who should prevail?

WITTER v. TAGGART

Court of Appeals of New York
78 N.Y.2d 234 (1991)

BELLACOSA, J., delivered the opinion of the court.

Plaintiff Witter and defendants Taggarts are East Islip neighboring property owners. Their homes are on opposite sides of a canal on the south shore of Long Island. . . . Champlin's Creek lies immediately west of both parcels. Their property dispute arose when the Taggarts erected a 70–foot long dock on their canal-side frontage. This was done after a title search revealed that their deed expressly permitted building the dock and reflected no recorded restrictions in their direct property chain against doing so. Witter complained of a violation of his scenic easement to an unobstructed view of the creek and an adjacent nature preserve, which he claims is protected by a restrictive covenant contained in his chain of title. He sued to compel the Taggarts to dismantle and remove the dock and to permanently enjoin any such building in the future.

Supreme Court granted the Taggarts' motion for summary judgment dismissing Witter's complaint and denied Witter's cross motion for summary judgment. Relying principally on Buffalo Academy of Sacred Heart v. Boehm Bros., 267 NY 242 (1935), the trial court held that the Taggarts are not bound by or charged with constructive notice of a restrictive covenant which does not appear in their direct chain of title to the allegedly burdened land. ... The Appellate Division affirmed....

We granted Witter's motion for leave to appeal to decide whether the covenant recited in Witter's chain of title to his purported "dominant" land, which appears nowhere in the direct chain of title to the Taggarts' purported "servient" land, burdens the Taggarts' property. We agree with the lower courts that it does not, and therefore affirm the order of the Appellate Division.

The homes of these neighbors are located on lots which have been separately deeded through a series of conveyances, originally severed and conveyed out by a common grantor, Lawrance. Lawrance conveyed one parcel of his land to Witter's predecessor in title in 1951. The deed contained the restrictive covenant providing that "no docks, buildings, or other structures [or trees or plants] shall be erected [or grown]" on the grantor's (Lawrance's) retained servient lands to the south "which shall obstruct or interfere with the outlook or view from the [dominant] premises" over the [creek.] That deed provided that the covenant expressly ran with the *dominant* land. William and Susan Witter purchased the dominant parcel in 1963 by deed granting them all the rights of their grantor, which included the restrictive covenant. In 1984, Susan Witter transferred her interest to William Witter alone.

After common grantor Lawrance died, his heirs in 1962 conveyed his retained, allegedly servient, land to the Taggarts' predecessor in title. Lawrance's deed made no reference to the restrictive covenant benefiting the Witter property and neither did the heirs' deed to the Taggarts' predecessors. The restrictive covenant was also not included or referenced in any of the several subsequent mesne conveyances of that allegedly servient parcel or in the deed ultimately to the Taggarts in 1984. Quite to the contrary, the Taggarts' deed specifically permitted them to build a dock on their parcel.

Restrictive covenants ... restrain servient landowners from making otherwise lawful uses of their property. However, the law has long favored free and unencumbered use of real property, and covenants restricting use are strictly construed against those seeking to enforce them. Courts will enforce restraints only where their existence has been established with clear and convincing proof by the dominant landowner. The guiding principle for determining the ultimate binding effect of a restrictive covenant is that [i]n the absence of actual notice before or at the time of ... purchase or of other exceptional circumstances, an owner of land is only bound by restrictions if they appear in some deed of record in the conveyance to [that owner] or [that owner's] direct predecessors in title." [*Buffalo Academy of Sacred Heart*.] Courts have consistently recognized and applied this principle, which provides reliability and certainty in land ownership and use.

In *Buffalo Academy*, we held that a restrictive covenant did not run with the dominant land, but added that even if it did, the servient landowners were not bound because the deed to the servient land did not reflect the covenant. We noted that this rule is "implicit in the acts providing for the recording of conveyances." The recording act ... was enacted to accomplish a twofold purpose: to protect the rights of innocent purchasers who acquire an interest in property without knowledge of prior encumbrances, and to establish a public record which will furnish potential purchasers with actual or at least constructive notice of previous conveyances and encumbrances that might affect their interests and uses.

The recording statutes in a grantor-grantee indexing system charge a purchaser with notice of matters only in the record of the purchased land's chain of title back to the original grantor. *Buffalo Academy* recognized that a "purchaser is not normally required to search *outside* the chain of title" (emphasis added), and is not chargeable with constructive notice of conveyances recorded outside of that purchaser's direct chain of title where ... the grantor-grantee system of indexing is used. This is true even if covenants are included in a deed to another lot conveyed by the same grantor.

To impute legal notice for failing to search each chain of title or "deed out" from a common grantor "would seem to negative the beneficent purposes of the recording acts" and would place too great a burden on prospective purchasers [*Buffalo Academy*.] Therefore, purchasers like the Taggarts should not be penalized for failing to search every chain of title branching out from a common grantor's roots in order to unearth potential restrictive covenants. They are legally bound to search only within their own tree trunk line and are bound by constructive or inquiry notice only of restrictions which appear in deeds or other instruments of conveyance in that primary stem. Property law principles and practice have long established that a deed conveyed by a common grantor to a dominant landowner does *not* form part of the chain of title to the servient land retained by the common grantor.

A grantor may effectively extinguish or terminate a covenant when, as here, the grantor conveys retained servient land to a bona fide purchaser who takes title without actual or constructive notice of the covenant because the grantor and dominant owner failed to record the covenant in the servient land's chain of title. One way the dominant landowner or grantor can prevent this result is by recording in the servient chain the conveyance creating the covenant rights so as to impose notice on subsequent purchasers of the servient land.

It goes almost without repeating that definiteness, certainty, alienability and unencumbered use of property are highly desirable objectives of property law. To restrict the Taggarts because of Lawrance's failure to include the covenant in the deed to his retained servient land, or for the failure by Witter's predecessors to insist that it be protected and recorded so as to be enforceable against the burdened property, would seriously undermine these paramount values, as well as the recording acts. . . . [We] hold that, consistent with long-standing precedents and property principles, the Taggarts did not have actual or constructive notice of this restrictive covenant because it was never included in their deed or direct chain of title. There being no other imputable constructive or inquiry notice, they are not bound by that covenant. [Affirmed.]

FINLEY v. GLENN

Supreme Court of Pennsylvania
303 Pa. 131 (1931)

SCHAFFER, J., delivered the opinion of the court.

. . . Mildred D. Rosekrans owned a tract of ground which had been divided into building lots. By deed dated March 16, 1926, and recorded April 13th of the same year, she and her husband conveyed three of the lots, with a dwelling house erected thereon, on the westerly side of Mildred Avenue to plaintiff Finley. Building restrictions, limiting the use of the property to dwelling house purposes, and providing that no factory or other building to be used or occupied for any commercial purpose whatsoever should be erected upon the lots were contained in the deed, and, in addition, a covenant in which it was agreed between the grantors and the grantee [and] "their respective heirs and assigns, that the said grantors, shall and will impose the same building restrictions as above set forth, upon all their other lots or pieces of land fronting upon both sides of Mildred Avenue [including] lots Nos. 7 and 10 to 19, inclusive on the west side of Mildred Avenue; and Nos. 20 to 29 inclusive, and No. 6 on the east side of Mildred Avenue." Subsequently on August 17, 1926, Rosekrans and his wife conveyed to defendant Joseph Glenn, lots Nos. 20 to 27 inclusive on the east side of Mildred Avenue. No restrictions were imposed by this deed. . . .

At the time defendants acquired title they had no actual knowledge of the building restrictions covenanted to be imposed by their grantors on the lots they had purchased. About six months thereafter, however, they learned of their existence and in June, 1928, when plaintiff was informed that they planned the erection of a factory on the lots opposite his dwelling, a notice in writing, referring to the restrictions and warning defendants against their violation, was sent to them and they acknowledged receipt. In July, 1928, defendants started the work of erecting a building for the manufacture of leather belting on the property conveyed to them and plaintiff began this proceeding. Notwithstanding its pendency, defendants proceeded with the erection of the factory.

The [lower court of equity enjoined] the use to be made of the building [but did] not extend it to an order for removal thereof. . . . We are of opinion that [this] is the correct [conclusion.]

The controlling factor in the decision of the case is that the immediate grantors of both plaintiff and defendants were the same. When the latter came to examine the title which was tendered to them, it was of primary consequence that they should know whether their grantors held title to the land which they were to convey. They could determine that question only by searching the records for grants from them. ... "The weight of authority is to the effect that if a deed or a contract for the conveyance of one parcel of land, with a covenant or easement affecting another parcel of land owned by the same grantor, is duly recorded, the record is constructive notice to a subsequent purchaser of the latter parcel. The rule is based generally upon the principle that a grantee is chargeable with notice of everything affecting his title which could be discovered by an examination of the records of the deeds or other muniments of title of his grantor." 16 Amer. Law Rep. 1013, and cases cited; 2 Tiffany's Real Property, 1920 edition, page 2188. So doing defendants would find the deed from Rosekrans and his wife to plaintiff which had been recorded. Coming upon this conveyance, it was their duty to read it, not ... to read only the description of the property to see what was conveyed, but to read the deed in its entirety, to note anything else which might be set forth in it. The deed was notice to them of all it contained; otherwise the purpose of the recording acts would be frustrated. If they had read all of it, they would have discovered that the lots which their vendors were about to convey to them had been subjected to the building restriction which the deed disclosed. It [matters not], so far as notice is concerned, that they did not acquaint themselves with the entire contents of the deed. It affected them to the same extent as though they had read it all. ... Were it otherwise, in the familiar instance where a grantor creates an easement on other property owned by him in favor of his grantee, the easement would not be effective against subsequent purchasers of the retained property....

The Recording Act ... provides, "all deeds and conveyances, which, from and after the passage of this act, shall be made and executed within this Commonwealth of or concerning any lands, tenements or hereditaments in this Commonwealth, or whereby the title to the same may be in any way affected in law or equity ... shall be recorded." The purpose in recording is to give notice and the notice given is not only of the land conveyed but "concerning" any lands. Certainly a restriction concerns the lands restricted. But in addition to this, recording is required so that notice may be given of anything "whereby the title may be in any manner affected" and manifestly it would be by restrictions placed on it. So not only by actual conveyance of the land they were purchasing would defendants be affected by the recording of a deed from their vendors but by anything placed of record "concerning" it or "whereby the title" to it might be affected. The record of a deed is notice of the existence of an equitable title or of an easement or servitude on land granted by the owner thereof. When plaintiff, the first grantee, recorded his deed, he did all that he could do to give notice of the restrictions. ... The record of a deed is constructive notice of its contents to those who are bound to search for it.

We do not see how defendants can complain of hardship to them in the decree. They had actual notice of the restriction six months after they acquired title and more than a year before they commenced building the factory. They also had written notice from plaintiff's attorney before they began building. They erected it with full knowledge that they were transgressing the covenant of their grantor which was equally binding upon them as upon him, as they were his "assigns."

NOTES AND QUESTIONS

1. Which Approach is Preferable? The New York court says *B* prevails, in Example 8–15. The Pennsylvania court says that *A* prevails. Which is preferable? Why? The states are nearly evenly divided on this question. Note that the New York court says that the common grantor can prevent the New York result "by recording in the servient chain the conveyance creating the covenant rights so as to impose notice on subsequent purchasers of the servient land." How can this be done?

The entire subject of servitudes—easements, irrevocable licenses, and restrictions on the use of land enforceable by legal remedies ("real covenants") or by equitable remedies ("equitable servitudes") is taken up in Chapter 10. It is the usual convention to speak of the estate benefitted by the servitude as the dominant estate, and to call the burdened estate the servient estate.

2. Tract Indexes. All the prior chain of title problems you have encountered thus far occur only in a name index—a grantor-grantee index—and do not occur in a tract index. Is that true with respect to this problem? If not, what must the searcher in a tract index do?

6. MARKETABLE RECORD TITLE ACTS

Marketable record title acts, which have been enacted by about 18 states, are designed to limit the number of years backward in time a title searcher must examine in order to establish a good title. These acts render void any claim not recorded within a time period extending backward from the present for specified number of years, often 30 or 40 years. The acts make some exceptions to this general principle, but except for the excepted interests, a person who can trace title back to a "root of title" that is older than the specified period has a good title, immune from attack. An example of a marketable record title act is Wyo. Stat. § 34–10–103.

> Any person having the legal capacity to own land in this state, who has an unbroken chain of title of record to any interest in land for forty (40) years or more, shall be deemed to have a marketable record title to such interest subject only to the matters stated in W.S. 34–10–104. A person shall be deemed to have such an unbroken chain of title when the official public records disclose a conveyance or other title

transaction of record not less than forty (40) years at the time the marketability is to be determined, which conveyance or other title transaction purports to create the interest, either in the person claiming the interest, or some other person from whom, by one (1) or more conveyances or other title transactions of record, the purported interest has become vested in the person claiming the interest, so long as nothing appears of record, in either case, purporting to divest the claimant of his purported interest.

Example 8–16: The jurisdiction has a marketable title act that makes void any claim not of record within 40 years from the present. In 2012, *O* intends to purchase Blackacre from *A*, who purchased Blackacre from *B* in 2000, who acquired it from *C* in 1985. *C* bought Blackacre in 1965 from *D*. Each of these deeds was recorded promptly at the time of the transaction. *O*'s title searcher need only trace the chain of title back to the 1965 *D* to *C* deed. This is an adequate root of title. Any prior interest that might otherwise be good but which is not of record in the 40 year period backward from 2012 to 1972 is void.

Marketable record title acts may seem simple, but imbedded in them are pitfalls. First, they are riddled with exceptions. For example, Wyo. Stat. § 34–10–104, which contains the exceptions referenced in the Wyoming marketable record title act, excepts interests recorded before the root of title if there is a specific mention of them in an instrument in the chain of title within the 40 year period, interests that might predate the root of title but which have been preserved by a notice of their existence recorded within the 40 year period, the rights of a possessor who has been in possession for more than 40 years, the rights of an adverse user or possessor whose interest arises from adverse use or possession within the prior 40 years, the rights of reversioners in leases, "apparent easements and interests in the nature of easements," water rights, mineral rights, and interests of either the state or federal government. Other statutes make exception for utility or railroad easements, whether or not they are apparent.

The scope of these exceptions dilutes the utility of marketable title acts. A searcher must extend his search well beyond a root of title to determine if any of the excepted interests are in the extended chain of title and must also conduct sufficient investigation to determine whether there are any apparent easements, adverse possessors, or adverse users. Claims of the state and federal governments may not be of record but found in tax liens or other public records that are not recorded in the realty records.

HEIFNER v. BRADFORD

Supreme Court of Ohio
4 Ohio St.3d 49 (1983)

CELEBREZZE, J., delivered the opinion of the court.

[In 1916, Elvira Sprague conveyed her interest in a tract of land in Muskingum County by deed to Fred H. Waters, in which she reserved the oil and gas rights in the land. The deed was recorded in 1916. Elvira Sprague died testate in 1931. Her will devised the reserved oil and gas rights in the land equally to her two daughters, Lottie E. Rogers and Sarah A. Bradford. In 1936, Fred H. Waters, without mention of the reservation of the oil and gas rights, conveyed the property by warranty deed to Charles B. Waters, Emma M. Waters, Sarah K. Waters, and William H. Waters. This deed was recorded in 1936. An authenticated copy of Elvira Sprague's will was filed in Muskingum County in 1957. An affidavit of transfer was filed and recorded in Muskingum County evidencing the transfer of the oil and gas rights by inheritance from Elvira Sprague to her daughters. However, both Lottie E. Rogers and Sarah A. Bradford had died intestate prior to this transfer. Thus, Lottie E. Rogers' one-half share in the oil and gas rights was divided equally among her four children and Sarah A. Bradford's share was equally divided among her three children. These transfers were evidenced by affidavits of transfer which were recorded in Muskingum County in 1957. In 1980, Charles B. Waters *et al.* conveyed their interest in the property to William H. Waters and his wife Shirley S. Waters. Appellants, Charlotte Heifner, Jean Stewart and Doris Schaevitz, who own three undivided fractional shares of the oil and gas rights in the property, sought to quiet title and partition the undivided fractional shares in the oil and gas rights. Defendants William H. and Shirley S. Waters, the record surface owners, claim also to be owners of the oil and gas rights in the land contrary to the claim of appellants, based upon Ohio's Marketable Title Act. The trial court ruled that appellants were owners of the oil and gas rights and ordered a partition of the undivided fractional interests. The court of appeals reversed, holding that the Marketable Title Act operated to extinguish appellants' interest and vest complete ownership of the property in William S. and Shirley H. Waters.]

. . . The question involved is one of first impression in this state and deals exclusively with the operation of R.C. 5301.47 through 5301.56, otherwise known as the Ohio Marketable Title Act. The issue presented by this appeal is whether appellees, who have an unbroken chain of title of record of forty years or more, have a marketable record title even though appellants' competing interest arose from an independent chain of title recorded during the forty-year period subsequent to appellees' root of title. . . .

[T]he Marketable Title Act sets forth several definitions germane to the instant cause. R.C. 5301.47(A) defines "marketable record title" as a "title of record, as indicated in section 5301.48 of the Revised Code, which operates to extinguish such interests and claims, existing prior to the effective date of the root of title. . . ." A "root of title" is defined in subsection (E) as "that conveyance or other title transaction in the chain of title of a person, upon which he relies as a basis for the marketability of his title, and which was the most recent to be recorded as of a date forty years prior to the time when marketability is being determined. . . ." Subsection (F) defines "title transaction" as "any transaction affecting title to any interest in land, including title by will or descent...." R.C. 5301.48 provides that one "who has an unbroken chain of title of record to any interest in land for forty years or more, has a marketable record title to such interest ... subject to the matters stated in section 5301.49 of the Revised Code." In relevant part, R.C. 5301.49 states: "Such record marketable title shall be subject to: ... (D) Any interest arising out of a title transaction which has been recorded subsequent to the effective date of the root of title from which the unbroken chain of title of record is started; provided that such recording shall not revive or give validity to any interest which has been extinguished prior to the time of the recording...."

Appellants' root of title is the 1916 deed from Elvira Sprague ... to Fred H. Waters which reserved to the grantors the oil and gas rights in the land. Appellees' root of title is the 1936 conveyance from Fred H. Waters ... to Charles B. Waters, Emma M. Waters, Sarah K. Waters, and William H. Waters which failed to mention the reservation of oil and gas rights. Consequently, unless subject to R.C. 5301.49, appellees hold a marketable record title to the oil and gas rights, as well as title to the surface land, by virtue of having an "unbroken chain" of record title for over forty years which extinguishes prior claims and interests, including that of appellants. R.C. 5301.47(A) and 5301.48.

The Act defines a "title transaction" to include the passage of "title by will or descent." Thus, the 1957 conveyance of the oil and gas rights which passed under the terms of Elvira Sprague's will must be considered a "title transaction" under R.C. 5301.49(D). Appellees argue that we should construe R.C. 5301.49(D) to require that a title transaction under that section arise from the same chain of title as that under which there is claimed to be a marketable record title. For the reasons to follow, we feel the proper construction should be otherwise.

Ohio's Marketable Title Act is taken primarily from the Model Marketable Title Act [and] R.C. 5301.49(D) is virtually identical to Section 2(d) of the Model Act. [We] are convinced that the General Assembly and the drafters of the Model Act intended that a title transaction under R.C. 5301.49(D) and Section 2(d), respectively, may be part of an entirely independent chain of title.

[The] drafters of the Model Act proposed comprehensive model title standards to accompany the Model Act. Standard 4.10 states: "The recording of an instrument of conveyance subsequent to the effective date of the root of title has the same effect in preserving any interest conveyed as the filing of the notice provided for in § 4 of the Act." Perhaps more significant is the comment to the above standard which provides that, "[t]his standard is operative both where there are claims under a single chain of title and where there are *two or more independent chains of title.*" (Emphasis added.) Moreover, the Ohio Standards of Title Examination drafted and adopted by the Ohio State Bar Association have embraced an identical approach....

Accordingly, a "marketable title," as defined in R.C. 5301.47(A) and 5301.48, is subject to an interest arising out of a "title transaction" under R.C. 5301.49(D) which may be part of an independent chain of title. Further, the effect of RC. 5301.49(D) is identical to that obtained by the filing of a preservation notice. R.C. 5301.51 provides for the preservation of interests by the filing of a notice of claim during the forty-year period. As a result, the recording of a "title transaction" under R.C. 5301.47(F) and 5301.49(D) is equivalent to the filing of a notice of claim during the forty-year period as specified in R.C. 5301.51 and 5301.52.[9]

We do recognize, as a practical matter, the difficulty faced by title examiners in locating these title transactions in a common title examination. We note that the General Assembly has mandated a "Notice Index" by which notices under R.C. 5301.51 are indexed under the description of the real estate. R.C. 5301.52. It would seem consistent to similarly require such an indexing procedure of at least the title transactions falling under R.C. 5301.49(D). However, that is in the nature of a legislative determination beyond the scope of our consideration.

Thus, the 1957 conveyance under the terms of Elvira Sprague's will was a "title transaction within the meaning of R.C. 5301.49(D), and appellants' interest was not extinguished by operation of the Marketable Title Act.[10] Accordingly, the judgment of the court of appeals is reversed.

NOTES AND PROBLEMS

1. Post–Root of Title Notices. As *Heifner* suggests, there are two ways that a pre-root interest can be kept alive after even after that root of title has been established. If the jurisdiction's Marketable Title Act permits, one method is to record within the statutory period a notice of an interest that arose under some pre-root instrument of record. The other method is the one at issue in *Heifner*: An instrument that is recorded within the statutory period that specifically refers to a pre-root interest serves to preserve that pre-root interest. Note that a title searcher in a grantor-grantee index would go back from 1983 to the 1980 deed from Charles Waters, *et al.* to William and

---

9. [Footnote relocated; ed.—] Appellees contend . . . that under the present grantor-grantee indexing system, in order to locate title transactions in an independent chain of title, the title examiner will have to search the title to its origin and then forward to discover such transactions. It is appellees' position that the purpose of the Act is to limit title searches to forty years. [This] approach . . . is not without support. See Barnett, Marketable Title Acts—Panacea or Pandemonium? 53 Cornell L. Rev. 45, 54–56 (1967). . . . [Professor] Barnett views the purpose of marketable title acts solely to shorten title examinations. We are not inclined to view the purpose of the Marketable Title Act so narrowly. The Supreme Court of Florida in Miami v. St. Joe Paper Co., 364 So. 2d 439, 442 (Fla. 1978), aptly stated that the purpose of marketable title acts is three-fold: "[to] reform [. . .] conveyancing procedures[, to] require[] stale demands to be asserted within a reasonable time after a cause of action has accrued[, and to] provide[] for a simple and easy method by which the owner of an existing old interest may preserve it. If he fails to take the step of filing the notice as provided, he has only himself to blame if his interest is extinguished. The legislature did not intend to arbitrarily wipe out old claims and interests without affording a means of preserving them and giving a reasonable period of time within which to take the necessary steps to accomplish that purpose."

10. The 1957 title transaction took place only twenty-one years from appellees' root of title, obviously within the forty-year period.

Shirley Waters, and then would search under Charles *et al.* to find the 1936 deed to Charles *et al.*, which would be the root of title (as it is over 40 years prior to 1983). That searcher would not find the 1957 transfer notice of the mineral rights from Lottie to her children, nor the 1957 transfer notice from Sarah to her children, nor the 1957 transfer notice from Elvira to Lottie and Sarah under Elivira's 1916 will. The only way a searcher would discover these notices would be if he went back to Elvira as the root of title and then searched forward in time. If a tract index were used, all of these notices and deeds would be indexed by the tract, and thus would be readily observable.

2. *Problems.*

a. In a jurisdiction with a 40 year statute such as the Ohio statute in *Heifner*, O conveys Blackacre for value to A in 1966. A fails to record the deed as he left for military service the next day. A is killed in action in Vietnam in 1967. His intestate heir is H. Upon learning of A's death, in 1968 O conveys Blackacre as a gift to B, who promptly records. In 1969 B conveys to C, who promptly records. In 2012 H learns that the estate of A included Blackacre and H sues C to recover possession. Who should prevail?

b. In a jurisdiction with a 40 year statute such as the Ohio statute in *Heifner*, in 1950 O conveys Blackacre for value to A, who records. In 1960 A conveys to B, who records. In 1970 F forges O's signature to a deed to Blackacre and delivers that deed to X. In 2012, who has title to Blackacre? Would the result be the same if in 1971 B had conveyed to C, who promptly records?

3. *Whimsy? Or a Lawyer's Frustration?* The marketable title acts are designed to prevent the necessity of tracing title to some original source, however far back in time. A legend that has persisted for at least half a century involves a lawyer who has painstakingly searched title to Louisiana property back to 1803, the date of the Louisiana Purchase, to secure a mortgage loan to his client, the current record owner. The lender responds that the title search is inadequate; title must be traced back to its original source. The lawyer supposedly replies:

> In 1803 the United States acquired Louisiana by purchase from France, which had acquired title from Spain by right of conquest. Spain acquired title through discovery by Panfilo de Narváez and Hernando de Soto, agents and proteges of Christopher Columbus, who was deputized by Isabella, Queen of Spain, to engage in his voyages of discovery. Isabella's authority to deputize Columbus was obtained from His Holiness, the Pope. The Pope is the living emissary on Earth of Jesus Christ, the Son of God, who sits at the right hand of God. God made Louisiana.

B. TITLE INSURANCE

Title insurance is a contract between an insurer and the owner of an interest in real property by which the insurer warrants that title is as stated in the policy as of the date of the policy, promises to defend the insurer against adverse claims, remove impediments to the title, and indemnify the insured for all losses incurred as a result of defects in the warranted title up to the policy amount. The insured makes a one-time premium payment at the time the policy is issued and the policy remains in effect for so long as the insured retains an interest in the property. Thus, when the property is sold, the new owner must obtain his own title insurance policy. There are two common insured interests under a title insurance policy—the owner's interest and the mortgagee's interest (assuming that the purchase is financed by a mortgage loan). In the case of the owner the policy amount is usually the purchase price. A mortgagee, however, usually obtains insurance in an amount equal to the principal of the loan. Title insurance policies need not be uniform, but the increasing presence of a secondary market in mortgages has produced almost universal use of one or both of two standard form contracts crafted by the American Land Title Association—an owner's policy and a mortgagee's policy. A mortgage lender will require issuance of a mortgagee's policy, which insures its interest (usually at the borrower's expense), but an owner who wants insurance must also purchase an owner's policy. The policy warrants title only as of the date of issuance; any later defects are outside the scope of the contract.

A title insurer examines the public records and concludes what the state of title is from its analysis of the records. The standard ALTA policy excludes a number of claims—persons in actual possession whose claims are not reflected in the public records, and easements and servitudes that are not recorded (including implied and prescriptive easements). The standard policy excludes any loss attributable to government regulations (such as zoning and building codes) unless the government has recorded a notice of violation and enforcement, and also excludes any defects that would be revealed by inspection and a survey.

Title insurance has largely replaced the prior practice of title abstracts followed by an attorney's opinion as to the state of title. A good description of the two practices follows, taken from the Kansas Supreme Court's opinion in Ford v. Guarantee Abstract & Title Co., Inc., 220 Kan. 244, 254–256 (1976):

> [If] the owner of real property desired to sell his property, he first entered into a preliminary agreement with the buyer and then arranged to prove his title by going to an abstractor to obtain an abstract.... The abstract was delivered to the buyer who then hired an attorney to examine it and give him a written opinion identifying the fee title holder, noting any liens or encumbrances and making exception as to any title defects or faults commonly known as clouds on title. If there were no clouds on title and no liens, the transaction was ready to close and the buyer's attorney prepared the deed, any other required instruments and a closing statement. Upon conveyance, payment and recording the transaction was complete. If there were liens not being assumed the owner either paid them or arranged for the buyer to pay them out of the purchase price and the transaction was ready for closing. If there were clouds on title, the owner hired an attorney to clear the title by such action as was necessary

and to represent the owner at closing, after one or both attorneys had prepared the required papers. Ofttimes the funds required for closing were placed in the attorney's hands to be held for subsequent distribution when the buyer was placed in title. [The] buyer's attorney . . . had a duty and professional responsibility to his client to examine the abstract skillfully, avoid any errors and omissions in his opinion and to avoid any mishandling of his client's money. In short, the buyer's attorney had the duty to either place his client in good title or advise against the purchase. The abstractor performed the essentially mechanical function of making a complete search of the appropriate records and preparing an abstract of all instruments or proceedings concerning the property, without opinion or judgment on his part as to their sufficiency or legal effect. His sole responsibility was to accumulate an accurate and complete title record of the property. . . .

Under the title insurance policy method [the insurer collects the] name of the seller, the name of the buyer, the description of the property and the purchase price [so that the insurer can] search for pending lawsuits, unpaid taxes, and judgments [in] the proper records. . . . [The insurer] is not making a search to accumulate the records in an abstract, but is in fact examining each instrument and proceeding, whether divorce, bankruptcy, tax foreclosure, mortgage foreclosure, probate estate, condemnation, partition or whatever to then and there form his opinion and judgment as to the sufficiency and legal effect of the same so as to pass good title in each instance. The former function of the buyer's attorney in examining the abstract of title is now performed by the title insurance company's examiner. The examiner also makes a search in the name of the record fee titleholder to determine if the property in question may be subjected to liens by reason of judgments, unpaid taxes or pending lawsuits.

The conclusions and findings of the examiner are then incorporated into the title insurance company's title report commitment to the buyer showing: The description, the name of the record fee titleholder, any liens or encumbrances, any title faults or defects which must be cleared before the title company will insure the title without exception from coverage, and the purchase price. The title report is then forwarded to the parties in accordance with directions given by the applicant for the title policy (usually the realtor, seller or buyer). If the title report indicates clouds on the title, they must be cleared to the title company's satisfaction before the transaction can be closed and the title insurance policy issued. One or more persons, usually attorneys, employed by the . . . title insurance company will have been authorized by the title company to make the determination as to what procedures or instruments will suffice to clear the clouds on the title and to actually issue the company's title policy.

In view of the foregoing practice it has become customary for realtors or lenders to place all or portions of the buyer's purchase price money in the hands of the title insur[er] with . . . written instructions to disburse the same for payment of mortgage liens, taxes, etc., only at such time as the authorized employees determine that clouds on the title have been cleared, the buyer is in title and the title company is prepared to issue its title policy.

As the foregoing description indicates, an insurer delivers a preliminary report to the prospective insureds, which indicates the state of title (including exceptions) that the insurer is prepared to insure. This report, sometimes called a binder, is the insurer's commitment to issue the policy on these terms. Note that a title insurer has considerably greater control over the risks that it is assuming than do insurers of other risks. A life insurer, a personal liability insurer, or a property casualty loss insurer has little control over the behavior of the insured, a key factor affecting the insurer's risk. But a title insurer controls the diligence with which it scours the records, and thus can limit its risk by the thoroughness of its search and the scope of the exceptions to the title it insures.

HEYD v. CHICAGO TITLE INSURANCE COMPANY

Supreme Court of Nebraska
218 Neb. 296 (1984)

SHANAHAN, J., delivered the opinion of the court.

Glen and Robin Heyd sued Chicago Title Insurance Company (Chicago) in two causes of action. Heyds' first cause of action relates to a loss claimed to be covered under Chicago's policy of title insurance, while Heyds' second cause of action alleges negligence regarding a title report prepared by Chicago. The district court ... sustained Chicago's demurrer ... and dismissed Heyds' lawsuit. We affirm in part and reverse in part.

In July 1978 Heyds contracted to purchase a home located on a lot designated as 5939 South 46th Street in Omaha, Nebraska. The seller was Gladys Smith. Heyds obtained a policy of title insurance from Chicago regarding the real estate being purchased from Smith. It was later discovered that the house being purchased was not entirely located within the boundaries of the tract described in the Smith–Heyd real estate contract. The house was in fact partially located on a public street of the city of Omaha.

The policy of title insurance issued by Chicago insures against any loss or damage by reason of "title to the [real] estate ... being vested [in one other than Smith]; any defect in or lien or encumbrance on such title; lack of a right of access to and from the land; or unmarketability of such title." The policy continues: "The estate or interest in the land described herein and which is covered by this policy is: Fee Simple ... in: GLADYS L. SMITH."

Chicago's policy was subject to certain stated and general exceptions specified in the policy, namely, "This policy does not insure against loss or damage by reason of the following exceptions: (1) Rights or claims of parties in possession not shown by the public records. (2) Encroachments, overlaps, boundary line disputes, and any other matters which would be disclosed by an accurate survey and inspection of the premises." ... Chicago's policy [defined "land" as] "the land described, specifically or by reference in Schedule A, and improvements affixed thereto which by law constitute real property; provided, however, the term 'land' does not include any property beyond the lines of the area specifically described or referred to in Schedule A, nor any right, title, interest, estate or easement in abutting streets, roads, avenues, alleys, lanes, ways or waterways...."

The policy issued by Chicago to Heyds also provided:

12. Liability Limited to this Policy. This instrument together with all endorsements and other instruments, if any, attached hereto by the Company is the entire policy and contract between the insured and the Company. Any claim of loss or damage, whether or not based on negligence, and which arises out of the status of the title to the estate or interest covered hereby or any action asserting such claim, shall be restricted to the provisions and conditions and stipulations of this policy.

In their first cause of action Heyds allege a loss covered by Chicago's policy of title insurance, that is, a defect in title to the real estate being purchased from Smith and unmarketability of title to the tract, because the house is not totally situated within the boundaries of the real estate described in the Smith–Heyd contract and Chicago's policy.

Heyds' second cause of action contains the allegation "That [Chicago] was negligent in preparing its title report and title policy for [Heyds]" in failing to correctly examine the records of title and in failing to report defects of title to Heyds.

The ... district court sustained Chicago's demurrer and held that "there is no defect in title to the described property, nor is there any unmarketability of title...." In their appeal Heyds maintain they should be allowed to prosecute their action based on contract, that is, the policy of title insurance, and based on Chicago's negligence regarding the title report.

[It] is settled that a standard policy of title insurance is a contract of indemnity which only insures against defects, discrepancies, or other impediments of record affecting title to the real estate designated in the policy or interfering with the marketability of title to the land described in the policy. Such indemnification does not protect the insured from matters dependent upon a survey or critical inspection of the property unless the policy provides for extended coverage or the insured requests special endorsements. See Contini v. Western Title Ins. Co., 40 Cal. App. 3d 536, 115 Cal. Rptr. 257 (1974). Unless agreed by a title insurance company or required by a provision of the policy of title insurance, an insurance company has no obligation to obtain a survey of the subject real estate before a policy of title insurance is issued. See Kuhlman v. Title Insurance Company of Minnesota, 177 F. Supp. 925 (W.D. Mo. 1959); cf. Offenhartz v. Heinsohn, 30 Misc. 2d 693, 150 N.Y.S.2d 78 (1956) (a title insurance company is not required to insure any title or interest to real estate beyond the boundaries of the property described in the policy of title insurance). "[I]nsurance policies should be construed as any other contract and should be given effect according to the ordinary sense of the terms used; and if those terms are clear, they will be applied according to their plain and ordinary meaning." Hemenway v. MFA Life Ins. Co., 211 Neb. 193, 199, 318 N.W.2d 70, 74 (1982)....

The policy issued by Chicago insures against any loss or damage resulting from a defect or unmarketability of Smith's title to the real estate being purchased by Heyds. The risk covered by Chicago's policy relates to a deficiency of the vendor's, Smith's, rights to or ownership in the land under contract to Heyds and described in the insurance policy. Loss or damage covered by the insurance policy might occur, for example, if Smith did not have absolute ownership (fee simple) in the described real estate. However, the loss or damage alleged by Heyds has resulted from the location of the house, namely, the house not being located within the boundary lines of the land described in the sale to Heyds and the insurance policy. There is no allegation that Smith does not own fee simple title in the real estate. Likewise, Heyds do not allege any aspect of Smith's title which has caused some doubt about or flaw in the validity of Smith's ownership so that marketability of title is impaired.

By general exception (2) in its policy, Chicago removed from the insurance coverage any loss due to "[e]ncroachments, overlaps, boundary line disputes, and any other matters which would be disclosed by an accurate survey and inspection of the premises." That survey exception is expressed in language having plain and ordinary meaning. Therefore, correct location of any structure on the described premises is not a risk or loss covered by Chicago's policy of title insurance. ... The district court was correct in dismissing Heyds' contract action based on the policy of title insurance.

The demurrer to Heyds' second cause of action is a different matter. The allegations in that second cause of action describe a situation in which Chicago made some type of title search and issued a title report regarding the Smith–Heyd sale. Presumably, the title report to Heyds stated the name of the person in whom title was vested (Smith) and listed taxes, liens, encumbrances, easements, restrictions, conditions, outstanding interests, and defects to which the title is subject—all as reflected in public records. Undoubtedly that title report was the basis on which the policy of title insurance was issued....

[In] Ford v. Guarantee Abstract & Title Co., 220 Kan. 244 (1976), [the] Supreme Court of Kansas concluded:

> [A] corporation organized for the purpose, among others, of examining and guaranteeing titles to real estate and which in all matters relating to conveyancing and searching titles holds itself out to the public, and assumes to discharge the same duties as an individual conveyancer or attorney, has the same responsibilities and its duty to

its employer is governed by the principles applicable to attorney and client. . . . Where a title insurer presents *a buyer* with both a preliminary title report and a policy of title insurance two distinct responsibilities are assumed; in rendering the first service, the insurer serves as an abstractor of title and must list all matters of public record regarding the subject property in its preliminary report. When a title insurer breaches its duty to abstract title accurately it may be liable in tort for all the damages proximately caused by such breach. [Id. at 256–258.]

Courts of other jurisdictions have recognized the duty of a title insurance company to use due care regarding inspection of public records and title reports. See . . . Dorr v. Massachusetts Title Insurance Co., 238 Mass. 490 (1921). . . .

The duty imposed upon an abstractor of title is a rigorous one: "An abstractor of title is hired because of his professional skill, and when searching the public records on behalf of a client he must use the degree of care commensurate with that professional skill . . . the abstractor must report all matters which could affect his client's interests and which are readily discoverable from those public records ordinarily examined when a reasonably diligent title search is made." Jarchow v. Transamerica Title Ins. Co., 48 Cal. App. 3d 917, 938–939 (1975).[11]

We now hold that a title insurance company which renders a title report and also issues a policy of title insurance has assumed two distinct duties. In rendering the title report the title insurance company serves as an abstracter of title and must list all matters of public record adversely affecting title to the real estate which is the subject of the title report. When a title insurance company fails to perform its duty to abstract title accurately, the title insurance company may be liable in tort for all damages proximately caused by such breach of duty. A title insurance company's responsibility for its tortious conduct is distinct from the insurance company's responsibility existing on account of its policy of insurance. Different duties and responsibilities imposed on the title insurance company, therefore, can be the basis for separate causes of action—one cause of action in tort and another in contract.

Heyds should have been permitted to amend their petition regarding Chicago's inspection of public records and the ensuing title report. It was error to deny Heyds the opportunity to amend their second cause of action and to dismiss Heyds' action.

Chicago has suggested some form of contractual merger to preclude any action by Heyds for negligent conduct of the insurance company. Chicago's suggestion is predicated on the language of paragraph 12 of its

---

11. [Ed.—] The duty imposed on title insurers by *Jarchow* was eliminated when in 1981 the California legislature enacted Calif. Ins. Code § 12340.11, which provides that a preliminary title report is not an abstract of title and that a title insurer does not owe the duties of an abstracter by issuing a preliminary title report. See also Siegel v. Fidelity National Title Insurance Co., 46 Cal. App.4th 1181 (1996).

policy: "Any claim of loss or damage, whether or not based on negligence
. . . shall be restricted to the provisions and conditions and stipulations of
this policy." In L. Smirlock Realty Corp. v. Title Guarantee Co., 52 N.Y.2d
179, 190 (1981), [the New York Court of Appeals held that the] implied
duty [that] arises out of the title insurance agreement that the insurer has
conducted a reasonably diligent search . . . may not be abrogated through
a standard policy clause which would . . . place the onus of the title
company's failure adequately to search the records on the party who
secured the insurance protection for that very purpose."

In any event, we believe that paragraph 12 of Chicago's policy and the
suggested merger of any negligence action at best relate to a matter of
defense, not to prohibition of a cause of action based on negligence.
Whether the language of paragraph 12 is proper and permissible as a
defense is another question and is not decided in the present appeal. . . .

Affirmed in part, and in part reversed and remanded for further
proceedings.

NOTES AND QUESTIONS

1. Tort or Contract Liability? The states are divided on the question of
whether title insurers owe a duty to search the records and disclose the
results to the prospective insured. Because most title insurers maintain their
own duplicate set of public records, usually organized by tract, it is entirely
possible that an insurer might rely on a prior search and merely update that
search, rather than re-examine the entire record. It is also possible that an
insurer might discover a defect that it considers sufficiently insignificant that
it is willing to insure title against the apparent defect, and thus does not
disclose it as an exception in the preliminary title report. Or the insurer might
not disclose the existence of a defect of which it knew, or would have known
had it done a dutiful search, but that came within one of the policy's
exceptions. While there would be no contractual liability in the latter instance, if the insurer is liable for its negligent search or failure to disclose, the
insured has an independent remedy in tort, where the measure of damages
might be considerably broader than in contract.

Some states mandate by statute that insurers conduct a search: Ariz Rev.
Stat. § 20–1567; Colo. Rev. Stat. § 10–11–106; Fla. Stat. § 627.7845; N.C.
Gen. Stat. § 58–132. These statutes do not expressly impose a duty to disclose
the results of the search, but that is probably implied as the point of imposing
a duty to search.

Some states hold that an insurer has no duty to examine the record or to
disclose the results of such a search. Accordingly, insurers in these states
incur no tort liability for their failure to search or disclose. See, e.g., Culp
Construction Co. v. Buildmart Mall, 795 P.2d 650 (Utah 1990); Brown's Tie &
Lumber Co v. Chicago Title, 115 Idaho 56 (1988); Houston Title Co. v. Ojeda
de Toca, 733 S.W.2d 325 (Tex. App. 1987), rev'd on other grounds 748 S.W.2d
449 (Tex. 1988); Walker Rogge, Inc. v. Chelsea Title & Guaranty Co., 116 N.J.
517 (1989) (no duty to examine and disclose unless insurer expressly agrees to
search and disclose results). Calif. Ins. Code § 12340.11 provides that a

preliminary title report is not an abstract of title and that a title insurer has none of the duties of a title abstracter. The statute was adopted in 1981 in reaction to judicial decisions imposing such a duty on title insurers.

If a buyer retains an attorney to search the records and prepare an abstract of title the attorney will, of course, be liable for his negligence in doing so. See Fleming v. Nicholson, 168 Vt. 495 (1998). But suppose that in a state that imposes no duty to search or disclose on an insurer, a title insurer retains an attorney to search the records and opine to the insurer upon the state of title. Would the attorney be liable to the purchaser of the title policy for his negligence?

2. *Scope of the Title Insurance Policy.* The standard policy insures title; it does not insure against physical defects in the property. One can have perfect title to worthless property. Title may be marketable, in the sense that the term is used in land sale transaction, while the physical property itself may not be marketable. Thus, in Hocking v. Title Insurance and Trust Co., 37 Cal.2d 644 (1951), a purchaser of unimproved property who was denied a building permit because the subdivision's streets did not comply with local law had no remedy under the title insurance policy. To similar effect is Title and Trust Co. v. Barrows, 381 So.2d 1088 (Fla. App. 1979), in which a street was so flooded in the wet seasons that the purchaser lacked vehicular access to the property. The purchaser's title was impeccable; the physical deficiencies of the property were irrelevant. The same principle holds true for toxic waste on the insured property. Though the presence of such hazardous material may render the property unsaleable the title remains marketable if there no record clouds on the title. Nor does the presence of such waste constitute an encumbrance of the property—a lien of some sort. See Lick Mill Creek Apartments v. Chicago Title Insurance Co., 231 Cal. App.3d 1654 (1991); Chicago Title Insurance Co. v. Kumar, 24 Mass.App. 53 (1987); South Shore Bank v. Stewart Title Guarantee Co., 688 F.Supp. 803 (D. Mass. 1988).

Title insurance does provide somewhat broader coverage than the warranties of title contained in a general warranty deed. The insurer must defend at its expense claims against the insured title. May the insured make a claim under the policy even when it has not been evicted, as required to sue for breach of the covenant of general warranty? Recall Brown v. Lober, in Chapter 7.D.2, in which the issue was whether the Browns had a cause of action for breach of the deed covenant of general warranty, and the court ruled that absent proof of constructive eviction no claim on that covenant could be made. If the Browns had purchased title insurance and the policy made no exception for the mineral rights at issue in Brown v. Lober, would the Browns have a cause of action against their title insurer?

3. *Exculpatory Clauses.* The court in *Heyd* treated the exculpatory clause is an affirmative defense, and expressed no opinion about its validity. Other courts have not been so shy. See, e.g. Somerset Savings Bank v. Chicago Title Insurance Co., 420 Mass. 422 (1995), in which the court held that a title insurance policy clause exculpating the insurer for its negligence was unconscionable and unenforceable as to a claim based on the duty to search and disclose.

C. REGISTERED TITLES: THE TORRENS SYSTEM

As you have no doubt gathered by now, the recording system is riddled with faults. In 1858, Sir Robert Torrens, a transplanted native of Ireland who had briefly been Premier of South Australia, shepherded the Real Property Act through the South Australian Assembly. This introduced a system of registered titles to replace the practice of public recording of deeds. To introduce the registration system it is first necessary to adjudicate title as residing in the plaintiff, the putative owner, subject to whatever interests (e.g., mortgages, tax liens, easements, or servitudes) are proven to exist. Once title is adjudicated it is registered in a conclusive certificate of title. Thereafter, when an owner holding the certificate of title transfers ownership the old certificate is extinguished and a new certificate of title is issued after the governmental agency responsible for administering the system has determined that title is indeed in the new owner. The certificate of title is supposed to be definitive, and eliminates all claimed interests other than those noted on the certificate. Thus, to deal with errors a governmental fund is usually established to compensate those people who have erroneously lost title because of human error. In brief, Torrens registration uses the government as the arbiter of title. By contrast, the recording system allows the private economy to produce good title through the maintenance of public records, the recording and marketable title acts, and reliance upon private title insurance.

In theory, Torrens registration offers a simplified and foolproof system. But as is often the case, there is a gap between theory and practice. First, establishing a registered title system is very expensive. Every title must be adjudicated, which may provide full employment for lawyers but empties the pockets of property owners.

Second, once the system is established title issuance is in the hands of bureaucrats. When public officials become incompetent or corrupt, this can produce serious repercussions. Cook County, Illinois, which encompasses Chicago, used Torrens registration until it took two years or more to get a title certificate, a condition that may have incited at least one public employee to accept forbidden payments to expedite issuance of title certificates. See United States v. Gannon, 684 F.2d 433 (7th Cir. 1981). The Illinois legislature finally repealed its law permitting Torrens registration and prohibiting further registrations. See 765 ILCS §§ 40/1 through 40/9.

Third, registration systems often contain a number of exceptions—typically tax liens, bankruptcy claims, mechanics' liens, short-term or residential leases, claims of actual possessors, claims by aboriginals, and visible servitudes. The exemption of such interests from the conclusive effect of a certificate of title undercuts the point of registration.

Finally, for all its faults the private recording system is probably more efficient than the governmentally run registration system. Title insurers invest in "title plants," which are computerized accurate replicas of the public records, and use those plants to issue policies of title insurance. Under a registration system, all of the functions that private parties perform under cost pressures to issue insurance at competitive rates are performed by government employees who have no competitive pressure to perform efficiently. Costs are thus shifted from users—through title insurance or title examinations—to taxpayers, and it is not at all clear that the taxpayer is getting value for the change. See John McCormack, Torrens and Recording: Land Title Assurance in the Computer Age, 18 Wm. Mitchell L. Rev. 61, 113 (1992). In addition, while it might be thought that Torrens registration eliminates the need for title insurance, in fact title insurance is purchased as frequently by buyers in a Torrens system as a recording system, and insurance of registered titles costs just as much as insurance of a recorded title. See Blair Shick and Irving Plotkin, Torrens in the United States (1978). This phenomenon is probably due to the exceptions that riddle Torrens statutes.

Perhaps this explains why Torrens registration is not widespread in the United States. Hawaii, Massachusetts, Minnesota, and Ohio are the only places where registered title is a continuing practice, and in some of them it is quite localized. In Minnesota, for example, it is confined to Hennepin and Ramsey Counties, which encompasses Minneapolis and St. Paul. Torrens registration has fared better elsewhere. It is mandatory in the United Kingdom, widespread in Canada, Australia, New Zealand and other members of the Commonwealth. A variety of western European countries have also adopted Torrens registration.

CHAPTER NINE

NUISANCE AND SUPPORT

■ ■ ■

Nuisance and trespass are each tort doctrines that involve the use of property. Trespass is concerned with acts that infringe upon a person's right of exclusive *possession* of his property. Nuisance is concerned with acts that interfere with a person's right to the *use and enjoyment* of his property. Of course, if *A* physically invades *B*'s property his action interferes with both *B*'s possession and use and enjoyment of his property. Thus, nuisance is limited to *non-trespassory* actions that interfere with a person's use and enjoyment of their property. Courts, however, do not always adhere to this distinction. Indeed, the term nuisance is bandied about with reckless abandon, so much so that Dean William Prosser, the *eminence grise* of tort law, once despaired that because nuisance "has meant all things to all people, and has been applied indiscriminately to everything from an alarming advertisement to a cockroach baked in a pie, . . . it is incapable of any exact or comprehensive definition." Prosser & Keeton on Torts, § 86 (5th ed. 1984). Nevertheless, in this chapter we shall try to corral and brand the beast.

Nuisances may be public or private. A public nuisance is an "unreasonable interference with a right common to the general public." Restatement (Second) of Torts § 821B. A private nuisance is a "nontrespassory invasion of another's interest in the private use and enjoyment of land." Of course, the same conduct may be both a private and public nuisance. The thrust of this chapter is private nuisances, although discussion of public nuisances occurs as it is germane to the central concern of this chapter: How do (and should) courts resolve incompatible land uses?

In general, when a person engages in a continuing activity that is unreasonable or wrongful—whether intentional or negligent—or is inherently dangerous, and that activity causes a non-trespassory interference with another's use of land, a question of nuisance arises. It is frequently said in the common law that one must use his property so not to injure the property of another. The Latin maxim *sic utere tuo ut alienum non laedas* is the expression of this idea. The problem with the maxim is that it is empty of useable meaning.

Example 9–1: A, a concert pianist, and *B,* a teacher of silent meditation, occupy two halves of a two-unit residence. *A* practices Rachmaninoff concertos in his home and *B* uses his home to hold silent meditations. The uses are incompatible. Each of *A* and *B* have a duty to use their property so as not to interfere with another person's use of his property. But which of *A* or *B* should yield, and why? Nuisance law purports to resolve this conflict.

Section A of this chapter describes the substance of the nuisance tort. Section B illustrates the range of remedies for nuisance and explores the question of when and why a particular remedy should be employed.

A. THE SUBSTANCE OF PRIVATE NUISANCE

For a private nuisance to exist there must be the union of several elements: 1) the acts of the defendant that interfere with the plaintiff's use and enjoyment of his property must stem from some form of liability-producing conduct, 2) the interference with the plaintiff's use and enjoyment of his property must be substantial, and 3) the defendant's acts must be the proximate cause of the defendant's injuries.

1. ACTIONS

The defendants' actions that interfere with another's use and enjoyment of their property may be either intentional or unintentional. Intentional actions are those in which a person acts for the purpose of interfering with another's use and enjoyment of property, or knows that such interference results from his actions, or knows that the interference is substantially certain to result from his actions. See Restatement (Second) of Torts, § 825. For nuisance liability to attach to intentional actions, the interference produced by such actions must be "unreasonable." Rest. (2d) Torts § 822(a). If those two conditions are met—intentional act and unreasonable interference—it is no defense to liability for the defendant to claim and prove that he has exercised the maximum possible skill and care to avoid inflicting the injury. Obviously, liability under this branch of nuisance depends heavily upon what constitutes an "unreasonable interference." In brief, an action constitutes an unreasonable interference when either "the gravity of the harm outweighs the utility of the actor's conduct" or "the harm caused by the conduct is serious and the financial burden of compensating for this and similar harm to others would not make the continuation of the conduct not feasible." Rest. (2d) Torts, § 826. We shall dwell in detail on this point shortly.

By contrast, unintentional actions that interfere with another's use and enjoyment of property must be "otherwise actionable under the rules controlling liability for negligent or reckless conduct, or for abnormally dangerous conditions or activities." Rest. (2d) Torts § 822(b). Note that negligence, standing alone, is quite different from nuisance. Negligence is the branch of tort law that imposes civil liability on persons for their unreasonable conduct. Nuisance, by contrast, is concerned with the effects produced by a person's conduct. Only if conduct results in an unreasonable interference with another's use and enjoyment of property and the harm is significant is a nuisance present. Because those effects might be unintentional, nuisance law asks the additional question of whether the unintended conduct posed an unreasonable risk of producing the harmful effects. Negligence or recklessness, in the context of nuisance, involves an assessment of whether the action poses an unreasonable risk that it will inflict an unreasonable interference with another's use and enjoyment of their property. The calculus of unreasonable interference requires determination of whether "the gravity of the harm outweighs the utility of the actor's conduct" and, if so, it must be determined whether the actions of the defendant posed an unreasonable risk of the occurrence of this harm. If nuisance is N, negligence is n, gravity of the harm is G, utility of the conduct is U, and the risk of occurrence of the harm is R, this might be expressed as $N = n + (G-U)$, where $G-U$ is a positive value. In this expression, $n = R \times (G-U)$, where $G-U$ is a positive value and the product of $R \times (G-U)$ exceeds some indefinite value that establishes the lower threshold of an unreasonable risk of occurrence of the harm. If this seems less than precise, it is. The temptation of courts is to conflate the two questions into a single question of whether the harm sufficiently exceeds the utility of the conduct so that the unintended conduct will be deemed to be negligent, but if this is done a form of strict liability results.

The concept of abnormally dangerous conditions or activities is indeed predicated on notions of strict liability. In Rylands v. Fletcher, LR 3 HL 330 (1868), the defendants constructed a reservoir on their own land, situated over underground mine shafts of which the defendants were unaware. When the reservoir was filled the water burst into the mine shafts and flooded the mine works of a nearby colliery to which the shafts led. In finding liability the House of Lords opined that the "person who for his own purposes brings on his lands and collects and keeps there anything likely to do mischief if it escapes, must keep it in at his peril. [If] he does not do so, [he] is *prima facie* answerable for all the damage which is the natural consequence of its escape" unless the damage was attributable to acts of God. This principle has been applied most strongly to obviously inherently dangerous activities or conditions such as blasting or storage of explosives, inflammables, or toxic substances. See, e.g., Laflin & Rand Powder Co. v. Tearney, 131 Ill. 322 (1890) (stored explosives); Cumberland Torpedo Co. v. Gaines, 201 Ky. 88 (1923) (stored explosives); Rotert v. Peabody Coal Co., 513 S.W.2d 667 (Mo.App. 1974) (blasting); Longtin v. Persell, 30 Mont. 306 (1904) (blasting); Gossett v. Southern R. Co., 115 Tenn. 376 (1905) (blasting); Patrick v. Smith, 75 Wash. 407, 134 P. 1076 (1913) (blasting); City of Bridgeton v. B. P. Oil, Inc., 146 N.J.Super. 169, 369 A.2d 49 (1976) (storage of ultrahazardous pollutants); Heeg v. Licht, 80 N.Y. 579 (1880) (storage of ultrahazardous pollutants).

Example and Problem 9–2: O keeps a German Shepherd dog on his well-fenced property. The dog has never been known to exhibit a

[handwritten margin notes, top: "unintentional + unreasonable? still NL" / "not neg + not abn. dangerous" / "unintentional + reasonable? NL" / "Just look parties not society" / "Gravity of harm dead llama" / "utility? Δ having the dog"]

dangerous temperament. The dog escapes the fence and kills a neighbor's prized and extremely valuable llama. Assess whether *O* should be liable for private nuisance. How, if at all, should the analysis differ if *O*'s animal was a wolf? *[handwritten: abn. dangerous]*

For a general discussion of the types of actions that might produce sufficient interference with the use and enjoyment of another's property to constitute a private nuisance, see Taylor v. Cincinnati, 143 Ohio St. 426, 435 (1944).

2. SIGNIFICANT HARM

According to Rest. (2d) Torts § 821F, nuisance liability runs "only to those to whom it causes significant harm, of a kind that would be suffered by a normal person in the community or by property in normal condition and used for a normal purpose." The harm must be "more than slight inconvenience or petty annoyance; ... there must be a real and appreciable invasion of the plaintiff's interests." Id., Comment c. A person seeking damages resulting from a public nuisance must prove that he has suffered an injury that is both substantial and "of a kind different from that suffered by other members of the public exercising the [public] right." Rest. (2d) Torts § 821C.

Example and Problem 9–3: From its office building *O* rang bells in a carillon for fifteen minutes each day, beginning at 12 noon. The sound could be heard for a distance of several miles. *A* heard the bells at his home, although the bells were rarely audible indoors. *A* found the sound to be highly annoying, but there was no diminution in property values due to the presence of the bells. Should *A* succeed in a claim of private nuisance against *O*? Should the result be different if, as a result of the bells, *A* sought and received medical and psychological treatment?

[handwritten margin: "prob will v prop. values"]

Example and Problem 9–4: *O* has a large lawn behind his home. He invites his friends to play croquet with him on the lawn. In the course of doing so they engage in conversation at a normal volume, punctuated by the clack of mallet upon ball, all of which produces a moderate amount of noise. *A*, an elderly neighbor who suffers from physical weakness and general nervous debility, is deeply distracted by the noise and becomes seriously ill. Nobody else complains of the noise. Should *A* succeed in her claim of private nuisance against *O*?

Example and Problem 9–5: *A* operates a foundry that emits extremely loud noises at all hours of the day and night. The foundry is sufficiently isolated that only a few houses are within earshot, only one of which is inhabited. That resident is *B*, who is stone deaf. Should *B* succeed in his claim of private nuisance against *A*?

[handwritten margin: "Look at Reasonable person not a deaf person! Would prob win"]

See also Amphitheaters, Inc. v. Portland Meadows, 184 Or. 336 (1948), in which the question was whether the lights emitted from a night-time race track were a substantial interference with an adjacent property owner's use of his property as a drive-in move theater. The movie theater owner had screened the site from adjacent streets to prevent lights from passing vehicles to penetrate the area, and had also constructed a "shadow box" to shield the movie screen from the light of the moon and stars. The effect of the lights from the race track on the theater, "when measured at [the movie] screen [was] approximately that of full moonlight."

Aesthetic injury has generally been regarded as insufficient to support a claim of nuisance. See, e.g., Ness v. Albert, 665 S.W.2d 1 (Mo. Ct. App. 1983) (the fact that the adjacent property was littered with old sinks, stoves, and a partially burned house trailer was insufficient interference). Beauty may be in the eye of the beholder, but appears to be beyond the ken of the judiciary, at least sometimes.

3.   UNREASONABLE INTERFERENCE

As noted above, the notion of unreasonable interference has a role to play in determining whether the defendant's conduct is intentional or unintentional. In each instance unreasonable interference hinges on the question posed by Rest. (2d) Torts, § 826(a): Does "the gravity of the harm outweigh[] the utility of the actor's conduct"? To measure the gravity of the harm, Rest. (2d) Torts, § 827, suggests that the extent and character of the harm are relevant, as well as the social value of the invaded use and the suitability of that use to the neighborhood. Also relevant is the burden that the person harmed would have to assume in order to avoid the harm. Rest. (2d) Torts, § 828, provides a similar set of factors to evaluate the utility of the actor's conduct: its social value, suitability to the character of the neighborhood, and "the impracticability of preventing or avoiding the invasion."

Despite the general rule that aesthetic injury is insufficient interference to support a nuisance claim, a few courts have suggested in dicta that aesthetic injury is a factor to be taken into account in assessing the gravity of the harm and the utility of the conduct. See, e.g., Robie v. Lillis, 112 N.H. 492 (1972); Hay v. Stevens, 271 Ore. 16 (1975) ("[W]e begin with the assumption that in the appropriate case . . . an interference with visual aesthetic sensibilities" will constitute a nuisance.).

Note that Rest. (2d) Torts, § 826(b) provides an alternative measure of unreasonable interference: If "the harm caused by the conduct is serious and the financial burden of compensating for this and similar harm to others would not make the continuation of the conduct not feasible." This is not the utilitarian assessment of harm v. utility, but involves some threshold of harm ("serious" harm) and a determination of whether compensation for that harm would be so onerous as to terminate the conduct. The compensation inquiry in this formula implicitly assumes that the conduct is of value, but the test is not an outright balancing of harm v. utility. The threshold approach acquires added force from Rest. (2d) Torts, § 829A: "An intentional invasion of another's interest in the use and enjoyment of land is unreasonable if the harm resulting from the invasion is severe and greater than the other should be required to bear without compensation."

A practical application of this principle is Jost v. Dairyland Power Cooperative, 45 Wis.2d 164 (1969). Sulphur particles and sulphur-dioxide gases were emitted from Dairyland's electric power generating plant, which caused ruinous damage to crops and trees downwind of the plant. Although Dairyland sought to introduce evidence that the utility of its conduct exceeded the gravity of the harm inflicted, the Wisconsin Supreme Court ruled that the exclusion of evidence on this point was proper: The trial "court properly excluded all evidence that tended to show the utility of the Dairyland Cooperative's enterprise. Whether its economic or social importance dwarfed the claim of a small farmer is of no consequence in this lawsuit. ... We know of no acceptable rule of jurisprudence that permits those who are engaged in important and desirable enterprises to injure with impunity those who are engaged in enterprises of lesser economic significance."

A variation on this theme is expressed in Rest. (2d) Torts, § 829: "An intentional invasion of another's interest in the use and enjoyment of land is unreasonable if the harm is significant and the actor's conduct is (a) for the sole purpose of causing harm to the other; or (b) contrary to common standards of decency." In Gorman v. Sabo, 210 Md. 155 (1956), the Maryland Court of Appeals upheld a a finding of nuisance and an award of damages, including punitive damages, on the basis of the following facts:

Mr. and Mrs. Sabo and their four children moved in next door to Mr. and Mrs. Gorman, ... who also had children. Trouble arose between the children which led to ill feeling on the part of Mrs. Gorman against the Sabo children, Mrs. Sabo, and eventually, Mr. Sabo. In the late summer or fall of 1952, Mrs. Gorman engaged in a deliberate and calculated effort to harass and annoy the Sabo family with the aim of making them move. She did this by deliberately turning up the radio in the Gorman house to an excessive and highly unreasonable volume, beaming it directly from a west window of the Gorman house into the east side of the Sabo house. This continued for hours each day over a period of several years. The radio was placed on a table in the middle bedroom on the second floor of the Gorman house right at the casement windows, which were opened and angled so that the sound was directed at the Sabo house. Closed was the door of the room in which the radio was so that other neighbors would not be annoyed. The window was kept open even in cold weather when normally the windows would have been closed. Mrs. Gorman also ordered her children to beat with sticks and stones on metal furniture and cans at strategic times to annoy the Sabo children and Mrs. Sabo. Mrs. Gorman's efforts to get rid of the Sabo family were known to the neighbors, many having seen the radio and heard its noise and other noises. Mrs. Gorman told various neighbors that she intended to make the Sabos move, that she would make life miserable for Mrs. Sabo, that she hoped Mr. Sabo would be struck down and never speak, and prayed that she would see Mrs. Sabo lie bleeding on the floor, that the Sabos would wish they were in hell before she was through with them, and on several occasions ... she said that she intended to see that Mrs. Sabo was carried out of the house either in a strait jacket or in a coffin. Soon after the campaign of noise began, Mr. Sabo asked Mr. Gorman to have his wife stop playing the radio. It continued to be played in the same loud and offensive manner for several years. Mr. Sabo complained to Mr. Gorman some five times about the noise. On one occasion Mr. Gorman turned the radio up loud in response to his wife's statement, "Louder, dear, it is not loud enough." ... There was testimony that as a result of the noise, life became miserable for Mr. and Mrs. Sabo, that their children could not sleep in the afternoon when they were supposed to take their naps, that it was necessary to move them from their room on the side of the house facing the Gormans and to shut the doors and windows of that room. Neighbors said that on innumerable occasions, too many to count, it was impossible to carry on a conversation in the Sabo home. There was medical testimony that Mrs. Sabo was suffering from an actual illness because of the constant harassment of the noise. Mr. Sabo testified that his wife's deterioration in physical and nervous condition, and the miseries they endured as a result of the Gorman's actions, made him irritable and nervous. Both Mr. and Mrs. Sabo said they had reached the point where they could not control themselves and could no longer stand the conditions to which they were subjected.

Id. at 159–161. Spite fences are a recurring example of this type of interference. See, e.g., Hutcherson v. Alexander, 264 Cal.App.2d 126 (1968), in which the appellate court upheld an injunction ordering removal of a fence erected by one business owner to block a neighboring business's view of the road, as part of general scheme of interference with the neighboring business's use and enjoyment of its property. The fence was "not necessary or essential to defendant's business and defendant's business motive [for the fence] was secondary or incidental." See also Norton v. Randolph, 176 Ala. 381 (1912), in which a 20 foot high fence located three to four feet from plaintiff's residence was treated as an unreasonable interference if the plaintiff could prove that it was useless and erected with malicious intent.

LANE v. W.J. CURRY & SONS

Supreme Court of Tennessee
92 S.W.3d 355 (Tenn. 2002)

DROWOTA, C.J., delivered the opinion of the court.

We granted review ... to determine whether a landowner can bring a nuisance action against an adjoining landowner when tree branches and roots from the adjoining landowner's property encroach upon and damage the neighboring landowner's property. The plaintiff asserts that encroaching branches and roots from the defendant's trees constitute a nuisance for which she is entitled to seek damages. The defendant responds that the plaintiff's sole remedy is self-help and, therefore, the plaintiff may not recover for any harm caused by the defendant's trees. The trial court and Court of Appeals agreed with the defendant, and held that an adjoining landowner's only remedy is self-help and that a nuisance action cannot be brought to recover for harm caused by encroaching tree branches and roots.

We have determined that self-help is not the sole remedy of an adjoining landowner and that a nuisance action may be brought when tree branches and roots from the adjacent property encroach upon and damage the neighboring landowner's property. Although encroaching trees and plants are not nuisances merely because they cast shade, drop leaves, flowers, or fruit, or just because they encroach upon adjoining property either above or below the ground, they may be regarded as a nuisance when they cause actual harm or pose an imminent danger of actual harm to adjoining property. If so, the owner of the tree or plant may be held responsible for harm caused by it and may also be required to cut back the encroaching branches or roots, assuming the encroaching vegetation constitutes a nuisance. We do not, however, alter existing Tennessee law that the adjoining landowner may, at his own expense, cut away the encroaching vegetation to the property line whether or not the encroaching vegetation constitutes a nuisance or is otherwise causing harm or potential harm to the adjoining property. We further find that the record in this case is sufficient to establish liability for nuisance. Accordingly, the judgment of the Court of Appeals affirming the trial court's dismissal of the case is reversed. The case is remanded to the trial court for a determination of damages and other appropriate relief.

Factual and Procedural Background. ... The plaintiff, Gloria Lane, owns a house in Memphis located next door to a house owned by the defendant, W.J. Curry & Sons. The plaintiff, who is 47–years old and unemployed, has lived in the house all of her life. Her disabled brother lives with her. The defendant's house is used as rental property and is occupied. The houses in the parties' neighborhood are at least fifty-years old and are situated close together.

The defendant has three large, healthy oak trees located on its property near the common boundary line with the plaintiff. The trees are much taller than the parties' houses and have limbs, described as "extremely protruding," that hang over the plaintiff's house. The defendant's trees were described as "overshadowing the [plaintiff's] entire house." The plaintiff has had problems with the trees' limbs and roots encroaching upon her property for many years. Her roof, for example, had to be replaced in the late 1980s because the overhanging branches did not allow the roof to ever dry, causing it to rot. The plaintiff testified that prior to that time "every roof and wall in [her] house had turned brown and the ceiling was just falling down. We would be in bed at nighttime and the ceiling would just fall down and hit the floor."

In 1997, a large limb from one of the defendant's trees located between the parties' houses broke off and fell through the plaintiff's roof, attic, and kitchen ceiling, causing rainwater to leak into the interior of her home. The water ruined the plaintiff's ceilings, floor, and the stove in her kitchen. The plaintiff is not physically able to cut the limbs back that hang over her house, and she cannot afford to hire someone else to do it. Nor can she afford to repair the damage to the exterior and interior of her home, including the hole in her roof.

Roots

In addition to the harm caused by the overhanging branches, roots from the defendant's trees have infiltrated and clogged the plaintiff's sewer line, causing severe plumbing problems. The plaintiff has tried to chop the encroaching roots over the years, but they keep growing back and causing more plumbing problems. The plaintiff has not been able to use her toilet, bathtub, or sink in two years because of the clogged sewer pipes. She must go to a neighbor's house to use the restroom. Raw sewage bubbles up into her bathtub, and her bathroom floor has had to be replaced because her toilet continually backs up and water spills onto her floor. Neighbors have complained to the plaintiff about the smell of sewage coming from her property. The plaintiff testified regarding the condition of her home that "everything is all messed up. I can't bathe. I can't cook. I don't want people coming to my house because it has odors in it, fleas, flies, bugs. It's just been awful for me." The plaintiff is under the care of a psychiatrist and takes medication for emotional problems. She testified that she may have to move out of her house because she "just can't take too much more."

After the defendant's branch fell through her roof, the plaintiff contacted Judith Harris, the owner of defendant W.J. Curry & Sons, to complain about the encroaching trees and to inform Harris of the damage caused by the fallen limb. Harris sent a tree trimming company to the property to cut back the overhanging limbs, but this proved unsatisfactory because branches high up in the trees were not cut, and those that were cut grew back. Harris eventually told the plaintiff that she, the plaintiff, could trim the branches or roots, but that Harris no longer felt any responsibility to remedy the situation.

Procedure

The plaintiff subsequently filed suit ... seeking damages to the exterior and interior of her house and plumbing system caused by the encroaching branches and roots. The ... trial court concluded that the plaintiff's sole remedy was self-help and that the defendant's trees could not constitute an actionable nuisance [because] "these three trees are alive and living and they do what trees normally do...." On appeal, the Court of Appeals agreed with the trial court's finding that the plaintiff was financially and physically unable to engage in self-help beyond what she had already tried without success. Nonetheless, after noting that "the three oaks at issue are viable, healthy, and innoxious trees whose natural growth is accompanied by the extension of their branches and roots over and into" the plaintiff's property, the intermediate court concluded that the plaintiff's only remedy was self-help and that her nuisance action could not be sustained. Accordingly, the Court of Appeals affirmed the trial court's dismissal of the case.

　　Analysis. . . . In finding that the plaintiff's only remedy was self-help and that a nuisance claim cannot be brought for harm caused by encroaching tree branches and roots, both lower courts relied on this Court's decision in Granberry v. Jones, 188 Tenn. 51 (1949). In *Granberry*, the parties owned residences on adjacent lots. The defendant planted a hedge row on her property near the common boundary line, which eventually grew to a height of twenty feet. Branches and foliage from the defendant's hedge encroached upon the plaintiff's property and rested against his house. The plaintiff alleged that the hedge row was a nuisance because its branches and foliage blocked the view from his windows and created a sanctuary for insects. He also alleged that damp conditions associated with the hedge caused the decay of his window sills, a wall, and a fence. . . .

　　This Court held in *Granberry* that the plaintiff had the legal right to cut any branches or foliage which to any extent hung over his soil from the hedge growing upon the adjoining land." In reaching this conclusion, we relied on the then prevailing rule that "no landowner has a cause of action from the mere fact that the branches of an innoxious tree, belonging to an adjoining landowner, overhang his premises, his right to cut off the overhanging branches being considered a sufficient remedy." The rationale for the rule was that a landowner has the "liberty to use his land, and all of it, to grow trees [and] their growth naturally and reasonably will be accompanied by the extension of boughs and the penetration of roots over and into adjoining property of others." We also noted that limiting a plaintiff's remedy to self-help would avoid subjecting landowners to the "annoyance, and the public to the burden, of actions at law, which would be likely to be innumerable and, in many instances, purely vexatious." However, we went on in *Granberry* to observe that "our conclusion . . . is without prejudice to whatever rights, if any, [the plaintiff] may have for recovery of the expense to which he may be put now or hereafter in cutting the overhanging branches or foliage." Thus, *Granberry* left open the possibility of the injured landowner recovering damages, or at least expenses, after the landowner availed himself to self-help remedies. . . .

　　[S]ince *Granberry* was decided in 1949, states considering the question of encroaching vegetation have taken a number of different approaches. The courts uniformly hold that a landowner has a remedy of self-help, meaning that the landowner has the right to cut encroaching branches, roots, and other growth to the property line, but may not enter the adjoining property to chop down the tree or plant or cut back growth without the adjoining property owner's consent. Some states apply this rule even if the encroaching limbs and roots are not causing any harm to the adjoining property. *See, e.g.,* Jones v. Wagner, 425 Pa. Super. 102, 624 A.2d 166, 168–69 (Pa. Super. Ct. 1993). These courts reason that from "ancient times" it has been the accepted rule that a landowner has the exclusive right to possess and use all of the landowner's property, including the air space above the ground, and therefore the redressable harm caused by encroaching trees is that of the trespass onto the neighboring property, not physical damage done to the neighboring land.

Although the jurisdictions uniformly agree that self-help is an appropriate remedy, they are divided on the availability of any remedy beyond self-help. In some states, for example, harm caused by encroaching branches and roots is not actionable at all, so self-help is the landowner's exclusive remedy. Courts adopting this approach, called the "Massachusetts rule," express the concern that "to grant a landowner a cause of action every time tree branches, leaves, vines, shrubs, etc., encroach upon or fall on his property from his neighbor's property, might well spawn innumerable and vexatious lawsuits." Melnick v. C.S.X. Corp., 312 Md. 511, 540 A.2d 1133, 1137 (Md. 1988). The Massachusetts rule, however, has been criticized as being outdated, having evolved in an earlier time when land was mostly unsettled and people lived predominately in rural settings. *See* Chandler v. Larson, 148 Ill. App. 3d 1032, 500 N.E.2d 584, 587, 102 Ill. Dec. 691 (Ill. Ct. App. 1986). The Massachusetts rule has also been criticized as fostering a "law of the jungle" mentality because self-help effectively replaces the law of orderly judicial process as the only way to adjust the rights and responsibilities of disputing neighbors. As one court has observed, "in the long run neighborhood quarrels and petty litigation will be minimized rather than magnified by a rule that does not require an exercise of self-help before permitting an action to enforce legal rights." Ludwig v. Creswald, Inc., 7 Pa. D. & C.2d 461, 464, 72 Mont. County L. Rep. 349 (1956). Finally, some courts have questioned whether the Massachusetts rule is fair given that it deprives deserving plaintiffs of any meaningful redress when their property is damaged. *See* Whitesell v. Houlton, 2 Haw. App. 365, 632 P.2d 1077, 1079 (Haw. Ct. App. 1981). A strict application of the Massachusetts rule to the present case, for example, would leave the plaintiff with no remedy for the hole in her roof or for being unable to use the only bathroom in her house for two years.

Criticism of MA rule

Other jurisdictions have adopted what is commonly called the "Restatement rule," which imposes an obligation upon a landowner to control the landowner's encroaching vegetation when the vegetation is "artificial" (i.e., planted or maintained by a person), but not when the encroaching vegetation is "natural." *See* Restatement (Second) of Torts §§ 839, 840 (1979). Although a few states follow the Restatement rule, most have rejected it because the distinction between artificial and natural vegetation is unworkable given the inherent difficulty of ascertaining the origin of a particular tree or plant. As one court has observed, "it would often be difficult to ascertain whether a tree of natural growth might not be in part the result of human activity, such as cultivating, fertilizing, trimming, etc. The distinction between purely natural conditions and conditions which in some degree are the result of man's activity ... cannot reasonably be made...." Finally, distinguishing between artificial and natural vegetation leads to the anomaly of imposing liability upon one who improves and maintains his property, while precluding liability of an adjacent landowner who allows the natural condition of his property to "run wild."

Another approach is the "Virginia rule," which provides that the injured landowner is limited to self-help unless the encroaching tree or plant is "noxious" and causes actual harm to the neighboring property. *See, e.g.,* Cannon v. Dunn, 145 Ariz. 115, 700 P.2d 502, 504 (Ariz. Ct. App. 1985); Smith v. Holt, 174 Va. 213, 5 S.E.2d 492, 495 (Va. 1939). Confusion exists over whether a tree or plant is noxious merely because it causes injury, or whether it must be inherently injurious or poisonous. Few jurisdictions follow the Virginia rule because of the inherent "difficulty of determining exactly what is a noxious tree or plant."

Several jurisdictions have adopted the "Hawaii rule," which holds that living trees and plants are ordinarily not nuisances, but can become so when they cause actual harm or pose an imminent danger of actual harm to adjoining property. Under this approach, "when overhanging branches or protruding roots actually cause, or there is imminent danger of them causing, [substantial] harm to property other than plant life, in ways other than by casting shade or dropping leaves, flowers, or fruit, the damaged or imminently endangered neighbor may require the owner of the tree to pay for the damages and to cut back the endangering branches or roots, and if such is not done within a reasonable time, the . . . neighbor may cause the cutback to be done at the tree owner's expense." Whitesell v. Houlton, 2 Haw. App. 365, 632 P.2d 1077, 1079 (Haw. Ct. App. 1981). However, the injured landowner "may always, at his own expense, cut away only to his property line above and below the surface of the ground any part of the adjoining landowner's tree or other plant life" that encroach upon the property. *Id.* The Hawaii approach thus addresses the flood of litigation concern expressed by some courts over the natural processes and cycles of trees, roots, and other vegetation, by imposing a requirement of actual harm or imminent danger of actual harm to the adjoining property. Hence, the mere fact that tree limbs or roots extend to another's property does not by itself constitute an actionable nuisance. Moreover, the Hawaii rule does not rely on distinctions made by the Restatement and Virginia rules that have been described variously as "unworkable," "vague," "difficult to apply," and "largely arbitrary." *Melnick*, 540 A.2d at 1138. At the same time, the rule provides a meaningful remedy in deserving cases, i.e., those involving actual harm or imminent danger of actual harm. The rule has been described as "realistic and fair" because the "owner of the tree's trunk is the owner of the tree, [and therefore] he bears some responsibility for the rest of the tree. . . ." *Whitesell*, 632 P.2d at 1079.

Finally, at least one court has gone so far as to permit the adjoining landowner to compel the owner of a tree to remove it to the extent of the encroachment, plus recover damages, including expenses incurred in the course of exercising a self-help remedy, in the absence of any actual harm to the property. *Jones*, 624 A.2d at 171. Under this view, a landowner "may avail himself of every available remedial avenue," self-help or a suit for damages or both, in the absence of harm or potential harm to the property in order to "protect the incidents of land ownership" and "freely enjoy unencumbered and exclusive use of property he rightfully possesses." *Id.* . . . As we see it, however, this approach is problematic because no actual harm or danger of harm to the property is required to bring suit. Permitting a cause of action every time a tree or plant so much as drops a leaf or casts shade upon another's land could well subject landowners to the "annoyance, and the public to the burden, of actions at law, which would be likely to be innumerable and, in many instances, purely vexatious." *Granberry*, 188 Tenn. 51, 216 S.W.2d 721 at 723. . . .

[We] have decided to join the growing number of states that have adopted the Hawaii approach. We do so for several reasons. First, the Hawaii approach strikes an appropriate balance between the competing rights of adjacent property owners. As stated by one court, "this approach voices a rational and fair solution, permitting a landowner to grow and nurture trees and other plants on his land, balanced against the correlative duty of a landowner to ensure that the use of his property does not materially harm his neighbor." . . . Second, we are persuaded that the Hawaii approach is stringent enough to discourage trivial suits, but not so restrictive that it precludes a recovery where one is warranted. Although some courts express the concern of spawning numerous lawsuits, we note that states which do not limit a plaintiff's remedy to self-help have apparently not suffered any such flood of litigation. Imposing a requirement of actual harm or imminent danger of actual harm to the adjoining property is a sufficient and appropriate gate-keeping mechanism. Third, we agree with the notion that limiting a plaintiff's remedy to self-help encourages a "law of the jungle" mentality because self-help replaces the law of orderly judicial process as the exclusive way to adjust the rights and responsibilities of disputing neighbors. It seems that more harm than good can come from a rule that encourages angry neighbors to take matters into their own hands. Fourth, the Hawaii rule does not depend upon difficult to apply or unworkable distinctions, a major disadvantage of the Restatement and Virginia approaches. We do not wish to place our courts in the difficult, and sometimes impossible, position of having to ascertain the origin of a particular tree or other vegetation. Nor should landowners who allow their property to run wild be shielded from liability while those who maintain and improve their land be subject to liability. The law should not sanction such an anomaly. Fifth, the Hawaii approach is consistent with the principle of self-help embraced in *Granberry*. The rule is also consistent with *Granberry*'s recognition that a landowner may recover the "expense to which he may be put now or hereafter in cutting the overhanging branches or foliage," assuming the encroaching vegetation constitutes a nuisance. Finally, the rule we adopt today is in keeping with the aim of the law to provide a remedy to those who are harmed as a result of another's tortious conduct.

Accordingly, we hold that encroaching trees and plants are not nuisances merely because they cast shade, drop leaves, flowers, or fruit, or just because they happen to encroach upon adjoining property either above or below the ground. However, encroaching trees and plants may be regarded as a nuisance when they cause actual harm or pose an imminent danger of actual harm to adjoining property. If so, the owner of the tree or plant may be held responsible for harm caused by it, and may also be required to cut back the encroaching branches or roots, assuming the encroaching vegetation constitutes a nuisance. We do not, however, alter existing Tennessee law that the adjoining landowner may, at his own expense, cut away the encroaching vegetation to the property line whether or not the encroaching vegetation constitutes a nuisance or is otherwise causing harm or possible harm to the adjoining property. Thus, the law of self-help remains intact as it has since 1949 when *Granberry* was decided.[1]

. . .

Depending on the surroundings, activities that constitute a nuisance in one context may not constitute a nuisance in another. Whether a particular activity or use of property amounts to an unreasonable invasion of another's legally protectable interests depends on the circumstances of each case, such as the character of the surroundings, the nature, utility, and social value of the use, and the nature and extent of the harm involved. . . . [A]ctions based on the unreasonable interference with another's interest in the private use and enjoyment of property date back to the twelfth century in England. Nuisance law has since developed over the centuries to the point where a nuisance may now consist of a physical condition on the land itself (i.e., vibrations, pollution, or flooding), cause discomfort or inconvenience to the occupants of the property (i.e., odors, dust, smoke, noise), or consist of a condition on adjoining property which impairs the occupier's tranquility (i.e., conducting an unlawful business or keeping diseased animals). So "long as the interference is substantial and unreasonable, such as would be offensive or inconvenient to the normal person, virtually any disturbance of the enjoyment of the property may amount to a nuisance." Thus, nuisance does not describe a defendant's conduct, but a type of harm suffered by the plaintiff.

A party who has been subjected to a private nuisance may be entitled to several types of remedies. [A] plaintiff may be entitled to injunctive relief, especially where the nuisance is likely to continue. Further, in cases involving a temporary private nuisance, which is one that can be corrected, damages may be awarded for the cost of restoring the property to its pre-nuisance condition, as well as damages for inconvenience, emotional distress, and injury to the use and enjoyment of the property. The typical way of measuring injury to the use and enjoyment of the property is the decrease in rental value of the property while the nuisance existed. Accordingly, courts provide an appropriate remedy in the form of either damages or injunctive relief or both. . . .

---

1. [D]ead or decaying trees that cause harm are in a category of their own and require a different analysis. Unlike the cases involving harm caused by live trees, which are based on nuisance or trespass principles, cases involving dead or decaying trees are typically analyzed according to negligence concepts. . . .

Applying the principles we have adopted to the present case, it is clear that the defendant's trees [constitute] a private nuisance. . . . of property." *Pate*, 614 S.W.2d at 47. The record reveals that . . . the defendant's encroaching trees have adversely affected the plaintiff's reasonable and ordinary use and occupation of her home, not to mention posing hazards to the plaintiff's health and safety. . . .

[T]he lower courts erred in finding that the plaintiff's sole remedy was self-help. [T]he record in this case is sufficient to establish liability for nuisance. Accordingly, the judgment of the Court of Appeals affirming the trial court's dismissal of the case is reversed. The case is remanded to the trial court for a determination of damages and other appropriate relief, such as ordering the nuisance abated (i.e., order the trees removed). . . .

NOTES, QUESTIONS, AND PROBLEMS

1. Nuisance or Trespass. Trespass is an intentional physical invasion of another's property, or causing a thing or third person to do so, or the failure to remove something from another's land when one is under a duty to do so. Rest. (2d) Torts, § 158. Trespass protects the right to exclusive possession of property. Thus, according to the Restatement, liability for trespass does not depend on the infliction of harm to "any legally protected interest" of the other party. Nuisance, of course, protects the right to use and enjoy one's property, so liability requires a significant harm as well as a substantial interference with that interest.

Some activities, such as various forms of air pollution, might constitute both a nuisance and trespass. Intolerable odors might be thought of as a trespass, because the molecules that compose the stench invade another's property, but such invasions have been treated as nuisances. See, e.g., Morgan v. High Penn Oil Co., 238 N.C. 185 (1953). But what about pollutants that consist of particles that settle on the ground? Jost v. Dairyland Power Cooperative, 45 Wis.2d 164 (1969), which involved severe sulphur dioxide emissions, was treated as a nuisance, but more recent cases have permitted plaintiffs to proceed under trespass as well as nuisance. The Alabama Supreme Court, in Borland v. Sanders Lead Co., Inc., 369 So.2d 523 (1979), permitted both theories to be advanced in a case in which the plaintiff alleged significant accumulation of lead particles and sulphur dioxides on his property resulting from the defendant's operation of a smelter to recover lead from used auto batteries, but limited trespass to instances where the particulate pollution actually interferes with possession (e.g., by remaining on the affected property) and inflicts substantial damages. Accord, Bradley v. American Smelting & Refining Co., 104 Wn.2d 677 (1985). See also, Martin v. Reynolds Metals Co., 221 Ore. 86 (1959), in which the court ruled that the same conduct—emission of invisible fluoride compounds from an aluminum reduction plant—could constitute both torts. The court noted that

> in an earlier day when science had not yet peered into the molecular and atomic world of small particles, the courts could not fit an invasion through unseen physical instrumentalities into the requirement that a trespass can result only from a *direct* invasion. But in this atomic age

even the uneducated know the great and awful force contained in the atom and what it can do to a man's property if it is released. In fact, the now famous equation $E=mc^2$ has taught us that mass and energy are equivalents and that our concept of "things" must be reframed. If these observations on science in relation to the law of trespass should appear theoretical and unreal in the abstract, they become very practical and real to the possessor of land when the unseen force cracks the foundation of his house. The force is just as real if it is chemical in nature and must be awakened by the intervention of another agency before it does harm. If . . . we must look to the character of the instrumentality which is used in making an intrusion upon another's land we prefer to emphasize the object's energy or force rather than its size. [We] define trespass as an intrusion which invades the possessor's protected interest in exclusive possession, whether that intrusion is by visible or invisible pieces of matter or by energy which can be measured only by the mathematical language of the physicist.

Id. at 93–94. The court's conclusion that the fluoride intrusions constituted a trespass enabled the plaintiff to proceed with the claim under the six year limitations statute applicable to trespasses. Had the plaintiff's suit been limited to nuisance it would have been time-barred under the two year statute applicable to nuisance claims.

Was the claim in *Lane* both a trespass and nuisance? What are the remedies for trespass and nuisance?

2. *Problem.* A and B own physically contiguous apartment houses. C, a tenant of A, permits his dog to defecate on the roof of B's building and, in violation of a local law, fails to remove the feces. Is this a trespass, private nuisance, public nuisance, or some combination of the three? What causes of action, if any, may B assert against C? Against A?

A news account, from which these facts are extracted, is "When the Dog Isn't Yours, But the Fine for its Waste Is," New York Times, Feb. 11, 2011, A23A (San Francisco Bay Area edition).[2]

3. *Light and Air.* The ancient rule in Anglo–American law is that a person has no legally enforceable right to continue to enjoy the light and air that naturally crosses the adjacent land of his neighbor. Thus, it has traditionally been held to be not a nuisance to erect a structure that blocks some of the light and air previously enjoyed by a neighbor. See, e.g., Fontainebleau Hotel Corp. v. Forty–Five Twenty–Five, Inc., 114 So.2d 357 (Fla. App. 1959) (14 story addition to Miami Beach's Fountainbleau Hotel, which would shade the pool and sunbathing area of the adjacent Eden Roc Hotel during winter afternoons, was not actionable as a nuisance); Sher v. Leiderman, 181 Cal.App.3d 867 (1986) (absent proof of malice, high trees shading neighbor's passive solar designed home was not an actionable nuisance); People ex rel Hoogasian v. Sears, Roebuck & Co., 52 Ill.2d 301 (1972) (new construction alleged to disrupt television reception was not actionable as a nuisance). But consider the following case.

---

2. A link to the online version of the article may be found at http://www.nytimes.com/2011/02/ 11/us/11bcjames.html?_r=1 & scp=1 & sq=WhentheDogIsn'tYours & st=cse

PRAH v. MARETTI

Supreme Court of Wisconsin
108 Wis.2d 223 (1982)

ABRAHAMSON, J., delivered the opinion of the court.

[Glenn Prah, the plaintiff, constructed a solar-heated home. Richard Maretti, the defendant, purchased the lot to the immediate south of Prah's home and began to design a home to be constructed on the lot. Prah informed Maretti that his design would block the sunlight needed to power Prah's heating system. Maretti began construction anyway. Prah sued to enjoin the construction, claiming that Maretti's design was a nuisance and that he was entitled to "unrestricted use of the sun and its solar power." The trial court denied the injunction and then granted summary judgment to Maretti.]

We consider first whether the complaint states a claim for relief based on common law private nuisance. ... The rights of neighboring landowners are relative; the uses by one must not unreasonably impair the uses or enjoyment of the other. When one landowner's use of his or her property unreasonably interferes with another's enjoyment of his or her property, that use is said to be a private nuisance. [This] court has recently adopted the analysis of private nuisance set forth in the Restatement (Second) of Torts. The Restatement defines private nuisance as "a nontrespassory invasion of another's interest in the private use and enjoyment of land." Restatement (Second) of Torts Sec. 821D (1977). The phrase "interest in the private use and enjoyment of land" as used in sec. 821D is broadly defined to include any disturbance of the enjoyment of property. The comment in the Restatement describes the landowner's interest protected by private nuisance law as follows:

> ... It comprehends not only the interests that a person may have in the actual present use of land for residential, agricultural, commercial, industrial and other purposes, but also his interests in having the present use value of the land unimpaired by changes in its physical condition. Thus the destruction of trees on vacant land is as much an invasion of the owner's interest in its use and enjoyment as is the destruction of crops or flowers that he is growing on the land for his present use. "Interest in use and enjoyment" also comprehends the pleasure, comfort and enjoyment that a person normally derives from the occupancy of land. Freedom from discomfort and annoyance while using land is often as important to a person as freedom from physical interruption with his use or freedom from detrimental change in the physical condition of the land itself. Restatement (Second) of Torts, Sec. 821D, Comment *b*, p. 101 (1977).

Although the defendant's obstruction of the plaintiff's access to sunlight appears to fall within the Restatement's broad concept of a private nuisance as a nontrespassory invasion of another's interest in the private use and enjoyment of land, the defendant asserts that he has a right to develop his property in compliance with statutes, ordinances and private covenants without regard to the effect of such development upon the plaintiff's access to sunlight. In essence, the defendant is asking this court to hold that the private nuisance doctrine is not applicable in the instant case and that his right to develop his land is a right which is *per se* superior to his neighbor's interest in access to sunlight. This position is expressed in the maxim "*cujus est solum, ejus est usque ad coelum et ad infernos*," that is, the owner of land owns up to the sky and down to the center of the earth....

The defendant is not completely correct in asserting that the common law did not protect a landowner's access to sunlight across adjoining property. At English common law a landowner could acquire a right to receive sunlight across adjoining land by both express agreement and under the judge-made doctrine of "ancient lights." Under the doctrine of ancient lights if the landowner had received sunlight across adjoining property for a specified period of time, the landowner was entitled to continue to receive unobstructed access to sunlight across the adjoining property. Under the doctrine the landowner acquired a negative prescriptive easement and could prevent the adjoining landowner from obstructing access to light.[3]

. . . American courts have not been as receptive to protecting a landowner's access to sunlight as the English courts.... American courts initially enforced the English common law doctrine of ancient lights, but later every state which considered the doctrine repudiated it as inconsistent with the needs of a developing country. Indeed, for just that reason this court concluded that an easement to light and air over adjacent property could not be created or acquired by prescription and has been unwilling to recognize such an easement by implication. Depner v. United States National Bank, 202 Wis. 405, 408, 232 N.W. 851 (1930); Miller v. Hoeschler, 126 Wis. 263, 268–69, 105 N.W. 790 (1905)....

This court's reluctance ... to provide broader protection for a landowner's access to sunlight was premised on three policy considerations. First, the right of landowners to use their property as they wished, as long as they did not cause physical damage to a neighbor, was jealously guarded. Second, sunlight was valued only for aesthetic enjoyment or as illumination. Since artificial light could be used for illumination, loss of sunlight was at most a personal annoyance which was given little, if any, weight by society. Third, society had a significant interest in not restricting or impeding land development. This court repeatedly emphasized that in the growth period of the nineteenth and early twentieth centuries change is to be expected and is essential to property and that recognition of a right to sunlight would hinder property development....

---

3. Pfeiffer, *Ancient Lights: Legal Protection of Access to Solar Energy*, 68 ABAJ 288 (1982). No American common law state recognizes a landowner's right to acquire an easement of light by prescription. Comment, *Solar Lights: Guaranteeing a Place in the Sun*, 57 Ore. L. Rev. 94, 112 (1977).

These three policies are no longer fully accepted or applicable. They reflect factual circumstances and social priorities that are now obsolete. First, society has increasingly regulated the use of land by the landowner for the general welfare. Second, access to sunlight has taken on a new significance in recent years. In this case the plaintiff seeks to protect access to sunlight, not for aesthetic reasons or as a source of illumination but as a source of energy. Access to sunlight as an energy source is of significance both to the landowner who invests in solar collectors and to a society which has an interest in developing alternative sources of energy. Third, the policy of favoring unhindered private development in an expanding economy is no longer in harmony with the realities of our society. The need for easy and rapid development is not as great today as it once was, while our perception of the value of sunlight as a source of energy has increased significantly. . . .

The law of private nuisance is better suited to resolve landowners' disputes about property development . . . than is a rigid rule which does not recognize a landowner's interest in access to sunlight. As we said in Ballstadt v. Pagel, 202 Wis. 484, 489, 232 N.W. 862 (1930), "What is regarded in law as constituting a nuisance in modern times would no doubt have been tolerated without question in former times."

We read State v. Deetz, 66 Wis. 2d 1, 224 N.W.2d 407 (1974), as an endorsement of the application of common law nuisance to situations involving the conflicting interests of landowners and as rejecting *per se* exclusions to the nuisance law reasonable use doctrine. In *Deetz* the court abandoned the rigid common law common enemy rule with respect to surface water[4] and adopted the private nuisance reasonable use rule, namely that the landowner is subject to liability if his or her interference with the flow of surface waters unreasonably invades a neighbor's interest in the use and enjoyment of land. Restatement (Second) of Torts, sec. 822, 826, 829 (1977). This court concluded that the common enemy rule which served society "well in the days of burgeoning national expansion of the mid-nineteenth and early-twentieth centuries" should be abandoned because it was no longer "in harmony with the realities of our society." . . .

Yet the defendant would have us ignore the flexible private nuisance law as a means of resolving the dispute between the landowners in this

---

4. [Ed.—] In its strict form, the "common enemy" doctrine held that "a possessor of land has an unlimited and unrestricted legal privilege to deal with the surface water on his land as he pleases, regardless of the harm which he may thereby cause to others." S. V. Kinyon and R. C. McClure, Interferences with Surface Waters, 24 Minn. L. Rev. 891, 898 (1940). The "common enemy" doctrine is of long duration, accepted by Wisconsin at least as early as Borchsenius v. Chicago, St. Paul, Minneapolis & Omaha R. Co., 96 Wis. 448 (1897). See also Gannon v. Hargadon, 92 Mass. 106 (1865). Two other doctrines are sometimes used to deal with surface water runoff. One is the "natural flow" rule, which imposes strict liability upon a landowner who alters the natural drainage patterns of water. This rule, exemplified by Powers v. Judd, 150 Vt. 290 (1988), increases development costs by requiring compensation to landowners harmed by the development. For that reason, some states that use the "natural flow" rule limit it to rural areas. First Lady, LLC v. JMF Properties, LLC, 681 N.W.2d 94 (S.D. 2004). Another approach is akin to the unreasonable interference rule of nuisance law. Originating in Armstrong v. Francis Corp., 20 N.J. 320 (1956), this test is now the most widely used approach. See, e.g., Locklin v. City of Lafayette, 7 Cal.4th 327 (1994).

case and would have us adopt an approach, already abandoned in *Deetz,* of favoring the unrestricted development of land and of applying a rigid and inflexible rule protecting his right to build on his land and disregarding any interest of the plaintiff in the use and enjoyment of his land. This we refuse to do.

Private nuisance law, the law traditionally used to adjudicate conflicts between private landowners, has the flexibility to protect both a landowner's right of access to sunlight and another landowner's right to develop land. Private nuisance law is better suited to regulate access to sunlight in modern society . . . than is an inflexible doctrine of non-recognition of any interest in access to sunlight across adjoining land. We therefore hold that private nuisance law, that is, the reasonable use doctrine as set forth in the Restatement, is applicable to the instant case. . . . That obstruction of access to light might be found to constitute a nuisance in certain circumstances does not mean that it will be or must be found to constitute a nuisance under all circumstances. The result in each case depends on whether the conduct complained of is unreasonable. [While] we hold that the plaintiff in this case has stated a claim under which relief can be granted . . . we do not determine whether the plaintiff . . . is entitled to relief. In order to be entitled to relief the plaintiff must prove the elements required to establish actionable nuisance, and the conduct of the defendant herein must be judged by the reasonable use doctrine.

CALLOW, J., dissenting.

. . . It is a fundamental principle of law that a "landowner owns at least as much of the space above the ground as he can occupy or use in connection with the land." United States v. Causby, 328 U.S. 256, 264 (1946). . . . [A] landowner's right to use his property within the limits of ordinances, statutes, and restrictions of record where such use is necessary to serve his legitimate needs is a fundamental precept of a free society which this court should strive to uphold. [It may] "fashionable to dismiss such values as deriving from a bygone era in which people valued development as a 'goal in itself,' but current market prices for real estate, and more particularly the premiums paid for land whose zoning permits intensive use, suggest that people still place very high values on such rights." Williams, Solar Access and Property Rights: A Maverick Analysis, 11 Conn. L. Rev. 430, 443 (1979). . . . The right of a property owner to lawful enjoyment of his property should be vigorously protected, particularly in those cases where the adjacent property owner could have insulated himself from the alleged problem by acquiring the land as a defense to the potential problem or by provident use of his own property.

. . . While the majority's policy arguments may be directed to a cause of action for public nuisance, we are presented with a private nuisance case which I believe is distinguishable. . . .[5] I would submit that any policy

5. I am amused at the majority's contention that what constitutes a nuisance today would have been accepted without question in earlier times. This calls to mind the fact that, in early days of travel by horses, the first automobiles were considered nuisances. Later, when automobile

decisions in this area are best left for the legislature. "What is 'desirable' or 'advisable' or 'ought to be' is a question of policy, not a question of fact. What is 'necessary' or what is 'in the best interest' is not a fact and its determination by the judiciary is an exercise of legislative power when each involves political considerations." In re City of Beloit, 37 Wis. 2d 637, 644, 155 N.W.2d 633 (1968)....

It is impossible for me to accept the majority's conclusion that Mr. Maretti, in lawfully seeking to construct his home, may be intentionally and unreasonably interfering with the plaintiff's access to sunlight. [It] is important to note that "[t]here is liability for a nuisance only to those to whom it causes significant harm, of a kind that would be suffered by a normal person in the community or by property in normal condition and used for a normal purpose." Restatement (Second) of Torts sec. 821F (1979). The comments to the Restatement further reveal that "[if] normal persons in that locality would not be substantially annoyed or disturbed by the situation, then the invasion is not a significant one, even though the idiosyncracies of the particular plaintiff may make it unendurable to him." *Id.* Comment d. ... I conclude that plaintiff's solar heating system is an unusually sensitive use. In other words, the defendant's proposed construction of his home, under ordinary circumstances, would not interfere with the use and enjoyment of the usual person's property....

NOTES AND QUESTIONS

1. Application of Unreasonable Interference. What factors are relevant to determination of whether Maretti's new house constitutes an unreasonable interference with Prah's use and enjoyment of his property? How do you assess whether the gravity of the harm to Prah is more or less than the utility of Maretti's conduct?

2. Unusual Sensitivity, Individual Rights, and Social Benefits. The dissenting judge concluded that Prah was an unusually sensitive user of his property. Would he be unusually sensitive if solar heating of homes were more common? How much more common must it be to destroy the claim that access to sunlight for heating purposes is an unusually sensitive use? The majority did not think that Prah's use was unusually sensitive. Why not? Was the majority view premised on the view that solar power is socially beneficial, and thus Prah's use should not be deemed unusually sensitive even though it was uncommon? Or did the majority think that Prah's use, while uncommon at the time, was bound to become more ordinary in the future? Or was it because the majority thought that, while solar heating may be uncommon, it is not an individual peculiarity like an unusual allergy, or a hyper-sensitive nervous condition?

If the perceived social benefit of solar power is the answer, note how the case involves a contest between the individual rights claims of Maretti—summed up by the *ad coelum* maxim—and the perceived social benefits of

---

travel became developed, the horse became the nuisance. Ellickson, Alternatives to Zoning: Covenants, Nuisance Rules, and Fines as Land Use Controls, 40 U. Chi. L. Rev. 681, 731 (1973)....

Prah's use as well as Prah's individual concern for continued access to sunlight. If this comparison is to be made, should the social benefits of Maretti's freedom to use his property be included in the calculus?

The majority asserted that "[t]he need for easy and rapid development is not as great today as it once was," yet the majority offered no reasons why that is so. Was the majority correct? Why or why not?

3. *First in Time?* The court mentions but does not rely upon the English doctrine of ancient lights, by which an early occupant of land may acquire a prescriptive easement for light and air across a neighbor's land. (Easements, which we consider in Chapter 10, involve some right to use another's property, and a prescriptive easement is one that is created by adverse use over a sufficiently long period of time. A prescriptive easement is the "use" analogue to adverse possession.) Suppose that Maretti had built his home first, and Prah had then designed his solar powered home, only to discover in the design process that Maretti's home blocks his access to sunlight. Same result as in the actual case?

First in time—or prior appropriation—is the principle used in some arid western states to govern water rights. See, e.g., Paug Vik v. Wards Cove, 633 P.2d 1015 (Alaska 1981). The first user of water is entitled to continue to receive his appropriation, leaving later users to take what is left over. Most eastern states, where water is more abundant, do not use this method, but instead allocate water rights by ownership of riparian land. Under riparian rights, each landowner abutting a stream has the right to reasonable use of the stream, so long as the use does not unreasonably diminish the flow or quality of the stream. Should prior appropriation apply to sunlight for solar power purposes? See the New Mexico Solar Rights Act, N.M. Stat. §§ 47–3–1 through 47–3–5, which declares access to solar energy to be a property right governed, in general, by prior appropriation for the beneficial use of solar energy production. Enforcement of a solar right is conditioned upon recording of the right in the public property records pursuant to the New Mexico Solar Recordation Act, N.M. Stat. §§ 47–3–6 through 47–3–12. See also Note, The Allocation of Sunlight: Solar Rights and the Prior Appropriation Doctrine, 47 Colo. L. Rev. 421 (1976). Should access to sunlight be treated on riparian principles, as a common resource that each may use so long as the flow of sunlight is not unreasonably diminished or exterminated by an "up-sun" user?

B. REMEDIES

The traditional remedy for a private nuisance is an injunction to prevent the continuation of the activity that has been found to be a nuisance. The reverse, of course, is the total absence of a remedy if the activity is not a nuisance. This duality is an expression of "property rules," those decision rules that treat property rights as inviolate. If *A*'s activity constitutes an unreasonable interference with *B*'s use and enjoyment of his property and inflicts significant harm on *B*, a property rule holds that *B* is entitled to his use and enjoyment; thus, *A* must be barred absolutely from continuing the offending activity. But if *A*'s activity is no nuisance he is entitled absolutely to continue it and *B* should have no remedy at all.

Along with property rules, earlier in this book you were introduced to the concept of liability rules. See Guido Calabresi & Douglas Melamed, Property Rules, Liability Rules, and Inalienability: One View of the Cathedral, 85 Harv. L. Rev. 1089 (1972). Liability rules compensate a person for the invasion of their interests, rather than treating the interests as inviolable. When a liability rule obtains, *A* may invade *B*'s interests so long as he pays damages to *B* for the intrusion. The corollary to this principle is that if *A*'s activity does not wrongly invade *B*'s interests but *B* wants *A* to stop the activity, *B* will have to pay *A* to stop. A theoretical question that will become quite practical in this section is: Under what circumstances should *B* be able to obtain an injunction to force *A* to stop so long as *B* is willing to pay damages to *A* for the forced cessation of his lawful activity?

Inalienability rules operate to prevent rights from being sold. Many property rights are completely inalienable, such as the beneficial interest in a spendthrift trust, or are partially inalienable, as is wild game that has been captured by a sportsman but which may not be sold but which can be given away.

The possibility of using liability rules and inalienability rules in addition to property rules to deal with claims of nuisance adds complexity to our consideration of remedies. We shall begin with the traditional use of property rules.

WHALEN v. UNION BAG AND PAPER COMPANY

Court of Appeals of New York
208 N.Y. 1 (1913)

WERNER, J., delivered the opinion of the court.

The plaintiff is a lower riparian owner upon Kayaderosseras creek in Saratoga county, and the defendant owns and operates on this stream a pulp mill a few miles above plaintiff's land. This mill represents an investment of more than a million dollars and gives employment to 400 or 500 operatives. It discharges into the waters of the creek large quantities of a liquid effluent containing sulphurous acid, lime, sulphur, and waste material consisting of pulp wood, sawdust, slivers, knots, gums, resins and fibre. The pollution thus created, together with the discharge from other industries located along the stream and its principal tributary, has greatly diminished the purity of the water.

The plaintiff brought this action to restrain the defendant from continuing to pollute the stream. The trial court granted an injunction. . . . The Appellate Division reversed . . . and eliminated that part of the trial court's decree granting an injunction. The plaintiff thereupon . . . appealed to this court. . . . The facts found by the trial court—which do not appear to have been disturbed by the Appellate Division—establish a clear case of wrongful pollution of the stream, and need not be set forth in detail.

The plaintiff is the owner of a farm of two hundred and fifty-five acres, and the trial court has found that its use and value have been injuriously affected by the pollution of the stream caused by the defendant. The defendant conducts a business in which it has invested a large sum of money and employs great numbers of the inhabitants of the locality. We have recently gone over the law applicable to cases of this character (Strobel v. Kerr Salt Co., 164 N. Y. 303 (1900); Sammons v. City of Gloversville, 175 N.Y. 346 (1903)), and it is unnecessary now to restate it.[6]

. . . The setting aside of the injunction was apparently induced by a consideration of the great loss likely to be inflicted on the defendant by the granting of the injunction as compared with the small injury done to the plaintiff's land by that portion of the pollution which was regarded as attributable to the defendant. Such a balancing of injuries cannot be justified by the circumstances of this case. . . . One of the troublesome phases of this kind of litigation is the difficulty of deciding when an injunction shall issue in a case where the evidence clearly establishes an unlawful invasion of a plaintiff's rights, but his actual injury from the continuance of the alleged wrong will be small as compared with the great loss which will be caused by the issuance of the injunction. [While] the damages to the plaintiff's farm amount to $100 a year [it] can hardly be said that this injury is unsubstantial, even if we should leave out of consideration the peculiarly noxious character of the pollution of which the plaintiff complains. The waste from the defendant's mill is very destructive both to vegetable and animal life and tends to deprive the waters with which it is mixed of their purifying qualities. It should be

---

6. [Ed.—] In *Strobel*, the operations of an upstream salt mine turned a fresh water creek into a salt water stream. The court declared:

A riparian owner is entitled to a reasonable use of the water flowing by his premises in a natural stream, as an incident to his ownership of the soil, and to have it transmitted to him without sensible alteration in quality or unreasonable diminution in quantity. While he does not own the running water, he has the right to a reasonable use of it as it passes by his land. As all other owners upon the same stream have the same right, the right of no one is absolute, but is qualified by the right of the others to have the stream substantially preserved in its natural size, flow and purity, and to protection against material diversion or pollution. This is the common right of all, which must not be interfered with by any. The use by each must, therefore, be consistent with the rights of the others, and the maxim of *sic utere tuo* observed by all. The rule of the ancient common law is still in force; *aqua currit et debet currere, ut currere solebat* [water runs and ought to run as it is has run]. Consumption by watering cattle, temporary detention by dams in order to run machinery, irrigation when not out of proportion to the size of the stream, and some other familiar uses, although in fact a diversion of the water involving some loss, are not regarded as an unlawful diversion, but are allowed as a necessary incident to the use in order to effect the highest average benefit to all the riparian owners. As the enjoyment of each must be according to his opportunity and the upper owner has the first chance, the lower owners must submit to such loss as is caused by reasonable use. Surrounding circumstances, such as the size and velocity of the stream, the usage of the country, the extent of the injury, convenience in doing business and the indispensable public necessity of cities and villages for drainage, are also taken into consideration, so that a use which, under certain circumstances, is held reasonable, under different circumstances would be held unreasonable.

164 N.Y. at 320–321.

borne in mind also that there is no claim on the part of the defendant that the nuisance may become less injurious in the future. Although the damage to the plaintiff may be slight as compared with the defendant's expense of abating the condition, that is not a good reason for refusing an injunction. Neither courts of equity nor law can be guided by such a rule, for if followed to its logical conclusion it would deprive the poor litigant of his little property by giving it to those already rich. It is always to be remembered in such cases that "denying the injunction puts the hardship on the party in whose favor the legal right exists instead of on the wrongdoer." (Pomeroy's Eq. Juris. vol. 5, § 530.) In speaking of the injustice which sometimes results from the balancing of injuries between parties, the learned author from whom we have just quoted, sums up the discussion by saying: "The weight of authority is against allowing a balancing of injury as a means of determining the propriety of issuing an injunction." To the same effect is the decision in Weston Paper Co. v. Pope, 155 Ind. 394 (1900). "The fact that the appellant has expended a large sum of money in the construction of its plant and that it conducts its business in a careful manner and without malice can make no difference in its rights to the stream. Before locating the plant the owners were bound to know that every riparian proprietor is entitled to have the waters of the stream that washes his land come to it without obstruction, diversion or corruption, subject only to the reasonable use of the water, by those similarly entitled, for such domestic purposes as are inseparable from and necessary for the free use of their land; and they were bound also to know the character of their proposed business, and to take notice of the size, course, and capacity of the stream, and to determine for themselves at their own peril whether they should be able to conduct their business upon a stream of the size and character of Brandywine creek without injury to their neighbors; and the magnitude of their investment and their freedom from malice furnish no reason why they should escape the consequences of their own folly."

This language very aptly expresses the rule which we think should be applied to the case at bar. The judgment of the Appellate Division, in so far as it denied the injunction, should be reversed and the judgment of the Special Term in that respect reinstated.... *injunction granted*

NOTES, QUESTIONS, AND PROBLEM

1. Property Rules, the Coase Theorem, and Transaction Costs. In this application of property rules, the court's conclusion is that an injunction should issue, despite the apparent wide disparity in the relative hardships that the injunction will impose. The injunction will deprive 400 to 500 people of employment and render an investment of "more than a million dollars" useless.[7] The plaintiff's annual damages are $100. Of course, there may be other parties affected by the pollution, and they may have damages of a similar (or greater) amount. For the sake of simplicity and illustration,

---

7. An investment of $1 million in 1900 would be the equivalent of about $25.5 million in 2009.

however, let's assume there is only one downstream user damaged—the plaintiff.

This appears to be an inefficient result; yet economic theory, in the form of the famous Coase Theorem,[8] declares that it does not matter that the injunction issues, and thus farmer Whalen is given the entitlement, because in the absence of any inalienability rules and any transaction costs, the entitlement will be transferred to the party who values it more—Union Bag. In theory, Union Bag will pay Whalen to purchase the injunction from him. Union Bag is better off financially to pay any price less than the present value of the sum of its investment of $1 million and the anticipated stream of profits from continued operations. (For simplicity, assume that maximum price is $1.5 million.) Whalen is economically better off to accept any offer greater than the present value of the stream of annual future damages of $100. (For simplicity, assume that Whalen's minimum price is $150.) Thus, in theory Whalen should sell the entitlement acquired by an injunction to Union Bag for a price in excess of $150 but less than $1.5 million. In theory.

There are several impediments to this transfer. First, there is only one seller (Whalen) and one buyer (Union Bag). Bilateral monopoly makes it harder to reach agreement because neither side can credibly threaten to make a better deal with a third party. Thus, there is a temptation to engage in whatever tactic might be thought likely to induce the other party to part with a disproportionate amount of the $1,499,850 that is at stake. Whalen may declare his desire to have clean water rush past his farm, and refuse to accept any payment, in the hope that Union Bag will become increasingly desperate and raise its offer price. Or Whalen may sincerely value clean water as worth more than $1,499,850. Not everyone is wholly economic. Union Bag may spend time and money investigating methods of pollution control, or at least signal to Whalen that the abatement cost is much lower than it actually may be. Information may be asymmetrical; Union Bag might have a decent idea of the diminution in value of Whalen's property but it might be harder for Whalen to acquire good information about Union Bag's abatement costs, particularly if Union Bag does unearth some lower cost alternatives to ceasing operations. Moreover, each of Whalen and Union Bag may spend money on lawyers or other experts as a part of the bargaining process. All of these things add up; they are transaction costs, whether they come in the form of bargaining costs or information acquisition costs.

Finally, the Coase Theorem rests on the assumption that what the party who owns the entitlement will ask for its sale will not wildly diverge from what the other party will offer for its purchase. The right may be valued more by its holder so the asking price may exceed the offer price by a modest amount, but the parties will bargain to a successful conclusion. But will they? Why should Whalen be willing to sell his entitlement? To part with what he possesses he must receive more than what he might pay to acquire the right in the first place. To see this, suppose that the pollution was not a nuisance. In theory, Whalen should be willing to offer the present value of the sum of his present and future losses to stop Union Bag's activity. That offer price is assumed to be $150. Union Bag will gladly pay much more than that sum, so

---

8. Ronald Coase, *The Problem of Social Cost*, 3 J.L. & Econ. 1 (1960).

a deal should ensue. But because Whalen owns the entitlement already, his asking price for sale of the entitlement may be far greater than $150; perhaps it will exceed $1.5 million. Now no deal will happen.

This hypothesized disparity between Whalen's asking and offer price is borne out by research into how people actually act. We value what we have more than what we would pay to acquire what we have. Suppose you buy a new sofa but decide to keep the old one in a seldom-used room. You could sell the old sofa for $50 at a garage sale but you would not pay any amount to purchase it if you did not already possess it. In essence you are giving up $50 for the sofa even though you would not pay $50 to acquire it if you did not already own it. Your offer price is zero (because you would not pay anything to acquire it) but your asking price is something in excess of $50 (because you will not part with it for $50). While this disparity may not be rational in economic terms, it is a common phenomenon. This adds yet another transaction cost—the irrational disparity between offer and asking prices based on who has the entitlement at the beginning of any negotiation. For more exploration of this point, see Mark Kelman, Consumption Theory, Production Theory, and Ideology in the Coase Theorem, 52 S. Cal. L. Rev. 669, 678–682 (1979).

2. *Why Nuisance?* If the gravity of the harm was measured at $100 per year, but the utility of the conduct is the combination of 500 jobs, a useful investment of $1 million, and the continuing production of paper bags for a bagless society, why was Union Bag's conduct a nuisance? Does this underestimate the gravity of the harm? A badly polluted stream may affect many others than Whalen. Although gravity of the harm may have a qualitative aspect to it, did the *Whalen* court fasten on that factor as the reason for its decision?

3. *Problem.*

A owns a single family home in a residential neighborhood that is a mix of single family residences and apartment buildings. In conformity with applicable laws, *B* constructs an apartment complex next door. Because the locale is extremely hot in the summer *B* provides air conditioning to each unit in the complex by means of a central cooling system, the generator of which is located on *B*'s property and within all applicable setback requirements, but only 50 feet from *A*'s home. The generator emits a constant high-pitched whine that is at the decibel level of a large passenger jet airplane with engines at full power just prior to the takeoff roll. The result is that *A* cannot converse in a normal tone within his home and cannot sleep without earplugs and noise-cancelling earphones. *A* brings suit, claiming the air conditioning unit is a nuisance. The court agrees, and hears uncontested testimony that the presence of the unit has reduced the value of *A*'s home from $50,000 to $20,000, and also that the cost to *B* of relocating the unit, or providing an alternate cooling system that would not interfere with *A*'s use and enjoyment of his home would be $125,000. Should the court enjoin *B* from continuing the nuisance? See Estancias Dallas Corp. v. Schultz, 500 S.W.2d 217 (Tex. Civ. App. 1973).

Based on union, yes

BOOMER v. ATLANTIC CEMENT COMPANY, INC.

Court of Appeals of New York
26 N.Y.2d 219 (1970)

BERGAN, J., delivered the opinion of the court.

Defendant operates a large cement plant near Albany. These are actions for injunction and damages by neighboring land owners alleging injury to property from dirt, smoke and vibration emanating from the plant. A nuisance has been found after trial, temporary damages have been allowed; but an injunction has been denied.

The public concern with air pollution arising from many sources in industry and in transportation is currently accorded ever wider recognition accompanied by a growing sense of responsibility in State and Federal Governments to control it. Cement plants are obvious sources of air pollution in the neighborhoods where they operate.

But there is now before the court private litigation in which individual property owners have sought specific relief from a single plant operation. The threshold question ... is whether the court should resolve the litigation between the parties now before it as equitably as seems possible; or whether, seeking promotion of the general public welfare, it should channel private litigation into broad public objectives. A court performs its essential function when it decides the rights of parties before it. Its decision of private controversies may sometimes greatly affect public issues. Large questions of law are often resolved by the manner in which private litigation is decided. But this is normally an incident to the court's main function to settle controversy. It is a rare exercise of judicial power to use a decision in private litigation as a purposeful mechanism to achieve direct public objectives greatly beyond the rights and interests before the court.

Effective control of air pollution is a problem presently far from solution even with the full public and financial powers of government. In large measure adequate technical procedures are yet to be developed and some that appear possible may be economically impracticable. It seems apparent that the amelioration of air pollution will depend on technical research in great depth; on a carefully balanced consideration of the economic impact of close regulation; and of the actual effect on public health. It is likely to require massive public expenditure and to demand more than any local community can accomplish and to depend on regional and interstate controls. A court should not try to do this on its own as a by-product of private litigation and it seems manifest that the judicial establishment is neither equipped in the limited nature of any judgment it can pronounce nor prepared to lay down and implement an effective policy for the elimination of air pollution. This is an area beyond the circumference of one private lawsuit. It is a direct responsibility for government and should not thus be undertaken as an incident to solving a dispute between property owners and a single cement plant—one of many—in the Hudson River valley.

The cement making operations of defendant have been found by the court at Special Term to have damaged the nearby properties of plaintiffs.... That court ... found defendant maintained a nuisance and this has been affirmed at the Appellate Division. The total damage to plaintiffs' properties is, however, relatively small in comparison with the value of defendant's operation and with the consequences of the injunction which plaintiffs seek. The ground for the denial of injunction, notwithstanding the finding both that there is a nuisance and that plaintiffs have been damaged substantially, is the large disparity in economic consequences of the nuisance and of the injunction. This theory cannot, however, be sustained without overruling a doctrine which has been consistently reaffirmed in several leading cases in this court and which has never been disavowed here, namely that where a nuisance has been found and where there has been any substantial damage shown by the party complaining an injunction will be granted.

The rule in New York has been that such a nuisance will be enjoined although marked disparity be shown in economic consequence between the effect of the injunction and the effect of the nuisance. The problem of disparity in economic consequence was sharply in focus in Whalen v. Union Bag & Paper Co., 208 N. Y. 1 (1913). A pulp mill entailing an investment of more than a million dollars polluted a stream in which plaintiff, who owned a farm, was "a lower riparian owner." The economic loss to plaintiff from this pollution was small. This court, reversing the Appellate Division, reinstated the injunction granted by the Special Term against the argument of the mill owner that in view of "the slight advantage to plaintiff and the great loss that will be inflicted on defendant" an injunction should not be granted. ... The rule laid down in that case, then, is that whenever the damage resulting from a nuisance is found not "unsubstantial," ... injunction would follow. [In] McCann v. Chasm Power Co., 211 N. Y. 301 (1914), [an injunction was denied because] the damage shown by plaintiffs was not only unsubstantial, it was non-existent. Plaintiffs owned a rocky bank of the stream in which defendant had raised the level of the water. This had no economic or other adverse consequence to plaintiffs, and thus injunctive relief was denied. ... [But if] the damage to plaintiffs ... from defendant's cement plant is "not unsubstantial," [according to Whalen] an injunction should follow.

[The] court at Special Term and the Appellate Division ... found that plaintiffs had been damaged in various specific amounts up to the time of the trial and damages to the respective plaintiffs were awarded for those amounts. The effect of this was, injunction having been denied, plaintiffs could maintain successive actions at law for damages thereafter as further damage was incurred. The court at Special Term also found the amount of permanent damage attributable to each plaintiff, for the guidance of the parties in the event both sides stipulated to the payment and acceptance of such permanent damage as a settlement of all the controversies among the parties. The total of permanent damages to all plaintiffs thus found was $185,000. This basis of adjustment has not resulted in any stipulation by the parties.

This result at Special Term and at the Appellate Division is a departure from a rule that has become settled; but to follow the rule literally in these cases would be to close down the plant at once. This court is fully agreed to avoid that immediately drastic remedy; the difference in view is how best to avoid it.[9]

One alternative is to grant the injunction but postpone its effect to a specified future date to give opportunity for technical advances to permit defendant to eliminate the nuisance; another is to grant the injunction conditioned on the payment of permanent damages to plaintiffs which would compensate them for the total economic loss to their property present and future caused by defendant's operations. For reasons which will be developed the court chooses the latter alternative.

If the injunction were to be granted unless within a short period— e.g., 18 months—the nuisance be abated by improved methods, there would be no assurance that any significant technical improvement would occur. The parties could settle this private litigation at any time if defendant paid enough money and the imminent threat of closing the plant would build up the pressure on defendant. If there were no improved techniques found, there would inevitably be applications to the court at Special Term for extensions of time to perform on showing of good faith efforts to find such techniques. Moreover, techniques to eliminate dust and other annoying by-products of cement making are unlikely to be developed by any research the defendant can undertake within any short period, but will depend on the total resources of the cement industry Nationwide and throughout the world. The problem is universal wherever cement is made. For obvious reasons the rate of the research is beyond control of defendant. If at the end of 18 months the whole industry has not found a technical solution a court would be hard put to close down this one cement plant if due regard be given to equitable principles.

On the other hand, to grant the injunction unless defendant pays plaintiffs such permanent damages as may be fixed by the court seems to do justice between the contending parties. All of the attributions of economic loss to the properties on which plaintiffs' complaints are based will have been redressed.

The nuisance complained of by these plaintiffs may have other public or private consequences, but these particular parties are the only ones who have sought remedies and the judgment proposed will fully redress them. The limitation of relief granted is a limitation only within the four corners of these actions and does not foreclose public health or other public agencies from seeking proper relief in a proper court. It seems reasonable to think that the risk of being required to pay permanent

9. Respondent's investment in the plant is in excess of $45,000,000. There are over 300 people employed there.

damages to injured property owners by cement plant owners would itself be a reasonable effective spur to research for improved techniques to minimize nuisance.

The power of the court to condition on equitable grounds the continuance of an injunction on the payment of permanent damages seems undoubted. . . . The present cases and the remedy here proposed are in a number of other respects rather similar to Northern Indiana Public Serv. Co. v. Vesey, 210 Ind. 338 (1936). . . . The gases, odors, ammonia and smoke from the Northern Indiana company's gas plant damaged the nearby Vesey greenhouse operation. An injunction and damages were sought, but an injunction was denied and the relief granted was limited to permanent damages "present, past, and future." Denial of injunction was grounded on a public interest in the operation of the gas plant and on the court's conclusion "that less injury would be occasioned by requiring the appellant [Public Service] to pay the appellee [Vesey] all damages suffered by it . . . than by enjoining the operation of the gas plant. . . ." [The award of permanent damages was grounded] "upon the general equitable principle that equity will give full relief in one action and prevent a multiplicity of suits." . . .

Thus it seems fair to both sides to grant permanent damages to plaintiffs which will terminate this private litigation. The theory of damage is the "servitude on land" of plaintiffs imposed by defendant's nuisance. (See United States v. Causby, 328 U.S. 256 (1946), where the term "servitude" . . . was used by Justice Douglas relating to the effect of airplane noise on property near an airport.) The judgment, by allowance of permanent damages imposing a servitude on land, which is the basis of the actions, would preclude future recovery by plaintiffs or their grantees. This should be placed beyond debate by a provision of the judgment that the payment by defendant and the acceptance by plaintiffs of permanent damages found by the court shall be in compensation for a servitude on the land. . . .

The orders should be reversed . . . and the cases remitted to Supreme Court, Albany County to grant an injunction which shall be vacated upon payment by defendant of such amounts of permanent damage to the respective plaintiffs as shall for this purpose be determined by the court.

JASEN, J., dissenting.

I agree with the majority that a reversal is required here, but I do not subscribe to the newly enunciated doctrine of assessment of permanent damages, in lieu of an injunction, where substantial property rights have been impaired by the creation of a nuisance. . . . In permitting the injunction to become inoperative upon the payment of permanent damages, the majority is, in effect, licensing a continuing wrong. It is the same as saying to the cement company, you may continue to do harm to your neighbors so long as you pay a fee for it. Furthermore, once such permanent damages are assessed and paid, the incentive to alleviate the wrong would be eliminated, thereby continuing air pollution of an area without abatement.

[When] courts have sanctioned the remedy here proposed by the majority [they have] grounded their decision on a showing that the use to which the property was intended to be put was primarily for the public benefit. Here, on the other hand, it is clearly established that the cement company is creating a continuing air pollution nuisance primarily for its own private interest with no public benefit. This kind of inverse condemnation may not be invoked by a private person or corporation for private gain or advantage. Inverse condemnation should only be permitted when the public is primarily served in the taking or impairment of property. The promotion of the interests of the polluting cement company has, in my opinion, no public use or benefit.

Nor is it constitutionally permissible to impose [a] servitude on land, without consent of the owner, by payment of permanent damages where the continuing impairment of the land is for a private use. This is made clear by the State Constitution (art. I, § 7, subd. [a]) which provides that "[private] property shall not be taken for *public use* without just compensation" (emphasis added). It is ... significant that the section makes no mention of taking for a *private* use....

I would enjoin the defendant cement company from continuing the discharge of dust particles upon its neighbors' properties unless, within 18 months, the cement company abated this nuisance....

NOTES AND QUESTIONS

1. Post–Decision Events. On remand, Atlantic Cement settled with many of the plaintiffs. There is only one reported decision of a permanent damage award to a single plaintiff, and that amount was $175,000, nearly the entire $185,000 in damages to all plaintiffs that the Court of Appeals assumed was the case. See Kinley v. Atlantic Cement Co., 349 N.Y.S.2d 199 (App. 1973). Investigation by Professor Daniel Farber revealed that the total of all permanent damages paid by Atlantic Cement was about $710,000. See Daniel A. Farber, Reassessing *Boomer*: Justice, Efficiency, and Nuisance Law, in Property Law and Legal Education 12 (Hay & Hoeflich, eds., 1988).

2. Why a Nuisance? Even considering the post-decision facts unearthed by Professor Farber, why was Atlantic Cement's activity a nuisance? From the Restatement view, the gravity of the harm ($710,000) was less than the utility of the conduct (the present value of maintaining over 300 jobs and a $45 million investment). From the Coase Theorem perspective the cost of abatement (cessation, given the technological unfeasibility of abatement and continuing production) probably exceeds the cost of avoidance to the plaintiffs (at a maximum, the present value of the sum of property losses and the cost of relocating to more tranquil environs). In a later New York case, involving facts similar to *Boomer*, the Court of Appeals found no nuisance. Copart Industries, Inc. v. Consolidated Edison Company of New York, Inc., 41 N.Y.2d 564 (1977). The court's rationale was that *Boomer* had involved intentional conduct that unreasonably interfered with the plaintiff's use and enjoyment, but that Consolidated Edison's actions were neither negligent, intentional, nor ultra-hazardous. Con Ed's smokestack emissions from an electric power generating plant apparently caused the paint of new autos that Copart was preparing for distribution to dealers to discolor and pit. The Court of Appeals upheld a jury verdict for Con Ed based on a jury charge that Copart must prove that Con Ed's emissions were resulted from negligence or knowledge (actual or imputed) that its emissions caused the harm of which Copart complained.

3. *Liability Rules.* When should liability rules displace property rules? If liability rules should be used whenever the cost of abatement grossly exceeds the harm, why were they not employed in *Whalen*?

Does an award of permanent damages provide adequate compensation? Suppose that before Atlantic Cement started operations, Boomer's property was worth $100,000. Suppose that at the time of the award of damages Boomer's property had declined in value to $40,000 as a result of Atlantic Cement's operations, and that the present value of his past and future damages from all other sources was $160,000. Boomer receives $220,000. Even assuming that the calculation of past and future non-economic damages is accurate and that the value of Boomer's property does not decline in the future, consider what happens when Boomer sells his property to Naif two years later for $40,000. If the award of permanent damages has imposed a servitude on the land, Naif receives nothing for the annoyance or other injury that he suffers after acquiring Boomer's property, but Boomer has $260,000 in his pocket. Perhaps Naif must negotiate with Boomer for an even lower price to obtain, in effect, some of the compensation awarded Boomer. If the award of permanent damages does not impose such a servitude, and Naif may maintain his own suit against Atlantic Cement, the damages are not permanent. Because the court's opinion appears to foreclose this possibility, does that suggest that the dissenting judge was correct that an award of permanent damages eliminates any incentive for Atlantic Cement to invest in abatement methods?

4. *Property Rules, Transactions Costs, and the Coase Theorem.* Suppose that the New York court had followed *Whalen*, applied property rules, and enjoined Atlantic Cement from continuing its nuisance. Would the entitlement be reassigned after the fact from Boomer and his seven fellow plaintiffs to Atlantic Cement? What obstacles might prevent such a post-judgment transfer? Would the obstacles be greater or lesser if the plaintiffs in *Boomer* consisted of several hundred persons instead of eight?

SPUR INDUSTRIES, INC. v. DEL E. WEBB DEVELOPMENT CO.

Supreme Court of Arizona
108 Ariz. 178 (1972)

CAMERON, VICE C.J., delivered the opinion of the court.

From a judgment permanently enjoining the defendant, Spur Industries, Inc., from operating a cattle feedlot near the plaintiff Del E. Webb

Development Company's Sun City, Spur appeals. Webb cross-appeals. Although numerous issues are raised, we feel that it is necessary to answer only two questions. They are:

1. Where the operation of a business, such as a cattle feedlot is lawful in the first instance, but becomes a nuisance by reason of a nearby residential area, may the feedlot operation be enjoined in an action brought by the developer of the residential area?

2. Assuming that the nuisance may be enjoined, may the developer of a completely new town or urban area in a previously agricultural area be required to indemnify the operator of the feedlot who must move or cease operation because of the presence of the residential area created by the developer?

The facts ... are as follows. The area in question is located in Maricopa County, Arizona, some 14 to 15 miles west of the urban area of Phoenix, on the Phoenix–Wickenburg Highway, also known as Grand Avenue. About two miles south of Grand Avenue is Olive Avenue which runs east and west. 111th Avenue runs north and south as does the Agua Fria River immediately to the west. . . .

Farming started in this area about 1911. In 1929, with the completion of the Carl Pleasant Dam, gravity flow water became available to the property located to the west of the Agua Fria River, though land to the east remained dependent upon well water for irrigation. By 1950, the only urban areas in the vicinity were the agriculturally related communities of Peoria, E1 Mirage, and Surprise located along Grand Avenue. Along 111th Avenue, approximately one mile south of Grand Avenue and 1 ½ miles north of Olive Avenue, the community of Youngtown was commenced in 1954. Youngtown is a retirement community appealing primarily to senior citizens.

In 1956, Spur's predecessors in interest ... developed feedlots, about ½ mile south of Olive Avenue, in an area between the confluence of the usually dry Agua Fria and New Rivers. The area is well suited for cattle feeding and in 1959, there were 25 cattle feeding pens or dairy operations within a 7 mile radius of the location developed by Spur's predecessors. In April and May of 1959, [Spur's predecessors were feeding approximately 7,500 to 8,500] head of cattle ... on [an] area of 35 acres.

In May of 1959, Del Webb began to plan the development of an urban area to be known as Sun City. For this purpose, the Marinette and the Santa Fe Ranches, some 20,000 acres of farmland, were purchased for $15,000,000 or $750.00 per acre. This price was considerably less than the price of land located near the urban area of Phoenix, and along with the success of Youngtown was a factor influencing the decision to purchase the property in question. By September 1959, Del Webb had started construction of a golf course south of Grand Avenue and Spur's predecessors had started to level ground for more feedlot area. In 1960, Spur purchased the property in question and began a rebuilding and expansion program extending both to the north and south of the original facilities.

By 1962, Spur's expansion program was completed and had expanded from approximately 35 acres to 114 acres....

Accompanied by an extensive advertising campaign, homes were first offered by Del Webb in January 1960 and the first unit to be completed was south of Grand Avenue and approximately 2 ½ miles north of Spur. By 2 May 1960, there were 450 to 500 houses completed or under construction. At this time, Del Webb did not consider odors from the Spur feed pens a problem and Del Webb continued to develop in a southerly direction, until sales resistance became so great that the parcels were difficult if not impossible to sell. [This occurred in about 1963.]

By December 1967, Del Webb's property had extended south to Olive Avenue and Spur was within 500 feet of Olive Avenue to the north. ... Del Webb filed its original complaint alleging that in excess of 1,300 lots in the southwest portion were unfit for development for sale as residential lots because of the operation of the Spur feedlot. Del Webb's suit complained that the Spur feeding operation was a public nuisance because of the flies and the odor which were drifting or being blown by the prevailing south to north wind over the southern portion of Sun City. At the time of the suit, Spur was feeding between 20,000 and 30,000 head of cattle, and the facts amply support the finding of the trial court that the feed pens had become a nuisance to the people who resided in the southern part of Del Webb's development. The testimony indicated that cattle in a commercial feedlot will produce 35 to 40 pounds of wet manure per day, per head, or over a million pounds of wet manure per day for 30,000 head of cattle, and that despite the admittedly good feedlot management and good housekeeping practices by Spur, the resulting odor and flies produced an annoying if not unhealthy situation as far as the senior citizens of southern Sun City were concerned. There is no doubt that some of the citizens of Sun City were unable to enjoy the outdoor living which Del Webb had advertised and that Del Webb was faced with sales resistance from prospective purchasers as well as strong and persistent complaints from the people who had purchased homes in that area.

Trial was commenced before the court.... [N]either the citizens of Sun City nor Youngtown are represented in this lawsuit and the suit is solely between Del E. Webb Development Company and Spur Industries, Inc.

May Spur be Enjoined?

The difference between a private nuisance and a public nuisance is generally one of degree. A private nuisance is one affecting a single individual or a definite small number of persons in the enjoyment of private rights not common to the public, while a public nuisance is one affecting the rights enjoyed by citizens as a part of the public. To constitute a public nuisance, the nuisance must affect a considerable number of people or an entire community or neighborhood.

Where the injury is slight, the remedy for minor inconveniences lies in an action for damages rather than in one for an injunction. Moreover, some courts have held, in the "balancing of conveniences" cases, that damages may be the sole remedy. [*Boomer.*] Thus, it would appear from the admittedly incomplete record as developed in the trial court, that, at most, residents of Youngtown would be entitled to damages rather than injunctive relief. We have no difficulty, however, in agreeing with the conclusion of the trial court that Spur's operation was an enjoinable public nuisance as far as the people in the southern portion of Del Webb's Sun City were concerned.

[Ariz. Rev. Stat.] § 36–601, subsec. A reads as follows:

§ 36–601. Public nuisances dangerous to public health

A. The following conditions are specifically declared public nuisances dangerous to the public health: 1. Any condition or place in populous areas which constitutes a breeding place for flies, rodents, mosquitoes and other insects which are capable of carrying and transmitting disease-causing organisms to any person or persons.

By this statute, before an otherwise lawful (and necessary) business may be declared a public nuisance, there must be a "populous" area in which people are injured:

[I]t hardly admits a doubt that, in determining the question as to whether a lawful occupation is so conducted as to constitute a nuisance as a matter of fact, the locality and surroundings are of the first importance. A business which is not per se a public nuisance may become such by being carried on at a place where the health, comfort, or convenience of a populous neighborhood is affected. ... What might amount to a serious nuisance in one locality by reason of the density of the population, or character of the neighborhood affected, may in another place and under different surroundings be deemed proper and unobjectionable....

MacDonald v. Perry, 32 Ariz. 39, 49–50, 255 P. 494, 497 (1927).

It is clear that as to the citizens of Sun City, the operation of Spur's feedlot was both a public and a private nuisance. They could have successfully maintained an action to abate the nuisance. Del Webb, having shown a special injury in the loss of sales, had standing to bring suit to enjoin the nuisance. The judgment of the trial court permanently enjoining the operation of the feedlot is affirmed.

Must Del Webb Indemnify Spur?

A suit to enjoin a nuisance sounds in equity and the courts have long recognized a special responsibility to the public when acting as a court of equity.... In addition to protecting the public interest, however, courts of equity are concerned with protecting the operator of a lawful, albeit noxious, business from the result of a knowing and willful encroachment by others near his business.

In the so-called coming to the nuisance cases, the courts have held that the residential landowner may not have relief if he knowingly came into a neighborhood reserved for industrial or agricultural endeavors and has been damaged thereby:

> [In] an area uncontrolled by zoning laws or restrictive covenants and remote from urban development ... plaintiffs cannot complain that legitimate agricultural pursuits are being carried on in the vicinity [that] depreciate the value of their homes. ... People employed in a city who build their homes in suburban areas ... beyond the limits of ... zoning regulations do so ... to avoid ... high taxation [or] to get away from the congestion of traffic, smoke, noise, foul air and the many other annoyances of city life. But with all these advantages in going beyond the area which is zoned and restricted to protect them in their homes, they must be prepared to take the disadvantages.

Dill v. Excel Packing Company, 183 Kan. 513, 525, 526, 331 P.2d 539, 548, 549 (1958). See also East St. Johns Shingle Co. v. City of Portland, 195 Or. 505, 246 P.2d 554, 560–562 (1952).

Were Webb the only party injured, we would feel justified in holding that the doctrine of "coming to the nuisance" would have been a bar to the relief asked by Webb, and, on the other hand, had Spur located the feedlot near the outskirts of a city and had the city grown toward the feedlot, Spur would have to suffer the cost of abating the nuisance as to those people locating within the growth pattern of the expanding city, [as when] "a business established at a place remote from population is gradually surrounded and becomes part of a populous center, so that a business which formerly was not an interference with the rights of others has become so by the encroachment of the population...." City of Ft. Smith v. Western Hide & Fur Co., 153 Ark. 99, 103, 239 S.W. 724, 726 (1922).

We agree, however, with the Massachusetts court that: "The law of nuisance affords no rigid rule to be applied in all instances. It is elastic. It undertakes to require only that which is fair and reasonable under all the circumstances. In a commonwealth like this, which depends for its material prosperity so largely on the continued growth and enlargement of manufacturing of diverse varieties, 'extreme rights' cannot be enforced...." Stevens v. Rockport Granite Co., 216 Mass. 486, 488, 104 N.E. 371, 373 (1914).

There was no indication in the instant case at the time Spur and its predecessors located in western Maricopa County that a new city would spring up, full-blown, alongside the feeding operation and that the developer of that city would ask the court to order Spur to move because of the new city. Spur is required to move not because of any wrongdoing on the part of Spur, but because of a proper and legitimate regard of the courts for the rights and interests of the public. Del Webb, on the other hand, is entitled to the relief prayed for (a permanent injunction), not because Webb is blameless, but because of the damage to the people who have been encouraged to purchase homes in Sun City. It does not equitably or legally follow, however, that Webb, being entitled to the injunction, is then free of any liability to Spur if Webb has in fact been the cause of the damage Spur has sustained. It does not seem harsh to require a developer, who has taken advantage of the lesser land values in a rural area as well as the availability of large tracts of land on which to build and develop a new town or city in the area, to indemnify those who are forced to leave as a result.

Having brought people to the nuisance to the foreseeable detriment of Spur, Webb must indemnify Spur for a reasonable amount of the cost of moving or shutting down. It should be noted that this relief to Spur is limited to a case wherein a developer has, with foreseeability, brought into a previously agricultural or industrial area the population which makes necessary the granting of an injunction against a lawful business and for which the business has no adequate relief.

It is therefore the decision of this court that the matter be remanded to the trial court for a hearing upon the damages sustained by the defendant Spur as a reasonable and direct result of the granting of the permanent injunction. Since the result of the appeal may appear novel and both sides have obtained a measure of relief, it is ordered that each side will bear its own costs. . . .

NOTES AND QUESTIONS

1. Public Nuisance, Private Nuisance, and Coming-to-the-Nuisance. Recall that a "public nuisance is an unreasonable interference with a right common to the general public." Rest. (2d) Torts, § 821B(1). Factors that may indicate an unreasonable interference include "conduct [that] involves a significant interference with . . . public health, . . . safety, . . . peace, . . . comfort or . . . convenience, or [that] is proscribed by a statute, ordinance or administrative regulation, or . . . is of a continuing nature or has produced a permanent or long-lasting effect, and, as the actor knows or has reason to know, has a significant effect upon the public right." Rest. (2d) Torts, § 821B(2). The conduct involved in operating Spur's feedlot violated an Arizona statute, so it was an easy decision to find that the feedlot constituted a public nuisance.

But the court also said that it was a private nuisance, even though it agreed that if Webb were the only party injured "the doctrine of 'coming to the nuisance' would have been a bar to the [injunction] asked by Webb." This apparent inconsistency is explained by the fact that the coming-to-the-nuisance doctrine does not operate as a complete defense to a claim of nuisance. In its formulation by Sir William Blackstone it appeared to be a complete bar: "If my neighbor makes a tan-yard so as to annoy and render less salubrious the air of my house or gardens, the law will furnish me with a remedy; but if he is first in possession of the air, and I fix my habitation near him, the nuisance is of my own seeking, and may continue." 2 Blackstone, Commentaries on the Laws of England *402–403. But American courts have been wary of so treating the doctrine, because "an absolute bar to a finding of nuisance would, in effect, give the offending activity a perpetual servitude upon the land of its neighbors without the payment of any compensation. [O]ne's coming to the nuisance is simply one factor that may be considered in determining whether or not a [person's] conduct was an unlawful interference with a neighbor's real estate." Weida v. Ferry, 493 A.2d 824, 827 (R.I. 1985). See also Jacques v. Pioneer Plastics, Inc., 676 A.2d 504, 508 (Me. 1996). Thus, the question of whether a party has come to the nuisance is a factor to be considered in determining whether there is a nuisance and, if so, what should be the remedy. In thinking about whether a plaintiff has come to the nuisance, courts have had to consider such things as the presence or absence of zoning regulations, the prior knowledge of the plaintiff of the pre-existing activity, whether the plaintiff's ownership of undeveloped property prior to the existence of the nuisance matters if the development occurs after the arrival of the nuisance, and the reasonable prospect of future development at the time the defendant commenced the activity.

A contemporary revival of the coming-to-the-nuisance doctrine as a complete defense inheres in so-called Right to Farm laws that have been enacted in a number of states. An example is S.D. Con. L. § 21–10–25.2:

> No agricultural operation or any of its appurtenances may be deemed to be a nuisance, private or public, by any changed conditions in the locality of the operation or its appurtenances after the facility has been in operation for more than one year, if the facility was not a nuisance at the time the operation began. Any agricultural operation protected pursuant to the provisions of this section may reasonably expand its operation in terms of acres or animal units without losing its protected status if all county, municipal, state, and federal environmental codes, laws, or regulations are met by the agricultural operation. The protected status of an agricultural operation, once acquired, is assignable, alienable, and inheritable. The protected status of an agricultural operation, once acquired, may not be waived by the temporary cessation of farming or by diminishing the size of the operation. The provisions of this section do not apply if a nuisance results from the negligent or improper operation of any such agricultural operation or its appurtenances.

As you see, this operates as a complete defense to an alleged nuisance arising out of intentional conduct that is said to be an unreasonable interference with another's property. However, the Idaho Supreme Court, in construing an identical statute as South Dakota's, ruled that it did not provide a complete shield to "an expanding agricultural operation surrounded by an area that has remained substantially unchanged." Payne v. Skaar, 127 Idaho 341, 344 (1995). Some states limit this statutory "right to farm" as a complete defense only to injunctions of the activity. See, e.g., R.I. Gen. L. § 2–23–5(a). The scope of these statutes is necessarily limited by the statutory definition of the agricultural activities protected. Some states limit protection to specific activities and others immunize a broad panoply of agricultural pursuits. Compare Iowa Code § 172D.2 (limiting protection to feedlots in compliance with applicable regulations) with Haw. Rev. Stat. § 165–2, which protects the non-exclusive categories of a commercial agricultural or aquacultural facility or pursuit conducted, in whole or in part, including the care and production of livestock and livestock products, poultry and poultry products, and apiary, horticultural, or floricultural products; the planting, cultivating, and harvesting and processing of crops; . . . the farming or ranching of any plant or animal species in a controlled salt, brackish, or freshwater environment[; as well as] marketed produce at roadside stands or farm markets; noises, odors, dust, and fumes emanating from a commercial agricultural or an aquacultural facility or pursuit; operation of machinery and irrigation pumps; ground and aerial seeding and spraying; the application of chemical fertilizers, conditioners, insecticides, pesticides, and herbicides; and the employment and use of labor. . . .

For discussion of these statutes, see Neil D. Hamilton, Right-to-Farm Laws Reconsidered, 3 Drake J. Agric. L. 103 (1998); Jacqueline P. Hand, Right-to-Farm Laws, 45 U. Pitt. L. Rev. 289 (1984); Margaret Rosso Grossman and Thomas G. Fischer, Protecting the Right to Farm, 1983 Wis. L. Rev. 95.

2. Liability Rules v. Property Rules, Again. Given the Arizona court's conclusion that Spur's feedlot was both a public and private nuisance, and that the coming-to-the-nuisance doctrine was not a complete defense, but would have barred injunctive relief had Webb been the sole injured party, the court was faced with the question of devising an appropriate remedy.

The Arizona court thought that Spur's feedlot was a lawful activity, though a nuisance, and that Webb and its senior citizen customers had come to the nuisance. Hence, it adopted a remedy that uses liability rules to require compensation to Spur for moving its feedlot and thus abating the nuisance. Note that the court opined that Webb's coming to the nuisance constituted a complete defense to an injunction, yet the court issued an injunction and ordered Webb to pay Spur's cost of abatement. In considering this result assume that the cost to relocate Spur was $5 million and that the damages to Webb were $4 million (the present value of the lost profits due to unsaleable lots); the damages to the residents of Sun City were $16 million (the present value of the sum of lost property values and the past and future damages due to the smell and insects). Assume that only 400 residents of Sun City[10] were affected. If Spur were not enjoined, economic theory posits a reassignment of the entitlement from Spur to the Sun City residents but not Webb (assuming Webb has no liability to the existing residents). Webb would only pay a maximum of $4 million and Spur would accept no less than $5 million. But the Sun City residents would pay something in excess of $4 million but less than $16 million to acquire the right from Spur. What is the largest component of the transaction costs that will likely prevent this outcome?

Continue to assume that the court had refused to enjoin Spur and that the damages are as set forth in the immediately preceding paragraph. In fact, the Sun City residents brought their own suit against Spur, seeking damages. In that proceeding, Spur filed a third party complaint against Webb, seeking indemnification from Webb for any liability Spur might have to the residents. In Spur Feeding Co. v. Superior Court of Maricopa County, 109 Ariz. 105

---

10. As of 2011 there were 9,802 residences in Sun City, housing a population of about 16,000 people. See http://www.grandinfo.com/spage.php?shw=100018 & m=htm.

(1973), the court ruled that Spur's complaint was not barred by *res judicata*. Suppose that Spur was entitled to indemnification from Webb. Would that make a material difference to the likelihood that Webb would successfully buy out Spur's entitlement?

For more background on *Spur Industries*, see Andrew P. Morriss, Cattle v. Retirees: Sun City and the Battle of *Spur Industries v. Del E. Webb Development Co.*, in Property Stories 337 (Korngold & Morriss, eds., 2d ed. 2009).

3. *A Matrix of Remedies.* You can now see that the combination of liability rules and property rules delivers four possible outcomes. Using property rules, (1) if a nuisance is present, it will be enjoined (and damages, if appropriate, will also be awarded); (2) if a nuisance is not present, there is no remedy available and the activity continues as before. Using liability rules, (3) if a nuisance is present, it may continue upon payment of permanent damages to those injured; (4) if a nuisance is present, it will be abated but the the injured party is required to pay the nuisance generator for the cost of abatement. *Whalen* is an example of category (1); the unduly sensitive user cases, such as *Portland Meadows*, are examples of category (2); *Boomer* is the exemplar of category (3); *Spur Industries* is the exemplar of category (4).

Problem: A constructs a cellulose pulp mill in an uninhabited area. It emits foul odors in the immediate vicinity. Years later, a real estate developer buys a large tract near the mill that is burdened by odors only when the wind is from a certain direction, about 60 days per year. The developer successfully constructs and sells houses to purchasers who are aware of the mill and that it emits odors. However, after living in the vicinity for an entire year, the residents find that even 60 days of the cellulose pulp aroma is intolerable. The residents (*R*) sue *A*, claiming that his intentional conduct constitutes an unreasonable interference with their use and enjoyment. The court concludes that because *R* came to the nuisance *A* has a complete defense. No nuisance, rules the court. Even so, should *R* be awarded an injunction if they pay *A*'s relocation costs?

4. *Nuisance and Environmental Preservation.* When environmental problems are local and their cause can be traced directly to an activity that is either negligent, abnormally dangerous, or the product of intentional conduct that unreasonably interferes with another's use and enjoyment, nuisance law is quite utile. But when the environmental problem is widespread—across regions, states, or even global—and the cause of the harm (whether considered in the aggregate or as experienced by an individual plaintiff) is necessarily the product of many actions, nuisance law is less useful. Nevertheless, various claims have been made by plaintiff groups that the emission of global greenhouse gases produced by the sale or consumption of fossil fuels constitutes a public nuisance. Current examples of these claims are Native Village of Kivalina v. Exxon Mobil Corp., 663 F. Supp.2d 863 (N.D. Cal. 2009) and Connecticut v. American Electric Power, 582 F.3d 309 (2d Cir. 2009), cert. granted sub nom. American Electric Power v. Connecticut, 131 S.Ct. 813 (2010). In *Kivalina* an Alaska native village alleged "that as a result of global warming, the Arctic sea ice that protects the Kivalina coast from winter storms has diminished, and that the resulting erosion and destruction will

require the relocation of Kivalina's residents." The plaintiff village alleged that the conduct of the defendants, twenty-four oil, energy, and utility companies, constituted "a federal common law . . . nuisance, based on their alleged contribution to the excessive emission of carbon dioxide and other greenhouse gases which they claim are causing global warming." 663 F. Supp.2d at 868. In *American Electric Power*, eight states, three land trusts, and New York City sued six electric utilities on a nuisance theory, claiming they were the largest emitters of carbon dioxide in the United States, that their conduct contributed to global warming, a phenomenon alleged to cause serious harm to human health and natural resources, and that they should be forced to abate their emissions. In *Kivalina*, the district court dismissed the complaint on grounds that the plaintiffs lacked standing and that the claims presented were not justiciable for want of judicially cognizable standards for decision as well as requiring an initial policy decision of the sort that is beyond the scope of the judicial power. As of September 2011, appeal is pending in the Ninth Circuit. In *American Electric Power* the Second Circuit reversed a district court's dismissal of the complaint on the ground that it presented a non-justiciable controversy. By an evenly divided court, the Supreme Court upheld the Second Circuit's ruling on justiciability, but concluded that the Clean Air Act and actions of the EPA displaced any federal common law rights that might otherwise be available. American Electric Power Co. v. Connecticut, 131 S.Ct. 2527 (2011).

Assuming that the plaintiffs in these cases have standing and that their claims are justiciable, how should nuisance law deal with them? Rest. (2d) Torts, § 821C, provides that the only individuals who can recover damages for a public nuisance are those who "have suffered harm of a kind different from that suffered by other members of the public exercising the right common to the general public that was the subject of interference." To abate such a nuisance, one must either "have the right to recover damages," or "have authority as a public official or public agency to represent the state or a political subdivision in the matter, or . . . have standing to sue as a representative of the general public, as a citizen in a citizen's action or as a member of a class in a class action." Of course, whether the plaintiffs have such standing is a matter of constitutional law. Finally, Rest. (2d) Torts, § 821F confines "liability for a nuisance only to those to whom it causes significant harm."

Is the activity complained of—selling petroleum products and generating electricity by burning fossil fuels—an abnormally dangerous activity in a world fueled by carbon? Can the conduct be found to be negligent when it is carried on in compliance with applicable laws and observes customary prudent standards of safety? Is it intentional conduct, because the companies knew or should have known that their conduct would contribute to greenhouse gases and global warming? If so, how does (or should) a court balance the gravity of the harm and the utility of the conduct? Assuming that such a balance produces a finding of unreasonable interference, can it be proven that the contributions of a single enterprise to global warming, or even a group of enterprises, is the cause of the significant harm? After all, global warming is the result of centuries of carbon emissions, and the contributions of all of the major American petroleum vendors and electrical energy producers is but a tiny fraction of the global output of greenhouse gases. And even if the problem of causation is overcome, what remedy is appropriate? How does one measure damages from a handful of generators when the harm is caused by billions of actors over centuries? How does one fashion appropriate injunctive relief when even a total bar to the activity will not have any discernible effect on the harm?

It is questions like these that lead most people to conclude that the judicial system is not well suited to resolution of major environmental problems. Legislative solutions—and in the case of global warming, transnational solutions—are more effective. Within the realm of environmental regulation, a topic outside the scope of this course, people may disagree about the optimal methods. Some prefer command-and-control regimes, which typically ban emissions of pollutants above a specified level. Others prefer market-based solutions, one of which is so-called cap-and-trade, in which a given amount of pollutants may be emitted, and individual polluters are free to buy or sell their rights to emit a given quantity of a specified pollutant. Courses in environmental law are a good introduction to these problems.

C. SUPPORT OF NEIGHBORING LAND

As the *ad coelum* maxim implies, an owner of real estate owns the surface, the air above the surface, and the earth beneath the surface. Obviously, there are practical limits to an owner's claim to the air and subsurface, but for our purposes in this section we can assume that a surface owner also owns the subsoil as far down as can be practically reached. Of course, if a surface owner has sold his mineral rights, the owner of those rights may remove minerals (e.g., coal, oil, or valuable ores) from beneath the surface. Ownership of the subsurface implies some obligations to use that right in a way that does not inflict injury on one's neighboring landowners. Those obligations are classified as *lateral support* and *subjacent support*.

1. LATERAL SUPPORT

Lateral support is the obligation not to remove the horizontal earthly support for a neighbor's land. The common law formulation of this obligation was to impose an absolute duty to refrain from withdrawing "naturally necessary lateral support"—the support that is provided to adjacent land in its natural, undeveloped, condition. See Rest. (2d) Torts, § 817, comment c: "Naturally necessary lateral support is that support which the supported land itself requires and which, in its natural condition and in the natural condition of the surrounding land, it would require. It does not include the support needed because of the presence of artificial additions to or other artificial alterations in the supported land or the surrounding land." Thus, if A excavates to his lot line, using the utmost care, but the result is that B's land tumbles into the excavation, A is strictly liable to B. But if B erects a structure on his land that requires more lateral support than would be naturally necessary, A is liable only if his excavation was conducted in a negligent manner.

Example 9–6: *B* erects a heavy structure that has is supported by concrete piles driven 20 feet onto *B*'s earth. *A*, a neighboring landowner, uses the utmost care to excavate to a depth of 10 feet on *A*'s land, immediately adjacent to the lot line. As a result *B*'s structure collapses. *A* is not liable to *B*; he used due care and experts agree that the collapse was not the result of removing the lateral support that would be required to support *B*'s land in its natural condition.

Example and Problem 9–7: *B* builds a home on his property that is supported by a foundation that extends three feet deep. Using reasonable care, *A* excavates along his property line that adjoins *B*'s property, but *B*'s home subsides due to the excavation, causing considerable damage to *B*'s home. *B* sues *A* for withdrawal of lateral support. At trial, the uncontroverted testimony of experts is that *A*'s excavation would have caused *B*'s property to subside even if *B* had not built his home. Who should prevail? Would the outcome be different if the uncontroverted testimony was that the subsidence would not have occurred had there been no home built on *B*'s property?

For an extended discussion of these issues, see Noone v. Price, 171 W.Va. 185 (1982).

Lateral support is a servitude created by operation of law. As you will learn in Chapter 10, servitudes are restrictions on the use of land for the benefit of other owners of land. There are two ways in which one can envision the lateral support servitude: It could be a restriction on the use of the supporting land for the benefit of the supported land in its natural condition, or it could be seen as a restriction on the use of the supporting land to maintain the integrity of the supported land, including structures erected upon it. The present law of the subject views the lateral support servitude as serving both interests, but does so in different ways: Strict liability for breach of the first part of the restriction, and negligence for breach of the second part. Thus, in "an action predicated on strict liability for removing support for the land in its natural state, the kind of lateral support withdrawn is material, but the quality of the actor's conduct is immaterial; however, in a proceeding based upon negligence, the kind of lateral support withdrawn is immaterial, and the quality of the actor's conduct is material." 171 W.Va. at 190.

This was not always so. In Thurston v. Hancock, 12 Mass. 220 (1815), the plaintiff in 1802 built a brick residence on the summit of Boston's Beacon Hill, supported by a foundation fifteen feet deep, the rear wall of which was two feet from the lot line. In 1811 the defendant purchased the adjacent downslope property, excavated to a depth of forty-five feet and within six feet of the lot line, causing soil to slip from plaintiff's property and rendering the foundation of his property sufficiently dangerous and unstable that he abandoned it. The court found no liability, reasoning that if the defendant "disturbs the natural state of the soil, he shall answer in damages; but he is answerable only for the natural and necessary consequences of his act, and not for the value of a house put upon or near the line by his neighbor." Id. at 229. Each owner had a right to develop his land as he saw fit, each did so, and the plaintiff was without remedy because "in so placing the house, the neighbour was in fault, and ought to have taken better care of his interest. ... It is, in fact, *damnum absque injuria*."[11] Id.

The question now would be whether Hancock's excavation was negligent. An "owner of land may be negligent in failing to provide against the risk of harm to his neighbor's structures. ... Although the law accords the owner of the supporting land great freedom in withdrawing from another's land support that is not naturally necessary ..., it does not excuse withdrawal in a manner that involves an unreasonable risk of harm to the land of another." Rest. (2d) Torts, § 819, comment e.

The lateral support duty runs with ownership of the land. For example, if A builds a retaining wall to maintain lateral support of his neighbor's property and then B buys the property, B is obliged to keep the retaining wall in sufficient repair to support the natural condition of the neighbor's land. If neighbor C constructs a heavy swimming pool that cannot be supported by B's well-constructed retaining wall, he is not liable to C. See, e.g., Klebs v. Yim, 54 Wn. App. 41 (1989). Accord, Gorton v. Schofield, 311 Mass. 352 (1942); Salmon v. Peterson, 311 N.W.2d 205 (S.D. 1981); Noone v. Price, 171 W.Va. 185 (1982).

Recoverable damages for breach of the duty to provide lateral support include diminution of value to the injured property, rehabilitation costs, and loss of use.

2. SUBJACENT SUPPORT

Subjacent support is the obligation not to remove the vertical earthly support for a neighbor's land. As with lateral support, there is an absolute duty to refrain from withdrawing "naturally necessary subjacent support"—the support that is provided underneath the land of another person in its natural, undeveloped, condition. Withdrawal of subjacent support that is not naturally necessary produces liability only when done in a negligent manner. See Rest. (2d) Torts, §§ 820, 821. You might wonder why this doctrine is needed, given that a trespass would occur if A burrowed under B's land to remove the earth supporting B's surface. There are at least two common ways in which subjacent support can be withdrawn without effecting a trespass.

First, A could own the mineral rights to B's land, and thus could be engaged in subterranean mining under B's land without committing trespass. Thus, if A lawfully removed coal from under B's property in a sufficient amount to cause B's property to subside, he might be liable to A.

11. Ed.—Literally, "loss without injury," better rendered as "loss without legally redressable injury."

Strict liability attaches to such withdrawal of subjacent support if the natural surface would have subsided as a result.

> *Example 9–8:* A owns the mineral rights under B's property. Using reasonable care, A mines ore under B's property and, in so doing, sufficient underground support is removed that B's home subsides, causing considerable damage. A is strictly liable if the surface would have subsided even without the structure B erected on it, but if the natural surface would not have subsided (and subsidence results from the added weight of B's home) B is not strictly liable. Rest. (2d) Torts, § 820, Illustration 1.

> *Example 9–9:* A owns the mineral rights under B's property. A mines ore under B's property and, in so doing, sufficient underground support is removed that B's home subsides, causing considerable damage. It is uncontested that the surface would not have subsided if there had been no structure on the surface. A's has liability to B only if A conducted his mining operations in a negligent manner. Rest. (2d) Torts, § 821.

Second, A could drill a well on his own property and extract groundwater. Although this would not be a trespass, if the result was to remove sufficient subjacent support from B's property to cause subsidence, A might be liable to B. See Rest. (2d) Torts, § 818: "One who is privileged to withdraw subterranean water, oil, minerals or other substances from under the land of another is not for that reason privileged to cause a subsidence of the other's land by the withdrawal."

The absence of immunity for subsidence of a neighbor's land caused by one's lawful pumping of water or oil does not end the matter. Rather, it merely raises the question of what standard determines liability for that subsidence. At one extreme is strict liability.

> *Example 9–10:* Using utmost care, A drills a water well on his own land and pumps substantial amounts of water, with the result that neighbor B's land subsides. A is liable to B. Rest. (2d) Torts, § 818, Illustration 2. See also Muskatell v. City of Seattle, 10 Wn.2d 221 (1941).

At the other extreme is a graft of negligence onto the ancient common law property right to pump water from one's own land in any amount. Acton v. Blundell, 152 Eng. Rep. 1223 (Ex. 1843) declared that "if a man digs a well on his own field and thereby drains his neighbor's [well], he may do so unless he does it maliciously." A dramatic expression of this principle is in Houston & T.C. Ry. Co. v. East, 98 Tex. 146 (1904), in which the court upheld the right of a railroad to pump 25,000 gallons daily from a well on its property, with the result that the neighbor's shallow well dried up completely. But these cases had nothing to do with subsidence. When the issue is subsidence and negligence is used as the standard defining liability, some courts hold that a landowner extracting water may do so without liability to adjacent owners if the extraction "is normally a legitimate and reasonable use of land." In such jurisdictions, there is no duty to refrain from otherwise reasonable and legitimate conduct that is reasonably foreseeable to cause subsidence of neighboring land. Precisely that interpretation of negligence was made in Finley v. Teeter Stone, Inc., 251 Md. 428, 439 (1968).

The more logical interpretation of negligence is to hold that negligence inheres in the failure to meet "the duty to produce water from his land in a manner that will not [cause reasonably foreseeable] damage [to] the lands of others." Friendswood Development Co. v. Smith–Southwest Industries, Inc., 576 S.W.2d 21, 30 (Tex. 1978).

CHAPTER TEN

SERVITUDES

■ ■ ■

This chapter deals with servitudes—private bargains that restrict land use. Servitudes may be divided into easements and covenants. Easements are rights to use another person's property in some manner. Their legal kin are profits, which entitle a person to take something from another's property (such as timber) and the irrevocable license. Covenants are restrictions that are imposed on a person's use of his own property, for the benefit of another estate in land. Covenants have traditionally been divided into real covenants, which are enforceable in suits seeking damages for breach of the use restriction, and equitable servitudes, which are enforceable by suits seeking to enjoin the owner of the land subject to the restriction from violating the use restriction. The principal issue in the common law of covenants is deciding when a covenant "runs with the land"—a hoary phrase that describes when a covenant may be enforced by or against an owner of an estate in land who was not a party to the agreement creating the covenant. At common law this task entails three main problems: defining the relationship that must exist between the landowners who created the covenant in order to bind future owners to its terms, defining the relationship that must exist between the subsequent holder of the benefit and the subsequent owner of the burdened estate in order for the benefit (or burden) to be asserted by (or against) those parties, and determining which covenants have a sufficient connection to land use that they should bind future owners. Those may be the main problems, but the common law of running covenants involves a number of ancillary issues as well.

A movement has arisen in recent years, exemplified by the Restatement (Third) of Property (Servitudes) to simplify and clarify the entire area by treating the entire body of law encompassing servitudes, whether easements, profits, or covenants, as a unified whole. Because that movement has not taken hold in the courts to any appreciable degree, the approach of this chapter is to present the common law taxonomy, and then to introduce the changes proposed by the Restatement (Third) of Property (Servitudes).

A. EASEMENTS, PROFITS, AND LICENSES

With few exceptions, easements are the affirmative right to use someone else's land, such as a right of *A* to use a defined strip of *B*'s land as a roadway for access to *A*'s land, or the right of *A* to run utility lines over or under *B*'s land. Negative easements are rights to prevent someone from using their own land in a certain way and, so defined, are functionally identical to covenants. While early English common law recognized a limited number of negative easements, American law has assimilated negative easements into the law of covenants and the law of nuisance. English law recognized, for example, a negative easement held by *A* to prevent *B* from blocking the natural light and air crossing *B*'s land and entering *A*'s windows. In American law, this right, if it exists at all, is likely to be found in the law of nuisance. See, e.g. Prah v. Maretti, discussed in Chapter Nine. Similarly, the right to demand lateral and subjacent support from one's neighbor, and the right to demand that one's upstream owner refrain from interfering with the flow of water in a natural stream are rights that are either subsumed into nuisance law or treated as its conceptual kin. All other rights to restrict the use of someone else's land are treated as aspects of the law of covenants.

Easements may be either *appurtenant* or *in gross*. An easement appurtenant is one that vests the right to use another's land in the owner of land that is benefitted by the easement. An easement in gross is one that vests the right to use another's land in a person, regardless of whether that person owns any land.

> *Example 10–1*: Blackacre and Whiteacre are adjacent parcels. *A*, owner of Blackacre, grants to "*B* and his successors in interest in Whiteacre an easement across Blackacre for foot passage to and from the ocean." This is an easement appurtenant. If *B* should transfer to *C* his interest in Whiteacre, *C* will be able to use the easement so long as he owns Whiteacre.

> *Example 10–2*: Blackacre and Whiteacre are adjacent parcels. *A*, owner of Blackacre, grants to "*B* and his assigns the personal right to enter upon and traverse Blackacre by foot to reach the ocean." This is an easement in gross. *B* has a personal right, unconnected to any ownership of an estate in land that is benefitted by the easement, for foot travel across Blackacre to the sea. Moreover, because the grant is to "*B* and his *assigns*," *B* has the right to assign this easement to *C*, who also need not own any land to enjoy the benefit of the easement.

Note that easements appurtenant are connected to estates in land. The land that is benefitted by the easement is called the dominant estate; the land that is burdened by the easement is called the servient estate. Easements appurtenant are generally transferable unless the easement specifies otherwise. As Example 10–2 indicates, easements in gross are entirely personal and thus create no dominant estate, although there will be a servient estate. Transferability of easements in gross depends on a number of factors that will be discussed in subsection A.2, below. Easements, like other interests in property, may endure for differing periods. For example, an easement can exist in perpetuity (as does a fee simple absolute), for life, a defined term, or be defeasible upon the occurrence of a specified event.

Profits, or *profits à prendre* in the law French of the post-Norman Conquest, are literally a "right of taking." The concept encompasses the right to take things from land, rather than to simply use land. Thus, the right to remove timber, minerals, fish, or game from land were all considered profits. In medieval England these rights generally extended to uncultivated wild lands and were typically thought of as common rights belonging to all. Of course, as population pressure increased and wild lands diminished, the idea of common profits began to fade, until it became a vestigial cousin of easements. Profits continue to exist but the most important species of profit—removal of minerals, such as oil and gas—has acquired its own distinctive body of law that is a blend of property law and governmental regulation.

Licenses are ubiquitous. Whenever someone is invited onto a business, for example, a license is created. When you enter a parking garage you receive a license to park. (Your parking ticket will probably also contain a disclaimer that no bailment is created, only a license to park is granted.) Such licenses are revocable at any time. If the bartender who has permitted you to enter his pub dislikes your attitude he may revoke your license to remain—perhaps by an unceremonious bum's rush. Licenses can become irrevocable, however, and when they do they assume the qualities of an easement. The conditions that cause a license to become irrevocable—usually some form of equitable estoppel—and the duration of irrevocable licenses are the subject of subsection A.1.b, below.

1. CREATION

Because easements and profits are interests in land their creation must comply with the Statute of Frauds, which requires a written instrument evidencing the easement or profit. Of course, the Statute of Frauds admits of various exceptions to the requirement of a writing—partial performance or equitable estoppel, for example. In addition to the exceptions within the Statute of Frauds, the common law recognizes several other ways in which an easement may be created. These include equitable estoppel (the irrevocable license), implication from prior use, implication from necessity, and prescriptive use (the easement cousin of adverse possession). These methods of creating easements are the topic of this subsection.

a. Grant

ASZMUS v. NELSON

Supreme Court of Alaska
743 P.2d 377 (Alaska 1987)

MOORE, J., delivered the opinion of the court.

John and Lillian Aszmus sued Mike Nelson to enjoin him from blocking a right-of-way easement they claimed over his land. The Aszmuses argued that a prior deed in Nelson's chain of title created an easement in their favor because it conveyed the land "subject to" a described right-of-way. The trial court held that, as a matter of law, the deed could not create an easement. Therefore, the court entered summary judgment in favor of Nelson. We reverse and remand for further proceedings.

Both Nelson's lot and the Aszmuses' lot were originally part of Government Lot 32, a larger tract once held by a single owner, Charles Swoboda. Nelson's lot occupies the northeast corner of Lot 32. The Aszmuses' lot occupies the southeastern part of Lot 32. The lots are not adjacent. Swoboda's estate first sold the property now owned by Nelson in 1965. Nelson acquired the land in 1977. The record does not disclose when the Aszmus lot was first separated from the original parcel; the Aszmuses acquired it in 1968.

A road along the northern boundary of Lot 32 provides access for Nelson's land. An access route, called "Swoboda Avenue," running along the east edge of Lot 32, has provided occupants of the southern portion of the lot with access to the road on the north since at least 1968. The Aszmuses and their tenants used Swoboda Avenue continuously from 1968 until Nelson blocked it off some time between 1978 and 1980. . . . In 1985, the Aszmuses sued Nelson to enjoin his blockage of Swoboda Avenue. The Aszmuses asserted that the original deed executed by Swoboda's estate to Nelson's first predecessor-in-interest created an easement over Nelson's land for their benefit. That deed (hereinafter called the Swoboda deed) stated that the land was sold . . . "subject to existing easements for power, light, and other utilities and restrictions of record and *subject to a 15 feet [sic] easement for an access roadway along the east boundary line of said Lot Thirty-two (32)*." (Emphasis added.) The Swoboda deed is in Nelson's chain of title. Subsequent deeds conveying the property to Nelson's predecessors-in-interest and to Nelson provided that the property was sold subject to easements of record. . . .

Nelson moved for summary judgment. He asserted that the "subject to" language of the Swoboda deed did not contain words of grant and so was ineffective to create an easement. . . . The trial court granted Nelson's motion and entered final judgment in favor of Nelson because it held that the Swoboda deed did not contain words of grant and so did not create an easement. . . . The Aszmuses appeal.

. . . The trial court apparently read our opinion in Hendrickson v. Freericks, 620 P.2d 205 (Alaska 1980), *opinion on rehearing,* 620 P.2d 213 (1981), as establishing that a deed which conveys land "subject to" an encumbrance cannot create a reservation in favor of the grantor or an interest in a third party. Therefore, the court held that Nelson was entitled to judgment as a matter of law. The trial court misconstrued *Hendrickson.* In *Hendrickson,* we held that a deed which conveyed real estate "subject to" a lease did not reserve the rights of the lessor in the grantor but merely qualified the estate that the grantee received. Although the opinion discusses cases from other jurisdictions in which the words "subject to" were held not to convey an interest, the opinion concludes that "the primary factor considered by the courts in determining how these phrases are to be interpreted in the individual situation is the intent of the parties." The *Hendrickson* court found that the grantor intended the deed to convey his entire interest in the property. Thus, the case simply affirms the general rule that deeds must be read to ascertain the intent of the grantor. Shilts v. Young, 567 P.2d 769, 773 (Alaska 1977). Under *Hendrickson,* the critical inquiry is whether the Swoboda estate intended to create an easement when it sold Nelson's lot. Because the grantor's intent presents an unresolved issue of material fact, the trial court erred in entering summary judgment.

We observe that the record discloses several factors suggesting that the grantor intended to create or retain an easement. For example, the easement provided the sole access for the southern portion of the property until 1984. . . . Additionally, the explicit description of the easement in the Swoboda deed is unlike prophylactic clauses intended merely to protect a seller from claims for breach of deed warranties. Typically such clauses recite simply that the property is sold subject to easements (or encumbrances) of record. On the other hand, the easement description fails to identify the dominant estate, or even to indicate with certainty that the easement was intended to be appurtenant to an estate rather than an easement in gross. . . .

Nelson argues that, even if the deed could create an easement by reservation to the grantor, the deed could not create an easement in favor of a third party. This argument assumes that the Aszmus property was separated from the original parcel before the Swoboda deed was executed, so the Aszmuses did not succeed to an interest originally created in the grantor. The record does not disclose whether this assumption is correct. In any case, we believe the question whether a deed could create an easement in favor of a third party can be resolved as a matter of law.

Nelson's argument is based upon the common law rule that a reservation or exception in a deed cannot create rights in third parties. Pitman v. Sweeney, 34 Wash. App. 321, 661 P.2d 153, 154 (Wash. App. 1983); *see generally* Annotation, *Reservation or Exception in Deed in Favor of Stranger,* 88 A.L.R.2d 1199, 1203–05 (1963). The rule is based on the technical definition of the terms "reservation" and "exception." "An 'exception' exists when some part of the ownership of the grantor is never parted with, while a 'reservation' is the term applicable when the instrument transfers all that the grantor had but recreates in him some specified interest in respect to the land transferred." 6 A R. Powell & P. Rohan, *The Law of Real Property*, para. 887[5] at 81–73. Since a stranger to the deed had no interest in the property conveyed, common law decreed that he could have no interest to be excepted from the grant, and none from which a reservation could be carved. Willard v. First Church of Christ, Scientist, 7 Cal. 3d 473, 498 P.2d 987, 989, 102 Cal. Rptr. 739 (Cal. 1972). "While a reservation could theoretically vest an interest in a third party, the early common law courts vigorously rejected this possibility, apparently because they mistrusted and wished to limit conveyance by deed as a substitute for livery by seisin." *Willard*, 498 P.2d at 989. The *Willard* court termed the rule's foundation "an inapposite feudal schackle;" it found the rule in conflict with the goal of effecting the grantor's intent, and it asserted that the rule produced an inequitable result because grantees paid less for encumbered property. *Id.* Accordingly, the court rejected the rule. *Id.* at 991.

The New York Court of Appeals recently upheld the rule on the grounds that the rule protects bona fide purchasers and avoids conflicts of ownership. Estate of Thomson v. Wade, 69 N.Y.2d 570, 516 N.Y.S.2d 614, 509 N.E.2d 309 (N.Y. 1987). The court stated that, in the area of property law, " 'stability and adherence to precedent are generally more important than a better or even a 'correct' rule of law. . . .' " We believe the view expressed by the California court in *Willard* represents the preferred position and therefore join the other jurisdictions which have similarly rejected the rule. *See, e.g.,* Malloy v. Boettcher, 334 N.W.2d 8, 9 (N.D. 1983); Medhus v. Dutter, 184 Mont. 437, 603 P.2d 669, 673 (Mont. 1979); Garza v. Grayson, 255 Ore. 413, 467 P.2d 960 (Or. 1970); Townsend v. Cable, 378 S.W.2d 806 (Ky. 1964). *See also* Restatement of Property § 472 comment b (1942). The rule clearly conflicts with our general view that a deed should be construed to effect the intent of the grantor. *Shilts,* 567 P.2d at 773. We find the justification for the rule articulated by the New York court unpersuasive. The rule has never been part of our case law and we perceive no policy reason for adopting it now.

Therefore, even if the Aszmuses acquired their property (or it was otherwise separated from the Swoboda property) before the Swoboda deed was executed, the Swoboda deed may have effectively created an easement across the Nelson lot for the benefit of the Aszmuses' lot. This case cannot be resolved without a factual determination as to the intent of Swoboda's estate at the time it sold the Nelson lot. Thus, summary judgment was improper. We reverse and remand for further proceedings consistent with this opinion.

NOTES, QUESTIONS, AND PROBLEM

1. *Grants, Reservations, Exceptions, and Third Party Beneficiaries.* There is no dispute that an easement may be created by an outright grant. In

Example 10–1 *A*, owner of Blackacre, grants to *B*, owner of the adjacent Whiteacre, an easement across Blackacre. Reservations, exceptions, and third party beneficiaries present related, but slightly different issues. As the court noted, when a grantor parts with some, but not all, of what he owns, he has "excepted" from the grant the portion that he retains. When a grantor conveys all that he owns, but the grant contains a reconveyance to the grantor of some portion of what he previously owned, the interest reconveyed to the grantor is a "reservation." The term "reservation" is a bit of a misnomer; it might be simpler to think of this a new interest created in the grantor, albeit created by the grantor's actions.

> *Example 10–3*: If *A*, owner of adjacent parcels Redacre and Greenacre, conveys Redacre to *B* "excepting therefrom an easement for access across Redacre to benefit Greenacre," *A* has created an easement by exception. Greenacre is the dominant estate; Redacre is the servient estate.

> *Example 10–4*: If *A*, owner of adjacent parcels Redacre and Greenacre, conveys Redacre to *B* "subject, however, to a reservation of an easement for access across Redacre to benefit Greenacre," *A* has created an easement by reservation. In a sense, *A* has conveyed his entire interest in Redacre to *B*, and *B* has simultaneously granted to *A* an easement in Redacre. Greenacre is the dominant estate; Redacre is the servient estate.

The traditional common law rule was that either of these methods of creating an easement was valid, because the owners of the dominant and servient estates were each a party to the deed. But a deed of Blackacre from *A* to *B* that purports to create an easement in Blackacre in favor of *C*, owner of Orangeacre, was invalid because *C* was not a party to the deed. Thus, the putative easement was neither an exception from the grant in favor of *A* nor the creation by *B* of a new interest in *A*. The traditional rule continues to be observed in some states. See, e.g., Estate of Thomson v. Wade, 69 N.Y.2d 570 (1987); Tripp v. Huff, 606 A.2d 792 (Maine 1992). In those states, how might *A* transfer Blackacre to *B* and still create an easement burdening Blackacre and benefitting Orangeacre? But the trend is toward the view expressed in *Aszmus*, and is expressly endorsed by the Restatement (Third) of Property (Servitudes) § 2.6(2).

2. *Queries.* a. Suppose that when Swoboda executed and delivered the deed to Nelson's predecessor in interest, Swoboda owned the parcel later acquired by Aszmus. Would the easement in favor of Aszmus be valid? On what does the answer to that question depend?

b. Suppose that when Swoboda executed and delivered the deed to Nelson's predecessor in interest, Swoboda had already conveyed to Aszmus's predecessor in interest all of his interest in the parcel later acquired by Aszmus. Would the easement in favor of Aszmus be valid? On what does the answer to that question depend?

3. *Problems.*

a. Suppose *A* owns Lot One, located at the intersection of Maple Lane and Oak Road. Across Maple Lane and at the same intersection is a private school, the Paine School, of which *A* is an alumnus. In 2000 *A* conveys Lot

One to *B* via a deed that recites that *A* conveys Lot One "subject to an easement for parking on Lot One on game day Saturday afternoons during football season for the benefit of the school at the intersection of Maple Lane and Oak Road, such easement to run with the land until the school ceases to use the property benefitted by this easement for school purposes." In 2012 Paine School moves to a new location, three blocks away, and sells its former location to the Charter Oaks School, a rival school. What is the status of the parking easement?

    b. Suppose that *A* and *B* own Blackacre in fee simple absolute as tenants in common. Without *A*'s knowledge or consent, *B* grants to "*C* and his heirs and assigns of Whiteacre," an adjacent parcel, an easement across Blackacre for purposes of connecting to a sewer on Blackacre. What rights and obligations have been created by that grant? See Restatement (Third) of Property, Servitudes § 2.3 (2000).

    4. Easement or Fee Simple? Grants of a "right of way" are most often construed as creating an easement but sometimes courts treat such a grant as conveying a fee simple absolute. The general rule is stated in Chevy Chase Land Co. v. United States, 355 Md. 110, 128 (1999): "[W]hen a deed conveying a right-of-way fails to express a clear intent to convey a different interest in land, a presumption arises that an easement was intended." See also Danaya C. Wright, Private Rights and Public Ways: Property Disputes and Rails-to-Trails in Indiana, 30 Ind. L. Rev. 723, 740 (1997): "The logical rule . . . is that where the deed is ambiguous *and* the granting clause is not specific, references to the interest being conveyed as a right-of-way gives rise to a presumption that an easement was intended." Swan v. O'Leary, 37 Wash.2d 533, 535 (1950) noted that "[t]he authorities are in hopeless conflict. . . . About the only common ground that can be found is that the intention of the parties to the conveyance is of paramount importance and must ultimately prevail in a given case." Thus, in City of Manhattan Beach v. Superior Court, 13 Cal.4th 232 (1996), the court construed a quit claim deed of a strip of land for a railroad right of way to convey a fee simple absolute. The court relied primarily on post-conveyance conduct of the grantor that suggested the landowner regarded the grant as conveying a fee simple absolute.

b. Estoppel

MUND v. ENGLISH

Court of Appeals of Oregon
69 Ore. App. 289 (1984)

ROSSMAN, J., delivered the opinion of the court.

    This case arises from a family dispute over the ownership of a well. Plaintiffs are the son and daughter-in-law of defendant. In 1977, plaintiffs and defendant, together with the deceased husband of defendant, purchased adjoining one acre parcels of property near Pendleton. In that year, a water well was drilled on defendant's property. Equipment and pipes were installed so that plaintiffs and defendant received water from the one well. In less than a year after the installation, the parties began to quarrel about their rights to the well and water. The fighting has continued since then, culminating in this suit for declaratory judgment and specific performance.

Plaintiffs contend that, from the beginning, their interest in the well was to have been a permanent and irrevocable interest. Defendant claims that plaintiffs' rights were not permanent and were subject to certain conditions. The trial court found for defendant. [Because] the facts clearly show that defendant did grant an irrevocable license to plaintiffs, . . . we reverse. . . .

Defendant argues that an irrevocable license can only be established when there is proof of an agreement for a permanent easement which is taken out of the Statute of Frauds (requiring a writing) by part performance. Defendant says that the proof is lacking here. Defendant's argument misses the basis of an irrevocable license. Although it is true that, in most jurisdictions, an oral license may be revoked, Oregon has consistently held that, when a licensee makes valuable improvements on the basis of a promise, the licensor will not be permitted to assert that the license could be revoked. An irrevocable license does not depend on proof of the agreement of the parties but arises by operation of law to prevent an injustice. *See* Powers et ux. v. Coos Bay Lumber Co., 200 Or 329, 415, 263 P2d 913 (1954); Shepard v. Purvine, 196 Or 348, 374, 248 P2d 352 (1952). . . . The situation before us is almost identical to Shepard v. Purvine. . . . There, the plaintiffs claimed to have been given an irrevocable license to use water from a spring on the Purvine property and for a right-of-way for the pipeline. The defendants claimed that the license was only temporary. The court, noting the hopeless conflicts in the testimony, looked at the circumstances of the case and concluded:

> All the undisputed circumstances of this case point directly to the fact that plaintiffs' oral license was intended to be, and was and is, permanent. In reliance upon this oral license, plaintiffs made valuable improvements on and in connection with their lands and in laying the pipeline. It would be wholly inequitable and unjust to now permit defendants to destroy plaintiffs' rights. Defendants, under all the facts and circumstances of this case, ought to be, and they are, estopped to deny plaintiffs' claims. 196 Or at 374.

The circumstances before us likewise show an irrevocable license. Defendant admits that she and her deceased husband granted plaintiffs the right to use the well and to install a pipeline to plaintiffs' property. The testimony of plaintiffs and defendant as to the permanency of this agreement is in direct dispute, and the testimony of the attorney who was to draft an agreement for the parties was [indeterminate]. The attorney admitted that he could not find a record of his meeting and that he had only a general recollection of the event. He recalled a lack of agreement as to whether the parties wanted a contract or a deed of easement, but he could not recall any specifics.

However, the circumstances here show a permanent arrangement. Plaintiffs and defendant shared the installation costs of the well and water system. Plaintiff Mr. Mund and defendant's husband worked together installing the system. The parties have continued to share operating expenses. Even more significantly, plaintiffs secured a $40,000 commercial loan in 1977 and constructed a residence on their property. There was, and is, no other source of domestic water for plaintiffs. The improvements made by plaintiffs clearly show their reliance on a permanent agreement. The law will not permit defendant to claim that she can withdraw the license to use the well.

Reversed and remanded for entry of a decree granting plaintiffs a one-half interest in the water well and water system on defendant's property, granting plaintiffs an easement over defendant's property for the purpose of access to the water system and requiring plaintiffs and defendant to share equally the cost of maintaining the system.

CROASDALE v. LANIGAN

Court of Appeals of New York
129 N.Y. 604 (1892)

ANDREWS, J., delivered the opinion of the court.

This case presents a question of importance from the principle involved, although the particular interest affected by the decision is not large. The action was brought to obtain [an] injunction to restrain the defendant from tearing down a stone wall erected on the defendant's land by the plaintiff, under an alleged parol license from the defendant, and in the erection of which the plaintiff expended in labor and materials a sum exceeding one hundred dollars. The parties are the owners of adjoining lots fronting upon a public street. The plaintiff's lot is west of the lot of the defendant. The land in its natural state descended toward the east. In 1886 the plaintiff graded his lot, and in so doing, raised an embankment several feet high along his eastern line, adjacent to the lot of the defendant, and erected a house on his lot. In 1887 the defendant graded his lot and excavated the earth up to his west line, adjacent to the embankment on the plaintiff's lot, to the depth of four or more feet, thereby removing the natural support to the lot of the plaintiff as it was in its original state. Before the defendant had completed his excavation, ... the question of the support of the plaintiff's embankment arose. The plaintiff claimed that the defendant was bound to build a wall where his excavation was. The defendant denied his obligation to do so and referred to the fact that the plaintiff had raised his land several feet higher than it was in its natural state. The plaintiff wanted the defendant to sell him two feet of his land to build a wall upon, which the defendant declined to do.

Both parties agree that the wall was spoken of. The plaintiff testified that nothing was said between them as to what kind of a wall the plaintiff would build, nor as to its height, dimensions or quality. The defendant on the other hand testified that the plaintiff stated he would build a wall laid up in mortar, pointed on the side facing the defendant's (proposed) house, and cement it on the top with Portland cement. Some days [later] and on the 13th day of April, 1887, the defendant addressed a letter to the plaintiff, in which, after referring to their previous interview, he said:

> While perfectly satisfied that I am justified in grading my lot as far as I have done, and that if at any time your embankment should topple over on my land, that I could claim damages, yet, perhaps, I was a little hasty and somewhat unreasonable with you the other night, and although I came away fully determined to stand on my rights and keep every inch of ground that belonged to me, since then I have thought the matter over seriously, put myself in your place, so to speak, and decided to give you two feet asked for to build your wall on.

The plaintiff on the same day replied in writing, saying:

> I will be glad to accept your offer in the spirit in which it was given, and thus end a disagreement, etc. I expect to go to work immediately to build the wall, and will go as far into my bank as is consistent with its safety. I will also modify as much as I can the grade of the bank along the side and the front.

The plaintiff thereupon proceeded to build a wall on the defendant's land, the building of which occupied four or five days. He first made a contract with a mason to build a mortared wall, and lime and sand were drawn upon the place to be used therefor. But for some reason he changed his mind, and he built the wall of "flat, ordinary building stone, not hewn into shape and not packed into regular courses, nor dressed at all," and without mortar or cement. The wall was ninety feet in length, two feet or less in width, and four to six feet high. It does not appear that the defendant saw the wall during the course of its construction, except that he was upon the lot on one occasion when the foundation was being laid, nor does it appear that he knew that the wall was to be laid up loose, or at any time consented to the erection of such a wall as was constructed. Within two weeks after the wall was completed he notified the attorney for the plaintiff, who, at the request of his client, had written him, demanding a deed of the two feet, that he had not agreed to give a deed, and that the wall was not built according to the understanding, and that he intended to tear it down.

This case was tried and decided upon the theory that the plaintiff had a license from the defendant to build the wall on his land, which, when executed, became in equity irrevocable. It was not claimed on the trial, nor is it now claimed, that there was any contract on the part of the defendant to sell the land occupied by the wall to the plaintiff, which, by reason of part performance, equity will enforce. The claim and the finding is that the license to enter upon the defendant's land, when acted upon by the plaintiff, conferred upon him a right in equity, in the nature of an easement, to maintain the wall on the defendant's lot. If this claim is well founded, there has been created, without deed and in violation of the

Statute of Frauds, an interest in the plaintiff and his assigns in the land of the defendant, impairing the absolute title which he theretofore enjoyed, and subjecting his land to a servitude in favor of the adjacent property. It is quite immaterial in result that this interest claimed, if it exists, is equitable and not legal. An encumbrance has been created upon the defendant's lot, and his ownership, to the extent of such interest, has been divested.

We are of opinion that this judgment is opposed to the rule of law established in this state. There has been much contrariety of decision in the courts of different states and jurisdictions. But the courts in this state have upheld with great steadiness the general rule that a parol license to do an act on the land of the licensor, while it justifies anything done by the licensee before revocation, is, nevertheless, revocable at the option of the licensor, and this, although the intention was to confer a continuing right and money had been expended by the licensee upon the faith of the license. This is plainly the rule of the statute. It is also, we believe, the rule required by public policy. It prevents the burdening of lands with restrictions founded upon oral agreements, easily misunderstood. It gives security and certainty to titles, which are most important to be preserved against defects and qualifications not founded upon solemn instruments. The jurisdiction of courts to enforce oral contracts for the sale of land, is clearly defined and well understood, and is indisputable; but to change what commenced in a license into an irrevocable right, on the ground of equitable estoppel, is another and quite different matter. It is far better, we think, that the law requiring interests in land to be evidenced by deed, should be observed, than to leave it to the chancellor to construe an executed license as a grant, depending upon what, in his view, may be equity in the special case....

The judgment should be reversed.

NOTES

1. Irrevocable Licenses. Most licenses are revocable. You acquire a license to use and occupy a portion of a theater when you buy a ticket, but if you insist on using your cell phone to converse loudly during the performance your license will probably be revoked. Similarly, if *A* invites you to picnic in his grove of balsam firs, *A* may revoke the license at his whim, But if the license is ancillary to your ownership of some chattel on *A*'s land, it is irrevocable. Thus, if you owned a profit—e.g., the right to cut the fragrant boughs from *A*'s balsam firs—the license to enter *A*'s land is *coupled with an interest*—your ownership of the profit—and is not revocable.

Neither *Mund* nor *Crosdale* involve that pattern. Each of those cases presents the question of whether principles of equitable estoppel should apply to the grant of a license otherwise revocable. Equitable estoppel requires a representation by *A* that is reasonably relied upon by *B* to his detriment. Once that is proven, *A* is estopped from denying the representation upon which *B* relied. Once a licensor is estopped from revoking a license, it becomes the functional equivalent and is so treated. See Restatement (Third) of Property (Servitudes) § 1.2(4).

Yet, easements are interests in real property and thus generally subject to the requirements of the Statute of Frauds. Should the Statute of Frauds be a barrier to easements by estoppel, as the *Crosdale* court held? Or, should judges and juries be free to create such easements on the strength of oral testimony and other evidence that bears on the question of what was promised, whether there was reliance on the promise, whether that reliance was reasonable, and whether there was sufficient detrimental reliance to support creation of an easement? What are the pros and cons of each approach?

2. *Property or Liability Rules?* In each of *Mund* and *Crosdale* the court applied property rules: An easement by estoppel was found in *Mund* and the servient estate owner was burdened with the easement. No easement was found in *Crosdale* and the owner of the putative dominant estate received nothing for his trouble. (Presumably, the wall was torn down.) Should liability rules have been used? If so, that would mean that the erector of the wall in *Crosdale* would be compensated for his loss, even though no easement was found to exist. In *Mund*, the servient estate owner would receive compensation for imposition of the easement. How should compensation be measured? Note that in *Mund* the servient estate owner was forced to cede ownership of a one-half interest in the well along with imposition of the easement, and both parties were required to share equally the costs of maintenance of the well.

3. *Problems.*

a. Suppose that *A*, owner of Blackacre, tells *B*, the owner of Whiteacre, an adjacent parcel, that he can use a roadway over Blackacre "to build your house" on Whiteacre. There is no other practical access to Whiteacre, although alternative vehicle access to Whiteacre from a public road could be created at great expense, involving considerable blasting through rocks and along cliff faces. *B* expends $200,000 to construct a home on Whiteacre, but does nothing to improve the roadway over Blackacre. *B* uses the roadway to bring in construction materials and workmen. Once the home is completed, *A* tells *B* that the license has "come to an end, because I granted it just to permit you to *build* your home." *B* contends that the license has become irrevocable. Who should prevail?

b. Suppose that in the prior problem, *B* is granted an irrevocable license to use the roadway over Blackacre to access his home on Whiteacre. Then *B*'s home is totally destroyed in an earthquake. Has *B*'s easement by estoppel expired? Would the answer be different if *B*'s home had been a yurt made of goatskins, costing $5,000, and had rotted due to exposure to natural elements? In considering this problem, note Restatement (Third) of Property (Servitudes) § 4.1(1): "A servitude should be interpreted to give effect to the intention of the parties ascertained from ... the circumstances surrounding creation of the servitude, and to carry out the purpose for which it was created." Consider also comment g to that section: "A servitude is created by estoppel ... when a party is led into a reasonably foreseeable and substantial change of position by actions of a landowner that lead to a belief that a license to use land will not be revoked or that the land is burdened by a servitude.

The expectations that create the servitude also define its scope and terms. The relevant expectations are those that reasonable people in the position of the landowner and the person who relied on the grant of permission or representation would have had under the circumstances.''

4. Cemetery Access. About a fifth of the states recognize an easement in gross in relatives of a dead person buried in a private cemetery. Some states do so by statute but some apply the common law, reasoning that the owner's permission to bury the deceased on his property implies permission to his or her relative to visit the grave, and that permission may not be revoked. This unusual version of an easement by estoppel is discussed in Alfred Brophy, *Grave Matters: The Ancient Rights of the Graveyard,* 2006 B.Y.U. L. Rev. 1469.

c. Implication

There are two methods by which an easement may be implied. An easement implied from prior use is one in which a landowner uses a portion of his land for the benefit of his remaining land, such as a roadway or utility line. By itself this creates no easement—the landowner owns all of the land—but when the owner divides the land by selling one part of it (either the benefitted or burdened portion) to another person, an easement may arise from the landowner's prior use. The other type of implied easement is limited to easements for access to a landlocked parcel—the necessity of access is the driving force in creating such an easement by implication. But as with an easement implied from prior use, the landlocked condition must be created by a common owner's severance of his parcel.

i. *Implied From Prior Use*

ROMANCHUK v. PLOTKIN

Supreme Court of Minnesota
215 Minn. 156 (1943)

PETERSON, J., delivered the opinion of the court.

In 1915 defendants acquired the real property at the northeast corner of Twelfth avenue north and Humboldt avenue north in Minneapolis, on which there was a duplex dwelling near the corner facing Twelfth avenue, known as 1312 Twelfth avenue north, and a small dwelling toward the rear facing Humboldt, known as 1206 Humboldt avenue north. Both houses were equipped with plumbing serviced by a common sewer drain which connected with the public sewer in Humboldt avenue. On February 23, 1921, defendants acquired the real property now owned by plaintiffs, located immediately east of the duplex and known as 1310 Twelfth avenue north. At that time this property was without plumbing and sewer connection. There has not been, nor is there now, a public sewer in Twelfth avenue north. In 1922 defendants installed plumbing in the house at 1310 Twelfth avenue, which they connected with a sewer drain they

Facts

laid below the basement floor and underground extending from the rear of the house across the properties of the parties into the basement of the duplex, where it was connected with the sewer drain from the duplex to the street. After this connection was made the one sewer drain connecting with the public sewer in Humboldt avenue serviced the three houses on defendants' property.

All the sewer drainpipes are four inches in diameter. The pipes became obstructed and clogged on numerous occasions, causing sewage to back up and thus creating an unsanitary and unhealthful condition. This condition is likely to recur periodically. A separate sewer drain connecting the property now owned by plaintiffs with the public sewer in Humboldt avenue could be installed at a cost of $175. This would have to be laid in Twelfth avenue north. A permit to use the street for that purpose is necessary. It was not shown that a permit could be obtained.

On February 25, 1921, two days after defendants became the owners of 1310 Twelfth avenue north and about one year before they installed the plumbing and made the sewer connection there, they executed a mortgage of the property . . . to one Margaret Roggeman. . . . In July 1936, Margaret Roggeman acquired title through foreclosure of the mortgage. She did not inspect the property either when she took the mortgage or when she foreclosed it. She dealt through an agent, who afterwards looked after the renting and who, out of rents collected, paid defendant Plotkin for cleaning and repairing the sewer.

On August 8, 1938, plaintiffs purchased the property from Roggeman. They dealt through Roggeman's agent. Plaintiff Nicholas Romanchuk testified that he observed the drainpipes in an unfinished and unused part of the basement [and] that the agent told him that the sewer drain connected with the public sewer in the street. Neither the mortgage to Roggeman nor the deed to plaintiffs mentions any easement in the sewer across defendants' land. In 1941 the common drain connecting these properties with the city sewer became clogged, necessitating repairs. Plaintiffs' proportionate share of the repairs was $25, of which they paid five dollars prior to trial and the balance during the trial. . . .

On October 22, 1941, defendant[] Samuel Plotkin notified plaintiffs that on November 5, 1941, the connection of the sewer drain serving their property with the drain to the sewer in the street would be severed. Plaintiffs then brought this action to enjoin defendants from disconnecting their sewer connection. . . . The court below found that plaintiffs had an easement for the use and maintenance of the sewer drain across defendants' property connecting with the sewer in Humboldt avenue north, subject to the requirement that they pay their proportionate share of the cost of repairing and maintaining the same. . . . [It] ordered judgment enjoining defendants to refrain from interfering with plaintiffs' use of the sewer drain and from severing the connection of their sewer drain with the sewer leading to the street. . . . Here, defendants contend that the finding that plaintiffs are entitled to an easement for the use and maintenance of the sewer drain across defendants' land is without basis, because (a) the severance of ownership occurred when the Roggeman mortgage was given, which was prior to the installation of the sewer drain on plaintiffs' property and the connection thereof with the one across their other property; (b) the use of the sewer drain across defendants' property to Humboldt avenue was not apparent but, on the contrary, was concealed by the fact that the sewer pipes were underground; and (c) the use thereof was not necessary to the beneficial use of plaintiffs' property....

The doctrine of implied grant of easement is based upon the principle that where, during unity of title, the owner imposes an apparently permanent and obvious servitude on one tenement in favor of another, which at the time of severance of title is in use and is reasonably necessary for the fair enjoyment of the tenement to which such use is beneficial, then, upon a severance of ownership, a grant of the dominant tenement includes by implication the right to continue such use. That right is an easement appurtenant to the estate granted to use the servient estate retained by the owner. Under the rule that a grant is to be construed most strongly against the grantor, all privileges and appurtenances that are obviously incident and necessary to the fair enjoyment of the property granted substantially in the condition in which it is enjoyed by the grantor are included in the grant. Prior to the severance and while there is unity of title, the use is generally spoken of as a quasi easement appurtenant to the dominant tenement. It is commonly said that three things are essential to create an easement by implication upon severance of unity of ownership, *viz.:* (1) a separation of title; (2) the use which gives rise to the easement shall have been so long continued and apparent as to show that it was intended to be permanent; and (3) that the easement is necessary to the beneficial enjoyment of the land granted.

Defendants contend that the sewer was not an apparent quasi easement at the time of severance of ownership, upon the theory that the severance took place when the mortgage was given, which was approximately one year before the sewer drain was installed on plaintiffs' property.... In [some] states a mortgage of real property conveys the title subject to defeasance upon payment of the mortgage debt or upon fulfillment of the conditions of the mortgage. We do not follow that rule. [By statute,] the rule that a mortgage of real estate conveyed the legal title was abrogated and the rule adopted that a mortgage creates a lien in favor of the mortgagee as security for his debt with right of ownership and possession in the mortgagor until foreclosure and expiration of the period of redemption. Where a mortgage on real estate creates a lien, the execution of the mortgage does not effect a severance of title, but the foreclosure of the mortgage does. Under the title theory, a use created after the giving of a mortgage does not give rise to an easement in favor of the mortgagee; but, under the lien theory, it does and passes to the purchaser at the foreclosure sale.

It cannot be seriously contended that the sewer in question was not continuous and permanent. It is urged, however, that, since the sewer, both in plaintiffs' house and outside in plaintiffs' and defendants' yards, was underground, it was not apparent. "Apparent" does not necessarily mean "visible." The weight of authority sustains the rule that "apparent" means that indicia of the easement, a careful inspection of which by a person ordinarily conversant with the subject would have disclosed the use, must be plainly visible. An underground drainpipe, even though it is buried and invisible, connected with and forming the only means of draining waste from plumbing fixtures and appliances of a dwelling house, is apparent, because a plumber could see the fixtures and appliances and readily determine the location and course of the sewer drain.

In 17 Am. Jur., Easements, p. 985, § 80, the text reads: "As a general rule, implied easements are restricted to servitudes which are apparent. . . . [T]he fact that a pipe, sewer, or drain may be hidden underground does not negative its character as an apparent condition, at least, *where the appliances connected with, and leading to, it are obvious.*" (Italics supplied.) In Larsen v. Peterson, 53 N.J. Eq. 88, 93, 94, 30 A. 1094, 1097 (1895), is an elaborate discussion of the principle as applied to underground water pipes leading from a well to a pump inside a house, where the pump was visible but the pipes were not. The court said: "[T]he controlling fact is that the pump was . . . visible and in use, and by its connection with the invisible pipe leading to *some* fountain the house conveyed to complainant was supplied with water. . . . [A]ll that is meant by 'apparent' . . . is that the parties should have either actual knowledge of the quasi-easement or knowledge of such facts as to put them upon inquiry."

In the instant case the plumbing fixtures and their connection with the sewer pipes were plainly visible. The pipes extended from the rear of plaintiffs' house toward defendants' duplex. A plumber easily could have ascertained that the pipes, although underground and invisible, extended under the duplex, where they connected with the drain leading from the duplex to the sewer in the street.

The authorities are in conflict as to what is meant by "necessary" in this connection. Some hold that "necessary" means substantially the same as indispensable. Others hold that it means reasonably necessary or convenient to the beneficial enjoyment of the property. . . . The weight of authority supports the view that "necessary" does not mean indispensable, but reasonably necessary or convenient to the beneficial use of the property. In 17 Am. Jur., Easements, p. 985, § 79, the text states:

[T]he prevailing rule . . . is that the necessity requisite to the creation of an easement by implication is not an absolute necessity, but that a reasonable necessity suffices. Generally, in order to support an easement as to drainage or sewage by implied grant the easement must be reasonably necessary or convenient to the beneficial enjoyment of the property. Where it appears that property is sold fully equipped with visible plumbing and appliances to carry off waste and water, it has been held that there can be no serious dispute that the use of the drainpipe is reasonably necessary for the convenient and comfortable enjoyment of the property and passes upon conveyance of the property without specific mention.

In the instant case the use of the drain was highly beneficial and convenient to the use of plaintiffs' property. The reasonable construction of the mortgage under which plaintiffs claim title in the light of the surrounding circumstances is that the use of the sewer drain was an appurtenance to plaintiffs' property which passed under the mortgage. Further, it appears that the parties placed a practical construction on their rights by which they in effect recognized plaintiffs' right to the easement. Plaintiffs were permitted to continue to use the sewer. Defendants charged them for repairs and maintenance, and plaintiffs paid the charges. A practical interpretation by the parties that an easement exists supports an inference that the easement is one of legal right.

As a word of caution, we do not hold that in all cases the existence of the three characteristics mentioned are necessary to create an easement by implication. Rules of construction are mere aids in ascertaining the meaning of writings.... [They] are neither ironclad nor inflexible and yield to manifestation of contrary intention. In 3 Tiffany, Real Property (3 ed.) p. 254, § 780, the author says:

> The rules declared by the courts as to the creation of easements corresponding to preexisting quasi easements, and of easements of necessity, constitute in reality merely rules of construction for the purpose of determining the scope of the conveyance. And the grant of the easement is implied only in the sense that the easement passes by the conveyance although not expressly mentioned, just as an easement previously created passes upon a conveyance of the land to which it is appurtenant without any express mention of the easement....

For present purposes, it is sufficient to hold that ... an implied easement to the use of the sewer across defendants' land passed under the mortgage and the foreclosure thereof and that plaintiffs became the owners of the easement as grantees of the purchaser at the mortgage foreclosure sale....

Affirmed.

NOTES, QUESTIONS, AND PROBLEMS

1. Why is an Easement Implied from Prior Use? There would be no reason to create an easement by implication if the common owner, who created the quasi-easement, had explicitly recited the existence of the easement in the deed that divided ownership of the property. In the absence of mention of the easement in the deed, is the best rationale for creating such an easement the notion that the easement must have been intended to be created by the grantor (and it was inadvertently omitted from the deed) or is it to prevent the possibility of deceit being practiced upon the buyer? Do the elements necessary for finding an easement by implication from prior use suggest one, both, or neither of these rationales?

2. *Benefit or Burden Retained by the Grantor.* In *Romanchuk*, the grantor, Roggeman, conveyed title to the parcel that was benefitted by the quasi-easement—an implied grant. What if the grantor had conveyed title to the parcel that was burdened by the quasi-easement—an implied reservation? Here are differing views of the matter. Which is best? Why?

Suffield v. Brown, 4 De G.J. & S 185, 190–192, 194, 46 Eng. Rep. 888, 89– 892 (1864).

A dock and an adjoining strip of land and coal wharf were held in fee by the same person, and whenever a ship of any size was taken into the dock to be repaired her standing bowsprit projected over and across the adjoining strip of land. All the properties were put up for sale by auction . . .; but nothing was stated to shew that the dock or its owners either then had or were intended to have any right or privilege over the adjoining premises. The strip of land and coal wharf were sold and conveyed to the purchaser in fee absolutely and in the most unqualified manner, and under such purchaser the Defendant claimed. Afterwards the dock was sold and conveyed to the purchaser thereof, under whom the Plaintiff claimed. [The Master of the Rolls issued] an injunction to restrain the Defendant from preventing or interfering with the Plaintiff's full use and enjoyment of the dock as the same had theretofore been used by allowing the bowsprit of any vessel in the dock to overlie or overhang the strip of land and coal wharf.

The Lord Chancellor, Lord Westbury:

It seems to me more reasonable and just to hold that if the grantor intends to reserve any right over the property granted, it is his duty to reserve it expressly in the grant, rather than to limit and cut down the operation of a plain grant (which is not pretended to be otherwise than in conformity with the contract between the parties), by the fiction of an implied reservation. If this plain rule be adhered to, men will know what they have to trust, and will place confidence in the language of their contracts and assurances. But this view of the case is not that taken by . . . the Master of the Rolls, [who concluded that an easement in favor of the grantor arose by implication because the implied reservation was] "essential to the full and complete enjoyment of the [property retained by the grantor.]" . . . The effect of this is, that if I purchase from the owner of two adjoining freehold tenements the fee-simple of one of those tenements and have it conveyed to me in the most ample and unqualified form, I am bound to take notice of the manner in which the adjoining tenement is used or enjoyed by my vendor, and to permit all such constant or occasional invasions of the property conveyed as may be requisite for the enjoyment of the remaining tenement in as full and ample a manner as it was used and enjoyed by the vendor at the time of such sale and conveyance. This is a very serious and alarming doctrine. . . . Suppose the owner of a manufactory to be also the owner of a strip of land adjoining it on which he has been for years in the habit of throwing out the cinders, dust and refuse of his workshops, which would be an easement necessary (in the sense in which that word is used by the Master of the Rolls) for the full enjoyment of the manufactory; and suppose that I, being desirous of extending my garden, purchase this piece of land and have it conveyed to me in fee-simple; and the owner of the manufactory afterwards sells the manufactory to another person; am I to hold my piece of land subject to the right of the grantee of the manufactory to throw out rubbish on it? According to the doctrine of the judgment before me, I certainly am so subject; for the case falls strictly within the rules laid down by His Honour, and it reduces them to an absurd conclusion. . . . But I cannot agree that the grantor can derogate from his own absolute grant so as to claim rights over the thing granted, even if they were at the time of the grant continuous and apparent easements enjoyed by an adjoining tenement which remains the property of him the grantor. [Reversed]

Howley v. Chaffee, 88 Vt. 468, 474 (1915)

[T]here is a clear distinction between implied grants and implied reservations, and . . . no question of public policy is here involved, as . . . is the case where a way of necessity is involved. To say that a grantor reserves to himself something out of the property granted, wholly by implication, not only offends the rule that one shall not derogate from his own grant, but conflicts with the grantor's language in the conveyance, which . . . is to be taken against him, and is wholly inconsistent with the theory on which our registry laws are based. If such an illogical result is to follow an absolute grant, it must be by virtue of some legal rule of compelling force. The correct rule is . . . that where . . . one grants a parcel of land by . . . a deed containing full covenants of warranty and without any express reservation, there can be no reservation by implication, unless the easement claimed is one of strict necessity, [rather than "superior convenience,"] Dee v. King, 73 Vt. 375, 378 (1901).

Van Sandt v. Royster, 148 Kan. 495, 500–501 (1938)

[T]he circumstance that the claimant of the easement is the grantor instead of the grantee, is but one of many factors to be considered in determining whether an easement will arise by implication. An easement created by implication arises as an inference of the intentions of the parties to a conveyance of land. The inference is drawn from the circumstances under which the conveyance was made rather than from the language of the conveyance. The easement may arise in favor of the conveyor or the conveyee.

The Restatement (Third) of Property, Servitudes § 2.12 (2000)

Unless a contrary intent is expressed or implied, the circumstance that prior to a conveyance severing the ownership of land into two or more parts, a use was made of one part for the benefit of another, implies that a servitude was created to continue the prior use if, at the time of the severance, the parties had reasonable grounds to expect that the conveyance would not terminate the right to continue the prior use. The following factors tend to establish that the parties had reasonable grounds to expect that the conveyance would not terminate the right to continue the prior use:

(1) the prior use was not merely temporary or casual, and

(2) continuance of the prior use was reasonably necessary to enjoyment of the parcel, estate, or interest previously benefited by the use, and

(3) existence of the prior use was apparent or known to the parties, or

(4) the prior use was for underground utilities serving either parcel.

Comment e to Rest. (3d) Property, Servitudes § 2.12 states that the rule "that reasonable necessity is required whether the implied easement is in favor of the grantor or grantee is the majority rule." States that continue to observe the minority rule of strict necessity where an implied reservation is at issue include Michigan, Montana, Nebraska, New York, Texas, and Vermont.

3. Scope of Easements Implied from Prior Use. Does an easement implied from prior use include uses not in existence at the time of severance? If so, what factor(s) should be relevant to determination of which new uses are included in such an easement?

> *Problem*: *O*, a farmer, owned two adjacent parcels. At the time *O* sold the parcels to two different purchasers, Parcel One consisted of farmland and an unoccupied farmhouse. Parcel Two consisted entirely of farmland. Both parcels were used exclusively for farming. Before severance, access to Parcel One was across Parcel Two. Later, *A*, the new owner of Parcel One, began to use Parcel One as his residence and claimed that the implied easement for access extended to residential use and utility services necessary for residential use. *B*, the owner of Parcel Two, objected, contending that the easement for access was limited to agricultural use of Parcel One. What result? See Stroda v. Joice Holdings, 288 Kan. 718 (2009).

ii. Implied From Necessity

An easement implied from necessity results when an owner of property (1) divides it into two parcels, one of which is landlocked by the division, (2) access to the parcel across the proposed servient estate is a necessity, not a convenience, and (3) the necessity of access existed at the time of the severance. The basis for this form of implied easement is *not* the same as that for an easement implied from prior use, but judges, as well as lawyers and law students, sometimes confuse the two forms of implied easements. There need be no prior use of an access easement to create an easement by necessity. See, e.g., Westover Sportsman's Association v. Broome County, 399 N.Y.S.2d 725 (1977).

KELLY v. BURLINGTON NORTHERN RAILROAD COMPANY

Supreme Court of Montana
279 Mont. 238 (1996)

NELSON, J., delivered the opinion of the court.

This is an appeal from the Montana Eighteenth Judicial District Court, Gallatin County. Following a nonjury trial, the District Court denied Plaintiffs' claims for the declaration of an easement by prescription, by necessity or by implication, and entered judgment for Defendants. From this judgment, Plaintiffs appeal. We reverse....

Plaintiffs own land in Sunny Bear Estates Subdivision, Gallatin County, Montana. Plaintiffs [Kellys] purchased Tract 1 on September 16, 1983, from ... Thompson and ... Hubbard. Plaintiffs [Smiths] purchased Tract 2 on June 26, 1989, from [the] Lefferts. Plaintiffs [Pipers] purchased Tracts 3–12 on May 8, 1990, from Sundance Realty & Investments, Inc. Defendant Burlington Northern Railroad Company (BN) is the owner of a 400' right-of-way in Section 24, Township 2 South, Range 6 East, M.P.M., Gallatin County, Montana. Defendant Montana Rail Link, Inc. (MRL) claims a leasehold interest in the right-of-way owned by BN.

Sunny Bear Estates is bounded on the west, north and east by rugged mountains and private property. To the south, Sunny Bear Estates is bounded by MRL's and BN's railroad right-of-way. Railroad tracks pass through the railroad right-of-way and have existed since March 1883. Running parallel to and south of the railroad right-of-way is the East Frontage Road. The East Frontage Road (old U.S. Highway 10) was originally part of the Bozeman Trail constructed in 1864. Just to the south of the East Frontage Road lies Interstate 90, a controlled access highway. The nearest public road to Sunny Bear Estates is the East Frontage Road. The East Frontage Road lies south of the railroad right-of-way. A gravel road leaves the East Frontage Road at its east end, runs north and crosses the railroad right-of-way at the planked crossing at issue, and enters Sunny Bear Estates. This railroad crossing is located in the SW 1/4 of the NW 1/4 of Section 24, Township 2 South, Range 6 East, M.P.M., Gallatin County, Montana. Frank King, a long time resident of the area, testified that he started using the crossing in 1926 and that he knew the crossing had been used for an undetermined time before 1926. The second closest road is Moffit Gulch Road, a county road, located one mile to the west of Sunny Bear Estates, over rugged mountain terrain and private property.

Ward I. Stone was the original predecessor-in-interest to part of the property owned by the Kellys, Smiths and Pipers (collectively Plaintiffs). Stone filed his homestead claim on the SW 1/4 of the NW 1/4 of Section 24 (the property) on November 1, 1880, and received his federal patent September 13, 1890. Stone conveyed the property to Lester Willson on January 30, 1882. On January 5, 1891, Willson conveyed the property to Northern Pacific Railroad Company (NP Railroad).... [On May 20, 1891 NP Railroad conveyed the property by quit claim deed to Northern Pacific Coal Company (NP Coal), and on June 4, 1891 NP Coal conveyed the 400' right-of-way back to NP Railroad by a quit claim deed. NP Coal retained title to the remainder of the property.]

[In 1984 Burlington Northern, the corporate successor to NP Railroad, insisted that the Sunny Bear Estates landowners execute a Private Roadway and Crossing Agreement, under which the landowners were required to pay a fee to BN and which permitted BN to terminate the road

Problem →

ρ

and crossing on 30 days written notice. Because no title company will insure title where access is subject to such an agreement, some of the plaintiffs were denied construction loans, which event prompted the suit.]

Plaintiffs filed their Complaint for Declaratory Judgment on February 25, 1991. Plaintiffs sought an order declaring that they held an easement for ingress and egress over and across Defendants' railroad right-of-way. Plaintiffs advanced four alternative theories upon which the relief could be granted: 1) public easement by prescription; 2) private easement by prescription; 3) private easement by implication; and 4) private easement by necessity. [After] a nonjury trial [the] District Court [denied] Plaintiffs' claims for declaration of an easement by prescription, necessity or implication . . . and entered judgment for Defendants. . . . Plaintiffs appeal from this judgment. . . .

[T]he District Court concluded, as a matter of law, that Plaintiffs did not establish easements by prescription, by necessity or by implication. In particular, the District Court concluded that Plaintiffs did not have an easement by necessity because at the time unity of ownership was severed, strict necessity did not exist. We review this conclusion of law to determine whether the District Court properly interpreted the law governing easements by necessity. . . .

We hold that Plaintiffs do have an easement by necessity and reverse the District Court's legal conclusion to the contrary. Because this issue is dispositive, we will not address the remaining three issues raised on appeal.

In Amended Conclusion of Law No. 7, the District Court stated in part:

> The requirements of an easement by necessity are 1) unity of ownership, and 2) strict necessity at the time the unified tract is severed. . . . Unity of title existed on the SW1/4 of the NW1/4 of Section 24 until Northern Pacific Railroad Company quitclaimed its interest in the section to Northern Pacific Coal Company, and the Coal Company quitclaimed the 400' right-of-wayback to the Railroad on June 4, 1891. There is no evidence in the record that prior to the separation of title, or even at the time the title was separated, that strict necessity existed for the grantor to have an "easement to the outside world" across its remaining lands.

Plaintiffs contend that the District Court erred when it concluded that Plaintiffs did not establish an easement by necessity because they failed to establish strict necessity at the time unity of ownership was severed. . . . Defendants argue that the District Court correctly concluded strict necessity did not exist. They support the court's conclusion by quoting Plaintiff Harry Piper's testimony that he had not negotiated to purchase an access easement from any neighboring property owners. We conclude that the District Court misinterpreted the strict necessity requirement for easements by necessity.

An easement by necessity is a subspecies of an implied easement. An easement by necessity arises through strict necessity for ingress and egress to a parcel of property. Graham v. Mack (1984), 216 Mont. 165, 175, 699 P.2d 590, 596. Strict necessity is defined by a lack of practical access to a public road for ingress and egress. Wangen v. Kecskes (1993), 256 Mont. 165, 169, 845 P.2d 721, 724. See also, Wagner v. Olenik (1988), 234 Mont. 135, 761 P.2d 822. That is, the purpose of an easement by necessity is "to permit communication with the outside world." Rathbun v. Robson (1983), 203 Mont. 319, 324, 661 P.2d 850, 853. We have defined an easement by necessity as follows:

> where an owner of land conveys a parcel thereof which has no outlet to a highway except over the remaining lands of the grantor or over the land of strangers, a way of necessity exists over the remaining lands of the grantor. Similarly, a way of necessity is found when the owner of lands retains the inner portion conveying to another the balance, across which he must go for exit and access.

Big Sky Hidden Village Owners v. HVI (1996), 276 Mont. 268, 915 P.2d 845, 850, 53 Mont. St. Rep. 379, 382 (quoting Schmid v. McDowell (1982), 199 Mont. 233, 237, 649 P.2d 431, 433). Furthermore, we have set forth two basic elements to establish an easement by necessity: 1) unity of ownership, and 2) strict necessity at the time the unified tracts are separated. *Graham*, 699 P.2d at 596.

[We] find two different explanations [by the trial court] as to how unity of ownership was severed in 1891: 1) NP Railroad reserved its 400' right-of-way when it quitclaimed the property to NP Coal or 2) NP Coal, after acquiring the property from NP Railroad, granted the 400' right-of-way back to NP Railroad by a separate quitclaim deed. In either case, the result is the same. Under the first explanation, NP Coal's land "had no outlet to a highway except over the remaining lands of the grantor [NP Railroad] or over the land of strangers, [therefore,] a way of necessity existed over the remaining lands of the grantor [NP Railroad]." See *Big Sky*, 915 P.2d at 850. Under the second explanation, "a way of necessity [existed] when the owner of lands [NP Coal] retained the inner portion conveying to another [NP Railroad] the balance, across which he [NP Coal] must go for exit and access." See *Big Sky*, 915 P.2d at 850. Therefore, as defined in *Big Sky*, a way of necessity existed over the railroad right-of-way whether NP Railroad reserved or was granted the right-of-way. See *Big Sky*, 915 P.2d at 850.

However, after reviewing the record, we conclude that unity of ownership was severed as noted in the second explanation above. On May 20, 1891, NP Railroad quitclaimed the SW 1/4 of the NW 1/4 of Section 24 to NP Coal. Subsequently, on June 4, 1891, NP Coal granted NP Railroad a 400' right-of-way across the SW 1/4 of the NW 1/4 of Section 24. As a result of these conveyances, unity of ownership was severed. Therefore, the District Court properly concluded that Plaintiffs satisfied the first element, unity of ownership, to establish an easement by necessity.

However, the District Court erred by concluding that strict necessity did not exist at the time unity of ownership was severed.

In 1891, NP Railroad possessed a 400' right-of-way through NP Coal's property, while NP Coal possessed title to the remainder of the property, and unity of ownership was severed. In 1891, NP Coal's property was surrounded to the west, north and east by rugged mountain terrain. The only possible way to access and exit the property was to the south. In fact, the nearest public road to NP Coal's property was the Bozeman Trail, which later became U.S. Highway 10, and currently is known as the East Frontage Road. The Bozeman Trail, constructed in 1864, ran along the same path as today's East Frontage Road which is located immediately to the south and adjacent to the railroad right-of-way. Because the railroad right-of-way separated NP Coal's property from the Bozeman Trail, the only way to reach this public road was to cross the railroad right-of-way. Without access across the railroad right-of-way, NP Coal's property would be landlocked and unable to "communicate with the outside world." That is, at the time unity of ownership was severed, the property lacked practical access to a public road for ingress and egress. Therefore, a strict necessity existed. Consequently, an easement by necessity arose.

Defendants attempt to bolster the District Court's conclusion that strict necessity did not exist by quoting Plaintiff Harry Piper's testimony that he had not negotiated with his neighbors for an alternative access easement. Defendants claim that this testimony "clearly indicates that strict necessity does not exist for an easement across the railroad right-of-way." We disagree. Whether Plaintiffs currently have the ability to obtain access easements over their neighbors' properties is irrelevant. Evidence of strict necessity must be shown to have existed *at the time unity of ownership was severed. Graham*, 699 P.2d at 596. Plaintiffs established that the property's unity of ownership was severed in 1891 and that strict necessity existed at that time. Defendants' evidence concerning Plaintiffs' easement options *at the time of trial* does not affect Plaintiffs' claim that an easement by necessity arose from land conveyances occurring in the last century. See State v. Cronin (1978), 179 Mont. 481, 488, 587 P.2d 395, 399–400.

[An] easement by necessity arose in 1891 because strict necessity existed at the time unity of ownership to the property was severed. Not only was NP Coal's property surrounded to the west, north, and east by rugged mountain terrain, but was also bounded to the south by the railroad right-of-way. This set of circumstances effectively left NP Coal's property landlocked, and the requirement of strict necessity was met because the property was without access to a public road. Logic dictates that the only practical means to access or exit the property was to cross the railroad right-of-way to reach the nearest public road, the Bozeman Trail. In fact, Frank King, a long time resident of the area, testified that in 1926 he started using the planked crossing at issue and that he knew the crossing had been used for an undetermined time before 1926.

Accordingly, we reverse the District Court and hold that Plaintiffs have an easement by necessity to cross Defendants' railroad right-of-way at the planked crossing at issue which is located in the SW 1/4 of the NW 1/4 of Section 24, Township 2 South, Range 6 East, M.P.M., Gallatin County, Montana. Reversed.

Notes, Questions, and Problems

1. The Basis for Easements by Necessity. Over time, courts have oscillated between two different rationales for finding easements to be implied by necessity. An ancient and fundamental maxim in the construction of conveyances of real property, said to date from the 13th century reign of Edward I, is quoted by Lord Coke as *Lex est cuicumque aliquis quid concedit, concedere videtur, et id sine quo res ipsa non esse potuit*—when anything is granted to someone, all the means to attain the thing granted that are within the power of the grantor to transfer are also granted. Liford's Case, 11 Coke Rep. 46b, 52a (1615). See also Lord v. Commissioners for City of Sydney, 12 Moore 473, 14 Eng. Rep. 991 (P.C. 1859). From this was derived the notion that an easement by necessity was implicitly intended to be a part of the grant, because otherwise the land conveyed would be rendered useless. By the mid–17th century, though, a different rationale was injected. In Packer v. Welsted, 2 Sid. 39, 111, 82 Eng. Rep. 1244 (1658), Chief Justice Glyn grounded the easement on the principle that it is "to the prejudice of the public weal, that land should lie fresh and unoccupied."[1] This difference of rationales becomes of significance only when a grantor specifically and explicitly refuses to provide access over his retained land to the parcel landlocked by the conveyance. Should public policy or the intent of the parties prevail? Compare Jackson v. Nash, 109 Nev. 1202, 1212 (1993); Murphy v. Burch, 46 Cal.4th 157, 163–164 (2009) with Ghen v. Piasecki, 410 A.2d 708, 712 (N.J. Super. App. Div. 1980).

2. The Degree of Necessity. Jurisdictions divide on the question of whether the necessity for access must be "strict" or "reasonable." According to the Restatement (Third) of Property, Servitudes § 2.15, comment d, necessity does not mean "essential to enjoyment of the property;" rather, it includes those rights that "are reasonably required to make effective use of the property. If the property cannot otherwise be used without disproportionate effort or expense, the rights are necessary... Reasonable enjoyment of the property means use of all the normally useable parts of the property for uses that would normally be made of that type of property."

While that may be the prevailing rule, some courts insist that the claimed easement must be absolutely necessary. See, e.g., Horowitz v. Noble, 79 Cal.App.3d 120, 131 n.4 (1978), quoting Kripp v. Curtis, 71 Cal. 62, 65 (1886): "The right of way from necessity ... cannot exist except in cases of strict necessity. It will not exist where a man can get to his property through his own land. That the way over his own land is too steep or too narrow, or that other and like difficulties exist, does not alter the case, and it is only where

---

1. The report of the case is in law French; the translation is taken from James W. Simonton, Ways by Necessity, 25 Colum. L. Rev. 571, 574 (1925).

there is no way through his own land that a grantee can claim a right over that of his grantor. It must also appear that the grantee has no other way."

Miller v. Schmitz, 80 Ill.App.3d 911, 912, 914 (1980):

> Plaintiff and defendant own adjoining farmland.... Defendant's land lies to the east of plaintiff's and is bordered on the east by a township road running north to south. To the west, another north-south road forms the western border of plaintiff's property. The eastern boundary of plaintiff's land and the western boundary of defendant's land abut. Plaintiff's land is bisected by Robinson Creek, separating her property into a western parcel and an eastern parcel. The western parcel is bordered by the township road on the west and the creek on the east. There is a 40–foot precipitous slope of the land to the creek bed. Plaintiff's eastern parcel is bordered by the creek on the west and defendant's land on the east. The creek's average depth is about four feet and its width averages approximately 40 feet. These figures vary seasonally. The township road to the west provides access to the western parcel of plaintiff's land, but the eastern parcel is inaccessible to a public road because it is bordered by the creek on one side and defendant's land on the other. In order to move farm machinery onto the eastern portion, plaintiff must traverse defendant's property or construct a bridge over the creek.

> Plaintiff and defendant derive their titles from a common grantor, Henry Williams.... In 1887 Williams divided his land, selling what is now plaintiff's property to John Kimlel and retaining the property owned by defendant until 1912, when he sold it to defendants predecessor in title....

> In order to satisfy the required element of necessity, it is sufficient if the claimed easement is highly convenient and beneficial. Plaintiff testified that her annual gross income from crops grown on the eastern portion ranged from $550 to $900 over the past 15 years. [An expert] estimated that it would cost plaintiff $24,790 to construct a low-water bridge across the creek and $1,000 annually to maintain it. The benefit to be enjoyed by plaintiff from the claimed easement is obvious; it allows her to have access to her otherwise landlocked eastern cropland without the necessity of substantial expenditures....

3. *Compensation?* A variation of sorts on strict necessity is the notion that governments seeking to impose an easement by necessity across private land lack strict necessity, even when all other elements are present and there is absolutely no other access route, because they can invoke the power of eminent domain to condemn such an access easement. See Leo Sheep Co. v. United States, 440 U.S. 668 (1979). Note that in such a case, the owner of the servient estate will receive "just compensation" for the easement, but that in ordinary cases of easements by necessity no compensation will be paid to the owner of the servient estate. Some states also provide that private landowners may impose easements by necessity across another private owner's land, even if there had been no common owner or if the necessity had not existed at the time of severance. See, e.g., Mont. Code § 70–30–107 (2010): "Private roads may be opened in the manner prescribed by this chapter, but in every case the

necessity of the road and the amount of all damage to be sustained by the opening of the road must be first determined by a jury, and the amount of damages, together with the expenses of the proceeding, must be paid by the person to be benefited." Wyoming has eliminated the common law easement by necessity in favor of a statutory private eminent domain procedure. See Wyo. Stat. §§ 24–9–101 *et seq.* (2011); Ferguson Ranch, Inc. v. Murray, 811 P.2d 287, 290 (Wyo. 1991).

Is there a justification for providing compensation to owners of servient estates whose property is subjected to an easement by eminent domain and not to those who bear an easement by necessity imposed by the common law?

4. Duration of Necessity. Easements implied from necessity terminate automatically once the necessity ceases. Thus, if the owner of the landlocked dominant estate acquires the servient estate, the easement comes to an end.

5. Problems.

a. O is the owner of a single 40 acre tract of ground that abuts a public highway on the south and is surrounded by National Forest land on the other three sides. Twenty feet before the western edge of the property the ground rises abruptly and almost vertically for about fifteen feet before sloping to the west at an angle of about 25 degrees. *O* constructed a home on the 20 acre portion of the land that is closest to the highway. In 2000 *A*, seeking utter seclusion and tranquility, purchased from *O* the rear 20 acres, including a 20 foot strip on the west that connected to the rear 20 acres, under a deed that made no mention of any easements. Instead of scaling the cliff on the western strip, *A* walked across the Forest Service land to reach the back 20 acres, where he built a yurt in which he lived with utter simplicity. In 2005, having decided that simplicity and tranquility was not what he had hoped, *A* sold the rear 20 acres to *B* for $20,000 under a deed that made no mention of easements. After learning that it would cost $500,000 to construct a road along the 20 foot strip, *B* contends that he has an implied easement by necessity for access to his property across *O*'s property. Is he correct? To what extent should the question of the degree of necessity required to establish an easement implied from necessity depend on the theoretical rationale for such an easement? Should the outcome be different if *A* had reached the back 20 acres by driving his Prius across a dirt road on *O*'s property? See, e.g., Oliver v. Ernul, 277 N.C. 591(1971); Schwab v. Timmons, 224 Wis.2d 27 (1999).

b. O owned a 20 acre parcel which he divided into two parcels, Lots 1 and 2. Lot 1 abuts a public road; Lot 2 is landlocked. In 2002 *O* sold Lot 2 to *A* under a deed that made no mention of any easements. *A* did not take possession. In 2010, *O* sold Lot 1 to *A*, and *A* took possession of both Lots. *A* borrowed money from *B* and to secure the loan gave *B* a mortgage on Lot 2. *A* defaulted on the loan and *B* foreclosed on Lot 2. Does *B* have an easement by necessity across Lot 1? See McClure v. Monongahela Southern Land Co., 263 Pa. 368 (1919); 3 Tiffany, Real Property § 822 (2010); 2 American Law of Property § 8.91 (1952).

d. Prescription

Acquisition of an easement by prescription is analogous to acquisition of title by adverse possession. The adverse possessor whose occupation has the requisite characteristics acquires title because the relevant limitations statute denies to the lawful owner any ability to recover possession of his land. Easements, however, do not involve possession of another's land; rather, they involve use of another person's land. The limitations statute that cuts off the true owner's right to recover *possession* says nothing about the true owner's right to enjoin an adverse *use* of his land. Nevertheless, courts universally recognize that adverse use for a sufficient period of time may ripen into a right—a prescriptive easement.

HESTER v. SAWYERS

Supreme Court of New Mexico
41 N.M. 497 (1937)

BRICE, J., delivered the opinion of the court.

... The question is whether the district court erred in holding that appellee has title by prescription to a right of way over appellant's land. If there is substantial evidence to support the findings and judgment of the court, it will not be disturbed by us. The evidentiary facts are practically undisputed and are as follows:

The parties are adjoining landowners. At the time and before appellee bought his property in 1920, appellant was the owner of the land over which the easement is claimed. Persons owning land on three sides had theretofore built fences around their own land, thus in effect placing fences on three sides of appellant's land; but the east side was open and all persons desiring so to do, could pass across it. The two tracts of land are separated by a fence belonging to appellee, which is appellant's west boundary. The original way had its beginning at appellee's house, passed an opening in the fence, and ran easterly across appellant's land to a road along her boundary, which at that time was unfenced.

In 1922 a golf club secured the consent of appellant to place a fence along the east boundary, thus inclosing the land; after which it was used in part as a golf course. Appellee claimed a right to pass over the land at that time, though he did not know who owned it. The golf club secured his consent to the building of the fence. He had no deed to the road, paid no taxes on it, and based his claim of right on the fact that "it was the only way to get in and out and had been used for years."

At the time the east fence was built the road was materially changed. From the west boundary it followed the old road a very short distance, then turned away to the south of it some distance, thereafter paralleling it for the greater distance across appellant's land, and terminated on the road at the east side in a lane south of "the old road." [The] "old road" and the "present road" ... are not substantially at the same location, though practically parallel. Since the east fence was built, appellee, his tenants, visitors, and those having business with him (and no other persons), have used the road daily and openly, without interruption or objection from any one until just prior to the filing of this suit in the district court. Appellee did not have the affirmative consent or authority of appellant, or any person, to use the road. When he gave his consent to the golf club to build the fence, he stated to its representative: "I don't lose my right to come down and out of this canyon." He sells lumber at his house and has no other way out. He did not buy his land from appellant. He testified: "My business is selling lumber at my claim up above my house, with no other way than this road to get to and from my place. I have rent houses and this road is the only way my tenants have to go back and forth. If the road is closed I will have to discontinue my business and move out of there. I claim this road as my right of way." Since the east fence was built, more than ten years prior to the filing of this suit, appellee has continuously graded and kept the road in condition for travel for his own use.

Just prior to the filing of this suit the appellant saw the appellee and insisted that he change the road to run further north so that it would interfere less with her property. Appellee agreed to do this, and to that end began the grading of a new road. This appellant claimed did not comply with her directions, so she closed appellee out with a fence, which was torn down by him. This suit followed.

There is no specific statute in this state under which title to an easement or other incorporeal hereditament[2] can be obtained by prescription, but appellant claims that section 83–122, Comp. St.1929, applies to corporeal and incorporeal hereditaments. It reads in part as follows: "No person or persons, nor their children or heirs, shall have, sue or maintain any action or suit, either in law or equity, for any lands, tenements or hereditaments, against any one having adverse possession of the same continuously in good faith, under color of title, but within ten years next after his, her or their right to commence, have or maintain such suit shall have come, fallen or accrued, and all suits, either in law or equity, for the recovery of any lands, tenements or hereditaments so held, shall be commenced within ten years next after the cause of action therefor has accrued: ... 'Adverse possession' is defined to be an actual and visible appropriation of land, commenced and continued under a color of title and claim of right inconsistent with and hostile to the claim of another." If this statute applies to easements, then appellee has no title for he does not claim, nor did he prove, color of title.

It was the ancient rule of law that the words "lands, tenements or hereditaments" comprehended only freehold estates and did not apply to easements or other incorporeal hereditaments; likewise statutes of limitation like that to which we have referred, which bar actions to recover

---

2. [Ed.—] Incorporeal hereditaments were traditionally those rights that were ancillary to the real property that descended by inheritance to the eldest son. Most relevant to us, they included easements and profits that were appurtenant to the inherited estate. Of no significance today are the incorporeal hereditaments that composed the bundle of rights relevant to medieval life as a landowner. That bundle included such things as titles of nobility (peerages), the right to appoint the parson for the church that served the manor (an *advowson*), various franchises (such as the right to hold a market or seize the personal possessions of convicted felons), and the assignable right to room and board in a monastery or other religious establishment (a *corody*). Corodies were useful patronage to deal with the unlucky or imprudent relative or friend who had lapsed into poverty.

lands held adversely under color of title for a period of years, are generally held to apply to corporeal hereditaments only.

Prescription may be defined to be a mode of acquiring title to incorporeal hereditaments by continued user, possession or enjoyment had during the time and in the manner fixed by law. The term properly applies only to incorporeal rights. An interest in the land of another greater than an incorporeal hereditament, such as the possession and use of a building thereon, cannot be established by prescription. Prescription is distinguished from custom in that the former is a personal usage or enjoyment confined to the claimant and his ancestors or those whose estate he has acquired, while the latter is a mere local usage, not connected to any particular person, but belonging to the community rather than to its individuals. Adverse possession is distinguished from prescription in that it is, properly speaking, a means of acquiring title to corporeal hereditaments only, and is usually the direct result of the statute of limitations; while prescription is the outgrowth of common-law principles, with but little aid from the legislature, and has to do with the acquisition of no kind of property except incorporeal hereditaments. 1 Thompson on Real Property, § 372.

Prescription applies only to incorporeal hereditaments. An interest in the land of another greater than an incorporeal hereditament, such as the possession and use of a building thereon, cannot be established by prescription. The statutes of limitations do not directly apply to actions in which incorporeal hereditaments, such as easements, are involved, but only to actions for the recovery of land. 1 Thompson on Real Property, § 375.

See ... Murray v. Scribner, 74 Wis. 602 [(1889)]; Boyce v. Missouri Pacific R. Co., 168 Mo. 583 [(1902)]. Appellant does not seriously contend that the statute of limitation applies to easements, but insists that if it does not, then the right is one at common law and that twenty years use is necessary to acquire title by prescription.

The courts of England and, with few exceptions, of the United States, have adopted the rule that the period of use for acquiring such title by prescription corresponds to the local statute of limitation for acquiring title to land by adverse possession.

The period for acquiring an easement in land corresponds to the local statute of limitation as to land. It would be irrational to hold that an easement may not be acquired by the same lapse of time required to confer title to the land by adverse possession. The period of limitation for the bringing of actions to recover the possession of land is generally adopted as the period for perfecting easements by prescription. This rule is based upon the assumption that if there had been no grant, the owner would have put an end to the wrongful occupation before the full period of limitation had expired. And while it is often said that from such user a grant will be presumed, the presumption in effect amounts to a positive rule of law, and evidence that no grant was made would not be material. ... 1 Thompson on Real Property, § 374.

Appellant ... insists that if, following the general rule, we adopt the period of time provided by statute under which adverse possession will bar an action to recover possession of real property, then we should hold that appellee must establish color of title and that he had paid taxes as required by the statute of limitation in question.... That an easement may be created by prescription, appellant agrees. If we should hold that one claiming an easement because of use for ten years is burdened further with proving he had color of title to such easement, and had paid taxes thereon if levied, then we would be applying the statute of limitation and not the law of prescription to easements, though we have just held the statute of limitation did not apply. Adverse possession of land could not apply to easements, for the use necessary to acquire them is not necessarily constant or exclusive. A prescriptive right is obtained by use alone and does not depend upon any statute. It is founded upon the presumption of a grant, though there may never have been one. The reason for the adoption by the courts of England and generally by those of the United States, of a time of use analogous to that required by statutes of limitation regarding adverse possession of land, is because the common law fixed no definite time. It was, "For a time whereof the memory of man runneth not to the contrary." The courts, through gradual change, ultimately adopted by analogy the time as that for the running of the statute of limitation in cases of lands held by adverse possession as the period of use necessary for a conclusive presumption of a grant. Statutes of limitation are not otherwise involved or material.

We hold that the period of use necessary to create an easement by prescription is ten years, following our statute of limitation with reference to adverse possession of lands. ... The use necessary to acquire title by prescription must be open, uninterrupted, peaceable, notorious, adverse, under a claim of right, and continue for a period of ten years with the knowledge or imputed knowledge of the owner.

Having disposed of these questions of law, we come to apply the facts, about which there is little dispute. [A]ppellee's use[] was continuous, open, uninterrupted, peaceable, notorious, and continued for a period of more than ten years; but it is contended by appellant that it was neither proven to be adverse under a claim of right, nor that it was with the knowledge, or imputed knowledge, of the owner. If the user was open, adverse, notorious, peaceable, and uninterrupted, the owner is charged with knowledge of such user, and acquiescence in it is implied. 1 Thompson on Real Property, § 462.

The real question in the case is whether the user was adverse under a claim of right or only permissive. A prescriptive right cannot grow out of a strictly permissive use, no matter how long the use. 1 Thompson on Real Property § 471.

A road existed across appellant's unenclosed land before the appellee bought his land; and after he acquired it he continuously used this road that others had used before his time, until the east boundary fence was built. But there was no substantial evidence of an adverse user under claim of right. Appellant quotes Boullioun v. Constantine, 186 Ark. 625, 54 S.W.2d 986, 987 [(1932)], as follows: "[T]he prevailing rule seems to be that, where the claimant has openly made continuous use of the way over occupied lands unmolested by the owner for a time sufficient to acquire title by adverse possession, the use will be presumed to be under a claim of right; but, where the easement enjoyed is across property that is unenclosed, it will be deemed to be by permission of the owner and not to be adverse to his title [although] those using a private way over unenclosed lands may, by their conduct, openly and notoriously pursued, apprise the owner that they are claiming the way as of right and thus make their possession adverse." In this state, where large bodies of privately owned land are open and unenclosed, it is a matter of common knowledge that the owners do not object to persons passing over them for their accommodation and convenience, and many such roads are made and used by neighbors and others. Under these circumstances it would be against reason and justice to hold that a person so using a way over lands could acquire any permanent right, unless his intention to do so was known to the owner, or so plainly apparent from acts that knowledge should be imputed to him.

[There] was no claim of right to the use of the road communicated to appellant, or evidenced by any acts that indicated a claim of right, prior to the inclosure of the lands by the building of the fence on the east side by the golf club in 1922. The substance of the evidence is that the road was there when appellee bought his place and he used it not knowing to whom it belonged. It is presumed that the original use of the road by appellee and others was permissive. A prescriptive right may be acquired, although the use was originally permissive, if in fact it became adverse. But the adverse user must be for the full ten years, which excludes the time under which the user was permissive. 1 Thompson on Real Property, § 472. If there was an adverse user by appellee, it must have begun at the time the east fence was placed around the property by Hahn in 1922.

If a use has its inception in permission, express or implied, it is stamped with such permissive character and will continue as such until a distinct and positive assertion of a right hostile to the owner is brought home to him by words or acts. . . . "A use acquired merely by consent, permission, or indulgence of the owner of the servient estate can never ripen into a prescriptive right, unless the user of the dominant estate expressly abandons and denies his right under license or permission, and openly declares his right to be adverse to the owner of the servient estate." Howard v. Wright, 38 Nev. 25, 143 P. 1184, 1186 [(1914)].

If the only evidence of an assertion by appellee of a hostile right to the use of a way across appellant's land after the fence was built was the fact that "he continually worked and graded" the road, it may be doubted (though we do not decide) whether this was sufficient to change a friendly and permissive use to a hostile and adverse one. . . . But after the fence was built a new road was established. A map introduced in evidence shows "the old road" used prior to the building of the fence and "the present road" made and used after the fence was built. The parties do not contend they are the same and all the evidence shows they are different. The two roads converge a short distance from appellee's land and pass through the same opening, otherwise they are entirely different roads. If appellee had used the present road for only eight years, he could not have tacked the use of the old road on it to give him a prescriptive right. A way claimed by prescription must be a definite, certain, and precise strip of land. . . . If in fact rights had been initiated in the first road, they would have been lost when it was abandoned. The two could not have been tacked together to make a prescriptive right, assuming that the first use was adverse. It was said in Peters v. Little, 95 Ga. 151, 22 S.E. 44, 45 [(1894)]: "She might have acquired a prescriptive right over the first strip if she had continued to use it; but when she voluntarily abandoned it . . . the prescription ceased to run in her favor as to that particular strip. As to the second strip, her use of the same did not continue for the requisite time to give a prescriptive right of way over it." . . .

The permissive right was to use the old road, not the new one. When appellee abandoned the old road, he established a new road over inclosed lands. He kept the road graded and in repair, exercising control over the strip of land as though his own, for more than ten years. In the absence of proof that this use was permissive (and there is no such proof), it is presumed, after ten years use, to have been hostile, adverse, and acquiesced in by appellant.

There is substantial evidence to support the judgment of the district court, and it is accordingly affirmed. . . .

NOTES, QUESTIONS, AND PROBLEMS

1. The Fictional Lost Grant. The opinion in *Hester* claims that prescriptive easements are "founded upon the presumption of a grant, though there may never have been one." This canard is a recurring trope in American law. It should be buried. At least from some time after the Norman Conquest English law permitted prescriptive use to ripen into right if the use had existed since the Conquest. Another version of this period was, as the *Hester* court alludes, usage for as long as anyone could remember. In 1275 Parliament enacted the First Statute of Westminster, which contained a limitations statute that barred claims to possession of land that arose prior to September 3, 1189, the day that Richard III (the Lionhearted) became King. As Richard III's accession faded into the mist of history courts created a rebuttable presumption that use "as far back as living witnesses could recall" was sufficient to establish use since 1189. Later, the courts shortened this period to 20 years, reasoning by analogy to a 1623 act, 21 Jac. I, c.16, which set 20 years as the limitations period for actions in ejectment. But the flaw in all of this was that the presumption was rebuttable; so long as the owner could show that at *some point* since 1189 there had been an interference with the use, suit to stop the use from continuing was permissible. To make the presumption conclusive, courts invented the complete fiction that there must have been a grant to the user, which has now been lost. The fictional and mysterious grant, of course, would cut off any claim by the owner of the servient estate to the contrary. It would have been more honest to simply declare that the limitations period applicable to claims to recover possession applies equally to claims to stop continuation of a use of one's land by another. In the end, that is what the *Hester* court did, but not after some folderol about lost grants. The definitive work on this hoary and unnecessary doctrine is William Stoebuck, The Fiction of Presumed Grant, 15 U. Kan. L. Rev. 17 (1966).

An unfortunate by product of the lost grant nonsense is the notion that the owner of the servient estate must acquiesce in the use, meaning that he does not object to the use (as one would expect of someone who has conveyed the use right to the user), but that he has not granted permission for the use. Acquiescence is evidence of the "lost grant;" a grant of permission is thought to be evidence of the absence of any such conveyance, and negates any claim that the use is adverse and thus can ripen into a prescriptive easement. The *Hester* court parrots this distinction, through its inclusion of an element of prescription that the use be with the "knowledge or imputed knowledge of the owner," thus creating an implication of acquiescence. Given the court's decision to import the 10 year limitations statute applicable to claims for recovery of possession, it need not have bothered with acquiescence. Permission, however, is another matter, for if the use is permissive it is not adverse and may never ripen into a prescriptive easement. But what kind of easement might be created by a permissive use?

The fiction of the lost grant may be nonsense, but some courts adhere to it, or at least its bastard offspring: acquiescence. See, e.g., Town of Manchester v. Augusta Country Club, 477 A.2d 1124, 1130 (Me. 1984). Where it exists it may be consequential, as Examples 10–5 and 10–6 illustrate.

Example 10–5: In 1970 *O* leases Blackacre to *A* for a 50 year term. In 1990 *B* enters Blackacre and grades a road across it, which *B* uses openly, notoriously, and continuously since then. The jurisdiction uses 20 years as the period of use and requires acquiescence to establish the fictional lost grant of the easement. In 2011, *B* has a prescriptive easement over Blackacre that is good against each of *A*'s leasehold and *O*'s reversion in fee simple absolute, because *it is possible* that *O* could have granted the right to *B*. See Restatement (Third) of Property, Servitudes § 2.17, comment f.

Example 10–6: Same facts as Example 10–5, except that the jurisdiction does not rely on the fictional lost grant and uses a 20 year limitations period for claims to recover possession, actions seeking ejectment, and for claims of trespass. In 2011, *B* has a prescriptive easement over Blackacre that is good only against *A*'s leasehold. *A*'s right to seek ejectment or remedies for trespass is time-barred, but *O*'s claim to recover possession has not yet arisen. See Dieterich Int'l Truck Sales, Inc. v. J.S. & J.

Services, Inc., 3 Cal.App.4th 1601 (1992); See Restatement (Third) of Property, Servitudes § 2.17, comment f.

2. *The Elements of Prescription.* The elements of the use necessary to acquire a prescriptive easement mimic those applicable to adverse possession, but there a few wrinkles in the doctrine when it is applied to use rather than possession.

Adverse, or under "claim of right." This means, in essence, that the use is not with the permission of the owner. Uses that are subordinate to the owner's title are permissive. Thus, if *O* leases Blackacre to *A* and, without violating the terms of the lease, *A* constructs a water line from a well on Blackacre to serve Whiteacre, a parcel *A* owns in fee simple, the use of Blackacre is subordinate to *O*'s title and cannot be adverse to *O*. See Restatement (Third) of Property, Servitudes § 2.16, comment f, Illustration 15.

Open and notorious. As in adverse possession cases, this element is designed to ensure that the owner has an opportunity to notice that an adverse use is occurring.

Problem: O owns Blackacre, which includes a body of fresh water known to *O* to contain eels. Because eels are active at night, *A*, an eel fisherman, regularly comes onto Blackacre during nocturnal hours to fish for eels. *O* is unaware of his presence, but does find occasional matted grass and other indications of an intruder on the land. *O* also notices that the eels are diminishing in abundance. *A* sells his eels to local connoisseurs of them and, like many fishermen, *A* does not reveal to others where he catches his eels, though he is widely known in the community as the "eel guy." *A*'s activity continues for the prescriptive period. Has *A* acquired an easement to enter Blackacre and a profit to take eels?

Exclusive. In slavish imitation of adverse possession law, some courts require that the use also be exclusive, but this element (which makes sense when the issue is title) has much less relevance to claims of adverse use. A roadway, for example, is likely to be used not only by the claimant of the easement, but also by his invitees, perhaps the owner of the putative servient estate, and the occasional stranger who is lost or nosy. Thus, courts that appreciate this fact hold that exclusivity, to the extent required at all, means that the use is exercised independently of others— that the claimed right is not dependent on use by others, as might be true of a prescriptive easement claimed by the general public. It does not mean that the use must be confined only to the claimant. See, e.g., Montana State Fish & Game Comm'n v. Cronin, 179 Mont. 481, 587 P.2d 395 (1978); Palisades Sales Corp. v. Walsh, 459 A.2d 933 (R.I.1983); Burks Bros. of Virginia, Inc. v. Jones, 232 Va. 238, 349 S.E.2d 134 (1986).

Uninterrupted. The use must be continuous for the period. A use may be interrupted by voluntary abandonment or by some action on the part of the owner. Obviously, a successful lawsuit to terminate the use is one such action, but what of various forms of self help? The Restatement (Third) of Property, Servitudes § 2.17, comment f, states that a "physical interference with the use is effective only if it brings about a cessation of use. If the adverse user resumes the use, the interruption has not been successful unless the cessation of use was long enough to indicate abandonment." But is this statement universally true? Consider the following problem:

Problem: O owns Blackacre, a summer home on the shore. Every summer *A*, his neighbor, beats the same path across Blackacre to reach the sea. Before the prescriptive period runs, *O* delivers a letter by hand to *A* that states: "Blackacre is mine. I own it in fee simple absolute. You have no right to enter upon Blackacre and, in particular, you commit trespass every time you use the path you have created to reach the sea. I expressly forbid you from using that path or entering upon Blackacre." *A* ignores the letter and continues to use the path. Has *A*'s use been sufficiently interrupted in 1) a jurisdiction adhering to the fiction of the lost grant, and 2) a jurisdiction that rejects the lost grant rationale? Would it make any difference in either type of jurisdiction if *O* had blocked the path with razor wire but *A* had promptly used wire cutters to remove the blockage and continued his use?

As with adverse possession, prescriptive easements may not be perfected against the government.

3. *Public Prescriptive Easements.* Prescriptive easements may arise in favor of the general public as well as a specific private user. The requirements for a public prescriptive easement are the same as for a private prescriptive easement, except that the use must be by the general public and that public use must be sufficiently open and notorious to provide actual or constructive notice to the owner of the public's adverse use. See, e.g., Auerbach v. Parker, 558 So.2d 900 (Ala. 1989). To prevent public use from ripening into a prescriptive easement, at common law a landowner must interrupt the use by physically blocking the public from the use for a period sufficient to establish abandonment of the use. However, by statute, some states prevent a public prescriptive easement from arising, no matter how long the use may continue without interruption, if the landowner posts notices that the right to pass is by permission of the owner and may be revoked at any time. See, e.g., Calif. Civil Code § 1008.

An alternative method of acquiring a public prescriptive easement is by dedication, which can be express or implied. Dedication requires an offer of public use by the owner and acceptance by the public. If a developer subdivides property and records a subdivision map to delineate the streets and lots thus created, and states that the streets are dedicated to public use, an express easement by dedication has arisen so long as the public accepts the offer. If the subdivision map says nothing about dedication of the streets to the public, a question of fact arises whether the developer has impliedly offered to dedicate the streets to public use and, if so, whether that offer has been accepted by the public.

Problem: O owns Green Acres, a 40 acre tract, that he subdivides into 40 lots, with four streets running through Green Acres, each connecting to a publicly owned thoroughfare. *O* constructs the streets at his expense and begins to sell lots. Has an easement by dedication been created under any of the following circumstances?

a. Before commencing construction, *O* records the subdivision map, which is silent about dedication. Without objection from *O*, the city cleans and repairs the streets within the subdivision.

b. Before commencing construction, *O* records the subdivision map, which is silent about dedication. Over *O*'s strenuous objections, the city cleans and repairs the streets within the subdivision.

c. Before commencing construction, *O* records the subdivision map, which states that the streets are dedicated to public use. *O* builds gates at each of the street entrances to Green Acres, and limits access to residents of Green Acres and their invitees. The city does not maintain the streets.

d. Before commencing construction, *O* records the subdivision map, which states that the streets are dedicated to public use. There is no observable difference between the publicly owned thoroughfares and the streets in Green Acres. The city does not maintain or clean the streets, but does use the streets for police patrols and emergency fire and medical responses.

e. Public Trust and Public Customary Usage

Another way for the public to acquire easements to use private property is through application of the public trust doctrine or its close kin, ancient customary use by the public.

RALEIGH AVENUE BEACH ASSOCIATION v. ATLANTIS BEACH CLUB, INC.

Supreme Court of New Jersey
185 N.J. 40 (2005)

PORITZ, C.J., delivered the opinion of the court.

This case raises a question about the right of the public to use a 480-foot wide stretch of upland sand beach in Lower Township, Cape May County, owned by respondent Atlantis Beach Club, Inc., and operated as a private club. We hold today that ... the public trust doctrine requires the Atlantis property to be open to the general public at a reasonable fee for services provided by the owner and approved by the Department of Environmental Protection [DEP].

I. Atlantis Beach Club, Inc. (Atlantis or Beach Club) is the successor in title to a Riparian Grant, dated January 17, 1907, from the State of New Jersey to the Cape May Real Estate Company. The grant encompassed a large area not relevant to this litigation except for certain submerged land that, in 1907, was located within the bed of Turtle Gut Inlet, a body of water that connected to the Atlantic Ocean. ... No longer submerged, [that land] extends to the mean high water line from a bulkhead running north/south along the western boundary of the property. That western boundary lies to the east of an unpaved section of Raleigh Avenue (which runs east/west), [and] consists of dry sand beach and protected dunes. The distance from the bulkhead ... to the mean high water line is about 342 feet. Persons using the beach for recreational purposes cross over the bulkhead by walking on a boardwalk pathway that traverses the dunes and curves southward to the beach. The dry sand beach area lies beyond the dunes and extends to the mean high water line. A pathway runs east/west along the unpaved section of Raleigh Avenue to the approximate midpoint of the bulkhead and then ... across the bulkhead and through the dunes....

[The] La Vida del Mar Condominiums (La Vida), a four-story, twenty-four-unit condominium structure along Raleigh Avenue [lies] immediately to the west of the bulkhead along the western boundary of the Atlantis property. [As a condition to granting a permit to build La Vida, the DEP (pursuant to a New Jersey law regulating coastal construction) required La Vida (then the owner of the Atlantis Beach Club property) to permit permanent public access to the foreshore along the boardwalk path through the dunes to the beach. Atlantis later acquired control of the beachfront property from La Vida.] Another four-story multiple unit condominium complex called the La Quinta del Mar sits to the south of La Vida and the path that runs from the end of the pavement on Raleigh Avenue and over the bulkhead. To the west of La Quinta del Mar are the Villa House and La Quinta Towers, both of which contain residential units. Seapointe Village (Seapointe) is located to the north of La Vida and consists of several structures, including a six-story, one-hundred-room hotel, and more than five hundred residential units. Seapointe occupies 63.4 acres, including the beach property to the north of the Atlantis beach....

When the Seapointe property was developed, the DEP, as a condition of [the building] permit, required the beach in front of Seapointe to be open to the public. Under the terms of the permit, Seapointe is allowed to sell daily, weekly, and seasonal beach passes at rates approved by the DEP, although residents can access the area beyond the mean high water line free-of-charge. Public access through Seapointe's beach along the water's edge is also free-of-charge, [as this wet sand foreshore is owned by the state of New Jersey,] and beach usage fees, regulations, and operations are subject to continued periodic review and approval by the DEP. Seapointe provides lifeguards on its beach, as well as public restrooms, outdoor showers, and parking facilities. In August 2002 when this litigation began, the rates for use of the Seapointe beach were, per person, $2.50 a day, $10 a week, and $40 a season....

The United States Coast Guard owns the property to the south of the Atlantis beach. That property is closed to the public from April 1 through August 15 to protect the piping plover, an endangered species, during breeding season. Although the Coast Guard beach is unavailable for most of the summer season, the property is open to the public the rest of the year.

Atlantis is located in the Diamond Beach neighborhood, a residential area of approximately three blocks by nine blocks that contains the only beach in Lower Township facing the Atlantic Ocean. In addition to the beach access point on the Atlantis property at the end of Raleigh Avenue, there are two other access points in Diamond Beach north of Atlantis.... [The] closest free entry to the beach is Dune Drive, a nine-block walk from Raleigh Avenue and a distance of approximately one-half mile. The beach access problem in Lower Township is further compounded by the limited number of parking spaces available in the Diamond Beach neighborhood.

Until 1996, the beach on the Atlantis property was open to the public free-of-charge. In the summer of 1996, however, Atlantis established a private beach club.... The club limited public access to its beach by charging a fee of $300 for six seasonal beach tags. As of July 2003, a sign posted on the gate at the entrance to the Atlantis beach read: "FREE PUBLIC ACCESS ENDS HERE/MEMBERSHIP AVAILABLE AT GATE." Atlantis's 2003 Rules and Regulations, also posted, provided the following warning:

> ANYONE ATTEMPTING TO USE, ENTER UPON OR CROSS OVER CLUB PROPERTY FOR ANY REASON WITHOUT CLUB PERMISSION OR WHO IS NOT IN POSSESSION OF A VALID TAG AND AUTHORIZED TO USE SUCH TAG WILL BE SUBJECT TO PROSECUTION, CIVIL AND OR CRIMINAL[,] TO THE FULL-EST EXTENT PERMITTED BY LAW[,] INCLUDING ALL COSTS AND LEGAL FEES INCURRED BY THE CLUB.

Prior to the commencement of this litigation, the membership fee for new members and members who had joined the beach club in 2002 was set at $700 for the 2003 summer season. Members were entitled to eight beach tags per household. Atlantis also sold "Access Easements" at $10,000 each, paid in cash. Easement holders were required to pay an annual membership fee [amounting to their pro rata share of the operating costs of] the beach club....

II. On June 22, 2002, Tony Labrosciano, a member of the Association, was issued a summons for trespassing when he attempted to leave the wet sand area and walk across the Atlantis property to the eastern terminus of Raleigh Avenue in order to take the most direct route back to his home. On July 26, 2002, Atlantis filed [suit] to enjoin Labrosciano and members of his class from "trespassing, entering onto and accessing" the Atlantis property, and declaring that Atlantis is not required to provide the public with access to or use of any portion of its property or the adjacent ocean. The Association, which consists of individuals who reside on Raleigh Avenue in the Diamond Beach neighborhood, filed a complaint on August 14, 2002 against Atlantis ... and the State of New Jersey. The Association claimed that Atlantis was in violation of the public trust doctrine and sought free public access through the Atlantis property to the beach, and to a sufficient amount of dry sand above the mean high water line to permit the public to enjoy the beach and beach-related activities. That Association action was subsequently consolidated with the Atlantis action....

[The] DEP moved . . . for partial summary judgment and dismissal of all claims against it. The [DEP] sought a ruling [that] the beach along the Atlantic Ocean in the Diamond Beach area is subject to the public trust doctrine such that an individual can walk along the ocean shore on the Atlantis property without fear of prosecution for trespassing. . . . [The trial court] held that the public was entitled to a right of horizontal access to the ocean by means of "a three-foot wide strip of dry sand, immediately landward of the mean high water line and extending from the northern to the southern boundaries of [the Atlantis] [p]roperty, which may be utilized by the public, at no charge, for the purpose of entering into and exiting from" the area located below the mean high water line. The trial court also held that the public was entitled to limited vertical access to the ocean, consisting [solely] of a path from the bulkhead through the dunes on the property. . . . Finally, Atlantis was prohibited from charging a fee or otherwise restricting the right of the public to horizontal or vertical ocean access. The [trial] court determined, however, that the provision of such services as lifeguards, equipment, or other facilities by Atlantis would entitle the Beach Club, on application to and with the DEP's approval, to charge a commercially reasonable fee to members of the public who use the horizontal access to swim in the ocean. The [trial] court denied without prejudice the Atlantis application to amend its pleadings so as to assert a regulatory takings claim.

The State and the Association appealed. . . . [The Appellate Division ruled] that "Atlantis cannot limit vertical or horizontal public access to its dry sand beach area nor interfere with the public's right to free use of the dry sand for intermittent recreational purposes connected with the ocean and wet sand," [but] could charge a fee to members of the public who remain on and use its beach for an extended period of time, as long as Atlantis cleans the beach, picks up trash regularly, and provides shower facilities. The panel ruled further that Atlantis was required to provide customary lifeguard services for members of the public who use the ocean areas up to the mean high water line, regardless of whether those individuals remain on the Atlantis beach area or merely pass through. Reasonable and comparable fees, approved by the DEP, would be allowed in an amount sufficient to cover operating costs, including an amount related to management services. . . . [We] granted certification. . . .

III.   The law we are asked to interpret in this case—the public trust doctrine—derives from the English common law principle that all of the land covered by tidal waters belongs to the sovereign held in trust for the people to use. Borough of Neptune City v. Borough of Avon-by-the-Sea, 61 N.J. 296, 303, 294 A.2d 47 (1972). That common law principle, in turn, has roots

> in Roman jurisprudence, which held that "[b]y the law of nature[,] . . . the air, running water, the sea, and consequently the shores of the sea," were "common to mankind." . . . No one was forbidden access to the sea, and everyone could use the seashore "to dry his nets there, and haul them from the sea. . . ." The seashore was not private

property, but "subject to the same law as the sea itself, and the sand or ground beneath it." [Matthews v. Bay Head Improvement Ass'n, 95 N.J. 306, 316–317, 471 A.2d 355, *cert. denied*, Bay Head Improvement Ass'n v. Matthews, 469 U.S. 821, 105 S. Ct. 93, 83 L. Ed. 2d 39 (1984),

In Arnold v. Mundy, 6 N.J.L. 1, 53 (E. & A.1821), the first case to affirm and reformulate the public trust doctrine in New Jersey, the Court explained that upon the Colonies' victory in the Revolutionary War, the English sovereign's rights to the tidal waters "became vested in the people of New Jersey as the sovereign of the country, and are now in their hands." [The] land on which water ebbs and flows, including the land between the high and low water, belongs not to the owners of the lands adjacent to the water, but to the State, "to be held, protected, and regulated for the common use and benefit."

Early understanding of the scope of the public trust doctrine focused on the preservation of the "natural water resources" of New Jersey "for navigation and commerce ... and fishing, an important source of food." In *Neptune City* the Court extended public rights in tidal lands "to recreational uses, including bathing, swimming and other shore activities." We invalidated a municipal ordinance that required non-residents of Avon-by-the-Sea to pay a higher fee than the residents of Avon were required to pay to access and use the town's beaches. The Court held:

> [A]t least where the upland sand area is owned by a municipality ... and dedicated to public beach purposes, ... the public trust doctrine dictates that the beach and the ocean waters must be open to all on equal terms and without preference and that any contrary state or municipal action is impermissible.

Later, in *Matthews*, we considered "the extent of the public's interest in privately-owned dry sand beaches," which, we noted, "may [include both] a right to cross ... privately owned ... beaches in order to gain access to the foreshore ... [and a] right to sunbathe and generally enjoy recreational activities" on the dry sands. We observed that New Jersey's beaches constitute a "unique" and "irreplaceable" resource, subject to increased pressure from population growth throughout the region and improved transportation to the shore. Concerned about the great demand and the limited number of beaches open to the public, we repeated:

> Exercise of the public's right to swim and bathe below the mean high water mark may depend upon a right to pass across the upland beach. Without some means of access the public right to use the foreshore would be meaningless. To say that the public trust doctrine entitles the public to swim in the ocean and to use the foreshore in connection therewith without assuring the public of a feasible access route would seriously impinge on, if not effectively eliminate, the rights of the public trust doctrine.

Matthews clearly articulates the concept already implicit in our case law that reasonable access to the sea is integral to the public trust doctrine. Indeed, as *Matthews* points out, without access the doctrine has no meaning.

That leaves the question raised in this case: whether use of the dry sand ancillary to use of the ocean for recreation purposes is also implicit in the rights that belong to the public under the doctrine. *Matthews* states unequivocally that a "bather's right in the upland sands is not limited to passage . . . [and that] [r]easonable enjoyment of the foreshore and the sea cannot be realized unless some enjoyment of the dry sand area is also allowed." Because the activity of swimming "must be accompanied by intermittent periods of rest and relaxation beyond the water's edge," the lack of an area available to the public for that purpose "would seriously curtail and in many situations eliminate the right to the recreational use of the ocean." Although the *Matthews* Court did not compare that use of the dry sand to use associated with ancient fishing rights, it did point out that under Roman law, "everyone could use the seashore 'to dry his nets there, and haul them from the sea . . . .'" (quoting Justinian *Institutes* 2.1.1) (T. Sandars trans. 1st Am. ed. 1876). It follows . . . then, that use of the dry sand has long been a correlate to use of the ocean and is a component part of the rights associated with the public trust doctrine.

The factual context in which *Matthews* was decided was critical to the Court's holding. *Neptune City* had held that the general public must be allowed to use a municipally-owned dry sand beach on equal terms with residents of the municipality. *Matthews* involved a private non-profit entity, the Bay Head Improvement Association (Improvement Association), that owned/leased and operated certain upland sand areas in the Borough of Bay Head for the recreational use of Bay Head residents only. The Improvement Association was closely connected with the municipality, which provided at various points in time, office space, liability insurance, and funding, among other things. That symbiotic relationship, as well as the public nature of the activities conducted by the Improvement Association, led the Court to conclude that the Improvement Association was in reality a "quasi-public body" bound by the *Neptune City* holding.

Although decided on narrow grounds, *Matthews* established the framework for application of the public trust doctrine to privately-owned upland sand beaches. The *Matthews* approach begins with the general principle that public use of the upland sands is "subject to an accommodation of the interests of the owner," and proceeds by setting forth criteria for a case-by-case consideration in respect of the appropriate level of accommodation. The Court's formulation bears repeating here:

> [We] perceive the public trust doctrine not to be "fixed or static," but one to "be molded and extended to meet changing conditions and needs of the public it was created to benefit." . . .
>
> Precisely what privately-owned upland sand area will be available and required to satisfy the public's rights under the public trust doctrine will depend on the circumstances. Location of the dry sand area in relation to the foreshore, extent and availability of publicly-

owned upland sand area, nature and extent of the public demand, and usage of the upland sand land by the owner are all factors to be weighed and considered in fixing the contours of the usage of the upper sand. Today, recognizing the increasing demand for our State's beaches and the dynamic nature of the public trust doctrine, we find that the public must be given both access to and use of privately-owned dry sand areas as reasonably necessary. While the public's rights in private beaches are not coextensive with the rights enjoyed in municipal beaches, private landowners may not in all instances prevent the public from exercising its rights under the public trust doctrine. The public must be afforded reasonable access to the fore-shore as well as a suitable area for recreation on the dry sand.

IV.   We turn now to an application of the *Matthews* factors to the circumstances of this case. . . . [The court noted that the Atlantis Beach Club property abutted the foreshore, there were no publicly-owned beaches in the vicinity,] there is enormous public interest in the New Jersey shore . . .; tourism associated with New Jersey's beaches is a $16 billion annual industry, [and the Atlantis Beach Club property had been used by the general public without fee until 1996.]

The private beach property held by Atlantis is an area of undeveloped upland sand and dunes at the end of a street in a town that does not have public beaches. The owner, after years of public access and use, and despite a condition in the La Vida [DEP] permit providing for access and, arguably use, decided in 1996 to engage in a commercial enterprise—a private beach club—that kept the public from the beach. Atlantis . . . asserts that it will lose one of the "sticks" in its bundle of property rights if it cannot charge whatever the market will bear, and, in setting fees for membership, decide who can come onto its property and use its beach and other services (lifeguards, trash removal, organized activities, etc.). But exclusivity of use, in the context here, has long been subject to the strictures of the public trust doctrine.

In sum, based on the circumstances in this case and on application of the *Matthews* factors, we hold that the Atlantis upland sands must be available for use by the general public under the public trust doctrine. In so holding we highlight the longstanding public access to and use of the beach, the La Vida . . . permit condition, the documented public demand, the lack of publicly-owned beaches in Lower Township, and the type of use by the current owner as a business enterprise. . . .

V.   [The court concluded that the New Jersey DEP had the power to regulate any fees charged by Atlantis for public use of its property.] Atlantis, as a private entity, should be allowed to include expenses actually incurred for reasonable management services (in addition to reimbursement for other costs) in the fee calculation. We add only that DEP-approved fees are unrelated to the independent and inherent right of Atlantis to provide cabanas for rent, at a rate determined by the Beach Club and after obtaining a permit to construct or place such buildings on its property, or to engage in other similar business enterprises for profit, *e.g.,* beach chair rentals, food concessions, etc.

VI. For the reasons expressed in this opinion, the decision of the Appellate Division is affirmed.

NOTES AND QUESTIONS

1. Regulatory Taking? In Chapter Twelve you will encounter the problem of regulatory takings. The takings clause of the U.S. Constitution requires that when private property is taken for public use the owner must be paid just compensation. U.S. Const., Amend V. In some circumstances, a regulation of property use may be so onerous that it is deemed to be a taking of the owner's property. The circumstances under which that occurs is the predominant subject of Chapter Twelve. One of the issues in regulatory takings is whether, and to what extent, a judicial decision can constitute a taking of private property. In Stop the Beach Renourishment, Inc. v. Florida Department of Environmental Protection, 130 S.Ct. 2592 (2010), the United States Supreme Court could not agree that such a judicial taking had occurred, or even whether it was necessary to address the issue. Four justices opined that judicial decisions could constitute a taking. The issue was whether the Florida Supreme Court had taken private property by its decision that the portion of a beach that consisted of newly created dry sand (as a result of governmental response to hurricane erosion) belonged to the state and not the littoral landowner. Assuming that judicial decisions can constitute takings, did the New Jersey Supreme Court, in *Raleigh Beach*, take the Atlantis Beach Club's property? Keep that issue in mind when you study Chapter Twelve.

2. Dedication, Prescription, and Customary Use. In addition to invocation of the public trust doctrine, courts have grounded public rights to use beaches in implied dedication, prescription, and ancient customary use. Decisions finding implied dedication include Gion v. City of Santa Cruz, 2 Cal.3d 29 (1970); Villa Nova Resort, Inc. v. Texas, 711 S.W.2d 120 (Tex. Ct. App. 1986). Decisions grounding access to and use of beaches on customary use by the public include City of Daytona Beach v. Tona–Rama, Inc., 294 So.2d 73 (Fla. 1974); State ex rel. Thornton v. Hay, 254 Ore. 584 (1969) (limited to ocean beaches only by McDonald v. Halvorson, 308 Ore. 340 (1989)); Pele Defense Fund v. Paty, 73 Haw. 578 (1992) (recognizing ancient and continuous customary rights of access and removal of items necessary for subsistence or cultural or religious purposes). Customary usage doctrine is a variant of prescription because it usually rests on a showing that the public use has existed from before the memory of living persons, and thus taps into the historical roots of prescription. Finally, cases finding the public right to be an application of the ordinary law of prescription include Concerned Citizens of Brunswick County Taxpayers Association v. Holden Beach Enterprises, Inc., 329 N.C. 37 (1991); Moody v. White, 593 S.W.2d 372 (Tex Civ. App. 1979) (also dedication).

3. Is the Earth's Atmosphere held in Public Trust? In 2011, an environmental group called Our Children's Trust filed a number of federal and state lawsuits alleging that the atmosphere is held in public trust and that, as a result, state and federal officials are obliged to take action to limit the extent of carbon emissions that contribute to global warming.[3] Is the atmosphere part of the public trust? If so, who holds it in trust?

2. TRANSFERABILITY OF EASEMENTS

By their nature, easements appurtenant are transferable. When the estate to which an easement is appurtenant is transferred the easement automatically follows, "like a dog's tail goes along with the sale of the dog." Cunningham, Stoebuck, and Whitman, The Law of Property 461, § 8.10 (2d ed. 1993). See Restatement (Third) of Property, § 5.1. An easement appurtenant may not be severed from ownership or possession of the property it benefits, unless the parties creating the easement intended to permit severance. Restatement (Third) of Property, Servitudes § 5.16 (3). *must be intent to sever*

But what about easements or profits in gross? If the use right granted is personal to the user, should the holder of the easement have the power to transfer the right? If so, may such a person subdivide the right by granting his use right to multiple people? These issues appear in the following case.

MILLER v. LUTHERAN CONFERENCE AND CAMP ASSOCIATION

Supreme Court of Pennsylvania
331 Pa. 241 (1938)

STERN, J., delivered the opinion of the court.

This litigation is concerned with interesting and somewhat novel legal questions regarding rights of boating, bathing and fishing in an artificial lake.

Frank C. Miller, his brother Rufus W. Miller, and others, who owned *Facts* lands on Tunkhannock Creek ... organized a corporation known as the Pocono Spring Water Ice Company, to which, in September, 1895, they made a lease for a term of ninety-nine years of so much of their lands as would be covered by the backing up of the water as a result of the construction of a 14–foot dam which they proposed to erect across the creek. The company was to have "the exclusive use of the water and its privileges." It was chartered for the purpose of "erecting a dam ..., for pleasure, boating, skating, fishing and the cutting, storing and selling of ice." The dam was built, forming "Lake Naomi," somewhat more than a mile long and about one-third of a mile wide.

By deed dated March 20, 1899, the Pocono Spring Water Ice Company granted to "Frank C. Miller, his heirs and assigns forever, the exclusive right to fish and boat in all the waters of the said corporation at Naomi Pines, Pa." On February 17, 1900, Frank C. Miller (his wife Katherine D.

---

3. See http://www.ourchildrenstrust.org/legal-action/lawsuits for links to the complaints.

Miller not joining) granted to Rufus W. Miller, his heirs and assigns forever, "all the one-fourth interest in and to the fishing, boating, and bathing rights and privileges at, in, upon and about Lake Naomi ...; which said rights and privileges were granted and conveyed to me by the Pocono Spring Water Ice Company by their indenture of the 20th day of March, A.D. 1899." On the same day Frank C. Miller and Rufus W. Miller executed an agreement of business partnership, the purpose of which was the erection and operation of boat and bath houses on Naomi Lake and the purchase and maintenance of boats for use on the lake, the houses and boats to be rented for hire and the net proceeds to be divided between the parties in proportion to their respective interests in the bathing, boating and fishing privileges, namely, three-fourths to Frank C. Miller and one-fourth to Rufus W. Miller, the capital to be contributed and the losses to be borne in the same proportion. In pursuance of this agreement the brothers erected and maintained boat and bath houses at different points on the lake, purchased and rented out boats, and conducted the business generally, from the spring of 1900 until the death of Rufus W. Miller on October 11, 1925, exercising their control and use of the privileges in an exclusive, uninterrupted and open manner and without challenge on the part of anyone.

Discord began with the death of Rufus W. Miller, which terminated the partnership. Thereafter Frank C. Miller, and the executors and heirs of Rufus W. Miller, went their respective ways, each granting licenses without reference to the other. Under date of July 13, 1929, the executors of the Rufus W. Miller estate granted a license for the year 1929 to defendant, Lutheran Conference and Camp Association, which was the owner of a tract of ground abutting on the lake for a distance of about 100 feet, purporting to grant to defendant, its members, guests and campers, permission to boat, bathe and fish in the lake, a certain percentage of the receipts therefrom to be paid to the estate. Thereupon Frank C. Miller and his wife, Katherine D. Miller, filed the present bill in equity, complaining that defendant was placing diving floats on the lake and "encouraging and instigating visitors and boarders" to bathe in the lake, and was threatening to hire out boats and canoes and in general to license its guests and others to boat, bathe and fish in the lake. The bill prayed for an injunction to prevent defendant from trespassing on the lands covered by the waters of the lake, from erecting or maintaining any structures or other encroachments thereon, and from granting any bathing licenses. The court issued the injunction.

It is the contention of plaintiffs that, while the privileges of boating and fishing were granted in the deed from the Pocono Spring Water Ice Company to Frank C. Miller, no bathing rights were conveyed by that instrument. In 1903 all the property of the company was sold by the sheriff under a writ of *fieri facias*[4] on a mortgage bond which the company had executed in 1898. As a result of that sale the Pocono Spring Water Ice Company was entirely extinguished, and the title to its rights and proper-

---

4. Ed.—A writ of *fieri facias* is a writ of execution to collect a judgment.

ty came into the ownership of the Pocono Pines Ice Company, a corporation chartered for "the supply of ice to the public." In 1928 the title to the property of the Pocono Pines Ice Company became vested in Katherine D. Miller. Plaintiffs therefore maintain that the bathing rights, never having passed to Frank C. Miller, descended in ownership from the Pocono Spring Water Ice Company through the Pocono Pines Ice Company to plaintiff Katherine D. Miller, and that Frank C. Miller could not, and did not, give Rufus W. Miller any title to them. They further contend that even if such bathing rights ever did vest in Frank C. Miller, all of the boating, bathing and fishing privileges were easements in gross which were inalienable and indivisible, and when Frank C. Miller undertook to convey a one-fourth interest in them to Rufus W. Miller he not only failed to transfer a legal title to the rights but, in attempting to do so, extinguished the rights altogether as against Katherine D. Miller, who was the successor in title of the Pocono Spring Water Ice Company. It is defendant's contention, on the other hand, that the deed of 1899 from the Pocono Spring Water Ice Company to Frank C. Miller should be construed as transferring the bathing as well as the boating and fishing privileges, but that if Frank C. Miller did not obtain them by grant he and Rufus W. Miller acquired them by prescription, and that all of these rights were alienable and divisible even if they be considered as easements in gross, although they might more properly, perhaps, be regarded as licenses which became irrevocable because of the money spent upon their development by Frank C. Miller and Rufus W. Miller. . . .

[It] is initially to be observed that no boating, bathing or fishing rights can be, or are, claimed by defendant as a riparian owner. Ordinarily, title to land bordering on a navigable stream extends to low water mark subject to the rights of the public to navigation and fishery between high and low water, and in the case of land abutting on creeks and non-navigable rivers to the middle of the stream, but in the case of a non-navigable lake or pond where the land under the water is owned by others, no riparian rights attach to the property bordering on the water, and an attempt to exercise any such rights by invading the water is as much a trespass as if an unauthorized entry were made upon the dry land of another.

It is impossible to construe the deed of 1899 from the Pocono Spring Water Ice Company to Frank C. Miller as conveying to the latter any privileges of bathing. It is clear and unambiguous. It gives to Frank C. Miller the exclusive right to fish and boat. *Expressio unius est exclusio alterius.* No bathing rights are mentioned. This omission may have been [an] oversight or it may have been deliberate, but in either event the legal consequence is the same. . . . But, while Frank C. Miller acquired by grant merely boating and fishing privileges, the facts are amply sufficient to establish title to the bathing rights by prescription. True, these rights, not having been granted in connection with, or to be attached to, the ownership of any land, were not easements appurtenant but in gross. There is, however, no inexorable principle of law which forbids an adverse enjoy-

ment of an easement in gross from ripening into a title thereto by
prescription. .... Certainly the casual use of a lake during a few months
each year for boating and fishing could not develop into a title to such
privileges by prescription. But here the exercise of the bathing right was
not carried on sporadically by Frank C. Miller and his assignee Rufus W.
Miller for their personal enjoyment but systematically for commercial
purposes in the pursuit of which they conducted an extensive and profitable business enterprise. The circumstances thus presented must be
viewed from a realistic standpoint. Naomi Lake is situated in the Pocono
Mountains district, has become a summer resort for campers and boarders, and, except for the ice it furnishes, its bathing and boating facilities
are the factors which give it its prime importance and value. They were
exploited from the time the lake was created, and are recited as among the
purposes for which the Pocono Spring Water Ice Company was chartered.
From the early part of 1900 down to at least the filing of the present bill
in 1929, Frank C. Miller and Rufus W. Miller openly carried on their
business of constructing and operating bath houses and licensing individuals and camp associations to use the lake for bathing. This was known to
the stockholders of the Pocono Spring Water Ice Company and necessarily
also to Katherine D. Miller, the wife of Frank C. Miller; no objection of
any kind was made, and Frank C. Miller and Rufus W. Miller were
encouraged to expend large sums of money in pursuance of the right of
which they considered and asserted themselves to be the owners. Under
such circumstances it would be highly unjust to hold that a title by
prescription to the bathing rights did not vest in Frank C. Miller and
Rufus W. Miller which is just as valid, as far as Katherine D. Miller is
concerned, as that to the boating and fishing rights which Frank C. Miller
obtained by express grant.

We are thus brought to a consideration of the next question, which is
whether the boating, bathing and fishing privileges were assignable by
Frank C. Miller to Rufus W. Miller. What is the nature of such rights? In
England it has been said that easements in gross do not exist at all,
although rights of that kind have been there recognized. In this country
such privileges have sometimes been spoken of as licenses, or as contractual in their nature, rather than as easements in gross. These are differences
of terminology rather than of substance. [T]hese privileges are easements
in gross, and we see no reason to consider them otherwise. It has
uniformly been held that a profit in gross—for example, a right of mining
or fishing—may be made assignable.... In regard to easements in gross
generally, there has been much controversy in the courts and by textbook
writers and law students as to whether they have the attribute of
assignability. There are dicta in Pennsylvania that they are non-assignable
[but] there is forcible expression and even definite authority to the
contrary. Learned articles upon the subject are to be found in 32 Yale Law
Journal 813; 38 Yale Law Journal 139; 22 Michigan Law Review 521; 40
Dickinson Law Review 46. There does not seem to be any reason why the
law should prohibit the assignment of an easement in gross if the parties

to its creation evidence their intention to make it assignable. Here, ... the rights of fishing and boating were conveyed to the grantee—in this case Frank C. Miller—"his heirs and assigns," thus showing that the grantor, the Pocono Spring Water Ice Company, intended to attach the attribute of assignability to the privileges granted. Moreover, as a practical matter, there is an obvious difference in this respect between easements for personal enjoyment and those designed for commercial exploitation; while there may be little justification for permitting assignments in the former case, there is every reason for upholding them in the latter.

The question of assignability of the easements in gross in the present case is not as important as that of their divisibility. It is argued by plaintiffs that even if held to be assignable such easements are not divisible, because this might involve an excessive user or "surcharge of the easement" subjecting the servient tenement to a greater burden than originally contemplated. The law does not take that extreme position. It does require, however, that, if there be a division, the easements must be used or exercised as an entirety. This rule had its earliest expression in Mountjoy's Case, [Earl of Huntingdon v. Lord Mountjoy, 1 And. 307, 123 Eng. Rep. 488, Godb. 17, 78 Eng. Rep. 11 (C.P. 1583),] which is reported in Co. Litt. 164b, 165a. It was there said, in regard to the grant of a right to dig for ore, that the grantee, Lord Mountjoy, "might assign his whole interest to one, two, or more; but then, if there be two or more, they could make no division of it, but work together with one stock." In Caldwell v. Fulton, 31 Pa. 475, 477, 478, and in Funk v. Haldeman, 53 Pa. 229, that case was followed, and it was held that the right of a grantee to mine coal or to prospect for oil might be assigned, but if to more than one they must hold, enjoy and convey the right as an entirety, and not divide it in severalty. There are cases in other jurisdictions which also approve the doctrine of Mountjoy's Case, and hold that a mining right in gross is essentially integral and not susceptible of apportionment; an assignment of it is valid, but it cannot be [alienated] in such a way that it may be utilized by grantor and grantee, or by several grantees, separately; there must be a joint user, nor can one of the tenants alone convey a share in the common right: ... Harlow v. Lake Superior Iron Co., 36 Mich. 105, 121; Stanton v. T. L. Herbert & Sons, 141 Tenn. 440, 211 S.W. 353.

These authorities furnish an illuminating guide to the solution of the problem of divisibility of profits or easements in gross. They indicate that much depends upon the nature of the right and the terms of its creation, that "surcharge of the easement" is prevented if assignees exercise the right as "one stock," and that a proper method of enjoyment of the easement by two or more owners of it may usually be worked out in any given instance without insuperable difficulty.

In the present case it seems reasonably clear that in the conveyance of February 17, 1900, it was not the intention of Frank C. Miller to grant, and of Rufus W. Miller to receive, a separate right to subdivide and sublicense the boating, fishing and bathing privileges on and in Lake Naomi, but only that they should together use such rights for commercial purposes, Rufus W. Miller to be entitled to one-fourth and Frank C. Miller to three-fourths of the proceeds resulting from their combined exploitation of the privileges. They were to hold the rights, in the quaint phraseology of Mountjoy's Case, as "one stock." Nor do the technical rules that would be applicable to a tenancy in common of a corporeal hereditament apply to the control of these easements in gross. Defendant contends that, as a tenant in common of the privileges, Rufus W. Miller individually was entitled to their use, benefit and possession and to exercise rights of ownership in regard thereto, including the right to license third persons to use them, subject only to the limitation that he must not thereby interfere with the similar rights of his co-tenant. But the very nature of these easements prevents their being so exercised, inasmuch as it is necessary, because of the legal limitations upon their divisibility, that they should be utilized in common, and not by two owners severally, and, as stated, this was evidently the intention of the brothers.

[We] are of opinion (1) that Frank C. Miller acquired title to the boating and fishing privileges by grant and he and Rufus W. Miller to the bathing rights by prescription; (2) that he made a valid assignment of a one-fourth interest in them to Rufus W. Miller; but (3) that they cannot be commercially used and licenses thereunder granted without the common consent and joinder of the present owners, who with regard to them must act as "one stock." It follows that the executors of the estate of Rufus W. Miller did not have the right, in and by themselves, to grant a license to defendant.

NOTES, QUESTIONS, AND PROBLEMS

✱ (1.) *The Common Law Rule.* English common law held that personal rights of the sort that American courts style as easements in gross were not transferable, and were extinguished by any attempt to transfer them. See Ackroyd v. Smith, 138 Eng. Rep. 68 (1850). The traditional rule of American common law was that commercial easements in gross were freely assignable, but the transferability of personal easements in gross was more problematic. A few cases held that personal easements in gross were not assignable unless the parties intended for the benefit to be assigned. See, e.g., Drye v. Eagle Rock Ranch, Inc., 364 S.W.2d 196 (Tex. 1962); Maw v. Weber Basin Water Conservancy District, 20 Utah 2d 195 (1968); Gilbert v. Workman's Circle Camp of the New York Branches, Inc., 282 N.Y.S.2d 293 (1967); Williams v. Diederich, 359 Mo. 683 (1949). The commercial/personal distinction was frequently challenged as unsupported by case law and ungrounded in any sound policy. See, e.g., Lewis Simes, Assignability of Easements in Gross in American Law, 22 Mich. L. Rev. 521 (1924); Charles E. Clark, The American Law Institute's Law of Real Covenants, 52 Yale L.J. 699, 715 n.52 (1943). For a summary of developments for the forty years after World War II, see Alan David Hegi, Note, The Easement in Gross Revisited: Transferability and Divisibility Since 1945, 39 Vand. L. Rev. 109 (1986). The Third Restatement makes the intent and expectations of the parties the determining factor, but provides two different default rules in the absence of evidence of a contrary intention: Non-personal easements in gross are transferable but personal easements in gross are not transferable. See Restatement (Third) of Property, Servitudes §§ 4.1, 4.6. An example of a non-personal easement is an easement for utility lines granted to an electrical utility.

2. *Divisibility.* The *Miller* court invoked *Mountjoy's Case* for the proposition that an easement in gross cannot be subdivided, but *Mountjoy's Case* involved a profit, not an easement. A profit, you will recall, is the right to remove something from the servient estate, such as timber or gravel, or peat. Should easements in gross and profits be treated equally with respect to their divisibility? Should the "one stock" rule of *Mountjoy's Case* apply to easements in gross? Consider these questions in analyzing the following problems.

3. *Problems.*

a. *O*, the owner of Blackacre, grants to *A* the exclusive right to enter Blackacre and remove gravel from a pit located on Blackacre, "until the gravel is exhausted." *A* transfers a one-third interest in this right to *B*, a one-third interest to *C*, and retains the remaining one-third interest. *B* and *C* are road-building contractors who have an unusually large demand for gravel. Should *A* be entitled to transfer and divide his right? Why or why not? Would it make any difference if *A*'s right was limited to "200 tons per year"? *O keeps right to give to others.*

b. Assume that *O*, in Problem 3a, had granted to *A* a non-exclusive right to enter Blackacre and remove gravel from the pit. *A* makes the transfers described in Problem 3a. Should *A* be entitled to transfer and divide his right? Why or why not? Is the "one stock" rule the best rule to apply here?

c. *X*, owner of Greenacre, grants to *Power Company* an easement to permit electrical power lines to cross Greenacre. *Power Company* erects poles carrying high voltage electrical transmission lines across Blackacre. Later, *Power Company* grants to *Telco*, a telephone company, and *Cableco*, a cable media provider, the right to use *Power Company*'s poles to string telephone and fiber-optic cables across Blackacre. Should *Power Company* be entitled to subdivide the easement? Why or why not?

Prohibited under 1-stock. But logically doesnt make sense

3. EXTENT OF EASEMENTS

What does an easement permit the easement holder to do? What property is entitled to benefit from an easement? To what extent may the owner of the servient estate alter the location of an easement?

FARMER v. KENTUCKY UTILITIES COMPANY

Supreme Court of Kentucky
642 S.W.2d 579 (1982)

STERNBERG, J., delivered the opinion of the court.

In 1978, Elva Skidmore Farmer ... acquired a small tract of land from her mother. In 1923, 55 years prior to [this acquisition], the respondent, Kentucky Utilities Company, constructed a transmission line which overhangs a portion of this property. The wires are attached to two poles which, themselves, are located on lands adjacent to the subject property but not on it. Since 1976, the premises have been unoccupied....

In 1980, Kentucky Utilities Company determined that the area beneath the wires . . . needed to be cleared. It . . . engaged the services of a tree, shrub, and undergrowth removal company who entered upon the subject premises, with men and equipment, and cut and removed trees and other growth of vegetation from beneath the wires and in close proximity thereto. The owners of the land filed a suit against the utility company charging trespass and sought damages by reason thereof.

This case was tried to the court without the intervention of a jury. . . . The trial court found that the Kentucky Utilities Company had a prescriptive easement as to the overhanging wires, but did not have any right to enter upon the land over which the wires were hung for the purpose of clearing. The Court of Appeals held that the prescriptive easement to hang lines necessarily includes as an incident thereof a right to enter the property underneath the lines for purposes of maintenance and repairs. This court . . . granted review.

[The] issue is one of first impression to this court. Even so, the general principle is so well recognized that it has been enforced in this jurisdiction for decades. The use of the land beneath the overhanging lines is . . . a secondary easement necessary for the enjoyment of the principal easement. It is ancient law that nothing passes under an easement but what is necessary for its reasonable use and proper enjoyment. The use of the easement must be as reasonable and as little burdensome to the landowner as the nature and purpose of the easement will permit. In Higdon v. Kentucky Gas Transmission Corporation, 448 S.W.2d 655 (Ky. 1970), this court [noted] that dominant and servient owners have correlative rights and duties which neither may unreasonably exercise to the injury of the other. . . .

[The] Kentucky Utilities Company could not use the primary easement for overhanging wires to the unreasonable detriment of the movants. Conversely, . . . the movants cannot use the servient estate to the detriment of the Kentucky Utilities Company. By using the servient estate so as to permit trees, shrubs, and other growth and vegetation to grow to heights as to interfere with the proper enjoyment of the primary easement, the movants inhibited the proper use of the overhanging wire easement.

[The] owner of an easement acquired by personal negotiations, by eminent domain, by prescription, or otherwise, for the erection of electric wires may enter upon the premises over which the wires are constructed for the purpose of removing vegetation, or other growth or substance, that interferes with the natural and reasonable use of the easement. . . . [However,] the Kentucky Utilities Company is limited in the manner and extent of its usage of the servient estate in that only so much thereof may be encroached upon as is necessary to the natural and reasonable use of its primary easement. To this extent, therefore, there is a factual issue to be determined by the fact finder.

We affirm so much of the decision of the Court of Appeals as holds that the Kentucky Utilities Company, by reason of its primary easement, has a right to enter upon the servient property beneath the lines and in the immediate vicinity thereof for the purpose of repairs and maintenance. However, we reverse and remand to the Harlan Circuit Court for a new trial on the issue of whether the Kentucky Utilities Company, in entering upon the servient estate, cut such trees, shrubs, and undergrowth as were necessary for the proper and natural and reasonable use of the primary easement or, if not, to respond in damages....

AKER, J., dissenting.

The majority ... fails to distinguish between easements arising by prescription and easements resulting from express agreement. Adverse possession can rest only upon "such open and notorious acts of physical possession as would put the owner upon notice of the assertion of a hostile claim." In this case, the appellants, and their predecessors in title, were willing to permit the two utility lines to overhang their property. However, on each occasion when Kentucky Utilities came upon the property to clear trees and shrubs, trespass actions were promptly initiated. It is my opinion that the prescriptive right of Kentucky Utilities is thus confined to the right to overhang two lines across the tract of land. As this court has stated, "an easement by prescription is limited by the purpose for which it is acquired and the use to which it is put for the statutory period." Williams v. Slate, 415 S.W.2d 616 (Ky. 1967). The easement "... will not ripen into a greater estate after the period of limitation has passed. The right is crystallized as to form during the waiting period and is of the nature of the use during that period." Baker v. Maggard, 255 S.W.2d 45 (Ky. 1953).

To now permit Kentucky Utilities to come upon the land and destroy property appears to me an unreasonable expansion of rights incident to the prescriptive easement. Therefore, I would reverse the Court of Appeals and affirm the judgment of the Harlan Circuit Court.

PROBLEM

A openly and continuously traverses O's land on foot to drive his cattle to and from other land owned by A, and does so for the prescriptive period without any permission from O. After A has acquired this prescriptive easement he begins to use it to drive his all-terrain vehicle across O's land. May A do so? Would your analysis be any different if O had granted A an easement for a "right of way" across O's property?

BROWN v. VOSS

Supreme Court of Washington
105 Wash.2d 366 (1986)

BRACHTENBACH, J., delivered the opinion of the court.

The question posed is to what extent, if any, the holder of a private road easement can traverse the servient estate to reach not only the original dominant estate, but a subsequently acquired parcel when those two combined parcels are used in such a way that there is no increase in the burden on the servient estate. The trial court denied the injunction sought by the owners of the servient estate. The Court of Appeals reversed. We reverse the Court of Appeals and reinstate the judgment of the trial court.... *Denied injnction of owners of servient estate*

In 1952 the predecessors in title of parcel A granted to the predecessor owners of parcel B a private road easement across parcel A for "ingress to and egress from" parcel B. Defendants acquired parcel A in 1973. Plaintiffs bought parcel B on April 1, 1977, and parcel C on July 31, 1977, but from two different owners. Apparently the previous owners of parcel C were not parties to the easement grant. When plaintiffs acquired parcel B a single family dwelling was situated thereon. They intended to remove that residence and replace it with a single family dwelling which would straddle the boundary line common to parcels B and C.

Plaintiffs began clearing both parcels B and C and moving fill materials in November 1977. Defendants first sought to bar plaintiff's use of the easement in April 1979 by which time plaintiffs had spent more than $11,000 in developing their property for the building. Defendants placed logs, a concrete sump and a chain link fence within the easement. Plaintiffs sued for removal of the obstructions, an injunction against defendant's interference with their use of the easement and damages. Defendants counterclaimed for damages and an injunction against plaintiffs using the easement other than for parcel B.

The trial court awarded each party $1 in damages. The award against the plaintiffs was for a slight inadvertent trespass outside the easement. The trial court made the following findings of fact:

> VI.   The plaintiffs have made no unreasonable use of the easement in the development of their property. There have been no complaints of unreasonable use of the roadway to the south of the properties of the parties by other neighbors who grant easements to the parties to this action to cross their properties to gain access to the property of the plaintiffs. Other than the trespass there is no evidence of any damage to the defendants as a result of the use of the easement by the plaintiffs. There has been no increase in volume of travel on the easement to reach a single family dwelling whether built on tract B or on [Tracts] B and C. There is no evidence of any increase in the burden on the subservient estate from the use of the easement by the plaintiffs for access to parcel C.

> VIII.   If an injunction were granted to bar plaintiffs access to tract C across the easement to a single family residence, Parcel C would become landlocked; plaintiffs would not be able to make use of their property; they would not be able to build their single family residence in a manner to properly enjoy the view of the Hood Canal and the surrounding area as originally anticipated at the time of their purchase and even if the single family residence were constructed on

parcel B, if the injunction were granted, plaintiffs would not be able to use the balance of their property in parcel C as a yard or for any other use of their property in conjunction with their home. Conversely, there is and will be no appreciable hardship or damage to the defendants if the injunction is denied.

IX.   If an injunction were to be granted to bar the plaintiffs access to tract C, the framing and enforcing of such an order would be impractical. Any violation of the order would result in the parties back in court at great cost but with little or no damages being involved.

X.   Plaintiffs have acted reasonably in the development of their property. Their trespass over a "little" corner of the defendants' property was inadvertent, and *de minimis*. The fact that the defendants counter claim seeking an injunction to bar plaintiffs access to parcel C was filed as leverage against the original plaintiffs' claim for an interruption of their easement rights, may be considered in determining whether equitable relief by way of an injunction should be granted.

Relying upon these findings of fact, the court denied defendant's request for an injunction and granted the plaintiffs the right to use the easement for access to parcels B and C "as long as plaintiffs['] properties (B and C) are developed and used solely for the purpose of a single family residence."

The Court of Appeals reversed [and remanded] "for entry of an order enjoining the use of the easement across parcel A to gain access to a residence any part of which is located on parcel C, or to further the construction of any residence on parcels B or C if the construction activities would require entry onto parcel C."

The easement in this case was created by express grant. Accordingly, the extent of the right acquired is to be determined from the terms of the grant properly construed to give effect to the intention of the parties. By the express terms of the 1952 grant, the predecessor owners of parcel B acquired a private road easement across parcel A and the right to use the easement for ingress to and egress from parcel B. [The] 1952 grant created an easement appurtenant to parcel B as the dominant estate. Thus, plaintiffs, as owners of the dominant estate, acquired rights in the use of the easement for ingress to and egress from parcel B.

However, plaintiffs have no such easement rights in connection with their ownership of parcel C, which was not a part of the original dominant estate under the terms of the 1952 grant. As a general rule, an easement appurtenant to one parcel of land may not be extended by the owner of the dominant estate to other parcels owned by him, whether adjoining or distinct tracts, to which the easement is not appurtenant. Plaintiffs, nonetheless, contend that extension of the use of the easement for the benefit of non-dominant property does not constitute a misuse of the easement, where as here, there is no evidence of an increase in the burden on the servient estate. We do not agree If an easement is appurtenant to a particular parcel of land, any extension thereof to other parcels is a misuse of the easement. Wetmore v. Ladies of Loretto, Wheaton, 73 Ill. App. 2d 454, 220 N.E.2d 491 (1966). *See also, e.g.,* Robertson v. Robertson, 214 Va. 76, 197 S.E.2d 183 (1973); Penn Bowling Rec. Ctr., Inc. v. Hot Shoppes, Inc., 179 F.2d 64 (D.C. Cir. 1949). ... Under the express language of the 1952 grant, plaintiffs only have rights in the use of the easement for the benefit of parcel B. Although, as plaintiffs contend, their planned use of the easement to gain access to a single family residence located partially on parcel B and partially on parcel C is perhaps no more than technical misuse of the easement, we conclude that it is misuse nonetheless.

However, it does not follow from this conclusion alone that defendants are entitled to injunctive relief. Since the awards of $1 in damages were not appealed, only the denial of an injunction to defendants is in issue. Some fundamental principles applicable to a request for an injunction must be considered. (1) The proceeding is equitable and addressed to the sound discretion of the trial court. (2) The trial court is vested with a broad discretionary power to shape and fashion injunctive relief to fit the *particular facts, circumstances, and equities of the case before it.* Appellate courts give great weight to the trial court's exercise of that discretion. (3) One of the essential criteria for injunctive relief is actual and substantial injury sustained by the person seeking the injunction. The trial court found as facts, upon substantial evidence, that plaintiffs have acted reasonably in the development of their property, that there is and was no damage to the defendants from plaintiffs' use of the easement, that there was no increase in the volume of travel on the easement, that there was no increase in the burden on the servient estate, that defendants sat by for more than a year while plaintiffs expended more than $11,000 on their project, and that defendants' counterclaim was an effort to gain ''leverage'' against plaintiffs' claim. In addition, the court found from the evidence that plaintiffs would suffer considerable hardship if the injunction were granted whereas no appreciable hardship or damages would flow to defendants from its denial. Finally, the court limited plaintiffs' use of the combined parcels solely to the same purpose for which the original parcel was used—*i.e.,* for a single family residence. ... Based upon the equities of the case, as found by the trial court, we are persuaded that the trial court acted within its discretion. The Court of Appeals is reversed and the trial court is affirmed.

DORE, J., dissenting.

The majority correctly finds that an extension of this easement to nondominant property is a misuse of the easement. The majority, nonetheless, holds that the owners of the servient estate are not entitled to injunctive relief. I dissent. ...

The majority grants the privilege to extend the agreement to nondominant property on the basis that the trial court found no appreciable hardship or damage to the servient owners. However, as conceded by the majority, any extension of the use of an easement to benefit a nondominant estate constitutes a misuse of the easement. Misuse of an easement is a trespass. The Browns' use of the easement to benefit parcel C, especially if they build their home as planned, would involve a continuing trespass for which damages would be difficult to measure. Injunctive relief is the appropriate remedy under these circumstances. In Penn Bowling Rec. Ctr., Inc. v. Hot Shoppes, Inc., 179 F.2d 64, 66 (D.C. Cir. 1949) the court states:

> ... It is true that where the nature and extent of the use of an easement is, by its terms, unrestricted, the use by the dominant tenement may be increased or enlarged. But the owner of the dominant tenement may not subject the servient tenement to use or servitude in connection with other premises to which the easement is not appurtenant. And when an easement is being used in such a manner, an injunction will be issued to prevent such use. Appellant, therefore, may not use the easement to serve both the dominant and nondominant property, even though the area thereof is less than the original area of the dominant tenement.

Thus, the fact that an extension of the easement to nondominant property would not increase the burden on the servient estate does not warrant a denial of injunctive relief.

The Browns are responsible for the hardship of creating a landlocked parcel. They knew or should have known from the public records that the easement was not appurtenant to parcel C. In encroachment cases this factor is significant. As stated by the court in Bach v. Sarich, 74 Wn.2d 575, 582, 445 P.2d 648 (1968): "The benefit of the doctrine of balancing the equities, or relative hardship, is reserved for the innocent defendant who proceeds without knowledge or warning that his structure encroaches upon another's property or property rights." In addition, an injunction would not interfere with the Browns' right to use the easement as expressly granted, *i.e.*, for access to parcel B. An injunction would merely require the Browns to acquire access to parcel C if they want to build a home that straddles parcels B and C. One possibility would be to condemn a private way of necessity over their existing easement in an action under RCW 8.24.010. *See* Brown v. McAnally, 97 Wn.2d 360, 644 P.2d 1153 (1982).

I would affirm the Court of Appeals decision as a correct application of the law of easements. If the Browns desire access to their landlocked parcel they have the benefit of the statutory procedure for condemnation of a private way of necessity.

Notes, Questions, and Problems

1.   Liability Rules or Property Rules? Brown v. Voss is a departure from the traditional rule that an injunction is the remedy for any misuse of an easement by the dominant estate owner. Is that departure justified? If so, is the award of damages preferable as a general matter? If a damage award is preferable in only some circumstances, what factors should be employed to identify those circumstances? In considering these questions in the specific context of *Brown*, you may wish to learn more about the parties and their behavior. To do so, see Elizabeth Samuels, Stories Out of School: Teaching the Case of *Brown v. Voss*, 16 Cardozo L. Rev. 1445 (1995). In short, Brown and Voss developed a deep mutual disdain, so pronounced that it degenerated into fisticuffs even before the lawsuit commenced.

    2. *Problems.*

    a. After the Washington Supreme Court's decision, suppose that Brown built his house and, years later, added a small structure (including a kitchen and bath) that housed his elderly parents? Would this violate the trial court's order, which was restored by the Washington Supreme Court? If so, what factors should be used to determine the remedy to the servient estate owner? Does it make any difference if the structure is physically attached to Brown's residence or standing alone? Should it make any difference if the structure is physically separate from Brown's residence and located entirely on Parcel B?

    b. *O*, owner of Blackacre, grants an easement across Blackacre for vehicular access to Whiteacre, a forty acre tract. Years later, Whiteacre is subdivided into 40 parcels, each of one acre. May the owners of each of those 40 parcels use the easement across Blackacre for vehicle access to their homes? Should it make any difference to the outcome if, at the time of the grant of the easement, Blackacre and Whiteacre were rural properties on the outskirts of a fast growing town and, at the time of the subdivision of Whiteacre, residential developments had popped up around Blackacre? Could the developer of Whiteacre place buried utility lines under the easement to serve the 40 subdivided parcels?

    c. Suppose that in Problem 2.b *O* and *W*, the owner of Whiteacre, had agreed on the location of the access easement. Years later, but before any subdivision had occurred, *O* decided to move the location of the easement, at his own expense and without *W*'s consent, in order to improve the drainage of water from Blackacre. Should *O* be entitled to do so? What factors should be relevant to your decision? Compare Davis v. Bruk, 411 A.2d 660 (Me. 1980), with M.P.M. Builders v. Dwyer, 442 Mass. 87 (2004). See also Restatement (Third) of Property § 4.8, comment f.

    d. Suppose that in Problem 2.c it was *W* who wished to relocate the easement and was willing to pay for the cost of doing so? Should *W* be permitted to do so without *O*'s consent? See Bradley v. Arkansas Louisiana Gas Company, 280 Ark. 492 (1983); Villager Condominium Association v. Idaho Power Company, 121 Idaho 986 (1992).

4. TERMINATION OF EASEMENTS

    Easements may be terminated in a number of ways: Expiration, release, estoppel, merger, abandonment, prescription (adverse use), and condemnation.

    Expiration. If the easement contains a limitation on its duration, it expires when the limitation is triggered. Thus, a 1995 grant of an easement for 20 years expires by its terms in 2015. Or, an easement for a railroad right of way "so long as the railroad maintains passenger rail service along the right of way" expires automatically when and if the railroad ceases passenger rail service along the line.

Release. The owner of the easement may extinguish it by a release of the easement, which is effectively a re-grant of the easement to the servient estate. As with other interests in real property, the Statute of Frauds applies and requires that a release be in writing, unless the circumstances of the release bring it within one of the exceptions to the Statute of Frauds. See generally Restatement (Third) of Property, Servitudes § 7.3.

Estoppel. Principles of equitable estoppel apply to the termination of easements as well as to their creation. If the servient estate owner relies to his detriment upon a representation or promise of the easement owner the easement owner will be estopped from denying the representation.

> *Example 10–7*: D, the dominant estate owner says to S, the servient estate owner: "I no longer need that easement for a right of way; I've acquired a better access route." S then constructs on the easement site a storage building at a cost of $50,000. D may not deny his representation, and the easement will be terminated.

See generally Restatement (Third) of Property, Servitudes § 7.6.

Merger. If the servient estate and the dominant estate are united in ownership the easement appurtenant is extinguished by merger of the two titles in a single owner. Similarly, if the owner of an easement in gross should acquire title to the servient estate the easement is extinguished by virtue of merger of the two formerly dissociated interests. After merger, the easement dies. There is no resurrection if the two estates are later severed in ownership. Any subsequent easement must be created anew by one of the available methods. See generally Restatement (Third) of Property, Servitudes § 7.5.

Abandonment. An easement may cease to exist if the easement owner abandons it. But what constitutes abandonment?

This issue has been frequently litigated in recent years as railway usage has declined and railway companies have gone out of business. Congress reacted to that trend by enacting the Rails-to-Trails Act, 16 U.S.C. § 1247(d). To preserve discontinued rail corridors and to permit the public to use those corridors for recreation the Act authorized the Interstate Commerce Commission (which has regulatory control over railroads) to either authorize abandonment of a rail line *or* discontinuance of the line and transfer of the right of way to a public or private organization willing to maintain it as a public recreational trail. In Preseault v. Interstate Commerce Commission, 494 U.S. 1 (1990), the United States Supreme Court ruled that the Act was a valid exercise of Congress's power to regulate interstate commerce, but noted that some conversions of railway easements to recreational trails might constitute a taking of private property, requiring just compensation to be paid. A taking of property owned by the servient estate owner would occur if the right of way was an easement (rather than a fee simple absolute), and either the scope of the easement did not include use as a public recreational trail or the easement had terminated by abandonment.

These issues were central to the disposition of *Presault v. United States,* 100 F.3d 1525 (Fed. Cir. 1996). Vermont law governed. The Presaults owned land near Burlington, Vermont which was bisected by an easement granted in 1899 to the Rutland–Canadian Railroad. Rail service ceased on the line in 1970. In 1986 the ICC approved an agreement between the railroad and the city of Burlington by which Burlington would maintain the corridor as a public recreational trail. The Presaults objected, contending that such use was outside the scope of the easement and, in any case, the railroad had abandoned the easement at least ten years prior to the transfer of the corridor to Burlington. The Court of Appeals agreed that the easement did not include the right to use the corridor for public recreational purposes, because the original grant was intended to permit the "transportation of goods and persons via railroad. . . . It is difficult to imagine that either party to the original [grant] had anything remotely in mind that would resemble a public recreational trail." But the Court of Appeals also ruled that the easement had been abandoned.

The Preseaults contend that under Vermont law the original easements were abandoned, and thus extinguished, in 1975. If that is so, the State could not, over ten years later in 1986, have re-established the easement even for the narrow purposes provided in the original conveyances without payment of the just compensation required by the Constitution. . . . Typically the grant under which such rights-of-way are created does not specify a termination date. The usual way in which such an easement ends is by abandonment, which causes the easement to be extinguished by operation of law. Upon an act of abandonment, the then owner of the fee estate, the "burdened" estate, is relieved of the burden of the easement. In most jurisdictions, including Vermont, this happens automatically when abandonment of the easement occurs.

Vermont law recognizes the well-established proposition that easements, like other property interests, are not extinguished by simple non-use. As was said in Nelson v. Bacon, 113 Vt. 161, 32 A.2d 140, 146 (1943), "one who acquires title to an easement [. . .] has the same right of property therein as an owner of the fee and it is not necessary that he should make use of his right in order to maintain his title." Thus in cases involving a passageway through an adjoining building (*Nelson*), or a shared driveway, the claimed easement was not extinguished merely because the owner had not made use of it regularly.

Something more is needed. The Vermont Supreme Court in *Nelson* summarized the rule in this way: "In order to establish an abandonment there must be in addition to nonuser, acts by the owner of the dominant tenement conclusively and unequivocally manifesting *either* a present intent to relinquish the easement *or* a purpose inconsistent with its future existence."(emphasis added). . . . The record here establishes that these easements, along with the other assets of the railroad, came into the hands of the State of Vermont in the 1960s. The State then leased them to an entity called the Vermont Railway, which operated trains over them. In 1970, the Vermont Railway ceased active transport operations on the line which included the right-of-way over the parcels at issue, and used the line only to store railroad cars. In 1975 the Railroad removed all of the railroad equipment, including switches and tracks, from the portion of the right-of-way running over the three parcels of land now owned by the Preseaults. In light of these facts, the trial court concluded that under Vermont law this amounted to an abandonment of the easements, and adjudged that the easements were extinguished as a matter of law in 1975. . . .

Under Vermont law, "the question whether there has been an abandonment . . . is one of fact," and "the fact that the question relates to a right of way taken by a railroad company does not make it one of law." Stevens v. MacRae, 97 Vt. 76, 122 A. 892 (1923). The underlying facts regarding this question are undisputed. . . . Abandonment . . . is a factual conclusion based on inferences to be drawn from the undisputed evidence regarding the historical events. . . . The question to be decided here is what was the intent or purpose of the Railroad in 1975, when, for all practical purposes, it ended railroad operations on this easement. . . .

As noted, in 1970 the Vermont Railway ceased using the easement for active transport operations and used the tracks solely to store railroad cars, as the only freight customer serviced on that portion of the line had moved from the area. In 1975, Vermont Railway removed the rails and other track materials from the segment of line crossing the Preseaults' property. . . .

The Government and the State argue that there are facts inconsistent with that determination, but we are not persuaded that any of them significantly undercut the trial court's conclusion. For example, when the Vermont Railway removed its tracks in 1975, it did not remove the two bridges or any of the culverts on the line, all of which remained "substantially intact." That is not surprising. The Railroad was under no obligation to restore the former easement to its original condition. Tearing out existing structures would simply add to its costs, whereas the rails that were taken up could be used for repairs of defective rails elsewhere on the line. It is further argued that, since the rail line continues to operate to a point approximately one and one-third miles south of the Preseaults' property, it is possible to restore the line to full operation. The fact that restoration of the northern portion of the line would be technically feasible tells us little. The question is not what is technically possible to do in the future, but what was done in the past.

Almost immediately after the tracks were removed, members of the public began crossing over the easement. Perhaps illustrating the difficulty in getting government paperwork to catch up with reality, or perhaps indicating that revenue collectors do not give up easily, the State of Vermont and Vermont Railway, as they had done before the removal of the tracks, continued to collect fees under various license and crossing agreements from persons wishing to establish fixed crossings. In January 1976, the Preseaults executed a crossing agreement with the Vermont Railway which gave the Preseaults permission to cross the right-of-way. In March 1976, the Preseaults entered into a license agreement with the State and the Vermont Railway to locate a driveway and underground utility service across the railroad right-of-way. As late as 1991, [the Presaults] paid a $10 license fee to "Vermont Railroad" (*sic*), presumably pursuant to one of the 1976 agreements. The Preseaults paid "under protest." Much of this activity suggests that, initially at least, the adjacent property owners decided it was cheaper to pay a nominal license fee to the State than to litigate the question of whether the State had the right to extract the fee. In view of all the contrary evidence of physical abandonment, we find this behavior by the State's revenue collectors unconvincing as persuasive evidence of a purpose or intent not to abandon the use of the right-of-way for actual railroad purposes.

One uncontrovertible piece of evidence in favor of abandonment is that, in the years following the shutting down of the line in 1970 and the 1975 removal of the tracks, no move has been made by the State or by the Railroad to reinstitute service over the line, or to undertake replacement of the removed tracks and other infrastructure necessary to return the line to service. The declarations in the 1985 lease between the State of Vermont, Vermont Railway, and the City of Burlington, which refer to the possible resumption of railroad operations at some undefined time in the future are of course self-serving and not indicative of the facts and circumstances in 1975....

The trial judge ... concluded that as a fact the Railroad had effected in 1975 an abandonment of the easement.... We affirm the determination of the trial court that abandonment of the easements took place in 1975. That determination provides an alternative ground for concluding that a governmental taking occurred.

See generally Restatement (Third) of Property, Servitudes § 7.4.

Prescription. This is the obverse of acquiring an easement by adverse use. If the servient owner physically obstructs the easement without any right to do so and thus prevents the easement owner from using the easement for the prescriptive period, the easement is extinguished by this adverse interference. In Simpson v. Fowles, 272 Ore. 342 (1975), the servient estate owner planted an orchard and maintained it for 35 years. Branches of the filbert trees encroached upon an easement for right of way "to such an extent that it cannot be used for the movement of vehicles without damaging the trees." That fact, together with the servient owner's cultivation activities around the trees, was observed by the dominant owner for the prescriptive period. The easement was extinguished. In Public Lands Access Association, Inc. v. Boone & Crockett Club Foundation, Inc., 259 Mont. 279 (1993), the public claimed to have acquired a prescriptive easement in an unimproved rough jeep trail. The servient owner blocked the road just prior to hunting season through the spring of the following year, and did this continually for the prescriptive period, although the servient owner allowed some permissive foot travel. The prescriptive easement, if it ever existed, was terminated by this adverse action. In Landgray Association v. 450 Lexington Venture, 788 F.Supp. 776 (S.D.N.Y. 1992), an easement for light and air was eliminated by a servient owner's open, notorious, continuous, and hostile erection and maintenance of a structure that interfered with light and air. Once terminated, the easement was not revived by the servient owner's removal of the structure in order to erect a different structure. However, in Nicholls v. Healy, 37 Mich.App. 348 (1971), the servient owner's interference with a five-foot wide access easement by planting a double row of trees, erection of a bathhouse, privy, and fence was insufficient to terminate the easement because none of these acts "seriously blocked passage on the strip." See Restatement (Third) of Property, Servitudes § 7.7.

Condemnation. If a government should condemn the servient estate through its eminent domain power and, as a result, has the power to use the property in a fashion inconsistent with the easement, the easement is terminated. Government condemnation of the dominant estate eliminates the easement only if that is the purpose of the condemnation. See Restatement (Third) of Property, Servitudes § 7.8.

Problems:

a. S, owner of Sweetgrass, borrows $100,000 from L and gives L a mortgage of Sweetgrass to secure the loan, which mortgage is promptly recorded. Later, S grants to D, an adjacent landowner, an easement for right of way across Sweetgrass. Then S defaults and L forecloses upon Sweetgrass. X buys Sweetgrass at the foreclosure sale. Has the easement in favor of D been terminated? Would it make any difference if S had granted the easement to D before mortgaging Sweetgrass, and D had promptly recorded the grant?

b. V, owner of Valhalla Acres, grants an easement for right of way across Valhalla Acres to T, an adjacent landowner. Then V fails to pay the property taxes and the City of Valhalla seizes and sells the property to P at a tax sale. Has the easement in favor of T been extinguished? What factors are relevant to determination of this problem?

5. PRESERVATION EASEMENTS

Preservation easements take the form of restrictions upon the use or development of land. Typically, a landowner grants to a public entity or a private charitable organization the right to prevent the landowner or his successors from developing the property in a manner inconsistent with the grant. As will become apparent in the next section, these easements would traditionally have been analyzed as a real covenant or equitable servitude. You will learn in that section that the common law imposed restrictions upon the enforcement and transferability of the benefit of such covenants, which are in gross rather than appurtenant. In an attempt to avoid these limits, conservation minded landowners and conservation organizations invented these easements. Moreover, because the transfer of valuable development rights to a charitable organization is a gift of the value of those rights, the owner making the transfer is generally entitled to deduct the value of the gift from his gross income for purposes of computing his income tax liability.

> *Example 10–8*: *O*, owner of the Ponderosa Ranch, grants to the Nature Conservancy, a charitable organization, an easement restricting any future development of Ponderosa Ranch. The value of Ponderosa Ranch without the easement is $5 million; its value burdened by the easement is $3 million. *O* may deduct from his gross income the gift of $2 million in development rights to the Nature Conservancy.

Of course, these easements may be made by people with less valuable property, and some owners may be motivated purely by preservation, but the combination of advancing preservation or conservation and reaping a reward in the form of a tax subsidy has spurred the growth of these easements. To ensure the validity of such easements, a number of jurisdictions have adopted the Uniform Conservation Easement Act, the purpose of which is establish statutory provisions that immunize restrictions designed to conserve natural resources from any impediments to their validity that might otherwise exist at common law.

Preservation easements are not without controversy. Their purpose is to restrict development and to do so in perpetuity. Thus, such easements impose costs on future generations by limiting the development of land that later generations may think is appropriate to develop. See, e.g., Julia D. Mahoney, Perpetual Restrictions on Land and the Problem of the Future, 88 Va. L. Rev. 739 (2002). Defenders of preservation easements may counter that these costs are offset by the benefit delivered to future generations in the form of preserved natural resources. One way to reconcile these costs and benefits is to permit future generations to modify these easements when they are no longer practicable. See, e.g., Nancy A. McLaughlin, Rethinking the Perpetual Nature of Conservation Easements, 29 Harv. Envtl. L. Rev. 421 (2005).

Preservation easements are not used only to conserve natural resources. They may also be used to restrict alteration of structures that have historical significance. For example, an owner of a structure that is registered on the national Register of Historic Places may grant to a charitable historic preservation group, such as the National Trust, an easement that restricts alteration of the facade of the structure. As with conservation easements, the value of the easement may be taken as a charitable deduction when computing the donor's federal income tax liability.

See also Restatement (Third) of Property, Servitudes § 1.6.

B. REAL COVENANTS AND EQUITABLE SERVITUDES

1. INTRODUCTION

The servitudes encountered thus far—easements—have all involved the creation of a right to use someone else's land. Easements need not be so limited; one could conceive of an easement that confers to *A* the right to prevent *B* from using *B*'s land, Blackacre, in a specified way. Thus, *B* could grant to *A* the right to ensure that *B* will never use Blackacre as an abattoir. When easements developed, English courts initially accepted such easements, but then stopped doing so. Why? First, the "negative easements" that they recognized—the right to prevent an adjacent land-owner from blocking his neighbor's light and air, removing support from his land, or interfering with water flowing through an artificial channel— could be acquired by prescription, which meant that later development was hindered or prevented. Second, England had no system of recorded titles, so the existence of these negative rights was not easily detectable. The existence of an affirmative easement—a right of way, for example— was obvious; but negative easements were not as readily apparent. Finally, because easements were interests in land, judges had a hard time conceiving of a right to prevent another from using his land in a certain way as an interest in that land. They perceived such a negative right, and its correlative obligation, to be personal: a species of contract. American courts generally accepted this dichotomy, and thus was born the branch of servitudes that we call real covenants and equitable servitudes.

The Third Restatment of Property, Servitudes, rejects the distinction between easements, real covenants, and equitable servitudes, and has created a unified doctrine that treats all of these interests as "servitudes." But because that approach has not yet been fully embraced by American courts, it is still important to understand the traditional distinctions. Only then can one appreciate the unification effort of the Third Restatement.

A covenant is, in general, a contractual promise. If *A*, owner of Coveside, for valuable consideration, promises *B*, owner of Blackacre, an adjacent property, that he will not erect a factory on Coveside, *B* may seek damages for breach of the promise if *A* should construct a factory on Coveside. However, *B* might prefer to obtain an injunction to restrain *A* from building the factory in the first place. So long as the parties consist of *A* and *B*, their rights and obligations with respect to this promise are matters of contract law. But what if *A* transfers his interest in Coveside to *C* and *B* conveys Blackacre to *D*? Because neither *C* nor *D* were parties to the contract, *D* may not enforce it and *C* is not bound by *A*'s promise.

However, if *A* and *B*, as owners of estates in land, are in *privity of estate*—they have a sufficient interest in each other's estates—the benefit and burden of the promise may run with the estates and future holders of those estates may assert the benefit and be bound by the burden of the original agreement. This relationship is called *horizontal privity*. But what constitutes an interest in land sufficient to create horizontal privity? There is no uniform answer, but here are the usual relationships that satisfy horizontal privity.

Landlord and Tenant: A covenant originating in a lease generally constitutes horizontal privity. Thus, if *A* leases Redacre from *B* and promises to use Redacre only for residential purposes, horizontal privity is satisfied.

Conveyances: A covenant contained in a deed transferring title to land from *A* to *B* is generally sufficient to create horizontal privity.

Prior Interests: In most states, a covenant created by a separate agreement at a time when one party holds an interest in the other party's land (e.g., an easement), or when both parties are co-owners of the land in question, constitute horizontal privity.

Note that a naked agreement—one made by two parties as landowners but with none of the relationships described above—does *not* constitute horizontal privity. Massachusetts adheres to a unique understanding of horizontal privity: Both parties must have a *prior mutual interest* in the affected land. Morse v. Aldrich, 36 Mass. 449 (1837).

The Third Restatement of Property (Servitudes), § 2.4, rejects horizontal privity altogether. The rationale for requiring horizontal privity was mostly to ensure that the covenant would be evidenced by some formal arrangement that would be recorded, but this rationale is fully satisfied by the Statute of Frauds. There is no need to limit running covenants to those that originate in conveyances or leases. In any case, it is a simple matter to create horizontal privity by the use of straw conveyances. As comment b to § 2.4 of the Third Restatement puts it: "The [horizontal privity] rule can easily be circumvented by conveyance to a strawperson, who imposes the covenant in the reconveyance. Since the rule serves no necessary purpose and simply acts as a trap for the poorly represented, it has been abandoned. As a matter of common law, horizontal privity between the covenanting parties is no longer required to create a servitude obligation." The flat assertion that horizontal privity is no longer necessary to create a servitude may be an overstatement, but that is certainly the trend.

Horizontal privity is the relationship between the creators of a covenant, but there is another form of privity, called *vertical privity*. This is the relationship between original parties to the covenant and their successors in interest to the estates burdened or benefitted by the covenant. To grasp vertical privity, consider the following example.

> *Example 10–9*: A, owner of Avondale and Blackacre, adjacent properties, conveys Blackacre to B for valuable consideration. In the deed A promises B, for himself and his successors in interest in Avondale, that he will never use Avondale as a cattle feedlot. Later, A conveys Avondale to C and B conveys Blackacre to D. Then C starts to construct a cattle feedlot on Avondale.

First, note that horizontal privity is present between A and B (except in Massachusetts). Thus, to the extent that horizontal privity is needed for the covenant to be enforceable by B against C, it is present. While the Third Restatement takes the position that horizontal privity is wholly unnecessary for a covenant to run for the benefit of or burden upon successors, the common law took two differing positions. Some states required horizontal privity to be present for either the benefit or burden of the covenant to run to successors. Other states held that horizontal privity was needed only for the burden to run, but not for the benefit to run to successors.

In Example 10–9, *vertical privity* is the relationship between A and C and also the relationship between B and D. Note that vertical privity can exist for either or both of the benefit or the burden of the covenant. Thus, if in Example 10–9 A had conveyed his entire interest in Avondale to C but B had remained the owner of Blackacre at the moment C began to construct his cattle feedlot, in order for B to enforce the covenant against C, B would be required to prove that C was in privity of estate with A ("vertical privity"). Similarly, if B had transferred his entire interest in Blackacre to D and A had begun to use Avondale as a cattle feedlot, D would be required to prove that he was in vertical privity of estate with B in order to assert the benefit of the covenant. In Example 10–9, D would be required to prove that vertical privity of estate exists for *both* the benefit and the burden of the covenant. As will be seen shortly, the common law generally imposed stricter requirements for vertical privity to exist with respect to the burden of a covenant than it did for the benefit of a covenant.

2. REAL COVENANTS

The law of running covenants (those enforceable by or against successors to the estates burdened or benefitted by the original covenant) began with real covenants. The essential feature of a real covenant is that it is enforceable by actions at law, resulting in an award of damages for breach of the covenant. Equitable servitudes, which are discussed in the next subsection, came later in time, and are simply covenants enforceable in equity, resulting in an injunction to restrain the owner of the estate burdened by the covenant from violating the terms of the covenant.

The traditional common law requirements for a real covenant to run with the estate were that 1) the covenant be in writing; 2) the creators of the covenant intended it to run with their respective estates; 3) the creators of the covenant were in privity of estate (horizontal privity); 4) a successor to an estate benefitted or burdened by the covenant was in privity of estate with the original creator of the covenant (vertical privity); and 5) the substance of the covenant "touched and concerned" the benefitted and burdened estates.

Intent. Intent is usually explicit in the written instrument creating the covenant. Language such as "for myself, heirs, and assigns" is enough to establish intent. If the instrument is silent on this matter, extrinsic evidence concerning the parties' intentions (such as the purpose of the covenant or the conduct of the parties) may be sufficient to establish intent.

Horizontal Privity. Horizontal privity (discussed above) was traditionally necessary for the *burden* of a covenant to run but not usually for the *benefit* to run. See, e.g., Shaber v. St. Paul Water Co., 30 Minn. 179 (1883). Some states required horizontal privity for either the benefit or burden to run. See, e.g, Albright v. Fish, 136 Vt. 387 (1978). Some states hold that horizontal privity is unnecessary for either the benefit or burden to run. As long ago as 1941, Judge Charles Clark, author of an influential treatise on covenants, argued that horizontal privity was "supported neither by ancient land law nor by modern policy." 165 Broadway Building v. City Investing Co., 120 F.2d 813, 817 (2d Cir. 1941). See also Orange & Rockland Util. v. Philwold Estates, 52 N.Y.2d 253 (1981); Gallagher v. Bell, 69 Md.App. 199 (1986); Rest. (3d) Property, Servitudes § 2.4. The function of horizontal privity was to prevent some covenants from enduring indefinitely, but horizontal privity is a crude and ill-suited device for doing so. A better approach, as we will see in subsection 4 and 5, is to identify those characteristics of covenants that disqualify them from coming into existence or warranting their termination.

Vertical Privity. Vertical privity traditionally meant something different for the burden to run with the estate than for the benefit to run with the estate. For the burden to run, the transferee had to own the *identical estate* that the transferor owned. Thus, if in Example 10–9 *A* owned Avondale in fee simple absolute, *C* must also own Avondale in fee simple absolute in order for the burden to run with *C*'s estate. However, for the benefit to run, the transferee need only own *some interest* in the land. If in Example 10–9 *B* owned Blackacre in fee simple absolute but had conveyed a life estate in Blackacre to *D*, vertical privity would be present because *D* owned some interest in Blackacre.

An implication of vertical privity is that the burden of a running real covenant attaches to an *estate* in land rather than the land itself. Professor Richard Powell's metaphorical description of this was that a real covenant was "like a bird riding on a wagon"—wherever the estate wagon went the bird remained perched on it, somewhat like Poe's ominous raven on the bust of Pallas or, more fancifully, Coleridge's fateful albatross. See 5 Powell on Real Property 670[2], at 60–6 (Patrick J. Rohan ed., 1996)

   Touch and Concern. The requirement that the covenant "touch and concern" the affected estates in land has bedeviled courts. The traditional approach was that only a "negative" covenant—one that imposes on the obligor the duty to refrain from using his property in a specified manner—could "touch and concern." But as affirmative covenants became more common, especially covenants in developments obliging owners to pay money for the upkeep of common areas, courts reconsidered the issue. In Neponsit Property Owners' Association v. Emigrant Industrial Savings Bank, 278 N.Y. 248, 256–258 (1938), the New York Court of Appeals held that such a covenant touched and concerned the burdened estate.

affirmative

> It has been often said that a covenant to pay a sum of money is a personal affirmative covenant which usually does not concern or touch the land. Such statements are based upon English decisions which hold in effect that only covenants, which compel the covenanter to submit to some *restriction on the use* of his property, touch or concern the land, and that the burden of a covenant which requires the covenanter to do an affirmative act, even on his own land, for the benefit of the owner of a "dominant" estate, does not run with his land. . . . [While it] may be difficult to . . . formulate a test of whether a particular covenant to pay money or to perform some other act falls within the general rule that ordinarily an affirmative covenant is a personal and not a real covenant, . . . we should at least be able to . . . find a reasonable method of approach. . . . It has been suggested that a covenant which runs with the land must affect the legal relations—the advantages and the burdens—of the parties to the covenant, as owners of particular parcels of land and not merely as members of the community in general, such as taxpayers or owners of other land. That . . . approach has the merit of realism. The test is based on the effect of the covenant rather than on technical distinctions. Does the covenant impose, on the one hand, a burden upon an interest in land, which on the other hand increases the value of a different interest in the same or related land? [Yet,] it still remains true that whether a particular covenant is sufficiently connected with the use of land to run with the land, must be in many cases a question of degree. A promise to pay for something to be done in connection with the promisor's land does not differ essentially from a promise by the promisor to do the thing himself, and both promises constitute, in a substantial sense, a restriction upon the owner's right to use the land, and a burden upon the legal interest of the owner. On the other hand, a covenant to perform or pay for the performance of an affirmative act disconnected with the use of the land cannot ordinarily touch or concern the land in any substantial degree. Thus, unless we exalt technical form over substance, the distinction between covenants which run with land and covenants which are personal, must depend upon the effect of the covenant on the legal rights which otherwise

would flow from ownership of land and which are connected with the land. The problem then is: Does the covenant in purpose and effect *substantially* alter these rights?

Does this formula help? Consider the following.

PROBLEMS

1. In the deed by which *A* conveys Brownacre (an oil refinery) to *B*, *B* promises (on behalf of himself and his successors in interest) never to seek indemnification or contribution from *A* for the cost of cleaning up any environmental contamination on Brownacre. Then *B* conveys Brownacre to *C*, who seeks to compel *A* to contribute to the cost of cleaning up environmental hazards on Brownacre. Does the covenant touch and concern? See Refinery Holding Co., L.P. v. TRMI Holdings, Inc. (In re El Paso Refinery), 302 F.3d 343 (5th Cir. 2002).

2. *A*, a developer, builds a condominium complex and includes in the deeds to each condominium a covenant that the owner and any successors in interest will pay annual dues of over $200 to a sports club adjacent to the condominium complex. The club is owned by the developer and is open to all condominium owners. Does the covenant touch and concern? See The Streams Sports Club, Ltd. v. Richmond, 99 Ill.2d 182 (1983).

Touch and Concern: Going, Going, Gone? One way to think about the touch and concern requirement is to consider why covenants are created in the first place. Each party thinks he is receiving a net benefit by agreeing to a land restriction. From an economic perspective a party might agree to limit his use of his property to residential use in exchange for his neighbor's agreement to do the same because he believes that the property's value will be enhanced if all of the surrounding properties are also residential. Assuming this is so, the increment in value will be unstable and short-lived unless the covenant will endure by binding all future owners as well. Thus, we might think about touch and concern as a term of art that seeks to identify those covenants that deliver net social or economic benefits. But because it is not always so easy to see whether that is in fact the case, perhaps touch and concern may be thought of as a description of the kind of promise about land use that *future owners* might reasonably agree to impose.

At bottom, touch and concern is simply a device to decide when covenants ought to bind future owners. For that reason the Third Restatement of Property, Servitudes, eliminates the touch and concern requirement. The Restatement presumes that any covenant is valid initially unless it is "illegal or unconstitutional or violates public policy." Rest. (3d) Prop., Servitudes § 3.1. But this raises more questions. Because covenants are private bargains about land use, they are not governmental regulations. In general, only government action is subject to invalidation as unconstitutional. Yet, in some circumstances, governmental enforcement of covenants triggers constitutional scrutiny, but not in all circumstances. This problem will be addressed in subsection 5, on modification and termination of servitudes.

 Which covenants violate public policy? According to Section 3.1 of the Third Restatement, a covenant violates public policy if it is "arbitrary, capricious, or spiteful," or "unreasonably burdens a fundamental constitutional right," or "imposes an unreasonable restraint on alienation, ... trade or competition," or is "unconscionable."

What about a covenant that prohibits exhibition or display of any religious icon or symbol? Or a covenant that prohibits hanging one's laundry out to dry on a clothesline? Or a covenant that prohibits any use of the property for music lessons for compensation?

3.   EQUITABLE SERVITUDES

TULK v. MOXHAY

High Court of Chancery
41 Eng. Rep. 1143 (1848)

In the year 1808 the Plaintiff, being then the owner in fee of the vacant piece of ground in Leicester Square, as well as of several of the houses forming the Square, sold the piece of ground by the description of "Leicester Square garden or pleasure ground, with the equestrian statue then standing in the centre thereof, and the iron railing and stone work round the same," to one Elms in fee: and the deed of conveyance contained a covenant by Elms, for himself, his heirs, and assigns, with the Plaintiff, his heirs, executors, and administrators, "that Elms, his heirs, and assigns should, and would from time to time, and at all times thereafter at his and their own costs and charges, keep and maintain the said piece of ground and square garden, and the iron railing round the same in its then form, and in sufficient and proper repair as a square garden and pleasure ground, in an open state, uncovered with any buildings, in neat and ornamental order; and that it should be lawful for the inhabitants of Leicester Square, tenants of the Plaintiff, on payment of a reasonable rent for the same, to have keys at their own expense and the privilege of admission therewith at any time or times into the said square garden and pleasure ground."

The piece of land so conveyed passed by divers mesne conveyances into the hands of the Defendant, whose purchase deed contained no similar covenant with his vendor: but he admitted that he had purchased with notice of the covenant in the deed of 1808. The Defendant having manifested an intention to alter the character of the square garden, and asserted a right, if he thought fit, to build upon it, the Plaintiff, who still remained owner of several houses in the square, filed this bill for an injunction; and an injunction was granted by the Master of the Rolls to restrain the Defendant from converting or using the piece of ground and square garden, and the iron railing round the same, to or for any other purpose than as a square garden and pleasure ground in an open state, and uncovered with buildings.

On a motion, now made, to discharge that order, ...

The Lord Chancellor [Cottenham], (without calling upon the other side).

That this Court has jurisdiction to enforce a contract between the owner of land and his neighbour purchasing a part of it, that the latter shall either use or abstain from using the land purchased in a particular way, is what I never knew disputed. Here there is no question about the contract: the owner of certain houses in the square sells the land adjoining, with a covenant from the purchaser not to use it for any other purpose than as a square garden. And it is now contended, not that the vendee could violate that contract, but that he might sell the piece of land, and that the purchaser from him may violate it without this Court having any power to interfere. If that were so, it would be impossible for an owner of land to sell part of it without incurring the risk of rendering what he retains worthless. It is said that, the covenant being one which does not run with the land, this Court cannot enforce it; but the question is, not whether the covenant runs with the land, but whether a party shall be permitted to use the land in a manner inconsistent with the contract entered into by his vendor, and with notice of which he purchased. Of course, the price would be affected by the covenant, and nothing could be more inequitable than that the original purchaser should be able to sell the property the next day for a greater price, in consideration of the assignee being allowed to escape from the liability which he had himself undertaken.

That the question does not depend upon whether the covenant runs with the land is evident from this, that if there was a mere agreement and no covenant, this Court would enforce it against a party purchasing with notice of it; for if an equity is attached to the property by the owner, no one purchasing with notice of that equity can stand in a different situation from the party from whom he purchased. . . .

I think . . . this decision of the Master of the Rolls perfectly right, and, therefore, that this motion must be refused, with costs.

NOTES

1. The Development of Equitable Servitudes. Prior to *Tulk* the only way a covenant could be enforced against successors in interest was by an action at law, with proof of the elements necessary for such a covenant to run with the affected estates. Under English law, Tulk and Elms lacked horizontal privity (a necessary element at the time of the case) because the covenant was in a conveyance rather than a lease. Thus, an action in the law courts would have been fruitless, and Tulk's only recourse was to seek the aid of the chancery courts. England maintained separate courts of law and equity at the time, so a plaintiff had to choose which remedy he preferred (or was eligible to receive). The distinction between law and equity has been nearly universally dissolved today, and courts may deliver either legal or equitable remedies, so the distinctions between real covenants and equitable servitudes should be of lesser consequence. The primary reason for observing any distinction is that damages (available for breach of a real covenant) exposes the party in breach to liability that could in theory be unlimited, while an injunction limits the exposure of the party in breach to the investment that he has made in the affected property. While that sum may be considerable, it is not unlimited. The Third Restatement of Property, Servitudes, eliminates the distinctions between real covenants and equitable servitudes.

2.) *More on "Touch and Concern."* While it is evident that the covenant at issue in *Tulk* touched and concerned Leicester Square, consider the differences between affirmative and negative covenants. Negative covenants, which directly limit land use, are easily seen as touching and concerning land. But affirmative covenants can be much less connected to land use. Suppose that in the Tulk to Elms deed, Elms had promised to conduct a fireworks display in Leicester Square on each anniversary of Guy Fawkes Night.[5] Would this touch and concern? Suppose that Elms had promised to entertain the residents surrounding Leicester Square with a hot air balloon arising from Leicester Square. Touch and concern? Suppose Elms had promised to entertain the surrounding residents by dressing as Father Christmas each Christmas Eve and appearing in Leicester Square that day? Recall *Neponsit*, in which the New York court concluded that an affirmative promise to pay money for the upkeep of commonly owned realty touched and concerned the burdened property. The possibility of very large expenditures to perform affirmative promises cautions some courts to be more willing to enforce such promises by damages than by injunctive relief. See, e.g., Oceanside Community Association v. Oceanside Land Company, 147 Cal.App.3d 166 (1983), in which a developer promised to build and maintain a golf course. He failed to do so, but instead of requiring him to perform (creating an uncertain liability and the likelihood of continuing judicial oversight of his performance) the court granted the homeowners collective damages of $9,320 for each month the course was not operable, and subjected the golf course to a lien upon which the homeowners could foreclose.

3. *The Aftermath.* Elms purchased Leicester Square in 1808 for £210. His devisee sold it in 1834 for £400 to Inderwick, who sold it five years later to Hyams for £451, who in turn sold it to Moxhay a year later for £531. Despite the covenant, ownership of Leicester Square was profitable, lending some doubt to the court's claim that the covenant affected the price and that it would be inequitable to permit Moxhay to purchase at a depressed price (due to the covenant) and sell at an enhanced price (free of the covenant). But there may be some bite to the court's comment, because the 1839 sale was by auction and the auction advertisement noted the unfortunate existence of the covenant, but suggested that an "Act of Parliament . . . might remedy the difficulty." After Tulk won, Moxhay died and his successors sold Leicester Square to James Wyld, who negotiated an agreement with Tulk's heirs to permit him to erect a "Great Globe," in which was exhibited a 60 foot high, 10,000 square foot replica of the world. After the agreement expired, the Globe was demolished in 1862 and the Square was vandalized and became thoroughly squalid. Tulk's heirs enclosed the garden by a 12 foot high wooden

---

5. On 5 November 1605 the plot of Guy Fawkes and his fellow conspirators to blow up Parliament with an enormous quantity of gunpowder was discovered and the plot foiled. The conspirators were Roman Catholics who intended to assassinate the Protestant King James I and replace him with his daughter, Princess Elizabeth of Scotland. The anniversary is commonly celebrated in the U.K. with bonfires and fireworks.

fence and sold advertising space on its exterior face. More litigation ensued. Finally, in 1874 a philanthropist, Albert Grant, purchased the garden and donated it for public use. Leicester Square is now a lovely spot amid London's theatre district and features a statue of William Shakespeare. This account is drawn from James Charles Smith, *Tulk v. Moxhay*: The Fight to Develop Leicester Square, Property Stories 171 (2d ed. 2009).

SANBORN v. McLEAN

Supreme Court of Michigan
233 Mich. 227 (1925)

WIEST, J., delivered the opinion of the court.

Defendant Christina McLean owns the west 35 feet of lot 86 of Green Lawn subdivision, at the northeast corner of Collingwood avenue and Second boulevard, in the city of Detroit, upon which there is a dwelling house, occupied by herself and her husband, defendant John A. McLean. The house fronts Collingwood avenue. At the rear of the lot is an alley. Mrs. McLean derived title from her husband and, in the course of the opinion, we will speak of both as defendants. Mr. and Mrs. McLean started to erect a gasoline filling station at the rear end of their lot, and they and their contractor, William S. Weir, were enjoined ... from doing so and bring the issues before us by appeal. Mr. Weir will not be further mentioned in the opinion.

Collingwood avenue is a high-grade residence street between Woodward avenue and Hamilton boulevard, with single, double and apartment houses[.] [P]laintiffs who are owners of land adjoining, and in the vicinity of defendants' land, and who trace title, as do defendants, to the proprietors of the subdivision, claim that the proposed gasoline station will be a nuisance *per se,* is in violation of the general plan fixed for use of all lots on the street for residence purposes only, as evidenced by restrictions upon 53 of the 91 lots fronting on Collingwood avenue, and that defendants' lot is subject to a reciprocal negative easement[6] barring a use so detrimental to the enjoyment and value of its neighbors. Defendants insist that no restrictions appear in their chain of title and they purchased without notice of any reciprocal negative easement, and deny that a gasoline station is a nuisance *per se.* We find no occasion to pass upon the question of nuisance, as the case can be decided under the rule of reciprocal negative easement.

This subdivision was planned strictly for residence purposes, except lots fronting Woodward avenue and Hamilton boulevard. The 91 lots on Collingwood avenue were platted in 1891, designed for and each one sold solely for residence purposes, and residences have been erected upon all of the lots. Is defendants' lot subject to a reciprocal negative easement? If the

---

6. [Ed.] The court's use of the term "reciprocal negative easement" may be confusing. While one could conceive of the asserted restriction as an easement, the court is really talking about an implied covenant which, since enforcement is sought by way of an injunction, is an equitable servitude.

owner of two or more lots, so situated as to bear the relation, sells one with restrictions of benefit to the land retained, the servitude becomes mutual, and, during the period of restraint, the owner of the lot or lots retained can do nothing forbidden to the owner of the lot sold. For want of a better descriptive term this is styled a reciprocal negative easement. It runs with the land sold by virtue of express fastening and abides with the land retained until loosened by expiration of its period of service or by events working its destruction. It is not personal to owners but operative upon use of the land by any owner having actual or constructive notice thereof. It is an easement passing its benefits and carrying its obligations to all purchasers of land subject to its affirmative or negative mandates. It originates for mutual benefit and exists with vigor sufficient to work its ends. It must start with a common owner. Reciprocal negative easements are never retroactive; the very nature of their origin forbids. They arise, if at all, out of a benefit accorded land retained, by restrictions upon neighboring land sold by a common owner. Such a scheme of restrictions must start with a common owner; it cannot arise and fasten upon one lot by reason of other lot owners conforming to a general plan. If a reciprocal negative easement attached to defendants' lot it was fastened thereto while in the hands of the common owner of it and neighboring lots by way of sale of other lots with restrictions beneficial at that time to it. This leads to inquiry as to what lots, if any, were sold with restrictions by the common owner before the sale of defendants' lot. While the proofs cover another avenue we need consider sales only on Collingwood.

[On] December 28, 1892, Robert J. and Joseph R. McLaughlin, who were then evidently owners of the lots on Collingwood avenue, deeded lots 37 to 41 and 58 to 62, inclusive, with the following restrictions: "No residence shall be erected upon said premises, which shall cost less than $2,500 and nothing but residences shall be erected upon said premises. Said residences shall front on Helene (now Collingwood) avenue and be placed no nearer than 20 feet from the front street line." [On] July 24, 1893, the McLaughlins conveyed lots 17 to 21 and 78 to 82, both inclusive, and lot 98 with the same restrictions. Such restrictions were imposed for the benefit of the lands held by the grantors to carry out the scheme of a residential district, and a restrictive negative easement attached to the lots retained, and title to lot 86 was then in the McLaughlins. Defendants' title, through mesne conveyances, runs back to a deed by the McLaughlins dated September 7, 1893, without restrictions mentioned therein. Subsequent deeds to other lots were executed by the McLaughlins, some with restrictions and some without. Previous to September 7, 1893, a reciprocal negative easement had attached to lot 86 by acts of the owners, as before mentioned, and such easement is still attached and may now be enforced by plaintiffs, provided defendants, at the time of their purchase, had knowledge, actual or constructive, thereof. The plaintiffs run back with their title, as do defendants, to a common owner. This common owner, as before stated, by restrictions upon lots sold, had burdened all the lots retained with reciprocal restrictions. Defendants' lot and plaintiff Sanborn's lot, next thereto, were held by such common owner, burdened with a reciprocal negative easement and, when later sold to separate parties, remained burdened therewith and right to demand observance thereof passed to each purchaser with notice of the easement. The restrictions were upon defendants' lot while it was in the hands of the common owners, and abstract of title to defendants' lot showed the common owners and the record showed deeds of lots in the plat restricted to perfect and carry out the general plan and resulting in a reciprocal negative easement upon defendants' lot and all lots within its scope, and defendants and their predecessors in title were bound by constructive notice under our recording acts. The original plan was repeatedly declared in subsequent sales of lots by restrictions in the deeds, and while some lots sold were not so restricted the purchasers thereof, in every instance, observed the general plan and purpose of the restrictions in building residences. For upward of 30 years the united efforts of all persons interested have carried out the common purpose of making and keeping all the lots strictly for residences, and defendants are the first to depart therefrom.

When Mr. McLean purchased on contract in 1910 or 1911, there was a partly built dwelling house on lot 86, which he completed and now occupies. He had an abstract of title which he examined and claims he was told by the grantor that the lot was unrestricted. Considering the character of use made of all the lots open to a view of Mr. McLean when he purchased, we think he was put thereby to inquiry, beyond asking his grantor whether there were restrictions. He had an abstract showing the subdivision and that lot 86 had 97 companions; he could not avoid noticing the strictly uniform residence character given the lots by the expensive dwellings thereon, and the least inquiry would have quickly developed the fact that lot 86 was subjected to a reciprocal negative easement, and he could finish his house and, like the others, enjoy the benefits of the easement. We do not say Mr. McLean should have asked his neighbors about restrictions, but we do say that with the notice he had from a view of the premises on the street, clearly indicating the residences were built and the lots occupied in strict accordance with a general plan, he was put to inquiry, and had he inquired he would have found of record the reason for such general conformation, and the benefits thereof serving the owners of lot 86 and the obligations running with such service and available to adjacent lot owners to prevent a departure from the general plan by an owner of lot 86.

While no case appears to be on all fours with the one at bar the principles we have stated, and the conclusions announced, are supported by Allen v. City of Detroit, 167 Mich. 464 (1911); McQuade v. Wilcox, 215 Mich. 302 (1921); French v. White Star Refining Co., 229 Mich. 474 (1924); Silberman v. Uhrlaub, 116 N.Y. App. Div. 869, 102 N.Y. Supp. 299 (1907); Boyden v. Roberts, 131 Wis. 659 (1907)....

We notice the decree in the circuit directed that the work done on the building be torn down. If the portion of the building constructed can be utilized for any purpose within the restrictions it need not be destroyed. With this modification the decree in the circuit is affirmed, with costs to plaintiffs.

NOTES, QUESTIONS, AND PROBLEMS

1. *Equitable Servitudes Distinguished from Real Covenants.* The obvious difference is that an equitable servitude is a covenant whose enforcement is sought by means of an injunction rather than damages. Less obviously, the requirements for enforcement of an equitable servitude by or against successors in interest differ from the requirements for enforcing a real covenant. For an equitable servitude to run with the land, 1) the covenant must be intended to bind successors; 2) the successors in interest must take with notice of the covenant; and 3) the substance of the covenant must touch and concern the affected land.

Because privity of estate is not required for the burden of an equitable servitude to run with the land, an equitable servitude does not attach to an *estate* in land, but to the *land itself*. To invoke and alter Professor Powell's metaphor of the real covenant as a "bird riding on a wagon," an equitable servitude is a badger burrowing into the soil to make a permanent home, or the rabbits in their warren of *Watership Down* after vanquishing General Woundwort.

But what if the *benefit* of an equitable servitude is held by an owner of an estate lacking vertical privity with the original covenantor? Most jurisdictions hold that if the benefit holder is a third party beneficiary of the covenant it may be enforced by that person. See Runyon v. Paley, 331 N.C. 293 (1992). But some states still cling to vertical privity as a device to limit standing to enforce covenants. See, e.g., Malley v. Hanna, 65 N.Y.2d 289 (1985).

2. *Creation by Implication from a General Plan.* Not every jurisdiction permits an equitable servitude to be created by implication from a general plan of development. California, for example, does not permit equitable servitudes to arise from implication. Riley v. Bear Creek Planning Commission, 17 Cal.3d 500 (1976). Neither does Massachusetts, although a general plan of development may be used as evidence that written covenants were intended to benefit owners of property in the development, and thus enforceable by them. Snow v. Van Dam, 291 Mass. 477 (1935). Virginia limits all equitable servitudes (whether written or implied) to those created as part of a general development plan. Barner v. Chappell, 266 Va. 277 (2003). In Virginia, covenants created apart from a general plan must meet the requirements for real covenants (including horizontal privity) but, once established, may be enforced by either damages or an injunction. The Third Restatement of Property, Servitudes, § 2.14, embraces servitudes implied from a general plan. Comment f to that section sets forth the considerations for finding the existence of a general plan: representations by the developer and the existence of similar restrictions in many deeds from a common owner. But the absence of any recorded development plat, significant differences in restrictions imposed, or the failure to impose restrictions on large portions of the putative development are all factors evidencing a lack of a general plan. See also Fong

v. Hashimoto, 92 Haw. 568, 573 (2000) (restrictions on three of fifteen lots insufficient to constitute a "common scheme or plan"); Olson v. Albert, 523 A.2d 585, 588 (Maine 1987) (restrictions on four of sixteen lots insufficient to establish a common scheme).

3. *Notice.* What sort of notice is necessary to the running of an equitable servitude? Notice may be *actual*, derived from the chain of title (*record notice*), or result from circumstances that would induce a reasonable person to inquire and thus learn of the existence of a covenant (*inquiry notice*). Which form of notice was present in *Sanborn*? inquiry notice

4. *Problems.*

a. *O* owns Green Acres, consisting of ten lots. *O* conveys Lots 1 through 5 to *A* under a deed limiting each lot to residential use and similarly burdening his retained land. Then *O* conveys Lot 6 to *B* under a deed containing no restrictions. Then *O* conveys Lots 7 through 10 to *C* under a deed limiting each lot to residential use. *B* lacks actual notice of the restrictions on any of the other lots in Green Acres. Does *B* have record notice? Inquiry notice? Why or why not?

b. *A* and *B* are friends and neighbors. *A* owns Alpha Acre and *B* owns Beta Block. As a birthday present to *B*, *A* delivers to *B* a written instrument in which he declares that, "on behalf of himself and his successors in interest in Alpha Acre, no plastic pink flamingoes shall ever be exhibited publicly on Alpha Acre." *B* records the instrument. Later, *A* conveys Alpha Acre to *C* and *B* conveys Beta Block to *D*. Then *C* places several plastic pink flamingoes on his front lawn. What remedies, if any, does *D* have?

4. LIMITATIONS ON SERVITUDES

a. Benefits and Burdens Held in Gross

in a person

A venerable principle of the law of servitudes is that the burden of a covenant will not run in *equity* if the benefit is in gross. The root of this principle is in English law. Because English courts regarded equitable servitudes as the functional equivalent of a negative easement, and because an easement could not exist without a dominant estate, the English courts fashioned this rule. See, e.g., London County Council v. Allen, 3 K.B. 642 (1914). American courts accepted the notion that an equitable servitude and a negative easement were analogues (recall the court's characterization of the implied equitable servitude in *Sanborn* as a "reciprocal negative easement"), but failed to appreciate that, in America, easements can be held in gross. A common example is an easement granted by property owner *O* to a utility company, permitting the utility to string its service lines over, under, or upon the property. The utility company is usually a corporation that does not own any land benefitted by the easement, but nevertheless the burden runs to *O*'s successor in equity so long as that successor takes with notice. Given the fact that the English root of this doctrine is not applicable in America, are there any reasons to adhere to the rule that the burden will not run in equity if the benefit is in gross? In thinking about this question, consider the ease or difficulty of

EIG

terminating such a servitude by agreement between the burdened estate owner and the in gross owner of the benefit.

The Third Restatement of Property, Servitudes, § 2.6, takes the position that the burden will run even when the benefit is in gross, but also provides that such servitudes may be modified or terminated if it becomes "impossible or impracticable locate the beneficiaries of a servitude held in gross." § 7.13. As noted in subsection A.5 of this chapter, concerning easements, many states have enacted statutes that expressly validate conservation easements that burden land but the benefit of which is held in gross.

There has never been any objection to the benefit of a covenant running with the land when the burden is in gross. An old New Jersey case explained the difference in this way:

> The reason assigned for [the rule that the burden will not run when the benefit is in gross] was the public inconvenience that would result if incidents could be annexed to land "as multiform and as innumerable as human caprice." But when we turn our attention to the consideration of those covenants, which, instead of being burthensome to the land, are beneficial to it, we perceive at once that such objection does not apply. Such covenants do not hinder, but rather facilitate, the transmission of land from hand to hand, and, therefore, with respect to their transmissibility, the question of public convenience has no place.

National Union Bank at Dover v. Segur, 39 N.J.L. 173 (Sup. Ct. 1877).

PROBLEMS

1. Frank, a famous architect noted for his innovative residential designs, enters into a partnership with Donald, a developer. Donald offers to prospective buyers of building lots that he owns the opportunity to have their house designed by Frank. *A* agrees, and the deed to Fallingrock, the lot that *A* purchases, contains a covenant that 20% of the profit on any resale of Fallingrock will be paid in equal portions to Donald and Frank. The covenant expressly purports to bind *A*'s successors and assigns and expressly limits the benefit to Frank and Donald personally. Frank designs and Donald constructs an architecturally acclaimed home on Fallingrock. *A* later sells it to *B* and remits 20% of his profit to Frank and Donald, in equal portions. Later, *B* sells Fallingrock to *C* but refuses to share any portion of his profit on the sale with either Donald or Frank, each of whom then sue *B* to enforce the covenant. What result?

2. Assume that Donald sells another lot, Wingspan, to *X* by a deed containing a covenant that the structure erected thereon may not be altered without the consent of Frank, who will design that structure. The covenant expressly purports to bind *X*'s successors and assigns. Frank designs and Donald constructs an architecturally acclaimed home on Wingspan. Later, *X* sells Wingspan to *Y*, who starts to construct an addition to the home on Wingspan. Frank sues to enjoin the modification. What result?

HILL v. COMMUNITY OF DAMIEN OF MOLOKAI

Supreme Court of New Mexico
121 N.M. 353 (1996)

FROST, J., delivered the opinion of the court.

Defendant–Appellant Community of Damien of Molokai (Community) appeals from the district court's ruling in favor of Plaintiffs–Appellees, enjoining the further use of the property at 716 Rio Arriba, S.E., Albuquerque, as a group home for individuals with AIDS. Plaintiffs–Appellees argue that the group home violates a restrictive covenant. The Community contends that the group home is a permitted use under the covenant and, alternatively, that enforcing the restrictive covenant against the group home would violate the Federal Fair Housing Act, 42 U.S.C. §§ 3601–3631(1988) [hereinafter FHA]. We ... reverse. *Grp home allowed*

I. *Facts*

The underlying facts of this case are not in dispute. The Community is a private, nonprofit corporation which provides homes to people with AIDS as well as other terminal illnesses. In December 1992 the Community leased the residence at 716 Rio Arriba, S.E., Albuquerque, located in a planned subdivision called Four Hills Village, for use as a group home for four individuals with AIDS. The four residents who subsequently moved into the Community's group home were unrelated, and each required some degree of in-home nursing care.

Plaintiffs–Appellees ... (hereinafter Neighbors) live in Four Hills Village on the same dead-end street as the group home. Shortly after the group home opened, the Neighbors noticed an increase in traffic on Rio Arriba street, going to and from the group home. The Neighbors believed that the Community's use of its house as a group home for people with AIDS violated one of the restrictive covenants applicable to all the homes in ... Four Hills Village. ... The applicable covenant provides in relevant part:

> No lot shall ever be used for any purpose other than *single family residence purposes*. No dwelling house located thereon shall ever be used for other than *single family residence purposes,* nor shall any outbuildings or structure located thereon be used in a manner other than incidental to such *family residence purposes.* The erection or maintenance or use of any building, or the use of any lot for other purposes, including, but not restricted to such examples as stores, shops, flats, duplex houses, apartment houses, rooming houses, tourist courts, schools, churches, hospitals, and filling stations is hereby expressly prohibited. [Emphasis added by the court.]

The Neighbors specifically argue that the term "single family residence" does not include group homes in which unrelated people live together [and sought] an injunction to enforce the covenant and to prevent further use of the Community's house as a group home. ... After hearing evidence ... the trial court held that the restrictive covenant prevented the use of the Community's house as a group home for people with AIDS and issued a permanent injunction against the Community. ... The Community appealed ..., and we granted a stay of the permanent injunction pending this appeal. We now review, first, the Community's claims regarding the proper interpretation of the restrictive covenant, and second, the applicability of the FHA.

II. *Four Hills Restrictive Covenants*

The first issue ... is the applicability of the Four Hills restrictive covenant to the Community's group home. [We] are guided by certain general rules of construction. First, if the language is unclear or ambiguous, we will resolve the restrictive covenant in favor of the free enjoyment of the property and against restrictions. Second, we will not read restrictions on the use and enjoyment of the land into the covenant by implication. Third, we must interpret the covenant reasonably, but strictly, so as not to create an illogical, unnatural, or strained construction. Fourth, we must give words in the restrictive covenant their ordinary and intended meaning.

A.   Operating a Group Home Constitutes Residential Use

... In reaching its conclusion that the group home violated the residential use restriction, the trial court made two specific findings regarding the nature of the current use of the home. The court found that the "Community uses the house ... as a non profit hostel for providing services to handicapped individuals" and that the "Community uses of the residence are much closer to the uses commonly associated with health care facilities, apartment houses, and rooming houses than uses which are commonly associated with single family residences." Thus the trial court apparently concluded that the property was being used for commercial purposes rather than residential purposes. However, we find that the trial court's conclusions are incorrect as a matter of law.

It is undisputed that the group home is designed to provide the four individuals who live in the house with a traditional family structure, setting, and atmosphere, and that the individuals who reside there use the home much as would any family with a disabled family member. The four residents share communal meals. They provide support for each other socially, emotionally, and financially. They also receive spiritual guidance together from religious leaders who visit them on Tuesday evenings.

To provide for their health care needs, the residents contract with a private nursing service for health-care workers. These health-care workers do not reside at the home, and they are not affiliated with the Community in any way. ... The in-home health services that the residents receive from the health-care workers are precisely the same services to which any disabled individual would be entitled regardless of whether he or she lived in a group home or alone in a private residence. The health-care workers do most of the cooking and cleaning. The residents do their own shopping unless they are physically unable to leave the home.

The Community's role in the group home is to provide oversight and administrative assistance. It organizes the health-care workers' schedules to ensure that a nurse is present twenty-four hours per day, and it provides oversight to ensure that the workers are doing their jobs properly. It also receives donations of food and furniture on behalf of the residents. The Community provides additional assistance for the residents at times when they are unable to perform tasks themselves. A Community worker remains at the house during the afternoon and evening but does not reside at the home. The Community, in turn, collects rent from the residents based on the amount of social security income the residents receive, and it enforces a policy of no drinking or drug use in the home.

The Community's activities in providing the group home for the residents do not render the home a nonresidential operation such as a hospice or boarding house. As the South Carolina Supreme Court noted when faced with a similar situation involving a group home for mentally impaired individuals:

> This Court finds persuasive the reasoning of other jurisdictions which have held that the incident necessities of operating a group home such as maintaining records, filing accounting reports, managing, supervising, and providing care for individuals in exchange for monetary compensation are collateral to the prime purpose and function of a family housekeeping unit. Hence, these activities do not, in and of themselves, change the character of a residence from private to commercial.

Rhodes v. Palmetto Pathway Homes, Inc., 303 S.C. 308 (1991). In Jackson v. Williams, 714 P.2d 1017, 1022 (Okla. 1985), the Oklahoma Supreme Court similarly concluded:

> The essential purpose of the group home is to create a normal family atmosphere dissimilar from that found in traditional institutional care for the mentally handicapped. The operation of a group home is thus distinguishable from a use that is commercial—i.e., a boarding house that provides food and lodging only—or is institutional in character.

... We agree ... that the purpose of the group home is to provide the residents with a traditional family structure and atmosphere. Accordingly, we conclude as a matter of law that, given the undisputed facts regarding how the Community operates the group home and regarding the nature of the family life in the home, the home is used for residential purposes in compliance with the restrictive covenant.

B. Residents of Group Home Meet Single Family Requirement

The Neighbors also argue ... that the four, unrelated residents of the group home do not constitute a "single family" as required by the restrictive covenant. The Neighbors contend that the restrictive covenant should be interpreted such that the term "family" encompasses only individuals related by blood or by law. We disagree.

The word "family" is not defined in the restrictive covenant and nothing in the covenant suggests that it was the intent of the framers to limit the term to a discrete family unit comprised only of individuals related by blood or by law. Accordingly, the use of the term "family" in the covenant is ambiguous. As we noted above, we must resolve any ambiguity in the restrictive covenant in favor of the free enjoyment of the property. This rule of construction therefore militates in favor of a conclusion that the term "family" encompasses a broader group than just related individuals and against restricting the use of the property solely to a traditional nuclear family.

In addition, there are several other factors that lead us to define the term "family" as including unrelated individuals. First, the Albuquerque municipal zoning ordinance . . . includes within the definition of the term "family" "any group of not more than five [unrelated] persons living together in a dwelling." The Neighbors argue that the zoning code definition is irrelevant to the scope of the covenant. They point to Singleterry v. City of Albuquerque, 96 N.M. 468, 470 (1981), in which this Court stated ". . . that zoning ordinances cannot relieve private property from valid restrictive covenants if the ordinances are less restrictive." However, we agree with the Colorado Court of Appeals which noted, "While [the zoning] statute has no direct applicability to private covenants, it is some indication of the type of groups that might logically, as a matter of public policy, be included within the concept of a single family." Turner v. United Cerebral Palsy Ass'n, 772 P.2d 628, 630 (Colo. Ct. App. 1988) (construing term "family" in covenant to include unrelated group home residents). . . . In the present case, we are not using the zoning ordinances to relieve the Community of its obligations under the restrictive covenant. We are instead looking to the definition of family within the zoning ordinance as persuasive evidence for a proper interpretation of the ambiguous term in the covenant. The Albuquerque zoning ordinance would include the residents of the group home within its definition of family.

Second, there is a strong public policy in favor of including small group homes within the definition of the term "family." The federal government has expressed a clear policy in favor of removing barriers preventing individuals with physical and mental disabilities from living in group homes in residential settings and against restrictive definitions of "families" that serve to exclude congregate living arrangements for the disabled. The FHA squarely sets out this important public policy. . . . [T]he Act "is intended to prohibit special restrictive covenants or other terms or conditions, or denials of service because of an individual's handicap and which . . . exclude, for example, congregate living arrangements for persons with handicaps." [United States v. Scott, 788 F. Supp. 1555, 1561 (D. Kan. 1992) (quoting H.R. Rep. No. 711, 100th Cong., 2d Sess. 23–24 (1988).] This policy is applicable to the present case because the FHA's protections for handicapped people extend to individuals with AIDS....

In New Mexico, the Developmental Disabilities Act, NMSA 1978, § 28–16A–2 (Cum. Supp. 1995), expresses a clear state policy in favor of integrating disabled individuals into communities....

Both the federal and state governments have expressed a strong policy encouraging locating group homes in single-family residential areas and treating them as if they constituted traditional families. This overwhelming public policy is extremely persuasive in directing us toward an expansive interpretation of the term "family." *See* Crane Neck Ass'n v. New York City, 61 N.Y.2d 154 (1984) (refusing to enforce restrictive covenant that contravened long-standing public policy favoring the establishment of group homes for the mentally disabled), *cert. denied,* 469 U.S. 804 (1984)....

Third, other jurisdictions have consistently held that restrictive covenants mandating single-family residences do not bar group homes in which the occupants live as a family unit....

Accordingly, we reject the Neighbors' claim that the term "family" in the restrictive covenants should be read to include only individuals related by blood or by law. We agree with the court in Open Door Alcoholism Program, Inc. v. Board of Adjustment, 200 N.J. Super. 191, 491 A.2d 17, 21 (N.J. Super. Ct. App. Div. 1985), which noted, "The controlling factor in considering whether a group of unrelated individuals living together as a single housekeeping unit constitutes a family ... is whether the residents bear the generic character of a relatively permanent functioning family unit." ... [T]he individuals living in the Community's group home do operate as a family unit. Much of the activities of the residents are communal in nature. More importantly, the residents provide moral support and guidance for each other and together create an environment that assists them in living with the disease that has afflicted them. We find that the Community's group home "exhibits [the] kind of stability, permanency and functional lifestyle which is equivalent to that of the traditional family unit." 491 A.2d at 22. We therefore conclude that the Community's use of the property as a group home does not violate the Four Hills restrictive covenant.

C. Findings Regarding Increased Traffic

The Neighbors strenuously argue that the covenant should be interpreted to exclude the group home because ... "the amount of vehicular traffic generated by [the] Community's use of the house ... greatly exceeds what is expected in an average residential area" and that, as a result, "the character of [the] residential neighborhood relative to traffic and to parked vehicles has been significantly altered to the detriment of this residential neighborhood and [its] residents." ... However, the Neighbors fail to appreciate that the amount of traffic generated by the group home simply is not relevant to determining whether the use of the house as a group home violated the covenant in this case. [The] restrictive covenants for the Four Hills Village ... are not directed at controlling either traffic or on-street parking. The various covenants and restrictions that attach to the neighborhood homes merely regulate the structural appearance and use of the homes. ... [Not] one ... of the covenants attempts to control the number of automobiles that a resident may accommodate on or off the property nor the amount of traffic a resident may generate....

[The] amount of traffic generated by the group home simply does not affect the threshold question whether Community's use of the property as a group home violates the restrictive covenant requirement that the property not be used for any purpose other than single-family residence purposes. Accordingly, because the covenants do not regulate traffic or off-street parking, and because the amount of traffic generated by the group home is irrelevant to whether the home is used for single-family residential purposes, we conclude that the Neighbors' argument is without merit.

III. Fair Housing Act

The Community's second contention is that the trial court erred in concluding that the FHA did not apply in the present case. Although we have already agreed with the Community on its first argument that it did not violate the restrictive covenants, given the importance of the issues raised, we review the Community's second claim in order to correct the trial court's erroneous ruling on the legal effect of the FHA. ... [Even] if we were to adopt the Neighbors' proposed definition that the term "family" only included individuals related by blood or by law, we would still find for the Community because such a restriction would violate the FHA....

[The] trial court believed that a facially neutral restriction which is equally applicable to both handicapped and nonhandicapped individuals does not implicate the FHA. However, this view of the FHA is incorrect.

TC incorrect

Section 3604(f)(1) of the FHA provides in relevant part that it is unlawful "to discriminate in the sale or rental, or to otherwise make unavailable or deny, a dwelling to any buyer or renter because of a handicap of ... a person residing in or intending to reside in that dwelling after it is sold, rented, or made available." Section 3604(f)(3)(B) states, "For purposes of this subsection, discrimination includes ... a refusal to make reasonable accommodations in rules, policies, practices, or services, when such accommodations may be necessary to afford such person equal opportunity to use and enjoy a dwelling...."

Courts have interpreted these provisions as creating three distinct claims for violations of § 3604(f) of the FHA: discriminatory intent, disparate impact, and reasonable accommodation. *See* Stewart B. McKinney Found., Inc. v. Town Plan & Zoning Comm'n, 790 F. Supp. 1197, 1210–11, 1221 (D. Conn. 1992) (discussing each of these theories). The first two are based on § 3604(f)(1), whereas the third arises out of

§ 3604(f)(3). The Community has raised each of these claims and we will address each of them in turn.

At the outset, we note that the Neighbors do not contest that persons with AIDS are considered handicapped under the FHA.

A. Discriminatory Intent   *None*

A discriminatory-intent claim focuses on whether a defendant has treated handicapped individuals differently from other similarly situated individuals. "To prevail on its claim of discriminatory [intent], ... the plaintiff is not required to show the defendants were motivated by some purposeful, malicious desire to discriminate against HIV-infected persons." "[The] 'plaintiff need only show that the handicap of the potential residents [of a group home], a protected group under the FHA, was in some part the basis for' the policy being challenged." Potomac Group Home Corp. v. Montgomery County, 823 F. Supp. 1285, 1295 (D. Md. 1993).

... [T]he Community argues that the Neighbors were aware of the Community's use of the property as a group home and decided to enforce the covenants, in part, because of antagonism to that use. The Community presented evidence that the Neighbors' traffic complaints began a few days after a newspaper article was published that described the group home and that the Neighbors inquired into the availability of other possible sites for the home outside of their neighborhood. The Community also identified several covenant violations by other landowners in the neighborhood that were not being prosecuted. However, this evidence is equivocal at best. Absent further evidence of an intent to enforce the covenant because of some animus toward the use of the property as a group home because the residents have AIDS, the Community's allegations are insufficient to support a claim for discriminatory enforcement of the covenant.

B. Disparate Impact   *effect*

To demonstrate a violation of the FHA under the disparate-impact analysis, a plaintiff need only prove that the defendant's conduct actually or predictably results in discrimination or has a discriminatory effect. "The plaintiff need make no showing whatsoever that the action resulting in ... discrimination in housing was ... motivated [by a desire to discriminate against the handicapped]. Effect, and not motivation, is the touchstone." *McKinney Foundation,* 790 F. Supp. at 1216 (quoting United States v. City of Black Jack, 508 F.2d 1179, 1184–85 (8th Cir. 1974), *cert. denied,* 422 U.S. 1042, 45 L. Ed. 2d 694, 95 S. Ct. 2656 (1975))....

[We] find that the Community has proved that enforcing the covenant as interpreted by the Neighbors would violate the FHA. First, the covenant, which attempts to limit group homes, has the discriminatory effect of denying housing to the handicapped. Individuals with disabling handicaps, such as the one suffered by the Community's residents, frequently require congregate living arrangements for physical assistance and psychological and emotional support in order to live outside of an institution and in a residential community. ... Without congregate living arrangements many disabled individuals would be unable to reside in traditional neighborhoods or communities and would be forced into hospitals and institutions. ... [The fact that] the negative effects of covenants that restrict congregate living arrangements are substantially more onerous for the disabled than for others ... weighs heavily in favor of the Community.

[The] Neighbors' interest ... to eliminate the increased traffic that ... detrimentally altered the residential character of the neighborhood ... is a legitimate interest which weighs in the Neighbors' favor. ... Accordingly, we must balance the Neighbors' interest in avoiding increased traffic against the Community's interest in providing housing to disabled individuals. ... We ... weigh in favor of the Community. A covenant that restricts occupancy only to related individuals or that bars group homes has a disparate impact not only on the current residents of the Community's group home who have AIDS but also on all disabled individuals who need congregate living arrangements in order to live in traditional neighborhoods and communities. ... [While] the trial court made a finding that the increased traffic generated by the Community's group home has negatively affected the residential character of the neighborhood [it] rejected the Neighbors' proposed finding of fact that this additional traffic posed any increased safety hazard to the neighborhood. ... Accordingly, we conclude that the negative effects of increased traffic, without any additional harms, are outweighed by the Community's interest in maintaining its congregate home for individuals with AIDS. Because the Community has proved a "disparate impact" under the FHA, the Neighbors cannot enforce the covenant against the Community....

C. Reasonable Accommodation

The Community's third claim under the FHA is that the Neighbors failed to make reasonable accommodations under § 3604(f)(3)(B). This section provides that "discrimination includes ... a refusal to make reasonable accommodations in rules, policies, practices or services when such accommodations may be necessary to afford [a handicapped] person equal opportunity to use and enjoy a dwelling." " 'Reasonable accommodation' has been defined [to include] 'changing some rule that is generally applicable so as to make its burden less onerous on the handicapped individual.' " North Shore–Chicago Rehabilitation, Inc. v. Village of Skokie, 827 F. Supp. 497, 508 (N.D. Ill. 1993) (quoting Oxford House, Inc. v. Township of Cherry Hill, 799 F. Supp. 450, 462 n.25 (D.N.J. 1992)); see also United States v. City of Philadelphia, 838 F. Supp. 223, 228 (E.D. Pa. 1993) (noting that cities must waive, change, or make exceptions in restrictive zoning rules to afford handicapped individuals equal opportunity to use and enjoy housing), aff'd, 30 F.3d 1488 (3rd Cir. 1994). In City of Philadelphia, the court explained that "an accommodation is not reasonable (1) if it would require a fundamental alteration in the nature of a program, or (2) if it would impose undue financial or administrative burdens on the defendant." Although § 3604(f)(3)(B) is more frequently applied to restrictive zoning ordinances, it is equally applicable to restrictive covenants. . . .

[T]he restriction does not need to be directed at the handicapped. It does not even need to have a disparate impact on handicapped groups in general. The restriction need only serve as an impediment to an individual plaintiff who is handicapped and is denied access to housing in order to implicate the "reasonable accommodation" requirement of the FHA. . . . [The Neighbors'] proposed interpretation of the Four Hills restrictive covenant . . . has the effect of denying housing access to the handicapped residents. Accordingly, § 3604(f)(3)(B) of the FHA is implicated, and the Neighbors would be required to reasonably accommodate the group home provided it would not require a fundamental alteration in the nature of the restrictions or impose undue financial or administrative burdens on the Neighbors.

The Neighbors do not suggest that allowing the group home to operate would impose any financial or administrative burdens on them. The Neighbors are not responsible for operating or maintaining the group home in any way, nor do they have to pay any additional costs as a result of the group home. Furthermore, nonenforcement of the single-family residence requirement against the Community's group home would not fundamentally alter the nature of the restrictions. As discussed above, the Four Hills restrictive covenants as a whole were designed to regulate the structural appearance of houses and to prevent the use of houses for business purposes. The Community's use of the property for a group home does not affect its structural appearance and is not a business use. The residents use the house like a traditional residential home and act as a second family for one another. Indeed, the Neighbors' stated reason for enforcing the restrictive covenant is not because of the nonresidential nature of the occupancy, but because of the additional traffic generated by the group home. However, traffic regulation is not a fundamental aspect of the Four Hills restrictive covenants.

Accordingly, we conclude that nonenforcement of the Four Hills restrictive covenants against the Community's group home would not impose an undue hardship or burden on the Neighbors and would not interfere with the plain purpose of the covenants. . . . "A reasonable accommodation would have been not to seek enforcement of the covenant." . . .

V. Conclusion

We conclude that the Community is entitled to continue operating its group home for individuals with AIDS both under the Four Hills restrictive covenants and under the Fair Housing Act. [The] trial court's ruling is reversed and the injunction is vacated. . . .

NOTE AND PROBLEMS

1. *Interpretation of the Scope of Covenants.* The New Mexico court stated that any ambiguity in a restrictive covenant should be resolved "in favor of

the free enjoyment of property and against restrictions." The rationale for that common law principle is that covenants tend to retard alienation and thus block the most efficient use of property. In contrast to the common law rule is the Third Restatement of Property, Servitudes, § 4.1, which asserts that a "servitude should be interpreted to give effect to the intention of the parties ascertained from the language used in the instrument, or the circumstances surrounding creation of the servitude, and to carry out the purpose for which it was created." Under the Restatement rule, the limits on covenants inhere in § 3.1, which invalidate covenants that are illegal, unconstitutional, or violate public policy. However, the New Mexico court's application of the common law rule of interpretation produced the same result that would have occurred had the Third Restatement rule been applied. But that is not necessarily the case. In Mains Farm Homeowners Association v. Worthington, 121 Wn.2d 810 (1993), the Washington Supreme Court relied on the "ordinary and common use" of language to determine "the intent of the parties" in imposing a covenant limiting use to "single family residential purposes." The court expressed doubt that the common law interpretive canon should apply to subdivision covenants because it thought that such covenants were likely to enhance, rather than inhibit, efficient land use. The court held that a homeowner's provision of continuous care to four adults in her residence for compensation was a commercial enterprise that violated the covenant, despite the fact that the owner also resided in the property.

2. *Problems.*

a. Blackacre, owned and occupied by *O*, is burdened by a covenant limiting use to single family residential purposes. *O* converts a spare bedroom into a room housing a number of computer servers, which he uses to offer computerized data storage and retrieval services to people who access his servers entirely on-line. *X*, a neighbor whose property is benefitted by the covenant, learns of *O*'s activity and seeks to enjoin *O* from conducting this activity on Blackacre. What result?

b. Whiteacre, owned and occupied by *K*, is burdened by a covenant limiting use to residential and recreational uses. *K* rents his bedrooms to transient visitors as a bed and breakfast and also raises and trains dogs for participation in the Iditarod sled dog race, 1150 miles from Anchorage to Nome, Alaska. *Z*, an owner of neighboring property benefitted by the covenant, seeks an injunction of this activity. What result?

SHELLEY v. KRAEMER

United States Supreme Court
334 U.S. 1 (1948)

CHIEF JUSTICE VINSON delivered the opinion of the Court.

These cases present for our consideration questions relating to the validity of court enforcement of private agreements, generally described as restrictive covenants, which have as their purpose the exclusion of persons of designated race or color from the ownership or occupancy of real property. ... On February 16, 1911, thirty out of a total of thirty-nine owners of property fronting both sides of Labadie Avenue between Taylor

Avenue and Cora Avenue in the city of St. Louis, signed an agreement, which was subsequently recorded, providing in part: "that hereafter no part of said property or any portion thereof shall be … occupied by any person not of the Caucasian race, it being intended hereby to restrict the use of said property … against the occupancy as owners or tenants of any portion of said property for resident or other purpose by people of the Negro or Mongolian Race." …

On August 11, 1945, pursuant to a contract of sale, petitioners Shelley, who are Negroes, for valuable consideration received from one Fitzgerald a warranty deed to the parcel in question. The trial court found that petitioners had no actual knowledge of the restrictive agreement at the time of the purchase. … On October 9, 1945, respondents, as owners of other property subject to the terms of the restrictive covenant, brought suit in the Circuit Court of the city of St. Louis praying that petitioners Shelley be restrained from taking possession of the property and that judgment be entered divesting title out of petitioners Shelley and revesting title in the immediate grantor or in such other person as the court should direct. The trial court denied the requested relief. … The Supreme Court of Missouri … reversed … and concluded that enforcement of its provisions violated no rights guaranteed to petitioners by the Federal Constitution.

[Petitioners] urge that they have been denied the equal protection of the laws. … Whether the equal protection clause [inhibits] judicial enforcement by state courts of restrictive covenants based on race or color is a question which this Court has not heretofore been called upon to consider. [It is] clear that restrictions on the right of occupancy of the sort sought to be created by the private agreements in these cases could not be squared with the requirements of the Fourteenth Amendment if imposed by state statute or local ordinance. [But] the present cases [do] not involve action by state legislatures or city councils. Here the [racial] discrimination and the [restrictive covenants are produced] by the terms of agreements among private individuals. Participation of the State consists in the enforcement of the restrictions.

Since [the] Civil Rights Cases, 109 U.S. 3 (1883), the principle has become firmly embedded in our constitutional law that the action inhibited by [the] Fourteenth Amendment is only such action as may fairly be said to be that of the States. That Amendment erects no shield against merely private conduct, however discriminatory or wrongful. [The] restrictive agreements standing alone cannot be regarded as violative of any rights guaranteed to petitioners by the Fourteenth Amendment. So long as the purposes of those agreements are effectuated by voluntary adherence to their terms, [there] has been no action by the State and the provisions of the Amendment have not been violated. But here there was more. [The] purposes of the agreements were secured only by judicial enforcement by state courts of the restrictive terms of the agreements. [Action] of state courts and judicial officers in their official capacities [has] long been established [as state action].

We have no doubt that there has been state action.... [Petitioners] were willing purchasers of properties upon which they desired to establish homes. The owners of the properties were willing sellers; and contracts of sale were accordingly consummated. [But] for the active intervention of the state courts, supported by the full panoply of state power, petitioners would have been free to occupy the properties in question without restraint. These are not cases [in] which the States have merely abstained from action, leaving private individuals free to impose such discriminations as they see fit. Rather, these are cases in which the States have made available to such individuals the full coercive power of government to deny to petitioners, on the grounds of race or color, the enjoyment of property rights in premises which petitioners are willing and financially able to acquire and which the grantors are willing to sell. The difference between judicial enforcement and non-enforcement of the restrictive covenants is the difference to petitioners between being denied rights of property available to other members of the community and being accorded full enjoyment of those rights on an equal footing. [State] action [refers] to exertions of state power in all forms. [We] hold that in granting judicial enforcement of the restrictive agreements in these cases, the States have denied petitioners the equal protection of the laws and that, therefore, the action of the state courts cannot stand.

NOTES AND PROBLEM

1. What was the State Action? In Barrows v. Jackson, 346 U.S. 249 (1953), the Supreme Court applied *Shelley* to hold that courts may not award damages for breach of a racially restrictive covenant. The Court said that a damages award would "coerce" a property owner "to observe a restrictive covenant that" could not be enforced "in equity. [If] the State may thus punish [the owner] for her failure to carry out her covenant, she is coerced to continue to use her property in a discriminatory manner. [It is no longer the owner's] voluntary choice but the State's choice that she observe her covenant or suffer damages." As was true in *Shelley*, the private parties wished to transfer the property in violation of the covenant; only the coercive hand of the state's judicial system frustrated them.

In Bell v. Maryland, 378 U.S. 226 (1964), Justice Hugo Black explained that "the reason judicial enforcement of the restrictive covenants in *Shelley* was deemed state action was not merely the fact that a state court had acted, but rather that it had acted 'to deny to petitioners, on the grounds of race, [the] enjoyment of property [that] petitioners are willing [and] able to acquire and which the grantors are willing to sell.' [But] when one party is unwilling," there is no state action.

2. Beyond State Action. While state action is necessary to invoke the Constitution, it is not the only way to invalidate racially restrictive covenants. Federal and state laws can and do make private racial discrimination in housing unlawful. See, e.g., the provisions of the Fair Housing Act, codified at 42 U.S.C. §§ 3601–3631. Moreover, the common law rules applicable to running covenants and equitable servitudes might have operated to prevent enforcement of the covenant. Do you see why? The Third Restatement approach to the invalidity of covenants would also prevent the enforcement of such a covenant. See Rest. (3d) Property, Servitudes § 3.1.

3. *Problem. A*, owner of Lots 1 and 2, located in Maine, conveys Lot 1 to *B* by a deed that restricts ownership or occupancy of Lot 1 to persons who have neither been born in Massachusetts nor ever resided in Massachusetts for more than one year. *B* enters into a contract to sell Lot 1 to *C*, a native of Massachusetts. *A* seeks an injunction to prevent the sale to *C*. What result? See Alfred L. Brophy and Shubha Ghosh, Whistling Dixie: The Invalidity and Unconstitutionality of Covenants Against Yankees, 10 Vill. Envtl. L.J. 57 (1999). *[handwritten: Restatement — wont enforce covenants against public policy]*

5. MODIFICATION OR TERMINATION OF SERVITUDES

As with easements, covenants may be terminated by release, merger, estoppel, abandonment, condemnation, prescription, or expiration (if a period of time specified in the covenant has elapsed). They may be modified by consent and, in the case of such common interest communities as condominiums or planned developments, even without unanimous consent. Finally, they may be modified or terminated if the conditions have changed sufficiently to warrant modification or termination.

WEST ALAMEDA HEIGHTS HOMEOWNERS ASSOCIATION v. BOARD OF COUNTY COMMISSIONERS OF JEFFERSON COUNTY

Supreme Court of Colorado
169 Colo. 491 (1969)

DAY, J., delivered the opinion of the court.

The West Alameda Heights Homeowners Association and certain individual homeowners, representatives in a class action for persons who reside in West Alameda Heights Subdivision, [appeal from a] decree of the Jefferson County district court, declaring null and void restrictive covenants on a number of lots in certain blocks in the subdivision. As plaintiffs below they brought an action to enjoin the construction of two large shopping facilities on the subject property by the F.W. Woolworth Company and Safeway Stores, Inc. . . . . . The three Newtons are made defendants as owners of the property. George Newton was the original developer of the subdivision who in 1947 filed the plat and created the covenants contained therein. The subdivision is bounded on the north by West First Avenue; on the east by Wadsworth Boulevard; on the south by West Alameda; and on the west by Cody Street. Outside of the subdivision, particularly to the east and to the southeast, there has been extensive commercial development, and both Wadsworth Boulevard and West Alameda are major four-lane highways.

The plat contains protective covenants restricting the use of the lands in the subdivision. Each covenant provides that, except as noted, all lots shall be Residential.... [The] subdivision is large and almost fully developed as planned, consisting primarily of single family residences. There are over 350 lots comprising the tract. Only 80 to 85 of these have not been developed. The only commercial uses presently situated in the subdivision are a service station and a garden center located on land originally reserved for commercial use in the plat. Apartments have been constructed on other land set aside for commercial purposes. The major portion of three blocks—numbers 13, 14 and 15—proposed to be used for the shopping facilities was platted as residential property and restricted to such use by the covenants which have never been amended. The original covenants provide that they would be in force until June 30, 1965 and automatically extended for successive ten-year periods unless the owners of a majority of the lots by vote change the covenants in whole or in part. There has been no attempt to amend or change them, no election has been called or held, and the present extension of the covenants does not expire until June 30, 1975.

The factor which precipitated this action was an application by George Newton to re-zone a portion of the blocks retained by him to permit the building of a Safeway Store and a Woolco Department Store. This property still owned by George Newton fronts on West Alameda and extends northward approximately 600 feet to an area zoned for single family homes. It was planned to erect a buffer consisting of a masonry wall not less than five feet nor more than six feet in height between the commercial enterprises and the residential property to the north.

The writ of error here involves only ... the restrictive covenants. [The] plaintiffs ... aver that the purchasers of the lots in the subdivision relied on restrictive and protective covenants which were designed for the protection of the neighborhood and of the property; and that the restrictions are applicable not only to the property in the development which has been sold but also to the property retained by the defendant George Newton for future sales. They allege they have invested large sums of money in lots and homes in the subdivision in reliance on the covenant.

In entering judgment against the homeowners on this claim, the trial court made the following findings, *inter alia*:

10. The character of this neighborhood has changed considerably since the West Alameda Heights was created. The subject land borders on West Alameda Avenue, a short distance from the intersection of Wadsworth Avenue. At the time of the imposition of the covenants, Alameda was mainly a residential avenue. Now it is a heavily traveled thoroughfare and the area is developing as a commercial area. Villa Italia Shopping Center is at the intersection of Alameda and Wadsworth.

11. The subject land is not suitable for residential use and is suitable only for commercial use. Plaintiffs will suffer no damage by commercial use. To deprive the defendants Newton of the right to use the property would not be equitable and if the restrictive covenants

are enforced, they would be deprived of the right to use their property. The enforcement of the restrictive covenants would impose an oppressive burden on defendants Newton without any substantial benefit.

The court declared the restrictive covenants to be null and void as to the subject property. . . .

We . . . hold that the covenants are valid and enforceable. The pertinent rule of law applicable to this case is most recently set out in Zavislak v. Shipman, 147 Colo. 184, 362 P.2d 1053, wherein this court adopted the language of McArthur v. Hood Rubber Co., 221 Mass. 372, 109 N.E. 162, as follows: ". . . When the purpose for which the restriction was imposed has come to an end, and where the use of the tract of land for whose benefit it was established has so utterly changed that no party to the bill could be heard to enforce it in equity or would suffer any damage by its violation, . . . a proper case is made out for equitable relief. . . ."

Parties plaintiffs and defendants all rely on our pronouncement in *Zavislak*. The court, in striking down the covenants, attempted to apply the same rule of law. We hold, however, that the court misconceived and misapplied the rule to changes and developments outside of and beyond the subdivision itself. This is made evident by the court's reference to the changed traffic patterns on Wadsworth and Alameda and the development of Villa Italia Shopping Center and other developments east of the Alameda and Wadsworth intersection.

The true test here, however, as to whether the purpose of the restrictions has come to an end, is the development of the subdivision which is the subject of the covenants subsequent to their creation. Thus the courts look to whether the original purposes of insuring maintenance of residential character for the subdivision has been abandoned or changed by acquiescence or passiveness of the subdivision residents.

Newton, in planning the property with the restrictions which he imposed, intended to insure the maintenance of the residential character for the subdivision. That purpose has continued to the present time, and the effect of it is demonstrated by what has happened to land outside of its perimeter over which the West Alameda Heights residents had no control. It is undisputed that in the subdivision wherein the covenants did control no change of the use contemplated when the plat was filed has occurred. Only the property originally platted for use of commercial enterprises thereon has been occupied as such.

Another test announced in the *Zavislak* case is whether the parties would suffer any damage by the removal of the covenant. [The] testimony of the individual plaintiffs was that their property would be subject to substantial decrease in value. One of plaintiffs' witnesses—a professional land planner—depicted the foreseeable increase in traffic to and from the proposed shopping facility with concomitant increase in noise, fumes, and hazard to children. The Traffic and Safety Engineer for Jefferson County stated that although he probably could control increased traffic through the residential area by the use of traffic signals and one-way streets, he candidly admitted that such a traffic pattern would inconvenience the homeowners as much as it might deter shoppers from driving through the area. There was testimony as to the present pleasant aspects of the neighborhood, undisturbed by the commercial activity beyond the borders. Contrariwise, the defendants did not prove that the purpose of the protective covenants had come to an end; that the land use within the tract had changed from what it was intended to be at the time the plat was filed; and that no person would suffer any damage by its violation. The evidence therefore is contrary to the court's finding that plaintiffs will suffer no damage from commercial use of the subject property.

Cases are numerous from other jurisdictions wherein covenants have been sought to be removed because subject lands would be more valuable for commercial than for residential purposes, and wherein there were conditions such as the presence of commercial uses nearby, heavy street traffic on the perimeter of the tract, and some commercial property within a primarily residential subdivision. But the weight of authority supports the view that *changes outside* of the tract will not warrant the lifting of restrictive covenants affecting property within the subdivision if the covenants are still a benefit to the owners of the property under the restrictions. Robertson v. Nichols, 92 Cal. App.2d 201, 206 P.2d 898; Batman v. Creighton, 101 So.2d 587 (Fla. App.); Cawthon v. Anderson, 211 Ga. 77, 84 S.E.2d 66; Redfern Lawns Civic Ass'n, et al. v. Currie Pontiac Co., 328 Mich. 463, 44 N.W.2d 8; Weinstein v. Swartz, 3 N.J. 80, 68 A.2d 865; Chuba v. Glasgow, 61 N.M. 302, 299 P.2d 774; Frey v. Poynor, 369 P.2d 168 (Okla.); Pitts v. Brown, 215 S.C. 122, 54 S.E.2d 538; Bullock v. Steinmil Realty, Inc., 1 Misc.2d 46, 145 N.Y.S.2d 331, *aff'd* 3 App. Div. 2d 806, 161 N.Y.S.2d 602.

Normal growth and change and the possibility of encroachment of commercial uses, we can infer, were contemplated when the covenants and the master plan of development were created by the original owner and platter. There would be no need for the covenants to protect the subdivisions from inroads of commercial expansion if it were not expected that such might take place. As long as the original purpose of the covenants can still be accomplished and substantial benefit will inure to the restricted area by their enforcement, the covenants stand even though the subject property has a greater value if used for other purposes. *See* 4 A.L.R. 2d 1111. A comment in Cowling v. Colligan, 158 Tex. 458, 312 S.W.2d 943, appeals to us:

> The reasoning of the courts is that if because of changed conditions outside the restricted area one lot or tract were permitted to drop from under the protective cover of residential-only restrictions, the owner of the adjoining lot would then have an equal claim on the conscience of the court, and, in due course, all other lots would fall like ten-pins, thus circumventing and nullifying the restriction and destroying the essentially residential character of the entire area.

In the case of protective covenants, it has sometimes been held that changes within the affected area may result in modification or removal of the covenant because the changes were within the control of those entitled to enforce the covenant. In other words, the doctrines of abandonment, estoppel and waiver are applicable. *See* Thodos v. Shirk, 248 Iowa 172, 79 N.W.2d 733; Mechling v. Dawson, 234 Ky. 318, 28 S.W.2d 18; Greer v. Bornstein, 246 Ky. 286, 54 S.W.2d 927; Tull v. Doctors Bldg. Inc., 255 N.C. 23, 120 S.E.2d 817. However, as to changes in conditions occurring outside the area restricted, the parties affected have no control whatever, and the doctrines of waiver, abandonment and estoppel are not applicable. Here, the problem presents itself as to whether the outside conditions affect the entire subdivision in a way that the restrictive purposes of the protective covenants would be defeated. As stated in *Thodos* ...:

> In both cases the factual situation largely governs as to whether or not equity will refuse to enforce the restrictions for the reason that by so doing the result would be oppressive and inequitable without any appreciable value to other property in the restricted area. It has been said that in order for this equitable defense of change of conditions to arise, there must be a change in the character of the surrounding neighborhood sufficient to make it impossible any longer to secure in substantial degree the benefits sought to be realized through the performance of the building restriction.

The construction of Villa Italia Shopping Center and of other commercial properties outside of West Alameda Heights, but in close proximity to it, have not changed the residential character of the subdivision. If the changed conditions outside the tract have made the particular property held by the owner since the original platting less desirable for residential use than it previously was, this is not to say that the whole tract has been made unfit for residential use. On the contrary, the evidence shows that the subdivision is a residential area of high quality, with expensive homes and quiet streets. The construction of commercial facilities nearby are all the more reason why the covenants for West Alameda Heights must be strictly enforced. The covenants have no meaning if external forces and pressures result in their removal.

The judgment is reversed and the cause remanded to the trial court with directions to enter a permanent injunction as prayed for in the complaint.

NOTES

1. Changed Conditions. As you see from *West Alameda*, termination of covenants due to changed conditions is not easy to do. An extreme example is Rick v. West, 228 N.Y.S.2d 195 (1962). In 1946 Chester Rick subdivided 62 acres of vacant land in Cortland, a town in suburban Westchester County, New York, and in 1947 recorded restrictions limiting its use to residential. In 1956, Rick sold a half-acre lot to Catherine West, who constructed a residence on the lot a year later. The town zoned the property residential in 1957.

Meanwhile, Rick agreed to sell 45 acres to an industrial developer if the property could be rezoned for light industrial use and the restrictive covenant could be released. The town acquiesced in the rezoning but West refused to release the covenant. The sale fell through, but in 1961 Rick sold the entire 62 acres (except the lot he had conveyed to West and a "few other plots sold by him") to a third party who contracted to sell 15 acres to the Peekskill Hospital. When West refused to release the covenant Rick and the new owner sued West, seeking a declaratory judgment that the covenant was no longer enforceable due to changed circumstances and, in the alternative, limiting West's remedy for breach of the covenant to money damages. The court refused to do so:

> There is no evidence of any substantial change in the general neighborhood since the last affirmation of the restrictions and there is no change at all within the parcel owned by the plaintiffs. . . . The parcel in question would doubtless by its topography and proximity to fast-growing suburban areas make a desirable location for the hospital. The hospital authorities would like to acquire it, and the plaintiffs would like to sell it, and it may be asked why should defendant owning a most respectable, but modest, home be permitted to prevent the sale, or in any event why should the . . . defendant [not be] relegated to pecuniary damages. Plaintiffs' predecessor owned the tract free and clear of all restrictions. He could do with the parcel as he saw best. He elected to promote a residential development and in the furtherance of his plan, and as an inducement to purchasers he imposed the residential restrictions. The defendant relied upon them and has a right to continue to rely thereon. It is not a question of balancing equities or equating the advantages of a hospital on this site with the effect it would have on defendant's property. Nor does the fact that defendant is the only one of the few purchasers from plaintiffs' predecessor in title who has refused to release the covenants make defendant's insistence upon the enforcement of the covenants no less deserving of the court's protection and safeguarding of her rights.

The court quoted Justice Cardozo in Evangelical Lutheran Church of Ascension v. Sahlem, 254 N.Y. 161, 168 (1930): "The defendant, the owner, has done nothing but insist upon adherence to a covenant which is now as valid and binding as at the hour of its making. His neighbors are willing to modify the restriction and forego a portion of their rights. He refuses to go with them. Rightly or wrongly he believes that the comfort of his dwelling will be imperiled by the change, and so he chooses to abide by the covenant as framed. The choice is for him only."

2. *What Remedy?* The common law approach to termination of covenants by changed conditions is to use a property rule: If conditions within the tract subject to the covenants have changed sufficiently to warrant termination, the covenant is eliminated; if conditions have not so changed the covenant is enforceable so long as any holder of the benefit refuses to release it. Under what conditions, if at all, should a liability rule be used instead? The plaintiffs in Rick v. West urged the court to use a liability rule: terminate the covenant and award West damages for her loss. Should the court have done

so? What information might you (or the court) need to know to make that judgment? Or do you need to know any more facts?

3. *The Third Restatement Approach.* Section 7.10 of the Third Restatement of Property, Servitudes, is entitled "Modification and Termination of Servitudes Because of Changed Conditions," and applies to all servitudes except "conservation servitudes held by public bodies and conservation organizations," which are subject to separate rules contained in § 7.11. Section 7.10 states:

(1) When a change has taken place since the creation of a servitude that makes it impossible as a practical matter to accomplish the purpose for which the servitude was created, a court may modify the servitude to permit the purpose to be accomplished. If modification is not practicable, or would not be effective, a court may terminate the servitude. Compensation for resulting harm to the beneficiaries may be awarded as a condition of modifying or terminating the servitude.

(2) If the purpose of a servitude can be accomplished, but because of changed conditions the servient estate is no longer suitable for uses permitted by the servitude, a court may modify the servitude to permit other uses under conditions designed to preserve the benefits of the original servitude.

Note that the Third Restatement approach permits use of a liability rule and grants to judges considerably greater power to modify or terminate covenants over the objections of a single holdout.

4. *Holdouts.* The lone covenant beneficiary is not the only sort of holdout. Owners of fees simple absolute may not be forced to sell (except by government condemnation). If the Peekskill Hospital had wished to construct a medical facility on a tract that included West's residence it could not have forced her to sell (unless the Hospital was a government entity armed with the condemnation power). The court's resolution of the covenant termination claim in Rick v. West produced the same result. Should property rules apply to forced transfer of fee ownership and liability rules apply to forced transfer of covenant benefits?

5. *Problem.* Swampacre, a lot in Grassy Acres, a common interest development, is subject to covenants requiring the owner to pay a monthly fee to the Grassy Acres Homeowners' Association and limiting its use to a "permanent single family residential structure." *O*, the owner of Swampacre, discovered that the lot's soil is incapable of sufficient percolation to permit him lawfully to construct anything on the lot. *O* seeks a judicial declaration that the covenants are no longer enforceable. What result?

In thinking about this problem, consider sections 3.7 and 7.12 of the Third Restatement of Property, Servitudes. Section 3.7 invalidates unconscionable servitudes. Comment c to that section indicates that an unconscionable servitude contains "an element of overreaching, unfairness, surprise, or harshness that leads to the conclusion that the servitude should not be enforced, even though the disadvantaged party could have protected him-or herself through the exercise of proper precautions." Section 7.12(1) provides that a "covenant to pay money," other than for "services or facilities concurrently provided to the burdened estate," shall terminate "after a reasonable time if the instrument that created the covenant does not specify the total sum due or a definite termination point." Section 7.12(2) provides that a "covenant to pay money or provide services in exchange for services or facilities provided to the burdened estate may be modified or terminated if the obligation becomes excessive in relation to the cost of providing the services or facilities or to the value received by the burdened estate...."

C. COMMON INTEREST ARRANGEMENTS

Common interest communities take two basic forms. One is the planned unit development; the other is the cooperative corporation. Planned unit developments consist of parcels that are separately owned in fee simple absolute but which also contain a tenancy in common interest in the common areas of the development. For example a subdivision may contain 100 lots, on each of which is a single family residence owned in fee simple absolute, and common areas consisting of open space and recreational areas that are shared by all lot owners. Thus each lot owner owns his home in fee simple and has a tenancy in common interest in the common areas. The same principle applies to condominium developments, which usually consist of units in a building or buildings that house the individual units. A condominium owner has fee simple title to his or her unit and a tenancy in common interest in the common areas, which may consist of hallways, the roof of the building, the exterior walls, the land on which the building is erected, and any shared amenities, such as a swimming pool. In the planned unit development, each owner arranges his own financing for purchase of the unit, and is individually responsible for his mortgage payments, property taxes assessed on the unit, and obtaining liability and casualty insurance for his unit.

The developers of planned unit developments record the conditions, covenants, and restrictions that they think purchasers may desire. Thus, when each unit is sold horizontal privity is present and when each unit is resold to a successor vertical privity is present. Because the CC & Rs, as they are commonly called, are recorded purchasers take with constructive notice of them. The nature of the CC & Rs are almost certain to touch and concern the land involved in the development. Once the developer has begun to sell units, a homeowners' association is formed. All unit owners are members and the association, through its elected board of directors, is empowered to enforce the CC & Rs, make regulations to implement the CC & Rs and to adopt new covenants if the CC & Rs so permit. The cost of maintaining the common areas is assessed to each owner as a monthly fee. This fee may well include some amount that is retained by the homeowners' association as a reserve fund for unexpected or even anticipated repairs or improvements. All of these details will be spelled out in the CC & Rs. Every state has a statute that regulates planned unit developments. These types of developments have become commonplace in America and provide the housing for approximately 60 million people in the United States.

Cooperative apartment corporations take a different form. An apartment building is owned by a corporation. A purchaser of a unit in the building acquires shares of capital stock in the corporation which entitles him to a lease of the unit he intends to occupy. Acquisition and maintenance of the building is done through the corporation. Thus, the lease rentals reflect the pro rata cost of these expenses: Mortgage interest and principal, property taxes, insurance, maintenance, doormen, elevator operators, and even a concierge in some buildings. Cooperative apartments are most common in New York's Manhattan borough, and can be very expensive. Because the financial fate of the residents is highly interdependent—much more so than in a planned unit development—different legal rules have developed to deal with this form of shared ownership.

1. HOMEOWNERS' ASSOCIATIONS

Because common interest communities are subject to special statutory regulations, a recurring issue is the interpretation of statutes that direct or limit enforcement of the CC & Rs that are created by developers and imposed on initial and subsequent purchasers as part of their decision to acquire the property subject to the CC & Rs. For example, California Civil Code § 1354(a) provides:

> The covenants and restrictions in the [developer's] declaration [of CC & Rs] shall be enforceable equitable servitudes, unless unreasonable, and shall inure to the benefit of and bind all owners of separate interests in the development. Unless the declaration states otherwise, these servitudes may be enforced by any owner of a separate interest or by the association, or by both.

There are two issues thus presented. First, what constitutes an "unreasonable" covenant and, in determining that question, should the covenant automatically be presumed to be valid? Second, no matter what the answer to that first question may be, should the same rules apply when a homeowners' association imposes a new covenant or regulation as it may be permitted to do under the original CC & Rs?

NAHRSTEDT v. LAKESIDE VILLAGE CONDOMINIUM ASSOCIATION, INC.

Supreme Court of California
8 Cal.4th 361 (1994)

[Natore Nahrstedt owned a unit in Lakeside Village, a 530 unit condominium complex in Culver City, part of the Los Angeles area, in which she lived with her three cats who stayed inside her unit. Once the Association learned of the cats' presence it demanded their removal because one of Lakeside Village's CC&Rs provided that "No animals (which shall mean dogs and cats), livestock, reptiles or poultry shall be kept in any unit." Nahrstedt contended that the cats never bothered her neighbors, and sought a declaration that the restriction was unreasonable as applied to her indoor cats, and to enjoin enforcement of the provision. She lost in the trial court and the intermediate California appeals court reversed. But the California Supreme Court reversed the Court of Appeal and held that the provision was reasonable and enforceable.]

KENNARD, J., delivered the opinion of the court.

. . . II. Use restrictions are an inherent part of any common interest development and are crucial to the stable, planned environment of any shared ownership arrangement. . . . The viability of shared ownership of improved real property rests on the existence of extensive reciprocal servitudes, together with the ability of each co-owner to prevent the property's partition. The restrictions on the use of property in any common interest development may limit activities conducted in the common areas as well as in the confines of the home itself. Commonly, use restrictions preclude alteration of building exteriors, limit the number of persons that can occupy each unit, and place limitations on—or prohibit altogether—the keeping of pets. . . . Natelson, *Consent, Coercion, and "Reasonableness" in Private Law: The Special Case of the Property Owners Association*, 51 Ohio St. L.J. 41, 48, fn. 28 (1990) [as of 1986, 58 percent of highrise developments and 39 percent of townhouse projects had some kind of pet restriction]; see also Noble v. Murphy (1993) 34 Mass.App. 452 [612 N.E.2d 266] [enforcing condominium ban on pets]. . . .

Restrictions on property use are not the only characteristic of common interest ownership. Ordinarily, such ownership also entails mandatory membership in an owners association, which, through an elected board of directors, is empowered to enforce any use restrictions contained in the project's declaration or master deed and to enact new rules governing the use and occupancy of property within the project. Because of its considerable power in managing and regulating a common interest development, the governing board of an owners association must guard against the potential for the abuse of that power.[7] . . . Therefore, anyone who buys a unit in a common interest development with knowledge of its owners association's discretionary power accepts "the risk that the power may be used in a way that benefits the commonality but harms the individual." Generally, courts will uphold decisions made by the governing board of an owners association so long as they represent good faith efforts to further the purposes of the common interest development, are consistent with the development's governing documents, and comply with public policy.

Thus, subordination of individual property rights to the collective judgment of the owners association together with restrictions on the use of real property comprise the chief attributes of owning property in a common interest development. As the Florida District Court of Appeal observed in Hidden Harbour Estates, Inc. v. Norman, 309 So.2d 180 (Fla.Dist.Ct.App. 1975), a decision frequently cited in condominium cases:

---

7. The power to regulate pertains to a "wide spectrum of activities," such as the volume of playing music, hours of social gatherings, use of patio furniture and barbecues, and rental of units. . . .

"[I]nherent in the condominium concept is the principle that to promote the health, happiness, and peace of mind of the majority of the unit owners since they are living in such close proximity and using facilities in common, each unit owner must give up a certain degree of freedom of choice which he [or she] might otherwise enjoy in separate, privately owned property. Condominium unit owners comprise a little democratic subsociety of necessity more restrictive as it pertains to use of condominium property than may be existent outside the condominium organization."

Notwithstanding the limitations on personal autonomy that are inherent in the concept of shared ownership of residential property, common interest developments have increased in popularity in recent years, in part because they generally provide a more affordable alternative to ownership of a single-family home. ... One significant factor in the continued popularity of the common interest form of property ownership is the ability of homeowners to enforce restrictive CC & R's against other owners (including future purchasers) of project units. Generally, however, such enforcement is possible only if the restriction that is sought to be enforced meets the requirements of equitable servitudes or of covenants running with the land....

When restrictions limiting the use of property within a common interest development satisfy the requirements of covenants running with the land or of equitable servitudes, what standard or test governs their enforceability? In California, ... our Legislature has made common interest development use restrictions contained in a project's recorded declaration "enforceable ... *unless unreasonable.*" Cal. Civ. Code § 1354(a) (italics added). In states lacking such legislative guidance, some courts have adopted a standard under which a common interest development's recorded use restrictions will be enforced so long as they are "reasonable." (See Riley v. Stoves, 22 Ariz.App. 223 (1974) [asking whether the challenged restriction provided "a reasonable means to accomplish the private objective"]; Hidden Harbour Estates, Inc. v. Norman, 309 So.2d 180, 182 (Fla.Dist.Ct.App. 1975) [to justify regulation, conduct need not be "so offensive as to constitute a nuisance"]. Although no one definition of the term "reasonable" has gained universal acceptance, most courts have applied what one commentator calls "equitable reasonableness," upholding only those restrictions that provide a reasonable means to further the collective "health, happiness and enjoyment of life" of owners of a common interest development. Note, *Community Association Use Restrictions: Applying the Business Judgment Doctrine,* 64 Chi.–Kent L.Rev. 653, 655 (1988). Others would limit the "reasonableness" standard only to those restrictions adopted by majority vote of the homeowners or enacted under the rulemaking power of an association's governing board, and would not apply this test to restrictions included in a planned development project's recorded declaration or master deed. Because such restrictions are presumptively valid, these authorities would enforce them regardless of reasonableness. The first court to articulate this view was the Florida Fourth District Court of Appeal.

In Hidden Harbour Estates v. Basso, 393 So.2d 637 (Fla.Dist.Ct.App. 1981), the Florida court distinguished two categories of use restrictions: use restrictions set forth in the declaration or master deed of the condominium project itself, and rules promulgated by the governing board of the condominium owners association or the board's interpretation of a rule. The latter category of use restrictions, the court said, should be subject to a "reasonableness" test, so as to "somewhat fetter the discretion of the board of directors." Such a standard, the court explained, best assures that governing boards will "enact rules and make decisions that are reasonably related to the promotion of the health, happiness and peace of mind" of the project owners, considered collectively. By contrast, restrictions contained in the declaration or master deed of the condominium complex, the Florida court concluded, should not be evaluated under a "reasonableness" standard. Rather, such use restrictions are "clothed with a very strong presumption of validity and should be upheld even if they exhibit some degree of unreasonableness. Nonenforcement would be proper only if such restrictions were arbitrary or in violation of public policy or some fundamental constitutional right. The Florida court's decision was cited with approval recently by a Massachusetts appellate court in Noble v. Murphy, 34 Mass. App. Ct. 452, 612 N.E.2d 266 (1993).

In *Noble*, managers of a condominium development sought to enforce against the owners of one unit a pet restriction contained in the project's master deed. The Massachusetts court upheld the validity of the restriction. The court stated that "[a] condominium use restriction appearing in originating documents which predate the purchase of individual units" was entitled to greater judicial deference than restrictions "promulgated after units have been individually acquired." The court reasoned that "properly-enacted and evenly-enforced use restrictions contained in a master deed or original bylaws of a condominium" should be insulated against attack "except on constitutional or public policy grounds." This standard, the court explained, best "serves the interest of the majority of owners [within a project] who may be presumed to have chosen not to alter or rescind such restrictions," and it spares overcrowded courts "the burden and expense of highly particularized and lengthy litigation."

Indeed, giving deference to use restrictions contained in a condominium project's originating documents protects the general expectations of condominium owners "that restrictions in place at the time they purchase their units will be enforceable." Ellickson, *Cities and Homeowners' Associations*, 130 U.Pa. L.Rev. 1519, 1526–1527 (1982) [stating that association members "unanimously consent to the provisions in the association's original documents" and courts therefore should not scrutinize such documents for "reasonableness."]. This in turn encourages the development of shared ownership housing—generally a less costly alternative to single-dwelling ownership—by attracting buyers who prefer a stable, planned environment. It also protects buyers who have paid a premium for condominium units in reliance on a particular restrictive scheme....

III. [W]hen enforcing equitable servitudes, courts are generally disinclined to question the wisdom of agreed-to restrictions. This rule does not apply, however, when the restriction does not comport with public policy. ... Nor will courts enforce as equitable servitudes those restrictions that are arbitrary, that is, bearing no rational relationship to the protection, preservation, operation or purpose of the affected land. See Laguna Royale Owners Ass'n. v. Darger, 119 Cal.App.3d 670, 684 (1981). These limitations on the equitable enforcement of restrictive servitudes that are either arbitrary or violate fundamental public policy are specific applications of the general rule that courts will not enforce a restrictive covenant when "the harm caused by the restriction is so disproportionate to the benefit produced" by its enforcement that the restriction "ought not to be enforced." ...

[We] now turn to section 1354, [which provides that] use restrictions for a common interest development that are set forth in the recorded declaration are "enforceable equitable servitudes, unless unreasonable." In other words, such restrictions should be enforced unless they are wholly arbitrary, violate a fundamental public policy, or impose a burden on the use of affected land that far outweighs any benefit....

When courts accord a presumption of validity to all such recorded use restrictions and measure them against deferential standards of equitable servitude law, it discourages lawsuits by owners of individual units seeking personal exemptions from the restrictions. This also promotes stability and predictability in two ways. It provides substantial assurance to prospective condominium purchasers that they may rely with confidence on the promises embodied in the project's recorded CC & Rs. And it protects all owners in the planned development from unanticipated increases in association fees to fund the defense of legal challenges to recorded restrictions....

When courts treat recorded use restrictions as presumptively valid, and place on the challenger the burden of proving the restriction "unreasonable" under the deferential standards applicable to equitable servitudes, associations can proceed to enforce reasonable restrictive covenants without fear that their actions will embroil them in costly and prolonged legal proceedings. Of course, when an association determines that a unit owner has violated a use restriction, the association must do so in good faith, not in an arbitrary or capricious manner, and its enforcement procedures must be fair and applied uniformly.

There is an additional beneficiary of legal rules that are protective of recorded use restrictions: the judicial system. Fewer lawsuits challenging such restrictions will be brought, and those that are filed may be disposed of more expeditiously, if the rules courts use in evaluating such restrictions are clear, simple, and not subject to exceptions based on the peculiar circumstances or hardships of individual residents in condominiums and other shared-ownership developments. . . .

Contrary to the dissent's accusations that the majority's decision "fray[s]" the "social fabric," we are of the view that our social fabric is best preserved if courts uphold and enforce solemn written instruments that embody the expectations of the parties rather than treat them as "worthless paper". . . . Our social fabric is founded on the stability of expectation and obligation that arises from the consistent enforcement of the terms of deeds, contracts, wills, statutes, and other writings. To allow one person to escape obligations under a written instrument upsets the expectations of all the other parties governed by that instrument (here, the owners of the other 529 units) that the instrument will be uniformly and predictably enforced. . . . Refusing to enforce the CC & Rs contained in a recorded declaration, or enforcing them only after protracted litigation that would require justification of their application on a case-by-case basis, would impose great strain on the social fabric of the common interest development. It would frustrate owners who had purchased their units in reliance on the CC & Rs. It would put the owners and the homeowners association in the difficult and divisive position of deciding whether particular CC & Rs should be applied to a particular owner. Here, for example, deciding whether a particular animal is "confined to an owner's unit and create[s] no noise, odor, or nuisance" is a fact-intensive determination that can only be made by examining in detail the behavior of the particular animal and the behavior of the particular owner. Home-owners associations are ill-equipped to make such investigations, and any decision they might make in a particular case could be divisive or subject to claims of partiality.

Enforcing the CC & Rs contained in a recorded declaration only after protracted case-by-case litigation would impose substantial litigation costs on the owners through their homeowners association, which would have to defend not only against owners contesting the application of the CC & Rs to them, but also against owners contesting any case-by-case exceptions the homeowners association might make. In short, it is difficult to imagine what could more disrupt the harmony of a common interest development than the course proposed by the dissent. . . .

V. Under the holding we adopt today, the reasonableness or unreasonableness of a condominium use restriction that the Legislature has made subject to section 1354 is to be determined *not* by reference to facts that are specific to the objecting homeowner, but by reference to the common interest development as a whole. As we have explained, when, as here, a restriction is contained in the declaration of the common interest development and is recorded with the county recorder, the restriction is presumed to be reasonable and will be enforced uniformly against all residents of the common interest development *unless* the restriction is arbitrary, imposes burdens on the use of lands it affects that substantially outweigh the restriction's benefits to the development's residents, or violates a fundamental public policy. . . .

We conclude, as a matter of law, that the recorded pet restriction of the Lakeside Village condominium development prohibiting cats or dogs but allowing some other pets is not arbitrary, but is rationally related to health, sanitation and noise concerns legitimately held by residents of a high-density condominium project such as Lakeside Village, which includes 530 units in 12 separate 3–story buildings. Nahrstedt's complaint alleges no facts that could possibly support a finding that the burden of the restriction on the affected property is so disproportionate to its benefit that the restriction is unreasonable and should not be enforced. Also, the complaint's allegations center on Nahrstedt and her cats (that she keeps them inside her condominium unit and that they do not bother her neighbors), without any reference to the effect on the condominium development as a whole, thus rendering the allegations legally insufficient to overcome section 1354's presumption of the restriction's validity. . . .

[We] discern no fundamental public policy that would favor the keeping of pets in a condominium project. There is no federal or state constitutional provision or any California statute that confers a general right to keep household pets in condominiums or other common interest developments. . . .

We reverse the judgment of the Court of Appeal, and remand for further proceedings consistent with the views expressed in this opinion.

ARABIAN, J., dissenting.

. . . I respectfully dissent. . . . [The] majority's analysis . . . reflects a narrow, indeed chary, view of the law that eschews the human spirit in favor of arbitrary efficiency. . . . Beyond dispute, human beings have long enjoyed an abiding and cherished association with their household animals. Given the substantial benefits derived from pet ownership, the undue burden on the use of property imposed on condominium owners who can maintain pets within the confines of their units without creating a nuisance or disturbing the quiet enjoyment of others substantially outweighs whatever meager utility the restriction may serve in the abstract. It certainly does not promote "health, happiness [or] peace of mind" commensurate with its tariff on the quality of life for those who value the companionship of animals. Worse, it contributes to the fraying of our social fabric. . . .

[The] the value of pets in daily life is a matter of common knowledge and understanding as well as extensive documentation. People of all ages, but particularly the elderly and the young, enjoy their companionship. Those who suffer from serious disease or injury and are confined to their home or bed experience a therapeutic, even spiritual, benefit from their presence. Animals provide comfort at the death of a family member or dear friend, and for the lonely can offer a reason for living when life seems to have lost its meaning.

What is gained from an uncompromising prohibition against pets that are confined to an owner's unit and create no noise, odor, or nuisance? To the extent such animals are not seen, heard, or smelled any more than if they were not kept in the first place, there is no corresponding or concomitant benefit. Pets that remain within the four corners of their owners' condominium space can have no deleterious or offensive effect on the project's common areas or any neighboring unit....

[The] majority's analysis ... simply takes refuge behind the "presumption of validity" now accorded *all* CC & Rs irrespective of subject matter. They never objectively scrutinize defendants' blandishments of protecting "health and happiness" or realistically assess the substantial impact on affected unit owners and *their* use of *their* property. ... In determining the "burden on the use of land," due recognition must be given to the fact that this particular "use" transcends the impersonal and mundane matters typically regulated by condominium CC & Rs, such as whether someone can place a doormat in the hallway or hang a towel on the patio rail or have food in the pool area, and reaches the very quality of life of hundreds of owners and residents. Nonetheless, the majority accept uncritically the proffered justification of preserving "health and happiness" and essentially consider only one criterion to determine enforceability: was the restriction recorded in the original declaration? If so, it is "presumptively valid," unless in violation of public policy. ... [It] is difficult to hypothesize any CC & Rs that would not pass muster. Such sanctity has not been afforded any writing save the commandments delivered to Moses on Mount Sinai, and they were set in stone, not upon worthless paper....

Owning a home of one's own has always epitomized the American dream. [It] represents the sense of freedom and self-determination emblematic of our national character. Granted, those who live in multi-unit developments cannot exercise this freedom to the same extent possible on a large estate. But owning pets that do not disturb the quiet enjoyment of others does not reasonably come within this compromise. Nevertheless, with no demonstrated or discernible benefit, the majority arbitrarily sacrifice the dream to the tyranny of the "commonality." ...

Pet ownership substantially enhances the quality of life for those who desire it. When others are not only undisturbed by, but *completely unaware of*, the presence of pets being enjoyed by their neighbors, the balance of benefit and burden is rendered disproportionate and unreasonable, rebutting any presumption of validity. [The majority's] view, shorn of grace and guiding philosophy, is devoid of the humanity that must temper the interpretation and application of all laws....

NOTES AND PROBLEMS

1. How much deference? Because the CC & Rs can be altered by the homeowners association, developers have a tendency to lard the CC & Rs with extensive restrictions. But even if the CC & Rs permit modification or elimination of restrictions by less than unanimity, it may still be very difficult to do so. Does this argue in favor of less judicial deference to the initial covenants? Does the fact that the directors of a homeowners' association are usually entitled to impose new restrictions without unanimous consent (and sometimes without any consent) argue for placing the burden of proving the reasonableness of such new restrictions on the directors?

2. *The Third Restatement.* The Third Restatement of Property, Servitudes treats most servitudes as indirect restraints on alienation. Such servitudes are valid unless they lack a "rational justification." By contrast, direct restraints on alienation (such things as requiring consent of the association to transfer title, limiting the people to whom a transfer can be made, or creating rights of first refusal should an owner wish to transfer title) are valid only if "reasonable." See §§ 3.4 and 3.5.

3. *The Legislative Reaction.* In 2000, the California legislature enacted Civil Code § 1360.5, which invalidates any common interest development restriction that prohibits the owner of a unit "from keeping at least one pet within the common interest development, subject to reasonable rules and regulations of the association." The term "pet" is defined to include "any domesticated bird, cat, dog, aquatic animal kept within an aquarium, or other animal as agreed to between the association and the homeowner."

4. *Problems.* Which of the following covenants are valid? What is (or should be) the standard of review? Do your answers differ if the covenant is an initial restriction or one adopted later?

a. *No Open–Air Laundry Drying.* "Use of a clothesline or other apparatus to dry or air laundry outside of the interior spaces of any unit is prohibited." See, e.g. Md. Real Prop. Code § 14–130.

b. *No Trucks.* "No motor-powered trucks of any kind (including pickups) may be parked at any spot in the common areas or separately owned spaces of the development." Suppose that *O*, an owner of a unit subject to the restriction, owns and uses a pickup truck that is essential to his landscaping business. Suppose that *X*, another unit owner, owns an SUV that is built on a pickup truck chassis and is treated as a truck for purposes of federal and state auto exhaust emission laws.

c. *Guinea Pig.* Suppose Lakeside Village enforces the restriction at issue in *Nahrstedt*, before enactment of California Civil Code § 1360.5, against *Z*, Natore Nahrstedt's neighbor, who keeps a guinea pig in her unit. The guinea pig, or cavy, is a species of rodent that was domesticated in South America for food consumption. Still consumed as food in South America, and to a limited extent elsewhere, the guinea pig is a popular pet in North America.

d. *No Sex Offenders.* "No individual who is required to register as a convicted sex offender may occupy any unit in the common interest development." See Mulligan v. Panther Valley Property Owners Association, 766 A.2d 1186 (N.J. Super. App. Div. 2001).

5. *The Business Judgment Rule.* Directors of corporations and of homeowners' association owe a fiduciary duty to their shareholders or members, respectively. It has long been settled that the duty of care of the directors of a cooperative apartment corporation is the business judgment rule, under which their duty is satisfied so long as they take action in good faith and exercising an honest judgment about the affairs of the corporation. The standard applicable to directors of homeowners' associations is less clear. Substantive

reasonableness is one possibility, but the California Supreme Court, in Lamden v. La Jolla Shores Condominium Homeowners' Association, 21 Cal.4th 249 (1999), ruled that, apart from enforcement of servitudes, the business judgment rule should control. Accord, Riverside Park Condominium Unit Owners Association v. Lucas, 691 N.W.2d 862 (N.D. 2005).

2. COOPERATIVE APARTMENTS

As noted above, directors of cooperative apartment corporations are held only to the deferential business judgment rule. One reason is the high financial interdependence of cooperative shareholder/tenants. Other reasons are given in Levandusky v. One Fifth Avenue Apartment Corp., 75 N.Y.2d 530 (1990).

> The difference between the reasonableness test and the [business judgment] rule we adopt is twofold. First—unlike the business judgment rule, which places on the owner seeking review the burden to demonstrate a breach of the board's fiduciary duty—reasonableness review requires the board to demonstrate that its decision was reasonable. Second, although in practice a certain amount of deference appears to be accorded to board decisions, reasonableness review permits—indeed, in theory requires—the court itself to evaluate the merits or wisdom of the board's decision. [C]ooperative board members will possess experience of the peculiar needs of their building and its residents not shared by the court. ... Allowing an owner who is simply dissatisfied with particular board action a second opportunity to reopen the matter completely before a court, which—generally without knowing the property—may or may not agree with the reasonableness of the board's determination, threatens the stability of the common living arrangement. Moreover, the prospect that each board decision may be subjected to full judicial review hampers the effectiveness of the board's managing authority. The business judgment rule protects the board's business decisions and managerial authority from indiscriminate attack. At the same time, it permits review of improper decisions, as when the challenger demonstrates that the board's action has no legitimate relationship to the welfare of the cooperative, deliberately singles out individuals for harmful treatment, is taken without notice or consideration of the relevant facts, or is beyond the scope of the board's authority.

The *Levandusky* court applied the business judgment rule equally to cooperative boards and to the directors of homeowners' associations.

In 40 West 67th Street Corporation v. Pullman, 100 N.Y.2d 147 (2003), the New York Court of Appeals applied the business judgment rule to insulate the board's decision to invoke a provision of a shareholder-tenant's lease that permitted termination of the lease for his "objectionable" conduct if two-thirds of the members so voted. Shortly after moving into the building defendant engaged in a course of behavior that, in the view of the cooperative, began as demanding, grew increasingly disruptive and ultimately became intolerable. After several points of friction between defendant and the cooperative, defendant started complaining about his elderly upstairs neighbors, a retired college professor and his wife who had occupied apartment 8B for over two decades. In a stream of vituperative letters to the cooperative—16 letters in the month of October 1999 alone—he accused the couple of playing their television set and stereo at high volumes late into the night, and claimed they were running a loud and illegal bookbinding business in their apartment. Defendant further charged that the couple stored toxic chemicals in their apartment for use in their "dangerous and illegal" business. Upon investigation, the cooperative's Board determined that the couple did not possess a television set or stereo and that there was no evidence of a bookbinding business or any other commercial enterprise in their apartment. Hostilities escalated, resulting in a physical altercation between defendant and the retired professor. . . . Defendant brought charges against the professor which resulted in the professor's arrest. Eventually, the charges were adjourned in contemplation of dismissal. . . . Following the altercation, defendant distributed flyers to the cooperative residents in which he referred to the professor, by name, as a potential "psychopath in our midst" and accused him of cutting defendant's telephone lines. In another flyer, defendant described the professor's wife and the wife of the Board president as having close "intimate personal relations." Defendant also claimed that the previous occupants of his apartment revealed that the upstairs couple have "historically made excessive noise." The former occupants, however, submitted an affidavit that denied making any complaints about noise from the upstairs apartment and proclaimed that defendant's assertions to the contrary were "completely false."

Furthermore, defendant made alterations to his apartment without Board approval, had construction work performed on the weekend in violation of house rules, and would not respond to Board requests to correct these conditions or to allow a mutual inspection of his apartment and the upstairs apartment belonging to the elderly couple. Finally, defendant commenced four lawsuits against the upstairs couple, the president of the cooperative and the cooperative management, and tried to commence three more. . . .

Despite [the] deferential standard [of the business judgment rule], there are instances when courts should undertake review of board decisions. To trigger further judicial scrutiny, an aggrieved shareholder-tenant must make a showing that the board acted (1) outside the scope of its authority, (2) in a way that did not legitimately further the corporate purpose or (3) in bad faith. [No such showing was made.] . . .

Levandusky cautions that the broad powers of cooperative governance carry the potential for abuse when a board singles out a person for harmful treatment or engages in unlawful discrimination, vendetta, arbitrary decisionmaking or favoritism. We reaffirm that admonition and stress that those types of abuses are incompatible with good faith and the exercise of honest judgment. While deferential, the *Levandusky* standard should not serve as a rubber stamp for cooperative board actions, particularly those involving tenancy terminations.

3. SOME POLICY CONSIDERATIONS

Are common interest communities good or bad? They provide choice, but as the proportion of housing units that are in common interest communities increases, effective choice may diminish. They provide security and tranquility (especially when they are gated communities) but they contribute to the atomization of civic life in America. They have the ability to do almost everything a local government could do, but they may reduce the incentive of their members to support the local government of which they are, at bottom, a part. Will this produce a nation of communities, each populated by people much like each other, and thus with a withered sense of a larger community? Or will these communities provide amenities that local governments fail to provide, and thus enhance the quality of life for their residents without material reduction of the quality of life of persons living in the old-fashioned community, where chance encounters with people who might be different adds to the spice of life?

CHAPTER ELEVEN

ZONING

■ ■ ■

This chapter deals with legislative control of land use. Nuisance, you will recall, is tort law's use of judicially enforced controls of land use, and the law of servitudes governs private bargains for controlling land use. Legislative control of land use, through comprehensive plans for land use and zoning laws that are enacted to implement those comprehensive plans, has become a ubiquitous feature of America.

A. SOME BASICS OF ZONING

1. HISTORY AND MECHANICS

Zoning was unheard of until the twentieth century, but a number of factors inspired its embrace in the first decades of that century. America was becoming more urban and the occasions for collisions between competing land uses became more frequent. Nuisance law was inefficient and, in any case, was of little help when both uses were independently benign and productive. Servitudes were useful only with respect to new subdivisions or developments, but were of little help in constraining a use of land unencumbered by any servitude. Thus, a commercial establishment might arise next door to a lovely residence, or the builder of an expensive residence might find his neighbor constructing shoddy shacks or a large tenement.

Perhaps because America was seen by European settlers as a boundless and virgin landscape, Americans have long idealized the rural landscape or its pygmy kin, the suburban or small town home surrounded by a garden, lawn, shade trees, and perhaps enclosed by a white picket fence. The city, by contrast, has often been thought to be the home of overcrowding, pestilence, crime, and vice. Thus, social reformers of the late nineteenth and early twentieth centuries began to champion the benefits of planned communities that separated different uses (e.g., industry in one quarter, commercial retailers and wholesalers in another, residences elsewhere), privileged the single-family residence, and fostered low density of population and buildings. These ideas caught on in the American political mind. By 1909 Los Angeles required industrial uses to be separated from residences, but it was New York in 1916 that enacted what might be called the first modern zoning law. The New York law divided the city into zones, classified various land uses, and assigned those uses to zones. In reaction to the new skyscraper movement, New York also limited the size and height of new buildings.

 In 1922 the U.S. Department of Commerce issued a report containing a Standard State Zoning Enabling Act,[1] the product of an advisory committee on zoning. A state zoning enabling act is deemed advisable, and in some cases may be necessary, to ensure that municipalities have the authority to enact local zoning ordinances. Following issuance of this report, a number of states adopted an enabling act, and cities rushed to adopt zoning ordinances. An enabling act empowers cities to regulate the height and uses of buildings, their location and density, and grants authority to regulate population density. Under the usual enabling act, a comprehensive plan must first be adopted by the political entity that proposes to engage in zoning. The comprehensive plan is a statement of the objectives and standards for future development. Most plans provide a narrative description of these matters and amplifies that description with maps that show the boundaries of the various zones—by land use, height, density, bulk, and any other criteria that may be relevant. Even so, only about half the state enabling acts mandate adoption of a comprehensive plan. Where plans do exist, they need not be as detailed as the prior description suggests. Many states regard the requirement of the comprehensive plan to be satisfied by highly informal statements or even by the zoning ordinance itself. The result is that comprehensive plans are often hortatory.

Model Act

Zoning ordinances can address a wide range of issues, but there are two main types. One is the cumulative ordinance, in which land uses are segregated from most protected to least protected. Typically, the most protected use is the single family residence. The next most protected is usually multiple family residences, then commercial, and then industrial. Under cumulative zoning only single family residences may be located in that zone, but single family residences may be located in a multiple family residential district, and both of those uses may be located in a commercial district, and all of them can be located in the least protected district, industrial. Of course, use districts can be much more finely drawn than these examples, but the essence of cumulative zoning is the notion that any more protected use can be located in a lesser protected district, but not the reverse. The other type of zoning is exclusive, in which each use district is limited exclusively to the uses permitted in that district. One can readily imagine a hybrid system in which, for example, commercial uses are permitted in an industrial zone but not any residential uses, or apartment buildings are permitted in a commercial zone, but not single family residences or industrial uses.

1. A copy of the report and Standard State Zoning Enabling Act may be accessed at http://law. wustl.edu/landuselaw/StndZoningEnablingAct1926.pdf

2. CONSTITUTIONAL CHALLENGES TO ZONING

As might be expected, the advent of zoning brought constitutional challenges to its validity. The test case follows.

VILLAGE OF EUCLID v. AMBLER REALTY COMPANY

Supreme Court of the United States
272 U.S. 365 (1926)

JUSTICE SUTHERLAND delivered the opinion of the Court.

The Village of Euclid is an Ohio municipal corporation. It adjoins and practically is a suburb of the City of Cleveland. Its estimated population is between 5,000 and 10,000, and its area from twelve to fourteen square miles, the greater part of which is farm lands or unimproved acreage. It lies, roughly, in the form of a parallelogram measuring approximately three and one-half miles each way. East and west it is traversed by three principal highways: Euclid Avenue, through the southerly border, St. Clair Avenue, through the central portion, and Lake Shore Boulevard, through the northerly border in close proximity to the shore of Lake Erie. The Nickel Plate railroad lies from 1,500 to 1,800 feet north of Euclid Avenue, and the Lake Shore railroad 1,600 feet farther to the north. The three highways and the two railroads are substantially parallel.

Appellee is the owner of a tract of land containing 68 acres, situated in the westerly end of the village, abutting on Euclid Avenue to the south and the Nickel Plate railroad to the north. Adjoining this tract, both on the east and on the west, there have been laid out restricted residential plats upon which residences have been erected.

On November 13, 1922, an ordinance was adopted by the Village Council, establishing a comprehensive zoning plan for regulating and restricting the location of trades, industries, apartment houses, two-family houses, single family houses, etc., the lot area to be built upon, the size and height of buildings, etc. The entire area of the village is divided by the ordinance into six classes of use districts, denominated U–1 to U–6, inclusive; three classes of height districts, denominated H–1 to H–3, inclusive; and four classes of area districts, denominated A–1 to A–4, inclusive. The use districts are classified in respect of the buildings which may be erected within their respective limits, as follows: U–1 is restricted to single family dwellings, public parks, water towers and reservoirs, suburban and interurban electric railway passenger stations and rights of way, and farming, non-commercial greenhouse nurseries and truck gardening; U–2 is extended to include two-family dwellings; U–3 is further extended to include apartment houses, hotels, churches, schools, public libraries, museums, private clubs, community center buildings, hospitals, sanitariums, public playgrounds and recreation buildings, and a city hall and courthouse; U–4 is further extended to include banks, offices, studios, telephone exchanges, fire and police stations, restaurants, theatres and moving picture shows, retail stores and shops, sales offices, sample rooms, wholesale stores for hardware, drugs and groceries, stations for gasoline and oil (not exceeding 1,000 gallons storage) and for ice delivery, skating rinks and dance halls, electric substations, job and newspaper printing, public garages for motor vehicles, stables and wagon sheds (not exceeding five horses, wagons or motor trucks) and distributing stations for central store and commercial enterprises; U–5 is further extended to include billboards and advertising signs (if permitted), warehouses, ice and ice cream manufacturing and cold storage plants, bottling works, milk bottling and central distribution stations, laundries, carpet cleaning, dry cleaning and dyeing establishments, blacksmith, horseshoeing, wagon and motor vehicle repair shops, freight stations, street car barns, stables and wagon sheds (for more than five horses, wagons or motor trucks), and wholesale produce markets and salesrooms; U–6 is further extended to include plants for sewage disposal and for producing gas, garbage and refuse incineration, scrap iron, junk, scrap paper and rag storage, aviation fields, cemeteries, crematories, penal and correctional institutions, insane and feeble minded institutions, storage of oil and gasoline (not to exceed 25,000 gallons), and manufacturing and industrial operations of any kind other than, and any public utility not included in, a class U–1, U–2, U–3, U–4 or U–5 use. There is a seventh class of uses which is prohibited altogether.

Class U–1 is the only district in which buildings are restricted to those enumerated. In the other classes the uses are cumulative; that is to say, uses in class U–2 include those enumerated in the preceding class, U–1; class U–3 includes uses enumerated in the preceding classes, U–2 and U–1; and so on. In addition to the enumerated uses, the ordinance provides for accessory uses, that is, for uses customarily incident to the principal use, such as private garages. Many regulations are provided in respect of such accessory uses.

The height districts are classified as follows: In class H–1, buildings are limited to a height of two and one-half stories or thirty-five feet; in class H–2, to four stories or fifty feet; in class H–3, to eighty feet. To all of these, certain exceptions are made, as in the case of church spires, water tanks, etc.

The classification of area districts is: In A–1 districts, dwellings or apartment houses to accommodate more than one family must have at least 5,000 square feet for interior lots and at least 4,000 square feet for corner lots; in A–2 districts, the area must be at least 2,500 square feet for interior lots, and 2,000 square feet for corner lots; in A–3 districts, the limits are 1,250 and 1,000 square feet, respectively; in A–4 districts, the limits are 900 and 700 square feet, respectively. The ordinance contains, in great variety and detail, provisions in respect of width of lots, front, side and rear yards, and other matters, including restrictions and regulations as to the use of bill boards, sign boards and advertising signs....

Appellee's tract of land comes under U-2, U-3 and U-6. The first strip of 620 feet immediately north of Euclid Avenue falls in class U-2, the next 130 feet to the north, in U-3, and the remainder in U-6. The uses of the first 620 feet, therefore, do not include apartment houses, hotels, churches, schools, or other public and semi-public buildings, or other uses enumerated in respect of U-3 to U-6, inclusive. The uses of the next 130 feet include all of these, but exclude industries, theatres, banks, shops, and the various other uses set forth in respect of U-4 to U-6, inclusive.

Annexed to the ordinance, and made a part of it, is a zone map, showing the location and limits of the various use, height and area districts, from which it appears that the three classes overlap one another; that is to say, for example, both U-5 and U-6 use districts are in A-4 area districts, but the former is in H-2 and the latter in H-3 height districts. . . .

The lands lying between the two railroads for the entire length of the village area and extending some distance on either side to the north and south, having an average width of about 1,600 feet, are left open, with slight exceptions, for industrial and all other uses. This includes the larger part of appellee's tract. Approximately one-sixth of the area of the entire village is included in U-5 and U-6 use districts. . . .

The enforcement of the ordinance is entrusted to the inspector of buildings, under rules and regulations of the board of zoning appeals. Meetings of the board are public, and minutes of its proceedings are kept. It is authorized to adopt rules and regulations to carry into effect provisions of the ordinance. Decisions of the inspector of buildings may be appealed to the board by any person claiming to be adversely affected by any such decision. The board is given power in specific cases of practical difficulty or unnecessary hardship to interpret the ordinance in harmony with its general purpose and intent, so that the public health, safety and general welfare may be secure and substantial justice done. Penalties are prescribed for violations. . . .

The ordinance is assailed on the grounds that it is in derogation of § 1 of the Fourteenth Amendment to the Federal Constitution in that it deprives appellee of liberty and property without due process of law and denies it the equal protection of the law. . . . The prayer of the bill is for an injunction restraining the enforcement of the ordinance and all attempts to impose or maintain as to appellee's property any of the restrictions, limitations or conditions. The court below held the ordinance to be unconstitutional and void, and enjoined its enforcement. 297 Fed. 307 [(N.D. Ohio 1924). The district judge found that the law's purpose was "to regulate the mode of living of persons" in Euclid and to make Euclid "develop into a city along lines now conceived by the village council to be attractive and beautiful." The district judge concluded that he need not decide whether these "purposes or objects would justify the taking of plaintiff's property . . . for a public use. . . . It is sufficient to say that . . .

it may not be done without compensation under the guise of exercising the police power." Id. at 316.]

The bill alleges that the tract of land in question is vacant and has been held for years for the purpose of selling and developing it for industrial uses, for which it is especially adapted, being immediately in the path of progressive industrial development; that for such uses it has a market value of about $10,000 per acre, but if the use be limited to residential purposes the market value is not in excess of $2,500 per acre; that the first 200 feet of the parcel back from Euclid Avenue, if unrestricted in respect of use, has a value of $150 per front foot, but if limited to residential uses, and ordinary mercantile business be excluded therefrom, its value is not in excess of $50 per front foot.

It is specifically averred that the ordinance attempts to restrict and control the lawful uses of appellee's land so as to confiscate and destroy a great part of its value; that it is being enforced in accordance with its terms; that prospective buyers of land for industrial, commercial and residential uses in the metropolitan district of Cleveland are deterred from buying any part of this land because of the existence of the ordinance and the necessity thereby entailed of conducting burdensome and expensive litigation in order to vindicate the right to use the land for lawful and legitimate purposes; that the ordinance constitutes a cloud upon the land, reduces and destroys its value, and has the effect of diverting the normal industrial, commercial and residential development thereof to other and less favorable locations.

The record [shows] that the normal, and reasonably to be expected, use and development of that part of appellee's land adjoining Euclid Avenue is for general trade and commercial purposes, particularly retail stores and like establishments, and that the normal, and reasonably to be expected, use and development of the residue of the land is for industrial and trade purposes. Whatever injury is inflicted by the mere existence and threatened enforcement of the ordinance is due to restrictions in respect of these and similar uses; to which perhaps should be added—if not included in the foregoing—restrictions in respect of apartment houses. [T]here is nothing in the record to suggest that any damage results from the presence in the ordinance of those restrictions relating to churches, schools, libraries and other public and semi-public buildings. ... For present purposes the provisions of the ordinance in respect of these uses may, therefore, be put aside as unnecessary to be considered. It is also unnecessary to consider the effect of the restrictions in respect of U–1 districts, since none of appellee's land falls within that class. . . .

We proceed, then, to a consideration of those provisions of the ordinance to which the case as it is made relates, first disposing of a preliminary matter. A motion was made in the court below to dismiss the bill on the ground that, because complainant [appellee] had made no effort to obtain a building permit or apply to the zoning board of appeals for relief as it might have done under the terms of the ordinance, the suit was premature. The motion was properly overruled. The effect of the allegations of the bill is that the ordinance of its own force operates greatly to reduce the value of appellee's lands and destroy their marketability for industrial, commercial and residential uses; and the attack is directed, not against any specific provision or provisions, but against the ordinance as an entirety. Assuming the premises, the existence and maintenance of the ordinance, in effect, constitutes a present invasion of appellee's property rights and a threat to continue it. Under these circumstances, the equitable jurisdiction is clear....

Is the ordinance invalid in that it violates the constitutional protection "to the right of property in the appellee by attempted regulations under the guise of the police power, which are unreasonable and confiscatory?"

Building zone laws are of modern origin. They began in this country about twenty-five years ago. Until recent years, urban life was comparatively simple; but with the great increase and concentration of population, problems have developed, and constantly are developing, which require, and will continue to require, additional restrictions in respect of the use and occupation of private lands in urban communities. Regulations, the wisdom, necessity and validity of which, as applied to existing conditions, are so apparent that they are now uniformly sustained, a century ago, or even half a century ago, probably would have been rejected as arbitrary and oppressive. Such regulations are sustained, under the complex conditions of our day, for reasons analogous to those which justify traffic regulations, which, before the advent of automobiles and rapid transit street railways, would have been condemned as fatally arbitrary and unreasonable. And in this there is no inconsistency, for while the meaning of constitutional guaranties never varies, the scope of their application must expand or contract to meet the new and different conditions which are constantly coming within the field of their operation. In a changing world, it is impossible that it should be otherwise. But although a degree of elasticity is thus imparted, not to the *meaning*, but to the *application* of constitutional principles, statutes and ordinances, which, after giving due weight to the new conditions, are found clearly not to conform to the Constitution, of course, must fall.

The ordinance now under review, and all similar laws and regulations, must find their justification in some aspect of the police power, asserted for the public welfare. The line which in this field separates the legitimate from the illegitimate assumption of power is not capable of precise delimitation. It varies with circumstances and conditions. A regulatory zoning ordinance, which would be clearly valid as applied to the great cities, might be clearly invalid as applied to rural communities. In solving doubts, the maxim *sic utere tuo ut alienum non laedas*, which lies at the foundation of so much of the common law of nuisances, ordinarily will furnish a fairly helpful [clue]. And the law of nuisances, likewise, may be consulted, not for the purpose of controlling, but for the helpful aid of its analogies in the process of ascertaining the scope of, the power. Thus the question whether the power exists to forbid the erection of a building of a particular kind or for a particular use, like the question whether a particular thing is a nuisance, is to be determined, not by an abstract consideration of the building or of the thing considered apart, but by considering it in connection with the circumstances and the locality. . . . A nuisance may be merely a right thing in the wrong place,—like a pig in the parlor instead of the barnyard. If the validity of the legislative classification for zoning purposes be fairly debatable, the legislative judgment must be allowed to control. . . .

There is no serious difference of opinion in respect of the validity of laws and regulations fixing the height of buildings within reasonable limits, the character of materials and methods of construction, and the adjoining area which must be left open, in order to minimize the danger of fire or collapse, the evils of over-crowding, and the like, and excluding from residential sections offensive trades, industries and structures likely to create nuisances. . . .

Here, however, the exclusion is in general terms of all industrial establishments, and it may thereby happen that not only offensive or dangerous industries will be excluded, but those which are neither offensive nor dangerous will share the same fate. But this is no more than happens in respect of many practice-forbidding laws which this Court has upheld although drawn in general terms so as to include individual cases that may turn out to be innocuous in themselves. . . . The inclusion of a reasonable margin to insure effective enforcement, will not put upon a law, otherwise valid, the stamp of invalidity. Such laws may also find their justification in the fact that, in some fields, the bad fades into the good by such insensible degrees that the two are not capable of being readily distinguished and separated in terms of legislation. In the light of these considerations, we are not prepared to say that the end in view was not sufficient to justify the general rule of the ordinance, although some industries of an innocent character might fall within the proscribed class. It can not be said that the ordinance in this respect "passes the bounds of reason and assumes the character of a merely arbitrary fiat." Purity Extract Co. v. Lynch, 226 U.S. 192, 204 [(1912)]. Moreover, the restrictive provisions of the ordinance in this particular may be sustained upon the principles applicable to the broader exclusion from residential districts of all business and trade structures, presently to be discussed.

It is said that the Village of Euclid is a mere suburb of the City of Cleveland; that the industrial development of that city has now reached and in some degree extended into the village and, in the obvious course of things, will soon absorb the entire area for industrial enterprises; that the effect of the ordinance is to divert this natural development elsewhere with the consequent loss of increased values to the owners of the lands within the village borders. But the village, though physically a suburb of Cleveland, is politically a separate municipality, with powers of its own and authority to govern itself as it sees fit within the limits of the organic law of its creation and the State and Federal Constitutions. Its governing authorities, presumably representing a majority of its inhabitants and voicing their will, have determined, not that industrial development shall cease at its boundaries, but that the course of such development shall proceed within definitely fixed lines. If it be a proper exercise of the police power to relegate industrial establishments to localities separated from residential sections, it is not easy to find a sufficient reason for denying the power because the effect of its exercise is to divert an industrial flow from the course which it would follow to the injury of the residential public if left alone, to another course where such injury will be obviated. It is not meant by this, however, to exclude the possibility of cases where the general public interest would so far outweigh the interest of the municipality that the municipality would not be allowed to stand in the way.

We find no difficulty in sustaining restrictions of the kind thus far reviewed. The serious question in the case arises over the provisions of the ordinance excluding from residential districts, apartment houses, business houses, retail stores and shops, and other like establishments. This question involves the validity of what is really the crux of the more recent zoning legislation, namely, the creation and maintenance of residential districts, from which business and trade of every sort, including hotels and apartment houses, are excluded. Upon that question, this Court has not thus far spoken. The decisions of the state courts are numerous and conflicting; but those which broadly sustain the power greatly outnumber those which deny altogether or narrowly limit it; and it is very apparent that there is a constantly increasing tendency in the direction of the broader view. . . . [These decisions] agree that the exclusion of buildings devoted to business, trade, etc., from residential districts, bears a rational relation to the health and safety of the community. Some of the grounds for this conclusion are—promotion of the health and security from injury of children and others by separating dwelling houses from territory devoted to trade and industry; suppression and prevention of disorder; facilitating the extinguishment of fires, and the enforcement of street traffic regulations and other general welfare ordinances; aiding the health and safety of the community by excluding from residential areas the confusion and danger of fire, contagion and disorder which in greater or less degree attach to the location of stores, shops and factories. Another ground is that the construction and repair of streets may be rendered easier and less expensive by confining the greater part of the heavy traffic to the streets where business is carried on. . . .

The matter of zoning has received much attention at the hands of commissions and experts, and the results of their investigations have been set forth in comprehensive reports. These reports, which bear every evidence of painstaking consideration, concur in the view that the segregation of residential, business, and industrial buildings will make it easier to provide fire apparatus suitable for the character and intensity of the development in each section; that it will increase the safety and security of home life; greatly tend to prevent street accidents, especially to children, by reducing the traffic and resulting confusion in residential sections;

decrease noise and other conditions which produce or intensify nervous disorders; preserve a more favorable environment in which to rear children, etc. With particular reference to apartment houses, it is pointed out that the development of detached house sections is greatly retarded by the coming of apartment houses, which has sometimes resulted in destroying the entire section for private house purposes; that in such sections very often the apartment house is a mere parasite, constructed in order to take advantage of the open spaces and attractive surroundings created by the residential character of the district. Moreover, the coming of one apartment house is followed by others, interfering by their height and bulk with the free circulation of air and monopolizing the rays of the sun which otherwise would fall upon the smaller homes, and bringing, as their necessary accompaniments, the disturbing noises incident to increased traffic and business, and the occupation, by means of moving and parked automobiles, of larger portions of the streets, thus detracting from their safety and depriving children of the privilege of quiet and open spaces for play, enjoyed by those in more favored localities,—until, finally, the residential character of the neighborhood and its desirability as a place of detached residences are utterly destroyed. Under these circumstances, apartment houses, which in a different environment would be not only entirely unobjectionable but highly desirable, come very near to being nuisances.

[These] reasons are sufficiently cogent to preclude us from saying, as it must be said before the ordinance can be declared unconstitutional, that such provisions are clearly arbitrary and unreasonable, having no substantial relation to the public health, safety, morals, or general welfare. ... It is true that when, if ever, the provisions set forth in the ordinance in tedious and minute detail, come to be concretely applied to particular premises, including those of the appellee, or to particular conditions, or to be considered in connection with specific complaints, some of them, or even many of them, may be found to be clearly arbitrary and unreasonable. But where the equitable remedy of injunction is sought, as it is here, not upon the ground of a present infringement or denial of a specific right, or of a particular injury in process of actual execution, but upon the broad ground that the mere existence and threatened enforcement of the ordinance, by materially and adversely affecting values and curtailing the opportunities of the market, constitute a present and irreparable injury, the court will not scrutinize its provisions, sentence by sentence, to ascertain by a process of piecemeal dissection whether there may be, here and there, provisions of a minor character, or relating to matters of administration, or not shown to contribute to the injury complained of, which, if attacked separately, might not withstand the test of constitutionality. In respect of such provisions, of which specific complaint is not made, it cannot be said that the land owner has suffered or is threatened with an injury which entitles him to challenge their constitutionality. ... Under these circumstances, therefore, it is enough for us to determine, as we do, that the ordinance in its general scope and dominant features, so far as its provisions are here involved, is a valid exercise of authority, leaving other provisions to be dealt with as cases arise directly involving them. . . .

In the realm of constitutional law, especially, this Court has perceived the embarrassment which is likely to result from an attempt to formulate rules or decide questions beyond the necessities of the immediate issue. It has preferred to follow the method of a gradual approach to the general by a systematically guarded application and extension of constitutional principles to particular cases as they arise, rather than by out of hand attempts to establish general rules to which future cases must be fitted. This process applies with peculiar force to the solution of questions arising under the due process clause of the Constitution as applied to the exercise of the flexible powers of police, with which we are here concerned. [Reversed.]

[JUSTICES VAN DEVANTER, MCREYNOLDS, and BUTLER dissented without writing an opinion.]

NOTES

1. The Constitutional Issues. The plaintiffs challenged the facial validity of Euclid's zoning law; that is, they asserted that by enacting the law Euclid had violated the Constitution—the law in its entirety was claimed to be unconstitutional. All that the Court did in *Euclid* was to conclude that the law was facially valid; it expressed no opinion on the validity of the law as it might be applied to some individual circumstance. Indeed, the Court was careful to suggest that it was possible that some applications of the law could be unconstitutional. Two years later, in Nectow v. Cambridge, 277 U.S. 183 (1928), the Court found an application of a Cambridge, Massachusetts zoning ordinance to be invalid. Cambridge had zoned Nectow's land for residential use only. The effect of the zoning was " 'that no practical use can be made of the land in question for residential purposes, because among other reasons . . ., there would not be adequate return on the amount of any investment for the development of the property.' " The adjacent properties were zoned for and devoted to industrial and railroad purposes and the fact finder had concluded that limiting Nectow's land to residential use did "not promote the health, safety, convenience and general welfare" of the city. Id. at 187. Because the application of the zoning law to Nectow's land was "a mere arbitrary or irrational exercise of power having no substantial relation to the public health, the public morals, the public safety or the public welfare," it was struck down as a violation of substantive due process.

Substantive due process is the unwieldy and somewhat oxymoronic term to describe the cluster of liberties that are not explicitly protected by the Constitution but which are so deeply rooted in the nation's history and tradition that they are regarded as constitutionally fundamental. Governmental invasion of such a liberty is presumed to be void and may be sustained only if the government can prove that its infringement is necessary to accomplish a compelling government objective. Liberties that are not constitutionally fundamental may be freely curtailed by governments unless the government either lacks a legitimate purpose or the means chosen are not rationally related to the accomplishment of a legitimate purpose. At the time of *Euclid* the doctrine was somewhat more obtuse—liberties, whether or not constitutionally fundamental, could be invaded so long as there existed a fair and substantial relationship to preservation of public health, morals, safety, or welfare.

An alternative constitutional argument by which zoning may be attacked as unconstitutional is that it constitutes an uncompensated taking of private property for public use. See U.S. Const., Amend. V. That basis was implicit in the trial court's conclusion that the Euclid ordinance was unconstitutional. See Ambler Realty Co. v. Village of Euclid, 297 F. 307, 316 (N.D. Ohio 1924). The law of takings, particularly regulatory takings—the taking of private property by regulations that effectively eviscerate the rights that constitute property—is the subject of Chapter Twelve. While some applications of zoning laws may constitute unlawful takings the overwhelming number of applications of zoning are valid exercises of the police power and do not constitute uncompensated takings. Proponents of a robust version of regulatory takings, such as Professor Richard Epstein, argue that zoning laws may be valid if they apply to all property in the polity and confer benefits on each affected landowner that are "a full and perfect equivalent" of the value lost due to imposition of zoning. See Richard A. Epstein, Takings: Private Property and the Power of Eminent Domain 273 (1986). Epstein argues that zoning regulations are compensable takings if they have a disproportionate impact on affected owners—leaving some owners better off than before and others worse off. Id. at 204–209. But if the impact of zoning is proportionate and each owner has received a full and perfect equivalent of the value lost in the form of benefits received by the imposition of zoning on every other parcel, the received benefits constitute a form of "implicit in-kind compensation." Id. at 195–215. Thus, in Eptsein's view, "the entire enterprise [of the Euclid ordinance was] an ill-concealed effort to transfer wealth from one set of landowners to another through the medium of regulation." Id. at 132. In part, this was because the means—the Euclid ordinance—were substantially over-broad in relation to the villages's objectives and in part because the restrictions imposed on Ambler Realty's property were not matched by restrictions on other properties in Euclid. Some Euclid landowners "remained free to develop their land as they saw fit, now without any competition from their regulated neighbors. The differential treatment, while neither a necessary or a sufficient condition to condemn zoning, is always a powerful telltale sign that the police power has become a cloak for illegitimate ends...." Id. at 133.

2. *Zoning Today.* Zoning is ubiquitous in 21st century America. Has it accomplished its goals? A study by Charles Haar and Jerold Kayden reached the following conclusions:

- Zoning helped establish the principle that the interests of private property owners must yield to the interests of the public.

- Zoning has delivered on its simpler promises such as keeping incompatible uses separated.

- Zoning has failed to deliver on its loftier promises of producing high-quality working and living environments.

• Innovative techniques such as incentive zoning have provided small-scale public amenities.

• Zoning has been misused by suburban communities to exclude low-income and minority families.

• Zoning engenders corruption, but so does all government exercise of power.

• Zoning has not dealt adequately with regional problems.

• Zoning can mandate only so much, and only in times of economic well-being.

Charles M. Haar and Jerold S. Kayden, "Foreword: Zoning at Sixty—A Time for Anniversary Reckonings," in *Zoning and the American Dream*, ix–xi (1989).

B. DISCRETIONARY APPLICATION OF ZONING

Because there so many different situations involving land use, zoning laws typically vest the administrators of zoning laws with some degree of discretion in the actual application of the law. Discretion, of course, may be abused, but may also introduce valuable flexibility into zoning. The following sections deal with these issues.

1. VARIANCES AND EXCEPTIONS

Zoning laws almost always create some administrative agency, sometimes called a zoning appeals board, or a board of adjustment, which is given the authority to grant variances, or waivers, of the applicable zoning provision where a literal reading of the provision would cause "unnecessary hardship" to the affected landowner and a variance would "not be contrary to the public interest." An example of such a law is Mass. Gen. Laws c.40A, § 10, the successor to the statute at issue in the next case, which provides that a zoning board may grant a "variance from the terms of the applicable zoning ordinance [when it] specifically finds [that due to] circumstances ... especially affecting such land or structures but not affecting generally the zoning district in which it is located, a literal enforcement of the provisions of the ordinance ... would involve substantial hardship, financial or otherwise, to the [applicant], and that desirable relief may be granted without substantial detriment to the public good and without nullifying or substantially derogating from the intent or purpose of such ordinance...." The usual application of variances is with respect to area requirements, e.g., minimum lot size, or setbacks from lot lines. Variances are addressed to individual cases of hardship.

An exception (sometimes called a conditional use, or a special use), by contrast, is a provision in the zoning law that permits certain uses in certain zones only after the zoning board has determined that criteria specified in the law have been met, and thus has granted an "exception" for the use. The general idea is that the use for which an exception is needed is thought to be generally compatible with the other uses in the zone, but which could cause problems unless some prior review of the particular impact of the use is made. Examples of uses that might be subject to an exception rule are a private school in a residential area, or an auto repair shop in a light commercial zone of small retail stores.

The problem with each of variances and exceptions is to provide sufficient flexibility to zoning administrators to address specific situations, but not to cede so much discretion to these powerful bureaucrats that abuse is invited.

ARONSON v. BOARD OF APPEALS OF STONEHAM

Supreme Judicial Court of Massachusetts
349 Mass. 593 (1965)

WHITTEMORE, J., delivered the opinion of the court.

This is an appeal by an aggrieved abutter from a decree of the Superior Court upholding the granting of a variance to the defendants Vincent A. and Irene T. De Pierro to permit them to add a porch to premises at 25 De Witt Road, Stoneham. The . . . northerly side line of the DePierros' house . . . is 6 1/2 feet from the lot line. The zoning by-law requires a side yard of not less than 10 feet. The variance would permit the construction of an 8' x 10' porch on the northeast corner of the house, so that its 8 foot northerly side line would be in the line of the house, and 6 1/2 feet from the lot line. . . .

The [trial] judge found that at the time of purchase by the De Pierros (July 12, 1961 . . .) and "up to [a] recent date they were unaware that the structure upon their land was in violation" of the zoning by-law. The judge found that the intended porch is for the use of an invalid child of the De Pierros, and that adding the porch "at the opposite side of said building" was not feasible because of bedrooms and a driveway along the south line of the building. Nothing in the plan or record shows that it would be infeasible to build the porch in about the same place as proposed, but with its north side line 10 feet from the lot line in conformity with the by-law. There is no express finding of hardship [by the trial court] although a finding of hardship by the [zoning] board is noted. The judge found that high shrubbery between the adjacent lots gives the parcels a great degree of privacy and that the intended addition will not detract from or affect the value of the adjoining properties. The judge ruled that the granting of the variance would not be detrimental to the public good.

The evidence did not permit the granting of the variance. That a zoning violation had existed was not a condition "especially affecting such parcel or such building but not affecting generally the zoning district in which it is located." (G. L. c. 40A, § 15). . . . A use which exceeds zoning limitations "cannot be made a fulcrum to lift those limitations." . . . We hold that where the proposal is to extend on the lot an existing violation the finding (required by § 15) may not be made that "desirable relief may be granted ... without nullifying or substantially derogating from the intent or purpose of such ... by-law." Even apart from the foregoing considerations, the variance would fail for want of a showing of sufficient hardship. See Winters v. Zoning Bd. of Review of Warwick, 80 R. I. 275, 279–280 ("hardship" does not refer to personal infirmity).

[Reversed.]

COMMONS v. WESTWOOD ZONING BOARD OF ADJUSTMENT

Supreme Court of New Jersey
81 N.J. 597 (1980)

SCHREIBER, J., delivered the opinion of the court.

We are again called upon to examine the proceedings before and findings of a board of adjustment which denied a zoning variance for construction of a single-family residence on an undersized lot. [Gordon and Helen Commons and Leo Weingarten were denied a variance. The New Jersey Superior Court and the intermediate appeals court upheld the denial.]

The facts [are] substantially undisputed. The property in question is a vacant lot, designated as Lot 20 in Block 208 on the tax map of the Borough of Westwood. Located in an established residential area consisting of one and two-family dwellings, this lot is the only undeveloped property in the neighborhood. Plaintiffs Gordon and Helen Commons are the present owners. They and their predecessors in title have owned this plot since 1927. Plaintiff Weingarten, a builder, contracted to purchase the property on the condition that he could construct a one-family residence on the lot.

A variance from the borough's zoning ordinance was necessary for two reasons. The land was located in a ... residential zone requiring a minimum frontage of 75 feet and a minimum area of 7500 square feet. The lot, however, has a frontage on Brickell Avenue of only 30 feet and a total area of 5190 square feet. When adopted in 1933, the borough's zoning ordinance contained no minimum frontage or area provisions. However, a 1947 amendment required that one-family houses be located on lots with a frontage of at least 75 feet and an area of no less than 7500 square feet. At the time the amendment was adopted there were approximately 32 homes in the immediate area. Only seven satisfied the minimum frontage requirement. The nonconforming lots had frontages varying from 40 to 74 feet.[2] This situation has remained virtually unchanged, only two homes having been constructed thereafter, one in 1948 with a frontage of 70 feet and one in 1970 with a frontage of 113 feet.

---

2. [Ed. Non-conforming uses will be discussed in subsection C.2 of this chapter. It is apparent from the court's discussion that the Borough of Westwood must have included a "grandfather clause" when it enacted its 1947 amendment, such that prior non-conforming uses were permitted to continue.]

Weingarten proposed to construct a single-family, one and one-half story "raised ranch" with four bedrooms, a living room, dining room, kitchen, two baths and a one-car garage. Weingarten had no architectural design of the proposed house, but submitted a plan for a larger home which he claimed could be scaled down. The proposed home would have an approximate width of 19 feet, 8 inches and a depth of 48 feet. It would be centered on the 30–foot lot so as to provide five-foot side yards, the minimum required by the zoning ordinance. The proposed setback would also conform with the zoning plan. Weingarten further explained that the proposed residence would be roughly 18 feet from the house belonging to Robert Dineen located on adjacent land to the north, and 48 feet from the two-family residence owned by David Butler on the property to the south. The Dineen property has a 50–foot frontage, and the Butler frontage measures 74.5 feet.

The proposed home would be offered for sale for about $55,000. That price compared favorably with the market values of other nearby homes which a local realtor, Thomas Reno, estimated at between $45,000 and $60,000. Reno testified that the proposed home would not impair the borough's zoning plan because the house would be new, its value would compare favorably with other homes, its setback from the street would be at least as great as others, and the distances between the adjoining houses on each side would be substantial.

In 1974, plaintiff Gordon Commons had offered to sell the lot to Dineen for $7,500. Negotiations terminated, however, after Dineen countered with a $1,600 proposal, the assessed value of the property. When Weingarten contracted to purchase the land, he sought, albeit unsuccessfully, to purchase from Butler a 10–foot strip, adjacent to the south side of the lot. Many neighbors opposed the application for a variance. Butler testified that a house on a 30–foot lot would be aesthetically displeasing, would differ in appearance by having a garage in front rather then alongside the dwelling, and would impair property values in the neighborhood. Another property owner, whose home was across the street, expressed her concern about privacy, reasoning that the occupants of a four-bedroom residence on a small lot would cause a spillover effect in terms of noise and trespassing.

The board of adjustment denied the variance, finding "that the applicant failed to demonstrate any evidence to establish hardship" and "that the granting of the variance would substantially impair the intent and purpose of the Zone Plan and Zoning Ordinance of the Borough of Westwood." The trial court ... affirmed because it felt that to permit the variance "would be detrimental to the entire area wherein the property in question is situated." The Appellate Division, holding that the board of adjustment had not acted arbitrarily, affirmed in a brief per curiam opinion.

The variance application was filed and heard when N.J.S.A. 40:55–39(c) was effective. That statute has been replaced with N.J.S.A. 40:55D–

70(c) of the Municipal Land Use Law.... Since these provisions are substantially the same and we are remanding this matter to the board of adjustment, we shall consider the issues in the light of the current statute.

I. N.J.S.A. 40:55D–70(c) provides that a board of adjustment shall have power to grant a variance where by reason of the narrowness of the land or other extraordinary and exceptional situation of the property, the strict application of a zoning ordinance would result in exceptional and undue hardship upon the developer of the property.[3] In addition, the statute's negative criteria must be satisfied, that is that the variance can be granted "without substantial detriment to the public good and will not substantially impair the intent and purpose of the zone plan and zoning ordinance." ...

"Undue hardship" involves the underlying notion that no effective use can be made of the property in the event the variance is denied. Use of the property may of course be subject to reasonable restraint. [A] property owner's use of the land is subject to regulation "which will promote the public health, safety, morals and general welfare...." N.J.S.A. 40:55D–2(a). Put another way an "owner is not entitled to have his property zoned for its most profitable use." However, when the regulation renders the property unusable for any purpose, the analysis calls for further inquiries which may lead to a conclusion that the property owner would suffer an undue hardship.

It is appropriate to consider first the origin of the existing situation. If the property owner or his predecessors in title created the nonconforming condition, then the hardship may be deemed to be self-imposed. ... Thus, if the lot had contained a 75–foot frontage and despite the existence of that requirement, the owner sold a 40–foot strip of the land, he or his successors in title would have little cause to complain. Likewise no undue hardship is suffered by an owner of a lot with a 35–foot frontage who acquired an adjoining 40–foot strip so that the lot complied with the ordinance and then sold a part of the land. These examples serve to illustrate the nature of a self-inflicted hardship which would not satisfy the statutory criteria.

Related to a determination of undue hardship are the efforts which the property owner has made to bring the property into compliance with the ordinance's specifications. Attempts to acquire additional land would be significant if it is feasible to purchase property from the adjoining property owners. Endeavors to sell the property to the adjoining landowners, the negotiations between and among the parties, and the reasonableness of the prices demanded and offered are also relevant considerations. See Gougeon v. Stone Harbor Bd. of Adjustment, 52 N.J. 212, 224 (1968),

---

3. The statute refers to situations in which a denial would "result in peculiar and exceptional practical difficulties to, or exceptional and undue hardship upon the developer of such property." N.J.S.A. 40:55D–70(c). In Chirichello v. Monmouth Beach Zoning Bd. of Adjustment, 78 N.J. 544, 552 (1978), we referred to the language as indicating "two different standards, difficulties or hardship," and noted that "the two in large measure are overlapping and complementary. Clearly, peculiar and exceptional practical difficulties may well bear upon the exceptional and undue hardship visited upon the owner of the property." ...

where it was held that if an owner of land refused to sell at a "fair and reasonable" price he would not be considered to be suffering an "undue hardship." If on the other hand the owner is willing to sell at a "fair and reasonable" price and the adjoining property owners refuse to make a reasonable offer, then "undue hardship" would exist.

When an undue hardship is found to exist, the board of adjustment must be satisfied that the negative criteria are satisfied before granting a variance. Thus the grant of the variance must not substantially impinge upon the public good and the intent and purpose of the zone plan and ordinance. As we observed in *Chirichello*, "the variance may be granted only if the spirit of the ordinance and the general welfare are observed." . . . In this respect attention must be directed to the manner in and extent to which the variance will impact upon the character of the area. We have frequently observed that the applicant carries the burden of establishing the negative criteria by a fair preponderance of the evidence, but that "[t]he less of an impact, the more likely the restriction is not that vital to valid public interests." *Chirichello*.

There lurks in the background of cases of this type the possibility that denial of a variance will zone the property into inutility so that "an exercise of eminent domain [will be] . . . called for and compensation must be paid." Harrington Glen, Inc. v. Leonia Bd. of Adjustment, 52 N.J. 22, 33 (1968). When that occurs all the taxpayers in the municipality share the economic burden of achieving the intent and purpose of the zoning scheme. Compared to this result is the denial of a variance conditioned upon the sale of the property at a fair market value to the adjoining property owners. They will perhaps receive the more direct benefit of the land remaining undeveloped and it may therefore be fairer for them to bear the cost. In this respect we made the following pertinent comments in *Chirichello*:

> It would certainly be consonant with the interest of all parties to deny a variance conditioned on the purchase of the land by adjoining property owners at a fair price. The immediate benefit to the adjoining property owners of maintenance of the zoning scheme and aesthetic enjoyment of surrounding vacant land adjacent to their homes is self-evident. The owner of the odd lot would suffer no monetary damage having received the fair value of the land. Of course, if the owner refused to sell, then he would have no cause for complaint. Or if the adjoining owners would not agree to purchase, then perhaps the variance should be granted, less weight being given to their position particularly when the land in question will have been rendered useless. In either event the use of a conditional variance, the condition bearing an overall reasonable relationship to the purposes of the zoning ordinance, may lead to a satisfactory solution. [. . .]

Hearings before the board of adjustment serve as the focal point for resolution of conflicting interests between public restraints on the use of private property and the owner's right to utilize his land as he wishes. A third interest which frequently makes its appearance is represented by other property owners in the immediate vicinity whose major objective is the more limited self-interest of taking whatever position they believe will enhance the value of their property or coincide with their personal preferences. The board of adjustment must settle these disputes by engaging in a "discretionary weighing," a function inherent in the variance process.

We have referred to the fair market value and the fair and reasonable price of the property with respect to considerations of offers to purchase and sell the property as well as the possibility of conditioning the variance. We believe that the preferred method to determine value is on the assumption that a variance had been granted so that a home could be constructed on the lot. . . . It is possible that other methods of valuation may be feasible. However, the parties have not briefed or argued the issue and accordingly we do not foreclose such possibilities.

II. Here, the board of adjustment concluded that "the applicant failed to demonstrate *any* evidence to establish hardship on the part of the applicant." (emphasis supplied) The record does not support that conclusion. Until the 1947 amendment to the zoning ordinance the plaintiffs or their predecessors in title could have constructed a one-family house on the lot. Ownership commenced in 1927 when the Borough of Westwood had no zoning ordinance. Furthermore, an attempt, albeit unsuccessful, had been made to acquire an additional ten-foot strip from Mr. Butler, owner of the property bordering to the south. A 40-foot frontage would have at least brought the property into conformity with one home in the neighborhood and within close proximity of the size of the lots of two other houses. In addition there had been discussions concerning the possible sale of the property to a neighbor, there being a substantial divergence in the offering and asking prices. Lastly, one could reasonably conclude that, if a variance were not granted, the land would be zoned into inutility. In view of all the above, it cannot be said that there was *not any* evidence to establish hardship.

Passing to the negative criteria, the board of adjustment made only the conclusive statement that the variance would substantially impair the intent and purpose of the zone plan and ordinance. The manner in which the variance would cause that effect is not explained. The board found that the lot was the only 30-foot parcel in the block, that the applicant builder had never constructed a house on a 30-foot lot, and that the proposed house would be 19 feet in width. How these facts relate to the zone plan is not made clear. The proposed use, side yards and setback meet the requirements of the ordinance. The proposed sales price of the home would be within the range of the value of the houses in the neighborhood. The total acreage of the land, exceeding 5,000 square feet, is comparable to 17 other properties in the neighborhood. Perhaps the proposed house would be smaller in size than others. But in and of itself that would not justify a denial of a variance. Size of the house does not violate any of the traditional zoning purposes of light, air and open space which are reflected in the ordinance. We have recognized that minimum lot size "may be closely related to the goals of public health and safety" but that minimum floor area requirements "are not *per se* related to public health, safety or morals." Home Builders League of South Jersey, Inc. v. Berlin Tp., 81 N.J. 127, 139, 142 (1979).

It is possible that the board of adjustment was concerned with the appearance of the house and its relationship to the neighborhood from an aesthetic and economic viewpoint. These are proper zoning purposes, for the appearance of a house may be related to the character of the district. N.J.S.A. 40:55D–62(a). In *Home Builders League of South Jersey, Inc.*, we recognized that conserving the value of the surrounding properties and aesthetic considerations are appropriate desiderata of zoning. Thus, if the size and layout of the proposed house would have adversely affected the character of the neighborhood, both with respect to a "desirable visual environment," N.J.S.A. 40:55D–2(i), and the value of the neighborhood properties, a board may justly conclude that a variance should not be granted.

The board's resolution does not address these problems. They are brought into sharp focus when an articulation of findings and reasoning must be made. We have frequently advised boards of adjustment to make findings predicated upon factual support in the record and directed to the issues involved. We refer again to Justice Francis's statements in *Harrington Glen, Inc.*, 52 N.J. at 28:

> Denial of a variance on a summary finding couched in the conclusionary language of the statute is not adequate. There must be a statement of the specific findings of fact on which the Board reached the conclusion that the statutory criteria for a variance were not satisfied. Unless such findings are recited, a reviewing court cannot determine fairly whether the Board acted properly and within the limits of its authority in refusing a variance.

[B]oards should be mindful that they may receive assistance from other municipal employees. The board would not have been amiss here in calling the municipal building inspector to testify to construction requirements. The board or its counsel may also have addressed inquiries with respect to the size and appearance of the other homes, and the aesthetic and economic impact upon those homeowners. We do not mean to imply that the burden of proof is not upon the applicant. It is, but in performing its function as a governmental body, the board may take some action which may be of assistance to it. The difficulty in this case also rests with the applicants. They did not submit a plan of the proposed house, demonstrate compliance with the municipality's building code, and adequately describe the appearance and type of the structure. It is essential in a case of this type that the proponent submit a detailed plan of the proposed house. Under all these circumstances we believe fairness calls for a remand to the board of adjustment so that the record may be supplemented, the matter reconsidered, and adequate findings made.

Reversed and remanded to the Borough of Westwood Zoning Board of Adjustment.

NOTES, QUESTIONS, AND PROBLEMS

1. *Area Variances and Use Variances.* In each of *Aronson* and *Commons* the problem was an area variance. The landowner in *Aronson* wanted a variance from a setback requirement and the landowner in *Commons* wanted relief from a minimum lot size requirement. Should the legal standard be different if the landowner sought a use variance? Suppose that an owner of property zoned for single family residential use wants a variance to permit conversion of a portion of his spacious single family residence into a so-called "mother-in-law" or "*au pair*" unit, which will function as a separate and independent residence. Should the applicant be subjected to a greater burden of proof of hardship than would be the case for an area variance? Or should the standards be different for each type of variance? Consider the possibility that the standard for obtaining a use variance is proof of hardship and lack of negative effects, and that the standard for an area variance should be proof of practical difficulty. Jurisdictions take each of these approaches. See, e.g., Hertzberg v. Zoning Board of Adjustment of Pittsburgh, 554 Pa. 249 (1998) (higher burden of proof of the general standard of hardship for use variances); Duncan v. Village of Middlefield, 23 Ohio St.3d 83 (1986) (employing "practical difficulties" as the test for an area variance). Are these standards really different? If not, and you think there should be a difference, how would you formulate the two standards?

2. *What is a Hardship?* The courts are in agreement that self-imposed hardships are not "hardships" for purposes of receipt of a variance. But what constitutes a self-imposed hardship? In *Aronson*, the De Pierros, parents of the invalid child, presumably did not create the medical condition that made their child an invalid. Yet, the court ruled that hardships resulting from personal circumstances are not legally cognizable as hardships. Note that in *Aronson* there was little if any harm that would occur from the variance. Why should personal circumstances that are not of one's making be ignored when alleviation of the condition by a variance would not adversely impact neighbors or the community? Is it an adequate answer to say that awarding variances to accommodate personal convenience would effectively eviscerate zoning? Or, even worse, would that create incentives for rampant corruption and favoritism in the award of variances? Courts generally hold that an applicant for a variance must demonstrate that strict compliance with area requirements (such as setback rules) denies the applicant the practical use of their dwelling.

3. *Problems.*

a. Suppose that when Gordon and Helen Commons acquired their lot in Westwood they were aware that the lot was too small to build on unless a variance was granted. Should their voluntary purchase of the lot with such knowledge constitute a self-imposed hardship that would disqualify them form obtaining a variance? Yes

b.) *D*, a developer, creates a residential subdivision of twenty-one lots. Each of Lots 1 through 20 comply with all area restrictions of the local zoning code applicable to building lots for residences. Lot 21 is too small in area to comply with those area restrictions. Indeed, Lot 21 has been designated by *D* as "open recreational space," even though title is held by *D* and none of the purchasers of Lots 1 through 20 have any legal interest in Lot 21. Nor is Lot 21 burdened by any servitude benefitting the purchasers of Lots 1 through 20. Needing cash, *D* sells Lot 21 to *A*, who is fully aware of the fact that Lot 21 does not comply with the area requirements. *A* then applies for a variance to permit him to build a residence on Lot 21 which will conform to the style and value of existing homes in the subdivision. Should *A* receive a variance?

NO!.

4. Exceptions, or Conditional Uses or Special Uses. The issue presented by zoning laws that contain an exception provision (or a conditional use or special use provision) is whether the legislative body has impermissibly delegated its legislative authority to the zoning board. Resolution of this question depends on whether the exercise of discretion granted to the zoning board is sufficiently bounded. There are two general boundaries: the state constitution's limits on delegation of legislative power and conformity of a local zoning law that provides for exceptions to the state's zoning enabling act.

In Westford v. Kilburn, 131 Vt. 120 (1973), the state's zoning enabling act provided that local zoning boards "may make special exceptions to the terms of the ordinance in harmony with its general purpose and intent and in accordance with general or specific rules therein contained." Two sections of the Town of Westford's zoning ordinance permitted the zoning board to grant exceptions so long as neighboring property owners consented and it "shall give due consideration to promoting the public health, safety, convenience and welfare of the inhabitants of the town of Westford, encouraging the most appropriate use of land and protecting and conserving property value, that it shall permit no building or use injurious, obnoxious, offensive or detrimental to a neighborhood and that it shall prescribe appropriate conditions and safeguards in each case." The Vermont Supreme Court held that the zoning enabling act did not permit the exercise of discretion in granting exceptions to be conditioned on neighbors' consent and that the standard of "public health, safety, convenience and welfare" was too general to comply with the zoning enabling act. In the exercise of discretion, said the court,

> guiding standards assure all parties concerned it has been exercised in a proper manner. When no such guiding standards are spelled out by the legislative body, the door is opened to the exercise of this discretion in an arbitrary or discriminatory fashion. As a consequence of a failure of a legislative body to spell out guiding standards, the applicant for a permit is left uncertain as to what factors are to be considered by the Board of Adjustment. ... On one hand the standards governing the delegation of such authority should be general enough to avoid inflexible results, yet on the other hand they should not leave the door open to unbridled discrimination. ... Because sections four and seven of the Protective Zoning Ordinance of the Town of Westford fail to prescribe appropriate conditions and safeguards to be followed in appropriate cases as they are

required to, they must be found invalid for their failure to comply with [Vermont's zoning enabling act].

Id. at 124–126.

In Waterville Hotel Corp. v. Board of Zoning Appeals, 241 A.2d 50 (Me. 1968), the Waterville zoning board denied an application to construct a gasoline filling station in a commercial zone that explicitly permitted such a use "subject to the approval of the Board of Zoning Appeals." The local zoning ordinance stipulated that the zoning board's discretion must be exercised "in harmony with the comprehensive plan for municipal development ..., in accordance with the public interest, and in support and furtherance of the health, safety and general welfare of the residents of the municipality." The Maine Supreme Judicial Court held that "where a zoning ordinance attempts to permit municipal officials to grant or refuse permits without the guidance of any standards, equal protection is denied the citizens." To similar effect is Osius v. City of St. Clair Shores, 344 Mich. 693 (1956), where the Michigan Supreme Court voided a zoning board's exercise of discretion under an ordinance containing no standards: "The ordinance is silent as to size, capacity, traffic control, number of curb cuts, location, or any other of the myriad considerations applicable to such business. ... a ready tool for the suppression of competition through the granting of authority to one and the withholding from another. ... The ordinance ... is unconstitutional and void ... since it fixes no standard for the grant (or refusal) of the certificate prayed. A zoning ordinance cannot permit administrative officers or boards to pick and choose the recipients of their favors." So, too, in State ex rel. Humble Oil & Refining Co. v. Wahner, 25 Wis.2d 1 (1964) ("Without standards both the board and Humble 'were at sea without chart, rudder, or compass' and this was bound to create a situation in which the board could do just as it pleased.") In accord are Taylor v. Moore, 303 Pa. 469 (1931), and North Bay Village v. Blackwell, 88 So.2d 524 (Fla. 1956). But see Coronet Homes, Inc. v. McKenzie, 84 Nev. 250 (1968), in which the Nevada Supreme Court upheld the validity of a local zoning ordinance that conferred discretion on the zoning board to grant special use permits only when the use was "necessary to the public health, convenience, safety and welfare and to the promotion of the general good of the community" and would "not result in material damage or prejudice to other property in the vicinity." The difference in result is attributable to Nevada's zoning enabling act, which provides: "For the purpose of promoting health, safety, morals, or the general welfare of the community, the governing bodies of cities and counties are authorized and empowered to regulate and restrict the improvement of land and to control the location and soundness of structures." The Nevada court did not address the issue of whether the Nevada statute violated the state constitution's guarantee of equal protection of the laws.

2. CONDITIONAL ZONING, CONTRACT ZONING, AND "SPOT ZONING"

Ordinarily, amendment of a zoning law poses no problems, but when a zoning law is amended to single out one small piece of land for either particularly advantageous or disadvantageous treatment, the re-zoning is susceptible to the following objections: 1) It is arguably not for the public interest but only for the benefit of the landowner (or, in the case of negative treatment, to punish or harm a landowner), and 2) the re-zoning fails to conform to a comprehensive plan. If these objections are valid, the re-zoning is almost certain to be invalid. This is often referred to as "spot zoning," but the term also encompasses some valid zoning amendments that target a small parcel for treatment different from surrounding parcels. If treatment of the affected parcel is demonstrably in the public interest and does no harm to a comprehensive plan, it may be an entirely legitimate use of the amending process.

A problem that has vexed courts in this area is the standard of review to apply to spot zoning. For a time some courts placed the burden of establishing the validity of spot zoning on the government, on the theory that the individualized nature of the re-zoning made it quasi-adjudicative, thus stripping the action of the normal presumption of legitimacy that attaches to legislation. See, e.g., Fasano v. Board of County Commissioners of Washington County, 264 Ore. 574 (1973). This approach had its own problems, however: When is the re-zoning sufficiently individualized to trigger this reversal of the burden of proof? What procedural rights and duties attach to the re-zoning process if it is "quasi-judicial" in nature? Eventually, this approach fell out of favor, being rejected outright in some states and even substantially overruled in Oregon, its place of origin. See State v. City of Rochester, 268 N.W.2d 885 (Minn. 1978); Neuberger v. City of Portland, 288 Ore. 155 (1979). Most states presume that re-zoning, even spot zoning, is valid unless the challenger can prove that the re-zoning produces little or no public benefit, confers special benefits to a small, discrete parcel, and is not consistent with the jurisdiction's comprehensive land use plan. A few jurisdictions require the proponent of spot re-zoning to prove that such re-zoning is either necessary to correct a mistake or to adapt to substantial changed neighborhood conditions since the zoning law was enacted. See, e.g., Stratakis v. Beauchamp, 268 Md. 643, 653 (1973) ("*strong* evidence of mistake in the original zoning or comprehensive rezoning or evidence of substantial change in the character of the neighborhood must be produced" to justify piecemeal rezoning).

Conditional zoning is the rezoning of a parcel to permit a use that would not be permitted under the prior classification, but subject to conditions that limit the permitted use to narrowly described uses that are designed to curb the possibility that the rezoning could result in a more intensive use that would inflict more damage on neighbors or produce fewer public benefits than those produced by the conditional rezoning. Contract zoning is rezoning pursuant to a private bargain, under which the zoning body abandons its responsibility to exercise independent judgement. Contract zoning is illegal, but the difference between contract zoning and conditional zoning is thin.

CHRISMON v. GUILFORD COUNTY

Supreme Court of North Carolina
322 N.C. 611 (1988)

MEYER, J., delivered the opinion of the court.

[Since 1948, on a three acre parcel adjacent to his home, defendant Clapp had operated a business as a dealer in grain and agricultural chemicals. In 1964 Guilford County adopted a zoning law, under which Clapp's property was zoned A–1, a classification permitting his grain dealing but not his sale of agricultural chemicals. Because the agricultural chemical business was a pre-existing use, Clapp was permitted to continue that business as a nonconforming use so long as it was not expanded. In 1969, Mr. and Mrs. Chrismon bought a tract of land across Gun Shop Road, an unpaved road, from Clapp's residence and built a home there. Immediately adjacent to the Chrismons' home was a five acre tract owned by Clapp that was used for cultivation of tobacco. In 1980, Clapp moved some of his business operations from the three acre to the five acre tract, built some new buildings on the latter parcel, and "generally enlarged his operation." The Chrismons complained to Guilford County about the increased noise, dust, and traffic caused by this expansion, and the County notified Clapp that his expansion of the agricultural chemical operation to the five acre tract was an impermissible expansion of a nonconforming use but that he could request a rezoning of the property.

[Clapp then applied to have both the three acre and five acre parcels rezoned from A–1 to CU–M–2, a "Conditional Use Industrial District," indicating in his application for the conditional use permit needed under the CU–M–2 classification that he would use the property as it was then being used and itemizing intended improvements. Issuance of the conditional use permit would make Clapp's agricultural chemical business a permitted use. The County Board of Commissioners held a public hearing on the application, at which Clapp, Chrismon, and Chrismon's attorney were heard. The Commissioners were made aware of the fact that members of the public had spoken in favor of Clapp's application at prior Planning Board hearings because Clapp's business provided a service to farmers in the immediate vicinity, and that the Board had received a petition favoring the rezoning signed by 88 persons. The Commissioners rezoned Clapp's parcels to CU–M–2 and approved the conditional use application.

[Chrismon sought judicial relief. The trial court ruled that the Commissioners had not acted arbitrarily, and that the rezoning was neither spot zoning nor contract zoning. The court of appeals reversed, finding that the rezoning constituted an illegal form of spot zoning and was also illegal contract zoning. The court of appeals thought it was illegal spot zoning] for three principal reasons: (1) the rezoning was not called for by any change of conditions on the land; (2) the rezoning was not called for by the character of the district and the particular characteristics of the area being rezoned; and (3) the rezoning was not called for by the classification and use of nearby land [even though the authorized uses] were not, in and of themselves, incompatible with the general area.... [The court of appeals thought the rezoning] constituted illegal "contract zoning" [because,] in essence, the rezoning here was accomplished through a bargain between the applicant and the Board rather than through a proper and valid exercise of Guilford County's legislative discretion....

The questions plainly before us are these: first, did the rezoning ... constitute illegal spot zoning; and second, did the same rezoning constitute illegal contract zoning. ... We conclude that the correct answer to both questions is "no."

I.   ... As an initial matter, ... because this Court has not previously been called upon to address the legal concept of conditional use zoning, and because the decision of the Court of Appeals virtually outlaws that practice, we pause now to address its place in the jurisprudence of this state. Specifically, we hold today that the practice of conditional use zoning is an approved practice in North Carolina, so long as the action of the local zoning authority in accomplishing the zoning is reasonable, neither arbitrary nor unduly discriminatory, and in the public interest....

Comprehensive zoning systems, though effective in preserving the character of ongoing uses, are often criticized for not allowing for the degree of flexibility needed to allow local officials to respond appropriately to "constantly shifting conditions and public needs." The practice of conditional use zoning—like that used by Guilford County in this case—is one of several vehicles by which greater zoning flexibility can be and has been acquired by zoning authorities. Conditional use zoning anticipates that when the rezoning of certain property within the general zoning framework ... would constitute an unacceptably drastic change, such a rezoning could still be accomplished through the addition of certain conditions or use limitations. Specifically, conditional use zoning occurs when a governmental body, without committing its own authority, secures a given property owner's agreement to limit the use of his property to a particular use or to subject his tract to certain restrictions as a precondition to any rezoning. D. Hagman & J. Juergensmeyer, *Urban Planning and Land Development Control Law* § 5.5 (2d ed. 1986).... It is indeed generally agreed among commentators that, because it permits a given local authority greater flexibility in balancing conflicting demands, the practice of conditional use zoning is exceedingly valuable....

> Conditional zoning is an outgrowth of the need for compromise between the interests of the developer seeking appropriate zoning changes for his tract, and the neighboring landowner whose property interests would suffer if the most intensive use permitted by the new classification were instituted. In an attempt to reconcile these conflicting pressures, the municipality will authorize the proposed change but minimize its adverse effects by imposing conditions.

Shapiro, *The Case For Conditional Zoning*, 41 Temp. L.Q. 267, 280 (1968)....

Without pausing at this juncture specifically to address the propriety of the zoning action in this case, we note that the action here is consistent with the observation[] of Shapiro.... Before the now-disputed zoning occurred, the tracts of land in question, and all of the surrounding land for some miles, were classified under the comprehensive zoning plan as A–1. While the A–1 classification allowed Mr. Clapp to engage in the storage and sale of grain, it did not allow him to store and sell agricultural chemicals, which was his desire. While the rezoning of the two tracts to M–2 Industrial would clearly allow the desired agricultural chemical operation, it would also clearly allow for activities substantially inconsistent with the surrounding A–1 areas.[4] Herein lies the usefulness of conditional use zoning. By rezoning these tracts CU–M–2, the desired activity becomes a conforming use, but by virtue of the attendant conditions, uses undesirable under these circumstances can be limited or avoided altogether.

Notwithstanding the manifest benefits of conditional use zoning, there has, over the course of time, been some divergence of opinion amongst courts and commentators alike as to the legal status of the practice. In fact, the initial judicial response to conditional use zoning was to condemn the practice as invalid per se. See, e.g., Hartnett v. Austin, 93 So. 2d 86 (Fla. 1956); V.F. Zahodiakin Eng'r Corp. v. Zoning Board of Adjustment, 8 N.J. 386, 86 A. 2d 127 (1952). Those courts falling into this category have objected to conditional use zoning on the several grounds that it constitutes illegal spot zoning; that it is not, on the specific facts, authorized by the state's zoning enabling legislation; and that it results in an improper and illegal abandonment of the local government's police powers.

The benefits of the additional zoning and planning flexibility inherent in conditional use zoning have apparently not escaped the attention of jurisdictions which have addressed the issue more recently. Many jurisdictions now approve of the practice of conditional use zoning, so long as the action of the local zoning authority in accomplishing the zoning is reasonable, neither arbitrary nor unduly discriminatory, and in the public interest.[5] These jurisdictions, which comprise a growing trend, have

---

4. For example, permitted uses in a district zoned under the M–2 Industrial classification would include, among other things, manufacturing facilities of virtually any kind, fuel oil dealerships, waste recycling facilities, and public utility storage depots.

5. See, e.g., Haas v. City of Mobile, 289 Ala. 16, 265 So. 2d 564 (1972); Transamerica Title Insurance Co. v. City of Tucson, 23 Ariz. App. 385, 533 P. 2d 693 (1975); J–Marion Co. v. County of Sacramento, 76 Cal. App. 3d 517, 142 Cal. Rptr. 723 (1977); City of Colorado Springs v. Smartt, 620 P. 2d 1060 (Colo. 1980); Warshaw v. City of Atlanta, 250 Ga. 535, 299 S.E. 2d 552 (1983); Goffinet v. County of Christian, 65 Ill. 2d 40, 357 N.E. 2d 442 (1976); Sylvania Electric Products, Inc. v. Newton, 344 Mass. 428, 183 N.E. 2d 118 (1962); Housing & Redevelopment Authority v. Jorgensen, 328 N.W. 2d 740 (Minn. 1983); Bucholz v. City of Omaha, 174 Neb. 862, 120 N.W. 2d 270 (1963); Collard v. Vil of Flower Hill, 52 N.Y. 2d 594, 421 N.E. 2d 818, 439 N.Y.S. 2d 326 (1981); Sweetman v. Town of Cumberland, 117 R.I. 134, 364 A. 2d 1277 (1976); City of Redmond v. Kezner, 10 Wash. App. 332, 517 P. 2d 625 (1973); Howard v. Elm Grove, 80 Wis. 2d 33, 257

concluded, among other things, that zoning legislation provides ample authority for the practice; that the use under the practice of carefully tailored restraints advanced, rather than injured, the interests of adjacent landowners; and that the practice is an appropriate means of harmonizing private interests in land and thus of benefitting the public interest. Today, we join this growing trend of jurisdictions in recognizing the validity of properly employed conditional use zoning. . . .

Having so stated, we hasten to add that, just as this type of zoning can provide much-needed and valuable flexibility to the planning efforts of local zoning authorities, it could also be as easily abused. We recognize that critics of the practice are to a limited extent justified in their concern that the unrestricted use of conditional use zoning could lead to private or public abuse of governmental power. . . . [C]onditional use zoning, like any type of zoning, must be reasonable, neither arbitrary nor unduly discriminatory, and in the public interest. It goes without saying that it also cannot constitute illegal spot zoning or illegal contract zoning. . . .

II.   We turn now to the question of spot zoning. . . . [The] rezoning accomplished in this case, while admittedly constituting a form of spot zoning, constituted a legal, and *not* an illegal form of spot zoning. . . . [We] find that, on the facts of this case, the county did show a reasonable basis for the rezoning at issue. . . .

We note as an initial matter that there is substantial disagreement amongst jurisdictions across the nation as to both the proper definition of and the legal significance of the term "spot zoning." Jurisdictions have essentially divided into two distinct camps. One group, the majority of jurisdictions, regards the term "spot zoning" as a legal term of art referring to a practice which is per se invalid. In such jurisdictions, a judicial determination that a given rezoning action constitutes spot zoning is, ipso facto, a determination that the rezoning action is void.

The position of this first group has been described by one commentator as follows:

> Spot zoning amendments are those which by their terms single out a particular lot or parcel of land, usually small in relative size, and place it in an area the land use pattern of which is inconsistent with the small lot or parcel so placed, thus projecting an inharmonious land use pattern. Such amendments are usually triggered by efforts to secure special benefits for particular property owners, without proper regard for the rights of adjacent landowners. These are the real spot zoning situations. *Under no circumstances could the tag of validity be attached thereto.*

N.W. 2d 850 (1977); 1982 Me. Laws ch. 598 (statute permits a municipality to include in its comprehensive plan provisions for conditional and contract rezoning); Va. Code § 15.1–491 (1988) (statute permits a municipality to impose reasonable conditions "as part of an amendment to the zoning map . . . in addition to the regulations provided for the zoning district by the ordinance, when such conditions have been proffered in writing, in advance of the public hearing before the governing body . . . by the owner of the [subject] property").

2 E. Yokley, *Zoning Law and Practice* § 13–3 at 207 (4th ed. 1978) (emphasis added).

A somewhat smaller group of jurisdictions, including our own, has taken a different approach. In these jurisdictions, it has been stated that "spot zoning" is a descriptive term merely, rather than a legal term of art, and that spot zoning practices may be valid or invalid depending upon the facts of the specific case. See Tennison v. Shomette, 38 Md. App. 1, 379 A. 2d 187 (1977); Save Our Rural Environment v. Snohomish County, 99 Wash. 2d 363, 662 P. 2d 816 (1983) (holding that the practice of spot zoning is not invalid per se). . . . [In] these jurisdictions, a spot zoning case poses, not merely the lone question of whether what occurred on the facts constituted spot zoning. It also poses the additional question of whether the zoning action, if spot zoning, was of the legal or illegal variety. We are firmly amongst this latter group of jurisdictions which has held that spot zoning is not invalid per se. . . . [In] Blades v. City of Raleigh, 280 N.C. 531, 187 S.E. 2d 35 (1972), we defined "spot zoning" as follows:

> A zoning ordinance, or amendment, which singles out and reclassifies a relatively small tract owned by a single person and surrounded by a much larger area uniformly zoned, so as to impose upon the small tract greater restrictions than those imposed upon the larger area, or so as to relieve the small tract from restrictions to which the rest of the area is subjected, is called "spot zoning."

[We] hastened to add that the practice is not invalid per se but, rather, that it is beyond the authority of the municipality or county and therefore void *only* "in the absence of a clear showing of a reasonable basis" [for the rezoning].

[Since] the action by the Board was . . . clearly spot zoning . . ., the lone question [is] whether there is a clear showing of a reasonable basis. . .

[The] Board did in fact clearly show a reasonable basis for its rezoning of Mr. Clapp's two tracts from A–1 to CU–M–2. We are particularly persuaded, first, by the degree of public benefit created by the zoning action here and, second, by the similarity of the proposed use of the tracts under the new conditional use zone to the uses in the surrounding A–1 areas. [A] judicial determination as to the existence or nonexistence of a sufficient reasonable basis in the context of spot zoning is, and must be, the "product of a complex of factors." . . . Among the factors relevant to this judicial balancing are the size of the tract in question; the compatibility of the disputed zoning action with an existing comprehensive zoning plan; the benefits and detriments resulting from the zoning action for the owner of the newly zoned property, his neighbors, and the surrounding community; and the relationship between the uses envisioned under the new zoning and the uses currently present in adjacent tracts. See . . . 1 R. Anderson, *American Law of Zoning* § 5.13 (3d ed. 1986). . . .

[We] find the latter two of the above-mentioned factors to argue forcefully for the proposition that the rezoning activity here was supported by a reasonable basis. . . . [The] true vice of illegal spot zoning is in its inevitable effect of granting a discriminatory benefit to one landowner and a corresponding detriment to the neighbors or the community without adequate public advantage or justification. Accordingly, while spot zoning which creates a great benefit for the owner of the rezoned property with only an accompanying detriment and no accompanying benefit to the community or to the public interest may well be illegal, spot zoning which provides a service needed in the community in addition to benefitting the landowner may be proper. Courts from other jurisdictions have held, for example, that the mere fact that an area is rezoned at the request of a single owner and is of greater benefit to him than to others does not make out a case of illegal spot zoning *if there is a public need for it.* See, e.g., Jaffe v. City of Davenport, 179 N.W. 2d 554 (Iowa 1970); Sweeney v. City of Dover, 108 N.H. 307, 234 A. 2d 521 (1967). The Supreme Court of New Jersey long ago announced a standard for properly weighing the various benefits and detriments created by disputed zoning activity. In a statement with which this Court agrees, that court stated as follows:

> The standard is not the advantage or detriment to particular neighboring landowners, but rather the effect upon the entire community as a social, economic and political unit. *That which makes for the exclusive and preferential benefit of such particular landowner, with no relation to the community as a whole, is not a valid exercise of this sovereign power.*

Mansfield & Swett, Inc. v. West Orange, 120 N.J.L. 145, 150, 198 A. 225, 233 (1938) (emphasis added).

[It] is manifest that Mr. Clapp . . . has reaped a benefit by the Board's action [in that] he will be able to carry on the otherwise illegal storage and sale of agricultural chemicals on both of his two tracts along Gun Shop Road in rural Guilford County. [The] Chrismons have simultaneously sustained a detriment. . . . [But] "[t]he evidence clearly shows that Mr. Clapp's operation is beneficial to area farmers." The record reveals that members of the farming community surrounding the disputed land spoke in favor of the rezoning action . . . [and that] the Board was presented with a petition signed by some eighty-eight area residents favoring the action. [We] note that it was the Chrismons, *and no one else,* who spoke up against the rezoning. [And] there is additional and more objective evidence that the operation constitutes a use valuable to the surrounding community. The area in the vicinity of Mr. Clapp's operation is zoned for some miles as exclusively A–1 and is used by many for farming activities. Quite independent of the indications from members of the community that they have a subjective need for Mr. Clapp's services, it cannot be gainsaid that services of this type—namely, the storage and sale of pesticides, lime, and fertilizer—are valuable in a farming community such as that here. It has been held elsewhere that community-wide need for commercial or industrial facilities usually takes precedence over the objections of several adjacent property owners. See Citizens Ass'n of Georgetown, Inc. v. D.C. Zoning Comm'n, 402 A. 2d 36 (D.C. App. 1979). We believe that to be the case here.

A second factor that we find important in the determination of a reasonable basis for the spot zoning here is the similarity between the proposed use of the tracts under the new conditional use zone and the uses already present in surrounding areas. . . . [Even] in the wake of the rezoning . . ., the uses present in the rezoned area and the surrounding A–1 area will remain, by virtue of the restrictions inherent in conditional use zoning, quite similar. At the very least, the differences in the uses will certainly not be vast, as is often the situation in a case of illegal spot zoning. The compatibility of the uses envisioned in the rezoned tract with the uses already present in surrounding areas is . . . an important factor in determining the validity of a spot zoning action. . . . One court has described the evil to be avoided as "an attempt to *wrench* a single small lot from its environment and give it a new rating *which disturbs the tenor of the neighborhood.*" Magnin v. Zoning Commission, 145 Conn. 26, 28, 138 A. 2d 522, 523 (1958) (emphasis added). We see no such disturbance on the facts before us. . . . [The] the rezoning of the tracts in question from A–1 to CU–M–2, with all of the attendant restrictions and conditions, really represents very little change. . . .

As we noted earlier in this section, cases involving a challenge to a rezoning action on the basis of possible illegal spot zoning are very fact specific; their resolution turns very heavily on the particular facts and circumstances of the case. This spot zoning case, in which the disputed action changed a general district zone to a *conditional use zone*, is, for that reason, a case of first impression. While . . . the rezoning of Mr. Clapp's two tracts constituted a form of spot zoning . . ., we find . . . that this activity was of the legal and not illegal variety. [B]ecause of the quite substantial benefits created for the surrounding community by the rezoning and because of the close relationship between the likely uses of the rezoned property and the uses already present in the surrounding tracts, there was a clear showing of a reasonable basis for the spot zoning in this instance. It is therefore not void. . . .

III   We turn finally to the question of contract zoning. . . . Illegal contract zoning properly connotes a transaction wherein both the landowner who is seeking a certain zoning action and the zoning authority itself undertake reciprocal obligations in the context of a *bilateral* contract. One commentator provides as illustration the following example:

> A Council enters into an agreement with the landowner and then enacts a zoning amendment. *The agreement, however, includes not merely the promise of the owner to subject his property to deed restrictions; the Council also binds itself to enact the amendment and not to alter the zoning change for a specified period of time.* Most courts will conclude that by agreeing to curtail its legislative power, the Council acted ultra vires. Such contract zoning is illegal and the rezoning is therefore a nullity.

Shapiro, *The Case for Conditional Zoning*, 41 Temp. L.Q. 267, 269 (1968) (emphasis added). As the excerpted illustration suggests, contract zoning of this type is objectionable primarily because it represents an abandonment on the part of the zoning authority of its duty to exercise independent judgment in making zoning decisions. . . .

[V]alid conditional use zoning, on the other hand, is an entirely different matter. Conditional use zoning, to repeat, is an outgrowth of the need for a compromise between the interests of the developer who is seeking appropriate rezoning for his tract and the community on the one hand and the interests of the neighboring landowners who will suffer if the most intensive use permitted by the new classification is instituted.

In our view, [there are two] principal differences between valid conditional use zoning and illegal contract zoning. . . . First, valid conditional use zoning features merely a unilateral promise from the landowner to the local zoning authority as to the landowner's intended use of the land in question, while illegal contract zoning anticipates a bilateral contract in which the landowner and the zoning authority make reciprocal promises. Second, in the context of conditional use zoning, the local zoning authority maintains its independent decision-making authority, while in the contract zoning scenario, it abandons that authority by binding itself contractually with the landowner seeking a zoning amendment. . . .

We conclude that the zoning authority neither entered into a bilateral contract nor abandoned its position as an independent decision-maker. Therefore, we find what occurred in the case before us to constitute valid conditional use zoning and *not* illegal contract zoning. . . . [We] find no evidence that the . . . Guilford County Board of Commissioners entered into anything approaching a bilateral contract with . . . Mr. Clapp. [When] the Guilford County Inspections Department . . . notified Mr. Clapp that his expansion of the agricultural chemical operation to the [five acre] tract . . . constituted an impermissible expansion of a nonconforming use, . . . the letter informed Mr. Clapp [that among] his various options "to resolve your Zoning Ordinance violations" was to "request rezoning of that portion of your land involved in the violations. *This is not a guaranteed option.*" . . .

[The] only promises made in this case were unilateral—specifically, those from Mr. Clapp to the Board in the form of the substance of his conditional use permit application. As the letter excerpted above makes clear, no promises whatever were made by the Board in exchange, and this rezoning does not therefore fall into the category of illegal contract zoning.

Second, and perhaps more important, the Board did not, by virtue of its actions in this case, abandon its position as an independent decision-maker. The . . . Board made its decision in this matter only after a lengthy deliberation completely consistent with both the procedure called for by the relevant zoning ordinance and the rules prohibiting illegal contract zoning. . . . In short, then, we find that the Board engaged here, *not* in illegal contract zoning, but in valid conditional use zoning. . . .

IV. ... Accordingly, the decision of the Court of Appeals is hereby reversed. The case is remanded to that court for further remand to the Superior Court, Guilford County, for reinstatement of the original judgment denying plaintiffs' action for a declaratory judgment and affirming the zoning action of the Guilford County Board of Commissioners....

NOTES

1. Conditional Zoning v. Contract Zoning. The line between permitted conditional zoning and illegal contract zoning is thin, indistinct, and dependent on the facts of each circumstance. If the legislative authority, by an agreement, has surrendered its independent judgment concerning a zoning alteration before it has made that decision it is illegal contract zoning. But if the landowner's offer of stipulations and concessions to entice the zoning change is honestly considered at the time of the zoning change decision it is conditional zoning. Cynics may note that agreement can be reached by winks and nods, to be implemented by the pretense of careful consideration by the zoning body. The possibility of such corrupt maneuvers is one reason why each case is dependent on the facts surrounding the decision.

2. Floating Zones. Another device to create flexibility in zoning is the creation of floating zones. A floating zone is a use designation that is not attached to any particular parcel, but which specifies the criteria that must be met for any parcel to receive the use designation.

Example 11–1: A city desires to promote recycling of consumer packaging, such as glass, cans, and paper, and creates a floating zone for the collection and temporary storage of such materials ("Z–1"). The floating zone specifies that it can be applied only to land that is at least one acre in size, accessible by a public road, and located at least 500 feet from the nearest property zoned for any residential use. A landowner who possesses property that meets these criteria may seek to have his property rezoned Z–1, although the usual considerations applicable to any zoning change also apply.

So long as the criteria for receipt of a floating zone classification are sufficiently precise the discretion permitted by floating zones is no more (and possibly less) than that exercised by variances and conditional uses. See, e.g., Rodgers v. Village of Tarrytown, 302 N.Y. 115 (1951).

3. Cluster Zoning. Yet another device to facilitate discretion is cluster zoning, in which a particular area is zoned for a particular use at a specified density, but which leaves the exact manner of achieving the density goal to the discretion of the zoning board.

Example 11–2: A city zones a 100 acre area for residential cluster zoning, stipulating that the density of residential units may be no greater than four units per acre. The zoning board has discretion to decide whether to permit 400 houses, each on lots of one-quarter of an acre, or 400 units in a single building standing on two acres, with the remaining 98 acres consisting of parkland and recreational uses, or some combination with an average density of four units or less per acre.

C. LIMITS ON THE EXERCISE OF ZONING

Although states possess an inherent police power—the authority to do whatever the people, through their legislative agents, think is wise—that power is limited by four principal sources: 1) the federal Constitution, 2) federal law that preempts local law, 3) the state constitution, and 4) state laws that limit state or local authority. Thus, the scope of zoning ordinances is curbed by each of these legal limits.

1. AESTHETICS

The traditional rule was that zoning to achieve aesthetic objectives is beyond the police power. This view was exemplified by Varney & Green v. Williams, 155 Cal. 318 (1909), overruled by Metromedia, Inc. v. San Diego, 26 Cal.3d 848 (1980). In *Williams*, the California Supreme Court struck down a San Jose ordinance prohibiting most billboards. The court concluded that the ban bore no "relation to the protection of passers-by from injury by reason of unsafe structures, to the diminution of hazard of fire, or to the prevention of immoral displays," and thus was a sufficiently "radical restriction of the right of an owner of property to use his property in an ordinary and beneficial way" to be outside of the police power. But this view has been largely repudiated.

PEOPLE v. STOVER

Court of Appeals of New York
12 N.Y.2d 462 (1963)

Fuld, J., delivered the opinion of the court.

The defendants, Mr. and Mrs. Stover, residents of the City of Rye since 1940, live in a 2 1/2-story 1-family dwelling, located in a pleasant and built-up residential district, on the corner of Rye Beach and Forest Avenues. A clothesline, filled with old clothes and rags, made its first appearance in the Stovers' front yard in 1956 as a form of "peaceful protest" against the high taxes imposed by the city. And, during each of the five succeeding years, the defendants added another clothesline to mark their continued displeasure with the taxes. In 1961, therefore, six lines, from which there hung tattered clothing, old uniforms, underwear, rags and scarecrows, were strung across the Stovers' yard—three from the porch across the front yard to trees along Forest Avenue and three from the porch across the side yard to trees along Rye Beach Avenue. In August of 1961, the city enacted an ordinance prohibiting the erection and maintenance of clotheslines or other devices for hanging clothes or other fabrics in a front or side yard abutting a street (General Ordinances, § 4–3.7). However, the ordinance provides for the issuance of a permit for the use of such clotheslines if there is "a practical difficulty or unnecessary hardship in drying clothes elsewhere on the premises" and grants a right of appeal to the applicant if a permit is denied.

Following enactment of the ordinance, Mrs. Stover, the record owner of the property, applied for a permit to maintain clotheslines in her yard. Her application was denied because, she was advised, she had sufficient other property available for hanging clothes and she was directed to remove the clotheslines which were in the yards abutting the streets. Although no appeal was taken from this determination and no permit ever issued, the clotheslines were not removed. Relying upon the ordinance, the city thereupon charged the defendants with violating its provisions. They were tried and convicted and their judgments of conviction have been affirmed by the County Court of Westchester County. [Defendants contend] that the ordinance, as it has been applied . . ., is unconstitutional both as an interference with free speech and as a deprivation of property without due process.

It is a fair inference that adoption of the ordinance before us was prompted by the conduct and action of the defendants but we deem it clear that, if the law would otherwise be held constitutional, it will not be stricken as discriminatory or invalid because of its motivation. Our problem, therefore, is to determine whether the law violates First Amendment rights or otherwise exceeds the police power vested in a city on the ground that it was enacted without regard to considerations of public health, safety and welfare.

The People maintain that the prohibition against clotheslines in front and side yards was "intended to provide clear visibility at street corners and in driving out of driveways, and thus avoid and reduce accidents; to reduce distractions to motorists and pedestrians; and to provide greater opportunity for access in the event of fires." Although there may be considerable doubt whether there is a sufficiently reasonable relationship between clotheslines and traffic or fire safety to support an exercise of the police power, it is our opinion that the ordinance may be sustained as an attempt to preserve the residential appearance of the city and its property values by banning, insofar as practicable, unsightly clotheslines from yards abutting a public street. In other words, the statute, though based on what may be termed aesthetic considerations, proscribes conduct which offends sensibilities and tends to debase the community and reduce real estate values.

There are a number of early decisions . . . which hold that aesthetic considerations are not alone sufficient to justify exercise of the police power. But . . . we have actually recognized the governmental interest in preserving the appearance of the community by holding that, whether or not aesthetic considerations are in and of themselves sufficient to support an exercise of the police power, they may be taken into account by the legislative body in enacting laws which are also designed to promote health and safety.

Once it be conceded that aesthetics is a valid subject of legislative concern, the conclusion seems inescapable that reasonable legislation designed to promote that end is a valid and permissible exercise of the police power. If zoning restrictions "which implement a policy of neighborhood amenity" are to be stricken as invalid, it should be, one commentator has said, not because they seek to promote "aesthetic objectives" but solely because the restrictions constitute "unreasonable devices of implementing community policy." (Dukeminier, Zoning for Aesthetic Objectives: A Reappraisal, 20 Law & Contemp. Prob. 218, 231.) Consequently, whether such a statute or ordinance should be voided should depend upon whether the restriction was "an arbitrary and irrational method of achieving an attractive, efficiently functioning, prosperous community—and *not* upon whether the objectives were primarily aesthetic." (Dukeminier, *loc. cit*.) And . . . this view finds support in an ever-increasing number of cases from other jurisdictions which recognize that aesthetic considerations alone may warrant an exercise of the police power. . . . As Mr. Justice Douglas, writing for a unanimous court in Berman v. Parker, 348 U.S. 26, 33 (1954), put it:

> The concept of the public welfare is broad and inclusive. . . . the values it represents are spiritual as well as physical, aesthetic as well as monetary. It is within the power of the legislature to determine that the community should be beautiful as well as healthy, spacious as well as clean, well-balanced as well as carefully patrolled. . . . If those who govern the District of Columbia decide that the Nation's Capital should be beautiful as well as sanitary, there is nothing in the Fifth Amendment that stands in the way.

Cases may undoubtedly arise . . . in which the legislative body goes too far in the name of aesthetics, but the present, quite clearly, is not one of them. The ordinance before us is in large sense regulatory rather than prohibitory. It causes no undue hardship to any property owner, for it expressly provides for the issuance of a permit for clotheslines in front and side yards in cases where there is practical difficulty or unnecessary hardship in drying clothes elsewhere on the premises. Moreover, the ordinance imposes no arbitrary or capricious standard of beauty or conformity upon the community. It simply proscribes conduct which is unnecessarily offensive to the visual sensibilities of the average person. It is settled that conduct which is similarly offensive to the senses of hearing and smell may be a valid subject of regulation under the police power, and we perceive no basis for a different result merely because the sense of sight is involved. . . .

Having concluded that the ordinance here in question is validly grounded on a proper exercise of the police power, we turn to the defendants' principal contention, that it is invalid as applied to them because it constitutes an unconstitutional infringement of their freedom of speech. The defendants erected the six clotheslines on their property as a protest against their tax assessment. This form of nonverbal expression is, we shall assume, a form of speech within the meaning of the First Amendment. However, it is perfectly clear that, since these rights are neither absolute nor unlimited, they are subject to such reasonable regulation as is provided by the ordinance before us. . . .

[The] ordinance here in question is ... a "precise and narrowly drawn regulatory statute evincing a legislative judgment that certain specific conduct be limited or proscribed." As the court aptly observed in [Schneider v. State, 308 U.S. 147, 160–161 (1939)], "a person could not exercise [his freedom of speech] by taking his stand in the middle of a crowded street, contrary to traffic regulations, and maintain his position to the stoppage of all traffic; a group of distributors could not insist upon a constitutional right to form a cordon across the street and to allow no pedestrian to pass who did not accept a tendered leaflet; nor does the guarantee of freedom of speech or of the press deprive a municipality of power to enact regulations against throwing literature broadcast in the streets. Prohibition of such conduct would not abridge the constitutional liberty since such activity bears no necessary relationship to the freedom to speak, write, print or distribute information or opinion."

This reasoning is equally applicable to the case before us. The prohibition against clotheslines is designed to prescribe conduct which offends the sensibilities and tends to depress property values. The ordinance and its prohibition bear "no necessary relationship" to the dissemination of ideas or opinion and, accordingly, the defendants were not privileged to violate it by choosing to express their views in the altogether bizarre manner which they did. It is obvious that the value of their "protest" lay not in its message but in its offensiveness....

Judgment affirmed.

VAN VOORHIS, J., dissenting.

My concern in this case is ... with the extent to which a municipality can go in restricting the use of private property....

What has happened here is that these defendants conceived the unusual idea of hanging what the majority opinion describes as "tattered clothing, old uniforms, underwear, rags and scarecrows" across their yard as a form of protest against the amount of their taxes. The city, at the instance of other residents in the area, fought back by adopting this ordinance from the operation of which almost every other property owner applying for a permit has been excepted. Although the origin of this dispute is evidently political in nature, the validity of this ordinance is sought to be upheld entirely on the basis of aesthetic considerations, e.g., that the eye is offended by what hangs from these clotheslines. ... Aesthetic considerations, in a certain sense, underlie all zoning, usually in combination with other factors with which they are interwoven. Lot area, setback and height restrictions, for example, are based essentially on aesthetic factors ..., but have been limited to specific situations and not extended to anything which offends the taste of the neighbors or of the local legislature. One may assume, for example, that a clothesline ordinance would be invalid which permitted the hanging of white but not red blankets, or allowed shirts to be put out to dry after washing but not underwear. Probably, at least until the next step in zoning law, a municipality would be held unauthorized to direct house owners what colors their homes should be painted, or what kinds of trees or shrubbery they should be allowed to grow and where they should be planted. Nevertheless if they can be told where to hang their clothes in their yards, these items would be but a small step beyond the present holding, or to prescribe what architectural designs should be adopted so as to harmonize with the designs of the neighbors. To direct by ordinance that all buildings erected in a certain area should be one-story ranch houses would scarcely go beyond the present ruling as a question of power, or to lay down the law that they should be all of the same color, or of different colors, or that each should be of one or two or more color tones as might suit the aesthetic predilections of the city councillors or zoning boards of appeal.

This ordinance is unrelated to the public safety, health, morals or welfare except insofar as it compels conformity to what the neighbors like to look at. Zoning, important as it is within limits, is too rapidly becoming a legalized device to prevent property owners from doing whatever their neighbors dislike. Protection of minority rights is as essential to democracy as majority vote. In our age of conformity it is still not possible for all to be exactly alike, nor is it the instinct of our law to compel uniformity wherever diversity may offend the sensibilities of those who cast the largest numbers of votes in municipal elections. The right to be different has its place in this country. The United States has drawn strength from differences among its people in taste, experience, temperament, ideas, and ambitions as well as from differences in race, national or religious background. Even where the use of property is bizarre, unsuitable or obstreperous it is not to be curtailed in the absence of overriding reasons of public policy. The security and repose which come from protection of the right to be different in matter of aesthetics, taste, thought, expression and within limits in conduct are not to be cast aside without violating constitutional privileges and immunities. This is not merely a matter of legislative policy, at whatever level. In my view, this pertains to individual rights protected by the Constitution. . . .

The avoidance by courts . . . of sustaining the constitutionality of zoning solely on aesthetic grounds has had its origin in a wholesome fear of allowing government to trespass through aesthetics on the human personality. . . . Individual taste, good or bad, should ordinarily be let alone by government. . . .

The judgments of conviction of appellants should be reversed and the charges against them dismissed.

NOTES

1. *Design and Architectural Approval.* As Justice Van Voorhis predicted in his dissent, judicial acceptance of aesthetic zoning has led to zoning laws that subject renovations or new construction to architectural and design review and approval by government bodies. These laws have met mixed fates.

In State *ex rel.* Stoyanoff v. Berkeley, 458 S.W.2d 305 (Mo. 1970), the Missouri Supreme Court upheld an ordinance of Ladue, Missouri, an upscale

St. Louis suburb, that conditioned a building permit upon approval of the plans by a city Architectural Board. The Board was charged by statute with the duty to approve plans that "conform to ... minimum architectural standards of appearance and conformity with surrounding structures" and to avoid approval of "unsightly, grotesque and unsuitable structures, detrimental to the stability of value and the welfare of surrounding property." In a neighborhood characterized by conventional neo-Colonial residences Stoyanoff wished to construct a home that was a flat-topped pyramid, ornamented by asymmetrical triangular window and door openings. The Board refused to approve the design and the Missouri Supreme Court upheld that action, concluding that the city had the authority under state law to adopt the ordinance and that it was neither vague nor an *ultra vires* exercise of the police power. In doing so, the court laid great stress on evidence that the unconventional design would have a "substantial adverse effect upon the market values of other residential property in the neighborhood." Such a decline in property values "affects not only the adjacent property owners ... but the general public as well because when such property values are destroyed or seriously impaired, the tax base of the community is affected and the public suffers economically as a result." Though it did not say so, the court accepted the notion that market values express societal notions of aesthetics. In accord are **Reid v. Architectural Board of Review of the City of Cleveland Heights**, 119 Ohio App. 67 (1963); Saveland Park Holding Corp. v. Wieland, 269 Wis. 262 (1955). *Reid* **is particularly instructive.** The neighborhood was composed of

> dignified, stately and conventional structures, two and one-half stories high. The house [in question] is a flat-roofed complex of twenty modules, each of which is ten feet high, twelve feet square and arranged in a loosely formed "U" which winds its way through a grove of trees. About sixty per cent of the wall area of the house is glass and opens on an enclosed garden; the rest of the walls are of cement panels. A garage of the same modular construction stands off from the house, and these two structures, with their associated garden walls, trellises and courts, form a series of interior and exterior spaces, all under a canopy of trees and baffled from the street by a garden wall. A wall ten feet high is part of the front structure of the house and garage and extends all around the garden area. It has no windows. Since the wall is of the same height as the structure of the house, no part of the house can be seen from the street. From all appearances, it is just a high wall with no indication of what is behind it. Not only does the house fail to conform in any manner with the other buildings but presents no identification that it is a structure for people to live in.
>
> The structure designed is a single-story home in a multi-story neighborhood; it does not conform to the general character of other houses; it would affect adjacent homes and three vacant lots; ... when viewed from the street, it could indicate a commercial building; ... it does not preserve property values; it would be detrimental to neighborhood on the lot where proposed; and it would be detrimental to the future development of the neighborhood.

By contrast, in Anderson v. City of Issaquah, 70 Wash.App. 64 (1993), a Washington appellate court concluded that the denial of a building permit for failure to win approval of the design by the city's Development Commission violated due process. The statute, both as written and applied, required people of ordinary intelligence "to guess at its meaning and differ as to its application." The statute limited approval to designs that were "compatible" with existing structures, harmonious in "texture, lines, . . . masses, . . . colors," and "lighting," using "appropriate proportions and relationships," not monotonous, and producing an "interesting project" that incorporates "complimentary details" and relates "the development to the site." When Anderson's initial design was rejected he was told the color was wrong and that the design was not "compatible with the image of Issaquah." A second design was rejected; Anderson was told to "drive up and down Gilman [Boulevard] and look at both good and bad examples." A third design, more in keeping with the perceived architectural *gestalt* of Issaquah, was then rejected because it failed to deliver the right "feeling"—the "feeling you get when you drive along Gilman Boulevard." Anderson may have lacked the "right stuff," to invoke Tom Wolfe, but the government had the obligation to make clear what constituted the "right stuff."

   2. Aesthetic Regulation and Free Speech. As *Stover* indicates, aesthetic regulation can sometimes pinch constitutionally protected free expression rights. Zoning laws that discriminate on the content of speech are presumed to be void; they are valid only if the government can meet the exacting burden of proving that the content based speech restriction is necessary to achieve a paramount, or compelling, government objective.

   Example 11–3: Mt. Ephraim, New Jersey's zoning law prohibited "all live entertainment." The law was invalid as applied to an "adult bookstore" that permitted its customers to view nude dancers through peepholes. The Supreme Court ruled that nude dancing was a protected form of expression, the law banned it on the basis of its content, and the village failed to sustain its burden of justification. Schad v. Borough of Mount Ephraim, 452 U.S. 61 (1981).

   However, some zoning laws that facially discriminate on the basis of the content of speech are treated differently. If the law's purpose is to regulate the *secondary effects* of speech—effects that are not produced by the content, or communicative impact, of the speech, but which are adventitiously associated with speech—the law is presumed to be valid and generally upheld.

   Example 11–4: Detroit's zoning law required the dispersal of theaters displaying non-obscene pornography, in order to eliminate the critical mass of sordid businesses that attract "an undesirable quantity and quality of transients, adversely affect property values, cause an increase in crime, . . . and encourage residents and businesses to move elsewhere." In Young v. American Mini–Theatres, 427 U.S. 50 (1976), the Supreme Court upheld the law because its purpose was not to suppress speech on account of its content, but to mitigate the secondary effects of businesses vending pornography. Accord, City of Renton v. Playtime Theatres, 475 U.S. 41 (1986).

unconst. if they're not narrowly tailored

Even though zoning laws that regulate speech without regard to its content are presumed to be valid, they are struck down if they are broader than reasonably necessary to achieve some significant government objective *or* fail to leave open ample alternative channels of communication.

Example 11–5: In order to minimize visual clutter, the city of Ladue, Missouri (the same city that nixed Stoyanoff's bizarre pyramidal house) enacted an ordinance banning all signs except signs identifying a home or business, "for sale" signs, and a few other types. Margaret Gilleo posted an 8 ½ by 11 inch sign in her front window, stating "For Peace in the Gulf." Local police told Gilleo her sign was not permitted and she sought a variance, which was denied. Gilleo then brought suit, contending that the law violated her free expression rights. The Supreme Court agreed. In a unanimous opinion the Court said that the "near-total prohibition" of signs did not leave open ample alternative channels of communication. The foreclosure of an entire venerable medium of expression was too broad. City of Ladue v. Gilleo, 512 U.S. 43 (1994).

By contrast, in City Council of Los Angeles v. Taxpayers for Vincent, 466 U.S. 789 (1984), the Supreme Court upheld an ordinance prohibiting the posting of signs on public property. Supporters of Vincent, a political candidate, affixed signs advocating his election to utility poles; the city removed them, and the ban was attacked as unconstitutional. The Court reasoned that the ban was content-neutral and left Vincent's supporters free to attach his signs to various bits of private property (such as bumper stickers, rented billboards, or via consent of property owners).

In *Stover*, the expression was symbolic. Governments may regulate symbolic speech if the regulation 1) is otherwise within the constitutional power of the government, 2) furthers an important or substantial government interest that is 3) unrelated to the suppression of expression, and 4) is no greater than essential to further the interest. United States v. O'Brien, 391 U.S. 367 (1968). Rye had the power to enact a zoning law; it furthered the interest of preserving aesthetic sensibilities and property values, interests unrelated to suppression of expression, and the ordinance was narrowly drawn to accomplish those interests. The court conceded that Rye was motivated by a desire to stamp out Stover's protest, but said (as did *O'Brien*) that a bad motive will not invalidate a law if it is otherwise valid. But should the motive to suppress speech be taken into account in assessing whether the asserted interests, while important, are really unrelated to the suppression of speech?

2. CONSTITUTIONAL RIGHTS

The collision between constitutional rights and zoning laws is not limited to free speech. In Chapter 12 we will consider the problem of regulations (including zoning laws) that so deprive property owners of the incidents of ownership that they should be treated as governmental takings of private property, requiring just compensation to the affected property owner. But apart from free expression and regulatory takings, there are a variety of ways in which zoning laws might offend either the

federal or state constitutions. For example, zoning laws can offend the federal Constitution's guarantee of equal protection of the laws, due process, or free exercise of religion. These issues are covered briefly in this section.

a. Non–Conforming Uses

When a zoning law is enacted that makes some existing use unlawful courts are required to deal with the issue of whether the law may validly force a prior lawful use to cease and, if so, to decide the terms on which the cessation must occur. Such cases often implicate either state or federal constitutional principles concerning governmental takings of private property. The following case, decided under Pennsylvania's constitution, is an example of the problem.

PA NORTHWESTERN DISTRIBUTORS, INC. v. ZONING HEARING BOARD

Supreme Court of Pennsylvania
526 Pa. 186 (1991)

Larsen, J., delivered the opinion of the court.

This appeal presents an issue of first impression to this Court, i.e., whether a zoning ordinance which requires the amortization and discontinuance of a lawful pre-existing nonconforming use is confiscatory and violative of the constitution as a taking of property without just compensation.

On May 4, 1985, after obtaining the necessary permits and certificates to conduct its business on leased premises, appellant, PA Northwestern Distributors, Inc., opened an adult book store in Moon Township, Pennsylvania. Four days later, the Moon Township Board of Supervisors published a public notice of its intention to amend the Moon Township Zoning Ordinance to regulate "adult commercial enterprises." On May 23, 1985, following a public hearing on the matter, the Moon Township Board of Supervisors adopted Ordinance No. 243, effective on May 28, 1985, which ordinance imposes extensive restrictions on the location and operation of "adult commercial enterprises." Section 805 of the ordinance provides as follows:

> *Amortization.* Any commercial enterprise which would constitute a pre-existing use and which would be in conflict with the requirements set forth in this amendment to the Moon Township Zoning Ordinance has 90 days from the date that the ordinance becomes effective to come into compliance with this ordinance. This 90–day grace period is designed to be a period of amortization for those pre-existing businesses which cannot meet the standards set forth in this amendment to the Moon Township Zoning Ordinance.

Appellant's adult book store, by definition, is an adult commercial enterprise under the ordinance, and it does not and cannot meet the place restrictions set forth in the ordinance in that it is not located within an area designated for adult commercial enterprises. The Zoning Officer of Moon Township notified appellant that it was out of compliance with the ordinance. Appellant filed an appeal to the Zoning Hearing Board of the Township of Moon, appellee herein. The appeal was limited to challenging the validity of the amortization provision set forth in the ordinance.

Following a hearing, the Zoning Hearing Board upheld the validity of the amortization provision as applied, and appellant filed an appeal to the Court of Common Pleas of Allegheny County. No further evidence was taken, and appellant's appeal was dismissed. On appeal, Commonwealth Court affirmed ..., basing its decision on Sullivan v. Zoning Board of Adjustment, 83 Pa. Commw. 228, 478 A.2d 912 (1984). We granted appellant's petition for allowance of appeal, and we now reverse.

Our scope of review in a zoning case, where the trial court has not taken additional evidence, is limited to determining whether the zoning hearing board committed an error of law or a manifest abuse of discretion. In ... *Sullivan*, the Commonwealth Court determined that provisions for the amortization of nonconforming uses are constitutional exercises of the police power so long as they are reasonable. ... To determine whether the amortization provisions are reasonable, the Commonwealth Court stated:

> Each case in this class must be determined on its own facts; and the answer to the question of whether the provision is reasonable must be decided by observing its impact upon the property under consideration. The true issue is that of whether, considering the nature of the present use, the length of the period for amortization, the present characteristics of and the foreseeable future prospects for development of the vicinage and other relevant facts and circumstances, the beneficial effects upon the community that would result from the discontinuance of the use can be seen to more than offset the losses to the affected landowner.

83 Pa. Commw. at 247, 478 A.2d at 920.

Following this standard, the Zoning Hearing Board herein heard evidence regarding the impact upon the property in question ... and determined that the amortization provision was reasonable as applied. [The] Zoning Hearing Board stated that the "real and substantial benefits to the Township of elimination of the nonconforming use from this location ... more than offset the losses to the affected landowner." If the Commonwealth Court opinion in *Sullivan* had been a correct statement of the law in this Commonwealth, we would be constrained to find that appellee herein had not committed an error of law or an abuse of discretion. For the following reasons, however, we find that *Sullivan* is not a correct statement of the law regarding amortization provisions in this Commonwealth.

In this Commonwealth, all property is held in subordination to the right of its reasonable regulation by the government, which regulation is clearly necessary to preserve the health, safety, morals, or general welfare of the people. Moreover, "a presumption of validity attaches to a zoning ordinance which imposes the burden to prove its invalidity upon the one who challenges it." This Court has noted, however, that the presumption of a zoning ordinance's validity must be tempered by the Court's appreciation of the fact that zoning involves governmental restrictions upon a property owner's *constitutionally guaranteed* right to use his or her property, unfettered by governmental restrictions, except where the use violates any law, the use creates a nuisance, or the owner violates any covenant, restriction or easement.

Many other jurisdictions have upheld the validity of amortization provisions in zoning ordinances, finding that it is appropriate to balance the property interests of the individual with the health, safety, morals or general welfare of the community at large, and that, where reasonable, amortization provisions succeed in effectuating orderly land use planning and development in a way that the natural attrition of nonconforming uses cannot. See cases collected at Annotation, *Validity of Provisions for Amortization of Nonconforming Uses*, 22 A.L.R. 3d (1968 & Supp.1990). *See also* Katarincic, *Elimination of Non–Conforming Uses, Buildings, and Structures by Amortization–Concept Versus Law*, 2 Duq. L.Rev. 1 (1963).

Although this Court has never before considered the validity of an amortization provision in a zoning ordinance, it has long been the law of this Commonwealth that municipalities lack the power to compel a change in the nature of an existing lawful use of property. See ... Bachman v. Zoning Hearing Board, 508 Pa. 180, 187, 494 A.2d 1102, 1106 (1985) ("continuance of nonconforming use is permitted to avoid a wrong notwithstanding that the use is an obstruction to a public purpose. The balance is settled by avoiding the injury to the property owner only so long as the governmental body fails to compensate for its loss."); Hanna v. Board of Adjustment, 408 Pa. 306, 312–13, 183 A.2d 539, 543 (1962) (continuance of nonconforming uses countenanced to avoid imposition of hardship on property owner and because refusal of continuance "would be of doubtful constitutionality."); Yocum Zoning Case, 393 Pa. 148, 152, 141 A.2d 601, 604 (1958) (municipality is without power to compel change in nature of use where property was not restricted when purchased and is being used for lawful purpose); Molnar v. George B. Henne & Co., Inc., 377 Pa. 571, 581, 105 A.2d 325, 329–30 (1954) ("rule as to nonconforming uses was evolved as a conceived element of due process"). In addition, municipalities may not prevent the owner of nonconforming property from making those necessary additions to an existing structure as are needed to provide for its natural expansion, so long as such additions would not be detrimental to the public welfare, safety, and health. *Yocum*.

A lawful nonconforming use establishes in the property owner a vested property right which cannot be abrogated or destroyed, unless it is a nuisance, it is abandoned, or it is extinguished by eminent domain. This determination is compelled by our constitution which recognizes the "inherent and indefeasible" right of our citizens to possess and protect property, Pa. Const. art. I, § 1, and requires that just compensation be paid for the taking of private property, Pa. Const. art. I, § 10. As we emphasized in Andress v. Zoning Board of Adjustment, 410 Pa. 77, 82–84, 188 A.2d 709, 711–12 (1963):

> The natural or zealous desire of many zoning boards to protect, improve and develop their community, to plan a city or a township or a community that is both practical and beautiful, and to conserve the property values as well as the "tone" of that community is commendable. But they must remember that property owners have certain rights which are ordained, protected and preserved in our Constitution and which neither zeal nor worthwhile objectives can impinge upon or abolish. . . . Neither the Executive nor the Legislature, nor any legislative body, nor any zoning or planning commission, nor any other Governmental body has the right—under the guise of the police power, or under the broad power of general welfare, or under . . . any other express or implied power—*to take, possess or confiscate private property for public use or to completely prohibit or substantially destroy the lawful use and enjoyment of property, without paying just compensation therefor.* . . . (citations omitted) (emphasis in original)

Although at times it may be difficult to discern whether zoning legislation is merely regulating as opposed to "taking," this Court has stated that "[a] 'taking' is not limited to an actual physical possession or seizure of the property; if the *effect* of the zoning law or regulation is to deprive a property owner of the lawful use of his property it amounts to a 'taking,' for which he must be justly compensated." Cleaver v. Board of Adjustment, 414 Pa. 367, 372, 200 A.2d 408, 412 (1964) (emphasis in original).

applied

The effect of the amortization provision herein is to deprive appellant of the lawful use of its property in that the ordinance forces appellant to cease using its property as an adult book store within 90 days. Appellee argues that appellant is free to relocate to one of the few sites in the Township of Moon that complies with the place restrictions of the ordinance, or to change its use to sell some other commodity, in an attempt to convince this Court that the ordinance has not effectuated a "taking" of appellant's property without just compensation. The Pennsylvania Constitution, Pa. Const. art. I, § 1, however, protects the right of a property owner to use his or her property in any lawful way that he or she so chooses. If government desires to interfere with the owner's use, where the use is lawful and is not a nuisance nor is it abandoned, it must compensate the owner for the resulting loss. A gradual phasing out of nonconforming uses which occurs when an ordinance only restricts future uses differs in significant measure from an amortization provision which restricts future uses *and* extinguishes a lawful nonconforming use on a timetable which is not of the property owner's choosing. . . .

Thus, we hold that the amortization and discontinuance of a lawful pre-existing nonconforming use is per se confiscatory and violative of the Pennsylvania Constitution, Pa. Const. art. I, § 1. There are important policy considerations which support this determination. If municipalities were free to amortize nonconforming uses out of existence, future economic development could be seriously compromised. As one commentator has noted: "The law of zoning should be designed to protect the reasonable expectations of persons who plan to enter business or make improvements on property. The possibility that the municipality could by zoning force removal of installations or cessation of business might serve to deter such investors." Note, *Nonconforming Uses: A Rationale and an Approach*, 102 U.Pa.L.Rev. 91, 103 (1953). This commentator also notes that forced destruction will often result in economic waste. *Id.* at 104.

It is clear that if we were to permit the amortization of nonconforming uses in this Commonwealth, *any* use could be amortized out of existence without just compensation. Although such a zoning option seems reasonable when the use involves some activity that may be distasteful to some members of the public, *no* use would be exempt from the reach of amortization, and *any* property owner could lose the use of his or her property without compensation. Even a homeowner could find one day that his or her "castle" had become a nonconforming use and would be required to vacate the premises within some arbitrary period of time, *without just compensation*. Such a result is repugnant to a basic protection accorded in this Commonwealth to vested property interests.

Accordingly, we find that the amortization provision, Section 805, of Ordinance No. 243 of the Township of Moon is unconstitutional on its face, and we reverse the order of the Commonwealth Court, which affirmed the order of the Court of Common Pleas of Allegheny County dismissing appellant's appeal from the decision of the Zoning Hearing Board of the Township of Moon.

NIX, CHIEF JUSTICE, concurring.

While I agree with the result reached by the majority, that Section 805 of Ordinance No. 243 is invalid in this case, I must disagree with the finding that any provision for the amortization of nonconforming uses would be *per se* confiscatory and unconstitutional. I would [rely] on Sullivan v. Zoning Board of Adjustment, 83 Pa. Commw. 228, 478 A.2d 912 (1984), and hold that a reasonable amortization provision is valid if it reflects the consideration of certain factors [identified in *Sullivan*.] The instant provision, however, falls short of the reasonableness requirements and therefore must be struck down.

The weight of authority supports the conclusion that a reasonable amortization provision would not be unconstitutional. See generally 22 A.L.R.3d. 1134 (1968). It has been stated that a blanket rule against amortization provisions should be rejected because such a rule has a debilitating effect on effective zoning, unnecessarily restricts a state's police power, and prevents the operation of a reasonable and flexible method of eliminating nonconforming uses in the public interest. Lachapelle v. Goffstown, 107 N.H. 485, 225 A.2d 624 (1967). The New Hampshire court found acceptable amortization provisions which were reasonable as to time and directed toward some reasonable aspect of land use regulation under properly delegated police power. *Id.* Other cases have considered several factors in determining the reasonableness of these provisions. Those factors weigh any circumstance bearing upon a balancing of public gain against private loss, including the length of the amortization period in relation to the nature of the nonconforming use, Gurnee v. Miller, 69 Ill.App.2d 248, 215 N.E.2d 829 (1966); Eutaw Enterprises, Inc. v. Baltimore, 241 Md. 686, 217 A.2d 348 (1966); length of time in relation to the investment, *id.;* and the degree of offensiveness of the nonconforming use in view of the character of the surrounding neighborhood. See City of Los Angeles v. Gage, 127 Cal.App.2d 442, 274 P.2d 34, 43–44 (1954); Grant v. Baltimore, 212 Md. 301, 129 A.2d 363 (1957); Lachapelle v. Goffstown, supra.

Our case law has expressed a preference for the protection of nonconforming uses in the face of changing zoning ordinances. That protection, however, is not absolute. It has long been recognized that a lawful, pre-existing, nonconforming use is permitted to continue notwithstanding that the use is an obstruction to a public purpose, provided that the use does not enlarge beyond its natural expectations or move from its original setting. The owner of property to which a lawful nonconforming use has attached enjoys a vested property right thereto unless it is a nuisance, or abandoned, or is extinguished by eminent domain. . . . I believe that a *per se* prohibition against amortization provisions is too restrictive. A community should have a right to change its character without being locked into pre-existing definitions of what is offensive. As this Court has also noted, "nonconforming uses, inconsistent with a basic purpose of zoning, represent conditions which should be reduced to conformity as speedily as is compatible with the law and the Constitution." Hanna v. Board of Adjustment of Borough of Forest Hills, 408 Pa. 306, 312–13, 183 A.2d 539, 543 (1962). I believe that amortization provisions are an effective method of reconciling interests of the community with those of property owners. Where the provisions are reasonable in consideration of the elements herein discussed, they provide adequate notice to the property owner so that no deprivation of property or use thereof is suffered, yet they simultaneously afford a township the opportunity to alter the character of its neighborhoods when the alteration takes the form of a reasonable land use regulation.

In this case, however, the amortization provision is not a reasonable one because it fails to provide adequate time for elimination of the nonconforming use. The period allowed for the dissolution of appellant's business is ninety days. Certainly ninety days is an insufficient period of time to allow a merchant to close a business. Any contractual obligations appellant has incurred in anticipation of operating the business probably cannot be terminated within such a short period of time without severe hardship on appellant's part. Three months also would not permit appellant to obtain an alternative means of income. Moreover, forcing appellant to liquidate his enterprise within ninety days could prevent him from obtaining a reasonable return on his investment. I therefore agree that the instant provision is confiscatory. . . .

NOTES, QUESTIONS, AND PROBLEM

1. *What's Reasonable?* The majority opinion declared any amortization period to be invalid, but Chief Justice Nix thought that the validity of amortization depended on its reasonableness. Why is any amortization period unreasonable? In Mugler v. Kansas, 123 U.S. 623 (1887), the Supreme Court held that a Kansas law prohibiting the manufacture, distribution, or sale of alcoholic beverages did not affect a taking of a brewer's property, even though his brewery was "of little value if not used for the purpose of manufacturing beer." The Kansas law provided for no amortization period at all, thus rendering the value of the brewery "very materially diminished." Said the Court:

> A prohibition simply upon the use of property for purposes that are declared, by valid legislation, to be injurious to the health, morals, or safety of the community, cannot, in any just sense, be deemed a taking or an appropriation of property for the public benefit. Such legislation does not disturb the owner in the control or use of his property for lawful purposes, nor restrict his right to dispose of it, but is only a declaration by the State that its use by any one, for certain forbidden purposes, is prejudicial to the public interests. Id. at 668–669.

Of course, the Pennsylvania Constitution is independent of the United States Constitution, in that the Pennsylvania Constitution can mean something different from the federal Constitution so long as the meaning of the state provision is not prohibited by the federal Constitution or federal law. Thus, the Pennsylvania Constitution's provisions governing takings can be more stringent than the federal analogue, but this technical fact does not answer the policy question of why *any* amortization period is void, or whether a *reasonable* amortization period is necessary to the validity of abatement of non-conforming uses.

 Assuming an amortization period is necessary, what factors make it reasonable? How much should the following factors matter: 1) The nature of the non-conforming use; 2) The investment in the non-conforming use; 3) The utility of the improvements for other uses; 4) The amount of time needed to recoup the investment; 5) The character of the neighborhood; 6) The public benefit produced by abatement; 7) The ability of the affected owner to find other sources of income? How should a court assess these diverse factors? Is there a common metric that enables easy and accurate comparison of these factors? How much deference should courts pay to statutory amortization periods, or to the determinations of zoning bodies applying criteria such as those outlined above?

2. *Apart from Amortization, When Does a Nonconforming Use End?* The Pennsylvania court suggested that a non-conforming use ends if it is a nuisance, is abandoned, or taken by eminent domain (and just compensation paid). Abandonment is generally found when the non-conforming use ceases to operate. See, e.g., Toys 'R' Us v. Silva, 89 N.Y.2d 411 (1996) (non-

conforming use as a warehouse abandoned when the owner emptied the warehouse even though he moved some material back in 19 months later and hired a property manager for the warehouse).

A non-conforming use also ceases if the owner changes the nature of the use. An example is Ka–Hur Enterprises, Inc. v. Zoning Board of Appeals of Provincetown, 424 Mass. 404 (1997). Certain property was used as a fuel storage and distribution facility by Holway Oil. After the zoning laws changed the use was a non-conforming use that was permitted to continue. In 1979 the property was sold to Nauset Trawling Co., which operated a fishing business and truck repair shop on the property in addition to the storage of 40,000 gallons of fuel oil for use by its fishing vessels and for sale to other fishing boats. Ka–Hur bought the property in 1987 and in 1993 sought permits to construct a new 25,000 gallon fuel storage tank and remove the old ones. The permit was denied on the ground that the non-conforming use had ceased due to abandonment or discontinuance. The Massachusetts Supreme Judicial Court ruled that Nauset's use of the property "to conduct a fishing business and store and repair trucks" constituted "a 'change or substantial extension' of the prior nonconforming use which caused the property to lose its protection as a preexisting nonconforming use." Note that the change in ownership did not cause a loss of the preexisting non-conforming use. That status runs with the land. But the reverse of that proposition is that the conversion of the use by a prior owner in the chain of title can cause a later owner to lose the protection of the non-conforming use.

3. *Estoppel Against the Government.* Relying on the notion of vested rights, some owners have attempted to assert estoppel against the government when they have reasonably relied to their substantial detriment on government representations (such as issuance of a building permit), only to learn later that the government made a mistake in issuing the permit. This gambit does not generally work. Courts are fairly uniform in rejecting claims of estoppel against the government. The usual rationale is that governments should not be prevented from rectifying their own errors, even though the expense of that correction falls on an innocent party who relied on the government's error. See, e.g., Parkview Associates v. New York, 71 N.Y.2d 274 (1988) (building permit erroneously issued for 31 story building in a zone permitting only 19 stories; estoppel denied and builder required to remove 12 stories at a cost of $1 million). It may be good policy to allow governments to enforce valid law even when the government errs in its application, but this does not explain why the government can avoid compensating the innocent citizen who would otherwise bear the loss. The usual answer to this suggestion is to say that such a rule would expose governments to unknown and unlimited liability. One retort would be to say that governments should get it right in the first instance.

4. *Problem.* In 2000 A pays $100,000 to acquire title to Blackacre. In 2010, the city in which Blackacre is located adopts an otherwise valid zoning ordinance that reduces the value of Blackacre to $30,000. In 2000 B pays $25,000 to acquire Whiteacre, on which property B expends $75,000 to construct and operate a dance hall. In 2010 the city in which Whiteacre is located adopts an otherwise valid zoning law that makes B's dance hall illegal

and provides for no amortization period. What remedies, if any, do *A* and *B* have?

b. Equal Protection, Federal and State

The Fourteenth Amendment prohibits states from denying those within its jurisdiction the equal protection of the laws and stipulates that no state may deprive any person of life, liberty, or property except by due process of law. The following case, decided on due process grounds at a time when the Supreme Court thought that equal protection was satisfied by laws requiring "separate but equal" treatment of the races, is better thought of as an early expression of what today is a fundamental principle of equal protection.

BUCHANAN v. WARLEY

Supreme Court of the United States
245 U.S. 60 (1917)

MR. JUSTICE DAY delivered the opinion of the court.

Buchanan . . . brought an action in the . . . Kentucky [courts] for the specific performance of a contract for the sale of certain real estate situated in the City of Louisville at the corner of 37th Street and Pflanz Avenue. The offer in writing to purchase the property contained a proviso: "It is understood that I am purchasing the above property for the purpose of having erected thereon a house which I propose to make my residence, and it is a distinct part of this agreement that I shall not be required to accept a deed to the above property or to pay for said property unless I have the right under the laws of the State of Kentucky and the City of Louisville to occupy said property as a residence." This offer was accepted by the plaintiff.

To the action for specific performance the defendant by way of answer set up the condition above set forth, that he is a colored person, and that on the block of which the lot in controversy is a part there are ten residences, eight of which at the time of the making of the contract were occupied by white people, and only two (those nearest the lot in question) were occupied by colored people, and that under and by virtue of the ordinance of the City of Louisville, approved May 11, 1914, he would not be allowed to occupy the lot as a place of residence. In reply to this answer the plaintiff set up, among other things, that the ordinance was in conflict with the Fourteenth Amendment to the Constitution of the United States, and hence no defense to the action for specific performance of the contract. [The Kentucky courts] held the ordinance valid and of itself a complete defense to the action.

The title of the ordinance is: " "An ordinance to prevent conflict and ill-feeling between the white and colored races in the City of Louisville, and to preserve the public peace and promote the general welfare by making reasonable provisions requiring, as far as practicable, the use of separate blocks for residences, places of abode and places of assembly by white and colored people respectively." By the first section of the ordinance it is made unlawful for any colored person to move into and occupy as a residence . . . any house upon any block upon which a greater number of houses are occupied as residences . . . by white people than are occupied as residences . . . by colored people. Section 2 provides that it shall be unlawful for any white person to move into and occupy as a residence . . . any house upon any block upon which a greater number of houses are occupied as residences . . . by colored people than are occupied as residences . . . by white people. Section 4 provides that nothing in the ordinance shall affect the location of residences . . . made previous to its approval; that nothing contained therein shall be construed so as to prevent the occupancy of residences . . . by white or colored servants or employees of occupants of such residences, places of abode or places of public assembly on the block on which they are so employed, and that nothing therein contained shall be construed to prevent any person who, at the date of the passage of the ordinance, shall have acquired or possessed the right to occupy any building as a residence . . . from exercising such a right. . . .

The assignments of error in this court attack the ordinance upon the ground that it violates the Fourteenth Amendment of the Constitution of the United States, in that it abridges the privileges and immunities of citizens of the United States to acquire and enjoy property, takes property without due process of law, and denies equal protection of the laws. . . .

This ordinance prevents the occupancy of a lot in the City of Louisville by a person of color in a block where the greater number of residences are occupied by white persons; where such a majority exists colored persons are excluded. This interdiction is based wholly upon color; simply that and nothing more. In effect, premises situated as are those in question in the so-called white block are effectively debarred from sale to persons of color, because if sold they cannot be occupied by the purchaser nor by him sold to another of the same color. This drastic measure is sought to be justified under the authority of the State in the exercise of the police power. It is said such legislation tends to promote the public peace by preventing racial conflicts; that it tends to maintain racial purity; that it prevents the deterioration of property owned and occupied by white people, which deterioration, it is contended, is sure to follow the occupancy of adjacent premises by persons of color.

The authority of the State to pass laws in the exercise of the police power, having for their object the promotion of the public health, safety and welfare is very broad as has been affirmed in numerous and recent decisions of this court. Furthermore, the exercise of this power, embracing nearly all legislation of a local character, is not to be interfered with by the courts where it is within the scope of legislative authority and the means adopted reasonably tend to accomplish a lawful purpose. But it is equally well established that the police power, broad as it is, cannot justify the passage of a law or ordinance which runs counter to the limitations of the Federal Constitution; that principle has been so frequently affirmed in this court that we need not stop to cite the cases. . . .

The Fourteenth Amendment protects life, liberty, and property from invasion by the States without due process of law. Property is more than the mere thing which a person owns. It is elementary that it includes the right to acquire, use, and dispose of it. The Constitution protects these essential attributes of property. Holden v. Hardy, 169 U.S. 366, 391. Property consists of the free use, enjoyment, and disposal of a person's acquisitions without control or diminution save by the law of the land. 1 Blackstone's Commentaries (Cooley's Ed.), 127.

True it is that dominion over property springing from ownership is not absolute and unqualified. The disposition and use of property may be controlled in the exercise of the police power in the interest of the public health, convenience, or welfare. Harmful occupations may be controlled and regulated. Legitimate business may also be regulated in the interest of the public. Certain uses of property may be confined to portions of the municipality other than the resident district, such as livery stables, brickyards and the like, because of the impairment of the health and comfort of the occupants of neighboring property. Many illustrations might be given from the decisions of this court, and other courts, of this principle, but these cases do not touch the one at bar.

The concrete question here is: May the occupancy, and, necessarily, the purchase and sale of property of which occupancy is an incident, be inhibited by the States, or by one of its municipalities, solely because of the color of the proposed occupant of the premises? That one may dispose of his property, subject only to the control of lawful enactments curtailing that right in the public interest, must be conceded. The question now presented makes it pertinent to enquire into the constitutional right of the white man to sell his property to a colored man, having in view the legal status of the purchaser and occupant.

Following the Civil War certain amendments to the Federal Constitution were adopted, which have become an integral part of that instrument, equally binding upon all the States and fixing certain fundamental rights which all are bound to respect. The Thirteenth Amendment abolished slavery in the United States and in all places subject to their jurisdiction, and gave Congress power to enforce the Amendment by appropriate legislation. The Fourteenth Amendment made all persons born or naturalized in the United States citizens of the United States and of the States in which they reside, and provided that no State shall make or enforce any law which shall abridge the privileges or immunities of citizens of the United States, and that no State shall deprive any person of life, liberty, or property without due process of law, nor deny to any person the equal protection of the laws.

The effect of these Amendments was first dealt with by this court in The Slaughter House Cases, 16 Wall. 36. The reasons for the adoption of the Amendments were elaborately considered by a court familiar with the

History of 14th amendment

times in which the necessity for the Amendments arose and with the
circumstances which impelled their adoption. In that case Mr. Justice
Miller, who spoke for the majority, pointed out that the colored race,
having been freed from slavery by the Thirteenth Amendment, was raised
to the dignity of citizenship and equality of civil rights by the Fourteenth
Amendment, and the States were prohibited from abridging the privileges
and immunities of such citizens, or depriving any person of life, liberty, or
property without due process of law. While a principal purpose of the
latter Amendment was to protect persons of color, the broad language
used was deemed sufficient to protect all persons, white or black, against
discriminatory legislation by the States. This is now the settled law. In
many of the cases since arising the question of color has not been involved
and the cases have been decided upon alleged violations of civil or property
rights irrespective of the race or color of the complainant. In *The Slaughter House Cases* it was recognized that the chief inducement to the passage
of the Amendment was the desire to extend federal protection to the
recently emancipated race from unfriendly and discriminating legislation
by the States.

In Strauder v. West Virginia, 100 U.S. 303, this court held that a
colored person charged with an offense was denied due process of law by a
statute which prevented colored men from sitting on the jury which tried
him. Mr. Justice Strong, speaking for the court, again reviewed the history
of the Amendments, and among other things, in speaking of the Fourteenth Amendment, said:

> It [the Fourteenth Amendment] was designed to assure to the colored
> race the enjoyment of all the civil rights that under the law are
> enjoyed by white persons, and to give to that race the protection of
> the general government, in that enjoyment, whenever it should be
> denied by the States. It not only gave citizenship and the privileges of
> citizenship to persons of color, but it denied to any State the power to
> withhold from them the equal protection of the laws, and authorized
> Congress to enforce its provisions by appropriate legislation. ... It
> ordains that no State shall make or enforce any laws which shall
> abridge the privileges or immunities of citizens of the United States.
> ... It ordains that no State shall deprive any person of life, liberty, or
> property, without due process of law, or deny to any person within its
> jurisdiction the equal protection of the laws. What is this but declar-
> ing that the law in the States shall be the same for the black as for
> the white; that all persons, whether colored or white, shall stand
> equal before the laws of the States, and, in regard to the colored race,
> for whose protection the amendment was primarily designed, that no
> discrimination shall be made against them by law because of their
> color? ... The Fourteenth Amendment makes no attempt to enumer-
> ate the rights it is designed to protect. It speaks in general terms, and
> those are as comprehensive as possible. Its language is prohibitory;

but every prohibition implies the existence of rights and immunities, prominent among which is an immunity from inequality of legal protection, either for life, liberty, or property. Any State action that denies this immunity to a colored man is in conflict with the Constitution.

... In giving legislative aid to these constitutional provisions Congress enacted in 1866, c. 31, § 1, 14 Stat. 27, [Rev. Stats., § 1978] that: "All citizens of the United States shall have the same right in every State and Territory, as is enjoyed by white citizens thereof to inherit, purchase, lease, sell, hold, and convey real and personal property." And in 1870, by c. 114, § 16, 16 Stat. 144 [Rev. Stats., § 1977] that: "All persons within the jurisdiction of the United States shall have the same right in every State and Territory to make and enforce contracts, to sue, be parties, give evidence, and to the full and equal benefit of all laws and proceedings for the security of persons and property as is enjoyed by white citizens, and shall be subject to like punishment, pains, penalties, taxes, licenses and exactions of every kind, and no other."

In the face of these constitutional and statutory provisions, can a white man be denied, consistently with due process of law, the right to dispose of his property to a purchaser by prohibiting the occupation of it for the sole reason that the purchaser is a person of color intending to occupy the premises as a place of residence? The statute of 1866, originally passed under sanction of the Thirteenth Amendment, 14 Stat. 27, and practically reenacted after the adoption of the Fourteenth Amendment, 16 Stat. 144, expressly provided that all citizens of the United States in any State shall have the same right to purchase property as is enjoyed by white citizens. Colored persons are citizens of the United States and have the right to purchase property and enjoy and use the same without laws discriminating against them solely on account of color. Hall v. DeCuir, 95 U.S. 485, 508. These enactments did not deal with the social rights of men, but with those fundamental rights in property which it was intended to secure upon the same terms to citizens of every race and color. Civil Rights Cases, 109 U.S. 3, 22. The Fourteenth Amendment and these statutes enacted in furtherance of its purpose operate to qualify and entitle a colored man to acquire property without state legislation discriminating against him solely because of color.

The defendant in error insists that Plessy v. Ferguson, 163 U.S. 537, is controlling in principle in favor of the judgment of the court below. In that case this court held that a provision of a statute of Louisiana requiring railway companies carrying passengers to provide in their coaches equal but separate accommodations for the white and colored races did not run counter to the provisions of the Fourteenth Amendment. It is to be observed that in that case there was no attempt to deprive persons of color of transportation in the coaches of the public carrier, and the express requirements were for equal though separate accommodations for the white and colored races. In Plessy v. Ferguson, classification of accommodation was permitted upon the basis of equality for both races....

In the recent case of McCabe v. Atchison & c. Ry. Co., 235 U.S. 151, where the court had under consideration a statute which allowed railroad companies to furnish dining-cars for white people and to refuse to furnish dining-cars altogether for colored persons, this language was used in reference to the contentions of the attorney general [that there was insufficient demand for dining-cars for blacks to warrant their provision]: "This argument with respect to volume of traffic seems to us to be without merit. It makes the constitutional right depend upon the number of persons who may be discriminated against, whereas the essence of the constitutional right is that it is a personal one." The effect of the ordinance under consideration was not merely to regulate a business or the like, but was to destroy the right of the individual to acquire, enjoy, and dispose of his property. Being of this character, it was void as being opposed to the due-process clause of the constitution.

That there exists a serious and difficult problem arising from a feeling of race hostility which the law is powerless to control, and to which it must give a measure of consideration, may be freely admitted. But its solution cannot be promoted by depriving citizens of their constitutional rights and privileges. ... It is urged that this proposed segregation will promote the public peace by preventing race conflicts. Desirable as this is, and important as is the preservation of the public peace, this aim cannot be accomplished by laws or ordinances which deny rights created or protected by the Federal Constitution. It is said that such acquisitions by colored persons depreciate property owned in the neighborhood by white persons. But property may be acquired by undesirable white neighbors or put to disagreeable though lawful uses with like results.

We think this attempt to prevent the alienation of the property in question to a person of color was not a legitimate exercise of the police power of the State, and is in direct violation of the fundamental law enacted in the Fourteenth Amendment of the Constitution preventing state interference with property rights except by due process of law. That being the case the ordinance cannot stand. ... Reversed.

NOTE

The federal equal protection and due process guarantees are not the only sources of limitation on zoning authority. State constitutions contain similar provisions, and the highest courts of the states are free to interpret those provisions more broadly than their federal analogues. In short, the federal Constitution establishes a floor beneath which state constitutions may not descend, but does not create a ceiling for a more expansive interpretation of these state constitutional provisions. The following case is a classic example.

SOUTHERN BURLINGTON COUNTY NAACP
v. TOWNSHIP OF MOUNT LAUREL

Supreme Court of New Jersey
67 N.J. 151 (1975)

HALL, J., delivered the opinion of the court.

This case attacks the system of land use regulation by defendant Township of Mount Laurel on the ground that low and moderate income families are thereby unlawfully excluded from the municipality. The trial court so found, and declared the township zoning ordinance totally invalid. [Appeal was taken directly to the Supreme Court.] . . . The implications of the issue presented are indeed broad and far-reaching, extending much beyond these particular plaintiffs and the boundaries of this particular municipality. . . .

Plaintiffs represent the minority group poor (black and Hispanic) seeking such quarters. But they are not the only category of persons barred from so many municipalities by reason of restrictive land use regulations. We have reference to young and elderly couples, single persons and large, growing families not in the poverty class, but who still cannot afford the only kinds of housing realistically permitted in most places—relatively high-priced, single-family detached dwellings on sizeable lots and, in some municipalities, expensive apartments. We will, therefore, consider the case from the wider viewpoint that the effect of Mount Laurel's land use regulation has been to prevent various categories of persons from living in the township because of the limited extent of their income and resources. In this connection, we accept the representation of the municipality's counsel at oral argument that the regulatory scheme was not adopted with any desire or intent to exclude prospective residents on the obviously illegal basis of race, origin or believed social incompatibility. . . .

I. *The Facts*

Mount Laurel is a flat, sprawling township, 22 square miles, or about 14,000 acres, in area, on the west central edge of Burlington County. . . . Part of its southerly side . . . is about seven miles from the boundary line of the city of Camden and not more than 10 miles from the Benjamin Franklin Bridge crossing the river to Philadelphia. In 1950, the township had a population of 2817, only about 600 more people than it had in 1940. It was then, as it had been for decades, primarily a rural agricultural area with no sizeable settlements or commercial or industrial enterprises. The populace generally lived in individual houses scattered along country roads. There were several pockets of poverty, with deteriorating or dilapidated housing (apparently 300 or so units of which remain today in equally poor condition). After 1950, as in so many other municipalities similarly situated, residential development and some commerce and industry began to come in. By 1960 the population had almost doubled to 5249 and by 1970 had more than doubled again to 11,221. . . . And 65% of the township is still vacant land or in agricultural use.

The growth of the township has been spurred by the construction or improvement of main highways through or near it. . . . This highway network gives the township a most strategic location from the standpoint of transport of goods and people by truck and private car. There is no other means of transportation.

The location and nature of development has been, as usual, controlled by the local zoning enactments. The general ordinance presently in force, which was declared invalid by the trial court, was adopted in 1964. . . . Under the present ordinance, 29.2% of all the land in the township, or 4,121 acres, is zoned for industry. . . . Only industry meeting specified performance standards is permitted. The effect is to limit the use substantially to light manufacturing, research, distribution of goods, offices and the like. Some non-industrial uses, such as agriculture, farm dwellings, motels, a harness racetrack, and certain retail sales and service establishments, are permitted in this zone. At the time of trial no more than 100 acres . . . were actually occupied by industrial uses. . . . The rest of the land so zoned has remained undeveloped. If it were fully utilized, the testimony was that about 43,500 industrial jobs would be created, but it appeared clear that . . . much more land has been so zoned than the reasonable potential for industrial movement or expansion warrants. At the same time, however, the land cannot be used for residential development under the general ordinance.

The amount of land zoned for retail business use under the general ordinance is relatively small—169 acres, or 1.2% of the total. . . . [The] greater part of the land so zoned appears to be in use. . . .

The balance of the land area, almost 10,000 acres, has been developed until recently in the conventional form of major subdivisions. The general ordinance provides for four residential zones, designated R–1, R–1D, R–2 and R–3. All permit only single-family, detached dwellings, one house per lot—the usual form of grid development. Attached townhouses, apartments (except on farms for agricultural workers) and mobile homes are not allowed anywhere in the township under the general ordinance. This dwelling development . . . has been largely confined to the R–1 and R–2 districts. . . . The result has been quite intensive development of these sections, but at a low density. The dwellings are substantial; the average value in 1971 was $32,500 and is undoubtedly much higher today.

The general ordinance requirements . . . realistically allow only homes within the financial reach of persons of at least middle income. The R–1 zone requires a minimum lot area of 9,375 square feet, minimum lot width of 75 feet at the building line, and a minimum dwelling floor area of 1,100 square feet if a one-story building and 1,300 square feet if one and one-half stories or higher. Originally this zone comprised about 2,500 acres. Most of the subdivisions have been constructed within it so that only a few hundred acres remain. . . . The R–2 zone . . . has been completely developed. ... The general ordinance places the remainder of the township, outside of the industrial and commercial zones and the R–1D district (to be mentioned shortly), in the R–3 zone. This zone comprises over 7,000 acres—slightly more than half of the total municipal area—[and] about 4,600 acres of it then remained available for housing development. Ordinance requirements are substantially higher, however, in that the minimum lot size is increased to about one-half acre (20,000 square feet). ... Lot width at the building line must be 100 feet. Minimum dwelling floor area is as in the R–1 zone. Presently this section is primarily in agricultural use; it contains as well most of the municipality's substandard housing.

The R–1D district was created by ordinance amendment in 1968. The area is composed of a piece of what was formerly R–3 land [and] is a so-called "cluster" zone. ... Here this concept is implemented by reduction of the minimum lot area from 20,000 square feet required in the R–3 zone to 10,000 square feet (12,000 square feet for corner lots) but with the proviso that one-family houses—the single permitted dwelling use—"shall not be erected in excess of an allowable development density of 2.25 dwelling units per gross acre." The ... developer must set aside and dedicate to the municipality a minimum of 15% and a maximum of 25% of the total acreage for such public uses as may be required by the Planning Board, including "but not limited to school sites, parks, playgrounds, recreation areas, public buildings, public utilities." Some dwelling development has taken place in this district [and about] 486 acres remained available in the district.

A variation from conventional development has recently occurred in some parts of Mount Laurel ... by use of the land use regulation device known as "planned unit development" (PUD). This scheme differs from the traditional in that the type, density and placement of land uses and buildings, instead of being detailed and confined to specified districts by local legislation in advance, is determined by contract, or "deal," as to each development between the developer and the municipal administrative authority, under broad guidelines laid down by state enabling legislation and an implementing local ordinance. The stress is on regulation of density and permitted mixture of uses within the same area, including various kinds of living accommodations with or without commercial and industrial enterprises. The idea may be basically thought of as the creation of "new towns" in virgin territory, full-blown or in miniature, although most frequently the concept has been limited in practice, as in Mount Laurel, to residential developments of various sizes having some variety of housing and perhaps some retail establishments to serve the inhabitants....

[Mount Laurel's four PUD projects] are very substantial and involve at least 10,000 sale and rental housing units of various types to be erected over a period of years. ... If completed as planned, they will in themselves ultimately quadruple the 1970 township population, but still leave a good part of the township undeveloped. ... While multi-family housing in the form of rental garden, medium rise and high rise apartments and attached townhouses is for the first time provided for, as well as single-family detached dwellings for sale, it is not designed to accommodate and is beyond the financial reach of low and moderate income families, especially those with young children. The aim is quite the contrary; as with the single-family homes in the older conventional subdivisions, only persons of medium and upper income are sought as residents. [Each] development will attract a highly educated and trained population base to support the nearby industrial parks in the township as well as the business and commercial facilities. The approvals also sharply limit the number of apartments having more than one bedroom. Further, they require that the developer must provide in its leases that no school-age children shall be permitted to occupy any one-bedroom apartment and that no more than two such children shall reside in any two-bedroom unit. The developer is also required, prior to the issuance of the first building permit, to record a covenant, running with all land on which multi-family housing is to be constructed, providing that in the event more than .3 school children per multi-family unit shall attend the township school system in any one year, the developer will pay the cost of tuition and other school expenses of all such excess numbers of children. In addition, low density, required amenities, such as central air conditioning, and specified developer contributions help to push rents and sales prices to high levels. These contributions include fire apparatus, ambulances, fire houses, and very large sums of money for educational facilities, a cultural center and the township library.

Still another restrictive land use regulation was adopted by the township through a ... new zone, R–4, Planned Adult Retirement Community (PARC) [of] perhaps 200 acres.... The extensive development requirements detailed in the ordinance make it apparent that the scheme was not designed for, and would be beyond the means of, low and moderate income retirees. The highly restricted nature of the zone is found in the requirement that all permanent residents must be at least 52 years of age (except a spouse, immediate family member other than a child, live-in domestic, companion or nurse). Children are limited to a maximum of one, over age 18, residing with a parent and there may be no more than three permanent residents in any one dwelling unit.

All this affirmative action for the benefit of certain segments of the population is in sharp contrast to the lack of action, and indeed hostility, with respect to affording any opportunity for decent housing for the township's own poor living in substandard accommodations.... In 1968 a private non-profit association sought to build subsidized, multi-family housing ... with funds to be granted by a higher level governmental agency. Advance municipal approval of the project was required. The Township Committee responded with a purportedly approving resolution, which found a need for "moderate" income housing in the area, but went on to specify that such housing must be constructed subject to all zoning, planning, building and other applicable ordinances and codes. This meant single-family detached dwellings on 20,000 square foot lots. (Fear was also expressed that such housing would attract low income families from outside the township.) Needless to say, such requirements killed realistic housing for this group of low and moderate income families.

The record thoroughly substantiates the findings of the trial court that over the years Mount Laurel "has acted affirmatively to control development and to attract a selective type of growth" and that "through its zoning ordinances has exhibited economic discrimination in that the poor have been deprived of adequate housing and the opportunity to secure the construction of subsidized housing, and has used federal, state, county and local finances and resources solely for the betterment of middle and upper-income persons."

There cannot be the slightest doubt that the reason for this course of conduct has been to keep down local taxes on *property* (Mount Laurel is not a high tax municipality) and that the policy was carried out without regard for nonfiscal considerations with respect to *people*, either within or without its boundaries. This conclusion is demonstrated not only by what was done and what happened, as we have related, but also by innumerable direct statements of municipal officials at public meetings over the years. . . . This policy of land use regulation for a fiscal end derives from New Jersey's tax structure, which has imposed on local real estate most of the cost of municipal and county government and of the primary and secondary education of the municipality's children. The latter expense is much the largest, so, basically, the fewer the school children, the lower the tax rate. Sizeable industrial and commercial ratables are eagerly sought and homes and the lots on which they are situate are required to be large enough, through minimum lot sizes and minimum floor areas, to have substantial value in order to produce greater tax revenues to meet school costs. Large families who cannot afford to buy large houses and must live in cheaper rental accommodations are definitely not wanted, so we find drastic bedroom restrictions for, or complete prohibition of, multi-family or other feasible housing for those of lesser income.

This pattern of land use regulation has been adopted for the same purpose in developing municipality after developing municipality. Almost every one acts solely in its own selfish and parochial interest and in effect builds a wall around itself to keep out those people or entities not adding favorably to the tax base, despite the location of the municipality or the demand for varied kinds of housing. There has been no effective inter-municipal or area planning or land use regulation. All of this is amply demonstrated by the evidence in this case. . . . One incongruous result is [that] developing municipalities render[] it impossible for lower paid employees of industries they have eagerly sought and welcomed with open arms (and, in Mount Laurel's case, even some of its own lower paid municipal employees) to live in the community where they work.

The other end of the spectrum should also be mentioned because it shows the source of some of the demand for cheaper housing than the developing municipalities have permitted. Core cities were originally the location of most commerce and industry. Many of those facilities furnished employment for the unskilled and semi-skilled. These employees lived relatively near their work, so sections of cities always have housed the majority of people of low and moderate income, generally in old and deteriorating housing. Despite the municipally confined tax structure, commercial and industrial ratables generally used to supply enough revenue to provide and maintain municipal services equal or superior to those furnished in most suburban and rural areas. The situation has become exactly the opposite since the end of World War II. Much industry and retail business, and even the professions, have left the cities. Camden is a typical example. . . . For various reasons, it lost thousands of jobs between 1950 and 1970, including more than half of its manufacturing jobs (a reduction from 43,267 to 20,671, while all jobs in the entire area labor market increased from 94,507 to 197,037). A large segment of retail business faded away with the erection of large suburban shopping centers. The economically better situated city residents helped fill up the miles of sprawling new housing developments, not fully served by public transit. In a society which came to depend more and more on expensive individual motor vehicle transportation for all purposes, low income employees very frequently could not afford to reach outlying places of suitable employment and they certainly could not afford the permissible housing near such locations. These people have great difficulty in obtaining work and have been forced to remain in housing which is overcrowded, and has become more and more substandard and less and less tax productive. There has been a consequent critical erosion of the city tax base and inability to provide the amount and quality of those governmental services—education, health, police, fire, housing and the like—so necessary to the very existence of safe and decent city life. This category of city dwellers desperately needs much better housing and living conditions than is available to them now, both in a rehabilitated city and in outlying municipalities. They make up, along with the other classes of persons earlier mentioned who also cannot afford the only generally permitted housing in the developing municipalities, the acknowledged great demand for low and moderate income housing.

II. *The Legal Issue*

The legal question . . . is whether a developing municipality like Mount Laurel may validly, by a system of land use regulation, make it physically and economically impossible to provide low and moderate income housing in the municipality for the various categories of persons who need and want it and thereby, as Mount Laurel has, exclude such people from living within its confines because of the limited extent of their income and resources. Necessarily implicated are the broader questions of the right of such municipalities to limit the kinds of available housing and of any obligation to make possible a variety and choice of types of living accommodations.

We conclude that every such municipality must, by its land use regulations, presumptively make realistically possible an appropriate variety and choice of housing. More specifically, presumptively it cannot foreclose the opportunity of the classes of people mentioned for low and moderate income housing and in its regulations must affirmatively afford that opportunity, at least to the extent of the municipality's fair share of the present and prospective regional need therefor. These obligations must be met unless the particular municipality can sustain the heavy burden of demonstrating peculiar circumstances which dictate that it should not be required so to do.

We reach this conclusion under state law and so do not find it necessary to consider federal constitutional grounds urged by plaintiffs. We begin with some fundamental principles as applied to the scene before us. Land use regulation is encompassed within the state's police power. . . . It is elementary theory that all police power enactments, no matter at what level of government, must conform to the basic state constitutional requirements of substantive due process and equal protection of the laws. These are inherent in Art. I, par. 1 of our Constitution,[6] the requirements of which may be more demanding than those of the federal Constitution. It is required that, affirmatively, a zoning regulation, like any police power enactment, must promote public health, safety, morals or the general welfare. (The last term seems broad enough to encompass the others). Conversely, a zoning enactment which is contrary to the general welfare is invalid. . . . Indeed these considerations are specifically set forth in the zoning enabling act [but their] inclusion therein really adds little; the same requirement would exist even if they were omitted. If a zoning regulation violates the enabling act in this respect, it is also theoretically invalid under the state constitution. We say "theoretically" because, as a matter of policy, we do not treat the validity of most land use ordinance provisions as involving matters of constitutional dimension; that classification is confined to major questions of fundamental import. We consider the basic importance of housing and local regulations restricting its availability to substantial segments of the population to fall within the latter category. . . .

The demarcation between the valid and the invalid in the field of land use regulation is difficult to determine, not always clear and subject to change. . . . This court has also . . . warned . . . of the inevitability of change in judicial approach and view as mandated by change in the world around us. . . . [This] implicates the matter of *whose* general welfare must be served or not violated in the field of land use regulation. Frequently the decisions in this state . . . have spoken only in terms of the interest of the enacting municipality, so that it has been thought, at least in some quarters, that such was the only welfare requiring consideration. It is, of course, true that many cases have dealt only with regulations having little, if any, outside impact where the local decision is ordinarily entitled to

---

6. The paragraph reads: "All persons are by nature free and independent, and have certain natural and unalienable rights, among which are those of enjoying and defending life and liberty, of acquiring, possessing, and protecting property, and of pursuing and obtaining safety and happiness."

NJ const.

prevail. However, it is fundamental and not to be forgotten that the zoning power is a police power of the state and the local authority is acting only as a delegate of that power and is restricted in the same manner as is the state. So, when regulation does have a substantial external impact, the welfare of the state's citizens beyond the borders of the particular municipality cannot be disregarded and must be recognized and served....

In recent years this court has ... stressed this nonlocal approach to the meaning of "general welfare" ... [In] Kunzler v. Hoffman, 48 N.J. 277 (1966), a case unsuccessfully attacking a use variance granted a private hospital to serve the emotionally disturbed in a wide area of the state, we rejected the contention that local zoning authorities are limited to a consideration of only those benefits to the general welfare which would be received by residents of the municipality, pointing out that "general welfare" in the context there involved "comprehends the benefits not merely within municipal boundaries but also those to the regions of the State relevant to the public interest to be served."

This brings us to the relation of housing to the concept of general welfare just discussed and the result in terms of land use regulation which that relationship mandates. There cannot be the slightest doubt that shelter, along with food, are the most basic human needs. ... It is plain beyond dispute that proper provision for adequate housing of all categories of people is certainly an absolute essential in promotion of the general welfare required in all local land use regulation. Further the universal and constant need for such housing is so important and of such broad public interest that the general welfare which developing municipalities like Mount Laurel must consider extends beyond their boundaries and cannot be parochially confined to the claimed good of the particular municipality. It has to follow that, broadly speaking, the presumptive obligation arises for each such municipality affirmatively to plan and provide, by its land use regulations, the reasonable opportunity for an appropriate variety and choice of housing, including, of course, low and moderate cost housing, to meet the needs, desires and resources of all categories of people who may desire to live within its boundaries. Negatively, it may not adopt regulations or policies which thwart or preclude that opportunity.

It is also entirely clear ... that most developing municipalities, including Mount Laurel, have not met their affirmative or negative obligations, primarily for local fiscal reasons....

In sum, we are satisfied beyond any doubt that, by reason of the basic importance of appropriate housing and the longstanding pressing need for it, especially in the low and moderate cost category, and of the exclusionary zoning practices of so many municipalities, conditions have changed ... to require ... the presumptive obligation on the part of developing municipalities at least to afford the opportunity by land use regulations for appropriate housing for all.

Rule/
Principles

We have spoken of this obligation of such municipalities as "presumptive." The term has two aspects, procedural and substantive. Procedurally, we think the basic importance of appropriate housing for all dictates that, when it is shown that a developing municipality in its land use regulations has not made realistically possible a variety and choice of housing, including adequate provision to afford the opportunity for low and moderate income housing or has expressly prescribed requirements or restrictions which preclude or substantially hinder it, a facial showing of violation of substantive due process or equal protection under the state constitution has been made out and the burden, and it is a heavy one, shifts to the municipality to establish a valid basis for its action or nonaction. ... The substantive aspect of "presumptive" relates to the specifics, on the one hand, of what municipal land use regulation provisions, or the absence thereof, will evidence invalidity and shift the burden of proof and, on the other hand, of what bases and considerations will carry the municipality's burden and sustain what it has done or failed to do. Both kinds of specifics may well vary between municipalities according to peculiar circumstances.

We turn to application of these principles in appraisal of Mount Laurel's zoning ordinance, useful as well, we think, as guidelines for future application in other municipalities. The township's general zoning ordinance (including the cluster zone provision) permits ... only one type of housing—single-family detached dwellings. ... [It is conceded that] low and moderate income housing has been intentionally excluded. ... [S]ingle-family dwellings are the most expensive type of quarters and a great number of families cannot afford them. Certainly they are not pecuniarily feasible for low and moderate income families, most young people and many elderly and retired persons, except for some of moderate income by the use of low cost construction on small lots. . . .

Mount Laurel has allowed some multi-family housing by agreement in planned unit developments, but only for the relatively affluent and of no benefit to low and moderate income families. And even here, the contractual agreements between municipality and developer sharply limit the number of apartments having more than one bedroom. ... The design of such limitations is obviously to restrict the number of families in the municipality having school age children and thereby keep down local education costs. Such restrictions are so clearly contrary to the general welfare as not to require further discussion.

Mount Laurel's zoning ordinance is also so restrictive in its minimum lot area, lot frontage and building size requirements, earlier detailed, as to preclude single-family housing for even moderate income families. ... The conclusion is irresistible that Mount Laurel permits only such middle and upper income housing as it believes will have sufficient taxable value to come close to paying its own governmental way.

[Mount Laurel has also zoned] very large amounts of land for industrial and related uses. Mount Laurel has set aside almost 30% of its area

. . . for that purpose; the only residential use allowed is for farm dwellings. . . . [It] seems plain that the likelihood of anywhere near the whole of the zoned area being used for the intended purpose in the foreseeable future is remote indeed and that an unreasonable amount of land has thereby been removed from possible residential development, again seemingly for local fiscal reasons. . . .

Mount Laurel's zoning ordinance is presumptively contrary to the general welfare and outside the intended scope of the zoning power in the particulars mentioned. A facial showing of invalidity is thus established, shifting to the municipality the burden of establishing valid superseding reasons for its action and non-action. We now examine the reasons it advances.

The township's principal reason [is] fiscal. . . . [Because] New Jersey's tax structure . . . substantially finances municipal governmental and educational costs from taxes on local real property, every municipality may, by the exercise of the zoning power, allow only such uses and to such extent as will be beneficial to the local tax rate. In other words, the position is that any municipality may zone extensively to seek and encourage the "good" tax ratables of industry and commerce, and limit the permissible types of housing to those having the fewest school children or to those providing sufficient value to attain or approach paying their own way taxwise. We have previously held that a developing municipality may properly zone for and seek industrial ratables to create a better economic balance for the community *vis-a-vis* educational and governmental costs engendered by residential development, provided that such was ". . . done reasonably as part of and in furtherance of a legitimate comprehensive plan for the zoning of the entire municipality." Gruber v. Mayor and Township Committee of Raritan Township, 39 N.J. 1, 9–11 (1962). We adhere to that view today. But we were not there concerned with, and did not pass upon, the validity of municipal exclusion by zoning of types of housing and kinds of people for the same local financial end. We have no hesitancy in now saying . . . that, considering the basic importance of the opportunity for appropriate housing for all classes of our citizenry, no municipality may exclude or limit categories of housing for that reason or purpose. While we fully recognize the increasingly heavy burden of local taxes for municipal governmental and school costs on homeowners, relief from the consequences of this tax system will have to be furnished by other branches of government. It cannot legitimately be accomplished by restricting types of housing through the zoning process in developing municipalities. . . .

By way of summary, what we have said comes down to this. As a developing municipality, Mount Laurel must, by its land use regulations, make realistically possible the opportunity for an appropriate variety and choice of housing for all categories of people who may desire to live there, of course including those of low and moderate income. It must permit multi-family housing, without bedroom or similar restrictions, as well as small dwellings on very small lots, low cost housing of other types and, in general, high density zoning, without artificial and unjustifiable minimum requirements as to lot size, building size and the like, to meet the full panoply of these needs. Certainly when a municipality zones for industry and commerce for local tax benefit purposes, it without question must zone to permit adequate housing within the means of the employees involved in such uses. ... The amount of land removed from residential use by allocation to industrial and commercial purposes must be reasonably related to the present and future potential for such purposes. In other words, such municipalities must zone primarily for the living welfare of people and not for the benefit of the local tax rate.[7]

[A] developing municipality's obligation to afford the opportunity for decent and adequate low and moderate income housing extends at least to "... the municipality's fair share of the present and prospective regional need therefor." ... Frequently it might be sounder to have more of such housing ... in one municipality in a region than in another, because of greater availability of suitable land, location of employment, accessibility of public transportation or some other significant reason. But, under present New Jersey legislation, zoning must be on an individual municipal basis, rather than regionally. So long as that situation persists under the present tax structure, or in the absence of some kind of binding agreement among all the municipalities of a region, we feel that every municipality therein must bear its fair share of the regional burden....

The composition of the applicable "region" will necessarily vary from situation to situation and probably no hard and fast rule will serve to furnish the answer in every case. Confinement to or within a certain county appears not to be realistic, but restriction within the boundaries of the state seems practical and advisable. (This is not to say that a developing municipality can ignore a demand for housing within its boundaries on the part of people who commute to work in another state.) ... The concept of "fair share" [relies on] the expertise of the municipal planning adviser, the county planning boards and the state planning agency, [to determine] a reasonable figure for Mount Laurel ..., which can then be translated to the allocation of sufficient land therefor on the zoning map. ... [I]nformation and estimates ... concerning the housing needs of persons of low and moderate income now or formerly residing in the township in substandard dwellings and those presently employed or reasonably expected to be employed therein, will be pertinent....

PASHMAN, J., concurring.

With this decision, the Court begins to cope with the dark side of municipal land use regulation—the use of the zoning power to advance the parochial interests of the municipality at the expense of the surrounding region and to establish and perpetuate social and economic segregation. ... The people of New Jersey should welcome the result reached by the

---

7. This case does not properly present the question of whether a developing municipality may time its growth and, if so, how. ... We now say only that, assuming some type of timed growth is permissible, it cannot be utilized as an exclusionary device or to stop all further development and must include early provision for low and moderate income housing.

Court in this case, not merely because it is required by our laws, but, more fundamentally, because the result is right and true to the highest American ideals.

NOTES AND QUESTIONS

1. Independent State Constitutions. As noted above, state constitutional guarantees can be interpreted more broadly than the analogous federal provision, so long as the state constitution does not violate the U.S. Constitution or federal law. Under the federal Constitution, state or local discrimination on the basis of wealth (or lack thereof) is presumptively valid. See, e.g., San Antonio Independent School District v. Rodriguez, 411 U.S. 1 (1973). In its interpretation of the New Jersey Constitution, the New Jersey Supreme Court reached the opposite conclusion. Thus, the identical practice—exclusionary zoning designed to fence out those of low or modest incomes—is presumptively valid under the federal Constitution but presumed to be invalid under the New Jersey Constitution. Nor is housing a constitutionally fundamental right under the federal Constitution. See Lindsey v. Normet, 405 U.S. 56 (1972). Did the New Jersey Supreme Court rule that housing was a fundamental right under the New Jersey Constitution?

Claims similar to that advanced in *Mount Laurel I* have met a rocky reception in the federal courts. In Warth v. Seldin, 422 U.S. 490 (1975), the United States Supreme Court ruled that plaintiffs asserting the same sort of exclusionary zoning claims lacked standing to bring the claims unless they could show some concrete, particularized, and personal injury in fact.

2. Exclusionary? Or Prudent Fiscal Policy? The New Jersey court conceded that Mount Laurel's motivation for its zoning scheme was to keep property taxes low. The optimal way to accomplish this is to have a rich tax base that does not demand much in the way of public services. Thus, a community with lots of non-polluting commercial or industrial uses and expensive homes on large lots dispersed to create low residential density will be ideal. The commercial and industrial tax base provides abundant revenue, the nature of the residential use virtually assures that only the affluent will live in the community, and the low density ensures that the number of school-age children is likely to be modest. Thus, demand for public water and sewer facilities is low, demand for fire and police protection is not overly high, there is no need to invest great sums in public education (though spending per pupil may be generous), and there is little need to fund welfare programs.

The devices used by local governments to create these conditions have met mixed reviews. Minimum lot sizes have survived judicial scrutiny when the community can justify them in terms of legitimate issues of historic preservation, water conservation, sanitation, or traffic congestion. See Ketchel v. Bainbridge Township, 52 Ohio St.3d 239 (1990); County Commissioners of Queen Anne's County v. Miles, 246 Md. 355 (1967). Minimum setback requirements, which ensure adequate light and air, are almost universally upheld. A number of other devices, such as limiting the number of new building permits or water connections, may be valid if the community has legitimate reasons to control growth. Similarly, environmental regulations and energy conservation building requirements are generally upheld, even though they can sharply increase the price of housing and thus have the effect of excluding the poor.

3. *The Aftermath.* The effect of *Mount Laurel I* was not dramatic, as it applied only to "developing communities." Contrary to Justice Pashman's concurring admonition, the people of New Jersey did not welcome the decision that followed: Southern Burlington County NAACP v. Township of Mount Laurel, 92 N.J. 158 (1983) (*Mount Laurel II*). In *Mount Laurel II* the New Jersey court extended the principles of *Mount Laurel I* to all communities in New Jersey, developing or not. New Jerseyans resisted this intrusion on local authority and planning, and the New Jersey legislature responded by enacting a Fair Housing Act that created an agency to identify and enforce *Mount Laurel II* requirements. The Fair Housing Act, N.J. Stat. Ann. § 52:27D–301 *et seq.*, permits communities, with agency approval, to pay other communities to provide up to half of the housing accommodations that *Mount Laurel II* imposes.

Other states have followed New Jersey's lead by legislation that is designed to provide housing access to most localities for those of law and modest incomes. See, e.g., Mass. Gen. Laws Ch.40B, §§ 20–23; Conn. Gen. Stat. § 8–30g.

c.   Substantive Due Process: Household Composition

Another zoning device is to limit the composition of households in the community. In Village of Belle Terre v. Boraas, 416 U.S. 1 (1974), the Supreme Court upheld a Long Island, New York suburb's regulation limiting occupation of single family residences to a "family," defined as including any number of people related "by blood, adoption, or marriage" but only two people not so related. The Court rejected a challenge to the ordinance by six unrelated college students who had rented a home in the community, reasoning that the ordinance did not impede the constitutional right to migrate from one state to another, noting that there was no constitutionally fundamental right to housing, and concluding that the ordinance was a rational means of accomplishing the legitimate ends of securing "the blessings of quiet seclusion and clean air."

MOORE v. CITY OF EAST CLEVELAND

Supreme Court of the United States
431 U.S. 494 (1977)

JUSTICE POWELL announced the judgment of the Court, and delivered an opinion in which JUSTICES BRENNAN, MARSHALL, and BLACKMUN joined.

East Cleveland's housing ordinance [limits] occupancy of a dwelling unit to members of a single family, [and] recognizes as a "family" only a few categories of related individuals. Because her family, living together in her home, fits none of those categories, appellant stands convicted of a criminal offense.[8] The question in this case is whether the ordinance

---

8.   [Footnote relocated] [The East Cleveland ordinance stated:]

violates the Due Process Clause of the Fourteenth Amendment. Appellant, Mrs. Inez Moore, lives in her East Cleveland home together with her son, Dale Moore, Sr., and her two grandsons, Dale, Jr., and John Moore, Jr. The two boys are first cousins rather than brothers; we are told that John came to live with his grandmother, [uncle, and cousin] after his mother's death. . . .

The city argues [that] Village of Belle Terre v. Boraas, 416 U.S. 1 (1974), requires us to sustain the ordinance attacked here. Belle Terre, like East Cleveland, imposed limits on the types of groups that could occupy a single dwelling unit; [we] sustained the Belle Terre ordinance on the ground that it bore a rational relationship to permissible state objectives. But [the] Belle Terre [ordinance] affected only unrelated individuals. It expressly allowed all who were related by "blood, adoption, or marriage" to live together, and in sustaining the ordinance we were careful to note that it promoted "family needs" and "family values." East Cleveland [has] chosen to regulate the occupancy of its housing by slicing deeply into the family itself. [When] a city undertakes such intrusive regulation of the family [the] usual judicial deference to the legislature is inappropriate. [We have] "long recognized that freedom of personal choice in matters of marriage and family life is one of the liberties protected by the Due Process Clause of the Fourteenth Amendment." [While] the family is not beyond regulation, [when] the government intrudes on choices concerning family living arrangements, this Court must examine carefully the importance of the governmental interests advanced and the extent to which they are served by the challenged regulation.

When thus examined, this ordinance cannot survive. The city seeks to justify it as a means of preventing overcrowding, minimizing traffic and parking congestion, and avoiding an undue financial burden on East Cleveland's school system. Although these are legitimate goals, the ordinance before us serves them marginally, at best. For example, the ordinance permits any family consisting only of husband, wife, and unmarried children to live together, even if the family contains a half dozen licensed drivers, each with his or her own car. At the same time it forbids an adult brother and sister to share a household, even if both faithfully use public

---

"Family" means a number of individuals related to the nominal head of the household or to the spouse of the nominal head of the household living as a single housekeeping unit in a single dwelling unit, but limited to the following:

(a) Husband or wife of the nominal head of the household.

(b) Unmarried children of the nominal head of the household or of the spouse of the nominal head of the household, provided, however, that such unmarried children have no children residing with them.

(c) Father or mother of the nominal head of the household or of the spouse of the nominal head of the household.

(d) Notwithstanding the provisions of subsection (b) hereof, a family may include not more than one dependent married or unmarried child of the nominal head of the household or of the spouse of the nominal head of the household and the spouse and dependent children of such dependent child. For the purpose of this subsection, a dependent person is one who has more than fifty percent of his total support furnished for him by the nominal head of the household and the spouse of the nominal head of the household.

(e) A family may consist of one individual.

transportation. The ordinance would permit a grandmother to live with a single dependent son and children, even if his school-age children number a dozen, yet it forces Mrs. Moore to find another dwelling for her grandson John, simply because of the presence of his uncle and cousin in the same household. We need not labor the point....

The city [suggests] that any constitutional right to live together as a family extends only to the nuclear family—essentially a couple and their dependent children. [Prior cases] did not expressly consider the family relationship presented here. They were immediately concerned with freedom of choice with respect to childbearing, or with the rights of parents to the custody and companionship of their own children, or with traditional parental authority in matters of child rearing and education. But unless we close our eyes to the basic reasons why certain rights associated with the family have been accorded shelter under the Fourteenth Amendment's Due Process Clause, we cannot avoid applying the force and rationale of these precedents to the family choice involved in this case....

Substantive due process has at times been a treacherous field for this Court. There are risks when the judicial branch gives enhanced protection to certain substantive liberties without the guidance of the more specific provisions of the Bill of Rights. [There] is reason for concern lest the only limits to such judicial intervention become the predilections of those who happen at the time to be Members of this Court. ... But it does not ... require what the city urges here: cutting off any protection of family rights at the first convenient, if arbitrary boundary—the boundary of the nuclear family. Appropriate limits on substantive due process come not from drawing arbitrary lines but rather from careful "respect for the teachings of history [and] solid recognition of the basic values that underlie our society." Our decisions establish that the Constitution protects the sanctity of the family precisely because the institution of the family is deeply rooted in this Nation's history and tradition. It is through the family that we inculcate and pass down many of our most cherished values, moral and cultural. Ours is by no means a tradition limited to respect for the bonds uniting the members of the nuclear family. The tradition of uncles, aunts, cousins, and especially grandparents sharing a household along with parents and children has roots equally venerable and equally deserving of constitutional recognition. Over the years millions of our citizens have grown up in just such an environment, and most, surely, have profited from it. Even if conditions of modern society have brought about a decline in extended family households, they have not erased the accumulated wisdom of civilization, gained over the centuries and honored throughout our history, that supports a larger conception of the family. Out of choice, necessity, or a sense of family responsibility, it has been common for close relatives to draw together and participate in the duties and the satisfactions of a common home. [In] times of adversity, such as the death of a spouse or economic need, the broader family has tended to come together for mutual sustenance and to maintain or rebuild a secure home life. This is apparently what happened here. Whether or not such a household is established because of personal tragedy, the choice of relatives in this degree of kinship to live together may not lightly be denied by the State. [The] Constitution prevents East Cleveland from standardizing its children—and its adults—by forcing all to live in certain narrowly defined family patterns.

Reversed.

JUSTICE STEVENS, concurring in the judgment.

[There] appears to be no precedent for an ordinance which excludes any of an owner's relatives from the group of persons who may occupy his residence on a permanent basis. ... Since this ordinance has not been shown to have any "substantial relation to the public health, safety, morals, or general welfare" of the city of East Cleveland, and since it cuts so deeply into a fundamental right normally associated with the ownership of residential property—that of an owner to decide who may reside on his or her property—[East Cleveland's] unprecedented ordinance constitutes a taking of property without due process and without just compensation ...

JUSTICE WHITE, dissenting.

[W]e must always bear in mind that the substantive content of the [Due Process] Clause [is] nothing more than the accumulated product of [its] judicial interpretation.... [This] Court has no license to invalidate legislation which it thinks merely arbitrary or unreasonable. [That] the Court has ample precedent for the creation of new constitutional rights should not lead it to repeat the process at will. [Under] our cases, the Due Process Clause extends substantial protection to various phases of family life, but none requires that the claim made here be sustained. I cannot believe that the interest in residing with more than one set of grandchildren is one that calls for any kind of heightened protection under the Due Process Clause. [The] present claim is hardly one of which it could be said that "neither liberty nor justice would exist if [it] were sacrificed." [Justice] Powell would apparently construe the Due Process Clause to protect from all but quite important state regulatory interests any right or privilege that in his estimate is deeply rooted in the country's traditions. For me, this suggests a far too expansive charter for this [Court]. What the deeply rooted traditions of the country are is arguable; which of them deserve the protection of the Due Process Clause is even more debatable. The suggested view would broaden enormously the horizons of the Clause; and, if the interest involved here is any measure of what the States would be forbidden to regulate, the courts would be substantively weighing and very likely invalidating a wide range of measures that Congress and state legislatures think appropriate to respond to a changing economic and social order....

NOTES, QUESTIONS, AND PROBLEM

1. *What is a Family?* The Supreme Court thought the Constitution includes a fundamental right of "extended families" to occupy the same

residential unit. But what is an extended family? Is it defined by "blood [genetics], marriage, or adoption." as the Belle Terre ordinance put it? Or is it the result of functional relationships between people?

Problem: Suppose that Anne and Bill live together for years without benefit of marriage, produce three children, and Anne dies. Then Bill falls in love with Grace, who moves in with her two children, although Bill and Grace do not marry. Bill, Grace, and the five children live together in the same residence for years. Do they have a constitutionally protected right to live together, assuming the East Cleveland ordinance applies to them?

Cf. Stanley v. Illinois, 405 U.S. 645 (1972).

2. State Constitutional Law. The high courts of various states have interpreted their state constitutions to provide constitutional protection to unrelated persons who wish to live together. See, e.g., City of Santa Barbara v. Adamson, 27 Cal.3d 123 (1980) (municipal limit of five unrelated persons living together infringed the California Constitution's guarantee of privacy, absent proof of necessity to achieve some compelling government interest); McMinn v. Town of Oyster Bay, 66 N.Y.2d 544 (1985) (Belle Terre-type ordinance invalidated as violating the New York Constitution's guarantee of due process).

3. STATUTORY CONTROLS

Zoning laws can also violate required statutory accommodations of religion, guarantees of access to housing (as under the Fair Housing Act), or limitations imposed by other superior laws.

CITY OF EDMONDS v. OXFORD HOUSE, INC.

Supreme Court of the United States
514 U.S. 725 (1995)

JUSTICE GINSBURG delivered the opinion of the Court.

The Fair Housing Act (FHA or Act) prohibits discrimination in housing against ... persons with handicaps [but] section 807(b)(1) of the Act entirely exempts from the FHA's compass "any reasonable local, State, or Federal restrictions regarding the maximum number of occupants permitted to occupy a dwelling." 42 U.S.C. § 3607(b)(1). This case presents the question whether a provision in petitioner City of Edmonds' zoning code qualifies for § 3607(b)(1)'s complete exemption from FHA scrutiny. The provision, governing areas zoned for single-family dwelling units, defines "family" as "persons [without regard to number] related by genetics, adoption, or marriage, or a group of five or fewer [unrelated] persons." ...

The defining provision at issue describes who may compose a family unit; it does not prescribe "*the* maximum number of occupants" a dwelling unit may house. We hold that § 3607(b)(1) does not exempt prescriptions of the family-defining kind, *i.e.*, provisions designed to foster the family character of a neighborhood. Instead, § 3607(b)(1)'s absolute exemption removes from the FHA's scope only total occupancy limits, *i.e.*, numerical ceilings that serve to prevent overcrowding in living quarters.

I. In the summer of 1990, respondent Oxford House opened a group home in the City of Edmonds, Washington (City), for 10 to 12 adults recovering from alcoholism and drug addiction. The group home, called Oxford House–Edmonds, is located in a neighborhood zoned for single-family residences. Upon learning that Oxford House had leased and was operating a home in Edmonds, the City issued criminal citations to the owner and a resident of the house. The citations charged violation of the zoning code rule that defines who may live in single-family dwelling units. The occupants of such units must compose a "family," and [because] Oxford House–Edmonds houses more than five unrelated persons [it] does not conform to the code. Oxford House asserted reliance on the Fair Housing Act, 102 Stat. 1619, 42 U.S.C. § 3601 *et seq.*, which declares it unlawful "to discriminate in the sale or rental, or to otherwise make unavailable or deny, a dwelling to any buyer or renter because of a handicap of . . . that buyer or renter." § 3604(f)(1)(A). The parties have stipulated, for purposes of this litigation, that the residents of Oxford House–Edmonds "are recovering alcoholics and drug addicts and are handicapped persons within the meaning" of the Act. . . .

Discrimination covered by the FHA includes a refusal to make reasonable accommodations in rules, policies, practices, or services, when such accommodations may be necessary to afford [handicapped] person[s] equal opportunity to use and enjoy a dwelling. § 3604(f)(3)(B). Oxford House asked Edmonds to make a "reasonable accommodation" by allowing it to remain in the single-family dwelling it had leased. Group homes for recovering substance abusers, Oxford urged, need 8 to 12 residents to be financially and therapeutically viable. Edmonds declined to permit Oxford House to stay in a single-family residential zone, but passed an ordinance listing group homes as permitted uses in multifamily and general commercial zones.

Edmonds sued Oxford House in the United States District Court for the Western District of Washington, seeking a declaration that the FHA does not constrain the City's zoning code family definition rule. Oxford House counterclaimed under the FHA, charging the City with failure to make a "reasonable accommodation" permitting maintenance of the group home in a single-family zone. The United States filed a separate action on the same FHA "reasonable accommodation" ground, and the two cases were consolidated. Edmonds suspended its criminal enforcement actions pending resolution of the federal litigation.

On cross-motions for summary judgment, the District Court held that [the Edmonds zoning rule] defining "family" is exempt from the FHA under § 3607(b)(1) as a "reasonable . . . restriction regarding the maximum number of occupants permitted to occupy a dwelling." . . . The United States Court of Appeals for the Ninth Circuit reversed; holding § 3607(b)(1)'s absolute exemption inapplicable. . . .

The Ninth Circuit's decision conflicts with an Eleventh Circuit decision declaring exempt under § 3607(b)(1) a family definition provision similar to the Edmonds prescription. See Elliott v. Athens, 960 F.2d 975 (1992). We granted certiorari to resolve the conflict and we now affirm the Ninth Circuit's judgment.

II.   The sole question before the Court is whether Edmonds' family composition rule qualifies as a "restriction regarding the maximum number of occupants permitted to occupy a dwelling" within the meaning of the FHA's absolute exemption.[9] In answering this question, we are mindful of the Act's stated policy "to provide, within constitutional limitations, for fair housing throughout the United States." § 3601. We also note precedent recognizing the FHA's "broad and inclusive" compass, and therefore according a "generous construction" to the Act's complaint-filing provision. Trafficante v. Metropolitan Life Ins. Co., 409 U.S. 205, 209, 212 (1972). Accordingly, we regard this case as an instance in which an exception to "a general statement of policy" is sensibly read "narrowly in order to preserve the primary operation of the [policy]." Commissioner v. Clark, 489 U.S. 726, 739 (1989).

A.   ... Land-use restrictions designate "districts in which only compatible uses are allowed and incompatible uses are excluded." D. Mandelker, Land Use Law § 4.16, pp. 113–114 (3d ed. 1993). ... In particular, reserving land for single-family residences preserves the character of neighborhoods, securing "zones where family values, youth values, and the blessings of quiet seclusion and clean air make the area a sanctuary for people." Village of Belle Terre v. Boraas, 416 U.S. 1, 9 (1974).... To limit land use to single-family residences, a municipality must define the term "family;" thus family composition rules are an essential component of single-family residential use restrictions. Maximum occupancy restrictions, [by contrast,] cap the number of occupants per dwelling, typically in relation to available floor space or the number and type of rooms. These restrictions ordinarily apply uniformly to *all* residents of *all* dwelling units. Their purpose is to protect health and safety by preventing dwelling overcrowding....

Section 3607(b)(1)'s language—"restrictions regarding the maximum number of occupants permitted to occupy a dwelling"—surely encompasses maximum occupancy restrictions. But the formulation does not fit family composition rules typically tied to land-use restrictions. In sum, rules that cap the total number of occupants in order to prevent overcrowding of a dwelling "plainly and unmistakably" fall within § 3607(b)(1)'s absolute exemption from the FHA's governance; rules designed to preserve the family character of a neighborhood, fastening on the composition of households rather than on the total number of occupants living quarters can contain, do not.

---

9.   Like the District Court and the Ninth Circuit, we do not decide whether Edmonds' zoning code provision defining "family," as the City would apply it against Oxford House, violates the FHA's prohibitions against discrimination set out in 42 U.S.C. §§ 3604(f)(1)(A) and (f)(3)(B).

B. ... [The] provisions Edmonds invoked against Oxford House ...
are classic examples of a use restriction and complementing family composition rule. These provisions do not cap the number of people who may
live in a dwelling. In plain terms, they direct that dwellings be used only
to house families. Captioned "USES," [it] provides that the sole "Permitted Primary Use" in a single-family residential zone is "single-family
dwelling units." Edmonds itself recognizes that this provision simply
"defines those uses permitted in a single family residential zone." A
separate provision caps the number of occupants a dwelling may house,
based on floor area.... This space and occupancy standard is a prototypi-
cal maximum occupancy restriction.

Edmonds nevertheless argues that its family composition rule ...
falls within § 3607(b)(1), the FHA exemption for maximum occupancy
restrictions, because the rule caps at five the number of unrelated persons
allowed to occupy a single-family dwelling. But Edmonds' family composition rule surely does not answer the question: "What is the maximum
number of occupants permitted to occupy a house?" So long as they are
related "by genetics, adoption, or marriage," any number of people can
live in a house. ... Family living, not living space per occupant, is what
[the family composition rule] describes....

Edmonds' zoning code provision describing who may compose a "family" is not a maximum occupancy restriction exempt from the FHA under
§ 3607(b)(1). It remains for the lower courts to decide whether Edmonds'
actions against Oxford House violate the FHA's prohibitions against
discrimination set out in §§ 3604(f)(1)(A) and (f)(3)(B). ... Affirmed.

JUSTICE THOMAS, with whom JUSTICE SCALIA and JUSTICE KENNEDY join,
dissenting.

Congress has exempted from the requirements of the Fair Housing
Act (FHA) "*any* reasonable local, State, or Federal restrictions regarding
the maximum number of occupants permitted to occupy a dwelling." 42
U.S.C. § 3607(b)(1) (emphasis added). [The] Court concludes that the
challenged provisions of petitioner's zoning code do not qualify for this
exemption, even though they establish a specific number—five—as the
maximum number of unrelated persons permitted to occupy a dwelling in
the single-family neighborhoods of Edmonds, Washington. Because the
Court's conclusion fails to give effect to the plain language of the statute, I
respectfully dissent.

I. ... [At oral argument the United States conceded that the effect
of Edmonds' zoning] provisions is to establish a rule that "no house in [a
single-family] area of the city shall have more than five occupants unless
it is a [traditional kind of] family." Tr. of Oral Arg. 46. In other words,
petitioner's zoning code establishes for certain dwellings "a five-occupant
limit, [with] an exception for [traditional] families." Ibid.

To my mind, the rule that "no house ... shall have more than five
occupants" (a "five-occupant limit") readily qualifies as a "restriction
regarding the maximum number of occupants permitted to occupy a

dwelling." In plain fashion, it "restrict[s]"—to five—"the maximum number of occupants permitted to occupy a dwelling." To be sure, as the majority observes, the restriction imposed by petitioner's zoning code is not an absolute one, because it does not apply to related persons. But § 3607(b)(1) does not set forth a narrow exemption only for "absolute" or "unqualified" restrictions regarding the maximum number of occupants. Instead, it sweeps broadly to exempt *any* restrictions *regarding* such maximum number. It is difficult to imagine what broader terms Congress could have used to signify the categories or kinds of relevant governmental restrictions that are exempt from the FHA.

Consider a real estate agent who is assigned responsibility for the city of Edmonds. Desiring to learn all he can about his new territory, the agent inquires: "Does the city have *any* restrictions regarding the maximum number of occupants permitted to occupy a dwelling?" The accurate answer must surely be in the affirmative—yes, the maximum number of unrelated persons permitted to occupy a dwelling in a single-family neighborhood is five. Or consider a different example. Assume that the Federal Republic of Germany imposes no restrictions on the speed of "cars" that drive on the Autobahn but does cap the speed of "trucks" (which are defined as all other vehicles). If a conscientious visitor to Germany asks whether there are "*any* restrictions regarding the maximum speed of motor vehicles permitted to drive on the Autobahn," the accurate answer again is surely the affirmative one—yes, there is a restriction regarding the maximum speed of trucks on the Autobahn.

The majority does not ask whether petitioner's zoning code imposes any restrictions regarding the maximum number of occupants permitted to occupy a dwelling. Instead, . . . the majority concludes that [Edmonds' rule] does not qualify for § 3607(b)(1)'s exemption because it "surely does not answer the question: 'What is the maximum number of occupants permitted to occupy a house?' " The majority's question, however, does not accord with the text of the statute. To take advantage of the exemption, a local, state, or federal law need not impose a restriction *establishing* an *absolute* maximum number of occupants; under § 3607(b)(1), it is necessary only that such law impose a restriction "regarding" the maximum number of occupants. Surely, a restriction can "regard"—or "concern," "relate to," or "bear on"—the maximum number of occupants without establishing an absolute maximum number in all cases.

I would apply § 3607(b)(1) as it is written. Because petitioner's zoning code imposes a qualified "restriction regarding the maximum number of occupants permitted to occupy a dwelling," and because the statute exempts from the FHA "any" such restrictions, I would reverse the Ninth Circuit's holding that the exemption does not apply in this case.

II.   The majority's failure to ask the right question about petitioner's zoning code results from a more fundamental error in focusing on "maximum occupancy restrictions" and "family composition rules." These two terms—and the two categories of zoning rules they describe—are simply irrelevant to this case. . . .

A. As an initial matter, I do not agree with the majority's interpretive premise that "this case [is] an instance in which an exception to 'a general statement of policy' is sensibly read 'narrowly in order to preserve the primary operation of the [policy].' " Why *this* case? Surely, it is not because the FHA has a "policy"; every statute has that. Nor could the reason be that a narrow reading of 42 U.S.C. § 3607(b)(1) is necessary to preserve the primary operation of the FHA's stated policy "to provide . . . for fair housing throughout the United States." Congress, the body responsible for deciding how specifically to achieve the objective of fair housing, obviously believed that § 3607(b)(1)'s exemption for "any . . . restrictions regarding the maximum number of occupants permitted to occupy a dwelling" is consistent with the FHA's general statement of policy. We do Congress no service—indeed, we *negate* the "primary operation" of § 3607(b)(1)—by giving that congressional enactment an artificially narrow reading. . . .

B. . . . [It] should be readily apparent that the category of zoning rules the majority labels "maximum occupancy restrictions" does not exhaust the category of restrictions exempted from the FHA by § 3607(b)(1). The plain words of the statute do not refer to "available floor space or the number and type of rooms;" they embrace no requirement that the exempted restrictions "apply uniformly to *all* residents of *all* dwelling units;" and they give no indication that such restrictions must have the "purpose . . . to protect health and safety by preventing dwelling overcrowding." . . .

The majority fares no better in its treatment of "family composition rules," a term employed by the majority to describe yet another invented category of zoning restrictions. . . . [The] majority's analysis consists *solely* of announcing its conclusion that "the formulation [of § 3607(b)(1)] does not fit family composition rules." This is not reasoning; it is *ipse dixit.* Indeed, . . . terms like "family character," "composition of households," "total [that is, absolute] number of occupants," and "living quarters" are noticeably absent from the text of the statute. Section 3607(b)(1) limits neither the permissible purposes of a qualifying zoning restriction nor the ways in which such a restriction may accomplish its purposes. Rather, the exemption encompasses "any" zoning restriction—whatever its purpose and by whatever means it accomplishes that purpose—so long as the restriction "regard[s]" the maximum number of occupants. [And] petitioner's zoning code does precisely that. . . .

NOTES AND PROBLEMS

1. Zoning and Group Homes. Whatever the merits of the dissent's statutory construction, *Edmonds* settled the question of whether ordinances such as Belle Terre's and Edmonds's, as applied to group homes for the handicapped, are exempt from the FHA.

Problem: City adopts an exclusive zoning scheme that limits one area to single family residences (R–1, defined as an unlimited number of people related by "blood, marriage, or adoption") and another area to multiple family or group residences, but limiting occupation of any residence to one person per 250 square feet of floor area (R–2). Cambridge House, an organization providing group housing for handicapped persons, establishes two such group homes, one in the R–1 area and the other in the R–2 area. The group home in the R–2 area is 2000 square feet and accommodates 9 people. City cites Cambridge House for a zoning violation for each of the group homes and Cambridge House defends by invoking the FHA. Does the FHA apply to either or both of these group homes? See, e.g., Oxford House v. City of St. Louis, 77 F.3d 249 (1996).

2. *Free Speech and Fair Housing.* 42 U.S.C. § 3617 makes it unlawful "to coerce, intimidate, threaten, or interfere with any person in the exercise or enjoyment of . . . any right granted or protected by" 42 U.S.C. §§ 3603 through 3606, which prohibit various forms of housing discrimination, including discrimination against the handicapped.

Problems:

a. Harvard House operates group homes for the mentally retarded. Harvard House agrees to purchase a home in the Sylvan Acres portion of Burbia, a city that has zoned Sylvan Acres exclusively residential, and limiting occupation of each residence to no more than eight persons. Neighbors who object to the sale gather signatures on a petition opposing the sale, which petition is filed with the Burbia city council, together with a request that the zoning of Sylvan Acres be changed to exclude any group homes comprised of more than three unrelated persons, a change that would make it uneconomic for Harvard House to operate its planned group home. The City Council declines to act, but the United States charges the objecting neighbors with a violation of § 3617. What result?

b. Assume the same facts as in *a*, but the neighbors then sue to enjoin the sale, on the ground that because Harvard House has announced it will house ten retarded persons in its home, the intended use will violate the zoning laws of Burbia. The United States charges the plaintiffs with a violation of § 3617. What result?

c. Assume the same facts as in *a*, except that Harvard House is in negotiations to purchase the home, but has not yet entered into a purchase contract. The objecting neighbors pool their resources and offer the seller of the home a higher price than Harvard House is willing to pay; indeed, a price that clearly exceeds the fair market value of the home. The seller accepts and Harvard House sues both the seller and the purchasers, alleging a violation of § 3617. What result?

See David K. Godschalk, Protected Petitioning or Unlawful Retaliation? The Limits of First Amendment Immunity for Lawsuits Under the Fair Housing Act, 27 Pepp. L. Rev. 477 (2000); Comment, Civil Rights v. Civil Liberties? The Legality of State Court Lawsuits under the Fair Housing Act, 63 U.Chi. L. Rev. 1607 (1996).

STS. CONSTANTINE AND HELEN GREEK ORTHODOX CHURCH v. CITY OF NEW BERLIN

United States Court of Appeals for the Seventh Circuit
396 F.3d 895 (7th Cir. 2005)

POSNER, CIRCUIT JUDGE.

This is a suit by a Greek Orthodox church (we'll call it the "Church") against a small town in Wisconsin (officially a "City") named New Berlin. There are additional parties on both sides, but there is no need to discuss them. The district court granted summary judgment for the defendants.

The suit is based on subsection (a)(1) of the cumbersomely titled Religious Land Use and Institutionalized Persons Act of 2000 (RLUIPA), 42 U.S.C. § 2000cc. That subsection forbids a government agency to "impose or implement a land use regulation in a manner that imposes a substantial burden on the religious exercise of a person, including a religious assembly or institution, unless the government demonstrates that imposition of the burden on that person, assembly or institution—(A) is in furtherance of a compelling governmental interest; and (B) is the least restrictive means of furthering that compelling governmental interest." 42 U.S.C. § 2000cc(a)(1). . . .

There is . . . no serious disagreement about the facts. By purchases made in 1995 and 1997 the Church acquired a 40-acre tract in a section of New Berlin zoned residential. It wanted to build a church on this land that would replace its existing church in the nearby city of Wauwatosa—a church that it was outgrowing because its congregation was getting larger. The tract it bought was bordered on one side by a Protestant church and on the other side by a parcel of land, belonging to another Protestant denomination, that the City had agreed to rezone to allow a church to be built on it.

In 2002 the Greek Orthodox Church applied to the City for permission to rezone a 14-acre chunk of its 40-acre property from residential to institutional so that it could build its church, which it estimated would cost $12 million. The New Berlin Planning Department, to which the application was first referred, expressed concern that should the parcel be rezoned for institutional use a school or other nonreligious facility might be built on it, instead of a church, were the Church unable to raise $12 million and as a result decided to stay put in Wauwatosa. To allay this concern the Church modified its application by coupling with the proposal for rezoning the 14-acre parcel a proposal that New Berlin promulgate a "planned unit development [PUD] overlay ordinance" that would limit the parcel to church-related uses. A specialized form of zoning ordinance, a PUD "differs from the traditional zoning in that the type, density and placement of land uses and buildings, instead of being detailed and confined to specified districts by local legislation in advance, is determined by contract, or deal, as to each development between the developer and the municipal administrative authority, under broad guidelines laid down by state enabling legislation and an implementing local ordinance." Old Tuckaway Associates Ltd. Partnership v. City of Greenfield, 180 Wis. 2d 254, 509 N.W.2d 323, 326 n. 1 (Wis. App. 1993).

The City's Director of Planning was satisfied with the revised proposal and recommended that the Planning Commission approve it, but the Commission disagreed and on its recommendation the New Berlin City Council voted the proposal down, precipitating this suit. Concern was expressed in the Commission's deliberations that if the Church didn't build a church on the property but instead sold the land, the purchaser would not be bound by the PUD. That was wrong. Nothing in the text of the PUD proposed by the Church, in the provisions of the New Berlin Municipal Code, or in the general property law of Wisconsin or elsewhere, suggests that the ordinance would lapse with the sale of the property. If the PUD said it was just limiting what *the Greek Orthodox Church* could do with the property, then a subsequent purchaser would not be bound. But since the PUD would restrict the use of the property, rather than just the conduct of its present owner, the Church's successors would be bound.

It is true that zoning ordinances are not the same as restrictive covenants that run with the land and so bind subsequent purchasers. A covenant is a contract and an ordinance isn't—though a PUD is very close to being a covenant because, as the passage that we quoted from the *Tuckaway* case explains, it is the product of a deal between a developer and a municipality. No matter; a zoning ordnance has the same effect as a covenant because, unless worded to bind only the current owner, it limits the use of the land by whoever owns it, not just whoever owned it when the ordinance was enacted. . . .

New Berlin's mayor suggested two possible courses of action that the Church might take. One was to apply for a conditional use permit, which would allow the building of the church without altering the zoning of the land. The problem was that the permit would lapse within a year unless construction began, New Berlin Municipal Code § 275–27(E), and it was infeasible for the Church to move that fast. If the Church waited to apply for the permit until it was within a year of starting construction, it would find it difficult to raise the necessary $12 million, since it could not assure donors that the church would actually be built. The statement in the City's brief that "it would not impose a substantial burden on the Church to wait to apply for a [conditional use permit] until it had its funds and plans in place" is unrealistic. Donors would be making contributions without any confidence that the contributions could be used for their intended purpose.

The City argues that the one-year deadline could be extended. Not true: "No extension shall be made to a conditional use permit." *Id.* The repeated legal errors by the City's officials casts doubt on their good faith.

The other alternative suggested by the mayor was that the Church apply for a PUD that would overlie not an institutional rezoning but instead the existing residential zoning, so that if the Church sold the parcel rather than building a church on it, and if the City were correct that such a sale would void the PUD, the buyer could not make an institutional use of the property because the property would revert to being zoned residential. The Church declined to follow this route too. It seemed obvious that the mayor, unless deeply confused about the law, was playing a delaying game. The PUD proposed by the Church would have had the same effect as the one proposed by the mayor, namely preventing a nonreligious institutional use of the property by either the Church or its successors.

To prevail in this suit, however, the Church has to show first of all that the denial of its application for the rezoning with the PUD overlay has imposed a "substantial burden" on the Church. ... The Church in our case doesn't argue that having to apply for what amounts to a zoning variance to be allowed to build in a residential area is a substantial burden. It complains instead about having either to sell the land that it bought in New Berlin and find a suitable alternative parcel or be subjected to unreasonable delay by having to restart the permit process to satisfy the Planning Commission about a contingency for which the Church has already provided complete satisfaction.

No doubt secular applicants for zoning variances often run into similar difficulties with zoning boards that, lacking legal sophistication and unwilling to take legal advice, may end up fearing legal chimeras. On that basis the City, flaunting as it were its own incompetence, suggests that the Church can't complain about being treated badly so long as it is treated no worse than other applicants for zoning variances. But that is a misreading of RLUIPA. A *separate* provision of the Act forbids government to "impose or implement a land use regulation in a manner that treats a religious assembly or institution on less than equal terms with a nonreligious assembly or institution." 42 U.S.C. § 2000cc(b)(1) ... The "substantial burden" provision under which this suit was brought must thus mean something different from "greater burden than imposed on secular institutions."

But if this provision is interpreted to place religious institutions in *too* favorable a position in relation to other land users, there is a danger that it will run afoul of the clause of the First Amendment that forbids Congress (and, by interpretation of the Fourteenth Amendment, state and local governments as well) to establish a church. Westchester Day School v. Village of Mamaroneck, 386 F.3d 183, 189–90 (2d Cir. 2004). But that is not argued; and if it were argued a counterargument would be the vulnerability of religious institutions—especially those that are not affiliated with the mainstream Protestant sects or the Roman Catholic Church—to subtle forms of discrimination when, as in the case of the grant or denial of zoning variances, a state delegates essentially standardless discretion to nonprofessionals operating without procedural safeguards.

[So construed,] the "substantial burden" provision backstops the explicit prohibition of religious discrimination in the later section of the Act, much as the disparate-impact theory of employment discrimination backstops the prohibition of intentional discrimination. ... If a land-use decision, in this case the denial of a zoning variance, imposes a substantial burden on religious exercise (the statute defines "religious exercise" to include the "use, building, or conversion of real property for the purpose of religious exercise," 42 U.S.C. § 2000cc–5(7)(B)), and the decision maker cannot justify it, the inference arises that hostility to religion, or more likely to a particular sect, influenced the decision.

The burden here was substantial. The Church could have searched around for other parcels of land (though a lot more effort would have been involved in such a search than, as the City would have it, calling up some real estate agents), or it could have continued filing applications with the City, but in either case there would have been delay, uncertainty, and expense. That the burden would not be insuperable would not make it insubstantial....

So the City was not entitled to summary judgment. Ordinarily the sequel to our ruling would be a trial. But as we said earlier, the facts are not in dispute. The only possible uncertainty is legal; and we acknowledge the possibility that some subtlety of the Wisconsin law of property has eluded us and that there is some danger after all that the 14–acre parcel may somehow end up with a school or hospital on it rather than a church. But since the Church is perfectly willing to bind itself by whatever means are necessary not to sell the land for a nonreligious institutional use, and the City has expressed no other concern about the use of the land, the only question is whether the Church's proposal may contain some loophole that might permit (though doubtless with low probability) the eventual putting of the property to a nonreligious institutional use. The closing of the loophole, if there is a loophole, does not require a trial in the district court or a further administrative proceeding of uncertain duration and, given the whiff of bad faith arising from the Planning Commission's rejection of a solution that would have eliminated the City's only legitimate concern, an uncertain outcome as well. All that is required is that we reverse, and instruct the district court to grant the relief requested by the plaintiffs but to stay its order for 90 days to give the City a chance to negotiate with the Church such arrangements as may be necessary to eliminate any possibility that the land might be put to a nonreligious institutional use without the City's consent. For example, if the City wants to substitute the mayor's second suggested alternative—the PUD ordinance overlaid on residential rather than institutional zoning—we assume that the Church would have no objection, at least no reasonable one, provided this is done promptly. Another alternative might be to make the institutional zoning with PUD overlay (the Church's proposal) conditional on the construction of a church on the property. We are sure that with the district judge's help the parties can work out a deal that will lift a substantial burden from the Church's shoulders without impairing any legitimate interest of the City.

Reversed and remanded, with directions.

NOTE

The Scope of RLUIPA. The portion of the RLUIPA that limits governmental actions pertaining to religious land uses is 42 U.S.C. § 2000cc:

Protection of Land Use as Religious Exercise

(a) Substantial burdens.

(1) General rule. No government shall impose or implement a land use regulation in a manner that imposes a substantial burden on the religious exercise of a person, including a religious assembly or institution, unless the government demonstrates that imposition of the burden on that person, assembly, or institution

(A) is in furtherance of a compelling governmental interest; and

(B) is the least restrictive means of furthering that compelling governmental interest.

(2) Scope of application. This subsection applies in any case in which—

(A) the substantial burden is imposed in a program or activity that receives Federal financial assistance, even if the burden results from a rule of general applicability;

(B) the substantial burden affects, or removal of that substantial burden would affect, commerce with foreign nations, among the several States, or with Indian tribes, even if the burden results from a rule of general applicability; or

(C) the substantial burden is imposed in the implementation of a land use regulation or system of land use regulations, under which a government makes, or has in place formal or informal procedures or practices that permit the government to make, individualized assessments of the proposed uses for the property involved.

(b) Discrimination and exclusion.

(1) Equal terms. No government shall impose or implement a land use regulation in a manner that treats a religious assembly or institution on less than equal terms with a nonreligious assembly or institution.

(2) Nondiscrimination. No government shall impose or implement a land use regulation that discriminates against any assembly or institution on the basis of religion or religious denomination.

(3) Exclusions and limits. No government shall impose or implement a land use regulation that—

(A) totally excludes religious assemblies from a jurisdiction; or

(B) unreasonably limits religious assemblies, institutions, or structures within a jurisdiction.

Note that there are two different types of claims that religious land users may make to thwart the application of zoning or other laws to their land uses. The usual claim is one made under 42 U.S.C. § 2000cc(a)—that some governmental action imposes a substantial burden on religious exercise and lacks the compelling justification required by § 2000cc(a). Although a substantial burden claim can be made with respect to government action that is part of a federally funded program or that has a substantial effect on interstate, foreign, or Indian commerce, challenges to zoning laws are rooted in § 2000cc(a)(2)(C)—the individualized application of zoning laws, such as variances and the like. The reason for the "individualized application" limit is that existing constitutional law presumes that individualized government decisions that substantially burden religious exercise are void but presumes that generally applicable rules that substantially burden religious exercise are valid. Compare Sherbert v. Verner, 374 U.S. 398 (1963) with Employment Division v. Smith, 494 U.S. 872 (1990).

The other type of claim is one of discrimination, but discrimination may take one of three forms: 1) unfavorable governmental treatment of the religious land user because of its religion; 2) governmental exclusion or unreasonable limitation of religious land use, or 3) treating religious land users unequally—failure to deal with religious land users on "equal terms."

RIVER OF LIFE KINGDOM MINISTRIES v. VILLAGE OF HAZEL CREST

United States Court of Appeals for the Seventh Circuit
611 F.3d 367 (7th Cir. 2010)

POSNER, CIRCUIT JUDGE.

The court granted rehearing en banc to consider the proper standard for applying the equal-terms provision of the Religious Land Use and Institutionalized Persons Act, 42 U.S.C. § 2000cc. That provision states that "no government shall impose or implement a land use regulation in a manner that treats a religious assembly or institution on less than equal terms with a nonreligious assembly or institution." § 2000cc(b)(1).

The appellant, River of Life, is a small church (it has 67 members, only about half of whom attend services on an average Sunday) that at present operates out of rented space in a cramped, dirty warehouse in Chicago Heights, a town 27 miles south of downtown Chicago. It wanted to relocate to a building in the Village of Hazel Crest, a town of some 15,000 people located two miles north and slightly west of Chicago Heights. The building, however, is in a part of the town designated by the town's zoning ordinance as a commercial district. The district is in the town's oldest part, which is run down; indeed the entire town has been in economic decline for years. The area designated as a commercial district is close to the train station, and the presence of commuters might enable the district to be revitalized as a commercial center. The zoning ordinance has therefore been amended to exclude new noncommercial uses from the district, including not only churches but also community centers, schools, and art galleries. River of Life sued the Village under the equal-terms provision and moved for a preliminary injunction against the enforcement of the zoning ordinance. The district judge denied the motion and a panel of this court affirmed, mainly on the ground that the church was unlikely to prevail when the case was fully litigated. 585 F.3d 364 (7th Cir. 2009). The existence of an inter-circuit conflict with respect to the proper test for applying the equal-terms provision, combined with uncertainty about the consistency of our decisions, persuaded the full court to hear the case in order to decide on a test.

Two of our sister courts of appeals have proposed tests. The Third Circuit in Lighthouse Institute for Evangelism, Inc. v. City of Long Branch, 510 F.3d 253, 266 (3d Cir. 2007), ruled that "a regulation will violate the Equal Terms provision only if it treats religious assemblies or institutions less well than secular assemblies or institutions that are similarly situated *as to the regulatory purpose*" (emphasis in original). The court must identify first the goals of the challenged zoning ordinance and second the secular assemblies (meeting places) that are comparable to the plaintiff's religious assembly in the sense of having roughly the same relation to those goals. If the reasons for excluding some category of secular assembly—whether traditional reasons such as effect on traffic or novel ones such as creating a "Street of Fun"—are applicable to a religious assembly, the ordinance is deemed neutral and therefore not in violation of the equal-terms provision. But if a secular assembly is allowed and the religious assembly banned even though the two assemblies don't differ in any way material to the regulatory purpose behind the ordinance, then neutrality has been violated and equality denied. That was the situation in the *Lighthouse* case. The zoning ordinance permitted meeting halls in the district in which the church wanted to locate and there was no way to distinguish between meeting halls and churches on the basis of the purpose of the ordinance. The Third Circuit therefore ordered summary judgment in favor of the church with respect to its challenge to the ordinance....

An alternative test was adopted by the Eleventh Circuit in Midrash Sephardi, Inc. v. Town of Surfside, 366 F.3d 1214, 1230–31 (11th Cir. 2004), and followed in Prima Iglesia Bautista Hispana of Boca Raton, Inc. v. Broward County, 450 F.3d 1295, 1308–10 (11th Cir. 2006), and Konikov v. Orange County, 410 F.3d 1317, 1324–29 (11th Cir. 2005) (per curiam). The Eleventh Circuit reads the language of the equal-terms provision literally: a zoning ordinance that permits *any* "assembly," as defined by dictionaries, to locate in a district must permit a church to locate there as well even if the only secular assemblies permitted are hospital operating theaters, bus terminals, air raid shelters, restaurants that have private dining rooms in which a book club or professional association might meet, and sports stadiums. In *Midrash* the court held that where private clubs are allowed, so must churches be....

Neither the Third Circuit's nor the Eleventh Circuit's approach, though in application they might yield similar or even identical results—and results moreover that would strike most judges as proper—is entirely satisfactory. We are troubled by the Eleventh Circuit's rule that mere "differential treatment" between a church and some other "company of persons collected together in one place ... usually for some common purpose" (the court's preferred dictionary definition of "assembly") violates the equal-terms provision. ... "Assembly" so understood would include most secular land uses—factories, nightclubs, zoos, parks, malls, soup kitchens, and bowling alleys, to name but a few (visitors to each of these institutions have a "common purpose" in visiting)—even though most of them have different effects on the municipality and its residents from a church; consider just the difference in municipal services required by different land uses, including differences in the amount of police protection. The land use that led the Eleventh Circuit in *Midrash* to find a violation of the equal-terms provision was, however, a private club, and it is not obvious that it has different effects on a municipality or its residents from those of a church. Thus our quarrel is not with the result in *Midrash* but with the Eleventh Circuit's test.

A subtler objection to the test is that it may be too friendly to religious land uses, unduly limiting municipal regulation and maybe even violating the First Amendment's prohibition against establishment of religion by discriminating in favor of religious land uses. ... The Supreme Court had held in Employment Division v. Smith, 494 U.S. 872, 878–80 (1990), that the clause of the First Amendment that guarantees the free exercise of religion does not excuse churches from having to comply with nondiscriminatory regulations, such as the prohibition of drugs believed to be dangerous, even if the regulation interferes with church rituals or observances: "we have never held that an individual's religious beliefs excuse him from compliance with an otherwise valid law prohibiting conduct that the State is free to regulate." If they were excused, this might be deemed favoritism to religion and thus violate the establishment clause.

Suppose a zoning ordinance forbids all assemblies except gymnasiums. Then because a gymnasium is an assembly as defined by the Eleventh Circuit, a church could locate in the district but a secular humanist reading room could not, unless secular humanist organizations (such as American Atheists, the American Humanist Association, the Freedom From Religion Foundation, the Godless Americans Political Action Committee, Internet Infidels, and the Skeptics Society—these are all real organizations) were defined as religions. (Nor could the local chapter of the Cat Fanciers' Association, which might have 67 dues-paying local members, only about half of whom show up on average at the chapter's meetings.) It was to avoid making its test overprotect religious assembles in comparison to their closest secular counterparts that the Eleventh Circuit added its "strict scrutiny" gloss—municipalities can bar religious land uses from particular zones if the regulation satisfies the "strict scrutiny" test for regulations that treat religious and secular activities differently.[10] There is no textual basis for the gloss, and religious discrimination is expressly prohibited elsewhere in the statute. The gloss was needed only to solve a problem of the court's own creation.

A further objection to the Eleventh Circuit's test is that "equality," except when used of mathematical or scientific relations, signifies not equivalence or identity but proper relation to relevant concerns. It would not promote equality to require that all men wear shirts that have 15-inch collars, or that the number of churches in a state equal the number of casinos, or that all workers should have the same wages. But it does promote equality to require equal pay for equal work, even though workers differ in a variety of respects, such as race and sex. If a church and a community center, though different in many respects, do not differ with respect to any accepted zoning criterion, then an ordinance that allows one and forbids the other denies equality and violates the equal-terms provision.

This understanding of the equal-terms provision is imperfectly realized by the Third Circuit's test as well. That test centers on identifying the zoning authorities' "regulatory purpose" in adopting an ordinance that excludes a church. Our concern is not that the equal-terms provision as drafted by Congress omits the term "regulatory purpose" or some cognate term. As we explained, "equality" is a complex concept. The fact that two land uses share a dictionary definition doesn't make them "equal" within the meaning of a statute. But the use of "regulatory purpose" as a guide to interpretation invites speculation concerning the reason behind exclusion of churches; invites self-serving testimony by zoning officials and hired expert witnesses; facilitates zoning classifications thinly disguised as neutral but actually systematically unfavorable to churches (as by favoring public reading rooms over other forms of non-profit assembly); and makes the meaning of "equal terms" in a federal statute depend on the intentions of local government officials....

The problems that we have identified with the Third Circuit's test can be solved by a shift of focus from regulatory *purpose* to accepted zoning *criteria*. The shift is not merely semantic. "Purpose" is subjective and manipulable, so asking about "regulatory purpose" might result in giving local officials a free hand in answering the question "equal with respect to what?" "Regulatory criteria" are objective—and it is federal judges who will apply the criteria to resolve the issue.

So let us consider those criteria, noting by way of background that originally zoning was "cumulative" [but cumulative] zoning soon gave way to noncumulative (or "exclusive") zoning, in which specified land uses were confined to specified districts and thus could be and often were separated. ... [As] Patricia E. Salkin, American Law of Zoning § 9:15 (5th ed. 2010), explains with specific reference to commercial districts:

---

10. [Ed.] Strict scrutiny requires the government to prove that its action is necessary to accomplish a compelling government objective—e.g., avoiding an unconstitutional establishment of religion.

"All commercial uses are not created equal. Some require pedestrian traffic; others create hazards for pedestrian traffic. Some commercial uses cause pedestrian traffic during the daylight hours; others operate at night and are quiet in the daytime. The list of characteristics could be extended, but this small sample suggests that residential uses in commercial neighborhoods will injure, as well as be injured by, the adjacent commercial uses. And it suggests further that some commercial uses will be incompatible with others.... The most common drafting answer to the problems sketched above is the 'exclusive' zoning ordinance.... Districts are established for named uses, or groups of uses, and all others are excluded. The chief virtue of such ordinances is that they create districts for commerce and industry, and exclude from such districts residential and other uses which are capable of interfering with the planned use of land." ...

Exclusion of churches from a commercial zone (though generally not from every commercial zone in the municipality), along with other noncommercial assemblies, such as exhibition halls, clubs, and homeless shelters, is thus not unique to the Village of Hazel Crest....

A reader might worry that "commercial" is a synonym for "secular." It is not. There are many secular noncommercial land uses, and if the Village of Hazel Crest were concerned for example about the sufficiency of parking space in some part of the village, the commercial or noncommercial character of land uses that generated similar vehicular traffic flows would be irrelevant. Suppose maintenance of regular (as opposed to sporadic and concentrated) vehicular traffic were the zoning objective. From that standpoint, a church is more like a movie theater, which also generates groups of people coming and going at the same time, than like a public library, which generates a smoother flow of traffic throughout the day. The equal-terms provision would therefore require the zoning authorities to allow the church in the zone with the movie theater because the church was more like the for-profit use (the movie theater) than the not-for-profit use (the public library).

Parking space and traffic control are not the only concerns of land-use regulation. Another is generating municipal revenue and providing ample and convenient shopping for residents, and can be promoted by setting aside some land for commercial uses only, which generate tax revenues. Hazel Crest has therefore created a commercial district that excludes churches *along with* community centers, meeting halls, and libraries because these secular assemblies, like churches, do not generate significant taxable revenue or offer shopping opportunities. See Robert C. Ellickson & Vicki L. Been, Land Use Controls: Cases and Materials 90–91 (3d ed. 2005). Similar assemblies are being treated the same. The permitted land use that is most like the plaintiff's is a commercial gymnasium, and that's not close enough because a commercial assembly belongs in an all-commercial district and a noncommercial assembly, secular or religious, does not.

Of course we can't be certain, or even confident, that a particular zoning decision was actually motivated by a land-use concern that is neutral from the standpoint of religion. But if religious and secular land uses that are treated the same (such as the noncommercial religious and secular land uses in the zoning district that River of Life wants to have its church in) from the standpoint of an accepted zoning criterion, such as "commercial district," or "residential district," or "industrial district," that is enough to rebut an equal-terms claim and thus, in this case, to show that River of Life is unlikely to prevail in a full litigation....

Indeed, this case is straightforward because ... Hazel Crest really was applying conventional criteria for commercial zoning in banning noncommercial land uses from a part of the village suitable for a commercial district because of proximity to the train station. ... But should a municipality create what purports to be a pure commercial district and then allow other uses, a church would have an easy victory if the municipality kept it out.

If the test we are adopting seems less than airtight, bear in mind that the equal-terms provision is not the only or even the most important protection against religious discrimination by zoning authorities. (Think of the religious clauses of the First Amendment.) It is not even the only protection in the Religious Land Use and Institutionalized Persons Act. For the Act provides that a land-use regulation "that imposes a substantial burden on the religious exercise of a ... religious assembly or institution" is unlawful "unless the government demonstrates that imposition of the burden ... is in furtherance of a compelling governmental interest; and is the least restrictive means of furthering that compelling governmental interest." 42 U.S.C. § 2000cc(a)(1). And it further provides that "no government shall impose or implement a land use regulation in a manner that discriminates against any assembly or institution on the basis of religion or religious denomination," § 2000cc(b)(2), or that totally excludes religious assemblies from a jurisdiction. § 2000cc(b)(3)(A). But as none of these other provisions is before us on this appeal, the appeal must fail. [Affirmed.]

NOTES

1. *State Laws.* A number of states have enacted statutes that invalidate any government action that substantially burdens any person's religious exercise unless the government can prove that the burden is necessary to accomplish a compelling government objective. These state "Religious Freedom Restoration Acts," or RFRAs, as they are commonly known, have broader application than the RLUIPA. Moreover, some states have interpreted their state constitutions to impose the same standard, even in the absence of a state RFRA. Thus, state RFRAs and state constitutions may impose stricter limits on zoning's control of religious land uses.

2. *Environmental Laws.* At least 17 states have adopted environmental planning statutes that, under some circumstances, require an assessment of

the environmental impact of governmental action before the action may be taken. These statutes may apply to changes in zoning laws. An example is Fisher v. Giuliani, 720 N.Y.S.2d 50 (App. Div. 2001). New York City amended its zoning laws governing the Theater District to permit transfer of the air rights from operating theaters to nearby properties, thus permitting the transferee to develop their property more intensively than would otherwise be allowed. New York City conducted an environmental assessment of the change, as required by New York law, for transfers as of right, but did no assessment of the impact of future discretionary transfers. The New York intermediate appeals court concluded that the failure to do so invalidated the discretionary transfer portion of the amended zoning law.

CHAPTER TWELVE

EMINENT DOMAIN AND THE PROBLEM OF REGULATORY TAKINGS

■ ■ ■

Eminent domain is the power of governments to take private property for public use. When a government decides to widen a public street it will likely be necessary to seize strips of privately owned land on either side of the highway to accomplish the job. This forced transfer of ownership is the exercise of eminent domain. But eminent domain is not absolute. The Fifth Amendment to the United States Constitution concludes its prohibitions of government conduct by stating: "nor shall private property be taken for public use without just compensation." The takings, or just compensation, clause is applicable to all governments in the United States, state and federal. See Chicago, Burlington & Quincy Railway v. Chicago, 166 U.S. 226 (1897).

There are two limits imbedded in the clause. Private property may only be taken for public use. It may not be used to force a transfer of property from *A* to *B* for the sole private benefit of *B*. But the meaning of "public use" is expansive. As you will see, the term public use has come to mean public benefit, and what is of public benefit is debatable. Even if private property is taken for public use, just compensation must be provided. This ensures that when governments take private property for public benefit the public pays for it, rather than foisting the cost of the benefit entirely on the individual whose property has been condemned.

Most takings are straightforward. If the government wants to widen a public road, it will declare its intentions, identify the property it needs, condemn that property, and then pay for it. The transfer is forced—so long as the taking is for a public use the landowner can do nothing to resist—but the issue of the amount of compensation can become a contested matter. If the government and the owner cannot agree on a fair price, the matter of just compensation will be resolved by the judicial system.

This chapter focuses on the problem of when regulations of property—which the government says are not takings of property—are in fact takings. As you have seen so far, property is subject to lots of regulations. The difficult question is to determine when any particular regulation is so invasive of the bundle of rights that constitutes property that it amounts to a *de facto* taking of that property.

The takings clause applies to all kinds of property, whether tangible or intangible, and applies to executive or legislative actions. See, e.g., Ruckelshaus v. Monsanto Co., 467 U.S. 986 (1984), in which the forced disclosure of proprietary trade secrets was held to be a taking. Whether judicial decisions can constitute a taking remains a matter of some controversy, and will be addressed on Section D of this chapter. Before we reach that topic, however, we will examine the public use requirement (Section A), the vexed question of when a regulation is a taking (Section B), and the problem of conditional regulatory takings (Section C).

A.   PUBLIC USE

HAWAII HOUSING AUTHORITY v. MIDKIFF

Supreme Court of the United States
467 U.S. 229 (1984)

JUSTICE O'CONNOR delivered the opinion of the Court.

The [takings clause of the] Fifth Amendment [provides] that "private property [shall not] be taken for public use, without just compensation." [Does] the Public Use [Clause], made applicable to the States through the Fourteenth Amendment, prohibit[] the State of Hawaii from taking, with just compensation, title in real property from lessors and transferring it to lessees in order to reduce the concentration of ownership of fees simple in the State[?] We conclude that it does not.

Issue

[The] Hawaii Legislature discovered that, while the State and Federal Governments owned almost 49% of the State's land, another 47% was in the hands of only 72 private landowners. [Eighteen] landholders, with tracts of 21,000 acres or more, owned more than 40% of this land. [On] Oahu, the most urbanized of the islands, 22 landowners owned 72.5% of the fee simple titles. The legislature concluded that concentrated land ownership was responsible for skewing the State's residential fee simple market, inflating land prices, and injuring the public tranquility and welfare. To redress these problems, the legislature decided to compel the large landowners to break up their estates [and] enacted the Land Reform Act of 1967 (Act), which created a mechanism for condemning residential tracts and for transferring ownership of the condemned fees simple to existing lessees. [Under] the Act's condemnation scheme, tenants living on single-family residential lots within developmental tracts at least five acres in size are entitled to ask the Hawaii Housing Authority (HHA) to condemn the property on which they live. When [a minimum number of tenants have so asked, and the HHA has determined that the] public purposes [of the Act] will be served, it is authorized to [acquire,] at prices set either by condemnation trial or by negotiation between lessors and lessees, the former fee owners' full "right, title, and interest" in the land. After compensation has been set, HHA may sell the land titles to tenants who have applied for fee simple ownership. [In] practice, funds to satisfy the condemnation awards have been supplied entirely by lessees.

[Midkiff] filed suit [in federal district court,] asking that the Act be declared unconstitutional and that its enforcement be enjoined. The District Court [upheld the Act]. The Court of Appeals for the Ninth Circuit reversed, [finding that the taking effected by the Act was not for "public use" but] was simply "a naked attempt on the part of the state of Hawaii to take the private property of A and transfer it to B solely for B's private use and benefit." . . .

The starting point [of] analysis [is] Berman v. Parker, 348 U.S. 26 (1954). In *Berman*, the Court held constitutional the District of Columbia Redevelopment Act of 1945. That Act provided both for the comprehensive use of the eminent domain power to redevelop slum areas and for the possible sale or lease of the condemned lands to private interests. In discussing whether the takings authorized by that Act were for a "public use," the Court stated:

> We deal [with] what traditionally has been known as the police power. [Subject] to specific constitutional limitations, when the legislature has spoken, the public interest has been declared in terms well-nigh conclusive. In such cases the legislature, not the judiciary, is the main guardian of the public needs to be served by social legislation. [This] principle admits of no exception merely because the power of eminent domain is involved. [The] power of eminent domain is merely the means to the end. [Once] the object is within the authority of Congress, the means by which it will be attained is also for Congress to determine. Here one of the means chosen is the use of private enterprise for redevelopment of the area. Appellants argue that this makes the project a taking from one businessman for the benefit of another businessman. But the means of executing the project are for Congress and Congress alone to determine, once the public purpose has been established.

The "public use" requirement is thus coterminous with the scope of a sovereign's police powers. [While there is] a role for courts to pay in reviewing a legislature's judgment of what constitutes a public use, [the] Court in *Berman* made clear that it is "an extremely narrow" one. [In] short, the Court has made clear that it will not substitute its judgment for a legislature's judgment as to what constitutes a public use, "unless the use be palpably without reasonable foundation."

To be sure, the Court's cases have repeatedly stated that "one person's property may not be taken for the benefit of another private person without a justifying public purpose, even though compensation be paid." [But] where the exercise of the eminent domain power is rationally related to a conceivable public purpose, the Court has never held a compensated taking to be proscribed by the Public Use Clause.

[We] have no trouble concluding that the Hawaii Act is constitutional. The people of Hawaii have attempted [to] reduce the perceived social and economic evils of a land oligopoly [that has] created artificial deterrents to the normal functioning of the State's residential land market and forced thousands of individual homeowners to lease, rather than buy, the land underneath their homes. Regulating oligopoly and the evils associated with it is a classic exercise of a State's police powers. We cannot disapprove of Hawaii's exercise of this power.

Nor can we condemn as irrational the Act's approach to correcting the land oligopoly problem. The Act presumes that when a sufficiently large number of persons declare that they are willing but unable to buy lots at fair prices the land market is malfunctioning. When such a malfunction is signalled, the Act authorizes HHA to condemn lots in the relevant tract. The Act limits the number of lots any one tenant can purchase and authorizes HHA to use public funds to ensure that the market dilution goals will be achieved. This is a comprehensive and rational approach to identifying and correcting market failure.

NOTE AND QUESTIONS

What's a Public Use? The Court declared that "[t]he 'public use' requirement [is] coterminous with the scope of a sovereign's police powers." The police power, when exercised by a state, is the state's inherent power to act for the health, safety, or general welfare of the people, bounded only by the state's constitution and federal constitutional or statutory law. The federal government's "police power," by contrast, is the sum of the federal government's enumerated powers, bounded by the constitutional limits on the exercise of those powers. Thus the police power "mark[s] the line between *noncompensable* regulation and compensable takings of property. [Legitimately] exercised, the police power requires no compensation." Thomas Merrill, The Economics of Public Use, 72 Cornell L. Rev. 61, 70 (1986). But does this dispose of the problem? Granted that the police power ends at the point that compensation is required; the question is whether a taking is for public use. Because the action taken by Hawaii in *Midkiff* was seen by the Court to be within Hawaii's police power (even though compensation was required and provided), does the police power have a dual quality—it is more confined when regulations effect an *uncompensated* taking than it is when the issue is whether a *compensated* taking is for public use? Or, was the Court simply confused when it equated public use with the police power?

There are alternatives to the Court's conception of public use. One suggestion is that the general public must actually *use* the taken property. Would this enable governments to compel the transfer of someone's home to McDonald's for conversion to a fast-food outlet on the ground that the general public is invited to use the facility? Cf. Jed Rubenfeld, Usings, 102 Yale L. J. 1077 (1993), arguing that the public use requirement should serve to define the point at which compensation is due: "[W]hen government conscripts someone's property for state use, then it must pay."

Professor Richard Epstein, *Takings: Private Property and the Power of Eminent Domain* 166–169 (1985), argues that the public use requirement is not satisfied unless the government devotes the taken property to the provision of what an economist would call "public goods." A pure "public good" is something from which nobody can be excluded from consuming and that remains available for consumption by anyone no matter how many people consume its benefits. National defense is a classic example. Epstein recognizes that there are very few pure public goods, and thus concedes that the public use requirement should be met so long as the property is devoted to attaining public benefits that are akin to pure public goods. Would Epstein's formula permit the government to condemn an entire neighborhood to be razed and devoted it to a General Motors factory that builds tanks for sale to the U.S. armed forces?

KELO v. CITY OF NEW LONDON

Supreme Court of the United States
545 U.S. 469 (2005)

JUSTICE STEVENS delivered the opinion of the Court.

In 2000, the city of New London approved a development plan that . . . was "projected to create in excess of 1,000 jobs, to increase tax and other revenues, and to revitalize an economically distressed city, including its downtown and waterfront areas." [The city] has purchased property from willing sellers and proposes to use the power of eminent domain to acquire the remainder of the property from unwilling owners in exchange for just compensation. The question presented is whether the city's proposed disposition of this property qualifies as a "public use" within the meaning of the Takings Clause of the Fifth Amendment to the Constitution.

Issue

[After Pfizer, a major pharmaceutical manufacturer, decided to build a large research facility adjacent to New London, Connecticut's Fort Trumbull area, a 90–acre peninsula jutting into the Thames River consisting of some 115 privately owned properties and a 32–acre state park, the city concluded that the Fort Trumbull area was ideally suited for redevelopment to improve the depressed economic conditions of the city. New London decided that Fort Trumbull should be converted into mixed uses, including a "waterfront conference hotel at the center of a 'small urban village' that will include restaurants and shopping," a pedestrian "riverwalk," recreational and commercial marinas, "approximately 80 new residences organized into an urban neighborhood," a parcel to "contain at least 90,000 square feet" of privately owned and occupied "research and development office space," a site reserved for future use "to support the adjacent state park, by providing parking or retail services for visitors, or to support the nearby marina," and other sites for privately owned "office and retail space, parking, and water-dependent commercial uses."] In addition to creating jobs, generating tax revenue, and helping to "build momentum for the revitalization of downtown New London," the plan was also designed to make the City more attractive and to create leisure and recreational opportunities on the waterfront and in the park. [Residents and property owners contended that condemnation to implement this plan was not for a public use. The Connecticut Supreme Court upheld the plan, and the Supreme Court affirmed.]

Two polar propositions are perfectly clear. On the one hand, it has long been accepted that the sovereign may not take the property of *A* for the sole purpose of transferring it to another private party *B*, even though *A* is paid just compensation. On the other hand, it is equally clear that a State may transfer property from one private party to another if future "use by the public" is the purpose of the taking; the condemnation of land for a railroad with common-carrier duties is a familiar example. Neither of these propositions, however, determines the disposition of this case.

[The] City would no doubt be forbidden from taking petitioners' land for the purpose of conferring a private benefit on a particular private party. Nor would the City be allowed to take property under the mere pretext of a public purpose, when its actual purpose was to bestow a private benefit. [These] takings [show] no evidence of an illegitimate purpose.... [The] City's development plan was not adopted "to benefit a particular class of identifiable individuals."

On the other hand, this is not a case in which the City is planning to open the condemned land—at least not in its entirety—to use by the general public. Nor will the private lessees of the land in any sense be required to operate like common carriers, making their services available to all comers. But ... this "Court long ago rejected any literal requirement that condemned property be put into use for the general public." [*Midkiff.*] [We have] eschewed rigid formulas and intrusive scrutiny in favor of affording legislatures broad latitude in determining what public needs justify the use of the takings power. [*Berman, Midkiff.*]

[The City's] determination that the area was sufficiently distressed to justify a program of economic rejuvenation is entitled to our deference. The City has carefully formulated an economic development plan that it believes will provide appreciable benefits to the community, including— but by no means limited to—new jobs and increased tax revenue. As with other exercises in urban planning and development, the City is endeavoring to coordinate a variety of commercial, residential, and recreational uses of land, with the hope that they will form a whole greater than the sum of its parts.... Given the comprehensive character of the plan, the thorough deliberation that preceded its adoption, and the limited scope of our review, it is appropriate ... to resolve the challenges of the individual owners, not on a piecemeal basis, but rather in light of the entire plan. [That] plan unquestionably serves a public purpose....

To avoid this result, petitioners urge us to adopt a new bright-line rule that economic development does not qualify as a public use. ... Promoting economic development is a traditional and long accepted function of government. There is, moreover, no principled way of distinguishing economic development from the other public purposes that we have recognized. In our cases upholding takings that facilitated agriculture and mining, for example, we emphasized the importance of those industries to the welfare of the States in question; in *Berman,* we endorsed the purpose of transforming a blighted area into a "well-balanced" community through redevelopment; [and] in *Midkiff,* we upheld the interest in breaking up a land oligopoly that "created artificial deterrents to the normal functioning of the State's residential land market...."

[P]etitioners maintain that for takings of this kind we should require a "reasonable certainty" that the expected public benefits will actually accrue. ... "When the legislature's purpose is legitimate and its means are not irrational, our cases make clear that empirical debates over the wisdom of takings ... are not to be carried out in the federal courts." *Midkiff.* ... A constitutional rule that required postponement of the judicial approval of every condemnation until the likelihood of success of the plan had been assured would unquestionably impose a significant impediment to the successful consummation of many [comprehensive redevelopment] plans....

We emphasize that nothing in our opinion precludes any State from placing further restrictions on its exercise of the takings power. [While] the necessity and wisdom of using eminent domain to promote economic development are certainly matters of legitimate public debate, [this] Court's authority ... extends only to determining whether the City's proposed condemnations are for a "public use"....

JUSTICE KENNEDY, concurring.

... [T]ransfers intended to confer benefits on particular, favored private entities, and with only incidental or pretextual public benefits, are forbidden by the Public Use Clause. A court applying rational-basis review under the Public Use Clause should strike down a taking that, by a clear showing, is intended to favor a particular private party, with only incidental or pretextual public benefits.... A court confronted with a plausible accusation of impermissible favoritism to private parties should ... review the record to see if it has merit, though with the presumption that the government's actions were reasonable and intended to serve a public purpose. Here, the trial court conducted a careful and extensive inquiry [and] concluded that "there is nothing in the record to indicate that ... [respondents] were motivated by a desire to aid [other] particular private entities." ... This taking occurred in the context of a comprehensive development plan meant to address a serious city-wide depression, and the projected economic benefits of the project cannot be characterized as *de minimus.* The identity of most of the private beneficiaries were unknown at the time the city formulated its plans. The city complied with elaborate procedural requirements that facilitate review of the record and inquiry into the city's purposes. In sum, while there may be categories of cases in which the transfers are so suspicious, or the procedures employed so prone to abuse, or the purported benefits are so trivial or implausible, that courts should presume an impermissible private purpose, no such circumstances are present in this case.

JUSTICE O'CONNOR, joined by CHIEF JUSTICE REHNQUIST and JUSTICES SCALIA and THOMAS, dissenting.

Over two centuries ago, just after the Bill of Rights was ratified, Justice Chase wrote:

> An act of the Legislature (for I cannot call it a law) contrary to the great first principles of the social compact, cannot be considered a rightful exercise of legislative authority.... A few instances will suffice to explain what I mean.... [A] law that takes property from A and gives it to B: It is against all reason and justice, for a people to entrust a Legislature with such powers; and, therefore, it cannot be presumed that they have done it."

Calder v. Bull, 3 Dall. [3 U.S.] 386, 388 (1798) (emphasis deleted).

Today the Court abandons this long-held, basic limitation on government power. Under the banner of economic development, all private property is now vulnerable to being taken and transferred to another private owner, so long as it might be upgraded—i.e., given to an owner who will use it in a way that the legislature deems more beneficial to the public—in the process. To reason, as the Court does, that the incidental public benefits resulting from the subsequent ordinary use of private property render economic development takings "for public use" is to wash out any distinction between private and public use of property—and thereby effectively to delete the words "for public use" from the Takings Clause of the Fifth Amendment.... *goes against words of 5th amend*

The public use requirement [means that] Government may compel an individual to forfeit her property for the *public's* use, but not for the benefit of another private person. This requirement promotes fairness as well as security. [While we] give considerable deference to legislatures' determinations about what governmental activities will advantage the public[,] were the political branches the sole arbiters of the public-private distinction, the Public Use Clause would amount to little more than hortatory fluff....

Our cases have generally identified three categories of takings that comply with the public use requirement, though it is in the nature of things that the boundaries between these categories are not always firm.... First, the sovereign may transfer private property to public ownership—such as for a road, a hospital, or a military base. Second, the sovereign may transfer private property to private parties, often common carriers, who make the property available for the public's use—such as with a railroad, a public utility, or a stadium. [Third,] in certain circumstances and to meet certain exigencies, takings that serve a public purpose also satisfy the Constitution even if the property is destined for subsequent private use. [*Berman, Midkiff.*]

This case ... presents an issue of first impression: Are economic development takings constitutional? I would hold that they are not. We are guided by two precedents about the taking of real property by eminent

Contradicting a prob in midkiff

domain. ... In both [*Berman* and *Midkiff*], the ... precondemnation use of the targeted property inflicted affirmative harm on society—in *Berman* through blight resulting from extreme poverty and in *Midkiff* through oligopoly.... [A] public purpose was realized when the harmful use was eliminated. Because each taking *directly* achieved a public benefit, it did not matter that the property was turned over to private use. Here, in contrast, New London does not claim that Susette Kelo's and Wilhelmina Dery's well-maintained homes are the source of any social harm. Indeed, it could not so claim without adopting the absurd argument that any single-family home that might be razed to make way for an apartment building, or any church that might be replaced with a retail store, or any small business that might be more lucrative if it were instead part of a national franchise, is inherently harmful to society and thus within the government's power to condemn.

[The] Court today ... holds that the sovereign may take private property currently put to ordinary private use, and give it over for new, ordinary private use, so long as the new use is predicted to generate some secondary benefit for the public—such as increased tax revenue, more jobs, maybe even aesthetic pleasure. But nearly any lawful use of real private property can be said to generate some incidental benefit to the public. Thus, ... the words "for public use" do not realistically exclude *any* takings, and thus do not exert any constraint on the eminent domain power.

[While] we said in *Midkiff* that "the 'public use' requirement is coterminous with the scope of a sovereign's police powers," [this] case ... demonstrates why ... the police power and "public use" cannot always be equated.... The trouble with economic development takings is that private benefit and incidental public benefit are, by definition, merged and mutually reinforcing. In this case ... any boon for Pfizer or the plan's developer is difficult to disaggregate from the promised public gains in taxes and jobs. ... If it is true that incidental public benefits from new private use are enough to ensure the "public purpose" in a taking, why should it matter ... what inspired the taking in the first place? How much the government does or does not desire to benefit a favored private party has no bearing on whether an economic development taking will or will not generate secondary benefit for the public. [The] effect is the same ...—private property is forcibly relinquished to new private owner-ship.... The specter of condemnation hangs over all property. Nothing is to prevent the State from replacing any Motel 6 with a Ritz–Carlton, any home with a shopping mall, or any farm with a factory....

slippery slope

Finally, in a coda, the Court suggests that property owners should turn to the States, who may or may not choose to impose appropriate limits on economic development takings.... States play many important functions in our system of dual sovereignty, but compensating for our refusal to enforce properly the Federal Constitution (and a provision meant to curtail state action, no less) is not among them....

Today nearly all real property is susceptible to condemnation on the Court's theory. In the prescient words of a dissenter from the infamous decision in *Poletown*, "now that we have authorized local legislative bodies to decide that a different commercial or industrial use of property will produce greater public benefits than its present use, no homeowner's, merchant's or manufacturer's property, however productive or valuable to its owner, is immune from condemnation for the benefit of other private interests that will put it to a 'higher' use." This is why economic development takings "seriously jeopardize the security of all private property ownership."

Any property may now be taken for the benefit of another private party, but the fallout from this decision will not be random. The beneficiaries are likely to be those citizens with disproportionate influence and power in the political process, including large corporations and development firms. As for the victims, the government now has license to transfer property from those with fewer resources to those with more. The Founders cannot have intended this perverse result. "That alone is a *just* government," wrote James Madison, "which *impartially* secures to every man, whatever is his *own*." For the National Gazette, Property, (Mar. 29, 1792), reprinted in 14 Papers of James Madison 266 (R. Rutland et al. eds. 1983).

Justice Thomas, dissenting.

... Today's decision is simply the latest in a string of our cases construing the Public Use Clause to be a virtual nullity, without the slightest nod to its original meaning. ... The most natural reading of the Clause is that it allows the government to take property only if the government owns, or the public has a legal right to use, the property, as opposed to taking it for any public purpose or necessity whatsoever. At the time of the founding, dictionaries primarily defined the noun "use" as "the act of employing any thing to any purpose." 2 S. Johnson, A Dictionary of the English Language 2194 (4th ed. 1773).... When the government takes property and gives it to a private individual, and the public has no right to use the property, it strains language to say that the public is "employing" the property, regardless of the incidental benefits that might accrue to the public from the private use. ... The Constitution's text ... suggests that the Takings Clause authorizes the taking of property only if the public has a right to employ it, not if the public realizes any conceivable benefit from the taking....

Early American eminent domain practice largely bears out this understanding of the Public Use Clause.... States employed the eminent domain power to provide quintessentially public goods, such as public roads, toll roads, ferries, canals, railroads, and public parks. [While] many States did have so-called Mill Acts, which authorized the owners of grist mills operated by water power to flood upstream lands with the payment of compensation to the upstream landowner[, those] early grist mills "were regulated by law and compelled to serve the public for a stipulated toll and in regular order," and therefore were actually used by the public. They were common carriers—quasi-public entities. These were "public uses" in the fullest sense of the word, because the public could legally use and benefit from them equally....

There is no justification ... for affording almost insurmountable deference to legislative conclusions that a use serves a "public use." ... We would not defer to a legislature's determination of the various circumstances that establish ... when a search of a home would be reasonable.... The Court has elsewhere recognized "the overriding respect for the sanctity of the home that has been embedded in our traditions since the origins of the Republic," when the issue is only whether the government may search a home. Yet today the Court tells us that we are not to "second-guess the City's considered judgments" when the issue is, instead, whether the government may take the infinitely more intrusive step of tearing down petitioners' homes. Something has gone seriously awry with this Court's interpretation of the Constitution. Though citizens are safe from the government in their homes, the homes themselves are not....

Berman and *Midkiff* erred by equating the eminent domain power with the police power of States. Traditional uses of that regulatory power, such as the power to abate a nuisance, required no compensation whatsoever, in sharp contrast to the takings power, which has always required compensation. The question whether the State can take property using the power of eminent domain is therefore distinct from the question whether it can regulate property pursuant to the police power.... To construe the Public Use Clause to overlap with the States' police power conflates these two categories. The "public purpose" test applied by *Berman* and *Midkiff* also cannot be applied in principled manner....

The consequences of today's decision are not difficult to predict, and promise to be harmful. So-called "urban renewal" programs provide some compensation for the properties they take, but no compensation is possible for the subjective value of these lands to the individuals displaced and the indignity inflicted by uprooting them from their homes. Allowing the government to take property [for] any economically beneficial goal guarantees that these losses will fall disproportionately on poor communities. Those communities are not only systematically less likely to put their lands to the highest and best social use, but are also the least politically powerful. If ever there were justification for intrusive judicial review of constitutional provisions that protect "discrete and insular minorities," United States v. Carolene Products Co., 304 U.S. 144, 152, n. 4 (1938), surely that principle would apply with great force to [such] powerless groups.... The deferential standard this Court has adopted for the Public Use Clause is therefore deeply perverse....

In the 1950s ... cities "rushed to draw plans" for downtown development.... Public works projects ... destroyed predominantly minority communities in St. Paul, Minnesota, and Baltimore, Maryland. In 1981, urban planners in Detroit, Michigan, uprooted the largely "lower-income and elderly" Poletown neighborhood for the benefit of the General Motors Corporation. J. Wylie, Poletown: Community Betrayed 58 (1989). Urban renewal projects have long been associated with the displacement of blacks; "in cities across the country, urban renewal came to be known as 'Negro removal.'" Pritchett, The "Public Menace" of Blight: Urban Renewal and the Private Uses of Eminent Domain, 21 Yale L. & Pol'y Rev. 1, 47 (2003). Over 97 percent of the individuals forcibly removed from their homes by the "slum-clearance" project upheld by this Court in *Berman* were black. Regrettably, the predictable consequence of the Court's decision will be to exacerbate these effects. . . .

NOTES, PROBLEMS, AND QUESTIONS

1.) *Poletown: A Case Study.* Justice O'Connor and Justice Thomas each referred to "Poletown," which was a thriving neighborhood in Detroit heavily populated by Americans of Eastern European, especially Polish, descent. In 1981, the cities of Detroit and Hamtramck, together with General Motors, agreed on a plan to condemn the entire neighborhood of some 4,200 people, 1,300 homes, 140 businesses, six churches, and one hospital for transfer to General Motors in order to permit GM to build an auto assembly plant on the site. Poletown residents resisted and brought suit, asserting the public use requirement. In Poletown Neighborhood Council v. City of Detroit, 410 Mich. 616, 304 N.W.2d 455 (1981), the Michigan Supreme Court found the public use requirement satisfied. The Michigan court said that "condemnation for a private use cannot be authorized whatever its incidental public benefit and condemnation for a public purpose cannot be forbidden whatever the incidental private gain. [Detroit and Hamtramck] presented substantial evidence of [their] severe economic conditions . . . , the need for new industrial development to revitalize local industries, the economic boost the project would provide, and the lack of other adequate available sites to implement the project. . . . [The power of eminent domain is to be used in this instance primarily to accomplish the essential public purpose of alleviating unemployment and revitalizing the economic base of the community. The benefit to a private interest is merely incidental."

Nearly a generation later, in County of Wayne v. Hathcock, 471 Mich. 445, 684 N.W.2d 765 (2004), the Michigan Supreme Court overruled *Poletown*. The court held that a proposed condemnation by Wayne County of land to create a business and technology park was not for public use within the meaning of the Michigan Constitution's takings clause. To satisfy the public use requirement when private property is condemned for transfer to another private owner, one of three elements must be present: (1) to obtain public benefits condemnation must be necessary; (2) after transfer to the new private owner, the property must be managed by and accountable to the public; (or) (3) the purpose of the condemnation itself, as distinguished from the later transfer and new use, must be to secure a public benefit independent of the benefits produced by the later transfer and new use. The Michigan court concluded that none of these elements was satisfied. The project could be accomplished by voluntary transfers; there would be no public oversight once the land was transferred to private businesses; nor was there any independent public benefit, such as improving public health and safety by eliminating a crime-ridden slum dotted with unsafe and unsanitary structures. The court held that a "generalized economic benefit" of the sort present in *Poletown* was insufficient to constitute a public use. "Every business ... contribute[s] in some way to the commonweal. To justify the exercise of eminent domain solely on the basis of the fact that the use of that property by a private entity seeking its own profit might contribute to the economy's health is to render impotent our constitutional limitations on the government's power of eminent domain. *Poletown's* 'economic benefit' rationale would validate practically *any* exercise of the power of eminent domain on behalf of a private entity."

For background on Poletown, see http://apps.detnews.com/apps/history/index.php?id=18

Michigan is not alone in its change of heart. In Norwood v. Horney, 110 Ohio St.3d 353 (2006), the Ohio Supreme Court relied on the Ohio Constitution to conclude that a taking for economic development purposes was invalid: "[A]lthough economic factors may be considered in determining whether private property may be appropriated, the fact that the appropriation would provide an economic benefit to the government and community, standing alone, does not satisfy the public-use requirement of ... the Ohio Constitution.... [A]ny taking based solely on financial gain is void as a matter of law and the courts owe no deference to a legislative finding that the proposed taking will provide financial benefit to a community."

2. *Legislative Reaction to* Kelo. After *Kelo* virtually every state has considered changes to its limits on eminent domain. By August, 2011, at least 43 states had adopted additional limits on the eminent domain power. Some of those changes are statutory, others are amendments to the state constitution. Some forbid most or all takings for economic development, others limit such takings to "blighted" properties, and still others impose more modest limits, such as requiring economic development takings to be authorized by the state legislature rather than municipalities. For an overview of this legislation, see <http://castlecoalition.org/index.php?option=com_content & task=view & id=57 & Itemid=113>.

3. *Problems.*

(a.) De Presse, an economically depressed small city of 20,000 people is approached by Omni, Inc., a global corporation which proposes to construct a customer service call center in the town. This proposal contains the credible prospect of hundreds of jobs—enough to lift the city from its moribund economic condition—but is conditioned upon condemnation (and payment by Omni of just compensation) of private property to be transferred to Omni to enable it to construct the call center on the condemned tract. The proposal is also conditioned on condemnation of a particularly handsome historic home, presently owned by De Presse's leading physician, which will be transferred to Omni for use as the residence of the call center manager after Omni has provided just compensation for the condemnation. After *Kelo*, are either of these proposed takings for public use?

a→b

helps w/ pretext prong

(b.) Assume the same facts as in Problem *a*, except that De Presse's City Council has searched diligently for other ways to spur economic development in De Presse and has unanimously concluded that the Omni proposal is by far the most feasible and economically stimulative. Should these additional facts change your conclusion in any way?

(c.) Assume the same facts as in Problem *b*, except that three of the five City Council members acquired several thousand shares each of the common stock of Omni just prior to voting in favor of the Omni proposal. Should these additional facts change your conclusion in any way?

(d.) The seacoast city of New Rotterdam has entered into a contract by which Waterman will act as the exclusive developer of a marina and associated support structures on city-owned land. New Rotterdam has validly rezoned the area as a redevelopment district, which facilitates the contemplated development. Archer owns a parcel that straddles the boundary of the redevelopment district. Archer enters into negotiations with ABC, a pharmacy chain, to construct an ABC outlet on the site. In order to do so, Archer sought the consent of Waterman to the development on the portion of Archer's site that is within the redevelopment zone. Unknown to Archer, Waterman had been negotiating with XYZ, a pharmacy chain that is the rival of ABC, to construct a pharmacy within the redevelopment district. Waterman demands either $800,000 to prevent a condemnation of the portion of Archer's parcel within the redevelopment zone or a 50% partnership interest in the ABC pharmacy project. Archer refuses both demands and a day later New Rotterdam condemns the portion of Archer's parcel within the redevelopment zone, thus making the ABC project infeasible. Waterman constructs an XYZ pharmacy within the redevelopment zone, on land that includes the condemned parcel. Is the taking for public use? Cf. Didden v. Village of Port Chester, 173 Fed. Appx. 931 (2d Cir. 2006).

4. *What Constitutes "Public Use"?* After reading these cases and notes, how would you formulate the public use requirement as a description of the present state of the law? What do you think *should* be the meaning of public use? Why?

B. REGULATORY TAKINGS

Regulation of property—how it may be used, who may possess it, when and how it may be transferred—is endemic to American law. But when regulation of property becomes so pervasive that it amounts to a *de facto* taking of that property, the government must either compensate the affected property owner or abandon the regulation. When is that point reached? There is no universal answer, but there are formulae and approaches that provide some guidance.

The Supreme Court has created three categorical rules and several balancing tests to assess whether a regulation is a *de facto* taking. The categorical rules purport to define when a taking has or has not occurred, but as you will see, the boundaries of these categories are imprecise, thus diminishing their utility as clear decision rules.

(1) No taking has occurred, says the Court, no matter what the economic impact of the regulation, if government regulation of property does no more than abate a previously recognized common law nuisance.

(2) A taking has occurred, says the Court, when a government regulation results in a permanent physical occupation of private property, no matter how minor that occupation may be.

(3) A taking has occurred, says the Court, when a government regulation does not abate a common law nuisance and strips the property owner of all economically viable use of his or her property.

When the categorical rules fail to provide an answer, the courts rely on a general balancing test, which holds that regulations are valid if the magnitude and character of the burden imposed on the property owner is not "functionally comparable to government appropriation or invasion of private property." To determine whether this standard is met, courts inevitably weigh the public benefits produced by the regulations against the harms imposed on the affected property owner or owners. If the harms outweigh the benefits the regulation is a taking. Of course, as always, the devil is in the details: How does one measure benefits and harms? What constitutes cognizable benefits or harms? Even so, the theoretical task is to ensure that the government has not "forc[ed] some people alone to bear burdens which, in all fairness and justice, should be borne by the public as a whole." Armstrong v. United States, 364 U.S. 40, 49 (1960). A fine sentiment, to be sure, but pitched at such a high level of generality that it is nearly useless in practice. More concrete criteria are needed to determine this issue.

Additional balancing tests apply when governments attach conditions to issuance of otherwise valid land use permits that would be takings if imposed alone. Such conditions are takings unless the government can prove both that (1) the condition is substantially related to the state's otherwise valid reason for restricting land use at all; and (2) the nature and scope of the condition are roughly proportional to the public impact of the proposed land use.

1. EARLY APPROACHES TO THE PROBLEM

PENNSYLVANIA COAL COMPANY v. MAHON

Supreme Court of the United States
260 U.S. 393 (1922)

JUSTICE HOLMES delivered the opinion of the Court.

This is a bill in equity . . . to prevent the Pennsylvania Coal Company from mining under [the Mahons'] property in such way as to remove the supports and cause a subsidence of the surface and of their house. [In 1878 the Coal Company conveyed] the surface, but in express terms reserve[d] the right to remove all the coal under the same, and the grantee [took] the premises with the risk, and waive[d] all claim for damages that may arise from mining out the coal. But [the Mahons] say that whatever may have been the Coal Company's rights, they were taken away by [Pennsylvania's] Kohler Act....

The statute forbids the mining of anthracite coal in such [a] way as to cause the subsidence [of] any structure used as a human habitation, [except] land where the surface is owned by the owner of the underlying coal and is distant more than one hundred and fifty feet from any improved property belonging to any other person. As applied to this case the statute is admitted to destroy previously existing rights of property and contract. The question is whether the police power can be stretched so far. [A state trial court had declared the Kohler Act unconstitutional but the Pennsylvania Supreme Court reversed.]

Government hardly could go on if to some extent values incident to property could not be diminished without paying for every such change in the general law. [S]ome values are enjoyed under an implied limitation and must yield to the police power. But obviously the implied limitation must have its limits, or the contract and due process clauses are gone. One fact for consideration in determining such limits is the extent of the diminution. When it reaches a certain magnitude, in most if not in all cases there must be an exercise of eminent domain and compensation to sustain the act. So the question depends upon the particular facts.

[The] act cannot be sustained as an exercise of the police power, so far as it affects the mining of coal under streets or cities in places where the right to mine such coal has been reserved. "[For] practical purposes, the right to coal consists in the right to mine it." What makes the right to mine coal valuable is that it can be exercised with profit. To make it commercially impracticable to mine certain coal has very nearly the same effect for constitutional purposes as appropriating or destroying it. This we think that we are warranted in assuming that the statute does....

The protection of private property in the [takings clause] presupposes that it is wanted for public use, but provides that it shall not be taken for such use without compensation. [When] this seemingly absolute protection is found to be qualified by the police power, the natural tendency of human nature is to extend the qualification more and more until at last private property disappears. But that cannot [constitutionally] be accomplished. The general rule [is] that while property may be regulated to a certain extent, if regulation goes too far it will be recognized as a taking. It may be doubted how far exceptional cases, like the blowing up of a house to stop a conflagration, go—and if they go beyond the general rule, whether they do not stand as much upon tradition as upon principle. In general it is not plain that a man's misfortunes or necessities will justify his shifting the damages to his neighbor's shoulders. [A] strong public desire to improve the public condition is not enough to warrant achieving the desire by a shorter cut than the constitutional way of paying for the change. [Reversed.]

JUSTICE BRANDEIS, dissenting.

[Coal] in place is land; and the right of the owner to use his land is not absolute. He may not so use it as to create a public nuisance; and uses, once harmless, may, owing to changed conditions, seriously threaten the public welfare. Whenever they do, the legislature has power to prohibit such uses without paying compensation; and the power to prohibit extends alike to the manner, the character and the purpose of the use. [Every] restriction upon the use of property imposed in the exercise of the police power deprives the owner of some right theretofore enjoyed, and is, in that sense, an abridgment by the State of rights in property without making compensation. But restriction imposed to protect the public health, safety or morals from dangers threatened is not a taking. The restriction here [is] merely the prohibition of a noxious use. The property so restricted remains in the possession of its owner. The State does not appropriate it or make any use of it [but] merely prevents the owner from making a use which interferes with paramount rights of the public. . . .

Restriction upon use does not become inappropriate as a means, merely because it deprives the owner of the only use to which the property can then be profitably put. [Nor] is a restriction imposed through exercise of the police power inappropriate as a means, merely because the same end might be effected through exercise of the power of eminent domain. [If] by mining anthracite coal the owner would necessarily unloose poisonous gases, I suppose no one would doubt the power of the State to prevent the mining, without buying his coal fields. And why may not the State, likewise, without paying compensation, prohibit one from digging so deep or excavating so near the surface, as to expose the community to like dangers? In the latter case, as in the former, carrying on the business would be a public nuisance.

It is said that one fact for consideration in determining whether the limits of the police power have been exceeded is the extent of the resulting diminution in value; and that here the restriction destroys existing rights of property and contract. But values are relative. If we are to consider the value of the coal kept in place by the restriction, we should compare it with the value [of] the whole property. [For] aught that appears the value of the coal kept in place by the restriction may be negligible as compared with the value of the whole property, or even as compared with that part of it which is represented by the coal remaining in place and which may be extracted despite the statute.

[It] is said that [the Kohler Act] cannot be sustained as an exercise of the police power where the right to mine such coal has been reserved. The conclusion seems to rest upon the assumption that in order to justify such exercise of the police power there must be "an average reciprocity of advantage" as between the owner of the property restricted and the rest of the community; and that here such reciprocity is absent. [Where] the police power is exercised [to] protect the public from detriment and danger there [is] no room for considering reciprocity of advantage. There was no reciprocal advantage to the owner prohibited from using his [brickyard in Hadacheck v. Sebastian,] 239 U.S. 394 [1915]; unless it be the advantage of living and doing business in a civilized community. That reciprocal advantage is given by the act to the coal operators.

NOTES AND QUESTIONS

1.) *How Far is Too Far?* Justice Holmes's enigmatic declaration that if a "regulation goes too far it will be recognized as a taking" is of little help by itself. Why was the Kohler Act a regulation too far? Holmes and the majority seemed to think that the Act completely eliminated the economic value of the coal required to be left in place. Brandeis emphasized the impact of the regulation on the value of the "whole property," and appeared to conclude that the Kohler Act had a negligible adverse impact on that value. This difference in perspective is sometimes referred to as "conceptual severance" problem. See Margaret Radin, The Liberal Conception of Property: Cross Currents in the Jurisprudence of Takings, 88 Colum. L. Rev. 1667, 1676 (1988). The idea is that the regulatory impact on the property owner may be envisioned as the numerator of a fraction, and the affected property is the denominator. Put crudely, if the regulatory impact is 20 and the property is also 20, the result is 20/20; i.e., the adverse impact precisely equals the property. But if the impact is 1 and the property is 20, the result is 1/20; i.e., the adverse impact is a modest fraction of the entire property. By itself, this might not answer completely the question of whether the regulation is a taking, but it does provide some guidance. However, the question that divided Holmes and Brandeis is: What property should compose the denominator? In Holmes's view it was the coal required to be left in place to support the surface, a conclusion reinforced by the fact that Pennsylvania law regarded the "support estate" as a legally separate piece of property. To Brandeis, it was the "entire property"—all of the coal that could potentially be mined— not just the remaining pillars of coal. Who was right? Should the answer depend on whether the affected property is legally separate, or on the functional impact of the regulation on all the property that is affected?

Sixty-five years later, in Keystone Bituminous Coal Association v. DeBenedictis, 480 U.S. 470 (1987), the Court appeared to side with Brandeis when it ruled that a modern version of the Kohler Act was not a taking. Pennsylvania's 1966 Subsidence Act required sufficient coal to be left in place to support the surface. The Court distinguished the Subsidence Act from the Kohler Act on two grounds. The Subsidence Act was intended to "arrest [a] significant threat to the common welfare," while the Kohler Act sacrificed the "private economic interests of coal companies" to benefit the "private interests of the surface owners." Is that a credible distinction? More significantly, the Court concluded that the coal that the Subsidence Act required to be left in place to support the surface did "not constitute a separate segment of property for takings law purposes" even though it was a separate legal estate under Pennsylvania law. Because the coal left in place was only a small fraction of the total amount of coal that could be removed the challengers had "not come close [to] proving that they have been denied the economically viable use of [their] property." Four justices dissented.

2) *What's "Average Reciprocity of Advantage"?* Justice Brandeis raised and rejected the applicability of this concept. The idea was that regulations of

property were not compensable if the regulation, while restricting a property owner's use of his property, also delivered roughly compensating benefits to the landowner. An example might be a zoning ordinance that limits all property uses to single-family residential. While each owner suffers the restriction, each owner also receives the benefit of the restriction on others— an "average reciprocity of advantage." A modern echo of this concept is articulated by Richard Epstein, who argues that redistributive regulations— those that impose costs and deliver benefits disproportionally—are takings. Epstein concedes that some regulations of this kind are fully compensated by "implicit in-kind compensation." Epstein, *Takings*, at 195–215. Brandeis thought that the presence of reciprocity of advantage was not necessary to support the validity of regulations that protect the public from harm.

But what are those regulations? Two early examples are Reinman v. Little Rock, 237 U.S. 171 (1915), and Hadacheck v. Sebastian, 239 U.S. 394 (1915). In *Reinman*, the Supreme Court upheld the validity of a Little Rock ordinance forbidding the operation of a livery stable within the central shopping and hotel district of the city. Although a livery stable was not a nuisance *per se*, the Court held that it was within the police power of the city to determine that, under the circumstances where 100 or so horses and mules were emitting noxious odors, the livery stable was a nuisance and thus could be abated without compensation. In *Hadacheck*, the Court held that Los Angeles could bar the operation of a brick kiln even though it was disputed whether the noise, dust, and smoke associated with the kiln was a nuisance, in part because the owner could still use the valuable deposits of clay on his land for brick manufacture, so long as he fired the bricks elsewhere. So far, so good; now consider the next case.

MILLER v. SCHOENE

Supreme Court of the United States
276 U.S. 272 (1928)

[After an outbreak of a type of "cedar rust" fungus that causes minimal damage to cedar trees but which inflicts major damage to apple trees that also host the fungus spores, Virginia enacted a law requiring the removal of all red cedar trees within two miles of an apple orchard whenever the cedars hosted cedar-apple rust fungus. Cedar owners were permitted to use the logs and received compensation for the cost of cutting the trees. No compensation was provided for the loss of the value of the standing cedar trees or for any decrease in the property's market value caused by the destruction of the trees. A property owner harboring infected cedars within two miles of an apple orchard challenged the law as an uncompensated taking. The Virginia courts upheld the validity of the order, and a unanimous Supreme Court affirmed.]

JUSTICE STONE delivered the opinion of the Court.

[C]edar rust is an infectious plant disease [that] is destructive of the fruit and foliage of the apple, but without effect on the value of the cedar. . . . It is communicated by spores from one to the other over a radius of at least two miles. It appears not to be communicable between trees of the same species but only from one species to the other, and other plants seem not to be appreciably affected by it. The only practicable method of controlling the disease and protecting apple trees from its ravages is the destruction of all red cedar trees, subject to the infection, located within two miles of apple orchards.

The red cedar, aside from its ornamental use, has occasional use and value as lumber. [Its] value throughout the state is shown to be small as compared with that of the apple orchards of the state. Apple growing is one of the principal agricultural pursuits in Virginia.

[The] state was under the necessity of making a choice between the preservation of one class of property and that of the other wherever both existed in dangerous proximity. It would have been none the less a choice if, instead of enacting the present statute, the state, by doing nothing, had permitted serious injury to the apple orchards within its borders to go on unchecked. When forced to such a choice the state does not exceed its constitutional powers by deciding upon the destruction of one class of property in order to save another which, in the judgment of the legislature, is of greater value to the public. It will not do to say that the case is merely one of a conflict of two private interests and that the misfortune of apple growers may not be shifted to cedar owners by ordering the destruction of their property; for it is obvious that there may be, and that here there is, a preponderant public concern in the preservation of the one interest over the other. And where the public interest is involved preferment of that interest over the property interest of the individual, to the extent even of its destruction, is one of the distinguishing characteristics of every exercise of the police power which affects property.

We need not weigh with nicety the question whether the infected cedars constitute a nuisance according to the common law; or whether they may be so declared by statute. For where, as here, the choice is unavoidable, we cannot say that its exercise, controlled by considerations of social policy which are not unreasonable, involves any denial of due process.

QUESTIONS

Was the Virginia law a valid regulation because maintaining red cedar trees that harbor cedar rust was a noxious use? If so, why wasn't underground coal mining that threatened to collapse the surface also a noxious use?

Or did *Miller* rest on the fact that the public economic benefits of preserving apple orchards from destruction substantially outweighed the burdens on affected owners of cedar trees? If that is so, why was the public benefit of preventing the collapse of the surface due to underground coal mining insufficient to outweigh the burdens on affected coal miners? Was it because the total economic loss to coal miners was greater than the total economic loss to surface owners? In *Miller* it was clear that the total economic loss to apple orchardists was much greater than the total economic loss to cedar tree owners. Assuming that is the answer, should the loss of cedar trees in *Miller* have been treated as a burden "which, in all fairness and justice, should be borne by the public as a whole"? Armstrong v. United States, 364 U.S. 40, 49 (1960).

2. THE CATEGORICAL APPROACH

LUCAS v. SOUTH CAROLINA COASTAL COUNCIL

Supreme Court of the United States
505 U.S. 1003 (1992)

JUSTICE SCALIA delivered the opinion of the Court.

[Lucas] paid $975,000 for two residential lots ... on the Isle of Palms, [a barrier island near Charleston,] on which he intended to build single-family homes. [Two years later,] the South Carolina Legislature enacted the Beachfront Management Act, which had the direct effect of barring petitioner from erecting any permanent habitable structures on his two parcels. A state trial court found that this prohibition rendered Lucas's parcels "valueless." This case requires us to decide whether the Act's dramatic effect on the economic value of Lucas's lots accomplished a taking of private property under the Fifth and Fourteenth Amendments requiring the payment of "just compensation."

[Under the Beachfront Management Act the South Carolina Coastal] Council was directed to establish a "baseline" connecting the landward-most "points of erosion [during] the past forty years" in the region of the Isle of Palms that includes Lucas's lots. [T]he Council fixed this baseline landward of Lucas's parcels. That was significant, for under the Act construction of occupiable improvements was flatly prohibited seaward of a line drawn 20 feet landward of, and parallel to, the baseline. The Act provided no exceptions.

[In South Carolina's courts Lucas argued that the] construction bar effected a taking of his property without just compensation. Lucas did not take issue with the validity of the Act as a lawful exercise of South Carolina's police power, but contended that the Act's complete extinguishment of his property's value entitled him to compensation regardless of whether the legislature had acted in furtherance of legitimate police power objectives. [The trial] court agreed. [The] Supreme Court of South Carolina reversed, [ruling] that when a regulation respecting the use of property is designed "to prevent serious public harm" no compensation is owing under the Takings Clause regardless of the regulation's effect on the property's value.

Prior to ... Pennsylvania Coal Co. v. Mahon, it was generally thought that the Takings Clause reached only a "direct appropriation" of property, or the functional equivalent of a "practical ouster of [the owner's] possession." Justice Holmes recognized in *Mahon*, however, that if the protection against physical appropriations of private property was to be meaningfully enforced, the government's power to redefine the range of interests included in the ownership of property was necessarily constrained by constitutional limits. If, instead, the uses of private property were subject to unbridled, uncompensated qualification under the police power, "the natural tendency of human nature [would be] to extend the qualification more and more until at last private property disappeared." These considerations gave birth in that case to the oft-cited maxim that, "while property may be regulated to a certain extent, if regulation goes too far it will be recognized as a taking." [But] *Mahon* offered little insight into when, and under what circumstances, a given regulation would be seen as going "too far" for purposes of the Fifth Amendment. In 70–odd years of succeeding "regulatory takings" jurisprudence, we have generally eschewed any "set formula" for determining how far is too far, preferring to "engage [in] essentially ad hoc, factual inquiries," Penn Central Transportation Co. v. New York City, 438 U.S. 104, 124 (1978).

[handwritten margin note: no standard yet]

We have, however, described at least two discrete categories of regulatory action as compensable without case-specific inquiry into the public interest advanced in support of the restraint. The first encompasses regulations that compel the property owner to suffer a physical "invasion" of his property. In general (at least with regard to permanent invasions), no matter how minute the intrusion, and no matter how weighty the public purpose behind it, we have required compensation. For example, in Loretto v. Teleprompter Manhattan CATV Corp., 458 U.S. 419 (1982), we determined that New York's law requiring landlords to allow television cable companies to emplace cable facilities in their apartment buildings constituted a taking, even though the facilities occupied at most only 1 cubic feet of the landlords' property [and consisted of a few wires and junction boxes largely obscured from view].

[handwritten margin note: ①]

The second situation in which we have found categorical treatment appropriate is where regulation denies all economically beneficial or productive use of land. As we have said on numerous occasions, the [takings clause] is violated when land-use regulation "does not substantially advance legitimate state interests or *denies an owner economically viable use of his land*." [Agins v. Tiburon, 447 U.S. 255, 260 (1980) (emphasis added).][1] . . .

[handwritten margin note: ②]

---

1. Regrettably, the rhetorical force of our "deprivation of all economically feasible use" rule is greater than its precision, since the rule does not make clear the "property interest" against which the loss of value is to be measured. When, for example, a regulation requires a developer to leave 90% of a rural tract in its natural state, it is unclear whether we would analyze the situation as one in which the owner has been deprived of all economically beneficial use of the burdened portion of the tract, or as one in which the owner has suffered a mere diminution in value of the tract as a whole. (For an extreme—and, we think, unsupportable—view of the relevant calculus, see Penn Central Transportation Co. v. New York City, 438 U.S. 104 (1978), where the state court examined the diminution in a particular parcel's value produced by a municipal ordinance in light of total value of the taking claimant's other holdings in the vicinity.)

Unsurprisingly, this uncertainty regarding the composition of the denominator in our "deprivation" fraction has produced inconsistent pronouncements by the Court. Compare Pennsylvania Coal Co. v. Mahon with Keystone Bituminous Coal Assn. v. DeBenedictis, 480 U.S. 470 (1987). [The] answer to this difficult question may lie in how the owner's reasonable expectations have been shaped by the State's law of property—i.e., whether and to what degree the State's law has accorded legal recognition and protection to the particular interest in land with respect to which

We have never set forth the justification for this rule. Perhaps it is simply [that] total deprivation of beneficial use is, from the landowner's point of view, the equivalent of a physical appropriation. Surely, at least, in the extraordinary circumstance when no productive or economically beneficial use of land is permitted, it is less realistic to indulge our usual assumption that the legislature is simply "adjusting the benefits and burdens of economic life," in a manner that secures an "average reciprocity of advantage" to everyone concerned. . . .

On the other side of the balance, affirmatively supporting a compensation requirement, is the fact that regulations that leave the owner of land without economically beneficial or productive options for its use—typically, as here, by requiring land to be left substantially in its natural state—carry with them a heightened risk that private property is being pressed into some form of public service under the guise of mitigating serious public harm. [The many state and federal] statutes [that] provide for the use of eminent domain to impose servitudes on private scenic lands preventing developmental uses, or to acquire such lands altogether, suggest the practical equivalence in this setting of negative regulation and appropriation. [In] short, [there] are good reasons [to conclude] that when the owner of real property has been called upon to sacrifice all economically beneficial uses in the name of the common good, that is, to leave his property economically idle, he has suffered a taking. . . .

The South Carolina Supreme Court [thought] the Beachfront Management Act [involved] an exercise of South Carolina's "police powers" to mitigate the harm to the public interest that petitioner's use of his land might occasion. [Because] "the erection of new construction [on the beaches and dunes contributes] to the erosion and destruction of this public resource" [South Carolina used] its "police powers" to enjoin a property owner from activities akin to public nuisances. See Mugler v. Kansas, 123 U.S. 623 (1887) (law prohibiting manufacture of alcoholic beverages); Hadacheck v. Sebastian, 239 U.S. 394 (1915) (law barring operation of brick mill in residential area); Miller v. Schoene, 276 U.S. 272 (1928) (order to destroy diseased cedar trees to prevent infection of nearby orchards); Goldblatt v. Hempstead, 369 U.S. 590 (1962) (law effectively preventing continued operation of quarry in residential area).

It is correct that many of our prior opinions have suggested that "harmful or noxious uses" of property may be proscribed by government regulation without the requirement of compensation. [But] the South Carolina Supreme Court was too quick to conclude that that principle decides the present case. The "harmful or noxious uses" principle was the Court's early attempt to describe in theoretical terms why government may, consistent with the Takings Clause, affect property values by regula-

the takings claimant alleges a diminution in (or elimination of) value. In any event, we avoid this difficulty in the present case, since the "interest in land" that Lucas has pleaded (a fee simple interest) is an estate with a rich tradition of protection at common law, and since the South Carolina [trial court] found that the Beachfront Management Act left each of Lucas's beachfront lots without economic value.

tion without incurring an obligation to compensate. [In] *Penn Central Transportation Co.*, in the course of sustaining New York City's landmarks preservation program against a takings challenge, we rejected the petitioner's suggestion that *Mugler* and the cases following it were premised on, and thus limited by, some objective conception of "noxiousness":

> The uses in issue in *Hadacheck, Miller*, and *Goldblatt* were perfectly lawful in themselves. They involved no blameworthiness, [moral] wrongdoing or conscious act of dangerous risk-taking which induce[d society] to shift the cost to a particular individual. [These] cases are better understood as resting not on any supposed noxious quality of the prohibited uses but rather on the ground that the restrictions were reasonably related to the implementation of a policy—not unlike historic preservation—expected to produce a widespread public benefit and applicable to all similarly situated property.

"Harmful or noxious use" analysis was, in other words, simply the progenitor of our more contemporary statements that "land-use regulation does not effect a taking if it 'substantially advances legitimate state interests.'"

The transition from our early focus on control of "noxious" uses to our contemporary understanding of the broad realm within which government may regulate without compensation was an easy one, since the distinction between "harm-preventing" and "benefit-conferring" regulation is often in the eye of the beholder. It is quite possible, for example, to describe in *either* fashion the ecological, economic, and aesthetic concerns that inspired the South Carolina legislature in the present case. One could say that imposing a servitude on Lucas's land is necessary in order to prevent his use of it from "harming" South Carolina's ecological resources; or, instead, in order to achieve the "benefits" of an ecological preserve. Whether one or the other of the competing characterizations will come to one's lips in a particular case depends primarily upon one's evaluation of the worth of competing uses of real estate. A given restraint will be seen as mitigating "harm" to the adjacent parcels or securing a "benefit" for them, depending upon the observer's evaluation of the relative importance of the use that the restraint favors. See Sax, Takings and the Police Power, 74 Yale L.J. 36, 49 (1964) ("The problem [in this area] is not one of noxiousness or harm-creating activity at all; rather it is a problem of inconsistency between perfectly innocent and independently desirable uses"). Whether Lucas's construction of single-family residences on his parcels should be described as bringing "harm" to South Carolina's adjacent ecological resources thus depends principally upon whether the describer believes that the State's use interest in nurturing those resources is so important that any competing adjacent use must yield.

When it is understood that "prevention of harmful use" was merely our early formulation of the police power justification necessary to sustain (without compensation) *any* regulatory diminution in value; and that the distinction between a regulation that "prevents harmful use" and that which "confers benefits" is difficult, if not impossible, to discern on an objective, value-free basis; it becomes self-evident that noxious-use logic cannot serve as a touchstone to distinguish regulatory "takings"—which require compensation—from regulatory deprivations that do not require compensation. *A fortiori* the legislature's recitation of a noxious-use justification cannot be the basis for departing from our categorical rule that total regulatory takings must be compensated. If it were, departure would virtually always be allowed.

Rule

[Where] the State seeks to sustain regulation that deprives land of all economically beneficial use, we think it may resist compensation only if the logically antecedent inquiry into the nature of the owner's estate shows that the proscribed use interests were not part of his title to begin with.[2] This accords, we think, with our "takings" jurisprudence, which has traditionally been guided by the understandings of our citizens regarding the content of, and the State's power over, the "bundle of rights" that they acquire when they obtain title to property. It seems to us that the property owner necessarily expects the uses of his property to be restricted, from time to time, by various measures newly enacted by the State in legitimate exercise of its police [powers]. And in the case of personal property, by reason of the State's traditionally high degree of control over commercial dealings, he ought to be aware of the possibility that new regulation might even render his property economically worthless (at least if the property's only economically productive use is sale or manufacture for sale). Andrus v. Allard, 444 U.S. 51 (1979) (prohibition on sale of eagle feathers). In the case of land, however, we think the notion pressed by the Council that title is somehow held subject to the "implied limitation" that the State may subsequently eliminate all economically valuable use is inconsistent with the historical compact recorded in the Takings Clause that has become part of our constitutional culture.[3]

Where "permanent physical occupation" of land is concerned, we have refused to allow the government to decree it anew (without compensation), no matter how weighty the asserted "public interests" involved—

---

2. Drawing on our [free exercise of religion clause] jurisprudence, [Employment Division v. Smith, 494 U.S. 872 (1990)] Justice Stevens would "look to the generality of a regulation of property" to determine whether compensation is owing. The Beachfront Management Act is general, in his view, because it "regulates the use of the coastline of the entire state." [The] equivalent of a law of general application that inhibits the practice of religion without being aimed at land is a law that destroys the value of land without being aimed at land. Perhaps such a law—the generally applicable criminal prohibition on the manufacturing of alcoholic beverages challenged in *Mugler* comes to mind—cannot constitute a compensable taking. But a regulation specifically directed to land use no more acquires immunity by plundering landowners generally than does a law specifically directed at religious practice acquire immunity by prohibiting all religions. . . .

3. [Justice Blackmun argues] that our description of the "understanding" of land ownership that informs the Takings Clause is not supported by early American experience. That is largely true, but entirely irrelevant. The practices of the States prior to incorporation of the [takings clause]—[which] occasionally included outright physical appropriation of land without compensation—were out of accord with any plausible interpretation of [the takings clause]. [And] the text of the Clause can be read to encompass regulatory as well as physical deprivations (in contrast to the text originally proposed by Madison [—] "No person shall [be] obliged to relinquish his property, where it may be necessary for public use, without a just compensation." . . .

though we assuredly would permit the government to assert a permanent easement that was a pre-existing limitation upon the landowner's title. We believe similar treatment must be accorded confiscatory regulations, i.e., regulations that prohibit all economically beneficial use of land. Any limitation so severe cannot be newly legislated or decreed (without compensation), but must inhere in the title itself, in the restrictions that background principles of the State's law of property and nuisance already place upon land ownership. A law or decree with such an effect must [do] no more than duplicate the result that could have been achieved [by] adjacent landowners (or other uniquely affected persons) under the State's law of private nuisance, or by the State under its complementary power to abate nuisances that affect the public generally, or otherwise.[4]

[On] this analysis, [the] corporate owner of a nuclear generating plant would not be entitled to compensation when it is directed to remove all improvements from its land upon discovery that the plant sits astride an earthquake fault. Such regulatory action may well have the effect of eliminating the land's only economically productive use, but it does not proscribe a productive use that was previously permissible under relevant property and nuisance principles. The use of these properties for what are now expressly prohibited purposes was always unlawful, and (subject to other constitutional limitations) it was open to the State at any point to make the implication of those background principles of nuisance and property law explicit.... When, however, a regulation that declares "off-limits" all economically productive or beneficial uses of land goes beyond what the relevant background principles would dictate, compensation must be paid to sustain it.[5]

The "total taking" inquiry we require today will ordinarily entail (as the application of state nuisance law ordinarily entails) analysis of, among other things, the degree of harm to public lands and resources, or adjacent private property, posed by the claimant's proposed activities, the social value of the claimant's activities and their suitability to the locality in question, and the relative ease with which the alleged harm can be avoided through measures taken by the claimant and the government (or adjacent private landowners) alike. The fact that a particular use has long been engaged in by similarly situated owners ordinarily imports a lack of any common-law prohibition (though changed circumstances or new knowledge may make what was previously permissible no longer so). So also does the fact that other landowners, similarly situated, are permitted to continue the use denied to the claimant.

---

4. The principal "otherwise" that we have in mind is litigation absolving the State (or private parties) of liability for the destruction of "real and personal property, in cases of actual necessity, to prevent the spreading of a fire" or to forestall other grave threats to the lives and property of others. Bowditch v. Boston, 101 U.S. 16 (1880).

5. Of course, the State may elect to rescind its regulation and thereby avoid having to pay compensation for a permanent deprivation. But "where the [regulation has] already worked a taking of all use of property, no subsequent action by the government can relieve it of the duty to provide compensation for the period during which the taking was effective." [First English Evangelical Lutheran Church v. County of Los Angeles, 482 U.S. 304, 321 (1987).]

It seems unlikely that common-law principles would have prevented the erection of any habitable or productive improvements on petitioner's land; they rarely support prohibition of the "essential use" of land. The question, however, is one of state law to be dealt with on remand. We emphasize that to win its case South Carolina must do more than proffer the legislature's declaration that the uses Lucas desires are inconsistent with the public interest, or the conclusory assertion that they violate a common-law maxim such as *sic utere tuo ut alienum non laedas* [use your property so as not to injure another]. [A] "State, by *ipse dixit*, may not transform private property into public property without [compensation]." Instead, as it would be required to do if it sought to restrain Lucas in a common-law action for public nuisance, South Carolina must identify background principles of nuisance and property law that prohibit the uses he now intends in the circumstances in which the property is presently found. Only on this showing can the State fairly claim that, in proscribing all such beneficial uses, the Beachfront Management Act is taking nothing.[6] [Reversed and remanded.]

JUSTICE KENNEDY, concurring in the judgment.

Where a taking is alleged from regulations which deprive the property of all value, the test must be whether the deprivation is contrary to reasonable, investment-backed expectations. ... The common law of nuisance is too narrow a confine for the exercise of regulatory power in a complex and interdependent society. The State should not be prevented from enacting new regulatory initiatives in response to changing conditions, and courts must consider all reasonable expectations whatever their source. ... Coastal property may present such unique concerns for a fragile land system that the State can go further in regulating its development and use than the common law of nuisance might otherwise permit....

JUSTICE BLACKMUN, dissenting.

[The] Beachfront Management Act [embodies findings by] the state legislature [that] the prohibition on building in front of the setback line prevents serious harm. ... "[A]ll property in this country is held under the implied obligation that the owner's use of it shall not be injurious to the community...." [*Keystone Bituminous Coal Assn.*] The Court consistently has upheld regulations imposed to arrest a significant threat to the common welfare, whatever their economic effect on the owner....

[Until] today, the Court explicitly had rejected the contention that the government's power to act without paying compensation turns on whether the prohibited activity is a common-law nuisance. [In] *Miller*, the Court

---

6. Justice Blackmun decries our reliance on background nuisance principles at least in part because he believes those principles to be [manipulable.] There is no doubt some leeway in a court's interpretation of what existing state law permits—but not remotely as much, we think, as in a legislative crafting of the reasons for its confiscatory regulation. We stress [that] eliminating all economically beneficial uses may be defended only if an objectively reasonable application of relevant precedents would exclude those beneficial uses in the circumstances in which the land is presently found.

found it unnecessary to "weigh with nicety the question whether the infected cedars constitute a nuisance according to common law; or whether they may be so declared by statute." ...

[The] "deprivation of all economically valuable use" [rule] cannot be [applied] objectively. [Whether] the owner has been deprived of all economic value of his property will depend on how "property" is defined. ... *Keystone* illustrates this principle perfectly. In *Keystone*, the Court determined that the "support estate" was "merely a part of the entire bundle of rights possessed by the owner," [and so] concluded that the support estate's destruction merely eliminated one segment of the total property. The dissent, however, characterized the support estate as a distinct property interest that was wholly destroyed.

[Even] more perplexing, however, is the Court's reliance on common-law principles of nuisance. [In] determining what is a nuisance at common law, state courts make exactly the decision that the Court finds so troubling when made by the South Carolina General Assembly today: they determine whether the use is harmful. [If] judges can [do this], why not legislators? ... Nor does history indicate any common-law limit on the State's power to regulate harmful uses even to the point of destroying all economic value. Nothing in the discussions in Congress concerning the Taking Clause indicates that the Clause was limited by the common-law nuisance doctrine.

JUSTICE STEVENS, dissenting. *— lot of ways around rule → makes rule not good.*

[The] categorical rule the Court establishes [is] unsound and unwise [, and] the Court's formulation of the exception to that rule is too rigid and too narrow.

The Categorical Rule. [The categorical] rule is wholly arbitrary. A landowner whose property is diminished in value 95% recovers nothing, while an owner whose property is diminished 100% recovers the land's full value.... The arbitrariness of such a rule is palpable. [Because] of the elastic nature of property rights, the Court's new rule will also prove unsound in practice. In response to the rule, courts may define "property" broadly and only rarely find regulations to effect total takings. [It] could easily be said in this case [that] Lucas may put his land to "other uses"— fishing or camping, for example—or may sell his land to his neighbors as a buffer. In either event, his land is far from "valueless."[7] [Developers] and investors may market specialized estates to take advantage of the Court's new rule. The smaller the estate, the more likely that a regulatory change will effect a total taking. Thus, an investor may, for example, purchase the right to build a multi-family home on a specific lot, with the result that a zoning regulation that allows only single-family homes would render the investor's property interest "valueless." In short, the categorical rule will likely have one of two effects: Either courts will alter the definition of the

___

7. [Ed.] Is it "far from valueless"? Why would a neighbor pay anything for land which may not be developed? What economic value attaches to beachfront fishing with rod and reel from a lot for which the owner paid $1 million?

"denominator" in the takings "fraction," rendering the Court's categorical rule meaningless, or investors will manipulate the relevant property interests, giving the Court's rule sweeping effect. To my mind, neither of these results is desirable or [appropriate].

The Nuisance Exception. The exception provides that a regulation that renders property valueless is not a taking if it prohibits uses of property that were not "previously permissible under relevant property and nuisance principles." [This] effectively freezes the State's common law, denying the legislature much of its traditional power to revise the law governing the rights and uses of property. [The] human condition is one of constant learning and evolution.... Legislatures implement that new learning; in doing so they must often revise the definition of property and the rights of property owners. [Of] course, some legislative redefinitions of property will effect a taking and must be compensated—but it certainly cannot be the case that every movement away from common law does so. [The] Court's categorical approach rule will, I fear, greatly hamper the efforts of local officials and planners who must deal with increasingly complex problems in land-use and environmental regulation....

NOTES AND QUESTIONS

1. *Permanent Physical Occupation.* As the *Lucas* opinion indicates, when a government physically occupies all or a part of private property, or authorizes a third party to do so, the government has taken the occupied property. The owner, however, has the burden of proving permanent physical occupation. See Loretto v. Teleprompter Manhattan CATV Corp., 458 U.S. 419 (1982). It does not matter whether the property permanently occupied is real or personal property. See Webb's Fabulous Pharmacies v. Beckwith, 449 U.S. 155 (1980). The occupation that constitutes a permanent occupation can, under the right circumstances, be constructive rather than actual. Continuous low-level government aircraft flights over private land rendered the land unusable for any purpose; thus, the resulting loss was "as complete as if the United States had entered upon the surface of the land and taken exclusive possession of it." United States v. Causby, 328 U.S. 256, 261 (1946). By contrast, in Yee v. City of Escondido, 503 U.S. 519 (1992), the Court found no permanent occupation by a "mobile home park" rent control ordinance that authorized a tenant to continue indefinitely to occupy the landlord's property at a below-market price. The permanent physical occupation requirement was not relevant because the initial decision of a landlord to permit the tenant to occupy his property was not compelled by the state, and the landowner could, upon 6 to 12 months notice, evict all tenants and put his land to another use.

As *Yee* suggests, temporary physical occupations of private property are not within this automatic takings rule. Whether a temporary occupation is a taking depends on application of the relevant balancing test.

2. *Loss of all Economically Viable Use.* Except when a regulation does no more than abate a recognized nuisance, it is a taking if it destroys all economically viable use of private property. The property owner has the burden of proving the loss of all economically viable use. The government has

the burden of proving that its regulation, in that circumstance, is nothing more than nuisance abatement.

This rule makes conceptual severance very important. In a footnote, the Court suggests (but does not hold) that separate legal titles might constitute the denominator in the conceptual severance fraction. Yet, that suggestion seems at odds with the Court's refusal, in *Keystone*, to attach any significance to Pennsylvania's recognition of the support estate as a separate fee title.

3. *Nuisance Abatement.* After *Lucas*, regulations that only abate common law nuisances are not takings, no matter how economically ruinous they may be. In so ruling, the Court rejected the idea that regulations of use that are "noxious" but not actionable nuisances are automatically not takings. Because the Court did not purport to overrule any of the "noxious use" cases, presumably regulations of noxious uses are considered under the balancing tests that you will soon encounter.

The dissenters argued that the nuisance rule transfers power from legislatures to courts, because it prevents legislatures from identifying new public harms and labeling them as nuisances. The majority said that courts must apply the pre-existing law of nuisance when ascertaining whether a regulation is a nuisance abatement measure. Moreover, the Court strongly hinted that the question of whether a regulation was a nuisance abatement was not exclusively a matter of state law. The Court noted that a state court's application of the nuisance abatement rule must comport with "objectively reasonable application of relevant precedents." Thus, in the event a state court invents a new, previously unheard of, nuisance a federal constitutional issue is created—whether a regulation that abates a new, judicially invented, nuisance is an "objectively reasonable application" of the relevant precedents of state nuisance law. Thus, it may be that *Lucas* does not so much transfer power from state legislatures to state courts as limit the power of each body to identify property uses as new nuisances.

Is it desirable to permit legislatures to identify property uses that pose new public harms, and then act to prohibit all economically viable use of property in order to prevent the newly identifiable harm? After *Lucas*, legislatures may continue to identify many new harms, and limit property use to address those harms, so long as they do not ban all economically viable use. Thus, a city might prohibit paving of more than some specified percentage of a parcel's surface area, to prevent runoff of polluted water into the city's streams and groundwater. Such a measure would likely not prohibit all economically viable use of the property. But a ban on all development to achieve the same end would probably kill all economically viable use and would likely not be a nuisance abatement measure under prior nuisance law.

William Fischel, in *Regulatory Takings: Law, Economics, and Politics* (1995), argues that a truly democratic legislative process will protect private property, and that judicial intervention is necessary only to ensure that the process is not abusive to people who lack representation in the polity or the ability to leave the jurisdiction. Landowners have no exit option, because they can't move their land, but they can sell their land. Fischel contends that local governments are prone to favor in-place landowners at the expense of outsiders. Thus, development restrictions are likely to be adopted that cater to the tastes of a majority of existing residents, even though some in-place owners might wish to develop their land intensively to accommodate newcomers (and reap a profit by doing so). Does the *Lucas* rule brake this propensity by ensuring that compensation must be paid if draconian anti-development measures are adopted?

3.   THE BALANCING APPROACH

PENN CENTRAL TRANSPORTATION COMPANY v. NEW YORK CITY

Supreme Court of the United States
438 U.S. 104 (1978)

[In 1965 New York City enacted a Landmarks Preservation Law, which empowered the city's newly created Landmarks Preservation Commission to designate certain buildings or sites as historic landmarks. Once so designated, the owner of a building is required to keep its exterior in "good repair" and may not make any exterior alterations without prior approval of the Commission. Penn Central's Grand Central Terminal was designated a landmark, and the Commission rejected Penn Central's proposal to erect a 55–story skyscraper on top of Grand Central. In New York state court, Penn Central contended that the Commission's refusal to permit the development constituted a taking. The New York courts ruled that the landmark regulations were not a taking. The Supreme Court affirmed.]

JUSTICE BRENNAN delivered the opinion of the Court.

. . . Although the designation of a landmark and landmark site restricts the owner's control over the parcel, designation also enhances the economic position of the landmark owner in one significant respect. Under New York City's zoning laws, owners of real property who have not developed their property to the full extent permitted by the applicable zoning laws are allowed to transfer development rights to [nearby] parcels. . . .

Grand Central Terminal . . . is one of New York City's most famous buildings. Opened in 1913, it is regarded not only as providing an ingenious engineering solution to the problems presented by urban railroad stations, but also as a magnificent example of the French beaux-arts style. The Terminal is located in midtown Manhattan. Its south facade faces 42d Street and that street's intersection with Park Avenue. At street level, the Terminal is bounded on the west by Vanderbilt Avenue, on the east by the Commodore Hotel, and on the north by the Pan–American Building. . . . The Terminal itself is an eight-story structure which Penn Central uses as a railroad station and in which it rents space not needed for railroad purposes to a variety of commercial interests. The Terminal is one of a number of properties owned by appellant Penn Central in this area of midtown Manhattan. The others include the Barclay, Biltmore, Commodore, Roosevelt, and Waldorf–Astoria Hotels, the Pan–American

Building and other office buildings along Park Avenue, and the Yale Club. At least eight of these are eligible to be recipients of development rights afforded the Terminal by virtue of landmark designation.

[In 1967] the Commission designated the Terminal a "landmark" and designated the "city tax block" it occupies a "landmark site." ... On January 22, 1968, appellant Penn Central, to increase its income, entered into a renewable 50–year lease and sublease agreement with appellant UGP Properties, Inc. (UGP), a wholly owned subsidiary of Union General Properties, Ltd., a United Kingdom corporation. Under the terms of the agreement, UGP was to construct a multistory office building above the Terminal. UGP promised to pay Penn Central $1 million annually during construction and at least $3 million annually thereafter. The rentals would be offset in part by a loss of some $700,000 to $1 million in net rentals presently received from concessionaires displaced by the new building.

Appellants UGP and Penn Central then applied to the Commission for permission to construct an office building atop the Terminal. Two separate plans, both designed by architect Marcel Breuer and both apparently satisfying the terms of the applicable zoning ordinance, were submitted to the Commission for approval. The first, Breuer I, provided for the construction of a 55–story office building, to be cantilevered above the existing facade and to rest on the roof of the Terminal. The second, Breuer II Revised, called for tearing down a portion of the Terminal that included the 42d Street facade, stripping off some of the remaining features of the Terminal's facade, and constructing a 53–story office building. The Commission denied ... this application as to both proposals.

The Commission's reasons for rejecting certificates respecting Breuer II Revised are summarized in the following statement: "To protect a Landmark, one does not tear it down. To perpetuate its architectural features, one does not strip them off." [In rejecting] Breuer I, which would have preserved the existing vertical facades of the present structure, ... the Commission stated:

> [We have] no fixed rule against making additions to designated buildings—it all depends on how they are done.... But to balance a 55–story office tower above a flamboyant Beaux–Arts facade seems nothing more than an aesthetic joke. Quite simply, the tower would overwhelm the Terminal by its sheer mass. The " 'addition" would be four times as high as the existing structure and would reduce the Landmark itself to the status of a curiosity. Landmarks cannot be divorced from their settings—particularly when the setting is a dramatic and integral part of the original concept. The Terminal, in its setting, is a great example of urban design. Such examples are not so plentiful in New York City that we can afford to lose any of the few we have. And we must preserve them in a meaningful way—with alterations and additions of such character, scale, materials and mass

as will protect, enhance and perpetuate the original design rather than overwhelm it.

[In the New York courts Penn Central and UGP] sought a declaratory judgment, injunctive relief barring the city from using the Landmarks Law to impede the construction of any structure that might otherwise lawfully be constructed on the Terminal site, and damages for the "temporary taking" that occurred between August 2, 1967, the designation date, and the date when the restrictions arising from the Landmarks Law would be lifted. The trial court granted the injunctive and declaratory relief, but severed the question of damages for a "temporary taking." . . . [The] New York Supreme Court, Appellate Division, reversed [and the] New York Court of Appeals affirmed.

Issue (1) only

The issues presented by appellants are (1) whether the restrictions imposed by New York City's law upon appellants' exploitation of the Terminal site effect a "taking" of appellants' property . . . and, (2), if so, whether the transferable development rights afforded appellants constitute "just compensation" . . . We need only address the question whether a "taking" has occurred. . . .

[While the takings clause is] "designed to bar Government from forcing some people alone to bear public burdens which, in all fairness and justice, should be borne by the public as a whole," this Court, quite simply, has been unable to develop any "set formula" for determining when "justice and fairness" require that economic injuries caused by public action be compensated by the government, rather than remain disproportionately concentrated on a few persons. Indeed, we have frequently observed that whether a particular restriction will be rendered invalid by the government's failure to pay for any losses proximately caused by it depends largely "upon the particular circumstances [in that] case." In engaging in these essentially ad hoc, factual inquiries, the Court [has] identified several factors that have particular significance. The economic impact of the regulation on the claimant and, particularly, the extent to which the regulation has interfered with distinct investment-backed expectations are, of course, relevant considerations. So, too, is the character of the governmental action. A "taking" may more readily be found when the interference with property can be characterized as a physical invasion by government than when interference arises from some public program adjusting the benefits and burdens of economic life to promote the common good.

[In] a wide variety of contexts, . . . government may execute laws or programs that adversely affect recognized economic values. Exercises of the taxing power are one obvious example. A second are the decisions in which this Court has dismissed "taking" challenges on the ground that, while the challenged government action caused economic harm, it did not interfere with interests that were sufficiently bound up with the reasonable expectations of the claimant to constitute "property". . . . United States v. Willow River Power Co., 324 U.S. 499 (1945) (interest in high-water level of river . . . to maintain power head is not property); United States v. Chandler–Dunbar Water Power Co., 229 U.S. 53 (1913) (no property interest can exist in navigable waters). . . .

More importantly for the present case, in instances in which a state tribunal reasonably concluded that "the health, safety, morals, or general welfare" would be promoted by prohibiting particular contemplated uses of land, this Court has upheld land-use regulations that destroyed or adversely affected recognized real property interests. Zoning laws are, of course, the classic example. . . .

"[T]aking" challenges have also been held to be without merit in a wide variety of situations when the challenged governmental actions prohibited a beneficial use to which individual parcels had previously been devoted and thus caused substantial individualized harm. [*Miller*; *Hadacheck*.] [Yet,] a use restriction on real property may constitute a "taking" if not reasonably necessary to the effectuation of a substantial public purpose or perhaps if it has an unduly harsh impact upon the owner's use of the property. Pennsylvania Coal Co. v. Mahon, 260 U.S. 393 (1922), is the leading case for the proposition that a state statute that substantially furthers important public policies may so frustrate distinct investment-backed expectations as to amount to a "taking." . . . Because the statute . . . had nearly the same effect as the complete destruction of rights claimant had reserved from the owners of the surface land, the Court held that the statute was invalid as effecting a "taking" without just compensation. Finally, government actions that may be characterized as acquisitions of resources to permit or facilitate uniquely public functions have often been held to constitute "takings." United States v. Causby.

[In] contending that the New York City law has "taken" their [property], appellants . . . first observe that the airspace above the Terminal is a valuable property interest. [They] urge that the Landmarks Law has deprived them of any gainful use of their "air rights" above the Terminal and that, irrespective of the value of the remainder of their parcel, the city has "taken" their right to this . . . airspace, thus entitling them to "just compensation" measured by the fair market value of these air rights. [T]he submission that appellants may establish a "taking" simply by showing that they have been denied the ability to exploit a property interest that they heretofore had believed was available for development is quite simply untenable. "[Taking]" jurisprudence does not divide a single parcel into discrete segments and attempt to determine whether rights in a particular segment have been entirely abrogated. In deciding whether a particular governmental action has effected a taking, this Court focuses rather both on the character of the action and on the nature and extent of the interference with rights in the parcel as a [whole].

[A]ppellants argue that New York City's regulation of individual landmarks is fundamentally different from zoning or from historic-district legislation because the controls imposed by New York City's law apply only to individuals who own selected properties. Stated baldly, appellants' position appears to be that the only means of ensuring that selected owners are not singled out to endure financial hardship for no reason is to hold that any restriction imposed on individual landmarks pursuant to the New York City scheme is a "taking" requiring the payment of "just compensation." Agreement with this argument would, of course, invalidate not just New York City's law, but all comparable landmark legislation in the Nation. We find no merit in it.

[A]ppellants emphasize that both historic-district legislation and zoning laws regulate all properties within given physical communities whereas landmark laws apply only to selected parcels. But ... landmark laws are not like discriminatory, or "reverse spot," zoning: that is, a land-use decision which arbitrarily singles out a particular parcel for different, less favorable treatment than the neighboring ones. In contrast to discriminatory zoning, which is the antithesis of land-use control as part of some comprehensive plan, the New York City law embodies a comprehensive plan to preserve structures of historic or aesthetic interest wherever they might be found in the city, and ... over 400 landmarks and 31 historic districts have been designated pursuant to this plan.

Equally without merit is the related argument that the decision to designate a structure as a landmark "is inevitably arbitrary or at least subjective, because it is basically a matter of taste," thus unavoidably singling out individual landowners for disparate and unfair treatment. ... But ... a landmark owner has a right to judicial review of any Commission decision, and, quite simply, there is no basis whatsoever for a conclusion that courts will have any greater difficulty identifying arbitrary or discriminatory action in the context of landmark regulation than in the context of classic zoning or indeed in any other context....

Next, appellants observe that New York City's law differs from zoning laws and historic-district ordinances in that the Landmarks Law does not impose identical or similar restrictions on all structures located in particular physical communities. It follows, they argue, that New York City's law is inherently incapable of producing the fair and equitable distribution of benefits and burdens of governmental action which is characteristic of zoning laws and historic-district legislation and which they maintain is a constitutional requirement if "just compensation" is not to be afforded. It is, of course, true that the Landmarks Law has a more severe impact on some landowners than on others, but that in itself does not mean that the law effects a "taking." Legislation designed to promote the general welfare commonly burdens some more than others. The owners ... of the cedar trees in Miller v. Schoene [were] uniquely burdened by the legislation sustained [there]. Similarly, zoning laws often affect some property owners more severely than others but have not been held to be invalid on that account. For example, the property owner in *Euclid* who wished to use its property for industrial purposes was affected far more severely by the ordinance than its neighbors who wished to use their land for residences.

In any event, appellants' repeated suggestions that they are solely burdened and unbenefited is factually inaccurate. This contention overlooks the fact that the New York City law applies to vast numbers of structures in the city in addition to the Terminal ..., many of which are close to the Terminal. Unless we are to reject the judgment of the New York City Council that the preservation of landmarks benefits all New York citizens and all structures, both economically and by improving the quality of life in the city as a whole—which we are unwilling to do—we cannot conclude that the owners of the Terminal have in no sense been benefited by the Landmarks Law. Doubtless appellants believe they are more burdened than benefited by the law, but that must have been true, too, of the property owners in *Miller, Hadacheck,* [and] *Euclid.*

Appellants ... would have us treat the law as an instance, like that in United States v. Causby, in which government, acting in an enterprise capacity, has appropriated part of their property for some strictly governmental purpose. Apart from the fact that *Causby* was a case of invasion of airspace that destroyed the use of the farm beneath and this New York City law has in nowise impaired the present use of the Terminal, the Landmarks Law neither exploits appellants' parcel for city purposes nor facilitates nor arises from any entrepreneurial operations of the city. The situation is not remotely like that in *Causby* where the airspace above the property was in the flight pattern for military aircraft. The Landmarks Law's effect is simply to prohibit appellants or anyone else from occupying portions of the airspace above the Terminal, while permitting appellants to use the remainder of the parcel in a gainful fashion. This is no more an appropriation of property by government for its own uses than is a zoning law prohibiting, for "aesthetic" reasons, two or more adult theaters within a specified area, or a safety regulation prohibiting excavations below a certain level.

[We] now must consider whether the interference with appellants' property is of such a magnitude that "there must be an exercise of eminent domain and compensation to sustain [it]." That inquiry may be narrowed to the question of the severity of the impact of the law on appellants' parcel, and its resolution in turn requires a careful assessment of the impact of the regulation on the Terminal site. [The] New York City law does not interfere in any way with the present uses of the Terminal ...: as a railroad terminal containing office space and concessions. So the law does not interfere with what must be regarded as Penn Central's primary expectation concerning the use of the parcel. More importantly, on this record, we must regard the New York City law as permitting Penn Central not only to profit from the Terminal but also to obtain a "reasonable return" on its investment.

[Moreover], to the extent appellants have been denied the right to build above the Terminal, [they have not] been denied all use of even those pre-existing air rights. Their ability to use these rights has not been abrogated; they are made transferable to at least eight parcels in the vicinity of the Terminal, one or two of which have been found suitable for the construction of new office buildings. [While] these rights may well not have constituted "just compensation" if a "taking" had occurred, the rights nevertheless undoubtedly mitigate whatever financial burdens the law has imposed on appellants and, for that reason, are to be taken into account in considering the impact of regulation.

Holding

[Application] of New York City's Landmarks Law has not effected a "taking" of appellants' property. The restrictions imposed are substantially related to the promotion of the general welfare and not only permit reasonable beneficial use of the landmark site but also afford appellants opportunities further to enhance not only the Terminal site proper but also other properties. Affirmed.

JUSTICE REHNQUIST, joined by CHIEF JUSTICE BURGER and JUSTICE STEVENS, dissenting.

Of the over one million buildings and structures in the city of New York, appellees have singled out 400 for designation as official landmarks. The owner of a building might initially be pleased that his property has been chosen [for] such a singular distinction. But he may well discover [that] the landmark designation imposes upon him a substantial cost, with little or no offsetting benefit except for the honor of the designation. The question in this case is whether the cost associated with the city of New York's desire to preserve a limited number of "landmarks" within its borders must be borne by all of its taxpayers or whether it can instead be imposed entirely on the owners of the individual properties. . . .

Typical zoning restrictions [so] limit the prospective uses of a piece of property as to diminish the value of that property in the abstract because it may not be used for the forbidden purposes. But any such abstract decrease in value will more than likely be at least partially offset by an increase in value which flows from similar restrictions as to use on neighboring properties. All property owners in a designated area are placed under the same restrictions, not only for the benefit of the municipality as a whole but also for the common benefit of one another. In the words of Mr. Justice Holmes, there is "an average reciprocity of advantage." Where a relatively few individual buildings, all separated from one another, are singled out and treated differently from surrounding buildings, no such reciprocity exists. The cost to the property owner which results from the imposition of restrictions applicable only to his property and not that of his neighbors may be substantial—in this case, several million dollars—with no comparable reciprocal benefits. And the cost associated with landmark legislation is likely to be of a completely different order of magnitude than that which results from the imposition of normal zoning restrictions. Unlike the regime affected by the latter, the landowner is not simply prohibited from using his property for certain purposes, while allowed to use it for all other purposes. Under the historic-landmark preservation scheme adopted by New York, the property owner is under an affirmative duty to preserve his property as a landmark at his own expense. To suggest that because traditional zoning results in some limitation of use of the property zoned, the New York City landmark preservation scheme should likewise be upheld, represents the ultimate in treating as alike things which are different. [The takings clause] bars the "Government from forcing some people alone to bear public burdens which, in all fairness and justice, should be borne by the public as a whole." . . . [The transferable development rights are relevant only to the question of whether those rights] constitute a "full and perfect equivalent for the property taken." . . . Because the record on [this point] is relatively slim, I would remand to the Court of Appeals for a determination of whether TDRs constitute a "full and perfect equivalent for the property taken."

NOTES AND QUESTIONS

1. Ad Hoc Inquiry: "Investment–Backed Expectations." The Court confessed that it has been "unable to develop any 'set formula' for determining when 'justice and fairness' require that economic injuries caused by public action be compensated by the government, rather than remain disproportionately concentrated on a few persons," and that the best it could do was to rely on "essentially ad hoc, factual inquiries." The categorical rules, however, provide a few bright-line formulae, so the ad hoc approach of *Penn Central* applies when the categorical rules fail to provide an answer. In this case, the landmarks law did not leave Penn Central with no economically viable use of Grand Central Terminal, did not dispossess Penn Central, and was not a nuisance abatement measure.

The Court said that Penn Central could still earn a "reasonable return" on its "investment-backed expectations." But how are those expectations to be determined? When Grand Central Terminal was being planned in 1903, the idea was to cover the tracks to facilitate real estate development above ground. Does that indicate that the "investment-backed expectations" were as much real estate development as operation of a rail terminal? But the Terminal was in fact used exclusively as a rail terminal from its opening in 1913. Does that indicate that the expectations were confined to use as a train station? By 1954, rail travel had declined sufficiently that the owners resolved to demolish the Terminal and replace it with an office tower. Nothing came of this plan but in 1958 the owners did combine with a developer to erect the 59 story Pan Am building at the north side of the Terminal. Does this bear on expectations?

What's a "reasonable return" on investment? Is there some objective measure? If one measure is the return on U.S. Treasury obligations, as of August 2011 the interest rate on short term (less than a year) Treasury notes was about 4/100 of one percent, or virtually zero. The rate on longer term Treasury notes varied from about 1/10 of one percent, for a one year note, to about 3 percent for a 20 year note. Do those yields suggest that a paltry return is reasonable? On the other hand, 10 year U.S. Treasury bonds in 1980 yielded almost 16%. So what's a reasonable return? And how is investment to be measured? Is it the historical cost, which was estimated to be about $80 million in 1904? Or, should it be historical cost adjusted to reflect inflation, in which case it is about $2 to $3 billion? Or, should it be replacement cost? The Court provides no answers to these practical questions.

2. *More on "Just Compensation."* The Court in *Penn Central* thought it was unnecessary to address the issue of whether the transferable air rights constituted just compensation. Instead, the majority saw those rights as simply another factor to be considered in its ad hoc balancing of interests. The dissenters, however, thought that issue was critical to disposition of the case.

What constitutes a "full and perfect equivalent for the property taken"? That question was central to Brown v. Legal Foundation of Washington, 538 U.S. 216 (2003). The Court had to decide whether Washington's practice of forcing lawyers and real estate escrow agents to deposit client funds into a pooled interest-bearing trust account, and then taking the interest earned on those accounts to pay for legal services provided by the state to indigents, denied just compensation to the clients whose funds earned the interest. In Phillips v. Washington Legal Foundation, 524 U.S. 156 (1998), the Court had held that the interest earned on such accounts was the property of the client, but did not decide the compensation issue. Washington required lawyers and escrow agents to deposit client funds into separate, individual interest-bearing trust accounts if the deposited funds would earn interest, net of transaction costs, and to pay the net interest to the client, but required all other client funds to be deposited into pooled trust accounts, with the interest earned to be paid to the Legal Foundation of Washington, a charitable foundation limited to financing legal services for the indigent ("IOLTA" accounts).

The Court, 5 to 4, ruled that no compensation was due to clients whose funds were deposited in pooled accounts, because the interest generated was so tiny in amount that the costs of computing and paying the interest would exceed the amount of earned interest. The majority reasoned that no compensation was due because the "pecuniary loss" to affected clients was "zero." Just compensation, said the Court, must be measured by the property owner's "net loss rather than the value of the public's gain."

Justice Scalia, writing for the four dissenters, contended that there was no difference between "the value the owner has lost [and] the value the government has gained." They "have lost the interest that *Phillips* says rightfully belongs to them—which is precisely what the government has gained.... The State could satisfy its obligation to pay just compensation by simply returning [the clients'] money to the IOLTA account from which it was seized, leaving others to incur the accounting costs in the event [clients] seek to extract their interest from the account." Justice Scalia cited with approval the observation of the Court in *Phillips* that "[t]he government may not seize rents received by the owner of a building simply because it can prove that the costs incurred in collecting the rents exceed the amount collected."

3. *Later Developments.* Because the categorical rule of *Lucas* applies when regulations deprive an owner of all economically viable use (except for nuisance abatement), its application hinges on the property affected. Compare *Mahon* and *Keystone*. This raises a number of thorny questions, some of which the Court has addressed.

In Palazzolo v. Rhode Island, 533 U.S. 606 (2001), the Court confronted the issue of whether a property owner lacks any reasonable expectation of investment return if he acquires property subject to existing regulations that would, if applied to him after acquisition of the property, constitute a taking. The majority rejected the idea that a landowner is barred from claiming that any regulations in effect at the time he acquires title constitute a taking. Embrace of that proposition would immunize extreme and unreasonable regulations against attack by future owners, would be capricious as it would allow owners with the will and means to hold property for a long time to challenge regulations but deny that ability to owners who have recently acquired property, and would deny to in-place owners the ability to transfer to others the same title they had. The Court concluded that the regulations did not deny to Palazzolo all economically viable use of his property and so remanded the case to the Rhode Island Supreme Court for a determination of whether the regulations effected a taking under the *Penn Central* balancing test. In a concurrence, Justice O'Connor suggested that regulations in place at the time an owner acquires property are relevant to the *Penn Central* issue of the owner's reasonable investment-backed expectations.

The question of whether a property owner has lost all economically viable use of his property if regulations absolutely forbid any development or use for a protracted period of time, but not for all time, is at the heart of the next case.

TAHOE–SIERRA PRESERVATION COUNCIL, INC. v. TAHOE REGIONAL PLANNING AGENCY

Supreme Court of the United States
535 U.S. 302 (2002)

JUSTICE STEVENS delivered the opinion of the Court.

The question presented is whether a moratorium on development imposed during the process of devising a comprehensive land-use plan constitutes a *per se* taking of property requiring compensation. . . . [Tahoe Regional Planning Agency (TRPA) imposed two moratoria, totaling 32 months (or nearly six years, as the dissenters contended), on development in the Lake Tahoe Basin while it created a comprehensive land-use plan for the area designed to address the threat of pollution of Lake Tahoe from increasing residential development. Petitioners, real estate owners affected by the moratoria and an association representing such owners, filed parallel suits, later consolidated, claiming that TRPA's actions constituted a taking of their property without just compensation.]

I.   The relevant facts are undisputed. . . . Lake Tahoe is "uniquely beautiful," [so much so] that Mark Twain aptly described the clarity of its waters as "not *merely* transparent, but dazzlingly, brilliantly so." [M. Twain, Roughing It 174–175 (1872), emphasis added by the Court]. Lake Tahoe's exceptional clarity is attributed to the absence of algae that obscures the waters of most other lakes. Historically, the lack of nitrogen and phosphorous, which nourish the growth of algae, has ensured the transparency of its waters. Unfortunately, the lake's pristine state has deteriorated rapidly over the past 40 years; increased land development in the Lake Tahoe Basin (Basin) has threatened the "noble sheet of blue water" beloved by Twain and countless others. "[D]ramatic decreases in clarity first began to be noted in the [1950s], shortly after development at the lake began in earnest." The lake's unsurpassed beauty, it seems, is the wellspring of its undoing. The upsurge of development in the area has caused "increased nutrient loading of the lake largely because of the increase in impervious coverage of land in the Basin resulting from that development," [a trend that, unless stopped, was predicted to cause the lake to] "lose its clarity and its trademark blue color, becoming green and opaque for eternity."

[The TRPA identified properties with steep slopes and] certain areas near streams or wetlands known as "Stream Environment Zones" (SEZs) [as] especially vulnerable to the impact of development because, in their natural state, they act as filters for much of the debris that runoff carries. [In order to implement an interstate compact concerning the Tahoe Basin, TRPA enacted two ordinances to suspend development until it adopted] the permanent plan required by the Compact.... In combination, [the two ordinances] effectively prohibited all construction on sensitive lands in California and on all SEZ lands in the entire Basin for 32 months, and on sensitive lands in Nevada (other than SEZ lands) for eight months. It is these two moratoria that are at issue in this case....

II.   ... [The District Court ruled that the moratoria constituted a taking under *Lucas* because they temporarily deprived petitioners of all economically viable use of their land. On appeal, the Ninth Circuit reversed, concluding] that because the regulations had only a temporary impact on petitioners' fee interest in the properties, no categorical taking [under *Lucas*] had occurred. [T]he moratoria involve only a "temporal 'slice'" of the fee interest. [The Ninth Circuit noted that] "a property interest may include a physical dimension (which describes the size and shape of the property in question), a functional dimension (which describes the extent to which an owner may use or dispose of the property in question), and a temporal dimension (which describes the duration of the property interest)." [It rejected the argument] "that we should conceptually sever each plaintiff's fee interest into discrete segments in at least one of these dimensions—the temporal one—and treat each of those segments as separate and distinct property interests for purposes of takings analysis." ... We now affirm.

III.   Petitioners make only a facial attack on [the moratoria]. They contend that the mere enactment of a temporary regulation that, while in effect, denies a property owner all viable economic use of her property gives rise to an unqualified constitutional obligation to compensate her for the value of its use during that period. [They] assert that our opinions in *First English* and *Lucas* have already endorsed their view, and that it is a logical application of the principle that the Takings Clause was "designed to bar Government from forcing some people alone to bear burdens which, in all fairness and justice, should be borne by the public as a whole." Armstrong v. United States, 364 U.S. 40, 49 (1960). ... [We] conclude that the circumstances in this case are best analyzed within the *Penn Central* framework.

IV. ... When the government physically takes possession of an interest in property for some public purpose, it has a categorical duty to compensate the former owner, regardless of whether the interest that is taken constitutes an entire parcel or merely a part thereof. [*Loretto; Causby.*] But a government regulation that ... bans certain private uses of a portion of an owner's property ... does not constitute a categorical taking. [*Keystone Bituminous Coal; Penn Central.*] "The first category of cases requires courts to apply a clear rule; the second necessarily entails complex factual assessments of the purposes and economic effects of government actions." Yee v. Escondido, 503 U.S. 519, 523 (1992)....

[Petitioners] rely principally on [*Lucas*] to argue that the *Penn Central* framework is inapplicable here. [But it was *Mahon*] that gave birth to our regulatory takings jurisprudence [and, after *Mahon*,] even though multiple factors are relevant in the analysis of regulatory takings claims, in such cases we must focus on "the parcel as a whole." [*Penn Central.*] This requirement ... explains why, for example, a regulation that prohibited commercial transactions in eagle feathers, but did not bar other uses or impose any physical invasion or restraint upon them, was not a taking, [Andrus v. Allard, 444 U.S. 51 (1979), and] clarifies why ... a requirement that coal pillars be left in place to prevent mine subsidence [was not a taking.] *Keystone.*

[However a regulation is to be determined to be a taking, it is a] separate remedial question of how compensation is measured once a regulatory taking is established. [In First English Evangelical Lutheran Church of Glendale v. County of Los Angeles, 482 U.S. 304 (1987), the Court ruled that] "once a court finds that a police power regulation has effected a 'taking,' the government entity must pay just compensation for the period commencing on the date the regulation first effected the 'taking,' and ending on the date the government entity chooses to rescind or otherwise amend the regulation." [While] nothing that we say today qualifies [*First English,*] we did not address in that case the quite different and logically prior question whether the temporary regulation at issue had in fact constituted a taking....

Petitioners seek to bring this case under the rule announced in *Lucas* by arguing that we can effectively sever a 32–month segment from the remainder of each landowner's fee simple estate, and then ask whether that segment has been taken in its entirety by the moratoria. Of course, defining the property interest taken in terms of the very regulation being challenged is circular. With property so divided, every delay would become a total ban; the moratorium and the normal permit process alike would constitute categorical takings. Petitioners' "conceptual severance" argument is unavailing because it ignores *Penn Central*'s admonition that in regulatory takings cases we must focus on "the parcel as a whole."

An interest in real property is defined by the metes and bounds that describe its geographic dimensions and the term of years that describes the temporal aspect of the owner's interest. Both dimensions must be considered if the interest is to be viewed in its entirety. Hence, a permanent deprivation of the owner's use of the entire area is a taking of "the parcel as a whole," whereas a temporary restriction that merely causes a diminution in value is not. Logically, a fee simple estate cannot be rendered valueless by a temporary prohibition on economic use, because the property will recover value as soon as the prohibition is lifted.... *Lucas* [and] *First English* ... make clear that the categorical rule in *Lucas* was carved out for the "extraordinary case" in which a regulation permanently deprives property of all value; the default rule remains that, in the regulatory taking context, we require a more fact specific inquiry.

V. [An] extreme categorical rule that any deprivation of all economic use, no matter how brief, constitutes a compensable taking surely cannot be sustained, [for it] would apply to [such normal matters as] orders temporarily prohibiting access to crime scenes, businesses that violate health codes, fire-damaged buildings, or other [issues] that we cannot now foresee.... A rule that required compensation for every delay in the use of property would render routine government processes prohibitively expensive or encourage hasty decisionmaking. [W]e are persuaded that the better approach to claims that a regulation has effected a temporary taking "requires careful examination and weighing of all the relevant circumstances." ... In rejecting petitioners' *per se* rule, we do not hold that the temporary nature of a land-use restriction precludes finding that it effects a taking; we simply recognize that it should not be given exclusive significance one way or the other.

[Moratoria] are used widely among land-use planners to preserve the status quo while formulating a more permanent development strategy [and] are an essential tool of successful development. Yet even the weak version of petitioners' categorical rule would treat these interim measures as takings regardless of the good faith of the planners, the reasonable expectations of the landowners, or the actual impact of the moratorium on property values.

[With] a temporary ban on development there is a lesser risk that individual landowners will be "singled out" to bear a special burden that should be shared by the public as a whole. At least with a moratorium there is a clear "reciprocity of advantage" because it protects the interests of all affected landowners against immediate construction that might be inconsistent with the provisions of the plan that is ultimately adopted.... In fact, there is reason to believe property values often will continue to increase despite a moratorium. Such an increase makes sense in this context because property values throughout the Basin can be expected to reflect the added assurance that Lake Tahoe will remain in its pristine state....

In our view, the duration of the restriction is one of the important factors that a court must consider in the appraisal of a regulatory takings claim, but with respect to that factor as with respect to other factors, the "temptation to adopt what amount to *per se* rules in either direction must be resisted." *Palazzolo*, [O'Connor, J., concurring]. We conclude [that] "fairness and justice" will be best served by relying on the familiar *Penn Central* approach when deciding cases like this, rather than by attempting to craft a new categorical rule.

[Affirmed.]

CHIEF JUSTICE REHNQUIST, with whom JUSTICE SCALIA and JUSTICE THOMAS join, dissenting.

For over half a decade petitioners were prohibited from building homes, or any other structures, on their land. Because the Takings Clause requires the government to pay compensation when it deprives owners of all economically viable use of their land, and because a ban on all development lasting almost six years does not resemble any traditional land-use planning device, I dissent.

I. "A court cannot determine whether a regulation has gone 'too far' unless it knows how far the regulation goes." [Although the Court] relies on the flawed determination of the Court of Appeals that the relevant time period lasted only from August 1981 until April 1984 [, in fact, because] respondent caused petitioners' inability to use their land from 1981 through 1987, that is the appropriate period of time from which to consider their takings claim.

II. I now turn to determining whether a ban on all economic development lasting almost six years is a taking. . . . [The] Court refuses to apply *Lucas* on the ground that the deprivation was "temporary." Neither the Takings Clause nor our case law supports such a distinction. For one thing, a distinction between "temporary" and "permanent" prohibitions is tenuous. The "temporary" prohibition in this case that the Court finds is not a taking lasted almost six years. The "permanent" prohibition that the Court held to be a taking in *Lucas* lasted less than two years ... because the law, as it often does, changed. Under the Court's decision today, the takings question turns entirely on the initial label given a regulation, a label that is often without much meaning. There is every incentive for government to simply label any prohibition on development "temporary," or to fix a set number of years. As in this case, this initial designation does not preclude the government from repeatedly extending the "temporary" prohibition into a long-term ban on all development. The Court now holds that such a designation by the government is conclusive even though in fact the moratorium greatly exceeds the time initially specified. . . .

More fundamentally, even if a practical distinction between temporary and permanent deprivations were plausible, to treat the two differently in terms of takings law would be at odds with the justification for the *Lucas* rule, [which is] that a "total deprivation of use is, from the landowner's point of view, the equivalent of a physical appropriation." The regulation in *Lucas* was the "practical equivalence" of a long-term physical appropriation.... The "practical equivalence," from the landowner's point of view, of a "temporary" ban on all economic use is a forced leasehold.... Surely that leasehold would require compensation. [What] happened in this case is no different than if the government had taken a 6–year lease of their property....

Lucas is implicated when the government deprives a landowner of "all economically beneficial or productive use of land." The District Court found, and the Court agrees, that the moratorium "temporarily" deprived petitioners of "all economically viable use of their land." [The] "temporary" denial of all viable use of land for six years is a taking.

III.   The Court worries that applying *Lucas* here compels finding that an array of traditional, short-term, land-use planning devices are takings. But since the beginning of our regulatory takings jurisprudence, we have recognized that property rights "are enjoyed under an implied limitation." ... When a regulation merely delays a final land use decision, we have recognized that there are other background principles of state property law that prevent the delay from being deemed a taking. We thus noted in *First English* that our discussion of temporary takings did not apply "in the case of normal delays in obtaining building permits, changes in zoning ordinances, variances, and the like." [The] short-term delays attendant to zoning and permit regimes are a longstanding feature of state property law and part of a landowner's reasonable investment-backed expectations.... But a moratorium prohibiting all economic use for a period of six years is not one of the longstanding, implied limitations of state property law. Moratoria [that] prohibit only certain categories of development, such as fast-food restaurants, or all commercial development, ... do not implicate *Lucas* because they do not deprive landowners of all economically beneficial use of their land. [But] moratoria that prohibit all development ... do not have the lineage of permit and zoning requirements and thus it is less certain that property is acquired under the "implied limitation" of a moratorium prohibiting all development....

But this case does not require us to decide as a categorical matter whether moratoria prohibiting all economic use are an implied limitation of state property law, because the duration of this "moratorium" far exceeds that of ordinary moratoria.... Because the prohibition on development of nearly six years in this case cannot be said to resemble any "implied limitation" of state property law, it is a taking that requires compensation.

Lake Tahoe is a national treasure and I do not doubt that respondent's efforts at preventing further degradation of the lake were made in good faith in furtherance of the public interest. But, as is the case with most governmental action that furthers the public interest, the Constitution requires that the costs and burdens be borne by the public at large, not by a few targeted citizens.

JUSTICE THOMAS, with whom JUSTICE SCALIA joins, dissenting.

I write separately to address the majority's conclusion that the temporary moratorium at issue here was not a taking because it was not a "taking of 'the parcel as a whole.' " ... *First English* put to rest the notion that the "relevant denominator" is land's infinite life. Consequently, a regulation effecting a total deprivation of the use of a so-called "temporal slice" of property is compensable under the Takings Clause unless background principles of state property law prevent it from being deemed a taking. . . .

A taking is exactly what occurred in this case. No one seriously doubts that the land use regulations at issue rendered petitioners' land unsusceptible of *any* economically beneficial use. This was true at the inception of the moratorium, and it remains true today. [The Court's] "logical" assurance that a "temporary restriction ... merely causes a diminution in value" is cold comfort to the property owners in this case or any other. After all, "*in the long run* we are all dead." John Maynard Keynes, Monetary Reform 88 (1924).

I would hold that regulations prohibiting all productive uses of property are subject to *Lucas*'s *per se* rule, regardless of whether the property so burdened retains theoretical useful life and value if, and when, the "temporary" moratorium is lifted. To my mind, such potential future value bears on the amount of compensation due and has nothing to do with the question whether there was a taking in the first place.

NOTES, QUESTIONS, AND PROBLEMS

1. Conceptual Severance Again. One impact of *Lucas* has been to heighten the importance of the denominator in the categorical takings analysis. The denominator is the property affected by the challenged regulation, but that property is not always so easily defined. Is it defined by interests that are legally recognized as separate? *Mahon* hinted as much, but *Keystone* thought that the legally separate support estate was of no consequence to takings analysis, yet the Court in *Lucas* also hinted that the denominator should be defined by legally separate estates. Property interests that are legally separated can be conceptually severed into two parcels, one of which bears the full force of the regulation and the other of which is untouched or only affected insignificantly. *Tahoe–Sierra* rejects the idea that a property interest can be temporally severed, at least conceptually. But what if a landowner had actually severed his interest temporally, creating two legally recognized and separate estates: A leasehold and a reversion in fee simple?

2. Problem: O, owner of a lot in the Tahoe Basin, enters into a 36 month lease of his lot to *A*. Then a total building and development moratorium 36 months is issued by the relevant authorities. Does the moratorium constitute a taking of all economically viable economic use of *A*'s leasehold?

3. Lingle v. Chevron U.S.A.: Clarification? Hawaii enacted legislation limiting the maximum rent payable by lessees of gasoline service stations owned by oil companies. The Legislature so acted because gasoline distribution in Hawaii was concentrated in the hands of the major oil companies. Chevron claimed the rent limit was an uncompensated taking of its property, and the Ninth Circuit agreed, relying on Agins v. City of Tiburon, 447 U.S. 255, 260 (1980), in which the Supreme Court declared that government regulation of private property "effects a taking if [such regulation] does not substantially advance legitimate state interests. . . ." In Lingle v. Chevron U.S.A., 544 U.S. 528 (2005), the Supreme Court rejected that standard "as a freestanding takings test," declaring that "it has no proper place in our takings jurisprudence." The Court reiterated its commitment to the *per se* regulatory takings rules, but asserted that "[o]utside these . . . relatively narrow categories (and the special context of land-use exactions discussed [in *Nollan* and *Dolan,* considered in the next section]), regulatory takings challenges are governed by the standards set forth in *Penn Central. . . .*"

The Court stated that each of the *per se* rules and the *Penn Central* ad hoc multi-factor approach "aims to identify regulatory actions that are functionally equivalent to the classic taking in which government directly appropriates private property or ousts the owner from his domain. Accordingly, each of these tests focuses directly upon the severity of the burden that government imposes upon private property rights." The Court contended that the " 'substantially advances' formula suggests a means-ends test: It asks . . . whether a regulation of private property is *effective* in achieving some legitimate public purpose." But this inquiry "reveals nothing about the *magnitude or character of the burden* a particular regulation imposes upon private property rights [nor] does it [illuminate] how any regulatory burden is *distributed* among property owners." Accordingly, the "substantially advances" test "does not help to identify those regulations whose effects are functionally comparable to government appropriation or invasion of private property." Instead, this "inquiry probes the regulation's underlying validity," but that issue "is logically prior to and distinct from the question whether a regulation effects a taking, for the Takings Clause presupposes that the government has acted in pursuit of a valid public purpose." The Court emphasized that its holding "does not require us to disturb any of our prior holdings."

Queries: Does the taking clause presuppose "that the government has acted in pursuit of a valid public purpose"? Isn't that what the "public use" requirement is designed to determine?

4. *Problem.* Suppose that the New York Landmarks law at issue in *Penn Central* had only applied to Grand Central Terminal in precisely the manner in which the law actually applied to the Terminal. Would (should) that change the result? If so, is the change due to some increase in the magnitude or character of the burden, or due to the poor fit between the end (preservation of New York City's numerous historical landmarks) and the means chosen (preservation of only one such landmark), or to some other reason? If the result would not change, why is that so?

C. CONDITIONAL REGULATORY TAKINGS

Suppose that a government adopts a regulation that is not itself a taking—such as a requirement that a property owner obtain a building permit before commencing construction. May the government then refuse to issue a building permit unless the property owner consents to some condition that, by itself, would be an uncompensated taking? That is the problem of "conditional regulatory takings." The problem is not confined to takings; it crops up repeatedly in constitutional law as the problem of unconstitutional conditions. We need not dwell on the various permutations of the larger problem; we need only consider when, if at all, a condition that standing alone would be a taking is a valid regulation because it is attached to some independently valid regulation.

The general answer, supplied by the next two cases, is that a government may not require a person to surrender his property without compensation "in exchange for a discretionary benefit conferred by the government where the property sought has little or no relationship to the benefit." Dolan v. City of Tigard, 512 U.S. 374 (1994). That standard embodies two elements: (1) there must be an "essential nexus" between the state's underlying legitimate regulatory interest and the condition imposed, so that the condition advances the state's legitimate reason for regulating in the first place; and (2) there must be "rough proportionality" between the condition and the impact of the owner's proposed action upon the state's legitimate regulatory interest. The government has the burden of proving each of these elements.

NOLLAN v. CALIFORNIA COASTAL COMMISSION

Supreme Court of the United States
483 U.S. 825 (1987)

JUSTICE SCALIA delivered the opinion of the Court.

James and Marilyn Nollan appeal from a decision of the California Court of Appeal ruling that the California Coastal Commission could condition its grant of permission to rebuild their house on their transfer to the public of an easement across their beachfront property....

The Nollans own a beachfront lot in Ventura County, California. A quarter-mile north of their property is Faria County Park, an oceanside public park with a public beach and recreation area. Another public beach area, known locally as "the Cove," lies 1,800 feet south of their lot. A concrete seawall approximately eight feet high separates the beach portion of the Nollans' property from the rest of the lot. The historic mean high tide line determines the lot's oceanside boundary.

The Nollans originally leased their property with an option to buy. The building on the lot was a small bungalow, totaling 504 square feet, which for a time they rented to summer vacationers. After years of rental use, however, the building had fallen into disrepair, and could no longer be rented out. The Nollans' option to purchase was conditioned on their promise to demolish the bungalow and replace it. In order to do so, under [California law] they were required to obtain a coastal development permit from the California Coastal Commission. On February 25, 1982, they submitted a permit application to the Commission in which they proposed to demolish the existing structure and replace it with a three-bedroom house in keeping with the rest of the neighborhood.

The Nollans were informed that . . . the Commission staff had recommended that the permit be granted subject to the condition that they allow the public an easement to pass across a portion of their property bounded by the mean high tide line on one side, and their seawall on the other side. This would make it easier for the public to get to Faria County Park and the Cove. The Nollans protested imposition of the condition, but the Commission overruled their objections and granted the permit subject to their recordation of a deed restriction granting the easement.

[The Commission defended] its imposition of the condition [because] the new house would increase blockage of the view of the ocean, thus contributing to the development of "a 'wall' of residential structures" that would prevent the public "psychologically . . . from realizing a stretch of coastline exists nearby that they have every right to visit." The new house would also increase private use of the shorefront. These effects of construction of the house, along with other area development, would cumulatively "burden the public's ability to traverse to and along the shorefront." Therefore the Commission could properly require the Nollans to offset that burden by providing additional lateral access to the public beaches in the form of an easement across their property. The Commission also noted that it had similarly conditioned 43 out of 60 coastal development permits along the same tract of land, and that of the 17 not so conditioned, 14 had been approved when the Commission did not have . . . regulations in place allowing imposition of the condition, and the remaining 3 had not involved shorefront property. . . .

Had California simply required the Nollans to make an easement across their beachfront available to the public on a permanent basis in order to increase public access to the beach, rather than conditioning their permit to rebuild their house on their agreeing to do so, we have no doubt there would have been a taking. To say that the appropriation of a public easement across a landowner's premises does not constitute the taking of a property interest but rather (as Justice Brennan contends) "a mere restriction on its use," is to use words in a manner that deprives them of all their ordinary meaning. Indeed, one of the principal uses of the eminent domain power is to assure that the government be able to require conveyance of just such interests, so long as it pays for them. Perhaps because the point is so obvious, we have never been confronted with a controversy that required us to rule upon it, but our cases' analysis of the effect of other governmental action leads to the same conclusion. [We] think a "permanent physical occupation" has occurred, for purposes of that rule, where individuals are given a permanent and continuous right to pass to and fro, so that the real property may continuously be traversed, even though no particular individual is permitted to station himself permanently upon the premises.

[Given that] requiring uncompensated conveyance of the easement outright would violate the [takings clause, made applicable to the states via the due process clause of the] Fourteenth Amendment, the question becomes whether requiring it to be conveyed as a condition for issuing a land-use permit alters the outcome. We have long recognized that land-use regulation does not effect a taking if it "substantially advance[s] legitimate state interests" and does not "den[y] an owner economically viable use of his land." Our cases have not elaborated on the standards for determining what constitutes a "legitimate state interest" or what type of connection between the regulation and the state interest satisfies the requirement that the former "substantially advance" the latter. They have made clear, however, that a broad range of governmental [purposes] satisfies these requirements. The Commission argues that among these permissible purposes are protecting the public's ability to see the beach, assisting the public in overcoming the "psychological barrier" to using the beach created by a developed shorefront, and preventing congestion on the public beaches. We assume, without deciding, that this is so—in which case the Commission unquestionably would be able to deny the Nollans their permit outright if their new house (alone, or by reason of the cumulative impact produced in conjunction with other construction) would substantially impede these purposes, unless the denial would interfere so drastically with the Nollans' use of their property as to constitute a taking.

The Commission argues that a permit condition that serves the same legitimate police-power purpose as a refusal to issue the permit should not be found to be a taking if the refusal to issue the permit would not constitute a taking. We agree. Thus, if the Commission attached to the permit some condition that would have protected the public's ability to see the beach notwithstanding construction of the new house—for example, a height limitation, a width restriction, or a ban on fences—so long as the Commission could have exercised its police power (as we have assumed it could) to forbid construction of the house altogether, imposition of the condition would also be constitutional. Moreover, [the] condition would be constitutional even if it consisted of the requirement that the Nollans provide a viewing spot on their property for passersby with whose sighting of the ocean their new house would interfere. Although such a requirement, constituting a permanent grant of continuous access to the property, would have to be considered a taking if it were not attached to a development permit, the Commission's assumed power to forbid construction of the house in order to protect the public's view of the beach must surely include the power to condition construction upon some concession by the owner, even a concession of property rights, that serves the same end. . . .

The evident constitutional propriety disappears, however, if the condition substituted for the prohibition utterly fails to further the end advanced as the justification for the prohibition. When that essential nexus is eliminated, the situation becomes the same as if California law forbade shouting fire in a crowded theater, but granted dispensations to those willing to contribute $100 to the state treasury. While a ban on shouting fire can be a core exercise of the State's police power to protect the public safety, and can thus meet even our stringent standards for regulation of speech, adding the unrelated condition alters the purpose to one which, while it may be legitimate, is inadequate to sustain the ban. Therefore, even though, in a sense, requiring a $100 tax contribution in order to shout fire is a lesser restriction on speech than an outright ban, it would not pass constitutional muster. Similarly here, the lack of nexus between the condition and the original purpose of the building restriction converts that purpose to something other than what it was. The purpose then becomes, quite simply, the obtaining of an easement to serve some valid governmental purpose, but without payment of compensation. Whatever may be the outer limits of "legitimate state interests" in the takings and land-use context, this is not one of them. [U]nless the permit condition serves the same governmental purpose as the development ban, the building restriction is not a valid regulation of land use but "an out-and-out plan of extortion."

... It is quite impossible to understand how a requirement that people already on the public beaches be able to walk across the Nollans' property reduces any obstacles to viewing the beach created by the new house. It is also impossible to understand how it lowers any "psychological barrier" to using the public beaches, or how it helps to remedy any additional congestion on them caused by construction of the Nollans' new house. We therefore find that the Commission's imposition of the permit condition cannot be treated as an exercise of its land-use power for any of these purposes.

[Our] cases describe the condition for abridgment of property rights through the police power as a "*substantial* advanc[ing]" of a legitimate state interest. We are inclined to be particularly careful about the adjective where the actual conveyance of property is made a condition to the lifting of a land-use restriction, since in that context there is heightened risk that the purpose is avoidance of the compensation requirement, rather than the stated police-power objective.

[The] Commission's [belief] that the public interest will be served by a continuous strip of publicly accessible beach along the coast ... may well be ... a good idea, but that does not establish that the Nollans (and other coastal residents) alone can be compelled to contribute to its realization. California is free to advance its [objective] by using its power of eminent domain for this "public purpose," but if it wants an easement across the Nollans' property, it must pay for it.

Reversed.

DOLAN v. CITY OF TIGARD

Supreme Court of the United States
512 U.S. 374 (1994)

[handwritten: Follow up to Nollan]

CHIEF JUSTICE REHNQUIST delivered the opinion of the Court.

Petitioner challenges the decision of the Oregon Supreme Court which held that the city of Tigard could condition the approval of her building permit on the dedication of a portion of her property for flood control and traffic improvements. We granted certiorari to resolve a question left open by our decision in *Nollan*[:] what is the required degree of connection between the exactions imposed by the city and the projected impacts of the proposed development[?] . . . *[handwritten: Issue]*

[After identifying congestion in the central business district as a problem,] the city of Tigard, a community of some 30,000 residents on the southwest edge of Portland, adopted a plan for a pedestrian/bicycle pathway intended to encourage alternatives to automobile transportation for short trips. The [city's Community Development Code (CDC)] requires that new development facilitate this plan by dedicating land for pedestrian pathways where provided for in the pedestrian/bicycle pathway plan. . . . *[handwritten: Facts]*

The city also adopted a Master Drainage Plan (Drainage Plan). The Drainage Plan noted that flooding occurred in several areas along Fanno Creek, including areas near petitioner's property. The Drainage Plan also established that the increase in impervious surfaces associated with continued urbanization would exacerbate these flooding problems. To combat these risks, the Drainage Plan suggested a series of improvements to the Fanno Creek Basin, including channel excavation in the area next to petitioner's property, . . . ensuring that the floodplain remains free of structures and that it be preserved as greenways to minimize flood damage to structures. The Drainage Plan concluded that the cost of these improvements should be shared based on both direct and indirect benefits, with property owners along the water-ways paying more due to the direct benefit that they would receive. . . .

Petitioner Florence Dolan owns a plumbing and electric supply store located on Main Street in the Central Business District of the city. The store covers approximately 9,700 square feet on the eastern side of a 1.67–acre parcel, which includes a gravel parking lot. Fanno Creek flows through the southwestern corner of the lot and along its western boundary. The year-round flow of the creek renders the area within the creek's 100–year floodplain virtually unusable for commercial development. The city's comprehensive plan includes the Fanno Creek floodplain as part of the city's greenway system.

Petitioner applied to the city for a permit to redevelop the site. Her proposed plans called for nearly doubling the size of the store to 17,600 square feet and paving a 39–space parking lot. The existing store, located on the opposite side of the parcel, would be razed in sections as construction progressed on the new building. In the second phase of the project, petitioner proposed to build an additional structure on the northeast side of the site for complementary businesses and to provide more parking. The proposed expansion and intensified use are consistent with the city's zoning scheme in the Central Business District.

The City Planning Commission (Commission) granted petitioner's permit application subject to conditions imposed by the city's CDC. . . . [T]he Commission required that petitioner dedicate [to the city] the portion of her property lying within the 100–year flood plain for improvement of a storm drainage system along Fanno Creek and that she dedicate an additional 15–foot strip of land adjacent to the flood plain as a pedestrian/bicycle pathway. The dedication required by that condition encompasses approximately 7,000 square feet, or roughly 10% of the property.

[Dolan applied for a variance, which the Commission denied.] The Commission made a series of findings concerning the relationship between the dedicated conditions and the projected impacts of petitioner's project. First, the Commission noted that "it is reasonable to assume that customers and employees of the future uses of this site could utilize a pedestrian/bicycle pathway adjacent to this development for their transportation and recreational needs." The Commission noted that . . . "it is reasonable to expect that some of the users of the bicycle parking provided for by the site plan will use the pathway adjacent to Fanno Creek if it is constructed." In addition, the Commission found that creation of a convenient, safe pedestrian/bicycle pathway system as an alternative means of transportation "could offset some of the traffic demand on [nearby] streets and lessen the increase in traffic congestion." The Commission went on to note that the required flood plain dedication would be reasonably related to petitioner's request to intensify the use of the site given the increase in the impervious surface. The Commission stated that the "anticipated increased storm water flow from the subject property to an already strained creek and drainage basin can only add to the public need to manage the stream channel and flood plain for drainage purposes." Based on this anticipated increased storm water flow, the Commission concluded that "the requirement of dedication of the flood plain area on the site is related to the applicant's plan to intensify development on the site." The Tigard City Council approved the Commission's final order. . . .

Without question, had the city simply required petitioner to dedicate a strip of land along Fanno Creek for public use, rather than conditioning the grant of her permit to redevelop her property on such a dedication, a taking would have occurred. *Nollan*. . . . Under the well-settled doctrine of "unconstitutional conditions," the government may not require a person to give up a constitutional right—here the right to receive just compensation when property is taken for a public use—in exchange for a discretionary benefit conferred by the government where the benefit sought has little or no relationship to the property. Petitioner contends that the city has forced her to choose between the building permit and her right under the Fifth Amendment to just compensation for the public easements. Petitioner does not quarrel with the city's authority to exact some forms of dedication as a condition for the grant of a building permit, but challenges the showing made by the city to justify these exactions. She argues that the city has identified "no special benefits" conferred on her, and has not identified any "special quantifiable burdens" created by her new store that would justify the particular dedications required from her which are not required from the public at large.

[We] must first determine whether the "essential nexus" [required by *Nollan*] exists between the "legitimate state interest" and the permit condition exacted by the city. If we find that a nexus exists, we must then decide the required degree of connection between the exactions and the projected impact of the proposed development. We were not required to reach this [latter] question in *Nollan*, because we concluded that the connection did not meet even the loosest standard. Here, however, we must decide this question.

☆Rule☆

[Unlike *Nollan*, no] gimmicks are associated with the permit conditions imposed by the city in this case. [T]he prevention of flooding along Fanno Creek and the reduction of traffic congestion in the Central Business District qualify [as] legitimate public purposes. It seems equally obvious that a nexus exists between preventing flooding along Fanno Creek and limiting development within the creek's 100–year flood plain. Petitioner proposes to double the size of her retail store and to pave her now-gravel parking lot, thereby expanding the impervious surface on the property and increasing the amount of storm water runoff into Fanno Creek. The same may be said for the city's attempt to reduce traffic congestion by providing for alternative means of transportation. In theory, a pedestrian/bicycle pathway provides a useful alternative means of transportation for workers and shoppers.

applied

The second part of our analysis requires us to determine whether the degree of the exactions demanded by the city's permit conditions bear the required relationship to the projected impact of petitioner's proposed development. [The] city required that petitioner dedicate "to the city as Greenway all portions of the site that fall within the existing 100–year flood plain [of Fanno Creek] and all property 15 feet above [the flood plain] boundary." [The] city relies on the Commission's rather tentative findings that increased storm water flow from petitioner's property "can only add to the public need to manage the [flood plain] for drainage purposes" to support its conclusion that the "requirement of dedication of the flood plain area on the site is related to the applicant's plan to intensify development on the site." The city [found that] "the proposed expanded use of this site is anticipated to generate additional vehicular traffic thereby increasing [traffic congestion]. Creation of a convenient, safe pedestrian/bicycle pathway system as an alternative means of transportation [could] lessen the increase in traffic congestion."

The question for us is whether these findings are constitutionally sufficient to justify the conditions imposed by the city on petitioner's building permit. Since state courts have been dealing with this question a good deal longer than we have, we turn to representative decisions made by them. In some States, very generalized statements as to the necessary connection between the required dedication and the proposed development seem to suffice. We think this standard is too lax to adequately protect petitioner's right to just compensation if her property is taken for a public purpose. Other state courts require a very exacting correspondence, described as the "specific and uniquely attributable" test. [Under] this standard, if the local government cannot demonstrate that its exaction is directly proportional to the specifically created need, the exaction becomes "a veiled exercise of the power of eminent domain and a confiscation of private property behind the defense of police regulations." We do not think the Federal Constitution requires such exacting scrutiny, given the nature of the interests involved. A number of state courts have taken an intermediate position, requiring the municipality to show a "reasonable relationship" between the required dedication and the impact of the proposed development. Typical is the Supreme Court of Nebraska's opinion in Simpson v. North Platte, 206 Neb. 240, 245 (1980), where that court stated:

> The distinction [which] must be made between an appropriate exercise of the police power and an improper exercise of eminent domain is whether the requirement has some reasonable relationship [to] the use to which the property is being made or is merely being used as an excuse for taking property simply because at that particular moment the landowner is asking the city for some license or permit.

Thus, the court held that a city may not require a property owner to dedicate private property for some future public use as a condition of obtaining a building permit when such future use is not "occasioned by the construction sought to be permitted." Some form of the reasonable relationship test has been adopted in many other jurisdictions. . . .

We think the "reasonable relationship" test adopted by a majority of the state courts is closer to the federal constitutional norm than either of those previously discussed. But we do not adopt it as such, partly because the term "reasonable relationship" seems confusingly similar to the term "rational basis" which describes the minimal level of scrutiny under the Equal Protection Clause of the Fourteenth Amendment. We think a term such as "rough proportionality" best encapsulates what we hold to be the requirement of the [takings clause.] No precise mathematical calculation is required, but the city must make some sort of individualized determination that the required dedication is related both in nature and extent to the impact of the proposed development. . . .

We turn now to analysis of whether the findings relied upon by the city here, first with respect to the flood plain easement, and second with respect to the pedestrian/bicycle path, satisfied these requirements. It is axiomatic that increasing the amount of impervious surface will increase the quantity and rate of storm water flow from petitioner's property. Therefore, keeping the flood plain open and free from development would likely confine the pressures on Fanno Creek created by petitioner's development. [But] the city demanded more—it not only wanted petitioner not to build in the flood-plain, but it also wanted petitioner's property along Fanno Creek for its Greenway system. The city has never said why a public greenway, as opposed to a private one, was required in the interest of flood control. The difference to petitioner, of course, is the loss of her ability to exclude others. As we have noted, this right to exclude others is "one of the most essential sticks in the bundle of rights that are commonly characterized as property." It is difficult to see why recreational visitors trampling along petitioner's flood plain easement are sufficiently related to the city's legitimate interest in reducing flooding problems along [the creek], and the city has not attempted to make any individualized determination to support this part of its request. [Imposition of] a permanent recreational easement upon petitioner's property [would strip petitioner of] all rights to regulate the time in which the public entered onto the Greenway, regardless of any interference it might pose with her retail store. Her right to exclude would not be regulated; it would be eviscerated. If petitioner's proposed development had somehow encroached on existing greenway space in the city, it would have been reasonable to require petitioner to provide some alternative greenway space for the public either on her property or elsewhere. [But] that is not the case here. We conclude that the findings upon which the city relies do not show the required reasonable relationship between the flood plain easement and the petitioner's proposed new building.

With respect to the pedestrian/bicycle pathway, we have no doubt that the city was correct in finding that the larger retail sales facility proposed by petitioner will increase traffic on the streets of the Central Business District. [But] on the record before us, the city has not met its burden of demonstrating that the additional number of vehicle and bicycle trips generated by the petitioner's development reasonably relate to the city's requirement for a dedication of the pedestrian/bicycle pathway easement. The city simply found that the creation of the pathway "could offset some of the traffic demand [and] lessen the increase in traffic congestion." As Justice Peterson of the [Oregon Supreme Court] explained in his dissenting opinion, "the findings of fact that the bicycle pathway system '*could* offset some of the traffic demand' is a far cry from a finding that the bicycle pathway system *will*, or is *likely to*, offset some of the traffic demand." (Emphasis in original.) No precise mathematical calculation is required, but the city must make some effort to quantify its findings in support of the dedication for the pedestrian/bicycle pathway beyond the conclusory statement that it could offset some of the traffic demand generated. [Reversed and remanded.]

NOTES, QUESTIONS, AND PROBLEMS

1. The "Essential Nexus" Requirement. The essential nexus test devised by the Court in *Nollan* limits the ability of governments to exact concessions from property owners by tying the permitted concessions to the reasons for imposing otherwise valid development restrictions. *Nollan* limits the exactions that governments may demand from owners as the price for a development permit to those that are substantially related to the purpose of the underlying regulation.

2. The "Rough Proportionality" Requirement. The rough proportionality test, articulated in *Dolan*, requires an adequate link between the condition imposed and the negative external effects of the owner's proposed activity. A development that imposes significant costs on the community may validly be conditioned upon the owner's taking action to absorb some of those external costs he is producing.

3. Problems.

a. Suppose that a City plagued by traffic congestion and a scarcity of on-street public parking adopts an ordinance that requires any applicant for a permit to construct new housing to provide one off-street parking place for each bedroom in the structure. Would the essential nexus requirement be met if City waives this requirement if the owner contributes money to the City's mass transit fund in lieu of off-street parking? Would a waiver conditioned upon the owner's dedicating the off-street parking to the public be valid? What about a waiver conditioned upon the owner donating $10,000 to the City Public Library?

b. Assume the existence of the same ordinance described in Problem *a*. Suppose that City conditions waiver of the requirement on a payment to City's mass transit fund of $10,000 per each off-street parking space waived. How would one determine whether this payment is roughly proportional to the impact of the proposed development on public on-street parking? What facts would you need (or desire) to know to make this assessment?

4. Takings Remedies. Several remedies are available once a regulation has been found to be a taking. First, a property owner may obtain damages in the form of just compensation for the property taken. Second, enforcement of the regulation may be enjoined; if the government wishes to proceed with the regulatory scheme, it must openly exercise its power of eminent domain and pay just compensation for its taking of property. But injunctive relief provides no redress for the time period during which the regulation (which was found to be a taking) was in place. For a long time the Court refused to provide a damages remedy for this "interim taking" of property, but since First English Evangelical Lutheran Church of Glendale v. County of Los Angeles, 482 U.S. 304 (1987), that is no longer the case. Temporary takings are no different from permanent takings, said the Court, save in their duration: "[W]here the government's activities have already worked a taking of all use of property, no subsequent action by the government can relieve it of the duty to provide compensation for the period during which the taking was effective." The affected property owner is entitled to damages for the loss of the use of his property during the period a regulatory taking was in effect.

D. JUDICIAL TAKINGS

STOP THE BEACH RENOURISHMENT v. FLORIDA DEP'T OF ENVIRONMENTAL CONSERVATION

Supreme Court of the United States
130 S.Ct. 2592 (2010)

[To restore beaches eroded by hurricane action Florida enacted the Beach and Shore Preservation Act, which governed the restoration of beaches by adding huge quantities of sand seaward of the mean high tide line that resulted from the erosion and maintaining that sand ("renourishment"). The effect of restoration and renourishment was that the mean high tide line moved seaward. Under Florida law the owner of beachfront property has title to the mean high tide line. However, the Beach and Shore Preservation Act stipulated that an "erosion control line"—the mean high tide line before beach restoration—would become the permanent boundary line regardless of any future shifting of the mean high tide line due to subsequent erosion.

[Under Florida common law the boundary of a beachfront property shifts with the mean high tide line so long as that line moves as a result of "accretion"—gradual and imperceptible movement that occurs "so slowly that one could not see the change occurring, though over time the difference [becomes] apparent." On the other hand, if the change occurs by a "sudden or perceptible loss of or addition to land by the action of the water" the movement is an "avulsion" and the prior boundary line remains as it was.

[The Florida Supreme Court ruled that the restoration and renourishment of beaches under the Beach and Shore Preservation Act, including the substitution of the "erosion control line" as the permanent boundary line, was not a taking. The Supreme Court agreed, concluding that the state's addition of sand seaward of the high tide line that had resulted from erosion was an avulsion, and that accordingly the erosion control line did not effect a taking. In the excerpt that follows, however, the justices debated whether and when judicial action can constitute a taking.]

JUSTICE SCALIA, joined by CHIEF JUSTICE ROBERTS, JUSTICE THOMAS, and JUSTICE ALITO:

... [We] discuss some general principles of our takings jurisprudence. The Takings Clause ... applies as fully to the taking of a landowner's riparian rights as it does to the taking of an estate in land. See Yates v. Milwaukee, 77 U.S. 497 (1871). Moreover, though the classic taking is a transfer of property to the State or to another private party by eminent domain, the Takings Clause applies to other state actions that achieve the same thing. Thus, when the government uses its own property in such a way that it destroys private property, it has taken that property. See

United States v. Causby, 328 U.S. 256, 261–262 (1946); Pumpelly v. Green Bay Co., 80 U.S. 166 (1872). Similarly, our doctrine of regulatory takings "aims to identify regulatory actions that are functionally equivalent to the classic taking." Lingle v. Chevron U.S.A. Inc., 544 U.S. 528, 539 (2005). Thus, it is a taking when a state regulation forces a property owner to submit to a permanent physical occupation, *Loretto*, or deprives him of all economically beneficial use of his property, *Lucas*. Finally (and here we approach the situation before us), States effect a taking if they recharacterize as public property what was previously private property. See Webb's Fabulous Pharmacies, Inc. v. Beckwith, 449 U.S. 155, 163–165 (1980).

The Takings Clause (unlike, for instance, the Ex Post Facto Clauses, see Art. I, § 9, cl. 3; § 10, cl. 1) is not addressed to the action of a specific branch or branches. It is concerned simply with the act, and not with the governmental actor ("nor shall private property *be taken*" (emphasis added)). There is no textual justification for saying that the existence or the scope of a State's power to expropriate private property without just compensation varies according to the branch of government effecting the expropriation. Nor does common sense recommend such a principle. It would be absurd to allow a State to do by judicial decree what the Takings Clause forbids it to do by legislative fiat.

Our precedents provide no support for the proposition that takings effected by the judicial branch are entitled to special treatment, and in fact suggest the contrary. PruneYard Shopping Center v. Robins, 447 U.S. 74 (1980), involved a decision of the California Supreme Court overruling one of its prior decisions which had held that the California Constitution's guarantees of freedom of speech and of the press, and of the right to petition the government, did not require the owner of private property to accord those rights on his premises. The appellants, owners of a shopping center, contended that their private property rights could not "be denied by invocation of a state constitutional provision *or by judicial reconstruction of a State's laws of private property*," *id.*, at 79 (emphasis added). We held that there had been no taking, citing cases involving legislative and executive takings, and applying standard Takings Clause analysis. We treated the California Supreme Court's application of the constitutional provisions as a regulation of the use of private property, and evaluated whether that regulation violated the property owners' "right to exclude others." Our opinion addressed only the claimed taking by the constitutional provision. Its failure to speak separately to the claimed taking by "judicial reconstruction of a State's laws of private property" certainly does not suggest that a taking by judicial action cannot occur, and arguably suggests that the same analysis applicable to taking by constitutional provision would apply.

Webb's Fabulous Pharmacies is even closer in point. There the purchaser of an insolvent corporation had interpleaded the corporation's creditors, placing the purchase price in an interest-bearing account in the registry of the Circuit Court of Seminole County, to be distributed in satisfaction of claims approved by a receiver. The Florida Supreme Court construed an applicable statute to mean that the interest on the account belonged to the county, because the account was "considered 'public money'" Beckwith v. Webb's Fabulous Pharmacies, 374 So. 2d 951, 952–953 (1979) *(per curiam).* We held this to be a taking. We noted that "[t]he usual and general rule is that any interest on an interpleaded and deposited fund follows the principal and is to be allocated to those who are ultimately to be the owners of that principal. ... Neither the Florida Legislature by statute, nor the Florida courts by judicial decree," we said, "may accomplish the result the county seeks simply by recharacterizing the principal as 'public money.'" [449 U.S. at 162, 164.]

In sum, the Takings Clause bars *the State* from taking private property without paying for it, no matter which branch is the instrument of the taking. To be sure, the manner of state action may matter: Condemnation by eminent domain, for example, is always a taking, while a legislative, executive, or judicial restriction of property use may or may not be, depending on its nature and extent. But the particular state *actor* is irrelevant. If a legislature *or a court* declares that what was once an established right of private property no longer exists, it has taken that property, no less than if the State had physically appropriated it or destroyed its value by regulation. "[A] State, by *ipse dixit*, may not transform private property into public property without compensation." . . .

Justice Breyer's concurrence says that we need neither (1) to decide whether the judiciary can ever effect a taking, nor (2) to establish the standard for determining whether it has done so. The second part of this is surely incompatible with Justice Breyer's conclusion that the "Florida Supreme Court's decision in this case did not amount to a 'judicial taking.'" One cannot know whether a takings claim is invalid without knowing what standard it has failed to meet. Which means that Justice Breyer must either (a) grapple with the artificial question of what would constitute a judicial taking if there were such a thing as a judicial taking (reminiscent of the perplexing question how much wood would a woodchuck chuck if a woodchuck could chuck wood?), or (b) answer in the negative what he considers to be the "unnecessary" constitutional question whether there is such a thing as a judicial taking. . . .

In sum, Justice Breyer cannot decide that petitioner's claim fails without first deciding what a valid claim would consist of. His agreement [that there has been no taking here] necessarily implies agreement with the test for a judicial taking ... which [the Court] applies: whether the state court has "declare[d] that what was once an established right of private property no longer exists." Justice Breyer must either agree with that standard or craft one of his own. ... But embracing a standard while being coy about the [constitutional] right is, well, odd; and deciding this case while addressing *neither* the standard *nor* the right is quite impossible.

Justice Breyer responds that he simply advocates resolving this case without establishing "*the precise* standard under which a party wins or loses." (emphasis added). But he relies upon no standard at all, precise or imprecise. He simply pronounces that this is not a judicial taking if there is such a thing as a judicial taking. . . .

Like Justice Breyer's concurrence, Justice Kennedy's concludes that the Florida Supreme Court's action here does not meet the standard for a judicial taking, while purporting not to determine what is the standard for a judicial taking, or indeed whether such a thing as a judicial taking even exists. That approach is invalid for the reasons we have discussed.

Justice Kennedy says that we need not take what he considers the bold and risky step of holding that the Takings Clause applies to judicial action, because the Due Process Clause "would likely prevent a State from doing by judicial decree what the Takings Clause forbids it to do by legislative fiat." He invokes the Due Process Clause "in both its substantive and procedural aspects," not specifying which of his arguments relates to which.

The first respect in which Justice Kennedy thinks the Due Process Clause can do the job seems to sound in Procedural Due Process. Because, he says, "[c]ourts, unlike the executive or legislature, are not designed to make policy decisions" about expropriation, "[t]he Court would be on strong footing in ruling that a judicial decision that eliminates or substantially changes established property rights" violates the Due Process Clause. Let us be clear what is being proposed here. This Court has held that the separation-of-powers principles that the Constitution imposes upon the Federal Government do not apply against the States. But in order to avoid the bold and risky step of saying that the Takings Clause applies to *all* government takings, Justice Kennedy would have us use Procedural Due Process to impose judicially crafted separation-of-powers limitations upon the States: courts cannot be used to perform the governmental function of expropriation. The asserted reasons for the due-process limitation are that the legislative and executive branches "are accountable in their political capacity" for takings and "[c]ourts . . . are not designed to make policy decisions" about takings. These reasons may have a lot to do with sound separation-of-powers principles that ought to govern a democratic society, but they have nothing whatever to do with the protection of individual rights that is the object of the Due Process Clause.

Of course even taking those reasons at face value, it is strange to proclaim a democracy deficit and lack of special competence for the judicial taking of an individual property right, when this Court has had no trouble deciding matters of much greater moment, contrary to congressional desire or the legislated desires of most of the States, with no special competence except the authority we possess to enforce the Constitution. In any case, our opinion does *not* trust judges with the relatively small power Justice Kennedy now objects to. It is we who propose setting aside judicial decisions that take private property; it is he who insists that judges cannot be so limited. Under his regime, the citizen whose property has been judicially redefined to belong to the State would presumably be given the Orwellian explanation: "The court did not take your property. Because it is neither politically accountable nor competent to make such a decision, it cannot take property."

Justice Kennedy's [Substantive Due Process arguments are] that [i]t is ... natural to read the Due Process Clause as limiting the power of courts to eliminate or change established property rights," ... the Due Process Clause imposes limits on government's ability to diminish property values by regulation," and ... that "the Due Process Clause would likely prevent a State from doing by judicial decree what the Takings Clause forbids it to do by legislative fiat." The first problem with using Substantive Due Process to do the work of the Takings Clause is that we have held it cannot be done. "Where a particular Amendment 'provides an explicit textual source of constitutional protection' against a particular sort of government behavior, 'that Amendment, not the more generalized notion of "substantive due process," must be the guide for analyzing these claims.' " Albright v. Oliver, 510 U.S. 266, 273 (1994) (four-Justice plurality opinion) (quoting Graham v. Connor, 490 U.S. 386, 395 (1989). The second problem is that we have held for many years (logically or not) that the "liberties" protected by Substantive Due Process do not include economic liberties. See, e.g., Lincoln Fed. Labor Union v. Northwestern Iron & Metal Co., 335 U.S. 525, 536 (1949). Justice Kennedy ... propels us back to what is referred to (usually deprecatingly) as "the *Lochner* era." See Lochner v. New York, 198 U. S 45, 56–58 (1905). That is a step of much greater novelty, and much more unpredictable effect, than merely applying the Takings Clause to judicial action. And the third and last problem with using Substantive Due Process is that either (1) it will not do all that the Takings Clause does, or (2) if it does all that the Takings Clause does, it will encounter the same supposed difficulties that Justice Kennedy finds troublesome. . . .

Justice Kennedy [asserts] that "it is unclear what remedy a reviewing court could enter after finding a judicial taking." Justice Kennedy worries that we may only be able to mandate compensation. That remedy is even rare for a legislative or executive taking, and we see no reason why it would be the exclusive remedy for a judicial taking. If we were to hold that the Florida Supreme Court had effected an uncompensated taking in the present case, we would simply reverse the Florida Supreme Court's judgment that the Beach and Shore Preservation Act can be applied to the property in question. ... Justice Kennedy ... warns that if judges know that their action is covered by the Takings Clause, they will issue "sweeping new rule[s] to adjust the rights of property owners," comfortable in the knowledge that their innovations will be preserved upon payment by the State. That is quite impossible. As we have said, if we were to hold that the Florida Supreme Court had effected an uncompensated taking in this case, we would not validate the taking by ordering Florida to pay compensation. We would simply reverse the Florida Supreme Court's judgment that the Beach and Shore Preservation Act can be applied to the ... property [in question]. The power to effect a *compensated* taking would then reside, where it has always resided, not in the Florida Supreme Court but in the Florida Legislature—which could either provide compensation or acquiesce in the invalidity of the offending features of the Act.

The only realistic incentive that subjection to the Takings Clause might provide to any court would be the incentive to get reversed, which in our experience few judges value.

Justice Kennedy, however, while dismissive of the Takings Clause, places no other constraints on judicial action. ... Moreover, and more importantly, Justice Kennedy places no constraints whatever upon *this* Court. Not only does his concurrence only *think about* applying Substantive Due Process; but because Substantive Due Process is such a wonderfully malleable concept, even a firm commitment to apply it would be a firm commitment to nothing in particular. Justice Kennedy's desire to substitute Substantive Due Process for the Takings Clause suggests, and the rest of what he writes confirms, that what holds him back from giving the Takings Clause its natural meaning is not the *intrusiveness* of applying it to judicial action, but the *definiteness* of doing so; not a concern to preserve the powers of the States' political branches, but a concern to preserve this Court's discretion to say that property may be taken, or may not be taken, as in the Court's view the circumstances suggest. We must not say that we are bound by the Constitution never to sanction judicial elimination of clearly established property rights. Where the power of this Court is concerned, one must *never* say never. The great attraction of Substantive Due Process as a substitute for more specific constitutional guarantees is that it *never* means never—because it never means anything precise.

Respondents ... argue that federal courts lack the knowledge of state law required to decide whether a judicial decision that purports merely to clarify property rights has instead taken them. But federal courts must often decide what state property rights exist in non-takings contexts. And indeed they must decide it to resolve claims that legislative or executive action has effected a taking. For example, a regulation that deprives a property owner of all economically beneficial use of his property is not a taking if the restriction "inhere[s] in the title itself, in the restrictions that background principles of the State's law of property and nuisance already place upon land ownership." *Lucas*. A constitutional provision that forbids the uncompensated taking of property is quite simply insusceptible of enforcement by federal courts unless they have the power to decide what property rights exist under state law....

For its part, petitioner proposes an unpredictability test. Quoting Justice Stewart's concurrence in Hughes v. Washington, 389 U.S. 290, 296 (1967), petitioner argues that a judicial taking consists of a decision that " 'constitutes a sudden change in state law, unpredictable in terms of relevant precedents.'" The focus of petitioner's test is misdirected. What counts is not whether there is precedent for the allegedly confiscatory decision, but whether the property right allegedly taken was established. A "predictability of change" test would cover both too much and too little. Too much, because a judicial property decision need not be predictable, so long as it does not declare that what had been private property under established law no longer is. A decision that clarifies property entitlements (or the lack thereof) that were previously unclear might be difficult to predict, but it does not eliminate established property rights. And the predictability test covers too little, because a judicial elimination of established private-property rights that is foreshadowed by dicta or even by holdings years in advance is nonetheless a taking. If, for example, a state court held in one case, to which the complaining property owner was not a party, that it had the power to limit the acreage of privately owned real estate to 100 acres, and then, in a second case, applied that principle to declare the complainant's 101st acre to be public property, the State would have taken an acre from the complainant even though the decision was predictable....

JUSTICE KENNEDY, with whom JUSTICE SOTOMAYOR joins, concurring in part and concurring in the judgment.

. . . [This] case does not require the Court to determine whether, or when, a judicial decision determining the rights of property owners can violate the Takings Clause of the Fifth Amendment of the United States Constitution. This separate opinion notes certain difficulties that should be considered before accepting the theory that a judicial decision that eliminates an "established property right" constitutes a violation of the Takings Clause....

[If] an authorized executive agency or official decides that Blackacre is the right place for a fire station or Greenacre is the best spot for a freeway interchange, then the weight and authority of the State are used to take the property, even against the wishes of the owner, who must be satisfied with just compensation. In the exercise of their duty to protect the fisc, both the legislative and executive branches monitor, or should monitor, the exercise of this substantial power. Those branches are accountable in their political capacity for the proper discharge of this obligation....

[The] power to select what property to condemn and the responsibility to ensure that the taking makes financial sense from the State's point of view [are,] as a matter of custom and practice, . . . matters for the political branches—the legislature and the executive—not the courts. . . . If a judicial decision, as opposed to an act of the executive or the legislature, eliminates an established property right, the judgment could be set aside as a deprivation of property without due process of law. The Due Process Clause, in both its substantive and procedural aspects, is a central limitation upon the exercise of judicial power....

The Takings Clause also protects property rights and it "operates as a conditional limitation, permitting the government to do what it wants so long as it pays the charge." Unlike the Due Process Clause, therefore, the Takings Clause implicitly recognizes a governmental power while placing limits upon that power. Thus, if the Court were to hold that a judicial taking exists, it would presuppose that a judicial decision eliminating established property rights is "otherwise constitutional" so long as the State compensates the aggrieved property owners. There is no clear authority for this proposition.

When courts act without direction from the executive or legislature, they may not have the power to eliminate established property rights by judicial decision. . . . Courts, unlike the executive or legislature, are not designed to make policy decisions about "the need for, and likely effectiveness of, regulatory actions." . . . The Court would be on strong footing in ruling that a judicial decision that eliminates or substantially changes established property rights, which are a legitimate expectation of the owner, is "arbitrary or irrational" under the Due Process Clause. . . .

To announce that courts too can effect a taking when they decide cases involving property rights, would raise certain difficult questions. . . . The evident reason for recognizing a judicial takings doctrine would be to constrain the power of the judicial branch. Of course, the judiciary must respect private ownership. But were this Court to say that judicial decisions become takings when they overreach, this might give more power to courts, not less. . . .

Consider the instance of litigation between two property owners to determine which one bears the liability and costs when a tree that stands on one property extends its roots in a way that damages adjacent property. If a court deems that, in light of increasing urbanization, the former rule for allocation of these costs should be changed, thus shifting the rights of the owners, it may well increase the value of one property and decrease the value of the other. This might be the type of incremental modification under state common law that does not violate due process, as owners may reasonably expect or anticipate courts to make certain changes in property law. The usual due process constraint is that courts cannot abandon settled principles. But if the state court were deemed to be exercising the power to take property, that constraint would be removed. Because the State would be bound to pay owners for takings caused by a judicial decision, it is conceivable that some judges might decide that enacting a sweeping new rule to adjust the rights of property owners in the context of changing social needs is a good idea. Knowing that the resulting ruling would be a taking, the courts could go ahead with their project, free from constraints that would otherwise confine their power. . . . And if the litigation were a class action to decide, for instance, whether there are public rights of access that diminish the rights of private ownership, a State might find itself obligated to pay a substantial judgment for the judicial ruling. Even if the legislature were to subsequently rescind the judicial decision by statute, the State would still have to pay just compensation for the temporary taking that occurred from the time of the judicial decision to the time of the statutory fix. *First English.*

The idea, then, that a judicial takings doctrine would constrain judges might just well have the opposite effect. It would give judges new power and new assurance that changes in property rights that are beneficial, or thought to be so, are fair and proper because just compensation will be paid. The judiciary historically has not had the right or responsibility to say what property should or should not be taken....

There are ... additional practical considerations that the Court would need to address before recognizing judicial takings. ... [It] is unclear what remedy a reviewing court could enter after finding a judicial taking. ... It is ... questionable whether reviewing courts could invalidate judicial decisions deemed to be judicial takings; they may only be able to order just compensation....

These difficult issues are some of the reasons why the Court should not reach beyond the necessities of the case to recognize a judicial takings doctrine....

JUSTICE BREYER, with whom JUSTICE GINSBURG joins, concurring in part and concurring in the judgment.

I agree that no unconstitutional taking of property occurred in this case.... I cannot join [the discussion of judicial takings], however, for [there] the plurality unnecessarily addresses questions of constitutional law that are better left for another day....

The plurality criticizes me for my cautious approach, and states that I "cannot decide that petitioner's claim fails without first deciding what a valid claim would consist of." But, of course, courts frequently find it possible to resolve cases—even those raising constitutional questions— without specifying the precise standard under which a party wins or loses. ... That is simply what I would do here.

In the past, Members of this Court have warned us that, when faced with difficult constitutional questions, we should "confine ourselves to deciding only what is necessary to the disposition of the immediate case." I heed this advice here. There is no need now to decide more than what the Court decides ..., namely, that the Florida Supreme Court's decision in this case did not amount to a "judicial taking."

NOTES AND QUESTIONS

1. Prior Opinions. In Hughes v. Washington, 389 U.S. 290 (1967), the question was whether a beachfront owner owned property added to the shore by accretion. Prior to Washington's admission to the Union in 1889 beachfront owners had the undisputed right, under federal law, to such lands. A 1966 decision of the Washington Supreme Court held that when Washington became a state its constitution changed that rule, and denied to beachfront owners any property added to their land by accretion. Because Hughes's predecessor in title acquired title prior to Washington's admission as a state the Court held that federal law governed. In a concurrence, Justice Stewart noted:

Surely, it must be conceded as a general proposition that the law of real property is, under our Constitution, left to the individual States to develop and administer. And surely Washington or any other State is free to make changes, either legislative or judicial, in its general rules of real property law, including the rules governing the property rights of riparian owners. ... To the extent that the decision of the Supreme Court of Washington on [this issue] arguably conforms to reasonable expectations, we must of course accept it as conclusive. But to the extent that it constitutes a sudden change in state law, unpredictable in terms of the relevant precedents, no such deference would be appropriate. For a State cannot be permitted to defeat the constitutional prohibition against taking property without due process of law by the simple device of asserting retroactively that the property it has taken never existed at all. Whether the decision here worked an unpredictable change in state law thus inevitably presents a federal question for the determination of this Court.

389 U.S. at 295–97 (1967) (Stewart, J., concurring).

In Webb's Fabulous Pharmacies, Inc. v. Beckwith, 449 U.S. 155 (1980), the Court found a taking had occurred by the Florida Supreme Court's conclusion that money deposited with a court clerk as an interpleader fund was "public money" and thus the interest earned on the sum belonged to the state, not the private parties for whose benefit the interpleader had been made. The Supreme Court reversed, after parsing Florida law to conclude that the Florida Supreme Court had erred in its reading of Florida's statutes. But because the Florida court had ruled that the seizure of the interest was constitutional, and that ruling rested on an interpretation of Florida law, the meaning of Florida law became a federal constitutional issue. *Webb's Fabulous Pharmacies* can thus be read as a instance of a judicial taking, or it can be understood as an erroneous reading of state law. But in each of *Hughes* and *Webb's Fabulous Pharmacies* the state supreme court changed the interpretation of state law to alter the prior understanding of property.

See generally, Barton Thompson, Judicial Takings, 76 Va. L. Rev. 1449 (1990).

2. Questions. If judicial takings are recognized, would judicial imposition of an easement by necessity be a taking? On what might resolution of this question depend? Would it make any difference if a state supreme court were to decide that easements by necessity must be imposed whenever any property is landlocked, and stipulating that the easement will be located over the last property conveyed by the party creating the landlocked condition, to the extent that can be determined, but otherwise to be located where "least intrusive"?

In Raleigh Avenue Association v. Atlantis Beach Club, Inc., 185 N.J. 40 (2005), the New Jersey Supreme Court ruled that the public had a right to cross the privately owned dry sand beach to reach the public shore and to use a six foot strip of the private dry sand. Suppose that New Jersey's legislature had decreed this result by new legislation. Would either action be a taking?

INDEX

References are to Pages

845

EMINENT DOMAIN—Cont'd
Public use requirement—Cont'd
    Economic development projects, 782, 786, 790
    Historical development, 787
    Incidental public benefit, 789
    Lessees, condemnations for benefit of, 779
    Oligopolies, exercise of eminent domain to eliminate, 781
    Public benefit as public use, 778, 785
    Redevelopment projects, 780, 782
    State law changes limiting eminent domain power, 790
Redevelopment projects, 780, 782
State law changes limiting eminent domain power, 790
Zoning variances, eminent domain as alternative, 705

ENCROACHMENTS
    Generally, 83
    See also Trespass, this index
Hawaii rule, 541
Marketable title, encroachments affecting, 406
Marketable title implications, 406
Nuisance liability, 535
Self-help alternatives to litigation, 538
Title insurance exceptions, 407
Tree branches and roots, 535

ENCUMBRANCES
Covenants against, 431
Disclosure obligations, 431
Further assurances, covenant of, 433
Open, visible, notorious physical encumbrances, 431
Zoning violations as, 432

ENVIRONMENTAL LAWS
Protected species laws, regulatory takings, 24
Takings challenges to regulations protecting ecological resources, 798, 801
Zoning amendments, 776

EQUITABLE CONTINGENT REMAINDERS
Generally, 181

EQUITABLE CONVERSION
Priority contests, 494
Risk of loss, 425

EQUITABLE ESTOPPEL
    Generally, 587
Irrevocable licenses created by, 578, 587
Statute of Frauds exception, 399

EQUITABLE SERVITUDES
    Generally, 647
Creation by implication from general plan, 653
Development, 648
Easements distinguished, 641
General plan implying, 653
Implication from general plan creation, 653
Injunctive remedies, 647
Law vs equity remedies, 648
Negative easements compared, 654

EQUITABLE SERVITUDES—Cont'd
Negative rights creations, 641
Notice, 654
Policy considerations, 641
Privity of estate, 653
Property rules and liability rules distinguished, 648
Real covenants distinguished, 641, 643, 653
Reciprocal negative easements, 650
Remedies
    Injunctions, 647
    Law vs equity, 648
    Property rules and liability rules distinguished, 648
    Real covenants distinguished, 653
Restatement simplification of servitude laws
    Generally, 576
    See also Servitudes, this index
Subdivisions as creating, 650
Touch and concern test, 646, 649

EQUITY
Contingent remainders, equitable, 181
Historical background of equity courts, 175
Injunctions, this index
Landlord and tenant damages, 343
Life estates, equitable and legal, 126, 143
Marital property, equitable division on divorce, 272
Mortgagors' equity interests, 445
Partition actions, 236
Remedies, transfers of real property, 425
Rule Against Perpetuities problems, cy pres resolutions, 214
Servitudes, this index

ESCHEAT
    Generally, 116
Tenure system, 120

ESCROW AGENTS
Transfers of real property, 383

ESTATE IN LAND
Definition, 115

ESTATE PLANNING
Role of future interests in, 164

ESTOPPEL
Deed, estoppel by, 437
Easements, termination by estoppel, 635
Equitable Estoppel, this index
Government regulations affecting vested rights, 736

EVICTION
See Landlord and Tenant, this index

EXCEPTIONS
Reservations distinguished, 580

EXCLUSIONARY RIGHTS
Property, bundle of rights, 24

EXECUTORY INTERESTS
    Generally, 173
Aggressive nature of, 168